Connecticut Town Meeting Records *during the* American Revolution

VOLUME I
ASHFORD–MILFORD

Jolene Roberts Mullen

HERITAGE BOOKS
2011

HERITAGE BOOKS
AN IMPRINT OF HERITAGE BOOKS, INC.

Books, CDs, and more—Worldwide

For our listing of thousands of titles see our website
at
www.HeritageBooks.com

Published 2011 by
HERITAGE BOOKS, INC.
Publishing Division
100 Railroad Ave. #104
Westminster, Maryland 21157

Copyright © 2011 Jolene Roberts Mullen

Other Heritage Books by the author:
*Connecticut Town Meeting Records during the Revolution
Volume I: Ashford–Milford*

*Connecticut Town Meeting Records during the Revolution
Volume II: New Fairfield–Woodstock*

All rights reserved. No part of this book may be reproduced or transmitted in any form or by any means, electronic or mechanical, including photocopying, recording or by any information storage and retrieval system without written permission from the author, except for the inclusion of brief quotations in a review.

International Standard Book Numbers
Paperbound: 978-0-7884-5314-4
Clothbound: 978-0-7884-8792-7

CONTENTS

Acknowledgements	v
Forward	vii
Ashford (ASHF)	1
Bolton (BOLT)	21
Branford (BRAN)	35
Canaan (CANA)	49
Canterbury (CANT)	63
Chatham (CHAT) see East Hampton	
Cheshire (CHES)	76
Colchester (COLC)	82
Colebrook (COLE)	97
Cornwall (CORN)	104
Coventry (COVE)	125
Danbury (DANB)	137
Derby (DERB)	149
Durham (DURH)	163
East Haddam (EHAD)	177
East Hampton/Chatham (CHAT)	191
East Hartford (EHAR)	209
East Windsor (EWIN)	211
Enfield (ENFD)	223
Fairfield (FAIR)	232
Farmington (FARM)	252
Glastonbury (GLAS)	284
Goshen (GOSH)	305
Greenwich (GREE)	325
Groton (GROT)	333
Guilford (GUIL)	346
Haddam (HADD)	368
Hartford (HARF)	384
Hartland (HARL)	405
Harwinton (HARW)	422
Hebron (HEBR)	437
Kent (KENT)	445
Killingly (KILY)	463
Killingworth (KILH)	481
Lebanon (LEBA)	491
Litchfield (LITC)	504

Mansfield (MANS)	518
Middletown (MIDD)	530
Milford (MILF)	567
Map of Connecticut Towns	578
Parent Towns	579
Index	584

ACKNOWLEDGEMENTS

I wish to especially thank my always patient husband, Peter; friends Sandy Slifka and Harlan Jessup of the Connecticut Professional Genealogists Council who pointed me in better directions; genealogist Sara Sukol, who passed my name around the Daughters of the American Revolution; the staff at the Connecticut State Library, especially Mel Smith, who helped me find all sorts of wonderful records; my ever present guardian angel; whoever invented the GPS; and Karon McGovern, the data expert who wrapped this all up.

I also wish to acknowledge Peter Harter, who started everything, and Ebenezer Burgess, who started this.

FOREWORD

These two volumes are a collection of extracts from the minutes of the town meetings of the towns that existed in Connecticut during the American Revolution. Town meeting records from April 1775 through November 1783 are included, with the addition of the Committees of Inspection, Correspondence and Safety in 1774.

Of the eighty towns that existed by November 1783, seventy-seven still have part or all of their meeting records available at a town clerk's office, the Connecticut State Archives or an historical society. A few of the town meetings for these years have been microfilmed by the Latter Day Saints; in these cases, the film numbers are noted and can be borrowed through a Family History Center.

All persons who were mentioned in the meeting records are included. Reasons to have been mentioned include: elected or appointed to a town office or committee, died or moved while in office, appointed to fill a vacant office, warned out, applied for permission to manumit a slave, became a manumitted slave, became sufficiently poor or ill as to require financial support, owned property along a new highway, lent money to the Cause, left for or returned from military service, took the freeman's oath, took the oath of fidelity/allegiance, and more. Lists of those who took the oath of fidelity/allegiance or the freeman's oath are included if I could find the original lists.

With few exceptions, annual meetings were held in December and often adjourned into January or February. Special meetings could be held at any time and could also be adjourned into the following months.

Meeting records may be continued into another volume, so there may be duplication of page numbers. After checking the meeting date, readers should check the first page of each town section to determine the town book containing that date's entry. Some town books were not paginated; in these cases, I assigned page numbers, identified by the use of brackets.

A person may be mentioned more than once on a page of the minutes. Duplicate entries have been removed from the index, so readers should be careful to read through the entire page of the minutes. Note also that the superscript feature has been removed from the index to save space; therefore, some names appear different in the index, i.e., Jos^h , an abbreviation for Josiah, appears as "Josh" in the index and W^o, an abbreviation for widow, appears as "Wo".

The parent town list gives the incorporation date of each town and from which town(s) each was created. Readers should consult this list if the town of interest is not included in these volumes.

Meeting records for Barkhamsted, Lyme and Waterbury could not be located. If readers have information on the present locations of these records or could assist in the retrieval and/or photocopying of these records, all discretion will be used.

Researchers may be familiar with *Non-Military Service in the Revolutionary War from Extracts Connecticut Town Council Minutes, 1774-1784,* prepared in the 1960's by Connecticut Daughters of the American Revolution. That work transcribed microfilmed reports made by town clerks in response to a request made in 1898 by the state librarian. The original request was not found, but it is clear that the towns were asked to provide names and duties of town officials during the Revolutionary War. However, seventeen of the original eighty towns presumably did not comply and are not included and many others only provided lists of those who were likely considered more important, such as town clerks or committees of inspection or safety. That work is not included here.

Undoubtedly, these pages contain errors. I'm sure I've misread, misunderstood, mistyped and mis-whatever elsed in these almost 75,000 entries. Still, my hope is that this will be seen as a good and lasting work.

Jolene Roberts Mullen
New Milford, CT
2011

Ashford

Ashford Town Records
1728-1804

Located at the Connecticut State Archives

Ashford

25 Aug 1774

Benj[a] Sumner Esq[r] Moderator	194
Voted that Cap[t] Jedediah Fay Cap[t] Ichabod Ward Cap[t] Elish Wales Benj[a] Sumner Esq[r] Amos Babcock Esq[r] and.. M[r] Ingolsbe Work be a Com[tee].. to Confer with the Com[tee] of Correspondants.. of this or the Neighbouring Colonies.. and to take in Subscriptions.. for our Distressed Bretheren at Boston	194
Benj[n] Sumner Esq[r] Moderator	199
Voted.. that Cap[t] Benj[n] Clark Cap[t] Caleb Hende &.. Samson Keyes Shall be a Com[tee] of Inspection	199

10 Apr 1775

Benj[n] Sumner Esq[r] Moderator	200
Voted.. that Cap[t] Ichabod Ward & Benj[n] Sumner Esq[r] Shall be Agents for the Town to Attend the General Assembly in May	200
Will[m] Knowltons Rate in W[m] Snows Hand shall be Abated	200

12 Sep 1775

Benj[n] Sumner Esq[r] Moderator	201
Voted.. that Benj[n] Sumner Esq[r] and Lef[t] Ezra Smith Shall be Agents.. to the General Assembly in October	201
Voted.. that M[rs] David Bolles Cap[t] Caleb Hende and Joseph Woodward Shall be a School Com[tee] to Provide School Masters	201

2 Dec 1775

Benj[n] Sumner Esq[r] Moderator	202
En[s] John Holmes Leu[t] Reuben Marcy M[r] Nath[ll] Loomis Cap[t] Simeon Smith Cap[t] Caleb Hende Chose Select Men	202
Meeting.. Adjour[nd] for a Quarter of an hour to the Hous of.. Isaac Perkins by Reason of y[d] Could	202
E[n] Bolles Chose Town Clerk and town Treas[r]	202
Cap[t] David Booles Chose Constable and to Gather the Colony Rate	202
W[m] Snow Leu[t] John Warren M[r] Jonah Rogers Constables Leu[t] John Warren Dismist by Vote from Being Constable	202
M[r] Joseph Kendal Chose Surveyor for the first Dist Mr Ephraim Lyon 2[d].. Mr John Frink 3[d] M[r] Frink Dism[st] and Ens[n] John Russell 3[d] John Frink 4th Amasa Watkins 5th John Knox 6th Cap[t] Ward 7th Cap[t] Ward Dism[st] Dan[ll] Lewis 7th Medina Preston 8th Ezekiel Holt 9th Cap[t] Ward 10th and Reconsid[rd] James Wheton 10th Calvin Eaton 11th James Whiton Chose for.. 11th & Reconsid[rd] Jacob Preston 12th Elisha Ellis 13th Leu[t] Marcy 14th of highways	202
Tho[s] Butler Stephen Johnson Chose fence Veiwors	202
Tho[s] Butler Elisha Ellis Je[d] Watkins Joel Ward Joseph Work John Frink Listers - Je[d] Watkins Dism[st]	202
Joseph Eaton Sealer of Leather	202
Job Robbins Ebe[r] Mason Ju[r] James Fitch Sumner Grand Juriors	202
Simeon Smith Ephraim Walker Sam[ll] Bicknell James Snow Jon[th] Chapman Ju[r] Tything Men	202
Simeon Smith Isaac Perkins John Holmes Ju[r] Tho[s] Stebbins Joseph Kendal Branders of Horses and Kee Keepers	202

Ashford

Sam^{ll} Snow Henery Lee Wm Chubb Sealer of Weights & Measures *202*

4 Dec 1775

1st Destrict Begins at the North East Corner of the Town Next to Pomfret.. West upon Woodstock Line to Still River .. Southerly Down Still River to Stoddards Soder Swamp Brook Including half the Bridges on S^d River.. Easterly up S^d Brook to Pomfret Line Including John Pitts & Excluding the Boens   *203*

2nd Destrict Begins at the South west Corner of the first Destrict: at the Soder Swamp Brook.. to Mr Sam^{ll} Snows Saw Mill on Biggalow River.. Down S^d River to Mansfield Line Including all East to Pomfret Line Excluding Ephraim Spaulding   *203*

3rd Destrict Begins at the North west Corner of the first Destrict.. to Daniel Allens Northwest Corner of his farm.. to the East End Buring Place.. South to Stoddards Line from thence So far West to Include the farm that was formerly Edward Watkins to Biggalow River.. Down the River to Samuel Snows Saw Mill.. up S^d River to the first Mentioned Bounds Including Half the Bridges on the Still River & Bungee   *203*

4th Destrict Begins at Daniel Allens North West Corner of his farm.. Runing Round upon Woodstock line to Christal Pond to Ephraim Peabody South line of his farm.. Westerly to the Road that Leads to Solomon Keyes.. Southerly on S^d Road Including Joseph Work Ju^r and Daniel Bartlet to Biggalow Bridge by the Potash viz) the whole of Said Road & the one half of the Bridge on Biggelow River & Still Down S^d River.. Southerly Down Biggalow River to Biggalow Bridge Including the whole of S^d Bridge & Still Down the River till it Comes to the 3rd Destrict.. Includi[*ng*] [ ] the Mill Road to Sam^{ll} Snows Mill   *203*

6th Destrict Begins at Westford North East Corner.. Runing to Ashford North West Corner.. Runing Southerly on the Town Line till it Comes to Henery Ammedowns Land.. Easterly to Samuel Springs Land.. to Westford Buring Place Near Samuel Knoxes.. to Job Tylers.. Runing Easterly to where Joseph Robbins South Line Crosses Biggelow River from thence up the River to the first Mentioned Corner Including Samuel Spring David Chaffee & Job Tyler   *204*

7th Destrict Beginning at Biggalow River East of John Masons.. Westerly 10 Rods North of Seril Browns House: Including John Mason: .. Northerly 10 rods West of Joshua Eatons House Still Northerly till it Strikes the South Line of the Sixth Destrict Including Jacob Chapman & Willm Rice and also the one Half of the Biggalow Bridge at the Potash   *204*

8th Destrict Beginning at Samuel Allens N.W. Corner of his farm.. Southerly to Capt Thomas Knowltons Including Capt Knowlton & Phineas Watkins.. Westerly So far as to Include the Bridge from thence to the Crotch of the Roads west of Amos Kendals that Leads to Capt Clarks from thence to Asa Davinsons Including Asa Davinson.. Westerly to the west Branch of Mount Hope River..   *204*

9th Destrict Begins at Willington Line.. Southerly on S^d Line to the Highway Leading by Widow Walkers House Including S^d Road till it Comes to Westford Meeting house.. Easterly till it Strikes the River to Include the House that was Daniel Eldriges.. Northerly by S^d River to the South LIne of the Sixth Destrict..   *205*

10th Destrict Begins at Willington Line the Northwest Corner of the 9th Destrict.. a Road that Leads from En^s Benjamin Walkers to Willington then Easterly on S^d Road to ye road that Comes from Union to Capt Clarks Including the fore Mentioned Road Excluding the Inhabitants South of the Road then to the Crotch of Mount Hope or 8th Destrict   *205*

11th Destrict Begins at the Southwest corner of the 10th Destrict on Willington Line.. South on S^d Line till it Comes to Mansfield Line thence by Mansfield Line East So far as to Exclude Mathew Road thence North Easterly to Exclude Jacob Preston and Inclule Calvin Eaton.. Northerly Including Josiah Chaffee thence to the Road Called Walkers Road ten rods East of Daniel Knowltons Including Thomas Wing thence to the first Mentioned Bounds   *205*

Ashford

12th Destrict Begins at the South East Corner of the 11th Destrict in Manfield Line on the Hill South of Mathew Road .. Easterly on S^d Line to Mount Hope River.. North on S^d River till it Comes to the BridgeWest of Capt Knowlton.. Westerly on the South Side of the Road Called Walkers till it Comes within ten Rods East of Daniel Knowltons this Destrict to Make & Maintain one Half of the two South Bridges on Mount hope River	205
13th Destrict Begins on Mount Hope River in Mansfield Line thence on Mansfield North Line till it Comes to a Road.. that Leads from Mr Boutwells to Ashford Meeting house thence by S^d Road North till.. the Road that Goes from Leu^t Marcy to Isaac Kendals then on S^d Road So as to Exclude S^d Kendal.. North so as to Exclude Capt Hende.. to the Road by Mr Eising then North by S^d Road till it Comes to the Country Road Excluding S^d Road & Capt Wales.. North by the Meeting house ten rods No[rth] of Cyrel Brown Including S^d Brown thence North westerly by the 7th Destrict to Mr Sam^{ll} Allens North Line so as to Include S^d Allen thence from the North west Corner of S^d Allens farm.. Westerly to Capt Knowltons Excluding S^d Knowlton.. to Mount hope River then on S^d River to the first Mentioned Bounds	206
14th Destrict Begins at Biggelow River East of John Mason .. Westerly on the 7th Destrict to Cyrel Browns.. Southerly to Isaac Kendals Including Capt Wales & Capt Hende & S^d Kendal then.. Southerly on S^d Road to Mansfield Line Including the Inhabitants on S^d Road then East on S^d line to Biggelow River then Northerly on S^d River to the first Mentioned Bounds Including the Bridges on S^d River So far	206
Ingolsby Work.. Reuben Marcy.. Josiah Spaulding.. Ebenezer Walker.. Ezra Smith.. Edward Sumner Ju^r.. John Holmes Ju^r Benjamin Clark } Com^{tee} [*gave Report to Divide the Town into Destricts for Highways*]	206
8 Apr 1776	
Benj^a Sumner Esqr Moderator	207
Capt Simeon Smith Chose Clerk pro tem^{ry}	207
Benja Sumner Esqr and Liu^t Ezra Smith be Agents to the General Assembly at Hartford in May	207
Josiah Spaulding be a One in Addition to the Com^{tee} of Correspondance	207
Capt Simeon Smith be one in Addition to the Above Com^{tee}	207
Meeting to Chuse 3 Men as a Com^{tee} to Examin.. State of ye Town Treas^y..Esqr Whiton Capt Clark & Lieut Spaulding be a Com^{tee} for the .. Purpose	207
Joseph Holmes be Appointed to take care of the wood and Timber on the Meeting house Green and Prosecute any Trespass	207
10 Apr 1776	
Benjn Sumner Esqr Moderator	208
Capt Benj^a Clark & Capt Elisha Wales Shall be Agents.. to the General Assembly in October	208
Joseph Woodward Chose a School Com^{tee} Man & Dismis^d	208
Leu^t John Warren.. Jonathan Chapman and.. Sam^{ll} Snow Shall be a School Com^{tee}	208
town will Dispose of.. Land Lying a Little E^s of Capt Benj^a Clarks Dwelling house to any Person by a Quit Clame Deed.. E^n Byles Shall be Agent for the town..	208
2 Dec 1776	
Elisha Wales Moderator	209
Meeting.. Shall be Adjornd to the house of Mr Isaack Perkins	209
Capt Caleb Hende Mr Nath^{ll} Lomis Capt Simeon Smith Mr Edward Sumner Ju^r Mr Josiah Spalding Chose Select Men	209

Ashford

E^{ns} Byles Town Clerk & Treas^r	209
Mr Ephraim Walker Chose Constable and Reconsidered	209
Mr Phinehas Birchard Chose Constable and to Gather the Colony Rate	209
Mr James F Sumner & Mr William Snow Constables	209
Mrs Joseph Kendal Jonth Chapman John Russell Ebe^r Bosworth Joseph Griggs Salvenus Shirtlif Sam^{ll} Eaton Medina Preston Asa Farnum Joseph Woodward John Uttley Josiah Chaffee Sam^{ll} Bicknell Thos Butler Capt Elisha Wales Surveyors of high Ways.. Mr Woodward Reconsidrd	209
Mr Stephen Johnson & Mr Thos Butler Chose fence Viewers	209
Mr Joel Ward Thos Butler Elisha Ellis John Frink Joseph Work Joseph Whiton Ju^r Chose Listors - Joel Ward Reconsidrd.. The Constables Chose Collectors of Rates	209
Capt Elisha Wales Chose Sealer of Leather	209
Mr Ephraim Walker Sam^{ll} Bicknell Dan^{ll} Allen Ju^r Chose Grand Juriors	209
Mrs Asa Eaton Jedediah Dana Ju^r Eben^r Eaton Francus Green Chaffee Asa Farnum Eben^r Wright Chose tything Men	209
Mrs Isaac Perkins Joseph Kendal John Utley Aaron Cook Chose Brandors of Horses	209
Mrs Sam^{ll} Snow & Henery Lee Sealers of weights & Measures	209
Mr Aaron Cook & John Utley Kee keepers	209
Voted.. that Mrs Sam^{ll} Snow Jonth Chapman John Warren be a Com^{tee} to take Care of the towns Loan Moneys	209
17 Feb 1777	
Capt Elisha Wales Moderator	210
Meeting Shall be Adjornd to Do^r Hows Chamber	210
Voted.. to Reconsider the former Votes that Were past last Decr in Chusing James F Sumner Constable and Collector	210
Voted.. that Mr Jonathan Chapman Shall be Constable.. and Collector for the Town Rate	210
Voted.. that Mr Jonth Chapman Shall be Collector to Gather the Remainder of.. Rates left in the hand of John Holmes Ju^r Deas^t	210
28 Mar 1777	
Benj^a Sumner Esqr Moderator	210
Meeting Shall be Abjornd to D^{or} Hows Chamber	210
Voted.. to Chuse a Com^{tee} for y^e Purpose Mentioned in y^e Governors Proclamation.. Voted.. that Benj^a Sumner Esqr.. Mr Simeon Dean Jonth Chapman Zachariah Bicknell Edward Sumner Ju^r Nath^{ll} Loomis Capt Eben^r Walker Jacob Preston Leu^t Ezra Smith Ingolsby Work Shall be a Com$^{[tee]}$ for that Purpose	210
Voted.. to Chuse a Com^{tee} of Inspection Mr Josiah Spauld[*ing*] and Ingolsby Work Chose.. Mr Edward Sumner Ju^r and Mr Spaulding Reconsidered & Capt John Work Thos Butler Zachariah Bicknell Elezar Warner Leu^t John Warren Leu^t Ezra Smith Chose as a Com^{tee}	210
Voted.. to Abate Mr John Pitts Rate for.. 1775	210
7 Apr 1777	
Jacob Dana Esqr Moderator	211
Meeting Shall be Adjor^d to the house of Nehemiah How	211

Ashford

Benj^a Sumner Esqr & Maj^r Benj^a Clark Shall be Agents.. to Attend ye Gen^{ll} Assembly in May	211

9 Sep 1777

Capt Elisha Wales Moderator	211
Capt Jedidiah Fay & Leu^t Ezra Smith Shall be Agents.. to Attend.. Gen^{ll} Assembly in October	211
Voted.. that Mrs Jonathan Chapman Sam^{ll} Snow and John Warren be a School Com^{tee} to Provide School Masters	211
Voted.. that Capt Eben^r Walker be one of ye Com^{tee} to Provide for Solgers' famalys	212
Voted.. that Mr Nath^{ll} Loomis be Dismist from Being one of s^d Com^{tee}	212
Voted.. that Mr Calvin Eaton be one of ye Com^{te} to Provide for Solgers' famalys	212
Granted.. the Balance of Maj^r Thos Knowltons Acmp^t Being £3:16.0 ~	212
Voted.. to Chuse a Com^{tee} to View the Places for a Road or Roads East & West of Byles land	212
Voted.. that Capt Caleb Hende Mr Samson Keyes & Joseph Woodward be a Com^{tee} for that Purpose	212
Voted.. to Chuse a Com^{tee} to Joyn the Listers in Assessing the Inhabitants.. Voted.. that Mrs Ingolsbe Work Maj^r Benjn Clark Leu^t John Warner be a Com^{tee} for that purpose	212

2 Oct 1777

Benjn Sumner Esqr Moderator	212
Meeting Shall be Adjorn^d to Do^r Hows Chamber	212
Voted.. that C$^{[ ]}$ Byles be Impower^d to Sell y^e Road Est of Maj^r Clarks Land that Sam^{ll} Woodcock Deeded to S^d Town	212

1 Dec 1777

Elijah Whiton Esqr Moderator	213
Isaac Perkins be Town Clark	213
Voted.. that Capt Caleb Hendee Mr Nat^l Loomis Capt Sim^n Smith Capt Reuben Marcy Lieu^t Josiah Spaulden and Maj^r Benj^a Clarke be Select Men Nat Lomis Reconsidered	213
Voted Isaac Perkins Town Tresurer	213
Voted Mr Elisha Ellis Constable to gather ye Country Tax Reconsi^d	213
Voted Mr Edward Sumner Jun: Counstable to gather the Country Tax and Mr Medinah Preston and Mr Jonathan Chapman Constables	213
Voted Mrss Joseph Kendel Aaron Tuffs Eben^r Write Jonath Chapman Robert Leach Jedad^h Dana Junr Capt Asaph Smith Jno Abbot Eben^r Mason Junr Jacob Preston Eleazar Warner Thos Chapman James Wheton David Chaffee and Hez^h Eldridge Surveyers	213
Voted Mrss Thomas Butler and Stephen Johnson Fence Viewers	213
Voted Mrss Elisha Ellis Thos Butlar Joseph Whiton Joseph Work Jno Frink & Solomon Keyes Leicesters Jno Frink Reconsidered	213
Voted Edward Sumner Junr Jona. Chapman & Medina Preston Collectors of Town Tax	213
Voted Capt Elisha Wales Leather Sealer	213
Voted Capt Elisha Wales Mess Elisha Ellis & Joseph Woodard Grand Juriors also Mr Job Tyler	213
Voted Mrss Cirel Brown Capt Asaph Smith Joseph Kendall Ephraim Spaulding Hez^h Eldridge & Thos Chapman Junr Tithing Men	213
Voted Mrss Joseph Kendell Aaron Cooke & Capt Sim^n Smith Brandors of Horses and Key	213

Ashford

keepers

Voted Mrss Samuel Snow & Henry Lee Sealers of Weights & Measures	213
Voted To Adjourn.. Meeting one quarter of an hour to Land^d Perkins on Acc^t of ye Cold	213
Voted To Choose a Com^{tee} to Settle with Mr Boyles ye Late Treasurer… Capt Wales Capt Fay & Maj^r Benj^a Clarke be S^d Comm^{tee}	213

8 Dec 1777

Voted ~~that~~ a Comm^{tee} of Nine men Jonath Chapman Joseph Work (Solo^n Keyes Recon^d) Joel Utley (Zeche^h Becknal Recon^d) Capt Asaph Smith Ephraim Walker Jno Warner & Capt Squire Hill & Capt Jno Work & Calvin Eaton to Supply the Families of those non Comm^d Officers and Soldiers now in Cont^l Service	214
Voted To Recons^r Mr Thomas Elisha Ellis and Joseph Work listers.. Voted in their room Joel Utley Wm Abbot and Clap Sumner	214
Voted To Adjourn'd the Meeting one quarter of an hour to Isaac Perkins on Acc^t of growing Dark	214
Voted To chose a Comm^{tee} Capt Elisha Wales Maj Benj^a Clark & Elijah Whiton Esqr to Enquire into all Matters relative to ye Moneys Sequestered to the Use of the Ministry	214
Voted That Phinehas Burchard be be remov'd from the district he now Lives in to that where ye School Stands near Land^d Utley	214
Voted That Thos Butler may build a Horse Shed in some Convenient place on the meeting House Green	214
Voted That Maj^r Benj^a Clark be a Comm^{tee} to take care of the Meeting House Green and Prosecute all Damage done	214
Voted that Capt Caleb Hendees Acc^t as Select Man to be Allow'd being £1 12-0	214
Voted To Allow Mr Nat Loomis Acc^t for Serving as Select Man £6 4-0	214

6 Jan 1778

Benjamin Sumner Esqr Moderator	215
Committee.. to Supply the Families of the non Commissioned Officers and Soldiers now in Cont^{al} Service provid for ye Family of Ephraim Spauldings Spaulding now in.. Service	215

13 Apr 1778

Benj^a Sumner Esqr Moderator	216
Voted Maj^r Benjamin Clark and Capt Simeon Smith Agents to Attend ye General Assembly	216
Voted to choose a Com^{tee} to Settle with ye Com^{tee} Appointed to provide for ye Families of ye Non Com^{ond} Oficers and Soldiers now in Contin^{al} Service .. Voted that Capt Elisha Wales Maj^r Benj^a Clark & Capt Simeon Smith be ye Com^{tee} Capt Smith Recon^{ded}.. Voted Isaac Perkins in ye room of Capt Sim^n Smith	216

27 Apr 1778

Voted That the Com^{tee} appointed to provide for ye Families of the Non Commisioned Officers and Soldiers provid for Elizabeth Knowlton	216

7 May 1778

Voted.. that they Except ye Report of ye Com^{tee} Capt Wales Maj^r Benj^a Clark Capt Fay appointed to Settle with ye former Treasurer Mr Byles	217
Voted to Allow Mr Brandon the meet that is in ye hands of Capt Asaph Smith which was purchased for Mr Brandon	217
Voted To Grant to Jonathan Chapman pay for what he had delt out to Mr Bowen	217

Ashford

We Report that y^e former Treasurer Mr Byles in our Oppinions owes the Town nothing, And hear are y^e Rec^{ts} we found with him.. Then Rece^d of Eben^r Byles town Treasurer £20-0-0 LM part of y^e fines for Draughted Men.. [*signed*] Caleb Hende } Select Man	217
Then Rec^d of Eben^r Byles town Treasurer £51=5.0 Part of the fines paid in to S^d Treas^r -- Edward Sumner Junr } Select Man *22 Dec 1777*	217
Then Rec^d of Eben^r Byles £15-0.0..part of y^e fines paid to S^d Byles as town treasurer -- Reuben Marcy } Select Man *7 May 1778*	217
Then Rec^d of Eben^r Byles town Treasurer £66=7-0.. Isaac Perkins Town Treasurer	217
We found Notes of hand in Mr Byles Custody.. Two Notes against Saml Holmes.. [ ]3.12.11.. One against Jno Sumner 5.12.6.. Rec^d Isaac Perkins town Treas^r { Elisha Wales.. Benj^a Clark.. Jedediah Fay { Committee *8 Sep 1778*	217
Benj^a Sumner Eq^r Moderator	218
Voted.. Maj^r John Keys and Capt Simeon Smith Agents to Attend ye General Court in October	218
Voted Mr Ebenezer Mason Junr Mr Abijah Brooks and.. Ephraim Lyon a School Com^{tee} *7 Dec 1778*	218
Benj^a Sumner Esqr Moderator	218
Voted Isaac Perkins Town Clerk and Treasurer	218
Voted Capt Simeon Smith.. Edward Sumner Junr Maj^r John Keys Benjamin Sumner Esqr and Capt Caleb Hendee Select Men	218
Voted Josiah Spaulding Constable Reconsidered	218
Voted Ephraim Lyon Constable to Collect ye Country Tax.. Ens^n Asa Eaton 2^d Constable & Joseph Woodard 3^d Constable	218
Voted Ingolsbe Work Caleb Grosvenor Capt Jno Work Jonathan Chapman Ens^n Joseph Burnham Elisha Ellis Joseph Woodard Junr Calvin Eaton Zepheniah Davison William Walker Daniel Dimock Abijah Brooks Thos Stibbins & Amasa Watkins Surveyor of highways	218
Voted Thos Butler Stephen Johnson fence Viewers	218
Voted Leiu^t Jno Warren Joseph Amadown Job Tyler Thos Butler Elisha Ellis Ens^n Joseph Burnham Inglesbee Work John Busect Joseph Kendall (Job Tyler Recons^d) & William Walker Listers	218
Voted Ephraim Lyon Asa Eaton & Joseph Woodard Collectors of town Taxes	218
Voted Capt Elisha Wales Leather Sealer	218
Voted Cyrel Brown Joseph Work and Peter Eastman Grand Juriors	218
Voted (Joseph Burnham Recon^d Joel Utley Recon^d) Benj^a Snow Amos Woodard Eben^r Bozworth Caleb Grosvenor Solomon Smith Joseph Chapman Tithingmen	218
Voted Joseph Kendall Aaron Cook Zepheniah Davison Brander of horses and Key keepers	218
Voted Saml Snow & Henry Lee Sealers of Weights & Measures	218
Voted Saml Snow William Chub Capt David Boles (David Chaffee Junr Recon^d) Maj^{or} Benj^a Clark Samuel Spring Lieu^t Josiah Spaulding Jonath Chaffee Junr Joel Ward Capt Asaph Smith John Kendell Ju^r & Benjamin Walker a Com^{tee} to Supply ye Officers and Soldiers Families	218

Ashford

now in Service	
Voted to Adjourn.. Meeting half an hour Night coming on to Land^d Perkins East Chamber	219
Voted Isaac Perkins Capt Elisha Wales & Cyrel Brown be a Com^{tee} to Settle with ye Com^{tee} Appointed to Supply ye Soldiers Famelies with Necesarys &c	219
Voted To Annex Sq^r Brown Elisha Ellis Cyrel Brown and Esqr Babcock to ye school District known by ye Name of Holmes District	219
Voted to Allow Leiu^t Josiah Spauldind [sic] for Service done ye Town [ ]^s/24^d/	219

1 Mar 1779

Benjamin Sumner Esqr Moderator	219
Voted to Allow James Brown Esqr eighteen Shillings for ye use of his House one Year and a half while ye Family of Mr Waterous lived in the [*House*]	219
Voted to allow Capt Asaph Smith £2 on Acc^t of a forty Shilling Connecticut Bill he Recv out of ye Treasury which was Counter^t	219

12 Apr 1779

Benjamin Sumner Esqr Moderator	220
Voted to choose Agents to Attend ye General Assembly next Sessions.. Voted Capt Simeon Smith & Maj^r Jno Keyes Agents	220

26 Apr 1779

Benjamin Sumner Esqr Moderator	220
Voted to pursue ye memorial that is now in ye General Assembly Relitive to Corbins heirs and this Town	220
Voted Mr Cyrel Brown Capt Elisha Eales & Capt Caleb Hendee a Com^{tee} to Settle with ye Treas^r	220
Voted That ye Town Agents Capt Simeon Smith and Maj^r Jno Keyes to prosecute ye above Memorial at ye General Assembly	220
Voted Edward Sumner £30.. for 4 Blankets that were Burnt at ye Mill that he paid his money for in behalf of ye Town	220

3 Sep 1779

Capt Elisha Wales Moderator	220
Voted To choose a Com^{tee} to send to Windham to meet ye County Convenon to Consult matters reletive to ye Courency & prices ~ ..Voted Maj^r Jno Keyes (Capt Simeon Smith Recond) Maj^r [ ] Benj^a Clark & Elisha Wales to be.. S^d Com^{tee}	220
Voted Eben^r Bozworth Surveyor of highways	220

14 Sep 1779

Benj^a Sumner Esqr Moderator	221
Voted Maj^r Jno Keys & Capt Simion Smith Agents to attend at ye General Assembly next Session	221
Voted The Town do Except ye Report of ye Com^{tee} Appointed to Settle with Mr Perkins ye Town Treas^r That ye Treas^r owes ye Town nothing	221
Voted To chose a Com^{tee} to send to Hartford to meet ye Conventions.. and that Maj^r Benj^a Clark should be the Man	221

6 Dec 1779

Benj^a Sumner Moderator	222

Ashford

Maj^r Benj^a Clarke, Capt Simeon Smith Mr Isaac Perkins Mr Edward Sumner Junr & Mr Jno Russel Selectmen	222
Voted Isaac Perkins Town Clerk & Treas^r	222
Voted Samuel Spring Constable to Collect ye Contry & town Tax Capt Wales Con^{ble} to Collect ye Town Tax & Capt Asaph Smith Constable to Collect ye town Tax	222
Voted Saml Whipple Frances Chaffee Tim^o Russ Benj^a Preston Sampson Keys Joseph Snow Junr Jno Smith Noah Payne Lieu^t Josiah Spaulding John Russell James Sumner Wm Snow Ephraim lyon Amasa Watkins Jacob Chapman Lieu^t Warner Oliver Hinchen and Maj^r Clark Surveyors of highways	222
Voted Thos Butler & Stephen Johnson Fenceviewers	222
Voted To have Seven listers Lieu^t Josiah Spaulding Joseph Burnham Wm Snow Squire Hill Dr Huntington Calvin Eaton & Eben^r Mason Junr	222
Voted Capt Asaph Smith Leather Sealer	222
Voted Dea^n Loomis Eben^r Walker Grand Jurors	222
Voted Tim^o Russ Tim^o Dimock Calvin Eaton & Capt Hendee tythingmen	222
Voted Joseph Kendall Aaron Cooke Calvin Eaton & Asa farnham Branders of horses	222
Voted Saml Snow Sealer of Weights & Measures	222
Voted Aaron Cooke Key keepers	222
15 Dec 1779	
Benj^a Sumner Moderator to Adjournd^d Meeting to land^d Perkins on Acc^t of ye Cold	222
Voted to have a Com^{tee} of three Men to Supply Soldiers Familys.. Voted Capt Reuben Marcy Timothy Dimock & Jonath Chapman S^d Com^{tee}	222
Voted Thos Wing Abijah Brooks Cyrel Brown Englesby Work & Saml Eaton be a Com^{tee} for ye Clothing	222
Voted Eben^r Mason Junr Ephaim Lyon & Abijah Broks School Com^{tee}	222
9 Mar 1780	
Benj^a Sumner Esqr Moderator	223
Voted Francies G. Chaffee one of ye Grandjuriors	223
Voted A Com^{tee} to move ye Impediments out of ye highway Leeding by Tim^o Russes Squire Hill Wm Warker Junr & Knox ye Com^{tee}	223
10 Apr 1780	
Elijah Whiton Esqr Moderator	223
Voted that Edward Sumner & Dea^n Nathaniel Loomis shall be Agents to attend ye General Assembly next May Session	223
Voted To Release to Capt Simeon Smith a Certain parcel of Land.. formerly S^d Capt Smiths land & was laid out as highway and is on ye West ~~part~~ End of his farm And to give to him 150 £ in Money In case.. Smith shall Execute a good Deed.. of that part of his land that was lately lade out as highway.. that leads from Jno Russels house to Asa Farnum [ ] house where it meets ye Road that leads from.. Farnams to Westford Meeting house	223
Voted That John Russel and Josiah Spaulding be a Com^{tee} to assist Peter Smith to Reckon with ye Com^{tee} of Supplies	223
Voted That Capt Elijah Babcock Capt Reuben Marcy & Leiu^t Jno Warren be a Com^{tee} to meet other Com^{tees} at Land^d Leavens Mansfield to Consult Matters Reletive to.ye late Acts passed by ye Gene^l Assm^y	223

Ashford

[ ] May 1780

Elijah Whiton Esqr Moderator	224
Voted To Choose a Com^{tee} to Settle with ye Com^{tees} of Supplys.. Voted Isaac Perkins & Capt Simeon Smith Com^{tee}	224
Voted Simeon Tiffany Surveyor of highways in lew of Sampson Keys	224

22 Jun 1780

Benj^a Sumner Esqr Moderator	224
Voted to give ye 19 Soldiers which this Town is Ordered to raise.. in Addition to ye State Encouragement 10^s/ p^r Month.. and to pay the at ye end of their 6 Months.. Voted a Com^{tee} of 19 to Assist ye Officers in Obtaining ye s^d 19 Soldiers Maj^r Clark, Capt Hendee, Benj^a Sumner Esqr, Capt Sim Smith Capt Hill Capt John Sumner Lieu^t Preston Lieu^t Walker Dr How Maj^r Keys Capt Babcock Ens^n Walker Lieu^t Spaulding Lieu^t Tyler lieu^t Warren Lieu^t Russel Capt Wales Ens^n Lyon Capt Marcy	

12 Sep 1780

Benj^a Sumner Moderator	225
Voted Maj^r Jno Keys & Capt Simeon Smith be Ag^{ts} to Attend ye General Assembly.. Octr next	225
Voted To choose an agent to attend ye Superior Court.. this Instant Sep^r .. Voted Elijah Whiton Esqr Ag^t	225
Voted That Capt Reuben Marcy Capt Simeon Smith Benj^a Turner Esqr be a Com^{tee} to look into ye Situation of ye Ministry Money	225
Voted Eben^r Mason Junr Abijah Brooks & Ephraim Lyon School Com^{tee}	225

14 Nov 1780

Benj^a Sumner Esqr Moderator	225
Voted to Raise a Tax of one Shilling L.M. on ye pound on ye list 1779 to be Collected for ye purpose of Purchasing Provisions Ordered to be Collected by ye Genl Assem^y.. Voted Dr Nehemiah How Mr Joel Ward lieu^t Jno Russel a Com^{tee} or Receivors to receive S^d Provisions	225
Voted Maj^r Clark Maj^r Keys Capt Hendee Capt Fay Esqr Sumner Capt Jno Sumner Ephra lyon Ens Kendall Capt Hill Capt Sim Smith Joseph Woodward Ens Wm Walker a Com^{tee} to Class ye Town	225

4 Dec 1780

Benj^a Sumner Esqr Moderator	226
Maj^r Benj^a Clark Edward Sumner Capt Simeon Smith Capt Squire Hill & Capt David Bolls Select Men	226
Voted Josiah Byles Town Clerk and Town Treas^r	226
Voted Capt Marcy Recons^d) Timothy Dimock & Joseph Kendall & Mathew Reed Constables, Reed to Collect ye Contry Tax	226
Voted Capt David Bolls Aaron Tuffs Jonathan Chapman Nathan Griggs Joseph Griggs Hez^h Smith Thos Butler Saml Eaton Josias Byles Stephen Snow Jabez Webb Medina Preston Tim^o Dimock Capt Squire Hill Calvin Eaton Asa Eaton Surveyors of highways	226
Voted Stephen Johnson & Thos Butler Fence Viewers	226
Voted listers Thomas Butler (Josiah Spaulding Recon^d) Capt Jno Work (Calvin Eaton Recond^d) Eben Mason Junr Wm Snow (Joseph Burnham Recons^d) Dr Huntington Medina Preston Ephraim lyon Capt Reuben Marcy listers	226

Ashford

Voted Capt Asaph Smith leather Sealer	226
Voted David Brown Phinehas Burchard Ephraim Spaulding Grand Juriors	226
Voted Eben^r Bozworth Joseph Griggs Manassih Farnam (Saml Johnson Recons^d) Eben^r Walker Junr Josiah Bugbee Asa Farnam Titheingmen	226
Voted Aaron Cooke Joseph Kendall Sim Smith Branders horses	226
Voted Dea^n Nat Loomis Capt Marcy a Com^{tee} to procure W^{ts} and Measures	226
Voted Isaac Perkins sealer of w^{ts} and Measures	226
Voted Aaron Cooke Key keeper	226
Voted Dea^n Nat Loomis Capt Hendee & Capt Marcy a Com^{tee} to move ye Town books and Settle with ye Treas^r	226
Voted that Simeon Smith and Isaac Perkins be a Committey to Recon with the Comittey of Supplyes	226

21 Dec 1780

Benjamin Sumner Moderator	227
Voted.. Ebenezer Sumner Constable & collector to gather the colony tax	227
Voted Joseph Byrnham Constable & collector to gather the town tax.. Dismist by Vote	227
Voted Capt Daniel Allen Constable & collector of Town tax.. Dismist by vote	227
Voted Joseph work Constable & collector of town tax.. Dismist by Vote	227
Voted Ebenezer Bosworth constable & collector of Town tax	227
Voted Ebenezer Sumner Collector of town rates	227
Voted Phineas Birchard Granjury man Dismist by vote	227
Voted Amos Kindall granjuryman	227
Voted Ephriam Lyon not Dismist from being Lister.. Dismist by vote	227
Voted Jonah Carpenter Lister	227
Voted Capt Simeon Smith be Desmist from being Select man	227
Voted Joseph Woodward Select man	227
Voted Nehemiah How Joel Ward Lieu^t John Rusell Collectors to collect the provision	227
Voted to Dismist Timothy Dimuck from being a from committee of Surplys	227
Voted Joseph Whiton committey of Surplys in Lieu^t of Mr Dimuck	227
Voted that the Select men Agest Joel Wards Accounts	227

15 Jan 1781

Benj^a Sumner Esqr Moderator	228
Voted to Chuse a Commity for to Ingage the Cota of men for this Town.. Voted Maj^r John Keyes Capt Simeon Smith Ephraim Lyon be the Commity	228
Voted to Chuse a Commity to Surply the Conennantal men of this Town now in the Army with Clothes.. Voted Joel Ward be the Commity	228
Voted that the Inhabitants pay one peney half peney on the pound in hard money or in Grain on the List 1779.. Do^r Nehemiah How Joel Ward Lieut John Russel Collectors and Receivers of the Same	228

Ashford

Voted Maj[r] John Keyes Agent for the Town to Draw the Wages which the Congress Allows	228
Voted Solomon Keyes Ephraim Lyon Cap[t] Marcy M[r] Perkins Joel Ward Solomon Wickwire Cap[t] John Sumner Sampson Keyes Cap[t] John Work William Hanfield David Bolls Samuel Eaton Abial Bugbe Stephen Snow Abil Simon Jun[r] Cap[t] Simeon Smith Be impowered with Aurthority for to Collect the money of Such persons as Shall be Delinquant or Refuse to pay.. their proportion of money	228

26 Feb 1781

Benj[a] Sumner Esq[r] Moderator	229
Voted to Chuse a Commity.. to Look up the Common and Undivided Lands -- Cap[t] Simeon Smith M[r] Benjamin Clark Edward Sumner Be the Comitty	229
Voted to take into Consideration.. the Title of Stodards Land..Voted to Chuse a Committy to Look into the Title.. Voted Cap[t] Simeon Smith M[r] John Keyes D[r] Nehemiah How Be the Committy	229

9 Apr 1781

Benjamin Sumner Esq[r] Moderator	229
Voted that Edward Sumner and Isaac Perkins be Agents to atend the General Assembly	229
Voted to Chuse a Commity.. to procure the men for the State Ser[vice] Voted Maj[r] John Keyes Cap[t] Marcy M[r] Benj[n] Clark Doc[r] How Cap[t] Hill Cap[t] Simeon Smith Insg[n] Will[m] Walker Joseph Woodward Insg[n] Lyon Cap[t] Allen Cap[t] John Sumner Cap[t] Bools be the Committy	229
Voted to Chuse an agent to meet the Committy at Windham Concerning the Continental men.. Voted Maj[r] Benj[a] Clark be the man	229

8 May 1781

Cap[t] Elisha Wales Moderator	230
Voted that the Town Accept a Deed of a Certain highway through Land of Joseph Prince David Robin David Chaffee Jun[r] David Chaffee Elias Chapman & Joseph Chapman	230

28 Jun 1781

Benjamin Sumner Moderator	230
Voted to Raise 4[d] on y[e] pound Either in Gold or Silver in Beaf.. Voted to Chuse three Collectors and Receivers of the Same.. Voted that Abel Dow Cap[t] John Sumner Lieu[t] Ebenezer Walker be the men for that purpose	230
Voted that the Town be att an Equal Expence and Shair an Equal Benefit in the Raising the Contenantal men for the present Campaign.. And Whereas their Being a Number of Contenantal men Listed into the Bay Stait from this Town.. Voted that Maj[r] John Keyes be Chosen as a Committey man.. to Look into the afair and to have Said men Count for the Town	230
Voted that the Town Look up and Sell their Sequested Land.. Voted that Maj[r] Benjamin Clark Edward Sumner Cap[t] Simeon Smith be a Committy for that purpose	230

16 Jul 1781

Benjamin Sumner Esq[r] Moderator	231
Voted to Chuse three Recevers to Receve Salt pack Secure &c the provision of those persons who Shall Chuse to pay y[e] 2/[ ] Tax Granted by the Assembly.. in S[d] Provision or other articles.. Voted Cap[t] Marcy Cap[t] Simeon Smith Cap[t] John Sumner be the persons	231
Voted that Each Class Shall procure 4 Shirts 4 pair of Overhalls and 2 Froks.. Voted Joel Ward be Chosen as a Committy man to Receve and forward the Same to the Commissary	231

Ashford

Voted to Release Cap[t] Smith from being Receiver	231
Voted that Elijah Whiton Esq[r] be Chosen in Lieu of Cap[t] Smith	231
11 Sep 1781	
Benj[a] Sumner Esq[r] Moderator	231
Voted M[r] John Keiyes D[r] Thomas Huntington Agents atend the General Assembly in October Next	231
Voted Insg[n] Lyon Ebn[r] Mason Jun[r] Joseph Woodard School Comity men	231
Voted Town accept the Doings of a Commity on certain highway through Land Belonging to David Millard.. Dec[t]	231
Voted M[r] Clark Edward Sumner Cap[t] Simeon Smith be Impourd as Agents to prosecute.. those that got the towns Comon Land in possesion	231
Whereas the town.. Laid out to Thomas Tiffany in.. 17[*18*] 200 Acres of land and to Joseph Olcutt 100 Acres which.. three hundred acres was afterward Sold to John [ ] of Barrington - Voted that the Town.. have had no Challengers.. over the 300 hund acres Since the Same was laid out.	231
3 Dec 1781	
Benj[a] Sumner Esq[r] Moderator	232
Cap[t] David Bools Edward Sumners Esq[r] Isaac Perkins Lieu[t] Will[m] Walker Joseph Woodard Select men Cap[t] Rubin Marcy Select men Edward Sumner Recons[d]	232
Voted Josias Byles town Clerk & Treas[r]	232
Voted Ebenezer Bosworth Ebenezer Sumner Timothy Dimuck Constables and Collectors Eben[r] Bosworth to Collect y[e] Colony Tax	232
Voted Thomas Butler Stephen Johnson fence viewers	232
Voted Joseph Works Jonathan Chapman Jonathan Bemas Eben[r] Wright David Allen Simeon Tiffany D[r] Howe Will[m] Snow Thomas Stibbins Calvin Eaton Moses Rodgers D[r] Joseph Palmer John Hanks Joseph Chapman Cap[t] Hill Joseph Snow Jun[r] Surveyors of highways	232
Voted Medinah Preston Jonah Carpenter Hezekiah Carpenter Aaron Cook Cap[t] Marcy James Howe Jun[r] Jabez Wee[ ] Listers	232
Voted Cap[t] Aseph Smith Leather Sealer	232
Voted Aaron Bosworth John Bosworth Eben[r] Mason Jun[r] Abel Simons Granjury men Eben[r] Mason Recons[d]	232
Voted Jonathan Chapman Eben[r] Bosworth John Pitts Daniel Dimuck Ransom Curtis Calvin Eaton Cap[t] Hendee Salvenus Shurtlif Samuel Johnston Tythingmen Eben[r] Bosworth Rec[d]	232
Voted Joseph Kindal David Brown Branders and Key keepers	232
Thomas Stebins Joel Ward Branders	232
Voted Dec[n] Nathanel Loomis Sealer of Weights and Measure	232
Voted Leiu[t] Job Tyler William Snow Lieu[t] Spaulding Francis Chaffe Comitys of Surplys Lieut Tyler Recon[d]	232
Voted to Chuse an Agent to atend the Next General Assembly.. Voted Elijah Whiton be the man	232
Voted D[r] Huntington & D[r] Palmer Inspect 2 Certain Bills of Account of D[r] Avriles and give their Opinion	232
Voted that the Select men Divide Destrict of highway in which [ ] Tifany and Joseph Snow Jun[r] are Serveyors	232

Ashford

Voted to Everidge ye money and Accounts Concerning ye Classes hiring Contenantal men -	232
Voted Major Clark Capt Bools Capt Marcy Capt Simeon Smith Lieu^t Spaulding be the Commity	
Voted Maj^r Clark be an Agent to Attend ye County Cort at Windham Concerning ye Case Between Gaven and Nathan Wales	232
Voted to Ajurn this meeting to Dr Hows	233
Voted that ye Town Accept of the Doings of a Commity on a Road through Land of Aaron Tufts and Esqr Babcock	233
Voted that ye Town Accept of a Road whare Joel Ward Offers to give in Lieu of one Laid out by a Commity through S^d Wards Land	233
Voted that ye Town Accept of ye Doings of a Commity on a Road from Solomon Smiths through Land of Dr Huntington to Joel Wards	233
Granted to Dr Thomas Huntington 5 pounds worth of Land.. for.. Land.. Huntington paid Capt Simeon Smith for a highway	233
Voted to Grant Mr Olds and other Liberty of a New Committy on a highway upon their own Cost Provided.. Commity Don't Asess more Damage than the former Committee	233
Voted to Accept of the Report and Doings of Mr John Russell and Mr Josiah Spaulding a Commity.. Chosen to Settle with Peter Smith and the Commity of Surplys	233
27 Feb 1782	
Benj^a Sumner Esqr Moderator	233
Voted to Chuse a Comitte .. to procure this Towns Quato of men.. Maj^r Keiyes Esqr Perkins Dr Howe Samuel Spring Capt Simeon Smith Capt Booles Insg^n Lyon Deacon Loomiss Maj^r Clark Joseph Kendall be a Comittee for the purpose.. Maj^r Keiys Esqr Perkins Capt Booles Reconsid^d	233
Voted to Chuse an agent to Wait on the Com^{tee} Appointed to meet Concerning the Continentall men.. Voted Capt Simeon Smith be the man	233
Voted to Chuse a Comitte to Settle the matter with Amos Dawset Concerning Sd Dawsets Working on the Comon Land.. Voted [*cut off*] Capt Wa[trus] Lieu^t Warren	233
Voted Mr Ebenezer Mason Junr be Impoured to collect the Money Due on School money Rates	234
8 Apr 1782	
Benj^a Sumner Esqr Moderator	234
Voted Esqr Whiton & Esqr Sumner be Agents.. to the General Assembly	234
Voted to Chuse a Com^{tee} to procure the 2 Soldiers.. wating for the Contenantall Armey.. Maj^r Clark Capt Simeon Smith Dr Howe be the Com^{tee}	234
22 Apr 1782	
Voted to Adjurn this meeting to Dr Howes west Room	234
Voted to Chuse a Com^{tee}.. to meet the Com^{tee} which are to meet at Tolland Concerning the Bill of Taxation.. Voted Dr Nemiah Howe & Maj^r Benj^a Clark be the Com^{tee}	234
10 Sep 1782	
Capt David Bolls Moderator	235
Voted Capt David Bolls & Capt Simeon Smith Agents to.. the General Assembly	235
Voted Esqr Clark Do^r Huntington Insg^n Lyon be a School Com^{tee}	235

15

Ashford

2 Dec 1782

Benj^a Sumner Esqr Moderator	236
Voted Capt David Bolls Esqr Perkins Capt Ruben Marcy Joseph Woodward Lieu^t Willm Walker Select men	236
Voted Josias Byles town Clerk & town Treas^r	236
Voted Joel Ward Constable and Collector and to Collect the Colony Tax	236
Voted Eben^r Sumner & Ebn^r Bosworth Constables and Collectors of Rates Eben^r Sumner Recons^d	236
Voted Abel Daw Constabel & Collector	236
Voted Joseph Works Joseph Peck Aaron Tuffts Josiah Spaulding Ebn^r Eaton Ebn^r Mason Ju^r Asa Eaton Stephen Johnston Jonathan Chaffee Moses Rodgers Mathew Reed Asa Farman Willm Knox John Warner Allen Bosworth Willm Bicknell Robert Leach Surveyors of highways Ebn^r Eaton Recons^d	236
Voted Thomas Butler Stephen Johnston fence Viewers	236
Voted Jabez Webb Medinah Preston Aaron Cook Abel Daw Jonah Carpenter Samuel Sumner James Hows Listers	236
Voted Capt Aseph Smith Leather Sealer	236
Voted Theday Dearning David Torrey Ebn^r Wright Lieu^t John Russell Grandjurymen Ebn^r Wright Recons^d	236
Voted Calven Eaton Joseph Whiton John Russell 2^d Jonathan Bemis Jonathan Chapman Ju^r David Brown Tythingmen	236
Voted Joseph Kindal Aaron Cook Joel Ward Branders and Key keepers	236
Voted Samuel Snow Decon Nath^{ll} Loomis Sealers of Weights and Measure	236
Voted Jeremiah Handley Abel Daw Moses Rodgers haywards - Recons^d	236
Voted that Bolls and Capt Clark be.. Impourd to Settel with Esqr Chandler and Esqr Wales and to give their Security to them.. for the Moneys Due from the town to them.. & to Ingage them..to Act as Atorneys for.. town in the case of Benj^a Marcey and the Town	237
Voted Ebn^r Bosworth Daniel Dimuck Capt Eleazer Warner Com^{tee} of Suplys for the soldiers familys	237

27 Jan 1783

Mr Joseph Woodward Moderator	237
Voted Ebenezer Mason Constabel and Collector of Town Tax.. Voted to Release Ebenezer Mason from being Surveyor of Highways	237
Voted David Brown Surveyor of Highways	237
Voted Timothy Dimuck a Committee of Surplys of the Continentals famelies	237

7 Apr 1783

Benjamin Sumner Esqr Moderator	238
Voted Benj^a Summner Esqr & Isaac Perkins Esqr be agents to.. the General Assembly	238
Voted to Chuse a Com^{tee} to Receve the accounts of those Classes that hired Continantal men.. Voted Esq^n Ephraim Lyon Lieu^t Willm Walker Capt Bools Capt Simeon Smith Capt Marcey be the Com^{tee}	238
Voted to Chuse a Com^{tee} to give Ebn^r Humphrey a Quit Claim Deed.. of Land where.. Humphrey now lives on Account of his Surcumstances &c.. Capt Simeon Smith Maj^r Clark	238

Ashford

Edward Sumner be the Com^tee	
Voted that the Selectmen be Desired to Receve.. the Accounts of Mr Kindal Mr Knox & Mr Russ for going to Boston after Salt	238
19 May 1783	
Maj^r Benjn Clark Moderator	238
Voted that Capt Dan^ll Allen Maj^r Benjn Clark and Simeon Smith be a Com^tee.. to adjust and Settle Acc^ts with the Soldiers that ware in the State Service the year past	238
Capt Dan^ll Allen Maj^r Benjn Clark and Simeon Smith be a Com^tee.. to Settle Acc^ts with the Soldiers.. in the State Service the year past	238
16 Jun 1783	
Mr Joseph Woodward Moderator	239
Voted to Rais 0/5^d on the pound on the List 1782 for to make an Everidge Between the Classes that hired Contenantal men and those that Did not - Voted to Chuse a Com^tee to Receive s^d money.. and make a final Settlemen.. Voted Capt Simeon Smith Lieu^t Willm Walker Insg^n Ephriam Lyon & Capt Ruben marcy be the Com^tee	239
Voted that the Town Accept the Doings of the Selectmen in giving an Order to M^srs Knox and Russ for bringing Salt from Boston	239
9 Sep 1783	
Elijah Whiton Esqr Moderator	239
9 Sep 1783	
Voted.. that Capt Simeon Smith and Isaac Perkins Esqr be Agents to Attend the General Assembley	239
Voted Dr Thomas Huntington Mathew Marcy and Joseph Kendall be a School Com^tee	239
3 Oct 1783	
Benjn Sumner Esqr Moderator	240
Voted to give the Deputys Sum Instructions.. Voted Dr Thos Huntington be a Com^tee to Draft the Instructions	240
Voted that the Town will go on Still further with the Case of Benjn Marcy and s^d Town	240
Voted Esqr Whiton be an Agent to Attend the General Assembley in Behalf of s^d Town in the Case of Marcy & the Town	240
Voted to Adjurn this meeting to Dr Hows	240
To Capt Simeon Smith and Isaac Perkins Esqr Representatives for the Town.. in the Next General Assembly The Adress & Instructions of the Inhabitants…	240
13 Apr 1778	
at a meeting of ye Freemen in Ashford ye following Persons took ye New freemans Oath Esqr Benj^a Sumner.. Jonathan Chapman.. Edd^d Sumner.. Dea^n Jeda. Dana.. Lieu^t Ezra Smith.. Esqr Elijah Whiton.. Saml Allen.. David Allen.. Saml Knox.. Lieu^t Jno Warren.. Lieu^t Jos: Spaulding.. Dea^n Nat Loomis.. Capt Icab^d Ward.. Ze[ ]^h Smith.. Samp^n Keyes.. Joel Utley.. Sam Spring.. Esqr Amos Babcock.. Calvin Eaton.. Jos: Chafee.. Ebn^r Wright.. Wm Knox.. Lieu^t Eleaz^r Warner.. Jon^th Chaffee.. Jed. Dana Junr.. Joel Ward.. Zep^h Davison.. Sol^n Keyes.. Abr^h Brooks.. Amos Bugbe.. Maj^r Ben^a Clark.. Silva^s Shirtleif.. Capt Caleb Hendee.. Wm Chub.. Maj Jno Keyes.. Ezeki. Tiffany.. Capt Eliph Babcock.. Capt Sim Smith.. Dr Neh. How.. Jno Russel.. Peter Eastman.. Joseph^h Burnham.. Henry Lee.. Hez. Eldridge.. Eben^r Fullar.. Capt Elisha Wales.. Capt Reu^n Marcy.. Midena Preston.. Elisha Ellis.. David Chaffee	308

Ashford

Ju^r.. Jno Preston.. Tim. Dimock.. Thos Butlar.. Wm Abbott.. Elias Burbank.. Joseph Woodard Ju^r.. Josiah Bubbe Junr.. Isaac Perkins.. Esqr Dana Jacob.. Clap Sumner.. Sam Eaton.. ..Nath. Wales.. Moses Rogers.. Jobe Tyler.. Jobe Robbins.. Capt Squire Hill.. Capt Asaph Smith.. Ens Jno Frink.. Inglos. Works.. Ephraim Walker.. Jno Utley.. Frances Chaffee.. Joseph Whiton.. JamesWhiton.. Thos Chapman Ju^r.. Joseph Woodward.. Capt Jno Palmer.. Saml Bugbee.. Josiah Bugbee.. Saml Whipple.. Lieu Preston.. Ezekiel Holt.. Dr Benj^a Palmer.. John Peck.. Manassah Farnam.. Zeche^h Bicknil   *308*

9 Apr 1781

att a meeting of ye Freemen .. ye following persons took ye freemans Oath.. James Hines.. Aaron Tufts.. James Howe..   *308*

11 Sep 1781

..Philip Pots.. John Lummis.. Rufus Tucker took the freemans Oath..   *308*

7 Apr 1783

..Thomas Russell.. John Mason.. Elias Underwood.. Olover Utley.. Samuel Sumner   *308*

9 Sep 1783

..Solomon Wickwire.. Lieu^t Benj^a Dimuck were Admited and Sworn freeman   *308*

9 Sep 1777

At a Meeting of ye Freemen in Ashford.. ye following Persons took ye oath of fidellity.. Jed^h Dana Benj^a Clark.. Josiah Chafee.. Ezra Smith.. Stephen Knot.. James Oulds.. Jacob Dana.. Zep^h Davinson.. David Chaffee Ju^r.. Nath^ll Loomis.. Calvin Eaton.. Ezek^l Holt.. Joseph Whiton Ju^r.. David Allen.. Timothy Robinson.. Wm Chubb.. Silvanus Shirtliff.. Jabez Webb.. John Smith.. Ephraim Walker.. Jonathan Abbe.. Eben^r Walker 3^d.. Smith Wales.. Caleb Hende.. Jed^h Dana Ju^r.. Job Tyler.. John Utley.. John Warren.. Joel Utley.. Jonah Carpenter.. John Bosworth.. Wm Walker.. Franceis Chaffe.. Joseph Chapman.. Benjn Russell..   *310*

.. Josiah Spaulding.. Squire Hill.. Wm Snow.. Joseph Amidown.. John Abbott.. Jonth Chapman.. Reuben Marcy.. Ingolsbe Work.. Nathan Wales.. Joseph Woodward.. John Russell.. Caleb Grosvenor.. Joseph Woodward Ju^r.. John Russell.. Isaac Perkins..   *310*

.. Eben^r Wright.. Eben^r Mason.. Phinehas Birchard.. Sam^ll Spring.. Simeon Smith.. Asa Farnum.. Isaac Burnham.. Jonth Chapman Ju^r.. Elisha Ellis.. Jedediah Fay.. Solomon Keyes.. Asa Eaton.. Stephen Johnson.. John Bicknell.. Thos Butler.. Benj^a Walker.. Asa Smith.. Zachariah Bicknell.. Medina Preston.. Eben^r Eastman.. ..Elijah Whiton.. Benj^a Sumner..   *310*

..Elisha Wales.. Thos Tiffany.. James Whiton.. Jonth Chapman Ju^r.. Samson Keyes.. Sam^ll Allen.. Job Robbins.. Robert Parry.. Sam^ll Abbott.. Cyrel Brown.. Peter Whitney.. Timothy Dimuck.. Benj^a Walker Ju^r *310*

ye following Persons took ye freemans oath.. Squire Hill.. Ephr^m Walker.. Joseph Chapman.. E^r Walker 3^d.. Jonth Carpenter.. Asa Farnum.. William Walker.. Jonth Chaffe Ju^r.. Job Robbins.. Timothy Dimuck   *310*

Ashford

Dec 1777

The following Persons took ye oath of Fidelity.. Thos Chapman.. Saml Whipple.. Jeremiah Standly.. Eben^r Warker.. Benj Preston.. Abijah Brooks.. Saml Walker.. Hez^h Eldridge.. Solo^n Smith.. Joseph Barny.. Jno Thompson.. David Hedges.. Benj^a Henfield.. Oliver Old.. Jno Russel.. Thos Willcox.. Reuben Johnson.. Asa Davison.. Matthias Button.. Joel Ward.. Jno Brooks.. Jno Knox.. Adam Knox.. Benj^a Chapman.. Elias Chapman.. Hez^h Smith.. Eben^r Mason Junr.. Robert Leach.. Capt Ward.. Moses Rogers.. Edward Sumner Junr.. Ephram Lyon.. Jno Frink.. Nathan Wright.. Stephen Snow.. Henry Lee.. Benj^a Snow.. Wm Becknal.. Joseph Kendell.. Saml Eaton.. Stephen Foster.. Abel Symmons..Clap Sumner.. Eben^r Bosworth.. James Fitch Sumner.. Joseph Work.. Robert Snow.. Jno Work.. Benj^a Coats.. Jno Pitts.. Nathan Griggs.. Jno Sumner.. Saml Perry.. Stephen Burges Junr.. Ezek. Badger.. Obediah Perry..   *311*

13 Dec 1777

..Thos Brigg, Dec^n Chapman.. Capt Warker.. David Chaffee.. Saml Knox.. Dr Huntington.. Wm Henfield.. Christo^r Bowen.. Tim^y Russ.. Thos Wing.. Eben^r Heath.. Joab Enos..   *311*

6 Jan 1778

..Benj^a Cheeney.. Saml Holmes.. Nehemah How..   *311*

8 Dec 1777

..Saml Bugbee.. Jason Woodward.. Jacob Preston..   *311*

7 Jan 1778

..Jonathan Beemis.. Samuel Snow.. Joseph Work Junr.. Timothy Eastman.. Ephraim Spaulding..   *311*

15 Dec 1779

..Matthew Reed.. Jacob Chapman..   *311*

13 Apr 1778

..Wm Knox.. Amos Bugbee.. Josiah Bugbe.. Jno Preston.. Peter Eastman.. Wm Abbott.. Joseph Burnham.. Capt Elijah Babcock.. Ezekiel Tiffany.. Maj^r Jno Keyes.. Thos Scott..   *311*

20 May 1778

..Simeon Dean.. Jonathan Hayward.. Joseph Griggs.. Icabod Griggs.. Amariah Winchester.. Joseph Chaffee.. Noah Paine.. [ ] Benj^a Palmer.. Jno Peck.. Manassah Farnam..   *311*

Dec 1778

Sworn in open Town Meeting.. Peter Smith.. Saml Snow Junr.. Eben^r Oles.. [ ] Obediah Brown.. Daniel Knowlton   *311*

7 May 1779

John Abbott took ye oath Fidelity as Certifyed per Nathan Frink Jus peace   *311*

1779

in Open Freemans Meeting took ye Oath Fidelity Thos Snell Saml Becknall   *311*

1779

Freemans Oath.. Timothy Russ Saml Snow Junr & Stephen Burges   *311*

6 Dec 1779

Open Town Meeting.. Saml Utley [*took an unnamed oath*]   *311*

Ashford

22 Mar 1777

This May Certifi that Hezekiah Carpenter.. is a Member of the Baptist Society and hath Attended.. with the Baptist Chh at Woodstock above three years.. Test Zebadiah Marcy.. Isaiah Bugbee } Ch^h Com^{tee}	312
This May Certifie.. that David Allen.. is a Member of the Baptist Society and hath Attended.. with the Baptist Chh at Woodstock above Seven years.. Test Zebadiah Marcy.. Isiah Bugbee } Ch^h Com^{tee}	312
This May Certifie.. that Olcutt Fisher.. is a Member of the Baptist Society and hath Attended.. with the Baptist Chh att Woodstock.. Test Zebadiah Morcey.. Isaih Bugbee Ch^h Com^{tee}	312
These may Sartify.. that Nathan Mors.. is a Baptized Person and Doth attend.. the Baptis Church att Woodstock.. Test Zebediah Marcey.. Isaiah Bugbee } Ch^h Committy	312

8 May 1777

This.. May Confirm that Mr Salvenus Snow.. Doth Belong to the Baptist Society in Ashford.. Certified.. First Day of May AD 1776 By Abr^m Knowlton Baptist Society Clerk	312

22 Dec 1779

Jonathan Avery took ye Oath of Fidelity before Benj^a Clark Justice of peace	313

10 Apr 1780

in open Town Meeting Oath Fidelity) Amos Kindell.. Saml Weed.. Abell Dow.. Eben^r Eaton	313

5 Jul 1780

before Esqr Whiton abel Coyt [*took the Oath of Fidelity*]	313

4 Dec 1780

in Town meeting [*took the Oath of Fidelity*].. Joseph Wright	313

9 Apr 1781

in freemans meeting Aaron Tafts took of Fidelity	313

1 Feb 1783

this Certify that Thomas Ewing has this Day taken the oath of Fidelity Before me Benj^a Clark Justice peace	313

10 Apr 1780

Oath freeman.. Eben^r Eaton Amos Kendall Jonath Avery Solomon Smith Abell Dow Wm Walkers Christo^r Bowen Benj^a Preston Elias Chapman Joseph Work Junr Thos Willcocks Jonth Beemis David Torry	313

11 Sep 1781

Philip Potes John Lummis took the Oath of Fidelity and also Thad^{us} Tucker	313

7 Apr 1783

the following Persons took the Oath Fidelity.. Ely Howe.. Joseph Peck.. Nathan Burnham.. Ingolsby Works.. Ephriam Lyon.. John Russell Ju^r.. Joseph Griggs	313

Bolton

Town Records
Volume 1
See also LDS microfilm # 1,376,044

Located at the Town Clerk's Office, Bolton

Bolton

12 Jul 1774

Joel White Esqr was Chosen Moderator	*138*
Voted That Thomas Pitkin Esqr Mr Ichabod Warner Isaac Fellowes Samuel Carver Ju^r & Benjamin Talcott Ju^r be a Commitee of Corispondance.. Certifyed by Benjamin Talcott Town Clerk	*139*
Benjamin Talcott Town Clerk	*139*

5 Dec 1774

Capt Joel White was Chosen moderator	*144*
Capt Benjamin Talcott was chosen Town Clerk	*144*

16 Jan 1775

Voted That Capt Thomas Pitkin Messrs Ichabod Warner Isaac Fellows Samuel Carver Ju^r Benjamin Talcott Ju^r Seth King and Capt Hezekiah King be a Commitee of Corispondence and inspection	*145*

10 Apr 1775

the Question being put whether the Select men.. Should prosecute the affair with regard to Enice Baker.. who appears to be with Child by fornication.. Voted in the affirmative and accuses Thomas Loomis of Bolton to be the father	*146*

4 Dec 1775

Seth King was Chosen moderator	*146*
Saul Alford was Chosen Town Clerk	*146*
The Select men Chosen were Capt Jonathan Birge M$^{[ ]}$ Saul Alvord and Charles King	*146*
Constables Chosen were Mr Samuel Carver Ju^r and to gather the Country Rate & Mr David West	*146*
Grandjurimen Chosen were Mr David Allis & David Taylor Jur	*146*
Tything men Chosen were { John Hutchens Ju^r John Howard Elijah Skiner and Phenehas Chapman	*146*
Capt Thomas Pitkin was Chosen Town Treasurer	*146*
Surveyers of Highways Chosen) Ezra Warterman John Howard David Webster Leiu^t Isaac Fellows Jonathan Smith Ruben Skinner Stephen King & Capt Ezekiel Olcott	*146*
Listers Chosen were Judah Strong Thom White Pitkin & Joseph Blish	*146*
Sealers of leather were Saul Alvord & David Dotchester	*146*
Branders of horses Mr Jonathan Darte & Ensign Edward Paine	*146*
Mr Saul Alvord was Chosen Pound keeper	*146*
fence veiwers Mr Elijah Hammond & Capt Joel White	*146*
Sealer of weights and Measures Benjamin Talcott	*146*
Hog Howards chosen were Charles Loomis Ju^r Jacob Lyman Liu^t Jared Cone Seth Talcott Daniel Ladd & John Daniels	*146*
Collectors of the Town Rate Chosen were David West and Mr Aaron Haskins	*146*
Voted that the place to Set up Notification to warn Town meetings in ye North part of Said Town Shall be Capt Kings house and Ensign Edward Paines Shop	*146*

Bolton

8 Apr 1776

Joel White Esq Chosen Modarator	*147*
Pound Keeper in North Bolton.. Gideon King	*147*
Ezra Waterman John Howard David Webster Leu^t Isaac Felllows Jonathan Smith Reuben Skiner Stephen King & Capt Ezekiel Olcott Chousen Colecters	*147*

27 Jun 1776

Joel white Esq was Chosen modarator	*147*
Nathan Strong was Chosen Constable to Colect Coloney Tax	*147*
John Skiner was Chosen Constable	*147*
Thomas Pitkin was Chosen Selectman	*147*

2 Dec 1776

Joel White Esq Chosen modarator	*148*
Benjamin Talcott Esq Chosen Town clark	*148*
Benjamin Talcott Esq Charles King & Saul Alvord Chosen Select men	*148*
Judah Strong to gather the Governments: tax & John Skiner Chosen Constable	*148*
Grandjurers.. Capt Ezekiel Olcott	*148*
Solomon Dewey David Webster oliver King and Able west Chosen Tithingmen	*148*
Saul Alvord En^s Abner Lomis John Howard Elijah olmsted Joshua Perl Mosis thrall Reuben Skiner & David Allis Chosen Survayers of ways & Colecters to Colect the Tax made for.. mending Highway	*148*
Joseph Blish Thomas White Pitkin & Jacob Lyman Listers	*148*
Saul Alvord & David Dochister Chosen Sealers of Lather	*148*
Jonathan Dart & Edward Pane Chosen Branders of Horses	*148*
Saul Alvord Chosen Poundkeeper	*148*
Joel White Esq & Mr Elijah Hammond Chosen fence vewers	*148*
Benjn Talcott Esq Chosen Sealer of waits & measuers	*148*
Thomas Pitkin Chosen Town treasuer	*148*
Hog Howard.. George Griswold Jacob Lyman John Daniels and Zachariah Cone	*148*

9 Dec 1776

Elaxander m^{c}Lane Chosen Grandjuriman	*148*

6 Feb 1777

Ensign Benjamin Trumbul was Chosen Moderator.. opend [sic] and adjour^d to Capt Joel Whites	*149*
Judah Strong & John Skiner were Cosen [sic] Colecters of the Town Rate	*149*
Voted that Capt Joel White Ensign Benjamin Trumbull Ichabod Warner Seth King David Allis Lieu^t Isaac Fellows & Saul Alvord be a Commitee of Inspection	*149*
David Allis Capt Hezekiah King and.. Elijah Hammond be appointed a Commitee.. to Recover and Receive the money.. for the Sale of the western Lands	*149*

Bolton

31 Mar 1777

Capt Joel White was Chosen Moderator	149
Voted Nem-con That a Comitee be appointed.. to Provid Necessarys for the Familyes of Soldiers.. who Shall engage and go into any of the Batalions to be Raised in this State.. Voted That Miss^{rs} Ichabod Warner Elijah White Capt Thomas Pitkin Capt Ezekiel Olcott and Capt Hezekiah King be a Commitee.. to Execut the Same	150

29 Apr 1777

Received of Benjamin Talcott Esqr one of the Select Men.. one Hundred and fifty Weight of Gun Powder Belonging to the Town Stock.. Received by me.. Thomas Pitkin Town Treasurer	150

22 Sep 1777

Joel White Esqr was Chosen moderator	150
Voted That Thomas Pitkin Esqr Lieu^t Elijah White &.. Judah Strong be a Commitee to Purchase Cloathing for the Contenential Non Commission officers and Soldiers	150

1 Dec 1777

Capt Joel White was Chosen Moderator	151
Capt Benjamin Talcott was Chosen Town Clerk	151
Select Men.. Saul Alvord David Allis & Leut Elijah White	151
Constables { Judah Strong & to gather the Country Rates and John Skinner and George Griswold	151
Grandjuriors { Ensign Joseph Carver Ezra Warterman & Daniel Fowler	151
Tything men { Jacob Lyman Jerijah Loomis Ju^r Nathan Jones and Joshua Pearl	151
Surveyors of Highways { Messrs Thomas White Jacob Lyman Samuel Whelding Ichabod Marshall Asahel Root Charles King David Dotchester and Pheniahs Chapman	151
Listers.. Oliver King Nathan Strong & Capt Ezekiel Olcott	151
Sealers of Leather Mr Saul Alvord & Mr David Dotchester	151
Brander of horses Mr Jonathan Darte & Lieu^t Edward Paine	151
pound keeper.. Ebenezer Carver	151
fence viewers Ms^{rs} Elijah Hammond & Saul Alvord	151
Sealer of weights and Measures Capt Benjamin Talcott & Measures only John Carver	151
Town Treasurer Lieu^t Elijah White	151

8 Dec 1777

Voted.. That Capt Joel White.. Benjamin Trumbull Mr Saul Alvord Do^t Ichabod Warner Decon Seth King & Mr David Dotchester be a Commitee of Inspection	152
Voted That the Town Salt be Divided unto the Inhabitants of the Town.. according to their Number of persons Equally They paying the Cost of bringing the Salt from Boston in propotion to what Each one receves of Said Salt - Voted That Benjamin Talcott Ju^r be a Committee to Deal out Said Salt	152

29 Dec 1777

David Allis was Chosen Moderator	152
Voted to Adjourn this Meeting for an hour & half and to.. David Dotchesters	152
Voted That Mr Benjamin Talcot Juner Dispose of the Town Salt.. Left after he has delt out to	152

the Inhabitants their.. propotion.. then to Sell the Rest to needy persons not more than half a peck to a person	
Voted That Lieu^t Abner Loomis & Mr John Skinner be Colecters of the Town Rats [sic]	153
Voted That Mr Saul Alvord Mr Benjamin Talcott Jur and Lieu^t Elijah White be a Commitee for to provide for non Comissioned officers and Soldiers familys that are gone into Continential Service	153

5 Mar 1778

David Allis was Chosen Moderator	153

16 Apr 1778

We the Subscribers being Appointed.. to Divide the Excise Money to the Different Parishes.. Find.. to the First Society to be Forty Pounds five Shillings And to the Second Society to be Twenty one Pounds Twelve Shillings and Six pence Mr Saul Alvord Received the money for the first Society And Mr David Alis Recev^d the Money for the Second Society.. [signed] { Saul Alvord.. David Allis.. Elijah White { Select Men	154

22 Jun 1778

David Allis was Chosen moderator	154
Voted That Mr Gideon King Lieu^t Abner Loomis Elijah Skinner Levi Loomis and Ensign Benjamin Risley be a Commitee to purchase Cloathing for the Soldiers.. in the Continential army	154

7 Dec 1778

Joel White Esqr was Chosen Moderator	155
Benjamin Talcott Esqr was Chosen Town Clerk	155
Select Men wer Lieu^t Elijah White Mr David Allis and Mr Saul Alvord	155
Constables Chosen { Ensign David Taylor and to geather the Country Rate Ensign George Griswold & Mr John Skinner	155
Grandjurymen Chosen { were Eliphalet Hendee Mr Andrus Minor & Mr Gideon King	155
Tything men { Chosen Saul Alvord Juner Mr Ebenezer Carver Abijah Johns and Mr Ruben Skiner	155
Surveyers of highways { were Aaron Strong Daniel Darte Levi Loomis Ichabod Marshall Capt Ezekiel Olcott Gideon King Caleb Talcott & Allixander m^{c}Lane	155
Listers Chosen were { Benjamin Talcott Ju^r Oliver King Lieu^t Abner Loomis Saul Alvord Ju^r & Ensign Benjamin Risley	155
Sealer of Leather { Mr Saul Alvord and Mr David Dotchester	155
Branders of Horse Kind Mr Jonathan Darte Capt Edward Paine	155
Sealer of weights and measures Capt Benjamin Talcott	155
Sealer of measurs only Mr John Carver	155
Liue^t Elijah White was Chosen Town Treasurer	155
Key keeper of the pound Mr Andrus Minor Chosen	155
Fence vewers Chosen Mr Elijah Hammond & Mr Saul Alvord	155
Voted That Mr Nathan Strong Nathaniel Hammond and Moses Thrall be a Commitee to Provide for the officers and Soldiers Families that are gone from Bolton into the Continential Service	155
Voted That Mr John Howard & Mr Allixander m^{c}Lane be Collectors of the Town Rates	155

Bolton

28 Dec 1778

Voted That M[r] Saul Alvord Cap[t] Benjamin Talcott and M[r] David Allis be a Commitee to Dispose of those usless [*sic*] High Ways.. And give Deeds to the Purchasers	156
Voted That the Selectmen Settle with Aaron Strong for his Service done in Supporting Sam[ll] Darte in his Sickness	156

21 Jun 1779

M[r] David Allis was Chosen Moderator	156
Voted.. That Ensign Benjamin Risley and M[r] Gideon King be a Commitee to provid Clothing for the Soldiers in the Continental Army	156
Voted to Raise a Tax of twelve pence on the pound on the Last August List.. to purchase Cloathing for Said Soldiers & pay town Debts &c - the Question being put whether John Howard Should be Excused from gathering or Collecting Said Tax voted in the Negitive	156

6 Dec 1779

Doct[r] Ichabod Warner was Chosen moderator	157
Benjamin Talcott Esq[r] Was Chosen Town Clerk	157
Select Men { were David Allis Doct[r] Icabod Warner & M[r] Nath[ll] Hammond	157
Constables Chosen { Ensign David Taylor and to gather the Contry Rate and M[r] George Griswold & M[r] John Skiner	157
Grand Jurymen { Lieu[t] Abner Loomis Jonathan Smith and Lieu[t] Smuel Carver Ju[r]	157
Tything men.. Levi Loomis Aaron Haskin Asahel Webster and James Lyman	157
Listers M[r] Oliver King Lieu[t] Abner Loomis & Saul Alvord Juner	157
Surveyors of Highways { M[r] Ichabod Marshall John Hutchen Ju[r] Jerijah Loomis Ju[r] Asa Bingham Daniel Ladd Thomas Chapman Ju[r] Samuel Roott & Hezekiah Loomis.. Voted that Said Surveyors be Collector of Rates for their Destricts	157
Voted That Jonah Strickland Juner & Elijah Skinner be Collectors of Said Town Rates	157
Voted M[r] Saul Alvord Juner be Town Treasurer	157
Leather Sealers M[r] Saul Alvord and M[r] Hezekiah Loomis	157
Brander of horse kind M[r] Anderson Miner & Cap[t] Edward Paine	157
Sealer of weights and measures Benjamin Talcott Esq[r] and M[r] John Carver Sealer of Measures only	157
Pound or Key Keeper M[r] Anderson Miner	157
fence vewers M[r] Elijah Hammond & M[r] Saul Alvord	157
Voted That Asa Hendee Joshua Pearl John Church Hutchens and Jeremiah Chapman be Hog Howards &c	157
Voted That.. Nathan Strong Nathaniel Hammond and Moses Thrall be a Commitee to take Care and Provid for the officers and Soldiers Wifes and Families in the Continental Service	158
the foregoing Meeting was part of it Held at M[r] Saul Alvords	158

27 Dec 1779

Joel White Esq[r] was Chosen moderator	158

13 Mar 1780

M[r] David Allis was Chosen Moderator	158

Bolton

Voted That Mesurer Judah Strong Abner Loomis Benjamin Trumbull Elijah White Benjamin Risley Joseph Carver David Taylor Ju^r Ruben Skinner David Allis Joshua Pearl John Payne Ozias Grant & Capt Edward Payne be a Comitee of Inspection	158
Voted that the Select men.. take Care and Provid Necessearys for John Clark and his Family	158

26 Jun 1780

Doc^t Ichabod Warner was Chosen Moderator	159
Voted that the place for the Seting up warnings for Town Meetings in the North Bolton Society.. Shall be Set up at Mr David Allises grist Mill and Mr William Hunts Dwelling House	159
Voted That Ensi^n Benjamin Trumbull Capt Edward Payne and Lieu^t Samuel Carver be a Comitee to See what is due to those Continental Soldiers to make the Ten pounds money good that.. Bolton promised to pay them yearly	159

13 Nov 1780

Mr David Allis was Chosen Moderator	159
Voted That Lieu^t Elijah White and Capt Edward Payne be a Comitee for the Receiving the Salt.. to procure Casks to Contain.. Provisions to recive and inspect the Same	159
Voted that a Rate of Six pence on the Pound be made on the Inhabitants.. on the List.. in the the year 1779 Exclusive of four fold Assessments to be paid in provisions.. Voted That Leiu^t Elijah White and Capt Edward Payne be Collectors of the afore Said Provisions	159

4 Dec 1780

Ensign Benjamin Trumbull was Chosen Moderator	160
Benjamin Talcott Esqr was Chosen Town Clerk	160
Ensign Benjamin Trumbull.. Saul Alvord & Mr David Allis were Chosen Select men	160
Voted to Choose a Comitee to Hire our Qota of Soldiers to fill up the Continental Army.. Chosen were Doct^r Ichabod Warner Capt Edward Payne Mr Judah Strong Liu^t Lemmy Thrall & Ens^n Benjamin Risley	160
Voted that .. David Taylor Ju^r be Costable and to gather the Country Taxes and also George Griswold and John Skinner were Chosen Constables	160
Grand Jury men { Jerijah Loomis Ju^r Abel West & John Hutchens Ju^r	160
Surveyors of highway { Benjn Risley George Griswold Charles Strong Sam^{ll} Whelden Daniel Fowler John Daniels Asahel Webster Elijah Skinner	160
Tything men { Simeon Griswold Thomas Loomis Samuel Root and Ruben King	160
Listers Oliver King Saul Alvord Juner Lie^t Loomis	160
Thomas Loomis and Ruben Skinner were Chosen Collectors of Town Rates	160
Saul Alford Ju^r was Chosen Town Treasurer	160
Mr Saul Alvord and Hezekiah Loomis Sealers of Leather	160
Benjamin Talcott Esqr Sealer of weights and Measures	160
Joel White Esqr was Chosen key keeper	160
Mr Oliver King was Chosen Collector in the Room of Capt Edward Payne to be Receiver of Provisions	160

[ ] Dec 1780

Voted That Mr Gideon King be a Comitte to Purchase or Provid Cloathing for the Soldiers.. in the Continental army and also for those that Shall be raised to fill up our Qota in the	160

Bolton

Continential army

hog howards Chosen were Jacob Lyman Saul Alvord Ju^r Anderson Minor & Ens^n Joseph Carver | 161

8 Dec 1780

Ensign Benjamin Trumbull was Chosen Moderator | 161

Voted That Capt Jared Cone and Mr Caleb Talcott be recevers and Collectors of the one peney half penny Tax which is to be paid in provision | 161

Voted That Zenas Skinner and Job Talcott Shall be allowed the three pounds p^r month promised by the Town.. for an Encoragement.. to fill up our Quota | 162

16 Feb 1781

Ensign Benjamin Trumbull was Chosen Moderator | 162

26 Feb 1781

Voted That Ens^n David Taylor Ju^r Judah Strong Ens^n Benjamin Risley and Ruben Skinner be a Commitee To Class the Town to Raise both the Continental Soldiers for three years and the States Soldiers for thirteen months | 162

voted to recall the Rate bill given out to Thomas Loomis and Ruben Skinner.. to hire Soldiers.. and to Return the Money to those that have paid the Same | 162

20 Mar 1781

Doct^r Ichabod Warner was Chosen moderator | 163

Voted That Ensign Benjamin Trumbull Mr David Allis and Leu^t Elijah White be a Commitee to See what is Due to those Soldiers that Inlisted into the Continental army upon the Encoruagement of the Town | 163

voted to give Uriah Skinner four pound State money pr month for his hireing an Enfield man for to go into the Army for 6-months | 163

Voted That Ens^n Benjamin Trumbull and Doc^t Ichabod Warner be a Commitee to make a Return of the Right to those men the Town.. have.. in the Continental Service to that Commitee appointed by the Assembly | 163

9 Apr 1781

Voted That Mr Ichabod Marshall be a Surveyor of High Ways in the Room of Ens^n Benjamin Risley who is going out of Town | 163

Voted That Benjamin Talcott David Allis and Saul Alvord be reappointed to Dispose of unnesary High ways | 163

30 Apr 1781

Joel White Esqr was Chosen Moderator | 163

21 Jun 1781

Doc^t Ichabod Warner was Chosen moderator | 163

voted to appoint an Agent to Settle with David Safford of Canterbury on the account of his bringing a writ against Said Town for his Three Pounds pr month.. promised to those Soldiers That Inlisted to fill up the.. Qota for the Continental Service for Six months Last Sumer: Voted That Mr Judah Strong be Agent | 163

Voted to Lay a Tax of four pence on the Pound.. to be paid in provisions.. Voted That Mr Judah Strong be a Collector | 164

16 Jun 1781

Voted That Saul Alford Ju^r and Caleb Talcott be Receivers of the Two Shilling and Six pence on the pound to be.. paid in money.. or flower Indian Corn or Cloathing on the List of Said | 164

Bolton

Town in the year 1780 &c Voted That Mr Nathan Strong & Mr Benjamin Talcott Juner be Collectors of Excise	
Voted That Saul Alford Ju^r Town Treasur Borrow.. Twenty hard Dollors to pay David Safford of Canterbury for his Last Sumer Service	164

3 Dec 1781

Docter Ichabod Warner was Chosen Moderator	164
Lieu^t Elijah White was Chosen Town Clerk	164
Deacon Saul Alvord Capt Ezekiel Olcott & Lieu^t Elijah White was Chosen Select Men	164
Constables { Capt Ezekiel Olcott and to geather the Country Tax or Rate Saul Alvord Ju^r & George Griswold	164
Grand Jurymen { Ichabod Marshall Capt Edward Payne & Thomas Loomis	164
Tything men { Samuel Carver Ju^r Jonah Strickland Jur. Lemuel Chapman & Barzillai Little	164
Surveyors of high ways { Jonah Stickland Juner Joshua Talcot Ju^r Capt Abner Loomis Samuel Carver Jur. Liu^t Zadock How Ezra Loomis Caleb Talcott and Abijah Johns	164
Listers Judah Strong Ruben Skinner and Nathaniel Hammond	164
Town Tresurer Saul Alvord Juner	165
Sealers of Leather Decon Saul Alvord & Hezekiah Loomis	165
Sealer of weights and Measures Benjamin Talcott Esqr	165
Hawards Simeon Spencer Jacob Lyman & James Thrall 2	165
Key Keepers of the Pounds Joel White Esqr & Moses Thrall	165
James Lyman was Chosen Collector of money Due for Raising a Soldier for the 13th Class	165
Ezra Loomis Elijah Skinner Elijah Tucker Aaron Haskins & William Willson were Chosen Collectors for the Classes to which they belonged.. for the Raising & paying.. Soldiers	165
Ensign Joseph Carver & Barzillai Little Chosen Collectors of the Town Rates	165
Fence Vewers Capt Jared Cone & Anderson Miner David Allis & Daniel Fowler	165

[ ] Dec 1781

Voted That Thomas Chapman Juner be Collector of Town Rates in Stead of Barzillai Little for the North Parish	165
Voted That Elijah Skinner be Constable in Stead of Capt Ezekiel Olcott and to gather the State Tax	165
Voted to give William Rock Six pounds.. for his past Services as a Soldier in the Continental Army	165

31 Dec 1781

Voted on Reconsideration That Mr Gideon King be Constable to gather the State Taxes in the Room of Elijah Skinner	165
Voted That the Select Men And Ichabod Marshall be a Comitee to Remove Incroachments off the High Ways.. And To Make Sale of the Useless Highways	166
Voted upon a Reconsideration That Benjamin Talcott Esqr be Town Clerk in the Room of Lieu^t Elijah White who was Chosen	166
Thomas White was Chosen Constable in the Room of Elijah Skinner and Refused to take the oath and paid the penalty	166

[ ] Mar 1782

Doct^r Ichabod Warner Chosen Moderator	166

Bolton

Messrs Judah Strong Saul Alvord Ju^r Moses Thrall Ruben Skinner And Abner Loomis were Chosen a Commitee to Class Said Town for Continental & State men	166
Mr Asahel Webster is appointed a Collector to the Class to which he belongs	166
Mr Benjamin Wells is appointed a Collector to the Class to which he belongs	166

2 Dec 1782

Mr David Allis was Chosen Moderator	166
Benjaminm Talcott Esqr was Chosen Town Clerk	166
Select men Chosen were Capt Ezekiel Octott Mr Judah Strong and Capt Abner Lomis	166
Constabels { Mr Saul Alvord Juner to gather the State Tax And.. John Skinner & Mr George Griswold	167
Grand jury men { Jonah Strickland Juner and Mr Aaron Hoskins and Allixander McLane	167
Tything men { Elijah Talcott Asahel Skinner Hezekiah Loomise and Seth King	167
Saul Alvord Juner was Chosen Town Treasurer	167
Leather Sealers Chosen were Decon Saul Alford & Hezekiah Loomise	167
Sealer of weights and Benjamin Talcott Eq^r was Chosen	167
Listers Chosen were Solomon Dewey Nath^{ll} Hammond & Ruben Skinner	167
Surveyors of highways { John Howard John Bishop Juner Liu^t Elijah White Liu^t Elijah Olmsted Daniel Root William Little Samuel King & Lemuel Chapman & to be Collectors of the one penny Tax to mend highways	167
Key keepers of the Pounds Ebenezer Carver and James Thrall	167
Fence vewers Mr David Allis Asahel Root & Ichabod Marshel	167
Voted to Except of the Doings of the Select Men and Commitee in Laying out a high Way from Ruben Carpenters to Ichabod Marshels & the Assessing Damages	167
Voted That Ezra Warterman & Seth King be Collectors of Town Rates	167
Voted that Town Treasurer pay.. Eight Pound in State money Bills And all the Continential Bills in Said Town Treasury To Liu^t David Taylor Ju^r .. to favor him for his Loss of Counterfit Bills he took for Taxes	167

[ ] Dec 1782

Voted That Samuel Carver Esqr And Mr David Allis be a Commitee… to.. Enquire.. of that affair wherein Ezra Loomiss.. was Commited to Prison by the Collectors of Publick Taxes of this State some of which ought to have been Collected many years agoe by David Taylor Ju^r when Said Loomis had Estate Enough in his hands & Said Committee are to Take.. Steps to find out the Elegallity or fraud in the affair and procure… an Efectual Remedy So that Said Town may not be Charged with an uriteous Debt	168

25 Aug 1783

Mr David Allis was Chosen Moderator	168
Voted That Capt Ezekiel Olcott Ens^n Benjamin Trumbull Doct Ichabod Warner Capt Jared Cone Samuel Carver Esqr and Mr David Allis be a Commitee to See what was Needfull to be done.. in Publick affairs	168
Voted that Joshua Pearl be a Surveyor of Highways in the room of Ezra Loomis which is gone out of the State &c and to take his rate bill and finnish the work at Highways as Loomis was to do	168
The oath of Fidelity which was made by the act of the Assembly in May 1777 was Taken by	180

Bolton

the Persons hereafter Named viz Benjamin Talcott Esqr and Mr Seth King had Said oth [sic] administred by Titus Hosmer Justice of the peace..
16 Sep 1777

..Said oth [sic] Administred to Joel White Esqr.. Thomas Pitkin Esqr.. Rever^d Ebenezer Kellogg.. Elijah Hammond.. Charles King.. Benjamin Talcott Ju^r.. Daniel Fowler.. Joshua Talcott.. Doc^r Ichabod Warner.. Capt Jared Cone.. William Huntt.. David Webster.. Liu^t Elijah White.. David Taylor.. Ezra Loomis.. Ebenezer Carver.. Asahel Root.. Abel West.. Stephen King.. Eliakim Roott.. Daniel Ladd.. Phenehas Chapman.. Joseph Carver.. Thomas White.. Samuel Roott.. Jerijah Loomis Ju^r.. John Howard.. Solomon Dewey.. Asa Bingham.. Zacariah Cone.. Asa Hendey.. Jonah Strickland.. Benjamin Trumbull.. John Darte.. Daniel Darte.. Gideon King.. Saul Alvord.. Caleb Talcott.. David Taylor Ju^r.. Jacob Lyman.. Judah Strong.. John Skinner.. Asahel Webster.. Elijah Skinner.. Elijah Olmstead.. Joshua Pearl.. Nathan Jones.. Capt Matthew Loomis.. Daniel Griswold.. George Griswold.. Crafts Goodrich.. John Hutchen Ju^r.. David Allis.. Ezra Warterman.. Jonathan Darte.. Levi Loomis Certifyed by Benjamin Talcott Just of the Peace
22 Sep 1777   *180*

And.. Richard Skinner.. James Fowler Sworn by me Benjn Talcott Just Peace   *180*

6 Oct 1777

And.. Joseph Blish.. Abner Loomis.. Nathan Strong.. John Talcott.. Charles Loomis Ju^r.. Aaron Strong.. Simeon Spencer.. Ebenezer Strong.. John Bishop Ju^r.. John Hale.. Jonah Strickland Ju^r.. Thomas Loomis.. Timothy Darte.. Abitha Man.. Samuel Carver ye 3^d .. Alexand McLane.. Asahel Skinner.. Aaron Hakins.. John Church Hutchens.. William Darte.. took the oath of fidelity before me Benjn Talcott Just Peace   *180*

1 Dec 1777

Ichabod Marshall too[k] the oath of fidelity and also Capt Ezekiel Olcott.. Jonathan Smith.. Moses Thrall.. Lemme Thrall.. Ruben King.. Hezekiah Loomis.. Isaac Brunson.. David Dotchester.. Oliver King.. Lieu^t Samuel Carver.. William Haskins.. Ozias Grant.. Ruben Skinner.. Daniel Roott.. James Nooney.. Robart Beebee.. James Lyman.. Rosel Paine Oath of Fidelity Administred unto the Persons following.. Ensign Joseph Tucker.. Elijah Tucker..   *180*
    181

5 Dec 1777

Benjamin Wells and the foregoing persons personall appeared and took the oath of Fidelity before me Benjn Talcott Jus^t of the Peace and also Decon David Strong.. John Bissell.. Eliphalet Hendee took the oath of Fidelity..   *181*

9 Dec 1777

William Little.. Josiah Whitney & Benjamin Blish took the oath of fidelity..   *181*

15 Dec 1777

..and also John Daniels had Said oath administred to him   *181*

16 Dec 1777

Silvanus Delino took Said Oath.. and Samuel Wheldon also   *181*

29 Dec 1777

Jabez Emerson.. Thomas Chapman and Jeremiah Chapman took the above Said oath   *181*

Jan 1778

Lieu^t Edward Paine took the oath of fidelity   *181*

Bolton

5 Mar 1778

Docᵗ John Gay, Elias Skinner Luther Skinner and Thomas Chapman Juʳ Took the oath of Fidelity before Jusᵗ White   *181*

14 Mar 1778

Benjamin Talcott 3ᵈ & Elijah Talcott took the oath of Fidelity.. Benjⁿ Talcott Jusᵗ Peace   *181*

3 Apr 1778

& John French took Said oath   *181*

4 Apr 1778

James Thrall and James Welch took Said oath..   *181*

13 Apr 1778

.. Then Andrew Emerson.. Prince Bruster.. Anderson Minor.. Revᵈ George Colton.. Moses Goodrich.. William Haskins.. John Bishop.. Samuel Carver.. Samuel Darte.. Abijah Johns Sworn   *181*

4 May 1778

Roger Loomis Juner.. John Tucker.. Charles Strong.. Timothy Isham.. Zepheriah Thare.. Samuel Talcott.. Sworn.. by me Benjⁿ Talcott Jusᵗ Peace   *181*

3 Sep 1778

Benjamin Risley Sworn by Esqʳ Pitkin.. then Saul Alvord Juʳ had the oath of Fidelity &c - by Joel White Jusᵗ Peace   *181*

7 Dec 1778

Jabez Emerson Juner.. Jerijah Loomis &c   *181*

23 Jan 1779

Daniel Daniels Sworn   *181*

2 Feb 1779

Jonathan Skinner Sworn &c .. before me Benjⁿ Talcott Jusᵗ Peace   *181*

Feb 1779

Benjamin Howard Sworn .. before me Benjⁿ Talcott Just Peace   *181*

1778

Patience Skinner Sworn by Joel White Esqʳ   *181*

Feb 1779

Simeon Griswold Sworn by Joel White Esqʳ   *181*

12 Apr 1779

Samuel Cooley took Said oth of fidelity &c before me Benjⁿ Talcot Jusᵗ Peace   *181*

5 Jul 1779

the oath of fidelity was &c to Charles King Jur .. Joseph Loomis.. Rachel Loomis.. Rachel Loomis Juner.. Temperance Fowler and Susannah Dutchester..   *181*

4 Oct 1779

..John Walker Juner.. David King.. Samuel King.. Enock Hyde   *181*

Bolton

24 Feb 1780

..Mary Welch.. Bezaleel Little.. Dorcas Olcott.. John Olcott and Lydia Welch took Said oath &c.. *181*

10 Apr 1780

..and also.. Liu^t Roger Loomis Joshua Talcott J^r & Seth King Juner *181*

16 Sep 1777

Freemen that took the oath of fidelity September 16th 1777 are a followeth ~ Benjamin Talcott Esqr Joel White Esqr Thomas Pitkin Esqr Rever^d Ebenezer Kellogg Elijah Hammond Charles King Saul Alvord, Seth King, Benjamin Talcott Ju^r Daniel Fowler Joshua Talcott Doc^r Ichabod Warner Capt Jared Cone William Hunt, David Webster Liu^t Elijah White David Taylor Ezra Loomis Ebenezer Carver, Asahel Root Abel West Stephen King Eliakim Root, Daniel Ladd Phenehas Chapman Joseph Carver Thomas White Samuel Root Jerijah Loomis Ju^r John Howard Solomon Dewey Asa Bingham Zacariah Cone Asa Hendey Jonah Strickland Ens^n Benjamin Trumbull John Darte Daniel Darte Gideon King Caleb Talcott David Taylor Ju^r Jacob Lyman Judah Strong John Skinner Asahel Webster Elijah Skinner Elijah Olmstead Joshua Pearl Nathan Jones Capt Matthew Loomis Daniel Griswold George Griswold Crafts Goodrich John Hutchens Ju^r David Allis Ezra Warterman Jonathan Darte Levi Loomis all admitted and Sworn in open freemens Meeting.. by me Sworn &c Benjamin Talcott Jus^t Peace *182*

14 Apr 1778

the Freemens oath appointed by the Law &c was administred to those who had Taken the oath of Fidelity as followeth viz Nathan Strong John Bishop Ichabod Marshall William Haskins Nathaniel Hammod Anderson Minor James Fowler Simeon Spencer Thomas Loomis Prince Bruster Ezra Loomis Andrew Emerson Allixander McLane Samuel Whelden Moses Thrall Edward Paine Richard Skinner John Talcott Jonathan Skinner Jeremiah Chapman Samuel Carver Capt Ezekiel Olcott Liu^t Samuel Carver Ju^r Benjamin Welles Joseph Blish John Gay Moses Goodrich & Eliphalet Hendee and were Sworn in open Freemans Meetinb by me Benjamin Talcott Justice of the Peace *182*

15 Sep 1778

oliver King and Saul Alvord Ju^r were Admitted as Free men and Sworn in open Meeting *182*

12 Apr 1779

the Rever^d Mr George Cotton Timothy Isham William Risley Simeon Griswold and Samuel Cooley were admitted freemen and Sworn in the open freemens meeting before me Benjamin Talcott Jus^t Peace *182*

21 Sep 1779

John Church Hutchens admitted a freeman and Sworn *183*

10 Apr 1780

Leu^r Roger Loomis Gorsom Risley Aaron Strong Seth King Ju^r, Jonah Strickland Ju^r Asahel Skinner and Joshua Talcott Ju^r were Admited Freemen & Sworn *183*

19 Sep 1780

Lieu^t Zadock How and Elijah Talcott were Admited Freemen & Sworn *183*

17 Sep 1782

Samuel Carver Ju^{nr} Joel King Daniel Badcock John Olcott and Phenehas Talcott were Admited Freeman and Sworn *183*

Bolton

8 Apr 1783

Eleazer Woodworth Lemuel Chapman David King and Samuel Talcott were Admitted Freemen and Sworn   183

16 Sep 1783

John Carver James Chapmen Joseph Davis John Daniels William Willson and John Skinner were admitted freeme[n] and Sworn   183

11 Jan 1780

oaths of Fidelity William Little Ju^r Samuel Benjaman Lemuel Chapman & Nathan Chapman Took Said oath Janury the 11th 1780 before me Benjamin Talcott Jus^t Peace   183

2 Mar 1781

John Rock of Munson Took the oath of Fidelity   183

21 Apr 1781

William Charles Warner a Resident in Bolton and Joel King of Said Bolton Took the oath of Fidelity   183

28 May 1781

Ichabod Gay & Uriah Skinner took Said oath before me Benjamin Talcott Jus^t Peace   183

4 Feb 1783

John Daniels Junr Took said oath of Fidelity   183

1[6] Sep 1783

John Skinner Ju^r Took Said oath   183

Branford

Vital Statistics
Vol. 3
1691-1788
Book 2 of 2

Located at the Branford Town Clerk's Office

Branford

[ ] Dec 1774

Josiah Rogers Esqr was chosen Moderator	*181*
Voted Unanimously that we do Approve of the Association entered into by the Continental Congress held at Philadelphia.. containing a Non-Importation Non-Exportation, & Non-Consumption Agreement.. chose the following Persons a Committe for the Purposes Specified in the 11th Article of said Associationviz Ebenezer Linsly Junr Stephen Potter, Cole W Gould, Samuel Barker, John Ford, Timothy Frisbie Capt Da[ ] Maltbie, Samuel Barker Ju^r Samuel Hoadly, John Linsly J[ ] Deac^n Barnabas Mulford, Aaron Baldwin, Deac^n Eben^r Russel Daniel Page, Phinehas Baldwin, Capt Josiah Fowler, Capt Wm Douglas & Thomas Rogers	*180*

15 May 1775

Samuel Barker was chosen Moderator	*180*
Voted a Rate of one half Penny on the Pound.. Chose Farrington Harrison, Israel Linsly Junr & Rufus Hoadly to collect said Rate	*180*
Saml Barker Town Clerk [*ed: entered minutes as Town Clerk; elected at Annual Meeting, Dec 1774*]	*180*

19 Sep 1775

Samuel Barker was chosen Moderator	*180*
Daniel Page One of the Constables.. chosen Collector of the Colony Tax.. in the Room of Stephen Potter, gone into the Army	*180*

17 Nov 1775

Samuel Barker was chosen Moderator	*180*
Voted that a Committe be chosen.. to distribute forthwith to such of the Inhabitants as are capable of bearing Arms.. a suteable Quantity of Ammunition out of the Town Stock.. Chose Capt Edward Russell, Capt John Russell, Lieu^t Timothy Frisbie, Mr Enoch Staples, Mr Peter Grant, Capt Reuben Rose Lieu^t Samuel Baldwin, Mr Ephraim Page Lieu^t Benjamin Baldwin Capt Josiah Fowler & Mr Elihu Baldwin	*179*
put to Vote whereas Samuel Barker hath some Time past borrowed.. of the Towns Stock, One quarter Cask of Powder, whether.. Barker should pay for said Powder.. (he now offering the same).. & voted that the Town would wait until he shall be able to purchase the Powder, & return the same into the Town Stock	*179*

[ ] Dec 1776

Deacon Josiah Rogers Esqr was Chosen Moderator	*179*
William Munro Town Clerk	*179*
James Barker Esqr Mersr^s Elnathan Beach Samuel Russell Aaron Baldwin Justis Rose Daniel Page Samuel Roose Junr Select men	*179*
James Barker Esqr Town Treasurer	*179*
Ebenezer Linsly Junr Constable	*179*
Roger Tyler Junr Constable to Geather the Collony Tax	*179*
Ithiel Russell Daniel Page Constables	*179*
Ebenezer Linsley Junr Steph: Foot Coll: William Gould Samuel Frisbie Enoch Staples Obediah Tyler Peter Harrison Bartholomew Goodrich William Monro Samuel Palmer Junr Titus Frisbie Abraham Rogers Samuel Rogers Able Page Artimious Johnson Jacob Frisbie Ebenezer Rogers Asahel Palmer Daniel Rose Samuel Ford Isaac Whedon Danl Hoadly	*179*

Branford

Gaushin Woodward Samuel Harrison Samuel Baldwin Jacob Barker Abijah Rogers Caleb Street Isreal Linsly Junr Jonathan Tyler Ozias Tyler Ebenezer Finch Timothy Hoadley Surveyors of Highways

Decon Elnathan Beach Samuel Russell Daniel Linsley Stephen Palmer Samuel Rose Junr Joseph Rogers Fence Vewers — *179*

John Gordon Samuel Frisbie Timothy Frisbie Jared Harrison Abraham Linsley Peter Tyler Ebenezer Hoadly Listers — *179*

Epharim Parrish Noah Baldwin Junr Edward Barker Daniel Rose Jonathan Russel Isaac Foot Josiah Linsley Grandjurors — *179*

Asher Sheldon Titus Frisbie Elijah Palmer Junr Dow Smith Ozias Tyler Ebenezer Hoadley Tythingmen — *179*

Jabish Palmer Israel Baldwin Joseph Chitsy Haywards — *179*

Deacon Elnathan Beach Packer of Provisions — *179*

Thomas Russell Edward Mulford Ebenezer Rogers Branders of Horses — *179*

Andrew Beach Sealor of Leather — *179*

Thomas Russel Sealer of waits & Decon Elnathan Beach Sealer of Measures — *179*

Samuel Tyler James Harrison Jonathan Bartholomew Keykeepers — *179*

Voted Lieu^t Stephen Foot should Receive all the Ear marks of Sheep brought to him and make Record of the Same — *179*

Stephen Palmer Junr for ye 2 Society Joseph Rogers for ye 3^d Society was Chosen for the Same Buisnes — *179*

Joseph Parmele Chosen Collector of 1st Society and Timothy Russel 2^d Society Caleb Street of ye 3^d Society — *179*

Voted that Ebenezer Linsley Junr Acc^t of 30/ or 40/ be allow^d for Charg of Drink &c when the Man of war was in this Harbour som Time in July Last — *179*

15 Jan 1776

James Barker Esqr was Chosen Moderator — *179*

Capt Edward Russell John Ford Joseph Barker Dec^n Barnabus Mulford Dec^n Ebenezer Russell Timothy Hoadley Jacob Bunnel was Chosen a Com^{tt} of Inspection — *179*

Voted a Rate of three Farthings on the Pound should be made on the List of year 1775.. Joseph Parmele Timothy Russel Caleb Street was Chosen Collectors of s^d Rate — *179*

meeting Granted Thos Rogers Liberty to prove the powder which he makes him self by Shooting — *179*

5 Feb 1776

Voted that an Addition should be made to the Commite of Inspection.. Chose Deac^n Elnathan Beach Richard Baldwin Aaron Baldwin Capt Benjamin Maltbie to assist the former Commity — *178*

Solomon Tyler was Chosen Collector of the town Rate.. (Capt Parmel Refuseing & p^d his fine) — *178*

8 Apr 1776

Voted that a comitte be appointed to apply to the Governer & Counsell to have the Priviledge of Building a Gally & that a Sufficient number of men be kept as a Gourd at the Expence of the Continent, Capt Samuel Russell was appointed & Chosen a Com^{tt} — *178*

[ ] Dec 1776

Josiah Rogers Esqr was chosen Moderator — *178*

Samuel Baker was chosen Town Clerk — *178*

Branford

James Barker Esq[r] Deacon Elnathan Beach Cap[t] Samuel Russell Aaron Baldwin Justus Rose Daniel Page & Samuel Rose the Second were chosen Selectmen	178
Ebenezer Linsly Jun[r] Roger Tyler Jun[r] & Isaac Foot were chosen Constables.. also Ithiel Russell was chosen a Constable.. and Also Collector of the Tax or Taxis.. Granted by the Gen[l] Assembly	178
Obed Linsly Samuel How, John Monro, Elnathan Beach, Ephraim Foot, John Barker, David Goodrich, Ebenezer Palmer, Thomas Gould, Pennock Howd, Edward Brockway, Samuel Rogers, Solomon Tyler, Eleazer Stent, Isaac Linsly Jonathan Foot, Roger Seymour, Ephraim Page, Elihu Stone, Ithiel Russell, Ephraim Baldwin, Daniel Baldwin Eli Rogers, Dow Smith, Jesse Street, Samuel Foot Isaac Ingraham Jun[r], Rufus Hoadly, Elihu Baldwin Edward Harrison Elihu Rogers were chosen Surveyors of Highways	178
Elnathan Beach Cap[t] Samuel Russell Stephen Palmer Daniel Linsly Samuel Rose 2[d] & Michael Tainter Fence Vewers	178
Obed Linsly Farrington Harrison Samuel Hoadly Peter Harrison Samuel Harrison Jon[th] Russell James Harrison Ebenezer Rogers & Elihu Baldwin Listers	178
Joseph Parmele, Thomas Norton, Bille Rose, Jesse Street John Palmer, Cap[t] Benj[n] Maltbie & John Blakeston Jun[r] Grandjurors	178
Samuel Barker John Ford Major Edward Russell Deac[n] Elnathan Beach Ephraim Parrish Joseph Barker, Deac[n] Barnabas Mulford, Cap[t] Josiah Harrison Deac[n] Ebenezer Russell, Samuel Rose 2[d] Isaac Foot & Cap[t] Josiah Fowler were chosen a Committe of Inspection	178
Hooker Frisbie William Frisbie, Joseph Smith Solomon Whedon, Elnathan Tyler & Peter Tyler Tythingmen	178
granted a Rate of Two penie farthing on the Pound to be made on the List of the present Year.. to defrey the Expence of purchasing Tents and Other Camp Furniture.. and Other necessary Expences of the Town and chose Cap[t] Daniel Olds, Cap[t] Reuben Rose & Jon[th] Tyler to collect said Rate	178
Thomas Russell Edward Mulford & Ebenezer Rogers Branders of Horses	178
Thomas Russell Sealer of Weights	178
Deac[n] E Beach Sealer of Measures	178

26 Feb 1777

Samuel Barker was chosen Moderator	177

7 Apr 1777

Voted that a Rate of Seven Pence on the Pound be granted and made on the List.. for the Year 1776.. for encouraging the enlistment of the Quota of Men Apportioned by the Governor & his Council of Safety.. for the light Battalions.. for Continental Service that is to Say, Ten Pounds to each Non-Commissioned Officer & Soldier, that either has, or Shall Enlist himself into said Service for & during the Term of Three Years or the Present War.. Chose Obed Linsley Collector.. for the first Society, Bille Rose for North Branford, & Elnathan Tyler for Northford Society [*ed: vote later repealed and Collectors to return the money already collected. See meeting 26 Apr 1777, same page.*]	177

26 Apr 1777

Samuel Barker was chosen Moderator	177

25 Jun 1777

Josiah Rogers Esq[r] was chosen Moderator	177
Voted that some suteable person be appointed.. to go forthwith to.. the Governor & lay before him our present very dangerous Situation, & request.. a suteable Number of the Levies now	176

Branford

raising.. to be stationed in this Town for our immediate Defence & Protection & chose..
Edmund Rogers, Ephraim Parrish Ebenezer Russell & Jonah Clark

29 Sep 1777

Samuel Barker was chosen Moderator	176
Voted, to chuse a Committe.. respecting the Towns providing sundry Articles of Clothing for the Non Commission Officers & Soldiers in the Continental Army.. & chose.. Edmund Rogers, Ephraim Parrish Ebenezer Russell & Jonah Clark	176
chose Messrs John Ford, Jesse Street Samuel Ford Samuel Rogers, Timothy Hoadley & William Whedon Assessors	176

[ ] Dec 1777

Josiah Rogers Esqr was chosen Moderator	176
Samuel Barker was chosen Town Clerk	176
Elnathan Beach, Ephraim Parrish, Maj^r Edward Russell, Aaron Baldwin, Justus Rose, Daniel Page & Samuel Rose the 2^d Selectmen	176
James Barker Esqr Town Treasurer	176
Isaac Foot Constable & Collector of the State Tax Roger Tyler Junr, Joseph Parmele, & Bille Rose Constables	176
Obed Linsly, Stephen Foot, Samuel Barker, Edmund Rogers, Stephen Blakiston, Timothy Goodrich, Peter Harrison, Roger Tyler Junr Ebenezer Palmer, Samuel Palmer Junr, Samuel Hoadly, Pennock Howd, Samuel Rogers, Eleazar Stent, John Linsly, Asahel Palmer Asahel Harrison, Solomon Rose, Capt Josiah Harrison, Gaskill Woodward, Timothy Harrison, Daniel Page, Wheeler Beers, Isaac Foot, Samuel Foot, Isaac Ingraham Junr Jonah Clark, Rufus Hoadly, Capt Josiah Fowler & Ebenezer Rogers Surveyors of Highways	176
Capt Saml Russell, Deac^n Elnathan Beach, Stephen Palmer, Daniel Linsly, Sam Rose 2^d & Michael Tainter, Fence Vewers	176
Capt James Barker, Eleazar Stent, Ebenezer Barker, Samuel Ford, Dec^n Ebenezer Russell, Isaac Ingraham Junr Jonah Clark, Stephen Palmer Junr and Josiah Howd Listers	176
Major Edward Russell, Daniel Page & Isaac Foot Assessors	176
Stephen Blakiston, Samuel Russell, Ebenezer Linsly Junr Reuben Rose, Solomon Rose Josiah Fowler & Benjamin Maltbie, a Committe for.. supplying the Families of such Officers & Soldiers belonging to this Town with such Provisions & Cloathing as may be necessary	176
Farrington Harrison Daniel Olds, Reuben Whedon & Timothy Hoadly, A Committe.. to procure one Shirt, either linnen or flannel, one hunting Shirt, or Frock, one pair of Woollen Overhalls, one or Two pair of Stockings, & one pair of good Shoes for each non-commission Officer & Soldier in the Continental Army belonging to this Town	176
Andrew Beach was chosen Sealer of Leather	175
Willford Johnson, Ephraim Foot, James Harrison, Nathl Page Junr, Capt Josiah Fowler, Phinehas Baldwin & Edmund Rogers Grandjurors	175
Ebenezer Linsly Junr Phinehas Tyler, Asahel Palmer, Dow Smith, John Page & Ebenezer Hoadly, Tythingmen	175
Chose Jabez Palmer, Joel Howd & David Rogers Haywards	175

9 Feb 1778

James Barker Esqr was chosen Moderator	175
Voted a Tax of Two Pence half Penny on the Pound to be Made on the List of the Year 1777.. chose Peter Harrison, Bille Tyler & Jairus Bunnel Collectors Collectors	175

39

Branford

Chose Ezekiel Hays Edward Mulford & Ebenezer Rogers Branders of Horses	175
Ezekiel Hays Sealer of Weights	175
voted that the Fine incurred by Benjamin Frisbie for neglecting to Join the Army when drafted in June last be refunded to him	175
chose Joseph Parmele Farrington Harrison & Stephen Palmer Junr to take care of the Stray Sheep	175

15 Sep 1778

Josiah Rogers Esqr was chosen Moderator	175
Voted that the Selectmen (if upon Enquiry they Jude it necessary) do afford such Assistance to Uzziel in supporting his son Isaac (being Affected with epileptick Fitts) as they Shall think Sufficient to enable him to provide for his Said Son	175

[ ] Dec 1778

Samuel Barker Moderator	175
Samuel Barker Town Clerk	175
Jonathan Beach, Ephraim Prrish, Col Edward Russell,. Justus Rose, Aaron Baldwin, Sam Rose 2^d & Isaac Foot Select Men	175
James Barker Esqr Town Treasurer	175
Roger Tyler Junr Constable & Collector of the State Taxes Joseph Parmele, Bille Rose, & Isaac Foot Constables	175
Joseph Tyler, James Barker Esqr, Samuel Barker, Abiel Page Enoch Staples, Timothy Goodrich, Edward Barker Abijah Hobart, Joseph Bartholomew, Noah Baldwin Josiah Howd, Samuel Hoadley, Timothy Barker, Samuel Rogers, Isaac Linsly, Asahel Harrison, Samuel Baldwin 2^d, Daniel Linsly, Joseph Smith, Abraham Harrison Bille Tyler, James Whedon, Levi Rogers Junr, Edward Meloy, Jairus Bunnel, Asahel Tyler Solomon Talmage James Maltbie Amos Harrison & Josiah Rogers Esqr Surveyors of Highways	175
Capt Samuel Russell, Deac^n Elnathan Beach, Stephen Palmer Daniel Linsly Samuel Rose 2^d & Michael Tainter Fence Vewers	175
Capt Daniel Olds, Capt John Rusell, Capt Edmund Rogers Lieu^t Saml Hoadly Deac^n Ebenezer Russell Capt Reubin Rose Capt Benjn Baldwin & Timothy Hoadley Listers & Assessors	174
Andrew Beach Leather Sealer	174
Lieu^t Stephen Foot, Hooker Frisbie Eli Rogers, Elihu Stone Jonah Clark, Ebenezer Rogers & Saml How Grand Jurors	174
Phinehas Tyler Capt Ebenezer Linsly, Edward Mulford Jonathan Foot, Ozias Tyler & Solomon Talmage Tythingmen	174
Enoch Staples, Eleazar Stent, John Ford, Willm Whedon Jonth Russell, Josiah Linsly & Elihu Baldwin, A Com^{tee} to procure Cloathing for the non Commissioned Officers & Soldiers in the American Army	174
Joseph Barker, Thomas Norton, Othniel Stent Daniel Linsly Lieu^t Samuel Baldwin Deac^n Phinehas Baldwin & Isaac Foot a Com^{tee} for Supplying the Families of the Officers & Soldiers	174
Ezekiel Hays, Edward Mulford & Ebenezer Rogers Branders of Horses	174
Ezekiel Hays Sealer of Weights	174
Deac^n Elnathan Beach Sealer of Measures	174
Voted a Tax of six Pence on the Pound to be mde on the List of the Year 1778; chose Joseph Wilford, Samuel Harrison & Ichabod Tyler Collectors of s^d Rate	174

Branford

chose Wellford Johnson, Joseph Parmele, John Russell, Timothy Goodrich, Joseph Willford, Elihu Stone Stephen Palmer Junr Edward Barker Daniel Baldwin Edmund Rogers David Rogers & Farrington Harrison Haywards	174
Lieu^t Stephen Foot, Stephen Palmer Junr & Ammaziah Rose were chosen a Com^{tee} to take up & take Care of all the Stray Sheep.. & Keep a Record of their Ear Marks, & to be allowed a Meet Reward for their Trouble *12 Apr 1779*	174
Chose.. Jonah Clark to make Application to s^d Assembly to lay before them our defenceless State & pray that a Guard may be granted *4 Jun 1779*	174
voted a Tax of One Shilling & Six Pence on the Pound, to be made on the List of the Year 1778.. to defrey the necessary expences of the Town. Chose Robert Olds Collector.. of the first Society, Timothy Harrison of the Second Society & Joseph Rogers of Northford Society *[ ] Dec 1779*	173
Col Edward Russell Moderator	173
Samuel Barker Town Clerk	173
Col Edward Russell, Ephraim Parrish, Isaac Foot, Samuel Ford, Capt Timothy Hoadley, Joseph Barker & Timothy Russell Selectmen	173
John Russell Town Treasurer	173
Bille Rose, Constable & Collector of the State Taxes, Eleazar Stent, Roger Tyler Junr & Isaac Foot Constables	173
Capt Ebenezer Linsly, Joseph Parmele, John Monro, Ezekiel Hays, Robert Olds, Ephraim Beach, John Baldwin Junr Bart^w Goodrich, Josiah Howd, Isaac Hoadley, Thomas Gould John Rogers Junr, Allen Smith, John Linsly Ju^r Asahel Palmer, Samuel Ford, Solomon Rose, John Palmer, Jared Harrison, Eber Beers, Daniel Barker Junr Daniel Foot Jonathan Tyler, Jonah Clark, Amos Harrison & Jacob Frisbie, Surveyors of Highways	173
Deacon E. Beach, Capt Saml Russell, Daniel Linsly Stephen Palmer, Samuel Rose, & Isaac Foot, Fence Vewers	173
Samuel Hoadley, Joseph Parmele, Enoch Staples, Captain Reuben Rose, Samuel Harrison, Capt Benjamin Baldwin & Stephen Williams, Listers	173
Timothy Goodrich, Farrington Harrison, Obed Linsly Daniel Rose, Asahel Palmer, Amos Harrison & Elihu Rogers Grandjurymen	173
Isaac Hoadley, Joseph Bartholomew, Israel Baldwin Moses Baldwin, Peter Tyler & Peter Augur Tythingmen	173
Ezekiel Hays, Edward Mulford, & Ebenezer Rogers Branders of Horses	173
Ezekiel hays Sealer of Weights	173
Deacon Elnathan Beach Sealer of Measures	173
Chose Samuel Frisbie, Levi Rose & John Foot Collectors	173
Chose Samuel Tyler, Stephen Palmer Junr & Samuel Rose Junr a Com^{tee} for.. taking Care of stray Sheep	173
Ephraim Parrish Constable & Collect^r of the State Taxes.. in the Room of Bille Rose who has refused & paid his Fine also William Whedon a Constable	173
Chose Willford Johnson, John Russell, Timothy Harrison, Stephen Palmer Junr, Peter Tyler Ju^r, Benjamin Maltbie 3^d, a Com^{tee} for Supplying the Soldiers Families	173
Edward Barker, Stephen Foot, Solomon Tyler, Daniel Rose, Solomon Whedon, Capt Josiah fowler. & Amaziah Rose a Com^{tee} for Supplying the Soldiers with Cloathing	173

Branford

9 Mar 1780

Edward Russell Esqr was chosen Moderator | 172

Voted that Twenty Four Persons be chosen Inspectors of Provisions, in Pursuance of an Act | 172
of the Genl Assembly.. Viz Ten in the first Society & Seven in each of the Other Societys & made Choice of Captain Ebenezer Lindsly, Alexander Gordon, Moses Hobart, Captain Samuel Barker, Joseph Parmele Samuel Hoadley Joseph Barker, Eleazar Stent Pennock Howd, Roger Tyler Junr James Hoadley Eli Rogers, Abijah Rogers, Samuel Harrison, Jonth Russell, Jonth Foot, Capt Reuben Rose, Jonah Clark Jesse Street, Phinehas Baldwin, Judah Howd, Capt Timothy Hoadley, Samuel Foot & John Augur Jun$^{[r]}$

This Town Sensible that all publick Bodies of Men.. are subject to be infested with | 172
unfriendly & evil designing Men And taking into Consideration the alarming Situation of our publick Interests.. from the State of our Medium of Trade, Depreciation of the Currency, evident Embarisment of the Legislative Power & feeble Exertion of the executive Branches of Government.. considering also the undeniable Right which every free & independent People have to be informed, & fully Acquainted with the Measures their Representatives adopt for the public Interest.. require that not only the Debates of our Representitives.. should be open, & free to be heard by any of the Inhabitants so disposed, but also that a correct & printed Journal of their Doings.. be made publick.. Voted that Capt Ephraim Parrish be desired to cause the foregoing Paper to be inserted in the next Connecticut Journal

..A Paper was presented to the Meeting by Mr Isaacs & the same being read, the Town Voted | 172
that the same be also published in the next Connecticut Journal

3 Jul 1780

Samuel Barker was chosen Moderator | 172

Voted that Capt Ebenezer Barker be desired to Attend this Meeting with the Commisison that | 172
he has lately received from.. the Govr & lay the same before the Meeting & that Two of the Select Men wait on Capt Barker and Desire his Attendance

it was put to Vote whether the Town do approve of the Doings of the informing Officers | 171
relative to the Seizure of certain Goods & Merchandize brought into this Town by Capt Ebenezer Barker & Company, and passed in the Affirmative

Voted that a Committee be chosen.. to exhibit a Complaint to.. the Governor against Capt | 171
Ebenezer Barker, for his Conduct under the Commission lately granted by his Excellency to s^d Barker, to raise against the Enemies of the United States of America.. chose.. Samuel Rose Junr Capt Ezekiel Hays, and Capt Timothy Hoadley

Voted that Asahel Harrison be recommended.. to.. the Governor as a Suteable Person to be | 171
commissioned to command an Armed Boat to cruise against the Enemy

10 Apr 1780

Whereas Application is made.. by Doct^r Willm Gould.. that he has.. Advanced.. Money for the | 171
Support & Cure of John Guy, a poor & impotent Person.. lately badly wounded.. Voted that s^d Sum be not paid out of the Town Treasury, but that the Select Men make Application to the County Court.. that the Court would Order that Mrs Mary Guy the Mother of.. John (who is of Sufficient Ability) pay s^d Debt

Voted that the Select Men make Representation to the.. County Court.. to compel the | 171
Children of Deborah Boyls.. to Support her.. she being by Age and Sickness become poor, & impotent & unable to Support herself.. and in the Mean Time to furnish her with necessary Supplies on the Cost of the Town

[ ] Sep 1780

A Rate.. of one Penny half Penny on the Pound to be made on the List of 1779.. to defray the | 171

42

Branford

Necessary Expences of the Town was granted.. Chose Caleb Frisbie Collector.. of the first Society Dow Smith for the North Society & Joshua Augur Jun[r] for Northford Society | 171

14 Nov 1780

Edward Russell was chosen Moderator	171
Voted that a Tax be levied.. for the Purpose of purchasing.. Provisions, with Liberty to any Person to pay in Provisions.. And Cap[t] Ezekiel Hays, Bille Rose & Amaziah Rose were chosen Collectors	171
Eleazar Stent, Asahel Harrison & Jonah Clark were chosen a Committee to be joined with the Collectors of the aforesaid Tax, to receive the Salt provided by the Government, procure Barrels, & to purchase & receive s[d] Provisions & to inspect & see the same put up	171
Voted that Captains Ebenezer Linsly, James Barker, Abraham Foot, Reuben Rose, Timothy Hoadley & Benj[n] Baldwin & Lieutenants Samuel Hoadley Joseph Willford, Samuel Baldwin Ebenezer Trusdel & Jairus Bunnel & Ensigns Farrington Harrison, Allen Smith, Asahel Harrison, Edward Mulford & Elihu Baldwin be a Committee to Ascertain the Number of Men now in Service that count for this Towns Quota & the Number.. to compleat.. this Towns whole Quota of Forty Four Men for the continental Army	170
Whereas Joseph Wilford informed the Meeting that he had.. the Expence of Twenty Spanish Milled Dollars in Obtaining the Knowledge of Thomas Osborn's being concealed in this Town, in Order to his being detected and brought to punished, requesting that he might be reimbursed.. it was voted that the Select Men.. make such Allowance as they Shall Judge Just	170

[ ] Dec 1780

Edward Russell Esq[r] was chosen Moderator	170
Samuel Barker Town Clerk	170
Mess[rs] Joseph Barker, Ephraim Parrish, Eleazar Stent Timothy Russell Samuel Ford Isaac Foot & Cap[t] Timothy Hoadley Select Men	170
Deac[n] Elnathan Beach Town Treasurer	170
Roger Tyler Jun[r] Constable & Collector of the State Taxes; Ephraim Parrish Eleazar Stent William Whedon & Isaac Foot Constables	170
Chose Cap[t] Ebenezer Linsly, Stephen Foot Ephraim Parrish Elnathan Beach Solomon Tyler, Bart[w] Goodrich Ebenezer Palmer, Enoch Staples, John Rogers, Benj[n] Palmer, Edw[d] Barker, Samuel Palmer, Rufus Linsly Dow Smith, Eli Rogers, Daniel Linsly, Jacob Harrison William Whedon, Bille Tyler, Hels Foot, Gasksill Woodward, Aaron Baldwin, Jesse Street, Joseph Augur, Joel Ives, Sam[l] Bartholomew Jun[r] Solomon Linsly James Smith & Cap[t] Josiah Fowler Surveyors of Highways	170
Cap[t] Samuel Russell, Deac[n] Elnathan Beach, Dan[l] Linsly Jonathan Foot, Samuel Rose Jun[r] Michael Tainter Fence Vewers	170
John Butler Jun[r] Cap[t] Ezekiel Hays Solomon Tyler, Stephen Blakiston, Asahel Harrison Edward Mulford, Warham Williams Jun[r] & Solomon Linsly Listers	170
Joseph Parmele, Samuel Frisbie, Zacheus Baldwin, Bille Tyler, Nathan Rose Jun[r] & John Potter Grandjurors	170
Cap[t] Ebenezer Linsly Enoch Staples, Solomon Whedon, Abijah Rogers, Michael Tainter Jun[r] & Stephen Williams, Tythingmen	170
Cap[t] Ezekiel Hays, Edward Mulford, & Ebenezer Rogers Branders of Horses	170
Cap[t] Ezekiel Hays Sealer of Weights	170
Deac[n] Elnathan Beach Sealer of Measures	170
Samuel Tyler James Harrison & Jonathan Bartholomew Key Keepers	170

Branford

Capt Daniel Olds, Ephraim Foot, Joseph Willford, Levi Rose, & Samuel Foot a Committee for Supplying the Families of the Soldiers	170
Capt Samuel Barker, Daniel Rose & Jonth Tyler A Committee for Procuring Cloathing for the Soldiers	170

1 Jan 1781

Col Edward Russell was chosen Moderator	169
Voted.. for providing a Quantity of Flour to the Amount of one Penny half Penny on the Pound o the List of the Year 1779 for the Use of the Troops of this State, a Rate, of Three Pence to the Pound on s^d List.. for the Purpose aforesd; & that each Inhabitant have Liberty to pay his Proportion.. in Flour.. Chose Edward Barker, Roger Seymour, Edward Harrison Collectors.. the s^d Edwd Barker refused to Serve.. & paid the Sum of Twenty Six Shillings.. as Penulty.. the Town then.. Chose Ephraim Beach to s^d Office	169
Chose Joseph Barker, Timothy Russell, & Isaac Foot a Committee to receive Flour, & to purchase such Quantities as Shall be wanting to compleat the Towns Quota	169
Voted a Rate or Tax of four Pence on the Pound in Bills emitted by the Genl Assembly of this State to be levied.. according to the List of 1780.. to be applied for Payment of the Necessary Charges arising within this Town and Chose Samuel Russell Junr Abraham Linsly & Solomon Linsly Collectors	169

30 Jan 1781

Samuel Barker was chosen Moderator	169
Chose Gideon Bartholomew Collector of the Rate.. in the rooom of Saml Russell Junr who hath refused to serve	169
Voted that an Agent be appointed.. to repair to.. the Governor, & represent.. the present defenceless & dangerous Situation of this Town.. & request.. a Guard of (at least) fifty Men properly Officered.. and Col Edward Russell was chosen	169

7 Feb 1781

Voted.. the Town do accept, & approve of the Arrangement made by the Civil Authority & Select Men.. of the Guard to be raised for the Defence of the same.. by our Agent Col Edward Russell	169
Voted.. the Proprietors of the Islands.. called Thimble Islands, be requested to consent that all the Timber & Wood growing thereon may be.. cut & carryed off.. Stephen Blakiston & John Blakiston Junr the s^d Owners.. being present consented.. Chose Samuel Hoadley, Samuel Barker Junr & Pennock Howd a Committee for the Purpose	169
whereas this Town.. have been divided into Seven Classes, each of which to procure One Able bodied, effective Man for the Defence of the Posts at Horse Neck & other Parts of this State, .. & that each Class tax themselves for s^d Purpose; .. made Choice of Obed Linsley for Class Number one, Papillon Barker for Class Number Two, Ja[ ] Rogers for Class Number Three; Jonathan Russell for Class Number Four, Jonth Foot for Class Number Five Medad Tainter for Class Number Six & John Page for Class Number Seven	169

9 Apr 1781

Voted that Col Edward Russell be desired.. to make Draffts from the several Militia Companys in this Town to compleat the.. Guards	168
Ralph Isaacs to Collect.. Rate of the Inhabitants of the first Society.. Daniel Hoadley of the North Society & Solomon Talmage of Northford Society	168

21 Jun 1781

Samuel Barker was chosen Moderator	168

Branford

Voted a Tax..in Silver, or Gold Coin, or Beef Cattle.. Chose Othniel Stent, Daniel Barker Junr & Deacon Phinehas Baldwin Collectors	168
25 Jun 1781	
Samuel Barker Chosen Moderator	168
Chose John Rogers Collector and Roger Tyler Junr Receivers of the Provisions	168
18 Sep 1781	
Coll Edward Russell Chosen Moderator	168
Voted a Tax.. for the purpose of supplying the Soldiers Families & the Town Guards.. Chose John Harrington Beach, Joseph Wilford & Timothy Bartholomew Collectors	167
27 Sep 1781	
Meeting Adjorned to the 2^d Day of Oct^r.. for the purpose of Choosing a Town Clerk in the Room of Sam^{ll} Barker Esqr Dec^d.. Certifyed.. Edward Russell Moderator	167
2 Oct 1781	
Edward Russell was (by one of the Select Men) Declared to be chosen Town Clerk	167
[ ] Nov 1781	
Chose Bille Tyler Collector of the 4^d Beef Tax.. in the room of Daniel Barker Ju^r Late Dec^d	167
[ ] Dec 1781	
Edw: Russell was Chosen Moderator and also Town Clerk	167
Deac^n Elnathan Beach was Chosen Town Treasurer	167
Eleaz^r Stent Ephraim Parrish Joseph Barker, Sam^{ll} Ford, Timothy Russell, Dea^n Phinehas Baldwin & Isaac Foot were Chosen Select-men	167
Willm Whedon, Roger Tyler Junr, Eleazr Stent Isaac Foot Ephraim Parrish were chosen Constables. and also Stephen Williams was Chosen Constable, & to Collect the State Tax	166
Willford Johnson, Timothy Bradley, Farrington Harrison Capt Ezekiel Hays Mason Hobart Bartholomew Goodrich, Thomas Norton, Eleaz^r Stent, Sam^{ll} Palmer, Sam^{ll} Hoadly, Thomas Frisbie, Zacheus Baldwin, Gideon Bartholomew, Jonathan Foot, Eli Rogers, Jacob Harrison, Bille Rose, Willm Russell Jonathan Byinton, Thomas Rogers, Timothy Harrison Junr Joseph Smith, John Linsley Ju^r Jesse Street, Jonathan Tyler, Sam^{ll} Bartholomew Ju^r Ichabod Foot, James Smith, Capt Ebenez^r Rogers, Jared Foot ware Chosen Survaiours of Highways	166
Capt Saml Russell Elnathan Beach, Daniel Linsley, Jonath^n Foot, Saml Rose, & Mical Taintor ware Chosen Fence Vewers	166
Capt Jam^s Barker, Elnathan Beach, Capt Sam^{ll} Russell, Sam^{ll} Hoadley, Joseph Willford, Willm Whedon, Benjn Maltbie Ju^r & Mical Taintor Ju^r ware Chosen Listers	166
Capt Gideon Bartholomew, Sam^{ll} Frisbie, Mason Hobart, Ruben Whedon, Solomon Rose, Jacob Bunnel, & Jared Foot ware Chosen Grand Jurimen	166
Joseph Bartholomew, Enoch Staples, Levi Rose, Justus Harrison, Elihu Baldwin, Isaac Foot ware Chosen Tytheing Men	166
Capt Ezekeil Hays, Edw: Mulford, & Elihu Baldwin ware Chosen Branders of Horses	166
Capt Ezekeil Hays Chosen Sealer of Weights	166
Dea^n Elnathan Beach Chosen Sealer of Measures	166
Sam^{ll} Tyler, Danl F Harrison and Jonathan Bartholomew Chosen Kee keepers	166
Andrew Beach Chosen Leather Sealer	166

Branford

19 Mar 1782

Ebenez^r Russell Esqr chose Moderator   166

Voted that a Guard.. of Twenty Men be.. Raised for the Defence of this Town.. and that an Officer be appointed in each Society. and to Rais their proportionable part of the Men by Inlistment, and chose Lt Jacob Bunnel, Lt Edw: Mulford & Ens^n Allen Smith for the purpose.. and to Command the Guard, each one his proportionable part of the time, and to take their Instructions from Col: Edw: Russell: and that they Receive the same pay & Rations as the soldiers in the Continental Army.. and to be allowed one shilling p^r Day for billiting themselves   166

8 Apr 1782

it being Represented to the Meeting that two Men, was this Towns Proportion to be procured for the Continental Army.. Voted a Com^{tee} be appointed to hire the Two Men on the Towns cost, for one Year, and chose Farrington Harrison & William Whedon   166

granted a Tax of one penney on the pound.. and chose Pennock Howd, Ephraim Baldwin and James Smith Collectors Collectors   165

7 Sep 1782

granted a Tax on the List 1781, of 2^d on the Pound.. to Defray the Necessary expences of the Town; and Chose Timothy Bradly, Jonathan Russell & Josiah Fowler Ju^r 165

28 Oct 1782

Joseph Barker was Chosen Moderator   165

4 Nov 1782

Chose John Baldwin Ju^r Collector of the 2^d Tax.. in the room of Timothy Bradly who refused, and s^d Baldwin also refused & paid his Fine; .. Meeting then chose Obediah Tyler in his room   165

11 Nov 1782

Chose Papillion Barker Collector of the 2^d TownTax, in the room of Obediah Tyler who Refused & paid his Fine   165

18 Nov 1782

mad Choice of Ebenez^r Palmer to Collect the 2^d Town Tax... in the Room of Papillon Barker who refuses   165

[ ] Dec 1782

Ebenez^r Russell Esqr chosen Moderator   165

Edw: Russell Clerk   165

made choice of Ephraim Parrish, C^t Sam^{ll} Russell, Willm Munro, Sam^{ll} Ford, Jonathan Russell, C^t Timothy Hoadley & Jesse Street Select-men   165

Chose Dea^n Elnathan Beach Town Treasurer   165

Ephraim Parrish, Sam^{ll} Hoadly, Roger Tyler Ju^r & Stephen Williams Constables, and also Ruben Rose Constable & to Collect the State Tax   165

Chose Willford Johnson, Tim^y Bradly, Farrinton Harrison, Ephraim Foot, Sam^{ll} Frisbie, John Barker, Willm Munro, James Hoadly, Isaac Palmer, Jos^h Bartholomew, Pennock Howd, Jonathan Towner Ju^r Sam^{ll} Page, Rufus Linsley, Asahel Palmer, Israel Linsley, Jona^n Hoadley, Dan^{ll} Foot Harrison, Edw: Mulford, Ebenez^r Russell Ju[ ] Jacob Barker, Jared Harrison, Tim^y Harrison Ju^r Joseph Willford, Jacob Bunnel, Peter Tyler, Charles Ford, Josiah Fowler Ju^r, and Jacob Frisbie Surveyours of Highways   165

Branford

C^t Sam^{ll} Russell, Dea^n Elnathan Beach, Dan^{ll} Linsley, Jonath^n Foot, Sam^{ll} Rose, and Micah Tainter, ware chosen Fence Veiwers	165
Joseph Barker, Sam^{ll} Whedon, Edmond Rogers, Doc^r Willm Gould, Solomon Whedon, Bille Tyler, Josiah Linsley, and Peter Augur ware chosen Listers	164
Andrew Beach chosen Sealer of Leather	164
Nicodemas Baldwin, John Butler, Willm Frisbie Sam^{ll} Harrison, Jacob Harrison, Amos Harrison, & Isaac Ingraham were Chosen Grandjury Men	164
C^t Ebenez^r Linsley, Joseph Bartholomew, Bille Rose, Abrah^m Linsley, Benjn Maltbie Junr & Elnathan Tyler were chosen Tything men	164
C^t Ez^l Hays, Edward Mulford, & C^t Ebenez^r Rogers chosen Branders of Horses	164
C^t Ez^l Hays Sealer of Weights	164
Dea^n Elnathan Beach Sealer of Measures	164
Josiah Tyler, James Harrison & Warham Williams Ju^r Chosen Key keepers	164
Sam^{ll} Ford moved to the Meeting to be excused from Serving as a Select-man.. & he was excused and Edward Muford chosen in his room	164

19 Dec 1782

Dea^n Aaron Baldwin (after long Debate) was chosen Moderator, and Edw: Russell was chosen Clerk	164
chose Edw: Russell & Jonah Clark Esqr Agents.. to represent to the next Genl Assembly their Grevances by Petition against the other part of the Town.. also chose C^t Sam^{ll} Barker, Enoch Staples Sam^{ll} Harrison, Joseph Willford, Jacob Bunnel, & Isaac Foot a Com^{tee} to Collect the Evidence Necessary to support the charge of those that moved for this Meeting against the rest of the Town	164
In behalf of themselves & the rest of s^d Inhabitants in favour of ye last meeting; (by their Agents Edw: Russel & Jonah Clark) brought their Petition to the Genl Assembly.. praying that the Doings of the s^d last Meeting might be Established, or that both Meetings might be made void, and an other Meeting Ordered by the Assembly	164

13 Feb 1783

proceeded to chose a Moderator, Dea^n Aaron Baldwin being Nominated.. past in the affirm^e and Edw: Russell was chosen Town Clerk	164
Eleaz^r Stent, Roger Tyler Ju^r Farrington Harrison, C^t Asahel Harrison, Willm Wheadon, Dea^n Phinehas Baldwin & Sam^{ll} Rose were chosen Select-men	164
Joseph Barker chosen Town Treasurer	164
C^t Rubin Rose was chose Constable & to Collect the State Taxes.. and Roger Tyler Ju^r Joseph Permele Isaac Foot & Stephen Williams were chosen Constables, Sam^{ll} Harrison also Chose Constable	164
John Ford, Benjn Plant, Farrington Harrison, Sam^{ll} Frisbie, Enoch Staples, Ephraim Beach, C^t Sam^{ll} Barker, James Hoadley, Willm Munro, Bartholomew Goodrich, Edward Barker, Rufus Linsley, Jonathan Foot, Israel Linsley, Danl Foot Harrison, Edw: Mulford Joseph Willford, Jonathan Russell, Jacob Barker, Ephraim Page, Timothy Harrison Ju^r, Jacob Bunnil, Peter Tyler, Isaac Ingraham, Benjn Maltbie Ju^r, Jonah Fowler Ju^r & Jacob Frisbie were chosen surveyours of Highways	164
John Ford, Joseph Parmele, Danl Linsley, Jonth Foot, Sam^{ll} Rose & Michael Taintor were chosen Fence Vewers	164
Edm^d Rogers, C^t Sam^{ll} Barker, Rufus Linsley, Sam^{ll} Harrison Solomon Whedon, Peter Augur, & Doc^r Jared Foot chose Listers	164

Branford

James Barker Esqr chose Lether Sealer	163
Ebenez^r Beach, John Gordon, Othniel Stent, Jacob Harrison, Dow Smith, Isaac Ingraham, & Amos Harrison chose Grandjurors	163
Enoch Staples, Joseh Bartholomew, Bille Rose, Joseph Baldwin Benjn Maltbie Ju^r, & Elnathan Tyler chose Tything-men	163
John Baldwin Ju^r C^t Ebenez^r Rogers & Edw: Mulford chose Branders of Horses	163
John Baldwin Ju^r sealer of weights & Elihu Stone sealer of Measures	163
Josiah Tyler, Danl F Harrison Jonth Bartholomew Kee keepers	163
C^t Edm^d Rogers, Sam^{ll} Harrison & Jonah Clark Esqr chose a Com^{tee} to settle with the Treasurer	163
Joseph Parmele, Enoch Staples, Edm^d Rogers, C^t Saml Barker, Solo^n Tyler, Elihu Stone, Reuben Whedon, Joseph Baldwin, Joseph Willford, Justus Rose, Jacob Bunnil, Judah Howd, Elihu Baldwin, C^t Ebe^r Rogers, Doc^r Jared Foot, Israel Baldwin & Wooster Harrison chose a Com^{tee} of inspection	163

10 Mar 1783

Voated that the Select-men apply to the Genl Assembly for Liberty to sell Willm Guy's Land (Exclucive of Hopyards plain Land) to Defray the Expence of his support	163

1 May 1783

Voated that a Tax of 4^d on the pound be granted for supplying the Treasury.. and chose C^t Reubin Rose Collector	163
Voated that the Select-men wright to Col: Ludington of York State to know wheather he will assist in the support of his Father in this Town, or not	163
Meeting Reconsidered their voat of the last Meeting respecting Willm Guys Land	163

30 Jun 1783

Dea^n Aaron Baldwin was chosen Moderator	163
Orders Drawn in favour of the Militia in this Town for their servises at the time the Enemy Landed at & burnt New London shall be received by the Collector.. & also the payroll of the Town Guards for ye last Year being properly made up & allowed by ye Select-men, and also the pay Roll of one certain £50 Order Drawn for Rotation Guards.. in.. 1781 and now in the hands of Capt Staples shall also be Rec^d	162

24 Sep 1783

Dea^n Aaron Baldwin was chosen Moderator	162
A motion was made that ye minds of ye Meeting be taken, whether this Town will appoint.. agents, to represent this Town at the convention.. and after many arguments used & a long Debate.., the Question was put & pas^d.. and they chose.. Barnabas Mulford & Aaron Baldwin	162

Canaan

Town Records
Vol. A
Pgs 8-29

Births, Deaths Marriages
Vol. A
Pgs 64 & 77
See also LDS film # 1,503,196 for Oaths of Fidelity.

Located at the Town Clerk's Office in Falls Village

Canaan

25 Oct 1774

a meeting.. held at the Dwelling house of Capt Isaac Lawrance	9
Chose Capt Tarbull Whitney be moderator	9
Voted that Capt Tarbull Whitney Capt Isaac Lawrance Timothy Moses Asahel Beebe John Whitney & Edward Sutton Shall be a Committee of Correspondance for the Town to Receve and Communicate Enteligence from and to.. the Neibouring Towns and Coloneys	9
Voted that Capt Tarbull Whitney & Asahel Beebe Shall be a Committee to meet Litchfield Countys Committee of Corrispondance	9

13 Dec 1774

Voted that Capt: Isaac Lawrance be moderator	10
Voted that John Whitney Nathaniel Dean Capt John Stevens Timothy Hurlburt Capt Tarbull Whitney Nehemiah Lawrence & John Watson be a Committee of Inspection	10

17 Aug 1775

Voted that Capt Isaac Lawrence be moderator	10
Voted that the Town will Raise three farthings on the pound on the Last List of Said Town to provide Amunition.. Voted that Lemuel Kingsbury Shall be a Collector Collector.. Voted that Elijah Holcomb Shall be a Colector	10

12 Dec 1775

Voted that Co^{ll} Charles Burrall be moderator	11
Voted that Co^{ll} Charls Burrall Capt Samuel Forbs Capt John Ensign Nehemiah Lawrence John Whitney be Select Men	11
Voted that Abiel Fellows be Town Clerk	11
Voted that Abiel Fellows be Town Treasurer	11
Voted that John Hollembeck be constable & Colletor of the Coloney Tax.. Voted that Lemuel Kingsbury be Constable.. the Constables be Collectors of Town Rates	11
Voted that Joshua Whitney Benjamin Sedgwick James Faning Medad Newel David Lucus Joseph Fellows Manus Griswold Edward Brownell Daniel Bebee Samuel Robbens Ruluff Dutcher Thomas Hosner Samuel Whitaker Elijah Holcomb Jeremiah How & David Rouland be Surveyors of Highways	11
Voted that Noah Wells James Faning Capt Daniel Horsford & Jonathan Belding be fence viewers	11
Voted that Thomas Hosmer Charles Burrall Ju^r Elisha Bebee Giles Hamlin Edward Brownell Joseph Fellows be Listers	11
Voted that Simon Tubbs & Bille Blin be Lother Sealers	11
Voted that Benajah Douglass Elisha Bebee Nehemiah Lawrence & Joseph Kellogg Ju^r be Grandjuriers	11
Voted that John Spaulding Capt Tarbull Whitney Jonas Lawrence James Stevens Abraham Bushnall Friend Phelps Jerediah Brown William Noys Abiel Fellows & Elijah Holcomb be Tything men	11
Voted that Elijah Cobb & Abraham Bushnall be Sealers of weights & measurs	11
Voted that Capt Benjn Stevens Jonathan Belding & John Whitney be Key keepers	11
Voted that the sign post Shall be at the Corner by Co^{ll} Burralls	11
Voted that the corner by Co^{ll} Burralls a place to Set up warnings for Town meetings	11

Canaan

Voted that Abraham Holcomb be a Collector to Colet the unpaid part of the Coloney and Town Rates in the hand of Timothy Holcomb Dces^d	11
Voted that Benjn Sedgwick Thomas Fellows Abiel Fellows Capt Ensign Ruluff Dutcher John Whitney & Asahel Beebe be a Com^{tte} of Inspection	11
Voted that the meeting be adjorned to Co^{ll} Burralls Dwelling house	11
Voted that the Selectmen Shall give Conveyance of an Allowance of highway from the brod Road between Capt John Beebes and Mr James Beebes	11
Voted that.. Ruluff Dutcher & Capt John Ensign be a Com^{tee} to take Care of the Bridges between Canaan and Salisbury	11
Voted that Jeremiah Horsford Benjamin Miller James Faning Capt Tarbull Whitney Capt Timothy Moses Joseph Bakley Ju^r Aaron Barns & Samuel Holembeck be Haywards	11

12 Feb 1776

Voted that Decon John Whitney be moderator	11
Voted that Samuel Robins be Constable and Collector of the Coloney Tax in the Room of John Hallembeck who is ingaged in the Continencial Service	11
Voted that Samuel Robbins be Collector of Town Rates	11
Voted that Thomas Fellows be Serveyor of highways	11

17 Sep 1776

Elisha Baker Esqr Moderator	11
Voted that Russell Hunt be An Agent for the Town to the County Court.. to Oppose the Suit of Jeremiah Hosford Against the Town for a highway from the Great Bridge below the falls by the grist mill and Sawmill on the falls to the Six rod highway Near Ozias Bordman	11

10 Dec 1776

Voted that Capt Isaac Lawrence be Moderator	12
Voted that Capt Samuel Forbs Asahel Beebe Nehemiah Lawrence John Whitney and Thomas Fellows be Select Men	12
Voted that Abiel Fellows be Town Clerk	12
Voted that Abiel Fellows be Town Treasurer	12
Voted that Benajah Douglass be Constable & Collector of the Coloney Tax	12
Voted that Samuel Robbins be Constable	12
Voted that Capt William Burrall Jonathan Belding Jeremiah Hogaboom William [ ]ugg Friend Phelps Joseph Henman Samuel Whitaker Daniel Stevens Nathaniel Lawrence Nathaniel Stanley Nathan Newell Capt Tarbull Whitney Manus Griswold Ruben Stevens & Ruben Darby be Serveyors of Highways	12
Voted that Benjamin Sedgwick Gorshum Hewit Hezekiah Deming & James Marsh be Fence Viewers	12
Voted that Joseph Fellows Edward Brownell Giles Hamlin Joshua Whitney Elisha Beebe Charles Burrall Junr & Thomas Hosmer be Listers	12
Voted that Benajah Douglass & Sam^{ll} Robbins be Collector of Town Rates	12
Voted that John Ensign & Joshua Whitney be Grandjurers	12
Voted that Samuel Kingsbury David Lucus Merinor Rood Junr Ashbill Lain Roswell Dean John Coleman Gideon Barns Junr and Jerediah Brown be Tythingmen	12
Voted that Elijah Cable & Abraham Bushnall be Sealers of weights & measurs	12

Canaan

Voted that Bille Blin & Manass Griswold be Lother Sealers	12
Voted that Benjamin Sedwick John Whitney Jonathan Belding be key keepers	12
Voted that Timothy Hulbut Nath^{ll} Dean Charles Belding Capt Tarbull Whitney Capt Timothy Moses James Faning and Lemuel Kingsbury be Com^{tee} of Inspection	12
Voted that Lemuel Kingsbury Benjamin Sedgwick Phinehas [ ] Abell Hansdell Elijah Holcomb Aaron [ ]rns Elisha Beebe & Elizur Wright be Hayards	12
Voted that the Sign post Shall be at the Corner by Capt Whitneys	12
a Warning for town Meetings Shall be put up by Nathaniel Stanleys	12
Voted that the Selectmen Shall Act Descrisonaly.. concerning Laying out the Road Svey^d for by Jeremiah Horsford	12

26 Mar 1777

Voted that John Whitney be moderator	12
Voted that Medad Newel be Serveyor of Highways	13

14 Apr 1777

Voted that Asahel Beebe be moderator	13

12 May 1777

Voted that John Whitney be moderator	13
Voted that the Select men Shall make a Rate.. Sufficient to pay all that have Inlisted or that Shall Inlist into the Eight Battallions Rasing in this State.. Voted that John Ensign Juner Shall be a Collector	13

2 Jun 1777

Voted that Co^{ll} Charles Burrall be moderator	14
Voted that Elisha Baker Esqr be Clerk pro tempore	14
Voted that Charles Burrall Junr be Constable for the Remainder of the present year in the place of Samuel Robbins Deces^d and Collector of the Coloney Rates.. be Collector of the Remainder of the Town Rates Left in the hands of Mr Robbins	14
Voted that Capt William Burrall be a Committee.. to take Care of the Lower Bridge	14
Voted that the Selectmen Endevour to Obtain Leave of the widow Esther Robbins to Cut a passage a Cross a Neck of Land a Little East of the Bridge over Hollenb[ ] River which will much Accommodate the Road	14

3 Jul 1777

Voted that John Whitney be Moderator	14

16 Sep 1777

Voted that Capt Sam^{ll} Forbs be moderator	14
Put to vote whether the Town will Establish the Doings of the Select men in Leying out a highway from the Great Bridge by Capt Burralls up by the mills on the great falls to the Six rod highway between John Beebe 2nd and Ozias Bordmans - Voted in the Negative	14

14 Oct 1777

Voted that John Whitney be moderator	15
Voted that Benajah Douglass be Clerk	15
Voted that Capt Timothy Moses James Stevens Edward Spaulding Manus Griswold Capt	15

Canaan

Benjamin Stevens Simon Tubbs Timothy Hulburt Capt John Ensign Hezekiah Andrus Charles Belding Elisha Yale David Holcomb be a Com^{tee} to act Descresonery with the Selectmen in Provideing Cloathing for the Continantial Soldiers

23 Oct 1777

John Whitney { moderator	15
John Walton Clerk Pro temp	15

4 Dec 1777

Voted that John Whitney be moderator	15
Voted that Samuel Whitaker be admited a Legall voter in Town Affairs	15
Voted that John Whitney Thomas Fellows Hezekiah Andruss Nehemiah Lawrence and Jonathan Belding be Select men	15
Voted that Abiel Fellows be Town Clerk	15
Voted that Abiel Fellows be Town Treasurer	15
Voted that Charles Burrall Ju^r be Constable and Collector of the Coloney Tax and Collector of Town Rates	15
Voted that Benjah Douglass be Constable & Collector of Town Rates	15
Voted that Simon Stevens And^w Bacon James Faning Manus Griswold David Lawrence Benajah Douglass Nathan Newell Ju^r John Spaulding Timothy Moses Elisha Beebe John Ensign Ju^r And^w Frank Joseph Kellogg Ju^r Hezekiah Deming Elisha Yale Samuel Whitaker & John Dean 2nd be Serveyors of Highways	15
Voted that Gersham Hewet Benjn Sedgwick Daniel Horsford Jonth Belding Joseph Kellogg Ju^r & Abel Hensdell be fence viewers	15
Voted that Elisha Beebe Charles Burrall Ju^r Thos Hosmer Joseph Fellows Benajah Douglass & Joshua Whitney be Listors	15
Voted that John Watson Ju^r Daniel Horsford Elijah Whitney & Noah Wells be Grand juremen	15
Voted that Ithamer Blakesley James Faning Merinor Rood Roswell Dean Abel Hensdell & David Johnson be Tithingmen	15
Voted that Abraham Bushnell & Elisha Cobb be Sealers of weights & measurs	16
Voted that Bille Blin & Manus Griswold be Lether Sealers	16
Voted that Jonathan Belding Capt Benjamin Stevens Elijah Whitney be Key keepers	16
Voted that Friend Phelps Abraham Holcomb Elisha Yale Sam^{ll} Hollembeck Da[ ] Beebe John Spaulding & Samuel Clark be Hayard	16
Voted that Timothy Hulbut Nath^{ll} Dean Hezekiah Andruss Abiel Fellow John Watson Ju^r & David Lucuss be Com^{tee} of Safety	16
Voted that And^w Bacon Capt Tim^y Moses Jonas Lawrence Abiel Fellows Co^{ll} Charles Burrall Tim: Hulbut Capt John Ensign & John Whitney be a Com^{tee} to provide Chlothing [sic] for the Soldiers belonging to this Town Now in the Continental Service.. Voted that the Last mentioned Com^{tee} be a Com^{tee} to provide Necessarys for the Soldiers familys	16
Voted that Capt Sam^{ll} Forbs Abiel Fellows & Capt John Watson Hezekiah Andruss Capt Wm Burrall & Jeremiah Andruss be a Com^{tee} to Divide the Salt	16

8 Jan 1778

Voted that Mr Timothy Hurlbut be moderator	16

Canaan

19 Mar 1778

Voted that Capt Samuel Forbs be moderator	16
Voted that Capt Daniel Horsford be Select man in the Room of our Jonathan Belding Decs^d	16
Voted that we will Add two Select men to the Number already chosen.. Voted that Capt John Watson be a Select man.. Voted that Nath^{ll} Dean be a Select man	16

24 Aug 1778

Voted that Capt Samuel Forbs be Moderator	17

9 Dec 1778

Voted that Co^{ll} Charles Burrall be moderator	17
Voted that Capt John Stevens.. John Whitney Capt Nehemiah Lawrence Hezekiah Andruss & Capt John Watson be Select men	17
Voted that Abiel Fellows be Town Clerk	17
Voted that Benajah Douglass be Town Treasurer	17
Voted that Joshua Whitney be Constable and Collector of the Coloney Tax	17
Voted t hat Charles Burrall Ju^r be Constable	17
Voted that Joseph Kingman And^w Kingsbury Job Rothbun Medad Newell Merinor Rood And^w Bacon Samuel Hide Russell Hunt Abraham Bushnall Elijah Kellogg Charles Belding Daniel Harriss David Holcomb Elisha Beebe Moses Marsh Daniel Stevens Sam^{ll} How 2^d and John Whitney Junr be Serveyors of Highways	17
Voted that Elisha Beebe John Ensign Ju^r John Whitney Ju^r Friend Phelps Capt John Watson & Edward Brownell be fence Viewers	17
Voted that Bille Blin Job Rothbun be Lother Sealers	17
Voted that Elijah Holcomb and Capt Jesse Kimbull be grandjurers	17
Voted that Capt Jesse Kimbull Capt Timothy Moses Capt William Burrall Benajah Douglass Nath^{ll} Dean Jeremiah Andruss David Holcomb and Abiel Fellows be Listers	17
Voted that Nathan Newell Rufus Marsh Sam^{ll} Bukley Nathan Hide be Hayards	17
Voted that Abraham Bushnall Elijah Cobb be Sealers of waits and measures	17
Voted that Elisha Beebe Elijah Whitney Eben^r Allin be Key keepers	17
Voted that Zebulon Stevens Benjamin Miller Lemuel Kingsbury Nathaniel Dean Elizur Wright and Joseph Kellogg jun^r be a Com^{tee} to Provide for the Continential Soldiers Famelys	18
Voted that Samuel Clark Noah Holcomb Isaac Beebe Joseph Kingman Henry Stevens ju^r Asahel Kellogg Ichabod Brownell & Abell Stevens be Tything men	18
Voted that the Sign post for the year.. be at the corner by Capt Whitings by the willow Tree	18

16 Feb 1779

Voted that John Whitney be moderator	18
Voted that Capt Ruluff Dutcher be a Serveyor of Highways	18
Voted that Asa North & David Lawrence be a Com^{tee} to Provide for the Soldiers Famelys	18
Voted that Edmon Graidy be Serveyor of Highways	18
Voted that Capt Nehemiah Lawrence be our Agent for the Town to Hire Money.. to Provid for the Soldiers famelys	18

Canaan

2 Sep 1779

Capt Samuel Forbs was Chosen Moderator	18
Voted.. a Rate of Eighteen Pence on the Pound to be made on the Town List 1778.. Voted that Joshua Whitney and Charles Burrall Junr be Colletors of Said Rate	18

6 Dec 1779

Capt Samuel Forbs was Chosen moderator	19
Voted that Timothy Hulbut Thomas Fellows Thomas Hosmer John Watson Ju^r And Charles Belding be Select men	19
Voted that Abiel Fellows be Town Clerk	19
Voted that Benajah Douglass be Town Treasurer	19
Voted that Charles Burrall Ju^r be Constable & Colletor of the State Tax and Town Rate	19
Voted t hat Joshua Whitney be Constable & Collector of Town Rates	19
Voted that Charles Belding John Peck 2nd Jacob Brown Joseph Bukby Ju^r Simeon Root Reuben Smith Roger Horsford Benajah Douglass Elisha Yale Samuel Clark Daniel Stevens David Lawrence Medad Newel Samuel Stow Joseph Fellows And Phinehas Darby be Serveyors of Highways	19
Voted that Elisha Beebe Roger Horsford James Faning and William Newel be fence Viewers	19
Voted that Jeremiah Horsford Capt William Burrall Jeremiah Andruss Nath^{ll} Lorey Elijah Holcomb Benajah Douglass Capt Timothy Moses and David Luciss be Listers	19
Voted that Bille Blin and Simon Tubbs be Lothersealers	19
Voted that Elisha Beebe & James Faning be Grandjurors	19
Voted that Roswell Fellows Abel Stevens Henry Stevens Ju^r Edward Brownell John Whitney Ju^r Ozias Bordman Noah Holcomb Asahel Kellogg and Roger Rood be Tythingmen	19
Voted that Capt Daniel Horsford Elijah Whitney & William Smith be Hayards	19
Voted that Abraham Bushnall and Elijah Cobb be Sealers of weights and measurs and Brandors of Horses	19
Voted that Elijah Whitney Elisha Beebe and Noah Wells be Key keepers	19
Voted that the Sign Post be at the Corner by Co^{ll} Burralls	19
Voted that the Selectmen be Directed to Settle the afair between Capt Ensign and the Town Respecting the Suplying Lieu^t Hollembecks famely with Neseserys for.. 1778	19

22 Dec 1779

At a meeting of the Inhabitants.. Conviend the Dwelling House of Abiel Fellows	20
Elisha Baker Esqr was Chosen moderator	20
Voted that Wee will add to the nomber of Grandjurors already Chosen.. Voted that Capt Watson be grandjurer.. Voted that the Last Vote be Reconsidered	20
Voted that Edward Brownell be Grandjurer	20
Voted that And^w Bacon be Grandjurer.. Voted that we will Not Reconsider the Last Vote	20
Voted that Hez^h Andruss be Grandjurer	20
Voted that Nath^{ll} Dean be Grandjurer	20
Voted that Moses Marsh be a Com^{tee} to take Care of the Bridge by Dutchers	20
Voted that John Ensign be a Com^{tee} to take Care of the bridge by Capt Burralls	20

Canaan

Voted that Capt Wm Burrall be Excused from being a Lister	20
6 Mar 1780	
Capt Samuel Forbs was Chosen moderator	20
Voted Each Seperately that Capt Ruluff Dutcher Capt William Burrall Asahel Beebe Capt John Ensign Daniel Beebe Elisha Yale Timothy Hulbut Charles Burrall Junr Abiel Fellows Joshua Whitney Timothy Wadsworth Jonas Lawrence And^w Kingsbury Nathaniel Lawrence Capt Uzziel Clark Asa North Capt Nehemiah Lawrence Capt Timothy Moses David Lucuss Capt John Stevens and Edward Brownell be a Com^{tee} of Inspection to Seise and Stop Provisions and other Articles forbidden by Law being Transported through this Town	20
10 Apr 1780	
John Watson Junr was Chosen Clerk Pro temp[ ]	20
Nathan Hale Esqr was chosen moderator	20
The Question being Put whether this Town will oppose the Petition of Elizer Wright and others Concerning the Highway from Ozias Bordman to Capt Burralls by the Great falls.. before the generall Assembly.. Voted in the Negetive	21
The Question being Put wheather this meeting will give in the fine Due from Thomas Peirce for killing four Dear Contrary to Law.. Voted in the Negetive	21
24 Jun 1780	
John Whitney was Chosen Moderator	21
Voted that the Select men Shall Receive and Adjust Capt Burralls Acc^t for going to Hartford to get our Choto of Continental Soldiers made Less	21
Voted that Capt John Watson & Abiel Fellows Shall (in the the absence of Co^{ll} Burrall muster the men who Shall Enlist or be Detached for the Service	21
10 Jul 1780	
Voted that Co^{ll} Charles Burrall be moderator	22
20 Nov 1780	
Voted that Co^{ll} Charles Burrall be moderator	22
Voted that we Will Chuse a Comtee to Procure Provisions for this town.. Voted that Capt John Watson be a Com^{tee} for the Purpose	22
Voted that Charles Burrall Junr be a Com^{tee} with Capt Watson	22
Voted that a town Rate be made of Eight Pence on the Pound to Enable Said Com^{tee} to Procure Said Provision.. and those that will Pay their Proportion in Pork beef or flower.. Shall Have their Said Rates Discharged by Paying Six Pence on the Pound.. Voted that Capt Watson & Charles Burrall Ju^r be Collectors of Said Rate	22
Voted that this meeting be Adjorned.. to the Dwelling House of Capt Isaac Lawrence	22
27 Nov 1780	
adjorned meeting.. held at the Dwelling House of Capt Isaac Lawrence	22
Voted that a Com^{tee} be Chosen to fill up this Towns Coto of Soldiers for the Continental Armey.. Voted that that John Hollembeck be one of Said Com^{tee}.. Voted that Capt Lemuel Kingsbury be one of Said Com^{tee}.. Voted that Abiel Fellows be one of Said Com^{tee}	23
11 Dec 1780	
Adjorned meeting was opened and Adjorned to the last Monday of December.. at the Dwelling House of Capt Isaac Lawrence	23

Canaan

Voted that Co[ll] Charles Burrall be moderator	23
Voted that John Watson Ju[r] Timothy Hulbut Nehemiah Lawrence Asahel Beebe & Benajah Douglass be Select men	23
Voted that Abiel Fellows be Town Clerk	23
Voted that Benajah Douglass be Town Treasurer	23
Voted that Joshua Whitney be Constable and Collector of the Coloney Tax	23
Voted that Charles Burrall be Constable	23
Voted that Joshua Whitney and Charles Burrall Ju[r] be Collectors of Town Rates	23
Voted that Isaac Beebe John Hollembeck Amasa Holcomb Elisha Yale Eben[r] Harriss Sam[ll] Forbs David Lucuss Timothy Moses And[w] Bacon Joshua Whitney Isaac Lawrence Hez[h] Andruss be Serveyors of Highways	23
Voted that Roswell Fellows James Faning John Peck 2nd and John Ensign Jun[r] be fence Viewers	23
Voted that Jeremiah Horsford Thomas Hosmer John Hollemback Jonas Lawrence David Lucuss & David Holcomb be Listers	23
Voted that Elijah Cobb & Abraham Bushnall be Branders of Horses and Sealers of Weights and measurs	23
Voted that Simon Tubbs & Bille Blin be Lother Sealers	23
Voted that Sam[ll] Hide Cap[t] Daniel Horsford Joseph Bukley Ju[r] and Joseph Bowman be Grandjurers	23
Voted that Giles Hamlin Meriner Rood Edmon Graidy John Whitney Sam[ll] Root & James Partridge be tythingmen	23
Voted that the Select men Draw an order on the Town Treasurer in favour of Joshua Whitney for.. a Counterfit bill Said Whitney took in Collecting Rates	24
Voted this meting be Adjorned till the Last Monday of Decem[r].. at the Dwelling house of Cap[t] Isaac Lawrance	24

25 Dec 1780

Adjorned meeting being opened at the Dwelling House of Cap[t] Isaac Lawrance..	24
Voted that the Signpost be.. at the Corner by Co[ll] Burrall[s]	24
Voted that Cap[t] William Burrall be a Com[tee] be to take Care of the Bridge by his House	24
Voted that ~~Capt~~ Jeremiah Andruss be a Com[tee] to take Care of the Bridge by Cap[t] Dutcher	24
Voted that Thomas Fellows be Serveyor of Highways	24
Voted that Ithamer Blakesley Benjamin Miller Joseph Henman and Abraham Bushnall by Hayards	24
an adjorned Town meeting.. at the House of Cap[t] Isaac Lawrance	24
Voted that Joseph Fellows Benjah Douglass Asahel Beebe Cap[t] Forbs Co[ll] Burrall John Hollembak Cap[t] Nat[h] Lawrence Elisha Baker Nath[ll] Lorey Tho[s] Hosmer Charles Burrall Jun[r] Eben[r] Harriss Cap[t] W[m] Burrall Cap[t] Ensign Cap[t] Lem[ll] Kingsbury Cap[t] And[w] Kingsbury Merinor Rood James Barber & Cap[t] Watson be a Com[tee] to Class the Town	24
meeting be Adjorned to the House of Esq[r] Hale	24

2 Jan 1781

an Adjorn[d] Town meeting Held at the Dwelling House of Nathan Hale	25
Benajah Douglass was Chosen Clerk for Said meeting	25

57

Canaan

Voted that Capt William Burrall Capt John Watson John Hallemback Capt Lem^{ll} Kingsbury David Holcomb Charles Burrall Junr Reubin Smith Capt Neh^h Lawrence and Abiel Fellows be a Com^{tee} to Recrute for the Town	25
meeting be adjorned to Capt Isaac Lawrances	25
15 Jan 1781	
adjorn^d meeting Conveined and opened at the House of Capt Isaac Lawrance at his House	25
Voted that Capt John Watson and Charles Burrall Junr be a Com^{tee} to Collect of the Inhabitants.. one Peney halfpeney on the Pound in Provision (viz) wheat flower Rye flower or Indian Corn	25
meeting be Adjorned to his the House of Nathan Hale Esqr	26
5 Feb 1781	
Town meeting Held by Adornment at the Dwelling house of Nathan Hale Esqr	26
meeting be Adjorned to the Dwelling House of Capt Isaac Lawrance	26
19 Feb 1781	
an Adjorned town meeting held at the Dwelling house of Capt Isaac Lawrance	26
meeting be adjorned to the Dwelling house of Nathan Hale	26
9 Apr 1781	
Voted that Capt Isaac Lawrences Barn Yard be for a Pound	26
Voted that Capt Nehemiah Lawrences Barn yard be for a Pound	26
Voted that the widow Sarah Beldings Barn Yard be for a Pound	26
Voted that Capt Timothy Moses Barn Yard be for a Pound	26
Voted that Mr Lem^{ll} Stows Barn yard be for a Pound	26
Voted that Asa North be a Serveyor of Highways	26
Voted that Elisha Beebe Roswell Dean Gideon Barns and Abel Hinsdell be Hayards	26
25 Jun 1781	
Voted that Mr Timothy Hulbut be modirator	26
Voted that We will Chuse a Comtee to Collect the Suplies for this town agreable to a Late act of Assembly.. Voted that the Select men Shall make the Severall Rates to Collect the above Suplies.. Voted that Capt Joshua Whitney be a Colletor to collect Said Rates.. Voted that Charles Burrall Ju^r be a Colletor of Said Rates	26
8 Oct 1781	
Voted that Nathan Hale Esqr be modirator	27
Voted that this meeting be Adjorn^d to the Dwelling house of Capt Isaac Lawrance	27
3 Apr 1781	
a town meeting.. Convened at the Dwelling House of Nathan Hale	27
Nathan Hale Esqr chosen modirator	27
Voted that Nathan Hale & Abiel Fellows be Agents.. to meet the Gentlemen Com^{tee} from the Severall towns in Litchfield County.. to Settle the Claims of the Soldiers in the Continental Service belonging to Each Town	27

Canaan

10 Dec 1781

Co^{ll} Charles Burrall Was Chose Moderator	27
Voted that Timothy Horlbut.. Benajah Douglas.. Capt John Ensign.. Jonas Lawrance.. Capt Thos Hosmer be } Select Men	27
That Benajah Douglas Be Town Clerk and Town Treasurer	27
That Elisha Bebee be Constable and Collector of the State Tax.. Joshua Whitney be Constable.. the Constables be Collectors of Town Rates	27
That Capt John Watson and Russel Hunt be A Committee to Prepare a Memorial for the General Assembly.. for Liberty to Do our Highway work by a Town Rate	27
Voted That Charles Belding Isaac Bebee Capt Thos Hosmar Russel Hunt Elisha Yale Elijah Holcomb Sam^{ll} Root John Deen 2nd Ebenezar Allin Ithamar Blakslee Nathaniel Stanley Roswel Fellows Ashbil Lane Sam^{ll} Hide Nathl How Ju^r Giles Hamlen Nathl Lawrance and Ira Rowlson be Surveyors of Highways	27
Voted that Capt Daniel Horsford Elisha Bebee Thos Fellows and Joseph Boman be Fence Viewers	27
Voted that Capt Timothy Moses Joseph Kingman And^w Bacon Capt William Burrall John Hollombeck John Whitney Junr and David Holcomb be Listers	27
Voted That Simon Tubbs and Billa Blyn be Leather Sealers	27
Voted That Roswel Fellows Abraham Bushnal Giles Hamlen and Elijah Kellogg Be Granjurors	27
Voted that Asahel Kellogg Isaac Bebee Aaron Brownell David Lucas James Stevens and Meriner Rood be Tything men	28
Voted that Nathaniel Marsh Benjn Phelps Ju^r Ichabod Brownell and And^w Frank Be Haywards	28
Voted that Elijah Cobb and Abraham Bushnell be Sealors of Weights and Measures	28
this Town Meeting be Adjournd to the House of Capt Isaac Lawrences	28

18 Dec 1781

an adjournd Meeting Legally Holden at Capt Isaac Lawrances.. (Bural being Moderator	28
Voted That the Several Barn Yards (Viz) Capt Isaac Lawrances Capt Neh^m Lawrances Capt Ruluff Dutchers Roger Horsfords Be Pounds.. and.. the Several Owners of S^d Yards Each be poundkeepers	28

21 Feb 1782

Co^{ll} Charles Burrall Was Chosen Moderator	28
Voted to Choose A Committee to Raise the Towns Quota of Soldiers for this States Guards.. Capt John Ensign Capt Lem^{ll} Kingsbury Mr Charles Burral Ju^r Capt Neh^m Lawrence and Mr Abiel Fellows Was Chosen	28
Voted that Co^{ll} Charles Burral be Agent for this Town To Apear Before the County Committee	28
Voted that Nathan Hale Esqr be A a Second Agent for the Above purpose	28

5 Apr 1782

Co^{ll} Charles Burral Was Chosen Moderator	28

9 Dec 1782

Co^{ll} Charles Burral Chosen Moderator	28
Benajah Douglas Timothy Hurlburt John Watson Charles Burrall Ju^r Jonas Lawrence Select	28

Canaan

Men	
Benajah Douglas Town Clerk and Town Treasurer	28
Elisha Beebe Constable and Collector of Town Rates	28
16 Dec 1782	
Jeremiah Hogeboom Daniel Beebe Russel Hunt Charles Burrall Junr John Whitney Ju^r Jesse Squire Elijah Buttles Elisha Yale Tim^o Wadsworth Jonas Lawrence Giles Hamlen Andrew Stevens Edward Brownell Mariner Rood Timothy Moses Ju^r Chosen Surveyors of Highways Abraham Bushnel Ozias Boardman James Fanning Noah Wells Fence Viewers	28 28
Joseph Kingman John Watson Joseph Fellows William Burrall John Holemback Elijah Holcomb and David Holcomb Listers	28
Billa Blyn & Simon Tubbs Leather Sealers	28
Amasa Holcomb John Spaulding Andrew Frank Asa North Joseph Kingman Grandjurors	28
Williams Hensdale Abraham Holcomb David Rood William Sol^n Lawrence Elijah Buttles James Fanning Abil Stevens Jacob How Tithing Men	28
Daniel Stevens Elijah Whitney Abraham Bushnell Zebulun Stevens Ju^r David Holcomb Hog hawyards	28
Elijah Cobb Abraham Bushnel Sealors of Weights and Measures and Branders of horses	28
Elijah Whitney Keekeeper for the pound	28
Roger Horsfords Yard to be a pound.. and also Capt Isaac Lawrence Capt Nehemiah Lawrence Tim^o Moses Ju^r Capt Ruluff Dutcher Yards and Each to be kee keeper for his yard	28
Meeting be adjournd to Esquire Nathan Hales; Capt John Watson Chosen Moderator for S^d Meeting	28
Voted Meeting be adjournd to the house of Capt Isaac Lawrences	28
19 Dec 1782	
an Adjournd Town Meeting.. holden at the Dwelling house of Capt Isaac Lawrences	29
Capt Lem^{ll} Kingsbury Was Chose Constable and Collector of State Taxes	29
Voted that Timothy Hurlburt & John Ensign be a Committee to Repair or Rebuild a Bridge below the Great falls	29
3 Mar 1783	
Esqr Sam^{ll} Forbes Chosen moderator	29
9 Sep 1783	
Samuel Forbes Esqr chosen moderator	29
Put to Vote Wheather the Town Were for half pay or Commutation of half pay for the officers of the Continental Army and Was fully Carryed in the Negative.. Voted that Co^{ll} Charles Burrall Esqr Nathan Hale Mr Tim^o Horlburt Abiel Fellows & Capt John Watson be a Committee To Draw Some proper Resolve To present to the Next Meeting Respecting half pay &c	29
Voted that Nathan Hale Esqr Sam^{ll} Forbes Esqr & Capt William Burrall Be a Committee To Meet the Com^{tees} from Other Towns in this State at a Convention to be at Middletown	29
Sep 1777	
The Names of those that Have Taken the oath of Fidelity.. Co^{ll} Charles Burrall.. Capt Samuel Forbs.. Capt Benjn Stevens.. John Whitney.. Benajah Douglas.. Joshua Whitney.. Edward Brownell.. Elisha Beebe.. John Green Junr.. Charles Burrall Junr.. Joseph Fellows.. Simon	64

Canaan

Stevens.. Ithamer Blakesley.. Benjn Miller.. And^w Bacon.. James Deming.. William Hegy..
Eben^r Harris.. Abraham Bushnall.. David Holcomb.. Abraham Holcomb.. Benjn Phelps..
Moses Marsh.. James Marsh.. Nath^{ll} Marsh.. Benjn Phelps Junr.. Benjn Carver.. Capt Daniel
Horsford.. Timothy Hurlburt.. Capt John Ensign.. Capt Jesse Kimbull.. John Franklin.. Elijah
Holcomb.. Edward Spaulding.. Amos [ ]ei[ ] Junr.. Elizur White.. Thomas Griswold.. Thomas
Barnes.. Gideon Barnes Junr.. Nath^{ll} Lorey.. Jeremiah Horsford.. Capt Isaac Lawrence..
Timothy Cowls.. Daniel Deming.. Giles Hamlin.. Jonas Marsh.. Simon Tubbs.. Friend
Phelps.. Sam^{ll} Clark.. Lem^{ll} Kingsbury.. Capt John Watson.. Jonathan Belding.. Jacob
Brown.. Abraham Hollembeck.. Roswell Deane..
.. John Lawrance.. Charles Belding.. Henery Stevens.. [ ]$^{[ ]}$ How.. Sam^{ll} Beckley.. Josiah   *64*
Hurlbut.. Asahel Beebe.. Nath^{ll} Dean.. Elijah Kellogg.. Joseph Horsdell.. Hezekiah Andruss..
David Johnson.. Jeremiah Hogoboom.. John Ensign Ju^r.. Joseph Kellogg.. Elisha Yale..
Jeremiah Andruss.. Daniel Beebe.. Nehemiah Marsh.. Joseph Beckley Ju^r.. Phinehas Root..
Elijah Whitney.. John Whitney .. Thomas Fellows.. Libies Fellows.. Joseph Beckley.. Noah
Holcomb.. Sam^{ll} Sedgwick.. Elizur Wright.. Samuel Whitaker.. Daniel Stevens.. Andw
Frank.. Abel Horsdell.. Capt William Burrall and Sarah Belding.. Asa Root.. Abner
Chamberlin.. Bille Blin.. John Morgan.. John Peck ye 2nd.. Jesse Bishop.. Thomas Paine..
John Dean 2nd.. John North.. Edmon Grandy.. William Gould.. Ozias Bordman.. Russell
Hunt.. Roswell Deming.. Daniel Hail.. Nathan Hale.. John Dobson.. Abijah Lee.. Nathaniel
Lawrance.. Jonathan Doolittle.. John Watson.. Abirem Peet.. [ ] Fellows..
.. Luke Knap.. Thedon Lee.. Eben^r Allin.. Reuben Smith.. Isaac How.. Daniel Stevens.. Eben^r *64*
Jackways.. William Peet.. Stephen Partredge.. Abil Fellows.. Henrey Stuart.. Elijah Cobb..
Timothy Moses jun^r.. David Rood.. Nathan Newel jun^r.. Merlain Mervin.. Mitchel Kingman..
William Smith.. Benjn Hewet.. John Hall.. Nath^{ll} How Ju^r.. Willard Green.. oliver Hurtwell..
James Dunham.. Thos Williams.. Eleazor Wells.. Isaac Lewis.. Benjn Griswold.. John
Rowbinson.. obadiah Smith.. William Rowbinson.. Zebulon Stevens Ju^r.. Elijah Babcock.
Revd Daniel Furrand.. Eben^r Murrell.. John Runford.. Sam^{ll} Darrow.. Simeon Root.. Joshua
Preston.. Capt Allin Curtiss.. Daniel Harriss..
.. Sarah Norton.. Capt John Stevens.. Nehemiah Lawrence.. Asa Kellogg.. Willard   *64*
Kingsbury.. William Noys.. Manus Griswold.. John Franklin.. David Lawrance.. Edward
Spalding.. David Lucas.. Joseph Kingsman.. Elisha Merrills.. Jonas Lawrance.. Thomas
Settle.. William Root.. Reuben Darby.. Stephen How.. Philip How.. Sam^{ll} How 2^d.. Isaac
Swain.. Jacob How.. Medad Newel.. Phinehas Peirce.. Asel Glens[on].. Nath^{ll} How.. Eben^r
Lee.. James Hanshaw.. Miles Bradley.. Charles Belding Ju^r.. James Stevens.. Henry Stewart..
Isaac Smith.. Thomas Nor[ ].. Aaron B[ ].. Stephen How.. Elijah Beckley.. Sam^{ll} Ba[ ]..
Jeremiah Lawrenc[e]..Roger Horsford.. Russell Hunt 2nd.. Sam^{ll} Hollom[ ].. Sam^{ll} Curti[ ]..
Jerediah [ ].. Isaac Hay[ ].. Joel Demm[ ].. John Coleman.. Benajah [ ].. August [ ]..
Lemm[ ] [ ].. William [ ].. Bartholom[ ] [ ].. Aaron [ ]
Sep 1777

A List of the Names of the Freemen that have taken the oath.. at the freemens meeting in   *77*
September 1779.. Co^{ll} Charles Burrall.. Capt Benjn Stevens.. Capt Sam^{ll} Forbs.. John
Whitney.. Thos Fellows.. Asahel Beebe.. Nathan Newel.. Simon Tubbs.. Elizur Wright.. John
Sprague.. Nehemiah Lawrence.. Sam^{ll} Hide.. Jonas Lawrence.. Nath^{ll} Dean.. And^w Bacon..
Capt Timothy Moses.. Lemuel Kingsbury.. Jonathan Lawrance.. Elisha Morrells.. Benjn
Miller.. Nath^{ll} Loroy.. Benjn Sedgwick.. Jonathan Doolittle.. John Lawrence.. William Hugg..
Jeremiah Andrus.. Capt William Burrall..
.. Jeremiah Hagaboom.. Russell Hunt.. Joshua Whitney.. Jeremiah Horsford.. John [ ] [ ]..   *77*
Charles Burrall ju^r.. Abiel Fellows.. Joseph Fellows.. Elijah Holcomb.. Elisha Yale.. Nath^{ll}
Lawrence.. David Lawrence.. Giles Hamlin.. Jesse Kimbull.. Zebulon Robbins.. Thomas

Canaan

Hosmer.. Simon Stevens.. James Deming.. Gershom Hewit.. Roswell Fellows.. Jacob Williams.. Edward Brownell.. David Lucass.. Sam^{ll} Clark.. Merinor Rood.. Charles Belding.. Roswell Deming.. Joseph Kingman.. Benajah Douglass..

Apr 1778

.. Nath^{ll} How Ju^r.. Eben^r [ ]ckways.. [ ] Dean ju^r.. Nathan Hail.. William Gould.. Revd Daniel Farrand.. Elijah Whitney.. Elisha [Hin]man.. Isaac Holcomb.. Elijah Kellogg.. Moses Marsh.. Abraham Bushwell.. Eben^r Merrell.. Capt Ruluff Dutcher.. Daniel Darrow.. Isaac Holcomb.. Ozias Bordman.. Nath^{ll} Dean ju^r.. Revd Daniel Farrand.. Isaac Beebe.. Abraham Hollemback.. John [ ]an[ ].. Bille Blin.. Benjn Barnes.. Abel Hansdell.. Ichabod Brownell.. Elijah Whitney.. Gideon Barnes Ju^r.. John Dean 2nd.. Capt Daniel Horsford.. [ ] Kellogg Ju^r.. John Peck 2nd Roswell Dean.. Daniel [ ].. Jonas Marsh..   77

Sep 1778

..Capt John Stevens.. Abijah Lee.. Asa Kellogg.. William Newell.. Nehemiah Lawrence jur.. Luke Knap.. Amos Peirce J^{ur}.. John Webster.. Willard Kingsbury..   77

Apr 1779

.. Oliver Dean.. Nehemiah Marsh.. Mitchel Kingsman.. [ ]   77

Sep 1780

.. Isaac Smith.. Abner Chamberlain..   77

.. Aaron Warner.. Roger Horsford.. Samuel Beckley.. Joshua Preston.. Samuel Peirce..   77

8 Apr 1782

.. William Lawrence.. Sam^{ll} Whitaker.. Benjn Hewit.. Sam^{ll} Curtice.. Russell Hunt 2nd.. Daniel Demming.. Levy Benton.. Sam^{ll} Holembeck.. Jeremiah Lawrence..   77

5 Aug 1782

.. ~~Joel Demming & John Coleman~~..   77

17 Sep 1782

.. ~~Benajah Andrus~~..   77

.. John Holembeck.. Lemmuel Demming..   77

8 Apr 1783

.. Joseph Kellogg.. John Dean.. Jonathan Burrall.. Ovid Burrall.. Bartholomew Belding.. Aaron Brownell.. Jacob How.. William Hinsdale   77

Canterbury

Selectmen's Journal
1768-1785
Pp 20-68

Town Book of Records of Town Acts
1717-1912
Pp 136-184

Located at the Town Clerk's Office

Canterbury

27 Jun 1774
Eliashib Adams Moderator [*ed: at meeting in which Committee of Correspondence chosen*]   *139*
Voted that Solomon Paine, John Felch, David Paine, Deac^n Eliashib Adams, Deac^n John   *139*
Herrick, Capt Eben^r Spalding & Asa Witter be a Committee to correspond with the
Committees of the Several Towns in this and the Neigbouring Colonies
14 Nov 1774
David Paine Moderator [*ed: at meeting in which a Committee of Inspection chosen*]   *140*
David Paine, John Herrick, Thomas Adams, Jz Fitch J^r, Jo^s Burgess, Capt Obadiah Johnson   *140*
& Capt Jo^s Cleaveland were chosen a Com^{tee} of Inspection
13 Feb 1775
Capt Asa Bacon, Sam^{ll} Ensworth & Thomas Adams were added to the Com^{tee} of   *143*
Correspondence
4 Dec 1775
Capt Asa Bacon Moderator   *144*

Capt Asa Bacon.. David Paine.. Capt Sherebiah Butt.. Capt Elkanah Cobb.. Asa Witter }   *144*
Select Men
John Felch Town Clerk.. D^o Town Treasurer   *144*
Jo^s Raynsford.. Danl Frost } Constables & Collectors   *144*
Saml Ensworth.. John Baldwin.. Gideon Ensworth.. John Carter Jr.. Wm Bingham.. Jo^s Clark..   *144*
Isaac Hide Jr.. Nehemiah Peirce.. Uriah Cady Jr.. Increase Hewett Jon^a Wheeler.. John
Adams Jr.. Richd Raynsford.. Lem^l Parrish.. Wm Foster.. Alexan^r Gordon.. Saml Parrish..
Henry Frost.. Nehem Adam.. James Delop.. Jo^s Leach.. Simeon Park.. Reuben Peck }
Surveyors of Highways
Tim^o Backus.. William Bingham.. Abner Bacon.. Wm Baldwin.. Capt Elijah Dyar.. Com^{tee} for   *144*
Quinabog River Bridges
John Adams Jr.. John Johnson } Fence Viewers   *144*
Thomas Buswell Jr.. John Felch.. John Barstow.. Thomas Adams.. William Foster.. Seth   *144*
Paine Jr.. David Baldwin } Listers
Capt Matthias Button.. David Paine } Leather Sealers   *144*
William Foster.. Nath^{ll} Clark.. Saml Butt 3rd.. Increase Hewett.. John Hough } Grandjurors   *144*
Jo^s Adams Jr.. Nathl Butt.. David Baldwin.. Darius Fish.. Jo^s Bacon.. Thos Dimmock.. Peleg   *144*
Brewster } Tythingmen
Tim^o Backus & William Bingham, Packers   *145*
Jonathan Davis Sealer of Weights aned measures   *145*
William Bond, Elihu Palmer Pound Keepers   *145*
Jabez Fitch Jr David Paine and Saml Ensworth were chosen a Com^{tee} to..examine William   *145*
Fosters Accompt against the Town
15 Jan 1776
Voted, that the power of Agency for this Town given to.. William Foster Decem^r 28th 1772 to   *145*
recover a maintenance for Jon^a Raynsford out of his fathers Estate be revoked & disannulled
Voted, that the Report of the Com^{tee}.. to examine William Foster's Accompts against.. town   *145*
be accepted
Jz Fitch Jr, David Paine & Saml Ensworth be a Com^{tee} to examine..Accompts of Richard   *145*
Raynsford & Jo^s Raynsford against the Town

Canterbury

Josiah Dewey, Sam¹ Ensworth & Silas Cleavland be a Com^tee to examine into the State of the town Stock of Ammunition & of the town treasury	145
Abner Bacon & Isaac Stevens were appointed to receive & keep the Town Stock of Ammunition	146
Abner Bacon, Solomon Paine, Eben^r Brown & James Adams were chosen Grandjurors	146
David Paine, Jabez Fitch Jr, Capt Asa Bacon, John Herrick, Eliashib Adams, Asa Witter & John Barstow were chosen Com^tee of Correspondence & Inspection	146
2 Dec 1776	
Eliashib Adams Esq Moderator	146
David Paine Esq.. Capt Benj Bacon.. John Herrick.. Asa Witter.. Sam¹ Ensworth } Select men	146
John Felch Town Clerk.. D° Town Treasurer	146
Jo^s Raynsford.. Dan¹ Frost } Constables & Collectors	146
Wm Bond.. Sam¹ Cleavland } Fence viewers	146
David Baldwin.. Jo^s Farnam Jr.. Wm Baldwin.. Asa Aspenwell.. Elisha Backus.. Jacob Bacon.. Asa Cleavland.. Squire Shepard.. Dan¹ Cady.. Reuben Harris.. Robert Ransom.. Benj^a Hide.. John Adams.. Simon Benjamins.. Levi Downing.. Sam¹ Henry.. Jo^s Safford.. John Park Jr.. Tim° Adams.. James Delop.. Elisha Leach.. Jo^s Adams Jr.. Jacob Fuller } Surveyors of Highways	146
x Isaac Stevens.. x Silas Cleavland.. x John Cleavland.. Reuben Peck.. x Davaid Baldwin.. Seth Paine.. Isaac Hide } Listers.. Those mark^d x were chosen by David Paine Esq	147
William Bradford.. Dan¹ Frost } Leather Sealers	147
Sam¹ Barstow Sealer of W^ts & measures	147
Capt Sherebiah Butt.. Nathan Waldo.. Andrew Winchester.. John Dyar Jr.. John Barstow.. Isaac Hide } Grandjurors	147
Thomas Buswell Jr.. David Baldwin.. Stephen Butt.. Sam¹ Barstow.. Gideon Carver.. Darius Fish } Grandjurors	147
2 Dec 1776	
Elihu Palmer.. Wm Bond } Pound keepers	147
Wm Bingham.. John Adams Jr } Packers	147
Josiah Dewey, Silas Cleavland & Sam¹ Ensworth be a Com^tee to collect the Ammunition delivered out of the Town Stock to particular persons in the late Alarms, or the money for it	147
Tim° Backus, William Bingham, Abner Bacon, William Baldwin & Capt Elijah Dyar were chosen a Com^tee to take Care of Quinabog River Bridges to cut away Ice &c to preserve them	147
3 Feb 1777	
Eliashib Adams Esq Moderator	147
Jz Fitch Jr, Eliashib Adams Esq, Elihu Palmer, Ephraim Lyon, David Baldwin, Reuben Peck, Uriah Cady Jr, John Cleavland & Wm Johnson were chosen a Com^tee of Safety	147
Richard Raynsford & Solomon Paine were chosen Select men in addition to those already chosen	148
Com^tee appointed to examine..Accompts of..Richard Raynsford and Joseph Raynsford against the Town on Acc^t of the Care of their Brother Jon^a Raynsford made their Report.. that they found due from s^d Town to..Raynsfords..£ 22.16.8	148
Selectmen reported.. at the desire of several Inhabitants.. and the better to accommodate	148

65

Canterbury

public travelling they had made an Alteration in the highway leading from Eph^m Lyon's westerly to the School House a little north of John Smith's viz. Beginning at a stake & heap of stones about a rod Southward of a large white oak tree in.. Jo^s Smith's Pasture the north Side of the old Road, then running W 27° N 16 rods to a stake & heap of stones, thence W 32 N 16 rods to the End of the wall by s^d Road the highway to lie South of s^d Lines & Monuments
27 Mar 1777

David Paine Esq Moderator	148
Capt Ebenezer Spaulding, Andrew Murdock, Col^o Aaron Cleavland, Robert Ransom, Elihu Palmer, Silas Cleavl^d, Josiah Dewey, Zachariah Waldo, Capt Elkanah Cobb, John Felch, Ephraim Lyon, Nathl Clark, and Thos Adams were chosen a Com^{tee}.. to provide Necessaries for the Families of.. Soldiers.. and.. enlist into the Continental Army for.. Three years, and deliver the.. Necessaries.. at the prices Stated by Law without any additional Expence; on.. Soldier's.. remitting money to.. Com^{tee} for that purpose	148

23 Jun 1777

David Paine Esq Moderator	149
Capt Benj^a Bacon was chosen Town Clerk and Town Treasurer.. in the room of John Felch appointed Commis^y in the Continental Army	149

2 Oct 1777

David Paine moderater	150
Voted to Chose a Committee of Nine Men to Provid Cloathing for our Coto of Sol^s in the Cont^l Army.. Viz 3 in the first Society 3 in westminster two in brokline one in hanover Viz Mr David Balden Mr^s John Felch Elihu Palmer Capt And^w Mordock Capt Aaron Fullar Elex Gordan Sam^{ll} Bestow Nathl Cleark Ruben Peck	150

16 Oct 1777

Col^{on} Aaron Cleavland Chose Moderator	150
Chose Mr John Berstow a Survayer of highways in the room of Mr John Parks he being abs^t in ye army	150

8 Dec 1777

John Felch Moderator	150
First a Committe to provide Cloathing for the Soldi^s: John Felch.. Elihu Palmer.. Capt An^w Mordoc.. Ruben Peck.. Sam^{ll} Bestow.. Nathl Cleark.. Lieut John Adams.. Ale^r Gordon	150
A Committe to provide for..families of those in ye army.. Solo^n Paine.. Colo Aar^n Cleaveland.. Doct Jabez Fitch.. Saml Ensworth.. Nathl Cleark.. Josiah Dewey.. Alex^r Gordon Benj Bacon.. Elihu Palmer.. Colo: Aaron Cleaveland.. Capt Elij Dyar.. John Felch.. Select Men	150

22 Dec 1777

Elis: Adams Esq Town Clerk and Town Treasurer	150
Constables Alex Gordon.. Daniel Frost	150
Distrs of highways Remain as they were the last Year Excepting that where Mr John Park & Mr Safford were Surv:^{s} the last year be made into one Dis.[ ]	150
David Baldwin.. Will: Ensworth.. Gide^n Ensworth.. John Sims.. Thom^s Buswel Jr.. Jos: Cleark.. Capt Asa Bacon.. Aaron Cleaveland Jr.. Israel Litchfield.. Capt Aaron Fullar.. Peter Woodward.. Moses Goodale.. Jos: Saford.. Steph Butt.. Lieut Jo^s Adams.. Co[ ]$^{[ ]}$ Adams.. Ric^d Raynsford.. Jos: Button.. Lieut Eph Lyon.. Silas Allen.. Nath^n Fish.. John Herrek Jr..	150

Canterbury

Ruben Peck Survayors of high Ways	
Fence Vewars Will: Bond.. Samuel Cleaveland	150
Lieut Eph^m Lyon.. Aaron Cleaveland Jr.. Will Bingham.. Josiah Dewey.. Asa Aspenwel.. Listers	150
Capt Jos: Cleaveland.. Nathan Waldo.. Stephen Butt.. Jacob Smith Jr.. John Dyar Jr.. Grand Jure	151
Alex Gordon.. Danl Frost.. Collectors of Rates	151
Danl Frost.. Capt Butten.. Lether Sealers	151
John Adams.. Peter Woodward.. Nathan Fish.. Gid. Ensworth.. Jedidiah Brewster.. Jos: Bacon.. Tything Men	151
Jes: Ensworth.. Seth Paine.. Hawards	151
John Felch Gager	151
Packers of Pork Beef and Tobaco Lieut John Adam.. Will Bingham	151
Brand^s of horses & toler.. Daniel Frost	151
Sealer of Wates and measures.. Jonathan Davice	151
Pound Kee keepers.. Will Bond Elihu Palmer	151
Com^e to take Care of the briges.. Will Bingham.. Capt Timo Backus New Brig.. Will Baldwin.. James Cobb Down Town Butts Bridge	151
voted to Give Up Peter Stevens his Note of five pounds taken for his Sons fine in Not going into ye army	151
12 Jan 1778	
John Felch Moderator	151
the Com^{te}..for Supplying the families of the Continantal Soldiers, be directed to Supply.. families of Sam^{ll} Adams 4th and Dan^{ll} Cushman So far as they Shall Judge Necessary, not to exceed.. Twelve pounds Each p^r year	153
2 Feb 1778	
Capt Asa Bacon was Chose Moderator.. in Stead of..John Felch who declined Serving	153
Chose the following persons to Serve as Com^{te} to provide Cloathing for the Continantal army in the room & Stead of Sundry persons heretofore Chosen who resined.. Viz.. John Hough in Stead of.. John Felch resined.. Eben^r Spalding Ju^r in Stead of Capt Andrew Mordock resined Capt Asa Bacon in Stead of.. Elihu Palmer, resin^d and.. Joseph Safford, in Stead of.. Sam^{ll} Barslow resined	154
Co^{ll} Aaron Cleaveland, Capt Elkanah Cobb, David Paine Esqr, Robert Ransom, and Sam^{ll} Ensworth, be a Com^{tt}.. to Examine.. accounts of.. Nath^{ll} Clark, and Sam^{ll} Barstow, respecting their purchesing Cloathing for the Continantal Soldiers	154
17 Aug 1778	
Capt Benjamin Bacon Modirator	154
Eliashib Adams, Benjamin Bacon, John Herrick, John Felch, & Wm Foster a Comm^{tt} to.. draw a Remonstrance & Petition Respecting the present mode of taxation.. to be prefered.. to the General Assembly	154
Voted that the Treasurer.. give to James Durfy.. a.. Note Executed by.. Durfy.. dated..24th.. of February 1778 for.. Ten pounds.. payable to Eliashib Adams.. Treasurer	155
Chose Eliashib Adams agent in name & behalf of Said Town to prefer Said Memorial to ye General Assembly	

Canterbury

7 Dec 1778

Capt Asa Bacon Moderator	155
Capt Benjamin Bacon.. Jabez Ensworth.. Dea^n Asa Witter.. Capt Sherebiah Butt.. Capt Asa Bacon ⸨ Selectmen	155
John Felch Town Clerk.. D^o Town Treasurer	155
Alex^r Gordon first Constable	155
Wm Bingham 2nd Constable	155
Surveyors of highways are as follows.. Joseph Devenport.. John Dyar Ju^r.. Wm Ensworth Ju^r.. Darias Fish.. Isaac Stevens.. Jacob Bacon.. Eben^r Spalding Ju^r.. Delceno Peirce.. Sam^{ll} Deains.. Increase Hewet.. Benj^a Jewet Ju^r.. Wm Hebbard Ju^r.. Eben^r Butt.. Sam^{ll} Bacon. Anthony Morse	155
Surveyors.. Capt Joseph Ransford.. Nath^{ll} Clark.. Abel Lyon.. Clark Herrington.. Isaac Backus.. John B. Adams.. Nathan Fish.. Barnabas Allen	156
Grandjurors are as follows.. Viz David Bauldwin.. Doc^r Jabez Fitch.. Eben^r Chafy.. Eph^m Lyon.. Wm Carew	156
Listers are as follows viz Capt Elijah Dyar.. Daniel Frost.. Sam^{ll} Bacon.. Joseph Safford.. Stephen Butt.. Sam^{ll} Butt 3^d.. Thomas Adams	156
Tytheing men are as follows viz Sam^{ll} Wright.. Elisha Leach.. Wm Aspenwall.. Josiah Cleaveland Ju^r.. Elisha Clark	156

14 Dec 1778

Chose Wm Bond, & Sam^{ll} Cleaveland fence Viewers	156
John Felch Gager	156
John Adams Ju^r, & Wm Bingham packers	156
Daniel Foster brander of horses	156
Jonathan Davis Sealer of Weights & Measures	156
Wm Bonds, & Elihu Palmer pound key keepers	156
Wm Bingham, & Alex^r Gordon Town Collectors	156
Thos Buswell Ju^r, Elisha Backus, Wm Bauldwin & James Cobb a Com^{tt} to take care of ye bridges over Quinabog River	156
Chose Nathan Waldo to take care of the town's guns Tents powder & ball, flints, canteenes &c	156
Chose Matthias Button & Dan^{ll} Frost Leather Sealers	156
a Com^{tt} to provid for ye Families of.. officers & Soldiers.. Inlisted into the Continantal army for three years or during the War viz Capt John Johnson Mes^{rs} Sam^{ll} Ensworth, Thos Buswell Ju^r, Zech^h Waldo, Barnabas Allyn, Wm Foster Ju^r, & Seth Paine	157
a Com^{tt} to provide Cloathing for ye Continantal Soldiers.. viz Mes^{rs} John Dyar Ju^r, Nathan Waldo, Isaac Hide, Thos Dimock, Eph^m Lyon, Lem^{ll} Parish, & Capt Wm Hebbard	157
vote passed.. the Year past.. (as it respects.. John Felch as.. Com^{tt}.. for procureing Cloathing.. for the army) be Eras^d & made Void	157

12 Apr 1779

Capt Asa Bacon Moder^r	157
John Felch and Asa Witter were chosen Agents to prefer a Memorial.. to the.. Genl Assembly.. to obtain Liberty for the Inhabitants.. to mend & maintain their highways.. by a general Rate or Tax	157

Canterbury

Capt Asa Bacon Moderator	158
Voted that this town are desirous .. to put a final stop to any further rise of the prices of the Necessaries and conveniencies of Life; and to prevent any further depreciation of the Currecy; .. Eliashib Adams & John Felch Esq^{rs} Col^o Aaron Cleavland, Mr Danl Frost and Capt Benj^a Bacon be a Com^{tee} to correspond.. with the Com^{ttes} of the.. Towns within this County. or.. State, or any.. of the united States on this interesting Subject, and to adopt Such measures as shall appear.. proper *12 Aug 1779*	158
Capt Benj^a Bacon was chosen Agent to procure or hire.. Money not exceeding £5000 - for.. purchasing Clothing for the Soldiers *19 Aug 1779*	158
Ephraim Lyon, Danl Frost and Capt Asa Bacon were chosen a Com^{tee} to enquire how the Fines of persons draughted for Tours of Duty in the Militia have been disposed of *6 Dec 1779*	159
Capt Asa Bacon Moderator	159
Capt Asa Bacon.. Jabez Ensworth.. Reuben Peck.. Zachariah Waldo.. Daniel Frost } Selectmen	159
John Felch Town Clerk & Treasurer	159
David Baldwin.. Stephen Butt } Constables	159
Capt Elijah Dyar, Thomas Dimmock, Wm Foster Junr, Capt Sherebiah Butt, Comfort Hide, Saml Bacon & Uriah Cady Junr were chosen a Committee to provide for ye Families of the Officers & Soldiers in.. the Continental Army	159
John Felch, Ephraim Lyon and Nathan Waldo were chosen a Com^{tee} to purchase Clothing for the Continental Army	159
John Adams Junr, Ephraim Lyon, David Baldwin, Col^o Aaron Cleavland & Eliashib Adams Esq were chosen a Committee to take into consideration.. repairing the highways *20 Dec 1779*	160
Surveyors of Highways.. Jacob Baldwin.. Gideon Ensworth.. Eben^r Baldwin.. Tim^o Backus Junr.. Nathan Waldo.. Capt John Johnson.. Josiah Cleavl^d Jr.. Timeus Peirce.. Thomas Merrit.. Abraham Snow.. Joseph Burgess.. William Foster Jr.. John Park Junr.. Benj^a Morse.. William Bradford.. Nathl Carver.. Thos Dimmock.. Ephraim Lyon.. John Brown.. John Herrick Jr.. Nehemiah Adams.. Reuben Parks.. Joseph Pellet Jr	160
Nehemiah Adams & Nathan Fish Fence viewers	160
Eliashib Tracy.. Thomas Buswell Jr.. Asa Cleavland.. Capt And Murdock.. Alex^r Gordon.. Elisha Leach.. Asa Witter.. Esq Felch.. Listers Sworn by } Esq Felch.. Esq Adams	160
David Baldwin.. Stephen Butt } Collectors &c	160
Danl Frost.. Capt Jos: Cleavl^d } Leather Sealers	160
Saml Ensworth.. Capt John Johnson.. Uriah Cady Jr.. Capt Jo^s Raynsford.. Thomas Adams } Grandjurors	161
Jacob Baldwin.. Darius Fish.. Saml Barstow.. David Raynsford.. Levi Adams.. Nathan Waldo.. Thomas Dimmock } Tything Men	161
Saml Barstow, Sealer of Weights and Measures	161
Benjamin Hide, Packer of Pork, Beef &c	161
William Bond & Elihu Palmer, Key keepers	161

Canterbury

Thomas Buswell Jun[r] and Elisha Backus were chosen to to cut away the Ice and make.. Repairs to Nevins Bridge	161
Eben[r] Baldwin & Paul Davenport were chosen to do the Same as above for Butts Bridge	161

14 Mar 1780

Eliashib Adams Esq Moderator	162
David Baldwin, Sam[l] Ensworth, Nathan Waldo, Isaac Stevens, Elihu Palmer, Col[o] Aaron Cleavland, Sam[l] Butt 3rd, Zachariah Waldo, Jo[s] Safford, William Foster Jun[r], Thomas Adams, Nath[l] Clark, and Cap[t] Aaron Fuller were chosen Inspectors of embargoed articles	162
Cap[t] Benjamin Bacon, Col[o] Aaron Cleavland and John Felch be a Com[tee] to meet.. with.. Com[tee] from.. Plainfield concerning building a Bridge over Quinabog river.. where Nevins Bridge lately stood; and.. building or hiring a Boat by the..Towns Jointly	162

21 Mar 1780

Voted, that this Town will Join with.. Plainfield in erecting a good Cart Bridge.. over Quinabog River at the place where Nevins's Bridge lately Stood.. Cap[t] Sherebiah Butt, .. Solomon Paine & Col[o] Aaron Cleavland be a Committee to Join..a Committee from Plainfield in building s[d] Bridge with.. power to employ.. persons.. to build s[d] Bridge	163
John Felch, John Adams, Sam[l] Ensworth & Jo[s] Safford were chosen a Committee to enquire into the Situation.. of the Cedar Swamp at the Southeast corner of.. town & other lands	163
Gideon Welles, Joseph Bacon and Cap[t] James Dyer were chosen Grandjurors	163

27 Jun 1780

Eliashib Adams Esq Moderator	164
Cap[t] John Johnson; Cap[t] Sherebiah Butt, Eph[m] Lyon, David Baldwin, Cap[t] Benj[a] Bacon, Dan[l] Foster, Joseph Safford, William Foster Jn[r] and Cap[t] William Hebbard be a Com[tee] to procure.. Nine Recruits	165

30 Jun 1780

Eliashib Adams Esq the former Moderator of this meeting not being present, Cap[t] Asa Bacon was chosen Moderator	165
Voted, that the Same Encouragements for enlisting into the Continental Army for three years or during the war as were offered.. June 27th be extended to three of the Troop in this town.. and that Doc[t] Jabez Fitch, William Bingham & David Paine Esq be added to the Com[tee]	165

12 Sep 1780

Cap[t] Asa Bacon Moderator	166

20 Nov 1780

Cap[t] Asa Bacon Moderator	166
Cap[t] Abner Bacon, Cap[t] Ephraim Lyon, William Foster Jun[r], John Cleaveland, John Adams, Cap[t] Benj[a] Bacon, Sam[l] Ensworth, Samuel Felch & Daniel Foster were chosen a Committee to procure.. Recruits to fill up the Quota.. in the Continental army	166
John Felch, John Hough & Nathan Waldo.. were appointed to apply for the Salt necessary [ed: *for provisions paid toward tax*].. procure Casks, receive & pack up s[d] Provisions	167
William Foster Jun[r] Eben[r] Spalding Jun[r], Cap[t] Eph[m] Lyon and Nathan Waldo were appointed a Com[tee] to purchase.. Provisions.. in case of Deficiency occasioned, or likely to be occasioned, by the Neglect of Individuals	167

4 Dec 1780

Col[o] Aaron Cleavland Moderator	167

Canterbury

Capt Benjamin Bacon.. Capt Jabez Ensworth.. Col^o Aaron Cleavland.. Alex^r Gordon.. Reuben Peck } Selectmen	167
John Felch Town Clerk.. Ditto Town Treasurer	167
David Baldwin.. Stephen Butt } Constables & Collectors	167
Jacob Baldwin.. Phin^s Kendall.. Jesse Ensworth.. William Aspenwall.. Tim^o Cleavland Jr.. Joseph Clark.. Nathan Hide.. Nathl Cogwell.. Saml Deans.. Benj^a Brown.. Joseph Burges.. Silas Cleavland.. John Parks Jr.. James Raymond.. William Carew.. John Smith.. Thos Dimmock.. Dea^c John Herrick.. Saml Henry.. Asa Smith.. Saml Adams Jr.. Jacob Smith Jr.. John Adams.. Surveyors of Highways	168
Nathan Fish.. Nehemiah Adams } Fence Viewers	168
Saml Ensworth.. John Felch.. Shubael Cleavland.. Zachariah Waldo.. Asa Witter } Listers	168
Danl Frost.. Capt Josiah Cleavland } Leather Sealers	168
Nathan Waldo.. Capt Sheremiah Butt.. John Adams.. Gideon Ensworth.. Isaac Stevens.. Gideon Carver.. Comfort Hide } Grand Jurors	168
Nathl Butt.. John Barstow Jr.. Eliashib Tracy.. Saml Bacon.. Levi Adams } Tything Men	168
John Felch Guager & Packer of Pork &c	168
Saml Barstow Sealer of weights & measures	168
William Bond & Elihu Palmer, Key-Keepers	168
Thomas Buswell Junr. & Elisha Backus to take care of Nevins' Bridge	168
Eben^r Baldwin & William Baldwin to take Care of Butts Bridge	168

8 Dec 1780

Samuel Bacon, Jacob Baldwin, Elihu Palmer James Delop and Saml Henry were chosen a Com^{tee} to provide for the families of.. Cont^l Officers and Soldiers	169

21 Dec 1780

William Foster Junr, Thomas Dimmock and Saml Bacon were chosen a Com^{tee} to procure Small Cloathing for the Continental Soldiers	169

16 Jan 1781

Capt Asa Brown Moderator	170
Granted a Rate of Two pence on the pound of the Lists of the Inhabitants.. for.. 1779.. in Silver money.. provided.. that any person may have Liberty to pay his.. Rate by by delivering.. either Wheat Flour at the rate of 24/ p^r C w^t Gross; or Rye Flour at.. 16/ p^r C Gross w^t; or Indian Corn at.. 4/ p^r Bushel; to the amount of Three fourths of that sum, or One penny half penny on the pound.. John Hough and Doc^r Gideon Welles were appointed Receivers or Collectors of the.. Rate	170
Upon the Representation of Timothy Backus Junr.. that he had procured.. David Enos a transient person to enlist into the Continental Army during the War, and that s^d Enos was now serving.., and might be reckoned in.. town's Quota, if.. town would allow.. Backus.. Thirty pounds in hard money, or Sixty pounds in States money.. Whereupon it was voted.. in favour of.. Backus for procuring.. Enos.. upon their being assured that.. Enos will answer in part of.. town's Quota of Soldiers in s^d Army	170
William Perkins was chosen Surveyor of Highways	171
Josiah Cleavland Junr Nath^ll Clark, Cornelius Adams and Zachariah Waldo were added to the Com^{tee}.. for Supplying the Families of the Officers & Soldiers	171

Canterbury

1 Feb 1781

Eliashib Adams Esq Moderator — 172

Cap[t] Asa Bacon, Gideon Ensworth and Will[m] Foster Jun[r] were chosen a Com[tee] to enlist.. — 172
Quota of non-commissioned officers & privates required for the Defence of this State
Cap[t] Ephraim Lyon was appointed to ascertain the exact number of Recruits for the — 172
Continental Army.. to compleat.. Town's Quota

8 Feb 1781

Cap[t] William Hebbard was appointed one the Com[tee] to procure.. Recruits for the State — 172
Troops in the Rooom of W[m] Foster Jr resigned and Cap[t] Ephraim Loyn, Dan[l] Frost, Deac[n] Asa Witter and Josiah Cleavland Jun[r] were added to s[d] Com[tee]

Moses Goodell was added to.. Victualling Com[tee] in the Room of Zachariah Waldo resigned — 172

John Hough was appointed to take Care of the Guns, Ammunition, Tents & other Camp — 172
Equipage

8 Mar 1781

David Paine Esq Moderator — 173

Voted, that.. Recruits may take the advantage of all the bounty allowed by the State and that — 173
the Town will pay one hundred Silver Dollars as a Bounty to each of s[d] Recruits; and will also at the end of Three years, in Case of Failure in the Public, make up their waqges as good as when the War begun. And will abate to Curtis Cleavland Nath[l] Gates and Silas Glass enlisted as afores[d] Rates on their estate for the three years: and in case sd Gates has not a Sergeant's Birth; or Liberty to drive the Teams, then the Town will allow him at the rate of £3.6.8 a year more than his Wages

5 Apr 1781

Col[o] Aaron Cleavland Moderator — 173

Chose .. Solomon Paine, Doc[r] Jabez Fitch, Cap[t] Asa Bacon, Ebenr Spalding Jun[r], Capt Aaron — 173
Fuller, Isaac Backus, Doc[r] Gideon Welles, Cap[t] Ephraim Lyon and Deac[n] Asa Witter a Comt[ee] to Class s[d] Town

9 Apr 1781

Cap[t] Asa Bacon and Col[o] Obadiah Johnson were Chosen Agents..to..Com[tee].. appointed by — 174
the General Assembly to.. Settle.. Claims of.. towns in the County.. to the Recruits lately enlisted in to the Continental Army

11 Jun 1781

Cap[t] Asa Bacon Moderator — 174

Voted, that this Town are willing.. to Submit to indifferent Judicious men to determine what — 174
is..due..to Doc[r] Jabez Fitch for doctoring Sarah Rogers - And..to.. James Raymond for nursing & providing for..Sarah; and Cap[t] Asa Bacon & .. Dan[l] Frost were chosen to agree with the s[d] Parties on the men for Arbitrators.. and to do whatever Shall be necessary to bring said matters to a Just and final Settlement

4 Jul 1781

Col[o] Aaron Cleavland Moderator — 175

Granted a Rate of four pence on the pound.. to be paid.. in Silver or Gold in order to — 175
purchase the Town's Quota of Beef Cattle.. David Baldwin, Eben[r] Spaulding Jr, Isaac Backus and Asa Witter were chosen Collectors.. and also to purchase Beef Cattle for the town's Quota

Canterbury

20 Sep 1781

Capt Asa Bacon moderator	175
Granted a Rate.. of Two pence half penny on the pound.. to be paid in Silver money.. Always provided that Indian Corn at 4/ p^r Bushel, Wheat at 8/ p^r Bushel, and Rye at 5/ p^r Bushel, Pork weighting 8 Score or upwards 5^d ½ & under that at 4^d pr lb, New milk Cheese at 8^d & Butter at 13^d p^r lb be rec^d in payment.. Mr Saml Ensworth, Mr Saml Bacon, Capt Sherebiah Butt and Mr Moses Goodell were chosen Collectors & Committee to collect s^d Rate & deliver the Same tp the Several Families of the Soldiers belonging to his town now in the Continental Army for whose Support and Benefit the above Rate is granted	175

3 Dec 1781

Eliashib Adams Esq Moderator	176
John Felch Esq.. Capt Asa Bacon.. Capt Sherebiah Butt.. Alex^r Gordon.. Joseph Safford } Selectmen	176
John Felch Town Clerk & Treas^r	176
David Baldwin.. Stephen Butt } Constables & Collectors	176
Granted a Rate of one penny lawful money on the pound.. for.. repairing the Highways. Voted.. the money raised by the foregoing Rate be laid out in the respective Districts in which it is raised. The following persons were chosen Surveyors of Highways and Collectors of the.. Rate for their respective Districts, viz: Jacob Baldwin.. Capt James Dyer.. Jesse Ensworth.. Saml Felch.. Capt Tim^o Backus.. Jacob Bacon.. Seth Paine.. Amos Pike.. Israel Geer.. Reuben Harris.. Zachariah Waldo.. Moses Goodell.. Amos Meach.. Moses Warren.. Capt Jo^s Raynsford.. Stephen Butt.. Thos Dimmock.. Capt Eph^m Lyon.. Solomon Adams.. James Delop.. Saml Adams Jr.. Jacob Smith Jr.. Saml Bacon.. Jacob Fuller	176

7 Dec 1781

Nathan Fish.. Saml Adams Jr } Fence Viewers	177
Reuben Peck.. Danl Frost.. Saml Parrish.. Eliphaz Perkins.. Col^o Obad^h Johnson } Grand Jurors	177
Doc^t Silas Allen.. John Brown.. Jacob Baldwin.. William Bacon.. Jed^h Brewster } Tything Men	177
Saml Ensworth.. Shubael Cleavland.. Saml Bacon.. Isaac Backus.. Nathl Butt } Listers	177
Capt Jonah Cleavland.. Danl Frost } Leather Sealers	177
John Felch Gager & Packer &c	177
Peter Kendall Brander &c	177
Wm Bond.. Elihu Palmer } Key Keepers	177
Saml Barstow Sealer of weights & measures	177
John Hough & Elishib Adams Esq were chosen Receivers of provisions & Clothing	177
Doc^t Gideon Welles Keeper of Town Arms & military Stores	177
Capt Timo Backus and Capt Benj^a Bacon Com^{tee} to take Care of Nevins's Bridge	177
Daniel Frost was chosen Agent.. in the suit brought by Nathan Waldo.. now depending before Windham County Court	177
a Com^{tee} of Supplies for the families of the Officers and Soldiers.. in.. the Continental Army, and especially for the family annexed to their names respectively, Capt Benj^a Bacon for James Duggen's family.. Ebenezer Brown for Danl Cushman's.. Reuben Peck for John	178

73

Canterbury

McCartee's.. Saml Bradford for John Cleavland's.. Capt William Hebbard for Silas Glass's.. Capt Jabez Ensworth for Benj^a Durfee's.. Cornelius Adams for Saml Adams's.. Deac^n John Herrick for Robt Herrick's.. Nathan Adams for Jon^a Symond's.. Capt John Johnson for Curtis Cleavland's.. Eben^r Dean's Jr for Nathl Gates's.. Benj^a Brown for Benj^a Brown Jr's Solomon Paine & Danl Frost were chosen Agents.. to prefer a Memorial to the Genl Assembly..for.. a Lottery for.. Building a Bridge.. acros Quinabog River at or near.. where Butt's Bridge.. lately stood	178
14 Dec 1781	
Capt Jz Ensworth, David Baldwin & Saml Ensworth were chosen a Com^{tee} to enquire into the State of the town Treasury	179
4 Mar 1782	
Capt Ephraim Lyon Moderator	179
John Adams, Saml Ensworth and Levi Downing were chosen a Com^{tee} to procure.. Recruits for the Continental Army	179
Capt Benjamin Bacon and Capt Asa Bacon were chosen Agents to Support the Claims of this town to Continental & State Recruits	179
Capt Ephraim Lyon, Daniel Frost and Capt Danl Foster were chosen a Com^{tee} to procure.. Recruits for the State Service	179
Zachariah Waldo was chosen one of the Com^{tee} of Supplies in the room of Capt John Johnson resigned, especially to provide for Curtis Cleavland's Family	179
18 Mar 1782	
Asa Bacon chosen Clerk pro tempore	179
2 Dec 1782	
Eliashib Adams Esq Moderator	180
Capt Asa Bacon.. Capt Sherebiah Butt.. Joseph Safford.. Deac^n Asa Witter.. John Adams } Selectmen	180
John Felch Town Clerk	180
John Felch Town Treas^r	180
David Baldwin.. Stephen Butt } Constables & Collectors	180
Granted, a Rate of one penny lawful money on the pound.. for.. repairing the highways.. Voted, .. Selectmen divide the money to be raised.. to the several Districts according to their Discretion. Surveyors of Highways & Collectors.. Saml Davenport.. Nathl Ensworth.. Jo^s Farnam.. Capt Abner Bacon.. Wm Bingham.. Benj^a Bacon Jr.. Isaac Hide.. John Stevens.. Elisha Bowman.. Eben^r Jewett.. Zachariah Waldo.. Eben^r Deans Jr.. Eben^r Butt.. Eben^r Adams.. John Bradford.. Gideon Carver.. Isaiah Williams Jr.. Elijah Parks.. Solomon Adams.. Jno Bradford Adams.. Nathan Fish.. Jacob Smith.. Jos Pellet Jr.. Wm Perkins Saml Adams Jr.. Nathan Fish } Fence Viewers	180
	180
Solomon Paine.. Eliphaz Perkins.. Zachariah Waldo.. Reuben Peck.. Seth Paine } Listers; all sworn by Eliashib Adams Esq	180
9 Dec 1782	
Danl Frost & Capt Josiah Cleavland Leather Sealers	181
Doc^t Gideon Welles chosen keeper of Military Stores	181
Capt Timothy Backus & Capt Benj^a Bacon Com^{tee} to take Care of Nevins's Bridge to cut away Ice &c	181

Canterbury

Wm Baldwin & Jacob Baldwin Com^{tee} for the same purpose for Butt's Bridge	181
a Com^{tee} of Supplies for the Families of the officers and Soldiers.. belonging to the Cont^l Army, & especially for the family annexed to their names.. Capt Wm Hebbard for Nathl Gates Family.. Joseph Adams for Silas Glass's d^o.. Isaac Backus for Benj^a Brown Jr's d^o.. Jacob Preston for Curtis Cleavland's d^o.. John Park for Benj^a Durfee's d^o.. William Foster Jr for Ens^n Jno Cleavland's d^o.. Capt Joseph Raynsford for Saml Adams's d^o.. Capt Aaron Fuller for Abial Farnam's d^o.. Capt Eben^r Spalding for Danl Cushman's d^o.. Comfort Hide for James Duggan's d^o.. Deac^n John Herrick for Robert Herrick's d^o.. Danl Frost for Andrew Hebbards d^o	181
John Felch, Danl Frost, Doc^t Gideon Welles, Deacon Asa Witter & Stephen Butt were chosen Managers of the Lottery.. for building Butt's Bridge	181
Capt Sherebiah Butt, Capt Jabez Ensworth & John Adams were chosen a Com^{tee} for building s^d Bridge	182

17 Dec 1782

Jos. Moore.. Moses Goodell.. Nathl Clark.. John Barstow.. Saml Butt Jr } Grand Jurors	182
Gideon Ensworth.. Elisha Payne.. Jno Barstow Jr.. Jed^h Brewster.. John Curtiss Jn^r } Tythingmen	182
Saml Barstow Sealer of Weights & Measures	182
William Bond Key keeper	182
Capt Sherebiah Butt ws chosen Moderator	182
William Foster Junr was chosen one of the Com^{tee} of Supplies especially for the Family of Nathl Gates in the room Capt Wm Hebbard resigned	182
Anthony Morse was chosen one of the Com^{tee} of Supplies especially for the Family of Ens^n Jno Cleavland in the room of William Foster Jn^r appointed for Nathl Gates's Family	182
Elisha Payne was chosen Agent for the town in the Case of Nathan Waldo against the Town	183

7 Feb 1783

Capt Asa Bacon Moderator	183
Voted that the Selectmen may draw an order on the Town Treasurer for.. Four pounds.. to enable William Cooper to remove himself, Family & Effects to Pownal	183
Daniel Frost was chosen Agent..to defend in a Suit.. by Timothy Backus Jr against Col^o Aaron Cleaveland, Capt Jabez Ensworth Reuben Peck & Alexander Gordon respecting an order drawn by them in the Capacity of Selectmen	183

7 Apr 1783

Capt Jz Ensworth Moderator	183
town do relinquish all claim to such part of the land formerly given by Richard Burt for an open highway as not now occupied & improved for that purpose	183

7 Oct 1783

Deacon Asa Witter Moderator	184
Accepted the Selectmen's return in laying out an open & public highway from Stephen Hewett's Southerly to Windham road.. near the Separate meeting house	184

Cheshire

Cheshire Town Records
1780-1790
Pgs 4-20
LDS microfilm # 1,412,760

[Oaths of Fidelity are unpaginated in town volume;
here paginated as "A" and "B"]

Located at the Town Clerk's Office

Cheshire

1777

Oaths of Fidellity 1777.. Ichabod Tuttle.. Isaiah Hall.. David Rice.. Rufus Lines.. Zachariah Ives.. Elnathan Beech.. Jason Hotchkiss.. John Peck Ju^r.. Obed Doolittle.. John Badger.. John Williams.. David Curtiss. Thomas Newton.. Henry Brooks J^r.. Samuel Tallmage.. Reuben Bristol.. William Clark.. Barnabus Lewis.. Samuel Tuttle.. Chancey Hall.. Ebenezer Hall.. Ebenezr Tuttle.. Thomas Underfield.. Isaac Bowers Moss.. Ruben Preston.. Samuel Doolittle.. John Beech.. Israel Bunnel.. Reuben Rice.. Elias Norton.. Gift Newton.. William Lewis.. Jonathan Hall J^r.. Andrew Hall J^r A

7 Jun 1780

Major Reuben Atwater was chosen moderator	4
Samuel Beach Esquire chosen Town Clerk	4
mr John Beach mr Timothy Hall and mr John Peck were chosen Selectmen	4
mr Lucious Tuttle mr Jonathan Hall and mr Reuben Rice were appointed Constables	4
Benjamin Hotchkiss Ju^r Mathew Bellamey Ebenezer Doolittle Bennoni Hotchkiss Benjamin Plumb and Ephraim Smith are appointed Grand Jurors	4
Capt Robert Rice Leu^t Benjamin Doolittle mr Josiah Tallmage mr John Bryan and mr Asa Brunson were chosen Listers	4
mr Amasa Hall and mr Seth Johnson were appointed Tything men	4
Dot^r Gold Gift Norton Amos Williams Abijah Hall Titus Moss Titus Hitchcock Israel Bunnell Jonathan Hall Ju^r Bennet Rice Dimon Barns Ebenezer Parker Moses Atwater Ju^r Jedediah Hall Isaac Brooks Junr Moses Blakesley were chosen Surveyors of highways	4
Dan Hitchcock was chosen Sealer of weights	4
Josiah Hotchkis was chosen Sealer of measures	4
Israel Bunnel was chosen Sealer of Leather	4
Asahel Hitchcock was chosen Recorder and Brander of Horses	4
mr Dan Hitchcock was chosen pound keeper and key keeper	4
Theophilous Moss and Amsas Hall were appointed to Erect pounds on their own Cost	4
mr Israel Bunnel G Gift Norton Capt Amos Hotchkiss Capt Ephraim Cook Erastus Lines Enos Tyler Jared Hall Job Yale Levi Rice Capt Enos Attwater Capt Robert Martin mr Andrew Hough Leu^t Joseph Norton mr Moses Attwater Aaron Bellamey David Brooks Nathan Gaylord and Jonathan Hall Ju^r have were chosen a Committee to Inspect provisions	4
mr Jonathan Hall was chosen Town Treasurer and Collector of the Tax	5
Major Reuben Atwater mr Israel Bunnel and mr Jonah Hotchkiss were chosen a Committee to Supply the Soldiers Families with provision	5

10 Jul 1780

Major Reuben Atwater was Chosen moderator at a town meting	5
Voted that the Town will Lay a tax of Six pence on the pount to Encorage the Inlistment of Soldiers & other Necessary Charges.. Voted also that andrew Hall Jur be appointed Collector to Collect said taxes	5
Voted that Capt Miles Hall Capt Amos Hotchkiss Capt Robert Martin Capt Nathaniel Bunnel & Capt David Hitchcock be appointed a Committee to hire men to Inlist in to the Continental Service for.. Six months three Years or Dureing the present War	5

Cheshire

26 Jun 1780

Major Reuben Atwater Chosen moderator	6
Voted that Miles Hall Nathaniel Bunnel and Robert Martin and David Hitchcock be a Committee for hireing the Soldiers to fill up the Continential army for.. three years or Dureing the present war	6
Voted that Andrew Hall Jur be a Collector to to Collect the tax of two pence on the pound	6
Voted Voluntine Hitchcok be a Collector of said Tax	7

15 Nov 1780

Major Reuben Atwater was chosen moderator	7

15 Nov 1780

Voted that mr Israel Bunnel Chose Collector to receive said tax of /6 pence on the Pound.. and also receive and Collect the assesment of the 4/ States money Granted by this Town by those who neglect to pay in provisions	7

15 Nov 1780

Voted that the Town will Divide into Classes for filling up the Continental army.. Voted that Nathaniel Bunnel David Hitchcok Miles Hall Robert Martin Amos Hotchkiss be Committee for that purpose	7

15 Nov 1780

Voted that Major Reuben Atwater & Samuel Beech Esqr be Committee for to assertain the Number of men now in the Continental Service and to Class the Inhabitants of the Town	7

[ ] Dec 1780

Major Reuben Atwater was Chosen moderator	8
Samuel Beech was Chosen town Clerk	8
Voted that John Peck Timothy Hall & John Beeche be Selectmen	8
Voted that Lucius Tuttle Reuben Rice and Jonathan Hull be Constables	8
Voted that Jonathan Hall be a Collector to Collect the States tax	8
Voted that Reuben Dorchester Amasa Hall Matthias Hitchcock Jonah Hotchkiss and Peter Munson be Grand Jurors	8
Voted that Enos Bunnel and Asa Brunson be appointed Tytheing men	8
Voted that John Bryan Leu^t Hotchkiss Andrew Hall Amos Bellamy and David Brooks be Listers	8
Voted that Erastus Lines Ezra Doolittle Jonathan Hall Ju^r Nicholas Russel Ephraim Cook Robert Martin Miles Hall William Parker David Hotchkiss Ambrose Doolittle Ju^r Ephraim Smith Ju^r William Hall & Andrew Clark Ju^r be Surveyors of Highways	8
Voted that Josiah Hotchkiss be Sealer of measures and Israel Bunnel Sealer of measures	8
Voted that Dan Hitchcock be Sealer of weights	8
Voted that Dan Hitchcock Theophilus Moss Amasa Hall Ebenezer Doolittle Samuel Hull the pound keepers	9
Voted to pay a tax of two pence.. on the pound to Defray the Incident Charges of the Town.. Voted that Leut Hotchkiss be appointed Collector	9
Voted that Benoni Hotchkiss Robert Brown Lucius Tuttle John Liness Thomas Newton Jur John Benhame Nicholas Russel Thomas Moss Amasa Hall David Hitchcock Amos Doolittle Thomas Gaylord Hezekiah Beecher Jacob Lewis and Dimon Barns be a School Committee	9

Cheshire

Voted that mr David Brooks Capt Robert Rice Aaron Bellamy Asa Brunson and Israel Bunnel be a Committee of Inspection	9
Voted that Reuben Rice Major Reuben Atwater Benoni Plumb be a Committee and Ephraim Smith to Supply the Soldiers families	9

2 Jan 1781

Major Reuben Atwater was Chosen Moderator	10
Voted.. that they approve of the Doings of the Committee of Wallingford and Chos[ ] to fill up the Continental army in appointing Oliver Stanley Esqr Agent to Repair to.. the Governor and Council of Safety for the Details of the Continental Army and Compare the Same with the Details from said Towns	10

15 Apr 1781

mr David Brooks was Chosen moderator	10
Voted.. that Capt Miles Hall and Capt Amos Hotchkiss be a Committee to repair to the County Committee now Setting at New haven for the purpose of Laying Claims to the Continental now in Service Belonging to this Town	10
Voted that Messr Robert and David Hitchcock be a Committee for the purpose of hireing the additional Number of men now to be Raised for the Defence of the Coast at horse neck	10
Voted.. to Lay a tax of one penny.. on the pound or other current money Equivalent for the purpose of Raiseing said Soldiers.. Voted that Gold Gift Newton be a Collector of said tax	10

11 Dec 1781

Capt Samuel Hall chosen moderator.. and Samuel Beech was Chosen Town Clerke	11
Voted that John Peck John Beech & Samuel Hull Jr be Selectmen	11
Voted that Lucius Tuttle Reuben Rice & Samuel Abernatha be Constables	11
Voted that Benjamin Doolittle Moses Pirkins Bennet Rice & Hezekiah Beecher & Thomas Moss be Grand Jurors	11
Voted that Ephraim Smith Jur & Jedediah Hall be tything men	11
Voted that William Law Dimon Burns Benoni Hotchkiss & Titus Moss be Listers	11
Voted that Major Reuben Atwater mr Timothy Hall John Sanford Asahel Andrews Henry Brooks Abijah Cornwell Ephraim Preston Jesse Moss Justus Bellamy Josiah Hotchkiss Ephraim Smith Jonathan Hall Jur & Andrew Hall be Surveyors of Highways	11
Voted that Lucius Tuttle be appointed a Collector to Collect the Country tax	11
Voted that mr Samuel Bunnel be Sealer of Leather & mr Josiah Hotchkiss Sealer of measures	11
Voted that Theophilus Moss Benjamin Atwater Israel Bunnel Amasa Hall Dan Hitchcock Ephraim Tuttle Andrew Hall & Henry Brooks be Pound Keepers.. to Build pounds at their own Expence	11
Vpted that mr Eliakim Hitchcock be Gager	12
Voted that Amos Parker Thomas Andrews Ebenezer Parker Gad Pond Uri Benham Elam Cook Henry Brooks Jesse Moss Samuel Atwater Israel Bunnel Amasa Hitchcock. Lucius Tuttle Jonas Hill Nicholas Russel John Bryan be a School Committee	12
Voted that Asa Brunson Munson Merriam John Bryan be a Committee to Supply the Soldiers families	12
Voted to Lay a tax of two pence two farthings on the pound to Defray the Several Charges of the Town.. Voted that Aaron Bellamy be a Collector of said tax	12
Voted that Capt Enos Atwater and David Brooks.. Nathaniel Moss mr Timothy Hall.. Henry Bellamy and Joseph Newton & mr Dimon Burns be a Committee to Remove Encroachments	12

Cheshire

from the Highways

27 Jun 1781

Major Reuben Atwater was Chosen moderator	*12*
Voted.. to Lay a tax of four pence Lawful money on the pound upon the List of 1780 to be paid in Beefe Cattle & Plank.. agreeable to an act of the General Assembly.. Voted that Israel Bunnel be a Collector to Collect said tax	*13*
Voted that mr Israel Bunnel be a Receiver of the Beefe & Pork	*13*
Voted that Capt Miles Hall & Capt Robert Martin be a Committee to hire men to fill up the three months State Service	*13*
Voted that major Nathaniel Bunnel & David Hitchcock be a Committee to hire the men in the three months Continential army	*13*
Voted to Lay a tax of two pence on the pound on the List 1780 to be paid in Silver or Grain.. for the purpose of raising men into the Service.. Voted that Joseph Newton be a Collector	*13*

4 Mar 1781

Voted.. to Lay a tax of three pence on the pound for the purpose of paying the States Guards and filling up the Continential to be paid half in Grain or Flore.. and half in money.. Voted that Asahel Hitchcock be a Collector	*13*

10 Dec 1782

Reuben Atwater was Chosen Moderator	*14*
Samuel Beech was Chosen Town Clerk	*14*
Samuel Beech was Chosen Town treasurer	*14*

12 Dec 1782

Voted that John Peck Esqr John Beech & David Budger be Selectmen	*14*
Voted that Lucius Tuttle Reuben Roys and Samuel Abenatha be Constables	*14*
Voted that Jonah Clark Hezekiah Beecher Titus Moss Erastus Lines and Thomas Andrews be Listers	*14*
Voted that Ebenezer Doolittle Enos Tyler Ephraim Timothy Hall Jur Daniel Hitchcock Nathaniel Rice be Grand Jurors	*14*
Voted that Thomas Andrews Oliver Bradley and John Miles be Tythingmen	*14*
Voted that Asa Blakesley Nathaniel Bunnel Thmas Bristol Moses Root Samuel [ ] Jur Job Parker Ephraim Doolittle John Miles John Bryan Waistil Hotchkiss Ephraim Smith Reuben Roys Joseph Doolittle Jeremiah [ ]d Jotham Ives and Ezra Doolittle be Surveyors of Highways	*14*
Voted that Dan Hitchcock Benjamin Atwater [ ] Moss Amasa Hall Andrew Hall Tonuel Bunnel Samuel Hall Jur Jonathan Hall Jur & Henry Brooks be pound keepers	*14*
Voted that Tonuel Bunnel be Sealer of Leather	*14*
Jonah Hotchkiss Sealer of measures	*14*
Dan Hitchcok be Sealer of weights	*14*
Voted that Lucius Tuttle be a Collector of the States tax	*15*
Voted to Lay a tax of two peney on the pound for a Town Rate.. Voted that Lucius Tuttle Collect said tax	*15*
Voted that David Badger Jared Hall Asa Blakesley Jonathan Wainwright Jonah Hotchkiss Oliver Bradley Samuel Atwater Jur Abner Bunnel Jur Amos Atwater Robert Rice Jere	*15*

Cheshire

Brooks Enos Tyler Nicholas Russel David Hotchkiss Jonas Hill Asa Willmott be School Committee and Collectors of the School tax in their Several Districts	
5 Feb 1782	
Major Reuben Atwater was Chosen moderator	15
25 Jun 1782	
Capt Enos Atwater was Chosen Moderator	16
Voted to Lay a tax of one penney on the farthing on the pound.. for the purpose of paying up the Execution against the Town for their Deficency in filling up the Continental army in the year 1781.. Voted that Erastus Lines be a Collector	16
22 Apr 1782	
Voted that Capt Enos Atwater be moderator	16
Voted that this Town will prefer a memorial to the General Assembly.. for the purpose of Obtaining their Proportion of men in the Continental Army belonging to the Town of Wallingford and Cheshire.. Voted that Reuben Atwater & Samuel Beach be.. Agents	16
26 Feb 1782	
Voted that John Beech John Peck and Samuel Hall Jur be a Committee to furnish the States Guards for the Defence of the post at Horseneck	16
Voted that John Beach John Peck and Samuel Hall Jur Robert Martin and Miles Hall be a Committtee for the purpose of ascertaining the Number of men in the Continental Army and to fill up the Deficency	16
8 May 1782	
Maj^{or} Reuben Atwater was Chosen moderator	17
30 Jul 1782	
Mr John Atwater was Chosen moderator	17
Voted.. to Lay a tax of one penny one Farthing.. on the pound.. Voted.. that David Hotchkiss be a Collector of said Tax	17
3 Mar 1783	
Major Reuben Atwater was Chosen Moderator	17
Voted.. to Lay a tax of Two pence.. on the pound to pay the Soldiers hired into the Continential Army and States Guards by the Committee and to pay the Incedint Charges of the Town.. Voted that Lucius Tuttle be a Collector of said Tax	17

Colchester

Town Meetings
1780-1829
Pgs 1-20

Records Births Marriages Deaths
No. 1
1713-1801
Pgs 140-272

Located at the Town Clerk's Office

Colchester

17 Jan 1775

Capt Dudley Wright was Chosen Moderator	241
Voated that this Town do Approve of the doings of the Continental Congress held at Philedelpha.. and Do Adopt the plan of Association and Corospondance.. the following Persons Were Chosen A Comitte of Inspection Agreeable to Eleventh Article of S^d Association Viz John Watrous & Peter Bulkley Esq^{rs} Capt Dudley Wright Mes^s Livi Wells Elias Worthington Moses Yeamons Asa Foot Charles Foot David Day James Ransom Capt Elijah Smith.. Silvanus Blish Pierpont Bacon Noah Pumroy Elijah Worthington	242

7 Dec 1775

Capt Asa Foot was Chosen Moderator	242
John Watrous Esqr Town Clerk	242
Capt Dudley Wright Town Treasurer	242
Elihu Clark.. David Yeamons.. David Miller } Constables and Collectors of the Town Rate	242
Jabez Rogers Constable to Collect the Coloney Tax and T: Tax	242
John Lomis.. Joshua Ransom Junr.. Wm Chamberlin.. Henry Daten.. Charles Bulkley.. John Worthington } Grand jurors	242
Noah Pumroy.. Hab: Foot } Fence Viewers	242
Aaron Gillit.. Jesse Day.. Samuel Lomis.. Elias Peck.. Eben Strong.. Stephen Otis.. Elij Williams Junr.. George Holmes } Tything Men	242
Stephen Otis.. Charles Foot.. Sam^{ll} Kellogg Junr.. David Purple.. Jeremiah Foot.. Nath^{ll} Chamberlin.. Nath Clark.. John Pratt.. Eliph: Chamberlin.. Elias Palmer.. Joseph Whay.. Elias Worthington Ju^r.. William Worthington.. Pierpont Bacon.. Samuel Dolbear.. Nath Chapmon.. Asahel Ransom.. Silvester Randal.. Samuel Holmes.. Joel Worthington.. Solomon Lomis.. Timothy Waters.. Ebenezer Carrier.. Benjamin Adams.. Joseph Day Junr.. Nath^{ll} Foot Junr.. James Sexton.. Daniel Judd Junr.. Elijah Buel.. Ezra Cartor.. Lazarus Waters.. Ebenezer McKall.. Oliver Bates.. Elizer Cartor [*ed: although the office is not written, these persons have likely been elected surveyors of highways, due to the number of persons elected and since this office is not otherwise included in the annual meeting.*]	243
Abner Dean.. John Worthington.. Aaron Foot.. Asa Daniels.. Roger Bulkley.. Samuel Kellogg Ju^r.. Asa Beebe.. Amos Wells.. Ebenezer Rogers } Listers	243
Noah Pumroy.. Capt Dudley Wright.. Elihu Clark } Select Men	243
Asa Daniels.. Noah Chapmon.. John Isham } L: Sealers	243
John Taintor P keeper	243
Elihu Clark Brander	243
John Johnson W^t Sealer	243
Elihu Clark W^t Sealer	243
Jonath: Deming Gager	243
Rich^d H: Huntley Packer	243
Daniel Bigelow.. Nath^{ll} Chamberlin.. Joseph Skinner.. Benjamin Curtis.. William Waters Ju^r.. Stephen Otis.. Nath^{ll} Foot Junr.. James Hamilton } Howards	243
John Olmstead a Com$^{[tt]}$ of Inspec^t in Leiu of Lieut David Day Dec^d	243
Voted that Ebenezer Rogers be a Collector of the Town Rate	243

Colchester

Meeting Voted to Relinquish to Elias Worthington his fine for not Serving as a Grandjuror the Last year	243
Voted that John Watrous Esqr: Mes^s Charles Foot and Asa Beebe be a Comittee to Settle Acct^s with the Mannagers of the Late.. Lottery and to Receive the Avails and Apply the Same towards paying the Publick Debt	243

24 Jan 1776

Elias Worthington Chosen Moderator	243
Capt Asa Foot Clerk of S^d Meeting	243
John Watrous Esqr Peter Bulkley Esqr Mess Charles Foot Pierpont Bacon Elias Worthington Jabez Jones Lieut John Isham Adonijah Foot Aaron Kellogg Capt Asa Foot David Miller Abner Dean Were Chosen to Districk the highways	243
Mess Charles Foot Zebulon Waterman Joseph Isham Junr John Olmstead and Asa Foot Were Chosen a Committe of Observation	244

11 Mar 1776

Voted that if David Foot Esqr will Leave out of his Land at the Northwest Part of his Lott So much as the Select men Shall think Necessary to Accomodate the Highway he Shall have Liberty to fence in and Improve the Lands Lying ye Opposite Side the highway & west of the Old parth Adjoyning to the Land formerly John Clarks and to the Road that goes Across the Rear of the home Lotts	244
Voted that John Watrous Esqr Mess Asa Beebe and Charles Foot be a Committe to Settle with the Mannagers of the Lottery the bad Debts that the Mannagers have Contracted	244
Voted - Epaphrodilus Champion Chosen Collector to Collect the Town Rate that Henry Champion Junr Was Chosen to Collect and Did not perform by means of his Absence in the Continantal Service	244
Voted that Capt Dudley Wright Elihu Clark and Jonathan Deming be a Comitte to Settle the Towns Acct^s	244

18 Mar 1776

Voted that John Watrous Esqr Mess Charles Foot and Asa Beebe be a Comitte to Inquire into the State of the Interest advanced by the Mannagers on prises in the Colchester Lottery and Wheather Any Interest Due to the Town	244

28 Mar 1776

Voted: David Yeamans Chosen ~~Collector~~ a Constable to Collect the Coloney Tax in Lieu of Henry Champion Junr who is now in the Continaltal Armey	244
Voted that the Settlement Made by the Comm^tt with the Mannagers of the.. Lottery.. is Accepted.. Voted That the Notes and Town orders.. and Also the Money which the Committe have Received of the Managers of the Lottery shall be.. handed Over to the Town Treasurer who is Directed to Remit the Avails.. to the Coloney Treasurer in Discharge of Capt Peter Bulkleys Bond given for Hopson Arearages	244
Voted to Sell the Horse Taken by Capt of Babcock for Tickets at Vandue and the avails to be.. Apply^d to the payment of the Arearage Due to the Colony from Colchester	244
Voted That the following be Accepted Viz.. Upon the Application.. of Noah Day & Joseph Taylor and a Number more of the Inhabitants.. to Lay a highway Across a Lott.. formerly Belonging to David Day Called Hopson Lott.. beginning at a Stake by the Stone wall a Little North of the Hopson House.. by the Road to Glastenbury then South 28 Deg: West 65½ rods to a highway by the Mill Brook the s^d Way Laid 2½ rods Wide the Southerly Side of s^d Line March 9th 1776 Laid by us.. Dudley Wright.. Noah Pumroy.. Elihu Clark } Select Men	245

Colchester

28 Mar 1776

We.. Freeholders and Inhabitants of.. Hebron being Appointed.. to Estimate the Damages to the Owners of S^d Farm by Laying the above highway.. Are of Opinion that five pounds L Money is a Meet Recompence.. Abner Jones.. Elihu Marvin.. John Kellogg }   245

16 Dec 1776

Capt Dudley Wright.. Elihu Clark } Select Men   245

Capt Asa Foot Moderator   245

Lieut Jonathan Deming Chosen Select Man in Lieu of Mr Elihu Clark   245

Joseph Isham Junr Chosen Select Man   245

John Watrous Esqr Chosen Town Clerk   245

Capt Dudley Wright Town Treasurer   245

Elihu Clark Constable to Collect the Colony Rate and a Collector of ye Town Tax   245

David Yeamons.. Elisha Lord.. Jabez Rogers } Constables and Collectors of the Town Rate   245

Samuel Kellogg Junr.. Nath^{ll} Chamberlin.. Prince Brewster.. Nehemiah Daniels.. John Otis.. Oliver Dodge.. David Kilborn.. Joseph Bulkley.. Samuel Lomis.. Aaron Gillit.. Nath^{ll} Clark.. William Bulkley.. Azariah Wright.. Deacon Israel Newton.. Elijah Williams Junr.. Jacob Lomis.. John Carrier.. Joseph Day Junr.. David Yeamons.. Jonath Dunham.. Ambros Niles.. Thomas Millor.. Asahel Ranson.. John Henry.. Jonah Dodge.. Silvester Randol.. Lieu^t John Cartey.. John Whay.. Ebenezer McCall.. Isaac Carrier.. Lazarus Waters.. Ezra Carter.. Daniel Judd Junr. Eliezer Carter } Surveyors of Highways   245

John Wright.. Solomon Wollcott.. Nath Clark.. Amos Wells.. Asa Beebe.. Aaron Foot.. Samuel Dolbear.. Amasa Ransom.. David Miller } Listers   245

Noah Pumroy.. Habb Foot } Fence Viewers   245

Jacob MacCall.. Habb Foot.. Abner Kellog.. Capt Noah Skinner.. William Chamberlin.. Zebulon Waterman } Grandjurors   246

Noah Day.. Asa Marriner.. Amos Ransom.. Alpheus Ransom.. Benjamin Randal Junr.. Timothy Waters.. Amasa Day } Tything Men   246

Noah Chapman.. Silvanus Blish.. Joseph Isham.. Capt John Chamberlin } L. Sealers   246

Elihu Clark } Sealer Weights   246

John Johnson } Sealer Measures   246

Elihu Clark.. Adonijah Foot.. Elijah Bewel } Branirs   246

Joseph Isham Junr Gager   246

Richard H: Huntley } Packer   246

Capt Charles Taintor.. Charles Foot.. Capt John Chamberlin } Comm^{tt} Inspection   246

10 Feb 1777

on the Motion of Mr Elihu Clark Voted And Abated Sundry Rates Aganst poor persons Absconded persons &c to the Amount of £8:14:7½   246

31 Mar 1777

Mr Elias Worthington Was Chosen Moderator   246

Voted that a Committe be Appointed.. to Provide Necessaries for the Support of the families of Soldiers.. who are or shall be Ingaged in any of the Continantal Battalions.. and Deliver.. to Such famelies at the.. Prises affixed by Law Without any Additional Expence.. on Such   246

Colchester

Soldiers Leaving Money with or Remitting Money to Such Comm^{tt} ..Voted that Mis^s Charles Taintor, Israel Wyatt Wells, Joshua Bulkley Amos Jones, Elias Worthington, Jabez Rogers John Olmstead Noah Skinner, Abner Dean and Amos Wells be a Committe Agreeable to the aforesaid vote

Voted that Israel Wyat Wells, Joshua Bulkley Capt Amos Jones, Elias Worthington Jabez Rogers John Olmstead Noah Skinner Abner Dean Amos Wells be Aded to the Committe of Inspection   246

Voted that Abner Dean be Chosen Constable in Lieu of Elisha Lord   246

30 Apr 1777

Mr Elias Worthington Chosen Moderator   247

Jonathan Deming Chosen Clerk Pro: Tem.   247

30 Sep 1777

Daniel Foot Esqr was Chosen Moderator   247

Voted that this Town Will Conform to the Requisition of his honour the Governor and Council of Safety Relative to providing Cloathing for the Soldiers &c.. Voted that Lieut Jonathan Deming John Hopson, EliasWorthington Junr John Worrthington Capt David Miller Capt Asa Foot Jabez Rogers Capt Zebulon Watermon Capt John Isham Capt Timothy Dutton William Brainard Asahel Ransom be a Committe for the Purpose afore Said   247

16 Dec 1777

Henry Champion Esqr Moderator   247

John Watrous Esqr Town Clerk   247

Elias Worthington Junr Constable to Collect the State Tax   247

Jabez Rogers.. Amasa Day.. Henry Deming } Constables   247

Jonathan Deming.. John Taintor.. Charles Foot.. Joseph Isham Junr.. Eph^m Little Junr } Select Men   247

Capt Dudley Wright Town Treas^r 247

Silvanus Blish.. John Wells Junr.. David Kilborn.. Azrariah Michel Arial Jones } Grandjurors   247

Jabez Jones.. Noah Chapmon.. Nath Foot Junr } L: Sealers   247

Solomon Woolcott.. Elijah Worthington.. William Gardner.. John Cartey.. Judah Scovill.. Jacob Fuller } Tything Men   247

Noah Pumroy.. Habakkuk Foot } F. Viewers   247

John Taintor.. Jabez Jones } K Keepers   247

Rich: H: Huntley - Packer   247

John Johnson: S: [*ed: Sealer, probably "of weights"*]   247

Elihu Clark: S: Measures   247

David Yeamons.. John Olmstead Junr.. John Wright.. Amos Wells.. Nath Clark.. Solomon Woolcott.. Epaphras Lord Junr.. Daniel Rogers Junr.. Alpheus Ransom } Listers   248

Rufus Randal..Benjamin Morgan.. Amasa Ransom.. Samuel Dolbear.. Joel Worthington.. Joshua Ranson Junr Silvester Randal.. Gershom Bulkley.. Jeremiah Foot.. William Worthington.. John Pratt.. Israel Lomis.. John Wright.. Hab: Foot.. Amos Wells.. Samuel Kellogg Junr.. Eliphalet Chamberlin Junr.. Bond Bigelow.. William Follet.. Joseph Skinner.. Henry Deming.. Silvanus Blish.. Theodore Lord.. Elisha Lord.. Isaac Carrier.. Ebenezer   248

Colchester

McKall.. David Yeamons.. Elijah Day.. Josiah Cridendon.. John Skinner 2nd.. Josiah Strong.. Capt Noah Skinner.. John Blish } Surveyors of Highways

Voted that Jabez Jones Junr his Barn Yard Near his Now Dwelling House be a Lawfull Pound — 248

29 Dec 1777

Elisha Lord Chosen Constable in Lieu of Henry Deming Who Refused	248
Jonathan Deming Tythingman	248
Elias Worthington Junr Collector of the Town Rates	248
Charles Bulkley.. Asa Treadway.. Daniel Coleman.. William Follet Chosen } Listers	248
Elisha Chapmon chosen a Committe in Addition to the Committe.. to Provide for the Soldiers famelies	248

15 Dec 1778

Daniel Foot Esqr Moderator	248
John Watrous Esqr Town Clerk	248
Miss Joseph Isham Junr.. Jonath Deming.. John Taintor.. Charles Foot.. Ephraim Little Junr } Select Men	248
Daniel Foot Esqr T: Treasurer	248
Elias Worthington Junr was chosen Constable to Collect the State Taxes	249
Jabez Rogers.. Henry Deming.. Stephen Day.. Aaron Kellogg } Constables	249
Charles Bulkley.. Daniel Kellogg.. ~~Joseph Bulkley~~.. Jonath Dodge Junr.. Samuel Holmes.. Libbeus Hills.. Lyman Crocker Joseph Knowlton } Tythingmen	249
Nathaniel Chamberlin.. Nath^{ll} Clark.. Jesse Billins.. William Bulkley.. Samuel Bridges.. Charles Bulkley.. Nath Warner.. John Pratt.. Ambros Strong.. John Caverley.. Elijah Northam.. David Purple.. John Carrier.. Noah Skinner Junr.. Ebenezer MacKall.. Isaac Carrier.. Ezra Carter.. David Strong.. Lazarus Waters.. Thomas Carrier.. Zebulon Waterman.. Simeon Ruthbun.. John Cartey.. Jeremiah Marshal.. John Whay.. Samuel Doulbear.. Jedediah Lothrop.. Stephen Day.. Timothy Dutton.. Samuel Isham.. Amasa Day.. Elisha Day.. John Bigelow Junr.. Solomon Lomis..Israel Kellogg } Surveyors of Highways	249
Daniel Isham.. Joseph Bulkley.. Henry Daton.. Joel Worthington.. John Whay.. Azariah Mitchel } Grandjurors	249
Israel Newton 3rd.. Abner Kellogg.. Jonathan Bigelow.. Gad Worthington.. David Yeamons.. John Olmstead Junr.. Elijah Buel.. Amos Jones.. Daniel Rogers Junr } Listers	249
Noah Pumroy.. Haba^k: Foot } Fence Viewers	249
Abner Kellogg.. Asa Daniels.. Nathaniel Foot Junr } Leath Sealers	249
Jonath Deming } Gager	249
Rich^d H: Huntly } Packer	249
Elihu Clark S: Weights	249
John Johnson S: Measures	249
John Taintor.. Jabez Jones } Key Keeper	249
Zeb Waterman.. Nath Clark.. Ezra Cartor.. Elias Palmer.. John Wright.. } Comm^{tt} To Supply The Soldiers famelies.. In Lieu of Elias Worthington.. Charles Taintor.. Abner Dean.. Amos Wells.. Israel Wyat Wills } Excused	249

Colchester

Silvanus Blish Comm^tt of Inspection	249
Voted.. a Tax of one Shilling on the Pound on all the Poles and Ratable Estate for Defraying the Necessary Charges of the Town.. Voted that Elias Worthington Junr be Collector	249
Voted That Co^ll William Whiting of Norwich Shall be Alowed for Supporting the Widdow Collit.. £ 0:12:0 p^r Week *15 Feb 1779*	249
Daniel Foot Esqr Was Chosen Moderator	250
Voted that we Will forthwith Collect and forward to the Com^tt for the Use of the Soldiers in the Connec^t Line of the Continental Army fifty woolen Blankets Seventy pair of Woolen Overhalls and Eighty Pair of Stockens.. Voted that Mess Jared Foot Adonijah Foot John Olmstead Junr Elias Worthing Esqr Capt Joseph Isham Junr John Wright Pierpont Bacon be the Committee	250
Granted a Tax of one Shilling on the Pound on All the Poles and Ratable Estate In the list 1778.. Voted that Elias Worthington Junr be a Collector *31 May 1779*	250
Capt Asa Foot Was Chosen Moderator	250
Voted that Some proper Method be Taken to Recover for Hannah Waters an Indigent Person a Support out of the Estate Left by her Deceased father.. the Select Men.. to Make Applycation to the Next County Court for.. a Conservator to Take Care of Hannah Waters.. an Aged Impotent Person now an Expence To the Town.. the Select Men.. to Pay Such Expences which May Arise in Searching out Hannah Waters Estate *1 Jul 1779*	250
Major Elias Worthington Was Chosen Moderator	250
Voted to Comply With the Requisition of the General Assembly Relative to Providing Cloathing for the Soldiers in the Continantal Armey.. Voted to Raise the Money.. by a TAx and Granted a Tax of five Shillings on the Pound.. Voted that Mess Asa foot.. James Ransom.. Nehemiah Gates.. Ephraim Little Jr } be a Committe to Purchase.. Cloathing for the Continantal Soldiers *13 Dec 1779*	250
Daniel Foot Esqr was Chosen Moderator	251
John Watrous Esqr Town Clerk	251
Capt John Isham Capt Stephen Day.. David Yeamons.. Capt Eliphalet Bulkley.. Aaron Kellogg } Select Men	251
Daniel Foot Esqr T: Treasurer	251
Elias Worthington Junr Constable to Collect the State Rates	251
Nath^ll Foot Junr.. Daniel F[ ] Junr.. Ebenezer Rogers.. Aaron Kellogg.. Ephraim Little Junr } Constables	251
John Bread.. Eliph: Chamberlin.. Nath^ll Otis.. John Worthington.. Gad Worthington.. Elijah Buel.. Asa Beebe.. Judah Scovil.. Simeon Rathbun.. Samuel Holmes } Listers	251
Jeremiah Foot.. Hab: Foot.. Abner Loweridge.. Dyer Lothrop.. Amasa Day.. Henry Daton } Grandjury Men	251
Noah Pumroy.. Hab Foot } F: Viewers	251
John Taintor.. Jabez Jones Key Keepers }	251
Israel Lomis.. William Worthington.. Peleg Ransom.. Amos Wells.. David Kilborn.. John	251

Colchester

Taintor.. Elihu Clark.. Elijah Northam.. Ambros Strong.. Abner Kellogg.. William Follet..
John Pratt.. Azariah Wright.. Stephen Day.. Adonijah Foot.. Samuel Isham.. John Isham 2nd..
Noah Skinner Junr.. Judah Lewis.. William Brainard and Richard Skinner Junr.. Jacob
Ingraham.. Theodor Lord.. Elizer Cartor.. Lazarus Waters.. Ebenezer MacKall.. Isaac
Carrier.. Edward Gustin.. Ebenezer Rogers.. Amos Jones.. John Whay.. Abel Rathbun.. John
Tenant.. Elijah Treadway } Surveyers of Highways

John Wright.. Samuel Lomis.. Joseph Skinner.. Robert Beeb.. William Welch.. Eben Strong.. *251*
Josiah Crittenden.. Jesse Day.. Samuel Isham } Tything Men

Noah Chapman.. Asa Daniels } L. Sealers *251*

Jonath Deming Gager *251*

Rich^d H: Huntley packer *251*

Elihu Clark S: Weights and Brander of Horses *251*

John Johnson Measur Sealer *251*

Voted that the Town do Accept of the Doings of the Select Men on the highways in *251*
Westchester, one Runing through John Holmes Land and the Other Runing by the School
house now Erecting S^d way as Laid in past Across Lieu^t David Days Land
20 Jan 1780

Vote to Chuse a Committe to Remoove Incroahments from Highway.. Voted that Daniel *251*
Judd.. Charles Food.. Peter Bulkley Esqr.. John Blish and Adonijah Foot be a Committe for
the Afore Said Purpose
23 Feb 1780

Daniel Foot Esqr was Chosen Moderator *251*

20 Mar 1780

Elias Worthington Esqr was Chosen Moderator *252*

Capt Eliphalet Bulkley.. Aaron Kellogg John Tenant John Whay James Ransom Job Rathbun *252*
Capt John Isham William Brainard John Cartey Jabez Rogors Rosel Chamberlin Henry
Deming Lieu^t Daniel Judd John Henry Stephen Day Joseph Carrier Were Chosen Committe
of Inspection

Voted that the Select Men be Directed to Agree with Timothy Waters and Lazarus Waters *252*
that Provided Said Timothy and Lazarus will Support Hannah Waters During her Natural
Life Clear from Charge to the Town.. then Said Town Agree that if any of the Hannah's
Breathren Shall become Chargable to the Town they Shall be Supported by the Town

Voted that Liberty be Granted to Daniel Dodge for his Nusserey of Apple Treas to Remain *252*
on the highway Near hebron Line in Colchester the Space of Six years
13 Apr 1780

Daniel Foot Esqr Chosen Moderator *252*

Voted to Accept the following Agreement Between the Select Men and the proprietors of the *252*
Lands on which the following highway is laid out and to Accept of s^d highway viz.. Highway
Laid out and Surveyed Part on Peter Bulkley and Rufus Randal and John Whay and [ ] the
heirs of Daniel Gardnor Deceased to Norwich Town Line.. Damages Apprised to Each
Proprietor.. To Peter Bulkley £ 8.16.. to Rufus Randal.. 5.13.. John Whay.. 4.7 LM.. Lawfull
Money as it went in the Year 1774 Jonath Gardner.. Silas Stark.. Jedediah Lothrop Apprisors
we the Subscribors Select Men of the Town.. Agree to Give the aforementioned Sums At *252*
which the Damages Are Apprised to.. the Proprietors of the Lands on which the .. Highway is
laid out.. Aaron Kellogg.. Eliph Bulkley.. John Isham 2nd } Select Men

Colchester

We the Subscribors.. Agree to Accept.. the Sums.. Alowed to us by the Apprisers of the Damages of Laying the.. highway on our Lands.. Peter Bulkley.. John Whay.. Rufus Randal	252
The following is the Survey of s^d Highway - Rufus Randal beginning half a Rod Eastward from the Northwest corner of Capt Peter Bulkleys Hide Lot by the Highway thence Running half a Rod on Said Hide Lott South.. to a Stake and Stones thence South East and a Strait LIne.. to the South East Corner of John Whays Land bought of Benjamin Randal thence a Strait LIne to a Stake Stones.. Eastward from the South East Corner of John Whays Land bought of James Gardner .. South to a Stake and Stones in Norwich Town Line.. Eastward from the Line of Land formerly Belonging to Daniel Gardner Disceased	252

29 May 1780

Daniel Foot Esqr Chosen Moderator	253
Capt Ephrain Little J^r and Elias Worthington Junr Appeared and Rufused to Serve as Collectors of the Town Rates	253
Voted to chuse Collectors in the Room of those that have Refused to Collect the Town Rate.. Elijah Northan Chosen Collector to Collect the Town Rate in the first Society	253

23 Jun 1780

Coll Elias Worthington Chosen Moderator	253

27 Jun 1780

Elisha Chapmon Chosen Collector to Collect the Town Tax	253

10 Jul 1780

Co^{ll} Elias Worthington Chosen Moderator	253
Voted that this Town will Give the Same Incoragement to those Soldiers that Shall be Drafted.. to fill up the Continental Armey.. as they have heretofore voted to Give to their proportion of the fifteen hundred heretofore Raised.. and Granted a Tax of hree [ ] on the pound in Silver or Gold.. for the Defraying the afore Said Charges.. Voted Elias Worthington Junr as Chosen Collector	253

14 Nov 1780

Daniel Foot Esqr Chosen Moderator	254
Voted that that this Town will Chuse a Committe.. to hire that Number of men to fill up the Continantal Armey that Shall be formed to be the Proportion for this Town.. Capt Joseph Isham Junr.. Capt Jonathan Deming.. Pierpont Bacon.. Co^{ll} Elias Worthington.. Capt Nath^{ll} Harris.. Capt John Isham.. Capt Stephen Day.. Capt Lazarus Waters } Were Chosen a Commi^{tt} for the Purpose	254
Voted to Tax the Inhabitants in Money to Raise the Money to Procure the Towns Quotoe of Provisions.. Voted and Granted a Tax of one Shilling State Money on the Pound for Defraying the afore Said And Other Charges Voted that that this Town will Chuse a Committe.. to hire that Number of men to fill up the Continantal Armey that Shall be formed to be the Proportion for this Town.. Capt Joseph Isham Junr.. Capt Jonathan Deming.. Pierpont Bacon.. Co^{ll} Elias Worthington.. Capt Nath^{ll} Harris.. Capt John Isham.. Capt Stephen Day.. Capt Lazarus Waters } Were Chosen a Commi^{tt} for the Purpose	254
Voted that Capt Joseph Isham Junr be a Committe to Receive the Cask and Salt from the State for Packing the Provisions to be by the Town provided for the Continantal Armey.. and to Receive Said Provisions and Pack the Same	254
Voted to Chuse a Commit^{tt} to Procure Said Provisions Co^{ll} Eliphalet Bulkley Mess John Blish Henry Deming John Henry Chosen a Committe for the Purpose	254

Colchester

Elias Worrthing Ju^r Chosen Collector to Collect S^d Tax	254
18 Dec 1780	
Capt Asa Foot was Chosen moderator	254
Dan^{ll} Foot Esqr Chosen Clerk	254
Charles Bulkly.. Israel Foot.. Nathan Williams.. Epaph^s Champin.. Israel Kellogg Ju^r.. Sam^{ll} Isham.. Sam^{ll} Morgan.. Elijah Treadway.. Elijah Buel Ju^r.. Hosea Foot.. Dan Worthington } Listers	254
Charles Foot.. Asa Daniels } Leather Sealers	254
Job Chamberlin.. Amasa Day.. Jedediah Lothrop.. Edward Gustin.. David Kilborn.. David Strong } Grandjurors	254
Simeon Rathburn.. Silas Stark.. Charles Hart.. Uriah Carrier.. Noah Skinner Ju^r.. John Eels.. Nath^{ll} Otis.. Jon^n Deming } Tything men	254
Dan^{ll} Foot Esqr.. Capt Jo^s Isham.. Capt Nath^{ll} Harris.. Capt Henry Champion.. Capt Asa Foot } Select men	254
Dan^{ll} Foot Chosen Tr^r	254
Elias Worthington Ju^r to Collect Colony tax.. Eben^r Rogers.. Nath^{ll} Foot Ju^r.. Theodore Lord.. Ep^m Little Ju^r } Constables	254
Noah Pumry.. Hab^k Foot } Fence viewers	254
John Johnson Sealer of Measures	254
Elihu Clark Sealer of Sealer of Weights	254
Nathan Warner.. Sam^{ll} Northum.. Zebulun Strong.. Jo^s Johnson.. Eliph^t Bulkley.. Jon^n Morgan.. Aaron Gillett.. Amos Ransom.. Sam^{ll} Church.. Aaron Kellogg.. Ariol Jones.. Bliss Ransom.. Jeremiah Marshal.. John Carty.. Freedom Chamberlin.. John Whay.. Elijah Northum.. John Blish.. Elijah Williams Ju^r.. Cephas Cone.. Jon^n Northum.. Jesse Day.. James Saxton.. Solomon Lomis.. Sam^{ll} Carrier.. Azariah Biglow.. Comfort Goff.. Elijah Buel.. Jacob Mackaul.. Charles Taintor.. Ep^s Lord Ju^r.. John Lord.. Dan^{ll} Bulkly.. Lebbeus Hills } Chosen Surveyors of Highways	255
John Taintor.. Jabez Jones Key Keepers	255
granted a Tax of :3^d: on ye Pound on ye List 1780 Elias Worthington Ju^r Chosen Collector	255
voted to Choose Dan^{ll} Foot agent for ye Town	255
voted that Capt Peter Bulkly Enquire into ye State of ye land Contained in New london old Road	255
22 Jan 1781	
Elias Worthington Esqr Was Chosen Moderator	255
22 Jan 1781	
Voted to have ye Town Classed as Intimated by ye Assembly in order to Raising men to fill up ye Continental army.. Voted that ye Captains of ye Several Companies in ye Town be a Com^{tee} to Class ye Inhabitants .. & that Ensign Wm Brainard Serve in ye Room of Capt Stephen Brainard he not belonging to this Town & that Lieu^t Josiah Gates Serve in ye Room of Capt Jesse Billings if he be not able to Serve himself	255
Voted that Capt Jo^s Isham be appointed to Collect ye Names of all ye Persons now in ye Continental army & transmit the Same to ye Govr	255
Voted to Grant a Tax of Six Pence State Money.. for ye Purpose of Procuring Corn flower &c for ye State Troops as Required by ye Assembly & to Defray ye Incident Chargs of ye Town..	255

Colchester

Voted that Elias Worthing Ju^r be Collector to gather ye forementioned Tax

Voted that Every Person that Shall Deliver Indian Corn at 4^s: p^r Bushel Rie flower at: 16^s: p^r 255
C: Weight: Wheat flower at :24: p^r C: w^t, to ye amount of 1 ½^d on ye pound on their Several
Lists of ye year 1780: Shall be allowed for ye 1^d ½ so paid in Grain & flower as afors^d: 4^d: on
ye pound on a Tax this Day Laid on ye Inhabitants.. for ye Purpose of Raising Grain &c: S^d
Corn & flower to be Delivered to Messrs Pierpont Bacon John Blish Dudly Wright or Asa
Foot.. & S^d Receivers are appointed to Receive S^d Corn & flower & Properly Pack & Store y^e
Same at ye Expence of ye Town
30 Jan 1781

Voted to Choose Gad Worthington in ye Room of John Blish one of ye Com^{tee} to Receive in 256
Provisions for ye Publick
26 Feb 1781

Noah Pumroy was Chosen Grandjuryman in ye Room of David Kilborn: & Dan^{ll} Judd was 256
Chosen Grandjuryman in ye Room of Job Chamberlin
Charles Bulkley & Eq^s Lord Ju^r Were Chosen Com^{tee} in ye Room of Capt Dudly Wright & 256
Asa Foot to Receive Grain & flower
voted to Choose Es^r Little Ju^r Collector of y^e :6: Tax granted in Jan^{ry} Last in ye Room of Elias 256
Worthington Ju^r..
Voted to Desire Col^l Bulkley & Capt Isham to make Enquiry at Hartford... Where ye Soldiers 256
that Inlisted in ye Continental Service for Six months Shall apply for their wages & in What
manner
voted that Bristow Johnson has Leave to Set up a Small house Between ye mill & Bohans 256

20 Mar 1781

Co^{ll} Elias Worthington Was Chosen Moderator 4

Voted to Direct.. Selectmen to agree with Silvanus Blish for a [ ] Way across his Land to 4
meet the Highway by Jacob Mackauls
voted to Grant a Tax.. to be Laid out to Procure Clothing for ye Soldiers.. & Ep^m Little Ju^r 4
Chosen Collector of s^d Tax
voted to Choose Sam^{ll} Kellogg Ju^r Grandjuryman in ye Room of Noah Pumry who Refuses to 4
Serve
voted that ye Pork & Beef Purchaed for ye Publick.. to be Conveyed to Hartford: be Carted to 4
East haddam & Conveyed from thence to Hartford by water & that Capt Jo^s Isham have
oversight of gitting it Done
16 Apr 1781

Capt Asa Foot Chosen Moderator 4

voted that Co^{ll} Henry Champion be Reimbursed ye money he Paid to Russel Day for Land 4
Included in ye Highway over Grassy hill
voted that Jon^n Morgans Rates in ye hands of Mr Worthing[*ton*] and Mr Clark be abated 4

4 May 1781

voted that a Tax be Laid.. on ye Inhabitants.. of one Penny on ye pound in State money for ye 5
purpose of Procuring Blankets for ye Continental & State Troops Newly Raised: & that Capt
Ep^m Little Ju^r Collect ye Same..

Colchester

18 May 1781

voted to appoint John Blish a Committee man in ye room of Dan^{ll} Foot to Provide for   5
Soldiers Families
31 May 1781
voted to Grant a tax one Peney on ye Pound Silver money on ye List 1780: .. to Purchase   6
Supplies for ye Soldiers Families.. voted to Choose Elias Worthington Ju^r Collector
voted to Choose Capt Jo^s Isham Com^{tee} for the Purpose of making S^d Supplies   6

18 Jun 1781

Elias Worthington Esqr Chosen Moderator   6

voted to Choose Elias Worthington Ju^r Collector of ye Tax granted ye Last meeting   6

6 Aug 1781

Elias Worthington Esqr Chosen Moderator   6

voted to Lay a tax.. of 4^d: on ye pound on ye List: 1780.. for ye Purpose of Procuring Beef   6
Cattle for ye use of ye Continental Army.. & Elias Worthington Ju^r Chosen to Collect
voted to Choose John Bliss Com^{tee} to purchase S^d Beef Cattle & Deliver the Same   6

voted to Choose Capt Elijah Worthington Nath^{ll} Harris James Ransom [ ] Noah Day Jo^s 6
Isham Ju^r & John Isham 2nd a Com^{tee} to hire six men to Serve in ye Continental army

voted that John Chamberlin have Liberty to move his Shop Six foot further into the Street   6

1 Oct 1781

Henry Champion Esqr Was Chosen moderator   7

Capt Jo^s Isham Ju^r Was Chosen to receive & Secure Provisions w^c shall be Delivered in   7
payment of taxes
8 Oct 1781
Elias Worthington Esqr Chosen moderator   7

voted to Grant Dan^{ll} Root ye Liberty of that Wedge of Land Between New london Road &   7
Lyme Road at ye South End of ye Town Street to Set a Shop on Provided it Does not Obstruct
Traveling
11 Dec 1781

Elias Worthington Esqr Was Chosen moderator   7

Dan^{ll} Foot Esqr Chosen Town Clerk   7

Israel Nuton 3rd.. Azariah Wright.. Dan^{ll} Bulkley.. John Chamberlin.. Joel Worthington..   7
Sam^{ll} Holms.. Zeb^n Waterman.. John Carrier.. Josiah Crittendon.. David Strong.. John Wright
} Listers
Jo^s Skinner. Jo^s Foot.. Edward Gustin.. George Holms.. Sam^{ll} Isham.. James Saxton.. Eben
Strong } Tything men
Dan^{ll} Foot Esqr.. Jo^s Isham Ju^r.. Elias Worthington.. John Isham 2nd.. Asa Foot } Select men   7
Elias Worthington Ju^r Collect State tax.. Nath^{ll} Foot Ju^r.. Theodore Lord.. Eben^r Rogers..   7
Jabez Rogers.. } Constables
Dan^{ll} Foot Town Tr^r 7

Benjn Beebe.. David Kilborn.. David Loweridge.. Rufus ~~Araunah~~ Randal.. Aaron Foot..   7
Eleazer Dunham.. Benjn Root } Grandjurors
Pierpont Bacon.. Jonath^n Biglow.. Jo^s Johnson.. Charles Bulkley.. Wm Follett.. Elisha   8

93

Colchester

Scoval.. Darius Clark.. Isaiah Mun.. Neh^h Daniels.. Nath^{ll} Chamberlin.. Azariah Wright.. Abner Chapman.. John Tennant.. Jabez Jones.. Jabez Rogers.. John Carty.. Thos Carrier Ju^r.. Rufus Randal.. Job Rathburn.. Ambrose Niles.. Amasa Day.. John Blish.. Simson Crocker.. Jon^n Dunham.. Stephen Skinner.. Dan^{ll} Williams.. Benjn Staples.. John Olmsted Ju^r.. Isaac Carrier.. Thos Carrier.. David Miller.. Eleazer Carter.. Sam^{ll} Finley.. Ezra Purple } Surveyors of Highways

Asa Daniels.. Noah Chapman } Leather Sealers	8
Hab^k Foot.. Noah Pumroy } fence viewers	8
Jon^n Deming: Gauger	8
Elihu Clark: Sealer of Weights	8
John Johnson: Sealer of measures	8
John Taintor.. Jabez Jones } Key Keepers	8
Granted a Tax 2^d on ye Pound Law^l money on ye List 1781.. Voted to Choose Elias Worthington Ju^r Collector	8
voted that ye Selectmen dispose Phebe Watsons Clothes in their hands to ye best advantage.. & Lodge ye money in ye Treasury	8
22 Jan 1782	
Capt Asa Foot Was Chosen Moderator	8
Jabez Rogers Chosen Constable in ye Room of Eben^r Rogers -- Resign^d	8
John Chamberlin Chosen Constable.. & Collector of Town tax in ye Room of Mr Worthington	8
Dan^{ll} Judd Chosen Grandjuryman in ye room of David Kilborn	8
Asa Foot Chosen Surveyor of Highways in ye room of Thos Carrier & Sam^{ll} Finley	8
voted to accept.. Laying a Highways across Silvanus Blishes Land	8
4 Mar 1782	
Col^l Elias Worthington Chosen Moderator	9
voted to Choose Capt Jo^s Isham J^r Agent to appear at Hartford before the Com^{tee} Now Sitting.. with Respect to ye Number of men Required for Continental Service & any other Case that shall be brought under Consideration	9
14 Mar 1782	
Henry Deming Chosen Grandjuryman in ye room of Benjn Root who Refuses to Serve	9
Charles Foot Chosen Grandjuryman in ye Room of Benjn Beedbe who Refuses to Serve	9
17 Dec 1782	
Capt Asa Foot was Chosen Moderator	9
John Watrous Esqr Town Clerk Town Clerk	9
John Watrous Esqr.. Capt Amos Jones.. Capt Asa Foot } Select Men	9
Voted to Chuse a Committe to Settel the Town Acct^s &c. Mess Asa Beebe.. John Caverley.. Elihu Clark } were Chosen a Committe for the.. Purpose	9
25 Dec 1782	
Capt Dudley Wright Town Treasurer	10
Daniel Watrous Constable to Collect the State Taxes	10

Colchester

John Chamberlin.. Jabez Rogers.. Nath Foot Jun[r].. Theodore Lord } Constables	10
John Carrier.. Eliphalet Gillit.. Elisha Lord.. Daniel Isham.. Exe[d]: Elisha Chapman.. Ref[d] John Whay.. Joseph Day Jun[r] } Grandjurors	10
Charles Bulkley.. William Follet.. Elisha Lord.. Abner Kellogg.. William Worthington.. Joseph Foot.. Elijah Williams J[r].. Israel Kellogg 2nd John Newton 3rd.. John Douglas.. Clark Cartey } Listers	10
Stephen Otis.. Excused Daniel Kellogg.. Bond Bigelow.. John Cartey.. Sylvester Randal.. Cephas Cone.. Jonath Dunham } Tythingmen	10
Remov[d] Noah Chapman.. John Chamberlin.. Jabez Jones } L Sealer	10
Remov[d] John Johnson M:S: [ed: sealer of measures]	10
Elihu Clark W[t] Sealer	10
John Taintor.. Jabez Jones } K: Keeper	10
David Purple.. Robert Beebe.. Samuel Gates.. John Whay.. John Henry.. Jeremiah Marshal.. David Wildes.. Joshua Bulkley.. Russel Kellogg.. Joseph Bulkley.. Amos Kellogg.. Solomon Woolcott.. Elisha Bigelow.. William Bulkley Excu[d].. Daniel Pratt Jun[r].. Joel Hinkley.. John Wright.. Joseph Isham J[r].. Nath Warner.. Sylvester Randal.. Ezra Purple.. David Strong.. David Skinner.. Laz: Waters.. Samuel Finley.. Thomas Carrier.. Uriah Carrier.. David Yeamons.. Thomas L: Hide.. Benjamin Hatch.. Thomas Smith.. Robert Shatuck.. Jacob Babbit.. John Isham 3rd.. Judah Scovill } Surveyors of Highways	10
Voted that Daniel Foot and Peter Bulkley Esq[r] be a Comm[tt] to Apply to the Next General Assembly for Information wheather the families of the Soldiers now in the Connecticut Line of the Continental Armey are by the Toun where they belong to be provided for any Longer *10 Feb 1783*	11
Elias Worthington Esq[r] was Chosen Moderator	11
voted to Adjorn this Meeting to the Dwelling House of M[r] Aaron Kellogg	11
Voted to Chuse Cap[t] Joseph Isham Jun[r] Agent for the Town	11
Voted to Chuse a Committe to Abate Such town Rates Against Such Poor people as are unable to pay.. Voted that Mess Pierpont Bacon David Yeamons Jabez Rogers and Asa Foot be a Committe for the Purpose *18 Mar 1783*	11
Cap[t] Asa Foot Chosen Moderator	11
Asa Bigelow Chosen Constable to Collect the State Rates in Lieu of Daniel Watrous who.. Refuses to Serve	11
Noah Pumroy and Hab Foot Fence Viewers	11
Silvester Randal Grandjuror - Excused	12
Joshua Morgan Surveyor of highways	12
Joseph Gillet Surveyor of Highways	12
Voted to Chuse a Comm[tt] to Supply for Soldiers famelies as Usual.. Adonijah Foot.. John Bulkley.. Thomas Gates } A Committe for the Purpose	12
whereas John Blish hath An Execution in his favour Against the Town for L Money and Cap[t] Ephraim Little Jun[r] is Collector of a Town Tax Granted for State Money that in Case S[d] Little Shall pay S[d] Execution that he shall be Alowed in Settling his S[d] Rate three Times the Sum Contained in S[d] Execution N.B. Little Collectd State Money	12
Voted that the Selecct Men Consider Some Abatements Requested by Jabez Rogers and	12

95

Colchester

Alow.. As they Judge Jus^t an Reasonable
Voted that Israel Holdridges Town Rate Due to Capt Chamberlin be Abated   12
Voted that the Select Men Alow Silas Dewey £ 3:10:0 L Money for a Gun the Town   12
Received of him
21 Aug 1783
Co^{ll} Champion Moderator   13
Whereas Mr Elias Worthington Junr had Lately Taken Benjamin Stapels Benjamin Mather   13
and Elisabeth Smithfield for their Rates and had them in Custody.. and whereas Sundery of
the Inhabitants Advised Said Collector Worthington to Suspend with Committing S^d Persons
to Goal untill after this Meeting voted that S^d Collector shall not come under Any Blame or
Loss for any Neglect of Committing Said three Persons Before this Time
*Editor's note: Duplicate entries show some discrepancies. Selectmen: p 254: "Jo^s Isham
Ju^r"; p 1 "Jo^s Isham Ju^r". Surveyors of Highways: p 255, "John Lord; p 1, John B: Lord".*

Colebrook

Town Meetings
1779-1825

See also LDS microfilm # 1,503,206, item 1

Located at the Town Clerk's Office

Colebrook

13 Dec 1779

Town Meeting.. Opened at the house of Capt Saml Rockwell	1
Capt Samuel Rockwell Chosen Moderator	1
Mr Elijah Rockwell Chosen Register Or Town Clerk	1
Mr David Pinney Mr Samuel Mills & Mr John Porter } Chosen Select Men	1
Mr Elijah Rockwell Chosen Town Treasurer	1
Mr Peletiah Mills Chosen Constable	1
Mr Moses Wright Chosen grandjury	1
Mr David Pinney Mr Samuel Mills & Capt Samuel Rockwell } Chosen Surveyors of Highways	1
Mr Jacob Ogden Mr John Rockwell & Capt Samuel Rockwell Chosen } Listers	1
Mr Peletiah Mills Chosen Collecttor	1
Mr Nathaniel Burr Chosen Brander of Horses	1
Mr Nathaniel Burr Chosen Sealer of Wates	1
Mr Moses Wright Chosen Sealer of Measures	1
Voted That their be a Pound Put on the South East Corner of Mr David Pinney Lot on the North Side of Norfolk Road	1
Voted That their be a Pound Bult on the South East Corner of Leu^t Mill's Lot the West Side of Sandersfield Road	1
Voted that Mr David Pinney be a Pound Keeper	1
Voted that Leu^t Mills be a Pound Keeper	1
Voted that Capt Samuel Rockwell be a Sealer of Leather	1

14 Mar 1780

Meeting.. Opened & held at Capt Saml Rockwells	2
Capt Samuel Rockwell Chosen Moderator	2
Mr Andrew Buckingham Mr Eleazer Bidwell & Mr John Porter } Chosen Inspectors of Provitions	2
Voted that Mr Elijah Rockwell be Directed to Procure a Town Book on the Towns Cost	2

10 Apr 1780

Town Meeting Held by ajurnment at Capt Saml Rockwells	2
Capt Saml Rockwell Moderator	2
Voted that Capt Samuel Rockwell.. Mr Samuel Mills.. And Mr Jacob Ogden be a } Commitee to hier Preching the Insuing year	2
Voted that Capt Samuel Rockwell be an agent for the Town to Apply To the general Assembly...to keep of a State Tax if Possable	2

26 Jun 1780

Town Meeting.. Opened at Capt Saml Rockwells	2
Capt Samuel Rockwell Chosen Moderator	2
Voted That the Thanks of this Meeting be Paid to Capt Sill and Capt Chipman for their generus Assistence to this Town towards filling up their Quota of Continental troops	3

Colebrook

Voted That the Treasurer.. be Directed.. to Pay an acknoledgment to Capt Sill and Capt Chipman of forty Shillings Each of Connecticut New Emition And twenty Shillings to Each Soldier who hath Ingaged for this Town By the Hand of Capt Sill	3

[ ] Oct 1780

Upon the Memorial of the Town.. by their Agent Capt Samuel Rockwell Shewing that this Assembly.. Directed Said Town to Return a list of the Polls and Rateable Estate.. in Order to their Contributing to the Publick Burthens of the State That the Memorialist haveing Now Complied With Said Order and also Laid Before this Assembly the State.. of Said Town that they are Destitute as yet of a minister of the gospel And of a meeting house.. That their Numbers are Small the Land rough & Stubborn to Subdue and have Many Other Difficulties to Incounter all which Renders their Cercumstancies inadequate to a Publick Tax at Present.. This Assembly Takeing their Case into Consideration Do Resolve.. that Said Inhabitants be Excused from Exhibeting any List of their Polls or Ratable Estate.. Whereby To be Subjected to any State Tax at this Time.. Examined By George Wyllys Secretary	3

19 Sep 1780

A Town Meeting held at Capt Samuel Rockwell	4
David Pinney Moderator	4

22 Sep 1780

A Town Meeting held at Capt Saml Rockwells.. By Ajurnment	4
Mr David Pinney Moderator	4
Voted That this Town Make Application to the Next County Court For a Committee to Set a Stake for A Meeting house Agre^d Without One Desenting Vote -- Voted that Capt Urial Homes of Hartland.. Col^o Seth Smith of New Hartford and Maj^r Giles Pettebone of Norfolk } be Nominated for a Committee	4
Voted that Capt Samuel Rockwell.. Mr Samuel Mills and Mr Jacob Ogden } be a Society Committee	4

4 Dec 1780

A Town Meeting Held at Capt Samuel Rockwells	4
Mr David Pinney Chosen Moderator	4
Capt Samuel Rockwell Mr David Pinney & Mr Samuel Mills } Chosen Select Men	4
Mr Elijah Rockwell Chosen Regestor or Town Clerk	4
Mr Elijah Rockwell Chosen Town Treasurer	4
Mr Nathaniel Burr Chosen Constable	4
Mr Aaron Griswold.. Mr John Porter.. Mr Joseph Bidwell.. Mr Elijah Rockwell.. Mr Hezekiah Simons } Chosen Surveyors of Highways	4
Mr John Rockwell Mr Jacob Ogden & Mr Eleazer Bidwell } Chosen Listers	5
Mr Nathaniel Burr Chosen Collecttor	5
Mr Joseph Tainter Chosen Grand Jury	5
Mr Joseph Bidwell Chosen Tythingman	5
Mr Nathaniel Burr Chosen Brander of horses	5
Mr David Pinney Chosen Pound Keeper	5
Voted that Mr Samuel Mills.. Mr David Pinney and Capt Samuel Rockwell } be a Committee	5

Colebrook

to Call Out the Committee Apinted by the County Court to Set a Meeting [ ]

22 Jan 1781

A Town Meeting.. Held at Capt Saml Rockwells	5
Capt Samuel Rockwell Chosen Moderator	5
Voted that Mr John Porter Mr Ebenezer Shepard & Mr Solomon Crisey } be a Committee to hier a Man for States Service	5
Voted Two Pence on the Pound on the List of the year 1780// in Hard Money Or Other Money at the Currant Exchang to be Collected By the 10 Day February 1781 Double to any Person that Shall Not Pay his Rate by the time.. Voted that Mr Joseph Taintor be a Collector	5
Voted that Capt Samuel Rockwell Mr John Rockwell and Mr Nathaniel Burr } be a Committee to hire Preching and Other Bisness for the Town	6

5 Feb 1781

Towm Meeting held at Capt Saml Rockwells	6
Capt Saml Rockwell Moderator	6
Voted that the School Destricks be two for the Town that the North District Extend from the State Line South as far as Capt Saml Rockwells Including the Whole of his List that the Inhabitants Living above two Miles from Winchester Line Shall Belong to Said North Destrict Excepting Mr John Porter and all that Live in the Said South two Miles to Belong to the South Destrict	6
Voted That Mr Aaron Griswold Collector Proceed to Collect by Destress or Other Wise the Several Sums.. of those Persons that have Not Settled the Same to Pay the Revd Mr Mills for Preching in.. 1778	7
Voted That the Treasurer.. be Directed to Pay unto Isaac Sharp John Willmore Thomas Stafford and George Hudson twenty Shillings Hard Money to Each.. when.. they have.. Joined the Contanental Army.. in Lieu of all former Bounties granted by this Town	7

10 Dec 1781

a Town Meeting Held at Capt Saml Rockwell	7
Capt Samuel Rockwell Chosen Moderator	7
Capt Samuel Rockwell Capt David Pinney & Mr Samuell Mills } Chosen Select Men	7
Mr Elijah Rockwell Chosen Town Clerk or Regestor	7
Mr Elijah Rockwell Chosen Town Treasurer	7
Mr Samuel Mills and Mr Nathaniel Burr Chosen Constables	7
Mr Samuel Mills and Capt David Pinney } Chosen Surveyors of Roads	7
Mr Hezekiah Simons & Ebenezer Shepard } fence Vewers	7
Mr Jacob Ogen Mr John Rockwell and Mr Eleazer Bidwell Chosen } Listors	7
Mr John Porter Chosen Collector	7
Edmond Howell Chosen Grand Jureman	7
Mr Joseph Seymour Junr Chosen tytheing Man	7
Mr Nathaniel Burr Chosen Sealer of Wates & Measurs and Brander of Horses	8
Voted That their be but One Town Pound and that that be ajineing the South end of Capt Samuel Rockwell garding	8

Colebrook

Mr Timothy Rockwell Chosen Pound Keeper	8
Mr Jacob Ogden & Mr Moses Wright } Chosen a School Committee for the South Destrict	8
Mr Samuel Mills and Capt Samuel Rockwell } Chosen a School Committee for the North Des^t	8
Voted That Mr John Porter Mr Aaron Griswold Mr Samuel Mills Capt David Pinney and Mr Edmond Howell } Be a Committee to Treet With Capt Rockwell about the Exchang of Lands	8
Voted That Mr Elijah Rockwell Make up the Rate Bill	8
Voted That Mr Nathaniel Burr be a grave Diger	8

10 May 1782

A Town Meeting.. Held at Capt Samuel Rockwells	9
Mr Samuel Mills Chosen Moderator	9
Voted That the Town Make Application to the.. Gene^{rl} Assembly.. Praying.. to Set aside the Doings of the.. County Cort held at Litchfield.. in Establishing the Doings of a Committe In Setting a Stake for a Meeting House.. And Likewise Appint An Other Comittee for Said Purpose.. Voted That Daniel Humphry Esqr of Simesbury Capt John Walson of Canaan and Hezekiah Fitch Esqr of Salisbury } be Nominated for the above Committee	9
Voted That Capt Samuel Rockwell be an Agent.. to Procure A Memorial and Manage the Same According to the above Vote	9

20 Aug 1782

At A Town Meeting.. Held at Capt Saml Rockwells	9
Mr John Rockwell Chosen Moderator	9
Voted That Capt Saml Rockwell Mr John Rockwell Mr Saml Mills Mr John Porter Mr Edmond Howell & Mr Eleazer Bidwell } Be a Committee to Call Out the Committee granted By the general Assembly.. to Set a Stake for a Meeting house.. To Victual & Provide for the Same	9
Voted That their be a Rate of One Penny on the Pound Raised.. on the List of the year 1781 to be applied by a Committee to be Chosen for that Purpose, in Procureing a Singing Master Sum time Next fall Or Winter in Order to Instruct the Inhabetants.. in the Art of Singing --	10
Voted That Mr Elijah Rockwell Make up the above Rate Bill	
Voted That Mr Timothy Rockwell be a Collector to Collect the above Rate	10
Voted That Mr John Rockwell Mr Saml Mills & Mr Eleazer Bidwell } Be a Committee to Procure a Singing Master	10
Voted That the Town Make Application by a Committee to be Chosen To Mr Roswel Cook to Preach hear the Next Summer With a vew To Settle with us as a gasspill Minister if We Can agree.. Voted That Mr Moses Wright Mr Edmond Howell & Capt Saml Rockwell } Be a Commmittee for the above Purpose	10

4 Oct 1782

a Town Meeting Held by ajurnment at Capt Saml Rockwells	10
Mr John Rockwell Moderator	10

2 Dec 1782

a Town Meeting.. held at Capt Saml Rockwells	10
Capt Saml Rockwell Chosen Moderator	10
Mr Sam^{ll} Mills Capt Sam^{ll} Rockwell Capt David Pinney Mr John Porter & Edmond Howell } Chosen Select Men or Townsmen	10

Colebrook

Elijah Rockwell Esqr Chosen Town Clerk and Treasurer	10
Mr Sam^{ll} Mills Chosen Constable	11
Voted Mr Jacob Ogden & Mr Joseph Seymour } Surveyors of Roads	11
Voted Mr Hezekiah Simons & Mr Andrew Buckingham } Fence Vewers	11
Voted Mr John Rockwell Mr Eleazer Bidwell Mr Jacob Ogden Mr Solomon Crisey & Mr Joseph Seymour Junr } Listers	11
Capt David Pinney Collecttor	11

23 Dec 1782

a Legal Town Meeting Held by Ajournment at Capt Saml Rockwell	11
Capt Saml Rockwell being Moderator	11
Voted Eleazer Bidwell grand-juror	11
Joseph Rockwell Tything-man	11
Edmond Howell Hayward	11
Nathaniel Burr Brander of Horses Sealer of Wates and Measurs	11
Selectmen be advised to lay Out a Road from Near the two Simons Acrost to their Sawmill	11
Selectmen be advised to Lay Out a Road from Ens^n Joseph Seymours to Norfolk Near Roger Orveses	11
Selectmen be advised to Lay out a Road from Near Mr Ogdens Sawmill to Sandersfield Road	11
Voted Mr Samuel Mills Capt Samuel Rockwell & Capt David Pinney } Be a Committee to Manage the Prudentials affairs of Building the .. Meeting House	11
Voted that Capt Samuel Rockwell be an agent for the Town to apply to the.. general Assembly.. for a Land Tax.. to help the Inhabitants in Building a meeting House	12
Voted That Esqr Rockwell Make up the Rate Bills	12
Voted That Nathaniel Burr be Saxton or grave Digger	12
Voted That John Rockwell be Released from Surveing as a Listor	12

28 Jan 1783

a Town Meeting Held by ajurnment at Capt Saml Rockwell	12
Capt Saml Rockwell Moderator	12
Voted that this Meeting give in to Mr David Werts 21/6 of his Rate Made on his List of... 1781	12

3 Feb 1783

a Town Meeting Held by ajurnment at Capt Saml Rockwell	12
Capt Saml Rockwell Moderator	12

7 Apr 1783

a Town Meeting Held at Capt Saml Rockwells	13
Mr Jacob Ogden Chosen Moderator	13
Votd that if Aaron Griswold Do not Return home by tomorrow that Hezekiah Simons be in his Room One of a Committee.. to See about Exchanging of Lands with Capt Saml Rockwell	13
Samuel Blaksly Eleazer Bidwell and Timothy Rockwell } Quaristers	13

Colebrook

Voted David Rockwell Rate on Mr John Porters Rate Bill Made On the List of.. 1781 given in by the Town	13
9 May 1783	
a Town Meeting.. Held at Capt Saml Rockwells	13
Mr Moses Wright Moderator	13
Voted That the Town take Sum Measure to Oppose a Certain Number of the Inhabetants of Colebrook and Winchester Pray[ing] To the general Asembly.. to be formed into an Eclesastical Society.. Voted That Capt Saml Rockwell.. to Apply to the general Assembly for the fore Mensioned Purpose	13
Capt David Pinney Mr Edmund Howell & Mr Samuel Mills } Be a Committee.. to Exchang Publick Lands for Roads &c	14
Capt Saml Rockwell Mr Moses Wright & Mr Edmund Howell } Be a Society Committee.. to provide Preaching & make Necessary Provision for the Same	14
13 Dec 1779	
A Roll of Parsons Names That hath Took the Oath of Fidellity.. Decem^r 13th 1779.. Samuel Phillips.. Nath^ll Burr.. Joseph Bidwell.. Eleazer Bidwell.. Samuel Mills.. John Stilman.. James Simons.. Moses Wright.. David Rockwell.. David Pinney.. John Porter.. Ebenezer Shepard.. Cary Pratt.. Solomon Crisey.. Stephen Russell.. Elijah Rockwell.. Aaron Simons.. William Simons.. Daniel Hall.. Benjn Horton.. Hezekiah Simons.. Joseph Rockwell.. Edmond Howell.. Francis Griswold.. Enos Martin.. Aaron Griswold.. Joseph Seymour..	113
18 Sep 1781	
..Edward Phelps..	113
8 Apr 1782	
..John Whiting..	113
7 Apr 1783	
..Timothy Rockwell.. Roger Stilman.. Elijah Hoskins	113
10 Apr 1780	
A Roll of Freemen Names Admitted as followes.. Elijah Rockwell.. Samuel Mills.. Peletiah Mills.. John Porter.. Eleazer Bidwell.. Nathl Burr.. Moses Wright.. Joseph Tainter.. Joseph Seymour.. Frances Griswold.. Daniel Hall.. Solomon Crisey.. David Pinney..	115
19 Sep 1780	
Aaron Simons.. David Rockwell..	115
18 Sep 1781	
.. Edward Phelps.. Edmond Howell.. Williams Simons..	115
8 Apr 1782	
.. Jacob Ogden.. John Whiteing.. Cary Pratt..	115
17 Sep 1782	
..Joseph Seymour Junr .. Charles Wright of Winchester..	115
7 Apr 1783	
.. John Stilman.. Roger Stilman.. Andrew Buckingham.. Joseph Rockwell.. Timothy Rockwell.. Elijah Hoskins	115

Cornwall

Town Meetings
1779-1828
Pgs 1-30

Cornwall's First Book to Record Town Votes in 1740-1780
Pgs a, 1-26, 76-91

Located at the Town Clerk's Office

Cornwall

22 Aug 1774

Heman Swift Esq Moderator	76
Thomas Porter and Heman Swift Esqr, Lieut Edward Rogers, Mr Andrew Young, and Lieut John Sedgwick a Committee to receive Such charitable Donations.. and them forward to the Select Men of.. Boston to be by them Distributed amongst the poor and needy.. And they are also Appointed a Committee of Correspondance	77

12 Dec 1774

the following votes were Pass'd.. That Heman Swift Esqr Should be moderator	79
That Heman Swift, Thomas Porter, Thomas Russell, John Sedgwick and andrew Young be a Committee of Inspection	9

11 Dec 1775

the following votes were Pass'd .. That Heman Swift Esq be Moderator	9
That Heman Swift, & Thos Porter, and John Pierce be Select men	9
That John Pierce be Town Clerk	9
That John Pierce be Town Treasurer	9
That Mr Judah Kellogg, & Edward Rogers be Constables	9
That Hez^h Carter, Abraham Payne, Jesse Buell, Sele Abbot, David Clark, Hez^h Foord, Asahel Alvord, William Pierce, Lemuel Hand, Noah Rogers, Timothy Scovil, & Benjamin Chandler be Surveyors of Highways	9
That Ketchel Bell, & Thomas Tanner be Fence-viewers	9
That Capt Joshua Pierce Ju^r, Judah Kellogg and Noah Rogers be Listers	10
That Mr Judah Kellogg be Collector of Rates	10
That Samuel Emons be Collector of the Rates of the Professors of the Church of England	10
That Silas Clark & Elijah Steele be Leather Sealers	10
That David Clark, Abel Abbott, and Sam^{ll} Sawyer be Grand Jurors	10
That Consider Tanner, Salmon Emons, Samuel Jones, Josiah Paterson, & John Hart be Tything-men	10
That Benjamin Chandler be Brander of Horses	10
That Lemuel Hnd be Sealer of Weights	10
That Lemuel Jennings be Sealer of Measures	10
That Joseph Bearse be Key Keeper	10
That Eben^r Simmons, Elijah Steele John Millard Ju^r, Roger Catlin, John Clother, Ketchel Bell, and Jesse Buell be a Committee to Provide Schools	10
That Capt Joshua Pierce Ju^r, be a Committee to take care of the School money belonging to the Town	10
That Joshua Pierce Ju^r, John Pierce and Seth Pierce be a Committee to take Care of the Parsonage Money	10
That Salmon Emons Shall have 84^s/ for Getting Ten Cords of Good Fire wood for Mr Gold	11
That Thomas Russell, Judah Kellogg, Andrew Young, Noah Rogers, Jesse Buell, Heman Swift and Thomas Porter be a Committee of Inspection	11
Salmon Emons agreed to Keep Abial Dudley one year.. for £ 6.. and Keep his Close in Good Repair &c	11

Cornwall

12 Feb 1776
Thomas Porter Esq was Chosen Moderator | 11
16 Dec 1776
The following votes were pass'd.. That Colonel Heman Swift Esq be Moderator | 11
That Cap[t] Thos Porter, Judah Kellogg, John Pierce Noah Rogers and Cap[t] Amos Johnson be Select Men | 11
That John Pierce be Town Clerk | 12
That John Pierce be Town Treasurer | 12
That Judah Kellogg & Noah Rogers} be Constables | 12
That Samuel Scovil, Benoni Pack, Abraham Hodgkins, Eben[r] Simmons, Timothy Brownson Consider Tanner, Nehemiah Bardsly, Daniel Stewart, Woodruff Emons, Samuel Wilcocks, Abraham Paine, Daniel Abbott be Surveyors of Highways | 12
That Sele Abbott & Jethro Bonney be Fence Viewers | 12
That Cap[t] Joshua Pierce Ju[r] & Noah Rogers and Judah Kellogg be Listers | 12
That Noah Rogers be Collector of Rates and Taxes | 12
That Elijah Allen be Collector of the Ministerial Rates of the Proffessors of the Church of England | 12
That Ithamer Sanders & Benjamin Dibble be Leather Sealers | 12
That Seth Pierce, Abraham Hogkins, and Woodruff Emons be Grandjurors | 12
That Sherman Patterson, David Clark, Daniel Abbott and Asahel Alvord be Tything men | 12
That Ebenezer Simmons be Brander of Horses | 12
That Abraham Hand be Sealer of Weights | 12
That Lemuel Jennings be Sealer of Measures | 12
That Joseph Bearse be Key Keeper | 13
That Joshua Pierce Ju[r], John Pierce, & Seth Pierce be a Committee to take Care of the Parsonage money | 13
That Cap[t] Joshua Pierce Ju[r], be Committee to take Care of the School money | 13
That Eben[r] Simmons, John Millard Ju[r], Timothy Brownson, Daniel Stewart, Cap[t] Thomas Porter, Nathan Millard, Daniel Harrison and John Clother be a Committee to Provide Schools | 13
That Lemuel Jennings be Grave Digger | 13
That Consider Tanner Shall Repair the Meeting House | 13
That Benoni Pack, John Dibble y[e] 3rd, Samuel Scovil, Doct[r] Benj[a] Dibble, & David Baldwin be appointed to Collect money of Such of s[d] Inhabitants as will freely bestow the Same for the use of Benjamin Marble, and that Elijah Steele, and Samuel Scovil be a Committee to lay out, and Dispose of the Same for the use & Relief of the s[d] Marble | 13
That John Dibble the 3rd Shall have £ 1-19-4 for gitting 10 Cords of good fire-wood for M[r] Gold | 14
M[r] Gold bid for abial Dudly £ 2=0=6 or 2=3=6 for the Year | 14
1 Apr 1777
Tho[s] Porter Esq was Chosen Moderator | 14

Cornwall

2 Apr 1777

the following Votes were pass'd.. That Cap[t] Joshua Pierce Ju[r], M[r] Elijah Steele, and M[r] Ketchell Bell be a Committee to Provide for the families of the Continental Soldiers   14

16 Dec 1776

That Elijah Steele, John Pierce & Josiah Patterson be a Com[tee] to Lease out the School Land in the Southerly Part of Town for 999 years   15

11 Dec 1777

Thomas Russell Esq[r] was chosen Moderator   15

M[r] Judah Kellogg was chosen Town Clerk or Register   15

M[r] Judah Kellogg.. Thomas Russell Esq[r] and Kitchel Bell } were chosen Select Men   15

M[r] Judah Kellogg was chosen Town Treasurer   15

Mess[rs] Noah Rogers and Joseph Bearce } were chosen Constables   15

Mess[rs] John Dibble 2nd David Baldwin Jun[r] (Sworn) Daniel Everest (Sworn) Jesse Buell ( ) Josiah Beach (Sworn) Benjamin Dibble (Sworn) Samuel Scovil (Sworn) David Dibble ( ) Thomas Dean (Sworn) Rufus Payne ( ) Timothy Brownson (Sworn) and Titus Bonny (Sworn) were chosen Surveyors of Highways   16

Mess[rs] Timothy Brownson and Daniel Abbot were chosen Fence Viewers   16

Mess[rs] Samuel Wadsworth, Joseph Bearce, Silas Clark, John Millard Jun[r] and Jesse Bewell were chosen Listers   16

M[r] Joseph Bearse was chosen Collector of Rates & Taxes   16

Mess[rs] Ithamar Saunders and Benjamin Dibble were chosen Sealers of Leather   16

Mess[rs] Andrew Young, Zechariah How Jones, Hezekiah Carter, Nathan Millard and Samuel Bassett were chosen Grand-Jurors.. M[r] Young and M[r] Carter were called upon to take the Oath, and refused and paid to this Town Treasurer Twenty five Shilling each.. M[r] Jones and M[r] Basset took the Oath in the Meeting   16

Mess[rs] Daniel Everest, Salmon Emmons, John Dibble 3rd and Daniel Harrison Jun[r] were chosen Tithing-Men.. M[r] Dibble & M[r] Harrison were sworn in the Meeting.. M[r] Emmons on Motion was excused.   16

M[r] Ebenezer Simmons was chosen Brander of Horses   17

M[r] Abraham Hand was chosen Sealer of Weights   17

M[r] Abel Abbot was chosen Sealer of Measures   17

M[r] Simeon Emmons was chosen Key-keeper   17

Capt Thomas Porter, Lieut John Peirce, Capt Amos Johnson .. Noah Rogers & .. Judah Kellogg, were appointed a Committee to procure and forward to the Soldiers.. now in the Continental Army, all the Articles of Cloathing required.. by the General Assembly
That Capt Joshua Peirce be a Committee to take Care of the School Monies   17

15 Dec 1777

That Capt Joshua Peirce, Lieut John Peirce & Ensgn Seth Peirce be a Committee to take Care of the Parsonage Monies   18

That Mess[rs] Ithamar Saunders, Thomas Porter Esq[r] Samuel Sawyer, Nathan Millard, Ebenezer Simmons, Zechariah How Jones and Noah Harrison be Committees of Schools   18

That Mess[rs] Kitchel Bell, Joseph Bearce, & Elijah Steele be a Committee, to provide for the Families of such Soldiers.. as are gone into the Continental Army   18

107

Cornwall

Mr Andrew Young ~~made~~ requested Liberty of the Town to Innoculate his Family with the Small Pox in his own House, or at a Place called the Elbow ~ Whereupon the Questin was put whether the Town would do anything about granting Liberty for any Person to Innoculate for the Small Pox and Voted in the Netagive.   *18*

Messrs Elijah Hopkins, John Carter, Reuben Fox & Rexford prefered a Petion.. seting forth the great Inconveniencies.. in attending public Worship and Schooling their Children on account of the great Distance at which they lived from the Town or Meeting Houses and Schools Praying Liberty to be set off from the Town.. & Annexed to the Town of Kent. Voted that they have not Liberty ~   *19*

15 Jan 1778

Thomas Russell Esqr was Chosen Moderator   *19*

A Memorial.. was prefered to Said Meeting.. by John Carter, Elijah Hopkins Reuben Fox and Daniel Rexford.. praying the Town to Grant them the Privilege of being let off from the Town.. to the Society of East Greenwich (in Kent) for.. Schooling their Children and other Society Privileges, Ecclesiastical and Military &c.. it was voted, that they.. have Liberty and Privilege.. and.. be excused.. from paying any Ministerial or School Rates   *19*

27 Mar 1778

Thomas Russel Esqr was chosen Moderator of a special Town Meeting   *20*

The Act Regulating the Prices of Labor &c .. was read in s^d Meeting as was also an Act requiring the Select Men.. or a Committee appointed by the Town to procure a Quantity of Cloathing.. for the Quota of Continental Soldiers required of said Town &c - Mr Joseph Bearce, Major John Sedgwick, Mr Abraham Payne and Mr John Millard Junr were chosen a Committee to procure said Cloathing ~   *20*

13 Apr 1778

Mr Abraham Payne one of the Committee appointed.. to procure Clothing &c represented.. that the Committee were unable to procure said Articles.. without Ready Money   *21*

3 Sep 1778

Thomas Porter Esqr was Chosen Moderator   *21*

A Letter from.. Litchfield directed to the Select Men.. notifying them that the Subscribers.. were appointed a Committee.. to meet with such Committee.. appointed by the Several Towns of this County to prepare a joint Petition to the Genl Assembly.. praying a more Equitable mode of Taxation was read.. The Question was put.. whether the Inhabitants.. are uneasy with the present Mode of Taxation.. Voted in the affirmative ~ Voted that Capt Edward Rogers and Mr Andrew Young be a Committee to meet Such Comittees as shall be appointed by the Several towns in this County..   *21*

21 Dec 1778

Voted, that Thomas Russell Esqr be Moderator   *22*

That Judah Kellogg, Ketchel Bell, Capt Edward Rogers Major John Sedgwick and Lieut Ebenezer Dibble, be Select Men   *22*

That Judah Kellogg beTown Clerk and Town Treasurer   *22*

That Capt Edward Rogers and Joseph Bearce be Constables   *22*

That Samuel Scovill Nathan Sawyer Levi Bonney Thomas Dean, William Tanner, Daniel Stewart Joseph Bearce Titus Bonny Matthew Beach and Daniel Everest be Surveyors of Highways   *22*

That Capt Joshua Pierce and Thomas Hart be Fence Viewers   *22*

Cornwall

That Joseph Bearce Matthew Patterson Major John Sedgwick Seth Pierce and Solomon Emmons be Listers	22
That Capt Edward Rogers be Collector of Rates & Taxes	22
That Silas Clark and Josiah Patterson be Sealers of Leather	22
That Ezra Cole Solomon Emmons and Matthew Beach be Grand Jurors	22
That Thomas Hart Nehemiah Beardslee Linus Beach and John Dibble 2nd be Tithing Men	22
That Ebenezer Simmons be Brander of Horses	23
That Samuel Sawyer be Sealer of Weights	23
That Abel Abbot be Sealer of Measures	23
That Capt Joshua Pierce, Samuel Sawyer, Ketchel Bell Ithamar Saunders, Capt Amos Johnson, Josiah Patterson, Solomon Hart, Daniel Harrison, Samuel Wadsworth, and Roger Catlin were chosen Committees of Schools	23
That Joseph Bearace be Key-Keeper	23
That Abraham Payne, Joseph Bearce and Noah Rogers be a Committee to provide for the Families of the Soldiers.. in the Continental Army	23
That Capt Joshua Pierce, Lieut John Pierce and Ensign Seth Pierce be a Committee to take Care of the School and Parsonage Monies	23

28 Dec 1778

voted that Ezra Cole & Solomon Emmon be excused from Serving as Grand Jurors	23
Voted, that Seth Peirce be Grand Juror.. who refused to serve & paid a Fine	23
That Rufus Payne be Grand Juror	23
That Salmon Emmons be Grand Juror	23
That Solomon Emmons have & receive fourteen Pounds ten Shillings for getting Ten Cords of good Firewood for the Revd Mr Gold	24

15 Feb 1779

Judah Kellogg was chosen Moderator	24
Question was put.. whether that in Consideration .. Revd Mr Gold abate Ten Pounds.. out of his Salary (which Salary is.. £ 64..16..4) and also abate one Twentieth.. of the Remainder.. to the Poor.. and also accept of the Nominal Sum of Money that is due to him and unpaid for his Service in the Ministry for the Year ending January 1st 1778 (all of which..Mr Gold offered to do.. upon Condition that The Town would pay him the Remainder after such Abatement & Deduction at the Rate of Six Pounds now for one Pound as Money was current in.. 1774) that then s^d Town would pay him.. the s^d Remainder of his Salary .. for the Year ending January 1st 1779 - Six Pounds for one Pound as Money was Current in the Purchase of the Necessaries of Life in.. 1774 ~ Voted in the Negative	24

28 Jun 1779

Major John Sedgwick ws chosen Moderator	25
The Question was put.. whether they would choose a Committee to procure Such Articles of Cloathing for the Soldiers belonging to the Continental Army as are required by.. the General Assembly Messrs Ebenezer Jackson, Capt Seth Peirce, Silas Clark & John Millard Junr be a Committee for the Purpose	25
Voted, that Messrs Andrew Young, Judah Kellogg & David Clark be a Committee to wait upon the Revd Mr Gold and know of him how he will Settle with the Town for his past	25

Cornwall

Services in the Ministry

Voted, That Major John Wedgwick & Lieut Jesse Buell be a Committee to agree with.. Ozias Hurlbut about the Exchange of Highway for a Burying Place in the North Part of the Town 25

26 Jul 1779

Committee appointed to wait upon the Revd Mr Gold, read a Paper.. receiv^d from of the Revd Mr Gold.. Whereupon The Question was put, whether if Mr Gold deduct his Proportion of extraordnary Taxes, the Town will.. pay him the Remainder of his Salary for his past Services in the Old Way, in the Necessaries of Living, as they were sold in.. 1774 or an Equivalence in Currency as it passes at the Time when they shall pay the same? Voted in the Negative ~ The Question was put, Whether the Inhabitants .. are Uneasy with, or under his Administration in the Work of the Ministry? Voted in the Affirmative~ 25

Voted, that Messrs Andrew Young, Noah Rogers, James Douglass, Phinehas Waller and David Clark, be a Committee, to Treat with the Rev^d Mr Gold.. whether he will.. receive his Salary for his past Services, according to the ~~Contract~~ Covenant made with him; and also agree with the Inhabitants.. to Call a Council, to dismiss him from his Pastoral Care and Charge of, and over the Congregation.. Voted, that if the Revd Mr Gold Refuse to Treat.. with the Committee; .. the above named Committee be impowered.. to call a Council for that Purpose 25

Judah Kellogg & Josiah Patterson, Protested against the three last Votes in open Town Meeting 26

The Question was put Whether the Inhabitants.. are Uneasy with the present Mode of Taxation? Voted in the Affirmative.. Voted That, Capt Edward Rogers Mr Josiah Patterson and Mr Ebenezer Jackson, be a Committee to point out the imagined Injustice & Oppression of the present Mode of Taxation;.. and consult with the.. Committees.. appointed for that Purpose, by any Town within this County 26

[ ] Sep 1779

The Question was put.. whether the Town would excuse the Committee appointed to Treat with the Revd Mr Gold concerning his Salary for his past Services & agree to join in Calling a Council to dismiss him &c from prosecuting the Matter any further ~ And Voted in the Negative. .. the Comittee appointed to Treat with the Revd Mr Gold be requested to call a Council 26

Capt Edward Rogers, Mr Josiah Patterson & Mr Ebenezer Jackson were Voted to continue a Committee for the Purposes for which they were appointed the last Town Meeting 26

21 Sep 1779

Samuel Gipson.. applyed to the Town to Release or forgive him two fines of ten Pounds each.. for refusing to serve in the Continental Army.. Voted that.. Gipson be released & forgien the Fines.. He paying all Costs that have or may arise upon the Prosecutions~ 84

18 Oct 1779

Major Jno Sedgwick was chosen Moderator 84

Voted That the Town will pay the Revd Mr Gold his Salary for his past Services until the first of January last in the Necessaries of living or in labour as they were current in.. 1774, or in Silver or Gold according to the Covenant Made with him, or in Continental Currency equivalent.. He deducting his Proportion for the extraordinary Expences of the War 84

Voted that Messrs Judah Kellogg Woodruff Emmons and Rufus Payne be a Committee to take a List of the Revd Mr Gold's Estate and determine how much shall be deducted for his Proportion of the extraordinary Expenses of the War 84

Cornwall

22 Aug 1777
These Certify That Mr John Pierce.. has Taken the Oath of Fidelity to this State, as by Law 86
Required before me Titus Hosmer Just Pac^s
16 Sep 1777
Noah Rogers.. Judah Kellogg.. Amos Johnson.. Thomas Porter.. Abel Judson.. Mathew 86
Beach.. Joseph Bearse.. Mr Hez^h Gold.. Caleb Jones.. Noah Bull.. Ketchel Bell.. Eben^r
Dibble.. John Millard Ju^r.. Samuel Bassett.. Joshua Pierce Ju^r.. Edward Rogers.. Sele Abbott..
Rufus Paine.. Daniel Abbott.. Hez^h Clark.. Christopher Grirnes.. John Millard.. Jacob
Brownson.. John Wright.. Thomas Dean.. Silas Clerk.. Benjamin Dean.. Samuel Scovil..
Edmond Beach.. Josiah Beach.. Nathan Millard.. David Clark.. Seth Pierce.. Trial Tanner..
John Pierce.. Daniel Harrison.. Josiah Patterson.. Eben^r Sherwood.. Samuel Butler.. These
Certify That all the above Named Persons Except my Self & John Pierce have Taken the oath
of Fidelity to this State as the Law Requires before me.. Thos Porter Jus^t of Peace.. all the
above Named Persons Except Esq Porter were admitted Freemen & took the Free- men's oath
as by Law Required before S^d Th^{o}s Porter Esq and Mr Judah Kellogg one of the Select- Men..
administred the two oaths afores^d to S^d Porter
11 Dec 1777
The following Persons, took the Oath of Fidelity to the Sate [sic] of Connecticut viz. Thomas 87
Russel Esqr was Sworn took the Oath before me.. Thomas Porter Justice of Peace
11 Dec 1777
Thomas Porter Esqr.. Woodruff Emmons.. Abraham Payne.. Hezekiah Carter.. David 87
Baldwin.. Ebenezer Bacon.. Simeon Emmons.. Ithamar Saunders.. William Tanner.. Elnathan
Patterson.. John Dibble 3rd.. Lemuel Hand.. Jacob Brownson.. James Sterling.. Samuel
Sawyer.. James Marsh Douglass.. Salmon Emmons.. John Wright.. Perez Bonney.. Daniel
Harrison Junr.. Zechariah How Jones.. Titus Bonney.. Hezekiah Ford.. Andrew Young..
Joshua Parmele.. John Bennedict.. Timothy Brownson.. Moses Knap.. Samuel Wadsworth..
James Wadsworth.. Samuel Lindsly.. Lemuel Jennings.. Reuben Fox.. John Carter.. Silas
Dibble.. Daniel Abbot.. Abel Abbot.. David Badwin Junr.. John How.. Stephen Miles..
Benjamin Dibble.. Daniel Everest.. Edward May.. Benjaman Jennings.. Jonathan Crocker..
James Griffis.. Ezra Cole.. Elijah Hopkins.. Timothy Scovill.. John Wright Junr.. Henry
Filmore.. Austin Bearce.. Titus Hart.. Ebenezer Simmens.. All the above named Persons took
the Oath of Fidelity as the Law requires before Thomas Russell Esqr Justice of Peace..
Certified p^r me Thomas Russell Just^{us} Pac^s
5 Jan 1778
This May Certify that.. Messrs Elijah Steele, Ebenezer Palmer aned Solomon Emmons, .. 87
appeared before me Thomas Porter Justice of the Peace for Litchfield County, and took the
Oath of Fidelity to the State of Connecticut
13 Apr 1778
Consider Tanner.. Ebenezer Jackson.. Nathan Saunders.. Thomas Hart.. Sherman Patterson.. 88
Nehemiah Beardslee.. John Dibble 2nd.. Solomon Hart.. Benoni Peck.. John Sedgwick.. Jesse
Buell.. David Dibble.. Joseph Wadsworth.. This may certify whom it may concern, that the
Persons whose Names are here on written, took the Oath of Fidelity to the State.. Before me
Thomas Porter Justice of Peace
18 Dec 1778
To Town Clerk of Cornwall, Sir, On the first Monday, I administered the Oath of Fidelity to 88
the following Persons, viz. Roger Catlin, Samuel Baldwin, Asa Morce, Stephen Baldwin,
Josiah Bartholomew, Jacob Green, Nehemiah Marvin Junr, and Since that Time to Darius

Cornwall

Hand ~ To Deacon Kellogg Town Clerk at Cornwall p' David Welch
21 Dec 1778

Lieut Matthew Patterson took the Oath of Fidelity to the State of Connecticut in open Town Meeting.. Before Thomas Rusell Esqr a Justice of the Peace *25 Mar 1779*	88
Linus Beach had the Oath of Fidelity to the United States administered to him p^r me Thomas Rusell Ju^s Pac^s *3 May 1779*	88
Litchfield.. This Day I administered the Oath of Fidelity to the State, to Elisha Dickinson.. Test David Welch Justice of Peace *18 Sep 1781*	88
The Oath of Fidelity to the State of Connecticut was administered to Samuel Brownson & Joel Harrison by me Jud^h Kellogg Jus Peace *8 Apr 1776*	88
At a Freemen's Meeting.. Thos Porter.. Heman Swift.. Judah Kellogg.. Andrew Young.. Abraham Paine.. Noah Rogers.. John Pierce } were by the Major Part of the Freemen then present Chosen Committee of Inspection *21 Sep 1779*	89
Phinehas Waller, John Jones Richard Lord Sill and Titus Hart .. took the Oath of Fidelity to the State of Connecticut before me Judah Kellogg Ju^s Pac^s *14 Mar 1780*	89
Lot Hart.. took the Oath of Fidelity to the State.. before me Judah Kellogg Jus. Pacis *10 Apr 1780*	89
Nathan Abbott, Samuel Butler Junr and Josiah Hopkins took the Oath of Fidelity to the State of Connecticut before me Judah Kellogg Justice of Peace *19 Sep 1780*	89
Josiah Bartholomew, Abraham Hochkin Uriel Lee, Asa Emmons, Isaiah Barce, Seth Hill and Nathan Sawyer took upon them the Oath of Fidelity.. before me Judah Kellogg Justice of Peace *6 Apr 1781*	89
Capt Thomas Tanner took the Oath of Fidelity to the State of Connecticut before me Judah Kellogg Ju^s Pac^s *9 Apr 1781*	89
Ketchel Bell Junr took the Oath of Fidelity.. before me Judah Kellogg Justice of Peace *10 Jul 1781*	89
Abraham Grimes took the Oath of Fidelity.. &.. Phinehas Hart and Elias Hart took said Oath before me Judah Kellogg Justice of Peace *15 Sep 1778*	89
A Roll of ye Freemen in the Town of Cornwall, .. in Open Freemens Meeting Legally Assembled.. Phinehas Waller.. Perez Bonney.. Timothy Brownson.. Abraham Hodgkins.. *21 Sep 1779*	90
.. Timothy Rogers.. Richard Lord Sill.. Reuben Fox.. Daniel Stewart.. Titus Hart.. Ezra Cole.. Ebenezer Bacon..	90

Cornwall

10 Apr 1780

..Samuel Butler Junr.. Josiah Hopkins.. Ebenezer Birdsey.. Col Heman Swift took the Freemans Oath prescribd by a late Act of the State of Connecticut also Nathan Abbott & Zelotes Saunders — 90

19 Sep 1780

Admitted.. Abel Butler.. Isaiah Barce.. Solomon Emmons.. Daniel Harrison Junr.. Asahel Alverd.. Asa Emmons.. Seth Hill.. — 90

9 Apr 1781

..William Stewart.. Ketchel Bell Junr.. Lot Hart — 90

10 Apr 1775

admitted free Men.. Consider Tanner.. — 91

19 Sep 1780

.. Sam^{ll} Willcocks.. Salmon Emons.. — 91

8 Apr 1776

.. Samuel Sawyer.. James Wadsworth.. — 91

7 Apr 1777

..Abraham Hodgkins.. Nathan Sawyer.. — 91

13 Apr 1778

*Stephen Miles.. *Samuel Lindsley.. Consider Tannor.. *Ebenezer Jackson.. *Nathan Saunders.. *Henry Filmore.. *Thomas Hart.. *Sherman Patterson.. *Nehemiah Beardslee.. *James Sterling.. *John Dibble 3rd.. * Solomon Hart.. *Benoni Peck.. John Sedgwick.. Jesse Buel.. *David Dibble.. Abraham Payne.. Zechariah A Jones.. *Lemuel Hand.. *Joseph Wadsworth.. *Ithamar Saunders.. *Daniel Everest.. Edward May.. Benjamin Dibble.. Abel Abbot.. James M Douglass.. Salmon Emmons.. Ebenezer Simmons..Sam^{ll} Wadsworth.. — 91

18 Sep 1781

.. Samuel Brownson.. Joel Harrison N.B. Those Persons whose names have this Mark (*) prefixed were admitted Freemen April 13 1778 the others were Freeman before but took the new Oath of Freemen — 91

19 Feb 1782

This may Certify whom it may concern that I administered the Oath of Fidelity.. to Mr Ozias Hurlbert.. February 19th 1782 Test Judah Kellogg Justice of Peace — a

21 Dec 1779

Voted that Capt Edward Rogers be Moderator — 1

Voted that Capt Edward Rogers, Mr Andrew Young, Major John Sedgwick, Ensign Joseph Barce, and Capt Seth Pierce be Select Men — 1

Voted that Judah Kellogg be Town Clerk & Town Treasurer — 1

Voted that Capt Edward Rogers be Constable — 1

Voted that Ensg^n Joseph Barce be Constable & Collector of Rates and Taxes — 1

Voted that Thomas Hart, Samuel Lindley, Rufus Payne, Sam^{ll} Scovel, James Wadsworth, Maj^r John Sedgwick, John Jones, John Wright, William Stewart, James Sterling and Josiah Patterson be Surveyors of Highways — 1

Voted that Solomon Emmons and Samuel Scovel be Fence Viewers — 1

Cornwall

Voted, That Doct: Isaac Swift, Capt Seth Pierce, Doct Rich^d L Sill, Rufus Payne & Silas Clark be Listers	1
Voted, That Josiah Patterson and Silas Clark be Sealers of Leather	1
Voted, That Nathan Millard and Daniel Stewart be Grandjurors	1
Voted, That Mathew Beach John Jones Ketchel Bell and David Clark be Tithing Men	1
Voted, That Ebenezer Simmons be Brander of Horses	1
Voted, That Lemuel Hand be Sealer of Weights	1
Voted, That Noah Rogers be Sealer of Measures	1
Voted, that Joseph Barce be Keykeeper	2
Voted, That Capt Joshua Pierce, Lieut John Pierce & Capt Seth Pierce be a Committee to take Care of the Bonds & Obligations of the Parsonage and School Monies	2
Voted, That Levi Bonney, Samuel Lindsley, Ketchel Bell Major John Sedgwick, Capt Edward Rogers, Nehemiah Beardslee Consider Tanner & Samuel Wadsworh be Committees of Schools	2
Voted, That Judah Kellogg, Andrew Young, Joseph Barce, Noah Rogers & Seth Pierce be a Committee to Wait upon the Revd Mr Gold, to knowof him how much Money or Currency he will accept for his past Services in the Ministry to the first Day of January next; and also to ask.. whether if the Majority of the Inhabitants.. and the Majority of the Church Members.. be desirous that he should be dismissed from the Work of the Ministry.. then he will agree.. for a Council to dismiss him	2

2 Mar 1780

Voted that Capt Edward Rogers be Moderator	2
Voted that Joseph Barce have.. one hundred and eight Pounds fifteen Shillings for cutting and getting ten Cords of good fire Wood for the Revd Mr Gold	3

13 Mar 1780

Voted, That Lieut Jesse Buell, .. Woodruff Emmons Lieut Mathew Patterson, .. Hezekiah Carter and David Baldwin be a Committee of Inspection or Inspectors of Provisions to stop, detain and Secure any Imbargoed Provisions which they or any of them shall Suspect are driving, carrying or transporting thro the Town with an Intention to carry or drive of this State contrary to Law	3
Voted, That an Accompt exhibited.. by Thomas Dean for repairing the Bridge across the South Hill Brook near Hezekiah Carter's Saw mill be left with the Select Men to adjust and settle.. according to their Judgment	3
The Revd Mr Gold came into the Meeting and delivered a Paper.. "Upon my receiving my just Dues for my ministerial Services.., I then ~~agree~~ concur with this Church and Congregation (if they choose it) that they call in a Candidate to preach with them .. for Settlement ~ When such Candidate Supplies the Pulpit, I will make no Demand of Pay from them - When the Pulpit is not Supplied in that Way, but by myself, I be paid according to Covenant. And when the Church and Congregation are agreed to Settle a Man.. I will relinquish my Salary.. they making no Demands of any Part of my Settlement" Hezekiah Gold.. The Question was put whether this Meeting are satisfied with said Paper. And Voted in the Negative	3
Voted.. one hundred and forty Pounds twelve Shillings in coined Silver at the Rate of six Shillings and eight Pence per Ounce or the Equivalence.. in Currency, or in Wheat, Rye or Indian Corn be levied.. upon the Inhabitants.. to pay and satisfy the Revd Mr Gold for his Service in the Work of the Ministry until the first Day of January last past; and that Messrs. Judah Kellogg Seth Pierce, Matthew Patterson and Joseph Barce be a Committee to..	4

Cornwall

ascertain the Par or Rate of Exchange between coined Silver and Currency or Wheat, Rye or Indian Corn from Time to Time monthly, until the whole be paid.. Also that the Vote passed at a Town meeting in October last respecting paying him for his past Services be, and it is hereby revoked

10 Apr 1780

Voted That the Revd Mr Gold be desired not to perform devine Service anymore in the Meeting house	5
Voted, That Messrs. Andrew Young and Seth Pierce be a Committee to wait upon the Revd Mr Gold and acquaint him with the foregoing Vote	5
Voted, that a Tax Sufficient to raise the Sum of Seventeen Pounds.. in Silver at 6/8 per Ounce or an Equivalence in Wheat, Rye, Indian Corn, Labour or Currency to pay the Revd Mr Gold for his Service in the Ministry.. since the first Day of January last.. be laid	5
Voted th at Messrs. Judah Kellogg, Seth Pierce, Matthew Patterson & Joseph Barce be a Commmittee to determine.. the Par or Rate of Exchange between coined Silver and Currency, or Wheat, Rye and Indian Corn from time to time until the whole be paid	5

4 May 1780

Voted that Capt Edward Rogers Collector of the Rate.. to pay the Revd Mr Gold for his Service in the Ministry, be desired.. to pay back to those Persons who have paid him the several Sums he has collected of them.. and not to collect any more, and be discharged	6

12 Jun 1780

Mr Phinehas Waller was Chosen Moderator	6
Voted, that two More Select Men be chosen in addition to those chosen in December last ~ The following Persons protested against said Vote, viz. Woodruff Emmons, Ebenezer Dibble, Elnathan Patterson Zechariah H. Jones, Daniel Everest, Josiah Patterson James Barce and David Dibble	6
Voted that Mr Elijah Steele be Select Man	6
Voted that Mr David Clark be Select Man	6

19 Jun 1780

The Question was put to the Meeting, Whether they are contented and satisfied with Mr Gold for their Minister? Voted in the negative.	6
Voted that the Inhabitants.. do at this Time declare themselves to be.. Congregationalists both in Doctrine and Discipline. Voted that the Revd Mr Gold be desired not to perform devine Service any more in the Meeting House	7
Voted, that Messrs. Andrew Young and Matthew Patterson be a Committee to wait upon the Revd Mr Gold and inform him of the foregoing Vote	7
Voted, that Capt Edward Rogers, Mr Elijah Steele, Mr Andrew Young, Mr Noah Rogers, and Lieut Matthew Patterson be a Committee to procure a Preacher to Supply the Pulpit	7
Voted, that Messrs. Elijah Steele, Ithamar Saunders and Noah Rogers be a Committee to take Care of the Meeting House	7

30 Jun 1780

Colo. Heman Swift was chosen Moderator	7
Voted, that the Select Men.. for the Time being.. are hereby appointed a Committee to assess the Inhabitants.. each their several Proportion of Grain, Money, &c to pay such able Bodied effective Men as shall enlist themselves into the Continental Army.. Joseph Barce be Collector	8

Cornwall

16 Nov 1780

Voted, that Major John Sedgwick be Moderator	9
Voted, that Seth Pierce receive the Votes of said Meeting	9
Voted, that Capt Edward Rogers receive Salt and Part of the rateable Part of Provisions.. Voted to excuse him from said Service.. Voted that Seth Pierce be appointed for that Purpose. Voted to excuse him from said Service ~ Voted that Seth Pierce be Receiver of public Salt, and all the rateable Part of Provisions	9

18 Nov 1780

Personally appeared Capt Seth Pierce and made Solemn Oath that he took the within written Votes in open Town Meeting before me Judah Kellogg Justice of Peace ~	9

4 Dec 1780

Voted, that Major John Sedgwick be Moderator	9
Voted, That Capt Edward Rogers, Messrs. Andrew Young, Samuel Scovel, Matthew Patterson and Silas Clark be Select Men	9
Voted, That Judah Kellogg be Town Clerk	9
Voted, That Mr Noah Rogers be Town Treasurer	9
Voted, That Lieut Matthew Patterson & Mr Noah Rogers be Constables	9
Voted, That Messrs. Sam^{ll} Scovel, Sam^{ll} Wadsworth, Levi Bonney, Capt Amos Johnson, Lieut Jesse Buell, Thomas Dean, Daniel Abbott, Jacob Brownson Junr, Lemuel Jennings, Nathan Sawyer, Daniel Stewart and Timothy Scovel be Surveyors of Highways	9
Voted, That Messrs. Woodruff Emmons and Henry Filmore be Fence Viewers	10
Voted, That Messrs. Andrew Young, Nathan Bristol Junr and Solomon Emmons be Listers	10
Voted, That Lieut Matthew Patterson be Collector of Rates and Taxes	10
Voted, That Messrs. Silas Clark and Daniel Abbott be Sealers of Leather	10
Voted, That Uriel Lee, Hezekiah Clark & Samuel Brownson be Grand Jurors	10
Voted, That Lieut Tyral Tanner, Salmon Emmons, Daniel Everest, Daniel Harrison Junr be Tything-Men	10
Voted, That Zelotes Saunders be Brander of Horses	10
Voted, That Samuel Sawyer be Sealer of Weights	10
Voted, That Abel Abbot be Sealer of Measures	10
Voted, That Asa Emmons be Key-keeper	10
Voted That Messrs. Samuel Scovel, Levi Bonney Benoni Pack, Daniel Stewart, Daniel Abbott, Nehemiah Beardslee, Matthew Beach, Daniel Harrison Junr Jacob Brownson Junr & James Sterling be Committees of Schools	10
Voted, That Capt Joshua Pierce Junr Lieut John Pierce & Capt Seth Pierce be a Committee to take Care of the Bonds, Obligations and Monies belonging to the Town.. both of the School & Parsonage	10
Voted, That Mr Joseph Barce be a Committee to procure collect and send.. to the Army, this Towns Quota of Cloathing	10

5 Dec 1780

Voted, That Capt Seth Pierce be excused from collecting the Provisions required	11
Voted, That Lieut Matthew Patterson be Collector, Receiver & Storer of the Provisions	11

Cornwall

required

Voted, That Capt Thomas Tanner, Capt Edward Rogers Roger Catlin, Lieut Jesse Buell, Capt 11
Seth Pierce, Ensign John Millard, Samuel Wadsworth & Lot Hart be a Committee to Class
the Inhabitants.. for raising and compleating this Towns Quota of the the Continental Army

Voted, that the Select Men.. Repair the High Bridge near Mr Birdsey's House..   11

23 Jul 1781

Major John Sedgwick was chosen Moderator   12

Voted, That Lieut Matthew Patterson be.. impowered to pay.. to Such Men in the Town as   12
are detached to Serve in the two State Regiments.. fifteen Pounds each

Voted, That Messrs. Woodruff Emmons, Joseph Barce, Capt Seth Pierce and Andrew Young   12
be a Committee to List the Estate of Revd Mr Gold for.. 1779 to determine his proportionable
Part of the extraordinary Public Expences of the Times

Voted, that Israel Dibble be excused.. from any Demands for a Gun & Bayonet, the Property   12
of the Town, taken from him by the Enemy when he was captured by them.. in 1777

27 Aug 1781

The Revd Mr Gold Signed the following, which was read in the Meeting, (viz.).. "I Hezekiah   13
Gold Pastor of the Church in Cornwall do.. agree to & with the Inhabitants.. who now attend
upon my Ministry, and who have lately Separated themselves from my Church &
Congregation, that in Consideration of.. forty one Pound nineteen Shillings & Seven Pence
and the Interest.. from the first Day of January last, to be paid in Silver or Wheat.. Rye..
Indian Corn.. I will discharge them.. from all Demands for any Servce.. except for ten Cords
of Fire~Wood - I further agree, that upon my receiving the Sum.. last committed to M^r
Joseph Barce to collect according to the.. Intention of the Vote for paying the Same.. I will
give a Discharge.. for all Services previous to.. 1780, except for five Cords of Fire Wood~"

Voted, That a Rate or Tax of one Penny on the Pound upon the LIst.. for the Year 1779, be   13
levied.. to pay & satisfy to the Revd Mr Gold.. forty-one Pounds nineteen Shilings and seven
Pence, & the Interest.. for his Services in the Ministry for.. 1780.. Voted, that Mr Joseph
Barce be Collector of the Rate

Mr Zelotes Saunders agreed to get ten Cords of good Fire Wood and deliver it to the Rev^d M^r 13
Gold at his House for £2..9..0 ~ by biding it off

Voted, that Mr Andrew Young be.. impowered to inspect the Bridges between Dean's   14
Gristmill & Carter's Sawmill & the Bridge at the Mouth of the Brook below Mr Carter's
Sawmill and make all necessary Repairs

22 Jan 1781

Major John Sedgwick was chosen Moderator   14

Voted that a.. Tax of three Pence in Money or one Penny-half penny in Wheat & Rye Flour   14
or Indian Corn.. be laid.. for collecting and storing a Quantity of Provisions for the Use of the
Forces raised for the Defence of this State.. Voted, That Lieut Matthew Patterson be
Collector, Receiver, Inspector and Packer of the.. Provisions and Monies ~

The Question was put.. whether the Inhabitants.. will at this Time Vote the Revd Mr Gold his   14
Salary for the Year past.. Voted in the Negative.

7 Feb 1781

Andrew Young was chosen Moderator   14

Voted, That the Inhabitants.. will procure.. three able bodied Men to Serve as Soldiers in a   14
Regiment to Serve at Horse neck &c for the Defence of this State until the first Day of March
1782.. Voted, That Capt Joshua Peirce, Lieut Jesse Buell and Capt Thomas Tanner be a

Cornwall

Committee to divide the Inhabitants.. into three equal Classes.. in order to procure the three Men	
Voted, That a Committee be appointed to Treat with a Committee that is already chosen by the Conso[ ]ated Church and Congregation, or those who adhere to the Revd Mr Gold, .. relative to an Accomodation of any Difficultie.. between said.. Church and Congregation and the Town	15
Voted, That Lieut Matthew Patterson, Mr Elijah Steele, Capt Edward Rogers Mr Andrew Young and Mr Silas Clark be a Committee for the Purpose.. [*and*] requested to procure.. a Minister for the Town.. to officiate according to the Congregational Constitution	15
Voted, That Ebenezer Jackson be abated the one half of all his Rates.. in his List for.. 1779	15

26 Mar 1781

Major John Sedgwick was chosen Moderator	16
Voted, That the Town.. will procure.. Six Men.. to Serve as Soldiers one Year.. Voted, That Capt Edward Rogers, Mr Andrew Young, Mr Rufus Payne, Maj^r John Sedgwick, Mr Lot Hart & Mr Thomas Hart be a Committee to procure the.. Six Men	16

25 Jun 1781

Lieut Matthew Paterson was chosen Moderator	16
Voted.. a Tax.. to be paid in Beef Cattle.. for raising supplies for the Use of this State and the Continental Army..Voted, That Lieut Mathew Patterson be Agent.. to procure the Beef Cattle.. or to collect each Inhabitants Proportion of said Tax	17

6 Dec 1781

Voted that Major John Sedgwick be Moderator	17
Voted, That Capt Edward Rogers, Major John Sedgwick, Capt Joshua Pierce, Mr Andrew Young & Elijah Steele, be Select Men	17
Voted, That Judah Kellogg Esqr be Town Clerk & Town Treasurer	17
Voted, That Mr Matthew Patterson be Constable	17

17 Dec 1781

Voted, That Mr Noah Rogers be Constable	17
Voted, That Daniel Hoskens, Levi Pierce, Amos Johnson Junr, Sam^{ll} Brownson, James M. Douglass, Trial Tanner, Abraham Hotchkin, Lemuel Jennings, Samuel Lindly, Salmon Emmons and Titus Hart, be Surveyors of Highways	17
Voted That Isaac Pierce and Silas Dibble be Fence Viewers	17
Voted, That Mr Noah Rogers be Collector of Rates & Taxes	17
Voted, That Messrs Andrew Young, Solomon Emmons and Nath^n Bristol Junr be Listers	17
Voted, That Messrs Elijah Steele and Beriah Hotchkin be Sealers of Leather	17
Voted, That Timothy Brownson & Silas Clark be Grand-Jurors	17
Voted That Messrs John Jones and Zelotes Saunders be Tithing Men	17
Voted, That Samuel Sawyer be Sealer of Weights	17
Voted, That Consider Tanner be Sealer of Measures	17
Voted, That Asa Emmons be Key-keeper	17
Voted, That Capt Thomas Tanner be excused from being Head of a Class for providing & paying a Continental Soldier & that Mr Seth Hill be Head of said Class	18

Cornwall

Voted, That Samuel Sawyer, Samuel Scovel, Capt Seth Pierce, Jacob Brownson Junr, Capt Amos Johnson, Titus Bonney, Daniel Harrison Junr, James Wadsworth, Joseph Bartholomew & Rufus Payne be Committees of Schools	18
Voted, That Capt Joshua Pierce, John Pierce Esqr & Capt Seth Pierce be a Committee to take Care of and Secure the Parsonage and School Monies, Bonds and Obligations	18
Voted, .. a Tax of four Pence upon the Pound upon the List.. for the year 1781 be laid.. to pay and satisfy all Ministerial Charges..Voted, That the Revd Mr Gold, Mr Cornwell & Mr Elijah Allen be impowered to discharge each individual Person's proportionate Part of the Rate.. such Person .. being their Adherents and paying the same to either of them respectively	18

21 Feb 1782

Voted, That Major Jno Sedgwick be Moderator	19
Voted, That Lieut Matthew Paterson, Mr Andrew Young, Mr Noah Rogers & Capt Seth Pierce be a Committee to procure four Men to serve for one Year as Soldiers for the Defence of this State	19
Voted, That a Rate or Tax of one Penny on the Pound upon the List.. For the Year 1781 - be.. Collected for procuring the above mentioned four Soldiers or Recreuits.. Voted, That Mr Noah Rogers be Collector	19
Voted, That Major John Sedgwick be Agent for this Town to Shew.. why the Town is deficient in their Quota of Men in the Continental Army	19
Voted, That the Select Men.. be a Committee to consider of, and abate the Rates and Taxes of such poor Inhabitants.. as are unable to pay the same to Mr Joseph Barce Collector	19

25 Mar 1782

Lieut. Matthew Paterson ws chosen Moderator	19
Voted, That the Town will appoint an Agent to oppose Capt Seth Pierce in an Action or Suit.. which he hath commenced against Messrs. Judah Kellogg & Ketchel Bell for £400 they borrowed of him in Augt 1779 as Select Men.. for the Use of said Town, to be tried at the next County Court	19
Voted, That Major John Sedgwick be Agent for the Town for the Purpose aforesaid	20
Voted, That the Select Men to be impowered.. to liquidate and settle with Mr Francis Brown the Value of a Sum of Continental Money borrowed of him by Mr Joseph Barce by Order of the Select Men, in Silver Money	20

1 Oct 1781

Voted, That Capt Seth Peirce be Moderator	20
Voted, That Lieut Matthew Patterson be Collector & Receiver of all Provisions & Cloathing required.. by an Act of the General Assembly.. and that he procure Barrels, receive and salt, pack and secure the Beef & Pork that shall be brought in to him, & store such other Articles as shall be delivered in payment of the Tax	20

8 Apr 1782

Voted, That Messrs Matthew Patterson and Noah Rogers be a Committee.. to procure two able bodied Soldiers to serve in the Continental Army	21
The Question was put.. whether the Inhabitants.. are willing in Case the Revd Mr Gold will resign his Office of Minister and Pastor.. and also relinquish his Salary, to unite and call and Settle a serious, pious, godly orthodox, learned Minister.. Voted in the Affirmative	21
Voted, that a.. Tax of four Pence upon the Pound.. be immediately laid.. and paid to the Revd Hezekiah Gold, Mr John Cornwell & to the Missionary of the Church of England who hath preached to the Inhabitants.. who are Professors of the Church of England the Year past; and each Individual Person.. pay his Proportionable Part of siad.. Tax to the Minister of that	21

Cornwall

Denomination of Christians whose Worship he attends..

Voted, That a Committee be appointed to wait upon the Revd Mr Gold to know.. whether he will to know whether he will consent to be dismissed from his Ministerial Office and pastoral Care.. And also relinquish his Salary.   21

17 Sep 1782

Lieut Matthew Patterson was chosen Moderator   22

Whereas the Widow Amy Squier hath become chargeable to the Town.. by Reason of Age and Infirmity; and whereas it is said that a considerable Interest in Lands does of Right belong to her at Colchester.. by Descent from her Father Mr Samuel Fuller, late of said Town deceased.. Judah Kellogg Esqr be a Committee.. to repair to Colchester.. and enquire into the Circumstances of said Estate, and of her Right thereto   22

Voted, That Messrs Judah Kellogg, Noah Rogers & Joseph Barce be a Committee to view the Road.. leading up the Great Hill by Mr Hindman's House to Litchfield and see whether the same shall be made repaired or amended in the Place where it now goes, or whether it is best if it should be exchanged or altered to some better and more convenient Place   22

2 Dec 1782

Major John Sedgwick was chosen Moderator   23

Solomon Emmons was chosen Clerk pro tempore   23

Voted, That Major John Sedgwick, Andrew Young, Matthew Patterson, John Millard Junr and Noah Rogers be Select Men   23

Voted, That Judah Kellogg be Town Clerk & Town Treasurer   23

Voted, That Noah Rogers and Seth Hill be Constables   23

Voted, That Thomas Dean, Joseph Bartholomew, Nathan Seward, Isaac Swift, Levi Bonney, Matthew Patterson, Jesse Buell, Abel Judson, Tryal Tanner, Zachariah H Jones, Nathan Millard, Amos Johnson, Elias Hart and Nathan Bristol Jr be Surveyors of Highways   23

Voted, That Daniel Stewart and Roger Catlin be Fence Viewers   23

Voted, That Andrew Young, Nathan Bristol Junr, Nathan Seward, Sawyer, Rufus Payne, and Solomon Emmons be Listers   23

Voted, That Noah Rogers be Collector of Rates & Taxes   23

Voted, That Silas Clark and Beriah Hochkin be Sealers of Leather   23

Voted, That Matthew Patterson and Andrew Young be Grand Jurors   23

Voted, That Consider Tanner, Jacob Brownson Junr, Joseph Barce & Silas Clark be Tything Men   23

Voted, That Zelotes Sanders and Samuel Sawyer be Branders of Horses   23

Voted, That Samuel Sawyer be Sealer of Weights and Oliver Foord be Sealer of Measures   23

Voted, That Nathaniel Seward, Joseph Barce, Solomon Emmons, Jesse Buell, Seth Pierce, Samuel Lindly, Samuel Wadsworth, James Sterling, Titus Bonney, Titus Hart, Andrew Young and Zachariah H Jones be Committees of Schools   23

Voted, That Joseph Barce be Key-keeper   23

Voted, That the Inhabitants.. impower Mr Joseph Barce to carry on a Suit commenced by Nathaniel Grey of Kent arisen on Account of defraying Ministerial Charges, and that Mr Matthew Patterson be appointed to assist in the Affair   24

A Question put.. whether a Committee be appointed to take Charge of the Parsonage & Shool Monies? Voted in the Affirmative: accordingly Major John Sedgwick Lieut Matthew   24

Cornwall

Patterson and Capt Joshua Pierce were chosen.

A Question put whether a Committee be appointed to treat with Mr Gold concerning his Salary? And Voted in the affirmative ~ accordingly Lieut Patterson, Capt Seth Pierce, Mr Joseph Barce and Mr Andrew Young were appointed
30 Dec 1782   24

Solomon Emmons appeared before me.. and made Oath that as he was chosen Clerk at a Town Meeting.. he made true Entries of all Notes past in said Meeting ~ Sworn before me Edward Rogers Justice of Peace
9 Dec 1782   24

Major John Sedgwick was chosen Moderator of a Town Meeting   24

Elijah Allen was chosen Town Clerk pro tempore   24

Voted, That Solomon Emmons deliver up to the Moderator of this Meeting, the Votes taken on the 2nd Day of Instant December   24

Voted, That John Sedgwick, Andrew Young, Matthew Patterson, John Millard Junr and Noah Rogers be Select Men   25

Voted, That Elijah Allen be Town Clerk   25

Voted, That Elijah Allen be Town Treasurer

Voted, That Noah Rogers and Seth Hill be Constables   25

Voted, That Thomas Dean, Joseph Bartholomew, Nathan Seward, Isaac Swift, Levi Bonney, Matthew Patterson, Jesse Buell, Abel Judson, Tryal Tanner, Zachariah How Jones, Nathan Millard Capt Amos Johnson, Elias Hart and Nathan Gristol Junr be Surveyors of Highways   25

Voted, That Daniel Stewart and Roger Catlin be Fence Viewers   25

Voted, That Andrew Young, Nathan Bristol Junr, Nathan Seward, Samuel Sawyer and Solomon Emmons be Listers   25

Voted, That Noah Rogers be Collector of Rates   25

Voted, That Silas Clark be Leather Sealer   25

Voted, That Andrew Young and Matthew Patterson be Grand Jurors   25

Voted, That Consider Tanner, Joseph Barce, Silas Clark and Zelotes Sanders be Tything Men   25

Voted, That Zelotes Sanders and Samuel Sawyer be Branders of Horses   25

Voted, That Samuel Sawyer be Sealer of Weights   25

Voted, That Joseph Barce be Key Keeper   25

Voted, That Oliver Foord be Sealer of Measures   25

Voted, That Nathan Seward, Salmon Emmons, Jesse Buell Seth Pierce, Samuel Lindly, Samuel Wadsworth, Consider Tanner, Titus Bonney, Titus Hart, Andrew Young, Zachariah How Jones and Ira Bartholomew be Committees of Schools   25

Voted, That Matthew Patterson Joshua Pierce and John Sedgwick be a Committee to take Care of the School and Parsonage and Parsonage Monies   25

Voted, That this Meeting will choose a Committee to treat with the Revd Mr Hezekiah Gold, to know how much he will accept and give a discharge for his Salary to the first of October last ~ Voted, That John Sedgwick Joseph Barce, Seth Pierce, Matthew Patterson, Edward Rogers, Andrew Young, Woodruff Emmons, John Pierce and Noah Rogers be said Committee ~   25

Cornwall

13 Dec 1782

Voted, That the Select Men be impowered to to carry on the Suit with the Revd Mr Hezekiah Gold at the adjourned County Court at Litchfield in instant December — 26

Voted, That if Stephen Trowbridge does join the Continental Army and count for a Soldier from the Town.. during the War, that then the s^d Town will pay him ten pounds Lawful Money — 26

Voted, That this Town will pay Edward Allen ten Pounds Lawful Money as a Gratuity for his inlisting into the Continental Army during the War, and counting for a Soldier from this Town — 26

28 Jan 1783

Voted, That Lieut Matthew Patterson be Moderator — 26

Vopted, That Major John Sedgwick and Lieut Matthew Patterson be Agents.. to.. defend the Town in a Suit commenced.. by the Revd Mr Gold — 26

a Rate or Tax of two Pence on the Pound upon the List of Polls and rateable Estate.. For the Year 1782 be.. laid.. to defray the Expences.. in defending the Town against a Suit now depending against said town in Favor of the Revd Mr Gold — 26

a Committee be appointed to treat with the Revd Mr Gold to know of him whether, and how he will Settle with the Town for the Arrearages due to him for his past Services in the Ministry.. Voted, That Messrs Joseph Barce, Tryal Tanner and Joshua Pierc Junr be a Committee for the Purpose aforesaid — 26

Lieut Matthew Patterson be appointed.. to take Care of and Dispose of all such Rie Flower as now lies at Hartford and not accepted by the Commissary in Payment of the Provision Rates.. to the best Advantage he can — 27

7 Apr 1783

Voted y^t John Pierce Esqr be Moderator — 27

Mr Joseph Barce agreed.. to take the Widow Amy Squier and keep her until the Annual Town Meeting.. to provide her with House Room, necessary Food and Washing for four Shillings & five Pence per Week ~ if she need doctoring or Cloathing he is to be paid for what he shall provide her, over and bove the 4/5 per Week — 27

Voted, that a Committee be appointed to wait upon the Revd Mr Gold to know of him how much Money and Wood are due to him for his Service in the Ministry.. previous to the 30th Day of October last past; and to know of him how much he is willing to deduct from such.. also to know of him upon what Considerations he will withdraw his Action now depending against the Town for Arrearages due to him — 27

Voted, That Matthew Patterson, Judah Kellogg and Jesse Buell be a Committee for the Purpose abovementioned ~ — 27

21 Apr 1783

Voted, That the Action Petition or Suit at Law commenced in March last against John Pierce Esqr for the Bonds Obligations and Securities for the Parsonage Monies..by the Select Men.. be by them them withdrawn and prosecuted no farther — 27

30 Apr 1783

Voted, That Lieut Matthew Patterson be Moderator — 28

On Motion.. whether this Town will petition the.. General Assembl .. respecting the Difficulties.. between Revd Hezekiah Gold and this town.. Voted in the affirmative — 28

Voted, That Major John Sedgwick Mr Andrew Young & Doct^r Timothy Rogers be a Committee or Agents to prefer a Petititon to the General Assembly.. relative to the Difficulties.. between the Revd Mr Hezekiah Gold & the Town, or to Settle all said — 28

Difficulties by any other legal Means.. that may be agreed on between said Mr Gold and said Committee or Agents

Voted, That a Vote passed in the last Town Meeting requesting the Committee appointed to take Care of the Parsonage Money to withdraw the Suit.. by them commenced against John Pierce Esqr for said Money or Obligations &c be now reconsidered and declared void, and the same is by this Meeting now reconsidered and declared to be null and void

Messrs Caleb Jones, Judah Kellogg & James Barce being the only Persons in this Meet who were of the Established Order or Denomination of Christians therein, protested against the preceeding Town Votes in open Meeting

Voted, That the Select Men be.. impowered to view the High Bridge near Mr Birdsey's House and see whether it is worth repairing

12 May 1783

Mr Andrew Young was chosen Moderator

Voted, That a Rate or Tax of two Pence on the Pound upon the List.. for the Year 1781, be.. levied.. to pay the Revd Mr Gold a Part of eighty nine Pounds five Shillings.. the Full of his Demand until the 30th Day of October last, provided he give the Town a Discharge in full to that Time; and that the Remainder of said Sum be paid him out of the Town Rate lately commited to Mr Noah Rogers Collector to collect, and that the Remainder of said Rate commited to Mr Rogers (after Mr Gold is satisfied, and the Expences of the Law Suit carried on by the Town are deducted, be divided between the two Societies ~

Voted, That the Revd Mr Gold shall.. receive all the Interest.. due upon the Bonds Obligations and Securities for the Parsonage Money.. previous to the 30th Day of October last past, except twenty Pounds.. provided Mr Gold and theTown settle

Voted, That Capt Joseph Barce be Collector of the two penny Rate last granted: and also to collect the two penny Rate granted in a former Meeting to defray the Costs of a Law Suit in defending the Town against.. Mr Gold for his Salary, and that Mr Rogers be excused from collecting the same

Voted, That Messrs Judah Kellogg, Andrew Young, Timothy Rogers and Beriah Hochkin be a Committee to wait upon Mr Gold's and see that his Dues from the Town are secured to him.. and procure of him a Discharge of all Demands for his Services in the Ministry to the Thirtieth Day of October last, and procure a Discharge for the Congregationalists

It is Proposed by the Revd Mr Gold.. That the Town Vote a Rate.. Sufficient to pay him.. eighty-nine Pounds five Shillings, without any.. Deduction.. viz. the whole Sum to be without Interest two Months after voted - then Interest for all that is unpaid until paid, the one half to be paid within five Months and the other half to be paid within ten Months.. in Consideration thereof Mr Gold to give the Town a Discharge for all former Dues previous to the 30th Day of October last.. ~ And to have no further Demand upon those Inhabitants.. who profess themselves to be Strict Congregationalists, and who lodged their Names with the Town Clerk in October last, so long as they continue to be of that Denomination and support that Worship; or who shall in future lodge their Names.. also proposed that Mr Gold have.. such Interest as hath arisen.. upon the Parsonage Money.. also proposed that Mr Gold shall have.. all the Interest that.. may arise.. upon the Parsonage Money.. so long as he continues to be a Minister in the Town, and Pastor of the first Church and Society therein

The within Proposals were made and agreed to by the Revd Hezekiah Gold and.. Andrew Young and Timothy Rogers, a Committee.. to prefer a Memorial or Petition &c in the last Town Meeting

16 Sep 1783

Colo John Sedgwick was chosen Moderator

Cornwall

Voted, That this Town will send a Delegate to meet the Delegates to convent at Middletown *30*
on the 30th Day of instant September.. Voted, That Edward Rogers attend the Convention..
as a Delegate from this Town

Coventry

Miscellaneous Town Records
Vol. 7
1782-1842

Located at the Town Clerk's Office

Coventry

15 Aug 1774

Phinehas Strong Esqr was chose Moderator	161
Ephraim Root Esqr Capt Ebenezer Kingsbery Leu^t William Willson Dr John Crocker & Capt Elas Buell was Chose A Cometee of Correspond	161

13 Sep 1774

.. Being Desirious of Keping up a mutual Corrispond With the Towns of this & the neighbouring Governments do appoint Ephraim Root Esqr Capt Ebenezer Kingsbery Dr John Crocker Capt Elias Buell and Mr William Willson a Commetee of Corrispon	163

11 Apr 1775

Voted that this Town will Prefer a Memorial to y^e.. General Assembly.. for Liberty to Mark Mend & Repair their Highway by a rate.. & that Capt Ebenezer Kingsbery and Jeremiah Riply be.. agents for & on behalf of this Town	164
Voted y^t Deac^n Richard Hale be a Comitee to Exchange So much of ye Highway with Mr Ephraim Deavenport as.. Nessesary to Accomidate.. Traveling	165

12 Sep 1775

Capt Ebenezer Kingsbery was Chose Moderator	165
Present Select men and Ephraim Kingsbery Dr Richard Hall Jonathan Porter Daniel Skinner Ichabod Jewett Moses Stanley Elipaz Hunt Elisha Jones Ju^r Samuel Robertson & Benajah Edwards was Chose a Come^{tt} to Divide ye Highways.. for ye Mending of ye Same	165

11 Dec 1775

Deacon Richard Hale was Chose Moderator	165
Noah Porter was Chose Town Clerk	165
Noah Porter was Chose Town Treasurer	165
Joseph Talcott Jeremiah Ripley Jacob Lyman were Chose Select Men	165
John Hale Amaziah Rust and Benjamen Jones was Chosen Counstables	165
Medad Root Ephraim Colman Ichabod Jewett Amariah Rockwell & Noah Jones was Chose Granuriors	165
Daniel Pomroy Ephram Cushman Robert Badcock & John Badcock was Chosen Tithingmen	165
Ephraim Dow Thomas Brigham Joshua Tildin Benjaman Case Ju^r was Chose Listors	165
James Parker & Jonathan Porter was Chose fence vewers	165
John Hale was Chose Colector to Colect ye Country Rate	165
Aron Blackman Samuel Ladd & Dudley Dor[ ] was Chose Colectors to Colect the Town Rate	166
Ephraim Deavenport Humphrey Dowe and Eliphalit Carpenter was Chose Sealors of leather	166
Abner White Amariah Rockwell and John Eansworth was Chose Sealors of weights and Measurs	166
Noah Porter was Chose Keykeper	166

Coventry

Noah Porter & Amos Richardson Jun[r] was Chose Branders & Recorder of Horses	166
Ephraim Root was Chose Gager of Casks	166
Ebenezer Wintworth Ju[r] was Chose packer	166
Jonathan Porter & Joseph Root was Chose School Cometee	166
Jeremiah Ripley & Ephraim Root was audators to audate with y[e] School Cometee	166
Richard Hale Ephraim Kingsbery Elipaz Hunt Thomas Brown Nathaniel Lad Benjaman Buell Samuel Daggit Zachariah Loomis Caleb Stanley Ju[r] Elias Buell Alerton Cushman Ju[r] Shobel Cook Thomas Judd Daniel Daniel Robertson was Chose Surveyer of Highways *25 Dec 1775*	166
Deacon Richard Hale was Chose Moderator	166

13 May 1776

Cap[t] William Willson was Chose Moderator	167

13 May 1776

Cap[t] Ebenezer Kingsbery & Ephraim Root Esq[r] was Chose agens to appear before y[e].. General Asembly.. to Defend in behalf of s[d] Town against y[e] Memorial of Cap[t] Eliphalet Carpenter & Sundrey others.. to be Exempt from a Tax.. for mending & Repairing y[e] Highways.. & also from aney further Impositions of Like Nature *10 Sep 1776*	167
Cap[t] Ebenezer Kingsbery was chose Moderator	167
Medad Root & Elijah Brown was Chosen Surveyers of highways & Colectors of y[e] Rate Granted for y[e] Mending of Highway.. in y[e] Room of Elias Buell & Nathaniel Ladd they being absent *23 Dec 1776*	167
Dec[n] Richard Hale was Chose Moderator	167
Noah Porter was Chose Town Clerk	167
Noah Porter was Chose Town Treasurer	167
Jeremiah Ripler Joseph Talcott & Jacob Lyman Chose Selectmen	167
John Hale Eliphas Hunt & Benjah Stron was Chose Constables	167
Eliphas Hunt was Chose Colector to Colect y[e] Country Rate	167
John Root Thomas Page Humphrey Dow Benjaman Buell & Eliphalit Hendy was Chose Granjuriors	167
Eleazer Pomroy Moses Stanley Justus Richardson Joseph Doubleday was Chosen Tithing Men	167
Thomas Brigham Ephraim Dowe John Badcock Paul Brigham & Jonathan Richardson was Chosen Listors & Enspectors	167
Eliphas Hunt Ephraim Kingbery Ephraim Colman Samuel Ladd Ju[r] Andrew Richardson Benjaman Jones Daniel White Eleazer Colman Daniel Robertson Enoch Larribee John	168

Coventry

Robertson ye 3rd D^n Richard Hale Buell Medad Root was Chosen Surveyers of Highway

James Parker & Ebenezer Stiles was Chose fence vewers	168
Matthew Duty & Robert Turner was Chose Sealors of Leather	168
Abner White Amariah Rockwell & John Ainsworth was Chose Sealors of whight & measures	168
Noah Porter Amos Richardson Ju^r was Chose brandors & Recorders of Horses	168
Noah Porter was Chose key kepor	168
Ephraim Root was Chose Gager of Casks	168
Ebenezer Wintworth was Chose Packer	168
Abner Fitch Ju^r Enoch Badger Ju^r James Carpenter was Chose Town Colectors	168
Daniel Pomroy was Chose a School Cometee Man	168

7 Apr 1777

Abraham Burnap Esqr was Chose Moderator	168
Richard Hale Daniel Polmroy Jonathan Porter Jonathan Porter Ju^r & Abraham Burnap Ju^r Was Chose a Commetee to Provide for ye Famelies of Such Persons as Shall inlist.. in ye armey	168
Jabez Edgerton Thomas Brown Joseph Root Samuel Doggit & Ritchard Hale was Chosen in addition to ye Commetee of Inspection	169

25 Sep 1777

Ephraim Root Esqr Capt Samuel Robertson Mr Ephraim Colman Deac^n Richard Hale Deac^n Jonathan Porter Ju[ ] Leut Ephraim Kingsbery Mr Ichabod Jewet Maj Thomas Brown Mr Daniel Pomroy Mr Ichabod Fowler Capt Thomas Terril Abraham Burnap Esqr & Mr Jacob Lyman was Chosen a Cometee to Provid ye articels of Clothing for the Solger	169

15 Dec 1777

Deacon Ebenezer Kingsbery was Chose Moderator	169

19 Dec 1777

Noah Porter was Chose Town Clerk	169
Noah Porter was Chose Town Treasurer	169
Jeremiah Ripley Josepoh Talcott & Jacob Lyman was Chose Select Men	169
John Hale Eliphas Hunt & John Badcock was Chose Constabels	170
Daniel Pomroy Joseph Root David Pattin Ebenezer Kingsbery & Jonathan Porter Ju^r was Chose Graniurmen	170
Asa Manley Jacob Willson John Waldow Daniel Turner was Chose Tithing Men	170
John Badcock was Chose Colector to Colect ye Country Rate	170
Samuel Robertson Ju^r Gold Hunt Daniel Loomis Otes Freman & Nathaniel Kingsbery was Chose Listors & Inspectors	170

Coventry

Noah Porter Ju[r] Thomas Porter Eleazer Pomroy Amos Dorman Moses Sanley Samuel Sprague James Hutchenson Samuel Allin Henry Curtis Humphry Taylor & Timothy Rose Ichabod Jewett Elijah Wrigh Amos Avary was Chose Surveyors of Highway	170
John Robertson y[e] 3r[d] Iaiah Porter & Asel Jones was Chose Colector	170
Robert Turner & Mathew Deuty was Chose Sealors of Leather	170
Abner White & Amoriah Rockwell was Chose Sealors of weights & measures	170
Ephraim Root Esq[r] was Chose Gager of Casks	170
Noah Porter & Amos Richardson was Chose brandors & Recorders of Horses	170
Jonthan Porter Ju[r] was Chose key keper	170
Jonathan Porter & Richard Hale was Chose fence vewers	170
Richard Hale Daniel Pomroy Jonathan Porter Abraham Burnap Ju[r] & Jonathan Porter Ju[r] was Chose a Cometee to Provid Nessaries for the Solders families	170
Thomas Brown Jeremiah Ripley Abraham Burnap Ju[r] William Willson Amariah Rust John Arnold Thomas Terril Ephraim Root & Richard Hale was Chose a Commetee to Examine.. what Measures aught to be taken with the Obligations Given to y[e] Treasurer.. for Military Dilnquancy	171
Jeremiah Ripley Joseph Talcott Jacob Lyman & Ephraim Root was Chose a cometee to Exammine Into y[e] Circomstances of y[e] Highway Leading from John Scriptures in Coventry to Ephraim Grants Ju[r] in Tolland & Settel with & agree with Simeon Scripture or otherwise conduct S[d] affair as they Judge best	171
Daniel Pomroy & Joseph Root was Chose a School Cometee	171

6 Jan 1778

D[n] Richard Hale was Chose Moderator	172
Joseph Hawkins was Chosen Granurior.. insted of Jonathan Porter Ju[r]	172

14 Dec 1778

Noah Porter was Chose Town Clerk	172
Noah Porter was Chose Town Treasurer	172
Joseph Talcott Jonathan Porter Ju[r] & Daniel White was Chose Selectmen	172
Caleb Stanley Ju[r] John Badcock & David Pettin was Chose Constables	172
Caleb Stanley Ju[r] was Chosen State Colector	172
Samuel Robertson Benajah Strong Elijah Wright Benjamin Lamb & Benjaman Jones was Chose Graniurimen	172
Allerton Cushman Grsham Colman John Grover Ju[r] Jessa Bruster was Chose Tithingmen	172
Elias Buell Thomas Porter Ephraim Kingsbery Jabez Edgerton Samuel Sprague Samuel Robertson Ju[r] Amos Avary & Samuel Kingsbery was Chose Listors & Inspectors	172

Coventry

Daniel Loomis Timothy Kimbal John Root Moses Woodward Timothy Cole Christopher Bennit Levi Dow Noah Grant Jeptha Fitch Israel Bruster Gershom Colman Humphrey Dowe Huphrey Taylor & Daniel Robertson was Chose Surveyors of highways	172
Benjaman Case Ju^r Nathaniel Kingsbery & Daniel Turner was Chose Colectors	172
Noah Porter was Chose Brandor and Recorder of Horses	172
Noah Grant Robert Turner & Matthew Duty was Chose Sealors of Leather	172
Abner White & Amariah Rockwell was Chose Sealors of weights & Measures	172
Jonathan Porter Ju^r was Chose Key keper	172
Ephraim Root was chose Packer	172
Joshua Edwards was Chose Packer	172
James Parker & Richard Hale was Chose fence vewers	172
Richard Hale Daniel Pomroy Abraham Burnap and Elijah Wright was Chose Cometee to Supply the famalies of ye offissers & Solders in ye Continen Servis	173
28 Dec 1778	
Ephraim Root Esqr was Chose Moderator	173
Ephraim Kingsbery was Chose School Cometee Man in addition to Joseh Root	173
Ephraim Root Esqr & Capt Jeremiah Ripley was chose audators to audit with ye School Cometee	173
12 Apr 1779	
Josiah Carpener was Chose a Surveyor of Highways in Sed of Jacob Bruster	173
14 Sep 1779	
Ephraim Root Esqr was Chose Moderator	173
Abraham Burnap Esqr & Coll Thomas Brown was chose a Cometee to Represent this Town at ye general State Meting	173
13 Dec 1779	
Ephraim Root Esqr was Chose Moderator	174
Noah Porter was chosen Town Clerk	174
Noah Porter was Chose Town Treasurer	174
Jonathan Porter Ju^r Choronal Thomas Brown & Leutent Daniel White was Chose Selectmen	174
Leu^{tt} Samuel Robertson Eleazer Pomroy & Daniel Patten were Chose Constables	174
Eleazer Pomroy was Chose Colector to Colect ye State Tax	174
Asa Manley Doct^r John Waldow Eli[ ] Palmer Noah Porter Ju^r & Nathaniel Kingsbery was Chose Graniurimen	174
Moses Stanley Elipas Hunt Abraham Badger Jehiel Rose & Josiah Carpenter was Chose	174

Coventry

Listors & Inspector

Daniel Robertson Thomas Deavenport Joseph Root Nathaniel Root Jabez Loomis Aaron Blackman Joshua Fildin Joseph Kingsbery Nathaniel Eels Samuel Parker Jacob Edgerton Robert Badcock Henry Curtis & Josiah Fuller was Chose Serveyers of Highway	174
Daniel Badger Ju^r Joseph Talcott Ju^r Elisha Jones & Jonathan Root was Chose Tithing men	174
Nathaniel Palmer Elijah Strong & Timothy Coles was Chose Town Colectors	174
Noah Porter & Amos Richardson was Chosen Brandors & Recorders of Horses	174
James Parker & Jonathan Porter was Chose Fence vewer	174
Hab^k Turner & Robert Turner was Chose Sealors of Leathor	174
Abner White & Amariah Rockwell was Chose Sealor of Wights & Measures	174
Ephraim Root was Chose Sealor of Casks	174
Joshua Edward was Chose Packer	174
Jonathan Porter Ju^r was Chose Key keper	174
Joseph Dubbeldy David Blackman & John Grover Ju^r was Chosen Howards	174
Ichabod Jewett was Chose a Cometee man to Suply the famalyes of ye Solders	174
10 Apr 1780	
Ephraim Root Esqr was Chose Moderator	175
Jabez Edgerton John Badcock John Hale Moses Stanley & was Chose Inspector of Provision	175
26 Jun 1780	
Con^l Jesse Root was Chose Moderator	175
Con^l Brown Mager Buell D^n Jonathan Porter & the Comissiened offesers of the Several Compenies of Melesha & alarm list be.. appointed to procure men to in List into the Continental armey	176
13 Nov 1780	
Chon^l Thomas Brown was Chose Moderator	176
Elijah Wright & Jonathan Porter Junr was Chose & appointed to Receive the Flower Requ[*ired*].. for ye use of ye armey	176
Thomas brown Calvin Mnning [*sic*] & David Pattin was Chose & appointed to Receive ye Beaf & Porck	176
21 Nov 1780	
Capt Ebenezer Kingsbery was Chose Moderator	177
voted to Chuse a Comt^{ee} to Procure ye Cota of Solders for this Town as Required.. toServe in ye Continental armey.. Majer Elias Buell Chon^l Thomas Brown Capt William Willson Capt Jeremiah Ripley Capt Samuel Robertson Ju^r Capt Thomas Terril & Capt Amazia Rust was Chose a Cometee for ye Purpos	177

Coventry

4 Dec 1780

Capt Ebenezer Kingsbery was Chose Moderator 177

Noah Porter was Chose Town Clerk 177

Chan^l Thomas Brown Benajah Strong & Benjaman Jones was Chose Select Men 177

Samuel Robertson Ju^r Eleazer Pomroy & Abner Badger was Chose Constables 177

Eleazer Pomroy was Chose Colector to Colect ye State Rate 177

Jehiel Rose Ephraim Colman Daniel Loomis Lemuel Long & Zachariah Lomis was Chose Graniurimen 177

Jeptha Fitch Henry Curtis Gad Hunt & Nathaniel Eells was Chose Tithing men 177

Nathaniel Root William Carpenter Calvin Manning John Root & Timothy Cole was Chose Listors & Inspector 177

Ozias Hawkins Andrew Crocker Levy Swetland Samuel Colman Thomas Page Eliphalet Hendee Jesse Cook Asel Jones Caleb Stanley Ju^r Ichabod Jewett Thomas Judd Oliver Boynton Jacob Willson was Chose Surveyers of Highways 177

Jonathan Porter & Richard Hale was Chose Fence vewers 177

Ephraim Root was Chose Gager of Casks 177

Joshua Edwards was Chose Packer 177

Amos Richardson & Noah Porter was Chose Brandors & Recorders of Horses 177

Amariah Rockwell Abner White & John Eansworth was Chose Sealors of weights & masures 177

Robert Turner & Matthew Deuty was Chose Sealors of Leather 177

Elias Buel Ephraim Kingsbery & Elipas Hunt was Chose School Cometee 177

Matthew Duty was Chose Keykeper 177

Ephraim Root Jeremiah Ripley ws Chose auditors to audate with ye School Cometee 177

Samuel Robertson Amos Richardson & Samuel Sprague was Chose a Cometee to Supply ye Solders Families 178

Elisha Jones Israel Bruster & Joseph How was Chose Colectors 178

8 Jan 1781

Ephraim Root Esqr was Chose Moderator 178

Cononal Thomas Brown.. Elias Buell Capt ~~Elias Buell~~ Capt Amaziah Rust Capt Jeremiah Ripley Abraham Burnap Capt Paul Brigham Capt Samuel Robertson.. Benjaman Jones Capt William Willson Ephraim Kingsbery Esqr Capt John Arnold Ephraim Root Esqr Mr John Badcock Capt Thomas Terril & Mr Daniel White was Chose a Cometee to Class ye Inhabitence.. to Rase ye Cota of Solders for ye Continental armey 178

John Loomis & Thomas Porter was Chosen a Comet^{ee} to Procure Clothing for the Continental Solders which.. belong to s^d Town 178

Coventry

voted to rais two Pence on ye pound in Silver or one penney half penney in flower or Corn at ye prises perfixed in the Law.. Jonathan Porter Ju^r & Elijah Wright was Chose to Receive & Colect the ye Tax *9 Apr 1781*	178
Ephraim Kingsbery Esqr was Chose Clerk for S^d Meting	178
Capt Ephraim Kingsbery was Chose Moderator *16 Apr 1781*	178
Daniel White ws Chose Clerk for S^d Meting	178
voted to procure those Men for the.. State Sarvis agreable to an act of General Assembly.. by a Cometee for that purpose.. Joseph Talcott Joseph Root Daniel White Eliphas Flint & Caleb Stanley were Chose a cometee to Inlist S^d Men	178
voted to Class ye Town for.. Raising ye Mentioned men.. Then Chononal Thomas Brown Leu^t Josep Talcott Maj^r Elias Buell Capt Jeremiah Ripley Leu^t Daniel White & Capt Samuel Robertson Ju^r was Chose a Cometee to Class ye Town	179
voted to Submit ye Mater Relative to Laying out a highway from Mr Enoch Badgers to Capt Paul Brighams to ye Select Men *27 Jun 1781*	179
Ephraim Root was Chose Moderator	179
voted to Rais 4 pence on ye pound on ye List of Augus 1781 to be paid in Lawfull Money or good Beaf Cattel at ye prises.. mentioned in a late act of ye General Assembly for a Supply of Beaf for our Line in ye Continental armey.. Then Capt Samuel Robertson Ju^r Colector & Receiver of s^d Tax Either in Money or beaf & also purcheser of Beaf if nead be & agent to Chuse apprise and Deliver Such Beef as he Shall So Colect Receive & Purchas to ye Comeseary	179
Enoch Badger Ju^r Samuel Lilley & Capt Timothy Dimock & Jethro Turner was Chose in adition to the Cometee appointed to Supply ye families of ye Solders that are in ye Continenal armey *31 Nov 1781*	179
Abraham Burnap Ju^r was Chose Moderator	179
Abraham Burnap was Chose to Receive ye provision required by a lat act of assembly *17 Dec 1781*	179
Capt Ebenezer Kingsber was Chose Moderator	180
Noah Porter was Chose Town Clerk	180
Thomas brown Benajah Strong & Benjaman Jones was Chose Select men	180
Eleazer Pomroy Samuel Robertson Ju^r & Abner Badger was Chose Constabels	180
Lemuel Long Josiah Carpenter Calvin Manning Samuel Walbridge & Joseph Howe was Chose Grajuriman	180
Samuel Robertson Ju^r was Chose Colector to Colect ye State Rate	180

Coventry

Abner Fitch Ju^r Levy Swetland Jacob Bruster & Dudley Dorman was Chose Tithing men	180
John Root John Badcock Samuel Lilley Humphrey Taylor & Timothy Coles was Chose Listors & Inspectors	180
Surveyers of Highways John Loomis Shobel Cook Jerijah Burnap John Walbridg Stephen How[ ] Thomas Thompson Joseph Hawkins Medad Root Josiah Brown Caleb Stanly Ju^r Thomas Judd ~~Medad Hunt~~ Gad Had Hunt Samuel Robertson & Daniel Robertson	180
Matthew Duty was Chose Key keper	180
Ephraim Root was Chose gager of Caskes	180
Abner White Amariah Rockwell & John Eansworth was Chose Sealors of wights & Measure	180
Matthew Duty Ephraim Davenport was Chose Sealors of Leather	180
Jonathan Porter & Jesse Cook was Chose fence vewers	180
Noah Porter Amos Richardson Ichabod Jewett was Chose Brandors & Recorders of Horses	180
Jonathan Richardson Joseph Root Thomas J[ ] Elipas Hunt & Christopher Bennit was Chose Hawards	180
Noah Porter was Chose Town Treasurer	180
Daniel Turner & Joseph Root was Chose a cometee to Suppy ye Familes of [ ] that are in ye Continental Armey	180
Joseph Root Daniel Turner Samuel Lilley Ju^r Eiphalit Hendee & John Loomis was Chose a Cometee to Suppy ye Familes of.. Solders that are in ye Continental armey	180
voted that Samuel Doggits yard be Demed as a lawfull Pound to Impound Cretures... Then.. was Chose key keper	180

8 Apr 1782

Benajah Strong was Chose Clerk for s^d Meting	181
Decon Richard Hale was Chose Moderator	181
Dniel Robertson Ju^r Josiah Brown & Billey Richardson Chose Colectors to Colect ye Town Rate	181
voted that Mr Ruben Stiles barn yard Shal be a Publick pound for ye use of ye Town without Cost to S^d Town & that Mr Ruben Stiles be the Keper	181

5 Jul 1782

Ephraim Root Esqr was Chose Moderator	181

10 Sep 1782

Deacon Richard Hale was Chose Moderator	181
Capt Joseph Root & Captain Joseph Talcott was Chose a Cometee to Joyn Mansfeld to repair or rebuil the Bridg over the River by John Turners	181
voted that Mr John Gove shal be Continewed in Capt Robensons Class in which.. he was first put by the Comet^{ee} appoynted to Class ye People in S^d town	181

16 Dec 1782

Coventry

Ephraim Root Esq[r] Chosen Moderator	314
M[r] Noah Porter Town Clerk and Treasurer	314
Benjamin Jones.. Benajah Strong.. Eliphas Hunt } Chosen Select Men	314
Jeremiah Fitch.. Justus Richardson.. Sam[ll] Sprague.. Moses Stanley.. Gad Hunt } Chosen Grand Jurors	314
Joseph Kingsbury Thomas Porter Elijah Strong John Robertson Jun[r] Chosen Tything Men	314
John Lomis, Gershom Brigham, Jeriah Burnap, Levi Swetland, and Daniel Turner, were Chosen Listers	314
Elijah Brown, Cap[t] Amos Richardson Jesse Brewster Joseph Kingsbury Ju[r] Elisha Sprague Eliphalet Carpenter Jun[r] Henry Curtis, Gershom Colman Elias Palmer Jacob Bruster Ephraim Colman Joseph Hale Elisha Jones Enoch Larrabe was Chosen Surveyors of Highways	314
John Fitch Benj[a] Carpenter Jun[r] Ebenezer Ainsworth were Chosen Collectors	314
Cap[t] Sam[ll] Robertson Ju[r] Eleazer Pomeroy John Badcock were Chosen Constables	314
John Badcock was Chosen Collector to Collect y[e] State Taxes	314
Ens[n] Jonathan Porter & Deacon Rich[d] Hale were Chosen fence Viewers	314
Jonathan Richardson William Badcock Christopher Bennet Cap[t] Joseph Root Ichabod Jewet Thomas Judd Zachariah Loomis, Amos Avery Cap[t] Jeremiah Riply were Chosen Hog howards	314
Ephraim Root Esq[r] Chosen gager	314
Joshua Edwards was Chosen Packer	314
Noah Porter & Cap[t] Richardson were Chosen Branders	314
John Ainsworth Amariah Rockwell Abner White were Chosen Sealers of Weights and Measures	314
Matthew Duty John Lomis Reuben Stiles Sam[ll] Dagget were Chosen Key Keepers	314
Ephraim Davenport and Matthew Duty were Chosen Leather Sealers	314
Noah Porter Ju[r] & Abner Fitch wer Chosen Committee for Supplying Soldiers Families	314

14 Feb 1783

Dea[n] Richard Hale Chosen Moderator	315
Benajah Strong Chosen.. Clerk of s[d] Meeting	315
Ephraim Kingsbury Esq[r] and Col[o] Thomas Brown Chosen Agents.. for the Town before the Adjourn[d] County Court at Windham.. to oppose and shew reasons why the.. Memorial of Ruben Stiles and others praying for a highway to be opened from M[r] Amariah Rockwells to Elijah Carpenters Should not be heard and granted	315

7 Apr 1783

Col[o] Jesse Root Chosen Moderator for a Town Meting	315

Coventry

voted the Selectmen be directed to go and Endeavour to accommodate with Mr Thomas Baxter about opening the Highway that he has inclosed.. and in Case they cannot accommodate the Matter then to resurvey the old Highway and warn the S^d Baxter to open the Same and on his refusing or neglecting.. to Prosecute S^d Baxter for not doing it *315*

Voted that Mr Sam^{ll} Spragues Barn Yard and Stable be A Pound for Publick use and S^d Sprague Key keeper *315*

Danbury

Town Records
Vol. 1
1777-1811

Located at the Town Clerk's Office

Danbury

1 Oct 1777
Capt Daniel Taylor chosen Moderator   38

1 Oct 1777
S^d Meeting was by vote adj^d.. Major Taylor Clerk   38

12 Nov 1777
To the Inhabitants of the Town of Danbury.. it being represented to the Genl Assembly.. in   39
May last that the public Records.. were consumed by Fire and s^d Assembly approved us the
Subscribers to look into the Matter and Acertain the Right of every individual owning Lands
in s^d Town - to facilitate the Matter beg leave to recommend.. to call a Town meeting and
appoint a Com^{tee}.. to collect all the necessary Deeds and Surveys and other Conveyances of
Lands.. and when any .. are lost of consumed by fire.. to bound out s^d Lands mentioning who
it adjoins upon also to Notify the Persons on whom such Lands do adjoin to be present at the
Time of bounding out the same and to adjourn your Town Meeting to the 29th Day of
December next when s^d Doings.. shall be publickly read.. Daniel Sherman.. Increase Mosely..
Nehemiah Beardsley.. Lem^l Sanford.. Caleb Baldwin Ju^r } Com^{tee}

18 Nov 1777
Capt Daniel Taylor chosen Moderator   39

voted to appoint three Men in each School District.. a Committee to assist Persons in   39
collecting the necessary Conveyances and bounding out their Land.. viz.. Messrs Daniel
Taylor Comfort Hoyt Benjamin Sperry, Nathan Gregory David Boughton Joseph Wildman
Benjn Boughton Ju^r David Wildman Saml Nicholls Alexander Stuart John Starr David Hoyt
Ju^r John Duning Benj Stevens John Gregory Richd Shute Noah Hoyt Ezra Stevens Joseph
Barnum Matt^w Linley Richard Barnum Saml Benedict David Perce Saml Weed, Thos Stevens
Thos Starr [ ]^d Eli Segar Benj$^{l\,l}$ Shove. Lemuel Benedict Daniel Wildman Daniel Wood
Thad^{us} Brownson Daniel Wood Ju^r Thos Taylor John Benedict Isaac Bene[ ] Joseph Starr
Eph^m Barnum Nathl Hoyt Joseph Beebe Nathl Benedict Thos Benedict Benjn Benedict James
Seely Nathan Taylor

voted to have one Com^{tee} man in each School District to procure Cloathing for the..   39
Continental Army - viz. Major Taylor Silas [ ] Justus Barnum Elisha Dibble Nathl Starr...
Ensign [ ] Wilks Nathl Gregory Nathl Benedict Thos S[ ] Daniel Wood Andrew Comstock
Eph^m Bar[ ]

15 Dec 1777
Capt Thos Stevens was chosen Moderator   40

Major Taylor Clerk   40

Constables Comfort Hoyt Ju^r & to Collect the Country Rate - Thos Taylor Justus Barnum   40

Grandjurors Zadok Benedict Eliphalet Barnum Andrew Comstock   40

Selectmen Major Taylor Daniel Hickok David Boughton Elijah Hoyt Ezra Dibble Ju^r Capt 40
Comfort Joseph Benedict

Listers Benjn Hickok Oliver Bened^t David Wood Danl Comstock Jonas Benedict Nathl Starr   40
Paul Hamilton

Tythingmen - Joshua Knap Eben^r Picket Ju^r Nath^n Gregory Joseph Elmoni Ezra Dibble   40
Matt^w Starr

Surveyors of Highways Comfort Hoyt Ju^r Joseph Wildman David Boughton Ju^r Eliakim   40
Starr Saml Benedt 4th Tim^o Benedict Eben^r Hickok Joseph Starr John McLean Alex^r Stuart
Saml Nicholls Saml Stevens Lem^l Linly Elea^r Bened^t Eli Segar Bracy Knap Thad^s Brounson

Danbury

Lem^l Wood Ju^r Benjn Stevens Ju^r Saml Sturdevent David Weed	
Fence Viewers - Daniel Hoyt Thad^s Barnum Caleb Church Josiah Vining Nathl Hoyt Matt^w Barnum	*40*
Sealer of Weights Jared Patchen	*40*
Sealer of Leather Joseph Bened^t	*40*
Sealer of Measure Ezra Dibble Thad^s Brownson	*40*
Pound Keeper Danl Church	*40*
the Town by vote grant a rate or Tax.. to defray the necessary Charges arising.. Benajah Starr Nathan Starr & David Judd appointed to Collect & pay in the same	*40*
the following persons were appointed to assist the Town Treasurer &c viz Capt Thos Stevens [ ] [ ] Joseph Beebe Thos Bened^t Richd Shute [ ] [ ] Richd Barnum	*40*
Committy of Inspection Messrs Lem^l Bened^t [ ] Benj Boughton Ju^r Thos Bened^t Joseph Beebe Thos Taylor J[ ] Hayes Matt^w Linley	*41*
voted that Major Taylor be appointed to receive the marks of Sheep	*41*
Voted that Saml Stevens be a Committy man in the Room of his Father	*41*

29 Dec 1777

voted to appoint the following Gentlemen a Com^{tee} to draw up a proper Survey of the highways throughout this Town viz: Zadock Benedict Thad^s Benedict & Comfort Hoyt Ju^r	*41*

19 Jan 1778

Capt Thos Stevens chosen Moderator	*41*
Eli Mygatt Joseph P Cooke Comfort Hoyt Justus Knap Andrew Comstock & Daniel Hickok were appointed a Com^{tee} to take Care of the free School	*41*
Eben^r Weed was appointed pound keeper	*41*

[ ] Jan 1778

A true Copy of Record examin^d by George Wyllys Secret^y	*42*

27 Feb 1778

Capt Thos Stevens Moderator of proprietors Meeting	*42*

10 Mar 1778

Fence Viewers - Jonathan Starr Eliphalet Barnum Robert Benedict Drake Hoyt Ju^r Ens^n Stephen Trowbridge Matt^w Starr	*43*

10 Mar 1778

W^t Sealer Jared Patchen	*43*
Leather Sealer Joseph Benedict	*43*
measure Sealers Thad^{u}s Brownson & Ezra Dibble Ju^r	*43*
Grand Jurors Matt^w Linsly Jonas Benedict Nathl Benedict	*43*
Pound Keeper David Wood	*43*
Town Treasurer Co^l Cooke	*43*
John McLean Noah Hoyt & Thos Benedict were appointed a Committy to prefer a memorial to the Genl Assembly	*43*
by vote grant a Rate or Tax.. to defray the Necessary Charges arising.. and Joshua Benedict Matt^w Gregory and Joseph Starr 3^d were appointed to Collect	*43*

139

Danbury

the Selectmen be impowered to sell as much of Lot on which Thomas Church lives as they shall judge best	43
22 Feb 1779	
Capt Thos Stevens was chosen Moderator	45
by vote grant a Rate.. for making & repairing Highways.. and James Stuart Tim^o Picket & Matt^w Wilkes were appointed to Collect	45
Lu^t Ezra Dibble Nathl Starr Saml Nicholds David Picket ~~Matt^w Linsley~~ Elnathan Knap Nathl Gregory Capt Thos Stevens Bracy Knap ~~David Boughton~~ Eben^r Gregory Eben^r Benedict Ju^r Capt Comfort Hoyt David Wood De^n Joseph Beebe Capt Eph^m Barnum John Andr[ ] and Dec^n Stephen Trowbridge were appointed a Com[ ] to take Care of the Soldiers Familys	45
9 Aug 1779	
Capt Thos Stevens was chosen Moderator	46
by vote grant a Rate.. to defray the necessary Expences arising.. Saml Wildman Danl Shove Ju^r & Eben^r Hickok were appointed to collect	46
Messrs Joseph P Cooke Noble Benedict and Daniel Taylor.. were appointed a Com^{tee} to meet the County Com^{tee} tomorrow morning at Reding to consult and adopt measures to prevent the further Depreciation of the paper money and raise its value	46
13 Dec 1779	
Eli Mygatt Esqr was chosen Moderator	46
Major Taylor was chosen Clerk	46
Town Treasurer; Col Joseph P Cooke	46
Constables Comfort Hoyt Ju^r to gather the Country Rate Lu^t John Trowbridge & Eliakim Starr	46
Selectmen Lu^t John Benedict Thad^{us} Barnum Nathan Gregory Saml Taylor Noah Hoyt Abijah Starr and Lem^l Benedict	47
Grandjurors Lu^t Caleb Church Capt Joseph Starr	47
Listers: Justus Barnum Benajah Starr Caleb Benedict Daniel Hoyt Thomas Taylor Nathl Hoyt	47
Tythingman: Capt Noble Benedict Paul Hamilton Saml Nicholds And^w Comstock Oliver Benedict and David Northrop	47
Surveyors of Highways { David Wood Daniel Comstock Ezra Dibble Ju^r Elijah Hoyt Jonas Benedict Eli Seger David Perce John Barnum Ju^r Justus Hoyt Elisha Dibble David Hoyt Saml Sturdevent Joseph Beebe Ju^r Joseph Platt Matt^w Barnum Silas Taylor Benjamin Hickok Joseph Wood Thad^{us} Brownson	47
Fence Viewers Jonth Starr Jabez Rockwell Levi Benedict Ma[ ] Starr David Boughton Ju^r Benjn Gorh[ ]	47
Sealer of Weights Jared Patchen	47
Sealer of Leather - Joseph Benedict	47
Sealer of Measures Thad^{us} Brownson & Ezra Dibble Ju^r	47
Pound Keeper -- David Wood	47
by Vote grant a Rate or Tax of six shillings on the pound on..the List last Computed to defray the necessary Charges arising.. Collectors Benjn Wood Saml Stevens and Saml Dibble	47
Nathl Starr Saml Nichols Caleb Baldwin Stephen Trowbridge Matt^w Wilkes Daniel Comstock & Capt Benjn Hickok were appointed a Com^{tee} to take Care of the Soldiers Familys	48

140

Danbury

21 Feb 1780

Thos Taylor Moderator	48
the Selectmen to Confer & settle with Major Starr for the Rent of the Town House & dispose of s^d House to the best advantage	48

28 Feb 1780

Thos Taylor Moderator	49
excused Capt Benjn Hickok from being Comitty man to take Care of the soldiers Familys and Elikim Starr Matthew Barnum David Boughton Ju^r & Jonas Ben[ ] were appointed	49
question was put whither the Town on Condition a Convenient House can be built by subscription for the accommodation of the Town poor they would instruct the Selectmen to appropriate it for them.. past in the affirmative - and Messrs Ezra Starr Daniel Taylor & Comfort Hoyt were appointed a Com^{tee} to assist the Selectmen	49

24 Mar 1780

Samuel Taylor ws chosen Moderator	49
Noble Benedict James Clark John McLean James Seely Bracy Knap Joseph Beebe Noah Hoyt Thos Starr Thos Taylor Saml Sturdevent Caleb Stevens Ju^r Nathan Taylor Ju^r Eli Segar Joseph Barnum Nathl Barnum Eben^r Picket Ju^r Thos Benedict Daniel Wood David Perce Ezra Dibble Ju^r Nathl Sillect Richard Shute & Major Taylor were appointed a Committy of Inspection to inspect Provisions	49

23 Jun 1780

Capt Thomas Stevens was chosen moderator	50
the Town by vote appointed the Commission Officers throughout this Town with Capt Noble Benedict Capt Comfort Hoyt Doct^r John Wood and Capt Daniel Hickok a Committy.. to procure the Towns Quota of Soldiers for the Continental Army both horse and foot	50
by Vote grant a Rate or Tax of /6^d lawful money or Contionental money at 40 for one on the pound on all the poles and ratable Estate.. to defray the Necessary Charges arising.. and Jonah Benedict Daniel Bougton & David Judd were appointed Collectors	50

23 Nov 1780

Capt Thos Stevens chosen Moderator	50
by vote grant a rate or tax of /6^d on all the poles & ratable Estate.. to be paid in Beef Pork & flour - .. & Doct^r John Wood was appointed to receive the same & also the salt and David Perce was appointed to collect what shall be then unpaid	50
Voted that the Commission Officers within this Town be a Com^{tee} to ascertain the Number of men in the Continental Service who count for this Town & Messrs Noble Bened^t Ezra Starr & John Wood are appointed a Com^{tee} to procure the Towns Quota for 3 years or during the war	50
voted that Lieu^t Ezra Dibbles Orders for surveying be accepted by the Collectors	51

11 Dec 1780

Capt Thos Stevens chosen Moderator & Major Taylor Town Clerk	51
Constables, Comfort Hoyt Ju^r to gather the Country Rates John Trowbridge & David Judd	51
Grandjurors - Jonth Hoyt Daniel Shove Ju^r Nathl Barnum Junr	51
Selectmen - Eli Mygatt Thos Taylor Caleb Benedict Benjamin Hickok Benjn Boughton Ju^r Justus Barnum & Danl Wildman	51
Listers - Major Taylor Eliphalet Barnujm Eliakim Starr Saml Cooke Eliasaph Kellogg James Stuart & John Andrews Ju^r	51

Danbury

Tythingmen - Matt^w Boughton Alexand^r Stuart David Boughton Danl Hickok	51
Surveyors - Joshua Benedict Matt^w Gregory David Boughton Ju^r Thad^{us} Morehouse Matt^w Linley Benjn Barber Thos Starr 3^d Theop[ ] Taylor Ju^r Stephen Curtiss Joseph Crofut Joseph Benedict Preserved Taylor James Seely Eph^m Barnum Jonth Benedict Isaac Gray Nathl Starr Jabez Rockwill Daniel Boughton	51
Fence Viewers - Noble Benedict Elijah Hoyt Ezra Dibble Ju^r Daniel Hoyt Saml Benedict 4th Robert Benedict	51
Sealer of Weights - Levi Stone	51
Sealer of Measures - Ezra Dibble Ju^r Thad^{us} Brownson	51
Sealer of Leather - Joseph Benedict	51
Pound Keeper - Jonah Benedict	51
Town Treasurer - Joseph Platt Cook Esqr	51
Selectmen be directed to give up the Effects of Comfort Stevens to Rebekah his Wife - if they judge it to be for the Towns Safety	51
by vote grant a Rate or Tax of /6^d on the pound on all the poles & Ratable Estate.. on the List of 1780 to defray the necessary Charges.. and Enos Hoyt Bracy Knap and James Trowbridge were appointed Collectors	51
Voted that Forward Stevens & Starr Hoyt be entitled to draw 40/ LM p^r month each out of the Town Treasury during their present Captivity	52
Lieu^t Thos Starr be added to ye Com^{tee} appointed to recruit the Army	52
by vote gave Mr David Judd the Towns money stolen out of his Possession being Eleven Pound^s	52
by vote grant Liberty to Mr Justus Barnum to fence the upper burying place he keeping two good Gates or pair of Bars during the Towns pleasure	52
25 Dec 1780	
At an adj^d Town Meeting.. Capt Thos Stevens present	52
by vote grant a Rate or Tax of three pence hard money or old Continental at the Exchange of seventy two for one on the pound.. on the List of 1780.. to recruit the Army - & Elijah Wood Matt^w Starr & Abijah Barnum were appointed Collectors	53
29 Dec 1780	
At an adj^d Town Meeting.. Capt Thos Stevens present	53
Alex^r Stuart was excused from the Office of Tything man & Jared Patchin	53
by vote release Co^l Mygat from the office of a Select man and appoint Capt Noble Benedict in his room	53
5 Feb 1781	
Capt Daniel Taylor Moderator	54
by vote grant a Rate or Tax of one penny half penny in silver on the pound on the List of 1779 to be paid in silver or wheat and Rye Flour & indian Corn.. and Doct^r John Wood is appointed to receive the provisions and Messrs Ezra Dibble Ju^r David Perce & Joseph Beebe Ju^r Collectors to collect what shall then be unpaid and pay the same to the select men to purchase provision	54
Jacob Judd & Joshua Starr Ju^r were appointed Collectors to collect the /3^d hard money Rate	54
Ezra Dibble Ju^r & Joseph Beebe Ju^r were appointed Collectors to collect the provision Rate granted before with David Perce	54

Danbury

Noble Benedict John Wood and Ezra Starr a Committee to procure the Towns Quota of Men for the horseneck service	54
Every person.. who has any stray sheep in possession and shall neglect to bring in the marks to Col^n Eli Mygatt by the first Day of March next shall be liable to loose the keeping and on entering them shall be intitled to receive of the owner 1/ each for his Trouble and 1/ per week after entering till taken away paying the Clerk /6 for his Trouble And if no owner appear by the first of May they are to be delivered to Capt Thos Starr and he is directed to sell them and turn the money into the Town Treasury	54
Daniel Boughton ws excused & Eli Boughton chosen Surveyor of highways	54

15 Feb 1781

Capt Daniel Taylor was chosen Moderator	55
Capt Eph^m Barnum was appointed to Collect the /3^d hard money Rate and Daniel Judd the /6d Rate	55
Question was put wheither the Town will do anything about the Class Money past in the affirmative - & Jonth Hayes Daniel Wood Leu^t Benjn Boughton & Joseph Benedict were appointed a Com^{tee} to look into the matter	55
voted to give Eben^r Benedict 3^d and Joseph Bunnell the same sums of the 40 p^r month for the Term of their service the last Campaign as others had who served	55
by vote appoint Messrs Joseph Wildman Noah Hoyt and Justus Barnum a Com^{tee} to procure a highway by Ens Nathan Gregorys fulling mill to the North River Road by exchanging for part of the Road a Cross the Great Pasture Hill	55
Thad^{us} Dikeman was appointed a surveyor of high[*way*]	55

26 Feb 1781

Capt Daniel Taylor Moderator	55
Voted to allow Eph^m Weed the same wages as others had who served the last Summer	55
Capt Eph^m Barnum was excused and James Trowbridge appointed to collect the three penny R[*ate*]	55
Voted to give Joseph Wildman Jabez Rockwells Note given to the Town	55

11 Apr 1781

Mr James Seely was chosen Moderator	56
appointed the following Gentlemen a Com^{tee} to procure the Cloathing required of this Town for the non Commission Officers and Soldiers the Continental Army viz Messrs Lem^l Benedict John Trowbridge and David Judd	56
by vote grant a Rate or Tax of six pence on the pound.. on the List last Computed to defray the necessary Charges arising.. and Messrs John Trowbridge Danl Wood Ju^r and David Judd were appointed to collect	56
Oliver Benedict appointed to collect the /3^d Rate	56

13 Apr 1781

Mr James Seely Moderator	56
by vote instruct the Select men to agree upon a price for.. Cloathing now to be purchas^d And the Cloathing Committy to give Certificates to the Selectmen for the Articles they buy and .. draw Orders on the Collectors in favour of the persons who have sold.. Mr David Judd was excus^d from being a Committy man and Collector	56
Mr Joseph Benedict appointed a Committy man to procure Cloathing	56

Danbury

Eliakim Benedict appointed to to Collect the Rate last granted	56
Question was put wheither the Town will approve the Memorial of Silas Hamilton and others praying for a highway past in ye aff^e	56
Co^l Cooke was appointed for that purpose	56
Major Taylor James Clark & Elijah Hoyt were appointed a Committee to procure the Towns Quota of men for the State Service	57
by vote release Capt Deforest from paying his /3^d hard Money Rate on account of his being taxed in Ridgfield	57

18 Jun 1781

Co^l Joseph P Cooke chosen Moderator	57

13 Jul 1781

Capt James Clark was chosen moderator	57
by vote grant a Rate or Tax of /4^d lawful silver Money on the pound.. on the List of 1780.. for the purpose of paying the State Troops and other Contingent Charges - And Daniel Com[ ] is appointed to Collect	57

15 Oct 1781

Capt Thom^s Stevens Moderator	58
Comfort Hoyt Ju^r ws appointed a Receiver to receive the Provision and Cloathing of the 2/6 Tax	58
by vote give Liberty to to Lu^t Wm Starr to set up a shop where the old Town house stood	58

17 Dec 1781

Lieu^t James Seely Moderator	58
Major Taylor Town Clerk	58
Constables - Eliphalet Barnum to Collect the State Taxes John Trowbridge & David Judd	58
Grand jurors Jonth Starr Nathan Hoyt & Elip$^{[ ]}$ Ferry	58
Select-Men Major Taylor James Clark Justus Barnum Benjamin Hickok & And^w Comstock	58
Listers Joshua Benedict Eliakim Starr Elisaph Kellogg Jonth Benedict Jacob Judd	58
Tythingmen - Jabez Rockwell Eliasaph Kellogg Elisha Dibble David Perce Thos Starr John Andrews	58
Leather Sealer - Joseph Benedict & Joshua Benedict	58
Horse Brander Daniel Church	58
W^t Sealer - Levi Stone	58
Meas^{re} Sealer Ezra Dibble Ju^r	58
Pound Keeper Jonah Benedict	58
Town Treasurer Col Cooke	58
Fence Viewers { Noble Benedict Elijah Hoyt Jonah Benedict David Wood Robert Benedict Saml Benedict 4th	58

31 Dec 1781

James Seely Moderator	59
James Hayes Jared Patchin Nathl Starr Jonah Stevens Elijah Wood Thad^{us} Barnum Nathan	59

Danbury

Gregory Benj[n] Gorham Judah Barnum Ju[r] Eli Segar Eben[r] Weed Theoph[s] Benedict Ju[r] Nath[l] Gregory Daniel Wood Nath[l] Sillick James Trowbridge Joseph Starr Joseph Dibble Ju[r] Dan[l] Crofut & Silas Taylor were appointed Surveyors of Highways	
by vote grant a Rate or Tax of six pence Lawful Money on the pound.. on the List of 1781.. one half may be paid in wheat Rye Corn or Oats.. and Joseph P Cooke Ju[r] is appointed Collector	59
22 Jan 1782	
M[r] James Seely chosen Moderator	59
Eliakim Benedict was appointed a Collector to collect the Town Rate	59
Voted to give Jakim Benedict 6/ for his Timber on Long Bridge	59
28 Jan 1782	
M[r] James Seely Moderator present	60
by vote grant Liberty to M[r] Eben[r] Munson to set up a house near the upper Burying place.. in such place as Noble Benedict & Benj[n] Barnum shall direct	60
by vote release the fines of Jon[th] Starr Nathan Hoyt & Eliph[t] Ferry	60
by vote appoint M[r] Daniel Church Eben[r] Munson & Isaac Benedict Grandjurors	60
28 Feb 1782	
Cap[t] James Clark chosen Moderator	60
appointed a Com[tee] to procure the Towns Quota of State Troops.. either by paying them in money or giving their obligations in the Towns Behalf viz - Mess[rs] Benj[n] Boughton Ju[r] Noble Benedict Benj[n] Hickok and Dan[l] Wildman	60
6 Mar 1782	
Cap[t] James Clark Moderator	61
Mess[rs] Noble Benedict Daniel Wildman Benj[a] Hickok & Benj[a] Boughton are appointed a Com[tee] to procure the Number of men wanted in the Continental Army	61
11 Mar 1782	
Cap[t] Clark moderator present	61
27 Mar 1782	
M[r] James Seely chosen Moderator	61
Mess[rs] Sam[l] Cooke Eliphalet Barnum James Stuart Eliasaph Kellogg Ju[r] Eliakim Starr & John Andrews Ju[r] are appointed a Com[tee] to make out the several Classes and each one of them to be included in a different Class	61
1 Apr 1782	
James Seely Moderator present	62
Question was put wheither the Town will direct the Selectmen to recommend M[r] David Osborn to the Commanding Officer at the Garison at Stanford to procure a flag to go to Long island to procure an Evidence from Josiah Stebbins late of Ridgfield	62
29 Apr 1782	
M[r] James Sely chosen Moderator	62
the question was put whither this Town will join with the adjoining Towns in prefering a Petition to the Gen[l] Assembly.. praying that this may be a half shire Town - past in the aff[ve] - And Col[n] Joseph Platt Cooke Major Taylor & Saller Pell were appointed a Com[tee] to meet the	62

Danbury

Committys of the adjoining Towns

Messrs James Seeley & Benj^a Hickok were appointed a Com^tee to wait on.. Samuel Staples of Fairfield and confer with him on a Motion he hath made respecting a Donation to the poor Children of this town and if they should think proper to join in a Memorial.. to the Genl Assembly praying that this Town might have the advantage of his propos^d Generosity for which s^d Com^tee are directed to present the Thanks of this Town   62

10 Aug 1782

Mr James Seely moderator   63

by vote appointed Messrs Daniel Taylor Benj^a Hickok & John Trowbridge a Com^tee to meet at Coun[cil] Convention.. to consult on proper measures to be taken to put a stop to the further progress of illicit Trade   63

9 Dec 1782

Mr James Seely chosen Moderator & Major Taylor Clerk   63

Constables - Mr Ezra Dibble Ju^r - & to collect the State Taxes - John Trowbridge & Eliakim Starr   63

Selectmen - Major Taylor James Clark Justus Barnum and Benj^a Hickok   63

Listers - Jon^th Bened^t Jacob Judd Eliakim Bened^t Ju^r Jabez Starr & Peter Hayes   63

Co^l Cooke Town Treasurer   63

Tything - Abner Osborn Wm Sone Hez^h Gray Eleazer Benedict Eben^r Gregory Danl Hickok Joseph Elmer   63

Grandjurors - David Picket Daniel Wood Eben^r Hickok   63

Surveyors of Highways - Thos Judd Ju^r Paul Hamilton And^w Akins Caleb Stevens Ju^r Benj^a Wood Comfort Hoyt Matt^w Gregory Benj^a Barnum John Barnum 3^d Thos Starr 3^d Elnathan Gregory Theop^us Taylor Samuel Benedict 3^d Nathan Whitlock Thad^us Dikeman Saml Benedict 4th David Beebe Moses Neal John Andrus Ju^r Silas Taylor   63

Fence Viewers - Oliver Lawrence Levi Starr Ezra Hubbel Amos Hoyt Robert Benedict Benj^a Platt   63

Leather sealer Joseph Benedict & Joshua Benedict   63

W^t Sealer Levi Stone   63

Horse Brander Daniel Church   63

Measure Sealer Ezra Dibble Ju^r   63

Pound Keeper Jonah Benedict   63

24 Dec 1782

Mr Seely Moderator present   64

Saller Pell Comfort Hoyt Ju^r Daniel Hickok & Noah Hoyt were chosen Grandjurors   64

Justus Barnum was appointed Constable to collect the State Taxes - also David Wood was chosen Constable   64

Nath^n Dunning was chosen Surveyor of highways   64

Noble Benedict & Elijah Hoyt were chosen fence Viewers   64

Eben^r Benedict Ju^r Eli Mygatt Matt^w Starr and Comfort Hoyt Ju^r were chosen Selectmen   64

Voted to give Wm Stone his Note in favour of the Town he paying the Cost that has arisen on acc^t of Comfort Raymond & his family   64

Danbury

30 Dec 1782

Mr Seely moderator present   64

6 May 1783

Capt Thomas Stevens chosen Moderator   65

Question was put whither the Town will do anything respecting those People who have gone off and joined the British Armay or have .. themselves under their pro[*tection*] on Supposition they do or.. should attempt to return.. Voted.. it is the Opinion of this Town not to permit any person or Persons of the above Description ever.. to return or be.. treated as wholesome Inhabitants of this Town - And Major Taylor Maj^r Ezra Starr Capt Richd Shute Capt Ezra Dibble Capt Benj^a Hickok Nathan Taylor Benedict Matt^w Wilkes & Dec^n John Duning were appointed a [*Com^{tee}*] to remove and keep out all such Persons   65

6 May 1783

Capt Noble Benedict & Doct^r Saller Pell were apppointed a Committy to examine.. John McLeans acc^t.. in 1776   65

6 May 1783

John Wood Major Taylor and Ezra Starr were appointed a Committy to nicker with the Committy of the free School   65

22 Sep 1783

Mr James Seely Chosen Moderator   65

The Town taking into Consideration the Distress to which a number of the Inhabitants are reduced by the Burning & plundering of the enemy during the late war.. and the great Injury done the Town.. during the Course of a war undertaken for the defence & Security of the Common Liberties.. in which it was understood & Expected the whole town should bear the Extraordinary Burdens accidentally thrown on any particular part.. and voted that Co^l Joseph P Cooke & Doct^r Saller Pell be agents for the Town for a Memorial in Conjnction with agents of the other Towns.. to Redress of the Towns Grievances.. and for a repair of the Damages done by the Enemy to be made to the individual Sufferers Excepting those Suffereres who are know to be inimical to the Libertys & Independence of the united States of America   65

2 Oct 1783

Capt James Clark Chosen Moderator   66

Comfort Hoyt Junr Chosen Clerk Pro Tem   66

Capt Clark Co^l Mygatt & Capt Shute were appoint^d a Committee to inform our Representatives that it is the Desire of the Town that they use every prudent Constitutional method for the non payment of Commutation   66

29 Dec 1780

by vote did appoint the Selectmen.. to designate the Town into ~~highways~~ Districts for the mending or repairing of the highways.. viz 1st.. beginning at the Brook runing between Mr Caleb Benedict & Mr Wm Porter then running a Cross Shetterock hill.. to that Road that runs from Crambury Bridge to Matthew Crofut Ju^r.. to the Road that runs from Bethel by Mr Jakin Benedict.. to where the Road that comes by Nathan Dibbles.. to the South Corner of Deacon John Dunings Land near Serg^t John Gregory.. to the Road that comes by Daniel Gregory.. and be called by the Name of Stony Hill Beaver Brook District..   68

..begining at the North End of Hays Hill.. onto where the Road that comes by Serg^t John Gregory &.. by Daniel Gregory.. a Cross the Road [ ] Silas Hamilton Ju^r.. into Benj^a 68

Danbury

Boughton Ju^r.. to where the Road parts that goes from Town to Jon^th Hayes.. and be Called by the Name of Great plain District..

..begining at the Brook runing a Cross the Road in Benj^a Boughton Ju^rs Land above Silas   69
Hamilton Ju^r.. runing North to New fairfield Line.. till it comes to the Road that pass by Mr David Pickets.. South to the Brook near Lem^l Linley.. to the Bridge a Cross said River near Mr Daniel Comstocks Land .. to the Brook above Silas Hamilton Ju^r.. & be called by the Name of Pembrook District..

..begining at the North River Bridge runing Northerly up the River till it comes to Mr Linleys   69
Sawmill.. up the little Brook by Lem^l Linleys House.. to the parting of the paths outh of Lockwood Gorhams.. to the parting of the paths South of Wm Combs.. then runing N E thr[ough] Eben^r Gregorys farm at Wigwam to the parting of the Paths [ ] Joseph Barnums near the Continental Pasture.. and be called by the Name of King Street District..

..begining at the parting of the Paths at Seths G[oround] runing to the parting of the Paths   69
South of Lockwood Gorums.. till it comes to a ltitle Brook that runs Easterly of Peter Castle.. Northerly through [ ] Whites & ~~Eben^r~~ Gregorys Swamp till it comes to the bend of the Road between John Gregory and W^o Gregory.. to the parting of the ~~Road~~ Paths at Seth [Gorund].. and be called by the Name of Mill plain bogs District..

..begining at fishware wi[ ] the little Brook that runs Easterly of Peter Castles empties into   69
fishware River.. till the Line turns East [ ] below Caleb Baldwin.. runing Northeasterly to Seth Shoves meadow South of W^m B Brooks.. & be called by the Name of Miry Brook District..

..begining at Sugar hallow Pond .. till it comes East of Mr Whitlocks house then runing   70
Northerly till it comes against the North part of Capt Taylors old field.. & be called by the Name of Starrs plain or Long Ridge District..

..begining at the parting of the paths at the foot of Thos mountain Ridge west of Daniel   70
Shoves.. runing East to the North part of Capt Taylors old field ..till it comes to Matthew Crofut Ju^rs.. to the little brook between Mr Caleb Benedict & Wm Porters.. till it comes to the parting of the paths by Mr Ezra Benedicts.. till it comes to the parting of the paths under Thomas Mountain Ridge.. and be Called by the name of the downtown District..

...beginning at the little brook between Mr Caleb Benedicts & Mr Wm Porters.. at the Crotch   70
of the paths by the north end of Eben^r Gregorys Lot.. to the parting of the path south of Joseph Barnums near the Continental pasture.. to the parting of the paths at Seths G[ ] near Wm Cobs.. South to the bend in the Road between John Gregorys and W^o Esther Gregorys from thence runing through Mr Whites & Gregorys Swamp.. to the parting of the paths at the foot of Thomas Mountain Ridge.. to the parting of the paths by Mr Ezra Benedeicts house.. leaving the Road to Caleb Benedicts till it comes to the brook between Caleb Benedicts and Wm Porters.. and be Called by the Name of the uptown District..

..begining at the meetinghouse.. till it comes to the Road that goes by Capt Beebes.. the Road   71
that goes by Deacon Beebes.. to where the Road that comes by Nathan Dibbles comes into the Road that comes by Jakin Benedicts.. and be called bethel Northern District..

..begining at the South Corner of Deac^n Dunings Land near Serg^t John Gregorys.. to where   71
Newbury Line crosses the Road that comes by Dec^n Beebes.. to be Called Newbury District

we the Subscribers upon the Desire of Saml Nicholds & Abijah Barnum did go to.. Stake out   198
a Highway at the East Swamp.. begin at Benjn Knaps Ba[ ] runing South two rods to Major Eli Mygatts Land and.. runing East to a heap of Stones at the North East corner of.. Mygatts Land leaving a two Rods highway South of Benjamin Knaps Fence then runing.. South to a Beach at the South East corner of.. Mygatts land and from s^d Beach two Rods East to a heap of Stones at Abijah Barnums Land then runing North untill it comes unto Benjamin Knaps Land.. - A true Record of the Original { Comfort Hoyt.. Nathan Gregory Select men.. Major Taylor Register

Derby

Town Meetings
Births Marriages Deaths
1722-1844

Located at the Town Clerk's Office

Derby

11 Dec 1775

Daniel Holbrook Esqr was Chosen Moderator	106
Charles French Esqr was Chosen Town Clerk	106
Col: Jabez Thompson Capt Nathaniel Johnson Capt Nathan Smith John Riggs Jn^r and Isaac Smith was Chosen Select men	106
John David Esqr was ChosenTown Treasurer	106
Edward Howd John Riggs Junr and John Humphry was Chosen Constables	106
John Riggs Ju^r was Chosen to Gether the Country Rate	106
Eben Hinman Abraham Person Ebenezer Durand Sheldon Clark Eben^r Plant Simeon Wheler Jeremiah Johnson Nehemiah Botchford Micah Pool Nathaniel French Abiel Fairchild Web Tomlinson Daniel Tucker Junr Isaac Beacher Caleb Cande Jn^r Levi Hotchkiss Jonathan Lum Jn^r Zachariah Hawkins Abijah Hide Robert Wheler Samuel Smith David Bassit & Noah Russell Lyman was Chosen Surveyors of Highways	106
Capt Joseph Riggs & Capt John Tomlinson Chosen Fence Vewers	106
Daniel Davis Enos Bradly Thomas Yale Abraham Beacher and Isaac Tomlinson Chosen Listers	106
Ephraim Harger & Andrew Smith Chosen Leather Sealers	106
Isaac Johnson Joseph Tomlinson James Perry Ruben Baldwin Benjn Bassit was Chosen Grand Jury men	106
Peter Johnson Levi Tomlinson Samuel Russell and Joseph Osborn Junr Chosen Tything Men	106
David Defoerst and Sheldon Clerk Gagers	106
Jonathan Lumm Nathan Person Abraham Smith Ebenezer Durand and Isaac Bunnel Chosen Packers	106
Abijah Hull & Isaac Bunel Chosen Sealers of Measurs	106
Enos Bradly Chosen Sealer of Weights	106
Zacka^h Hawkins & Nath^{ll} French Chosen Kee keepers	106
Daniel Holbrook Jn^r Dan^{ll} Tucker Jn^r John Tomlinson Samuel Wooster Jn^r Isaac Johnson and Levi Hotchkiss Chosen Branders of Horses	106
the Town.. do Grant a Rate.. to Defray Town Charges.. Eleazer Hawkins Chosen Collector	107
Capt John Holbrook Mr Henry Tomlinson Coll: Jabez Thompson Mr Joseph Picket Capt Thomas Clark Mr Abraham Smith Mr Thomas Yale Mr John Coe Capt Nathan Smith Lieut John Bassit Capt Joseph Riggs Lieut Bradford Steel and Capt Ebenezer Buckingham Charles French Esqr John Davis Esqr Eliphelet Hotchkiss Esqr Capt John Tomlinson Daniel Holbrook Esqr Capt Zackariah Hawkins Sheldon Clark Mr Noah Tomlinson Capt Nathl Johnson Capt Timothy Baldwin Mr John Howd Mr John Humphry Mr John Riggs Junr Mr Ebenezer Keeney Capt Ebenezer Graccey James Beard Esqr Mr Agur Tomlinson Mr Benjn Tomlinson & Saml Wheler Jn^r were Chosen a Committe of Inspection	107

9 Dec 1776

John David Esqr was Chosen Moderator	113
Charles French Esqr Chosen Town Clark	113
Capt Nathan Smith Mr James Beard Abraham Hawkins Isaac Smith and John Riggs Jn^r Choosen [*sic*] Select men	113
John Davis Esqr Chosen Town Treasurer	113

150

Derby

John Riggs Jn^r Edward Howd Oliver Curtis Joseph Riggs Jn^r and Levi Tomlinson Choosen Constables and Levi Tomlinson Chosen to Gether the Country Rate	113
Philo Johnson John Coe Oliver Curtiss Joseph Picket Saml Hull Jn^r Gideon Johnson Ranford Whitney Abiel Fairchild Abraham Beacher Gideon Tucker David Woodruff John Basit Nathan Buckingham Eleazer Lewis Cristepher Smith Isaac Tomlinson Webb Tomlinson Ruben Lumm Josiah Smith William Burit Nehemiah Botchford Saml Wheler Jn^r and Capt Nathan Smith Chosen Surveyrs of Highway	113
Abraham Beacher Thomas Yale Enos Bradly Isaac Tomlinson and Daniel Hoolbrook Jn^r Chosen Listers	113
John Davis & Ashbell Loveland Chose Leather Sealers	113
Cristopher Smith Noah Russel Lyman Abraham Downs Noah Durand ye 2^d Elijah Hotchkiss and Ethiel Perkins Chosen Grand Jurors	113
Freegift Hawkins Eben^r Durand & Nathan Person Chosen Packers	113
Enos Bradly Chosen Sealer of Weights	113
Capt John Tomlinson Andrew Smith Daniel Holbrook Junr and Daniel Tucker Jn^r Chosen Branders of Horses	113
Abijah Hull Chosen Sealer of Measures	113
Nath^ll French Chosen Kee keeper of the Pound	113
the Town.. grant a Rate.. on the List of.. 1776.. David DeForest Chosen Collector of Said Rate	113
Thomas Clark Esqr and Lieut Bradford Steel appointed a Committee to Take Care and Keep the Bridge near Castle Rock in Repare	114
Abraham Hawkins & Sam^ll Hull appointed to take Care & Keep the Bridge Near S^d Hulls House in Repare	114
Capt Joseph Riggs Capt John Tomlinson.. Eben^r Keeney .. Joseph Picket Leiu^t John Basit & Leiu^t Bradford Steel & Leiu^t Daniel Chatfield chosen a Com^{tee} of Inspection	114

10 Feb 1777

John Davis Esqr Chosen Moderator	114
Vaoted.. the Town will Repare the Bridge across Naugatiuck River Near.. Sam^ll Hulls Dwelling House at the Same place where the Bridge Stood that was in past Lately Carried away by an Ice Flood	114
Samuel Hull to be a Committee.. to take Care of and Repare Said Bridge	114

16 Sep 1777

The Persons Hearafter Named have taken the oath of Phidelity as by Law Provided - Viz - the Revd Mr Daniel Humphry, the Revd Mr David Bronson, Charles French Esqr, John Davis Esqr Eliphelet Hotchkiss Esqr James Beard Esqr, Thomas Clark Esqr, Capt John Holbrook, Agur Tomlinson, Joseph Durand, Benjn Tomlinson, Capt Joseph Riggs, Abraham Bassit, David D^{e}Forest, Philo Johnson, John Coe, Daniel Chatfield, Ruben Baldwin, Gideon Johnson Nathan Mansfield, Joseph Pickit, Bradford Steel, Turel Whitemore, Henry Whiteny Abraham Beacher, Enos Bradly, Jonathan Hitchcock, Noah French, Daniel Todd. Joseph Person, Ebenezer Gracy, Nathaniel French, David Person, Samuel French, Joseph Chatfield, ..	120
.. John Howd, David Johnson, John Riggs Junr, Noah Tomlinson, Thomas Yale, Decon Daniel Holbrook, Capt John Tomlinson, Abraham Hawkins, Isaac Smith, Capt Nathaniel Johnson, Capt Nathan Person, Daniel Todd, Levi Tomlinson, Peter Johnson, Webb Tomlinson, Isaac Tomlinson, Doc^r Edward Croft, Eleazer Hawkins, Capt William Clark, Capt Timothy Baldwin, Amos Bassit, Sam^ll Wheler Jn^r Joseph Davis Junr, Jeremiah Johnson,	120

Derby

John Botchford.. Joseph Riggs Junr, Samuel Allen, Ashbel Love Land, Timothy Baldwin Ju^r, Benjamin Basit, John Edee, Elijah Hotchkiss, Asahel Johnson, Abraham Downs, Sam^{ll} Johnson Junr Lieu^t Oliver Curtis, David Hitchcock, Joseph Canfield, Jonathan Lumm, Doct^r Silas Baldwin, Samuel Smith, Ensign John Humphrey, Nathan Person Davis Junr, Capt Nathan Smith, Micah Pool Jehiel Spencer Joseph Canfield Ethiel Perkins John Roe.. Isrel French Junr Hezekiah Johnson Thaddeus Baldwin Joseph Shearwood Capt Joseph Lumm Joseph Wheler Ebene^r Hitchcock Ruben Perkins Samuel Botchford Ju^r Eleazer Lewis Enock Smith Ebenezer Keeney Ebenezer Durand Thomas Yale Henry Tomlinson Isaac Johnson Noah Durand Junr James Pritchard Junr Benjn Carpenter Glad Bartolome Richard Smith Elisha Griffin William Burrit Freegift Hawkins.. Capt Jeremiah Gillitt Josiah Smith Isaac Durand Joseph Johnson Joseph Hawkins Nathan Buckingham Lemuel Lum Ebenezer Basit John Crawford Eben^r Johnson Dan Tomlinson David Tomlinson Nehemiah Botchford Jonathan Lumm Ju^r Daniel Davis Joseph Russell Nathan French John Prindle Abel Person Francis French Zeph^h Tucker Rodert Pope Beman Hale Moses Clark Moses Wheler..

.. Leu^t Edward Howd Gideon Tuttle James Humphry Doctor Elijah Baldwin Abijah Hull Andrew Smith Lewis Hubbel Noah Durand Nathaniel Johnson Moses Riggs Noah Durand 3^d Samuel Tomlinson
8 Apr 1782   *121*

Took the oath of Fidelity.. Charles Whitelsey Jonathan Lyman Saml Person Wm Grinnil Nehe^{ah} Candee Eleazer Wooster John Churchol Edmond Clark Abra^m Smith Jn^r Jonas Tomlinson James Basit Joseph Fairchild Joseph Moss
16 Sep 1777   *121*

the Persons here after Named had the Oath Provided by Law for freemen Administred to them in open Freemens Meeting Viz the Revd Mr Daniel Humphry, the Revd Mr David Bronson, Charles French Esqr, John Davis Esqr Eliphelet Hotchiss Esqr James Beard Esqr, Thomas Clark Esqr, Capt John Holbrok, Agur Tomlinson Joseph Durand, Benjamin Tonlinson, Capt Joseph Riggs, Abraham Basit David D^{e}Forest, Philo Johnson, John Coe, Daniel Chatfield, Ruben Baldwin, Gieon Johnson, Nathan Mansfield, Joseph Picket, Bradford Steel, E. Turel Whitemore, Henry Whitney, Abraham Beacher, Enos Bradly, Jonathan Hitchcock, Noah French, Daniel Todd, Joseph Person, Ebenezer Gracey, Nathaniel French, David Person Sam^{ll} French Joseph Chatfield, John Howd, David Johnson, John Riggs Junr Noah Tomlinson, Thos Yale, Decon Daniel Holbrook Jn^r, Capt Nathaniel Johnson, Abraham Hawkins, Isaac Smith, Capt John Tomlinson Capt Nathan Person, Daniel Todd, Levi Tomlinson, Peter Johnson, Webb Tomlinson, Isaac Tomlinson, Doc^r Edward Croft, Elezer Hawkins Capt William Clark, Capt Tiimothy Baldwin, Amos Bassit, Sam^{ll} Wheler Jn^r Joseph Davis Jn^r Jeremiah Johnson, John Botchford, Joseph Riggs Jn^r Sam^{ll} Alin Ashbel Loveland, Tim^o Baldwin Jn^r, Benjn Bassit John Edee, Elijah Hotchkiss, Asahel Johnson, Abraham Downs, Samuel Johnson Jn^r
13 Apr 1778   *122*

the following Persons Took the Freemans Oath Viz Capt Joseph Lumm William Hine Joseph Loveland Lemuel Lumm Elezer Lewis Enoch Smith Ebenezer Basit John Crawford John Humphry Ranford Whitney Isaac Durand Jehiel Spencer Capt Nathan Smith Thadeus Hine Ebenezer Johnson Glad Bartholomue Samuel Russell Joseph Tomlinson Nathan Buckingham Zachariah Fairchild Nathan Mansfield Freegift Hawkins Edward Howd Joseph Bassit Eleazer Hawkins Eli Hawkins Levi Hotchkiss Dan Tomlinson David Tomlinson Eben Hinman Joseph Shearwood Nehemiah Botchford Saml Hull Jn^r David Hitchcock Noah French Jonathan Lumm Jn^r Elijah Davis David Basit Ruben Perkins Thomas Horsey Joseph Canfield Silas Baldwin Abijah Hull Andrew Smith James Humphry Lewis Hubbel Nathl *122*

Derby

Johnson Moses Riggs Saml Wheler Robert Wheler Andrew Smith Beman Hale Philo Holbrook
8 Apr 1782

the following Persons took the freemans oath Charles Whitelsey Jon^n Lyman Saml Person Wm Grinnel Nehemiah Candee Eleazer Wooster John Churchel Edman Clark Abraham Smith Jn^r Jonah Tomlinson James Basit	*122*

8 Dec 1777

John Davis Esqr Chosen Moderator	*124*
Charles French Esqr Chosen Town Clerk	*124*
Select Men } Abraham Beacher James Beard Esqr Abraham Hawkins Capt Nathan Smith and Ens^n John Humphry	*124*
John Coe David D^{e}Forest & Capt Thomas Clark Chosen a Com^{tte} to Take Care of the Famelies of the Soldiers in the Army	*124*
John Davis Esqr Chosen Town Treasurer	*124*
Levi Tomlinson Joseph Riggs Junr David Person Timothy Baldwin Junr & Edward Howd Chosen Constables.. and Said David Person Chosen to Gether the Country Rate	*124*
Joseph Person Joseph Wheler Abraham Smith Philo Johnson John Edee Eliphelet Hotchkiss Esqr Saml Wheler Junr Abraham Beacher Noah Russell Lyman David Johnson Ruben Perkins Cristepher Smith Caleb Candee Jeremiah Durand Saml Russell Micah Pool David Woodruff Thomas Horsey Elezer Hawkins Dan Tomlinson Elisha Griffin & Richard Smith Chosen Surveyers of Highways	*124*
Capt Joseph Riggs and Capt John Tomlinson Chosen Fence Vewers	*124*
Thaddus Baldwin Ruben Baldwin Ebenezer Riggs Juner Micah Pool Ethiel Perkins & Josiah Smith Chosen Listers	*124*
Ashbel Loveland Edward Howd & John Davis Esqr Chosen Leather Sealers	*124*
Jonathan Hitchcock Benjn Bassit Daniel Tood Saml Russell and Daniel Chatfield Chosen Grandjurors	*124*
John Humphry Noah Russell Lyman John Goodshall Jonathan Lumm Jn^r & Josiah Smith Chosen Tything Men	*124*
Abraham Smith & & Ebenezer Durand Chosen Packers	*124*
Capt John Tomlinson Daniel Holbrook Jn^r Sam^{ll} Russell and Isaac Johnson Chosen Branders of Horses	*124*
Enos Bradly Chosen Sealer of Weights	*124*
Abraham Smith Chosen Sealer of Measures	*124*
Abraham Smith Chosen School Committee in the Room of Eliphlet Hotchkiss	*124*
Nathaniel French Chosen Kee Keeper	*125*
Capt Joseph Riggs Thomas Yale Ebenezer Keeney Joseph Picket Bradford Steel John Bassitt and Daniel Chatfield Chosen a Com^{tee} of Inspection	*125*
Town by their Voate Grant a Rate or Tax of three pence ~~on the~~ Lawfull Money on the pound on the List of the Yeat 1777 to Defray Town Charges.. Ruben Baldwin Chosen Collector	*125*
Town by their Voate Grant Liberty to Capt John Holbrook & Mr Henry Tomlinson to Erect and Build a Pound Near the School House on the Great Hill.. on their own Cost.. Eleazer Lewis Chosen to be Kee keeper	*125*

Derby

14 Dec 1778

James Beard Esqr was Chosen Moderator	126
Charles French Esqr Chosen Town Clerk	126
Select Men } Abraham Hawkins, Capt Nathan Smith, James Beard Esqr Ensign John Humphry & Abraham Beacher	126
Town Treasrer } John Davis Esqr	126
Constables } Levi Tomlinson Davis Person Joseph Loveland Thadus Baldwin and Josiah Smith Chosen Constable all Sworn but Said Thadeus Baldwin.. Said Joseph Loveland Chosen to Colect the Country Rate	126
Survaers of Highways } Capt Ebenezer Gracey Enos Bradly Joseph Loveland Stephen Whitney Ashbel Loveland William Burrit Noah Durand Jn^r Dan Tomlinson Elezer Lewis Zachariah Fairchild Jonathan Lumm Jn^r Ethiel Perkins John Basit Isaac Beacher Daniel Davis Ebenezer Plant Joseph Riggs 3^d Gideon Tuttle Ebenezer Buckingham & Ruben Tucker	126
Fence Vewers / Capt John Tomlinson & Capt Joseph Riggs	126
Listers } Eliphalet Hotchkiss & Thomas Clark Esqr Capt John Holbrook Daniel Holbrook Jn^r John Howd James Beard Esqr and Bradford Steel	126
Leather Sealers } John Davis Esqr & John Howd & both Sworn	126
Surveyors of [*Shoes*] } John Davis Esqr and Capt Nathan Smith & Ashbel Loveland	126
Grandjurors } Isaac Smith David Woodruff Daniel Todd Abraham Person & Gideon Johnson	126
Tything Men } Eben Hinman David Bassit Robert Wheler Isaac Beacher and Zachariah Fairchild	126
Packers / Eben^r Durand Freegift Hawkins and Nathan Person	126
Branders of Horses } Capt John Tomlinson Decon Daniel Holbrook Jn^r Daniel Tucker Jn^r & Isaac Johnson	126
Sealer of Weights / Enos Bradly	127
Sealer of Measurs / Abraham Smith	127
Kee keeper / Nathaniel French	127
Com^{tte} to take Care of ye Soldiers Cloathing } Sam^{ll} Hull David D^{e}Forest Abraham Becher Capt John Tomlinson Capt Timothy Baldwin Nathan Buckingham Capt John Riggs Leiu^t Samuel Wheler Saml Bassit Danl Holbrook Jn^r Capt Joseph Riggs Isaac Smith Ruben Tucker Eben^r Gracey Capt Nathl Johnson Jo^s Russell Elip^t Hotchkiss Esqr Noah Tonlinson Thomas Clark Esqr John Howd & Capt John Holbrook	127
Com^{tee} to Provid Cloathing for the Soldiers } Joseph Chatfield Edward Howd Daniel Chatfield and Samuel Russell & Thadeus Baldwin	127

28 Dec 1778

Town by their Voate Grant a Rate of one Shilling and Nine pence Lawfull Money on the Pound on the Grand List of the Year 1778 to pay the Bounty Granted to the Soldiers and to Defray Town Charges.. Mr Micah Pool Chosen to Collect Said Rate	127
Ensign John Humphry appointed to Recive the money Granted to the Soldiers and to pay out the Same	127
Leiu^t Bradford Steel appointed to take Care of the Bridg at ye falls	127
Capt Joseph Riggs Capt John Tonlinson & Leiu^t Steel appointed a Com^{tee} to make Such olterations in in the School Districts.. as they Judge Needfull	127

Derby

13 Dec 1779

James Beard Esqr Chosen Moderator	131
Charles French Esqr Chosen Town Clerk	131
Abraham Hawkins James Beard Esqr John Humphrys Abraham and Henry Tomlinson Chosen Select Men	131
John Davis Esqr Chosen Town Treasurer	131
Capt Joseph Loveland Ebenezer Plant Samuel Hull Jn^r David Tomlinson Abraham Beecher and Levi Hotchkiss Chosen Constables.. Said Abraham Beecher Chosen to Collect the Country Rate	131
Surveyors of Highways } Joseph Chatfield Ruben Baldwin John Coe Nathan Davis Jn^r Ruben Tucker Eben^r T Whitmore Elijah Davis Bowers Washbond Moses Wheler Wil^m Burrit Joseph Smith Ruben Lumm Abra^m Bassit Jn^r Webb Tomlinson Cristepher Smith Bradford Steel Ebenezer Johnson Abial Canfield Isaac Beecher Nathan Fairchild David Woodruff Samuel Candee and Ethiel Perkins	131
Fence Vewers - Capt John Tomlinson & Capt Joseph Riggs	131
Listers } DanTomlinson Joseph Riggs Jn^r David D^{e}Forest David Person Saml Russell all Sworn by Esqr Hotchkiss	131
Leather Sealers } John Davis Esqr & Capt Joseph Loveland	131
Grandjurors / Eben Henman Ruben Perkins David Basit David Woodruff & Nathan Buckingham	131
Tything Men } Joseph Pees Cristepher Smith Isaac Durand and Joseph Riggs the 3^d	131
Packer / Freegift Hawkins & Eben^r Durand	131
Branders of Horses } Capt Daniel Holbrook Capt John Tomlinson and Capt John Riggs	131
Sealer of Weights / Enos Bradly	132
Sealer of Measures / Abraham Smith	132
Kee keeper / Nathaniel French	132
Comite for Soldiers } Benjamin Bassit Isaac Smith Capt Timothy Baldwin Joseph Chatfield Amos Basit Agur Tomlinson Capt John Tomlinson Eli Hawkins Abiel Fairchild Jn^r Robert Wheler Jonathan Lumm Jn^r Saml Basit Moses Wheler Joseph Wheler Capt Bradford Steel James Pritchard Saml Hull Capt Daniel Holbrook Noah Tomlinson John Coe Nathan Buckingham Isaac Beecher Abraham Basit Capt John Riggs and Joseph Russell	132
Commitee for Cloathing for the Soldiers } Mr Ebenezer Keeney Capt John Holbrook David Person Capt Nathaniel Johnson and Mr Isaac Johnson	132
School Committee / Levi Tomlinson	132
Bridge Com^{tee} / Capt Bradford Steel & Samuel Hull	132
by their Voate Grant a Rate of Six Shillings Lawfull Money on the Pound on the List of the year 1778 Mr Ebenezer Keeney Chosen Collector	132
Voated that James Humphry & Michal Clark which Came from the Enemy be Permitted to Stay.. under the Care of the Select men	132
Lieu^t Isaac Smith be a Commi^{tee} in addition to Capt John Tomlinson & James Beard Esqr to Exchange Highways for Highways and alter Highways	132
Considering the Distance that a Considerable Number of the Inhabitants of the 4th and 5th Districts Live from the Scenter of Said Districts.. we.. whose Names are under written Desire to be Set off to be an entire District.. Joseph Davis Joseph Davis Abraham Bassit Saml Smith	133

155

Derby

Jn^r David Person John Davis John Church Isaac Beecher Abraham Beecher Ebenezer Riggs John Riggs Bradford Steel } Comm^{te}.. ..Begining at the Stone Bridge at the Lower end of.. Abraham Basits Little River Meadow.. Runing East to the Top of the Hill South of Said Basits, then runing North with the High way to Capt Joseph Davises.. Runing East to the High way that runs West of Tobies rock.. North to the Head of the Bounds between Derby & Waterbury Including W^d Abigail Gunns farm.. West with the Line to Waterbury Road.. South with the Road Down to Mr Miles Barn.. west to Touantick brook.. South with the Brook to the Bridge over S^d Brook Southeast of David Twitchels.. Southerly Down to the Roade to the firrst mentioned Bounds Including wid^w Ruth Bunnell Pased in the Affirmative *27 Dec 1779*	*133*
Thomas Yale Chosen Constable	*134*
Elijah Davis Chosen Grand Juryman	*134*
Doctor Elijah Baldwin Chosen Constable	*134*
Timothy Baldwin Jn^r appointed a Com^{tte} for Soldiers Famelys	*134*
We.. whose Names are under written Desire the Town.. permitt us to be formed into a School District.. begining at the mouth of Hassekee Meadow Brook runing Northerly by Naugatuck River till it Comes to the upper end of Long plain.. Westerly to the North Side of the Park.. Southerly to the west Side of John Botchfords farm.. Southerly to.. Joseph Canfields Barn.. Southerly to the Highway Twenty Rods North of Nehemiah Botchfords House then Runing with the High way to Hassekee Meadow Brook.. to the first mentioned Corner.. Bradford Steel.. Ashbell Steel.. Hezekiah Woodin.. Ruben Perkins.. Ranford Whitney.. Lowis Riggs.. John Wooster.. Eunis Pritchard.. James Pritchard Jn^r.. Samuel Wooster.. Wm Gordin.. John Botchford.. Edward Harger.. Josiah Washbond.. Abra^m Wooster.. Daniel Davis.. Benjn Davis.. Eben^r Keeney.. Wm Keeney.. Theo^{us} Miles.. Jona^n Miles.. John Riggs.. John Tomlinson } Com^{tee} Pased in the Affirmative *8 Mar 1780*	*134*
Eliphelet Hotchkiss Esqr Chosen Moderator	*135*
Capt John Tomlinson, Capt Daniel Holbrook, Mr Ruben Baldwin Capt Bradford Steel, Capt Nathan Person, Lieu^t Joseph Riggs, Mr Josiah Smith, Mr Turel Whitemore Mr Gideon Johnson Mr Agur Tomlinson Lieu^t John Basit Webb Tomlinson Abiel Fairchild Jn^r Mr Samuel Basit, Capt Daniel Chatfield, Capt John Riggs, Lieu^t Levi ~~Tomlinson~~ Hotchkiss Ethiel Perkins Capt Henry Whitney Leu^t Abraham Smith and David Tomlinson was Chosen Inspectors of Provisions	*135*
by their Voate appoint Capt Bradford Steel and Mr Gideon Johnson a Committee.. to take Care of the Indians Lands.. and Let out the Same.. for the Support of Said Indians	*135*
Abraham Hawkins James Beard Esqr Mr John Humphry Capt Nathan Person Mr Noah Tomlinson Maj^r Nathan Smith David Tomlinson Leiu^t Levi Hotchkiss Walter Wooster and Ebenezer Warner be a Committe to Assist the Officers of the Several Companies in the Town.. in Raising there Cota of Men.. for the Contental and State Service	*135*
by their Voate grant a Rate of Two Shillings Lawfull Money on the Pound on the List of the year 1779 again Mr Ebenezer Keeney Chosen Collector	*135*
Abial Fairchild Junr Chosen a Com^{tee} man in addition to the former Com^{tee} to Provid Cloathing for the Soldiers *27 Jun 1780*	*135*
Abraham Hawkins Chose Moderator	*137*

Derby

3 Jul 1780

by their Voate Grant a Rate of Six pence Lawfull Money on the pound on the List of the year 1779 to pay the Bounty to the Contenental Soldiers and to Defray Town Charges.. Mr Joseph Wheler Chosen Collector	137
Capt John Riggs Capt Daniel Holbrook & Capt Bradford Steel are appointed a Com^{tee} to Inlist Contental Soldiers and to pay them their Bounty	137
The Following Persons Names have taken the Oath of Phidelity (Viz) Ruben Davis Dan^{ll} Holbrook Medad Cande William Mansfield David Smith Samuel Wheler J^r	138

13 Nov 1780

Eliphelet Hotchkiss Esqr Chosen Moderator	139
by their Voate appointed Eliph^t Hotchkiss Esqr to Receive the States Salt and to Receive & put up the Provisions for the Army	139
by their Voate Grant a Rate of Six pence half penny on the Pound in good pork Beaf & Wheat Flower on the List 1779 Beaf of the best Quality to be Computed at /5 p^r Pound and that of an inferior Quality being good & Marchantable at 4½ p$^{r\,[lb]}$ the pork not Exceeding five Score p^r Hog at /5 p^r lb] & between five & Eight Score /5½ and that above Eight Score at /6 p^r [lb] and the Flower at 24 /p^r Hundred Grose Wieght.. .. Amos Basit Chosen Collector	139
by their Vote appoint Mr Jonathan Hitchcoct Capt Thos Clark Capt Micah Pool Mr John Howd Capt John Tomlinson Mr Jonathan Lum Jn^r & Liu^t John Bassit a Com^{tee} to Class the People.. for filling up & Compleating the States Cuotes of the Contenantal Army	139

11 Dec 1780

James Beard Esqr Chosen Moderator	140
Charles French Chosen Town Clerk	140
Mr Abraham Hawkins James Beard Esqr Mr John Humphry Mr Abraham Beecher & Capt Micah Pool Chosen Select Men	140
John Davis Esqr Chosen Town Treasurer	140
Mr Thomas Yale Mr Abraham Beecher Ebenezer Plant Elijah Baldwin and David Tomlinson Chose Constables.. Said Yale & Beecher Sworn.. Thomas Yale Chosen Colector the Country Rate	140
Peter Johnson Joseph Shearwood Glad Bartholomew Jabez Thompson Moses Wheler Joseph Hawkins Nehemiah Botchford Samuel Basit Webb Tomlinson Eli Hawkins Josiah Strong Naboth Osbon Isaac Beecher Nathan Person Nathan Fairchild Samuel Russel Gideon Cande Hezekiah Johnson Capt John Riggs Isaac Smith Ebenezer Warner & John Basit Chosen Survyers of Highway	140
Capt Joseph Riggs & Capt John Tomlinson Fence Vewers	140
Leiu^t Joseph Riggs Mr David Deforest Samuel Russell David Person & Dan Tomlinson Chose Listers.. & all Sworn by Esqr Hotchkiss	140
John Davis Esqr Ashbel Loveland & Gideon Cande Chose Leather Sealers	140
Elijah Davis Ruben Perkins and Zachariah Fairchild Chosen Grand Jury men	140
Levi Hotchkis Joseph Washbond Samuel Basit Noah Tomlinson & William Burrit Chosen Tything Men	140
Freegift Hawkins Nathan Person & Ebenezer Durand Chosen Packer	140
Capt Daniel Holbrook Capt John Tomlinson and Capt John Riggs Chosen Branders of Horses	140
Enos Bradly Chosen a Sealer of Weights	141

Derby

Abraham Smith Chosen a Sealer of Measurs	141
Nathan French Chosen a Kee keeper	141
Josiah Smith Chosen a School Com^{tee} man in the Room of Edward Howd	141
the Comittee to take Care of the Soldiers Famelies } Peter Johnson Joseph Russell Thadeus Baldwin Daniel Holbrook Isaac Smith Benjn Basit, Jabez Thompson Cristepher Smith Andrew Smith Jonathan Lum Jn^r John Basit, Josiah Strong, Robert Wheler, Isaac Beecher, Ebenezer Johnson Abiel Fairchild Jn^r, and Noah Tomlinson	141
the Inspecting Committee of Provisions Daniel Holbrook, Joseph Pickit, Li^t Jos: Riggs John Tomlinson Levi Hotchkiss Levi Tomlinson David Tomlinson Ruben Baldwin Abra^m Smith Turel Whitemore Bradford Steel Gideon Johnson Abra^m Downs Webb Tomlinson Eben^r Plant and Peter Johnson	141

25 Dec 1780

Voted that the following Persons be Collectors.. to Collect the Rates & Assessments in Each Class to Raise Recrutes for the Contenental Army Viz: for the first Class David Hitchcock , for the 2^d Class Glad Bartholeme, 3^d Class John Howd, 4th Class, Levi Tomlinson 5th Class Dan Tomlinson 6th Class Bradford Steel 7th Class Webb Tomlinson 8th Jonathan Lum Jn^r 9th Abraham Downs 10th Ebenezer Plant 11th Robert Wheler 12th Naboth Candee	141
Joseph Wheler Chose a Com^{tee} Man in addition to the Last Years Commite for Cloathing	141
Charles French James Beard Thomas Clark Esq^{rs} and Capt Micah Pool appointed a Com^{tee} to Class the People	141

8 Jan 1781

by their Voate Grant a Rate or tax of one peney half peney on the Pound on the List 1779 to be paid in Flowers and Indian Corn - Elip^t Hotchkiss Esqr Chosen to Receive Provisions	142
Amos Basit Chosen Collector of Tax	142
Capt Eben^r Buckingham Chosen Colector of the 11th Class in the Room of Robert Wheler and Said Wheler to be Dismissed	142

15 Jan 1781

Voted that the Town will Class the Inhabitants into 41 Classes.. to Procure Cloathing for the Soldiers.. Elip^t Hotchkiss Esqr appointed to Class the Town into 41 Classes	142
by their Vote Grant a Rate or Tax of Two pence in hard money or an Equevilent in other money on the Pound on the List of the year 1780.. Isaac Smith Chosen Collector	142
Voated that the.. Select Men be Impowered.. to give Certificates to Capt Daniel Holbrook and Capt John Wooster to free and Emancipate their Servants Negro Men on the Condition that the Said Negro men Inlist into the State Reg^t to be Raised for the Defence of this State for.. one year	142
Voted that Charles French Thomas Clark Esq^{rs} and Capt Micah Pool be appointed a Com^{tee}.. to Doom Such Inhabitants that have not paid the full of the 6½ Tax in Provision.. and take out Warrants for Said Collector who is to Collect the Same.. and to abate Such of the Inhabitants which they Shall Judge to be unable to pay the Said Provisions or an Equivelent in Value.. for the Relief of the Needy and Indegent Inhabitants	142

2 Apr 1781

Thomas Clark Esqr Chosen Moderator	144
John Humphry Chosen Town Clerk	144
Voated that Amos Basit be appointed a Collector for the furfeture of the Neglecting Classes	144
Voted that Each Class.. be Notified of Such Persons as are Classed for the Purpose afore	144

Derby

Said.. and the number of Cloathing and when Notified they are to Furnish and Procure the.. Cloathing Required of them.. and in Case any Class or any Individuable of Either Clas Shall Neglect or Refuse.. they Shall be.. Doomed to Pay Double.. in Gold or Silver.. Which forfiture from each Neglecting Clas Shall be Dlievered to Mr John Howd Treasurer
10 Dec 1781

John David Esqr Chosen Moderator	145
Charles French Esqr Chosen Town Clerk	145
Select Men } Abraham Hawkins James Beard Esqr John Humphrys Capt Abraham Basit & Capt Micah Pool	145
Town Treasurer - John Davis Esqr	145
Constables } Mr Thomas Yale Mr David Hitchcock Mr Abraham Beecher, Ebenezer Plant and Mr Philo Holbrook.. Mr Thomas Yale Chosen to Gether the Country Rate	145
Surveyrs of High Ways } Joseph Chatfield Henry Whitney Levi Hotchkiss Saml Hull, Joseph Person, Joseph Sherwood Ashbel Loveland Moses Clark, Ranford Whitney Isaac Beecher Abraham Beecher Sam^{ll} Candee Nathan French Robert Wheler Naboth Osborn Josiah Strong John Basit Jonathan Lumm Jn^r Micah Pool Joseph Basit Isaac Smith and David Canfield	145
Fence Vewers } Capt Joseph Riggs & Capt John Tomlinson	145
Listers } David D^{e}Forest Joseph Riggs Jn^r David Person Sam^{ll} Russell and Dan Tomlinson } all Sworn Except Russel	145
Lather Sealers } John Davis Esqr Capt Joseph Loveland	145
Grand Jurors } Edward Howd Jeremiah Johnson Levi Hotchkiss and Samuel Basit	145
Tything Men } Eleazer Lewis Thadeus Baldwin William Burrit and Daniel Tucker Jn^r	145
Sealer of Weights - Enos Bradly	145
Sealer of Measurs - Abraham Smith	145
Gagers - David Deforest	145
Packers } Abraham Smith Freegift Hawkins Eben^r Durand Philo Holbrook & Noah Russel Lyman	145
Branders of Horses } John Tomlinson Daniel Holbrook Capt John Riggs Andrew Smith and Hezekiah Woodin	145
Kee Keeper } John Howd & Josiah Strong	145

31 Dec 1781

Select Men are ~~Directed~~ Desired to give to the Revd Mr Daniel Humphrys a Certificate or Liberty to Manumit His Servants Cambridge & Cate his Wife & past	146
Capt Ebenezer Gracey and the Rest of the Inhabitants of the first District for Schooling have Liberty to Build a Shool House on the New Highway that Leads from Stephenses ferry Down to Milford	146
Voated that on Reconsideration Mr David Hitchcock is Chosen to Collect the Country Rate in the Room of Mr Thomas Yale	146
Voated that Capt Bradford Steel be A Committee to keep the Upper Bridge in Repare	146
Voated that Mr Samuel Hull be a Committee to keep the Lower Bridge in Repare	146

28 Jan 1782

by Voate Grant a Rate of two Pence Lawfull Money on the Pound on the List of the year 1781 to Defray Town Charges.. Chosen Nethaniel Collector of the above Rate for the Old Society up to Oxford Line	147

159

Derby

Abiel Fairchild Chosen Colector of the above Rate for Oxford to the old Line of Said Society	147
Capt Abraham Bassit and and his Neighbours have Liberty to Erect and keep in Repare a pound on Shefurt Tree Hill.. in Oxford Society.. Capt Abraham Basit Chosen Kee keeper of said Pound	147
Ruben Baldwin and John Coe Chosen Grand Jurors	147
Beers Tomlinson Chosen Constable	147

25 Feb 1782

Eliphalet Hotchkiss Esqr Chosen Moderator	147
Voted that the Town.. be Classed into Seven Classes to Raise Seven Men to be State Gard for the Post at Horse Neck and Stanford.. Eliphalet Hotchkiss Esqr be appointed.. a Committee to Class the Town.. into Seven Classes for the Purpose of Raising Seven State Gard as above S^d.. Eliphelet Hotchkiss Esqr is appointed a Superintending Committee over Said Classe	147

11 Mar 1782

Voated that a Two Peney Rate on the Pound one [sic] the List 1781.. to be paid in Lawfull Money or in Wheat.. Rye.. Indian Corn.. for the Payment of the Bounties of the Recruits Required to be Raised.. to fill up Said Towns Cota of the Contenental Line in the Contental Army for the year 1782.. Capt Nethaniel Johnson be a Collector of the Said Tax in the old Society and a Committee to Hire the Soldiers and Capt Daniel Holbrook Likewise to be a Committee for Said Soldiers	148
George Beard Chosen Collector of the above Said Tax in the Great Hill Society and Committe for Said Soldiers and Capt Micah Pool be a Com^{tee} Likewise for Said Soldiers	148
Abraham Beecher Chosen Collector of Said Tax in Oxford Society and a Commitee to hire Said Soldiers, Capt Ebenezer Riggs Likewise Chosen a Committe to Hire Said Soldiers	148

14 Mar 1782

Mr Ebenezer Plant appointed Colector of the Town Rate in the Parish of Oxford Laid for Procuring Soldiers for the Contental Army	148
Mr Gideon Tucker Chosen Collector of the Town Rate.. in the Room Abiel Fairchild	148

9 Dec 1782

Eliphet Hotchkiss Esqr Chosen Moderator	167
Charles French Chosen Town Clerk	167
John Davis Esqr Chosen.. Town Treasurer	167
Select Men } John Humphry Mical Pool Abraham Bassit John Howd and Samuel Hull	167
Constables } Thomas Yale David Hitchcock David Tomlinson Josiah Strong and Philo Holbrook	167
Surveyors of High Ways } Capt Nathaniel Johnson Jeremiah Gillit Abraham Smith Elezer Durand Eleazer Hawkins George Beard John Holbrook Jn^r Isaac Tomlinson Abel Hull Theophiles Miles Ranford Whitney John Crawford Abiel Fairchild John Church Joseph Fairchild Thad^s Baldwin Eliphet Wooster Ruben Tucker Ebenezer Plant Justice Candee Dan Tomlinson James Perry Benjn Davis Nathan Smith	167
Fence Vewers } Capt Joseph Riggs Capt John Tomlinson	167
Listers } M^{ss} Joseph Riggs David Person Samuel Russell Noah Russell Lyman Joseph Hawkins Capt Thomas Horsey in the Room of Joseph Riggs	167
Capt Isaac Smith Capt Daniel Holbrook Capt John Tomlinson appointed a Com^{tee} to view the Circumstances of the High way from Woodby to Derby by the Great Island in Naugatuck	167

Derby

River
16 Dec 1782

Capt Danl Holbrook Chose Select man in the Room of John Humphry	167
Grand Jurors } Capt Bradford Steel Capt John Tomlinson Capt John Riggs Major Nathan Smith & Mr Benjamin	167

23 Dec 1782

Tything Men } Caleb Candee Zacheriah Fairchild Ruben Baldwin Isaac Elott Marshall Jos Davis Jn^r and Benjamin Twichel	168
Leather Sealers } Capt Joseph Loveland Mr Andrew Smith and Edwar in the Roon [sic] of Esqr Davis	168
Packers /Abraham Smith Abram Smith Eben^r Durand & Saml Tucker Jn^r	168
Branders of Horses } Capt John Tomlinson Capt Daniel Holbrook Daniel Tucker Junr and George Beard	168
Listers } Levi Hotchkis & Thomas Farmer	168
Sealer of Weights / Enos Bradly	168
Sealer of Mesures } Abraham Smith	168
Keepers } Capt Zachh Hawkins John Howd & Capt Abraham Bassit	168
Constables } Naboth Osborn in the Room of Josiah Strong Elezer Lewis in the Room of Philo Hobrook	168
Grand Jurors } Philo Johnson and Charles Whitellsey	168
Town Rate / Voated a Rate of 2^d Lawfull Money on the Pound on the List of the year AD 1782.. Eli Hawkins Chosen Collector	168
Considering the Great Expense.. in Building and Supporting two Large Bridges acros Naugatuck river.. and Said Bridge Now wants to be ReBuilt also a New High way from Woodbury to Derby by Housatunack River all which.. will amount to five Hundred.. Pounds this in addition to the other Burdains Lying on S^d Town in Supporting High ways & other Public Burdens the Town feels thems Selves very unable to bare thereon Voated that Capt Thomas Clark & Capt Daniel Holbrook be appointed.. to Petition the General Assembly for Liberty to Set up a Lottery for.. five Hundred Pounds for the Purpose of Building Said Bridges & making Said High ways	168

20 Jan 1783

Listers } Mr Philo Holbrook Mr Josiah Strong	169
Grand Jurors } Mr Gideon Johnson Mr Joseph Riggs the rd	169
Lifers [sic] [ed: listers] Capt Thomas Horsey Mr Levi Hotchkis Mr Philo Holbrook & Mr Josiah Strong. the oath administerd by Eliphelet Hotchkis Esqr	169

17 Feb 1783

Capt Daniel Holbrook Chosen Moderator	169

24 Feb 1783

Voated that the Town will appoint the Managers of the Lotery Granted by the General Assembly.. by their Voat appoint Mr Samuel Hull to be one of the Managers of Said Lotery	169
Chose Capt Daniel Holbrook another of the Managers of Said Lotery	169
Mr David Deforest was Chosen the other of Said Managers of Said Lotery	169

Derby

by their Voat appoint Mr Ashbel Loveland a Committee to over See and Build a Bridge over Naugatuck River in Derby below the falls	169
Mr Samuel Hull was.. appointed a Committee to over See and Build a Bridge over Naugatuck River where the old Bridge now Stands Called the Lower Bridge	169
Capt Zecheriah Hawkins is appointed a Committee to over See and Make a New Highway from Woodbury to Derby by Howsotunak River	169

18 Mar 1783

James Beard Esqr Chosen Moderator	170
Mr John Humphrys Chosen a Maneger of the Lottery	170
Lieu^t Joseph Riggs chosen A Nother of Said manegers	170

Durham

Town Records
1769 – 1835

Located at the Town Clerk's Office

Durham

17 Nov 1774

Moderator [ed: in meeting at which Committee to observe the Conduct of all Persons in this Town is chosen]	8
Col° Chauncey Col° Wadsworth.. Daniel Hall Capt Israel Camp &.. John Newton be a Com^{tee} to observe the Conduct of all Persons	8
Phinehas Spelman Elnathan Camp Samuel Camp & Elias Camp be a Com^{tee} to receive.. Contributions.. to be sent to the Overseers of the Poor.. of Boston	8

12 Dec 1775

Col° Chauncey was chosen Moderator	10
Col° James Wadsworth Ju^r was chosen Town Clerk	10
Col° Elihu Chauncey Col° James Wadsworth Ju^r & Capt Ebenezer Garnsey were chosen Select Men	10
Benjamin Picket and Samuel Camp were chosen Constables.. also voted that Samuel Camp be Collector of the Colony Tax	10
Simeon Parsons Ju^r & Joseph Chidsey were chosen Grandjurors	10
Phinehas Spelman was chosen Town Treasurer & Collector of the Town Rate	10
John Curtiss was chosen Collector of the Minister's Rate	10
Abr^m Scrantom Ju^r was chosen Collector of the School Rate	10
Daniel Wright Lemuel Garnsey Sam^{ll} Sutlief Ashur Robinson Levi Parmele John Crane & Thos Lyman were chosen Surveyors of Highways	10
Abraham Bartlet Elnathan Camp Abraham Scrantom Ebenezer Tibbals & Abial Baldwin were chosen Listers & Ratemakers	10
Ambrose Field Henry Crane Sam^{ll} Bates & Charles Norton were chosen Tythingmen	10
Bryan Rosseter & Joseph Hull were chosen Fenceviewers	10
Capt Garnsey was chosen Sealer of Leather	10
Abial Baldwin was chosen Sealer of Weights	10
Capt Curtiss was chosen Sealer of Measures	10
Elnathan Camp was chosen Gauger	10
Danll Hall ye 3^d was chosen Keykeeper	10
John Johnson Ju^r John Jones Thos Cook John Coe Ju^r Eli Crane Timothy Coe Ithamar Parsons Ju^r & Phin^s Canfield were chosen Haywards	10
Tax of seventy Two Pounds to be paid in lawfull money or Provisions at the ready money market Price to be paid to the Revd Mr Elizur Goodrich for his Sallary the current Year	10
Town voted that the Bond given by Prosper Hubbard & Dan^{ll} Whitmore to the loan Com^{tee} be put on Suit next April Court if not paid up before the Time	11
Benjn Picket Caleb Fowler John Canfield & Abial Baldwin were chosen a School Com^{tee}	11

13 Dec 1775

Elihu Crane was chosen Surveyor of Highways	11
Abr^m Bartlet was excused from the Office of Lister and Elias Camp was chosen Lister & Rate maker	11
John Canfield was excused from swerving as School Com^{tee} and Capt Camp was chosen as one of the School Com^{tee}	11

Durham

Town.. Determined that the School shall be kept the current Year in the various Parts of the Town.. viz six months at the School House near the Meeting House five & a half Months near Eben^r Robinsons House five & a half months at the School House near Jess Austin's House four months at the School Houses on the west Side the great Swamp four months at the School House at the south End of the Town and one month at the School House near John Newton's House	11
Nathan Curtiss Simeon Parsons Ju^r Israel Camp Elihu Crane Sam^{ll} Camp John Newton & John Johnson were chosen a Com^{tee} to seat the Meeting House anew	11
Town gave to Rowland Rosseter the old School House which lately stood near the Meeting House	11
Town.. [vot]ed to Dan^{ll} Merwin School Collector James Hinman's Rate being 4/6 ¼ and ordered him to be paid out of the Town Treasury	11
Town orderd that James Wadsworth.. Col^o James Wadsworth Ju^r & wife be allowed to sit in the Pew at the right Hand the Pulpit	11

15 Feb 1776

Col: Elihu Chauncey was chosen Moderator	11
Benjn Pickett Lieu^t Sam^{ll} Parsons Elias Camp Capt James Robinson Jesse Crane John Coe & Dan^{ll} Wright were chosen a Com^{tee} to seat the Meeting House anew according to Directions given.. last Town Meeting	11
Capt James Arnold & .. Lemuel Garansey were chosen to be of the Com^{tee} of Inspection	11

10 Dec 1776

Col^o Chauncey was Chosen Moderator	12
General Wadsworth ws chosen Town Clerk	12
Elnathan Camp was chosen Town clerk Protemporay to Serve in the Absense of General Wadsworth	12

30 Dec 1776

General Wadsworth Capt Ebenez^r Garnsey Capt Israel Camp Capt Stephen Norton & Elnathan Camp were chosen Select men	12
Capt Ebenezer Garnsey was Excused from Serveing as a Selectman	12
Ens^n Danl Hall was chosen Select Man	12
Benjamin Pickitt & Capt Samuel Camp were chosen Constables.. and.. Benjamin Pickitt to be Collector of the Colony Rate	12
Thomas Strong and Thomas Lyman was Chosen Grandjurie men	12
Leu^t Simeon Parsons was Chosen Town Treasurer & Collector	12
Noah Baldwin was Chosen Collector of the Ministers Rate	12
Ithamar Parsons Ju^r was chosen School Collector	12
Eliphas Parmele Israel Burritt: John Canfield: Leu^t Eliakim Strong: Ephraim Coe: John Coe: Capt Job Camp Ely Crane & Dan Parmele were chosen Surveyors of Highways	12
Ebenezer Tibbals Sam^{ll} Bates Moses Bates Joseph Chidsey & Elihu Crane were chosen Listers & Rate makers	12
Jonathan Wakeley Abraham Bishop: Asher Robinson: & Daniel Wright were chosen Tything men	12
Leu^t Bryan Rosseter and Joseph Hull were chosen fence Veiwers	12
Capt Ebenezer Garnsey was chosen Sealer of Leather	12

Durham

Abial Baldwin was chosen sealer of Weights	12
Deac[n] James Curtiss was chosen sealer of Measures	12
Daniel Hall Jun:[r].. was chosen Key keeper	12
Elnathan Camp was chosen Gauger	12
Ambrous Field: Abraham Bartlet: Samuel Sutlief Gurdon Hull & Phinehas Canfield were chosen Haywards	12
Cap[t] Samuel Camp Thomas Lyman & Ephraim Coe were Chosen School Committe	12
Determined that the schools Shall be kept the currant year in the various parts of the Town.. six months att the school house near the Meeting house: five months & half att the school house near Jacob Clarks House: five months & half att the school house near Josiah Parsons house, five months att the school Houses on the west side the Great Swamp four months att the school House att the south End of the town & one month att the school house near John Newtons house	12

30 Dec 1776

Town.. Granted a Rate.. of seventy two Pounds.. to be paid to the Rev[d] M[r] Elizur Goodrich for his sallary the currant year	13
Town ordered: .. cloathing Belonging to Ann Stephens Late Deceased should be Given to her sisters and divided.. by the Select men as they Judge Best	13
select men were appointed to be a committe of Inspection.. and.. Co[ll] James Arnold and Phinehas Spelman were added to them	13

10 Feb 1777

Dan[ll] Hall was chosen Moderator	13

24 Mar 1777

Daniel Hall was chosen Moderator	13
It is voted that the Families of such Soldiers belonging to this Town as shall engage in s[d] Service [ed: in the Continental Battallions] on their reasonable Request shall be supplyed in their Absence with necessaries at the Prices stated by law and that a Com[tee] be appointed.. to see them provided for & supplyed.. on such Soldiers lodging or from Time to Time remitting money to s[d] Com[tee] for that Purpose.. Lemuel Garnsey Samuel Parsons & Caleb Fowler were chosen a Com[tee]	13

16 Sep 1777

Daniel Hall Esq[r] was chosen Moderator	13

9 Dec 1777

Dan[ll] Hall Esq[r] was chosen Moderator	14
Gen[l] James Wadsworth was chosen Town Clerk	14
Gen[l] James Wadsworth Daniel Hall Esq[r] Cap[t] Israel Camp Cap[t] Stephen Norton and .. Elnathan Camp were chosen Select Men	14
Thomas Lyman and Cap[t] Sam[ll] Camp were chosen Constables.. and Cap[t] Sam[ll] Camp was chosen Collector of the Colony Tax	14
Phinehas Spelman and Abraham Bartlet to be Grandjurors	14
Lieu[t] Simeon Parsons Ju[r] was chosen Town Treasurer & Collector of the Town Rate	14
John Canfield Elihu Crane John Johnson Ju[r] Dan Parmele & Samuel Bates were chosen Listers & Ratemakers	14

Durham

Noah Norton Eliphaz Parmele Joseph Parsons Phin^s Camp James Bates Dan^{ll} Wright & John Johnson were chosen Surveyors of highways	14
Lemuel Moffitt David Talcott Abr^m Scrantom Ju^r and Joseph Chidsey were chosen Tythingmen	14
Capt Charles Norton was chosen Collector of the Minister's Rate	14
Jeremiah Butler was chosen Collector of the School Rate	14
Joseph Chidsey was excused from serving as a Tythingman and Joseph Wright Ju^r was chosen Tythingman	14
Phin^s Spelman & Abraham Bartlet were excused from serving as Grandjurors	14
Lemuel Garnsey and John Johnson were chosen to be Grandjurors	14
John Johnson was excused from Serving as Surveyor of high ways and John Crane was chosen Surveyor of High ways	14
Bryan Rossetter and Joseph Hall were chosen Fence viewers	14
Dan^{ll} Wright was excused from serving as Susrveyor of Highways and Henry Crane was chosen Surveyor of Highways	14
Capt Garnsey was chosen Sealer of Leather	14
Abial Baldwin was chosen Sealer of weights	14
Capt Curtiss was chosen Sealer of Measures	14
Danll Hall Jur was chosen Keykeeper	14
Abial Baldwin Phin^s Spelman & Capt Job Camp were chosen School Com^{tee}	14
Genl James Wadsworth Dan^{ll} Hall Esq Capt Israel Camp Capt Stephen Norton .. Eln^n Camp Capt Ja^s Robinson Col^o Arnold & .. Phin^s Spelman were chosen a Com^{tee} of Inspection	14
Robert Smithson Jesse Crane Elah Camp Tim^o Parsons Heth Camp Elias Camp & Abel Coe were chosen a Com^{tee} for supplying the Families of the Officers & Soldiers of the Continental Army belonging to this Town with Cloathing & Provissions	14
Capt Garnsey Itha^r Parsons & Capt Curtiss were chosen a Com^{tee} to procure the Meeting House on the north Side to be shingled anew	15
Town.. Granted a..Tax of £72 to be paid in lawfull Money or Provissions.. to the Revd Elizur Goodrich [for] his Sallary the current Year	15
Lemual Johnson Morris Col Thos Strong Ju^r Jesse Cook Noah Lyman & Ashur Robinson were chosen Haywards	15
Elnathan Camp was chos[en] Gauger	15
Meeting voted that the Salt.. be divided to each Family in Proportion to the Number of Souls and.. each Head of a Family shall return to a Com^{tee}.. the Name of each Person in his Family.. Eben^r Tibbals Joseph Chidsey and Phin^s Spelman were chosen a Com^{tee} for the Purposes	15
5 Jan 1778	
Daniel Hall Esqr was chosen Moderator	15
9 Feb 1778	
Dan^{ll} Hall Esqr was chosen Moderator	15
18 Aug 1778	
Daniel Hall Esqr was chosen Moderator	16

167

Durham

8 Dec 1778

Daniel Hall Esqr was chosen Moderator	16
Genl James Wadsworth was chosen Town Clerk	16
Genl James Wadsworth Daniel Hall Esqr Capt Stephen Norton Capt Samuel Camp & Phinehas Spelman were chosen Select men	16
Daniel Hall Esqr was excused from serving as Select man	16
Col^o James Arnold was chosen Selectman	16
Dan Parmele was chosen Constable.. and Collector of the State Tax	16
Capt Charles Norton was chosen Constable	16
Phinehas Camp was chosen Constable	16
Jonathan Wackley & Jeremiah Butler were chosen Grandjurors	16
Lieu^t Simeon Parsons Ju^r was chosen Town Treasurer & Collector of the Town Rate	16
Amos Fowler John Jones Joseph Parsons & Phinehas Parmele were chosen Tythingmen	16
Caleb Fowler Samuel Bates Benjn Pickett Ebenezer Tibbals & Jabez Chalker were chosen Listers & Rate makers	16
Caleb Fowler and Samuel Bates were excused from serving as Listers	16
Amos Fowler & James Bates were chosen Listers & Ratemakers	16
Ithamar Parsons Ju^r Lemuel Garnsey Daniel Wright Levi Parmele John Canfield William Burrit Lemuel Johnson Moses Seaward & Abraham Scranton Ju^r were chosen Surveyors of Highways	16
Abijah Curtiss was chosen Collector of the Minister's Rate	16
Robert Smithson was chosen Collector of the School Rate	16
Bryan Rossetter & Caleb Fowler were chosen Fenceviewers	16
Capt Garnsey was chosen Sealer of Leather	16
Abial Baldwin was chosen Sealer of Weights	16
Capt Curtiss was chosen Sealer of Measures	16
Daniel Hall Ju^r was chosen Keykeeper	16
Capt Chauncey John Johnson & Abial Baldwin were chosen School Com^{tee}	16
Thos Lyman Thos Strong & Lemuel Garnsey were chosen a Com^{tee} of Inspection	16
Eliphaz Parmele Abel Lyman Noah Norton Gideon Canfield Caleb Fowler Ithamar Parsons & John Curtiss were chosen a Com^{tee} to provide for the Families of the Officers & Soldiers belonging to continental Army from this Town	16
Thos Lyman & Ashur Robinson were chosen Assessors	17
Capt Garnsey Daniel Hall Esqr & Capt Curtiss be a Com^{tee} to confer with the Revd Mr Goodrich touching the advanced Prices the necessarys of Life now bear from what they were at at the Time of his Settlement in the Ministry	17
Whereas Col^o Arnold having excused himself from serving as Selectman by paying his Fine .. Simeon Parsons Ju^r was chosen Selectman	17
Phin^s Camp having excused himself from serving as Constable by paying his Fine.. Jesse Cook was chosen Constable.. who likewise excused himself by paying his Fine	17

Durham

Benjn Pickett was chosen Constable	17
Eliphaz Parmele was excused from serving as one of the Com^{tee} to provide for the Families of the Officers & Soldiers.. And.. Samuel Parsons was chosen.. one of s^d Com^{tee}	17
Phinehas Spelman was chosen Assessor	17
Jess Austin Ambrose Field Eli Crane Simeon Coe Ju^r Sam^{ll} Bates Jacob Clark Heth Camp & Daniel Coe were chosen Haywards	17
On the Report of the Com^{tee}.. to confer with Mr Goodrich.. Voted that the Rate granted by the Town.. to pay Mr Goodrich's Sallery which became due on the 24th of Novr last and yet remains unpaid be paid in Provissions at the Prices regulated by a Law of this State.. And that a Tax of £432 be levied on.. the Inhabitants of this Town and of Tim^o Bishop of Guilford.. on Consideration of the advanced Prices of the Necessaries of Life.. to be.. paid to the Revd Mr Goodrich.. not to be considered as a Precedent in future.. Town.. granted a.. Tax of £72.. to be paid to the Revd Mr Elizur Goodrich for his Sallary the Current	17
voted there be paid.. to Simeon Parsons Ju^r Collector of the Town Rate in.. 1777 Elihu Hinman's rate being £0-5-9 and John Dunawon's rate being £0-4-6 and in.. 1778 Sam^{ll} Seaward's rate being £0-1-7¼ and John Loas's rate being £0-8-9 to Abr^m Scrantom Ju^r Collector of the School rate 1776 Charles Bishop's rate being £0-4-1¾ John Loas's rate being £0-2-3[½] and Sam^{ll} Seaward's rate being £0-10-10 -- To Ithamar Parsons Ju^r Collector of the School rate 1777 Sam^{ll} Seaward's rate being £0-19-0¾ and John Loas's rate being £0-3-0-2	17
voted there be paid.. to Simeon Parsons Ju^r Collector of the Town Rate in.. 1777 Elihu Hinman's rate being £0-5-9 and John Dunawon's rate being £0-4-6 and in.. 1778 Sam^{ll} Seaward's rate being £0-1-7¼ and John Loas's rate being £0-8-9 to Abr^m Scrantom Ju^r Collector of the School rate 1776 Charles Bishop's rate being £0-4-1¾ John Loas's rate being £0-2-3[½] and Sam^{ll} Seaward's rate being £0-10-10 -- To Ithamar Parsons Ju^r Collector of the School rate 1777 Sam^{ll} Seaward's rate being £0-19-0¾ and John Loas's rate being £0-3-0-2	17

11 Jan 1779

Daniel Hall Esqr was chosen Moderator	18
Question was put whether the Town would reconsider the Vote.. touching the Revd Mr Goodrich's Sallary the last Year.. voted in the negative	18

18 Oct 1779

Daniel Hall Esqr was chosen Moderator	18
Whereas Capt John Noyes Wadsworth claims a Right to the Pew in the Meeting House next the Pulpit Stairs and whereas the Town have ordered the Pew to be filled up by seating other Persons therein.. And whereas.. Wadsworth has offered to submit his Right to s^d Pew to the Judgment of the Honble Mathew Griswold Eliphalet Dyar & William Pitkin Esq^{rs} to be determined according to Law.. Voted that the Town do agree to s^d Proposal.. And.. Thomas Lyman & Elnathan Camp are appointed Agents.. to appear before.. Honble Mathew Griswold Eliphalet Dyar and William Pitkin Esq^{rs} to defend against the the Right of.. Wadsworth to s^d Pew	18

14 Dec 1779

Daniel Hall Esqr was chosen Moderator	18
Genl James Wadsworth was chosen Town Clerk	18
Genl James Wadsworth Capt Stephen Norton Lieu^t Simeon Parsons Ju^r Capt Samuel Camp & Mr Phinehas Spelman were chosen Selectmen	18
Elnathan Camp & Mr Dan Parmele were chosen Constables	18

169

Durham

Phinehas Camp & Abraham Scranton Ju^r were chosen Grandjurors	18
Moses Bates Samuel Bartlet John Johnson Ju^r Abijah Curtiss were chosen Tythingmen	18
Capt John N: Wadsworth Ashur Robinson Elias Camp Joseph Smith Thos Strong Samuel Hart Curtis Bates Joseph Parsons & Capt Job Camp & Henry Crane were chosen Surveyors of Highways	18
Elnathan Camp was chosen Collector of the State Tax	18
Capt John N Wadsworth was chosen Town Treasurer & Collector of the Town Rate	18
Thomas Strong Ju^r was chosen Collector of the Minister's Rate	18
Jesse Crane was chosen Collector of the School Rate	18
Capt Curtiss was chosen Sealer of Measures	18
Abial Baldwin was chosen Sealer of weights	18
Capt Garnsey was chosen Sealer of Leather	18
Joseph Hull & Noah Baldwin were chosen Fenceviewers	18
Dan^{ll} Hall Ju^r was chosen Keykeeper	18
Thomas Strong Thomas Lyman & Capt Charles Norton were chosen a Com^{tee} of Inspection	18
Jeremiah Butler David Talcott & Abraham Bartlet were chosen School Com^{tee}	19
Samuel Parsons Ju^r Ithamer Parsons Ju^r Eben^r Tibbals Isaiah Cox Eliphaz Parmele John Canfield Curtis Bates & Lemuel Garnsey were chosen a Com^{tee} to provide for the Families of the Officers & Soldiers belonging to this Town in the Continental Army	19
Dan^{ll} Hall Ju^r Lemuel Moffatt Giles Rose Caleb Fowler Simeon Coe Ju^r Benjn Ames & Phin^s Canfield were chosen Haywards	19
Town.. granted a.. Tax of seventy two Pounds to be paid in lawfull money or Provisions.. to the Revd Mr Elizur Goodrich for his Sallary the current Year	19
Phin^s Spelman Thos Lyman & Capt Sam^{ll} Camp be a Com^{tee} to confer with the Revd Mr Goodrich.. touching his Sallary the last Year	19
22 Dec 1779	
Whereas.. £72 was granted to the Revd Mr Goodrich for his Sallary the then current Year which ended the 24th Nov^r.. which remains unpaid -- And whereas the Necessaries of Life have been greatly enhanced in their Prices by Reason of the present War and Increase of public Expences -- A Part of which Mr Goodrich is willing.. to bear..Voted.. Tax of £72 of which Abijah Curtiss is Collector be paid to.. Goodrich by the first day of January..	19
Jacob Clark was chosen Collector of the School Rate.. Jesse Crane having paid his fine	19
Thos Lyman Capt Job Camp Simeon Parsons Ju^r Capt Charles Norton Joseph Chidsey Lemuel Johnson Elnathan Camp Dan Parmele Israel Burritt Benjn Picket & Jesse Crane were chosen a Com^{tee} to seat the lower Part of the Meeting House anew	19
Capt John N Wadsworth was excused from serving as Town Treasurer & Collector of the Town Rate	19
John Johnson was chosen Town Treasurer & Collector of the Town Rate	19
Whereas Josiah Coe refused to serve as a Com^{tee} for supplying the Families of the Soldiers in the Continental Army and paid the Fine by Law imposed.. Heth Camp was chosen one of the Com^{tee}	19
28 Feb 1780	
Daniel Hall Esqr was chosen Moderator	19

Durham

Capt Charles Norton Phinehas Spelman Dan Parmele Jesse Crane Capt Stephen Norton Thomas Lyman Phinehas Camp Jabez Chalker James Bates Thomas Strong Capt Samuel Camp Capt John Noyes Wadsworth Jeremiah Butler Joseph Chidsey Abial Baldwin & Israel Burrit were chosen Inspectors of Provisions
24 Apr 1780

Daniel Hall Esqr was chosen Moderator

Whereas Capt John Noyes Wadsworth hath set up a Claim to a certain Pew in the Meeting House next the Pulpit Stairs which Claim has been endeavoured to be terminated amicably .. Disputes & Controversies do still subsist respecting the Same - Voted that we will defend the Right of the Town.. against the Claim of.. Wadsworth or any other Person.. and will indemnify.. all such Persons as are seated in s^d Pew against any Damages.. that may accrew to them by.. any Suit.. brought.. against them.. Lemuel Garnsey Thomas Lyman & Elnathan Camp be.. appointed Agents.. to appear in Behalf of the Town
7 Jul 1780

Daniel Hall Esqr was chosen Moderator

Voted.. £6 in new Bills be paid.. to Capt Sam^{ll} Camp to enable him to fullfil the Agreement he made with Elihu Crane & Sutlief Seaward for their inlisting to serve in the Connecticut Battalions in the Continental Army
13 Nov 1780

Capt Stephen Norton was chosen Moderator

Ithamar Parsons Ju^r was chosen Collector of [*a tax for procuring Provissions for the Continental Army*].. who excused himself by paying his Fine of 26/

James Wadsworth & Phin^s Spelman were chosen to receive inspect & put up the Provissions to be purchased.. for the Use of the continental Army

Capt Charles Norton was chosen to collect the Tax granted this Meeting also to purchase the Provissions

Capt Sam^{ll} Camp Capt Charles Norton Capt Parsons Lt Smith Lt Butler Lt Scrantom Ens^n Scrantom Ens^n Johnson Ens^n Strong & Corn^t Baldwin were chosen a Com^{tee} to procure Recruits for the Continental Army
12 Dec 1780

Daniel Hall Esqr was chosen Moderator

Genl James Wadsworth was chosen Town Clerk

Genl James Wadsworth Capt Stephen Norton Capt Simeon Parsons Capt Samuel Camp & .. Phinehas Spelman were chosen Selectmen

Dan Parmele was chosen Constable and Collector of the State Tax

Elnathan Camp was chosen Constable

John Johnson Ju^r & Medad Strong were chosen Grandjurors

John Curtiss Thos Strong and Elnathan Camp are appointed to confer with Mr Goodrich touching his Sallary

James Hickcox Titus Loveland Noah Lynch & Israel Burrit were chosen Tythingman

Charles Burrit Joseph Parsons Joseph Smith Eben^r Tibbals Abraham Bartlet Jesse Crane Benjn Pickett Thos Stevens Abraham Scrantom & Joseph Camp were chosen Surveyors of Highways

Thos Lyman Charles Norton Phinehas Camp Israel Burrit Noah Norton Thos Strong & Joseph Chidsey were chosen Listers & Ratemakers

Durham

Thos Lyman & Charles Norton were excused from serving as Listers & Ratemakers	21
John Johnson was chosen Town Treasurer & Collector of the Town Rate	21
James Hickcox was chosen Collector of the Minister's Rate	21
Moses Bates was chosen Collector of the School Rate	21
Eln^n Camp was chosen Sealer of Measures	21
Abial Baldwin was chosen Sealer of Weights	21
Capt Garnsey was chosen Sealer of Leather	21
Bryan Rossetter & Job Camp were chosen Fenceviewers	21
Daniel Hall Ju^r was chosen Keykeeper	21
Jeremiah Butler Capt Charles Norton & Lemuel Garnsey were chosen a Com^{tee} of Inspection	21
John Johnson Ju^r Dan^{ll} Dimock and Timothy Coe were chosen School Com^{tee}	21
Voted that Thos Strong Ju^r Collector of Minister's Rate the last Year may receive of the Inhabitants who have not paid their Rates two Shillings in new bills emitted on the Credit of this State or seventy two Shillings in old Continental Currency for one Shilling charged in the Rate Bill or Provissions at the Prices regulated by an Act.. passed in.. 1777	21
Town..granted a.. Tax of £72 to be paid in lawfull money or Provissions.. to the Revd Mr Elizur Goodrich for his Sallary the current Year.. levied on the Poles & rateable Estate in this Town and of Tim^o Bishop of Guilford	21
Levi Parmele Tim^o Hall and Capt Job Camp were chosen a Com^{tee} to provide for the Families of the Soldiers in the Continental Army	21

21 Dec 1780

Ashur Canfield Frederick Crane Nath^{ll} Hickcox Ithamar Parsons Ju^r & Timothy Hall were chosen Haywards	22
Selectmen.. exhibited an Account of Expenditures.. Amounting to..£2107-4-2 in Continental Currency and.. £100-15-6 in New bills of Credit on this State and.. a Balance in favour of the town in the hands of.. John Johnson Town Treasurer the Sum of £484-19-10 Continental Currency and.. £7-13-10 in new bills of Credit	22
Capt James Robinson Capt Simeon Parsons Phin^s Spelman Elah Camp & John Canfield were chosen a Com^{tee} to treat with Capt John N Wadsworth relating to the Pew in the Meeting House which.. Wadsworth claims a Right to exclusive of the Town	22

1 Jan 1781

Elnathan Camp was chosen one of the Com^{tee} to collect hold & loan the Monies granted for the Support of the Schools in the room of Dea^n James Curtiss resigned and.. John Canfield in the Room of Deac^n Ezra Baldwin resigned	22
Com^{tee} appointed to treat with Capt John N Wadsworth relating to a Pew in the Meeting House which .. Wadsworth claims a Right to.. having made their Report.. which Report contains two Proposals made by s^d Wadsworth.. voted that the Town do not accept of the Same	22
Town granted a Tax of one penny half penny on the Pound.. to be paid in.. wheat flour at the Rate of twnety four Shillings per Hundred gross weight.. rye Flour at sixteen Shillings per hundred gross weight or Indian Corn at four Shillings per Bushel.. Jonathan Wackley was chosen Collector of the Tax.. & also to procure Casks recieve inspect & pack s^d Flour & Indian Corn	22

Durham

21 Jun 1781

Capt Stephen Norton was chosen Moderator	22
Capt Ja^s Robinson was chosen Purchaser of beef Cattle for Supplies of the Army	23
Elias Camp was chosen Collector of the Tax [*for raising Supplies for the Use of this State and the Continental Army*]	23

6 Aug 1781

Ja^s Wadsworth Esqr &.. Phin^s Spelman were appointed to procure Barrels receive & salt pack & secure the Beef & Pork.. brought in and.. store such other Articles as shall be Delivered in Payment of a State Tax	23

11 Dec 1781

Dan^{ll} Hall Esqr was chosen Moderator	23
Genl James Wadsworth ws chosen Town Clerk	23
Genl James Wadsworth Capt Simeon Parsons.. Elnathan Camp Capt Stephen Norton &.. John Johnson were chosen Selectmen	23
Thomas Lyman & Dan Parmele were chosen Constables	23
Joseph Parsons & James Hickcox were chosen Grandjurors	23
Benjamin Picket was chosen Constable & Collector of the State Tax	23
Tim^o Coe Ashur Canfield Abijah Curtiss & Dan^{ll} Dimmock were chosen Tythingmen	23
Lemuel Garnsey Chareles Norton Sam^{ll} Bates Charles Burrit & David Scrantom were chosen Listers & Ratemakers	23
Levi Parmele Noah Lyman Ashur Robinson Sam^{ll} Camp John Coe Eliakim Strong Phinehas Spelman & Joseph Chidsey were chosen Surveyors of Highways	23
Abial Baldwin was chosen Town Treasurer & Collector of the Town Rate	23
Abel Lyman was chosen Collector of the Minister's Rate	23
Capt Garnsey was chosen Sealer of Leather	23
Abial Baldwin was chosen Sealer of weights	23
Tim^o Hall was chosen Sealer of Measures	23
Job Camp & Bryan Rossetter were chosen Fence viewers	23
Dan^{ll} Hall Ju^r was chosen Keykeeper	23
Stephen Norton Ju^r Tim^o Parsons Tim^o Coe Ju^r Thos Cook Jno Noyes Wadsworth Ju^r & John Curtiss Ju^r were chosen Haywards	23
Capt James Robinson Thos Lyman Jesse Crane & Joseph Camp were chosen a Com^{tee} to provide for the Families of the Soldiers in the Continental Army	24
Jeremiah Butler Charles Burrit Joseph Smith John Johnson Ju^r & Abr^m Scrantom were chosen a Com^{tee} of Inspection	24
Lemuel Johnson Abr^m Scrantom and Jacob Clark were chosen School Com^{tee}	24
Saml Fenn Parsons was chosen Collector of the School Rates	24
Town.. granted a.. Tax of £72.. to be paid to the Revd Mr Elizur Goodrich for his Sallary the current Year.. levied on the .. rateable Estate in this Town and of Tim^o Bishop of Guilford	24
Town.. abated Sam^{ll} Seaward's School Rate of 6/ Shillings State Bills and also John Loas's School Rate of 3/9 State Bills and ordered them to be paid to Jacob Clark Collector out of the Town Treasury	24

Durham

Town.. abated Sam^{ll} Seaward's School Rate of £2-8-11 Continental Currency & ordered the Sum of 7/10.. to be paid to Jer^h Butler Collector out of the Town Treasury	24
Town ordered.. 7/11 to be paid.. to Thos Strong Collector of Mr Goodrich's Rate in part Payment of s^d Rate	24
Town.. abated Sam^{ll} Seaward's School Rate of £2-8-11 Continental Currency & ordered the Sum of 7/10.. to be paid to Jer^h Butler Collector out of the Town Treasury	24

21 Feb 1782

Dan^{ll} Hall Esqr was chosen Moderator	24
Capt Simeon Parsons Capt Samuel Camp Capt Charles Norton.. Elnathan Camp Lieu^t Jeremiah Butler Lt Abr^m Scrantom Lt Joseph Smith Ens^n John Johnson Ens^n Medad Strong & Ens^n David Scrantom were chosen a Com^{tee} to procure five able bodied Men to serve in a Regiment ordered by the Genl Assembly.. to be raised for the Defence of Horseneck or western Frontiers	24
Hezekiah Camp was chosen Collector of the School Rate	24

10 Dec 1782

Dan^{ll} Hall Esqr was chosen Moderator	24
Genl James Wadsworth was chosen Town Clerk	24
Genl James Wadsworth Simeon Parsons.. Capt Stephen Norton.. Elnathan Camp & Capt Sam^{ll} Camp was chosen Selectmen	24
James Hickcox was chosen Constable & Collector of the State Tax	24
Capt John Johnson was chosen Constable	24
Noah Lyman & Charles Burritt were chosen Grandjurors	24
Lt Jeremiah Butler was chosen Town Treasurer and Collector of the Town Rate	24
John Coe Simeon Cox Fredrick Crane & David Scrantom were chosen Tythingmen	25
Charles Norton Israel Burritt Samuel Bates Phin^s Spelman & Dan Parmele were chosen Listers & Ratemakers	25
Thos Lyman Eben^r Tibbals James Bates Capt John N Wadsworth Heth Camp Tim^o Coe Jesse Crane Abijah Curtiss & Jabez Chalker were chosen Surveyors of Highways	25
Ithamar Parsons Ju^r was chosen Collector of the Minister's Rate	25
Abel Tibbals was chosen Collector of the School Rate	25
Capt Garnsey was chosen Sealer of Leather	25
Abial Baldwin was chosen Sealer of weights	25
Tim^o Hall was chosen Sealer of Measures	25
Elias Camp & John Canfield were chosen Fenceviewers	25
Dan^{ll} Hall Ju^r was chosen Keykeeper	25
Lemuel Johnson Lemuel Garnsey Abr^m Bartlett & John Johnson were chosen a Com^{tee} of Inspection	25
Tim^o Hall Phin^s Camp & Medad Strong were chosen a School Com^{tee}	25
Town granted a.. Tax of £72 to be paid.. to the Revd Mr Elizur Goodrich for his Sallary the current Year.. levied on the.. Poles & rateable in this Town and of Tim^o Bishop of Guilford	25
Town.. abated to Capt Char^s Norton the following Persons Rates in State bills viz Willm Bishop 23/ Tim^o Dunn 23/ Elihu Hinman 36/ Wm Johnson 9/1 John Loas 44/ David Squire	25

Durham

11/2 Charles White 13/ Joseph Wright 6/6

Town.. ordered.. 19/10¾ to be paid.. to Hez^h Camp being Elihu Hinman's School Rate	25
Town.. ordered 3/8 LM and.. 11/6 State Bills to be paid.. to John Johnson being sundry of John Loas's Town Rates	25
Town.. ordered.. 19/7 to be paid.. to James Hickcox Collector of the Minister's rate being.. sundry Persons Rates	25
Richd Spelman Phin^s Canfield John Crane Aaron Parsons & Sam^{ll} Bartlet were chosen Haywards	25
On the Petition of Alexander Linn Thos Franses & Daniel Franses of Killingworth praying Liberty of attending public Worship in Durham &c voted.. shall have Liberty of attending public worship in this Town and be seated in the Meetinghouse.. provided.. [they].. give bond to the Selectmen.. and pay their proportionable Part of the Ministerial Charges *11 Dec 1782*	25
Whereas the Selectmen of Wallingford have made Application to the County Court to have a highway layed out near the House of Joseph Camp to Wallingford Line by Pistopauge Pond -- voted that the Selectmen lay out s^d Highway at their best Discretion	25
Town.. ordered.. 2/10 to be paid.. (being an Abatement made to Abel Tibbals) to James Hickcox Collector of the Minister's Rate	26
Town voted to pay.. ten Shillings p^r Month to Sam^{ll} Seaward Tim^o Dunn Ju^r Josiah Hull Elihu Crane John Norton Ju^r Gilbert Kirtland Phin^s Meigs & David Ward during the Time they served in Maj^r Shipman's Reg^t in.. 1781 provided they Deliver to the Selectmen the Obligations given to them	26
Capt Robinson Jesse Crane & Thos Lyman were chosen a Com^{tee} to shingle the Meeting House	26
Capt Charles Norton Benjn Picket Capt Johnson Charles Burrit Capt Sam^{ll} Camp & Sam^{ll} Bates were chosen a Com^{tee} to seat the Meeting anew	26
Meeting voted that 7/6 be paid to Abial Baldwin.. being Elihu Hinman & John Loas's Town Rates	26
Meeting voted that 5/6 be paid to Abijah Curtiss.. being sundry Rates and for Mr Goodrich's Sallary 1779	26
Daniel Hall Esqr was chosen Moderator	26
whereas a Controversy & dispute in Law has long subsisted between Capt John Noyes Wadsworth and the Town.. respecting a certain Pew adjoyning the Pulpit Stairs in the Meeting House.. and now undetermined in the Honble Superior Court and the Town being now called together for the.. Purpose.. of an amicable Settlement..Do now move.. as a final Settlement.. that he.. & Esther his wife.. have their Choice.. to set either in the fore Seat where they are now seated or in the Pew in Dispute which they please during their natural Life or Residence in.. Durham.. and so long as.. Wadsworth and his heirs lives up to s^d Agreement never hereafter to renew or commence any suit of Action.. concerning the s^d Pew.. and that hereafter we endeavour to live in Peace & Harmony *25 Aug 1783*	26
Capt Simeon Parsons was chosen Moderator	26
Genl Wadsworth Capt Parsons Dan^{ll} Hall Esqr Capt Wadsworth & .. Elnathan Camp are appointed a Com^{tee} to report to this Meeting a proper vote expressing their disapprobation of the giving halfpay for Life to the Officers of the Army or a Commutation *1 Sep 1783*	26
This Town being advised by a late Publication of Genl Washington's last official Address to	27

Durham

the Legislatures.. of the Halfpay & Commutation of Halfpay given by Congress to the Officers of the Army -- Think it a Duty they owe to the Public themselves & Posterity to shew their disapprobation of the various Arts & Practices made use of to induce Congress to give the Same..
Dan[ll] Hall Esq[r] & Cap[t] Simeon Parsons were chosen Delegates to attend a Convention to be held at Middletown.. to consider what ought to be done upon the Subject of Commutation

East Haddam

Votes of the Town
1766 – 1822

Located at the Town Clerk's Office

East Haddam

5 Jan 1775

Mr Israel Champion Was Chosen Moderator	43
the Committee of Inspection Chosen November 17th 1774 Made Report Relateing to a Complaint.. Exhibitted to them by Sundry Inhabitents.. against Doc^{tr} Abner Beebe.. for being Enimical to the Liberties of these American Colonies Which Report being Read Voted.. that We.. shall hold him to be Enimical to these Colonies & Will Break of all Connections..with Said Beebe & all those that Shall have any Connection With him untill.. Beebee Shall Comply & Sign the Confession.. & then we will Restore him to his former favour and We Desire S^d Com^{tt} to Advertise What is Done in the New London Gazette	43

4 Dec 1775

Capt William Cone was Chosen Moderator	44
Daniel Brainerd Esqr Was Chosen Town Clerk	44
Mesr^{es} Israel Champion Timothy Gates Capt William Cone Mr Barzillai Beckwith and Mr Jabez Comstock Ware Chosen Select Men	44
Daniel Brainerd Esqr Was Chosen Town Treasurer	44
Mr Joseph Fowler Was Chosen Constable and to gather the Country Rate.. & also Capt James Green Mesrs Ebenezer Emmons Isaac Spencer and Robart Hungarford Ware Chosen Constables	44
Mesrs Noadiah Gates Jonathan Booge Benjamin Fuller John Chapman and Mr Samuel Willey Ware Chosen Grand Jurors	44
Mr Ozias Chapman Mr Joshua Gates Junr Mr William Steward Mr Richard Sparrow and Mr Asael Andrews Ware Chosen Tything men	44
Mesres John Percivel Charles Williams Thomas Knowlton Abner Hall Joel Cone Bezaleel Gates Caleb Gates Amos White J[ ] Selby Job Spencer Ashbel Olmsted Phillip Williams Abraham Williams Reuben Beebee James Dixson Jared Brainard Nathan Tiffeny Nathanael Cone John Annabel David Burnham John Driggs William Baker Silvanus Cone 2nd Phineas Palmerly Samuel Marsh Luri Crosby & Joseph Willey 2nd Ware Chosen Surveyors of Highways	44
Misers Amos Booge Amasa Brainerd Sam^{ll} Arnold Nathan Burnham and Capt Eliphelet Holmes 2nd Ware Chosen Listers	45
Mesres Thomas Fuller and John Percivel Junr Ware Chosen fence Viewers	45
Mesr^s Zacheriah Cone William Cone 2nd and John Spencer Ware Chosen Colectors	45
Mes^{res} Jonathan Booge Capt Aaron Cleavland and Capt Christopher Holmes Ware Chosen Leather Sealers	45
Missers John Warner Thomas Fuller Amos Randal Ignatious Smith Capt Elijah Atwood ~~Timothy~~ William Fox & Jonathan Willey Ware Chosen Haywards	45
Mr Eleazer Brainerd Was Guager	45
Mesres Elijah Metcalf and Thomas Daneals Ware Chosen packers	45
Mesres John Willey Junr Ira Church & Joseph Church Ware Chosen Branders of Horses	45
Mr William Selby Was Chosen Sealer of Weights & Measures	45
Mr Daniel Cone & Mr James Dixson Ware Chosen Key keepers	45
Mr Elijah Metcalf Was Chosen Culler of Staves	45
Mr Ephraim Ackly Was Chosen Town Colector in the Room of Zacheriah Cone Released	46
Mr Nathan Hungerford Was Chosen Grand Jury man in the Room of John Chapman Excused	46

East Haddam

Mr Timothy Chapman Was Chosen a Grand Jury Man in the Room of Noadiah Gates Excused	46
upon the Request of Mr Amos Randal.. Shewing that he Lived Remote from any Town Pound.. and that he Might have the Privilege of having his yard a Lawful pound,...Said Request.. Was Granted.. provided Said Randal Would procure and keep in good order a good Lock and Key...also Voted that Said Randal to be Key keeper to Said Pound	47
Mesres Jehiel Fuller Daniel Fox Joseph Gates Nehemiah Tracy Jeremiah Cone John Watson Green Hungerford and Ezekiel Brockway Beckwith Ware Chosen Listers	48
Capt William Cone Docter Gibbon Jewett and Mr Green Hungerford Ware Chosen a Committe to Repair to the Burying yard Near to Mr Green Hungerford and Make a proper Survey.. also to View the Burying place in the Land that was lately Capt Jared Spencers.. Dec^d Make Report.. how that ought to be Surveyed and how it may be Obtained of Said Capt Spencers Heirs	48

10 Jan 1778

Mr Timothy Gates Was Chosen Moderator	48
Mr Humphry Lyon Capt Samuel Gates Docter Gibbon Jewet Capt Ichabod Throop and Deacon Christopher Holmes Was Chosen Com^{tt} of Inspection	48
Voted that they Would take the powder that Dan^{ll} Brainerd & Jabez Esqr Was to have of Capt Munford	48
Upon the Petition of Major Dyer Throop Jabez Chapman Esqr Capt Elijah Attwood and Mr Nathan Goodspeed Requesting that they might have Liberty to Erect Suitable Buildings for.. Manufacturing salt Petre somewhere in the Town Street Between Daniel Brainerd Esq^{rs} and .. Israel Spencer's Where they Can find a Convenient place for the Works and not Discommode the Publick the Town Voted that they might Have Liberty as Requested	49

2 Dec 1776

Mr Jabez Comstock Was Chosen Moderator	49
Daniel Brainerd Esqr Was Chosen Town Clerk.. & Town Treasurer	49
Mes^{rs} Israel Champion Capt James Green Capt William Cone Capt John Willey Mr Jabez Comstock Ware Chosen Select men	49
Mes^{rs} Joseph Fowler & Mr Robart Hungarford Was Chosen Constables & Said Robart Was Chosen to Gather the Colony Tax and Mr Ebenezer Emons Was Chosen Constable	49
John Percivel Jn^r Capt Matthew Smith Mr Daniel Lord Mr Nathaniel Sparrow & Mr Increase Crosby Ware Chosen Grand Jury men	49
Mes^{rs} Elkanah Higgins Zachariah Cone William Church 2^d Mr Samuel Emons & John Beebe Ware Chosen Tythingmen	49
Mes^{rs} Matthew Smith J^r Timothy Cone Thomas Fuller Sam^{ll} P Lord John Andrews Thomas Marshall Capt Jonathan Olmsted Eliphelet Fuller Joseph Annabel Robart Hurd J^r Timothy Booge Hezekiah Usher George Cone [ ] David Jewitt Green Hungarford Jeremiah Cone Enoch Brainerd James Cone Joseph Arnold 2^d Samuel Hungarford Daniel Fuller Thomas Emons John Watson Samuel Cone Ezra Willey Joseph Beckwith 2^d Levy Crosbee Ware Chosen Surveyors of Highways	49
Mes^{rs} Amos Booge Amasa Brainerd Nathan Barnham Capt Ichabod Olmsted & Lt Elijah Cone Ware Chosen Listers	50
Mesr^{es} Thomas Fuller John Percival Junr Ware Chosen fence Viewers	50
Mes^{rs} Joseph Gate 3^d Danl Olmsted 2^d & Sam^{ll} Cone 2^d Ware Chosen Town Colectors	50
Mr Jonathan Booge Capt Christopher Holmes Joseph Arnold 2^d ware Chosen Leather Sealers	50

East Haddam

Messr Humphry Tiffeny John Warner Stephen Scovel James Booge Jonathan Willey & Medad Thornton Ware Chosen Haward	50
Lt Eleazer Brainerd was Chosen Guager	50
Mr John Willey 2^d & [ ] Church Ware Chosen Branders of Horses	50
Mr William Selby was Chosen Sealer of Weights & Measures	50
Capt Daniel Cone & Mr James Dixson & David West was Chosen key keepers	50
Lt Joseph Gate Mr Jehiel Fuller Daniel Fox John Watson Green Hungarford Jeremiah Cone 2^d Ezekiel B Beckwith & Nehemiah Tracy Ware Chosen Sextons	50
Mr Humphry Lyon Capt Samuel Gates and Doct^r Gibbin Jewett Ware Chosen Committee of Inspection	51
Mr Ebenezer Emmons was Chosen Lister in the Room of Capt Ichabod Olmsted excused	51

30 Jan 1777

Mr Israel Champion was Chosen Moderator	51
Timothy Gates was Chosen Register and also Treasurer	51

24 Mar 1777

Mr Israel Champion was Chosen Moderator	51
Silvanus Tinker was Chosen Clerk Pro Tempore	51
Voted that Samuel Huntington Esqr Timothy Gates Israel Spencer Matthias Fuller Capt Jonah Cone Be a Committee to Provide Necessusaries as The Families of any Such Soldiers.. as have or Shall Inlist in the Continental Service Shall want During the absence of Such Soldier	51
At the Same meeting was Chosen Capt Daniel Cone In an addition to the Committee of Inspection	52

7 Apr 1777

Mr Israel Champion was Chosen Moderator	52

16 Sep 1777

Co^{ll} Dyar Throop was Chosen moderator	53
Capt Samuel Gates: Mr Silvanus Tinker: Samuel Huntington Esqr Doc^t Gibbon Jewett: Capt Christopher Holmes: Capt William Cone: Mr Job Spencer: Capt Matthew Smith: Lieu^t David: B: Spencer: Dea^n Thomas Fuller: Capt Ebenezer Spencer: Mr George Cone ju^r: Capt Ichabod Olmsted: Ens^n Increase Crosby: Capt John Willey: Mr Nathan Gates: Mr Levi Palmer: and Lieu^t Nathan Jewett Be a Committee to provide the following Articles for for every Non Comissioned Officer and Soldier in the Continental army, Belonging to this Town: (viz) one Shirt or more Either Linnen or flannel one hunting Shirt or frock, one pair of wollen over halls one or two pair of Stockings, and one pair of Shoes, to be transmitted to Capt Eliphalet Holmes, as Soon as May be	53
Said Holmes is Desired To Dispose of Said articles, to Said Soldiers at the prises following (viz) Shoes at 8/6 p^r pair: Stockings at 6/ p^r pair: Shirts Hunting frock and over halls according to their quality and in proportion To Good yard wide tow Cloth at 2/9 p^r yard and good yard wide Check^d or Striped flannel at 3/6 p^r yard: and that Capt Holmes be Desired To transmit the money.. to Samuel Huntington Esqr one of S^d Committee: and that this Town Pay the Cost of Said articles and Transportation	53
Mr Caleb Gates was Chosen Collector to Gather the Town Rate in the [ ] of Mr Joseph Gates 3^d	53

East Haddam

1 Dec 1777

Mr Israel Champion was Chosen Moderator	54
Timothy Gates was Chosen Town Clerk.. and also Town Treasurer	54
Mr Israel Champion Capt James Green: Capt Ebenezer Dutton: Capt John Willey: and Mr Jabez Comstock: were Chosen Select men	54
Mr Ebenezer Emons: Mr Joseph Fowler and Mr Robert Hungerford were Chosen Constables.. Said Ebenezer was Chosen to Gather The Colony tax	54
Deac^n Thomas Fuller: Capt Matthew Smith: Mr Nathaniel Cone: Mr Daniel Emons: and Mr Levi Crosby: were Chosen Grandjury Men	54
Mr Amasa Ackley: Mr Jehial Fuller: Mr Enoch Brainerd: Mr David West and Mr Abraham Willey were Chosen Tything men	54
Messrs Timothy Chapman: Noadiah Gates; Bezaleel Brainerd Jonah Brainerd: Amos White Ephraim Ackley: Thomas Knowlton nd Samuel Wright Joel Cone: Job Spencer: Bezaleel Gates: Nathan Jewett Barzillai Beckwith: Joshua Burnham: Joseph Arnold: Dan[ ] Gates: John Arnold 2nd John Driggs: Solomon Cone: Stephen Scovel Samuel Emons: Joseph Selden: Joseph Beckwith: Increase Crosby and John Spencer: were Chosen Surveyors of Highways	54
Messrs Thomas Fuller: and John Parsivel 2nd were Chosen fence Viewers	54
Messrs Phineas Gates; David: B Spencer: Gibbon Jewett: Amasa Dutton: and Robert Hungerford 2nd were Chosen Listers	54
Messrs Eliphalet Fuller Daniel Southmaid and Ebenezer Holmes: were Chosen Town Collectors	55
Capt Christopher Holmes: and Messrs Jonathan Booge: and Joseph Arnold: were Chosen Leather Sealers	55
Messrs Medad Thornton: Timothy Booge: Matthias Fuller & Jeremiah Cone: were chosen Haywards	55
Mr Elijah Medcalf: was Chosen Packer.. and also Culler of Staves	55
Mr Eleazer Brainerd was Chosen Guager	55
Mr William Selby: was Chosen Sealer of weights & measures	55
Capt Daniel Cone: and Mr James Dixson: were Chosen Key keepers	55
Messrs Joseph Gates: Jehiel Fuller: Nehemiah Tracy: Daniel Fox: John Watson: Ira Church: Green Hungerford: and Ezekiel B: Beckwith were Chosen: Sextons	55
Samuel Huntington Esqr Capt Israel Spencer: Mr Matthias Fuller: Capt Jonah Cone: and Capt Matthew Smith: were Chosen: a: Com^{tt} to: To: Provide: Nessasaries: for the Families of those Soldiers That are in the Continental Service	55
Mr Joseph Church: was Chosen Brander of horses	55

6 Jan 1778

Mr Israel Champion Was Chosen Moderator	56
Capt Samuel Gates Lieu^t Humphry Lyon: Doc^t Gibbon: Jewett and Capt Daniel Cone were Chosen a Committee of Inspection	56
Mr William Selby was Chosen: a: Grand jury man .. in The room of Capt Matthew Smith: Excused	56

9 Feb 1778

Mr Israel Champion Was Chosen Moderator	57

East Haddam

Capt Samuel Gates: Mr Silvanus Tinker: Samuel: Huntington: Esqr Doc^t Gibbon jewett --- Capt Christopher Holmes: Capt William Cone: Mr Job: Spencer: Capt Matthew Smith: Lieu^t David: B: Spencer: Deac^n Thomas Fuller Capt Ebenezer Spencer: Mr George Cone 2nd: Capt Ichabod Olmsted: En^s Increase Crosby: Capt John Willey: Mr Nathan Gates: Mr Levi: Palmer: and Lieu^t Nathan jewett --- Were Chosen a Committee: to Provide Blankets: Shoes and Other Articles as Pointed out By an Act of Assembly.. for the Benefit of the Soldiers in the Continental Army	57
Voted that Jonathan Shepard Ju^r Should have five poinds money.. for the Support of his family	57

19 Mar 1778

Mr Israel Champion Was Chosen Moderator	58

15 Sep 1778

Mr Israel Champion Was Chosen Moderator	58
Mr Silvanus Tinker Doc^t Daniel Southmaid: Capt Nathan Jewett: Capt Zachariah Hungerford Mr James Dixson: and Mr John: Percival ju^r were Chosen Assessors to Assist the Listers	58
Voted that: Mr David Willey Should be Paid.. £ 7:4:10 for the Loss of Cloathing Sent to his Sons in the Army	58

7 Dec 1778

Capt James Green was Chosen Moderator	58
Timothy Gates was Chosen Town Clerk.. and also Treasurer	58
Capt Daniel Cone Mr Ebenezer Cone: ju^r Mr Enoch Brainerd Capt Nathan Jewett: and Capt Ebenezer Spencer: were Chosen Select men	59
Messrs Joseph Fowler Ebenezer Emons and Robert Hungerford: were Chosen Constables.. S^d Joseph was Chose to Gather the Coloney Rate	59
Messrs Bezaleel Gates Elkanah Higgins: Matthias Spencer: David Jewett and Phineas Parmerly: were Chosen: Grand jury men	59
Messrs Eliphalet Fuller Ozias Chapman: Richard Church: Joseph Arnold and Israel Andrewes: were Chosen Tythingmen	59
Messrs Thomas Fuller Joshua Gates 2nd Doc^t Gibbon Jewett: Simeon Chapman and Robert Hungerford 2nd were Chosen Listers	59
Messrs John Peek: Obadiah Gates: Ephraim Gates: Gabriel Ely: Aaron Chapman Elijah Atwood: Ephraim Selby: Amos White: David Willey: Joseph Gates 3^d: Joseph Andrewes: -- Abraham Ackley Thomas Beckwith: Benajah Willey: Ephraim Arnold: Lemuel Willey: Hezekiah Usher: Asa Harvy: Reuben Spencer: William Cone ju^r: William Church ju^r John Parker: Joseph Beckwith ju^r: Ezra Willey & Edmund Marsh: were Chosen Surveyor^s of Highways	59
Messrs Thomas Fuller and John Percival 2nd were Chosen: Fence Viewers	59
Messrs Noadiah Cone: Solomon Cone: and Ephraim Fuller: were Chosen: Collectors	59
Messrs Job Spencer and Amasa Dutton were Chosen Seallers of Leather	59
Mr William Selby was Chosen Sealer of weights & Measures	60
Messrs Gideon Spencer: Elihu Beebe: Joseph Stewart: Isaac Chapman" were Chosen: Haywards	60
Mr Eleazer Brainerd was Chosen: Guager	60
Messrs Joseph Church and Ira Church: were Chosen Branders of Horses	60

East Haddam

Capt Daniel Cone: And Mr Ira Church: were Chosen Key keepers	60
Messrs Jehiel Fuller: Joseph Gates: Daniel Fox: Nehemiah Tracy: John Watson -- Zechariah Gates: Green Hungerford: Isaiah Brockway And Nathaniel Beckwith: were Chosen: Sextons	60
Mr John Percival ju^r Capt Samuel Gates: and Mr Humphry Lyon: were Chosen Com^{tt} of Inspection	60
Mr James Olmsted Messrs Lemuel Griffing ju^r Matthias Fuller: and Abraham Willey: were Chosen: a Com^{tt} to Provide for the Soldiers Families	60
Mr Thomas Fuller: Mr Timothy Chapman: Capt Jonathan Olmsted: Mr Bezaleel Gates: Mr William Selby: Mr Matthew Sears Mr Samuel: [ ]: Lord: Mr Abner Hall: Mr Sam^{ll} Emons Mr Amasa Dutton: Capt Ebenezer Dutton: Mr Silvanus Cone Mr Asa Harvey: Mr George Griffing: Deac^n Benjamin Fuller Capt Zechariah Hungerford: Mr Elijah Cone and Mr James Dickson were Chosen a Committee to provide.. Cloathing for the Soldiers in Continental Service	60

14 Dec 1778

voted that the Select men Shall have Liberty to Draw out of the Town Treasury: five Hundred pounds:.. to Purchace Grain with: for the Support of the Poor of the Town that need: and also for the Soldiers Families which are to be provided for: Mr James Olmsted was Chosen a Com^{tt} man to Lay Out Said Money	61
Mr Reuben Beebe: was Chosen a tything man.. in the room of Mr Joseph Arnold	61
Voted that Mr Robert Hungerford.. Shall have Six pounds.. for the Same Sum Lost by Counterfeit money Collected for the Colony tax for.. 1777	61
voted that Mr Joseph Fowler upon his request Shall have £2:8:0.. for that Sum Lost by Counterfeit money: Collected for the Colony tax in this Town in: 1776	61
Mr Jehiel Fuller: was Chosen a Com^{tt} man To provide for the Soldiers Families	61
Voted that: Timothy Gates: Treasurer.. Should have £12:00: .. for his trouble in S^d office the year past	61

11 Jan 1779

Capt Daniel Cone was Chosen Moderator	62
Voted to Raise by Rate or Tax The Sum of three Hundred pounts money: to purchase Cheese And Butter for the Soldiers in the Continental Army that Belong to this Town.. Capt Samuel Gates: Mr Thomas Fuller Capt Daniel Cone: Capt Ebenezer Dutton: Capt Israel Spencer Capt John Willey: Mr Nathaniel Sparrow and: Capt Zachariah Hungerford: were Chosen a Committe to Lay out the Said three Hundred pounds in Butter and Cheese for S^d Soldiers use and to transport the same to them as Soon as may be	62

26 Jul 1779

Capt Daniel Cone was Chosen Moderator	62

6 Dec 1779

Mr Ebenezer Cone 2^d was Chosen Moderator	63
Timothy Gates was Chosen Town Clerk	63
Capt Daniel Cone: Mr Ebenezer Cone 2nd Capt Nathan Jewett: Mr Ebenezer Emons: and Capt Ithamer Harvy was Chosen Select men	63
Mr Joseph Fowler Mr Ebenezer Emons and Mr Robert Hungerford 2nd was Chosen Constables.. and Said Hungerford was Chosen to Gather the State Tax	63
Timothy Gates was Chosen Treasurer	63
Messr^s Joel Cone Silvanus Tinker; Capt Jonah Cone: Mr Amasa Dutton and Increase Crosby:	64

East Haddam

were Chosen Grand jurors

Messr^s Abner Hall: Elijah Ackley 2nd Isaac Spencer: John Annable and Joseph Selden were Chosen Tything men 64

Messr^s Joshua Gates 2nd Timothy Chapman: Richard Sparrow: Daniel Emons and John Spencer: were Chosen Listers 64

Messr^s Job Winslow: Caleb Gates Elisha Cone: Levi Palmer: Thomas Fuller: Matthew Smith 3^d Amasa Brainerd: Amasa Ackley: Elijah Medcalf: Eliphas Spencer: David Jewett: Joseph Gates 2^d: John Annable -- Nathaniel Ackley: 3^d: Reuben Spencer: Capt Jonathan Kilborn Daniel Shaw: Robert Harvy: Zachariah Harvy: James: Dixson Roswell Cone: Joseph Comstock: Elijah Hungerford: Ephraim Willey: and Israel Comstock: were Chosen Surveyors of Highways 64

Messr^s Thomas Fuller and John Persival 2^d: were Chosen fence Viewers 64

Messr^s Samuel Fuller Nathan Gates and Judah Cone: were Chosen Collectors of Rates 64

Messr^s Job Spencer: and Amasa: Dutton were Chosen Leather Sealers 64

Mr William Selby was Chosen Sealer of weights & measures 64

Messr^s Daniel Warner: Joseph Arnold Francis Chapman: Samuel Stewart: Lemuel Marsh: and Joseph Gilbert: were Chosen Haywards 64

Mr Eleazer Brainerd was Chosen Guager 65

Mr Joseph Church was Chosen Brander of Horses 65

Capt Daniel Cone: and Mr Zachariah Gates: were Chosen Key keepers 65

Messr^s Jehiel Fuller: Nehemiah Tracy: Joseph Gates: Isaiah Rogers: John Watson: Green Hungerford: Joseph Beckwith 3^d: Nathaniel Gates: and Amos Randol: were Chosen Sextons 65

Messrs Thomas Hall 2^d: Thomas Smith 2^d Joseph Emons: Simeon Ackley 2^d: and Asael Andrewes: were chosen: a Committee to provide for the Soldiers Families 65

13 Dec 1779

Mr Elijah Medcalf was Chosen Packer.. And also Culler of Staves 65

Messrs Thomas Fuller: Timothy Chapman: Ephraim Ackle: Capt Jonathan Olmsted Isaac Ackley: Samuel: P. Lord: Matthew Sears: Matthew Smith 2^d: - George Griffing: Capt Ebenezer Button: Doc^t Augustus Mather: Daniel Lord: Silvanus Cone: Samuel Emons Phineas Parmerly: Abraham Willey: Joseph Willey 2^d: - and Thomas Beckwith: were Chosen a Committee to provide Cloathing for the Soldiers in the Continental Army.. Also Doc^t Thomas Mosley was Chosen for one of S^d Com^{tt} in the Room of Capt Jonathan Olmsted 65

16 Mar 1780

Capt Daniel Cone was Chose Moderator 66

Capt James Green Mr Elijah Atwood Mr Elijah Medcalf Mr Eliphas Spencer: Mr Abner Hall: Mr Jehiel Fuller: Mr Joseph Church: Mr Barzillai Beckwith: Mr Matthias Fuller: Mr Richard Sparrow: Mr Samuel Emons Mr Enoch Arnold: Mr Asa Harvy: Mr Joseph Selden Mr Jabez Comstock: Capt Ebenezer Spencer: Capt Zechariah Hungerford: & Mr Samuel Willey: were Chosen Inspector of Provisions 66

Col^o Dyar Throop Esqr was Chosen Agent for the Town 66

10 Apr 1780

Mr Ebenezer Cone 2^d: was Chose Moderator 66

Mr Zechariah Gates: was Chose: Collector.. in the room of Mr Nathan Gates: who refuses to Serve 66

East Haddam

26 Jun 1780

Mr Ebenezer Cone 2^d: was Chose Moderator   67

16 Nov 1780

Mr Ebenezer Cone 2^d: was Chose Moderator   67

Voted that Co^{lo} Jabez Chapman Capt Samuel Gates: Doc^t Gibbons Jewett: Capt Enoch Brainerd: Capt Eliphalet Holmes: Capt Israel Spencer and Capt Jonathan Kilborn Be a Committee .. for Dividing and Classing all the Inhabitants of the Town   67

Voted: That Mr Samuel [?] Lord: Capt Ebenezer Dutton: and Capt Eliphalet Holmes: Be a Committee To Receive the Governments Salt: To Procure Barrels: faithfully To Receive: Inspect: and put up: all Such Provisions as Shall be Raised Collected and Deliver^d to them by a rate or tax on the List.. for.. 1779   68

4 Dec 1780

Maj^r Daniel Cone was Chosen Moderator   68

Timothy Gates Esqr was Chosen Town Clerk .. also was Chose Treasurer   68

Maj^r Daniel Cone: Mr Ebenezer Cone 2nd: Mr Barzillai Beckwith: Capt Ebenezer Emons: and Capt Ithamer Harvy were Chosen Selectmen   68

Mr Joseph Fowler: Capt Ebenezer Emons and Mr Robert Hungerford 2^d: were Chosen Constables.. and Said Joseph was Chose to Gather the State Tax   68

Mr Jehiel Fuller: Capt David: B: Spencer Mr Silvanus Cone 2^d: Mr Samuel Emons: and Mr Jabez Comstock: were chosen Grand jurors   68

Mr Bezaleel Brainerd: Mr Amasa Brainerd Mr Ephraim Arnold: Mr James Cone and Capt Zachariah Hungerford were Chosen Tything men   69

Messrs Caleb Gates Jonah Scovel: Amos White Ozias Chapman: Joseph Warner: Joseph Annable Eleazer Rowley: Thomas Olcott Ephraim Gates: Nehemiah Tracy: Bezaleel Gates: Job Spencer: Simeon Ackley Solomon Cone Simon Starlin: Levi Beebe: Joseph Arnold Samuel Stewart: Lemuel Griffing 2^d Nathaniel Ackley 3^d: Joseph Ackley: Richard Sparrow: Nathaniel Hungerford: Zachariah Gates: Joseph Beckwith 2^d: Abraham Willey Noah Willey 2^d: John Warner 2^d: Dan^{ll} Hall Edward Dixson: & Joshua Chapel were Chosen Surveyors of Highways   69

Messrs Joshua Gates: 2^d: Timothy Chapman John Spencer: Daniel Emons: and Nathaniel Sparrow: were Chosen: Listers   69

Messrs Ezekiel Fox: David Willey: were Chose Haywards   69

Messrs Isaac Ackley and James Olmsted were Chose fence Viewers   69

Mr William Selby was Chose Sealer of weights & measures   69

Mr Eleazer Brainerd was Chose Guager   69

Mr Joseph Church was Chose Brander of horses   69

Messrs Joseph Gates: Jehiel Fuller Nehemiah Tracy: Isaiah Rogers; Green Hungerford: John Watson Ezekiel: B: Beckwith: and Jeremiah Cone were Chose Saxtons   69

Maj^r Daniel Cone and Mr Zachariah Gates were Chose Key keepers   69

Messrs David Brainerd: Isaac Spencer 2^d and Stephen Beckwith: were Chose Collector of Rates   69

Messrs Thomas Fuller: George Griffing: and Phineas Parmerly were Chosen: a Cloathing Committee to provide Cloathing for the Soldiers in the Continental Army   70

Messrs David West: Nathan Goodspeed: Increase Crosby and: Stephen Scovel: were Chosen a Com^{tt} of Supply^s for the Soldiers Families   70

East Haddam

Voted to Give the Second Division of Soldiers: that was Called for: and that went into the continental Service.. last July The Same addition to their Bounty and wages: as those that Inlisted by the first of July as by their vote at a Town Meeting.. on the 26th Day of June Last.. voted that Joseph Willey 2^d a Detach^d Soldier: for the Continental Service: Should have the Same Additional Bounty as the above Soldiers are Intitled	70
19 Dec 1780	
Colonell Dyar Throop Esqr was Chosen Agent for the Town	70
Mr Daniel Lord 2^d was Chosen Collector of Rates.. in the room of Mr Isaac Spencer 2^d Excus^d	70
Mr Levi Palmer was Chosen Leather Sealer	70
Mr Elijah Medcalf was Chosen Packer: and also Culler of Staves	70
Mr Nehemiah Cone was Chosen a Surveyor of Highways	71
26 Dec 1780	
Mr Silvanus Tinker was Chosen a Com^{tt} Man to Assist S^d Classing Com^{tt} in the Room of Capt Samuel Gates Excused -- also Capt James Green: was Chosen a Com^{tt} man for S^d purpose of Classing in the Room of Col^o Jabez Chapman Excus^d	71
9 Jan 1781	
Mr Judah Cone was Chosen Surveyor of Highways	72
Mr Noadiah Gates Shall be a Com^{tt} to receive in and put up.. Towns quota of flour And Grain for the State	72
16 Apr 1781	
Maj^r Daniel Cone was Chosen Moderator	73
Doc^t Zachariah Chapman: Do^{ct} Gibbons Jewett: and Capt Eliphalet Holmes: were Chosen a Committee To Divide & Class the Inhabitants.. to Raise: the Six Soldiers or Infantry for the Defence of this State	73
Mr George Cone 2^d: was Chosen a Lister.. in the Room of Mr Nathaniel Sparrow Excus^d	73
Mr Timothy Cone was Chosen a Lister.. in the room of Mr Joshua Gates 2^d: Dec^d	73
Mr Edward Chapman was Chosen Surveyor of Highways.. in the room of Mr Joseph Annable who is Excus^d by reason of Age	73
23 Apr 1781	
Messrs Joseph Emons and Daniel Emons and Capt Eliphalet Holmes: were Chosen a Com^{tt} to purchase provisions to make up S^d Towns Deficiency as their Quota	73
25 Jun 1781	
Mr Ebenezer Cone 2^d: was Chose moderator	74
Messrs Silvanus Tinker Noadiah Gates Capt Ebenezer Dutton and Capt Eliphalet Holmes was Chosen a Committee to Receive and put up for S^d Town their Quota of Beef, Pork, Flour: &c: for the use of theArmy	74
Mr Joseph Emons was Chosen a Purchaser of Beef	74
Mr Jedadiah Higgins was Chosen Surveyor of Highways.. in the room of Mr Edward Chapman: Going into Continental Service	74
8 Nov 1781	
Maj^r Daniel Cone was Chosen Moderator	75

East Haddam

13 Nov 1781

Mr Joseph Emmons and Capt Eliphalet Holmes were Chosen purchasers & Receivers of Beef and flour: and Capt Ebenezer Dutton was Chosen a Purchaser and Receiver of Beef: and Messrs Noadiah Gates and Daniel Lord ju^r were Chosen Receivers of flour -- all for Said Towns quota of provisions for the Army	*78*
Capt Eliphalet Holmes was Chosen a Committee to procure Salt for Said Town to put up S^d Beef &c	*79*

3 Dec 1781

Maj^r Daniel Cone was Chose Moderator	*79*
Timothy Gates Esqr was Chosen Town Clerk	*79*
Messrs Joseph Church Joseph Emmons Daniel Emmons Simeon Chapman and Capt Zachariah Hungerford: were Chosen Select men	*79*
Timothy Gates Esqr was Chosen Treasurer	*79*
Mr Joseph Fowler: Capt Ebenezer Emmons and Mr Robert Hungerford 2^d: were Chosen Constables.. and S^d Capt Emmons was Chosen to Collect the State Tax	*79*
Messrs Eleazer Rowley Isaac Chapman Elijah Ackley 2^d Jedadiah Higgins Zachariah Cone Nathan Stedman: Co^{lo} John Hurlbut: John [ ] Albertson Samuel Wright: William: W: Fuller: Matthew Smith 2^d Amasa Dutton Nathaniel Lord: Ens John Arnold: Lemuel Griffing 2^d: Nathaniel Hungerford: Amos Randol: Joseph Gates 2^d: Green Hungerford: Silas Beebe Hobart Eastabrook Reuben Spencer: Lt George Cone: Joseph Selden: John Parker and Ezekiel: B: Beckwith - - - - - were Chosen Surveyors of Highways	*79*
Mr Isaac Ackley and Capt Jonathan Olmsted were Chos fence viewers	*80*
Messrs Abner Hall Lt Amasa Brainerd Daniel Olmsted 2^d William Cone 2^d and Ebenezer Holmes were Chosen Listers	*80*
Messrs Amos White: Isaac Spencer 2^d and Levi Crosby 2^d: were Chosen Collectors of Rates	*80*
Capt David: B: Spencer and Mr Joseph Arnold were Chose Leather Sealers	*80*
Messrs Joel Cone Elijah Ackley Noadiah Fuller: Lt Isaac Spencer: and Phineas Parmerly were Chosen Grand juror	*80*
Messrs Levi Palmer Nathan Goodsped John Watson: John Annable and John Beebe were Chose Tything men	*80*
Messrs Joseph Andrewes: Noadiah Cone Caleb Beebe &: John Driggs were Chosen Haywards	*80*
Messrs Eleazer Brainerd and Gideon Cook were Chosen Guagers	*80*
Mr Elijah Medcalf: was Chosen Packer	*80*
Mr Joseph Church was Chosen Brander of Horses	*80*
Mr William Selby was Chose Sealer of weights and Measures	*80*
Maj^r Daniel Cone and Mr David Burnham were Chos Key Keepers	*80*
Messrs Jehel Fuller Joseph Gates Nathaniel Hungerford John Watson: Nathaniel Gates Samuel Clark: Joseph Beckwith 3^d Nehemiah Tracy and Isaiah Rogers were Chosen Saxtons	*81*
Deac^n Thomas Fuller /~~En^s John Arnold~~/ Hezekiah Usher and Benajah Willey: were Chosen a Com^{tt} of Supply^s for the Soldiers Families.. Said Willey was Chose in the room of Said Arnold Excusd	*81*
Mr Thomas Fuller: was Chose a Com^{tt} to provide Cloathing for the Soldiers in the Continental Army: /if Called for by the State/	*81*

East Haddam

28 Feb 1782

Mr Joseph Church was Chose Moderator 82

Voted to Divid or Class the Inhabitants.. into as many Classes as there are Soldiers Required 82
for Said Towns quota of men for the post of Horse neckL or western frontiers.. Capt James
Green Maj^r Daniel Cone: Capt Ichabod Omsted Capt Willm Cone and Capt Ithamer Harvey:
were Chosen a Committee.. for Classing the Inhabitants

Capt Eliphalet Holmes and Israel Spencer Esqr were Chosen Agents: to Represent S^d Town at 82
Hartford Before the Committee appointed By the General Assembly to Ascertain the
Deficiency of Continental and State Soldiers in the Several Towns in the County of Hartford

Messrs Thomas Fuller and Silvanus Cone 2^d were Chosen a Committee to Supply the Soldiers 82
familys

Mr Joseph Arnold was Chosen Tything man 82

12 Mar 1782

Mr Joel Cone: was Chosen a Com^{tt} to Supply the Soldiers familys.. in the room of Mr Thomas 83
Fuller Excus^d

Mr Jehiel Fuller: Mr Amos White Mr Joseph Fowler: Mr Jabez Comstock: Mr Joseph Arnold 83
Mr Nathan Gates: Mr Amasa Dutton Doc^t Gibbon Jewett and Mr George Griffing: were
Chosen Committy^s or fore men: of Each Class to which they Respectively Belong To give
notice to the Individuals in their S^d Classes to meet.. to Raise a Recruit &c

Capt Eliphalet Holmes Mr Joseph Fowler and Mr Noadiah Gates were Chosen a Committee to 83
Examin into the Towns accounts

Doc^t Zachariah Chapman Doc^t Daniel Southmayd and Mr Robert Hungerfor 2^d were Chosen a 83
Com^{tt} To Class the Inhabitants.. Into as many Classes as Said Town Shall be found Deficient
of their Quota of Soldiers to fill up the Continental army

26 Mar 1782

voted that: Doc^t Gibbon Jewett and Capt Eliphalet Holmes be a Committee to examin into the 84
affair of the Class N° 1 that neglected Raising their State Soldier for the Last year: and also to
Examin.. that Class that hired a Horseman for the State Service the year past and Neglected
to Send Said Horseman into Service and to Sue: if they Judge Proper To Recover Such Sum..
as Shall avaridge with other Classes that hired State Soldiers the Same year - Together with a
Reasonable part of Said Horsemans Bounty to be by him returned

Mr Thomas Fuller Mr Nath[ ] Goodspeed Mr John Warner 3^d Mr Eliot Beckwith Mr Abraham 84
Ackley Mr Nathaniel Gates Mr Daniel Shaw Mr Joseph Andrewes and Mr Nathaniel Baker:
were Chosen Collectors for the Classes to which they Respectively Belong

Mr George Cone 2^d: and Mr Amos Randol were Chosen a Committee of Supplys for Soldiers 84
familys.. S^d George was Chosen in the room of Mr Silvanus Cone 2^d Excus^d

Voted that Capt Eliphalet Holmes Be a Committee (or Superintendant) To Inspect Take Care 84
and See that Soldiers in the Army Belonging to this Town (That Come home on furloughs or
otherwise) Be Sent on to Camp at a proper time to Return as he Shall Judge fit: and also to
take up Deserted Soldiers that Belong To this Town: and to Send Such Deserters on to Camp
when Ever they may be found

Voted that Capt Eliphalet Holmes S^d Towns Com^{tt} Man: for to Look up Deserted Soldiers &c: 84
to Send them on to the Army: Shall have Liberty.. to Draw his just Cost out of the Town
Treasury

8 Apr 1782

Messrs Silvanus Tinker: Zachariah Chapman: Joseph Fowler: Jabez Comstock: Nathan Gates: 85
Gibbons Jewett: Amasa Dutton: Joseph Arnold: and George Griffing - were Chosen

East Haddam

Committee^s or fore men of Each Class to which they Respectively Belong: to give notice to Said Classes to meet.. to raise a Continental Recruit or Soldier for Each Class	
Messrs Thomas Fuller: Nathan Goodspeed: Ambrose Dutton Nathaniel Lord: Elijah Clark: Jabez Comstock 2^d: Timothy Spencer Joseph Andrewes: and Lemuel Griffing 2^d: were Chosen Collectors for the Clases to which they Belong: for Raising the Continental Soldiers	85
Voted: that provided Pierce Mobs: Cannot be held as a Continental Soldier /for this Town/ that Capt Eliphalet Holmes Hire one in S^d Mobs room on the Towns Cost	85
Mr Joseph Church was Chosen Moderator	85

29 Aug 1782

Mr Joseph Church was Chosen Moderator	86

2 Dec 1782

Timothy Gates Esqr was Chosen Town Clerk	86
Messrs Joseph Church: Joseph Emmons: Daniel Emmons: George Griffing: and Capt Eliphalet Holmes: were Chosen Select Men	86
Timothy Gates Esqr was Chosen Town Treasurer	86
Messrs Joseph Fowler: Capt Ebenezer Emmons and Robert Hungerford 2^d were Chosen Constables.. and the Said Robert was Chose to Collect the State Taxes	86
Messrs Eleazer Rowley: Phineas Gates: John Brainerd: Jonathan Booge: Hezekiah Mack Gideon Cook Reuben Champion: Ephraim Ackley: Capt James Green: Levi Beebe: Joseph Gates 2^d: Hobart Eastabrook Jabez Swan: Samuel Olmsted: Abraham Williams: Hezekiah Usher Noadiah Emmons: Gideon Bailey: Isaac Spencer: Edward Dixson Job Beckwith: Roswell Cone: Eliot Beckwith Philip Williams Asa Harvey & Asael Andrewes: were Chosen.. Surveyors of Highways.. also William Giltson was Chose a Surveyor	86
Messrs Crippen Hurd: Timothy Cone: Nathan Burnham: Samuel Emmons: and Increase Crosby: were Chosen Grand jurors	86
Messrs Thomas Hall 2^d: Elijah Medcalf: Daniel Fuller: Reuben Spencer: and Judah Cone were Chosen Tything men	86
Mr Noadiah Gates: Capt David B:Spencer: Capt Enoch Brainerd: Mr Richard Sparrow: and Mr Ebenezer Holmes: were Chosen Listers	87
Messrs Isaac: C: Ackley: Noadiah Fuller 2^d and Elijah Hungerford: were Chosen Collectors of Town Rates	87
Capt David: B: Spencer: and Mr Joseph Arnold were chosen Leather Sealers	87
Messrs John Persivel 3^d: Robert Hurd 2^d: John Warner 3^d: Ithamer Fuller: Joseph Dutton: James Booge: Matthias Gates: and Jabez Warner 2^d Noah Willey 2^d were Chosen Haywards	87
Messrs Eleazer Brainerd and Gideon Cook were Chosen Guagers	87
Mr Joseph Church was Chosen Brander of Horses	87
Mr William Selby was Chosen Sealer of weights & Measures	87
Maj^r Daniel Cone was Chosen Key keeper also Messrs Nathaniel Gates: & Amos Randol were Chosen key keepers	87
Messrs Jehiel Fuller: Joseph Gates Nehemiah Tracy: Robertson Williams: John Watson: Nathaniel Gates: Joseph Beckwith 3^d: Nathaniel Hungerford: Samuel Clark were Chosen Saxtons	87
Mr Ozias Chapman Deac^n Benjamin Fuller: Capt Ichabod Olmsted: Nathaniel Sparrow were Chosen a Committee of Supplys for Soldiers Familey's	88
Capt Ebenezer Dutton was Chosen a Com[*mittee*] to provide Cloathing for the Soldiers in Continental Service if Called for	88

East Haddam

Voted that Capt Eliphalet Holmes Messrs Noadiah Gates and Joseph Fowler: a former Com^{tt} for odditing accounts with the Select Men &c — 88

Voted that Mr Samuel Booge by reason of his aged Mother Being Bedrid for a number of years Shall have Liberty of a Contribution throughout this Town as Soon as may be — 88

Mr Joseph Church was Chosen Moderator — 88

24 Dec 1782

Messrs Joseph Arnold: Matthias Fuller and Asa Harvey: were Chosen a Com^{tt} of Supplys for Soldiers Familys.. in the Room of Capt Ichabod Olmsted Deac^n Benjamin Fuller and Mr Nathaniel Sparrow - Excused — 89

Capt Eliphalet Holmes was Chosen Moderator — 89

7 Apr 1783

Mr Bezaleel Brainerd and Capt Ithamer Harvey: were Chosen Select Men — 89

Mr Silvanus Tinker was chosen Lister — 89

East Hampton/Chatham

Records and Accounts of the Selectmen
February 2 – 1781 – September 27, 1798

Located at the Connected State Archives

East Hampton/Chatham

19 Dec 1774

Voted that this Town Do accept and approve of The Doings of the Continental Congress held at Philadelphia in September Last and agree To Keep .. the Same.. and the following Persons are appointed as a Com^{tee} of observation According To the Eleventh Article of Said Association .. (Viz) Eben^r White Esqr John Cooper Capt Moses Bush Charles Goodrich Capt John Penfield Enoch Smith Doct^r Jer^h Bradford Capt George Stocking Capt Stephen Olmsted Capt Abijah Hall & Capt Silas Dunham   29

10 Apr 1775

this May Certify that the persons Whose Names Are Under Written are of a peaceable and Civil Conversation and otherwise Qualified According To Law To Take the freemans oath (viz) John Washburn Aaron Willcox Stephen Stocking Nathan Brainerd Moses Willcox Eben^r Hall Noadiah White Ju^r Abraham Schillenx Jonathan Brown John Bidwell Fisk Bartlit John Ward Edward Shepard Stephen Hosmer Timothy Cornwell Jon^th Ufford Joseph White Joel Hall Thomas Rogers Timothy Smith Josiah Cook Ju^r Daniel Shepard Ju^r Thomas Stevenson Moses Higgins Ezra Purple Charles Goodrich Warren Green Ju^r Jabez Hall Thomas Johnson & Simeon Penfield........ David Sage Jer^h Bradford Elisha Cornwall John Penfield Silas Dunham } Select Men   29

19 Sep 1775

this May Certify that the Persons Whose names are Under Written Are of a peaceable and Civil Conversation and otherwise Quallifyed.. To take the freemans oath (Viz) David White Solomon Goodrich Moses Cornwill John White George Ranney Ju^r John Bartlit Eliakem Ufford Joseph Pelton Ju^r Samuel Lewcas Joseph Washborn Thomas Cornwell & Daniel Lee..... David Sage.. Jon^th Penfield.. Silas Dunham.. John Penfield } Select Men   30

4 Dec 1775

Capt Sam^ll Hall Chosen Moderator   30

David Sage Esqr Eben^r White Esqr Maj^r John Penfield Capt George Stocking Enoch Smith Capt Abijah Hall and Capt Stephen Olmsted Chosen Select Men   30

Hezekiah Goodrich Sam^ll Taylor & Bryan Pamerlee Were Chosen Constables   30

Benjamin Bowers John Ufford John Mighells Abner Stocking Jonathan Clark Ju^r James Bill Othnail Brainerd and Samuel Acley Chosen Grand jury Men   30

Doct^r Moses Bartlit David Robinson Jer^h Goodrich Ju^r Hezekiah Sears John Giddings John Norton Ju^r Gideon Arnold and Thomas Williams Chosen Listers   30

John Pelton John Washborn Daniel Shepard Ju^r Seth Hubbard Sam^ll Young Moses Cook Titus Carrier Chosen Tything Men   30

Voted this Meeting be adjourned.. to the Third Monday of this Instant December at nine of the Clock in the Morning.. Test Jon^th Penfield Town Clerk   30

18 Dec 1775

Aaron Clarke Chosen Grandjuryman.. And James Bill above is Released   30

Capt Joseph Blague Lt Noadiah Russel John Cooper Leiu^t Joseph Churchel Nath^ll Brown Aaron Willcox Elijah Stocking Jese Johnson Enoch Smith Lemuel Smith Richard Mayo Simon Brainerd Benjamin Smith Joseph Dart Capt Abijah Hall Capt Stephen Olmsted Thomas Cowdery Deacon John Clark Moses Cole Rowland Percivil and Stephen Brainerd Chosen Surveyors of Highways   31

David Robinson Lt Daniel Shepard Capt Sam^ll Hall Warren Green Capt Daniel Brainerd Capt Abijah Hall and John Norton Ju^r Chosen Town fence Viewers   31

David Robinson Nath^ll Mott and Thomas Hubbard Chosen Sealers of Leather   31

East Hampton/Chatham

Whereas Hez^h Goodrich haveing Made Sufficient Excuse for not Serving as a Constable..To the acceptance of this meeting there was chosen in his Room James Wilton	31
Gideon Hall Ithamer Pelton Stephen Penfield Nath^{ll} Cornwell Zoeth Smith Ozias Brainerd Seth Hubbard Dewey Hall Ezra Purple Nath^{ll} Clark Nathan Lewis and Stephen Brainerd Are Chosen Hog Haywards	31
Abraham Schellinx Cristopher Van sant Jedediah Hubbard and Richard Cook Chosen Key Keepers of pounds	31
John Mighells Chosen Sealer of Weights	31
Elisha Shepard Chosen Sealer of Dry measures	31
Sam^{ll} Hall Chosen Sealer of Liquid measurs	31
Robert Stevenson & Enoch Smith Chosen Gagers	32
Sam^{ll} Taylor and Robert Stevenson Chosen packers	32
John Bidwell and Isaac Smith Ju^r Chosen Cullers	32
Jonathan Penfield Chosen Brander of Horses	32
Sam^{ll} Taylor Chosen Collector To Gather the Two Last Town Rates in Middle haddam parrish which were Granted in 1773 and 1774	32
Bryan Pamerlee Chosen Collector to Gather the last Town Rate in East Hampton parrish Granted in.. 1774	32
Enoch Smith Sam^{ll} Abby and John Norton Ju^r Chosen .. a Com^{tee} to Settel Some affairs with Lt David Smith in Middle haddam parrish Concerning the Colony School money Taken out of the Treasury Some years Past	32
James Wilton Chosen Collector To gather the Colony Rate	32
Jonathan Penfield Chosen as a School Com^{tee} To Recive the Colony School money.. out of the Treasury and To Divide in proportion To the Severall Schools	32

8 Apr 1776

this may Certify that the Person whos name is under Written is of of a Peaceble and Civil Conversation and otherwise Qualified By law To take ye freemans oath viz Joshua Grifeth.. David Sage.. Stephen Olmsted.. Eben^r White.. Abijah Hall.. Enoch Smith } Select Men	32

2 Dec 1776

Capt Stephen Olmsted Chosen Moderator	33
Ebenezer White Esqr David Sage Esqr and Maj^r John Penfield Were Chosen Select Men.. voted this Meeting To be adjorned .. for one hour.. the meeting the Proceded To Chuse the Rest of the Select Men.. (viz) Enoch Smith Deac^n David Smith Capt Abijah Hall and Capt Stephen Olmsted	33
James Wilton Samuel Taylor and Bryan Parmelee Were Chosen Constables	33
Hezekiah Goodrich Ezra Bevin Capt Daniel Stewart Seth Doane Amasa Daniels and John Bates were Chosen Grandjuriers	33
Doc^t Moses Bartlit David Robinson Jer^h Goodrich Ju^r Hezekiah Sears John Giddins Gideon Arnold John Nortons Ju^r and Thomas Williams were Chosen Listers	33
David White Jonth Brown Israel Higgins Ju^r Samuel Fuller Dewey Hall and Nathan Lewis were Chosen Tything Men	33
Surveyors of highways.. William Dixon Noah Smith Thomas Cooper Abel Strickland Jeremiah Goodrich Ju^r Capt Daniel Brainerd Benjamin Smith Elijah Abel Warren Green Ju^r John Giddings Sam^{ll} Youngs Bryan Parmelee Nathaniel Clark Isaac Kneeland Thomas Goodrich Othniel Brainerd Nathan Lewis David Martin Nathaniel Brown John Ufford David	33

East Hampton/Chatham

Robinson and Ebenezer Hall

James Wilton Chosen a packer of meat	33
Doctor Moses Bartlit Enoch Smith and William Clark Are Chosen as a Com[tee] to Settle acouts with the Town Treasurer	33
Voted this be adjorned.. To Monday the 16th Day of this Instant Decemr.. Test Jonath[n] Penfield Town Clerk	33

16 Dec 1776

fence viewers.. David Robinson Leiu[t] Daniel Shepard Cap[t] Sam[ll] Hall Warren Green Cap[t] Daniel Brainerd Cap[t] Abijah Hall John Norton Ju[r] and Bryan Parmelee	34
Benjamin Stocking Nicholas Ames Thomas Hubbard and Nathaniel Mott were Chosen Sealers of Leather	34
John Crosby Daniel Lee Beriah Bacon Joseph Makham Tim[t] Smith Alexander Case John Hubbard Ju[r] Rich[d] Cook Jabez Clark Moses Cole John Johnson Ju[r] Samuel Killborn and Ephraim Harding were Chosen Hog Hayards	34
Abraham Schellenx Cristopher Van sant Mahetable Youngs and Richard Cook are Chosen Key keepers of Pounds	34
Abraham Schellenx Cristopher Van sant Mahetable Youngs and Richard Cook are Chosen Key keepers of Pounds	34
John Mighells Chosen Sealers of Weights	34
Elisha Shepard Chosen Sealer of Dry Measurs	34
Cap[t] Sam[ll] Hall Chosen Sealer of Liquid Dito	34
John Bidwell and Enoch Smith Chosen Gagers of Cask	34
Samuel Taylor Chosen paker of meat	34
John Bidwell and Sam[ll] Taylor Chosen Cullers of Staves	34
James Wilton Released from Serving as a Constable.. and Hez[h] Goodrich Chosen in his Room and Released from Serving as a Grandjury man .. and Moses Willcox chosen Grandjury Man in his Room	34
Samuel Taylor Chosen Collector To Gather the Colony Rate.. and to Settle the Same with the Colony Treasurer	34
Enoch Smith and Cap[t] Abijah Hall were Chosen as a Commitee To abate Rates	35
Jonathan Penfield Chosen as a Comtee To Receve the Colony School money …And To Distribute the Same to the Severall Schools	35

16 Dec 1776

We the Subscribers Being appointed.. To Enquire into and Settle the acount of S[d] Town with Cap[t] Sam[ll] Hall Teasurer.. Do find as folloeth viz.. To Cash by Doc[t] Bradford for y[e] Sale of Lands } 09=17-4.. To Dito James Rich.. 13-2-0.. To Dito by Lucy Knowlels 3-16-2.. Examined p[r] us John Clark.. Enoch Smith.. Moses Bartlit } Com[tee]	35
Whereas there appeared To be a Mistake in the Making the Rate on the Grant of the year 1774 which Consequently Made an Error in the above Sittlement which Error To Rectify.. we the Subswcribers.. Do find that the Bills on the List of 1774 were made £21-9-10 1/2 Less then was Granted.. p[r] Enoch Smith William Clark.. Moses Bartlit } Com[tee]	36

1 Apr 1777

Cap[t] Abijah Hall Chosen Moderator	36
Voted that a Commitee be appointed.. To provide Necessarys for the famelies of the Soldiers.. who Shall Engage and Go into any of the Continental battalions to be Raised in this	36

194

East Hampton/Chatham

State.. John Cooper David Robinson Charles Goodrich Moses Willcox George Stocking Chancey Bulkley John Giddins James Bill Bryan Parmelee Thos Cowdery Thomas Williams and Joseph Dart Be a Commitee
16 Sep 1777

in open freemans Meeting.. The following Persons.. appeared and had the oath Provided for freemen.. administered to them (Viz) Jeremiah Goodrich Ju^r.. John Giddings.. Edward Purple.. Thomas Cooper.. Elkanah Sears.. Seth Doane.. Nath^{ll} Brown.. Ebenez^r Hall.. Joseph White.. Jabez Clark.. Benjamin Goff.. Colo^n John Penfield.. Capt Sam^{ll} Hall.. Ezra Bevin.. John Hinkley.. Andrew Carrier.. Jonth Clark.. Darius Addams.. Gideon Arnold.. Aaron Horsford.. Christopher Vansant.. James Bill.. Richard Mayo.. Nath^{ll} Cornwell.. Noadiah White Ju^r.. Abijah Hall.. Hezekiah Goodrich.. Capt Moses Bush.. Joseph Kellogg.. John Bidwell.. Rever^d Cyprian Strong.. Revd John Norton.. David Sage Esqr.. Eben^r White Esqr.. John Shepard.. Warren Green.. David Robinson.. Elisha Taylor.. Enoch Smith.. Capt Daniel Brainerd.. Jonth Bush.. Lt Noadiah Russell.. Moses White.. Robert Stiles.. Jonth Pamerlee.. James Acley Ju^r.. Moses West.. Nathan Lewis.. Ezra Purple.. James Stanclift.. David White.. Thomas Johnson.. John White.. Jonathan Penfield.. Sam^{ll} Taylor.. Bryan Pamerlee.. Capt Jeremiah Goodrich.. Capt Stephen Olmsted.. Capt John Cooper.. Capt Abijah Hall.. Thomas Cowdery.. Chancey Bulkley.. Elisha Shepard.. Thomas Williams

37

22 Sep 1777

personally appeared Nath^{ll} Freeman Esqr.. To Whom the oath of Fidelity.. was administred By Me Ebenez^r White Jus^t Peace

37

30 Sep 1777

Warren Green Chosen Moderator

38

Voted.. that the Soldiers Inlisted into the Continental army Shall Be provided with Necessarys.. Voted that there Should be a Commite Chosen.. in Each Parrish of S^d Town To procure Said Necessarys.. Chosen as Said Com^{tee} in the first Society Joseph Sage Hezekiah Goodrich Thomas Cooper Lt Noadiah Russel Capt Joseph Churchel Elisha Shepard Jesse Johnson Joshua Goodrich Nicholas Ames John Ufford & William Dixon & Jeremiah Goodrich

38

In Middle haddam Elisha Taylor Capt Joseph Dart Enoch Smith Josiah Strong Chancey Bulkley John Giddings Gershom Rowley Benjn Smith Hezekiah Sears Elisha Hurlbut Sam^{ll} Young Lemuel Higgins and Jonathan Smith Ju^r

38

in East Hampton John Hinkley John Bates Benjn Goff Elkanah Sears Isaac Kneeland Thomas Cowdery Stephen Brainerd & John Clark Ju^r

38

1 Dec 1777

Capt Stephen Olmsted Chosen Moderator

39

in open Town Meeting the following persons.. appeared and Took the oath of Fidelity.. which Was administered To them by Ebenez^r White Esqr (viz) Capt Stephen Olmsted.. Capt Abijah Hall.. William Welch.. Capt Jeremiah Goodrich.. Noah Smith.. Noadiah White Ju^r.. Capt Sam^{ll} Hall.. Joseph Pelton.. Jonathan Bush.. Nicholas Ames.. Nathan Brainerd.. James Stanclift.. Hezekiah Goodrich.. Jonth Brown.. Thomas Johnson.. John Ward.. Fisk Bartlit.. Timothy Smith.. Joseph Kellogg.. Moses Bush.. E^n Benjamin Bidwell.. David Sage Esqr.. David Smith Ju^r.. William Clark.. C^o John Penfield.. Robert Usher.. Bryan Pamerlee.. Edward Purple.. Daniel Shepard Ju^r.. David White.. Sylvanus Freeman..

39

.. Gideon Arnold.. Enoch Smith.. Jeremiah Goodrich Ju^r.. John Hinckley.. John Giddings.. Capt John Cooper.. David Robinson.. John Gains.. Thomas Williams.. Josiah Strong.. Chancey Bulkley.. Sam^{ll} Ackley.. Lt David Smith.. Ezra Bevins.. Moses Bartlit.. Nath^{ll}

39

East Hampton/Chatham

Brown.. James Rich.. George Ranney Ju^r.. Capt Silas Dunham.. Sam^{ll} Taylor.. Warren Green.. Elisha Taylor.. Thomas Cowdery.. Stephen Brainerd.. Nathan Brainerd.. Samuel Brown.. Ezra Purple.. Gideon Hall.. Dewey Hall.. Capt Joseph Churchel.. Jonathan Penfield.. Isaac Kneeland

Ebenezer White Esqr David Sage Esqr Colon^l John Penfield Enoch Smith D^n David Smith John Hinckley and William Welch were Chosen Select men	39
Capt Sam^{ll} Hall Chosen Town Treasurer	39
Joseph Sage Samuel Taylor and Bryan Pamerlee Were Chosen Constables	39
Job Bates Capt Joseph Churchel Nathan Brainerd Josiah Strong Isaac Smith Ju^r and Eben^r Sears Ju^r Were chosen Grandjurymen	40
Highway Surveyors.. Noah Smith David White En^s George Ranney Nicholas Ames Daniel Shepard Ju^r Josiah Pelton John White Jeremiah Goodrich Ju^r Edward Shepard Richard Mayo Thomas Selden Moses Higgins Samuel Young Timothy Smith Gideon Arnold Moses Cook Amos Morgain Edward Purple Sam^{ll} Sexton Sam^{ll} Brown Samuel Ackly Othniel Brainerd and Elkanah Sears	40

15 Dec 1777

Capt Stephen Olmsted the Moderator Being abstent Capt Sam^{ll} Hall was Chosen Moderator	40
in open Town Meeting the following persons.. Took the oath of fidelity Provided by Law before Eben^r White Esqr (viz) Capt George Stocking.. Capt Joseph Dart.. Amos Morgain.. Israel Whitcomb.. James Acley.. John Bates.. Abraham Baley.. Dea^n John Clark.. Ens^n George Ranney and John Bidwell	40
Doct^r Moses Bartlit David Robinson Jeremiah Goodrich Ju^r John Giddings Hezekiah Sears John Norton Ju^r Gideon Arnold and Thomas Williams were Chosen Listers	40
John Bidwell Daniel Shepard Ju^r Daniel Crittendon Joshua Strong Sam^{ll} Fuller Jonath^n Pamerlee Ju^r and Moses Cole were Chosen Tything Men	40
Noah Smith and Benjamin Bidwell were Chosen Grandjurymen	40
John Bidwell and Samuel Taylor Chosen Packers of meet	40
David Robinson Lt Daniel Shepard Capt Sam^{ll} Hall Warren Green Capt Joseph Dart Capt Abijah Hall And Bryan Pamerlee Chosen fence Viewers	40
Bryan Pamerlee Chosen a Collector To Gather the State Rate And also To Settle with Treasurer	41
David Sage Esqr Capt John Cooper Eben^r White Esqr David Robinson Jesse Johnson John Shepard Enoch Smith Thomas Seldon John Eddy Ju^r Capt Joseph Dart Chancey Bulkley Jonathan Clark Ju^r Thomas Cowdery Capt Abijah Hall James Bill Moses Cook Jonth Pamerlee Ju^r Stephen Knowlton and John Giddins were Chosen as a Commitee of Supplys	41
Doc^t Moses Bartlit Chosen as a Com^{tee} To Settle with the Town Treasurer	41

22 Dec 1777

David Robinson Thomas Hubbard and Benjamin Goff were Chosen Sealers of Leather	41
Capt Sam^{ll} Hall Chosen Sealer of Liquid Measurs	41
Elisha Shepard Chosen a Sealer of Dry Measures	41
Job Bates Chosen a Sealer of Weights	41
William Dixon Cristopher Vansant Mahiteble Young and Richard Cook Chosen Key keepers of Pounds	41
William Dixon Beriah Bacon Nath^{ll} Cornwell Sam^{ll} Bortun Solomon Goodrich Wait^{ll} Cary Joseph Hurd John Goff Timothy Smith John Hubbard Ju^r Nathaniel Markham Samuel Sexton	41

East Hampton/Chatham

Amos Morgain Thomas Goodrich Stephen Knowlton Ju[r] and Timothy Rogers are Chosen Haywards

Voted that There Should Be four pence on the pound on the present List Raised in order To Defray the Necessary Charges of the Town.. Joseph Sage Samuel Taylor & Bryan Pamerlee are Chosen Collectors To Gather Said Rait in their Respective Parrishes 42

5 Jan 1778

Isaac Smith Ju[r] and Eben[r] Sears Ju[r] Took the oath of Fidelity.. in my presents: before Eben[r] White Esq[r].. Test Jon[th] Penfield Town Clerk 42

9 Mar 1778

William Welch Esq[r] Chosen Moderator 42

the following persons.. apeared and Took the oath of fidility.. which was administerd To them by Eben[r] White Esq[r] (Viz) George Lewis.. D[r] Isaac Smith.. John Casswel.. Elijah Dean.. David Hale.. Noadiah White.. David West.. Sam[ll] Lewcas.. Nath[ll] Kies.. Warren Green Ju[r].. Richard Mayo.. Thomas Ackley.. Abel Sheperd.. Elisha Cornwell.. William Norcott.. David Bazell.. Thomas Ranney.. Sam[ll] Hodge.. John Shepard.. Jabez Hall.. John White.. Ens[n] Sam[ll] Aken.. John Fox.. Jonas Wright.. Sam[ll] Bordman.. Benjamin Stocking.. Elijah Stocking.. Daniel Cruttendon.. David Hale Ju[r].. Abel Strickland.. Isaac Hall Ju[r].. Thomas Selding.. Ens[n] Hezekiah Sears.. Joel Hall.. Jonathan Clark Ju[r].. John Ufford.. Noadiah Taylor.. Jesse Johnson.. John Eddy Ju[r].. Francis Ranney.. Joseph Shepard.. Thomas Goodrich.. Elisha Shepard.. David Bates.. Daniel Bidwell 42

Doc[t] Moses Bartlit Cap[t] Joseph Dart and Deac[n] John Clark Were Chosen a Com[tee] to Settle with the Town Treasurer 42

Voted To Chuse a Com[tee] to provide Clothing For the Continental Soldiers.. the persons Whose names are hereafter Inserted are.. appointed for the Com[tee].. (viz) L[t] Joseph Sage William Dixon Joseph Kellogg Cap[t] Joseph Churchel Nocholas Ames Elisha Shepard John Ufford Jesse Johnson Jeremiah Goodrich Ju[r] Thomas Cooper Chancey Bulkley Elisha Taylor Elisha Hurlbut Josiah Strong Hez[h] Sears John Eddy Ju[r] Amasa Daniels Sam[ll] Young Jonth Clark Ju[r] Benj[n] Smith Tho[s] Seldling Jacob Hurd Cap[t] Jo[s] Dart John Giddings William Wright Stephen Hurlbut Jonathan Smith Ju[r] Cap[t] Daniel Brainerd Warren Green Ju[r] Enoch Smith y[e] 3[d] Edward Shepard Doc[t] Jeremiah Bradford Reuben Stocking Jedediah Hubbard Seth Doane Josiah Purple James Bill John Clark Ju[r] Oren Alvord Nathan Lewis Benjamin Goff Andrew Carrier Rowland Percivil Thomas Williams & Sam[ll] Kilburn 43

Ezra Bevin Chosen as a Com[tee] of Supplys 43

Jonathan Penfield was Chosen as a General School Com[tee] To Draw the School Money out of the State Treasury that is now become Due and Distribute the Same to the Severall Schools in the Town 43

13 Apr 1778

in open freemens meeting the following persons.. appeared and Took the oath of Fidility Provided by Law Before Eben[r] White Esq[r] Rev[d] Cipryan Strong George Lewis Ju[r] Robert Stiles John Clark Ju[r] Joseph Daley Moses Cook Cap[t] Daniel Brainerd Elkanah Sears William Bevins Ju[r] Moses Cole Moses White Cap[t] Daniel Stewart William Bartlit Daniel Churchell Israel Higgins Tho[s] Cornwell William Bevin Benjamin Smith Gideon Hurlbut Josiah Pelton WIlliam Dixon Charles Goodrich Samuel Sexton Jared Pamerlee Moses West 43

This may Certify that the persons whose names are under Written are of a of a peacable and Civil Conversation and otherwise Qualified by Law to Take the freemans oath (viz) Daniel Shepard George Lewis Ju[r] Samuel Brown Jared Pamerlee Joseph Sage William Welch Esq[r] Nicholas Ames } David Sage.. William Welch.. John Hinkley.. Enoch Smith.. John Penfield.. 43

East Hampton/Chatham

Eben' White } Select men

15 Sep 1778

This may Certify that the persos Whos names are under Written are of a of a peacable and 44
Civil Conversation and otherwise Quallified by Law To take the freemans oath (viz)
Benjamin Johnson Doc' Thomas Welles John Hubbard Ju' and Seth Allvord   David
Sage.. Enoch Smith.. Will'" Welch.. John Hinkley.. John Penfield.. Eben' White } Select men
in open freemans meeting the followig Persons Whos Names are under Written appeared and 44
Took the oath of fideiity Provided by Law Before Ebenezer White Esq' (viz) Nicholas
Ames.. Hezekiah Sears.. John Hubbard Ju'.. Daniel Mackall.. John Johnson.. Isaac Bevin.. L'
George Hubbard.. Ralph Smith.. Benjamin Johnson.. Thomas Cooper.. Doct' Jeremiah
Bradford.. Elkanah Fuller.. Phinehas Dean.. Aaron Clark.. Joshua Griffeth.. Cap' Tim°
Percivil.. Oren Alvord.. John Markham.. Doct' Thos Welles.. Seth Alvord

7 Dec 1778

in open Town meeting the following persons Who' names are under Written appeared and 44
Took the Oath of Fidility Provided by Law Before Eben' White Esq' (viz) Joshua Cook
Thomas Cooper L' Elijah Cook and Sam" Hill

15 Dec 1778

Nath" Markham Took ye same 44

4 Jan 1779

appeared Titus Carrier and Took the oath of fidlity.. before Eben' White Esq' 44

21 Dec 1778

Middletown in the County of Hartford.. then and There the oath of fidility To this State as 44
perscribed by Law was Duely administered To M' Eliakim Ufford of Chatham.. by me Elijah
Treadway Justice Peace

7 Dec 1778

Doct' Jeremiah Bradford was Chosen Moderator 45

Doct' Moses Bartlit Colo" John Penfield Cap' Joseph Kellogg Dea" David Smith Cap' Joseph 45
Dart Cap' Silas Dunham And Cap' Timothy Percivel were Chosen Select Men

Voted.. that Cap' Sam" Hall Should Receive Ten pounds.. for His Service As Treasurer the 45
Year Ensueing

David White Sam" Taylor and Bryan Pamerlee Were Chosen Constables 45

William Dixon Cap' Daniel Stewart Jeremiah Goodrich Ju' Joshua Strong John Giddins 45
James Bill John Norton And Thomas Williams were Chosen Listers

15 Dec 1778

Hezekiah Goodrich Thomas Johnson Daniel Shepard Ju' Lieu' David Smith Cap' Daniel 45
Brainerd Titus Carrier And Sam" Brown were Chosen Grandjuriors

Leiu' Joseph Sage En" Jon'" Belcher Thomas Bliss Cap' Joseph Churchel John Shepard Enoch 45
Sage Ens" Sam" Abby Jacob Hurd Jedediah Hubbard Elisha Hurlbut Benj" Smith Simon
Brainerd Will'" Bradford Gershom Rowley John Bates Isaac Smith Ju' Nathan Lewis Moses
West Darius Addams Cap' Stephen Brainerd Rowland Percivil and L' Marcus Cole in the
Room of John Bates were Chosen Surveyors of Highways

Lieu' David Robinson L' Daniel Shepard Cap' Sam" Hall Warren Green Cap' Joseph Dart Cap' 45
Abijah Hall and Bryan Pamerlee Chosen Fence Viewers

David Bates Gideon Hurlbut Tho' Selden Timothy Smith Oren Alvord and Thomas Acley 45
were Chosen Tything men

198

East Hampton/Chatham

John Bidwell George Bush Daniel Lee Solomon Goodrich Benjamin Hunt Richard Mayo William Hurlbut Caleb Strong Capt Abijah Hall John Norton Daniel Clark Othniel Brainerd and Moses Cook were Chosen Haywards	46
John Bidwell Sam^{ll} Taylor and John Norton Chosen Gagers and Packers	46
Jabez Hall Lem^{ll} Higgins and Benjn Goff were Chosen Sealers of Leather	46
Willim Dixon Cris^{tr} Vansant widow Young & Richd Cook were Chosen Key keepers of pounds	46
David Bates Chosen a Sealer of Weights	46
Capt Sam^{ll} Hall Chosen a Sealer of Liquid Measurs	46
Elisha Shepard Chosen a Sealer of Dry measurs	46
Capt Joseph Churchel Doc^t Jer^h Bradford and John Norton Are Chosen as a Commitee of Supplys.. and Each one To provide for s^d Soldiers families in the Respective Parrishs To which they Belong	46

22 Dec 1778

Eben^r White Chosen a Com^{tee} To adjust and Exchange Highways	46
Thomas Cooper Chosen a Constable and also To Collect the State Rate and also the Town Rate in the first Parrish	46
Sam^{ll} Taylor Chosen Collector To Collect ye Town Rate in Middle haddam parrish	46
Abijah Hall ye 3^d Chosen To Collect the Town Rate in East Hampton Parrish	46

12 Apr 1779

This may Certify the persons hereafter Named are of a peaceable & Civil Conversation and otherwise Qualified by Law to Take the freemans oath (Viz) Ens^n Jonathan Belcher Abel Strickland Charles Davis & Joshua Woolcott John Penfield.. Moses Bartlit.. Joseph Kellogg.. David Smith.. Timothy Percivil.. Joseph Dart } Select men	47
in open freemans meting Ithamer Pelton and Edward Shepard appeared and Took the oath of Fidelity.. Before Eben^r White Jus^t Peace	47

19 Apr 1779

in open Town meeting Abijah Hall the 3^d Took the oath of Fidility before Ebenez^r White Esqr	47

21 Sep 1779

in open freemans meeting the following Persons Took the oath of Fidility Before Ebn^r White Esqr (viz) Thomas Hubbard Sylvanus Waterman & Constant Welch	47

15 Dec 1778

We the Subscribers being appointed.. To Settle acounts with the Treasurer.. have proceeded To Examine and adjust s^d acounts and Do finde Due from the Treasurer: To Said Town the Sum of one Hundred thirty three Pounds Seventeen Shillings & Eight Pence.. John Clark.. Joseph Dart.. Moses Bartlit } Com^{tee}	47

19 Apr 1779

Capt Sam^{ll} Hall Chosen Moderator	48
Voted that the Treasurer.. Should pay out of the Treasury a Balence Due To Middletown Which hath arrisen by the Deficiency of Stephen Blake a former Collector of a Colony Rate he had To gather when Middletown and Chatham were one Town	48
Voted that there Should be one Shiling o the pound Raised.. To Defray the Necessary Charge of the Town.. Daniel Shepard Ju^r Timothy Smith and Stephen Clark are chosen Collectors To Gather the above Said Rate Each one in Their Respective Parrishes	48

East Hampton/Chatham

Jonathan Penfield Chosen as a School Com[tee] To Draw the Publick School money out of the State Treasury and Distrubute the Same To the Severall School Commitees	48
29 Jun 1779	
David Sage Esq[r] Chosen Moderator	48
1 Oct 1779	
Cap[t] Sam[ll] Hall Chosen Moderator	49
It being Put To vote .. whether or not They would appoint one or more as Deligades To a Meeting or Convention To be held at Hartford on Tuesday Next.. Voted in the Afirmative.. David Sage Esq[r] only was Chosen To attend Said Convention	49
6 Dec 1779	
Cap[t] Abijah Hall was Chosen Moderator	50
Colo[n] John Penfield Doc[t] Moses Bartlit Cap[t] Joseph Kellogg Deac[n] David Smith Cap[t] Joseph Dart Cap[t] Silas Dunham and Cap[t] Timothy Percivil were Chosen Select men	50
Thomas Cooper Sam[ll] Taylor and Bryan Pamerlee were Chosen Constables	50
Robert Waterman L[t] Noadiah Russel Gideon Hurlbut Enoch Smith Reuben Stocking and Moses White were Chosen Grandjurymen	50
William Dixon Cap[t] Daniel Stewart Jer[h] Goodrich Ju[r] John Giddins Chancey Bulkley James Bill John Norton and Thomas Williams were Chosen Listers	50
Survayors of Highways.. L[t] Joseph Sage Noah Smith Ezra Bevin L[t] David Robinson Jonath[n] Brown John Washburn Josiah Pelton Ens[n] Sam[ll] Abby Chancey Bulkley Josiah Purple Moses Higgins Jacob Hurd Seth Hubbard Eben[r] Rowley Samuel Acley James Acley Gideon Arnold Sam[ll] Hill Thomas Cowdery John Johnson Ju[r] Moses Cook and Amos Morgain	50
Leiu[t] Joseph Sage James Bill and Chancey Bulkley were Chosen a Com[tee] To Settle with the Town Treasurer	50
20 Dec 1779	
Bryan Pamerlee Chosen a Colector To Gather the State Rate	50
David White Chosen Constable.. and also To Colect the Town Rate in the first parrish	50
Sam[ll] Taylor Chosen To Collect the Town Rate in Middle haddam	50
Amos Clark Chosen To Gather the Town Rate in East hampton	50
Voted.. there Should be Chosen a Commity of Supplys To provide for the Soldiers familys as many as one To Each family the persons Chosen for Said Com[tee] are.. William Dixon Cap[t] Joseph Blague Hez[h] Goodrich Jesse Johnson L[t] Joseph Sage Jeremiah Goodrich Ju[r] Sam[ll] Bordman John Shepard Johnson Pelton Nicholas Ames Joel Hall Tho[s] Rogers Daniel Shepard Ju[r] Elkanah Sears Richard Cook Nath[ll] Clark John Hinkley Doc[t] Robert Usher Jonath[n] Smith Ju[r] Elisha Taylor Josiah Strong Stephen Hurlbut Thomas Seldin and Reuben Stocking	51
Tything men... Joseph Washborn Gideon Hall Stephen Stocking Ju[r] Nath[ll] Spencer Jonath[n] Bowers Benjamin Goff and Richard Cook	51
Jabez Hall Thomas Hubbard and Benjamiin Goff were Chosen Sealers of Leather	51
Elisha Shepard Chosen Sealer of measurs	51
David Bates Chosen Sealer of Weights	51
Cap[t] Sam[ll] Hall Chosen Sealer of Liquid measures	51
Cap[t] Samuel Hall David Robinson Daniel Shepard Daniel Smith Enoch Smith Cap[t] Abijah Hall and Gideon Arnold Chosen fence viewers	51

East Hampton/Chatham

John Bidwell and Samuel Taylor Chosen packer Gagers and Cullers	51
David Bates Christopher Vansant Nath^{ll} Spencer and Richd Cook Chosen Key Keepers of Pounds	51
Joseph White Timothy Russel Abner Pelton John Ufford Benjamin Abby Sam^{ll} Cornwell Amasa Daniels Enoch Smith Ju^r Jonath^n Bowers Josiah Purple Ezekiel Goff Garshom Rowley Joseph Johnson Dewey Hall Ebenezer Harding Thomas Acley and Sam^{ll} Acley were Chosen Hog hayards	51
Voted that Capt Sam^{ll} Hall Receiv Thirty Pounds out of the Town Treasury the ensuing year for his Service in the Capacity of as Treasurer	51
Jonath^n Penfield Chosen as a Com^{tee} To Draw the Publick School money out of the State Treasury and Distribute the Same To the Several Schools	51

13 Mar 1780

David Sage Esqr Chosen Moderator	52
the Commitee Chosen for for Enspection.. their Names are as follows (Viz) George Lewis Ju^r Jeremiah Goodrich Ju^r Eliakem Ufford Jonath^n Bush John Shepard Cristopher Vansant Ithamer Pelton Joseph Parke Caleb Strong Gideon Arnold Cristopher Comstock Isaac Kneeland and Joshua Cook	52
Chancey Bulkley Chosen a Select man	52

10 Apr 1780

this may Certify the persons whose name are under Written are of a peaceble and Civil Conversation and otherways Qualifyed by Law To Take the freemans oath (Viz) Nath^{ll} Kies Samuel Lewcus David Bates Constant Welch Stephen Stocking Ju^r Sam^{ll} Bortun Nath^{ll} White Stephen Hosmer Gideon Schallenx Capt Elijah Smith Daniel Clark & Nath^{ll} Clark	52
then the following persons appeared in open reeman meeting and Took the oath of Fidility Provided by Law (Viz) Capt Elijah Smith Stephen Hosmer Nath^{ll} Clark Daniel Clark Jabez Wood David Bates and John Washburn	52

26 Jun 1780

David Sage Esqr Chosen Moderator	53
Put To Vote.. whether the Town would Raise a rate or Tax.. as a bounty To Encorage Soldiers To List To fill up the Continentiall Army for three Years or Dureing the war.. Voted in the afirmitive.. Voted To appoint a Com^{tee} Instantly To Confer.. how much To Raise and in what maner To proceed:.. the Comitty chosen & appointed are (viz) Capt Abijah Hall Leiu^t David Smith and Colo^l John Penfield	53
Voted.. To Raise A rate two pence on the Pound this State money on the present List .. to Defray the above Said Charge.. Collectors Chosen.. are Enoch Smith ye 3^d John Willcox and Isaac Sears	53
Recruting officers Chosen and appointed To inlist Said Soldiers are Capt Joseph Kellogg Capt Joseph Blague Capt Abner Stocking Capt Silas Dunham Capt Abijah Hall Capt Daniel Stewart and Leiu^t David Smith	53
then appeared the persons whose names are under Written and Took the oath of fidility taken Before Eben^r White Esqr (viz) Zacheus Cook Jacob Hurd Jedediah Hubbard Thos Smith Enoch Smith Ju^r Simon Brainerd Eben^r Harding Ruel Alvord Reuben Stocking Richd Cook Isaac Sears David Kneeland Ezra Ackley Benjn Hale Sam^{ll} Young Sam^{ll} Wood Seth Hubbard Willm Wright William Clark Jer^h Wood Abijah Fuller Othniel Brainerd Jonath^n Hale Sylvanus Eaton Henry Wetheril Nehemiah Gates Asa Foster Ju^r Lemuel Tubs & Stephen Ackley	54

East Hampton/Chatham

6 Jul 1780

Doct[r] Jer[h] Bradford Chosen Moderator   *54*

it being put to vote to appoint a Commitee.. To Raise the Recruits now wanted for to fill up the army voted in Negative.. Voted to appoint a Com[tee] 'meadiately To Consult and Confer what Sum To Grant for Each Solder who Shall inlist into the Service voted in the affirmative.. the Com[tee] Chosen.. are Col[n] John Penfield Cap[t] Silas Dunham & Cap[t] Elijah Smith   *54*

Voted that Each able Bodied Effective man that Shall or has inlisted or ben attached to Serve in the State Service for three months from the fifteenth of July instant Shall be intitled To four Bushel of what for Each month whilst in Service Exclusive of all other premiums: or So much State money as to purchase the Same at the Time he Returns from Service.. Voted.. To Raise a Rate on the present List of four pence on the pound this State money to Defray the above Said Charges.. Collectors Chosen to Gather the above S[d] Rate are John Willcox Enoch Smith y[e] 3[d] and Isaac Sears   *55*

then appeared John Welch Sam[ll] Cassell and Amos Ranney and Took the oath of Fidility.. before Eben[r] White Esq[r]   *55*

19 Sep 1780

this may Certify that the person whos name is under Written is of a peacable Conversation and otherwise Qualified by Law To Take the freemans oath… (viz) Daniel Smith.. Said Smith Took the oath of Fidility at the Same Time   Silas Dunham.. Timothy Percivil.. Moles Bartlit } Select men   *55*

4 Dec 1780

Amasa Daniels Selah Jackson Recompence Baley Abner Pelton Nath[ll] Cone Sam[ll] Fuller & Joseph Pelton Ju[r] appeared and Took the oath of Fidility   *55*

11 Dec 1780

John Willcox Benjamin Abby Tho[s] Abby Jesse Sexton Frances Ranney and David Hall appeared and Took the oath of Fidility   *55*

14 Nov 1780

Doct[r] Jeremiah Bradford Chosen Moderator   *56*

John Bidwell Samuel Taylor and Gideon Arnold are Chosen To Receive the Salt provided by the State.. and also To Recive the provision as they Shall Be brought in and To inspect procure the Cask and put up the Same.. And allso To Receive the money so Brought in of Such person or persons if any Such there be who Chuse To pay in money.. and.. to Collect S[d] assessment on the Inhabitats and Tax on the nonresidents   *56*

Voted further.. To Chuse a Commitee.. To assertain the Number of Soldiers already in Service and also To Class the Town if Need Be.. the Commitee.. are as follows (viz) Colo[ll] John Penfield Cap[t] Joseph Brague Hezekiah Goodrich Doct[r] Jer[h] Bradford Cap[t] Daniel Brainerd Leiu[t] David Smith Cap[t] Elijah Cook Cap[t] Bryan Pamerlee and Cap[t] Stephen Brainerd   *56*

4 Dec 1780

Doc[t] Jeremiah Bradford Chosen Moderator   *58*

Jonathan Penfield Doc[t] Moses Bartlit Cap[t] Joseph Kellogg Joseph Dart Esq[r] Chancey Bulkley Cap[t] Silas Dunham and Cap[t] Timothy Percivil were Chosen Select men   *58*

David White Sam[ll] Taylor and Bryan Parmelee Were Chosen Constables   *58*

Cap[t] Sam[ll] Hall Chosen Treasurer   *58*

East Hampton/Chatham

Joseph Sage James Bill and Chancey Bulkley were Chosen.. As a Com[tee] to Settle with the Town Treasurer	58
William Dixton Cap[t] Daniel Stuart Jer[h] Goodrich Ju[r] Moses Cook Doc[t] Robert Usher Benjamin Goff Nathan Brainerd and Seth Doane were Chosen Listers *11 Dec 1780*	58
William Bartlit Daniel Cruttendon Joshua Cook Sam[ll] Fuller Thomas Cowdery John Clark Ju[r] and Thomas Bliss were Chosen Grand jury men	58
Hezekiah Goodrich Eben[r] Chipman Tho[s] Ranney Elisha Shepard Cap[t] Joseph Churchel Abel Strickland Benj[n] Hunt Cap[t] Abner Stocking L[t] David Smith James Brainerd Jonathan Bowers Ithamer Rowley Ezekiel Goff Reuben Stocking Isaac Bevin Sam[ll] Sexton Henry Wetherel Joshua Baley Amos Clark Nath[ll] Cone Benjamin Trobridge Nath[ll] Markham Ens[n] Sam[ll] Abby and Gideon Hurlbut are Chosen Surveyors of Highways	58
Ithamer Pelton Chosen Constable.. and also a State Collector To Gather the State Rates	58
Joseph White Benj[n] Johnson John Eddy Ju[r] Josiah Strong Jared Parmelee and Ezra Ackley are Chosen Tythingmen	58
Jabez Hall Lemuel Higgins and Benj[n] Goff were Chosen Sealers of Leather	58
David Bates Chosen a Sealer of weights	58
Elisha Shepard Chosen a Sealer of measurs	58
John Bidwell & Sam[ll] Taylor chosen Gagers Cullers and Packers	58
Moses Lewis John Shepard Ju[r] Frances Ranney Solomon Goodrich John West Thomas Aken Ju[r] Ephraim Harding Sam[ll] Hill David Allen Randale Shattuck John Polley Ju[r] and Ralph Smith were Chosen Hog hayards	59
Voted.. To appoint a Com[tee].. To purchase Cloathing for Chathams Quota of Continental Soldiers the Com[tee] Chosen and appointed are (viz) Doct[r] Thomas Welles Jer[h] Goodrich Ju[r] Cap[t] Abijah Hall and Cap[t] Seth Doane *25 Dec 1780*	59
Com[tee] of Suplies for Soldiers famelies.. William Dixon Doct[r] Thomas Welles Jer[h] Goodrich Ju[r] Cap[t] Daniel Stow Nicholas Ames Cap[t] Daniel Stewart Jedediah Hubbard Cap[t] Abner Stocking Sam[ll] Ackley Andrew Carrier Isaac Smith Ju[r] and Isaac Bevin	59
The Question being put whether the Survey Bill of a Highway Through Lands of the Heirs of L[t] Stphen White Dces[d] Eben[r] White and M[r] Robinson Should be excepted and Recorded voted in the Negative	59
Elkanah Sears Chosen for a Com[tee] of Cloathing in the Room of Cap[t] Abijah Hall *2 Jan 1781*	59
Voted to.. appoint a Com[tee] To Class the Town into Eight Classes.. To Rais our Quota of State Soldiers To Guard this State the Com[tee] Chosen.. are as follows (viz) Joseph Sage Ithamer Pelton Cap[t] Daniel Stewart Cap[t] Elijah Smith Doct[r] Jer[h] Bradford Cap[t] Bryan Parmelee L[t] James Bill and Cap[t] Stephen Brainerd *2 Jan 1781*	59
Voted.. To Reconsider a Certain vot pased the Last adjorned Meeting.. whether the Survey Bill of a Highway Through Lands of the Heirs of L[t] Stephen White Dces[d] Eben[r] White Esq[r] and M[r] Robinson Should be Excepted and Recorded & voted in the Negative *15 Jan 1781*	60
Voted.. To Grant L[t] Sam[ll] Aken as a Bounty.. Twelve pounds this State money upon Condition that he undertakes to Go into the States Service	60

East Hampton/Chatham

At Meeting of the Com^tee .. To Devise ways and Means To Carry into Execution a Late Act of the General Assembly.. for Raising Men for the Defence of Horsneck and other parts of the State Did agree to Give Each able Bodied Effective Man who Shall Voluntary Inlist himself into the Service of this State.. Twelve pounds State money as a bounty to be paid Each Soldier before He Shall march and forty Shillings wages p^r month the one Half in provisions to be paid Quarterly at the prices Stipulated for Continental Soldiers the other half.. to be made Good in L Current money of this State.. Likewise if any Soldier shall find himself a Blanket Gun Catridge box & Knapsack Shall be Entitled to the premium By Law Allowed.. Com^tee } Elijah Smith.. Jeremiah Bradford.. Bryan Parmerlee.. James Bill.. Ithamer Pelton.. Daniel Stewart.. Joseph Sage   60

Voted To Raise a Rate of one peny half peny on the pounds To be paid in flower and Corn.. to Suply this States Soldiers.. the persons Chosen and appointed to Receive and Collect the above Said Rate are (viz) John Bidwell Samuel Taylor and Jared Parmelee   61

Voted.. To Raise a Rate of Six pence on the pound on the pound.. To provide for Soldiers families and other Necessary Charges in the Town.. Collectors Chosen to gather Said Rate are (viz) Capt Ithamer Pelton Noadiah Taylor Ju^r and Benjamin Goodrich   61

Gideon Hall Joseph Pelton Enoch Sage Chancey Bulkley Capt Daniel Brainerd Samuel Hill Nehemiah Gates and John Markham are Chosen as a Com^tee To Suply the State Soldiers families   61

The Question Being put whether the Survey Bill of a Highway through Lands of the Heirs of Stephen White Eben^r White Esqr and Mr Robinson Should be Excepted and Recorded voted in the afirmative   61

Jonath^n Penfield Chosen To Draw the State School Money out of the Treasury and pay it in proportion To the Severall School Com^tees   61

9 Apr 1781

this may Certify the persons under Writen are of a of a peaceble and Civil Conversation and otherwise Qualified by Law to Take the freemans oath (viz) Revd Lemwill Persons James Rich Sam^ll Cornwell Thomas Eddy Nath^ll Cone and Enoch Smith ye 3^d..... Jona^n Penfield.. Silas Dunham.. Tim^o Percivil.. Chancey Bulkley.. Joseph Dart.. Joseph Kellogg.. Moses Bartlit } Select Men   61

Eben^r Hall took the oath of Fidility the Same Time   61

12 Apr 1781

Doc^tr Jer Bradford Chosen Moderator   62

Voted to appoint a Com^tee to procure Cloathing for the Soldiers.. the Com^tee Chosen and appointed are Gideon Hall Thomas Rogers John Eddy Ju^r and Dewey Hall   62

Voted to Raise Six pence on the pound State money .. To Defray the Charge of the Town.. Collectors Chosen.. are Nicholas Ames Noadiah Taylor Ju^r And Benjn Goodrich   62

5 Jan 1781

John Polly Junr appeared and.. Took the oath of Fidility Before Joseph Dart Esqr   62

11 Jan 1781

Oliver Acly appeared and Took the oath of Fidility Before Joseph Dart Esqr   62

5 Jul 1781

David Sage Esqr Chosen Moderator   63

Voted.. To Raise four pence on the pound Through the Town for Suply in Beef for the army.. Capt Ithamer Pelton Chosen a Collector.. Voted.. To pay Said Pelton 5 p^r Cent provided he   63

East Hampton/Chatham

Can Receve no pay from the State for Collecting Said Tax

John Bidwell Gideon Arnold and Enoch Smith ye 3 are Chosen Receivers of provision and Clothing — 63
3 Dec 1781

Capt Joseph Kellogg Chosen Moderator — 64

Jonath^n Penfield Doct^r Moses Bartlit Capt Joseph Kellogg Joseph Dart Esqr Chancey Bulkley Lt James Bill and Capt Bryan Parmelee Chosen Sellect men — 64

Ithamer Pelton Sam^{ll} Taylor and Capt Bryan Parmelee were Chosen Constables — 64

David White Noadiah Russell Benjamin Johnson Edward Shepard Sam^{ll} Young Capt Elijah Cook John Clark Ju^r and Doct^r Thomas Welles were.. Chosen Grandjury men — 64

William Dixson Capt Daniel Stewart Jeremiah Goodrich Ju^r Seth Doane Nathan Brainerd Moses Cook Benjn Goff and Doct^r Robert Ussher were Chosen Listers — 64

Joel Hall Gideon Hall John Gains Benjn Johnson Daniel Shepard Ju^r John Washburn Ens^n Sam^{ll} Abby Enoch Smith Ju^r Jonathan Clark Thomas Seldin Capt Abner Stocking Benjamin Smith Sam^{ll} Fuller Daniel McCall Jared Parmelee David Kneeland Lt John Johnson Robert Stiles Jesse Sexton Stephen Knowlton Jabez Clark and Capt Stephen Brainerd Chosen Surveyors of Highways — 64

Maj^r Joseph Blague Ebn^r White Esqr and Joseph Sage were Chosen a Com^{tee} to Settle with ye Town Treasury — 64
18 Dec 1781

Jonath^n Brown Aaron Willcox Josiah Strong Jedediah Hubbard John Eddy Junr Daniel Clark and Nath^{ll} Cone Were Chosen Tything men — 64

John Bidwell & Sam^{ll} Taylor Chosen Cullers Gagers & Packers — 64

David Bates Nath^{ll} Spencer Richd Cook & Capt Vansant Chosen Key keepers of pounds — 64

Lt David Robinson Capt Sam^{ll} Hall Lt Daniel Shepard Enoch Smith Joseph Dart Esqr Capt Abijah Hall & Gideon Arnold Chosen fence viewers — 64

Abner Bates John Washborn Daniel Lee John Wood Solomon Goodrich Elijah Johnson John Goff John Hubbard Ju^r Daniel Miller Dewey Hall John Markham Ju^r Recompence Baley and Edward Purple were Chosen Hog hawards — 65

Elisha Shepard Chosen Sealer of Dry measurs — 65

Capt Sam^{ll} Hall a Sealer of Liquid measurers — 65

David Bates a Sealer of weights — 65

Jabez Hall Lemuel Higgins and Nath^{ll} Mott Sealers of Leather — 65

Capt Ithamer Pelton Chosen Collector to Gather the State Rates — 65

Voted To Continue Capt Sam^{ll} Hall in the office of a Treasurer in the Town untill the first Day of May Next.. Voted that Capt Sam^{ll} Hall have Liberty to Draw Thirty Shillings.. out of the Treasury or Equivelent in State money for his Service.. untill May Next.. Voted To add Thirty Shillings.. to this Last Grant — 65

Thomas Bliss Gideon Hall Hez^h Goodrich William Dixson Elijah Stocking John Bates and Ralph Smith were Chosen Commitee of Suplies for the Soldiers families — 65

Voted.. To Raise a Rate of one peny on the Pound on the Grand Levy of.. 1781 To Defray the Necessary Charge of this Town.. Ithamer Pelton Thomas Cowdery and Amasa Daniels were chosen Collectors To Gather the above Said Town Rates and Settle the Same with the Town Treasurer — 65

Voted.. that the Select men.. Should Be appointed as a Com^{tee} To Review.. a Certain — 65

East Hampton/Chatham

Highway Laid out from John Shepards To David Robinsons which was laid across Eben[r] White Esq[s] land
21 Feb 1782

David Sage Esq[r] Chosen Moderator	66
Eben[r] White Esq[r] and Col[n] John Penfield were Chosen as a Com[tee] to Represent the Town.. with a Com[tee] appointed by the Generall Assembly in Respect To Delinquents and Claims to State and Contenential Soldiers	66
Cap[t] Joseph Sage Cap[t] Joseph Kellogg Ithamer Pelton Josiah Strong Chancy Bulkley Cap[t] Bryan Parmelee and L[t] James Bill are Chosen as a Com[tee] To procure this Towns Cota of State Soldiers and also the Continentall Soldiers When the Number is ascertained	66
Voted.. To Raise two pence on the Pound on the Common List.. to Defray the Charge of procureing and paying Said Soldiers the one half of which may be paid in Grain at the following prices (Viz) Wheat at 6/ p[r] Bushel Rye at four and Corn at three.. Collectors Chosen To Gather Said Rate are Amasa Daniels Thomas Cowdery and Jesse Johnson	66

8 Apr 1782

This may Certify the persons Whos names are under Writen Are of a of a peaceble Civil Conversation and otherwise Qualified By Law to Take the freemans oath (Viz) Gosuirus Erklins & Ephraim Whitaker   66
17 Sep 1782

this may Certify the persons whos Names are under Writen are of a peaceble & Civil Conversation and otherwise Qualified to Take the freemans oath (viz) Josiah White & Thomas Acly also Josiah White Took the oath of fiielity at the Same Time...... Joseph Dart.. Chancey Bulkley.. Moses Bartlit.. Jona[n] Penfield } Select men   66
2 Dec 1782

David Sage Esq[r] Chosen Moderator	67
Jonathan Penfield Cap[t] Daniel Stewart Maj[r] Joseph Blague M[r] Chancey Bulkley Joseph Dart Esq[r] Cap[t] Bryan Parmelee and M[r] James Bill were Chosen Select men	67
Ithamer Pelton Sam[ll] Taylor & Bryan Parmelee Chosen Constables	67
David Bates Thomas Cooper Cap[t] Jo[s] Churchel Jedediah Hubbard Elisha Hurlbut Thomas Acly and Jared Parmelee Chosen Grandjury men	67
Leiu[t] Robert Waterman Jesse Johnson Daniel Shepard Ju[r] Seth Doane Doct[r] Jer[h] Bradford Moses Cook Benjamin Goff and Abner Brainerd were Chosen Listers	67
Josiah White L[t] Noadiah Russel Tho[s] Cooper Nicholas Ames Joseph Pelton Ju[r] Aaron Willcox John Washborn Edward Shepard Cap[t] David Smith Amasa Daniels Thomas Seldin Jedediah Hubbard Jared Parmelee Tho[s] Cowdery John Markham Ju[r] Moses Cole Nath[ll] Clark Thomas Williams Rowland Percivil Nehemiah Lord Nath[ll] Cone and John Ufford Chosen Surveyors of Highways	67
John Crosbe Sam[ll] Cornwell Noadiah Taylor Ju[r] Moses Higgins Lemuel West and Nathan Lewis Chosen Tything men	67
Joseph Sage Maj[r] Joseph Blague and Hezekiah Goodrich Chosen a Commitee To Settle with the Town Treasurer	67

East Hampton/Chatham

16 Dec 1782

Voted.. Maj^r Joseph Blague Joseph Sage aned Hezekiah Goodrich be Continued As a Com^{tee} To Settle with the Town Treasurer	67
Voted.. Col^o John Penfield Capt Bryan Parmelee & Chancey Bulkley be a Commitee to Settle with the Towns Comtee which were appointed formerly To lay out and Exchange Highways	67
Voted.. Joseph Dart Esqr David Sage Esqr Eben^r White Esqr Doct^r Jer^h Bradford Capt Abijah Hall John Norton & Jonath^n Penfield Should be a Com^{tee} To Lay out Highways.. where they Shall find it Necessary and also to Exchange the Towns Land for Necessary Highways and also to Sell the Towns land to purchase Highways as they Shall Se fit	68
Ens^n Sam^{ll} Abby Charles Goodrich David Robinson Thomas Ranney Joseph Dart Esqr Capt Daniel Brainerd Capt Elijah Smith John Hinckley Isaac Kneeland & John Norton are.. appointed to Enspect into the Highways through the Town and .. To Remove Incrochments or if the Se fit to Leave out the Land taking the Rent fo the use of the Town	68
Jabez Hall Nath^{ll} Mott & Hezekiah Sears are Chosen Sealers of Leather	68
David Robinson Leiu^t Daniel Shepard Capt Abijah Hall Gideon Arnold Elisha Taylor & Jona^n Clark Ju^r were Chosen fence Viewers	68
David Bates Chosen a Sealer of Weights	68
Elisha Shepard a Sealer of Dry measurs	68
Capt Sam^{ll} Hall a Sealer of Liquid measurs	68
John Bidwell & Sam^{ll} Taylor were Chosen Packers Cullers and Gagers	68
David Bates Richard Cook and Capt Elijah Smith Chosen Kee Keepers of Pounds	68
Persons Chosen Hayards.. are Abner Bates Fransis Ranney John Washborn Benjamin Hale Solomon Goodrich Thos Smith John Hubbard Ju^r Capt Abijah Hall John Norton Jesse Sexton John Johnson Ju^r Isaac Kneeland Nathan Lewis Capt Stephen Brainerd and John Ward	68
David White Noah Smith Thomas Cooper Josiah White Joseph Pelton Hezekiah Sears Capt Stephen Brainerd Isaac Bevin and Benjamin Smith are Chosen a Com^{tee} of Supplies	68
Voted.. To Raise a Rate of one peny on the pound on the Present List To Defray the Necessary Charges of the Town.. Voted the three Constables of the Town (viz) Ithamer Pelton Sam^{ll} Taylor & Bryan Parmelee Should Collect the aford S^d Rate Each in his Respective parrish	69
Samuel Taylor Chosen Colector To Colect the State Rate and Settle with the Treasurer	69

10 Mar 1783

David Sage Esqr was Chosen Moderator	69
David Robinson and Josiah Stronge were Chosen Howards	69
Thomas Williams was Chosen a Commitee of Suplies	69

7 Apr 1783

This may Certify the persons whose names are under Writen are of a Peaceble and Civil Conversation and otherwise Qualified by Law to Take the oath of Freemen (viz) Elizur Chapman Richard Cook Nath^{ll} Markham Amos Clark John Welch & Amos Morgan.......... Chancey Bulkley.. Joseph Blague.. James Bill.. Jonath^n Penfield } Select Men	69

19 Mar 1783

Lemuel Smith.. Took the oath of fidelity Before Joseph Dart Esqr.. as appears by a Certificate Signed by Said Esqr Dart	69

25 Sep 1783

East Hampton/Chatham

David Sage Esqr was Chosen Moderator

East Hartford

Town Meetings Record
February 10, 1784 thru 1842

Located at the Town Clerk's Office

East Hartford

[ ] Oct 1783

Upon the Memorial of John Pitkin &c Inhabitants of the Town of Hartford on the East Side of Connecticutt River Shewing that by Reason of the Distance many of them Live from the place of Transacting publick Bussiness.. and the Difficulty of passing the Great River at Various Seasons of the Year, they Labour under Great Burdens and are often prevented attending and Enjoying their Legal Priviledges -- also that they are of Sufficient Ability and Numbers to be Constituted into a Destinct Town and praying for the Same.. A true Copy of Record Exaamin^d By George Wyllys Seccret^y.. the foregoing is a true Copy Tes^t Jonathan Stanly Junr Reg^t *1*

18 Nov 1783

The Inhabitants of the town of East Hartford are hereby Notifyed and Warned to Meet and Convene together at the Meeting House in the first Society in East Hartford on the Second Tuesday of December Next.. to Chuse the Town Officers by Law Required and to transact any Other Bussiness proper to be Done in Town Meeting.. George Pitkin Justice of ye Peace..... Daniel Pitkin.. Richard Pitkin } Select Men of East Hartford   *2*

[ ] Dec 1783

In pursuance to the foregoing Waring I proceeded and Warned the Inhabitants of the Town of East Hartford to Convene and Meet at the Meeting House in the first Society.. to Chuse Town Officers by Law Required and Transact all Other Bussiness proper to be Done in Town Meeting.. Daniel Pitkin Select Man for the Town of East Hartford   *2*

Voted that William Pitkin Esqr be Moderator   *3*

Voted that Jonathan Stanly Junr be Register or town Clerk Register   *3*

Voted that Daniel Pitkin Capt Richard Pitkin and Capt Samuel Smith be Select men   *3*

Voted that Jonathan Stanly Junr be town Treasurer   *3*

Voted that Mr John Wyles be Constable   *3*

Voted that Mr Timothy Bryant be Constable   *3*

Voted that Mr John Wyles be Collector of the Country taxes   *3*

Voted that Mr Ashbel Pitkin be Grand Juryman for this town and County   *3*

Voted that Capt Moses Forbs be Grand Jury man for this town and County   *3*

Voted that Mr Timothy Stedman be Grand Jury man for this town and County   *3*

Voted that George Gilman be Surveyor of Highways   *3*

Voted that Theodore Stanly be Surveyor of Highways   *3*

Voted that Joseph Arnold be Surveyor of Highways   *3*

Voted that Russell Kilbourn be Surveyor of Highways   *3*

Voted that John Cadwell be Surveyor of Highways   *3*

Voted that Timothy Braynard be Surveyor of Highways   *3*

Voted that Elisha Buckland be Surveyor of Highways   *3*

East Windsor

Town Meetings
Vol. 1
1768 – 1826

Located at the Town Clerk's Office

East Windsor

[ ] Aug 1774

Erastus Wolcott Esqr was Chosen Moderator	6
Voted that William Wolcott Erastus Wolcott Charles Elsworth Ju^r Esqr Capt Ebnezer Grant Messieurs Benoni Olcott Lemuel Stoughton Daniel Elsworth Junr and Edward Chapman Grant be a Committee to Keep a Corrispondence with the Towns of this and the Neighbouring towns and.. forward Such Contributions that Shall be made.. for the Relief of the poor in Boston under their present Distress	7

20 Sep 1774

Erastus Wolcott Esqr was Chosen Moderator [*ed: at Meeting in which "it is Judged advisable that a Meeting of Delegates from all the Towns in this Colony be held to consult Measures to carry the Resolves of said General Assembly at Phyladelphia into Execution"*]	7

[ ] Dec 1775

William Wolcott Esqr was Chosen Moderator	8
Aaron Bissell was chosen Town Clerk or Register	8
Selectmen are Benoni Olcott.. Daniel Elsworth Ju^r.. Edward Chapman Grant.. Joseph Allin Ju^r	8
Constables are Samuel Tuder.. Hezekiah Bissell.. Andrew McKinney & to gather ye Colony Tax	8
Grandjurors are Nathaniel Strong.. Samuel Allin.. Jabez Chapman.. Timothy Skinner	8
Tythingmen are Luke Lomis.. Daniel Osborn.. Lamson Wells Ju^r.. James Thomson 3^d.. James McKinney Ju^r.. Thatcher Lothrop	8
Surveyors of highways.. Charles Bissell.. John Stoughton.. Thomas Bancroft Ju^r.. Roswell Elmer.. Sam^{ll} Rockwell Grant.. Jeremiah Fitch.. Jabez Rogers.. Obadiah Dickinson.. Andrew McKinney.. Samuel King.. Simeon Belknap.. Caleb Lyon.. Paul McKinstry.. Oliver Hills.. John Bancroft.. Nathaniel Stoughton Ju^r.. Solomon Elsworth.. Fredric Elsworth.. Joshua Wells.. Timothy Meklewain.. Jonathan Munsell.. Joseph Stoughton.. Roger Lomis.. Col Erastus Wolcott	8
Listers are Warham Moor.. David Trumbull.. Jeremiah Fitch.. James Fitch 2nd.. Daniel Rockwell	8
Collectors are Alex^r Stoughton.. Job Belknap.. Eli Moor.. Eben^r Watson Junr	8
Packers of Tobacco.. Joel Lomis.. Azariah Grant.. Noah Bissell.. Ebenezer Watson Ju^r	8
Branders of Horses.. Benjamin N [ ]ry.. Daniel Elsw[ ] Ju^r.. David Trumbull	8
Fence Viewers.. Mathew Bi[ ]ll.. John Smith	8
Sealers of Leather.. Ebenezer Read.. Joel Pease.. Thomas Sexton	8
Key Keepers.. Moses Wells.. David Trumbull.. Silas Drake	8
Aaron Bissell Treasurer	8

East Windsor

[ ] Feb 1776

William Wolcott Esqr ws chosen Moderator	8
Voted to apply to the General Assenbly.. to grant Liberty & Enable the Town.. to Mend and Maintain their highways by a Rate.. Dec^n Benoni Olcott chosen Agent to prefer a Memorial for that purpose	8

[ ] Dec 1776

William Wolcott Esqr was chosen Moderator	8
Aaron Bissell was chosen Town Clerk or Register	8
Dec^n Benoni Olcott.. Daniel Elsworth Ju^r.. Joseph Allin Ju^r.. Ed^{w}d Chap. Grant.. Capt Eben^r Grant.. Capt Lem^l Stoughton.. Capt Nathl House } are Selectmen	8
Constables.. Samuel Tuder.. Andrew McKinney.. Hezekiah Bissell & to Collect Colony Tax	8
Grandjurors.. Capt Ebenezer Grant.. Capt Jonathan Bartlett.. Samuel Sessions.. James McKinney Ju^r.. Abner Rockwell	8
Tythingmen are Eliphalet Chapin.. Fredric Elsworth.. Samuel Bartlett.. Gurdon Elsworth.. Noah Barber.. Jonathan Porter Ju^r	8
Listers.. Erastus Wolcott Ju^r.. David Trumbull.. Ezekiel McKinstry.. Jeremiah Fitch.. Daniel Rockwell	8
Collectors.. Abiram Skinner.. Samuel Allin.. W^m McKinney.. Obadiah Dickinson	8
Packers of Tobacco.. Capt Joel Lomis.. Azariah Grant.. Noah Bissell.. Eben^r Watson Junr	8
Branders of Horses.. Benjamin Newberry.. David Elsworth Junr.. David Trumbull	8
Sealers of Leather.. Ebenezer Read.. Joel Pease.. Thomas Sexton.. David Dorchester	8
Fence Viewers.. Matthew Bissell.. John Smith	8
Key Keepers.. Moses Wells.. Samuel Wolcott.. David Trumbull.. Silas Drake	8
Aaron Bissell was chosen Treasurer.. & also Sealer of Weights and Measures	9
Capt Joel Lomis Lieu^t Edward Chapman Grant Jeremiah Fitch Jabez Chapman William Shurtliff Nathaniel Stoughton Junr John Prior & Henry Wolcott were chosen Surveyors of highways	9
William Wolcott Esqr Moderator	9
Capt Ebenezer Grant Capt Lemuel Stoughton and Mr Fredric Elsworth be a Committee to build the Scantick Bridge	9
Voted that William Bissell be a Tythingman in the Stead of Fredric Elsworth who is Excused	9
Voted that James Slade be one of the Tythingmen.. in the Stead of Jonathan Porter Ju^r	9
Voted that Andrew McKinney be a Collector of Town Rates.. in the Room of William McKinney	9

2 Apr 1777

Dec^n Benoni Olcott was Chosen Moderator	9
Voted to Supply the Families of Such Inhabitants of this Town as Shall Inlist as Soldiers into the Continental Service with the Necessaries of Life at the prises at which they are affixed by Law on thier applying to & leaving with the Committee.. the money for S^d Necessary^s -- Voted that Dec^n Benoni Olcott Capt Eben^r Grant Capt Nathl House Capt Lemuel Stoughton Mess^s Joseph Allin Ju^r Edward Chapman Grant & Danl Elworth Ju^r be a Committee appointed.. to make provision for the purpose aforesaid	9

East Windsor

Voted William Wolcott Ju^r be one of the Listers	9
7 Apr 1777	
Dec^n Benoni Olcott Moderator	9
22 Sep 1777	
William Wolcot Esqr was Chosen Moderator	9
[ ] Dec 1777	
General Erastus Wolcott ws Chosen Moderator	10
Aaron Bissell was chosen Town Clerk or Register	10
Capt Ebenezer Grant Dec^n Benoni Olcott Joseph Allin Daniel Elsworth Ju^r Esqr Edward Chapman Grant Fredric Elsworth & Capt Nathl House chosen Selectmen	10
Aaron Bissell chosen Town Treasurer	10
Constables are { Samuel Tudor & to gather the Colony Tax.. Hezekiah Bissell.. Andrew McKinney	10
Grandjurors { Joseph Allin.. Ebenezer Grant.. Medina Fitch.. William Grant	10
Tythingmen { Azariah Grant.. Alexander King.. Lamson Welles.. Zacheus Munsell.. Silas Read.. Joseph Pinney Ju^r.. Saml Rockwell	10
Listers are { Samuel Wolcott.. David Trumbull.. Ezekiel McKinstry.. Jeremiah Fitch.. Danl Rockwell	10
Collectors { Samuel Tuder Hezekiah Bissell.. Silas Read.. Joseph Smith	10
Tobacco Packers are { Capt Joel Lomis.. Azariah Grant.. Noah Bissell.. Eben^r Watson Ju^r	10
Sealers of Leather { Ebenezer Read.. Joel Pease.. Pelatiah Foster.. David Dorchester	10
Fence Viewers { Matthew Bissell.. John Smith	10
Key Keepers { Moses Wells.. Samuel Wolcott.. David Trumbull.. Silas Drake	10
Sealer of Weights and Measures { Aaron Bissell	10
Surveyors of High ways &c { Capt Joel Lomis.. Ed^{wd} Chapman Grant.. Jabez Chapman.. Wm Shirtliff.. Henry Wolcott.. Eben^r Watson Ju^r.. John [ ]nor	10
26 Jan 1778	
William Wolcott Esqr chosen Moderator	10
Voted that Wm Wolcott Esqr Capt Eben^r Grant Dec^n David Skinner Gen^{rl} Erastus Wolcott Maj^r Lemuel Stoughton Danl Elsworth and Dec^n Benoni Olcott be a Committee to Consider.. the Several Articles of Consideration proposed by Congress and Report	10
[ ] Feb 1778	
Gen^{rl} Erastus Wolcott Moderator	10
Warham Moor was Chosen Constable.. and also to gather the Colony Tax	10
[ ] Dec 1778	
Gen^{rl} Erastus Wolcott was Chosen Moderator	10
Aaron Bissell was chosen Town Clerk or Register	10
Mr Edward Chap. Grant.. Mr Frederick Elsworth.. Danl Elsworth Ju^r Esqr.. Capt Ebenezer Grant } Selectmen	10
Aaron Bissell Treasurer	10

East Windsor

Samuel Bancroft.. Nathl Stoughton Ju^r.. Gurdon Elsworth & Collect^r of State Tax } Constables	10
Ebenezer Read.. Thomas Ladd.. John Bancroft.. Edwd Kneeland } Grandjurors	10
Aaron Grant.. Phinehas Strong.. W^m McKinney.. Aaron Frost.. Hezekiah Allin.. Gideon Lomis.. Capt Ichabod Wadsworth } Tythingmen	10
Wareham Moor.. Thos White Pitkin.. Caleb Booth Ju^r.. James McKinney 3^d } Collect^{rs} of Town Rate	11
Joel Lomis.. Nathl Porter Ju^r.. Azariah Grant.. Noah Bissell. Eben^r Watson Ju^r } Packers of Tobacco	11
Ebenezer Read.. Pelatiah Foster.. Joel Pease.. Ed^{wd} Kneeland } Sealers of Leather	11
Matthew Bissell.. John Smith.. Ed^{wd} Kneeland.. David Johnson } Fence viewers	11
Joel Lomis.. Elisha Bisell.. Zachariah Allin.. Simon Wolcott.. Hezekiah Welles.. Ed^{wd} Chap. Grant.. Jeremiah Fitch.. Nathl Newhall.. Abraham Wallace.. James McKinney Ju^r } Surveyors of High Way	11
Aaron Grant.. David Trumbull } Key Keepers	11
Oliver Day Sealer of Weights & Measures	11
Capt Amasa Lomis.. Frederick Elsworth.. Ed^{wd} Chap. Grant.. Danl Elsworth Jr Esqr } Listers	11

12 Apr 1779

a Town Meeting.. Legally holden.. att the Dwelling House of Mr Justus Day	11
Wm Wolcott Esqr was Chosen Moderator	11
Lieu^t Samuel Tudor & Samuel Bartlett Chosen Constables	11
John Hall ws Chosen Tythingman	11

[ ] Dec 1779

Capt Ebenezer Grant was Chosen Moderator	12
Aaron Bissell was Chosen Town Clerk	12
Selectmen are Capt Ebenezer Grant.. Daniel Elsworth Ju^r Esqr.. Edwd Chap Grant.. Frederick Elsworth	12
Constables are Gurdon Elsworth.. Eli Bissell.. Samuel Allin & to gether State Taxes	12
John Bancroft.. Nathaniel Porter.. David Johnson.. Noah Barber chosen Grandjurors	12
John Bartlett.. Benoni Thomson.. Ezekiel Lomis.. James McKinney Jr.. Medinah Fitch.. Phinehas Strong.. Jonathan Chapman chosen Tythingmen	12
Surveyors of highways.. Capt Hezekiah Bissell.. Zaccheus Munsell.. Nathan Pelton.. Noah Allin.. Joel Lomis.. Elisha Bissell.. James McKinney Ju^r.. Abraham Wallace.. Nathl Newhall.. Jeremiah Fitch.. Edward Chap. Grant.. William Grant.. Eleazer Pinney.. Timothy Holton.. Samuel Sessions.. Adonijah Day.. Levi Fish.. Asahel Stiles.. Roger Lomis.. Joshua Wells	12
Listers are Capt Amasa Lomis.. Ebenezer Watson Ju^r.. Daniel Elsworth 3^d.. Simeon Drake	12
Collectors are Hezekiah Allin.. Asahel Olcott.. Silvenus Rockwell.. Ezekiel McKinstry	12
Tobacco Packers are Capt Joel Lomis.. Azariah Grant.. Ebenez^r Watson Ju^r	12
Key Keepers.. Aaron Grant.. David Trumbull	12
Sealer of weight & Measures.. Oliver Day	12
Sealers of Leather.. Ebenezer Read.. Pelatiah Foster.. Joel Pease.. Edward Kneeland	12

East Windsor

Fence Viewers.. Matathew Bissell.. Alexander Smith..Samuel Sessons	12
6 Mar 1780	
a Town Meeting.. Legally holden at the Dwelling House of Mr Justus Day	12
General Erastus Wolcott was Chosen Moderator	12
Maj^r Lemuel Stoughton Capt James Harper Mr Joseph Allin Mr Zachariah Allin Mr John Prior Mr Aaron Grant Capt Joel Lomis Lt Saml Tuder Ens Chap. Grant Mr White Pitkin Capt Jed^d Wadsworth $Mess^s$ Jabez Chapman James McKinney Ju^r Abraham Wallace & Ebenezer Nash } were Chosen Inspectors of $Imbargon^d$ Provisions	12
Mr David Allin was chosen Constable and to gather the State Taxes (in Room of Hezekiah Allin who.. is Released)	12
Oliver Chapman Chosen $Collect^r$ (in Sted of Ezekiel McKinstry who by this meeting is Excused)	12
Elijah Lomis and Edmond Bartlett Chosen Grandjurors	12
22 Jun 1780	
Genl Erastus Wolcott was Chosen Moderator	12
10 Jul 1780	
Dec^n Benoni Olcott was Chosen Moderator &c	13
19 Sep 1780	
Genl Erastus Wolcott was Chosen Moderator	13
Voted that Zachariah Allin be one of the Town Collectors (in the Room of Hezekiah Allin)	13
15 Nov 1780	
Dec^n Benoni Olcott was Chosen Moderator	13
Voted to Chuse a Committee to purchase the provision Required from the Town by a Late Act of the General Assembly -- Voted a Tax of Ten pence of the new Emitted Bills of this State on the pound.. to Defray Town Expences and purchase Said Provisions.. Voted that Maj^r Lemuel Stoughton Capt Simon Wolcott Capt James Chamberlin Timothy Holton Capt Amasa Lomis Eli Bissell & Lt Simeon Drake be a Committee to purchase S^d Provisions and also to Receive the Salt Necessary for Salting the meat part of provisions procure Casks Inspect the Same & put it up in good order and.. to Collect above Tax	13
[ ] Dec 1780	
Genl Erastus Wolcott was Chosen Moderator	13
Aaron Bissell was chosen Town Clerk or Register	13
Capt $Eben^r$ Grant.. Danl Elsworth Jr Esqr.. Mr Edwd Chap. Grant.. Mr Fred. Elsworth } Selectmen	13
Eli Bissell & to gather the Tax.. David Allen.. Gurdon Elsworth } Constables	13
Saml Tuder.. Saml Bartlett.. Abiel Abott.. Elijah Lomis.. Jabez Chapman } Grandjurors	13
Aaron Bisell } Town Treasurer	13
Saml Bancroft.. Wareham Moor.. Hezi. Allen.. Oliver Barber.. W^m McKinney.. Eph^m Ladd.. Timothy Bissell.. David Johnson } Tythingmen	13
Amasa Lomis.. $Eben^r$ Watson Ju^r.. Simeon Drake.. Danl Elsworth 3^d.. Ephraim Ladd } Listers	13
Oliver Dau Sealer of Weights & Measures	13

East Windsor

Joel Lomis.. Az^h Grant.. Eben^r Watson Jr. . Nathl Porter Jr } Tobacco Packers	13
Aaron Grant.. David Trumbull } Key keepers	13
Eben^r Read.. Pel^h Foster.. Joel Pease.. Dan Hibbard } Leather Sealers	13
Mathew Bissell.. Alex^r Smith. Saml Sessions.. Silas Read } Fence Viewers	13
Nathl Porter Ju^r.. Zac^h Allen.. Eleaz^r Pinney Thos Ladd Ju^r Collect^{rs}	13

Voted to Mend and Repair the high ways.. by a Tax and voted a Tax of two pence State Mony on the List 1780 for the purpose of Repairing & Mending Sd Highways.. Voted that the Roads Called Wolcotts and Bissells Roads Leading from the River to the Street be taken under the Surveyors Charge & Care 13

Voted that Capt James Chamberlin Capt Joel Lomis Saml Sessions Thomas Foster Ed^{wd} Chap. Grant Wm Grant Capt Hezekiah Bissell Levi Fish Noah Allen Elijah Lomis and Wm Shirtliff be the Repairers & Menders of the highways.. and to Collect the above Tax granted for that purpose 13

Capt Amasa Lomis Capt Roswell Grant Capt Hezekiah Bissell Capt Hez: Wells Capt James Chamberlin Capt Ichabod Wadsworth Capt David Johnson and Capt Noah Baber Genl Erastus Wolcott & Maj^r Lem^l Stoughton be a Committee to Inlist men for the Continental Army 14
15 Jan 1781

Genl Erastus Wolcott was chosen Moderator 14

Voted to Raise a Tax of one penny half penny on ye pound.. on the List 1780 to be paid in wheat flower at 24^s/0^d a hundred gross weight and Rye flower at 16^s/0 and Indian Corn at 4^s/0^d p^r Bushel.. Voted that Eli Bissell Maj^r Lemuel Stoughton Lt Simeon Drake & Capt James Chamberlin be the persons appointed to Collect Receive put up & Store the above mentioned flower & Corn 14
19 Feb 1781

Genl Erastus Wolcott Moderator 14

voted to Class the Inhabitants of this Town to Raise the Ten Men Required by the Act of the General Assembly for the Defence of this State -- Capt Amasa Lomis Capt Hez: Bissell Cap^l Roswell Grant Capt Hez: Wells Capt David Johnson Capt Jeh^d Wadsworth Capt James Chamberlin Capt Noah Barber Cp^t Alex^r McKinney Maj^r Lem^l Stoughton Danl Elsworth Esqr Lt Simeon Drake Capt Aaron Bissell be a Com^{tee} to Class as aforesaid 14

Voted that the Selectmen Eliquedate adjust and pay the Debt of the Town to Capt James Chamberlin & others for finding Lodging &c for Capt Webbs Troop of Dragoons &c 14
9 Apr 1781

General Erastus Wolcott chosen Moderator 14

Voted to Class the Inhabitants of the Town in order to Raise Eight men for the State Service -- further voted that Maj^r Lem^l Stoughton Capt Hez: Bissell Capt Hez: Wells Danl Elsworth Esqr Capt Ichabod Wadsworth Capt David Johnson Capt James Chamberlin Capt Alex^r McKinney Capt Amasa Lomis Capt Roswell Grant Capt Aaron Bissell Capt Noah Barber Lt Simeon Drake be a Com^{tee} for the purpose 14
25 Jun 1781

Genl Erastus Wolcott was Chosen Moderator 14

Voted to Raise a Tax.. to be paid in.. Mony or in good Merchantable Beef.. Voted that Mr Eli Bissell be the Collect^r to gather S^d Tax pay the mony he Shall Collect to ye Treasurer of this State and take his Receipt therefor & Dispose the Beef he Shall Receive for S^d Tax 14

East Windsor

Voted that to Raise the Twons [sic] Quota of men to fill the Continental Army the Town be Classed into 40 Classes and Maj Lem^l Stoughton Capt Hez: Bissell Capt Hez: Wells Danl Elsworth Esqr Capt Ichabod Wadsworth Capt David Johnson Capt James Chamberlin Capt Alex^r McKinney Capt Amasa Lomis Capt Roswell Grant Capt Aaron Bissell Capt Noah Barber Lt Simeon Drake Capt Simon Wolcott Mr Joseph Allin & Mr Jabez Chapman be the Committee for S^d Classing 14

Voted the Mr Daniel Osborn & Mr Silas Drake be Town Collect^{rs} (in the Room of Zac^h Allin & Thos Ladd Jr who have Refused to Serve) 14

18 Sep 1781

Genl Erastus Wolcott Chosen Moderator 15

2 Nov 1781

Genl Erastus Wolcott Chosen Moderator 15

Voted that Eli Bissell be the Receiver of the Sundry articles allowed by Law for the payment of the present 2^s/2^d State Tax 15

Voted that Genl Erastus Wolcott and the Selectment take Effectual Measures to Settle up the Six penny Tax of Beef and the penny half penny tax of Flower assessed.. by the Assembly 15

Voted that the Treasurer.. Pay to Mr Eli Bissell Collect^r of the State Tax the Sum of £539 - 4^s State money.. in Discharge of one half of a five penny & a four penny tax by him to be Collected from the Inhabitants 15

3 Dec 1781

Genl Erastus Wolcott was chosen Moderator 15

Aaron Bissell was chosen Town Clerk or Register 15

Genl Erastus Wolcott.. Capt Amasa Lomis.. Daniel Elsworth Jr Esqr.. Capt James Chamberlin.. Mr Joseph Allin.. Lt Simeon Drake } Selectmen 15

David Allen.. Danl Elsworth 3^d & to gather State Tax.. Eli Moore } Constables 15

Jabez Rogers.. Wareham Moor.. Samuel Allin.. Ebenezer Nash.. Abiel Abbott } Grandjurors 15

Samuel Osborn Jr.. John Morton.. Justus Day.. Gideon Grant.. Andrew McKinney.. Hosea Chapman } Tythingmen 15

Capt Amasa Lomis.. Ebenezer Watson Ju^r.. Simeon Drake.. Oliver Chapman.. Ephraim Ladd } Listers 15

Capt Hezekiah Bissell.. Noah Allin.. Levi Fish.. Capt Joel Lomis.. Thomas Foster.. Ed^{wd} Chap. Grant.. Samuel Sessions.. Capt James Chamberlin.. William Shirtliff.. William Grant.. Elijah Lomis } Surveyors of Highways 15

Capt Joel Lomis.. Ebenezer Watson Ju^r.. Azariah Grant.. Nathl Porter Ju^r } Tobacco Packers 15

Aaron Grant.. David Trumbull } Key keepers 15

Ebenezer Read.. Pelatiah Foster.. Eben^r Nash.. Caleb Parsons } Leather Sealers 15

Matthew Bissell.. John Smith.. Samuel Sessions.. Silas Read } Fence Viewers 15

Oliver Day Sealer of weights & measures 15

Aaron Bissell Town Treasurer 15

Eli Bissell Town Collect^r 15

Voted that if Mess^s Nathaniel Porter Junr Eleazer Pinney Daniel Osborn & Silas Drake the Collectors who were chosen to Collect the tax of two pence on the pound.. do within one Week Deliver to the Treasurer their Respective Rate Bills together with the Mony they have Collected (if any)... that they be Excused from Collecting Said Rate and that the Treasurer 16

East Windsor

Deliver S^d Rate Bills to Mr Eli Bissell who is chose to collect Said Tax

11 Mar 1782

Genl Erastus Wolcott was Chosen Moderator	16
Voted that the Several Classes formed the Last Year for filling up this Town^s Quota of the Continental Army be continued and that those Classes that did not git their men for three years or During the war proceed to procure their men.. And that Maj^r Lemuel Stoughton Capt James Chamberlin Capt Amasa Lomis be a Committee to procure the Remainder	16
Voted that in order to Raise the Towns Quota of men for the State Service the Town be Classes according to their lists for.. 1781 and that Capt Amasa Lomis Lt Simeon Drake.. Ebenez[er] Watson Junr and.. Daniel Elsworth Junr be a Committee to Class the Town accordingly	16

26 Aug 1782

Maj^r Lem^l Stoughton was chosen Moderator	16
whereas this Town is [ ]ed by the Genl Assembly in the Sum of £210.. for the Deficiency of providing fourteen Soldiers.. to make their Quota to fill up the Continental Army for.. 1781.. and whereas the Town is Enabled by Law to Tax Each deficient Class £15 for their deficiency.. voted to Lay a Tax.. on the.. Rateable Estate of the Individuals.. of S^d Classes..in proportion to their Respective Lists for the year 1781.. Collect^rs Chosen as follows Elisha Bissell for the first Class in the first Society: Capt Roswell Grant for the third Class Lt Eli Moor for the fifth Class Chauncey Newberry for the Sixth Class --	16
Ens Alex^r King for the Seventh Class Lt Samuel Tuder for the Tenth Class Eben^r Holmen for the Eleventh Class and Benjamin Gillett for the Twelvth Class and Lt Saml King for the Eleventh Class in the Second Society and David Smith for ye first Class in North Bolton part of the Town and Capt Hezekiah Bissell for the Seventh Class in the 3rd Society	16
Voted that Wm Wolcott Esqr Capt Aaron Bissell Capt Amasa Lomis and Mr Daniel Elsworth Ju^r be a Committee to make the Rate Bills for the Several Collect^rs on each Class &c	16

[ ] Dec 1782

Capt James Chamberlin was Chosen Moderator	17
Aaron Bissell was chosen Town Clerk	17
Lt Simeon Drake.. Capt James Chamberlin.. Mr Joseph Allin.. Capt Amasa Lomis.. Mr Wm Shirtliff } Selectmen	17
Samuel Treat.. Caleb Booth Ju^r & to gather State taxes.. Eleazer Pinney } Constables	17
Ebenezer Read.. Silas Read.. David Smith.. Capt Hezekiah Wells.. Thatcher Lothrop } Grandjurors	17
Benajah Lomis.. Eleazer Pinney.. Eliakim Hitchcok.. Alex^r Vining.. Thomas Ladd Ju^r.. Roger Lomis.. W^m McKinney } Tythingmen	17
Lt Eli Moor.. James Steel.. Timothy Bissell.. Saml Bartlett.. Amasa Lomis } Listers	17
Wareham Foster.. Caleb Booth.. Aaron Bissell Jr.. Stephen Stedman Jr } Collect^rs	17
Capt Joel Lomis.. Thomas Foster.. Andrew McKinney.. Timothy Holton.. Samuel King.. Eben^r Brown.. Capt Hezekiah Bissell.. Noah Allin.. David Trumbull.. Wm Grant.. Sylvenus Rockwell.. Elijah Pember } Surveyors of Highway	17
Capt Joel Lomis.. Nathl Porter Jr.. Azariah Grant.. Eben^r Watson Ju^r } Packers of Tobacco	17
Aaron Grant.. David Trumbull } Key Keepers	17
John Smith.. Charles Bissell.. Samuel Sessions.. W^m McKinney.. Robert Watson.. Saml Watson Jr } Fence Veiwers	17

East Windsor

Pelatiah Foster.. Caleb Parsons.. Ebenezer Nash.. Azel Bowers } Leather Sealers	17
Oliver Day Sealer of Weights & Measures	17
Aaron Bissell Town Treasurer	17
Dec^n Benoni Olcott Collect^r for the 6th Class in the first parish in Chauncey Newberrys Stead	17

2 Sep 1783

Capt James Chamberlain Chosen Moderator   17

2 Sep 1783

This Meeting Considering the Commutation or five years pay to the Officers of the   17
Continental Army given them by Congress oppressive and unjust.. voted that Mr John
Watson be a Committee.. to meet the Committee^s from the Neighbouring Town^s.. to advise
and Seek for Redress

2 Sep 1783

Voted that Mr Jabez Chapman and Joseph Allin Esqr be a Com^{ttee} or Delegates.. to meet and   17
attend the Convention of Delagates for the Several Town^s in this State

16 Sep 1777

The Names of the Persons who took the Oath of Fidelity to this State.. William Wolcott   85
Esqr.. Erastus Wolcott Esqr.. Revd Joseph Perry.. Capt Ebenezer Grant.. Thomas Skinner..
Dec^n David Skinner.. Capt Matthew Grant.. Maj^r Lemuel Stoughton.. Joseph Allin.. Ens E^{dwd}
Chap. Grant.. Dec^n Benoni Olcott.. Lt Samuel Tuder.. Capt Nathl House.. John Prior..
Andrew McKinney.. John Watson.. Ezekiel Sexton.. David Smith.. Danl Elworth Ju^r Esqr..
John Lomis.. Doc^{tr} Charles Mather.. Edward Kneeland.. Eliphalet Bartlett.. Jonathan Brown..
Joseph Kneeland.. Aaron Bissell.. Ebenezer Bissell.. Thomas Drake.. Elijah Hills.. Moses
Wells.. Stephen Lee.. Capt Hezekiah Bissell.. Jonathan Barber.. Zachariah Allin.. Simeon
Barber.. Oliver Stoughton.. Abiel Abbott.. David Bissell.. Abrah^m Foster.. Capt Simon
Wolcott.. Paul Simons.. Ens Fredric Elsworth.. Ens Roswell Grant.. Samuel Webster..
Eliphalet Chapin.. Lt Samuel Watson.. Ens Joseph Diggers.. Danl Rockwell.. Danl Elmer..
Shadrach Barber.. Ebenezer Read.. Capt James Harper.. Zebedee Orsborn.. Nathan Day.. Mr
Nathan Day.. Joseph Chapin.. Jacob Elmer.. Hezekiah Crane.. Ashbel Barber..

26 Jan 1778

.. Augustus Fitch.. Caleb Booth Ju^r.. Robert Watson.. Ebenezer Nash.. Abraham Wallace..   85
Nathl Strong.. Ephraim Ladd.. Thomas Foster.. Noah Barber.. Jeremiah Fullar.. Oliver Hills..
John Lomis Ju^r.. Wm Stoughton.. Capt Amasa Lomis.. Joel Drake.. Lt Thomas Ladd..
Benjamin Newberry.. Elijah Lomis.. Jerijah Bissell.. Benajah Lomis..

16 Feb 1778

..Dec^n Ezekiel Ladd Sworn.. as by Certificate appear[ed]..   85

13 Apr 1778

.. Capt Joel Lomis.. John Craw Ju^r.. Ebenezer Watson Ju^r.. Archelus Flynt.. Dan Bissell..   85
Wareham Moor.. Levi Booth.. Samuel Watson Ju^r.. Isaac Phelps.. Gideon Lomis.. David
Trumbull.. Abner Blodgett.. George Burnham.. Nathan Pelton.. Ashbel Barber.. Isaac
Rockwell.. Oliver Barber.. Henry Wolcott.. Timothy Elmer.. Jonathan Chapman.. Matthew
Bissell.. Danl Bissell.. Saml Bartlett.. Aaron Grant.. Alex^r Elmer.. Danl Osborn.. Noah
Bissell.. Jacob Munsell.. Abijah Skinner.. John Thomson 3^d.. Ezekiel Osborn.. Abiel

East Windsor

Gaylord.. George Cummings.. Ethemar Pelton.. Ebenezer Allin.. Hezekiah Munsell.. Alexander Vining.. Cyrenus Webster.. Joseph Smith.. Lamson Wells..

4 May 1778

.. Elisha Ladd Sworn.. as p^r Certificate..   85

15 Sep 1778

.. Nathaniel Porter.. Eliakim Hitchcock.. Abijah Skinner.. Zebulon King.. Stephen Paine.. Noah Allin.. Benjamin Wolcott.. Hezekiah Porter..   85

12 Apr 1779

.. Samuel Allin.. Wm Lewis.. Abiram Skinner.. Robert Wood.. Benjamin Carver.. Benjamin Cook.. Capt Jonath^n Bartlett.. Abijah Jones.. Abner Rockwell.. Simeon Belknap.. Jabez Fox.. Henry Wolcott.. Lamson Wells.. Azariah Grant..   85

21 Sep 1779

.. Benoni Thomson.. Phinehas Strong.. Thatcher Lothrop.. Eli Bissell.. Samuel Smith.. Alex^r Elmer.. Charles Bissell.. Hezekiah Wells..   85

10 Apr 1780

.. Ezra Rockwell.. John Bancroft.. Elisha Munsell.. Titus King.. Isaac Newton.. Ezekiel Ladd Ju^r.. David Ladd.. Justus Grant.. Daniel Carpenter.. William McCray.. Eleazer Pinney.. Lemuel Pinney.. Silvenus Rockwell.. Jonathan Stoughton.. Alex^r Stoughton.. Nathl Rockwell.. Gideon Chapin.. Nathaniel Lomis.. Joel Rockwell.. Lt Solomon Elsworth.. Jonath^n Bissell Ju^r.. Barzilla Green..   85

9 Apr 1781

.. Eben^r Holman Sworn..   85

18 Sep 1781

.. David Allin.. Nathaniel Allin.. Joseph Pinney Ju^r..   85

17 Sep 1782

.. Daniel Elsworth Junr.. Oliver Chapman.. Levi Gibbs.. Hezekiah Allin.. James Steel.. Jonathan Butten..   85

7 Apr 1783

.. Eben^r Chubbuck.. James Burnham.. Eph^m Wolcott..   85

16 Sep 1783

.. Chaunsey Newberry.. Amasa Newberry.. Russell Stoughton.. Capt Erastus Wolcott.. David Shaw.. John Stoughton.. William Stoughton.. Arodi Wolcott.. Aaron Chapin.. Eben^r Rockwell 3^d.. Albert Wolcott.. Benjamin Skinner.. Aaron Bissell Ju^r.. Benajah Lomis.. Obadiah Dickinson.. Timothy Bissell.. Ephraim Parker.. Oliver Day   85

[ ] Sep 1777

A Role of Freemen.. Admitted & Sworn in open Freemen^s Meeting.. William Wolcott Esqr Gen^{rl} Erastus Wolcott Revd Jos: Perry Capt Eben^r Grant Thomas Skinner Dec^n David Skinner Capt Matthew Grant Maj^r Lemuel Stoughton Joseph Allin Edwd Chap. Grant Dec^n Benoni Olcott Lt Saml Tuder John Prior Capt Nathl House Andrew McKinney John Watson Ezekiel Sexton David Smith Daniel Elsworth Ju^r Esqr John Lomis Doc^{tr} Charles Mather Edward Kneeland Eliphalet Bartlett..Jonathan Brown Joseph Kneeland Aaron Bissell Eben^r Bissell Thomas Drake Elijah Hills Moses Wells Stephen Lee Capt Hez: Bissell Jonathan Barber Zacheriah Allin Simeon Barber Oliver Stoughton: Abiel Abbott David Bissell Araham Foster Capt Simon Wolcott Paul Simons: Ens Fredric Elsworth Ens Roswell Grant Samuel Webster   88

East Windsor

Eliphalet Chapin Lt Samuel Watson Ens Joseph Diggens Dan[l] Rockwell Daniel Elmer Shadrach Barber Ebenezer Read Cap[t] James Harper Zebedee Osborn Nathan Day Joseph Chapin Jacob Elmer Hezekiah Crane Ashbel Barber..

13 Apr 1778

.. Cap[t] Joel Lomis John Craw Ju[r] Benj[n] Newberry Archelus Flynt Dan Bissell Wareham Moor Levi Booth Eben[r] Watson Jun[r] Samuel Watson Ju[r] Isaac Phelps Gideon Lomis Caleb Booth Jun[r] David Trumbull Abner Blodgett Cap[t] Amasa Lomis George Burnham Nathan Pelton Dec[n] Ezekiel Ladd Ashbel Burnham Isaac Rockwell Oliver Barber Henry Wolcott Timothy Elmer.. Jonathan Chapman Matthew Bissell Daniel Bissell Samuel Bartlett Aaron Grant Alex[r] Elmer Daniel Osborn Noah Bissell Joel Prior Jacob Munsell Abijah Skinner George Cummings Ethemar Pelton Ebenezer Allin Hezekiah Munsell Alex[r] Vining Cyrenus Webster Joseph Smith Lamson Wells Abiel Gaylord Ezekiel Osborn John Thomson 3[d].. 88

15 Sep 1778

.. Nathaniel Porter: Eliakim Hitchcock: Abijah Skinner: Zebulon King: Stephen Paine Noah Allin Benjamin Wolcott: Hezekiah Porter.. 88

12 Apr 1779

.. Samuel Allin: William Lewis: Abiram Skinner: Robert Wood: Benjamin Cook: Benjamin Carver Eph[rm] Parker Daniel Warner: Jonathan Damon Cap[t] Jonathan Bartlett Abijah Jones Abner Rockwell Simeon Belknap Jabez Fox Aaron Frost Henry Wolcott Lamson Welles Azariah Grant.. 89

21 Sep 1779

.. Benoni Thomson Phinehas Strong Thatcher Lothrop Eli Bissell Sam[l] Smith Alex[r] Elmer Charles Bissell & Cap[t] Hezekiah Wells.. 89

9 Apr 1781

.. Eben[r] Holman.. 89

18 Sep 1781

.. David Allin Nathaniel Allin & Joseph Pinney Jr.. 89

17 Sep 1782

.. Daniel Elsworth Jr Oliver Chapman Levi Gibbs Hez: Allin James Steel and Jonathan Butten.. 89

7 Apr 1783

.. Simeon Drake Eli Moor Roswell Paine Noah Wells Eben[r] Chubbuck James Burnham Ephraim Wolcott.. 89

16 Sep 1783

.. Chaunsey Newberry Amasa Newberry Russell Stoughton W[m] Stoughton Erastus Wolcott Ju[r] David Shaw John Stoughton Arodi Wolcott Aaron Chapin Eben[r] Rockwell 3[d] Albert Wolcott Benj[n] Skinner Aaron Bissell Jr Benajah Lomis Obadiah Dickerson Timothy Bissell Ephraim Parker Oliver Day.. 89

16 Sep 1783

Sworn [*freeman*] in open Freemen Meeting 89

Enfield

Town Meeting
Vital Records
Vol 2
1762 - 1813
1761 - 1824

See also LDS film # 1,317,124

Located at the Town Clerk's Office

Enfield

11 Jul 1774

Mr Isaac Kibbe was Chosen Moderator 16

Messrs Ephraim terry peter Raynolds Edward Collins Ephraim Pease Nath^{ll} Terry Isaac Kibbe and thomas Parsons be a Committee to Correspond with the Comittes of the other towns in this Colony to Consult and adopt such measures as shall appear to be most safe & salutery.. for the Relief of those persons in those towns of Boston [and] Charlestown &c who are distressed by the unhappy Consequences of the Boston post Bill 17

4 Dec 1775

Isaac Kibbe Moderator 18

Select men Ezekiel peese Edward Collins thomas parson[ ] 18

Town Clerk Edward Collins Esqr 18

Town treasurer Eliphalet terry 18

Constables Nehemiah Chandlor & Jehial Markham 18

Granjurors Daniel Booth & Shadrack terry 18

Surveyors of highways Isaac pease 2^d Joseph olmsted phinehas Lovejoy Sam^{ll} Eaton Junr Jacob hills Thomas Root Simeon olmsted Christopher parsons Junr Sam^{ll} pease 2^d Eldad parsons Capt Daniel perkins 18

fence viewers Selah terry oliver Bush 18

Listors Sam^{ll} Jones Joseph Booth Junr and Jehiel markham 18

Collectors Sam^{ll} Jones David Meacham 18

Leather sealer Joseph olmsted 18

tythingmen moses pease Benjn pease Aaron Bush Ephraim terry Junr Sam^{ll} Eaton Benjn King 18

Gager Isaac Kibbe 18

packer peter parsons 18

brander Shadrach terry 18

sealer of weights & measures Joseph Booth Ju^r 18

key keeper Eliphalet Chapen 18

Voted that Bugbe Sam^{ll} pease & downes for Benjn Roots be set to waymoth for schooling 18

Voted to Chuse a Comittee to Regulate the schools in all parts of the town.. & Chose Maj^r terry John Booth Junr thomas parsons Selah terry Isaac Kibbe timothy pease Junr Edward Collins John parsons Capt pirkins Joseph Gleason Sam^{ll} Gowdy to be a Comittee 19

18 Dec 1775

Voted that Sam^{ll} pease and others set off to weymoth at the Last Meeting be set back again to London Street as they were before 19

voted y^t James firman Jonathan terry & David terry be set to Capt Daniel pirkinss District for Schooling 19

voted that James peas be set to that District Called Jabbock for Schooling 19

School Committee John Reynolds Nehemiah Chandler Isaac Kibbe Edward parsons Elijah parsons Zaccheus prior Sam^{ll} Gowdy James farrington Capt pirkins Sam^{ll} pease Junr timothy pease Junr &c 19

Chose david terry Granjuror in Stead of Shadrack terry who Refused to serve 19

Enfield

Committee of Inspection Capt pirkins Joseph Kingsberry Selah terry Thomas peas Joseph Booth Junr Joseph olmsted & John Booth Junr	19
Committee to view the highway proposed.. from Miah Chandlers out East & Chose Joseph Kingsbury Stephen Chandler & Isaac Kibbe	19
Chose Joseph Kingsberry peter Reynolds & Sam^{ll} pease a Committee to Reck[on] with the Select Men for the Year past	19
Chose Justus Markham Aaron pease & John Reynolds a Committee to Reckon with the Select Men the year to come	19
Voted that Ensign Ely terry prepare and Send a petition to the Assembly to Get Liberty to do the highway work by a Rate	19

15 Jun 1782

Levi Sterns enters his name here that he Chuses to belong to and Join with the 2^d Society in Enfield	20

2 Dec 1776

Edward Collins Esqr was Chosen moderator	24
Ezekiel pease Edward Collins & thomas parsons were Chosen Select men	24
Eliphalet terry was Chosen town treasurer	24
Edward Collins was Chosen town Clerk	24
agustus Diggins Nehemiah Chandler Constables	24
Lemuel Kingsberry oliver Bush Isaac pease fence viewers	24
Sam^{ll} Jones Selah terry Liu^t Ephraim terry Listors	24
Daniel Booth Daniel terry Collectors	24
Joseph olmsted Sealer of Leather	24
Sam^{ll} Jones & Thomas Root Granjurors	24
Elijah parsons John Kingsberry Junr Joseph Knight david Meacham & John Morrison tythingmen	24
Maj^r terry Gager	24
peter parsons packer of meat	24
Justus Markham Brander of horses	24
Joseph Booth Junr Sealer of weights & measures	24
Benjn parsons Key keeper	24
Liu^t Ephraim terry John Raynolds Sam^{ll} pease 2^d Sam^{ll} pease Edward parsons Sam^{ll} Jones Sam^{ll} Gowdy Cap pirkins John Booth Junr & Jacob terry School Committee	24
the Committee of Inspection the same that was in last year with the addition of Nath^{ll} Chapen Eliphalet terry & John Raynolds [*ed: see Dec 18, 1775 meeting*]	25
voted that Selah terry John Booth Junr & Isaac pease be a Committee to Straighten the town street	25

31 Mar 1777

Edward Collins Esqr was Chosen moderator	25
voted to Chuse a Committee to take Care of the families of those that Shall Engage in the Service of the War in their absence and Chose peter Raynolds Sam^{ll} Warriner Capt pease Selah terry Joseph Gleason & Isaac pease a Committee for that purpose	25

Enfield

7 Apr 1777

voted that Joseph Knight Capt pirkins & Ens^n Eliphalet terry be a Committee to prefer a memorial to the assembly in May next pray that the Negrows in this State be Released from their Slavery and Bondage	25

24 Sep 1777

moderator Isaac Kibbe	25
voted to Chuse a Committee to purchase Cloathing for the Soldiers and that they borrow mony if need be for that purpose the Committee Chosen were Capt pease John Reynolds and Moses allen	25
Chose Eliphat terry John Raynolds Edward Collins & Nath^{ll} Chapin to assist the Listers in making up the List	26

1 Dec 1777

moderator Capt Joseph Booth	26
Capt Booth peter Raynolds & Selah Terry [*ed: voted to unnamed position, most likely Selectmen*]	26
Edward Collins Esqr town Clerk	26
Eliphalet terry town treasurer	26
Constables Jonathan Bush & Sam^{ll} pease 2^d	26
Listers Sam^{ll} Jones Augustus Diggins Le^t John Booth	26
Colectors Elijah holkins & Asahel parsons	26
Granjurors Elijah parsons & Eli Bush	26
Tythingmen Timothy pease Junr Aaron Bush David meacham and John french	26
Leather Sealer Joseph olmsted and packer also	26
Gager John Raynolds	26
Branders Eldad parsons Shadrack terry	26
Sealer of weights & measures Capt Booth	26
surveyors of highways Ebenezer Chapen John french Sam^{ll} gowdy eliphalet terry Richard Abbe Oliver Bush Joseph olmsted John Kingsberry Junr Ebenezar terry Junr Eldad phelps Daniel Abbe	26
fence viewers Joseph olmsted Barzillah markham	26
Committee to take Care of the families of the Soldiers in their absence Edward Collins Esqr David Bullin Moses allen Isaac Kibbe david Chandler Isaac pease & Asa olmsted	26
School Committee Eliphalet terry Sam^{ll} Jones Ebenezer terry Junr Eli Bush Sam^{ll} pease 2^d Sam^{ll} Gowdy timothy holten Liu^t John Booth Liu^t abbe Jonathan Bush David terry	26
Committee of Inspecttion denis Bement Ju^r David moses allen Nath^{ll} Chapen John Raynolds Eliphalet terry	26
Ezekiel pease was Chosen to measure out the salt Come from Boston to Each family according to their number in Equal propotion	27
the Select men shall see about the highway by hubbards and Exchange the Road with hubbard that it may Go where the path now Goes	27

14 Jan 1778

moderator Capt Joseph Booth	27

Enfield

Chose Isaac Kibbe Doctor field Eliphalet terry Capt hezekiah parsons & Edward Collins Esqr a Committee to take in to Consideration the articles of Confederation	27
Denis Bement a Committee man to take Care of Jonathan parsons wife	27

13 Apr 1778

moderator Capt Joseph Booth	27
Chose Eliphalet terry a Lister in the Room of Sam^{ll} Jones Removed	27
voted that the Select men shall take Care of Elizar wrights and his family according to their discretion	27
voted to abate Joseph peases Rate to Mr Diggins and John halls Rates to pay the Soldirs	27

7 Dec 1778

Capt Joseph Booth moderator	28
Capt Ephraim pease Edward Collins Esqr peter Raynolds Selah terry Eliphalet terry Capt Booth and John Booth were Chosen Select men	28
Edward Collins Esqr Town Clerk	28
Town treasurer Eliphalet terry Esqr	28
Constables moses allen David terry & Daniel Burbank	28
Survayors of highways John parsons david Meacham Darias Markham Edward pease Sam^{ll} Gowdy Benjn parsons Thomas Root Noadiah pease Amos Alden Daniel Burbank daniel terry david terry Nathan pease 2^d & Ebenezar Chapen	28
fence viewers Mathew thomson Joseph Markham	28
Listors Co^{ll} Nath^{ll} terry Isaac Kibbe david Chandler david meacham & Sam^{ll} Gowdy	28
assessors Aaron pease Nehemiah Chandler and John parsons	28
Colectors Sharon pease Ebenezar terry 3^d	28
Leather Sealer Joseph olmsted	28
Grandjurors Edward parsons daniel Burbank	28
Tythingmen Zachariah Booth Benjn King Ebenezar parsons John Booth James farrington & Isaac Chandler	28
John Raynolds Gager	28
peter parsons packer	28
Capt Booth Sealer of weights & measures	28
Eliphalet Chapen Chosen Brander	28
Schooll Committee Joseph Knight sam^{ll} pease 2^d simeon olmsted Eliphalet Collins Lemuel Kingsberry thomas Root Isaac pease 2^d Ebenezar terry Junr John booth Isaac Kibbe & matthew thomson	28
Voted that the South part of London Street be Set to weymouth for Schoolling as far north as to take in bugbe & Sam^{ll} pease & John Kingsberry & John Junr to be Set to London Street for Schooling	28

21 Dec 1778

the Question was put Wheither the town would do anything about the ferry now in the hands of Isaac Kibbe voted in the affirmative then Chose Mr Joseph Kingsberry to Go to the General Assembly to try to Get the ferry now in Isaac Kibbes hands to be Established for the use of the town	28

Enfield

12 Apr 1779

Capt Joseph Booth moderator	29
voted that the town Book of Records of Land be trancescribed as soon as may be and the town Clerk Shall Invite the town of Somers to pay their part of the Cost.. voted that Edward Collins Esqr Ezekiel pease Augustus diggins and Eliphalet terry Esqr Shall do the same and that Somers have Liberty if they Se Cause to Send a man to write part of the time	29
Chose Eliphalet terry Esqr to to Join with and assist Mr Joseph Kingsberry at the Assembly.. to Get the ferry on the north Side of freshwater Established to and for for the use of the town	29
voted that the Select men Straiten the Road that Goes out by Ebenezar Chapens.. and that out by John Me[]tons	29

25 Jun 1779

Isaac Kibbe moderator	29

6 Dec 1779

Capt Joseph Booth moderator	29
Select men Eliphetlet terry Esqr Capt Booth Peter Raynolds Esqr Edward Collins Esqr	29
town Clerk Eliphalet terry Esqr	29
Town treasurer Eliphalet terry Esqr	29
Constables moses allen David terry and Daniel Burbank	29
voted to Chuse a Comittee to purchase Cloathing for the Soldiers to take Care of their families and Chose John Raynolds David meacham david Chandler and John Parsons	29
Listers John parsons John Raynolds and Augustus Diggins	29
Collectors Cummis pease Junr and Gustus markham	30
Leather Sealer Joseph olmsted	30
Granjurors Asahel parsons and Sam^{ll} pease 2^d	30
tythingmen John Gains Junr asa olmsted Daniel Booth Edward pease & asa pease	30
Survayors of highways Eldad phelps Rufus Bush Stephen Chandler Cumins pease Junr Elijah holkins Sam^{ll} Godowy Eli hale denis Bement Junr Elisha Kibbe John Morrison John pease 3^d John Booth Zacheus prior	30
fence viewers Nathan pease 2^d John abbe 2^d	30
Gager Isaac Kibbe packer peter parsons	30
Brander Shadrack terry	30
Sealer of waits and measures Capt Joseph Booth	30
key keeper Benjn parsons	30
Schooll Comittee John french Jehiel markham moses allen Zacheus prior Ebenezer terry 2^d Eliphalet Collins Sam^{ll} pease 2^d Joseph markham James farrington Shadrach terry	30

13 Mar 1780

Capt Joseph Booth moderator	30
Chose Capt Richard abbe Nehemiah Chandler moses allen Joseph gleason Selah terry david terry asa olmsted and Capt Jonathan Bush to be Inspectors	30
Chose Capt Ephr^m pease a Select man	30

Enfield

21 Jun 1780

moderator Co[ll] Nath[ll] terry	31
voted that whenever any of the milia are Cald and in Service they shall Receive So much mony out of the town treasury as a Comm[tee] Shall think just for their Expence going out & Coming home Both foot and horse both officers and soldiers Equally alike and Chose Doc[r] field Selah terry & Joseph Knight for that purpose	31

16 Nov 1780

Cap[t] Booth moderator	32
Voted 10[d] on the pound upon the List 1779 for provision for the armie or pay it in provision.. and Chose Joseph Knight & Eli Bush to Receive the provision & Colect the mony	32

4 Dec 1780

Cap[t] Joseph Booth	32
Cap[t] Pease Cap[t] Booth & John Raynolds were chose Select Men	32
Edward Collins Esq[r] was Chosen Town Clerk	32
& Eliphalet Terry Esq[r] town treasurer	32
and Augustus Diggins Jehiel Markham & Cap[t] Bush Listers	32
& John Kingsberry & Nathan Markham Grandjurors	32
& Solomon Chandler Isaac Pease Sam[ll] Gowdy John parsons & James farrington Tything men	32
& Chose Selah terry Rogor Griswould Jun[r] asahel parsons John morrison Gustus Markham david Bullen Elias Pease vashni hall oliver Bush amos alden Elijah parsons Benj[n] king Ebenezar Chapen & Cap[t] pirkins Surveyors of highways	32
fence viewers John abbe 2[d] & nathan pease 2[d]	32
& Joseph olmsted Leather Sealer	32
& John Raynolds Gager	32
& Justus markham Brander	32
& Key keeper Benj[n] parsons	32
Colectors Edward pease & Eli parsons	32
voted to.. Chuse a Committee to take Care of the Soldiers wifes & to purchase Cloathing & Chose Nehemiah Chandler Jehiel Markham & Simeon olmsted	32
School Committee moses allen Shubael Griswould John Booth david Chandler darias markham John morrison asa pease Zacheus prior John parsons & thomas pease	32

6 Jan 1781

Co[ll] terry moderator	33
voted that one peny half peny on the pound be paid in Grain.. or two pence half peny on the pound in States mony to purchase Corn and flower & Chose Eli Bush and Joseph Knight to Colect the same and a Committee to Receive and Store the Grain & pack it	33
Eliphalet Killam School Comittee	33

12 Mar 1781

Moderator Cap[t] Daniel pirkins	33
voted to Excuse david meacham from his office as Constable and Chose Jehiel markham in	33

Enfield

his Stead	
then Chose Capt pease Capt Booth Joseph Kingsberry John Raynolds and John Booth a Committee to Settle with the Soldiers that were in the Continental armie last Sumer	33
18 Mar 1782	
Capt pirkins being Chose moderator	33
voted to divide the town into four Clases to Raise the men for the State Regiment & Chose Capt Bush Esqr terry Selah terry & Elisha Kibbe for that purpose	33
3 Jul 1781	
moderator Capt Booth	34
Eli Bush Was Chosen to Receive the Sundry articles.. in Lieue of the hard mony and to Raise four pence on the pound in hard mony to Be paid in Beaf & Cattle at four pence p^r pound & the Cost to be made in purchasing the Beef	34
voted to divide the town in Classes to Get 2 men for the State Service Esqr terry david Chandler & Isaac peas to Class the town	34
18 Sep 1781	
moderator Capt Booth	34
voted to Chuse a Comittee to Settle with the Six Mmonths men & Chose Eliphalet terry Esqr asahel parsons & Eli Bush	34
Chos Christopher parsons Junr & Nathan pease 2^d Collectors to Collect the 4^d tax of live Beef	34
3 Dec 1781	
Capt Booth moderator	34
town Clerk Edward Collins Esqr	34
Select men John Raynolds Capt pease & moses allen	34
Eliphalet terry Esqr treasurer	34
Constables John Booth & Benjn parsons	34
Listers Augustus diggins Capt Bush & Capt Booth	34
Survayers of highways Eldad phelps daniel Booth denis Bement Junr James pease amos alden david terry Sam^{ll} Gowdy daniel Burbank thomas pease Joel Simons hezekiah parsons Benjn Simons & Isaac Gleason	34
fence viewers John abbe Junr & nathan pease 2^d	34
Collectors david terry & Eliphalet Collins	34
Granjurors Benjn pease Isaac pease	34
tythingmen timothy pease Junr Ebenezar Chapen Wareham parsons & oliver Bush	34
Gager John Raynolds	34
Brander Eliphalet Chapen	34
Sealer of weights Joseph Booth Junr	34
Leather Sealer thomas parsons	34
key keeper Benjn parsons	34
Schooll Committee asa peas Joseph olmsted Ebenezar Chapan Roger Griswould david Chandler John Booth daniel Booth Eliphalet Collins Elisha Kibbe eliphalet Killam & Capt	34

Enfield

pirkins

2 Dec 1782

moderator Capt Booth	35
Select men John Raynolds Capt pease Eliphalet terry Esqr	35
Edward Collins Esqr town Clerk	35
Eliphalet terry Esqr town treasurer	35
Constables Eli Bush moses allen	35
Survayors of highways John Raynolds hezekiah parsons david hall Junr heman peas abner meacham Joseph parsons James farrington daniel abbe Joseph Knight Simeon olmsted John pease 3^d & Elisha Kibbe	35
fence viewers denis Bement Joseph olmsted	35
Listors augustus diggins Selah terry Capt Booth	35
Collectors John peace 2^d Isaac peace 3^d	35
Leather Sealer Joseph olmsted	35
Gran jurors John parsons daniel	35
tything men Lemuel Kingsbery Elijah parsons	35
haywards John Raynolds augustus diggins Joseph Kings[ ] Ebenezar terry Eli Bush Isaac terry daniel abbe	35
Gager John Raynolds	35
packer Joseph Knight	35
Branders Eldad parsons Shadrack terry	35
Sealer of Weights Capt Booth	35
key keeper Ben parsons	35
School Committee Eliphalet terry Esqr Simeon olmsted Elijah parsons Sam^{ll} pease 2^d Isaac pease Eliphalet Killam Eben^r terry 2^d Eliphalet Collins Sam^{ll} Gowdy John Booth	35
voted to appoint a Committee to Survey the town Street or Country Road through the town.. & Cause all Incumbrances.. to be Removed or Receive the Worth of the Land which are now Enclosed by any person or persons.. if s^d Committee Shall think it be for the publick good also dispose of.. land belonging to S^d highway if they Shall think it Best.. the Comittee for that purpose Eliphalet terry Esqr Capt pease Edward Collins Esqr John Raynolds	35

Fairfield

Town Minutes 1601 – 1826
Typed transcript, unpaginated
Located at the Town Clerk's Office

Fairfield Town Meetings
Located at the Connecticut State Archives

Fairfield

29 Dec 1774

Ebenezer Silliman Esqr Moderator	269
having duly considered the.. Association entred into by the Continental Congress Lately held at Philadelphia do heartily approve thereof and adopt the Same:. And.. make choice of the following Gentlemen to be a Committee for the purposes therein mentioned (viz) Gold Selleck Silliman Jonathan Sturges Job Bartram Andrew Rowland Samuel Squier Jonathan Bulkley Elijah Abel Increase Bradley Eliphalet Thorp Aaron Jennings Benjamin Lacy Daniel Wilson Azariah Odell David Hubbell Zalmon Bradley John Hubbell Thomas Cable Joseph Hanford Stephen Gorham Thaddeus Burr Jonathan Lewis David Dimon John Wilson Joseph Strong Albert Sherwood Moss Kent Samuel Wakeman John Squier Ichabod Wheeler Ebenezer Bartram Jonathan Dimon Jabez Hill George Burr Hezekiah Hubbell Benjamin Wheeler Josepih Hide Jeremiah Sherwood Daniel Andrews Hezekiah Bradley Joseph Bradley Ephraim Lyon and John Allen	269
Voted.. it is expedient a County Congress be held.. Voted that Col^o Gold S. Silliman Jonth Sturges Andrew Rowland Esqr Mr Job Bartram & Thad^s Burr Esqr be a Committee to attend the Same	269
Voted.. Col^o Gold S. Silliman Jonth Sturges Andrew Rowland Esqr Mr Job Bartram & Thad^s Burr Esqr be a Committee of Correspondence	269

16 Jun 1775

Jonathan Sturges Esqr be Moderator	268

14 Dec 1775

Voted that Joseph Bradley Esqr be Moderator	267
Agreed that Nathan Bulkley be Town Clerk	267
Agreed that Doctor John Allen Thad^s Burr Jospeh Strong Eben^r Banks Sam^{ll} Wakeman Esq^{rs} Mr Joseph Wakeman and Mr Daniel Andrews be Selectmen	267
Voted y^t Doc^r John Allen be Town Treasurer	267
Agreed y^t Jonth Silliman Benj^a Rumsey Dan^{ll} Sherwood 2^d Richard Hubbell Ju^r Seth Down and Dan^{ll} Duncan be Constables	267
Voted y^t Richard Hubbell Ju^r be Collec^r to Collect ye Country Rate	267
Agreed y^t And^w Wakeman Joseph Wakeman James Hall Jonth Squier David Hubbell and Silas Haines be Grandjurors	267
Agreed y^t And^w Jennings Moses Jennings Reuben Beers Nathan Seely John Allen Ju^r Jehiel Whitehead Ezra Williams Jehiel Thorp Aaron Whitney and David Beers be Tythingmen	267
Agreed y^t Ichabod Wheeler Elijah Abell Hez: Nichols Hez: Sturges Isaac Jennings Deodate Silliman Dan^{ll} Wilson Seth Morehouse Elip^t Thorp -- John Nichols Ju^r Tim^y Wheeler Dan^{ll} Lacy Benjamin Hubbell Esbon Hall -- Stephen Morgan Hez: Fanton Augustus Hill David Bradley Sam^{ll} Prince Azariah Odell David Silliman Solomon Burton Silvenus Morehouse Sam^{ll} Baker Nath^{ll} Seely Ju^r -- Hum^y Ogden Eben^r Bixby Jonth Squier David Godfrey Thos Banks Lemuel Wood -- Jeremiah Sherwood Moss Kent Thos Nash Richard Elwood Stephen Gorham Stephen Wakeman Hez: Coley John Andrews Dan^{ll} Hull Eph^m Burr Gideon Wakeman -- Dan^{ll} Sherwood 2^d Oliver Middlebrook John Stratton Gershom Hubbell George Burr Noah Sherwood Moses Ogden John Bradley 2^d Thad^s Wakeman Tim^y Wakeman Thos Wheeler Ju^r Gershom Jennings Dan^{ll} Meaker 2^d and Elip^t Wakeman be Surveyors of Highways	267
Agreed y^t Hez: Sturges John Smedly Eben^r Jesup Jos: Hide Stephen Wakeman David Adams Dan^{ll} Andrews -- Eph^m Lyon Eben^r Hill Dan^{ll} Banks John Wakeman Ju^r Jabez Hill Nath^{ll}	267

Fairfield

Seeley Ju^r Elnath^n Williams Hez: Hubbell and Seth Seely be fence viewers

Agreed y^t Eben^r Silliman Sam^{ll} Burr Thos Nash Dan^{ll} Duncan Seth Down Nathan Bennitt Ju^r 267
Thad^s Bennitt Hez: Bradley and Daniel Banks be Listers

Voted y^t Joseph Bradley Esqr & Mr David Allen be Sealers of Leather   267

Voted y^t ye laying out a Highway already Done from ye Country Road Across by Dan^{ll} 267
Wheeler.. Meeting House by ye Selectmen be Accepted

Agreed y^t Jonth Bulkley be Gauger & Sealer of Measures   267

Voted y^t Hez: Nichols be Sealer of weights   267

Voted y^t David Osborn & Jehiel Whitehead be Packers   267

Agreed y^t Abel Gold Deliverance Bennitt John Olmsted Ju^r Hez: Hubbell Josiah Brinsmaide   267
and Hez: Bradley be branders of horses

Voted y^t Solomon Sturges Hez: Bradley Simon Couch Ju^r Eben^r Ogden Dan^{ll} Duncan and   267
Obadiah Platt be Key keeper

Agreed y^t Benj^a Dean Dan^{ll} Duncan Jeremiah Sherwood Jos: Hide Job Bartram And^w 267
Rowland Jos: Strong Hez: Hubbell Jonth Dimon George Burr Sam^{ll} Seely Nathan Bennitt Ju^r
and Elijah Abell be a Com^{tee} to remove Incroachments off from ye Highways

Voted y^t Mr John Olmsted and Sam^{ll} Wakeman Esqr be a Com^{tee} to Exchange part of   267
Newtown Road So Called with Sam^{ll} Thorp Ju^r for other Lands near said Thorp's Barn & to
be at said Thorp's Cost

28 Dec 1775

The former Moderator Joseph Bradley Esqr being present   267

Voted y^t Capt Elijah Abell be Lister   267

Voted y^t David Tredwell be Surveyor of Highways   267

Voted y^t Jonth Silliman Richard Hubbell Ju^r Noah Taylor Hanford Dan^{ll} Sherwood 2^d Dan^{ll} 267
Duncan and Azariah Odell be Collectors of ye Town Rate Each one to Collect in the Society
wherein they live and Each Collector to have forty Shilings for his Service Except Richard
Hubbell Ju^r he to have twenty Shillings for his Service in Collecting

Voted y^t Noah Taylor Hanford be Constable   267

Voted y^t John Smedly be Constable   267

Voted y^t Dan^{ll} Andrew Eben^r Squier and Dan^{ll} Duncan be a Com^{tee} to purchase Some Lands   267
adjoining to Sturges Highway near Norfield Meeting House for.. a Highway provided they
purchase no more than the value of four pounds

Voted y^t Sam^{ll} Wakeman Esqr Capt Jabez Hill and Mr Elnathan Williams be a Com^{tee} to Sell   266
part of ye Cross Highway leading from the Country Road to Francis Bradley Ju^{rs} old House &
part of upright Highway adjoining near said House and the money to be laid out in
purchasing land for a Highway to go to Gershom Bradley's Grist Mill

Voted y^t David Williams John Bradley Ju^r and Elip^t Wakeman be a Com^{tee} to view a place for   266
a Highway to run Across from from Burrs Highway Easterly to Wilsons Highway

Voted y^t Benj^a Lacy be Constable   266

Voted y^t Elnath Williams be added to.. the former Com^{tee} Appointed to to procure a place of   266
Parrade in Northfairfield Parish

Voted y^t Sam^{ll} Wakeman Esqr Capt Jabez Hill and Mr Elnath Williams be a Com^{tee} to   266
Exchange part of ye upright Highway between the Mile Comon and Dimon's Long lott near
Redding bounds with Gershom Bradley for other Lands for a Highway

Voted y^t Thad^s Burr Jonth Sturges Esq^{rs} and Cap^{ts} Elijah Abell Abra^m Gold Jonth Dimon   266

234

Fairfield

David Hubbell Jabez Hill and Mess[rs] Elip[t] Thorp Jeremiah Sherwood Tho[s] Nash Joseph Bennitt George Burr Eben[r] Squier Benj[a] Dean Azariah Odell Hezekiah Hubbell and Benj[a] Lacy be a Com[tee] of Inspection	
Voted y[t] Gold Selleck Silliman Thad[s] Burr Jon[th] Sturges and And[w] Rowland Esq[rs] and Mr Jon[th] Lewis be a Com[tee] to attend the County Congress and also.. be a Com[tee] of Correspondence	266
Voted y[t] And[w] Rowland Esq[r] M[r] Job Bartram and Cap[t] Elijah Abell be a Com[tee] to Exchange Highways in the first Society	266
Voted y[t] Mess[rs] Jeremiah Sherwood Joseph Hide & Joseph Wakeman be a Com[tee] to Sell or Exchange part of y[e] Highway near John Morehouse 2[ds] House with him	266
31 Oct 1776	
Voted y[t] Jonathan Sturges Esq[r] be Moderator	266
Voted y[t] there be a guard of Twenty Six men to guard the Town Nightly and Every Night to be Set in manner following viz: four to patrol from Saugatuck River to Cable's Mill and four to patrol from said Mill to Sasco River and four from said Sasco River to the Mill River and four from s[d] Mill River to the Pine Crrek and Six to patrol from s[d] Pine Creek to the Ash house Creek so Called and in the Town Streets and four at Stratfield	266
11 Dec 1776	
Voted y[t] Jonathan Sturges Esq[r] be Moderator	266
Agreed y[t] Nathan Bulkley be Town Clerk	266
Agreed y[t] Jonathan Lewis Thad[s] Burr Benjamin Dean Eben[r] Banks Joseph Strong Joseph Wakeman and Nath[ll] Seely Ju[r] be Selectmen	266
Voted y[t] Doct[r] John Allen be Town Treasurer	266
Agreed y[t] Richard Hubbell Ju[r] Eben[r] Wakeman Ju[r] Jon[th] Silliman Dan[ll] Sherwood 2[d] Dan[ll] Duncan Benjamin Rumsey Noah Taylor Hanford and Seth Down be Constables	266
Voted y[t] Richard Hubbell Ju[r] be Collector to gather y[e] Colony Tax	266
Agreed y[t] Benj[a] Wheeler John Nichols Ju[r] Dan[ll] Lacy Benj[a] Hubbell Ezbun Hall Ichabod Wheeler Job Bartram And[w] Rowland Seth Morehouse Sam[ll] Wilson Hez: Sturges And[w] Wakeman Will[m] Bulkley Joseph Hide David Burr Gideon Wakeman Eben[r] Morehouse Noah Taylor Hanford Eben[r] Godfrey Solomon Gray David Lyon Dan[ll] Meaker Seth Meaker David Banks Joseph Smith Albert Sherwood John Banks Joseph Frost George Burr Eben[r] Hill Amos Williams Seth Lyon Gershom Jenning John Wakeman Ju[r] Abel Bradley Eben[r] Burr Eben[r] Squier Humphrey Ogden Lem[ll] Wood Eben[r] Bixby David Godfrey Elip[t] Coley Jeremiah Oakly Sam[ll] Thorp Ju[r] Gershom Bradley Seth Murwin Obadiah Platt Tho[s] Sherwood Dan[ll] Bennitt Isaac Seely Francis Jackson Nath[ll] Hubbell Sam[ll] Baker & Nath[ll] Seely Ju[r] be Surveyors of Highways	266
Agreed y[t] Seth Seely Hez: Hubbell John Smedly Hez- Sturges Joseph Hide Jeremiah Sherwood Dan[ll] Andrews David Adams Eph[m] Lyon Eben[r] Hill Joseph Smith Dan[ll] Banks Elna[th] Williams and Josiah Brinsmaide be fence viewers	265
Agreed y[t] David Allen Ju[r] Eben[r] Silliman Richard Hubbell Ju[r] Jeremiah Sherwood Dan[ll] Duncan Dan[ll] Banks Nathan Bennitt Ju[r] and Elna[th] Williams be Listers	265
Voted y[t] David Allen Ju[r] & Elisha Bradley be Sealers of Leather	265
Agreed y[t] Moses Jennings Joseph Smith Moses Burr Ju[r] Seth Seely Dan[ll] Burr Ju[r] & David Silliman be Grandjurors	265
Agreed y[t] Tho[s] Staples Eben[r] Bulkley Benj[a] Wheeler Zalmon Bradley Joseph Lyon Lem[ll] Wood John Philips Asa Disbrow and John Olmsted be Tythingmen	265

Fairfield

Voted y^t Jerem^h Jennings Ju^r & Eben^r Wakeman Ju^r be Haywards	265
Voted y^t And^w Rowland Esqr be gauger	265
Voted y^t John Parrit be Packer	265
Voted y^t Abel Gold Hez: Bradley Jos: Rumsey John Olmsted Ju^r Hez: Hubbell & Peter Nichols be branders of horses	265
Voted y^t Hez: Nichols be Sealer of weights	265
Voted y^t David Allen Ju^r be Sealer of Measures	265
Agreed y^t Hez: Bradley Eben^r Ogden Simon Couch Ju^r Dan^{ll} Duncan Obadiah Platt Judgson Sturges be Keykeepers of Pounds	265
Agreed y^t Jonath Sturges & Thad^s Burr Esq^{rs} Col^o Abra^m Gold Capt Jabez Hill & Messrs Job Bartram John Smedly Moses Jennings Eben^r Bulkley Hez: Hubbell Nathan Seely David Hubbell George Burr Jonath Lewis Eben^r Hill Jerem^h Sherwood Thos Nash Eben^r Squier Humphrey Ogden Azariah Odell David Silliman & Joseph Bennitt be a Com^{tee} of Inspection	265
Voted y^t Richard Hubbell Ju^r Azariah Odell Dan^{ll} Duncan Noah Taylor Hanford & Dan^{ll} Sherwood 2^d be Collec^{rs} of Town Rate Each one to Collect in the Parish in which they live: Richard Hubbell Ju^r to have Twenty Shillings for his Service & the Rest to have forty Shillings Each	265

26 Dec 1776

Voted y^t Thad^s Burr Esqr be Moderator	265

31 Dec 1776

The former Moderator Jonth Sturges Esqr being present	265
Voted y^t Jonth Silliman Collect ye Town Rate in the Prime Society	265
Voted y^t Deodate Silliman be a Surveyor of Highways	265
Voted y^t Eben^r Bulkley be Constable	265
Voted y^t Sam^{ll} Wakeman Esqr Capt Jabez Hill & Mr Elnath Williams be a Com^{tee} to view the Highway running from Moses Dimon's Door Downwards, & to make Sale of such part thereof as will not be Detrimental to ye Publick	265

17 Feb 1777

Voted y^t Thad^s Burr Esqr be Moderator	265
Voted y^t Nathan Wheeler Ju^r be Constable.. in the room of Seth Down Deceased	264
Voted y^t Nathan Wheeler Ju^r be Collector of ye Town Rate.. in ye Parish of Northfairfield in ye room of Azariah Odell Deceased and have forty Shillings for his Service	264

2 Apr 1777

Voted y^t Jonth Sturges Esqr be Moderator	264
Voted yt Gershom Hubbell be Selectman.. in the room of Eben^r Banks Esqr Dec^d	264
Voted y^t Thad^s Burr Esqr and those Pesons that are with him in like Circumstances.. infected with the Small Pox, have Liberty to return to Such place in this Town as the Selectman shall Appoint, and there remain until released	264

14 Aug 1777

Voted y^t Thad^s Burr Esqr be Moderator	264
Voted y^t Deodate Silliman be Constable.. in the room & Stead of his Brother Jonth Silliman Dec^d	264

Fairfield

Voted y^t Deodate Silliman Richard Hubbell Ju^r Noah Taylor Hanford Dan^{ll} Sherwood 2^d Dan^{ll} Duncan & Nathan Wheeler Ju^r be Collectors of ye Town Rate Each one to Collect in the Society wherein they Dwell.. Each Collec^r have forty shillings.. Except Richard Hubbell Ju^r and he to have Twenty Shillings *18 Sep 1777*	264
Voted that Thad^s Burr Esqr be Moderator	264
Voted y^t Moses Sherwood be Lister in the room of his Father Jer: Sherwood Dec^d	264
24 Sep 1777	
The former Moderator Thad^s Burr Esqr being present	264
Voted y^t Joseph Hide be Lister in ye room of Jeremiah Sherwood Dec^d	264
Voted y^t the Selectmen be a Com^{tee} to procure Cloathing for the Soldiers in the Continental Service.. according to an order of ye Govr and Council of Safety.. Also Voted.. Capt David Hubbell Capt John Andrews Hez: Hubbell Major Jabez Hill; Dan^{ll} Duncan and Nath^{ll} Wilson be a Com^{tee} to assist ye Selectmen in procuring the.. Cloathing	264
Voted y^t Seth Seely Major Jabez Hill Jonth Lewis Eben^r Jesup Capt Eben^r Hill Daniel Andrews and Thad^s Burr Esqr be Assessors	264
Voted y^t Gold Selleck Silliman Esqr, as agent for the Town prefer a Memorial to ye General Assembly in October next, praying said Assembly to appoint a Com^{tee} to Enquire into the Damages Done to the Inhabitants of this Town by the Ministerial Army when they went to Danbury in April last past *19 Dec 1777*	264
Voted y^t General Gold Selleck Silliman be Moderator	264
19 Dec 1777	
Voted y^t Nathan Bulkley be Town Clerk	264
19 Dec 1777	
Agreed y^t Thad^s Burr Esqr Jonth Lewis Capt Hez: Hubbell Capt Thos Nash Gershom Hubbell Esqr, Benjamin Dean and Capt Nath^{ll} Seely be Selectmen *19 Dec 1777*	264
Voted y^t Doct^r John Allen be Town Treasurer	264
Agreed y^t Deodate Silliman, Richard Hubbel Ju^r Benj^a Rumsey, Dan^{ll} Sherwood 2^d, Dan^{ll} Duncan, Nathan Wheeler Ju^r Walter Budington and Noah Taylor Hanford be Constables and y^t s^d Richd Hubbell Ju^r be Collector to Collect ye State Tax	264
Agreed y^t Capt Ichabod Wheeler, Major Elijah Abel, Deodate Silliman, Isaac Jennings, Seth Morehouse, Dan^{ll} Wilson, Jabez Thorp, Capt Stephen Thorp, Capt Job Bartram, John Nichols Ju^r Dan^{ll} Lacy, Sam^{ll} Sherwood Ju^r Benj^a Wheeler, Noah T. Hanford, Eben^r Godfrey Nathan Godfrey, Benj^a Wynkoop, Stephen Gwier, Eben^r Odgen, John Crosman, Gideon Wakeman, Isaac Oysterbanks, Capt David Banks Albert Sherwood, Seth Sherwood, Amos Williams, Justice Bradley, Nathan Gold, David Gold, John Staples, Eben^r Burr, Seth Bradley, Chauncey Down Joseph Frost, Abel Bradley, John Banks, Hez: Ogden Dan^{ll} Duncan Eben^r Bixby, Thos Banks, Joseph Smith, Lemuel Wood, David Godfrey, Daniel Silliman Dan^{ll} Bennitt, Najah Bennitt, Jabez Rowland, Silvenus Morehouse, Sam^{ll} Thorp Ju^r Elnath Williams, Peter Osborn, Seth Murwin and Benj^a Jennings be Surveyors of Highways	264
Agreed y^t Capt Hez: Sturges, John Smedly, Wm Dimon, Seth Seely Capt Hez: Hubbell, Dan^{ll} Lacy, Joseph Hide, Capt Thos Nash, Capt Eben^r Hill, Albert Sherwood, John Hull, Hum^y Ogden, Nehem^h Beers, Benj^a Dean, Dan^{ll} Bennitt and Nath^{ll} Seely 3^d be fence viewers	263

Fairfield

Agreed y^t Capt Hez: Hubbell, Nathan Seely, Capt Job Bartram, Dan^{ll} Osborn, Joseph Hide, Thos Couch, John Bradley, Elisha Bradley, Lemuel Wood, Joseph Smith, David Silliman and Elnathan Williams be Grandjurymen	263
Agreed y^t David Allen, Major Elijah Abel, Dan^{ll} Lacy, Joseph Hide, Gershom Wakeman, Dan^{ll} Duncan, David Silliman and Nathan Wheeler Ju^r be Listers	263
Voted y^t David Allen & Elisha Bradley be Leather sealers	263
Voted y^t Eben^r Bulkley, Jabez Thorp, Dan^{ll} Lacy, Eben^r Lewis, John Crosman, David Bradley, Hez: Price, David Morehouse and Josiah Brinsmaide be Tythingmen	263
Voted y^t David Patchin, Paul Nichols & Sam^{ll} Beers Ju^r be Pounders	263
Voted y^t Samuel Penfield be Gauger	263
Voted y^t Sam^{ll} Squier Ju^r & David Osborn be Packers	263
Voted y^t Abel Gold, Capt Hez: Hubbell, Hez: Bradley, Deliv: Bennitt and Joseph Rockwell be branders of horses	263
Voted y^t Hezekiah Nichols be Sealer of weights	263
Voted y^t David Allen be Sealer of Measures	263
Voted y^t Eben^r Ogden & Thos Couch be Keykeepers	263

29 Dec 1777

The former Moderator Gen^{ll} G Sellect Silliman being present	263
Voted y^t Major Elijah Abel, Amos Hubbell, Eben^r Jesup, Capt Eben^r Hill Hum^y Ogden and David Silliman be a Com^{tee} of Inspection	263
Voted y^t Eben^r Jesup be Grandjuryman	263
Agreed y^t Capt Hez: Hubbell, John Wilson & Sam^{ll} Odell be a Com^{tee} to remove Incroachments off from ye Highways.. in particular off from the Highway on ye East Side of ye Long Lotts next to Stratford Line	263
Voted y^t Richard Hubbell Ju^r Deodate Silliman, Moses Sherwood Dan^{ll} Sherwood 2^d Dan^{ll} Duncan and Nathan Wheeler Ju^r be Collec^{rs} of the Town Rate Each one to Collect in Society in which they Dwell & Each to have three pounds for his Service except Richard Hubbell Ju^r and he to have thirty Shillings	263
Voted y^t the Selectmen procure an Account of all.. Inhabitants.. that have Inlisted into the Continental Service & for how long a time & also of all foreigners: And of all ye Inhabitants.. & foreigners y^t have been hired into s^d Service and for how long a time and also of the Persons who hired them.. Voted y^t Capt George Burr & Capt Eben^r Hill assist	263
Agreed y^t a Memorial be prefered to the next Sessions of the Gen^{ll} Assembly praying.. to Tax themselves.. for defraying the Expence of Making & Maintaining and repairing Bridges and for mending Highways & y^t Sam^{ll} Squier Esqr and Major Elijah Abell be Appointed to prefer Such Memorial	263
Voted y^t Isaac Seely, Sam^{ll} Prince & Dan^{ll} Hull be Surveyors of Highways	263

2 Jan 1778

The former Moderator Gen^{ll} G Selleck Silliman being present	263
Voted y^t Isaac Bennitt and Hez: Bradley be a Com^{tee} to Assist the Selectmen in providing for the families of Soldiers in the Continental Service	263

2 Feb 1778

Voted y^t Gold Selleck Silliman Esqr be Moderator	263
Town do desire that the Alarm post, for the Militia to Repair to in Case of an Alarm, be the	263

Fairfield

places of Parrade in the first Society and in Stratfield: And at Jesup Wakeman's in Greensfarms
25 Mar 1778

Voted y^t Capt Hezekiah Hubbell be Moderator	262
Agreed y^t Justin Jenning be Constable & Collec^{rs} to Collect ye Town Rates in the first Society	262
Voted y^t Hez: Bradley & Jere: Oakley be Surveyors of Highways	262

27 Apr 1778

Voted y^t Thad^s Burr Esqr be Moderator	262
Voted y^t Sturges Lewis, Capt Job Bartram Seth Seely, Joseph Hide, Moses Sherwood, David Hubbell Increase Bradley Esqr Sam^{ll} Wakeman Esqr and Isaac Bennitt be a Com^{tee} to provide Cloathing for the officers and Soldiers in the Continental Army	262

15 Dec 1778

Voted y^t Gold Selleck Silliman Esqr be Moderator	262
Voted y^t Nathan Bulkley be Town Clerk	262
Agreed y^t Thad^s Burr Esqr Mr Jonathan Lewis Capt Hez: Hubbell Capt Thos Nash Gershom Hubbell Esqr Capt Benj^a Dean and Capt Nath^{ll} Seely be Selectmen	262
Voted y^t Doct^r John Allen be Town Treasurer	262
agreed y^t Justin Jennings Richard Hubbell Ju^r Benj^a Rumsey Dan^{ll} Sherwood 2^d Dan^{ll} Duncan and Nathan Wheeler Ju^r be Constables.. Also voted y^t Richard Hubbell Ju^r be Collector of ye State Tax	262
Agreed y^t Peter Perry, Wakeman Burr, Seth Morehouse, Elip^t Thorp Ichabod Wheeler, Eben^r Silliman, Abel Gold, Eph^m Jennings, Isaac Jennings, Benj^a Hubbell, Benj^a Wheeler, Sam^{ll} Sherwood 2^d, Nathan Seely, Stephen Godfrey, Jos: Wakeman, Moses Sherwood, John Hide, James Bennitt, Deliv^e Bennitt; Elip^t Hull, Benj^a Sherwood, Albert Sherwood, Hez: Bradley Jos: Frost, John Banks, George Burr, John Bradley, Chauncey Down, John Wakeman 2^d, Wm Wakeman, John Staples, Eben^r Hill, Elnath Bradley Increase Bradley, Nehem^h Beers, Eph^m Lyon, John Silliman Andrews, David Godfrey, Benj^a Dean, Nathan Adams Ju^r: Josiah Gold Leavitt, Dan^{ll} Bennitt, Sam^{ll} Thorp Ju^r, David Bradley Ju^r Seth Murwin and Peter Osborn be Surveyors of Highways	262
Agreed y^t Hez: Sturges, Job Bartram, Deodate Silliman; Seth Seely, Dan^{ll} Lacey, Hez: Hubbell; Eben^r Morehouse, John Hide, Stephen Wakeman; Eben^r Hill, Dan^{ll} Banks John Hull: Eph^m Lyon, Nehemiah Beers: Nath^{ll} Seely 3^d and Josiah Brinsmaide be fence viewers	262
Agreed y^t Elijah Abell, Ezekiel Hull: Joseph Strong, Benj^a Wheeler: Joseph Hide, Gideon Wakeman: Gershom Wakeman, David Bradley: Dan^{ll} Duncan, Increase Bradley: David Silliman and Nathaniel Wheeler Ju^r be Listers	262
Agreed y^t Justin Jennings, James Bennitt, Dan^{ll} Sherwood 2^d Dan^{ll} Duncan and Nathan Wheeler Ju^r be Collec^{rs} of the Town Rate.. Each one to have £12: for his Service - Richard Hubbell Ju^r to Collecr of said Rate & have £6: for his Service	262
Voted y^t David Allen be Sealer of Leather	262
Agreed y^t David Allen, Deodate Silliman: Seth Seely: John Philips, Joseph Bennitt: Dan^{ll} Banks, Silvenus Middlebrook: Avery Baker, Daniel Godfrey: Josiah Brinsmaide. Peter Osborn and Daniel Lacy be Grandjurymen	262
Agreed y^t Joseph Down, Isaac Jennings: Gideon Hubbell: Moses Sherwood, Stephen Godfrey: Aaron Jennings. David Hubbell: Nehemiah Beers: Samuel Staples and Samuel Thorp Ju^r be Tythingmen	262

Fairfield

23 Dec 1778

The former Moderator G Seleck Silliman Esqr being present	262
voted y^t Abel Gold Ju^r John Smedly David Patchin & Benj^a Fayerweather be Howards	262
voted y^t Sam^{ll} Penfield be Gauger	262
voted y^t David Osborn & John Parrit be Packers	262
voted y^t Abel Gold Hez: Hubbell Hez: Bradley Dan^{ll} Andrews Ju^r Thos Nash and David Silliman be branders of horses	262
voted y^t Hez: Nichols be Sealer of weights	262
voted y^t David Allen be Sealer of Measures	262
voted y^t Solomon Sturges Dan^{ll} Duncan Hez: Bradley, Eben^r Ogden Eliz: Couch & Obadiah Platt be Key Keepers	262
voted y^t Dan^{ll} Lacy be Surveyor of Highway	262
Agreed y^t Increase Bradley Esqr Messrs John Hide Del: Bennitt Stephen Wakeman James Bennitt Sam^{ll} Squier Esqr Thad Wakeman John Wakeman Ju^r Peter Smith Col^o Jonth Dimon David Silliman Nathan Wheeler Ju^r Benj^a Lacy & Seth Seely be a Com^{tee} to provide for officers & Soldiers wives & families who are in the Continental Service	261
Agreed y^t Capt Job Bartram Messrs Seth Seely Richard Hubbell Ju^r Joseph Hide Moses Sherwood Increase Bradley Esqr David Williams Sam^{ll} Wakeman Esqr and Mr Isaac Bennitt be a Com^{tee} to provide Clothing for officers & Soldiers.. in the Continental Service	261
Voted y^t Col^o Jonth Dimon and Gershom Hubbell Esqr be a Com^{tee} to Exchange part of a Cross Highway with Dan^{ll} Squier of Greenfield for other Lands, said Highway Lyes near s^d Squier's Dwelling House	261

17 May 1779

voted y^t Tha^{ds} Burr Esqr be Moderator	261
Voted the Selectmen prefer a Memorial to the General Assembly requesting that the Guards at Greensfarms under Lieu^t Joseph Bennitt may be Established on the Same footing at those.. under Capt Elip^t Thorp	261

1 Jul 1779

Voted that Jonathan Sturges Esqr be Moderator	261
Voted that Mr John Morehouse Ju^r & Capt Nath^{ll} Seely be a Com^{tee} to provide Cloathing for the Soldiers.. in the Continental Service	261
Voted y^t Thad^s Burr, Jonth Sturges and Samuel Squier Esq^{rs} be a Com^{tee} to represent.. this Town to the Governour and Council of Safety to order Some vessels of force to guard our Sea Coast against the designs of the enemy during the Summer Season	261
Voted y^t Thad^s Burr, Jonth Sturges, Sam^{ll} Squier & George Burr Esq^{rs} be a Com^{tee} to call a County Convention & to represent this Town.. to Consider of some Method to prevent the depreciation of our Paper Currency	261

20 Jul 1779

Voted that Andrew Rowland Esqr be Moderator	261
Voted y^t George Burr, Thad^s Burr & Abraham Andrews Esq^{rs} & Mr Sam^{ll} Odell be a Com^{tee} to wait upon Col^o Jonathan Dimon and desire him to appoint 50 men to keep guard in the prime Society & 25 men to keep guard at Greensfarms and 15 men to keep guard at Stratfield: Also to request him to appoint Such men as are friendly to the United States of America	261

Fairfield

Voted y[t] Jon[th] Lewis, Thad[s] Burr, George Burr, Sam[ll] Wakeman & Jon[th] Sturges Esq[rs] & Mess[rs] Joseph Wakeman, Richard Hubbell Ju[r] Dan[ll] Duncan & David Silliman be a Com[tee] to put about Subscriptions to raise.. Money as a reward for.. Persons that Shall Captivate and take Prisoner General William Tryon, who Commanded the Brittish Trops when they burnt this Town on the Seventh and Eighth Days of this Instant July	261
Voted y[t] Major Elijah Abell M[r] Sam[ll] Odell Doct[r] Eben[r] Jesup Cap[t] David Hubbell Mess[rs] Dan[ll] Duncan & David Silliman be a Com[tee] of Inspection	261
Voted y[t] And[w] Rowland, Jon[th] Sturges & Thad[s] Burr Esq[rs] be a Com[tee] to draw a narrative of the proceedings of General William Tryon on the destruction of this Town	261

31 Aug 1779

voted y[t] Jonathan Sturges Esq[r] be Moderator	260
voted y[t] Major Elijah Abel be Town Treasurer	260
voted y[t] Cap[t] Sam[ll] Squier M[r] Hezekiah Bradley Major Elijah Abel & Cap[t] Thomas Nash be a Com[tee] to build the Town House	260
voted y[t] this meeting disapprove of importing goods into this Town that are plundered from the Inhabitants on Long Island.. voted y[t] Thad[s] Burr Esq[r] write to the.. Gov[r].. & Council of Safety & inform them of this practice & Especially of one Bishop lately belonging to Hartford importing goods here from Long Island & Selling them at Vandue without libelling the Same	260

21 Sep 1779

The former Moderator Jon[th] Sturges Esq[r] being present	260
voted y[t] Thad[s] Burr Esq[r] Mess[rs] Peter Perry, Eben[r] Silliman, Sam[ll] Odell, Nathan Seely, Tho[s] Nash, Joseph Wakeman, James Bennitt, David Williams, Hez: Bradley, Albert Sherwood, Daniel Duncan, Benj[a] Dean, Eph[m] Lyon, Nathan Wheeler Ju[r], David Silliman and Elnathan Williams be a Com[tee] of Inspection	260

18 Oct 1779

Voted that Hezekiah Hubbell be Moderator	260
Voted y[t] an Agent be Appointed to represent this Town at the General Assembly.. with regard to the Doings of the Cvil Authority of the County of Fairfield.. respecting the building a Court House and Gaol in said County.. Voted y[t] Major Elijah Abel be Agent for the purpose	260
Voted y[t] Jonathan Sturges Esq[r] Major Elijah Abel and Sam[ll] Squier Esq[r] be a Com[tee] to represent this Town before the Com[tee] to be Appointed by the General Assembly to view the County of Fairfield.. to fix a place for building a Court-House and Gaol	260
voted y[t] Sam[ll] Squier and Sam[ll] Wakeman Esq[rs] be a Com[tee] to prefer a Memorial to the Gen[ll] Assembly.. praying said Assembly to appoint a Com[tee] to Ascertain the Losses.. this Town Sustained by the Enemy in July last past by by burning and plundering	260
Voted y[t] Doct[r] David Rogers Mess[rs] Seth Sherwood Benj[a] Banks Ju[r] Hez: Bradley Dan[ll] Bennitt Josiah Brinsmaide and Sam[ll] Thorp Ju[r] be a Com[tee] to provide Cloathing for the Soldiers.. in the Continental Service	260

20 Dec 1779

Voted y[t] Thad[s] Burr Esq[r] be Moderator	260
Voted y[t] Nathan Bulkley be Town Clerk	260
Voted y[t] Thad[s] Burr Esq[r], M[r] Jonathan Lewis, Hezekiah Hubbell Esq[r] Cap[t] Thomas Nash, M[r] Gershom Hubbell, Cap[t] Benjamin Dean and M[r] David Silliman be Selectmen	260

Fairfield

Voted y⁺ Major Elijah Abel be Town Treasurer	260
Voted y⁺ Justin Jennings, Richard Hubbell Juʳ, Benjᵃ Rumsey, James Bennitt, Danˡˡ Sherwood 2ᵈ Danˡˡ Duncan and Nathan Wheeler Juʳ be Constables	260
Voted y⁺ Richard Hubbell Juʳ be Collector of the State Tax	260
Voted y⁺ Ichabod Wheeler Abel Gold, Peter Perry, Elipᵗ Thorp, Isaac Jennings Ebenʳ Silliman, Ephᵐ Jennings: John Odell, John Nichols Juʳ, Samuel Sherwood 2ᵈ Timothy Wheeler: Ebenʳ Banks, Benjᵃ Sherwood, Benjᵃ Banks Juʳ John Banks, Samˡˡ Whitney Juʳ, Aaron Jennings, Elipᵗ Lyon, Thadˢ Wakeman, Ebenʳ Burr, Moses Bradley, John Wakeman Juʳ Gershom Jennings, Elnathan Bradley: Josiah Gold Leavitt, Danll Bennitt Jabez Rowland, James Crowfoot, Isaac Seely, Samˡˡ Thorp Juʳ, Peter Osborn, Enos Bradley Benjᵃ Dean, Lemuel Wood, David Godfrey, Joseph Smith Nehemiah Beers, Ephᵐ Lyon Ebenʳ Bixby: Thoˢ Cable, Stephen Godfrey, Moss Kent, Danˡˡ Burr, Hez: Coley, Jehiel Whitehead, Ebenʳ Morehouse and Moses Sherwood be Surveyors of Highways	260
Voted y⁺ Hez: Sturges, Jabez Thorp: Danˡˡ Lacy, Joseph Strong: John Hide Stephen Wakeman, Ebenʳ Morehouse: Ebenʳ Hill, Benjᵃ Sherwood: Ephᵐ Lyon, Joseph Smith, Nehemiah Beers: Samˡˡ Thorp Juʳ & Jabez Wheeler be fenceviewers	260
Voted y⁺ Elijah Abel, Ezekiel Hull: Joseph Strong, Benjᵃ Wheeler: Joseph Hide, Gideon Wakeman: Gershom Wakeman: David Bradley: Danˡˡ Duncan, Jonᵗʰ Squier: Nathan Wheeler Juʳ and Josiah Brinsmaide be Listers	260
Voted y⁺ David Allen & Elisha Bradley be Leather Sealers	259
Voted y⁺ Justin Hobart, Samˡˡ Beers Juʳ, Seth Seely, Nathˡˡ Adams Juʳ Thadˢ Wakeman & Aaron Whitney be Grandjurymen	259
Voted y⁺ Isaac Jennings, Amos Hubbell, Moses Nichols, John Hide, Danˡˡ Burr, Thoˢ Wheeler Juʳ, Moses Odgen, John Olmsted & Isaac Seely be Tythingmen	259
Voted y⁺ Abel Gold, Isaac Jennings and John Nichols Juʳ be Haywards	259
Voted y⁺ Major Elijah Abell be gauger	259
Voted y⁺ John Parrit be Packer	259
Voted y⁺ Abel Gold, Hez: Hubbell Esqʳ, Hez: Bradley, Joseph Rumsey, Jonah Rockwell & Abijah Gregory be branders of horses	259
Voted y⁺ Isaac Jennings be sealer of weights	259
Voted y⁺ Stephen Turney be Sealer of Measures	259
Voted y⁺ Judson Sturges, Ebenʳ Jesup, Ebenʳ Ogden, James Bennitt, Hez: Bradley, Danˡˡ Duncan & Capᵗ Nathˡˡ Seely be Keykeepers	259
Voted y⁺ Ansel Truby have Liberty to build a dwelling House in the Town Street near Applegates gate and to Set it on the Same Spot of ground where his former house Stood and there to Stand during the Towns pleasure or untill the first Society Shall order a removal of the Same	259

27 Dec 1779

The former Moderator Thads Burr Esqʳ being present	259
Voted y⁺ Danˡˡ Lacy be Grandjuryman	259
Voted y⁺ John Squier Juʳ, Gideon Hubbell, John Hide, Deliverance Bennitt, James Bennitt, Ebenʳ Morehouse, Thadˢ Wakeman, Benjᵃ Banks Juʳ, Hez: Bradley, Increase Bradley Esqʳ, David Silliman & Capᵗ Nathˡˡ Seely be a Comᵗᵉᵉ for supplying Soldiers families with provisions	259
Voted y⁺ James Bennitt, Richard Hubbell Juʳ Nathan Wheeler Juʳ Danˡˡ Sherwood 2ᵈ Danˡˡ	259

Fairfield

Duncan & Eph^m Jennings be Collec^rs of the Town Rate & Eph^m Jennings be Constable	
Voted y^t Lyman Jennings be Constable	259
Voted y^t Col^o Jon^th Dimon, Francis Jackson, Seth Morehouse, John Wilson & Nath^ll Wilson be Surveyors of Highways	259
Voted y^t Capt Nath^ll Seely & Mr David Silliman be a Com^tee to remove Incroachments from off Highways	259
Agreed y^t Sam^ll Odell, Major Elijah Abel, Eben^r Jesup, Eben^r Hill, Sam^ll Thorp Ju^r and Dan^ll Duncan be a Com^tee of Inspection	259
Agreed y^t Eph^m Jennings, Eben^r Silliman, Nathan Seely, Amos Hubbell, Joseph Wakeman, Joseph Bennitt, Benj^a Banks Ju^r, Seth Sherwood, Dan^ll Duncan, Dan^ll Andrews and Dan^ll Bennitt be a Com^tee to provide Cloathing for the Soldiers.. in the Continental Army	259
Voted y^t Capt Nath^ll Seely have Liberty to build a pound near his Dwelling House	259

6 Mar 1780

Voted y^t Thad^s Burr Esqr be Moderator	259
The Town Clerk Nathan Bulkley being absent by reason of Sickness voted y^t Daniel Osborn be Clerk during said meeting	259
Voted y^t Mr Deodate Silliman and Mr Sam^ll Burr be a Com^tee to Assist Hez: Hubbell Esqr in Collecting Witnesses in the Case against Mr Jon^th Bulkley	259
Voted y^t Sam^ll Odell, Ichabod Wheeler, Eben^r Bartram, Abijah Morehouse, James Penfield, Judson Sturges, James Bulkley, Joseph Bennitt, Thos Nash, Nathan Seely: Joseph Wakeman, Samuel Pearsall, Benjamin Wynkoop, Dan^ll Duncan, Jonathan Squier, Eben^r Banks, John Stratton, Sam^ll Thorp Ju^r Gershom Wakeman, Elnathan William, Capt Daniel Bennitt, William Wakeman, Dan^ll Lacy, Eph^m Lyon, William Bennitt, Gershom Thorp, John Gray and John Wakeman be Inspectors of provisions	259

10 Apr 1780

Voted y^t Jonathan Sturges Esqr be Moderator	259

19 Jun 1780

Voted y^t Thad^s Burr be Moderator	259

13 Nov 1780

Voted y^t G Selleck Silliman Esqr be Moderator	258
Voted y^t Mr Nathan Seeley, Maj^r Elijah Abel, Mr Moses Sherwood, George Burr Esqr, Mr Daniel Duncan and Mr David Silliman be the Persons to receive the Salt, procure Casks and receive the Provisions and inspect the Same.. for the use of the Continental Army and the forces raised for the Defense of this State	258

13 Dec 1780

Voted that Jonathan Sturges Esqr be Moderator	258
Voted y^t Nathan Bulkley be Town Clerk	258
Agreed y^t Hez: Hubbell & Thad^s Burr Esq^rs Messrs Jonathan Lewis, Thos Nash, Nehemiah Banks, Benj^a Dean and David Silliman be Selectmen	258
Voted y^t Maj^r Elijah Abel be Town Treasurer	258
Voted y^t Richard Hubbell Ju^r James Bennitt Dan^ll Duncan Nathan Wheeler Ju^r Dan^ll Sherwood 2^d and Eph^m Jennings be Constables	258
Voted y^t Benj^a Wheeler, Seth Seeley, Ezra Seeley, Amos Hubbell, Dan^ll Lacy, Ichabod Wheeler, James Penfield, Peter Jennings, Peter Whitney, Howes Osborn, Abijah Morehouse,	258

Fairfield

Nathan Adams, Seth Silliman, And^w Wakeman, Ezra Jennings, Elip^t Thorp, Josiah Gold Leavitt, Aaron Whitney, Nath^{ll} Seeley 3^d, Jabez Rowland, Gershom Lyon, Jabez Wheeler, Obadiah Platt, Gershom Bradley, Seth Murwin, Silvenus Morehouse, Sam^{ll} Prince, Silliman Godfrey, John Gray, Sam^{ll} Rowland Ju^r, Lemuel Wood Thos Banks, Eben^r Squier, Dan^{ll} Duncan, Thos Cable, Stephen Gwier, Joseph Wakeman, Benj^a Wynkoop, Thad^s Whitlock, Amos Gray, John Hull, John Stratton, Oliver Middlebrook, David Rogers, Dan^{ll} Banks, Hez: Ogden, Thos Goodwell, John Bradley, John Wakeman Ju^r, Gershom Jennings, Eben^r Burr, Eben^r Hill, David Williams and Amos Williams be Surveyors of Highways

Voted y^t Joseph Strong, Dan^{ll} Lacy, Hez: Sturges, Jabez Thorp, Peter Osborn, Elnath Williams, Dan^{ll} Godfrey Dan^{ll} Duncan, Jonth Squier, Joseph Bennitt, Eben^r Morehouse, Dan^{ll} Meaker, Dan^{ll} Banks, Eben^r Banks, and Silv^s Middlebrook be fenceviewers 258

Voted y^t Joseph Strong, Ezekiel Hull, Elijah Abel, Joseph Hide, Gideon Wakeman, Dan^{ll} Duncan, Jonth Squier, Nathan Wheeler Ju^r, Josiah Brinsmaide, Gershom Wakeman, David Bradley and Benj^a Wheeler be Listers 258

Voted y^t David Allen be Sealer of Leather 258

Voted y^t Eben^r Bulkley, Zebulon Fanton, Thad^s Wakeman, Nathan Beers, John Jones and Amos Hubbell be Grandjurymen 258

Voted y^t Peter Jennings, Nathan Seeley, Walter Hubbell, Jos: Seeley, Thos Wheeler Ju^r Nathan Bradley Ju^r, Dan^{ll} Osborn, Talcott Bulkley, David Morehouse, Eben^r Morehouse and Noah Taylor Hanford be Tythingmen 258

Voted that Joseph Hill Ju^r and Jeremiah Jenning be Haywards 258

Voted y^t Sam^{ll} Penfield be Gauger 258

Voted y^t John Parritt be Gauger 258

Voted y^t Abel Gold, Hez: Bradley, Joseph Rumsey, John Olmsted Ju^r, Abijah Gregory, Nath^{ll} Hubbell and Hez: Hubbell Esqr be branders of horses 258

Voted y^t Abel Gold be Sealer of weights 258

Voted y^t Stephen Turney be Sealer of Measures 258

Voted y^t Judgson Sturges, Hez: Bradley, Obadiah Platt Nath^{ll} Seeley 2^d and Jonathan Squier be Keykeepers of pounds 258

Voted y^t Richard Hubell Ju^r, Jos: Strong, And^w Wakeman, Eben^r Burr Ju^r, Moses Sherwood, Jos: Hide, Aaron Jennings, David Hubbell, Nath^{ll} Seeley 2^d, Josiah Brinsmaide, John Silliman Andrews, and Eben^r Bixby be a Com^{tee} to remove Incroachments from off the Highways 258

Voted y^t Capt Benj^a Dean be a Receiver of provisions to assist Dan^{ll} Duncan 258

28 Dec 1780

The former Moderator Jonathan Sturges Esqr being present 257

Voted y^t Sam^{ll} Odell be Lister instead of Ben^a Wheeler 257

Voted y^t Richard Hubbell Ju^r be Collec^r of State Tax 257

Voted y^t Richard Hubbell Ju^r, Eph^m Jennings, Dan^{ll} Sherwood 2^d James Bennitt, David Morehouse and Nathan Wheeler Ju^r be Collec^{rs} of the Town Rate 257

Voted y^t Capt David Wheeler be Constable 257

Voted y^t Joseph Strong, Joseph Hide, Isaac Jennings, Moses Burr David Hubbell and Josiah Brinsmaide be Grandjurymen 257

Voted y^t David Jennings 2^d be Constable 257

Fairfield

Voted y^t John Squier 3^d Benj^a Banks Ju^r, Wm Bennitt, Deliverance Bennitt, Humphrey Ogden, Silv^s Middlebrook, Peter Perry, John Silliman Andrews, Nathan Seeley and John Hide be a Com^{tee} to Supply necessaries for ye families of Such Soldiers as belong to this Town that are in the Continental Army	257
Voted y^t Nathan Seeley, Eph^m Jennings, James Bennitt, Dan^{ll} Sherwood 2^d David Morehouse, Dan^{ll} Bennitt and Samuel Wakeman Esqr be a Com^{tee} to purchase Cloathing for the Soldiers.. in the Continental Army	257
Voted y^t Dan^{ll} Wilson have Liberty to build a Pound near his Dwelling House	257
Voted y^t Moses Jennings be Tything man	257
Voted y^t John Lyon and David Patchin be Haywards	257

9 Jan 1781

Voted y^t Thad^s Burr Esqr be Moderator	257
Voted y^t the penny halfpenny Tax ordered to be paid in provision by the Gen^{ll} Assembly be paid in kind.. Also voted y^t Sturges Lewis, Moses Sherwood, Eben^r Burr 2^d Nathan Seeley, David Silliman and Dan^{ll} Duncan be receivers of s^d Tax	257

13 Mar 1781

voted y^t Thad^s Burr be Moderator	257
Voted y^t Elijah Abel be Clerk P.T. [*ed: pro tempore*]	257
Voted y^t Maj^r Elijah Abel be.. Appointed a Collector of the provision Tax for the Continental Army Nathan Seeley, Moses Sherwood, George Burr, Dan^{ll} Duncan & Nathaniel Seeley J^r are Appointed Collec^{rs} in their Several Societies respectively for the above purpose	257
Voted y^t Dan^{ll} Duncan, Nathan Seeley, Eben^r Burr 2^d Moses Sherwood, Nath^{ll} Seeley & Sturges Lewis be Collec^{rs} to Collect the penny halfpenny Provision Tax	257
Voted y^t Richard Hubbell Ju^r be Appointed a purchasing Commissary for the Town.. to supply the Coast Guards with provision of the Meat kind	257

27 Mar 1781

Voted y^t Thad^s Burr Esqr be Moderator	257
Voted y^t Maj^r Elijah Abel take the Minutes of the proceedings of this Meeting	257
Voted y^t Capt Seth Silliman, David Allen, Doct^r David Rogers, Nathan Wheeler, David Morehouse and Jonth Squier be a Com^{tee} in addition to them already appointed to purchase Cloathing for Soldiers in ye Continental Army	257
Voted y^t Dan^{ll} Banks & Josiah Brinsmaide be a Com^{tee} in addition to them already appointed to provide for Soldiers families	257
Voted y^t Nehemiah Beers be a Surveyor of highways	257
Voted y^t Hez: Hubbell Esqr be agent.. to attend the Assemblys Com^{tee} to lay in the claims for Disputed Soldiers in the Continental Army	257
Voted y^t Maj^r Abel be the Officer to Conduct the Recruits for the Continental Army to Danbury	256
Voted y^t the Resolves now read in this Meeting, Draughted by Thad^s Burr Esqr be Approved of, and said Burr.. to cause s^d Resolves to be Printed or Inserted in the Publick News Papers	256

18 May 1781

Voted that George Burr Esqr be Moderator	256
Voted y^t Nathan Adams be Collec^r of the Town Rate in the Prime Society.. in the room of Eph^m Jennings Dec^d	256

Fairfield

Voted y^t Capt Benj^a Dean be a receiver of Provisions on the penny halfpenny Tax in the room of Mr Dan^{ll} Duncan

Put to vote whether Inhabitants.. are willing that the Assessment laid on David Adams.. for his having a Son gone over to the Enemy of the United States; Shall be Abated -- and passed in the negative

Put to vote whether Inhabitants.. are willing that the Assessment laid on Thomas Turney.. for his having a Son gone over to the Enemy of the United States; Shall be Abated -- and passed in the negative

Put to vote whether Inhabitants.. are willing that the Assessment laid on Hezekiah Jennings.. for his having a Son gone over to the Enemy of the United States; Shall be Abated -- and passed in the negative

Put to vote whether Inhabitants.. are willing that the Assessment laid on Increase Burr.. for his having a Son gone over to the Enemy of the United States; Shall be Abated -- and passed in the negative

19 Jun 1781

Voted y^t G Selleck Silliman Esqr be Moderator

Voted y^t there be a Tax of four pence in hard money on the pound or in beef Cattle.. for the purpose of raising Supplies for the Use of this State and Continental Army.. Voted y^t one person be a Collec^r of the above Tax and also a purchasing Commissary.. Voted y^t Mr Nathan Seely be the person to Collect the above Tax and to purchase the Cattle & that he have Six p^r Cent for his trouble

Voted y^t Jonth Sturges and Thad^s Burr Esq^{rs} be a Com^{tee} to write to the Govr and Council of Safety respecting ye Complaints of ye Coasts guards about their Wages

Voted y^t Daniel Banks be Lister in ye room of Gershom Wakeman Dec^d

20 Aug 1781

Voted y^t Thad^s Burr Esqr be Moderator

Voted y^t Richard Hubbell Ju^r, procure barrels receive and Salt, pack and Secure the beef and pork that Shall be brought in, .. also to store Such other Articles as Shall be delivered in payment of the Two Shilling and Sixpenny Tax granted by the General Assembly in May last

19 Dec 1781

Voted that G Selleck Silliman Esqr be Moderator

Voted that Nathan Bulkley be Town Clerk

Voted that Hezekiah Hubbell Esqr Thad^s Burr Esqr Mr David Allen Capt Thos Nash Mr Nehemiah Banks Capt Daniel Duncan and Mr David Silliman be Selectmen

Voted that Major Elijah Abel be Town Treasurer

Voted y^t Richard Hubbell Ju^r be Constable & Collec^r of ye State Tax and also Collec^r of ye Town Rate in Stratfield Society

Voted y^t Israel Bibbins James Bennitt Dan^{ll} Sherwood 2^d Dan^{ll} Duncan and Nathan Wheeler Ju^r be Constables.. and Collec^{rs} of the Town Rate in the society wherein they Dwell & that Each of s^d Collec^{rs} have the Customary fees for Collecting

Voted y^t Amos Hubbell Ezra Seely John Odell Seth Seely Benj^a Wheeler: James Penfield G Selleck Silliman Esqr Capt Ichabod Wheeler Matthew Jennings Capt Seth Silliman Seth Morehouse Eben^r Burr 2^d Capt Ezekiel Hull Hez: Nichols Howes Osborn Jonth Sturges Esqr Capt Stephen Thorp: Capt Thos Nash David Burr Ju^r Talcott Burr Andrew Sturges Thos Cable Sam^{ll} Pearsall Joseph Mill Stephen Wakeman: Col^o Jonth Dimon Hez: Bradley Nehemiah Banks Ju^r Lewis Goodsell George Burr Esqr Sam^{ll} Whitney Ju^r Hez: Price Isaac Bradley

Fairfield

Lyman Wakeman John Staples Tim^y Burr Amos Williams David Gold Seth Sherwood: Capt Ebne^r Coley: Capt Eph^m Lyon John Olmsted Ju^r Nathan Beers Silliman Godfrey Capt Daniel Godfrey Daniel Silliman Joseph Seely Gershom Lyon Zac: Jennings Ju^r Sam^ll Thorp Ju^r John Gilbert Peter Osborn Seth Murwin Sam^ll Prince and Capt Daniel Bennitt be Surveyors of Highways

Voted that Sam^ll Odell Walter Hubbell Eben^r Burr 2^d Isaac Jennings Joseph Bennitt Eben^r Morehouse Dan^ll Banks Silv^s Middlebrook Eben^r Banks Dan^ll Andrews Ju^r Sam^ll Rowland Ju^r Squier Adams Dan^ll Bennitt and Nath^ll Seely 3^d be fence viewers — 255

Voted y^t Sam^ll Odell Joseph Strong Esqr Major Elijah Abel Capt Ezekiel Hull Joseph Hide Gid: Wakeman Dan^ll Banks David Bradley Capt Dan^ll Duncan Jon^th Squier Nathan Wheeler Ju^r and Nath^ll Seely 3^d be Listers — 255

Voted y^t David Allen Elisha Bradley Elna^th Williams and Noah Taylor Hanford be Leather sealers — 255

Voted y^t Joseph Strong Esqr Capt Andrew Wakeman Eben^r Morehouse Thad^s Wakeman Joshua Adams and Jabez Rowland be Grandjurymen — 255

Voted y^t Seth Seely Abel Gold David Burr Ju^r Simon Couch Ju^r Joseph Bulkley Peter Bradley John Olmsted Ju^r Dan^ll Bennitt Elna^th Williams and Ezra Seely be Tythingmen — 255

Voted y^t Benj^a Fayerweather John Lyon Abel Gold Isaac Jennings John Burr Delivernce Bennitt Joseph Rumsey Benj^a Smith Ju^r Moses Ogden Dan^ll Wheeler Ju^r Jonah Rockwell Brush Marvin Isaac Bennitt and John Olmsted be Haywards — 255

Voted y^t Sam^ll Penfield be Gauger — 255

Voted y^t Sam^ll Cable and David Osborn be Packers — 255

Voted y^t Abel Gold Hez: Hubbell Esqr Joseph Rumsey Hez: Bradley Dan^ll Andrews Ju^r and Jabez Rowland be branders of horses — 255

Voted y^t Stephen Turney be Sealer of Measures — 255

Voted y^t Isaac Jennings be Sealer of weights — 255

Voted y^t Judgson Sturges Daniel Wilson Eben^r Ogden Eben^r Jesup Hezekiah Bradley Jonathan Squier and Capt Nath^ll Seely be Key keepers of Pounds — 255

28 Dec 1781

Voted y^t Hezekiah Hubbell Esqr be Moderator — 255

Voted y^t Ezra Seely James Knap Walter Hubbell Capt And^w Wakeman Lewis Goodsell Deliverance Bennitt Capt Dan^ll Bennitt and Gershom Hubbell Esqr be a Com^tee for Supplying Soldiers families — 255

Voted y^t Capt Benj^a Dean be a Constable.. and also Collec^r of ye Town Rate in the Parish of Norfield in the Room of Capt Dan^ll Duncan — 255

Voted y^t Capt David Wheeler be Constable — 255

26 Feb 1782

Voted that G Selleck Silliman Esqr be Moderator — 255

Voted y^t Thad^s Burr Esqr be agent..before the Com^tee Appointed by ye last Gen^ll Assembly to Enquire into.. the deficiencies of the Continental Army in the Several Towns in this County — 255

Voted y^t Hez: Hubbell Esqr be agent.. before the Com^tee Appointed by ye last Gen^ll Assembly to Enquire into.. the deficiencies in the State guards (on the Western frontiers under the Command of General Waterbury) in the Several Towns in this County — 255

Voted y^t Thad^s Burr Esqr Hez: Hubbell Esqr G Selleck Silliman Esqr Capt Thos Nash Jonathan Sturges Esqr George Burr Esqr be a Com^tee to Agree upon some.. Plan for keeping Coast guards in this Town — 255

Fairfield

Voted y^t Sam^{ll} Rowland Ju^r John Silliman Andrews and Capt Daniel Duncan be a Com^{tee} to Exchange parts of Applegates Highway with the Adjoining Proprietors — 254

Voted y^t Capt Thomas Nash and his family and Sush other persons (to be one Class only).. have Liberty to innoculate for the Small Pox at s^d Capt Nash's House — 254

25 Mar 1782

Voted y^t G Selleck Silliman Esqr be Moderator — 254

Voted y^t a Com^{tee} be Appointed to to Enquire into the number of the Deficient Classes (ordered to provide Men for the Continental Army the year last past for this Town) and the reasons of Such deficiencies and to do everything in their power in a Legal way to Oblige such Classes to do their Duty.. Also voted y^t Jonathan Sturges & George Burr Esq^{rs} and Mr Seth Seely be a Com^{tee} for ye purpose — 254

Voted y^t a Com^{tee} be Appointed to hire Men for one Year to fill up the Quota of Soldiers.. for the Continental Army.. and y^t Major Elijah Abel, Messrs Albert Sherwood, Deliverance Bennitt, Capt Benj^a Dean and Mr David Silliman be a Com^{tee} for that purpose — 254

Voted y^t ye Report of the Com^{tee}.. to agree upon Some.. Plan for keeping Coasts guards in this Town.. is approved.. by the Town Excepting out of said plan ye appointing of Capt Josiah Lacy Captain of said guards — 254

25 Jun 1782

Voted y^t G Selleck Silliman Esqr be Moderator — 254

Voted y^t a Com^{tee} be appointed to Enquire into the facts that laid a foundtion for granting Two Executions against ye Town by the Gen^{ll} Assembly.. respecting the deficiency of the Town in raising Soldiers for Sundry Services the last Year.. Agreed y^t Gen^{ll} Silliman, Jonth Sturges Esqr Thad^s Burr Esqr and Hez: Hubbell Esqr be a Com^{tee} for that purpose — 254

Agreed y^t a Com^{tee} be appointed to hire men to fill up our Quota of ye Continental Army.. and that Such men as have Inlisted into ye Continental Service this Year or have been draughted.. and have joined the Army or have hired others to Serve in their place be entitled to receive the Same bounty from ye Town as those shall have that may be hired by the Com^{tee}.. Capt Dan^{ll} Lacy, Capt And^w Wakeman Capt Jos: Bennitt Capt George Burr Capt Dan^{ll} Duncan and Mr David Silliman be a Com^{tee} for purpose aforesaid — 254

30 Aug 1782

Voted y^t Jonth Sturges Esqr be Moderator — 254

Voted y^t a Com^{tee}..be Appointed to inspect the behavior of persons respecting the carrying on an illicit Trade with the Enemies of the United States of America: .. Voted y^t Mr Nathan Seeley, Capt Dan^{ll} Lacy, Mr Seth Seely, Mr David Allen, Capt And^w Wakeman, Mr Peter Perry, Mr Albert Sherwood Mr Nehemiah Banks, Mr Hezekiah Bradley, Capt Ichabod Wheeler, Mr Eben^r Banks, Mr Stephen Gwier, Capt Thos Nash, Capt Joseph Bennitt, Mr Moses Sherwood, Mr Jehiel Whitehead, Mr Sam^{ll} Hazard, Mr John Chapman, Mr Dan^{ll} Meaker of Greensfarms, Major Albert Chapman, Capt Eben^r Hill, Capt Elip^t Thorp, Mr Samuel Rowland, Capt Eph^m Lyon, Mr Dan^{ll} Andrews Ju^r, Mr Nehemiah Beers, Mr David Silliman, Mr Sam^{ll} Bennitt 3^d, Capt Dan^{ll} Bennitt, Mr Nath^{ll} Seeley 3^d, Mr Elnath Williams, Mr Sam^{ll} Thorp Ju^r Mr David Bradley Ju^r Mr Sam^{ll} Taylor and Mr Simon Couch be a Com^{tee} of inspection for ye purpose aforesaid — 254

25 Sep 1782

Voted that Hezekiah Hubbell Esqr be Moderator — 253

Voted y^t Elijah Abel and Hezekiah Hubbell Esq^{rs} be Agents.. to prefer a Memorial.. to the Gen^{ll} Assembly.. respecting the Dooms against the Town for neglecting to raise or forward their Quota of Men for the Service of the last Year — 253

Fairfield

16 Dec 1782

Voted that Hezekiah Hubbell Esqr be Moderator	253
Agreed that Nathan Bulkley be Town Clerk	253

20 Dec 1782

The former Moderator Hezekiah Hubbell Esqr being present	253
Agreed y^t Thad^s Burr Esqr Mr David Allen Hez: Hubbell Esqr Capt Thos Nash Mr Nehemiah Banks Capt Daniel Duncan & Mr David Silliman be Selectmen	253
Voted y^t Col^o Elijah Abel be Town Treasurer	253
Agreed y^t Israel Bibbins Richard Hubbell Ju^r Deliverance Bennitt Dan^{ll} Sherwood 2^d Capt Benjamin Dean & Nathan Wheeler Ju^r be Constables & Richard Hubbell Ju^r be also Collec^r of the State Tax	253
Agreed y^t David Wheeler: John Wason David Allen Jonathan Sturges Esqr Eben^r Burr 2^d Howes Osborn Peter Perry G Selleck Silliman Esqr Nathan Adams David Jennings: Eben^r Jesup David Jennings 3^d Eben^r Morehouse John Philips Corn$^{[ ]}$ Stratton John Hide Dan^{ll} Meaker Joshua Oysterbanks James Chapman Deliverance Bennitt Moss Kent Eben^r Gorham: Eben^r Banks John Stratton Silvenus Middlebrook Gershom Hubbell Esqr Daniel Banks Joseph Lyon Benjamin Banks Ju^r Seth Bradley Chauncey Down Lyman Wakeman Gershom Jennings David Hubbell Eben^r Hill: Moses Burr Squier Adams Albert Lockwood Isaac Godfrey John Fanton Ju^r Elijah Gray John Lockwood Ju^r: Zachariah Lacy Josiah Brinsmaide Capt Nath^{ll} Seely Jonathan Lyon Sam^{ll} Prince John Olmsted Obadiah Platt Peter Osborn Enos Bradley Isaac Seely: Walter Hubbell Benj^a Wheeler Josiah Lacy, Dan^{ll} Lacy & Ezra Seely be Surveyors of highways	253
Agreed y^t Capt Andrew Wakeman Eben^r Burr 2^d Jabez Thorp: Joseph Strong Timothy Wheeler: Capt Joseph Bennitt Eben^r Morehouse Daniel Meaker: Daniel Banks Capt Eben^r Hill Silvenus Middlebrook: Sam^{ll} Rowland Daniel Andrews Ju^r Squier Adams: Nath^{ll} Seely 3^d and Elnathan Wheeler be fence viewers	253
Voted y^t Thad^s Whitlock be Packer	253
Agreed y^t Abel Gold: Hez: Bradley: Deliverance Bennitt: Hez: Hubbell Esqr: John Olmsted 2^d: & John Olmsted: be branders of horses	253
Voted y^t James Penfield be Sealer of Measures	253
Voted y^t Isaac Jennings be Sealer of weights	253
Agreed y^t Col^o Elijah Abel Capt Ezekiel Hull: Seth Seely Josiah Lacy: Gideon Wakeman Joseph Hide Daniel Banks: Capt Dan^{ll} Duncan: Jeremiah Rowland: Nath^{ll} Seely 3^d & Nathan Wheeler Ju^r be Listers	253
Agreed y^t William Silliman Eben^r Squier: Joseph Strong: Eben^r Banks Thos Wheeler Ju^r: Eben^r Ogden: Nathan Gray Ju^r: Najah Bennitt be Grandjurors	253
Agreed y^t Jabez Perry James Penfield Eben^r Bulkley Isaac Jennings: Timothy Wheeler: Joseph Bulkley 3^d Gershom Bulkley 3^d: Andrew Sturges John Hide Ju^r: Dan^{ll} Andrews Ju^r: Sam^{ll} Rowland: David Bradley 2^d & Jabez Wheeler be Tythingmen	253
Voted y^t David Allen & Elisha Bradley be Leather Sealers	253
Agreed y^t Peter Jennings Joseph Hill Ju^r Gideon Hubbell: Jehiel Whitehead Deliverance Bennitt Joseph Rumsey: Nehemiah Banks Ju^r Silvenus Middlebrook Moses Ogden Willm Wakeman & Josiah G Leavitt be Haywards	253
Voted y^t Abigail Sturges Daniel Wilson: Hez: Bradley: Eben^r Ogden: Stephen Godfrey: Capt Dan^{ll} Duncan: Capt Nath^{ll} Seely & Obadiah Platt be Key keepers	253

Fairfield

Voted y^t Sam^{ll} Penfield be Gauger	253
Agreed y^t Hez: Hubbell Esqr Messrs Joseph Strong & John Wilson be a Com^{tee} to view the Highway laid out through John Odells Land at Stratford and Consider what the Same may be worth	253

30 Dec 1782

The former Moderator Hezekiah Hubbell Esqr being present	252
Voted y^t Moses Sherwood be Lister in ye room of Jos: Hide	252
Voted y^t Benj^a Lacy be Constable.. & Collec^r of ye Town Rate in ye Prime Society & Stratfield Parish	252
Voted y^t Deliverance Bennit be Collec^r of ye Town Rate in Greensfarms Parish	252
Voted y^t Dan^{ll} Sherwood 2^d be Collec^r of ye Town Rate in Greenfield Parish	252
Voted y^t Benj^a Dean be Collec^r of ye Town Rate in Norfield Parish	252
Voted y^t Nathan Wheeler Ju^r be Collec^r of ye Town Rate in Northfairfield Parish	252
Voted y^t James Knap be a Surveyor of highways	252
Agreed y^t Eben^r Burr 2^d Seth Morehouse Benj^a Lacy Eben: Morehouse Eben^r Ogden Deliv: Bennitt: Benj^a Dean and Nathan Wheeler Ju^r be a Com^{tee} to provide for Soldiers families	252
Agreed y^t Seth Seely and Talcott Burr be Grandjurymen	252
Agreed y^t ye Selectmen pay to John Odell Six pounds.. provided he.. Execute a good and lawful Deed.. of ye Land now used for a Highway from ye front of ye long Lott up to his house where he now lives	252

10 Apr 1783

Voted y^t Jonathan Sturges Esqr be Moderator	252
Voted y^t a Com^{tee} be Appointed to remove all Persons from this Town who are now in it, or may hereafter come into it, who have gone to & Joined the Enemy & put themselves under their protection during the War between Great Brittain and the United States of America.. Also voted y^t David Allen Daniel Osborn Capt Thomas Nash, Albert Sherwood Daniel Lacy Daniel Wilson Capt Joseph Bennitt Moses Sherwood Nathan Seely Ezra Seely Hezekiah Hubbell Esqr Nehemiah Banks Col^o Jonathan Dimon Dudley Baldwin Esqr Ebenezer Banks Capt Benj^a Dean John Squire 3^d Joseph Smith Daniel Andrews Ju^r Capt Ephraim Lyon Zebulon Fanton Nathaniel Seely 3^d David Silliman Nathan Wheeler Ju^r Samuel Wakeman Esqr Samuel Bennitt 3^d Robert Wilson and Peter Perry be a Com^{tee} for the purpose	252
Voted y^t Capt Eph^m Lyon and Thomas Banks be a Com^{tee} to view Capt Joseph Bennitts proposals for Exchanging of other Lands for part of ye Highway running up the Mile Commons on the West side of Saugautuck River to Prince's Saw Mill	252

8 May 1783

Vote y^t G Selleck Silliman Esqr be Moderator	252

14 May 1783

The former Moderator G Selleck Silliman Esqr being present	252
Voted y^t a Memorial be preferred to ye Gen^{ll} Assembly.. respecting those Persons y^t have gone to and joined the Enemy & put themselves under their protection during the War between Great Brittain and the United States of America and have already returned or may herafter come back to reside among us.. Voted y^t the Memorial drawn and now read in this Meeting by Dudley Baldwin Esqr be preferred to the Gen^{ll} Assembly	252

Fairfield

Voted y^t G Sellect Silliman Esqr the Moderator of this Meeting be desired to Sign said Memorial in behalf of the Town and forward and lay the same before the Gen^{ll} Assembly	252

26 Jun 1783

Vote y^t G Selleck Silliman Esqr be Moderator	251
The Town taking into Consideration the Distress to which a number of the Inhabitants are reduced by the burning and plundering of the Enemy during the late War.. and the great Injury done the Town thereby.. voted that Jonathan Sturges Esqr be Agent for the Town to make use of Such Measures by Memorial to the General Assembly or otherwise to obtain redress of the Town's Grievances.. for a repair of the Damages done by the enemy to be made to the individual Sufferers; Excepting to those Sufferers who are known to be inimical to the Liberties & Independance of the United States of America	251
Voted y^t George Burr Esqr Doctor David Rogers Mr Richard Hubbell Ju^r and Mr Joseph Hide be a Com^{tee} to.. make out a List of the Sufferers of this Town who are friendly to the Liberties and Independance of the United States of America within the meaning of the foregoing vote	251
Agreed y^t Mr Israel Bibbins be Collector of State Taxes.. in the room of Mr Richard Hubbell Ju^r	251

18 Aug 1783

Vote y^t G Selleck Silliman Esqr be Moderator	251

251

Farmington

Town Records
Vol. 2, Part 1
Pages 1 – 35

Town Records
Vol. 1, part 2
Pages 423 – 456

Located at the Town Clerk's Office

Farmington

15 Jun 1774

Colonel John Storng [sic] Moderator — 427

Voted.. That Wm Judd Fisher Gay, Selah Heart, & Stephen Hotchkiss, Esq^{rs}, Mes^{rs} John Treadwell, Asahell Wadsworth, Jon$^{[\,]}$ Root, Sam^{ll} Smith, Ichabod Norton, Noadiah Hooker, & Gad Stanly be.. a Com^{tee} to Keep up a Correspondence, with the Town of this and the Neibouring Colonys — 427

12 Dec 1774

Col John Strong was Chosen Moderator — 430

Com^{tee} of Inspection } Mes^{rs} Willm Judd John Treadwell Noadiah Hooker Stephen Dorchester Tim^o Root Peter Curtis Asahel Wadsworth Kensington Mathew Cole Stephen Norton Joseph Welles Elijah Hooker ~ Worthington John Allyn John Lee ~ Southington Jon^a Root Eldad Lewis Timothy Clark Danl Lankton Capt Josiah Cowles Asa Bray Eliakin Peck ~ New Cambridge Asa Upson Amos Barns Hez^h Gridley Ju^r Dan Hill Joseph Byington ~ Northington Tim^o Thomson Capt Norton Jos$^{[\,]}$ Miller Noah Hart ~ New Brittain Gad Stanly Lodwick Hotchkiss John Lankton Noah Stanly Farmingbury Stephen Barns Thomas Upson Aaron Harrison Joseph Beacher ~ West Brittain Simeon Hart Titus Bunnell Simeon Strong Seth Wiand ~ — 430

Whereas Upon a Vote of the Town.. to Adopt the Doing of the Continenta^{ll} Congress one Matthias Looming and Nehemiah Royce Utterly Refused to Vote for the Same, we do Therefore Consider them as Open Enemies to their Country & as Such we will.. withdraw all Connection from them Untill they Shall Make public Retraction of their Principles & Sentiments in ye matters afores^d — 430

26 Dec 1774

there was by Vote Added to the Inspecting Com^{tee} Jon^a Pa[ ] Willm Whealer Royce Lewis Asa^{ll} Barns Eben^r Hamblin Hez^h Wadsworth Thos Lewis Rezin Gridley Timothy Hosmer Martin Bull & Jos^h St[ ] — 431

[ ] Apr 1775

Clement Gridley Wm Lee & Stephen Sedgwick were by Vote Chosen Surveyors of Highways — 432

Voted that Seth Lee John Treadwell Willm Judd Thos Lewis and Noadiah Hooker be Com^{tee} of Coresspondince with the Towns of this & the Neibouring Colonies — 432

11 Dec 1775

Col John Strong was Chosen Moderator — 433

Solomon Whitman Esqr was Chosen Town Clerk — 433

Selectmen } Ens^n Noah Porter Timothy Root Isaac Gleason Noah Cowles Capt Obadiah Andrus Capt Amos Barns Ens^n Elijah Frances — 433

Constables } Capt Sol^n Cowles & he to Collect the Rate &c: John Newel Ju^r Elijah Hooker John Stoughton Dan^{ll} Lankton Asahel Barns Elnathan Smith Capt Ichabod Norton John Goodrich Stephen Barns Ju^r Asa Yale Ju^r — 433

Town Treasurer Capt Solomon Cowles — 433

Grandjurors } Ezek^{ll} Cowles Nehemiah Street Marvin Clark Eli North Asahel Hooker Mathew Cadwell Thomas Stanly Caleb Hopkins Hez^h Winchell Eliazer Peck Timothy Lee William Barns Elisha Root William Lewis Nathl Churchel Thomas Hooker David North Joseph Hart Ju^r Jacob Bartholemew Joseph Andrus Luther Atkins Titus Bunnell & Sam^{ll} Culver — 433

Tythingmen } Sam^{ll} North Ju^r Thos Lewis Martin Bull Daniel Root Luther Stockin Ezra — 433

Farmington

Scovell John Clark Dan^{ll} Woodruff Ju^r Josiah Newel J[ ] David Neal Dan Hill Joseph Heyford Josiah Ives Wm Hart Ju^r Joseph Bishop Elijah Woodruff Lamuel Hotchkiss Abel Clark Jared Harrison Heman Hall David Robbards Simon Clark & Enoch Johnson Surveyor of Highways } John Porter Gad Wadsworth Thomas Cowles Danl Rowe Sam^{ll} North Isaiah Post Elnathan Gridley Samuel Scott Aaron Carrington Salmon Root Moses Merrills Ju^r for Tallcots Road & the Road Adjacent Reuben Cases Moses Dickerson Oliver Heart Titus Brownson Sam^{ll} Cowles Ju^r Capt Obad Andrus Elihu Moss Nath^{ll} Barns Jonth^n Barns John Hart John M[ ] Ju^r Abra^m Winston James Hasington John Woodruff Ju^r Howkins Hart Capt Elisha Warren Capt Amos Barns Capt David Barns Capt Asa Upson.. 433

.. Surveyors } Thos Hungerford Benj$^{l\,l}$ Lindsley Jesse Gaylord Math^w Hungerford Josiah Lewis Ju^r Leu^t Joseph Woodford Ens Willm Woodford David Bristall Joseph Woodruff Ju^r Leu^t John Lankton Capt Gad Stanly Elnathan S[ ] Josiah Kilborn Stephen Barns Ju^r Thos Upson Daniel Fince Jesse Alcox Isaac Hart Moses Deming Ezra Yale Daniel Bunnell Eben^r Burdick Eldad Hart & Jacob Robbards 433

Listers } Gideon Cowles Leu^t Peter Curtis Wm Wadsworth Sol^n Whitman Ju^r Asahel Woodruff Elnathan Hooker Wm Webster Joseph Peck Elijah Cole Gamaliel Cowles John Stoughton Josiah Andrus Ju^r Isaac Hall Zebulun Peck Ju^r Wm Woodford Ju^r David Gleason Jonath^n Belding Seth Stanly Jacob Car[ ] Sam^{ll} Harrison Joseph Bacon Ju^r Joseph Lankton & Joseph Stone Seth Duning 433

Town Collectors } Capt Solomon Cowles Hezekiah Stanly Timothy Lewis Zebulun Frisbee Jedediah Norton Joseph Heart Moses Pond Hooker Gilbert 433

Fence Vewers } Mathew Clark Ens^n Noah Porter Barnabas Dunham Gideon Williams Eben^r Scott Whitehead Howd Luke Gridley Benj^a Lindsley Elisha Miller Job Miller !ohn Judd Ju^r James Booth & Nath^{ll} Hitchcock John Dean 433

Sealers of Leather } Capt Ephra^m Treawell Jon^a Lankton Jon^a Barns Jabez Robbards Joseph Hart Esqr Capt Josiah Lee 434

Sealers of Weights } Capt Isaac Bidwell David Peck James Lee Ezekiel Woodford James North Seth Wiard 434

Sealer of Measures } Leu^t Elijah Porter Sam^{ll} Burr Capt Joseph Porter Daniel Lankton Wm Lee Ruben Miller James Booth Gideon Andrus Aaron Harrison 434

Brander of Horses } Thomas Cowles Stephen Norton Timothy Lee Samuel Bouge James Lee Lodwick Hotchkiss Dan^{ll} Johnson 434

Key Keepers } Timothy Porter Ju^r Stephen Norton Timothy Lee Sam^{ll} Bouge Royce Lewis James North Asa Yale Ju^r 434

Packer Solomon Thomson 434

Rate Makers } Sol^n Whitman Esqr Capt Sol^n Cowles Thos Lewis & Leu^t Elijah Porter 434

a Com^{tee} for Exchanging Highways } in ye Parish of Farmingbury Thomas Upson.. in the Parish of West Britain Simeon Hart Titus Bunnell and Seth Wiard 434

the Town by Vote abated to Oliver Gridley Collector the following Town Rates (Viz) Eben^r Wettens 1/6^d Micall Mitchels 1/6 also to Doc^r Joshua Porter Collector Nath^{ll} Messenger Rate 2/0 Sam^{ll} Root 1/7:2: also to Thos Barn Collector Asa Porter Rate 1/10 434

Upon the Moriall of Martin Bull & John Treadwell praying the Town to Grant them Liberty to Set up in the Highway adjacent to s^d Treadwells Pott Ash works a Building.. for.. Manufacturing Salt petre &c.. Voted that ye s^d Martin Bull & John Treadwell have Liberty to Erect and Set up a Building as prayed for and to Continue ye Same Dureing the Towns pleasure 434

Upon the Memoriall of Asher North praying for Liberty to Remove a Small House Standing in the Highway belonging to Judah Hart and up Set ye Same Upon About half an Acre of Lane at the parting of the paths Near the Burnt Swamp &c: Voted that y^t Mes^{rs} Moses Andrus 434

Farmington

David Marther & Thos Hart be a Com^{tee} to Vew the place above.. and Make Report	
Voted that Asahel Cowles Noah Cowles & Stephen Norton be a Com^{tee} to Vew on the the place prayed for by the wid^w Sary Flagg to Set a House in the Highway and to Report	434
25 Dec 1775	
Surveyor of Highways } Viz Eli Andrus Simeon Hart Thomas Lankton	434
Grandjuryman Leu^t Elisha Strong	434
Voted that the Highway in Southington Parish Between Dan^{ll} Porter Lott & John Brounson shall be four Rods wide at ye East End & no more	434
Voted to Give to Eli North & Elnathan Hart ye Rate of hand in favour of ye Town in the hand of the Town Treasurer for.. £4:1:0	434
Voted that Jedediah Norton Ju^r be a Com^{tee} to Exchange Highways & to Remove Nusances	435
Chosen Hogg Haywards (Viz) Asahel Wadsworth Thos Lewis Leu^t Peter Curtis Joseph Lankton Ens^n Joseph Porter Eliakim Deming Capt Dan^{ll} Sloper Isaac Newel Job Lewis Tim^o Lee John Upson Josiah Newel Ju^r Hez^h Gridley Ju^r Asahel Barns Seth Stanly Jon^a Belding John Judd Ju^r Capt Ichabod Norton Timothy Thomson Wm Wadsworth	435
Noah Woodruff was by Vote Chosen Tythingman in ye Room of Sam^{ll} North Ju^r	435
Voted that Roger Norton Ju^r be a Tythingman in the Room of Thos Root	435
Voted that they would Leave Discresinary with ye Com^{tee} to Settle with Scot & Lankton Respecting their Incroachments on ye Highway	435
Voted that the the Incroachments on the Highways in the Possession of Jon^a Edward be Removed	435
Voted that Col^o Fisher Gay Mes^{rs} Elijah Porter Seth Lee John Treadwell Noah Porter Selah Hart Esqr Noah Cowles Oliver Hart Elisha Root John Curtiss John Stoughton Amos Barns James Stoddard Da[ ] Hills Ichabod Norton Joseph Hart Ju^r Joseph Woodruff Gad Stanly Col Isaac Lee David Mather Simeon Hart Seth Weard Titus Bunnel Thomas Upson Joseph Beacher be an Inspecting Com^{tee}	435
Voted to Remit to John Brownson Collector Wm Minor Town Rate 2/3	435
Simon Hart Seth Woodruff & Titus Bunnell was.. Chosen a Com^{tee} to Vew and find a place for a Burying Yard in the Parish of West Britain	435
[ ] Apr 1775	
Voted that Capt Hotchkiss have Liberty to Set up a Shop and Horse House in the Highway Near the Dwelling House belonging to ye the Heirs of Capt Moses Hills Dec^d and Mr John Root & Leu^t Noad^h Hart be a Com^{tee} to fix the place for Seting s^d Shop & Horse House	435
Dan^{ll} Johnson was.. Chosen Key Keeper for the Parish of Farmingbury	435
Timothy Andrus was.. Chosen Grandjuror	435
Voted that James Judd Timothy Root & Dec^n Noah Porter be a Com^{tee} to Vew and find a place for Erecting a New Pound	435
Ser^t Thomas Newel Shall have Liberty to Improve about An Acre of Land in the Highway for Sowing of flax	436
Rhoderick Cadwell & Elijah Smith.. Chosen Haywards to Impound Swine in the Parish of New Britain	436
Voted that Wm Woodford be a Grandjuror.. in the Room of David North	436
Thos Newel Ju^r was.. Chosen Surveyor of Highway in ye Room of Isaiah Post	436
Voted that Nathan Barns be abated from the appraisement of the freeholder of the Stray Colt in his Custody	436

Farmington

Voted that Capt Isaac Bidwell Shall have the Use of the Land he has fenced in the Highway for one year	436
9 Dec 1776	
Solomon Whitman Esqr ws Chosen Town Clerk or Reg^r	436
Selectmen } Mes^{rs} Isaac Gleason Timothy Root Dan^{ll} Curtiss Oliver Heart Obadiah Andrus Amos Barns William Woodford	436
Constables } Capt Solomon Cowles and he to Gather the County Rate & Settle with ye Treasurer John Newel Ju^r Elijah Hooker John Stoughton Amos Root Asahel Barns William Woodford Ju^r John Richard Asa Yale Ju^r Stephen Barns Ju^r John Goodrich	436
Town Treasurer Capt Solomon Cowles	436
Grand Jurors } Elisha Scott Isaac Buck Abel Thomson Asa North Jonathan Lankton Hez^h Judd Elijah Thompson William Lewis Sam^{ll} Curtiss Sol^n Bell Thomas Peck Hez^h Gridley Jacob Bartholomew James Lee Elnathan Hart Noah Gillet - David Mather Lott Stanley Justice Peck - Sam^{ll} Warner Jeremiah Griswould Gideon Andrus	436
Tythingmen } Reuben Dec^n North Eben^r Hawley Sam^{ll} Stedman Ju^r Amos Clark Luke Brownson John Brounson Amos Wilkinson Solomon Newel Jon^a Brounson Linds Thorp Eleazer Heart Nathan Booth Ju^r Elihu Smith Thomas Hungerford James Lee Medad Hart Thos Thomson Dudley Woodford Zadock Brounson Calvin Cowles Ephr^m Boardman Joseph Bacon Ju^r Daniel Darren Abell Humphry Jon^a Lee	436
Surveyors of Highways } Sam^{ll} Smith Josiah North Ju^r Abijah Portter Wm Wadsworth Capt John Porter Abner Curtis Wm Portter Sam^{ll} North Ju^r Morgain Goodwin Lodwick Hotchkiss Thos Gridley Gideon Judd Joseph Stockin Calvin Hurlburt Obadiah Andrus James Hasington Silas Clark Isaac Woodruff Reuben Hart Lemuel Lewis Noah Gridley Hez^h Root Abell Carter Ju^r Benoni Atkins - Stephen Hungerford Jacob Hungerford David Newel Jesse Gaylord Nath^{ll} Carrington Mathew Hungerford Sam^{ll} Lewis Moses Cogswell Jared Butler Reuben Hawley Dan^{ll} Woodford Josiah Wittens Ju^r Nath^{ll} Lewis Joseph Beace Danl Johnson	436
Surveyor of Highways } Elijah Smith Samuel Smith Thos Hart Ezek^{ll} Wright Elisha Tubbs Gideon Belding Abill Humphry Bartholomew Driggs Asa Woodruff and Stephen Brounson Jonathan Carrington John Root Eph^m Hollester	438
Listers } Peter Curtis Wm Wadsworth Sol^n Whitman Ju^r Asahell Woodruff Elnathan Hooker William Webster Ju^r Stephen Cole Ju^r Sam^{ll} Cowles Ju^r John Stoughton Gamaliall Cowles Josiah Andrus Ju^r Isaac Hall Zebulon Peck Ju^r David North David Gleason Jon^a Belding Seth Stanley Jacob Carter Ju^r Jesse Alcox Joseph Bacon Ju^r Joseph Lankton Seth Deming	438
Sealers of Leather } Capt Ephraim Treadwell Jon^a Lankton Jon^a Barns Jabez Robbard Joseph Hart Esqr Timothy Merrills Stephen Barns Ju^r	438
Sealer of Waits } Capt Isaac Bidwell Ezra Scovell David Peck James Lee Ezek^{ll} Woodford James North Seth Wiard	438
Sealer of measures } Elijah Portter Sam^{ll} Burr Capt Joseph Porter Dan^{ll} Lankton Willm Lee James Booth Aaron Harrison Gideon Andrus Reuben Miller	438
Fence Vewers } Mathew Clark Noah Porter Barnabas Dunham Gideon Williams Eben^r Scott Whithead Howd Luke Gridley Benjn Lindsley James Booth Isaac Lee 3^d Gideon Hart Job Miller Nath^{ll} Hitchcock John Brounson Dan^{ll} Bunnell Justis Webster	438
Key Keeper } Timothy Porter Ju^r Stephen Norton Timothy Lee Royce Lewis Sam^{ll} Cook Bouge Dan^{ll} Johnson James North Sam^{ll} Brockway	438
Brander of Horses } Thomas Cowles Ezra Scovell Tim^o Lee James Lee Ezek^{ll} Woodford James North Dan^{ll} Johnson	438
Colectors for the Town Rate } Thomas Cowles Allyn Smith Thomas Barns Lemuel Andrus Elijah Woodford Timothy Stanly Noah Neal Gershom Tuttel Seth Gelbart	438

Farmington

Packer Solomon Thomson	*438*
Rate Maker } Sol[n] Whitman Esq[r] Cap[t] Sol[n] Cowles Leu[t] Elijah Porter and Thomas Lewis	*438*
Timothy Lee a Com[tee] for Exchanging Highways for Southington Parish	*438*
A Com[tee] for Exchanging Highways in the Parish West Briton ~ Simion Hart Seth Wiard Ebenezer Hamblin	*438*
the following Persons were.. Chosen Haywards to Impound Swine at Large on the Common Not Ring[d] and Yoked (Viz) Joseph Porter Tho[s] Lewis William Lewis Miles Cramton Isaac Buck Elijah Smith Ju[r] Joshua Webster Gideon Hart Stephen Norton Seth Brounson Asa Upson Hez[h] Gridley Sam[ll] Lowree Luther Atkins & Stephen Hitchcock	
Voted that a a Pound be Erected in the Parish of West Brittain Near Tar Kill Brook by Litchfield Road in the Room of that by M[r] Yales	*438*
Voted to Remit to David Leaming the Town part of the fines for Killing two Dear for which Judg[t] Lyeth against him before Esq[r] Hotchkiss	*438*
Voted to Remit to Isaiah Post Dec[d], his fine Twelve Shilling for a Breach of Peace and that Esq[r] Strong Discharge the Judg[t]	*440*
Voted that Aaron Neal Should have the 4 Load of Stone he had of Towns property	*440*
Voted to Remit to Josiah Kilborn 13/3 which he owed to the Town	*440*
Granted to Sam[ll] Steadman Ju[r] Liberty to Erect a Sawmill on the fulling Mill Brook	*440*

26 Mar 1777

the Rev[d] Sam[ll] Newel & Timothy Pitkin Mes[rs] John Treadwell Noah Porter Hez[h] Wadsworth Jon[a] Root Josiah Cowles Timothy Clark Noah Cowles Oliver Hart Elijah Hooker Asa Upson Amos Barns Ichabod Norton Tim[o] Thomson Jacob Foot Joseph Woodford Cal Lee Maj[r] Stanley Stephen Barns Ju[r] Simeon Hart and Moses Deming be a Com[tee] to take into Consideration the Request.. of the Govenour & Counsell of Safety the 15th day of March 1777 and Report their Opinion	*440*
Voted that Mes[rs] John Treadwell Noah Porter & Solomon Whitman be.. appointed a Com[tee] to draw on the Treasury.. in favour of such Solders.. as have or Shall Inlist into the Continentall Battalions for three years or During the present War	*440*
Voted that Sam[ll] Smith Martan Bull Cap[t] Treadwell Noah Cowles Elijah Hooker Jon[a] Root John Curtiss Asahel Barns Stephen Hotchkiss Esq[r] Cap[t] W[m] Woodford Timothy Thomson Elnathan Smith John Richard Simeon Heart John Wiard Stephen Barns Ju[r] Jacob Foot & Tho[s] Upson be a Com[tee] To take Care of the Severall families of the Solders that have or may Inlist into the Continental Army when they Shall be properly Applied to & See that they are Supplied with Nessesarys at y[e] price fixd by Law without any Aditionall Cost	*440*
Voted that Mes[rs] John Treadwell Sam[ll] Smith & Martin Bull Was by Vote Cosen [sic] Rate makers	*441*

7 Apr 1777

M[r] Jonathan Bull was.. Chosen a grand juror	*441*
Zachariah Hart was Chosen Lister in the Room of Seth Deming	*441*
Cap[t] Amos Barns was.. Chosen Com[tee] for y[e] Exchange of Highways in the parish of New Cambridge	*441*
At the same Meeting were Chosen Collectors to Collect the /4[d] Rate for Incoragemint of Inlisting Solders into the Continentall Service for the first Society Amos Cowles Kensington Eben[r] Heart Southington Eliakim Deming New Cambridge Seth Robbards Northington Elisha Miller New Brittain Josiah Dewey Farmingbury Stephen Barns Worthington Moses Deming West Brittain Seth Wiard and he to Collect the Town Rate	*441*

Farmington

Voted that Stephen Hotchkiss Lodwick Hotchkiss & Sam^{ll} Smith be A Com^{tee} to Repair to the House Lately Belonging to Dan^{ll} Tuttel in the Parish of New Cambridge where there is Now Inoculation Carrying on for the Small pox and to Inquire Strickly into the Circumstances & Regulations of s^d & See if their be any admitted that are Not Inhabitants of this Town and Lett them Know that the Town Highly Disappproves of their admitting any more Into s^d House to Take s^d Infection   *441*

Upon the Report of James Judd Noah Porter & Timothy Root a Com^{tee} appointed to find a Convenant place for Creating a Pound in the first Society.. Report As followeth that in their Judgment the Most convenient place was on the Green East of the meeting House.. Adjoining to Capt Sol^n Cowles Lott   *441*

15 Sep 1778

at a Freemans Meeting.. Samuel Culver Elnathan Smith Noah Andrus Jonah Barns Nath^{ll} Churchel Levi Thomson & Joseph Booth were Admitted & Sworn   *441*

22 Sep 1777

Col Isaac Lee was Chosen Moderator   *442*

Upon the Reading the Requition of the Consell of Safety for the provideing Cloathing for the Continentall Army.. Voted that Sam^{ll} Smith Thomas Lewis Martin Bull Capt John Allyn Capt Mathew Cole Noah Cowles Roger Norton Ju^r Jon^a Andrus Capt Timothy Clark Simeon Newel Capt Hez^h Gridley Capt James Stoddard Royce Lewis Capt Ichabod Norton Elisha Miller Jared Butler Timothy Stanley Step^n Hollester Ens^n Lemuel Hotchkiss Step^n Barn Joseph Beacher Capt Simeon Hart Seth Wiard and Ens^n Titus Bunnel be A Com^{tee} to procure the articles mentioned in the above Requition   *442*

Capt James Stoddard and Sam^{ll} Curtis were.. Chosen Constables   *442*

16 Sep 1777

Att a Freemans Meeting.. the Oath of Fidellity and ye Oath provided for freemen was Administred to ye Persons whose Name Are underwritten (Viz) Revd Tim^o Pitkin Revd Sam^{ll} Newel Rev^n Rufus Hawley Revd Alexander Gillet Ensq^r Lee John Allyn Josiah Lewis Josiah Cowles Jon^a Lewis Asa Upson Step^n Hotchkiss Esqr Thos Smith Thos Upson Eldad Lewis Jon^a Root Isaac Lee Ju^r Esqr Step^n Dorchester Ephraim Treadwell Sol^n Whitman Esqr Zeb^n Peck.. Aaron Day Thos Cowles Amos Gridley Hez^h Gridley Elisha Monross.. Jos^h Bacon..   *442*

.. Phinehas Lewis Jon^a Bull John Gridley Dan^{ll} Lankton Amos Barns Dan^{ll} Curtis Dan^{ll} Gridley John Lankton Mathew Cowles Stephen Norton Sam^{ll} Stanley Noah Woodruff David Peck Stephen Cole Jacob Carter Ju^r Elizur Hart Asa Goodrich Gideon Cole Eliakim Deming Gamaliel Cowles David Cogswell John Porter Amos Upson Jesse Curtis Jos^h Beecher.. John Treadwell Esqr Peter Curtis Jed^h Goodrich Elijah Frances Zealous Atkins David Smith Benj^a Andrus Wm Lewis Benj^a Dutton John Lewis Tutor Obadiah Andrus Thos Hungerford..   *442*

..Sam^{ll} Lewis Seth Wiard Re[ ] Lewis Lemuel Hotchkiss Elisha Booth James North Isaac Lee 3^d Heman Hall Amos Root Moses Dickinson Tim^o Gridley Luke Gridley Jared Harrison Da[ ] Wiskell Step^n Hollester.. Hez^h Beardsley Nath^{ll} Lewis Elijah Heart Sam^{ll} Smith New Brittain Noah Stanley Elijah Hooker John Richard John Newel John Goodrich Eben^r Fish Dan^{ll} Rowe Tim^o Stanley James Judd Matt^w Clark Abner Curtis Sam^{ll} Hitchcock Simeon Hart Asa Johnson Tim^o Clark Moses Andrus..   *442*

.. Sam^{ll} Smith Oliver Peck Jos^h Porter Rezin Gridley Asa Bray Titus Bunnel Sam^{ll} Thomson Tim^o Porter.. Abel Clark David Mather Amos Hawley Tim^o Lee Sam^{ll} Cowles Sol^n Newel Calvin Cowles Abel Yale Elijah Porter Seth Lee John Root Oliver Phiney Lemuel Lewis Sol^n Whitman Ju^r Isaac Buck Ezek^{ll} Cowles J[ ]s Hooker Eben^r Gridley David Newel Sam^{ll} Hooker Ju^r Thos Hooker Wm Wadsworth Fenn Wadsworth Gad Wadsworth Ichabod Norton Thomas Lewis   *442*

258

Farmington

.. Joseph Lee Sam^{ll} North Isaac Newel Dan^{ll} Bunnel Zach: Gillet James Stoddard Ambrose Sloper Jas Porter Joshua Phelps David Gleason Bartholemew Driggs Josiah Newel Job Cole Phin^s Judd John Hungerford Elnathan Gridley Nath^n Lewis Ju^r Doc^t Jos Wells Judah Hart Ju^r Mark Harrison Seth Wadsworth Nehe^h Street..   *442*

.. Zeb^n Peck Ju^r Tim^n Upson Josiah Upson Hez^h Wadsworth Jas Heyford Noah Porter Benjn Bishop Oliver Heart Jon^a Bull Sam^{ll} Goodrich Tim^o Woodruff Hez^h Scott Josiah Andrus   *443*
1 Dec 1777

The oath of Fidelity to the State of Con^t was administered to the following persons by John Curtis Jus^t Peace.. James Smith Eben^r Barns Wm Barns Sam^{ll} Woodruff David Hitchcock Abell Carter Ju^r Robert Cook Jon^a Barns Wm Day John Clark Elisha Bell Ashbel Cowles Thos Barns Asa Barns Jening Johnson Joel Potter Philip Farnsworth Nathan Barns Ju^r Joseph Dutton Jon^a Woodruff Aaron Webster Eliathah Rew Benj^a Dutton Ju^r John Dutton Eleazer Peck.. Thos Andrus Pomroy Newel Thos Peck John Upson Ju^r Jacob Carter Ju^r Joseph Gridley.. Hawkins Hart Noah Woodruff Phinehas Woodruff Abell Carter Sol^n Curtis..   *443*

.. Eliakim Peck Step^n Hitchcock Jon^a Andrus Hez^h Root Sam^{ll} Shepard Dan^{ll} Sloper Jon^a Brounson Isaac Woodruff James Beckwith Ju^r Charles Thorp Timothy Lewis Elisha Woodruff Wm Dickinson John Carter Job Lewis John Woodruff.. James Bradley Isaac Smith Joel Atkin Sam^{ll} Curtis Amos Beacher Aaron Harrison Dan^{ll} Allen Dan^{ll} Byington Stephen Pratt Benony Atkins Nath^{ll} Hitchcock Jon^a Carter Jacob Talmage Joseph Benham Gideon Fince Eleazer Fince Sam^{ll} Harrison Tim^y Bradley Noah Neal Giles Porter John Barret Elijah Lain Israel Clark Eben^r Johnson Elisha Horton Abell Beacher Chales Hall Justice Peck Amos Hall Jeremiah Smith Josiah Hart Philemon Bradley John Beacher Zacheous Gillet Ju^r Isaac Gleason Tim^o Root Wm Woodford Asahel Hooker John Lewis Elnathan Hooker Isaac Bidwell Dan Clark   *443*
16 Sep 1777

At A Fremans Meeting.. Sam^{ll} Byinton Levi Andrus Calvin Hurlburt Joseph Woodruff Robert Webster Elijah Rose Sam^{ll} Cook Caleb Smith Stephen Cook Jonathan Carrington Joshua Woodruff Elisha Scott Dan^{ll} North Ju^r Jon^a Belding & Jon^a Hart were all admitted Freemen & Sworn   *443*
1 Dec 1777

Elisha Strong John Horsford Sam^{ll} Culver Asahel Lewis Mr Webster Sam^{ll} Burr Mathew Cadwell Reuben Case Eben^r Tillotson Abell Thomson Barnebas Thomson James Thomson Zac: Hart Thos Barns Step^n Sedgewick Elijah Andrus Eben^r Meriam Heman Judd   *443*
1777

The Oath of Fidellity to the State of Connecticut as Required by Law was administred to ye following persons by Isaac Lee Ju^r Jus^t of Peace (Viz) Nath^{ll} Cole Roger Norton Abra^m Gridley Chreles Brounson Isaac Hurlburt Roger Gridley Jon^a Lankton Hez^h Winchel Eben^r E[ ]ten Hez Judd Amos Wilkinson Thos Stanly James Percevall Luke Brounson Nath^{ll} Brounson Jos Stocken Math^w Heart Asahel Cowles Noah Cowles John Stanly Jos^h Peck Dan^{ll} Smith Oliver Stanly Elihu Heart Gideon Judd Job Gridley Luther Stockin Joseph Wells Ju^r John Cowles Elisha Cole Titus Brounson Roger Norton Ju^r Elijah Cole Benjn Hopkins Ezra Scovell Dan^{ll} Cowles Ju^r Dan^{ll} Peck Ju^r Rogers Maj^r Gad Stanly Ezra Belding Jere H: ozgood Ezek^{ll} Wright Jehuda Heart Leonard Belding Thos Heart Lott Stanly John Kilborn Josiah Kilborn Jos Hart Levy Judd Seth Stanly Jos Smith Elijah Smith Judah Hart John Judd Ju^r Sam^{ll} Dickerson Rhodrick Cadwell Nathan Booth John Judd   *443*

Farmington

1777

The Oath of Fidellity to this State was Administred by Jared Lee Esqr to the following Persons (Viz) Richard Porter To John Curtiss Esqr & Mr Dan^{ll} Root & Nathaniel Crittenten	443

1777

The Oath of Fidellity to this State was administred by Solomon Whitman Esqr to the following Persons (Viz) Maj^r Rogor Hooker & John Hart Timothy Hosmer Gad Wadsworth Simeon Newel Amos Cowles & Martin Bull Ens^n Joseph Byington	443

8 Dec 1777

Col Isaac Lee was Chosen Moderator	444
Sol^n Whitman Esqr was Chosen Town Clerk or Register	444
Selectmen } John Treadwell Esqr Amos Cowles William Wadsworth Stephen Norton Dec Timothy Clark Dec Elisha Manross Elijah Frances Capt Wm Woodford	444
Constables } Solomon Cowles he to Collect ye Country Rarte & acc^t with the Treasurer Martin Bull Roger Norton Ju^r Job Lewis Amos Root James Stoddard John Richards Wm Woodford Ju^r Stephen Barns John Goodrich Joseph Bacon Ju^r	444
Town Treasurer Capt Sol^n Cowles	444
Grandjurors } Asahel Wadworth Sol^n Whitman Ju^r John Deming Joshua Woodruff Eli North Isaac Lankton Sam^{ll} Burr Dr Joseph Wells Titus Brounson Dr Amos Gridley David Smith Josiah Newel Amos Upson Sol^n Curtis Benj$^{[ ]}$ Lindsly Joseph Byinton Thos Barnes Elijah Heart Abell Clark Ambros Hart Job Miller Jared Harrison John Gilbert Jon^a Wait Smith Sam^{ll} Brockway Joseph Stone Ezra Dowd	444
Tythingmen } John Thomson Seth Wadsworth Amos Tubbs Roger Gridley Eben^r A: Brounson John Gilbert John Newel Ozias Andrus Chauncy Merriman Wm Rich Josiah Ives: Reuben Wright Rhoderick Cadwell Eldad Woodruff Sol^n Woodford Eben^r Tillotson Jon^a Carrington John Barret Ensign Hamblin Jabez Wetmore	444
Surveyors of Highways } Phinehas Lewis Eli Andrus Ma[ ]en Clark Eneas Cowles Hez Wadsworth Amos Hawley John Root Eliphalet Wadsworth Reuben Hawsley Wm Webster Sam^{ll} Burr John Lusk: John Gridley Eldad Peck Jas Peck Job Gridley John Lee Wm Day Wm Dickinson James Bradley Sam^{ll} Smith Joel Allen Eliather Rew Elnathan Judd Pomroy Newel Isaac Smith Whitehead Howd Abell Hawley Jacob Bartholomew Wm Elton Jesse Gaylord John Carrington Dan Hill Thos Hungerford Joseph Heyford Stephen Bushnel Josiah Lewis J^r John Judd J^r Gideon Hollester Levi Andrus John Lusk Wm Woodford J^r Joseph Woodford Sam^{ll} C: Booge	444
Surveyors &c } Thos Upson Stephen Barns Joel Gra[ ]s Josiah Burnham Eph^m Bordman Sam^{ll} Warner Amos Dowd Othniel Moses Seth Wiard Sam^{ll} Culver: Sam^{ll} Lowree John Wells Ju^r for Tallcott Road	444
Listers } Wm Wadsworth Sol^n Whitney Ju^r Elnathan Hooker Noah Porter Abell Thomson Wm Webster Sam^{ll} Cowles Caleb Hopkins Stephen Hitchcock Josiah Andrus Ju^r Gamaliel Cowles: Eli Lewis Gideon Seth Stanly Elizur Heart Isaac Lee 3^d Thos Thomson David Gleason Jesse Alcox Mark Harrison Zac^h Heart Joseph Bacon Joseph Lankton	444
Sealer of Leather } Capt Eph^m Treadwell Jon^a Lankton Jon^a Barns Jabez Robard Timothy Merrills Jon^a Miller	444
Sealer of Waits } Isaac Bidwell Ezra Scovell David Peck James Lee James North Ezekiel Woodford Dr Aaron Harrison Seth Wiard	444
Sealer of Measures } Elijah Porter Sam^{ll} Burr Dan^{ll} Lankton Wm Lee James Booth Reuben Miller Gideon Andrus	444
Fence Vewers } Mathew Clark D^n Noah Porter Barnabas Dunham Gideon Williams Eben^r	445

Farmington

Scott Whitehead Howd Royce Lewis James Booth Isaac Lee 3^d Gideon Hart Reuben Miller Nath^{ll} Hitchcock John Brounson Dan^{ll} Bunnel Justis Webster

Town Collectors } Sol^n Cowles Joseph Wells Ju^r Ashbel Cowles Amasa Hart Elijah Smith Levi Thomson Samuel Byington John Lee Joseph Bacon

Key keepers } Timothy Porter J^r Stephen Tim^o Lee Royce Lewis James North Sam^{ll} C: Bouge Dan^{ll} Johnson Isaac Hall

Branders of Horses } Thos Cowles Ezra Scovel Tim^o Lee James Lee James North Ezek^{ll} Woodford Seth Wiard

Packer Solomon Thomson

Ratemakers } Sol^n Whitman Esqr Capt Sol^n Cowles Leu^t Elijah Porter Thos Lewis John Treadwell Esqr and Martin Bull

Com^{tee} for Exchange of Highway in Southington } Capt Josiah Cowles Jon^a Barns and Timothy Lee

Com^{tee} To provide for the Solders Families } James Judd Jos^h Porter Thos Cowles John Thomson Noah Cowles Hez^h Judd Elijah Hooker Capt Josiah Cowles Aaron Day John Curtiss Esqr Capt Asa Upson Capt Hez Gridley

Com^{tee} To provide for the Solders Families } Thos Hart Tim^o Stanly Moses Andrus Jacob Foot Jos^h Woodford Stephen Barns Zacheus Gillet Thomas Upson Simeon Hart Titus Bunnel Seth Wiard ~ John Root

Voted that John Porter Amos Cowles Joseph Porter Timothy Root Wm Wadsworth Dan^{ll} North Ju^r Josiah North Elnathan Hooker Rezen Gridley Asahel Hooker Asa Upson Abell Lewis John Newel Silas Clark Ju^r Asa Bray Levi Judd Joshua Webster Dr Jos^h Wells C^t John Allyn Dr Amos Gridley Reuben Miller Jos^h Woodford & Jacob Foot be Haywards to Impound all Swine that Should be found at Large on the Highways

Voted that Col Hooker Maj^r Stanley Capt Bray Dan^{ll} Lankton Hez^h Wadsworth Capt Bidwel John Treadwell Esqr Capt Upson Capt Josiah Cowles Jacob Foot Noah Cowles be a Com^{tee} to Inquirewhat.. into Moneys have been paid by the Solders that have Been Draughted and Did Not Enter Into the Service

Josiah Cowles Hez^h Wadsworth Dan^{ll} Lankkton Noah Porter Stephen Barn and Isaac Bidwell were appoin^d a Com^{tee} to Enquire into and Devise a Method to Repair the Road at the South End of Farmingbury Society

Voted that Step^n Barns Sam^{ll} Smith & Eber Merriman be a Com^{tee} to Repair s^d Road

upon the Memorial of Joseph Wright praying that Town would See or Lease to him.. Land adjoining to the House where he Now Dwells it was Voted that Maj^r Gad Stanly Ens^n Samuel Hotchkiss & David Mather the Com^{tee} for the Exchange of Highways in the Parish of New Brittain be Impowred to Lease out the Land Above

23 Dec 1777

Voted that Daniel Thomson Elijah Cowles Nath^{ll} Wadsworth & John Curtiss Esqr be added to the Com^{tee} for provideing Nessesarys for the Solders Families &c

Voted that Benj^a Churchell be a Tythingman

Voted that Isaac Bidwell Lt Elijah Porter Thomas Lewis Dec^n Noah Porter Maj^r Roger Hooker Asa Barns Moses Andrus & Jon^a Belding be Grandjurors

Voted that Mes^{rs} Elijah Porter John Treadwell Asahel Wadsworth Asahel Cowles Oliver Hart Jon^a Root Dan^{ll} Lankton Asa Upson Royce Lewis Hez^h Gridley Dan Hill Ichabod Norton Joseph Woodford Ju^r Noah Stanley David Mather Thos Upson Simeon Hart Seth Wiard & John Allyn be Com^{tee} of Inspection

Voted that Elijah Hooker Seth Wiard Stephen Barns & Aaron Harrison be added to the Com^{tee} to Inquire what is Become of the money paid by the Solders that were Draughted and

Farmington

Did Not Go into ye Service

Voted That John Treadwell Esqr Wm Judd Esqr Col Noadiah Hooker & Solomon Whitman be a Com^tee to Inspeck the Vote proposed & Exhecuted by Mr Judd   446

Voted that Elijah Porter & Dan^ll Lankton be Added to the Com^tee of Inspection   446

13 Jan 1778

Capt Peter Curtis.. Chosen Constable   447

Voted that Timothy Root Thos Smith Ju^r Capt Obadiah Andrus Eleazer Peck & Eli Lewis be Grandjurors   447

Amos Clark was by Vote Chosen Tythingman   447

Voted that John Richards & Jon^a Belding be a Com^tee in addition to the former Com^tee to provide Nessessarys for the Solders Familys   447

Voted that the Salt Belonging to the Town shall be Devided to Each Society According to their List and that the Selectmen with Sol^n Whitman be Com^tee to Devide the Same   447

[ ] Apr 1778

Voted that James North be.. added to ye Com^tee to provide for the Solders Families   447

Voted that Sol^n Whitman Ju^r Dec^n Noah Porter & Lt James Judd be a Com^tee to Lay out a Burying place in Lovely Town (so called)   447

Voted that Sam^ll Stand and Dan^ll Allin be Surveyors of Highways   447

voted that Capt Isaac Biwell Shall have Liberty to Improve About the Acres of Land in the Highway for a Reasonable Rent   447

Upon the Memoriall of Elijah Andruss praying that the Town would grant him.. Land.. Butting Partly on Esqr Whitman Land and partly on Noah Stanley's Land.. for Seting Up a Small Dwelling House and Conveniency of Taning at the Brook &c: Voted that Maj^r Gad Stanley Elijah Frances & Sol^n Whitman Ju^r be a Com^tee to.. Examine the Situation   448

[ ] 1778

To Isaac Lee Ju^r and John Treadwell Esq^rs Repre[sen]tatives.. in the Generall Assembly.. You are.. Directed to Use Your Influence in the Generall Assembly of this State by proper ways & means that the Articles of Confederation may be Amanded and Altered.. if such Emendations Can be made without manifestly endangering the Independence and Liberties of the United States..   448

14 Dec 1778

Col Isaac Lee was Chosen Moderator   449

Sol^n Whitman was chosen Town Clerk or Reg^r   449

Selectmen } Amos Cowels Asahel Wadsworth Elijah Porter Capt Mathew Cole Capt Dan^ll Lankton Elisha Manross Timothy Thomson Capt Norton in the room of Thomson   449

Constables } Seth Porter Roger Norton Ju^r Job Lewis Amos Root Capt James Stoddard William Woodford Ju^r John Richards John Goodrich Stephen Barns Joseph Bacon & Isaac Cowles Capt Sol^n Cowles to Gather ye Rate & make up with ye Treas^r   449

Treasurer Capt Solomon Cowles   449

Grandjurors } John Porter Isaac Lee John Thomson Dec^n Stephen Dorchester Joseph Lankton Elisha Scott Capt Judah Woodworth Elisha Woodruff Ruben North Benj^a Kenedy Luther Stockin Mathew Heart Oliver Peck Ambross Sloper Sam^ll Woodruff Josiah Andrus Asahel Lewis Timothy Lee Capt Asa Upson Hez^h Grieley Jared Butler Micah Woodruff Thos Heart Jon^a Belding Calvin Cowles Zadock Brounson Simon Hart Titus Bunnel Bartholemew Drigg Seth Gilbert   449

Farmington

Tythingmen } James Merrills John North Joseph Root Himan Judd Noah Woodruff Bennoni Brounson Benj^a Hopkins Elisha Bell David Pardy Eber Merriman Abell Yale Reuben Ives Medad Woodruff Isaac Woodruff Barnabas Thomson James Booth Lott Stanley Zacheus Gillet Amos Beacher Eldad Brounson Moses Bacon & Joseph Stone   *449*

Surveyors of Highways } Capt John Porter Abner Curtis Azell Hills Isaac Gridley Timothy Porter Ju^r Willm Smith Wm Porter Tim^o Andrus Sam^{ll} Gridley Joseph Hooker James Percivall Asa Goodrich Dan^{ll} Smith John Stanley Joseph Dutton Abr^m Winstone Amos Hart Robert Hazard Tim^o Upson John Woodruff Ju^r Sam^{ll} Thorp Ju^r Silvanus Dunham David Newel Amos Barns Benj^a Churchel Mathew Hungerford Benj^a Willcox Abell Peck Lament Peck Sam^{ll} Adams Isaac Norton Nath^{ll} Carrington Jedediah Norton Ezek^{ll} Woodford Thos Thomson Eldad Woodruff Livi Andrus Elnathan Smith Charles Edy Judah H[ ] Judah Hart Ju^r Heman Hall John Brounson Justus Peck Joel Graniss Thos Upson Seth Deming Wait Smith Noadiah Heart Stephen Cooke Edward David Robbards Elisha Rust Hez^h West   *449*

Listers } Col Noadiah Hooker Timothy Root ~~Isa[ ] Bidwell~~ Peter Curtis Elnathan Gridley Hez^h Judd Elijah Hooker Stephen Norton Roswell More Obadiah Andrus John Curtiss Esqr Jesse Gaylord David North David Gleason Wm Woodford Seth Stanley Eleazer Heart Isaac Lee 3^d Jesse Alcox Mark Harrison Zachariah Heart Joseph Bacon Joseph Lanton Jude Clark   *449*

Constable to Collect the Colony Rate & Settle with the Treasurer Capt Sol^n Cowles   *449*

Town Collectors } Capt Sol^n Cowles Ezra Scovell Thomas Cowles Judah Barns Solomon Woodford Juday Joseph Dunham Jon^a Lee Seth Wiard   *449*

Sealer of Leather } Capt Treadwell Moses Dickerson Josiah Cowles Jabez Robbard Jon^a Miller Ju^r Thos Heart Stephen Barns ~~Gideon Andrus~~   *449*

Sealer of Measures } Elijah Porter Sam^{ll} Burr Joseph Porter Dan^{ll} Lankton Willm Lee Reuben Miller James Booth Aaron Harrison Gideon Andrus   *449*

Sealer of Weights } Isaac Bidwell Ezra Scovell David Peck Ezekiel Woodford James North   *449*

Key Keepers & Branders } Timothy Porter Ju^r Thos Cowles Brander Ezra Scovel Tim^o Lee Ezekiel Woodford James North Royce Lewis Dan^{ll} Johnson Zebulon Frisby Samuel C: Bouge Key Keeper   *449*

Fence vewers } Noah Porter Math^w Clark Barnabas Dunham Gideon Williams David Cogswell Asa Barns Elisha Miller Gideon Hart Sam^{ll} Dickerson Joshua Webster Royce Lewis Luke Gridley Nath^{ll} Hitchcock John Brounson Dan^{ll} Bunnel Justis Webster   *450*

Packer Solomon Thomson   *450*

Rate Makers } Solomon Whitman Esqr Solomon Cowles John Treadwell Esqr Elijah Porter Thomas Lewis & Martin Bull   *450*

Com^{tee} to provide for Solders Families } Ezek^{ll} Cowles Elijah Cowles Dan^{ll} Thomson Elnathan Gridley Nath^{ll} Wadsworth James Judd Thomas Cowles Elisha Strong Asahel Cowles Roger Norton Olver Heart Jon^a Root Asa Upson Amos Barns Seth Woodruff Lott Stanley Elijah Heart Charles Edy David Dewey   *450*

Com^{tee} For the Exchange of Highways } For Kensington Sealah Hart Noah Cowles.. For Southington Timothy Lee Ashbell Cowles Amos Root.. For New Cambridge Elisha Manross Asa Upson & Royce Lewis   *450*
28 Dec 1778

Daniel North Ju^r Roger Hooker Zadock Orvis Luke Thomson & Seth Woodruff were Chosen Tythingmen & Roger Hooker in the Room of Joseph Root   *450*

in Addition to the Com^{tee} for Solders Familys } Joseph Woodruff Solomon Whitman Ju^r Abner Curtiss   *450*

Listors Capt Asa Upson Dec^n Elisha Manross Mathew Cadwell   *450*

Farmington

Surveyors of Highways Capt Isaac Bidwell Willm Webster Elisha Deming Rezen Gridley	450
Grandjurors Noadiah Burr James Lee John Upson Ju^r Dan^{ll} Sloper Dan Hills & Timothy Lewis in the Room of Timothy Lee	450
Hog Howards Col Hooker Amos Cowles Asahel Wadsworth Capt Bidwell Timothy Root Heman Judd Jos Wright Capt John Allyn Hez^h Wadsworth Joseph Booth Levi Judd	450
Voted that Col Selah Heart & John Treadwell Esq^{rs} be Ajents.. to perfer a Memoriall to the Generall Assembly.. to obtain Liberty for s^d Town to Support & Maintain their Highways by a Rate	450
Voted Major Stanly Col Hooker Dan^{ll} Lankton Col^o Heart & Capt Norton be Com^{tee} to Examin Audit & Settle the Accounts With Solomon Cowles Town Treasurer for the Years past	450
Upon the Petision of Solomon Cowles Thos Cowles Isaac Bidwell Amos Cowles And Phinehas Cowles praing that the Town would Grant.. full Liberty to Erect one or more grist mills on the fulling Mill Brook.. the Question was put.. and Voted in the Afirmative	451
[ ] Feb 1779	
Voted to Abate to Peter B Gleason the Town Rates Now Lying Against him	451
Voted that Col: Heart James Percivall & Capt Mathew Cole be a Com^{tee} to Vew the Road Called the Blew House Road where it Crosses the River and See whether theyShall Judge it Nessesary to Move s^d Highway	451
Voted that Col Hooker Asahell Wadsworth be a Com^{tee} to provide for the Solders Families.. in the Room of the present Com^{tee}	451
Voted that John Treadwell Esqr Maj^r Stanley & Hez^h Wadsworth by a Com^{tee} to make a Set of Instructions for the Representatives.. Chosen to Attend the Generall Assembly in May	451
Voted that Capt Josiah Cowles Jon^a Root John Curtiss Esqr Dan^{ll} Lankton & Eleazer Peck be a Com^{tee} of Inspection	451
Voted that John Treadwell Esq^{rs} Cal: Heart & Mes^{rs} Jon^a Root Josiah Lewis Capt Norton Maj^r Stanley Stephen Barns Capt Simeon Heart be A Com^{tee} to Up a plan.. for maintaining the Highways	451
Voted that Thos Smith Ju^r & Elisha Strong & Timothy Wadworth be Haywards	451
Voted that Sam^{ll} Smith Elisha Miller Elijah Hooker Roger Norton Dan^{ll} Sloper Ambrose Sloper Timothy Stanley Hez^h Gridley James Stoddard Stephen Hollester Joseph Beacher Noadiah Heart Bartho^w Driggs & Thomas Upson be A Com^{tee} to procure Cloathing for the Solders	452
Upon the Petision of Josiah Lewis Abell Yale James Hadsell & Joseph Byington praying for Liberty to Set a part of a Sawmill and A part of a Dam in the four rod Highway Runing East & west on the South Side of Abell Yale Farm in the parish of New Cambridge	452
Selah Heart Ichabod Norton Noadiah Hooker Esq^{rs} Dan^{ll} Lankton & Maj^r Gad Stanley being Auditors to Settle the acc^{ts} with the Town Treasurer and with the Severall Com^{tees} to provide Cloathing for the Solders And to Take Care of the Solders Famylies Made their Report as follows (Viz) Capt Sol^n Cowles Treasurer Debt Against the Town Amounts to £9828.15.4.2	452
We find A Ballance in Favour of the Town from the following Com^{tee} (Viz) Leu^t Joseph Beacher - £0.8.6 .. Capt James Stoddard - 1.15.9 .. Leu^t Jon^a Andrus - 11.2.9 .. Mr Saml Smith - 6.15.8 .. Ens^n Stephen Barns - 1.7.6 .. Mr Elijah Hooker - 3.16.7	452
We find a Ballance in Favour of the following Com^{tee} (Viz) Capt Simeon Heart - £0.10.3 .. Capt John Allyn - 0.17.4	452
We find A Balance in favour of ye Town from the following Com^{tee} paid into the Treasury before Settelment (Viz) Leu^t Simeon Newel - £8.11.6 .. by Mr Noah Cowles - 4.13.9 .. by Capt Tim^o Clark - 57.0.0 .. by Mr Jon^a Belding - 2.0.0. ... by John Curtiss Esqr - 0.10.5 .. by	452

Farmington

Mr Hez Judd - 0.7.6 .. by Mr Roger Norton - 1.2.0 .. by Capt Asa Upson - 23.10.3..

8 Feb 1779

..Selah Heart.. Daniel Lank.. Gad Stanley.. Ichabod Norton.. Noadiah Hooker } Auditors — 453

[ ] Apr 1779

Voted that Ichabod Norton Esqr Wm Ford & Jacob Foot be a Com^{tee} to Vew the Land in the 20 rod Highway.. prayed for in the Memoriall of Elnathan Hart.. to Sell the s^d Land.. the s^d Hart paying all the Cost — 453

Voted that Major Stanley David Mather & Ens^n Hotchkiss be A Com^{tee} to Vew the forty rod Highway prayed for by Eben^r Steel and if they Judge that Not incomode the publick.. to Sell ye Same to s^d Steel.. s^d Steel paying all the Cost — 453

Voted that Maj^r Stanley David Mather & Ens^n Hotchkiss be a Com^{tee} to Vew the Land in the Horse plain where Two 20 rod Highways Cross one another prayed for in the memorial of Eben^r Steel Ju^r and they Shall Judge that the Same may be Spared.. to Sell the Same to s^d Steel.. the s^d Steel paying all the Cost — 453

Voted that Maj^r Gad Stanley and David Mather be Listers in the Room of Seth Stanley & Isaac Lee the 3^d — 453

Voted that Ichabod Norton Esqr Wm Ford & Jacob Foot be Com^{tee} for ye Exchange of Highway & Removeing of Nusances in the Society of Northington — 453

Voted that Aaron Webster & Jon^a Woodruff be A Com^{tee} to provide for the families of the Noncomision Offercers & Solders in the Room of Jonathan Root & Josiah Cowles — 453

Voted that the wid^w Achsa Brounson Should be provided for in the Same Manner as the families of the Solders Are proved for — 454

Martin Bull & Gideon Hart & Willm Hart were Chosen Listers.. & Martin Bull to be in the room of Col Hooker — 454

Voted that Col Hooker & James Cowles be A Com^{tee} to Fix a place for Mr Sam^{ll} North and his Confederates to Build a Horse House on the Meeting House Green — 454

Selah Heart Esqr Capt John John Allyn & Capt Mathew Cole were Chosen a Com^{tee} to vew the place in the Highway Refered to in the Memoriall of John Hewlet — 454

5 Aug 1779

Col Isaac Lee was Chosen Moderator — 454

there was by Vote Chosen for A Com^{tee} of Inspection .. (Viz) in ye first Society John Treawell Esqr Capt Isaac Bidwell Mes^{rs} Timothy Root Noah Porter & Elijah Porter In Kensington Gen^{ll} Selah Heart Elijah & Stephen Norton In New Cambridge Mr Robert Cogswell Capt James Stoddard Capt Asa Upson & Capt Hez^h Gridley for Northington Major Ichabod Norton Elisha Miller Capt Joseph Woodford for New Brittain Col Isaac Lee Col Gad Stanley & David Mather For Farmingbury Capt Zacheus Gillet Capt Joseph Beacher West Brittain Simeon Hart Esqr Capt Asa Yale & Joshua Phelps For Worthington John Goodrich — 454

Voted to Give to John Curtiss Esqr 18 Dollars.. for his Troble in Purchasing Tents &c — 454

[ ] Sep 1779

The Oath of Fidellity to this State was Administred to Stephen Graniss Enos Clark Ju^r George Dickerson Lines Thorp Abraham Persson Nath^n Judd Luke Hart Eph^m Clark Joel Graniss Rusell Graniss Stephen Granniss Ju^r John Newel John Whitman Ju^r Thos Wm Tamage James Smith Ju^r Isaac White Sam^{ll} Thorp Ju^r Thos Kirk Hez^h Woodruff Ju^r Thomas Smith 3^d By John Curtiss Jus^t Peace — 455

25 Sep 1779

Revd Benoni Upson Zach^h Heart Abel Thomson Benoni Brounson Wm Rich Ju^r Zadock — 455

Farmington

Brounson Saml Plumb Joseph Smith Saml Smith Nathl Cridendon Asa Yale Job Frisby Jesse Allcox Eneas Tubbs Joseph Benham Step^n Brounson Jude Clark Saml Clark Math^w Cadwell Elijah Cowles Joseph Wells were all admitted Freemen & Sworn
[ ]

The oath of Fidellity to the State was Administred to Amos Clark Simon Plump Ephraim Boardman   Before me Simeon Heart Jus^t Peace   455
[ ]

The Oath of Fidelity to the State was adminis^d to y^e following Persons (Viz) Zerubable   455
Jeroms Sam^{ll} Adams Caleb Mathews Ju^r Joseph Rowe Dan^{ll} Rowe Sam^{ll} Adams Asa Upson Ju^r Joel Benham Luke Hill David Robbards Abram Brook Zebulon Frisbee James Benham John Lewis Ju^r Abijah ____ [sic] Robert Jerom Amasa Smith Asahell Mathews Caleb Mathews Noah Andrus Joseph Smith Ebenezer Hamblin Jeames Benham Ju^r J[ ] Larcom John Weard Abell Humprey Moses Persons Ichabod Andrus Jos^h Stone Ezra Dowd Zebulun Frisbee Asa Yale Ju^r John Pecks Justis Webster Phenihas Smith Jere^h Griswould Jude Clark OthnielMoses Edwd Ward Hez^h West Job Parkes Amos Dowd Stephen Brounson David Robbard Nath^{ll} Warner Noadiah Hart   By me Stephen Hotchkiss Jus^t Peace
[ ]

The Oath of Fidellity was Administred Unto Sam^{ll} North Ju^r Capt John Porter Sam^{ll} Cook   455
Bouge Eben^r Porter Miles Cramton Appleton Woodruff David North James Gridley Mica[ ] Woodruff James Northway Seth Porter Isaac Gridley Tim^o Wadsworth Abner Whittelsey Elijah Brounson Miles Andrus Robert Woodruff Nath^n Booth James Booth Joshua Webster Benj^a Heart David Dewey Samuel Brounson Charles Edy Samuel Smith Antony Judd Simeon Brounson Elijah Brounson Ju^r and Elisha Booth Ju^r By Isaac Lee Ju^r Jus^t Peace
[ ]

The Oath of Fidellity to this State was Administred to Col Selah Heart Elnathan Hooker   455
Gideon Andrus Noah Andrus William Woodford Levi Thomson Elijah Root Abraham Gillet John Fuller John Cook   p^r Sol^n Whitman Justice Peace
[ ]

The Oath of Fidellity was administerd to Gideon Belding Moses Peacom Jesse Fuller Jesse   455
Woodruff Benj^a Belding Josiah Rob[ ]ards Job Whitcomb Abijah Gillet Enoch Johnson Jonah Griswould
15 Dec 1777

The Oath Fidellity was Administred to the following Persons.. by John Curtiss Jus^t Peace..   456
Mr Jeremiah Curtiss Reuben Munson Moses Mathews Dan^{ll} Carter Nathan Barns Cornelious Dunham Jacob Buck Robt Woodruff James Hasington Dan^{ll} Allin Silas Clark Ju^r Amos Hart John Dorson Immer Judd Ju^r Sam^{ll} Beckwith John Newel Levi Woodruff Silvanus Dunham Oliver Woodruff Robert Hazzard Nathan Lewis Eben^r Allin Brounson Eldad Peck
[ ]

The oath of Fidelity was Administred to Thomas Gridley Rowlen Hooker by Isaac Lee Ju^r 456
Jus^t Peace
[ ]

The oath of Fidellity was Administred to Levi Lankton & Jon^a Ingham Jeremiah Frank Isaac   456
Lankton Amos Peck Asahell Wadsworth Timothy Porter Ju^r Aaron Lindsly Capt Sol^n Cowles J[on^a] Hill & Math^w Mann Miles Marks Before me Sol^n Whitman Jus^t Peace
[ ]

The Oath of Fidelity to this State was Administred to Moses Deming Seth Deming Jedediah   456

Farmington

Norton Asahell Goodrich and Wait Smith Sam^ll Williams Joseph B[ ] Judah Wright & to Revd John Smalley Gideon Hollester Leu^t Nath^ll Churchill Eleazer Whaples By Isaac Lee Ju^r Justice of Peace
[ ]

The oath of Fidellity was Administred to Timothy Andrus Joseph Lankton Eli North Asa North Dan^ll Thomson Sam^ll Brockway Ju^r Amos Clark Jon^a Bull Elnathan Hubbard Joseph Root Elisha prat Eliakim Marshall Abel Peck Abel Lewis Elisha Newel Jesse Curtiss Sam^ll Brockway Nath^ll Carrington Thos North Seth Gilbert James Cowles Reuben Miller J[ ]^n Cart[er] John Barns Ju^r John Case Sam^ll Deming Silvanus Dunham Josiah Willcox Sam^ll Smith Zebulon Cole Elijah Stanley   Andrus Col Selah Heart Elnathan Hooker Gideon Andrus Noah Andrus Wm Woodford Ju^r Levi Thomson By John Treadwell Jus^t Peace *456*
[ ]

The Oath of Fidelity was Administred to Jon^a Lee Selah Cole Abner Curtiss Ju^r Sam^ll Hale David Smith Ju^r Joseph Bunell Ju^r Abraham Winston Asa Woodruff Robert Kinkead Andrew Kinkead Apha^m Winstone Amos Hart Ju^r Amos Hitchcock Moses Moss David Cogswell Ju^r Sam^ll [ ] [ ] Seth Lankton *456*
6 Jan 1778

The Oath of Fidelity was Administred to the following persons.. By Stephen Hotchkiss Jus^t Peace.. Thomas Hart Wm Jerome Jon^a Crampton John Willcox Math^w Hungerford Tim^y Hungerford Gideon Robbards Lemuel Peck Wm Rich Jacob Hungerford Dan Hill Freeman Upson Theod[ ] Root Jesse Gaylord Step^n Hungerford Dan^ll Johnson Abel Hawley Jon^a Lindsly Joseph Spencer Joel Hitchcox James Lee Eli Lewis Wm Lee Lem^ll Andrus Josiah Ives Jesse Mathews John Gaylord J^r Wm Rich J^r Wm Elton David Lewis Josiah Peck Benj[ ] Lindsley Robert Cogswell Isaac Norton Josiah Lewis J^r Jacob Bartho^w Josiah Holt Step^n Rowe Gershom Tuttel Tim^o Hotchkiss *456*
[ ]

The oath of Fidellity to ye State was Administred to Capt Reuben Hart Ozias Andrus Robert Foot Jon^a Root Ju^r Roswell moor & Jabez Robbard Benjn Chapman Eben^r Barns 2^d Thos Wendon Enos Clark Sam^ll Root Ezek^ll Andrus Josiah Andrus 2^d & Benj^a Andrus David Hill Frederick Humphry By John Curtiss Jus^t Peace *456*
[ ]

The oath of Fidelity was Adm^d to John Belding Silas Clark Obed Clark Immer Judd   By Jared Lee Jus^t Peace *456*
18 Apr 1778

At a Freemans Meeting.. Simeon Newel Amos Cowles Josiah Holt Seth Gilbert Jon^a Brounson David Heart Elijah   were admited and Sworn and also Took the Oath of Fidelity to this State *456*
[ ]

The Oath of Fidelity was Adminstred to Collens Luddington John Morrish a Brittish Prisoner Job Brounson James Merrill Isaac Cowles Daniel Johnson Samuel Peck Ezra Belding Ju^r Salmon Root Isaac Hall Stephen Johnson John Fuller   By Salomon Whitman Jus^t Peace *456*
12 Oct 1780

The Oath Fidellity to State was Administred Thomas Wells Elias Frances Elisha Wells Moses Merrill and G[ ]ore Wells p^r Noah Webster Jus^t Peace *1*
13 Dec 1779

Gen^ll Selah Heart was Chosen Moderator *2*

Farmington

Solomon Whitman was Chosen Town Clerk of Reg^r	2
Selectmen } Capt Isaac Bidwell in the Room of Dec^n Porter James Judd in the Room of Asa^{ll} Wadsworth Jonathan Lankton Stephen Hotchkis Esqr Col Gad Stanley Ichabod Norton Esqr Eben^r Hamblin	2
Town Treasurer Capt Solomon Cowles	2
Constables } Solomon Cowles Ju^r to Collect the State Tax & Setel with ye Treasurer… Simeon Newel Gideon Cowles Roger Norton Capt James Stoddard James North Willm Woodford Ju^r Titus Bunnell & John Goodrich	2
Grandjurors } Leu^t Jon^a Bull Dec^n Seth Lee Hawkins Woodruff Roger Woodford Salmon Root Mathew Cadwell Hez^h Winchell Clement Gridley Jacob Hungerford Abell Lewis Thomas Hungerford Levi Andrus Joseph Heart Levi Judd Jacob Foot Gideon Hart David Bristoll Jabez Whitmore Stephen Cook Noadiah Heart Moses Deming	2
Tythingmen } Eben^r Hawley Martin Woodruff Dan Clark Oliver Gridley Selah Cowles Seth Brounson Jesse Gaylord Zeb^n Peck Ju^r Joseph Gaylord Ezek^{ll} Wright Benj^a Heart Wm Lewis Isaac Woodford Moses Woodruff Levi Thomson Moses Bacon Ichabod Andrus Edward Word Zeb^n Cole Samuel Lee	2
Surveyors of Highways } Dan^{ll} Rowe Jesse Curtiss Richard Porter Jno Hamblin James Cowles Eben^r Porter Elisha Strong Joseph Porter Eben^r Lankton Reuben Woodruff Asa North Joseph Selden Tim^o Wells Frederick Humphry Jos^h Wells Ju^r Thos Gridley John Cole Nath^{ll} Brounson Lemuel Andrus Freman Upson Thos Barns Eben^r Scott James Hadsdell Jos^h Gaylord Sam^{ll} Hickox Dan^{ll} Lowree Joshua Webster Elijah Frances Elijah Hensdale Josiah Kilborn Capt Jos^h Woodford Wm Heart Ju^r Ezra Willcox	2
Surveyors } Josiah Kilborn Capt Jos^h Woodford Wm Heart Jur Ezra Willcox John Tillotson Nath^n Bayley Tim^o Woodruff Othniel Moses Gideon Belding Elisha Tubbs Ezra Dowd Amos Heart Ephraim Hollester Hooker Gilbert	2
Listers } Peter Curtiss Isaac Cowles Roger Hooker Sam^{ll} Smith Sam^{ll} Stanley Stephen Cole Calvin Hurlburt Luke Gridley Judah Barns Elizer Heart Seth Stanley Jon^a Belding Wm Woodford Ju^r David Gleason Jude Clark Seth Wiard Jeremiah Griswould Zachariah Heart	2
Com^{tee} for Solders Families } Timothy Root Isaac Gleason Wm Wadsworth Mathew Heart Sam^{ll} Goodrich Joseph Peck Oliver Stanley Amos Barns Jehudah Heart Joseph Smith Isaac Lee 3^d	2
Collectors } Solomon Cowles Ju^r Job Gridley James Stoddard Lott Stanley Josiah Willson Ju^r Titus Bunnel Joseph Gilbert	2
Sealer of Leather } Ephraim Treadwell Moses Dickerson Jabez Robbards Thomas Heart Micah Woodruff	3
Sealer of Weights } Capt Isaac Bidwell Ezra Scovell James Lee James North Ezekiel Woodford	3
Sealer of Measures } Elijah Porter Sam^{ll} Burr Ju^r Joseph Porter Willm Lee James Booth Reuben Miller Ichabod Andrus	3
Key Keepers } Timothy Porter Ju^r Stephen Norton Royce Lewis James North Sam^{ll} Cook Booge Zebulen Cole	3
Branders of Horses } Thomas Cowles Ezra Scovell James Lee James North Ezekiel Woodford Seth Wiard	3
Packer Solomon Thomson	3
Rate Makers } Solomon Whitman Esqr John Treadwell Esqr Isaac Cowles Solomon Cowles Ju^r Martin Bull Capt Solomon Cowles	3
Com^{tee} of Cloathing } Samuel Smith James Persivall Oliver Peck Capt Hez^h Gridley Timothy Stanley	3

Farmington

Com^{tee} for Exchange of Highways} Ichabod Norton William Woodford Jedediah Norton Ju^r Titus Bunnel Eben^r Hamblin Jeremiah Griswould	3
Voted that John Treadwell Esqr Gen^{ll} Selah Heart Col Gad Stanley James Stoddard Ichabod Norton Esqr & Simeon Heart Esqr be a Com^{tee} to Join with the Com^{tee}.. of Southington to Liquidate and Adjust the Accounts Originall of.. Farmington and Make a proper and Just.. Distribution of the Poor.. and Come to.. a finall Settlement of all Open & Current Accounts.. and also to preambulate between.. Farmington & Southington and.. fix Monuments or Points that Shall be Durable & permanent between s^d Towns	3
Voted that Col Noadiah Hooker be allowed 2^d ½ p^r cent for the Money they have Expended in providing for the Solders Families	3

[ ] Dec 1779

Voted that the Town Approve of the Selectmen Giving an Order to Doct^r Grayham for £26 for for Doctring P[ ] Kilborn	4
Voted that Gabriel Curtiss Elijah Woodford & Ezekiel Cowles be Grandjurors.. & Ezekiel Cowles in ye Room of Dec^n Seth Lee	4
Voted that Titus Burr and Robert Padden be Surveyors of Highways	4
Voted that William Ford be a Com^{tee} for the Exchange of Highways & Removeing of Nusances in the Parish of Northington	4
Voted that ye Com^{tee} for Exchanging Highway &c be Directed.. to Sell to Isaac Gridley about forty Square foot of Land for the Coveniency of Setting a Barn	4
Voted that John Treadwell Esqr John Hamblin & Isaac Gleason be A Comt^{ee} to fix A place for a Pound	4

5 Jan 1780

Voted that John Treadwel Esqr & Col Noadiah Hooker Be Agents for the Town.. at the Generall Assembly.. at Hartford on ye 6th Day of Jany instant	4
Voted that the Town Com^{tee} for Exchanging Highways.. to Agree with Luke Thomson for So much of the Corner of his Home lott Called the Thomsons Corner as to make it Convenient Turning s^d Corner with Teams &c	4
that Timothy Stanley one of the Colectors be allowed three pounds out of the Town Treasury for Rates that he paid to the Treasurer & Could Not Collect	5
Voted that Asahel Wadsworth Col Noadiah Hooker Col Isaac Lee Col: Gad Stanley Generall Heart Stephen Norton Elisha Manross James Stoddard Ichabod Norton Esqr Wm Woodford Simeon Heart Esqr & James Lusk be A Com^{tee} to assist Capt Solomon Cowles in Takeing the Names of the poor people in his Several Rate Bills that they Judge Unable to pay their Rates	5

[ ] Apr 1780

Capt William Woodford was Chosen Grandjuror	5
Eldad Peck was Chosen A Com^{tee} to Take Care of the Solders Families I the Room of Oliver Stanley	5
David Mather Seth Deming & Roger Norton Ju^r was by Vote Chosen A Com^{tee} of Inspection of provision	5
Voted that Martin Bull And Gideon Cowles be Listers	5
Voted that if Mes^{rs} Sol^n Cowles Isaac Bidwell Thomas Cowles And Amos Cowles Do Not Erect A well Constructed Gristmill on the fulling Mill Brook by the first of Decr 1781 that Any Other person may apply	5

[ ] Sep 1779

At A Freemans Meeting.. Sam^{ll} Brounson Wm Hart Ju^r Barnabas Thomson Joel Hart John Tillotson Charles Woodford Sol^n Woodford Abell Woodruff Simeon Marshall John Upson	5

Farmington

Ju^r Thomas Thomson Philemon Bradley Levi Lankton Seth Marshall And Micah Woodruff where all Admitted freemen & Sworn by Ichabod Norton Jus^t Peace
10 Apr 1780

At a Freemans Meeting.. Mes^{rs} Abell Hawley Nathan Booth Rhoderick Cadwell Joseph Selden Salmon Root Stephen Hart Dan^{ll} Ames Memucan Rew Jon^a Cowles Chauncy Deming Luke Wadsworth John North Daniel Gridley Abner Whittlesey Elizur Andrus Eben^r Hasington John Hayford & David Carrington were all Admitted Freemen & Sworn By Ichabod Norton Jus^t Peace 5

the Oath of Fidellity to this State was Adminstred Unto Chauncy Deming Sam^{ll} Bird Luke Wadsworth Joseph Selden John North Memucan Rew Dan^{ll} Gridley Ezekiel Woodford Elijah Woodford Thomas Lee Jon^a Cow[*les*] Oliver Marshall Asa Thomson John Hayford James Root Daniel Ames Eben^r Horsington Marvin Clark Asa Hart By John Treadwell Jus^t Peace 5
19 Sep 1780

At a Fremans Meeting.. Mes^{rs} Elijah Woodruff David Lewis Noah Stanley Stephen Hungerford Lott Woodruff Palmer Sweett Baizel Wells Amos Hinman were All Admitted Freeman & Sworn And Also Took the oath of Fidellity to the State By Ichabod Norton Jus^t Peace 5
1 Mar 1780

At a meeting of the Inhabitants of Farmington Held.. in Compliance with the Order of his Excellency Governour Trumble 6

John Treadwell Esqr was Chosen Moderator & Thomas Lewis to minute the Votes of s^d meeting and to Deliv^r them to Solomon Whitman Esqr Town Clerk 6

Amos Cowles was Chosen Key Keeper of ye Town pound in ye Room of Timothy Porter Ju^r 6

Jacob Byington was Chosen Grandjuror & Joseph Root Surveyor of Highways 6

there was Cosen [*sic*] A Com^{tee} of Inspectors of provisions Mes^{rs} Elnathan Gridley Sam^{ll} Smith Roger Hooker Noah Porter Wm Wadsworth Timothy Root Asahel Wadsworth Thos Lewis Heman Judd Joseph Hooker Marvin Clark James Lusk Gad Stanley Elizur Heart Jon^a Belding Lemuel Hotchkiss Seth Stanley Elath^n Smith Elisha Miller Wm Ford Joseph Woodford Jacob Foot Thos Thomson Seth Wiard Step^n Cook Zebulin Frisbie Ju^r Titus Bunnel James Persevall Step^n North Elijah Hooker Stephen Cole Math^w Heart John Allyn John Root Amos Barns James Lee Eli Lewis Thos Hungerford Joseph Byington Josiah Holt and Benj^a Willcox 6

Voted that Gideon Porter of New Brittain have his Rates Abated that Arose on the List for 1778 6
21 Jun 1780

Col Isaac Lee was Chosen Moderator 6

Voted that Samuel Smith be A Com^{tee} to procure the Shirts for the Solders 7

Granted by Vote a Rate or Tax of Ten pence on the pound to be paid in one Month in bill of the New Emision.. to be paid out to the Solders that Shall Inlist Into the Army.. they briging [*sic*] A Certificate of their Inlist[*ment*] from the officer that Inlisted them.. also Voted that Seth Wadsworth Job Gridley Samuel Lewis Elijah Woodford Rhoderick Cadwell Zebulun Frisbee & Samuel Lee be Collectors in ye Society to which they Belong to Collect ye Tax Above Granted 7
13 Nov 1780

Col Isaac Lee was Chosen Moderator 7

Farmington

John Treadwell Esqr Col Hooker Generall Heart [ ] Norton David Mather Leu^t Byington W^m 7
Woodford Capt Allyn He[ ] Mr Percivall Barth^w Driggs Hez^h Wadsworth be a Com^{tee} to take
into Consideration the Acts of Assembly that have Now Been Read and Report
Mr Thomas Lewis James Percivall Hezakiah Gridley Wm Ford Elnathan Smith & Seth   7
Wiard.. be hereby Appointed to procure Casks to Contain.. Provisions to receve & Inspect
the Same.. Thomas Lewis is specially appointed to Receve ye Salt provied for [the] Public to
preserve s^d provision
Voted that James Lusk Col Hooker John Treadwell Esqr Capt Gridley Capt Porter W^m 8
Wadsworth Timothy Root Tim^o Gridley Gen^{ll} Heart Nath^n Cole Elijah Hooker Stephen
Norton Seth Deming John Allyn Jason Gaylord Thos Hungerford Capt Upson Step^n Hotchkiss
Esqr Leu^t Byington Maj^r Norton Elisha Miller Jacob Foot Tim^o Thomson Mathew Cadwell
Jedediah Norton Ju^r James Lee Col: Stanley Col: Lee Capt Hotchkiss David Mather Leu^t
Booth Elnathan Smith Seth Stanley Simeon Hart Esqr Titus Bunnel Joseph Bacon Ju^r Barth^w
Driggs Eben^r Hamblin Woodford Jere^h Griswold [ ] Wiard Lodwick Hotchkiss be a Com^{tee} to
make out the Credits.. of Such as Are already engaged in ye Continental Army.. and Class the
Inhabitants persu[ant] to an Act of the Generall Assembly passed in their Sessions in Octob^r
.. Col: Hooker Col Stanley & Major Norton are Appointed to Settle with Southington
Concerning the Quotas & Credits of the Two Towns
Voted that Sol^n Whitman John Treadwell Martin Bull Wm Wadsworth & Elijah Porter be   8
Rate makers to make Rates Now Granted & Deliver them to the Severall Collectors
Voted that Mr Wm Wadsworth John Allyn Hez^h Gridley William Woodford Abell Clark &   8
Timothy be.. Appointed Collectors to Collect the Provision Tax.. in ye societys to which they
Respectively belong.. Taking their Receipt & the Money they Shall so Collect to Mr Thomas
Lewis taking his Receipt who is Hereby Appointed to Receve the Same & to Account
therefore when Required
11 Dec 1780

Generall Selah Heart was Chosen Moderator   8
Voted that Solomon Whitman Esqr be Town Clerk   8
Select men } James Judd Capt Isaac Bidwell Elijah Hooker James Lee Willm Ford Col Gad   8
Stanley Eben^r Hamblin
Town Treasurer Capt Solomon Cowles   8
Constables } Isaac Cowles & he to Collect the State Taxes & Settel with the Treasurer [ ]   8
Newel & Gideon Cowles Stephen Norton Dan^{ll} Barns Ens^n Willm [ ] Titus Bunnell & John
Goodrich
Surveyors of Highways } Joseph Woodruff Amos Cowles Ezekiel Scott Isaiah Rowe Sam^{ll} 9
Smith Dan^{ll} North Ju^r James Cadwell Eli North Thos Gridley Dan^{ll} Gridley Ju^r Zadock Orvis
Palmer Sweet Elisha Hasington Dan^{ll} Thomson Moses Dickerson Luther Stockin Oliver
Heart Sam^{ll} Peck Ju^r Jacob Bartholomew Capt Amos Barns Amasa Hart Reuben Barns W^m
Rich Reuben Hungerford Nath^{ll} Mathews Ezra Dorman Josiah Lewis Ju^r John Lounsboury
Nath^{ll} Churchell Tim^o Stanley Stephen Hollester Sam^{ll} Dakeson Nath^{ll} Bull Stephen Darren
Wm Ford Elijah Woodford John Tillotson Zachariah Heart Jabez Whitmore Joshua Phelps
Seth Peck Thos Brooks Noadiah Heart Elisha Covey Jude Clark Sam^{ll} Deming in the Room
of Richard Porter Morgan Goodwin
Grandjurors } Martin Bull Elijah Lewis Hawkins Woodruff Wm Porter James Bishop Baize   9
Wells Sol^n Winchel Caleb Hopkins Jon^a Lindsley Sam^{ll} Brooks Theodore Root Capt John
Lankton Elisha Booth Ju^r Jon^a Miller Ju^r Job Miller Reuben Hawley John Root Sam^{ll} Culver
and Sam^{ll} Warner John North & Eliphalet Wadsworth
Tythingmen } Amos Hawley Lott Woodruff Isaac Gridley Tim^o Root Isaac Gleas[ ] Marvin   9

Farmington

Clark Jabez Cowles Ezra Scovel Amos Peck Ju^r Capt Hez Gridley Benj^a Willcox Joseph Gaylord Joseph Booth Abell Elijah Smith Elnathan Hart Isaac Woodford Levi Thomson Salmon Hollester Eli Catlin Isaac Hall Benj^a Ray Abell Humph[ry]

Listers } Sam^{ll} Stanley Martin Bull Roger Hooker Gideon Cowles Isaac Co[ ] Capt James Lusk Stephen Cole Calvin Hulburt Capt Seth Deming L[ ] Gridley Judah Barns David Gleason Ezek^{ll} Woodford Thos Thomson J[ ] Heart Elnathan Smith Levi Andrus Seth Wiard Benj^a Belding B[ ] Driggs — 9

Fence vewers } Mathew Clark Noah Porter Barnabas Dunham Gideon Williams John Judd Ju^r James Booth Luke Gridley Roice Lewis Capt Jos^h Woodford Elisha Miller Dan^{ll} Bunnel Justiss Webster — 9

Sealer of Leather } Nath^{ll} Wadsworth Moses Dickerson Hezekiah Gridley Jon^a Miller Ju^r Thos Heart — 9

Sealer of Weights } Isaac Gleason Ezra Scovell James Lee Ezek^{ll} Woodford James [ ] Seth Wiard — 9

Sealer of Measures } Elijah Porter Joseph Peck Jesse Brounson Wm Lee James Booth Reuben Miller Ichabod Andrus — 9

Key Keepers & Branders of Horses } Amos Cowles Key Keeper Stephen Norton Brander Ezra Scovell Riyce Lewis James North Sam^{ll} Bouge Kee Keeper) Ezek^{ll} W[ ] Brander) Zebulon Cole — 9

Com^{tees} for Solders Families } Nehe^m Street Thos Smith Ju^r Simeon Newel Thoms Stanley Silas Brounson Abr^m Gridley Hez^h Andrus Eli Lewis & Lemuel Andrus James Frances James Booth — 9

Collecttors Town Rate } Wm Smith Oliver Stanley Dan^{ll} Barns Josiah Dewey David B[ ] Wm Woodford John Goodrich Eli Lewis Samuel Andrus — 9

Voted that Antony Judd be A Colector in ye Room of Josiah Dewey — 9

Com^{tee} to Exchange Highways } Titus Bunnel Seth Wiard Jeremiah Griswould — 9

Voted that John Treadwell Esqr Capt Upson & Asahel Hooker be A Com^{tee} to Examine the Selectmens Acc^{ts} — 10

25 Dec 1780

Voted that Col Hooker Maj^r Norton Hez^h Wadsworth be A Com^{tee} to Take Into Consideration the Memorial of Abner Curtiss Ju^r Respecting his Sons in the Continentall Army praing that the Town would Grant to them the Same Sum that was Given to them that Inlisted in Service in June Last.. the s^d Com^{tee} Reported that Twas there Opinion that ye Town Grant to.. Sons.. Ten Pounds State Money Each — 10

Voted that Abner Curtiss Ju^r be Abated of the Towns part of the fore fould Asesments.. on the List 1779 — 10

Voted that Selah Cole be A Collector.. in the Room of Job Gridley — 10

Voted that Col Hooker be A Com^{tee} to Procure one Light Horsman Required in the present Requitision — 10

Voted a Rate or Tax of one peney half peney on the pound on ye List 1779.. Voted that Willm Wadsworth James Percivall & Elijah Heart Capt Hez^h Gridley Wm Ford and Seth Wiard be Collectors & Recevers of the foregoing Rate — 11

[ ] Jan 1781

Voted that Asa Upham Ju^r And Gideon Roberts be Listers.. Voted that on Reconsideration they Revoke the Vote for Electing or Choseing Asa Upson Lister — 11

Voted that Lt Elijah Porter Col: Stanley & Hez^h Wadsworth be a Com^{tee} to Look into the Circumstances of the Highway Laid Through the Mead[ow] — 11

Farmington

Voted that Asa Hart be Kee Keeper in ye Room of Amos Cowl[ ]	11
Voted that Thos Lewis by [sic] A Tytheingman	11
Voted that the Com^{tee} Appointed to Settle with Capt Cowles & the Town of Southington.. Make Such Abatements As May be Nessesary in Order to Make A finall Settlement of All such Acc^{ts}	11
Voted Hez^h Wadsworth & Timothy Root be Joined to the former Co[m^{tee}]	11
Voted that the Accounts with Capt Cowles be Settled with ye Com^{tee}.. by the first Day of Aprill Next and that after that No Abatements to be Allowed	11
Voted that Generall Heart be A Com^{tee} to Confer with Class of Worthington to procure A Solder to Join the Army for one year and to Draw two third of the Money out of the Town Treasury that be Nessesary to Procure s^d Solder	11
Voted that Hez^h Wadsworth Phenihas Lewis Amos Cowles C[l] Hez^h Gridley Joshua Webster James Judd Ju^r Abell Clark Thos Thomson Seth Heart John Brounson Ezekiel Woodford Benj^a Andrus John Tillotson Phenihas Penfield be Hog Howard to Impound Swine that may be found at Large	12
Voted that Asahell Wadworth be a Com^{tee} to Take Care of the Tents Guns & Kettles Returned belonging to ye Town	12
Voted that Eli Lewis & David Gleason be Tythingmen	12
Voted Seth Hart be A Surveyor of Highways	12
Voted that Col Hooker Maj^r Norton & Hez^h Wadsworth be A Com^{tee} to Examine Mott & Couch: and to Draw orders on the Town Treasurer for Such Sums As they Judge Just & Reasonable	12
Voted that Simeon Newel be a Collector & Receiver of the provision Tax in the Room of Wm Wadsworth	12
Voted that Doct^r Jon^a Bird be paid 7/6.. for Doctoring Rufus Barns	12

[ ] Apr 1781

voted that Col Gad Stanley be A Com^{tee} to Join with the Class to Hire half a Solder Wanted to Make out our Quota in ye Last Requisition of Assembly	12
Voted that Col Noadiah Hooker Col: Gad Stanley & Maj^r Ichabod Norton be A Com^{tee} to Hire Two Lite Horsemen in Complying with s^d Last Requision Afores^d	12

16 Apr 1781

Voted that the Com^{tee} for Exchangeing Highways in the Parish of New Cambridge be Directed to Convey half An Acre of Land to Doct^r Isaac Camp for Debt Against the Town for Doctoring John Lewis	12
Voted that John Treadwell Hez^h Wadsworth Gen^{ll} Selah Heart Stephen Norton James Lee Maj^r Norton Col Lee Col Stanley Simeon Heart Esqr Titus Bunnel be A Com^{tee} to Examine the provisions Tax And to postpone the payment of Such of the poor As they Judge Unable to pay their Rates	12

12 Oct 1780

The oath of Fidellity to this State was Administred to Thomas Wells Elias Frances Elisha Wells Moses Merrill & George Wells By Noah Webster Jus^t Peace	13

24 Jan 1781

The Oath of Fidelity was Administred to Jonathan Gridley Wm Ford Tim^o Thomson Joel Hart Selah Heart Elihu Heart Antony Heart Ezra Willcox Oliver Bouge Jeffery Bouge Seth Heart Eben^r Tillotson Sam^{ll} Root & Sam^{ll} Booge.. By Ichabod Norton Jus^t Peace	13

Farmington

9 Apr 1781

At A Freemans Meeting.. the following Persons were admitted Freemen And Sworn (Viz) Elihu Heart Antony Heart Ezra Willcox Oliver Booge Seth Heart Jeffery Booge Sam^{ll} Gleason Amos Tubbs Selah Cole Eben^r Tillotson Amos Heart Sam^{ll} Root Sam^{ll} Richards Selah Heart Eben^r Hamlin 13

13 Jul 1781

The oath of Fidellity to this State was Administred to Nathan Covey & Naomi Dawis By oliver Humphries Jus^t Peace 13

19 Mar 1782

The oath of fidellity was Administred to Joseph Woodruff.. 13

28 Mar 1782

.. To Samuel Burr John Woodford Ju^r.. 13

9 May 1782

.. To Elnathan Hart.. 13

8 Jul 1782

.. To Amos Bunnell Thomas Morriss 13

3 Mar 1783

The Oath of Fidelity was Administred to Solomon Lankton.. by John Treadwell Jus^t Peace 13

8 Sep 1783

The oath of Fidelity was Administred to Martin Woodruff.. By Sol^n Whitman Jus^t Peace 13

6 Jun 178[1]

The oath of Fidellyty to this State was Admistred to Joseph Archer 13

16 Apr 1781

Voted that Maj^r Norton Hez^h Wadsworth Timothy Root be a Com^{tee} to Vew the Curcumstance of the Land proposed to be Exchanged by the Twons [sic] Com^{tee} with John Portter 14

Voted that Capt Peter Curtiss & Thomas Lewis be A Comt^{ee} to hire Recruits for the Defitient Classes &c 14

Voted Upon the Report of Mes^{rs} Elijah Porteer Hez^h Wadsworth & Gad Stanley that the Selectmen.. be Desired to Take Speciall Care that the Intterest of the Town Do Not Suffer in the Matters Reffered to in said Report 14

Apr/Ma 1781

Voted that Joseph Lankton John Heyford & John Deming be Surveyors of Highways 14

Voted that Gen^{ll} Selah Heart Noah Cowles & Stephen Cole be A Com^{tee} to Fix A place for A Town Pound in the Society of Kensington 14

Voted that Hez^h Wadsworth Maj^r Norton & Timothy Root be A Com^{tee} to Compleat the Bargain with John Porter Began by the Standing Com^{tee} And to Give him A meet Recompence for ye Land Conveyed to the Town and Compleat A Deed of Conveyence 14

Voted that Eben^r Allyn Brounson be A Collector to Collect the Hard money Tax in the Society of Kensington & Worthington 14

Voted that Capt Peter Curtiss be A Costable [sic] 14

Voted that Benj^a Ives be Assessed.. 3/11 Lawfull Silver money and Abraham Waters.. 10/9 14

Farmington

½ like money assessed for Refuseing to pay their Rates for Raising a Solder

Whereas the Class of Which Capt Titus Bunnel is A member have Neglected to procure An Able bodied Recruit to Join the Continentall Army.. And whereas this Town have Procured Such Recruit.. & have paid and Advanced to Such Recruit.. £48 Hard Money.. Voted that the s^d Class be.. Assessed £96 Hard money and.. £60 in bills of this State 14

28 May 1781

Voted that Col Hooker Col: Stanley & Maj^r Norton be A Com^{tee} to Hear the Individuall Members.. of the Class of Which Capt Bunnel is A Member And Also the Indevidualls of the Class of Which Capt Bacon is A Member which Are Doomed Agreable to ye Law.. & to put Such Abatements.. to Such Individuals As Shall Appear to have Done their Duty 15

Voted that Thomas Thomson be A a Com^{tee} to Join with other Com^{tees} for the Exchange of Highways &c: in the Society of Northington 15

[ ] Sep 1781

Votead that Thomas Lewis Joseph Stockin William Lee Gideon Heart David Mather & Simeon Heart Esqr be Receivers & Packers of the Provisions to be Collected by the 2/6^d Tax 2/2^d of which is to be paid in provision and Cloath &c 15

Voted that Samuel Smith be A Recever & Storer of the Cloath^s that be Collectted by the Tax Aboves^d 15

Voted that Zebulun Frisbee Ju^r be a Collector to Collect the /4^d Tax Allready Laid 15

Voted that William Smith by A Collector of ye peney Tax for the first Society Luther Stockin for Kensington & Worthington Lemuel Andrus for N: Cambridge David Gleason for Northington Ashbell Griswould for N: Brittain Bartholemew Driggs for West Brittain 16

Voted that This Town will No further interpose to Suspend the Operation of Law Against Joseph Smith Upon A Judgement rendered Against him.. for Aiding & Assisting one of his Sons in Going Over to the Enemy as he has had Sufficient opportunity to be heard on the Subject 16

26 Jun 1781

Gene^{ll} Selah Heart was Chosen Moderator 16

Voted that the Twon Clerk Now Enter the vote that Passed in the Last Town Meeting which Through Mistake was Mist Entring - (Viz) Voted that Elijah Porter Dec^n Noah Porter & Sol^n Whitman Ju^r be a Com^{tee} to Ascertain the Highway from the Two Mile Bound by Mathew Woodruff (so Called) Runing North to the Sequestred Corner on the Mountain Near Tillotsons Agreable to Newburys Line so Called ~ 16

Voted that Mr Thomas Lewis A Purchaser & Recever of the Beaf Cattle for the paying Taxes 16

Voted that Dec^n Noah Porter be A Colector of Taxes for the first Society Thomas Heart for Kensington Society Eli Lewis for the Society of New Cambridge Levi Thomson for the Society of Northington Timothy Stanley for ye Society of New Brittain and Seth Peck for the Society of West Brittain 16

Voted that Col: Noadiah Hooker be a Treasurer to Receive Money Upon ye Taxes.. And to Delever the Same Mr Thos Lewis Purchaser Upon Order of the Selectmen 16

Voted that Mr Thos Lewis be Directed to Take the Advice of the Governour & Counsell of Safety Respecting the Cattle he may Purchase where & to whom he must Delever so As may be Safe for the Town & the State 16

Voted that the Othority & Selectmen be Desired to Suspend the Exec^n Against Joseph Smith Untill he Can have A fair Hearing 17

Voted that Daniel Tyler Have Liberty.. to Build a grist mill on his own Land At Smith falls so Called at his own Cost 17

Farmington

10 Dec 1781

Voted that Gen^{ll} Selah Heart be A Moderator	17
Voted that Sol^n Whitman Esqr be A Town Clerk	17
Voted that Capt Sol^n Cowles be A Town Treasurer	17
Selectmen } Col Noadiah Hooker Timothy Root Elijah Hooker James Lee Col Gad Stanley Wm Ford & Seth Wiard	17
Constables } Isaac Cowles And he to Collect the State Tax & Settle with ye Treasurer.. Capt Peter Curtis Stephen Norton Daniel Barns David Gleason James North Zebulun Frisbee John Goodrich	17
Grandjurors } Dan Clark Gideon Cowles Elijah Root Thos Newel Ju^r Hawkins Woodruff Amos Gridley Abraham Gridley Willm Wheler Theodore Root Josiah Ives Amos Woodruff Benj^a Heart Reuben Wright Capt Jos^h Woodford Elnathan Hart Micah Woodruff Zebulun Cole Stephen Bronson John Spencer & Salmon Hollester & Dudley Woodford	17
Tythingmen } Reuben North Elijah Lewis Miles Cramton Eliphalet Wadsworth Benoni Brounson Benj^a Hopkins Sol^n Winchel Reuben Ives Thos Barns Lemuel Carrington Timothy Mix James Frances James Ames Isaac Woodford Josiah Willcox Ju^r Eleazer Willcox Eph^m Boardman Capt Jos^h Bacon Joseph Gilbert	17
Listers } Isaac Cowles Joseph Hooker Josiah Hotchkiss James Lusk Beze[ ] Wells Calvin Hurlbut Roger Norton Ju^r Jos^h Wells Ju^r Thos Hungerford Jos^h Byington Josiah Peck Elna^n Smith Jos^h Hart Levi Andrus David Gleason Thos Thomson Ezekiel Woodford Seth Wiard Bartho^w Driggs Benj^a Belding & Seth Stanley	17
Surveys of Highways } Jas: Portter Sam^{ll} Peck Elisha Scott Abner Whittlesey Amos Hawley Abell Thomson Jon^a Thomson Josiah Gillet Palmer Sweet Luke Br[ ] Jos^h Stocking Job Gridley Allin Smith Step^n Hungerford Isaac Br[ ] Asa Upson John Gaylord Benj^a Churchel Lament Peck Josiah Lewis Nath^{ll} Mathews Benj^a Willcox Jos^h Heyford Step^n Hart Jere^h H: osgood James Booth Thos Hooker James Hollester Gideon Hart Dudley Woodford John Tillotson Sam^{ll} Gleason Seth Hart Jos Bacon Thos Beckwith Eben^r Barington Jere^h Griswould Ep^m Boardman Abra^m Pettibone Titus Bunnell Noadiah Hart & Seth Gilbert	17
Colectors } Eleazer Curtiss Elihu Hart Asa Upson Ju^r David Hill David Gleason Elisha Covey Elizur Andrus	17
Sealers of Leather } Nath^{ll} Wadsworth Noah Cowles Hez^h Gridley Thos Hart Gideon Hart Zebulun Frisbee	17
Sealer of Waits } Capt Isaac Bidwell James Lee James North Ezek^{ll} Woodruff Ezra Scovel Seth Wiard	17
Sealer of Measures } Elijah Porter Jos^h Peck Jesse Brounson Wm Lee James Booth Reuben Miller	18
Brander of Horses } Thos Cowles Ezra Scovell James Lee James North Ezek^{ll} Woodford Seth Wiard Oren Lee	18
Key Keeper } Asa Hart Thos Stanley Royce Lewis James North Samuel Booge Zebulun Cole	18
Fence vewers } Mathew Clark Noah Portter Barnabas Dunham Gideon Williams Luke Gridley Royce Lewis Dan^{ll} Bunnel Justis Webster Reuben Miller Sam^{ll} Booge John Judd James Booth	18
Com^{tee} for Solders Farmilies } James Percivall Clement Gridley Sam^{ll} Peck Ju^r Sam^{ll} Smith Thos Hart Jon^a Belding Lemuel Andrus Seth Wiard	18
Hogg Hayward } Collens Ludington Phinehas Penfield Rhoderick Cadwell Jos Andrus	18
Voted that Col: Gad Stanley & John Treadwell be A Com^{tee} to Look into the Record of the County Court & Return of the Jury in Laying Out A Highway Across the Common Field	18

Farmington

Voted that Seth Wadsworth be a Collector for the penny Tax in the Room of Wm Smith	18
Voted that John Treadwell Esqr Col Gad Stanley & Ichabod Norton Esqr be A Com^{tee} with the Com^{tee} from Southington to the Exe^{ns} Against Severall Individualls for Neglecting Millitary Duty & Some Note of hand and See what ought to be Abated and Also See what Can be Collected	18

[ ] Dec 1781

The Com^{tee} Appointed.. At a Meeting.. Held on the 13th Day of Decr 1779 to meet ye Com^{tee}.. of Southington to Determine on Certain Matters.. beg Leave to Report that Com^{tees} At their first meeting & Also At Some future Meetings produced their Commissions which.. Are as follows (Viz) .. John Treadwell Esqr Gen^{ll} Selah Heart Col: Gad Stanley James Stoddard Ichabod Norton Esqr & Simeon Heart Esqr Be A Com^{tee} to Join the Com^{tee}.. of Southington to Liquidate the Accounts Originall of the Town and Make a proper Just Decision & Distribution of the poor.. & Come a Just and finall Settelment of open & Current Accounts.. And Also to preambulate between.. Farmington and Southington And At proper Distances to fix Monuments or Bounds that Shall be Durable & Lasting Between s^d Towns   18

At a Meeting of.. Farmington held Decr 11 17[ ] Voted that the Com^{tee} Appointed to Settle with Capt Cowles And .. Southington be Impowred to make Such Abatements As may Nessary.. To make a finall Settlement of such Accounts   19

.. Voted that Hezekiah Wadsworth & Timothy Root be jointed to the former Com^{tee} with the Same Power   19

At a Meeting.. of Southington.. Holden by speciall order of the Generall Assembly the 11th Day of Novr 1779.. Mr Jonathan Root Capt Josiah Cowles Capt Daniel Lankton Majo^r Asa Bray & Capt Zacheus Gillet were appointed a Com^{tee} to adjust Accounts with the Town of Farmington and to Receve our proportion of the Town Stock And to Set the Bounds of.. Southington   19

At a Meeting.. of Southington Holden by Adjournment on the 10th Day of Aprill 1780 ~ Voted That the Com^{tee}.. to Join a Com^{tee}.. of Farmington be instructed to adjust Accounts with Capt Solomon Cowles respecting the Country & Town Rates.. to find who Are the proper Subjects of An Abatement & to make Abatements Accordingly And Also to Divide the poor of s^d Towns   19

Pursuent to s^d Commission we Did on the 26th Day of June *[ed: 1780]* .. Agree with ye Com^{tee} of..Southington to A.. Distribution of the Poor in manner following (Viz).. To the Town of Farmington.. Mathew Parsons Martha Tillotson Mary Orvis Anne Brounson Phebe Ashbell Phillis Buck Asher North Daniel Tailbourn Thankfull Smith Mercy Smith the Child of Thankfull Stephens Theodore Stedman Lucina Sted[man] Ester Barns And Martha Tailbourn..   19

.. To the Town of Farmington,, Rachel Parsons William Parsons Mary Evans Andrew Kinkead Eunice Buck Amos Parsons & wid Mary Byington..   19

Your Com^{tee} beg Leave Further to report that.. they Did proceed in Union with Southington Com^{tee} to preambulate Between the Towns to Ascertain ye Devision Line And to Erect monument which Business Completed.. on the 27th Day of Novr Last.. being Assisted by Solomon Whitman Ju^r County Surveyor..   19

..s^d Line is as follows (Viz) we Erected A Large Monument of Stone at the Northwest Corner of the Division Called the Long Lotts.. Erected on Samuel Lewis Lott a Monument of Stone.. & Erected in Thos Parsons Mowing Lott a Monument of Stones.. & Erected about one rod west of William Parsons House a Momument of Stone.. and Erected in Cornelious Dunhams Lott A monument of Stones, Thence South.. in Isaac Smith Lott a monument of Stones, Thence South.. & Erected in Silvanus Dunhams Lot A monument of Stones, Thence South.. and erected in Roswell Mores Lot a Monument of Stones, Thence South.. and Erected About   20

Farmington

10 rods South of Solomon Munsons House a Monument of Stones.. and Erected in Esqr Darling Lott a Monument.. and Erected in Isaac Woodruffs Lott a Monument of Stones..
4 Apr 1781

I the Subscriber in Consequence of An Abatement.. made by the Committees of.. Farmington And Southington Appointed to Settle & Adjust Accounts between the Towns of the Rates & Taxes.. Whether of the State or Town Laid Upon the Several Lists Anteceedent to the List of 1779.. to the Sum of £250 in Bills of Credit of this State Do.. fully & forever Discharge.. Farmington and Southington of.. Claims and Demands that I have.. Against s^d Towns... Solomon Cowles
the Com^{tee} after much Labour & Care Did Come to A Liquidation & Adjustment of the Accounts of the Originall Town of Farmington.. And find there is due from s^d Town the Sum of £487..0..4.. which being proport[ ] to.. Farmington & Southington.. there Appears to be Due from.. Southington.. £130..15..5.. Your Com^{tee} However beg Leave to say that there are Sundry Matters .. that Cannot be Determined at this Time And.. Suggest.. it would be Advisable to Defer a finall & Compleat Settlement.. Hez: Wadsworth.. Gad Stanley.. Ichabod Norton.. John Treadwell.. Timothy Root } Committee
6 Dec 1781

21

21

We the Subscribers the Com^{tee} of.. Southington do fully agree to the matters & things Contained in the foregoing Report.. Jonathan Root.. Josiah Cowles.. Daniel Lankton } Commitee of Southington
4 Apr 1781

21

Whereas we the Subscribers being.. A Com^{tee} to Ascertain a 20 Rod Highway lying on the East Side of the Sequestered Land.. formerly Drawn by the Agreement of three Surveyors to wit Mes^{rs} Wells Newberry and & Burnham And Approved by s^d Town.. from the Dweling House of Marvin Clark.. then we Began At the first Station and Ran a Course of North Two Degrees West as we found that the proper Course by Mr Solomon Whitman Ju^r Compose as he was Surveyor for Hartford County.. we found the Antient Monument placed by the s^d Surveyors Demolished but as there being a well Erected Monument A Stake & Stone About it placed by Elijah Porter formerly County Surveyor when the old Monument was in being Twenty East of s^d Corner in the place Called Harts Meadow.. Elijah Porter.. Noah Porter.. Solomon Whitman Ju^r } Com^{tee}
[ ] Feb 1781

22

Voted that they Abate to Thomas Shepart his /4^d Tax that was to be paid in Beaf Cattle At that Dec^n Noah Portter be Excused from Collecting the Same

22

Voted to Abate to Stephen Gridley the Town part of the Tax on his four fold of which Dec^n Porter is Collector on his paying A Single Part without Any Trouble

23

Voted that the Motion of Nehemiah Royce Respecting his four fold be Refered to the Selectmen

23

Voted on Reconsideration that Isaac Cowles be Exchused from being Constable & from Collecting the state Tax &c: And that William Wadsworth be Appointed Constable in his Room & to Gather the State Tax & Settle with Treasurer

23

Voted that Tim^o Root Thos Lewis Wm Wadsworth Hez^h Wadsworth Sam^{ll} North Ju^r in Northington Eldad Woodruff & Micah Woodruff in Kensington Elijah Hooker be.. Appointed A Com^{tee} in Adition to those allready Appointed .. to Inspect the State & Curcumstances of the Town and to Remove Incroachments & Nusances.. And they are hereby Required & Injoined to Exert themselves with Vigilence & Activity in the Business of their Commission particularly to Remove all Enchroachments on Such Highway that have Taken place within.. Fifteen years.. and to Institute proper Suits in the Law Against Some

23

Farmington

Individuals who Claim by Virtue of Fifteen Years Possession

Voted that Col: Noadiah Hooker John Treadwell Esqr Martin Bull Elijah Hooker Stephen Cole Gen[ll] Selah Heart Zeb[n] Peck Ju[r] Cap[t] Upson Cap[t] Grisley Col Stanley Cap[t] Jos[h] Woodford Jacob Foot Maj[r] Norton Jon[a] Belding James North Seth Wiard Jeremiah Griswould & Cap[t] Bunnel be A Com[tee] for the purpose of Classing the People	23
Voted that Col Hooker be A Com[tee] to Represent the Town Before the County Com[tee]	23
Voted that Sam[ll] Deming Daniel Gridley & Joshua Woodruff & Cap[t] Jos Woodford be Surveyors of Highways	23
Voted that Sol[n] Whitman Esq[r] John Treadwell Esq[r] Martin Bull & Seth Porter be Rate Makers	23
Voted to Abate to Abner Curtiss Ju[r] the Town part of the forefold Assessment Set to him in the Year 1780	23
Voted that the Liberty Granted to Cap[t] Bidwell to Set up a grist mill on the fulling mill Brook be Continued untill October Next & if he Shall Not Compleat A Mill by that Time then the Mill Place to be Sold by the Selectmen to the Highest Bidder	23

[ ] Apr 1781

Voted that Cap[t] John Allyn Joseph Byington & Cap[t] Peter Curtiss be A Com[tee] to Hire the Solders Wanted to fill Up the Continentall and to Settle the Dispute with Col: Hooker and other Deficient Glasses	23
Voted that Bithiah Dewey be A Lister	24
Voted that Roger Hooker be A Surveyor	24

Apr 1781

Voted to Remit the Following Rates on the 1½ Tax Simeon Newel Collector.. To Robert Booth 6/0[d] To Robert Rowel 2/5: wid[w] Eunice Burr 2/3 To Eleazer Fisher 2/7 Sam[ll] Stedman 1/1 Sam[ll] Sears 3/4…. Fourfould Assesments.. Sam[ll] Bird 5/0 Kitt a Negro /8	24
Voted that the Selectmen be Impowred to Settle Acc[ts] with Col: Hooker As Treasurer for the /4[d] Tax Beaf Cattle	24
Voted that the.. Selectmen be Directed to Give An Order on the Treasurer.. to pay the Officers and Evidences Improved in y[e] Case Against Joseph Smith out of the moneys to be Collected of s[d] Smith	24
Upon the Memorial of John Lewis Ju[r] praying that the Note in the Towns favour Against himfor the Sum of Ten Pounds might be Abated Voted that they Grant the prayer of s[d] Memorial	24
Upon the Memorial of Simon Lincoln praying that the Town would order the Com[tee] for the Exchange of Highways in the parish of New Britain to Sell to him.. Land in the Highway Lately Occupied by Moses Barns, Dec[d] for a meet Recompence &c Voted to Grant the prayer	24

21 Jun 1782

Generall Selah Hert was Chosen Moderator	25
Voted that John Treadwell Esq[r] Cap[t] W[m] Judd Col Gad Stanley Generall Selah Heart be.. Appointed to attend the proposed Convention to Represent this Town	26

26 Aug 1782

Generall Selah Heart Moderator	26
Voted that Hez[h] Wadsworth Isaac Bidwell William Judd Esq[r] Noah Porter James Lusk For Kensington Parish James Percivall & Elijah Hooker For New Cambridge Royce Lewis & James Lee For Northington Joseph Woodford & W[m] Ford For New Britain Jon[a] Belding &	27

Farmington

Abell Clark For West Brittain Seth Wiard & Stephen Hotchkiss Esqr be Appointed A Com^{tee}
of Inspection and to Detect and Bring to Justice all Violators of the Laws of ye State
Respecting Illicit Trade &c:
Voted that John Treadwell William Judd and Noadiah Hooker Es^{rs} be A Com^{tee}.. of   27
Correspondence Upon the principles and for the Purposes in the Doings of the s^d Convention
[ ] Sep 1782
Voted that Col Noadiah Hooker Capt Tim^o Root Thos Lewis Asahel Wadsworth Martin Bull   27
Capt Peter Curtiss Ichabod Norton Maj^r Roger Hooker Doc^r Timothy Hosmer Reuben Hart
Esqr & Zeb^n Frisbee be added to Former Com^{tee} of Inspection
Voted that Ezra Yale be A Collector in the Room of Elisha Covey who Refused to Serve   27
Voted that the Com^{tee} for Exchangeing Highways.. to.. mark out the Limmitts of a   28
Convenient Plott of Ground.. in or Near the Town Plott Sufficient to Erect a Small House
Upon for the Use of Obadiah Andrus And Family with Small Garden Plott Adjoining
9 Dec 1782

Generall Selah Heart be A Moderator   28

Voted that Solomon Whitman Es^{qr} be Town Clerk   28

Selectmen } Noadiah Hooker Esqr Capt Timothy Root Elijah Hooker Leu^t James Lee Col Gad   28
Stanley Capt Joseph Woodford Seth Wiyard
Constables } Capt Peter Curtiss & he to Collect the State Tax & Settle with ye Treasurer   28
Daniel Barns Capt Stephen Nortton Leu^t James North David Gleason John Goodrich Zebulun
Frisbee
Grandjurors } Solomon Lankton Elijah Lewis John North Dan^{ll} North Ju^r Josiah Gillit   28
William Porter Timothy Wells Elihu Smith Sam^{ll} Hall David Newel Samuel Lowrey Robert
Barret Benj^a Andrews Judah Heart Ju^r Seth Stanley Leonard Belding Benj^a Bishop Eliakim
Marshell Eldad Woodruff Zachariah Heart Jeremiah Griswould Asa Yale & Timothy Wells
Tythingmen } Gabriel Curtiss Elnathan Whitman Gad Wadsworth John Brounson Elijah   28
Gridley Ju^r Gideon Roberts Judah Barns Sam^{ll} Heacox Abraham Brooks James Judd Ju^r
Elijah Heart Ju^r Joseph Woodruff Dudley Woodford Ezra Willcox Samuel Norton Joseph
Lankton Sam^{ll} Peck Amos Tubbs David Markas
Listers } Thomas Lewis Joseph Hooker Asahel Hooker Roger Woodford Capt William Judd   28
Baze Welles Asahel Wadsworth Josiah Norton Joseph Wells Ju^r Roger Norton Ju^r Thos
Hungerford Joseph Byington Josiah Peck David Gleason Levi Thomson John Tillotson
Josiah Dewey Elizur Heart Seth Stanley Seth Stanley Benj^a Belding Seth Peck Zeb^n Frisbee
Ju^r
Surveyors } Capt John Porter Isaac Cowles Samuel Smith John Woodruff Eli North   28
Carrington John Hamblin Elip^t Wadsworth Dan^{ll} Lowrey Martin Woodruff Elijah Cowles
Math^w Cadwell John [ ] Belding Jon^a Hart Abner Curtiss Ju^r Phinehas Cowles John Cowles
Dan^{ll} Root Jesse Brounson Elisha Fox James Stone Caleb Matthews [ ] James Beckwith
Dan^{ll} Johnson Sam^{ll} Carrington Noah Andrews Jacob Bartholomew Stephen Bushnell Enos
Ives Jos^h Chidsey Munson Hart Anthony Hart Seth Marshell Calvin Judd Capt Nath^{ll}
Churchel Thomas Hart Noah Stanley David Dewey Zachariah Heart Sam^{ll} Lounsbury Sam^{ll}
Hotchkiss Joel Hitchcock James Prichard Sam^{ll} Warner Jesse Fuller Ichabod Andrus John
Lowrey Benj^a Lewis Zeb^n Cole
Town Collectors } Elijah Cowles Ju^r Seth Deckerson Elijah Gaylord David Gleason James   29
Francess John Goodrich Goodrich Cornelious Cornwell
Fence vewers } Mathew Clark Noah Porter Barnabas Dunham Gideon Williams Dan^{ll} Bunnel   29
Justiss Webster Reuben Miller Sam^{ll} B: Bouge Isaac Lee Ju^r Joseph Booth Luke Gridly
Royce Lewis

Farmington

Sealers of Leather } Nath[ll] Wadsworth Noah Cowles Cap[t] Hez[h] Gridley Thomas Heart Micah Woodruff	29
Sealers of Measures } Elijah Porter Joseph Peck Jesse Brunson William Lee James Booth Reuben Miller Gideon Andrus	29
Sealers of weights } Cap[t] Isaac Bidwell Ezra Scovell Jeames Lee Ezek[ll] Woodford James North Seth Wiard	29
Brander of Horses } Tho[s] Cowles Ezra Scovill James Lee James North Ezekiel Woodford Timothy Woodruff	29
Key Keepers } Asa Hart Thomas Stanley Royce Lewis Sam[ll] C Bouge James North Zebulun Frisbee Ju[r]	29
Supply of Solders Families } Lemuel Andrus Levi Andrus Abell Clark Thomas Heart Jonathan Belding	29
Hog Haywards } Job Gridley Lemuel Smith Josiah Kilborn Robert Booth Elijah Rose	29
Voted that William Judd John Treadwell Esq[r] Gen[l] Selah Heart Col Isaac Lee Zebulun Peck Ju[r] Col Gad Stanley Maj[r] Ichabod Norton Simeon Hart Esq[r] be A Com[tee] to Devise Some plan or Means whereby the Expinces of the Town May be Retrenched or Lessened	29
Voted that Col Noadiah Hooker be Town Treasurer	29

[ ] Feb 1782

The Com[tee] Appointed.. to Join the Com[tee].. of Southington to Examine Adjust & Settle the Accounts Between the S[d] Towns.. report that Haveing Met.. on .. 31st Day of Decem[r] Last they Took into Consideration the State .. of the Notes & Executions of Melitia Delinquents & Liquidated & Settled the Same so far As related to the the Subject of our Commission All y[e] curcumstances of the Highways in the North Meadow And of Two Other Highways in.. Southington Laid out Before the Devision of s[d] Towns and Not yet fully paid for, also the Curcumstances of the Town Stock.. and do find that the Balance of Accounts Contained in our former Report is so Near the Truth that it will be for the Interest of the Town Except it.. Submitted by your most Obedient Humble Servants { Gad Stanley.. Ichabod Norton.. John Treadwell.. Timothy Root } Committee	30
We the Subscribers do Hereby fully Consent and Agree to the foregoing Report Containing the Result of our joint Determination { Jonathan Root.. Josiah Cowles.. Daniel Lankton Committee of Southington }	30

23 Dec 1782

The Com[tee] Appointed to Devise Ways & Means for the More prudent and aconomicall Management of Business of the Town.. beg Leave to Report.. { Selah Heart.. Gad Stanley.. John Treadwell.. Ichabod Norton } Committee	30
Voted that John Treadwell Esq[r] & Col Gad Stanley be A Com[tee] to Examine the Accounts of the Com[tee] for the Exchange of Highways in the Parish of New Cambridge	31

30 Dec 1782

Voted that Col Noadiah Hooker be A Constable and Collector of the State Tax in the Room of Cap[t] Peter Curtiss And to Settle with the Treasurer	31
Voted that Roger Hooker be A Constable and Collector of the Town Rate.. Voted that Roger Hooker be A Colletor of the Town Rate in the Room of Elijah Cowles Ju[r]	31
Voted that a Town Pound be Erected Near the Dweling House of Ens[n] John Wells under the Direction of Cap[t] Joseph Woodford	31
Voted that Leu[t] Baze Wells be a Key Keeper	31
Voted that Ezekiel Cowles Samuel Smith & Elizur Hart be a Com[tee] for the Supply of Solders Farmiylies	31

Farmington

Voted that Solomon Whitman Ju^r Dec^n Noah Porter Elnathan Hooker Capt Timothy Root & James Cowles be A Com^{tee} to Exchange Highways & to Remove Nusances	31
Voted that Ezekiel Cowles Ju^r be A Collector of the Town Rate in the Room of Roger Hooker	31
Voted that Col Hooker be Joined to the Com^{tee} Appointed to Look Into the Accounts of Com^{tee} of the Parish of New Cambridge for the Exchange of Highway &c	31
Upon the Memorial of Lemuel Wiard praying 4 or 5 rods in wedth for a Building Spott at the Southwest Corner of Ezra Scovills Lott to Extend the whole wedth of s^d Lott for a Building Spott.. Voted that the Com^{tee} for Exchanging Highways in the Parish of Kensington be Directed to Take the Subject.. into their Consideration	31

Apr 1782

Voted that Luke Gridley Elijah Lewis & John Goodrich Job Miller be Surveyors of Highway	31
Voted that Martin Bull & Samuel Richard Ju^r be Listers	31

30 Dec 1782

Voted that the Sellectmen be Directed to Vew.. the place Near where Capt Bidwell has Erected a Grist Mill and Grant to Stephen Brounson the Liberty he prays for if it may be and Not Incomode the Publick Nor Capt Bidwell	32
Upon the Petision of Noah Gillit Elijah Andrus & Others praying that the Doings of Com^{tee} for Exchanging Highways in Exchangeing A Certain Highway in the Parish Northington Under the Mountain With Maj^r Norton & that the Deed Conveying the Same May be made Void &c: Voted that Hez^h Wadsworth Timothy Woodruff & Dan^{ll} Curtiss be A Com^{tee} to Repair to the Society of Northington And to Vew the Curcumstances Hear the parties.. & Report	32

24 Feb 1783

Voted that Hez^h Wadsworth be A Moderator	32
Voted that Isaac Cowles be Constable & he to Collect the State Tax & to Settle with the Treasurer	32
Voted that Generall Selah Heart Col Noadiah Hooker & Col: Gad Stanly be A Com^{tee} to Vew the Ground proposed for A New Road in the Parish of Northington that may Serve the Publick as well as s^d Society in Room of Talcotts Road so as to Save the Expence of Building two Bridges Across the River	32
Voted that Joshua Finney be A Surveyor of Highways	32
Voted that William Smith be A Grandjuror	32
Voted that Solomon Whitman Ju^r be A Constable.. And to Collect the State Taxes & Settell with Treasurer	32

6 May 1783

Voted that Col: Isaac Lee & John Treadwell Esqr be Appointed a Com^{tee} or Agents.. at the Generall Assembly.. to Oppose the Memorial of Thomas Goodman & Others praying to the s^d Assembly to Appoint A Com^{tee} to Rebuild Called Talcott Bridge	33
Voted that Upon Joseph Smith paying.. within one month.. the Cost Arising on the Suit on which An Exe^n Now Lyeth Against him in favour of the Town that then the s^d Selectmen Stop all further proceeding on s^d Execution	33
Voted that Amos Clark be A Tything Man	33
Voted that John Treadwell Esqr Col Isaac Lee Hez^h Wadsworth Gen^{ll} Selah Heart & Col Gad Stanly be A Com^{tee} to Take Into Consideration the Act of Congress Granting to the Officers of the Army full pay for.. five years after a general peace Shall Take place	33

Farmington

Generall Selah Hart - - - Moderator	*33*
Voted that this Town do Approve of foregoing Draught as Containg the Sence of the Town on the Subject of Extra pay of the Officers of the Army and that it Committed into the Hand of Col: Isaac Lee and John Treadwell Esq' Representitives of the Town to be them Laid before the Generall Assembly *30 Jun 1783*	*34*
Voted tht John Treadwell Esq' be A Moderator	*34*
Voted that Col Noadiah Hooler Maj' Ichabod Norton & Col Gad Stanley be.. Appointed A Com^tee.. to take all proper Measures to Build a Bridge Over Farmington River Near the Center of Northington Parish	*34*
Voted y^t William Ford be Surveyor of Highways.. and his power to Extend through the whole parish with full power to Warn out the Inhabitants to work in the New Road so much As May be Nessesary to Make it feasible for the Publick Travall	*35*

Glastonbury

Town Meetings
1739-1837

Located at the Town Clerk's Office

Glastonbury

23 Jun 1774

Col⁰ Elizu' Talcott Chairman	59
Voted that Colonel Elizur Talcott William Welles Elisha Hollister Ebenezer Plummer Isaac Moseley Thomas Kimberly and Josiah Hale be a Committe of Correspondence	60

27 Dec 1774

Voted that Mes'ˢ Elizur Talcott William Welles Elisha Holister Elijah Hollister Elijah Smith Josiah Hale Thomas Kimberly Aron Hubbard & David Blush Chosen a Com^tee of Correspondence to See all Persons in this Town do Conform themselves to the doings of the Congress held at Philadelphia on the 5th of September 1774	63

20 Nov 1775

Aron Bayley a Transient Person was warned to Depart this Town	64

2 Mar 1775

James Patterson was warned to Depart this Town by Mr Howel Woodbridge one of the Selectmen	64
Allex' Mc Dowel was warned to Depart this Town	64

5 Sep 1775

Jonath Weaver was warned to Depart this Town	64

16 Oct 1775

Deliverance Warner was Warned to Depart this Town by Mr Howel Woodbrick, one of the Selectmen	64
one of the Selectmen.. warned Deliverance Warner to Depart this Town	64

30 Apr 1778

These may certify that Mr Hezekiah Wright who was formerly an Inhabitant.. has many Years last past lived in... East Windsor with his Family ceryifyed by Wm Wolcott.. Erastus Wolcott } the peace officers of.. East Windsor.. Benoni Olcott.. Ebenezer Grant.. Nathl House } Select men.. Edward Chapman Gran' .. a true Copy.. Test Wm Wells Reg'	64

9 Aug 1779

This may Certify that We the Subscribers.. Acknowledge Eunice Stark late of Colchester to be an Inhabitans.. & will Receive her as Such when ever She becomes Chargeable.. Jonathan Deming.. Joseph Isham Jun'.. Ephm Little Jun'.. John Taintor Selectmen.. John Waters Jus' Peace.. A true Copy Tes' Wm Welles Reg'	64

3 Jul 1778

This may Certify that Mr Daniel Harris, his Wife & Six Children are proper Inhabitants of New London and are desireous of Removing to Glastonbury.. John Hemsted Jus' Peace.. Martin Wait.. Edward Hallarn.. Thoˢ Harding Select-men.. a true Copy.. Test Wm Welles T Clerk	65

1 Feb 1780

Benjn Simson was warned to depart this Town	65

14 Feb 1780

then was John Strong warned to depart this Town	65

8 Sep 1780

then was W⁰ Rachel Strong & John Condly were warned to depart this Town	65

Glastonbury

1 Dec 1780
then Hendrick Tembleton was warned to depart this Town 65

5 Feb 1781
This is to certifie that David Robertson is an Inhabitant of.. Middletown.. Ch^y Whittelsy.. Hugh White.. Thomas Goodwin.. Isaac Miller } Selectmen of Middletown.. A true Copy Tes^t Josiah Hale Reg^r 65

13 Dec 1775
William Welles Esqr was Chosen Moderator 66
William Welles Esqr was Chosen Clerk 66
Elisha Hollister Jonathan House Samuel Welles Howel Woodbridge & Daid Blush ware Chosen Selectmen 66
Ebenezer Plummer was Chosen Town Treasurer 66
Gideon Hale Isaac Goodrich & Isaac Smith ware Chosen Constable.. & Gideon Hale & to gather the Country Rate 66
Jonathan Hubbard Joseph Bidwell & William House ware Chosen Grandjurors 66
Elijah Smith Thomas Kimberly Josiah Hale Aron Hubbard Thomas Hollister Ju^r & William Charmberlin ware Chosen Listers 66
Elizur Talcott Ju^r Samuel Welles Ju^r John Wickham Pelitiah Loveland & John Findley ware Chosen Collectors of Rates 66
Philip Selew Samuel Bidwell Joseph Churchel & Charles Andrews Junr ware Chosen Tythingmen 66
David Hale & David Wickham Chosen fence Viewers 66
Thomas Stevens Chosen Sealer of Waits & Measures 66
Thomas Loveland & Peter Treat Chosen Sealers of Leather 66
David Loveland & Samuel Bidwell Chosen Packers of Pork Beaf Tobacco &c 66
John Selew Timothy Hale Junr Benjamin House Theodore Hale Joel Brooks Peter Treat Elisha Goodrich Jonah Chapman Ashbel Algor Samuel Hills Benjamin Hodge Thomas Dickiinson Richard Skinner John Wyar & Ruben Risley ware Chosen Surveyors of Highways 66
Elizur Talcott William Welles Elisha Hollister Elijah Smith Thomas Kimberly Josiah Hale Elijah Hollister Aron Hubbard & Peter Huxford ware Chosen a Committe of Inspection to See all Persons in this Town do Conform themselves to the doings of the Continentall Congress 67
Voted to Axcept.. Laying out a Highway from Samuel Smiths House in Eastbury by Samuel Brooks House to Hartford Line 67
Voted that the Select men lay out a Highway from the Bridge by John Cabless Mill to the Bridge by Timothy Eastons 67
Vtoed that the Selectmen Lay out a Highway from Samuel Stratton House Southeast a Crost the forescore acre lotts to the Highway on the South Side of Said Lotts 67
Voted that Thomas Matson Junr Cow Yard may Serve to be a pound 67
Voted to Axcept of a Survey of a Highway made.. in the Year 1774 and now.. of a Highway from Samuel Treats House by Williams Tryons House to Chatham line 67

22 Jan 1776
Capt Elisha Hollister Chosen Moderator 68

Glastonbury

Voted that the Selectmen Vew.. a Highway from the Dwelling House of Henry Huxford.. near the Dwelling House of W^o Mary Kimberly & Hez^h Hubbard & in the most Convenient place to Bolton Line	68
Voted that the Selectmen Settle the Cost with the Charmberlins that Sued this Town (for a Highway) to the County Court	68
Voted that Mes^{rs} Joseph Moseley Wait Goodrich & Eleazer Wright be a Com^{te} to Vew.. where their Can be an alternation of a Highway in any other place than where the Select men have Layd out Through Samuel Smiths lot in Eastbury	68
Voted to Give Stephen Taylor the Two Last Rates	68
Voted to Aron Roberson forty Shillings for what Elisha Loveland Junr Stold from him	68

2 Sep 1776

Jonathan Welles Esqr Chosen Moderator	69
Voted that Mr Joseph Moseley be added to the Selectmen	69
Voted that Mes^{rs} Joseph Moseley Thomas Kimberly Eleazur Wright Elijah Hollister Benjn Hodge Joseph Goodale Nehemiah Strickland Thomas Hunt & Nathan Dickinson Chosen a Com^{tee} to Inspect Each able Bodied man in this Town and See wheather Each man is aquipt with a good Gun and if any man has a Gun not fixed.. to warn Such Person to get Such Gun well fixed within one week.. and if any Person is poor and not able to fix their Gun Then Such Person immedeadiately to Deliver Such Gun to the Selectmen.. to appoint Two Juditious freeholders to Apprize.. and fix Such Gun at the Cost of this Town, and if the owner.. Shall pay.. for fixing Said Gun within Six months, then the person to have his Gun otherwise the Selectmen to pay Said Person what Said Gun Shall be apprized at, and keep Said Gun	69
Voted that the Select men to purchas bullet molds of Serj^t Anderson for the benefit of this Town	69

11 Dec 1776

Jonathan Welles Esqr chosen Moderator	70
William Welles Esqr Chosen Clerk	70
Maj^r Howel Woodbridge Elisha Hollister Joseph Moseley Timothy Hale Ju^r Wait Goodrich Aron Hubbard & David Blush Chosen Selectmen	70
Ebenezer Plummer chosen Treasurer	70
Gideon Hale Isaac Goodrich & Isaac Smith Chosen Constables & Gideon Hale to gather the Country Rates	70
Joseph Bidwell & John How chosen Grandjurors	70
Daniel Hale Jonath Smith Mathew Miller Samuel Gibson Sam^{ll} Stratton Jonah Chapman Ashbel Algor Benjn Hodge Joseph Simons Amos Strong Abra^m Skinner Junr Samuel Hills John Wyar & Noah Tryon chosen Surveyors of Highways	70
David Hale & David Wickham Chosen fence Vewers	70
Elijah Smith Thomas Kimberly Josiah Hale Thomas Hunt Ruben Risley & John Findley ware Chosen Listers	70
Thomas Loveland & Peter Treat chosen Sealers of Lether	70
Timothy Easton David Loveland Solo^n Loveland & Samuel Bidwell Chosen Packers of Pork Beaf fish &c	70
Edward Benton George Stocking Junr Israel Brewer & Isaac Fox Chosen Tythingmen	70

Glastonbury

David Loveland Junr Eleazer Hubbard Junr Isaac Fox & William Charmberlin Chosen Collectors of Rates	70
Joseph Fox Stephen Hollister Thomas Hunt & Samuel Findley chosen Kee keeper of Pounds	70
Silvester Pulsefor Timothy Easton Samuel Welles Junr Jehiel Goodrich Richard Skinner & Thomas Dickinson ware Chosen Town Howards	71
Voted to Axcept of the Report of the Com^{tee} of altering the Highway Through Samuel Smiths lot in Eastbury	71
The Questin was put whether the Inhabitants.. would mend the Highways.. by a Rate made on the Ratable Estate &c Resolved in the affirmative And Mr Elijah Hollister was Chosen a Com^{tee} to prefer a Memorial to the General Assembly.. for a Confirmation of the Same	71

20 Jan 1777

Jonathan Welles Esqr Chosen Moderator	71
Col^o Elizur Talcott William Welles Thomas Kimberly Elijah Smith Eben^r Plummer Joseph Talcott Elijah Hollister Howel Woodbridge Elisha Hollister & Aron Hubbard ware Chosen a Com^{tee} of Inspection	71

28 Mar 1777

Jonathan Welles Esqr was Chosen Moderator	71
Isaac Moseley Thomas Kimberly Josiah Hale Eben^r Plummer Samuel Hills & Isaac Hale Chosen a Com^{tee} to provide provisions for the families of those Soldiers that Shall inlist in the Continentall Service	71

7 Apr 1777

Thomas Kimberly be a Committe to acquaint.. the Governor that this Town has made Choice of Mr Isaac Goodrich to be Captain in the Continentall Service for the incorageing of Soldiers to Enlist	72

23 Sep 1777

Jonathan Welles Esqr Chosen Moderator	72
William Welles Eleazer Wright Josiah Hale John Findly Asa Talcot Samuel Hills & Ruben Risley Chosen a Committe to provide Shirts Frocks Stockings Shews & overhalls for the Soldiers in the Continentall Army	72

7 Apr 1777

Voted that Mr Thomas Kimberly be a Committe to acquaint.. the Governor that this Town has Made Choice of Mr Isaac Goodrich to be their Captain	73
Voted that Mes^{rs} Noah Tryon Eleazer Wright William Stevens Thomas Hollister Junr & Amos Strong be a Com^{tee} to Joyn the Lister in assessing the Inhabitants	73

10 Dec 1777

Jonathan Welles Chosen Moderator	74
William Welles Esqr Chosen Clerk	74
Elizur Talcott Timothy Hale Junr and Eleazer Wright Chosen Selectmen	74
Eben^r Plummer chosen Town Treasurer	74
Gideon Hale & Isaac Smith Chosen Constables and Gideon Hale Chosen together the Country Rate	74
Elisha Hale Jonathan Smith Josiah Hale Joseph Simons Benjamin Hodge Aaron Hubbard John Hodge Nathan Dickinson John Findly & Elizur Loveland Chosen Surveyors of Highways	74

Glastonbury

Josiah Hale Elisha Hale Samuel Welles Junr Ruben Risley Aaron Hubbard Stephen Goodrich & Amos Strong Chosen Listers	74
Solomon Loveland & Samuel Bidwell Chosen packers of Beaf Pork Tobacco &c	74
Thomas Stevens Chosen Brander of Horses & Sealer of Waits & measures	74
Ambr^s Neckolson Stephen Hollister Thomas Hunt Chosen kee keepers to Pounds	74
Voted that the Selectmen make no Rate on the poles of George Stocking & his 3 Sons that are Deceas^d	74
Voted that David Hollister John Hollister Asa Goodale & David Blush be Collectors of Rates	74
Voted Thomas Loveland & Peter Treat Chosen Sealers of Leather	75
David Hale & David Wickham Chosen fence Vewers	75
Joseph Bidwell & Malatiah Nye Chosen Grandjurors	75
William Moseley George Talcott Gideon Hollister Junr & Isaac Fox Chosen Tythingmen	75
Elijah Hollister Jehiel Goodrich Joseph Moseley & Daniel Hale Chosen Hawards	75
Edward Benton Elisha Hale & Isaac Smith Chosen a Committe to provide Clothing and provisions for the non Commission Officers & Soldiers Families that are in the Continentall Service that are poor	75
Voted that the Selectmen Lay out or make the Highways by Joseph Goodales House and the Highway Leading to the Meeting House Wider	75
Elijah Smith Joseph Talcott Joseph Moseley John Welles Elisha Hollister Elizur Hubbard & Wait Goodrich Chosen a Com^{tee} of Inspection	75

21 Dec 1777

Voted to Give Martha Kilborn her Town Rate on the List 1775 2/10^d and Edward Potter his Rate that Year 3/9	75
Voted that the Town Clerk represent Peter Peas & & the Rest that Listed under him to.. the Govonor the State of their Case &c	76
Voted that the Selectmen View the new Highway Layd out by Samuel Strattons and if they do not alter to have it Seettled according to Law	76

7 Jan 1778

William Welles Esqr Chosen Moderator	76

14 Jan 1778

Voted that William Welles Esqr & Aaron Hubbard Chosen Selectmen	76
Voted that the Selectmen Tender to Thomas Hunt 3/ p^r Yard for 27 Yards of Toe Cloth that Said Hunt Left with Capt Elisha Hollister one of the Selectmen the Last fall or Summer for the benefit of this Town, and if Said Hunt Shall Refuse to Axcept the Same and Sue, the Selectmen are to Defend the Same at the charge of this Town &c	77

20 Apr 1778

Jonathan Welles chosen Moderator and William Wells Town Clerk	77
Voted that the Selectmen be impowered to Sell.. a piece of common Land lying near Abraham Skinners	77

20 Mar 1778

Col^o Elizur Tallcott chosen Moderator and Isaac Goodrich Clarck	77
Voted that Mes^{rs} Theodore Hale.. Philip Selew.. Elisha Hollister.. Nathan Dickerson.. Joseph Goodale.. Thomas Hollister } be a Committee to purchase Cloathing for the Officers &	77

Glastonbury

Soldiers of the Continental Army	
Voted that the Select-men settle with Elisha Goodrich for a Highway	77
14 Dec 1778	
Jonathan Welles Esq[r] Chosen Moderator at a Town Meeting	78
Eleazer Wright Timothy Hale Jun[r] Samuel Wells Aaron Hubbard & Maletiah Nye be Selectmen	78
William Wells Chosen Town Clark	78
Ebenezer Plummer chosen Town Treasurer	78
Gideon Hale & Isaac Smith Chosen Constables.. Said Gideon Hale was chosen to Collect the Country Rates	78
Jonathan Smith, Elisha Hale, Josiah Hale, Joseph Bidwell, Stephen Goodrich, Noah Tryon, Israel Hollister, Benjamin Andrews, Job Risley, Samuel Hills, David Blush Ju[r], David Bigelow & Charles Andrews Ju[r] Chosen Surveyors of Highways	78
David Hale, John Stevens & David Wickham Chosen Fence Viewers	78
Josiah Hale, Benoni Smith, Joseph Mosely Elizur Hubbard & John Fiendly Chosen Listers	78
Elijah House, Joseph Wells & Samuel Hills Ju[r] & W[m] Chamberlin Chosen Collectors of Town Rates.. and Joseph Goodale Ju[r] is also Chosen to collect the remainder of those Rates which his Brother Asa omitted	78
Israel Smith & Thomas Loveland chosen leather-Sealers	78
Joseph Bidwell, Elisha Hollister and Joseph Simons Chosen Grandjurors	78
Samuel Smith, John Gains, Levi Loveland and John Wiar Chosen Tythingmen	78
Solomon Loveland, Samuel Bidwell & Nehemiah Hollister chosen Packers of Pork, Beef & Tobacco &c	79
Thomas Stevens chosen Brander of Horses and Sealer of Weights & Measures	79
Ambrose Nickolson, Stephen Hollister, Thomas Hunt & W[m] Chamberlin chosen Key Keepers	79
Elezur Hubbard & John Wells Chosen a Com[tee] to provide for the Soldiers Families	79
Elisha Hale, Philip Selew, Elijah Hollister, Joseph Goodale & Nathan Dickerson Ju[r] chosen a Committee to provide Clothing for the Continental Army	79
Voted to pay Moses Lott for his Snapsack & Blanket worn out in the Continental Service	79
Voted that the Selectmen order about a Highway at the East end of the Three Mile Lots agreeable to M[r] Joseph Mosely's Request	79
Voted that Mis[rs] Ebenezer Plummer, Joseph Mosely, Wait Goodrich, Aaron Hubbard, Elisha Hollister & David Bigelow be a Committee to take Care of the Town Moneys and pay to Each Society their Proportion	80
Voted that the Selectmen act their Judgment with regard to the Highway by Hubbards Mill	80
Voted that the Selectmen order about opening the Highway west of Benjamin Andrews House	80
Voted to give Wid[o] Martha Fox her Rate being 5/1[d] and Edward Potter his Rate 12/ and Benoni Dwolf his Rate 1/7[d]	80
Voted that the Highway by Elizur Loveland & Lemuel Tubbs, Shall run North of both of their Houses according to the old Survey	80
Voted to pay Cap[t] Elisha Hollister, the Debt & Cost which Tho[s] Hunt has recovered against him for a Piece of Toe Cloth	80

Glastonbury

25 Jan 1779

Colonel Elizur Talcott Chosen Moderator	80
Voted that the Town pay to Mr Elijah Hollister £39..17..6, with the Interist from May last, for Two Barrels and a half of Pork, that s^d Holister dealt out to the Melitia when called out upon Duty, which Pork Mr Shaw of New london Claims, as being his Property	80
Voted that the Town pay to Mr Nathaniel Hollister Fifteen Shilling per Yard for a Piece of Toe Cloth that he let Mesu^r Joseph Mosely & Capt Wait Goodrich have when Selectmen	81
Voted to pay Capt Elisha Hollister 3/ per Yard for about 22 Yards of Toe Cloth that he let the Selectmen have for making a Tent	81
Voted to let Mrs Sarah Lyman have those Tools & Cloths that her Father Bartlet gave her	81
Voted that Mess^{ur} Joseph Mosely, Matthew Miller & Elisha Hale be a Committee to prevent Cutting Timber on public Highways, and to prosecute all Offenders	81
Voted that Capt Samuel Wells, Timothy Hale & Eleazer Wright be a Committee to Settle with Capt Jon^n Wells about some Town Deeds now in his possession	81

18 Jun 1779

Col^n Elezur Talcott Chosen Moderator	81
Voted .. that a Rate of 1/6 upon the Pound be made for the raising of money in order to purchase Cloathing for the Continental Soldiers of this State.. & voted that David Hale Ju^r George Tallcott Benj[ ] Hale Abra[ ] Skinner Ju^r & John How Ju^r be Collectors	81

6 Aug 1779

Co^l Elizur Tallcott Chosen Moderator	82
Voted that Capt Wait Goodrich, Lieu^t Colo^l Howel Woodbridge, Capt Joseph Moseley, Aaron Hubbard & Capt Elizur Hale Ju^r be a Committee of Inspection	82
[*Voted*] to Set up a House.. for Prince a free Negro, & Family and also to Examin, in order to find out who was to set up the said Princes House, at the Time the s^d Prince Enter[ ]d the Continental Service, and how the s^d Prince's House became pulled down, afer being set up.	82

13 Dec 1779

Jonathan Welles Esqr Chosen Moderator	82
Capt Samuel Welles, Timothy Hale Junr Capt Elisha Hollister, Josiah Hale, & David Blush chosen Select-men	82
Wm Welles Chosen Town Clerk	82
Ebenezer Plummer Chosen Town Treasurer	82
Gideon Hale, Isaac Smith & Elisha Hale Chosen Constables.. and s^d Elisha Hale was Chosen to Collect the State Taxes	82
Melitiah Nye, Jonath Smith, Elisha Hale, Liu^t Wm Miller, Joseph Bidwell, John Hodge, Noah Tryon, Benjn Hodge, Samuel Hills, Nathan Dickerson, Charles Andrews Junr, Joseph Churchel, Wm Chamberlin & Samuel Covel Chosen Surveyors of Highways	83
David Hale, David Wickham & John Stevens Chosen Fence Viewers	83
Capt Elizur Hubbard, John Findley, Capt Elizur Hale, Doc^t Isaac Moseley & Jonath Brace Chosen Listers	83
John Hale, Elizur Miller, Elisha How, Benjamin Hodge Junr & Thomas Dickerson Chosen Collectors of Town Rates	83
David Wickham, Israel Smith, & Thomas Loveland Junr Chosen Leather Sealers	83
Samuel Stratton, & Samuel Brooks Chosen Grandjuri-men	83

Glastonbury

George Hollister, John Shipman, David Dickerson Junr & Daniel Miles Junr Chosen Tything-men	83
Solomon Loveland & Samuel Bidwell Chosen Packers of Beef Pork Tobacco &c	83
Thomas Stevens Chosen Brander of Horses and Sealer of Weights & Measures	83
Ambrse Nickleson, Stephen Strickland, Stephen Hollister & Thomas Hunt chosen Kee Keepers	83
Capt Wait Goodrich, Capt Joseph Moseley Lie^t Col^n Howel Woodbridge, Aaron Hubbard Esqr, & Capt Elizur Hale Chosen a Committee of Inspection	83
Voted.. that the Select-men view the land upon the Green & make Report.. at Y^e Request of Ambse Nickleson	83
Voted that Thomas Materson Ju^r have Liberty to erect a Grist-mill near the House of Joseph Hollister	83

22 Dec 1779

Voted that the Select-men view the Land upon the Green & agreeable to Ambrose Nicklesons Request to give him.. a Lease of Ten or Twelve Rods of Land for a Term not exceeding 999 Years	84
voted that Elizur Tryon be a Tything-man in the room of John Shipman who has not taken the Oath of Fidelity, and the said Tryon took the Oath accordingly	84
voted that a Committee be Chosen to provide for the Soldiers Families and Mes^{surs} Joseph Moseley, Edward Benton, Elijah Hollister, Melitiah Nye Elizur Hubbard, Job Risley, Noah Tryon & Ephraim Hubbard Ju^r be a Committee for that purpose	84
Voted that the Survey of a Highway from Joseph Churchels Land to Samuel Brooks Land.. be accepted	84
Voted that the Select-men Turn the Road on Thomas Mattersons Land below the Rocks where it used to Run, or was once thrown out for a Highway & open the same immediately, & also appoint a Committee to assess the Damages in this Turning of it, and make Report.. to the next annual Town Meeting, all which Damages & Cost to be at the Expence of Doc^t Isaac Moseley & Amos Matterson	84
Voted that the Select-men order about turning the Road where it Runs up a Steep Hill near the West End of Elijah Hodges Lot	85
George Tallcott Capt Benoni Smith and Nathan Dickerson Chosen Chosen Listers in addition to those before Chosen.. & Doc^t Isaac Moseley excused	85
voted that a Committee be Chosen to prevent Wood & Timber being needlessly carried out of Town, and that none shall be carried out, without the .. Consent of the Committee Chosen for that Purpose.. Voted that Elijah Hollister, Joseph Bidwell, Wm Stevens, Hosea Fox & Benjn Smith be a Committee for the above Purpose	85
Voted that the Select-men open that Road by Aaron Robersons House	85
Voted that Benjn Smith & Samuel Smith have Liberty to Erect a Saw-mill between Capt Goodrich's Grist-mill & Colo^l Tallcott's Saw-mill, they taking a Skilful man to examin the Place & to say whether or no the Erecting of a Mill.. will.. damage either of the above s^d mills	85
Voted that the Selectmen Settle with Doc^t Elizur Hale & Samuel Smith for a Highway throught their Land	86
Voted that the Highway leading from Molbury by Wid^o Kimberley be opened	86
Voted that the following Rates be given (viz) Eliphalet Foxs £1..13.0 Joseph Scotts £1..7..0 W^o Mary Treat £1..10..0 Sonny Negros £1..7..0 Eliphalet Foxs £1..2..0 Thomas Eddys £0..4..0 Sonny Negro 18/ Joseph Scotts 18/ Jabez Lewis 2/1^d Ezekiel Wilcoxs 4/7^d Edward Potter £1..3..0 Felix Lindsley 18/	86

Glastonbury

6 Mar 1780

Jonathan Welles Esq[r] Chosen Moderator	86
Eleazer Wright, Peter Treat, Cap[t] Wait Goodrich, Col Howel Woodbridge, W[m] Stevens, Cap[t] Elizur Hale, John Findley, Lieu[t] Thomas Hollister, Theodore Hale, Reuben Risley & Lieu[t] Stephen Goodrich be a Committee, or Inspectors of Provisions	86

17 Apr 1780

Cap[t] Isaac Goodrich Chosen Moderator	87
Voted.. that a Memorial be present,d to the General Assembly.. to get Liberty to make a Rate.. to Raise Money.. to furnish all Supplies of Men that, Shall be Called to actual Service.. and voted that Jonathan Welles Esq[r] draw the s[d] Memorial & that M[r] Ebenezer Plummer present the same	87
Voted that the Selectmen adjust the Accounts with Jonathan Hollister for keeping Thomas Scott	87
Voted that the Select-men Settle with Ezekiel Tubbs for the Building of a Bridge on his Land	87
Voted that the Select-men Settle with Elisha Treat for a Carriage & Horse that he employ,d in transporting the Baggage for the Militia	87
Voted that the Select-men lay-out a Highway.. across Lieu[t] Timothy Hales, Eleazur Hubbards & Elizur Hubbards Land, agreeable to Joseph Tallcott's Request	87
Voted that the Select-men Settle with Levi loveland for Two Highways lay,d out on his Father's Land	87
Voted that the Select-men alter the Road leading from John Millers to Elijah Hodges House	87

2 May 1780

Voted.. that a Petition.. be presented to the General Assembly.. for Liberty to make a Rate.. to raise money as an extraordinary Encouragement for men to go into the Service when called, and to enable us to collect the same, as other Taxes are.. Jonathan Welles Esq[r] & M[r] John Welles be Agents for this Town to present the s[d] Petition	88
Voted that M[r] Gideon Hale have Liberty to do acrost the Highway.. to drain the Pond South of his House, he making a Bridge over the Ditch	88
Voted that Samuel Smith have Liberty to move his Fence West of Richard Crarys House	88
Voted that a Committee be appointed to give Instructions to our Representatives to use their utmost influence in the General Assembly to have the Mode of Taxation alter,d, that each one may pay in proportion to what he possesses.. and also voted that M[r] Elijah Smith, Cap[t] Elizur Hale & W[m] Welles be a Com[tee] for the above purpose	88

2 May 1780

Voted that the Selectmen.. see whether Warren,s Family, who is a Continental Soldier be provided for & also whether he counts for this Town	88

12 Jun 1780

voted that Cap[t] Stephen Goodrich, Cap[t] Benoni Smith, Cap[t] Timothy Hale, Cap[t] Elizur Hubbard, Cap[t] Elizur Hale & Ensign Amos Strong be a Committee to hire and procure so many Men, as shall be called.. to Serve in the State, or Continental Service	89
and voted that the Select-men make a Rate adequate for the above Purpose.. And voted that Elizur Miller, John Hale, Elisha How & Thomas Dickerson be Collectors	89
Voted that Mes[urs] Gideon Hale, Stephen Goodrich, Nathan Dickerson & Josiah Benton Ju[r] be added to the Committee who provide for the Soldiers Families	89
Voted that the Select-men act their Discretion, with regard to selling too or exchanging with W[m] Willes, the South End of that Highway Runing by W[m] Heldreths House	89

Glastonbury

Voted that Col Elizur Tallcott have a Committee to view a Highway on his Land agreeable to a former Vote.. supposed to be illegal for such Business, which Vote is as follows --- Voted that Capt Wait Goodrich, Eleazer Wright & Elijah Hollister be a Com^{tee} to view a Highway Runing acrost his Land agreeable to his Request, and at his Expence, and make a Report.. to the next annual meeting 89

23 Jun 1780

Capt Isaac Goodrich Moderator 90

Voted that Capt Stephen Goodrich, Capt Timothy Hale, Capt Benoni Smith, Capt Elizur Hubbard, Capt Elizur Hale & Ensign Amos Strong be a Committee to procure what Men shall be called from this Town, to the State or Continental Service 90

Voted that Mess^{urs} Joseph Hide, Isaac Plummer Elisha How & Thomas Dickerson be Collectors to collect the Rates order'd 90

20 Nov 1780

Jonathan Welles Esqr Chosen Moderator 90

Colo Newel Woodbridge, Capt Wait Goodrich Capt Elizur Hubbard & Nathan Dickerson Chosen a Committee to hire Men to fill up our Quota of Recruits in the Continental Army 90

Voted that Wm Wells be appointed to purchase & put up the Town's Quota of Provisions 91

Stephen Strickland Junr Nathaniel Tallcott Junr & David Blush Junr were Chosen Collectors to Collect those Rates, which were order'd to be Raised by this Meeting 91

Voted that Wm Welles have Liberty to borrow.. Money for the purchasing of Provisions 91

19 Sep 1775

Samuel Bidwell Elizur Hale Junr Jonathan Hale Junr John Welles Elizur Tryon John Shipman Elizur Talcott Junr John Jopp & Ezekiel Tubbs were admitted Freemen & Sworn 92

15 Sep 1778

the following persons (viz) Captain Samuel Wells, Jonathan Brace Thomas Hollister & Philip Perce took the Oath of Fidelity, and the Freemans Oath also, excepting Philip Perce, before Elizur Tallcott Jus^t Peace 92

Elizur Tryon, Benjamin Chamberlin & Steven Shipman Ju^r took the Freemans Oath 92

30 Apr 1779

Nehemiah Hollister, Charles Rieley, Benjn Hodge Ju^r Adonijah Scott Simion Strickland & Plenny Hollister have taken the Oath of Fidelity before me.. Elizur Tallcott Jus^t Peace 92

1779-80

The following Persons took the Oath of Fidelity before Elizur Tallcott Jus^t Peace (viz) Samuel Hills Ju^r Aaron Hollister John Stratton Elijah Hubbard David Smith Felix Lindsey Amos Fox & Barnabas Fuller 92

10 Apr 1780

the following Persons took the Freemans Oath (viz) Samuel Brooks Wm Holmes, Jonathan Treat, Philip Covel Elijah Covel Wm Hale Elizur Loveland Joseph Temple Aaron Robinson Hezekiah Hubbard Junr, Joseph Buel Levi Loveland Joseph Matson Isaac Tallcott 92

8 Apr 1781

the following Persons were admitted Freeman (viz) Ebenezer Goodale, Eliphalet Rice, & Joseph Welles 92

16 Sep 1777

An account of those Persons that Took the Oath of Fidelity and the freemans Oath.. (viz) 93

Glastonbury

Elizur Talcott William Welles Jonathan Welles Eben^r Plummer David Goodrich Josiah Benton Asa Talcott George Talcott Gideon Hale Isaac Smith Joseph Mosely Timothy Hale Wait Goodrich Elisha Hollister David Dickinson Benjamin Hodge Benoni House Benjamin House Samuel Wright Thomas Hunt Benjamin Stevens Joseph Kilborn Ambrous Nickolson Jonathan House John How Benoni Smith John Taylor Eleazer Wright Solomon Loveland Joseph Goodale Richard Fox Abraham Hollister Junr William House Asaph Colman Stephen Shipman John Findly Jabez Whelden John Hodge Peter Huxford.. David Bluss..

.. Bluss George Welles Josiah Hale Benjamin Risley David Hale Samuel Rice Edward Benton Benjamin Hale Jonathan Hubbard John Jopp Wm Charmberlin John Welles Daniel Charmberlin Isaac Fox Timothy Hale Junr Benjamin Wetherel Amos Hollister Jonathan Hollister Eben^r Benton Samuel Stratton John Brook Ephraim Hubbard Samuel Peas Timothy Morley Hosea Fox Joseph Goodale Junr Nathaniel Hollister Jonah Chapman Gideon Hollister Junr Peter Treat Noah Tryon Eph^m Hubbard Junr John Hodge Ju^r John Goodrich Samuel Welles Ju^r Elisha Hale Elijah Hodge Jonath Taylor Elijah Hollister Samuel Gibson Elizur Talcott Junr Daniel Andrews Elijah Stevens William Miller Elijah Smith Samuel Price Stephen Hollister.. Benjn Smith Stephen Strickland Nehe^h Strickland Malatia Nye.. 93

.. Ruben Risley Nez^h Hubbard Elizur Hubbard Aaron Hubbard Matthew Miller David Biglow Daniel Hale Samuel Smith Hezekiah Bidwell Ruben Sparks Israel Brewer Abijah Miller Thaddeus Welles Nathan Dickinson Benjn Tryon Nathl Talcott Amos Matson Jonath Webster William Moseley Philip Slew Stephen Shipman Junr Daniel Ward Joseph Talcott Amos Strong all the above Named are Freemen And all Sworn (but Wm Welles) before me William Welles Justice Peace.. 93

.. the Same day Wm Welles Esqr was Sworn before me Jonathan Welles Justice Peace 93

7 Dec 1778

The following Persons (viz) Job Risley, Gideon Hollister, Thomas Hollister Wm Welles and John Follon.. took the Oath of Fdelity to the United States of America before Jonathan Welles Jus^t Peace 94

13 Jan 1779

.. Then Elizur Bell & Caleb Tennant Elisha Hills took the Oath of Fidelity before Jonathan Welles Jus^t Paces 94

This certify that Timothy Stevens has taken the the Oath of Fidelity to this State before me.. Jonth Welles Jus^t Pac^s 94

This certify that David Loveland has taken the Oath of Fidelity to this State before me Jonath Welles Jus^t Peace 94

Oath of Fidelity taken by Ezra Tryon Elizur Hale, Howel Woodbridge, Stephen Fox, Joseph Bidwell, Aaron Gool, Joel Brook, Henry Huxford, David Dickinson Ju^r Charles Andrews Benjamin Andrews, Jonathan Bidwell, Jonathan Peas, Asa Goodale, Jonathan Smith Hez^h Wickham Theodore Hale, Joseph Hollister Wm Stevens, Stephen Goodrich, Joseph Simons, John Wickham, Thomas Risley, Amos Matson, John Selew, Theodore Hollister, Elizur Tryon, Levi Loveland, Ashbel Algar, Peleg Seldon, Elizur Loveland, Peletiah Loveland, Benjn Hunter, Samuel Bidwell, George Hollister, Abiathur Camp, Wm Heldreth, Wm Fox, Jonah Fox, Thomas Loveland Ju^r, Eben^r Scott, Ezek^l Tubbs, David Daniels, Elisha How. Silvester Pulsefer, John Webster, Isaac Goodale.. Abraham Skinner Ju^r, Benjn Skinner.. 94

..Benjn Chamberlin, Thomas Dickinson, Thomas Hollister Ju^r, Isaac Mosely, Elisha Goodrich, Nehemiah Wyar, Samuel Covel, John Wyar, Pheneas Grover, Gehiel Goodrich, Joseph Bewel, John Miller, Ephraim Wyllys, Eze^l Skinner, John Wyllys, Joseph Tryon, Charles Andrews Ju^r, John How Ju^r, Edward Potter, Lemuel Tubbs, Eleazer Hubbard, Philip Cove, John Stevens, John Cross, Lemuel Peas, Samuel Brooks, James Wyar, Malin Woodruff, Eben^r Goodale, James Wright, Appleton Holms, Lemuel Jones, Eben^r Fox, Elijah 94

Glastonbury

Covel, ..

.. Thomas Brooks Ju^r, John Covel, Demick Morley Israel Fox, Wm Holms, Jeduthun Smith, Nathl Gains, Thomas Stevens, Isaac Goodrich, George Goodrich, Jon^o Gains 95
12 Apr 1779

At a Freema[n]s Meeting.. took the Oath of Fidelity the following Persons (viz) Hezekiah Wright, Richard Chamberlin and Jeremiah Wright. Also at s^d Meeting the Freemans Oath was administred to Richard Chamberlin, Hezekiah Wright, David Loveland Wm Wells, Hezekiah Wickham Jeremiah Wright Jonathan Peas, Martin Woodroof, Timothy Morley, Samuel Bidwell, Joseph Hollister, Joel Brooks, David Wickham Isaac Moseley, Phineas Grover Isaac Goodale Thomas Dickenson, and Samuel Covel 95
21 Sep 1779

Took the Oath of Fidelity & Freemans Oath Thomas Matson and Richard Skinner 95

19 Oct 1780

This certifies that Wm Dutton, once a British Prisoner, has taken the Oath of Fidelity to this State Certified p^r Jonathan Welles Jus^t Pac^s 95

This certifies that John Hotchkiss has taken the Oath of Fidelity to this State.. Jonathan Welles Jus^t Peace 95

These Certify that Samuel Nouland has taken the the Oath of Fidelity.. Jon^a Welles Just Peace 95

1 Jun 1780

the following Persons took the Oath of Fidelity (viz) David Loveland Ju^r Elijah Hill, Abraham Tallcott, Thaddeus Welles Junr Richard Smith Lazarus Wheeler David Fox & Nathaniel Tallcott Junr Elezarus House 95

The Oath of Fidelity by Joseph Churchel and Josiah Brooks taken before Jonth Wells Jus^t Peace 95

18 Sep 1781

At a Freemans Meeting.. The following Persons took the Freemans Oath Nathaniel Tallcott Ju^r Benjn Hodge Ju^r Joseph Churchell Samuel Treat Dorotheus Treat George Hollister 95

20 Nov 1780

Then the Oath of Fidelity.. was Administered to David Goodrich.. Certified p^r Elizur Tallcott Justicei Peace 95

15 Jan 1782

The Oath of Fidelity Taken by Elizur Goodrich Benjn Hale Ju^r & Lazarus Loveland before Elizur Tallcott Jus^t Peace 96

8 Apr 1782

At a Freemans Meeting.. Then the Freeman Oath was taken by Dimock Morley & Josiah Benton J^r & Josiah Benton J^r took the Oath of Fidelity before me Elizur Tallcott Jus^t Peace 96

7 Apr 1783

At a Freemans Meeting.. Then the Oath of Fidelity & Freemans Oath was taken by Theodore Woodbridg & Isaac Welles before Elizur Tallcott Jus^t Pac^s 96

16 Sep 1783

Then the Freemans Oath was taken by George Stevens & the Oath of Fidelity by Oliver Tallcott before Elizur Tallcott Jus^t Pac^s 96

11 Dec 1780

Jon^a Welles Esqr Chosen Moderator 98

Glastonbury

Capt Samuel Wells, Mr Josiah Hale, Capt Elisha Hollister, Mr David Blish & Capt Stephen Goodrich Chosen Select-men	98
Wm Welles Chosen Town Clerk	98
Mr Ebenezer Town Treasurer	98
Gideon Hale & Isaac Smith Chosen Constables.. & Said Gideon chosen to Collect the State Taxes	98
Josiah Fox, Joseph Bidwell & Thomas Stevens Chosen Grand-jurors	98
Jon^a Smith Elisha Hale, Elisha Goodrich, Joel Brooks, Isaac Fox, Benjn Hodge, Samuel Hills, Joseph Churchel, James Wiar, Wm Chamberlin, Joseph Goodale, Nathan Dickerson & David Holllister Chosen Surveyors of Highways	98
Aaron Gool, Benjn Hodge Ju^r, John Hodge & Eleazer House Chosen Tythen-men	98
David Hale & David Wickham chosen Fence-viewers	98
George Tallcott, Nathaniel Tallcott Junr, Elisha Hale, Joseph Churchel & Isaac Tallcott chosen Listers	98
Ezekiel Skinner, George Hollister, Wm Goodrich & Joseph Hollister Junr chosen Collectors of Rates	98
Solomon Loveland & Samuel Bidwell Chosen Packers of Beef, Pork &c	98
Lieu^t Thomas Stevens chosen Brander of Horses & Sealer of Weights & Measures	98

11 Dec 1780

Vieto Forrest, Stephen Strickland, Stephen Hollister & Thomas Hunt Chosen Kee keepers	98

11 Dec 1780

Israel Smith David Goodrich & Wm Chamberlin Chosen Leather Sealers	98

19 Dec 1780

Voted that Jabez Wealding be a Lister	99
Voted that Col Howd Woodbridge, Capt Wait Goodrich, Capt Elizur Hubbard & Mr Nathan Dickerson be a Committee to procure what men Shall be called.. to fill up the Battallions.. for the Defence of our Sea Costs	99
Voted that Capt Isaac Goodrich be a Com^{tee} to provide for the Soldiers Families Such necessaries as they are entitled to..	99
Voted that Charles Andrus Junr be a Com^{tee} man to assist in Purchasing & Receiving our Quota of Provisions	99
Voted that the Report of the Com^{tee} appointed at Request of Col Elizur Tallcott to view a Highway lay,d out on his Land be accepted	99
Voted that the following Rates be given, at the Request of John Hale, (viz) Richard Crarys £0..11..0 Tim^y Stevens £0..18.11 W^o Mary Treat £2..2..0 Wm Tryon £4..19..11 at the Request of Isaac Plummer (viz) David Fox £0..9..0 Tim^y Stevens £0..2..9 W^o Mary Treat £0..5..10 at the Request of N Tallcott (viz) David Fox £0..18..0 Tim^y Stevens £0..5..9 W^o Mary Treat £0..11..9 Wm Tryon £1..7..3 at the Request of George Tallcott [ ] at allins [ ] (viz) Timothy Stevens £1..5..6 Joseph Chubb £1..7..0 at the Request of David Hollister (viz) Hugh Casey £0..11..6 Eliphalet Fox £0..11..0 Eliphalet [ ] 9/Josiah Stevens 9/ Elisha Stevens 9/1 Joseph Scott 9/ James Stevens 9. Wm Taylor 9/..	99
.. At the Request of Elisha How (viz) Wo Martha Fox Con^l 1..2..0 State money 0..3..1 Alexander Ramsey [Con^l] 3..6..0 [State money] 0..9..0 Charles Riley [Con^l] 3..1..0 [State money] 0..9..9 Edward Potter [Con^l] 0..18..4 [State money] 0..2..8	100

Glastonbury

Voted that Joseph Moseley, Samuel Hills & Wm Wells be a Comit^{ee} to look up Common Land belonging to this Town,.. and prevent Trespassing on the same	100
Voted that the Select-men view the Road Runing by Wm Chamberlins to Henry Huxford,s and layout the same to Bolton Line	100
Voted that Ebenezer Plummer, Wait Goodrich and Elizur Hale Junr be a Committee to Settle with that Com^{tee} who provided for the Soldiers Families the year past	100
Voted that Israel Hollister draw £9..0..0 out of the Town Treasurrer to ballance a mistake made by him	100
Voted that Elijah Hollister, Stephen Goodrich & Elizur Hale Junr be a Com^{tee} to view the Highway on Ebenezer Scotts Land	100
Voted tht Gideon Hale be be allowed for making the Rate Bills, his accounts to be adjusted by the Select-men	100
Voted that Isaac Mosely, Elizur Hale Junr & Jonah Fox be a Com^{tee} to call the Select-men..to Render unto them an account of their doings & moneys expended by them	101
9 Jan 1781	
Jon^a Wells Esqr Chosen Moderator	101
Voted that there be a Com^{ee} to Class the Inhabitants of this Town, in order to raise men to fill up the Contine^l Army.. Voted that Capt Wait Goodrich, Mr Ebenezer Plummer Col Howel Woodbridge & Aaron Hubbard Esqr be a be a Com^{tee} to for the above Purpose	101
Voted that there be Raised a Tax of one Penny & an half Penny in hard money on the Pound, Three Pence States Money or an equivalency the hard money to procure this Town,s Quota of Grain.. for the use of the Forces Raised for the Defence of this State.. Voted that Capt Wait Goodrich, Wm Stevens & Elijah Hubbard Goodrich be a Com^{tee} to Purchase Receive & Collect the same	101
Voted that this Town will indemnify Isaac Goodrich in providing for the Soldiers Families	101
Voted that a former Voted taken at Eastbury with regard to Asaph Colmans Bill for doctrin Elizabeth Tryon, be Reconsider,d and render,d null & void	101
Voted that Do^t Isaac Mosely Do^t Elizur Hale & Mr Nathan Dickerson be a Committee to examine the Bills.. of Do^t Asaph Colman for taking care Elizabeth Tryon	102
Voted that the Select-men adjust Wm Wells,s accounts and Settle with him for procureing the this Town,s Quota of Provisions	102
Voted that the following Rates be given (viz) at the Request of ~~Steven~~ Stephen Strickland Ju^r.. W^o Martha Fox £0..6..3 Edward Potter £0..5..3 Lot Loveland 0..2..3 Charles Riley 0..19..6 Thomas Brooks 1..2..6 John Holding Junr 0..9..0 W^o Martha Kilbourn 0..7..9 ..	102
..at the Request of Elisha How.. Lemuel Tubbs £5..6..4 States Money 0..14..5 ..	102
..at the Request of John Hale viz Samuel Lymen £3..9..8	102
At the Request of Stephen Strickland Junr.. Lem^l Tubbs £1..9..0 Elisha Loveland Ju^r 0..7..0 Lemuel Jones 1..6..0	102
26 Mar 1781	
Capt Isaac Goodrich Chosen Moderator	102
Voted that Capt,s Timothy Hale, Stephen Goodrich Benoni Smith Elizur Hale Elizur Hubbard & Lieu^t William Miller be a Committee to hire this Towns Quota of Troops	102
Voted that Cap^{ts} Wait Goodrich & Isaac Goodrich be a Com^{tee}.. to meet the Com^{tee} for this County.. that the Claims of several Towns to men in the Continental Service may be adjusted	103
Voted to allow the Ballance due to Richard Skinner as Colle^r of Rates for 1772 & 1773	103
Voted that Joseph Mosely, Samuel Hills and Wm Wells be a Committee to sell what Common Land they find in this Town	103

Glastonbury

30 May 1781

Deacon Josiah Hale Chosen Moderator	103
Voted that Samuel Welles Junr & Hosea Fox be a Committee.. to hire an able Bodyed Recrute to Serve for Three Years or dureing the War in the Continental Service	103
Voted that the Inhabitants.. be Class'ed into Eleven Classes, and that each Class hire a Recrute to Serve for the Defence of this State.. also voted that Col Howel Woodbridge, Doc^r Asaph Coleman and Edward Benton be a Committee to Class said Inhabitants for that Purpose	104
Voted to give Phineas Wheeler's Provision Rate which Eighteen Shillings	104

2 Jul 1781

Jonathan Welles Esqr Chosen Moderator	104
Voted that Capt Wait Goodrich be Appointed to Receive the 2/6^d Rate	104
Voted that Thaddeus Welles, Ashbel Hollister, Charles Andrus J^r & Nathan Dickinson be Collectors of the 4^d Rate	104
Voted that Jonah Fox Capt Elizur Hale & Dr Isaac Moseley be a Committee to call the Several Captains of this Town to account for the several Fines they have.. Received of Persons refusing to go into the Service	104

27 Aug 1781

Capt Isaac Goodrich Chosen Moderator	105
Voted that Ashbel Hollister Charles Andrus Ju^r & Nathan Dickinson be Excused from being Collectors of the four penny Tax	105
Voted that John Dewey Stephen Shipman Ju^r & Benjn Hodge J^r be Collectors to Collect the four penny Rate	105
Voted that all Taxes due to this Town in Continental Curency be Immediately Collected.. & Mr Eben^r Plummer give Directions to the Collectors to Collect it Accordingly	105
Voted that Josiah Hale be a Committee with Joseph Moseley in the Room of Wm Wells Absent	105

2 Oct 1781

Voted at the Request of John Hale the following Rates be given viz Hez^h Bidwell £8-3-4 Constant Baker £3-17- Roswell Fox £3-17-0 Daniel Harris £4-0-8 Hez^h Wright £0-11-0 Phinehas Wheeler £3-6 Continental Money	105
Voted at the request of Nath^{ll} Tallcott Ju^r the following Rate be given in States Money viz James Cable £0-9- Roswell Fox £0-10-6 Phinehas Wheeler £0-9-0	105

10 Dec 1781

Jonathan Welles Esqr Chosen Moderator	105
Capt Elisha Hollister Capt Samuel Welles Capt Stephen Goodrich Josiah Hale & Wm Chamberlain Chosen Selectmen	105
Josiah Hale Chosen Town Clerk	105
Eben^r Plummer Chosen Town Treasurer	105
Gideon Hale Isaac Smith & Philip Selew Chosen Constables & Philip Selew to Collect the State Tax	105
Eleazer Wright, Elisha Hale, Elisha Goodrich John Miller, John Hodge, Benjamin Hodge, Isaac Fox, Sam^{ll} Hills, Melatiah Nye, John Wier, Abraham Skinner, John Findley Chosen Surveyors of Highways	106

Glastonbury

David Hale & David Wickham chosen fence vewers	106
George Tallcott, Nath[ll] Tallcott Ju[r], Elisha Hale, William Steens, Tho[s] Hunt, & Elijah Covel Chosen Listers	106
Benjamin Hale Ju[r] Roswell Goodrich, Levi Loveland, James McLane & Jabez Wheelding Chosen Collectors of the Town Rate	106
Israel Smith, David Goodrich Peter Treat Richard Chamberlain chosen Leathers-Sealers	106
Jehiel Goodrich Samuel Rice & Israel Brewer chosen Grand Jurors	106
John Hodge Josiah Benton Ju[r] Appleton Homes & Elijah H Godrich chosen Tything Men	106
Solomon Loveland Sam[ll] Bidwell & Lemuel Jones chosen Packers of Beef Pork & Tobacco &c	106
Thomas Stevens chosen Sealer of Weights & Measures	106
Stephen Strickland, Ambrose Nicholson, Stephen Hollister & Tho[s] Hunt Chosen Keekeepers	106
Meeting be the 24th Day of Instant Dec[r].. Adjourned.. to the School House near Gideon Hales	106

4 Jan 1782

William Richardson was Warned to Depart this Town by Josiah Hale, one of the Selectmen	106

17 Oct 1782

Then David Wiles was Warned to Depart this Town by Sam[ll] Welles	106

12 Mar 1782

Then Tim[th] Brainard was Warned to Depart this Town by the Selectmen	106

19 Oct 1782

Then Philip Squire was Warned to Depart this Town by the Selectmen	106

7 Dec 1778

We Guy Richards & Richard Dishon.. of New London Administrators on the Estate of Cap[t] Peter Harris late of New London, deces[d] by & with the Consent of the Heirs.. for.. Forty Pounds in Money & Ten Bushels Corn & Ten bushels Rye to us in Hand paid by Venture Smith of East Haddam have Bargained, Sold.. & deliver unto the said Venture Smith a Certain Negro Man Named Sawney which was the Property of said Cap[t] Peter Harris.. [*Signed*] Guy Richard.. Rich[d] Dishon.. Signed, Sealed & delivered in Presence of Marvin Wait	107

26 Oct 1779

The within Bill of Sale was given upon condition, in Nature of Mortgage for a small sum that I was bound in for Sawney, & he having paid the Same, I do this Day Deliver this Bill of Sale to Sawney, having no furthrer Claims upon him [*signed*] Venture his X mark Smith.... In presence of Dyar Throop.. Tho[s] Moseley	107

24 Dec 1781

Voted the Select men agree with Thankfull Freeman for keeping of the Wid[w] Bartlett & make a Rate Accordingly	108
Voted Eben[r] Plummer be a Committee.. in Disposing of the Wid[w] Bartlets Estate if any can be found	108
Voted.. Josiah Benton Ju[r] & Joseph Churchill be Surveyors of Highways	108
Voted.. Joseph Tallcott William Moseley & Nathan Dickinson be a Committee to Settle with M[r] Elijah Hollister Joseph Mosely and Noah Tryon &c	108

Glastonbury

Voted.. Timothy Hale & Theodore Hale be a Committee to bring the Deficient Classes to.. Punishment.. for not hiring a Man for the State Service	108
Voted the Selectmen lay out the Road by Lieu^ت Joseph Churchell.s to Hartford Line	108
Voted the Selectmen Compleat the Road across Eben^r Scotts Lot & Hubbards to the Grist Mill	108
Voted..Theodore Hale be a Committee to Supply the Soldiers families	108
Voted the Selectmen open the Road from the Town Street to.. Daniel Pratts Ferry & remove of all Incroachments	108
Voted the Selectmen do what they think proper upon.. Joseph Bidwells motion Concerning a Piece of Land he is Desirous of Buying of the Town	108
Voted Capt Joseph Moseley Capt Sam^{ll} Welles Mr David Hale Mr Elijah Hollister Capt Elizur Hubbard Capt Elisha Hollister Capt Stephen Goodrich Amos Strong & Sam^{ll} Hills be places Appointed to Carry Stray Sheep to	108
Voted the following Rates be given at the Request of George Tallcott viz To Joseph Chubb the Sum of £1-7- Timothy Stevens £1-5-6 Samuel Lyman £1-11- Continental Money..	108
..At the request of Nath^{ll} Tallcott Ju^r Samuel Lyman £0-19-..	109
..At the request of Capt Benoni Smith Samuel Lyman £0-3-	109
..At the request of Elijah H. Goodrich Simeon Strickland £0-5-0 State Money	109
..At the request of John Wickham to Thomas Smith Sterne £0-3-4	109
Voted Joseph Goodale Ju^r be Grand Juror	109

15 Jan 1782

Doct^r Isaa[c] Moseley Chosen Moderator	109
Voted the Selectmen Compleat the Road by Lieu^t Joseph Churchells if they find it is not already done	109
Voted Samuel House a Surveyor of Highways	109
Voted Samuel Hoiuse be a Tything man	109
at the request of Samuel Welles Ju^r Voted to give the following Rates viz to Benjn Tryon Jur 3/4½ Thos Lamb 1/3..	109
..At the request of Elisha How Lot Loveland 1/2 John Holden Ju^r 4/6..	109
..At the request of Nath^{ll} Tallcot Ju^r Constant Baker 1-11 John Strong 1-11-..	109
..At the request of Isaac Plummer Constant Baker 15/6	109

25 Feb 1782

Jonathan Welles Esqr Chosen Moderator	109
Voted Capt Wait Goodrich, Capt Timothy Hale & Mr Eben^r Plummer be a Committee to Class the Town into Six Classes	109
Voted Col Howell Woodbridge & Capt Wait Goodrich be a Committee to Represent this Town before the Committee at Hartford	109
Voted.. Timothy Hale Theodore Hale & Isaac Mosely be a Committee to bring that Class that is Deficient in hiring a Recruit for the last Years State Service to Punishment	109
Voted Daniel Loveland be Collector of the Town Tax in the Room of Jabez Wheelding Excused	109
Voted Mr Theodore Hale have Liberty to Draw Money out of the Town Treasury.. to Supply the Soldiers families.. & also that he have Liberty to take in Rye at Nine Shilings p^r Bushel State Money on the Two shilling Tax	110

Glastonbury

18 Mar 1782

Voted Jonathan Welles Esqr Mr Eben^r Plummer & Capt Wait Goodrich be a Committee to Confer Immediately with the Soldiers that Engaged as Artificers that are now at Home Absent from the Army & make Report	110
Voted James McClean be Excused from being Collector of the Town Tax & David Nye be appointed in his Room	110
Voted Capt Wait Goodrich Mr Eben^r Plummer & Ambrose Nicholson be a Committee that whenever their is Orders for Detaching Men to go into the Service the Committe Immediately through the Town into as many Classes as there are Men to be Detached	110
Voted Capt Timothy Hale be a Committee to wait on Capt Granger at Hartford Concerning the Soldiers Wages that went into the State Service last year	110

1 Apr 1782

Voted Philip Covel be Collector of the Town Tax in the Room of David Nye Excused	111
Voted at the request of [*blank*] Thomas Bidwell Rate be given him the Sum of £3-6-0	111
Voted that the Selectmen give Order to take Care of the Highways & that particularly by Sam^{ll} Williams	111
Voted Capt Wait Goodrich & Aaron Hubbard Esqr be a Committee to Divide this Town into Classes.. to furnish Men for Three Years or During the War	111

28 May 1782

Jonathan Welles Esqr chosen Moderator	111
Voted Mes^r Joseph Temple & Sam^{ll} Smith be a Committee to hire a Man to Serve as a Soldier in the Continattal Army untill the first Day of January next	111
Voted the Selectmen make a Rate upon the Inhabitants.. to procure & pay s^d recruit.. Voted Mes^r Isaac Welles Abraham Tallcott Eben^r Goodale & Wm Findley be Collectors to gather said Rate	111

9 Dec 1782

Jonathan Welles Esqr chosen Moderator	111
Voted Messrs Wm Chamberlain Gideon Hale & Elizur Hollister be Selectmen	111
Josiah Hale chosen Town Clerk	111
Eben^r Plummer chosen Town Treasurer	111
Gideon Hale Philip Sellew Isaac Smith chosen Constables Philip Sellew to gather the State Tax	111
Messrs Wait Goodrich Elijah Stevens Elisha Goodrich Jonathan Treat George Hollister & David Bigelow be Surveyors of Highways	111
Messrs David Hale & David Wickham chosen fence viewers	112
Messrs John Sellew Sam^{ll} Welles Ju^r John Hollister Benjn Tucker & Jabez Wheelding chosen Listers	112
Eleazer House Sam^{ll} Stratton tert. Elizur Loveland & Amos Strong chosen Collectors	112
Israel Smith Peter Treat Wm Chamberlain Leather Sealers	112
Sam^{ll} Rice & Joseph Goodale chosen Grand Jurors	112
Capt Joseph Moseley Stephen Shipman Ju^r Capt Sam^{ll} Covell and Sam^{ll} Hill Ju^r chosen Tythingmen	112
Lieu^t Thomas Stevens chosen Sealer of Weights & Measures	112

Glastonbury

Ambrose Nicholson Stephen Hollister Benjn Hodge Ju^r Stephen Strickland te[ ]t chosen Kee keeper	112
Solomon Loveland & Nehemiah Hollister chosen Packers of Beef Pork & Tobacco	112

16 Dec 1782

Voted at the request of Elisha How to give Isaac Tubbs 16/ S.M.	112
Voted at the request of Isaac Plummer & Joseph Hale to give unto the Estate of John Strong 18/3 also to Amasa Brown 17/	112
Voted that no Man Shall Inocolate but Doc^t Elizur Hale Dr Asaph Coleman & that they shall not before they are put under Bonds	112
Voted to accept of the doings of the Selectmen in laying a Road from Sam^{ll} Brooks to Hartford Line & pay Sam^{ll} Brooks £5-0-0 for the Road that runs across his Land	113
Voted Matthew Miller be a Committee to provide for the Soldiers families	113
Voted Josiah Hale procure a Record Book & give Acc^t to the Selectmen	113
Elijah Hollister Jehiel Goodrich Daniel Hale David Hale Ju^r Wm Moseley Stephen Strickland tert. Peter Huxford Thomas Hollister Ju^r & Wm Goodrich Ju^r be Haywards	113
Voted Capt Wait Goodrich & Mr Eleazer Wright be Selectmen	113
Voted Thomas Hunt be Lister	113

12 Mar 1783

Jonathan Welles Esqr chosen Moderator	113
Sam^{ll} Stratton chosen Collector.. in the room of Sam^{ll} Statton Ju^r Excused	113
Voted the Selectmen Compleat the Road that runs through Sam^{ll} Hills land at Eastbury & all other Roads that they shall think necessary	113
Voted Sam^{ll} Hills be Surveyor of Highways in addition to those already chosen	113
Voted at the request of Levi Loveland to forgive Edward Potter 7/3½	113
Voted Elisha How be Lister.. in the room of Thos Hunt Excused	113
Voted Mr Eben^r Plummer pay Elisha Hale the Sum of £4-12-8 State Money	113
Voted Joseph Kilborn have Liberty to Build a Saw mill on his own Land on Roaring Brook	114
Voted Wm Chamberlain have Liberty to build a Grist mill on his own Land on a Stream called Blackleaches River	114
Voted Gideon Hale be paid.. 32/ State Money out of the Town Treasury	114
AT the request of Capt Benoni Smith voted to give the following persons their Rates Moses Pierce 1/11¾ Sam^{ll} Pratt 2/6½ Israel Smith Ju^r 1/10½ Nath^{ll} Tory 1/10½ Benjn Tryon Ju^r 1/10½ Ezra Tryon 2/3½ Simeon Alger 2/8½ Sam^{ll} Bidwell [ ] 5^d John Brooks Ju^r 2/1¼ Richard Crary 2/3¾ Dennis Cuningham 2/6 Elisha Goff 1/10½ Elisha Hale Chatham 2^d ½ John Ketchum 1/10½ Joseph Lamb 1/10½ Sam^{ll} Lamb 2/3½ Sam^{ll} Lyman 3/3½	114
Voted Isaac Smith pay up his Receipt he gave Eben^r Plummer for money he drew out of the Treas^{ry} when he Supplied Soldiers families	114
Voted Reuben Risley Sam^{ll} Hills & Elijah Smith be a Com^{tee} to look up all the Powder & Ball. Guns & Catouch be [ ] fines & forfitures paid to the Commanding Officers of the Military Companies & all other Things that belong to this Town & has been Receipted out Since the present War	114

21 Apr 1783

Capt Timothy Hale Chosen Moderator	114

Glastonbury

Capt Wait Goodrich Clerk *114*

Voted Mr Eben^r Plummer Capt Timothy Hale & Capt Joseph Moseley be a Com^{tee} to Inspect Mr Theodore Hales Acc^t for Supplying the Soldiers families last Year *114*

21 Aug 1783

Capt Jonathan Welles chosen Moderator *115*

The Question being moved & Seconded whether the Inhabitants of this Town approve of the Act of Congress call the Commutation Act & Voted in the Negative.. The Question being moved & Seconded whether this Town will appoint a Committee to correspond with the Committees of other Towns on the above Subject & Voted in the Affirmative and the following Persons wer chosen.. viz Capt Wait Goodrich Col Elizur Tallcott Capt Jonth Welles Mr Wm Welles & Mr Sam^{ll} Smith *115*

Goshen

Town Records
Vol. 1

Located at the Town Clerk's Office

Goshen

11 Dec 1775

Lt Hurlbut was Chosen Moderator	102
Sam^{ll} Nash ws Chosen town Clerk	102
Select men } Isaac Pratt Capt Beech David Humphry Asaph Hall Silas Richmond	102
Constables Fisk Beech head Constable Abel Phelps Ju^r 2^d Constable	102
Grandjurors Sam^{ll} Hopkins Stephen Thomson Ens Wadhams Jacob Beech John Riley Moses Lyman	102
Listers Miles Norton Moses Lyman Lt Elisha Thomson David Hudson Sam^{ll} Baldwin Jabez Wright	102
Surveyors of Highways Lt Matthew Smith Ebenez Norton Ju^r Philemon Sanford Dan^{ll} Miles John Munson Leu^t Elisha Thomson Step^n Tuttle Jos Butler Jonath Kollet Jabez Wright Lines Beech	102
Tythingmen Jabez Norton Thomas Converse Philemon Sanford Giles Griswold Sam^{ll} Barthollomew	102
treasurer Sam^{ll} Nash	102
School Com^{tte} } Abel Butler Capt Stanly John Wadhams Elisha Hurlbut Josiah Royce David Thomson Nehe Lewis Ju^r Aaron Norton	102
Sealer of Measures Col Norton	102
Weights D^o Sam^{ll} Nash	102
[Sealer] of Leather Josiah Royce	102
Horse Branders Sam^{ll} Nash Capt Beech John Rily Isaac Pratt	102
Pound Keepers Adna Beech ~~David~~ Isaac Humphry	102
fence viewers Thos Lucas Step Smith	102
voted to Give the Revd Mr Nevil 65 L money for his Salary for the year past	102
Sam^{ll} francis was Chosen Collector for s^d Rate	102
voted to Raise one ½ on the pound.. for Defraying town Charges -- Amasa Cook was chosen Collector of s^d Rate	102
voted to Give to Col Norton 2/ to Fisk Beech 6/ and to the jurymen 2/ Each for their trouble about the bones found of Some person who perished in s^d town	102
voted that Step thomsons Bard Yard be a town pound.. and Stephen thomson be pound Keeper	102

8 Apr 1776

Gideon Hurlbut was Chosen Moderator	103
Josisah Nash Chosen a Collector to Collect Revd Mr Nevels Rate in the Room of Sam^{ll} Francis.. who has Refused S^d trust	103
Sam^{ll} Barthol^w was Chosen Surveyor of high Ways in the room of Jos- Butler Gone into the war	103
voted that the Selectmen Directed.. to Seat Lt Ashman Vancy other persons who Need a Seat in the Meetinghouse	103

[ ] Dec 1776

Town Clerk Sam^{ll} Nash	104
Town treas[urer] Sam^{ll} Nash	104

Goshen

Selectmen } David Thompson Cyprian Collens Silas Richmond Capt Stanly Capt Buel	104
Constables } Fisk Beech head Constable and to Collect the Cuntry Rate James Thomson 2^d Constable	104
Grand Jurors } Philimon Sanford Ens Miles Norton Lt Maltbie Sam Stephens Moses Lyman Westil Willoby Ep^h Starr	104
Listers } Lt Elisha Thomson Moses Lyman Ens Miles Norton David Hudson Sam^{ll} Baldwin Jabez Wright	104
Surveyors of Highway } Lt Matthew Smith Dan^{ll} Miles Leu^t Nehe Lewis Leu^t Step Tuttle Nath^a Newill Josiah Nash Dr Elias Deming Step^n Thomson Barna Richm^d Seth Wadhams Amasa Cook	104
Tythingmen } Abel Philips Ju^r Josiah Royce Ebenz Norton Ju^r Phinehas Hinman Amasa Cook Jesse Jud	104
School Com^{tee} } Aaron Norton Capt Stanly John Wadhams Josiah Royce Abel Butler Lt Thomson Ebenz Norton Ju^r Elisha Hurlbutt	104
Sealer of measures &c } of measures Col Norton of weights Sam^{ll} Nash of Leather Josiah Royce	104
Horse Branders } Sam^{ll} Nash Capt Beech Isaac Pratt Lt Riley	104
Pound Keepers } Adna Beech Isaac Humphry Step Thomson	104
Voted to New Seat the meeting house.. Col Norton Capt Nash Capt Beech Lt Parmalee Lt James Thomson Moses Lyman Dan^{ll} Miles Was Chosen a Com^{tee} for that purpose	104
Voted to Raise a tax of 2^d on the pound.. for Defraying town Charges Voted that Charls miles Be a Collector	104
Voted to Give the Revd Mr Nevel 70 L money for his Service in the Ministry in the Year past	104
Voted that John Carington be a Collector	104
Voted that Col Norton Lt Hurlbut who are a Com^t to Exchange highways.. also a Com^t.. to Exchange the Road from Mr Lucases to the Land of Capt Beech.. and the Road Runing between.. for other Land to Accomodate a Road Between s^d Lucas & Mr Stanlys land to Run North to the Road Across Ives montain & also a Road Across Cases Lot So Called	104
13 Mar 1777	
Capt Buel Chosen Moderator	105
Voted to ad five pounds to what the town have already Voted to give Mr Nivel for his Salary for the Year past	105
Voted to Choose a Com^{te} to treat with Mr Nivel about Setling his Salary for the future.. Voted that Col Norton Sam^{ll} Nash Esqr Baird Tyler David Thomson Cyprian Collins Sam^{ll} Kellogg & Ens Wadhams be a Com^{te} for that purpose	105
1 Apr 1777	
Sam^{ll} Kellogg was Chosen Moderator of a town Meeting	105
Capt Asaph Hall Step^n Thomson Cyprian Collins Abel PhelpsJu^r were Chosen a Com^{tee} to procure the tents & other Necessaries Required by Law	105
[ ] Apr 1777	
this town Do.. promise all Such able Bodied Afective Soldiers that Inlist & Goe into the Continental army.. to Supply the Quoto of men Demanded of this town att this time and may not have time Before their march to Supply their famelies (of any they have) with Necessary Provision in their absence.. on their Lodging or from time to time Remitting to a Certain Com^{te}.. money for purchasing the Same.. Voted that Capt Beul Capt Beech & Lt James Thomson be a Com^{te} for that purpose	105

Goshen

Select men.. are to Lay a Rate or tax.. for Raising the Sum of ten pounds Lawful to Each Soldier who Shall Inlist.. and Continue there in one Year after his Inlisment and to Lay a Rate or tax.. for Raising Such Sum of money as is Sufficient to pay Each of s^d Soldiers ten pounds Lawfull money who Shall Continue in s^d Service att the End of two years.. Eph^m Starr was Chosen Collector to Collect Each of s^d Rates	106

10 Sep 1777

Leu^t Hubbel was Chosen Moderator	106

25 Sep 1777

Capt Beul was Chosen Moderator	109
Each able Bodied Soldier.. who shall Enlist or Volunteer Under General Olliver Woolcott.. to Assist Gen Gates in the Northern Department Shall be paid five pounds	109
Danl Miles Capt Beech and Sam^{ll} Kellogg be a Com^{te} to transport the Salt.. Now att Boston in the most prudent Manner they Can.. and when the s^d Salt is Delivered here to Distribute the Same to Each family.. according to their Number	109
Voted that Eph^m Starr Dan^{ll} Miles Capt Stanley Capt Buel Ens Collins Silas Richmond fowlor Merwin & Sam^{ll} Kellogg be a Com^{te}.. to purchase.. for Each Non-Commission officer and Soldier Now in the Continental army which are of the Quota of Soldiers Required of this Town..one Shirt either Linnen or flax mill one hunting Shirt or frock one p^r of Woollen Overhulls one or 2 p^r of Stockintgs & one p^r of Good shoes and Deliver the Same to the Commissary	109
Voted that Sam^{ll} Nash town treas^r is.. Impowred to [ ] the Notes Given to him by Sundry persons for not Going into the Service.. for which they have Been Draughted	109
Voted that fisk Beech be Quoristor to tune the psalm & be head quorestor	109
Voted that Wait Hinman be Assistant Quorestor	109
Voted that Mr How Capt Beul & Ens Moses Lyman have Liberty to build a Sabbath Day house in Some part of the Green Round the meeting house	110

8 Dec 1777

Leu^t Hurlbut was Chosen Moderator	110
Sam^{ll} Nash Town Clerk & town treasr	110
Selectmen { Capt Beul David Thomson Sam^{ll} Kellog Capt Goodwin Capt Stanley	110
Constables Eph^m Starr head Constable and to Collect the Cuntry Rate - Fisk Beech 2^d Constable	110
Listers Miles Norton Moses Lyman Elisha Thomson Sam^{ll} Baldwin wistill Willoby	110
Surveyors of highways { Capt Beech Capt Hall Sam^{ll} Bishop Linus Beul Chauncy Beech Capt Beul John Munson Elisha Munson Step^n Tuttle Chuliab Smith Thos Dickenson	110
Grand Jurors Sam^{ll} Norton Ju^r Zach Grisw^d Ju^r Step^n Thomson Aaron Norton Silas Richmond	110
Tything men Nath^{ll} Baldwin Capt Beech Capt Goodwin Ens Wadhams	110
School Com^{te} { Dr Sill Jos How Elisha Hurlbut Westill Willoby Cyprian Collins Josiah Benton Abel Butler	110
Sealer of Waits Sam^{ll} Nash of Measures Col Norton of Leather Josiah Royce	110
Horse Branders Sam^{ll} Nash Capt Beech Isaac Pratt Lt Riley	110
fence viewers Thos Lucas & Step Smith	110
Com^{te} of Inspection Capt Jabez Wright Sam^{ll} Hopkin Ens Wadhams Capt Hall Capt Francis	110

Goshen

Com^{te} to provide for the Soldiers famelies Ens Wadhams Lt Riley & Dan^{ll} Miles	110
Voted to Raise a tax of 3 pence ½.. for Defraying town Charges Charls Miles was Chosen Collector of s^d Rate	110
the Select men Reported that they Could not agree with the Revd Mr Nevel as to the Sum of his Salary for the Year past and that he Chose to Refer the matter to A Com^{te}	110
Voted to Give the Revd Mr Abel Nevel £130 Lawful money for his Service in the ministry in the Year past Philip Cook was Chosen Collector to Collect s^d Rate	110

6 Jan 1778

Col Norton was Chosen Moderator	111

16 Mar 1778

Capt Jonath Buel was Chosen Moderator	111
Voted to Chose a Com^{te} to purchase Articles of Cloathing for the officers and Soldiers.. now in the Service of the Continental army.. Dan^{ll} Miles Eph Starr Jonath Kelleg Chosen a Com^{te} for the purpose	111
Voted that Capt Halls Yard by his new Barn be a town pound.. and s^d Hall was Chosen key keeper	111
Dan^{ll} Miles was chosen a School Com^{te} man for the midle District on the East Side	111
David tyler was Chosen key keeper.. and his yard was voted to be a pound	111
Capt Jabez Wright & Elisha Hurlbut were Chosen Com^{te} men to provide for the famelies of the Soldiers	111

24 Aug 1778

Gideon Hurlbut Was Chosen Modorator	111

[ ] Sep 1778

Voted that Leu^t Giles Griswold be a Com^{te} man in the room of Capt Geb Wright to provide for Zeb pecks wife	111
Voted that John Medcalf be a Com^{te} man in the Room of Elisha Hurlbut to take care of John Goulds wife	111

14 Jan 1778

Capt Edmund Beech was Chosen Moderator	112
Town Clerk Sam^{ll} Nash	112
head Constable Eph Starr	112
2^d Constable fisk Beech	112
Select men } Capt Jonath Buell Capt Asaph Hall Lt John Riley David Thomson & Capt Step Goodwin	112
Grand Jurors } John Doud Dan^{ll} Miles [*Sworn*] James Thomson fowler Merwin Giles Griswold	112
Tythingmen } Capt Matthew Smith Chauncy Beech John Carington Jonath Beul Ju^r Wait [ ]	112
Listers } Ens Wadhams Lt Dan^{ll} Miles Sam^{ll} Ovitt Col Ebenz Norton	112

21 Jan 1778

Voted that Lt Moses Lyman William Stanly Aaron Norton and Stephen Thomson be a Com^{te} to take Care of the officers & Soldiers families while they are in the Continental Service	112
Surveyors of highways } Lt Moses Lyman Ebenz Norton Ju^r Barnabas Richmond Capt Matthew Smith Stephen Tuttle Lt Elisha Thomson John Wadhams Aaron Norton Fisk beech	112

Goshen

Elisha Hurlbutt Lt Parmerlee	
Horse Branders Sam^{ll} Nash Capt Beech Gideon Pratt Lt Rily	112
Sealers of Weights Sam^{ll} Nash.. of Measures Col Norton.. of Leather Josiah Royce	112
School Com^{te} Josiah Royce Seth Wadhams Step Hudson Dan^{ll} Baldwin David Tyler Cheliab Smith Westil Willoby Capt Wright	112
Pound Keepers Capt Hall Adna Beech David tyler	112
Voted Capt Halls Barn Yard be a town pound	112
fence viewers Thos Lucas & Step^n Smith	112
Voted to Chose a Com^{tee} to Examine the affair of Alvords family beem introduced into this town by the owner of the mill Called Norton & Barkers mill.. Capt Hall & Lt Hurlbut were Chosen	112
Voted to Rise a tax of two Shillings on the pound.. for Defraying town Charges.. Ens Jonath Kellog be a Collector to Collect s^d Tax	112
Selectmen Confered with Mr Revd Nevel Concerning the Sum he Demanded for his Sallary for the Current Year.. and that s^d Mr Nevel proposed to Refer the matter to be adjudged by indifferent men.. the Question was put whither the town would join with Mr Nevel in Choosing a Com^{te} for that and itt pased in the Negative	113

21 Jan 1779

Capt Asaph Hall was Chosen Moderator	113
Voted that Daniel Miles to refer a memorial to the General Assembly for Liberty to Repair the highways.. by a Rate or tax	113
Voted to give the Revd Mr Abel Nevel 400 £ L money for his Service in the ministry AD 1778 and to Satisfy him for.. for 1777 & 1776 in which Years he is desputing what this town has Given him provided Mr Nevel is willing.. to abate as much as the public taxes [*in*] 1778 would amount too had his Estate been taxed	113
Voted to Choose a Com^{te} to treat with Mr Nevel.. Capt Buel Capt Beech Lt Hurlbut Col Hill & Capt Goodwin be a Com^{te}	113
Voted that Solomon Wadhams be a Collector to Collect Mr Nevils Rate	113

11 Mar 1779

Capt Jonath Buel was Chosen Moderator	113

16 Mar 1779

Voted the Selectmen withdraw an Action [*against*] Augustus Hill for Breaking the Meetinghouse Glass & Voted that Capt hall	113
Voted that Capt Hall be an Agent.. to prosecute any and all perons for trespassing on the parsonage or School Land	113
Voted to Give the Revd Mr Nevel Six hundred & Eighty pounds Continental money for his Services in the ministry	114

26 Apr 1779

Capt Asaph Hall was Chosen Moderator	114
Voted to Reconsider the Vote.. to Give the Revd Mr Nevel 680 Continental money for his Service	114
Voted to Give the Revd Mr Abel Nevel £65.0.0 Lawfull money for his Service in the Ministry AD 1778	114
Voted that the.. Covenant with Mr Nevel att his Settlement Respecting his Stated Sallary be	114

310

Goshen

altered
24 Jun 1779

Capt Jonath Buel was Chosen Moderator	*114*
James Thomson Silas Richmond & Ens John Doud were Chosen a Com^{te} to purchase Cloathing for the officers and Soldiers of the Continental Army & of the Line of Connecticut Sent out of this Town.. and to Borrow money on the towns Credit for that purpose	*114*
Voted to Raise a tax of 2/ on the pound.. for Defraying the Charge of mending high ways..	*114*
Solomon Moss was Chosen Collector of s^d Rate	
Capt Jabez Wright Giles Griswold & Capt Matthew Smith were Chosen Listers	*114*

[ ] Sep 1779

Capt Buel was Chosen Moderator	*114*

13 Dec 1779

Capt Asaph Hall was Chosen Moderator	*115*
Town Clerk Sam^{ll} Nash.. Town treas^r Sam^{ll} Nash	*115*
Select men { Isaac Pratt Capt Hall John Riley James Thomson	*115*
Constables { Ephraim Starr head Constable and to Collect the ~~Cuntry~~ State tax & fisk Beech 2^d Constable	*115*
Grand Jurors { Coll Medad Hill Capt Asa Francis Ens Collins Robert Rood Nath$^{[ ]}$ Newill Lt Moses Lyman	*115*
Listers { David Thomson Ebenz Norton Ju^r Jonath Buel Stephen Thomson Ens Aaron Norton Dan^{ll} Baldwin	*115*
Surveyors of highways Stephen Thomson Wm Nash Fisk Beech Ebenz Norton Ju^r Lt Theod Parmalee Andrew Baily Ambrose Collins	*115*
Tything men { Elisha Hurlbutt Westill Willoby Joseph How Sam^{ll} Ovit Theophilus Mix Sam^{ll} Lyon Sam^{ll} Bishop Titus Gailord Sam^{ll} Norton Ju^r Wm Brown Nehe Lewis John Munson	*115*
Sealer of weights Sam^{ll} Nash of measures Col Norton.. Do of Leather Thos Ens Munson	*115*
horse Branders Sam^{ll} Nash Capt Edmond Beech Lt Pratt Lt Rily David Tyler	*115*
pound Keepers Adna Beech Jur David Tyler Capt Hall	*115*
School Com^{te} } Wm Nash Philemon Sanford Elisha Hurlbutt Fowler Merwin Abell Butler Roger Lomis Sam^{ll} Hopkis Nehe Lewis	*115*
Voted that Sam^{ll} Nash Col Norton Lt Parmelee & James Thomson be a Com^{te} to treat further with the Revd Mr Nevel as to his Salary	*115*

27 Dec 1779

Samuel Hopkins & Silas Richmond were Chosen fence viewers	*115*
David Tyler was chosen in Room of Stephen Thomson [ed: *office is unstated*]	*115*
~~Chileab Smith & Elisha Thomson~~ were Chosen fence viewers	*115*
Com^{te} to take Care of and provide for the famalies of the Soldiers in the Continental Service were Giles Griswold John Carington Oliver Bech & ~~John Carington~~ Amasa Cook	*115*
Voted to Raise a tax of two Shillings on the pound.. for Defraying the Charges of Repairint highways.. Miles Norton was Chosen Collector to Collect the Rate	*116*
Adino Hale was Chosen Collector to Collect.. Rate.. voted to Give the Revd Mr Abel Nevel for his Service in the Mnistry 114 pounds money put to wheat att 4/ p^r Bushel Rye and 3/ p^r [ ] & Indian Corn .. 2/p^r bushel and those who pay their Rates to Mr Nivel to pay in money an	*116*

Goshen

Equivelent theretoo in Continental money which Equivelent is to be Determined by a Com^{te} to be Chosen by Mr Nevel and the town s^d Com^{te} to be of the Inhabitants of s^d town

Voted that Col Norton Sam^{ll} Nash Capt Beech Lt Parmalee and James Thomson be a Com^{te} to wait on Mr Nevel and Acquaint him with the Vote and if he Accepts to Report the same and if Shall.. Voted the Town will Refer the matter of his Sallary for his past Service.. to be adjudged & Determiend by a Com^{te} to be Chosen by Mr Nevel & the town   116

Voted that Chileab Smith Elisha Thomson Giles Griswold Capt Matthew Smith and Westill Willoby be a Com^{te} to Remove Nusances in highways   116

7 Feb 1780

Capt Beech was Chosen moderator   116

the Com^{te} appointed.. to treat with Mr Nevel about his Salary and to acquaint him with the offers and votes of the town.. Report that.. Mr Nevel Declined Accepting of Either of them   116

Samuel Norton Ju^r was Chosen a Com^{te} man to take Care of Capt Converses family   116

Voted to Choose a a Com^{te} to treat with the Rev^d M^r [*Nevel*] and to know of him.. on what terms he is willing to Lay down the Work of the ministry in this town and Abraham Parmelee Capt Edmund Beech Capt Buel Lt James Thomson and Dan^{ll} Miles were Chosen   116

21 Feb 1780

the afores^d Com^{te} Reported that Mr Nevel would Come into the meeting.. & Mr Nevel.. Represented that he was not prepared to Give a Definitive answer to the proposal of the town Respecting his Laying down the work of the Ministry and was of the opinion that the matter of his Salary Ought to be first Setled.. whereupon the Question was put whether the town would Leave the affair of what Mr Nevel Should have for his past Service to be Determined by a Com^{te} to be Chosen by Mr Nevel and the town and itt passed in the affirmative   117

23 Mar 1780

Capt Hall was Chosen moderator   117

Capt Buel Capt Goodwin Capt Matthew Smith Liu^t James Thomson Lt John Rily were Chosen Inspectors to Inspect the transporting provisions of all Sorts out of this town   117

the Question was put whether the town Desires the Revd Mr Abel Nevel to.. Lay down the Work of the Ministry in this town and itt passed in the Affirmative. 28 in the Affirmative and 13 in the Negetive.   117

Voted to Choose a Com^{te} to Lay before Mr Nevel the foregoing vote and to Desire him to Joyn with the town in Calling an Ecclesiastical Com^{te} to Give him a.. Loyal Dismission.. Capt Buel Nath^{ll} Baldwin Sam^{ll} Hopkins & Lt James Thomson were Chosen for s^d Com^{te} 117

29 Jun 1780

Capt Edmund Beech was Chosen Moderator   118

19 Sep 1780

Liu^t Isaac Pratt was Chosen moderator   118

Voted that Capt Asaph Hall be an Agent.. to prefer a Memorial.. to the General Assembly.. praying s^d Assembly to Grant.. such money as they have advanced for the Supply of [*the*] families of Soldiers.. who went into the Continental Army which money was Raised.. on the Re[*quision*].. of the Govr and Councill of Safety   118

[ ] Oct 1780

Voted that allyn Lucas be Collector (in the Room of John Wadhams.. who Refused to Serve)   119

Voted to New Seat the meetinghouse -- and the Seaters to Seat the Same According to their Age and the List AD 1779.. Capt Sill Dan^{ll} Miles Sam^{ll} Hopkins Silas Richmond Capt Wright   119

Goshen

Lt James Thomson & Lt Moses Lyman were Chosen Seaters

13 Nov 1780

Capt Hall was Chosen Moderator	119
Voted to Give the Revd Mr Abel Nevel Sixty five pounds Silver money Counting a Spanish mill^d Dollar att 6/ or in Gold Equivalent.. for his Service in [the] Ministry in AD 1778 and the Like Sum for 1779.. to be adjudged.. by Messrs ~~Andrew A~~ Lynd Capt Bradly & Capt Seymour, all of Litchfield	119
Leu^t Moses Lyman was Chosen Collector of the Rate to Raise s^d Sums	119
Voted that Fisk Beech and Ep^h Starr be a Com^{te} to provide Casks and Receive Salt of the publick Stores and Receive in pork & Beef and Salt it up for the Service of the army	119
the Question was put.. whether the town Desire the Rev^d Mr Nevel to Desist in the Work of the ministry in this town and itt passed in the affirmative	119
Ep^h Starr who was Chosen a Receiver and packer of provisions Refusing to Serve voted that he be Excused	119
Voted that James Thomson be a Receiver & packer of provisions and he Refusing was Excused and Elisha Thomson appointed in his Room	119
Voted the Money Granted to be paid to Mr Nevel for his Service in 1778 & in 1779 be Raised one half on the List 1778 & the other half on the List 1779	120
Voted to Devide the inhabitants.. into as many Clases as s^d town are by Law Required to Raise Recruits to fill up the Continental Army for 3 years or During the war.. Voted that the present Selectmen and Capt Wright & Capt Matthew Smith be a Com^{te} for s^d purpose	120

11 Dec 1780

Capt Edmund Beech was Chosen Moderator	120
Select men Capt Goodwin Capt Hall Liu^t pratt Capt Sill Capt francis Lt Rily & Lt James Thomson	120
Town Clerk Sam^{ll} Nash	120
Constables Fisk Beech head Constable and to Collect the State tax 2^d Constable Ephraim Starr	120
town treasr Capt Sill	120
Grand Jurors William Stanly Josiah Benton David Thomson Josiah Nash	120
Tything men Barnabas Richmond Chileab Smith William Beech Eph Towner	120
Listers Dan^{ll} Baldwin Jonath Buel Jur Eben Norton Jur Aren Norton Ens Jonath Kellel	120
Surveyors of highways Fisk Beech Capt W[ ] Capt Goodwin Josiah Willoby heman Smith Jacob Beech John medcalf Step^n Thomson abel Butler Capt Buel Nath^{ll} Norton Col Hill Amasa Cook Ens Katell	120
Leather Sealer Nehemiah Lewis of measures Col Norton of Weights Sam^{ll} Nash	120
School Com^{te} Lt Lyman Sam^{ll} Barthollomew Neh Lewis Eph Starr Josiah Royce fowler murvin Chauncy Beech	120
pound Keepers David Tyler Capt Hall & adna Beech Jur	120
fence viewers Silas Richmond & Sam^{ll} Hopkins	120
Horse Branders S Nash Capt Beech L^t pratt Lt Rily David Tyler	120
Voted that Jonah Case [&] Sam^{ll} Bishop be taken out of the west Side School District and aded to the Joy mountain District	121

Goshen

[ ] Dec 1780

Voted to Lay a Rate or tax of /2^d on the pound State money.. for Defraying town [*Charges*]   *121*
Robert Rood was Chosen Collector
Dan^{ll} Miles was Chosen in the Room of Ens Lewis to [ ] with Lt Hurlbut and Ens Collins who   *121*
were Chosen to the Com^{te} who Built the meeting house to a Settleme[*nt*] [ ] Building the
new meetinghouse and James Thomson aded to s^d Com^{te}
Voted that Miles Norton Lt Moses Lyman Sam^{ll} Baldwin [ ] be a Com^{te} to procure Shoes &   *121*
other Cloathing for the Men Now in the Service of the Continental Army
Westil Willoby Capt frances & John Carington & Seth [ ] were Chosen a Com^{te} to procure   *121*
provisions & other Necessaries for the Supply of the famalies of the officers & Soldiers in
the Service of the Continental Army
Selectmen Reported.. Revd Mr Nevel having Signifyed his willingness to Accept.. 65£ Silver   *122*
money Accounting a Spanish milld Dollars.. or the Equivelent.. for his Sallary for 1778 &
1779.. Question was put whether the town would Give Mr Nevel s^d Sum for his Service.. AD
1780 and itt pas'd in the Negative itt was then moved that as the town had twice Voted that
they Desired Mr Nevel to Dessist the ministry.. and.. he thought itt not fitt to Give a
Definitive Answer.. untill Sallary affairs were Setled itt was moved that the minds of the
town should be layed to see if they Give him 65 pounds money as afors^d on Condition he
would.. Dessist the ministry in this town and itt pas'd in the affirmative
Voted that Sam^{ll} Nash Eph Starr & Amos Beech be a Com^{te} to Report to Mr Nevel the   *122*
afores^d votes of the town

3 Jan 1781

Voted to Lay a tax.. to be paid in State money or 1 penny ½ penny to be paid in wheat or Rye   *122*
flower or Indian Corn.. to be Delevered to Elisha Thomson or fisk Beech..[*and*] to Receive
and pack and Store s^d articles
Moses Lyman was Released from being Collector and Sundry others were Chosen in [*his*]   *122*
Room and Released and finally Capt Buel was Chosen Collector who Accepted
Chauncy Beech was Chosen Lister   *122*
Mr Nevel.. Reported an answer to the proposals of the town.. that he was willing to Accept of   *122*
a Dismission from his pastoral [ ]
.. a Disinterested Councill.. Chosen & Agreed upon by Mr Nevel and [ ] church (with the   *123*
Concurrence.. of the town) Should be Called in to hear & Consider Certain matters of
Grievance.. the Councill to Consist of the following Revd Messrs viz Jonath Marsh of New
Hartford Timo^y Pitkin of farmington Enoch Huntington of Middleton Benj Trumble of North
haven & Andrew St[ ] of Northbury
Fisk Beech Sam^{ll} Hopkins James Thomson Dan^{ll} Miles & Eph Starr were Chosen a Com^{te} to   *123*
Call s^d Councill & to prepare matters of the.. Complaint to be Laid before s^d Councill and to
Give Mr Nevel a Coppy

15 Jan 1781

Capt Goodwin was Chosen moderator   *124*
Voted to Choose a Com^{te} to procure.. 5 Soldiers in the best manner they Can.. Capt Matthew   *124*
Smith Ens Collins & ens Kettel were Chosen for s^d Com^{te}
In the Representation of L^t E: Thomson & Fisk Beech that Sundry persons have Neglected to   *124*
pay their Respective parts of the tax of 6¼.. to be paid in pork beef wheat or Rye flour.. voted
that s^d Elisha and Fisk be appointed Collectors

15 Feb 1781

Capt Hall was Chosen Moderator   *124*

Goshen

voted that Capt francis Silas Richmond Stephen Thomson and Ebenez Norton Ju^r be a Com^{te} to Examine what Classes Shall be Deficient in hiring a Recruit	124
Voted to Give the Revd Mr Abel Nevel for his Service in the Ministry Since his Year Service AD 1780 was Ended until he was Dismissed.. and to be paid in the Same money & manner as the town have Voted to Give him for.. 1779.. Voted that Mr Nevels Sallary for 1780.. be Raised on the List 1780	125
voted that Capt Buel be a Collector to collect Mr Nevels Rate for 1780 and for what is Voted to Give Mr Nevel for his Service Since 1780 till he was Dismissed	125
Voted that Col Norton Sam^{ll} Nash Stephen Thomson James Thomson & Dan^{ll} Miles be a Com^{te} to procure an Orthodox Learned Candadate or Gospel Minister to preach.. until the Annual town Meeting in Decem[ber]	125
Robert Rood being Chosen Collector to Collect the town Rate Granted in December Last Desiring to be Released Voted that s^d Robert be Released	125
Voted that Theodore Parmerlee be Collector to Collect s^d Rate	125
Voted that Earl Stanly be a Collector to Collect the Ministers Rate for the Church men	125
Voted that Adna Beech Sitt in the high pew Next to the pulpit Stairs & Capt Edmund Bech Sitt in the oposite pew	125

22 Mar 1781

Capt Hall was Chosen moderator	125
Voted to Lay a Rate or tax of one Shilling on the pound State money.. for Defraying the Charges Arisen.. Voted that William Goodwin be Collector to Collect the afores^d Rate	126
Voted that fisk Beech be Collector to collect the money Assessed that was assessed on particular persons in the Several Classes.. who Refuse or neglect to pay their proportion of the Cost in hireing a man to Serve in the Continental Army for 3 Years or During the war	126
Voted that Dan^{ll} Miles James Thomson & Capt Hall be a Comte to Collect Evidence of the number of Soldiers this town hath in the Continental Army and to appear Before the Com^{te} appointed to Ascertain the Same	126
Es Collins & Ens Kettil were appointed a Com^{te} to hire Such Soldiers or Light horse as are Required to be Raised	126
Voted that a Bill.. of the Cost of Calling Entertaining and prosecuting before An Ecgliastical Council Sundry matters of Grievence Relating to Mr Nevel which Cost amounted to £23 -5- 10 State money be allowed	126
Voted that the Lt Miles Norton be Quorister for this town for the future	126

23 Jun 1781

Capt Buel was Chosen Moderator	126
Voted to Raise a Rate.. of one penny on the pound in hard money or Other money Equivelent.. for the Support of a preacher of the Gospel.. Westill Willoby was Chosen Collector of s^d Rate	126
Voted to Lay a Rate.. to be paid in merchantable Beef Cattle at the prices and att the Several periods Named in a Resolve of the General Assembly.. fisk Beech was Chosen Collector and Receiver of s^d tax & he Refusing was Excused & Ens Collins Chosen in his Room	126
Dan^{ll} Miles was Chosen Chosen Receiver to Receive the 2/6 tax.. to be paid in provisions or Cloathing	127
Voted that Capt Hall Capt Wright & Lt Miles Norton be a Com^{te} to hire the two Recruits Required.. And that they Act Descritionary as to Lending Caleb Miles and Bonny to the army to Serve During the war in Room of the 2 men to Serve till the Last Day of ~~Jan[ ]y~~ Decemr	127

315

Goshen

23 Aug 1781

Capt Hall was Chosen Moderator — *127*

Voted to Lay a Rate or tax of [ ] 2 pence on the pound..on the List AD 1780 William Beech was Chosen Collector — *127*

the Question was put whether the town Desire the Com^{te} to Hire the Revd Mr Sherman to preach.. for a Certain term hereafter on Condition he Can be hired on Reasonable terms and itt passed in the affirmative — *127*

Voted that Capt Buel L^t pratt Capt francis & Capt Goodwin & Silas Richmond be a Com^{te} to Enquire if a Suitable house and a Small Lott of Land Can be Purchased Near the meetinghouse for a Glebe Lot for a minister.. also to Enquire of the Vallue of the parsonage lot Laying Near Mr Ovits and whether the Same Can be Sold .. to procure s^d Glebe Lott — *127*

[ ] Aug 1781

Question was put whether the town would proced to Give the Revd Mr Sherman a Call to Settle in the Gospel ministry in this town & itt passed in the affirmative — *128*

Voted that Col Norton Sam^{ll} Nash Stephen Thomson & others be a Com^{te} to wait on Mr Sherman.. to Invite or Desire him to Settle in the work of the Gospel ministry in this town — *128*

Voted that James Thomson with Dan^{ll} Miles.. to Receive.. the 2/6 tax.. to be paid in provisions and Cloathing & to pack Store and Deliver the same.. Voted that the Receivers afores^d be paid a Reasonable Reward for their Cost & trouble — *128*

Voted that Elisha Thomson & Fisk Beech who they had Chosen Receivers & Collectors of the 2 taxes ordered to be paid in provisions in Case any person Should neglect to pay their proportion of s^d taxes by the time stated by Law.. are Directed.. to Collect of Such persons as are in arrears.. the whole there of Either in hard money or in wheat flower — *128*

[ ] Sep 1781

Voted that Col Norton James Thomson & Sam^{ll} Miles be a Comte to make further Enquiry Concerning purchasing a Convenient Gleb Lott near the meeting house — *128*

Voted that Capt Buel be an agent for the town to prosecute any person or persons who.. trespass on any of the highways.. by Diging Clay — *128*

8 Oct 1781

Sam^{ll} Kellogg was Chosen moderator — *129*

the Question Being put Whether this town are Desirous to Give the Revd Mr Josiah Sherman a proper Call to Settle in the work of the Gospel Ministry in this town and itt passed in the affirmative.. Voted to Give the Revd Mr Josiah Sherman.. for a Sallary one hundred and fifteen pounds Lawful hard money p^r Annum.. fifty pounds in provisions and Articles for Cloathing.. and 10£ of S^d Sum to be paid in Wood.. the use and Improvment of a Convenient Dwelling house & a Glebe Land att a Reasonable price and the Remainder of s^d 115 pounds to be paid in hard money — *129*

Voted that Daniel Miles Silas Richmond & Lt James Thomson be a Come to Lay Before the..Revd Mr Sherman the.. votes of the town Relating to his Setling in the work of the Gospel ministry in this town and Desire his Answer — *129*

Voted that Silas Richmond Dan^{ll} Miles & James Thomson be a Com^{te}.. to purchase a Convenient parsonage Lott near the meeting house and to Sell so much of the parsonage Land Lying near Mr Ovitt as Shall be Suffecient to Raise money to procure a Small Glebe Lott — *129*

Voted that fisk Beech be an Agent.. to apply to a proper Board for So much Salt of the State as needed to Salt the Beef and pork.. for the use of the Soldiers this fall and the Ensuing winter — *129*

Goshen

Voted that James Thomson be Released from being a Receiver of provisions	130
voted to Reconsider a former Vote.. proposing Silas Richmond Lt James Thomson and Daniel Miles as a Com^{te} to Sell part of the parsonage Land	130
Voted that Daniel Miles Receiver of provisions be allowed to Credit those persons who Shall be willing to have their Beef Cattle Drove to hartford and killed and Weighted there 4^d p^r pound if he Cannot agree with them on better terms.. to pay their provision tax and s^d Reciever is to Deliver over to fisk Beech So many Beef Cattle as Shall be needed	130
Voted that all those persons.. as Shall neglect to pay their provision tax Collected by Elisha Thomson and fisk beech in provision by 3^d Day of Decembr Next Should be liable to pay in the Same hard money only	130

10 Dec 1781

Capt Jonath Buel was Chosen Moderator	130
Town Clerk Sam^{ll} Nash	130
Town treasurr Capt Elisha Sill	130
Select men } Capt Sill Dan^{ll} Miles Silas Richmond Capt pratt Capt Matthew Smith	130
Constables Fisk Beech & Collector of the Cuntry Rate Ephraim Starr 2^d Do	130
Grand Jurors} Cheliab Smith Heman Smith Wait Hinman Barnabas Richmond Chauncy Beech	130
Listers } Aaron Norton Lt Collins Ens Kettell Dan^{ll} Baldwin Jonath Buel Jur Ebenez Norton Jur Capt Wright	130
Surveyors of highways } Elisha Mayo Lt Collins Eph^m Starr Seth Hill Capt Stanly Giles Griswold Ens Norton Theoph Mix Sam^{ll} Logon John Medcalf Lt Rily Sam^{ll} Hopkins Titus Gailord	130
Tything men } Sam^{ll} Norton Jur Westill Willoby Asa Bonny Abraham Wadhams	130
Sealers of Weights Sam^{ll} Nash of Measures Col Norton of Leather Nehe Lewis	130
Pound Keepers Capt Hall Adna Beech Jur David Tyler	130
School Com^{te} } Thos Ens Munson Ebenez Norton Jur Josiah Royce Capt pratt Benj Ovitt Capt Wright Dan^{ll} Baldwin John Medcalf	131

14 Dec 1781

Voted that whereas the parsonage Land.. Remote from the meetinghouse and Cannot be used to proffitt for the use of the ministry.. therefore the town will.. Exchange 100 Acres of s^d Land for Land near the meeting house for.. Accomodating a minister the Land to be Exchanged.. Lying near Mr Ovitts	131
And Dan^{ll} Miles Silas Richmond & James Thomson were Chosen a Com^{te}.. to Exchange s^d 100 Aceres for Other Land Lying Near the meeting house.. and to Give Leases of s^d 100 Acres for 999 Years	131
Voted to Lay a Rate.. of 2^d on ye pound hard money.. for paying the Cost of preaching Sam^{ll} Hopkins was Chosen Collector of s^d taxes	131
Voted that Col Norton Sam^{ll} Nash Capt Goodwin Sam^{ll} Miles & James Thomson be a Com^{te} to hire preaching	131

7 Jan 1782

Capt Beech was Chosen Moderator	132
the Question was put whether the town Desire the Revd Mr Josiah Sherman Should Settle in the Work of the Gospil Ministry.. and itt passed in the affirmative.. Question was then put whether the town Would Give s^d Mr Sherman for a Sallary.. the Sum of one hunred and	132

Goshen

fifteen pounds hard money..

Voted that James Thomson & Danˡˡ Miles be a Comᵗᵉ to Lay Before Mʳ Sherman the foregoing vote.. Relating to his Setling in the Ministry and Desire his Answer   *133*
[ ] Feb 1782

Capᵗ Beech the moderator of sᵈ Meeting being unable to attend Liuᵗ Hurlbut was Chosen moderator   *133*

a Great Majority.. being Still Desirous that the Revᵈ Mʳ Josiah Sherman Should be their pastor and that Everything Should be Removed that is a Di[ ] in sᵈ Mʳ Shermans mind.. Voted to Desire sᵈ Mʳ Sherman to Remove himself and family into this town to preach a few months for the purpose aforesᵈ.. this vote passed with but 3 Dissenting votes   *133*

Voted that Lᵗ James Thomson & Ens Danˡˡ Miles be a Comᵗᵉ to Lay before sᵈ Mʳ Sherman the foregoing Desire   *133*
28 Feb 1782

Capᵗ E Beech was Chosen Moderator   *133*
[ ] Feb 1782

Voted that Ens Danˡˡ Miles & Capᵗ Hall be a Comᵗᵉ to appear before the Comᵗᵉˢ appointed by the General Assembly to Aportion the Number of Recruits to be Raised for the filling up the Continental army & to Show the Number of men we have now in Actual Service   *134*

Voted that the Comᵗᵉ .. to Supply the pulpit with preaching Do out of the Rates already Granted.. procure for the Revᵈ Mʳ Sherman with the Necesaries he Shall Need for the present Support of his family   *134*
[ ] Mar 1782

Voted to Lay a Rate or tax of on the pound hard money on the List 1781.. Fisk Beech Was Chosen Collector of sᵈ Rate and to be allowed the Same fees for Collecting sᵈ Taxe as Constables Receive for Collecting public taxes   *134*

Voted that Capᵗ Pratt Lᵗ Collins & Lᵗ Rily be a Comᵗᵉ to Remove Incroachments & Nucencies out of yᵉ highways   *134*
27 Mar 1782

Capᵗ Edmund Beech was Chosen moderator   *134*

Capᵗ francis & Danˡˡ Miles were Chosen a Comᵗᵉ to Joyn Samˡˡ Nash to Settle it Mʳ Starr about his Acctˢ of yᵉ meeting house   *134*

Voted to proceed to Build a parsonage house 38 feet in Length & 28 feet wide upright 2 Stories high.. by next fall.. Voted that James Thomson Danˡˡ Miles & Jonaᵗʰ Kettel be a Comᵗᵉ to Build sd house   *134*

Sᵈ Comᵗᵉ to purchase Land of Mʳ heatin Land on the North Side of the Road Leading from the meetinghouse to Elisha Thomsons   *134*
2 Apr 1782

Perez Bonny Delivered to me the Subscriber a paper in these Words.. We the Subscribers Being Inhabitants of.. Goshen Do this Day profess Our Selves to hold with & Belong to a Sell or Denomination of Christians Called & Known by the Name of baptists.. Test Peres Bonny.. Asa Bonny   *135*

These may Certify whom it may Concern that Mʳ John Munson hath been a member of the Strict Congregational meeting att Cornwell for 10 months past   *135*
[ ] Jun 1782

Capᵗ Beech was Chosen moderator   *136*

the Question was put whether the town Do Still Continue their Desire that the Revd Mr Josiah Sherman Would Settle in the Work of the Gospel ministry.. and it passed in the affirmative 54 or 9.. Voted to Give the Revd Mr Sherman (in Case he Should Settle.. in this town to be paid to him annual the Sum of one hundred and fifteen pounds Lawful Silver Money.. [*ed: see original record for full description of payment method*]	136
Voted that Capt Beech James Thomson & Sam^{ll} Hopkins be a Com^{te} to Lay Before Mr Sherman the foregoing votes of the town Relataling to his Setling in the work of the Gospel ministry and deliver his answer	136
Dan^{ll} Miles was Chosen Collector	137
the Com^{te} appointed to Lay before Mr Sherman the Call and votes of the town Relating to his Setling in the mnistry.. Reported.. Mr Shermans Answer	137
Voted that Capt Buel & Silas Richmond & Aaron Norton & Capt Jabez Wright & Miles Norton be .. Added to the Com^{te} to build the parsonage house	137

17 Jun 1782

.. I Signify to You my Willingness to Accept Your Call.. Josiah Sherman.. To the Town and Church in Goshen: a true Coppy of the Original Test Sam^{ll} Nash	137

2 Sep 1782

Capt Edmund Beech was Chosen Moderator	137
Voted to Lay a tax of 3^d on the pound L money.. for the purpose of paying the Revd Mr Sherman	137
Voted that Nath^{ll} Baldwin Ens Wadhams Barnabas Richmond John Carington and Capt Jabez Wright be a Com^{te}.. to Collect S^d Rate.. Voted that s^d Com^{te} Ascertain the price of the provisions.. which we are to pay Mr Sherman and those who Decline [*or*] Neglect to pay their part.. to pay the whole in money	137
Voted to Dignify the Seats in the meeting house anew.. to be Seated According to what they Agree to pay toward the Support of preaching to Mr Sherman	138
Voted that Col Norton Capt Buel Capt Beech Capt pratt Capt Wright Silas Richmond Lt James Thomson Ens Miles Ens Kettell & Sam^{ll} Hopkins be a Com^{te} for s^d purpose	138
Voted that Dan^{ll} Miles & Ens Kettell be a Com^{te} to take in Subscriptions for hireing a Singing Master	138
Voted to use 5° of the money Coming to the town for the parsonage Land Sold to Ovit &c for.. furnishing the parsonage house	138

2 Dec 1782

Capt Edmund Beech was Chosen moderator	138
Town Clerk Sam^{ll} Nash town treasr Capt Sill	138
Select men Capt E: Sill Capt A: Hall Ens Wadhams Silas Richmond & Dan^{ll} Miles	138
Constables Adino Hale 1st Constable & to Collect the Cuntry rate… 2^d Constable Fisk Beech	138
Grand Jurors Jonath Buel Jur Giles Griswold David Tyler Sam^{ll} Hopkins Ezekiel North	138
Tything men } Ens Doud Ens Kettell Nehe Lewis Seth Wadhams	138
Listers Ens Kettell Dan^{ll} Baldwin Jonath Buel Jur Ens Kellog A: Norton Ebenz Norton Jur Chauncy Beech	138
Surveyors of highways } Elisha Mayo Elisha Thomson Miles Norton Fisk Beech Brewen Baldwin Timoth Buell Noah Tuttle John Rily Moses Barthollomew Wait Hinman Erl Stanly Robert Rood	138
Key Keepers Adna Beech Jur Jos Baily D Tyler	138

Goshen

School Com^te the Same as Last Year Except John Wadhams in Stead of Capt Pratt	138
fence viewers Fisk Beech & Sol Wadhams	138
Com^te to Remove Nusances on Highways Fisk Beech & Lt Moses Lyman	138
Voted that Jos Brooks be as: Assisting Quoristor	139

[ ] Dec 1782

Capt Hall was Chosen Moderator	139
Adino hale Being Chosen Collector of the publick tax Decemr Last past and he making his Excuse was by vote Released and Fisk Beech Chosen in his Stead	139
S^d Adino was Chosen Constable	139
Jonath Buel Jur Being Chosen Grandjuror in Decemr Last and he made his plea to be Excused which was by vote Accepted & Sam^ll Logan was chosen in his Room	139

24 Mar 1783

Capt Hall was chosen moderator	139
Voted to choose a a Com^te to treat with Mr Nevil about a Settlement Relating to an action he has Commenced	139
Committee to treat with Mr Nevil about a Settlement Relating to an action he has Commenced.. for his Salary Since 1760 to the time of his Dismission and also for money the town have Borowed of him.. Sam^ll Kelleg Capt Beul Capt pratt Capt Goodwin & Capt Sill were Chosen for this Com^te	139
Voted to Choose an Agent to answer Before the County Court in the 2 Actions above Named & to Defend thereon in the Best manner he Can.. and therein Dan^ll Miles was Chosen for s^d Agent	139
Voted that the Select men pay Mr Nevel the Money the town have Borowed of him In hard money	139
Voted that Silas Richmond be a Collector of the Rate for Mr Shirmans Sallary in the Room of Barnabas Richmond gone out of town	139

23 Jun 1783

Capt E Beech was Chosen Moderator	140

16 Sep 1783

Capt Asaph Hall was Chosen moderator	140
Question was.. put whether the town would Send a Deligate to Joyn the proposed Convention at Middleton the 30th of Inst Septr and itt passed in the afirmative.. Capt Elisha Sill was Chosen a Deligate for the purpose afores^d	140

[ ] Oct 1783

on the Motion of Wm Brown Shewing that Some Years Since he provided 26 prs of Shoes for the Soldiers in the Continental Army and Delivered the Same to Eph^m Starr a Com^te man Chosen to provide the Same and he had never Rec^d any Reward therefore	140
Voted tht Capt Goodwin Ens Wadhams & Sam^ll Hopkins be a Com^te to look into that affair and Settle the matter between Brown and Eph Starr	140

6 Oct 1783

Capt Buel was Chosen Moderator	141
Voted to Lay a Rate or tax of three pence on the pound on the List of s^d town AD 1782) Churchmen and Bubli[ ] Excepted for the purpose of paying the Revd Mr Sherman his Annual Sallary Stephen Thomson & Ebenez Norton were Chosen Collectors of s^d Rate	141

Goshen

Voted that Cap[t] Goodwin James Thomson & Cap[t] francis be a Com[te] to Call the Several Collectors appointed to Collect former Rates Granted for M[r] Shermans sermon Sallaries and to Examine how the town Accts Stand with M[r] Sherman Respecting his Sallary [ ] 1777	141
An Acc[t] of those who took the Oath of fidelity 1777.. Seth Lockwood.. Thos Dickenson.. Sam[ll] Norton Jur.. Step Tuttle.. W[m] Goodwin.. Theody Parmele.. W[m] Brown.. George Deer.. Jona[th] Mayo.. Cheliab Smith.. Olliver Beech.. David Humphry.. [ ] 1778	183
.. John Munson.. Levi Carr.. Titus Allyn.. Aug 1778	183
.. Zach Griswold Jur.. Giles Griswold.. Rev[d] M[r] Heaton.. Theophilus Mix.. Nehe Lewis Ju[r].. L[t] Parmelee Sen[r].. Abel Phelps Ju[r].. Sam[ll] Jones.. Noah Tuttle.. W[m] Beech.. Charls Miles.. Caleb Munson.. Munson Winchel. Thos Ens Munson.. Abel Butler.. John Carr.. Caleb Carr.. Stephen Lee.. 31 Mar 1778	183
.. Elisha Andrus.. Sep 1778	183
.. Munson Beech.. Jona[th] Buel Jnr Nov 1778	183
.. Brewen Baldwin.. 30 Nov 1778	183
.. James Glass.. 19 Dec 1778	183
.. L[t] John Rily.. 20 Jan 1779	183
.. Ens Lewis 9 Dec 1778	183
.. Cap[t] Hinman.. 26 Jan 1779	183
.. Olliver Willcox.. 10 Feb 1779	183
.. Seth Nash.. Noah Malbie.. 12 Mar 1779	183
.. W[m] Nash.. Abel Butler Jur.. 14 Dec 1778	183
.. Sam[ll] Ovit.. Jun 1779	183
.. Asa offiria..	183

Goshen

2 Aug 1779
.. Dr Deming..   *183*

21 Sep 1779
.. Adino hale ..   *183*

27 Dec 1779
..Apleton Kulberis..   *183*

10 Apr 1780
.. Josiah Nash..   *183*

9 Apr 1781
.. Seth hill.. Jos Norton.. Joel Clemins   *183*

18 Sep 1781
in open freemens meeting the following persons were admited and took the freemans Oath and also took the Oath of fidelity.. + Andrew Baily Timoth Buel Heman + Smith Benj + Ovitt Allyn + Lucas Ambrose Collins Timoth Hudson those marked this + had taken the Oath of fidelity before   *183*

1 Dec 1781
Jonah Case Solemnly affirmed the Oath of fidelity.. before me S Nash J pece   *183*

5 Dec 1781
Abijah Munson took the oath of fidelity before Ebenz Norton Esqr.. and brought me a Certificate there[*to*]..   *183*

6 Dec 1781
.. Asher Smith also.. the Same Oath Before s^d Norton and produced a Ce[*rtificate*]   *183*

16 Sep 1777
A List or Roll of the freeman .. who took the Oath of fidelity to the State of Connecticut.. and also the Oath appointed for freemen by a Late Act of Assembly.. Revd Mr Nevil.. Col Ebenezer Norton.. Sam^{ll} Nash Esqr.. Thos Lucas.. Step Smith.. Capt Buell.. Capt Cook.. Nath^{ll} Baldwin.. Sam^{ll} Baldwin.. Capt Sill.. Capt Stanly.. Capt Hall.. Capt Goodwin.. Capt Beech.. Capt Francis.. Adna Beech.. David Thomson.. James Thomson.. Elihu Norton.. Ebenez Norton Jur.. Aaron Norton.. Isaac Pratt.. Chileab Smith.. Fisk Beech.. ~~Elisha Tuttle~~.. Philip Cook.. Jonath Kettle.. Amasa Cook.. Sam^{ll} Norton.. Lazarus [ ].. Joel Hinsman.. .. Chauncy Beech.. Philemon Sanford.. Sam^{ll} francis 2^d..   Clemons.. David Tyler.. Jos Baly.. Ens Munson.. Sam^{ll} Logon.. Fowler Munson.. Thos Lucas.. Jno Doud.. Nevil Hinman.. B[ ] Richmond.. Linus Beech.. Jonath Buel Jur.. Sam^{ll} Norton Jur.. Theophilus Mix.. Capt Pettibone.. Silas Richmond.. Sam^{ll} Hopkins.. Josiah Royce.. Dan^{ll} Miles.. Capt Smith John.. Col Hill.. Sam^{ll} Bishop.. Ep^{hm} Starr.. Jared Jones.. Josiah Benton.. ~~Dan^{ll} Baldwin~~ + not Sworn.. Lieu^t Hurlbut.. Josiah Willoby.. Westil Willoby.. Amos Beech.. John Willcox.. Ens Wadhams.. Ens Collins.. Elisha Hurlbut.. Elisha Tuttle.. Lt Miles Norton.. Lt Jabez Wright.. Step Thomson.. Ens Lyman.. Robert Rood.. Capt Matthew Smith.. Titus Gailord.. John Carington.. Sam^{ll} Kellogg.. Jos Howd.. John Hay   *184*

Dec 1777
these took ye Oath of freemen in the Same meeting.. ~~Thos Dickenson~~.. Sol Wadhams B[ ] Richmond.. Jacob Beech.. John Wadhams.. Ezekiel North.. Sam^{ll} Barthol.. Jonath Mayo..   *184*

Goshen

Abel phelps Ju^r.. Nehe Lewis Ju^r.. Noah Tuttle.. Thos Dickenson.. Thos Ens Munson.. Minius Beech.. George D[ ] Wm Heaton.. Theodore parmalee.. John Medcalf.. Abel phelps Ju^r.. Nehe Lewis Ju^r.. Noah Tuttle.. Thos Dickenson.. Thos Ens Munson.. Minius Beech.. George D[ ] Wm Heaton.. Theodore parmalee.. John Medcalf
Sep 1780

Abell Butler.. [ed: *on the Roll of freemen who took the Oath of fidelity and also the oath for freemen*]   *184*
1 Jul 1782

Jacob Williams took ye Oath of fidelity   *184*
12 Apr 1779

Att the freemans meeting.. Sam^{ll} Ovitt Lt Rily & Wm Nash took the freemans Oath   *185*
20 Apr 1779

Nathan Carter Do [ed: *"ditto"*]   *185*
28 Apr 1779

Sollomon Moss took the oath of fidelity & Sam^{ll} Woodman   *185*
29 Apr 1779

do Eber Norton [ed: *"ditto"*]   *185*
3 May 1779

Wm Stanly Thos Humphry Noah Humphry Mat Lockwood Aaron Tuttle Asa Bonni Dan^{ll} Humphry Dan^{ll} Baldwin Allyn Lucas Heman Smith Timo Stanly Jur Elisha Mayo Elijah Jur Will[ ] Amos Beech Jur Sam^{ll} Kellogg Jur [ed: *took the oath of fidelity*]   *185*
21 Sep 1779

Att the freemans meeting.. Step Lee ~~was~~ took the freemans oath & Solomon moss William Beech Wm Goodwin & Adino hale   *185*
26 Jan 1780

I Rec[ ]d a Certificate from the town Clerk of Waterbury.. Certifying that Abraham L[ ] Now Living in Goshen had taken the oath of fidelity and freemans Required by Law.. Test S Nash Clerk   *185*
29 Feb 1780

Stephen North took the oath of fidelity   *185*
[ ] Oct 1779

Phinehas Hinsman took the Oath of fidelity to the State.. Before Ebenez Norton Esqr as pr s^d Nortons Certificate   *185*
[ ] 1780

Gid Hurlbut took the oath of fidelity before Ebenez Norton Just of peace   *185*
9 Apr 1781

Att a freemans meeting.. Seth Hill Ebez Norton Adna Beech Jur Jos Norton.. took the freemans oath.. Do Joel Clemons   *185*
19 Nov 1781

Libeus Holms took the Oath of fidelity to this State Before Ebz Norton Esqr.. as by s^d Norton Certificate Shown me S Nash Clerk   *185*

Goshen

29 Dec 1781

Ens Jere How Brought to me a Certificate under the hand of Ebenz Norton Esqr that he had taken the Oath of fidelity to the State of Connecticut before s^d Norton *185*

27 Apr 1782

John Norton took the oath of fidelity *185*

16 Sep 1783

att a freemens meeting.. the following persons were admitted to the Oath of fidelity.. John Thomson Jnr.. Elisha Stanly.. Elihu Lewis.. Elijah Towner.. Isaac Miles.. Jonath Deming *185*

6 Sep 1783

the following persons were sworn freemen.. David Douglas.. Jos Butler.. Elihu Lewis.. Isaac Miles.. Elisha Stanly.. Elijah Towner.. Jonath Deming *186*

10 Apr 1780

Att a freemens meeting.. the following persons took the Oath of fidelity to this State viz Noah Humphry Sam^{ll} Hinsman Darias Griswold Elisha Thomson Jur Elisha Baldwin Simeon Humphry David Hart Nath^{ll} Pease David Humphry Jur Sam^{ll} Baldwin Jur Brewin Baldwin and all of them took the freemens oath & Seth Perler Moses Beech & Lemuel Hill took the freemens Oath all before S Nash Just of peace *186*

Greenwich

Commonplace Book 3
1703 – 1797

Located at the Town Clerk's Office

Greenwich

[ ] Dec 1774

Make Choice of Mr Bezaleel Brown to be Moderator	118
make Choice of Jesse Parsons to be Town Clerk	118
Order that A Com^{tee} be Chosen According to the 11th Article of the Assocation of the Continental Congress at Philadelphia [*ed: Committee of Inspection*].. And the Town.. do appoint Messrs Amos Mead Nehemiah Mead Titus Mead with Jno Mackay	118

8 Feb 1775

Proposed to this Meeting Whether they will Send Delegates to Attend A County Congress at Fairfield.. Resolved in the Affirmative and that Doc^r Amos Mead and John Mackay be their Delegates	119
the Town further Order Benjamin Mead Junr Bezaleel Brown & Jeremiah Lockwood be Aded to their Com^{te} of Inspection	119

[ ] Dec 1775

made Choice of Lieu^t Bezaleel Brown to be Moderator	119
Make Choice of Mr Jesse Parsons To be Town Clerk	119
Selectmen { Peter Mead & John Mead Esq^{rs} Messrs John Mackay Benjn Mead Junr Lieu^t Bezaleel Brown	119
Constables { Maj^r Thomas Hobby and Abraham Lockwood to be Constable and to Collect the Country Rate if any be	119
Listers { Saml Peck Silas Betts Joseph Hobby Junr John Hobby Simon Ingersol Saml Peck Junr Benjn Mead Jr	119
Grand Jurors { Joshua Ferris Saml Seymour Caleb Lyon Junr Abr^m Mead Obadiah Banks	119
Surveyors of Highways { John Palmer Junr David Brown Jesse Hallock Israel Knapp Junr Denham Palmer Elijah Mead James Lyon Richard Titus Thomas Lewis James Brown Nathan Merrit Oliver Sherwood Thos Cromwell Jehiel Mead Benjamin Mead Junr Sylvanus Knapp Jonah Smith Moses Husted Ju^r Eben Knapp Saml Palmer Junr Reuben Holmes Holmes Horton Reynolds Gershom Lockwood 3^d Tim^o Ferris John Mackay Coll John Mead ~	119
Fence Viewers { Joseph Peck Joshua Ferris James Ferris Nathaniel Ferris John Palmer Junr Seth Palmer Nehemiah Mead Daniel Lyon Junr Mathew Mead John Hobby Capt Solomon Purdy Willm Brundige Uriah Knapp John Knapp Jn^r Saml Palmer Junr Willm Rundall David Wood Gersh^m Lockwood Joseph Hobby Junr Eli Rundall Jabez Ferris Henry Rich	119
Keykeepers { Sylvanus Jezup of his own Pound Which Pound he is to provide on his own Capt Samuel Seymour of the Town Pound Saml Palmer of his own Pound Gershom Lockwood 3^d of his own Pound	119
Tythingmen { James Ferris Joshua Smith David Wood	119
Leather sealers Jeduthan Ferris Peter Mead Jonathan Hobby ~	119
Sealer of Weights & Measures Nehemiah Mead Isaac Holmes Junr Packer of Meat Culler of Staves	120
Brander & Toller of Horses Saml Seymour & Jacob Lockwood	120
Agent { Coll^o John Mead	120
Com^{te} of Safety & Inspection { Saml Peck James Ferris John Mackay Amos Mead Benjamin Mead Junr Nehemiah Mead Coll^o John Mead Roger Brown Bez^l Brown David Wood Maj^r Thos Hobby Odell Close Nathl Mead Junr	120
Liberty p^r the Town is Given to the Daughter of Mr John Palmer the Wife of Phillip Reynolds to Erect a House and Fence in a Small Garden on the Highway and to have the Use of the	120

Greenwich

Same During the Towns Pleasure

15 Jan 1776

The Town p^r vote Add to their Com^{te} of Safety and Inspection the following persons viz Israel Knapp Junr Saml Seymour John Hobby Messenger Palmer & Peter Mead Esqr	120
In this Meeting Comes Jesse Hallock and presents himself to Set up the Salt Petre Works in this Town	120

26 Jul 1776

At Special Town Meeting.. Called on Acount of the Death of Mr Jesse Parsons the Late Town Clerk &c.. Made Choice of Mr Benjamin Mead to be Moderator	120
Made Choice of Co^l John Mead to be Town Clerk untill the Next Annual Town Meeting in December.. the town p^r vote Made Choice of Col John Mead to be Town Treasurer	120
also p^r vote Made Choice of Capt Jabez Sherwood also Peter Mead Esqr to be Sevears of Highweys untill the Next Town Meeting	120

[ ] Dec 1776

made choice of Bezaleel Brown to be Moderator	120
made choice of Jabez Fitch to be Town Clerk	120
made choice of Col John Mead Mr John Mackay Benjamin Mead Junr Bezaleel Brown and Capt John Grigg to be Selectmen	120
made choice of Col Thomas Hobby Abraham Lockwood Edmond Mead Constables by vote Also made choice of Mr Josiah Ferris Constable and Collector of the Country Rate and to Settle with the Treasurer of the Colony	121
made choice of Jonathan Lockwood ye 3^d Abraham Hays & Jonathan Coe Grand Jurymen	121
made choice of Capt Matthew Mead Samuel Peck Josiah Ferris Bezaleel Brown Samuel Peck Junr Benjamin Mead Junr David Wood Esqr and Daniel Merrit to be Listers	121
made choice of John Palmer Junr Jonth. Lockwood ye 3^d Jacob Lockwood Nehemiah Mead Joseph Sackett Justus Sackett Capt John Grigg James Banks Daniel Merrit Andrew Miller John Ogden Silas Mead Junr Ebenezer Holmes Joshua Knapp Nathaniel Mead Junr Samuel Rundall Benjamin Peck Caleb Mead Junr Edmond Brown Richard Webb Nathaniel Jesup Titus Palmer Solomon Phiney Jonathan Finch Junr Thomas Cromwell Stephen Davis and Col John Mead to be Surveyors of highways	121
made choice of Nehemiah Mead Daniel Lyon Junr John Hobby Matthew Mead David Wood Esqr Gershom Lockwood Junr to be Fence Viewers	121
made choice of Gershom Lockwood Junr Samuel Palmer Samuel Seymour Silvanus Jesup and Capt Solomon Purdy to be Keykeepers of their own Pound	121
made choice of Nathaniel Mead ye 3^d to be Leather Sealer	121
made choice of Nehemiah Mead to be Sealer of Weights & Measures	121

11 Mar 1777

made choice of Lieu^t Bezaleel Brown to be Moderator	121
made choice of Nehemiah Mead to be Town treasurer	121
made choice of Dr Amos Mead to be Agent	121
made Choice of Messrs Josiah Ferris Robert Peck Nehemiah Mead Capt Matthew Mead Thadeus Mead Lieu^t Seth Palmer & Gershom Lockwood to be a Committee of Inspection	121
made Choice of Capt Josiah Ferris to to Collect the remainder of the two penny Country Rate that was in the hands of Col Thomas Hobby and Settle with the Colony Treasurer	121

Greenwich

made choice of Messrs Saml Peck Ebenezer Peck Nehemiah Mead Daniel Lyon jun^r Joshua Smith Jered Mead Thaddeus Mead Edmund Mead Nathaniel Mead jun^r & John Knapp junr to be Fence viewers	123
made choice of Sam^{ll} Peck to be Keykeeper of his own pound .. & Jered Mead of the Town pound & Messrs John Mead Sam^{ll} Palmer jun^r Gershom Lockwood jun^r Reuben Merrit & Roger Brown to be Keykeepers of their own pounds	123
made choice of Joshua Smith & Silvanus Ferris to be Tythingmen	123
made choice of Messrs Nathaniel Mead jun^r & John Knapp Junr to be Leather Sealors	123
made choice of Nehemiah Mead to be Sealor of weights & measures	123
made choice of Bezaleel Brown to be Packer of meat & Culler of Staves	123
made choice of Titus Mead to be Brander & Toller of Horses	123
made choice of Col John Mead to be Agent for the town	123
made choice of Bezalel Brown to Collect the Town Rate	123
made choice of Titus Mead to be Town treasurer	123
Eben Knapp agrees to keep Nathaniel Acerly for twelve shillings.. for six months	123

12 Jan 1778

made choice of Bezaleel Brown to be Moderator	123
made choice of Bezaleel Brown to be Barrackmaster to Supply the Troops with wood & other nuessances	123

20 Mar 1778

made choice of Lieut Bezaleel Brown to be Moderator	124
It is propossed whether the Town are willing that the moneys that were loaned by the General Assembly for the use of Schools be divided among the Several Societies of this Town according to the List 1776 Voted in the Affirmative.. made choice of David Mead Esqr Peter Mead Esqr Josiah Ferris to be a Committee to devide s^d moneys	124

14 Dec 1778

made choice of Bezaleel Brown to be Moderator	124
made choice of Jabez Fitch to be Town Clerk	124
The Town further voted as follows (viz) for Col John Mead Benjamin Mead jun^r John Mackay Bezaleel Brown & Capt Samuel Lockwood to be Selectmen..	124
.. for Seth Palmer to be Constable & Collector to collect the State rates & Settle with the Treasurer of the State.. and for Caleb Finch to be Constable.. Both refuse to accept..	124
..For Titus Mead Stephen Ferris & Peter Mead jun^r to be Grandjurors..	124
.. For Seth Palmer Jeremiah Rundall Robert Peck James Ferris Daniel Lyon jun^r Ezra Marshall Solomon Finney Abraham Heusted Peter Mead Thomas Peck John Mead James Banks Daniel Merrit Joseph Palmer Jehial Mead Caleb Lyon jun^r Isaac Howe jun^r Eben Knapp Roger Sutherland Gershom Lockwood jun^r Silvanus Ferris William Hubbard Eli Rundall jun^r Samuel Rundall Jonah Knapp & Jered Mead to be Surveyors of Highways..	124
.. For John Wood Palmer Ebenezer Mead Josiah Ferris Silas Betts Capt Abraham Mead Daniel Merrit Eliphalet Mead jun^r Nathaniel Mead jun^r Nathaniel Reynolds jun^r & Benjamin Hobby to be Listers & assessors.. John Wood Palmer refused to take it..	124
.. For Joseph Hubby jun^r & Nath^{ll} Meade ye 4th to be a Committee of Supplies for the Soldiers Families	124

Greenwich

voted For Capt Silvanus Mead to be Barrackmaster..	125
.. For John Palmer Jeremiah Palmer Josiah Ferris Sam^{ll} Lockwood Nehemiah Mead Daniel Lyon jun^r Jered Mead Matthew Mead John Knapp Uriah Knapp Gershom Lockwood ye 3^d Eli Mead to be Fenceviewers..	125
..For Samuel Peck to be Key keeper of his own pound Jared Mead Keykeeper of the Town pound & Odle Close & David Wood Keykeepers of their own pound..	125
..For Mr Nehemiah Mead to be Sealer of weights & measures..	125
..For Reuben Holmes & John Knapp to be leather Sealers..	125
..For Samuel Seymour Caleb Lyon jun^r & Stephen Mead jun^r to be Branders of Horses..	125
..For Bezaleel Brown to be Town Treasurer..	125
.. For Messrs Silvanus Mead Isaac Howe jun^r Reuben Rundall Abraham Mead Josiah Ferris Matthew Mead & Edmund Mead to be a Committee of inspection	125

[ ] Dec 1778

voted for Capt Josiah Ferrris to be their Moderator	125
..For Josiah Ferris to be Constable & Collector to collect the State taxes & Settle with the Treasurer of the State..	125
..For Bezaleel Brown to be Constable..	125
..For Cornelious Van Randts to be Gauger..	125
..For Bezaleel Brown to be Culler of Staves & Packer of meat	125
..That there be a Town rate raised of a Shilling on the pound.. Josiah Ferris to be Collector to Collect s^d Rate & Settle with the Treasurer of the Town for Thirty pounds	125

13 Dec 1779

This Town voted as follows viz For Mr Bezaleel Brown to be their Moderator	126
..For Mr Jabez Fitch to be their Town Clerk..	126
..For Benjamin Mead jun^r Col John Mead John Mackay Bezaleel Brown Sam^{ll} Lockwood jun^r Capt John Grigg & Messenger Palmer Esq to be Selectman..	126
.. For Bezaleel Brown to be Town Treasurer..	126
..For Capt Josiah Ferris to be Constable & Collector to collect the State rate & Settle with the State Treasurer..	126
..For John Knapp & John W^d Palmer to be constables..	126
..For James Ferris Philip Lockwood Enos Knapp Ebenezer Peck Seth Palmer Thos Johnson Silas Betts Andrew Marshall Justus Sackett Peter Mead jun^r John Mead ye 3^d Caleb Finch Moses Heusted jun^r David Brown Benjamin Green Thaddeus Mead Isaac Ferris Thaddeus Lockwood Edmund Mead Eli Rundall jun^r Reuben Holmes Gold John Silleck Eliphalet Mead jun^r & Daniel Merrit Benjamin Sutton Jonathan Coe Wm Rundall & Denham Palmer to be Surveyers of highways..	126
..For Messrs Sam^{ll} Peck Ebenezer Peck Eli Rundall jun^r Horton Reynolds Jared Mead Joshua Smith Thaddeus Mead & Gershom Lockwood jun^r to be Fence viewers..	126
..For Messrs Ebenezer Peck Jabez Fitch Elkanah Mead Bezaleel Brown Nath^{ll} Mead jun^r Daniel Merrit David Wood Roger Brown Nath^{ll} Reynolds jun^r & John Hobby to be Listers..	126
..For Jeduthan Ferris Nath^{ll} Mead 3^d & John Knapp to be Leather Sealers..	126
..For Messrs Eben Knapp Benjamin Peck Ebenezer Peck Edmund Mead & Matthew Mead to be Grandjurors..	126

Greenwich

..For the Town house to be sold for the benefit of the Town   For Sam[ll] Peck & Benjamin Peck to to appraise the Town house.. — 126

..For Col Mead to have the Town house the appr[ ] which is Year 1774 £7 Lawful money or in Continental money at 12 for one at that rate.. — 126

..For Joshua Smith to be Tythingman.. — 126

..For Bezaleel Brown to be Culler of Staves & packer of meat.. — 126

..For Nehemiah Mead to be sealer of weights & measures.. — 126

..For Sam[ll] Seymour & Samuel Peck to be branders of horses.. — 126

..For Jared Mead to be Keykeeper of the Town pound.. — 126

..For Messenger Palmer Col John Mead Odle Close David Wood W[m] Rundall & Sam[ll] Peck to be key keepers of their own pound.. — 126

..For a Town rate to be laid & Collected on the List 1779 of three shillings on the pound For Captain Josiah Ferris to be collector to collect said Town rate for £249. — 126

11 Dec 1780

The meeting voted as follows.. (viz) For M[r] Bezaleel Brown to be their Moderator.. — 126

..For Jabez Fitch Esq for Town Clerk.. — 126

..For Messenger Palmer Esq Benjamin Mead jun[r] Esq Bezaleel Brown Sam[ll] Lockwood jun[r] & Col Tho[s] Hobby to be Selectmen.. — 126

..For Capt Josiah Ferris to be Constable & Collector to collect the State rates & Settle with the State Treasurer.. — 126

..For M[r] John Wood Palmer & Andrew Mead to be Constables.. — 126

..For Bezaleel Brown to be Town Treasurer.. — 126

..For a rate to be laid & collected of 4[d] on the pound in hard money or provisions or grain at the going price on the List 1779 For Capt Josiah Ferris to be collector to collect s[d] Town rate & Settle with the Selectmen for £12..0..0.. — 126

..For M[r] Seth Palmer & Edmund Mead to be a Committee to receive the monies or grain for said rate.. — 126

.. For James Ferris Robert Peck Joseph Knapp Nehemiah Mead Titus Mead Ezra Marshall Daniel Merrit Zacheus Mead Sam[ll] Peck jun[r] Joshua Knapp David Wood John Mackay Edmund Mead & Benjamin Peck to be Surveyors of highways.. — 126

..For Thomas Ferris Capt Sam[ll] Lockwood John Palmer Jeremiah Palmer Josiah Utter Silas Betts Joshua Smith & Jabez Fitch to be fence viewers.. — 127

..For Oliver Ferris Josiah Utter Jabez Fitch Edmund Mead Sam[ll] Peck jun[r] Roger Brown & Jonathan Coe to be Listers.. — 127

..For John Knapp Humphrey Denton & George Lockwood to be Leather Sealers.. — 127

..For Nehemiah Mead jun[r] to be Sealer of weights & measures.. — 127

..For Robert Peck Abr[m] Hays Edmund Mead & Benjamin Peck to be Grandjurors.. — 127

..For Jared Mead to be Key keeper of the Town Pound   For Jonathan Jesup Jeremiah Palmer David Wood & Joshua Knapp to be Keykeepers of their own pound.. — 127

..For M[r] Bezaleel Brown to be Agent — 127

2 Mar 1780

The Meeting voted as follows (viz) For Benjamin Mead jun[r] Esq to be their Moderator.. — 127

..For Roger Brown Gershom Lockwood junr Nath[ll] Mead jun[r] Cap[t] Odle Close Abraham Heusted Stephen Davis Peter Mead jun[r] Caleb Finch Andrew Marshall Sam[ll] Lockwood jun[r] — 127

Greenwich

Robert Peck Timothy Reynold Jehial Mead Caleb Lyon jun^r Jonathan Coe & Silas Mead jun^r to be inspectors of provisions

5 Dec 1781

a Meeting of the Inhabitants.. Legally warned and [*held*] at Mr Seth Palmers	127
The meeting voted.. as follows viz For General John Mead to be Moderator..	127
..For Jabez Fitch to be Town Clerk..	127
Benjamin Mead jun^r proposed to be Selectman and negatived Messenger Palmer nominated for Selectman & negatived	127
..For Col Thos Hobby Capt Sam^{ll} Lockwood Bezaleel Brown Josiah Ferris Seth Palmer Nath^{ll} Mead & Jabez Fitch to be Selectmen..	127
..For Bezaleel Brown to be Town Treasurer..	127
..For Mr John Wood Palmer to be Constable and collecter to collect the State taxes and Settle with the Treasurer For Capt Josiah Ferris to be Constable For Josiah Utter to be Constable who was excused from taking the Oath..	127
..For David Brown Joseph Heusted Robert Peck Jeremiah Palmer Andrew Marshall Titus Mead Edmund Brown Abraham Heusted Capt Matthew Mead James R[ ] Daniel Merrit Capt Solomon Purdy Frances Nash Jehial Mead Moses Heusted jun^r Jonah Knapp Joshua Knapp Benjamin Peck Samuel Palmer Isaac Ferris Capt David Wood Jeremiah Chapman Daniel Lyon jun^r Nehemiah Mead & James B[ ]sh to be Surveyors of highways..	127
..For Sam^{ll} Peck Ebenezer Peck Daniel Lockwood Joseph Peck Nehemiah Mead Ezra Marshall Matthew Mead Nath^{ll} Mead jun^r Nath^{ll} Mead & John Knapp Capt David Wood Gershom Lockwood Joseph Hubby jun^r Horton Reynolds James Pine & Isaac Anderson to be Fence viewers..	128
..For Oliver Ferris Jabez Fitch John Mackay Daniel Merrit & Nath^{ll} Mead to be Listers..	128
..For Jeduthan Ferris Reuben Holmes & Henry Waring to be Leather Sealors..	128
..For Sam^{ll} Peck Peter Mead (nominated & ~~objected to~~/negatived) Eli Rundall & Nehemiah Mead to be Grandjurors..	128
. For Joshua Smith Jonathan Jesup & William Hubbard to be Tythingmen..	128
..For Nehemiah Mead to be Sealor of weights & measures..	128
..For Capt John Wyllys to be gager..	128
..For Sam^{ll} Seymour & Jacob Lockwood to be brander of horses..	128
..For Jonathan Jesup Gershom Lockwood jun^r & Sam^{ll} Seymour to be Keykeepers of their own pounds..	128
..For Capt Josiah Ferris to be collector to collect the Town rate & Settle with the Town Treasurer for fourteen pounds..	128
..For Jabez Fitch to Agent..	128
Joseph Banks bid off Wm Ross to board a year a two dollars p^r week	128
Jeremiah Palmer bid off Abner Hutchings to board him a year at 12/ p^r week	128
Solomon Finney bid off the boarding Nat Aucly for a year at two dollars p^r week	128

9 Dec 1782

The Meeting voted for Genl John Mead to be their Moderator	128
..For Jabez Fitch to be Town Clerk..	128

Greenwich

..For Col Thos Hobby & Captains Josiah Ferris & Jabez Fitch to be Selectmen..	128
..For Seth Palmer to be Town Treasurer..	128
..Capt Josiah Ferris to be Constable & Collector to collect the State Taxes & Settle with the Treasurer..	128
..For Thos Hobby & Abraham Lockwood to be Constables John Wood Palmer nominated to be Constable & negatived..	128
..For James Ferris Charles Knapp John Wood Palmer Robert Peck Joseph Peck Nehemiah Mead Titus Mead Doctor William Bush Thos Hobby Andrew Marshall Moses Heusted jun^r Jonathan Coe Drake Seymour Thos Clapp Eliphalet Mead jun^r Charles Brundage Jonah Knapp Joshua Knapp Gershom Lockwood jun^r Solomon Rundall John Mackay David Mead Joseph Hobby jun^r Jeremiah Mead Eben Knapp & Nath^{ll} Reynolds jun^r to be Surveyors of highways..	128
..For Messrs Enos Lockwood Joseph Heusted Sam^{ll} Peck Ebenezer Peck John Hobby Matthew Mead Elkanah Mead Jeremiah Mead jun^r David Wood Gershom Lockwood jun^r John Knapp Sam^{ll} Peck jun^r to be Fence viewers..	128
..For Messrs Oliver Ferris Bezaleel Brown John Mackay Sam^{ll} Peck jun^r & Thos Hobby to be Listers..	128
..For Reuben Holmes & George Lockwood to be Leather Sealers..	128
..For Enos Lockwood Nath^{ll} Mead jun^r & Wm Hubbard to be Grandjurors..	128
..For John Wyllys to be gauger..	128
..For Nehemiah Mead to be Sealers of weights & measures..	128
..For Messrs Enos Lockwood Titus Mead Jeremiah Mead & John Mackay to be Key keepers of their own pound	128
Proposed whether this meeting are willing to give the widow Mary Peck keep her note voted in the negative	128

[ ] Apr 1783

Voted that Messrs William Bush Israel Knapp Junr and Joseph Hubby Junr be appointed a Committee to call to an account and settle with all Selectmen Town Treasurers collectors and others who have received any monies or specifick articles in behalf of the Townin since the year 1775	129
Voted that there be laid a tax of six pence on the pound on the List 1780.. Voted that Jonathan Coe be a collector to collect said Town rate	129
Voted that the Selectmen get places for the poor of the Town Voted that Jabez Fitch Esq be their Agent	129

12 Aug 1783

voted for Benjamin Mead Junr Esq to be their Moderator	129
The town taking into consideration the distress to which the inhabitants thereof are reduced by the.. plundering of the enemy and the constantly quartering of troops for the defence of this State.. during the late war with Great britain and the great injury done thereby.. voted that Brigadier Genl John Mead be agent for the town to make use of such measures by Memorial to the General Assembly.. to obtain redress of the towns grievances in this behalf and for a repair of the damages to the sufferers occassioned by the war excepting to those sufferers who are known to be inimical to the liberties and independence of the United States of America..	129

Groton

Town Meetings
1730 – 1821
Unpaginated

Located at the Town Clerk's Office

Groton

20 Jun 1774

William Williams Esqr Moderator [1]

Voted that Capt William Ledyard Thomas Mumford Benadam Gallup Esqr Dot^r Amos Prentice Mess^s Charles Eldredge Junr Deac^n John Hurlbut and Amos Geer be a Committe to Correspond with the Committees of the Several Towns of this and the other Brittish Colonies [1]

12 Dec 1774

William Williams Esqr be Moderator [2]

Ebenez^r Ledyard Esqr Thomas Mumford Esqr William Williams Esqr Benadam Gallup Esqr William Avery Esqr Capt Solomon Perkins David Avery William Morgan Esqr John Elderkin Joseph Packer Deac^n John Hurlbut Ebenez^r Avery 2^d Amos Geer; were Chosen Commi^{te} of Inspection [3]

10 Apr 1775

William Williams Esqr Chosen Moderator [3]

Voted that the Doings of the Selectmen Respecting the Alteration of the Highway from Paucatanuck to the Highway near the Dwelling House of Joseph Mallison be Accepted [3]

Voted that the Selectmen take care of Sarah Brown [3]

Voted that Thomas Mumford Esqr and Mr Nathan Gallup be a Committe to prefer a memorial to the General Assembly.. to Settle the Excise Money [3]

4 Dec 1775

Co^l Ebenezer Avery Chosen Moderator [4]

Thomas Mumford Esqr Capt Ralph Stoddard Deac^n John Hurlbut Ens^n Joseph Packer Capt Thomas Fanning Selectmen [4]

William Avery Esqr Town Clerk and Town Treasurer [4]

Benadam Gallup Junr firs Constable to Collect Town and Country Rates [4]

Parke Avery Junr: Second Constable [4]

Isaac Avery Joseph Allyn Daniel Avery Joseph Stanton William Ledyard Elijah Avery Capt Daniel Packer: were Chosen Grandjurymen [4]

Elisha Williams Thomas Fish Peleg Williams Benajah Avery and William Starr were Chosen Listers [4]

Richard Starr Benajah Chester Robert Allyn Allyn Samuel Mallison Nathan Crary Junr Elisha Packer were Chosen Tythingmen [4]

12 Dec 1775

Co^l Eben^r Avery Chosen Moderator [4]

Ebenez^r Avery 3^d Thomas Lester James Lamb Caleb Haley John Hix Nathan Crery Thos P: Gallup Nehemiah Smith Isaac Geer John Bellows James Worden John Perkins Joseph Lewis Shapley Morgan Agrippa Newton Sam^{ll} Andrews Thomas Pelton Isaac Avery Abel Sholes James Avery 2^d Rufus Allyn Chris Allyn Joshua Elderkin Obadiah Baley Obadiah Perkins Benjn Bill Walter Buddington Amos Allyn Ezekiel Turner Bethuwel Baley Chris^r Morgan Jonathan Faning Jonas Avery William Williams 2^d John Gardiner Benjn Brown Jos: Packer & Jonathan Fish Were chosen Surveyors of Highways [4]

Capt Jasper Latham and James Street Fence Viewers [4]

Thos Mumford Esqr Gager & Capt Jabez Smith Packer [4]

Groton

Jesse Gallup Sealer of Weights and Measures	[4]
Tho[s] Mumford Esq[r] Benadam Gallup Esq[r] William Ledyard Amos Prentice Amos Geer Deac[n] John Hurlbut Charles Eldredge Jun[r] Committe of Correspondance	[4]
William Williams Ebenezer Ledyard Tho[s] Mumford Esq[r] William Morgan Esq[r] John Elderkin David Avery Benadam Gallup Esq[r] Ebenez[r] Jun[r] Simeon Avery Joseph Packer Stephen Billings Parke Avery Nathan Gallup William Avery Esq[r] and Cap[t] Solomon Perkins Were Chosen Committe Of Inspection	[4]
Voted that Tho[s] Mumford Esq[r] and Lieu[t] Nathan Gallup be Agents for Said Town.. to the Honn[l l] General Assembly.. Respecting their Need and Necessity of Erecting a fortification near the Ferry and to Obtain an Order to Draw Money ought of the Colony Treasury.. for the purposes	[5]

11 Jan 1776

Robert Geer Esq[r] Chosen Moderator	[5]

5 Feb 1776

William Williams Esq[r] Chosen Moderator	[5]
Voted that the Selectmen Signify to the Honnour: County Court to be Hoden at Norwich that Robert Stoddard is not this Towns Agent	[5]

8 Apr 1776

Co[l] Ebenezer Avery Chosen Moderator	[5]
Voted that Richard Starr be Released from the Bond he Gave to the Town for the Supporting William Buttolph: upon his Returning what he Receiv'd of Said Buttolphs Estate to the Selectmen	[5]

9 Dec 1776

Thomas Mumford Esq[r] Deacon John Hurlbut Joseph Packer Cap[t] Thomas Fanning and Samuel Allyn were Chosen Selectmen	[6]
William Avery Esq[r] Chosen Town Clerk and Town Treasurer	[6]
Lieu[t] Parke Avery Jun[r] first Constable to Collect Town and Country Rates	[6]
Benadam Gallup Jun[r] Second Constable	[6]
Youngs Morgan John Elderkin John Spicer Peleg Williams William Starr Allyn Whitman Richard Starr were Chosen Grandjurors (Jonath[n] Fanning Excused & Nathan Crery paid his fine)	[6]
David Avery William Avery Co[l] Benadam Gallup William Morgan Esq[r] and Charles Eldredge were Chosen Listers	[6]
Thomas Lester James Morgan Bethuwil Baley David Chapman Samuel Mallison William Brown John Morgan 2[d] Were Chosen Tythingmen	[6]
John Williams 3[d] David Palmer John Burrows Nathan Smith Jun[r] Jonathan Randall Thomas Prentice Gallup Giles Capron Cap[t] Henry Williams Cap[t] Thomas Fanning John Perkins Abel Newton James Avery 2[d] Deac[n] Nathan Allyn 2[d] Rufus Hurlbut John Lester Joseph Woodmansey John Woodmansey Ezekiel Turner Jesse Gallup Jasper Avery Daniel Avery Thomas Lester Allyn Whitman Charles Eldredge Thomas Morgan Jonathan Fanning James Worden Deac[n] John Hurbut James Ally Jun[r] Samuel Androus Isaac Avery John Elderkin Joshua Chapman Vine Stoddard John Wood Amos Allyn Joseph Lewis Benadam Gallup Jun[r] - were Chosen Surveyors of Highways	[6]
Co[ll] Benadam Gallup Thomas Mumford Parke Avery William Williams Maj[r] Nathan Gallup Simeon Avery Stephen Billings John Elderkin Cap[t] Solomon Perkins David Avery Amos	[6]

335

Groton

Prentice Elijah Avery Deac[n] John Hurlbut Joseph Packer Amos Geer Were Chosen Comm[tte] of Inspection

Thomas Mumford Benadam Gallup Esq[rs] William Ledyard Charles Eldredge Jun[r] Deac[n] John Hurlbut Were Chosen Committee of Correspondance *[6]*

1 Apr 1777

William Williams Esq[r] Moderator *[7]*

Voted that this Town will Supply the Families of those Soldiers on their Reasonable Requests who Shall Voluntarily Engage and go into any of the Continental Battalions for the Term of Three Year or During the Warr with the Necessarys of Life as Stated by Law so far as those Soldiers that List into the Said Continental Service shall Lodge with or Remit Money with a Committee to be Chosen.. Voted that Mes[rs] Tho[s] Mumford David Avery Joseph Starr William Avery Robert Geer Tho[s] Fanning Co[ll] Benadam Gallup John Hurlbut Jonathan Fish Thomas Np: Niles be a Committee *[7]*

7 Apr 1777

William Williams Esq[r] Moderator *[7]*

28 Apr 1777

William Williams Esq[r] Moderator *[7]*

Voted: Capt[ns] Joseph Gallup Ralph Stoddard Hubbard Burrows Jun[r] John Morgan Oliver Spicer Elijah Avery Stephen Billings Abel Spier be a Com[tte] to Enquire how many Soldiers have Inlisted into the Continental Army Since the 7th April Last *[7]*

6 May 1777

A Report of the Comm[tee] Chosen.. to.. make Report.. of the Number of Men that have Inlisted into the Continental Army Since the 7th Day of April Last.. the Number is Twenty Seven } Elijah Avery.. Stephen Billings.. Abel Spicer.. Joseph Gallup.. Ralph Stoddard.. Hubbard Burrows Jun[r].. John Morgan.. Oliver Spicer } Committee *[7*

[ ] May 1777

William Williams Esq[r] Moderator *[8]*

16 Jun 1777

Co[l] Ebenezer Avery Moderator *[8]*

9 Sep 1777

William Williams Esq[r] Chosen Moderator *[8]*

Voted that Col Nathan Gallup and Deac[n] John Hurlbut be a Committee to Purchase as many of those Guns that are Co[l] Motts as can be obtained *[8]*

30 Sep 1777

M[r] Parke Avery Chosen Moderator *[8]*

Voted that Mess[rs] David Avery Stephen Billings Samuel Allyn Joseph Packer and Thomas Fanning be a Committee to.. take in Subscriptions and Recieve those Articles.. to furnish those Non Commitioned Officers and Soldiers.. now in the Continental Army.. with.. Articles of Cloathing agreeable to the Request of.. the Governour and Counsel of Safety *[8]*

9 Dec 1777

William Williams Esq[r] Chosen Moderator *[9]*

Thomas Mumford Esq[r] Samuel Allyn Daniel Avery Stephen Billings and Isaac Geer Chosen Selectmen *[9]*

Groton

William Avery Chosen Town Clerk and Town Treas^r	[9]
John Lester Chosen first Constable to Collect Town and Country Rates	[9]
Parke Avery Junr Second Constable	[9]
John Kennady Benajah Avery Christopher Morgan David Palmer Richard Starr Junr Samuel Williams 2^d Nathan Crery Junr Chosen Grand Juriors	[9]
Ebenez^r 3^d Edward Spicer Abel Sholes Walter Buddington Junr Samuel Labmb David Brown Jabez Smith Junr Tything men	[9]
Elijah Avery Simeon Allyn Co^l Nathan Gallup Isaac Avery and John Avery 2^d Chosen Listers	[9]
Co^l Benadam Gallup and Thomas Lester Leather Sealers	[9]
Jesse Gallup Sealer of Weights and Measures	[9]
Daniel Avery and Isaac Geer be a Com^{tte} to Assist the former Com^{tte} in getting Cloathing for the Soldiers	[9]
Surveyors of Highways.. are as follows (viz) John Williams 3^d Walter Buddington Junr John Barber Thos Np: Niles Hubbard Burrows Junr Charles Eldridge Thos P Gallup John Morgan Abel Spicer Ebenezer Brown Asa Avery Theophilus Avery Abel Sholes Richard Arthur Chris^r Avery Junr Nathan Lester Amos Turner Ezekiel Turner Amos Allyn Oliver Spicer Abel Newton Joseph Worden Tryal Allyn Joshua Chapman Amos Lester Obadiah Baley Junr John Wood Benjn Bill Joseph Woodmansey Simeon Avery David Fanning John Dixon John Gardiner David Palmer Joseph Packer Nathan Stark Jessee Gallup Shapley Morgan Comfort Brown Walter Buddington Jonathan Randal Ichabod Stoddard	[9]
Thomas Mumford Thos Np: Niles Co^{ll} Benadam Gallup George Geer and Capt Joseph Morgan be a Com^{tte} to provide for the Soldiers Families	[9]
12 Dec 1777	
William Williams Esqr Moderator	[9]
Thomas Mumford Ebenezer Ledyard Amos Prentice David Avery John Elderkin Sam^{ll} Allyn Dan^{ll} Avery Thos N:P: Niles Co^{ll} Benadam Gallup Stephen Billings Amos Geer and Co^{ll} Nathan Gallup were Committee of Inspection	[9]
Thomas Mumford William Ledyard Charles Eldredge Junr and Co^{ll} Benadam Gallup be a Comm^{tte} of Correspondance	[10]
Voted that John Elderkin Shall be agent.. to Appear at the County Court and Oppose the Petetion of Capt Jonas Belton and Others Respecting the Alteration of the Highway near the Mill Brook Westward	[10]
30 Dec 1777	
Voted that Sam^{ll} Edgcomb and Uriah Wilbour be Grandjurors	[10]
Voted that James Geer be Surveyor of Highways	[10]
Voted that Oliver Spicer and Nathan Smith Junr be Comm^{tte} of Inspection	[10]
18 Mar 1778	
William Williams Esqr Chosen Moderator	[10]
David Avery Esqr Capt Josep Morgan Mr Hubbard Burrows Co^l Benadam Gallup Lieu^t Theophilus Avery be a Committee to Supply the Continental Officers and Soldiers	[10]
3 Jun 1778	
Capt Joseph Morgan Chosen Moderator	[11]
Voted that Ebenez^r Ledyard Esqr be this Towns Agent.. at the County Court... to Oppose a	[11]

Groton

Writt brought against Said Town by Thomas Fanning as he Shall be Advised by Counsel Learned..

8 Sep 1778

Co[ll] Benadam Gallup Esq[r] Moderator	[11]
Tho[s] Mumford Esq[r] Clerk Protemporary	[11]
Voted.. do Accept the Doings of the Selectmen.. in Laying Out the Public Highway from Captain Daniel Packers to the road Leading from M[r] Joseph Packers to New London Ferry	[11]
Voted.. do Except of the doings of the Selectmen in Laying Out A Tent way from Joseph Parke's to Elder Timothy Wrightman's Meeting house and Also a Drift way from Narrow Passage so called on Mistick river to the Tent way begining at Joseph Park's	[11]
Voted that Mess[rs] Thomas Mumford James Avery Daniel Packer Coll[n] Benadam Gallup and George Gere be a Comittee to Procure Provisions and Cloathing for the Soldiers Families from this Town Belonging to the Continental Army	[11]

15 Dec 1778

William Williams Esq[r] Moderator	[11]
Ebenezer Ledyard Esq[r]s Capt[n] John Morgan Deac[n] Peter Avery Lieu[t] Isaac Gere and Lieu[t] Robert Allyn were Chosen Selectmen	[11]
William Avery Esq[r] was Chosen town Clerk & Treasu[r]	[11]
Vine Stoddard Constable to Collect Town & Country rates	[12]
John Avery 2[nd] Second Constable	[12]
James Gere Elisha Niles Nathan Allyn 2nd Samuel Edgecomb Joseph Packer Jun[r] Nicholas Starr Jesse Barns Chosen Grand Jurors	[12]
Charles Eldredge Jun[r] Samuel Allyn Tho[s] P Gallup Tho[s] N Niles and Captain Abel Spicer were Chosen Listers	[12]
Benajah Chester Daniel Eldredge Gilbert Smith Ralph Stoddard Jun[r] Tisdale Eddy & Park Avery Jun[r] were Chosen Tythingmen	[12]
Ebenezer Avery 2nd Cap[t] Elijah Avery Cap[t] Jonas Belton Nathaniel Niles Caleb Haley David Fanning John Dixon Joseph Latham Jun[r] Sylvester Worden Joseph Lee Shapley Morgan Isaac Crery Chris[r] Morgan Simeon Capron Isaac Morgan Hubbard Burrows Benadam Gallup Jun[r] Amos Allyn John Avery Oliver Spicer Robert Rose Jun[r] Constant Edy Theophilus Avery Samuel Lester James Avery Cap[t] Ralph Stoddard Jona[th] Baley John Woodmansey Rufus Hurlbut Amos Lester John Gates Joseph Allyn James Lamb Joseph Lewis John Gardiner Daniel Packer Daniel Avery Abel Newtown Joshua Chapman were Chosen Surveyors of highways	[12]
Jesse Gallup Sealer of Weights & Measures	[12]
Coll[n] Benadam Gallup & Thomas Lester.. were Chosen Leather Sealers	[12]
Jasper Latham Jun[r] & John Woodmansey were chosen fence Viewers	[12]
Thomas Mumford Esq[r] Guager & Charles Eldredge Jun[r] Packer	[12]
Hubbard Burrows Brander of Horses	[12]
Samuel Lester Jun[r] Peter Avery Jonathan Randall Obadiah Perkins Thomas Pelton Nathaniel Niles Benad[m] Gallup Theophilus Avery John Lester Samuel Androus Robert Gere 2nd Pound Keepers	[12]
Nathan Morgan Comittee of Supply	[12]

Groton

2 Feb 1779

Co[ll] Ebenezer Avery Chosen Moderator [13]

Voted: That this Town Approve of Inoculation for a Month or Six weeks under the Direction of a Committee.. Voted } That Co[ll] Benadam Gallup Parke Avery Ebenez[r] Ledyard Esq[r] Cap[t] John Morgan Parke Avery Jun[r] Benajah Chester and Charels Eldredge Jun[r] be a Committe for the above Said Business [13]

Voted } That William Avery Morgan be One of the Comm[te] of Supplies for Soldiers Families [13]

17 Feb 1779

William Williams Esq[r] Chosen Moderator [13]

12 Apr 1779

William Williams Esq[r] Moderator [13]

Voted that } Tho[s] Mumford Esq[r] and Co[ll] Nathan Gallup be Agents… to Prefer a Memorial to the General Court.. and see if Said Assembly will Relieve the Town from the Cost.. made by the Prisoners being Sent in here [13]

William Williams Esq[r] Moderator [13]

15 Jun 1779

William Williams Esq[r] Moderator [13]

Voted } That Cap[t] Thomas Chester Deac[n] Joseph Allyn Elisha Niles Chris[r] Morgan and Isaac Avery be a Comm[te] to Procure Clothing for the Soldiers [13]

6 Jul 1779

Co[ll] Benadam Gallup Chosen Moderator [14]

25 Aug 1779

William Williams Esq[r] Chosen Moderator [14]

Voted that the Selectmen Allow the whole of Co[ll] Benadam Gallups Acc[t] which was not Allow'd by the General Assembly for his being a Committee of Supples [14]

21 Sep 1779

Co[ll] Benadam Gallup Chosen Moderator [14]

Voted: that William Avery Esq[r] be a Committee to Represent Said Town…at the proposed General Convention [14]

Voted: That William Ledyard Ebenez[r] Ledyard and Co[ll] Benadam Gallup be a Committee to meet a proposed County Convention [14]

Voted: That Nathan Morgan James Avery Dan[ll] Packer William Avery Morgan and George Geer be a Committee to Supply the Soldiers Families [14]

7 Dec 1779

William Williams Esq[r] Chose Moderator [14]

Cap[t] John Morgan Doc[t] Peter Avery Leutenant Isaac Geer Leu[t] Robert Allyn Cap[t] Elijah Avery ware Chosen Select Men [14]

William Avery Esq[r] Town Clerk and Town Treas[r] [14]

Leut John Avery Collecting Constable for town & Colony Taxes [14]

Vine Stoddard 2[d] Constable [14]

Lieu[t] Park Avery 3[d] Constable [14]

Groton

Benj[n] Chester William Morgan Sam[ll] Edgecomb Amos Lester Jonathan Burrows Ebenezer Avery ware Chosen Grand Jurymen [14]

Cap[t] John Williams 3[d] Leu[t] William Williams Jun[r] Cap[t] Oliver Spicer Ralph Stoddard Jun[r] Elisha Niles were Chosen Listers [14]

Charles Eldredge Jun[r] Leu[t] Park Avery John Barber Nathan Niles Daniel Eldredge Nathan Crary Thomas P: Gallup Christopher Morgan Cap[t] Abel Spicer Robert Geer Esq[r] Leu[t] John Bellows Robert Rose Jun[r] Abel Newton Joshua Chapman John Gates James Avery 3[d] Israel Morgan Lieu[t] Samuel Allyn John Lester Obadiah Baly Joseph Woodmansy Nicholas Starr John Wood Noah Baley John Daboll Jun[r] Henry Gallup David Fanning Simeon Avery Sam[ll] Lamb Jabez Waterhous Joseph Packer Ens[n] Daniel Avery John Morgan Nathan Lester Rusul Hurlbut Cap[t] Simeon Allyn Ichabod Stoddard ware Chosen Surveyors of Highways [15]

Leu[t] Ebenezer Avery Isaac Whitman Rufus Fish Josiah Morris Nicholas Starr Tho[s] Allyn Amous Alley Jasper Avery ware Chosen Tythingmen [15]

Thomas Lester Cap[t] Benadam Gallup Leather Sealors.. the same Persons Brandors of Horses the same Persons key keepers the same Persons fence Vewers that ware Last Year [15]

Jesse Galllup Sealor of Weights & Measures [15]

Voted That Charles Eldredge Jun[r] be a Com[te] of Supplies for Soldiers Families [15]

21 Feb 1780

William Williams Esq[r] Chosen Moderator [15]

Voted that Co[ll] Nathan Gallup William Avery and Amos Geer Esq[rs] be a Com[te] to Exammine into the Town Acc[t] [15]

13 Mar 1781

Co[ll] Benadam Gallup Chosen Moderator [15]

Voted That Cap[t] John Williams Amos Prentice Elder Parke Avery Lieu[t] Thomas Avery Cap[t] Solomon Perkins John Elderkin Dean Thomas N P Niles Daniel Eldredge Daniel Avery Nathan Fish Jun[r] Cap[t] Stephen Billings Cap[t] Abel Spicer Lieu[t] Sam[ll] Williams John Bellows George Geer Committee of Inspectors to take care no Provisions be Carryed out of this State [15]

Co[ll] Nathan Gallup Co[ll] William Ledyard Capt[n] Elijah Avery Stephen Billings Abel Spicer John Morgan Oliver Spicer Hubbard Burrows Simeon Allyn and John Williams be a Comm[te] to Adopt Some Plan.. to Engage the Quoto of Men... to Serve in the Continental During the War [16]

22 Mar 1780

Co[ll] Benadam Gallup Chosen Moderator [16]

Voted that this Town Accept and Approve of the Method proposed by the above Comm[tee] in Order to Engage the Quoto of Men to be furnished by this Town to Serve in the Continental Army.... { Nathan Gallup.. W[m] Leyard.. Abel Spicer.. Elijah Avery.. Stephen Billings.. John Morgan.. Oliver Spicer.. Hubbard Burrous.. John Williams 3[d].. Simeon Allyn } Committee [16]

6 Jun 1780

W[m] Williams Esq[r] Moderator [16]

18 May 1780

Elder Parke Avery Chosen Moderator [17]

Voted that Lieu[t] Robert Allyn be this Towns agent to Prosecute Obadiah Baley at the County Court for his turning two Old Negroes on this Town for their Support (viz:) Sharper and Silva his Wife as he shall be Advis'd by Counsel Learned [17]

Groton

26 Jan 1780

William Williams Esqr Chosen Moderator	[17]
Voted that this Town will give in Addition to all other Bounties to those Soldiers.. who Shall Inlist.. and Join the Continental Army £6.0.0 in Silver or Gold to those who Shall Inlist till the 1st of January Next; and £8.0.0 in like Money Annually for 3 three Years or during the Warr.. Voted that Capt John Williams William Avery Esqr Lieu^t William Williams Capt Oliver Spicer & Thomas N:P: Niles Esqr be a Comm^{te} to Assess the Inhabitants.. to raise a Bounty for the above purpose	[17]
Voted that Thomas Mumford David Avery Esq^{rs} Charles Eldridge Junr Co^{ll} Nathan Gallup Lieu^t John Avery Capt Asa Avery Nathan Crery be a Comm^{te} to Supply Soldiers Families	[17]

10 Jul 1780

Co^{ll} Benadam Gallup Esqr Chosen Moderator	[17]

14 Nov 1780

William Williams Esqr Moderator	[18]

14 Nov 1780

Voted that Co^{ll} Benadam Gallup Lieu^t Parke Avery Junr Ens^n John Lester Charles Smith and Joseph Latham be a Commi^{te} to Recieve this Towns proportion of Salt for.. Securing this towns Quota of Provisions	[18]

4 Dec 1780

William Williams Esqr Chosen Moderator	[18]
Capt John Morgan Decon Peter Avery Lieu^t Isaac Geer Lieu^t Robert Allyn were Chosen Selectmen	[18]
Wiliam Avery Esqr Chosen Town Clerk and Town Treas^r	[18]
Lieu^t Parke Avery Chose Constable & Collector to Collect Town and Country Rates	[18]
Lieu^t John Avery and James Geer Constables	[18]
Doct^r Amos Prentice Ens^n John Lester William N Morgan Ens^n Edward Packer and Lieu^t John Bellows Chosen Listers	[18]
Daniel Avery Samuel Lamb Joseph Whipple were Chosen Grandjurors	[18]
Edward Jeffery John Barber Nathaniel Niles Daniel Eldredge Jesse Gallup Chris^r Morgan Nehemiah Smith Robert Geer Esqr Oliver Spicer Luther Whipple Marke Newton Sam^{ll} Androus Isaac Avery Theophilus Avery Samuel Mallison Vine Stoddard Joseph Woodmansey Thomas Starr Amos Allyn Lieu^t John Avery Joseph Allyn Rufus Hurlbut Co^{ll} Benadam Gallup Nathan Allyn 2^d Isaac Gallup Abel Newton Lieu^t Samuel Williams John Dixon Simeon Avery Shapley Morgan Samuel Stanton Nathan Lester Capt Joseph Morgan John Morgan Gilbert Smith David Palmer Elisha Packer were Chosen Surveyors of highways	[18]
Voted that.. Jedediah Leeds Junr and Simeon Smith be a Committee to Supply the Soldiers Families	[19]
Voted that Benadam Gallup and William Avery Esq^{rs} be a Committee to Search the Records to See if their be any Lands.. formerly Set of for Publick Uses or any other Land that belongs to this Town: and make Sale	[19]

14 Dec 1780

Co^{ll} Benadam Gallup Chosen Moderator	[19]
Voted That Jasper Latham Junr and John Woodmansey be fence Viewers	[19]

Groton

Co[ll] Benadam Gallup and Thomas Lester were Chosen Leather Sealers [19]

Amos Allyn Shapley Morgan Jabez Smith Youngs Morgan Caleb Haley Thomas Fish Cap[t] Elijah Avery Tythingmen [19]

Thomas Mumford Gager and Packer [19]

Coo[ll] Benadam Gallup and Cap[t] Jasper Latham Branders of Horses [19]

Jesse Gallup Sealer of Weights and Measurs [19]

Cap[t] John Fish Co[ll] Benadam Gallup Elisha Perkins Sam[ll] Lester Ju[r] Nathaniel Niles Lieu[t] Thephilus Avery Robert Geer Jun[r] Dec[n] Peter Avery Nathan Lester (making Good and Sufficient Pounds at their own Cost are to be keykeepers of the same [19]

Doct[r] Amos Prentice to be the fifth Selectman [19]

Joseph Packer Jun[r] and Walter Buddington Chosen Grandjuros [19]

Voted that William Avery Esq[r] Cap[t] John Williams Tho[s] N: P: Niles Esq[r] Cap[t] Oliver Spicer and Lieu[t] William Williams be a Comm[tee] to Asess the Inhabitants [19]

28 Dec 1780

William Williams Esq[r] Chosen Moderator [20]

Voted: That Joseph Latham be a Committee of Supplys for Soldiers Families: and Surveyor of Highways.. that Charles Smith and William Williams Jun[r] be Surveyors of highways [20]

10 Jan 1781

M[r] Parke Avery Chosen Moderator [20]

Amos Prentice Chosen Clerk Pretompory [20]

16 Jan 1781

M[r] Parke Avery Moderator [20]

Voted that Cap[t] Elijah Avery Joseph Starr and M[r] Daniel Eldredge Cap[t] Stephen Billings and Cap[t] Oliver be a Committee to purchase and Supply Cloathing for the Soldiers in the Continental Army.. and to hire Money of M[r] Mumford and others.. to purchas the.. Cloathing [20]

1 Feb 1781

William Williams Esq[r] Moderator [21]

Voted = that their be a Rate or tax of One penny Three farthings on the Pound made on the Pound List 1779; to be paid in hard Money or three pence halfpenny in State Money or Continental Bills Equivilent thereto; = Voted that Co[ll] Benadam Gallup Joseph Latham Lieu[t] Park Avery Jun[r] John Lester and Gilbert Smith be a Committe to Receive.. this Towns part of Grain and Flower for use of the Continental Army [21]

Voted = that Lieu[t] Park Avery be a Comm[te] to purchase what Grain and Flower shall be needful [21]

3 Mar 1781

Co[ll] Benadam Gallup Chosen Moderator [21]

9 May 1781

William Williams Esq[r] Chosen Moderator [21]

Voted: That Cap[t] Stephen Billings be a Committee to make out this Towns Claim to the.. Soldiers Inlisted.. in the Connecticut Line in the Continental Army During the Warr [21]

Voted } That Lieu[t] Ebenezer Avery Ralph Stoddard Gilbert Smith Abel Spicer Amos Geer Esq[r] be a Comm[te] to Collect Cloathing for the Continental Army [21]

Groton

14 May 1781

Co^{ll} Benadam Gallup Chosen Moderator	[21]
Voted Thomas Mumford Esqr & Capt John Morgan be Agents to.. Oppose a Memorial.. to the.. General Assembly.. by Jonathan Bruisters and others praying for part of this Town to be set to a part of Norwich and Preston for the forming a new Town as they Shall be Advised by Counsel Learned	[21]

26 Jun 1781

William Williams Esqr Chosen Moderator	[22]

31 Oct 1781

Capt Stephen Billings Chosen Moderator	[22]
Voted that the doings of the Selectmen in Laying out a Bridle or pentway through Daniel Knowles land be Accepted	[22]

7 Nov 1781

Voted: Co^{ll} Benadam Gallup Joseph Latham Elisha Niles Lieu^t Robert Allyn Nathan Morgan be a Committee to Receive in Provisions and Cloathing on the half Crown^d Tax	[22]
Voted that the Selectmen be Desired to Settle Acc^{ts} with the W^d Lester Respecting the Provision that now lies on Hand	[22]
Voted that the Vote respecting the pentway through Daniel Knowles land be Reconsidered and not accepted	[22]

30 Jan 1782

Voted } that William Williams Esqr be Moderator	[22]
That Lieut Robert Allyn be this Towns Agent to Appear at the Adjourn'd County Court.. wherein Obadiah Baley.. is Plain^t.. as he Shall be Advised by Counsel Learned	[22]

17 Dec 1781

William Williams Esqr Chosen Moderator	[23]
Amos Prentice Esqr Deac^n Peter Avery Lieu^t Robert Allyn Mr Elisha Williams and Mr Robert Geer 2^d were Chosen Selectmen	[23]
William Avery Esqr was Chosen Town Clerk and Town Treasurer	[23]
Nathan Morgan first Constable and Collector for Town & State Rates Parke Avery Junr Second Constable and James Geer Third Constable	[23]
Allyn Whitman William A Morgan and Gilbert Smith were Chosen Granjurors	[23]
Gilbert Smith Capt Thomas Avery Thomas Lester William Morgan and Joseph Latham were Chosen Listers	[23]
Ebenezer Avery James Baley Charles Smith Nathaniel Niles Daniel Eldredge John Morgan 2^d Simeon Smith Elisha Packer Benjamin Brown Isaac Crery Thomas Prentice Gallup Christopher Morgan Epraim Allyn Robert Geer Junr John Williams Robert Rose Junr Capt William Williams ~~Lt~~ Samuel Stanton Squire Lee John Daboll John Avery Leiu^t Abel Newton John Power Shapley Morgan Israel Morgan Lieu^t Theophilus Avery Simeon Avery Joshua Chapman Samuel Androws Amos Lester Nathan Lester Vine Stoddard Joseph Woodmansey Samuel Lester Junr Jasper Latham Junr John Kennedy Joseph Allyn Ichabod Stoddard [ ] Addam Gallup Junr & Samuel Lamb were Chosen Surveyors of Highways	[23]
Starr Chester William Starr Samuel Lamb Caleb Williams Elisha Packer Edward Spicer Asa Button Agrippa Newton were Chosen Tythingmen	[23]
Sealer of Weights and Measurs	[23]

Groton

Co[ll] Benadam Gallup and Thomas Lester Leather Sealers	[23]
John Womansey and Jasper Latham Jun[r] Fence Viewers	[23]
Lieu[t] Parke Avery Gager and Benajah Lester Packer	[23]
Co[ll] Benadam Gallup & Cap[t] Jasper Latham Branders of Horses	[23]
Co[ll] Banadam Gallup Peter Avery Nathan[l] Niles Samuel Lester Jun[r] Cap[t] John Fish Robert Geer Jun[r] Nathan Lester Ephraim Allyn and Samuel Androus were Chosen Key keepers	[23]

8 Apr 1782

William Williams Esq[r] Chosen Moderator	[24]
Voted: that the Laying a pent or Bridle way through Daniel Knowles Land be Acepted	[24]
Voted that Lieu[t] Robert Allyn be this Towns Agent to Accommodate the Matter with Obadiah Baley for not Supporting or pay the charge & Expense of two Old Negros (viz) Sharper and Silva who were Sent to the Selectmen.. by the said Baleys Father Since Dec[d] the 22[d] January 1780 as he Shall be Advised by Counsel learned in the Law	[24]
Liberty Granted to Cap[t] William Wyllys for carrying on Enoculation	[24]

16 Dec 1782

William Williams Esq[r] was Moderator	[24]
Amos Prentice Esq[r] Deacon Peter Avery and Mes[r] Robert Allyn Elisha Williams Robert Gere 2[d] were Chosen Selectmen	[24]
William Avery Esq[r] Town Clerk and Town Treasurer	[24]
Nathan Morgan Chosen first Constable and Collector for Town & State Taxes he procuring Sufficent Bonds	[24]
Parke Avery Jun[r] Second Constable	[24]
James Gere Third Constable	[24]
Deac[n] Joseph Chapman Isaac Whitman William Smith 3[d] Grand Jurors	[24]
Parke Avery Jun[r] Ichabod Stoddard Peleg Williams Daniels Eldredge and David Gere were Chosen Listers	[24]
William Starr Starr Chestor Joseph Chapman Jun[r] John Avery [ ] Niles John Dabool Jun[r] Eisha Packer Tythingmen	[24]
William Starr Joseph Latham Walter Buddington Jun[r] Nathan[l] Niles Nathan Crery Sam[l] Eldredge John Morgan Nehemiah Smith Elijah Brown Robert Rose Jun[r] John Williams Elisha Hurd John Powers William Williams Jun[r] Benadam Gallup Jun[r] Abial Lamb Shapley Morgan Cap[t] Ralph Stoddard John Kenady Thomas Allyn Nathan Allyn 2[d] Nathan Lester Ralph Stoddard Jun[r] Theophilus Avery Ezrael Morgan Abel Newton Sam[ll] Androus Deac[n] Peter Avery Sam[l] Williams 4th Cap[t] Stephen Billings Obadiah Baley Walter Buddington Joshua Chapman John Baley Daniel Knowles Joseph Packer Jun[r] Gilbert Smith Jos: Packer Jesse Brown Isaac Gere Simeon Capron Surveyors of Highways	[25]
Co[ll] Benadam Gallup & Thomas Lesters: Leather Sealors	[25]
Jasper Latham Jun[r] John Woodmansey John Bellows and James Allyn Fence Viewers	[25]
Parke Avery Gager: Jesse Gallup Sealer of weights & Measures	[25]
Co[ll] Benadam Gallup Nathan[ll] Niles Sam[ll] Androus Robert Gere Sam[ll] Lester Jun[r] Jo[s]: Allyn Peter Avery and John Fish Keykeepers	[25]

Groton

26 Dec 1782

Amos Prentice Esq[r] Chosen Moderator [25]

30 Dec 1782

Co[ll] Benadam Gallup Chosen Moderator [25]

Voted That Co[ll] Benadam Galup and William Avery Esq[s] be a Comm[te] to view the Lott.. near the Ferry called the Building Yard and find the Situation.. and make Report [25]

Voted That the Highway from James Gere to Lieu[t] Theophilus Avery's be Accepted: Ebenezer Ledyard Jun[r] Chosen Gager: William Morgan & Cap[t] Jesse Gere Surveyors of Highways [25]

Guilford

Guilford Miscellaneous
1773 – 1828

Located at the Connecticut State Archives

Guilford

14 Dec 1774

Col Andrew Ward was chosen Moderator at a full Special Meeting	259
Eben^r Parmele Junr was chosen Clerk of the Meeting	259
This Meeting.. agree.. & strictly abide by the Association, Entered in to by the s^d Congress. And Samuel Brown Esqr Mr Solomon Leete Capt Andrew Ward, Mr Samuel Robinson Junr, Mr Abraham Fowler Mr David Landon, Mr Nath^{ll} Stone, Mr Bilious Ward Timothy Todd Esqr Mr Isaac Knight Capt Timothy Hill Mr Eben^r Fowler, Oliver Dudly Esqr Mr Robert Griffing Mr Caleb Mungar Lieu^t John Hopson and Mr Nehemiah Griswold are appointed a Committee, to see.. the Same every Part carried into Execution	260
Voted that Tim^o Tod Esqr Sam^{ll} Brown Esqr Mr David Landon, Capt Andrew Ward & Mr Sam^{ll} Robinson Junr be a Committee to Corrispond with the Committees of other [*Towns*] or Governments, and to Recieve Charitable Donations for the Distressed Poor, in Boston	260

12 Dec 1775

Col: Andrew Ward, was chosen Moderator	269
Eben^r Parmele Junr was chosen Town Clerk	269
Thos Burgis Junr.. Abraham Chittenden.. Nath^{ll} Eliot.. Sam^{ll} Lee.. Elias Grave.. Benjn Rosseter.. David Dudley 2^d { were chosen Select Men	269
Mr Thos Burgis Junr was chosen Town Treasurer	269
Sam^{ll} Johnson, Elihu Bartlet.. Jared Chittenden & Miles Munger { were Chosen Constables	269
Reuben Shelby.. Thos Hotchkin.. Joseph Fyler.. David Field & Thos Hart { were chosen Grand Jurors	269
Dan^{ll} Leete was chosen Constable to Collect the Country Rate	269
John Hall Caleb Dudly Junr Josiah Scranton John Bishop Stephen Fowler Jesse Bishop Nath^{ll} Steevens 2^d Benj: Crampton Joseph Parmele and Tim^o Norton { were chosen Tithingmen	269
Eli Foot Sam^{ll} Benton Sam^{ll} Lee Junr Dan Collens Lieu^t Jehiel Meigs Timothy Hill Junr Capt Agustus Collens Lot Benton Lieu^t John Hopson and Timothy Mungar were chosen Listers	269
Abraham Fowler, Elon Lee John Leete John Hotchkiss Westal Scovil Miles Hall, Jonathan Evarts Junr Abner Stone Joseph Cruttenden Junr John Starr John Hill Josiah Bishop Lieu^t Robt Griffing Gilbert Dudly Timothy Field John Stone Thos Adkins Junr John Fowler John Stone 2^d Ebenezer Hall Lieu^t Robt Griffing Philemon French Eliakim Steevens and David Field were chosen Surveyors of Highways	270
Thos Hart Nath^{ll} Eliot Lieu^t Jehiel Meigs Josiah Scranton Sam^{ll} Bishop David Fowler Caleb Mungar and John Hopson, were chosen Fence Viewers	270
Caleb Benton Benjamin Hart John Hill Thos Fitch Lieu^t Joshua Blatchly and Ashbil Norton, were chosen Pound keepers	270
Col: Andrew Ward Capt Timothy Hill Selah Dudley & Lieu^t Josh Blatchly were chosen Branders of Horses	270
Thelus Ward was chosen Sealer of Aberdupois Weight	270
Capt Sam^{ll} Parmele was chosen Sealer of Troy Weight	270
Joseph Chittenden Simeon Munger and Philemon French were chosen Sealers of Measures	270

15 Dec 1775

Voted that the Town Rates of Eben Ki[ ]um 2/3 Of the widow of Simeon Norton dec^d 2/10½ and Of Amaziah Joselin 2/3 on Collector Dudlys Rate Book for last year be released by the Town	271

Guilford

Thos Burgis Thos Willcox and Nehemiah Griswold were chosen Sealers of Leather	271
Sam^{ll} Brown Esqr was chosen Guager of Cask	271
Joseph Weld Nath^{ll} Hall Nath^{ll} Allis and Abraham Scranton were chosen Cullers of Staves & Surveyors of Timber	271
Simeon Chitenden Junr was chosen Titheingman	271
Voted that Reuben Parmele's Cow Yard near his House shall be deemed.. a lawful Town Pound, for Impounding Creatures taken Damage feasant.. Reuben Parmele was chosen Pound Keeper	271
Increase Pendleton was chosen Constable	271
David Landon was chosen Grandjuror in the room of Thomas Hart, released from serving	271
Caleb Stone was chosen Surveyor of Highways	271
Timothy Leete, Eber Parmele Nath^{ll} Johnson 3^d Simeon Sexton, Eber Hall, Amos Dudley Abraham Hubbard Abel Norton, Elihu Meigs Moses Blatchly Junr Jonathan Willcox Jared Willard Junr Josiah Cramton Junr Noadiah Norton & Didymus French were chosen Haywards	272
Voted that the Cowyard of Sam^{ll} Chittenden shall be deemed.. a lawful Town Pound for impounding Creatures liable to be taken and pounded by Law.. chosen Pound Keeper	272
Mes^s Abraham Chittenden Thos Burgis Junr Sam^{ll} Lee and Nath^{ll} Eliot were chosen Committee of the Mill	272
Noah Hotchkiss Junr was chosen Lister	272
Elias Cadwell was chosen Collector to collect the Town Rate within the Limits of the first & fourth Societyes	272
Sealah Murray was chosen Collector of the Town Rate within the Limits of East Guilford Society	272
Benj^a Graves was chosen Collector of the Town Rate with the Limits of North Guilford Society	272
31 Jul 1776	
Coll: Andrew Ward was chosen Moderator	273
Voted that the Committee of Inspection.. be released from their Services ~ and that a new Committee of Eleven persons be chosen in their Room - Nath^{ll} Ruggles Esqr.. Sam^{ll} Brown Esqr.. Solomon Leete.. Nath^{ll} Stone.. Sam^{ll} Lee Junr.. Timothy Todd Esqr.. Tim^o Hill Esqr.. Capt Ag^t Collens.. Eben^r Fowler.. Capt Jno Hopson & Ens^n Nathl Steevens were chosen a Committee of Inspection	273
10 Dec 1776	
Coll Andrew Ward was chosen Moderator	273
Thos Burgis Junr was chosen Town Clerk	273
Mr Sam^{ll} Lee Mr Sam^{ll} Scranton, Lieu^t Eben^r Hopson Ensg^n Abr^m Fowler Mr Elias Grave Mr Benjamin Rossetter & Capt John Hopson were chosen Select Men	273
Thos Burgis Junr was chosen Town Treasurer & Excused from Serving	274
Nath^{ll} Bishop 2nd was chosen Constable to Collect the Country Rate	274
Increase Pendleton.. Elihu Bartlet.. Jared Chittenden.. Miles Munger } were chosen Constables	274
Lieu^t Eben^r Hopson was chosen Town Treasurer	274
Abr^m Dudley.. Philemon Hall.. Eben^r Field.. Simeon Grave.. Peter Tallman } were chosen Grandjurors	274

Guilford

Cap⁺ David Seaward.. Mʳ Miles Hotchkiss.. Joseph Doud.. Levi Ward.. Jairus Chittenden.. Thoˢ Adkins Junʳ.. Eber Benton.. Danˡˡ Handy.. Philemon French.. Moses Doud } were chosen Tithing Men	*274*
Samˡˡ Robinson, David Seaward Junʳ.. Abrᵐ Chittenden Junʳ, Noah Hodgkin Junʳ.. Nathˡˡ Stone, Timothy Hill Junʳ.. Daniel Miegs, Selah Dudley Junʳ.. Timothy Baldwin, Timothy Munger.. Noah Benton } were chosen Listers	*274*
Surveyors { Thoˢ Burgis Samˡˡ Evarts, Timothy Fowler, Thoˢ Hart, Nathˡˡ Crittenden, Daniel Stone Ebenʳ Hodgkin, Joseph Evarts, Abrᵐ Stone Timothy Meigs, Timothy Field, Elihu Meigs	*274*
Philemon French was chosen Collector of the Town Rate within the Limits of North Bristol Society	*275*
Voted that fifty five shillings of this Town's Mony stolen from Collector Jairus Chittenden be released out of the arrears of the Rate he Collected	*275*
Samˡˡ Brown Esqʳ Col: Andrew Ward Junʳ, Mʳ John Redfield Col John Eliot, Lieu⁺ Ebenʳ Hopson, Mʳ Nathˡˡ Stone Ensⁿ Abraham Fowler, Nathˡˡ Ruggles Esqʳ, John Burgis Esqʳ Mʳ Solomon Leete Cap⁺ David Landon, Mʳ Wᵐ Chittenden Mʳ Samˡˡ Lee Junʳ Cap⁺ Jasper Griffing, Ensⁿ Thoˢ Willcox Timothy Hill Esqʳ Mʳ Nathˡˡ Allis, Timothy Todd Esqʳ Oliver Dudly Esqʳ Cap⁺ Augustus Collens, Lieu⁺ Robᵗ Griffing, Mʳ Ebenʳ Fowler, Mʳ Caleb Mungar, Lieu⁺ John Hopson & Mʳ Nathˡˡ Caldwell were chosen a Committee of Inspection to see that the Rules and Orders of the Honourable Continental Congress be carried into Execution	*275*
Timothy Todd Esqʳ Samˡˡ Brown Esqʳ Cap⁺ David Landon Col: Andrew Ward Junʳ & Doctʳ John Redfield were chosen a Committee of Correspondence	*275*
Mʳ Aaron Evarts Oliver Dudly Esqʳ Ensn Thoˢ Willcox Col: Andrew Ward Junʳ & Mʳ Samˡˡ Robinson Junʳ were appointed a Committee to view & consider the Circumstances of the Causey at Jones Bridge	*275*
Selah Murray was chosen a Collector of the Rate… for Building the Town House within the Limits of East Guilford Society	*276*
Benjᵃ Graves was Chosen a Collector of the Rate… for Building the Town House within the Limits of North Guilford Society	*275*
Philemon French was chosen a Collector of the Rate… for Building the Town House within the Limits of North Bristol Society	*276*
Ensign Ebenʳ Dudley, Benjⁿ Rossetter, Deaⁿ Simeon Chittenden Enˢ John Hubbard, Hull Cruttenden, Oliver Dudley Esqʳ Benjⁿ Crampton, Deaⁿ David Dudley 2ⁿᵈ, Asher Fowler Deaⁿ Caleb Munger, Deaⁿ Selah Dudley were Chosen Surveyors of Highways	*277*
Thoˢ Hart Nathˡˡ Eliot Josiah Scranton James Munger Junʳ, Samˡˡ Bishop David Fowler Caleb Munger, & Cap⁺ John Hopson were Chosen Fence Viewers	*277*
Caleb Benton.. John Hill.. Lieu⁺ Joshua Blatchley.. Ashbill Norton.. Benjⁿ Hart.. Thoˢ Fitch.. Samˡˡ Chittenden.. Reuben Parmele } were chosen Pound keepers	*277*
Col Andrew Ward Cap⁺ Timothy Hill Deaⁿ Selah Dudley Lieu⁺ Joshuah Blatchly } were chosen Branders of Horses	*277*
Thelus Ward was chosen Sealer of Averdupois Weight	*277*
Cap⁺ Samˡˡ Parmele was chosen Sealer of Troy Weight	*277*
Joseph Chittenden Simeon Munger, Philemon French were chosen Sealers of Measures	*277*
Thoˢ Burgis, Thoˢ Willcox, Selah Dudley were chosen Sealers of Leather	*277*
David Landon was chosen Gauger of Cask	*277*
Joseph Weld.. Nathˡˡ Hall.. Nathˡˡ Allis } were chosen Cullers of Staves & Surveyors of Timber	*277*

Guilford

Abr^m Fowler.. Eben^r Hopson.. Sam^{ll} Lee } were chosen Committee of the Mill	278
31 Dec 1776	
Mulford Coan & Timothy Benton were Chosen Haywards	278
Eliphalet Hall Junr was chosen a Collector to collect the Town Rate within the Limits of the first & fourth Societyes	278
Simri Bradly was chosen a Collector to collect the Town Rate within the Limits of East Guilford Society	278
Luther Dudley was chosen a Collector to collect the Town Rate within the Limits of North Guilford Society	278
Phineas Johnson was chosen a Collector to collect the Town Rate within the Limits of North Bristol Society	279
James Bishop was chosen a Collector to collect the Rate… for Building the Town House in the Limits of the East Guilford Society	279
Caleb Benton Junr was chosen Pound keeper	279
Col John Eliot was chosen Surveyor of Highways	279
Voted that Aaron Evarts, Thos Burgis & Philemon French be a Committee to View for Some Convenient place to Set a Water or Wind Mill	279
28 Mar 1777	
Col Andrew Ward was Chosen Moderator	280
Thos Burgis, Sam^{ll} Chittenen, David Bishop Gilbert Dudley Thos Willcox, John Hubbard Medad Dudley David Dudley 2nd Caleb Munger & Reuben Stone, were chosen a Committee to provide for the Soldiers Families	280
Voted, That a Bounty of ten Pounds be paid out of the Town Treasury to each soldier that shall Inlist into the Continental Army for three Years, or dureing the War.. John Leete was chosen Collector to Collect the above within the Limits of the first & fourth Societys	280
Jospeh Doud was Chosen Collector to Collect s^d Rate within the Limits of East Guilford Society	280
John Bartlet was Chosen Collector to Collect s^d Rate within the Limits of North Guilford Society	280
Miles Munger was chosen Collector to Collect s^d Rate within the Limits of North Bristol Society	280
7 Apr 1777	
Wm Chittenden was chosen Grandjuror & refused to Serve	282
John Grave was chosen Collector to collect the town Rate.. in the room of Joseph Doud excused from Serving	282
Joel Tuttle was Chosen Grandjurors	282
Voted That this Town will Build a Wind Mill upon the towns cost.. Thos Burgis.. Aaron Evarts.. Philemon French & Sam^{ll} Brown Esqr were Chosen a Com^{tee} to take the Care & oversight of Building s^d Mill	282
24 Jun 1777	
Col Andrew Ward was Chosen Moderator	283
Capt David Seaward was Chosen Constable to collect the Country Rate	283
the Civil Authority, Select Men & Genl Ward are desired to hire such a number of Men for a Guard as they shall Judge Sufficient for the Safety of the Town	283

Guilford

Voted, That in Case of an Attack.. at North Bristol the fireing of three small Arms & Beat of the Drum on the Hill by Cap[t] Hopsons House be an Alarm	283
5 Aug 1777	
Andrew Ward was chosen Moderator	284
16 Sep 1777	
Aaron Evarts, Tho[s] Burgis Jun[r] Elihu Benton Dea[n] Caleb Munger & Levi Ward were Chosen Assessors	285
Tho[s] Burgis.. Nath[ll] Stone & Sam[ll] Lee Jun[r] { were chosen a Committee to take the Care & oversight of Seting the Salt Works	285
29 Sep 1777	
Col John Eliot was Chosen a Committee Man for the Salt Works	285
9 Dec 1777	
John Burgis Esq[r] was Chosen Moderator	286
Tho[s] Burgis Jun[r] was Chosen Town Clerk	286
Mess[r] David Bishop, W[m] Starr Nathan Chittenden Nath[ll] Allis, Lieu[t] John Hubbard & Cap[t] John Hopson were Chosen Select Men	286
John Leete was Chosen Constable to Collect the Country Rate	286
David Hoit, Sam[ll] Fitch & Miles Munger were Chosen Constables	286
Nath[ll] Hall, Miles Griswould, Eben[r] Grave Jun[r] & Timothy Benton were Chosen Grandjurors	286
Joseph Bartlet, Jonathan Evarts Jun[r], Benj[n] Hall, Lieu[t] W[m] Rosseter Elihu Benton Noadiah Norton, Philemon French Reuben Bartlet, & Ambrose Leete were Chosen Tythingmen	286
Sam[ll] Robinson David Seaward Jun[r] Abra[m] Chittenden Jun[r] Timothy Field Selah Dudley Jun[r] David Dudley 3rd Aaron Stone Ambrose Evarts John Hotchkiss, Peletiah Leete Jun[r] & Stephen Fowler, were Chosen Listers	286
Lieu[t] Ebenezer Hopson was Chosen Town Treasurer	286
David Bishop.. W[m] Starr & Nathan Chittenden { were Chosen Mill Committee	287
16 Dec 1777	
W[m] Chittenden, Paul Dudley, Ens[n] Joseph Crittenden Timothy Bartlet, Eleazer Evarts, Caleb Stone, Tho[s] Griswould Jun[r] Jon[th] Evarts Jun[r] Benj[n] Bartlet, Dec[n] Tho[s] Stone Nath[ll] Allis, John Hill, Jedediah Coe, Benj[n] Rosseter Oliver Dudley Esq Eben[r] Hall, Peter Tallman, Phineas Fowler Nath[ll] Steevens Jun[r] Phinehas Johnson, Noadiah Norton, Joarib Field, & Sam[ll] Benton were Chosen Surveyors of Highways	287
Eber Norton was Chosen Tythingman	287
Tho[s] Hart Lu[t] Eben[r] Hopson, Josiah Scranton, James Munger Jun[r] Lieu[t] Robert Griffing Sam[ll] Fitch, Dec[n] Caleb Munger & Cap[t] John Hopson were Chosen Fence Viewers	287
Col Andrew Ward, Benj[n] Hart John Hill, Tho[s] Fitch, Lieu[t] Joshua Blatchley, Sam[ll] Chittenden, Reuben Parmele, & John Burgis Esq[r] were Chosen Pound keepers	287
Col Andrew Ward Cap[t] Timothy Hill Tho[s] Fitch Lieu[t] Joshuah Blatchley - were Chosen Branders of Horses	288
Cap[t] Sam[ll] Parmele was Chosen Sealer of Troy Weight	288
Thelus Ward was chosen Sealer of Averdupois Weight	288
Philemon French was chosen Sealer of Measures	288

Guilford

Thos Burgis & Joseph Doud { were chosen Sealers of Leather	288
Sam^{ll} Brown Esqr was chosen Gauger	288
Nath^{ll} Hall, Joseph Weld, & Nath^{ll} Allis were Chosen Cullers of Staves & Surveyors of Timber	288
Capt Noah Fowler was Chosen a Select Man	288
Thos Adkins Junr.. Sam^{ll} Field Junr { were Chosen Grandjurymen	288
Sam^{ll} Chittenden Junr & Abra^m Fowler Junr { were Chosen Constables	288

23 Dec 1777

Aaron Evarts, Thos Burgis Junr Levi Ward Elihu Benton, & Dec^n Caleb Munger - were Chosen Assessors	288
Miles Hall was Chosen Collector to Collect the Town Rate.. within the Limits of the 1st & 4th Societys	289
Joshuah Field was Chosen Collector to collect the Town Rate.. within the Limits of North Bristol Society	289
Simeon Chittenden Junr was chosen Collector to Collect the Town Rate.. within the Limits of North Guilford Society	289
Reuben Stone, Miles Hotchkiss, Eben^r Hodgkin Paul Dudley, Timothy Meigs, Joseph Doud, Lieu^t Gilbert Dudley, Medad Dudley, Peter Tallman, David Dudley 2^d Dec^n Caleb Munger - were Chosen a Committee to provide for the Soldiers Families	289
Abra^m Chittenden was Chosen a Committee Man for the Salt Works	289

31 Dec 1777

Daniel Leete & Jared Chittenden { were Chosen Surveyors of Highways	290
Joseph Chittenden was Chosen Sealer of Measures	290
Theo. Scranton was Chosen Collector to Collect the Town Rate within the Limits of East Guilford Society	290
Increase Pendleton, Eben^r Hopson, & Thos Hart were chosen a Committee to inquire into the damages that Tim^o Shelley has sustained in his House & Goods	290

5 Jan 1778

the Com^{tee} that was chosen the last meeting to inquire into the Damages that Tim^o Shelley had sustained in his House & Goods Reported that the damages were five pounds ten Shillings... Voted, That the Town Treasurer pay s^d Shelley his damages out of the Town Treasury	290
Simeon Munger was Chosen Sealer of Measures	291
Timothy Field, Dec^n Peletiah Leete, Thos Hart, & Thos Fitch were chosen to be joyned with the Com^{tee} to provide for the Soldiers Families	291
Sam^{ll} Robinson, Solomon Leete, Nath^{ll} Stone Dec^n Simeon Chittenden, Elias Grave, & Capt John Hopson were Chosen a Com^{tee} to State the Prices of the necessary Articles of Life	291

10 Feb 1778

Wm Chittenden was Chosen Clerk Pro Temp$^{[\ ]}$	291
Nath^{ll} Stevens Ju^r was Chosen a Committee Man to Supply the Families of the Soldiers in the army	291
Voted that Catling Griffings Town Rate in John Leetes Rate Book be abated	292
Voted that Catling Griffings and Archelus Parmeles Town Rates in Eliphalet Hall Ju^r Rate Book be abated	292

Guilford

13 Apr 1778

Voted that Wid^o Sarah Waterous De^{cd} Town Rate 12/ and Thos Walstones Town Rate in Miles Halls Rate Book be abated	293
Whereas Judgment has been given by the County Court of N Haven against James Bishop 2^d for Neglecting to March with the Militia in October last… Voted that this Town is willing to Release S^d Bishop from paying S^d fine	293

8 Dec 1778

John Burgis Esqr was Chosen Moderator	293
Thos Burgis Junr was Chosen Town Clerk	293
David Bishop, Wm Starr, Nathan Chittenden Capt Noah Fowler Josiah Scranton, Liu^t John Hubbard, & Capt John Hopson - were Chosen Select Men	293
Mr Wm Starr was Chosen Town Treasurer	293
Ens^n David Hoit was Chosen Constable to gather the Country Rate	293
David Seaward Junr Sam^{ll} Scranton Junr Sam^{ll} Fitch, & Miles Munger were Chosen Constables	293
John Starr was chosen a Grandjuror & refused to Serve	294
John Norton Junr, Phineas Fowler, Samuel Field Junr & Capt Daniel Hand were Chosen Grandjurors	294
Nathan Johnson, Nath^{ll} Ruggles Junr, Eben^r Munger, Joel Rose, Mulford Coan, Eber Norton Zebulon Hail & Eliakim Steevens were Chosen Tithingmen	294
Lt Eben^r Hopson, Col John Eliot, Ens^n Abraham Fowler, Lt Tim^o Field, Ens^n Ambrose Evarts, Lt Robert Griffing, Simeon Chittenden Junr David Dudley 3^d & Miles Munger were Chosen Listers	294
David Bishop, Wm Starr, & Nathan Chittenden were chosen Committee of the Mill	294
Joseph Crittenden Junr Sam^{ll} Chittenden Junr Abra^m Chittenden, Elias Cadwell, Beriah Norton, Benjn Johnson, Benjn Hall Junr Nath^{ll} Stone, Peletiah Leete Junr Nath^{ll} Cruttenden, Benjn Hart, Levi Ward, Edmund Willcox, Ens^n Eben^r Dudly Benjn Rosseter, Dec^n Simeon Chittenden, Joel Rose, Phineas Fowler, Capt Jared Dudley, Liu^t John Hubbard, Benjn Cramton, Noadiah Norton, Joarib Field, & Eben^r Bragg - were Chosen Surveyors of Highways	294
Thos Hart, Lu^t Eben^r Hopson, Josiah Scranton, James Munger Junr, Liu^t Robert Griffing, Sam^{ll} Fitch, Dec^n Caleb Munger & Capt John Hopson were Chosen Fence Viewers	294
Andrew Ward, Benjn Hart, John Hill, Thos Fitch, Liu^t Joshuah Blatchley, Sam^{ll} Chittenden Reuben Parmele & John Burgis Esqr were Chosen Pound Keepers	295
Col Andrew Ward, Timothy Hill Esqr Thos Fitch & Liu^t Joshuah Blatchley were Chosen Branders of Horses	295
Capt Sam^{ll} Parmele was Chosen Sealer of Troy Weight	295
Thelus Ward was chosen Sealer of Averdupois Weight	295
Joseph Chittenden, Simeon Munger & Philemon French were chosen Sealers of Measures	295
Thos Burgis, & Joseph Doud { were Chosen Sealers of Leather	295

11 Dec 1778

Mr Sam^{ll} Brown was chosen Gauger	295
Ens^n Nath^{ll} Hall.. Joseph Weld & Nath^{ll} Allis { were Chosen Cullers of Staves & Surveyors of Timber	295

Guilford

Miles Hotchkiss, Daniel Leete, Nath^{ll} Stone Nath^{ll} Lee, Simri Bradly, Simeon Munger Daniel Meigs, Timothy Baldwin, Stephen Fowler, Eben^r Fowler Junr, Aaron Stone Phineas Johnson, & Timothy Munger, were Chosen a Comittee to provide for the Soldiers families & Cloathing for the Soldiers	295
Voted, that the Town Treasurer pay the town Rate upon Wm Johnsons Pole to Mr Miles Hall	296
Voted, That Icabud Bartlets, Eben^r Dudley Jun^{rs} John Maltbeys & Thos Cruttendens Town Rates be abated out of Theophilus Scrantons Rate Book	296
Silas Benton, Jabez Benton, Capt Dan Collins & Jared Benton were Chosen to be Joyned with the Committee to provide for the Soldiers families & Cloathing for the Soldiers	296
Levi Ward was Chosen Tything man	296
Hooker Bartlet was Chosen Constable	296
Ambrose Chittenden was chosen Collector of the Town Rate within the Limits of the 1st & 4th Societys	296
Ambrose Dudley was chosen Collector of the Town Rate within the Limits of North Guilford Society	297
Josiah Cramton was Chosen Collector of the Town Rate within the Limits of North Bristol Society	297
Eliu Meigs was Chosen Collector of the Town Rate within the Limits of East Guilford Society	297
Darius Collens was Chosen Grandjury Man	297
Voted, That the Town Treasurer pay Deac^n Peletiah Leete 30/ for Building a Guard House at a Place commonly called Leets Island	297
12 Apr 1779	
Jonathan Todd Junr was Chosen Constable to gather the Country Rate	297
Joseph Stone & Eli Grave { were Chosen Grandjurors	297
Voted, That the Town Treasurer pay Mr Reuben Stone (in behalf of the Committee to provide for the Soldiers &c) £4..7..6 for two journeys to New Haven & One Journey to Hartford	298
Timothy Meigs was chosen Tythingman	298
Voted that there Shall be £1..6..6 paid.. to Aaron Evarts for Plank & Labour done at the Bridge across Neck River near Hooker Nortons House	298
21 Sep 1779	
Ens^n Nath^{ll} Hall was chosen Pound Keeper	298
Ens^n Nath^{ll} Hall was chosen Brander of Horses	298
Voted, that 3 Dozen of Cartridges and two pounds of Powder that Solomon Leete Drew out of the Town Stocks be given to S^d Leete	298
John Burgis Esqr Deac^n Simeon Chittenden Deac^n Caleb Munger, & Capt Elias Grave were Chosen a Committee to Remove Enroachments & Incumbrances from the Highways	299
14 Dec 1779	
John Burgis Esqr was Chosen Moderator	299
Thos Burgis Junr was Chosen Town Clerk	299
Liu^t James Munger, Deac^n Caleb Munger, Mr David Bishop, Mr William Starr were Chosen Select Men	299
Hooker Bartlet, David Seaward Junr, Liu^t Timothy Field, & Miles Munger were Chosen Constables	299

Guilford

Mr Willm Starr was chosen Town Treasurer	*299*
Deac^n John Hall, Thos Hotchkin, Philomon French & Joseph Cruttenden Junr were Chosen Grandjurors	*299*
Capt Peter Vail, Eber Dudley, Miles Johnson Timothy Hill Junr Elijah Crane, Abra^m Grave Eben^r Hall, Gideon Hoppin, Nathan Dudley, & Richard Bristol were chosen Tythingmen	*299*
Nath^{ll} Ruggles Junr Sam^{ll} Chittenden Junr Henry Hill Abra^m Fowler, The^o Fowler, Jairus Chittenden, David Dudley 3rd Timothy Munger Capt David Seaward, James Bishop, & Jonathan Willcox were Chosen Listers	*299*

21 Dec 1779

Increase Pendleton, Thos Hart, Caleb Stone Jno Parmele, Tim^o Evarts, Solomon Leete Junr Capt Noah Fowler Daniel Stone, Sam^{ll} Benton Elihu Meigs, Aaron Blatchley, Nath^{ll} Allis, Nath^{ll} Lee, Eleazer Evarts Deac^n Simeon Chittenden, Benjn Rosseter, Ens^n Daniel Chittenden, Abra^m Grave, Liu^t Robert Griffing, Joseph Chidsey Philemon French, Aaron Stone, Tim^o Scranton Caleb Munger, & Benjn Johnson were Chosen Surveyors of Highways	*300*
Thos Hart Eben^r Hopson, Josiah Scranton James Munger Junr Liu^t Robert Griffing, Sam^{ll} Fitch, Deac^n Caleb Munger, & Capt John Hopson were Chosen Fence Viewers	*300*
Benjn Hart John Hill, Thos Fitch, Joshua Blatchly Sam^{ll} Chittenden, Reuben Parmele, & John Burgis Esqr were Chosen Pound Keepers	*300*
Ens^n Nath^{ll} Hall, Timothy Hill Esqr Thos Fitch & Liu^t Joshua Blatchly, were chosen Branders of Horses	*300*
Hooker Baratlet was Chosen Constable to gather the Country Rate	*300*
Jared Chittenden was Chosen Constable	*301*
Mr Joel Tuttle, Mr Eben^r Fowler, & Col John Eliot were Chosen Select Men	*301*
Nathan Johnson, Ens^n Daniel Norton, Joseph Bartlet Miles Griswould, Liu^t Moses Blatchly, Eben^r Munger, Theophilus Scrantom, Lot Benton John Hopson Junr & Liu^t Joshua Blatchly were Chosen a Committee to provide for the Soldiers Families & Cloathing for the Soldiers	*301*
Nathan Fowler was Chosen Grandjuror	*301*
Joel Tuttle was chosen Committee Man for the Mill	*301*
Capt Sam^{ll} Parmele was chosen Sealer of Troy Weight	*301*
Thelus Ward was chosen Sealer of Averdupois Weight	*301*
Joseph Chittenden, Simeon Munger & Philemon French were Chosen Sealers of Measures	*301*
Thos Burgis & Joseph Doud } were Chosen Sealers of Leather	*301*
Ens^n Nath^{ll} Hall was chosen Pound Keeper	*301*
Sam^{ll} Brown Esqr was chosen Gauger of Cask	*301*
Ens^n Nath^{ll} Hall, Joseph Weld & Nath^{ll} Allis were chosen Cullers of Staves & Surveyors of Timber	*301*

28 Dec 1779

Benjn Norton was chosen Fence Viewer	*301*
Daniel Evarts & Eleazer Evarts Junr were chosen to be Joyned with the Committee for provideing for the Soldiers Families & Cloathing for the Soldiers	*302*
Ambrose Leete was chosen Collector to Collect the Town Rate within the Limits of the 1st & 4th Societys	*302*
Benjn Norton was chosen Collector to Collect the Town Rate within the Limits of North Guilford Society	*302*

Guilford

Elias Munger was chosen Collector to collect the Town Rate within the Limits of North Bristol Society	302
Benjn Hart was chosen Collector to Collect the Town Rate within the Limits of East Guilford Society	302
David Bishop & William Starr } were chosen Committee of the Mill	302
Voted that there be a Committee appointed to provide Timber for the Town Mill & to keep her in Repair, Nathan Chittenden & Darius Collens were Chosen a Committee for that purpose	302
Voted that the Wid^o Rebecca Letes, Wid^o Mary Nortons & Mr Edmund Wards Town Rates be Abated out of Ambrose Chittendens Rate Book	302
Voted that the Town Rates of Martha Wing 4/ Joshua Cook 8/ Jedidah Cook 3/ & Oliver Collens £1..3..0 be Abated out of Ambrose Dudleys Rate Book	302
Granted to the Widow Rebecca Hill the Sum of £22..4..0 Continental Currency to pay Doct^r Foot for doctering her Son in his last Sickness	302
Jonathan Evarts, Joseph Cruttenden & Timothy Bartlet were Chosen Surveyors of Highways	303

14 Feb 1780

John Burgis Esqr was Chosen Moderator	303
Timothy Cruttenden Miles Hall Daniel Leete Aaron Jones Eben^r Doud Junr Tim^o Baldwin Miles Hotchkiss, & Phineas Johnson were chosen to be Joyned with the Committee to provide for the Soldiers Families & Cloathing for the Soldiers	303
Jehiel Willcox was chosen Collector to Collect the Town Rate within the Limits of East Guilford Society in the Room of Benjn Hart excused from Serving	303
Elias Meigs was Chosen Grandjuror	303
Voted, That there be a Sufficient Covr^d Bridge Built & maintained across the West River in the Highway Northward of Henry Bartlets home Lot upon the Towns Cost	303
Jairus Handy was chosen Surveyor of Highways	303

7 Mar 1780

John Burgis Esqr was Chosen Moderator	303
Solomon Leete, Nath^{ll} Hall, Noah Hotchkin Junr Peletiah Leete Junr, Sam^{ll} Chittenden Capt Dan Collens Capt Noah Fowler Elias Cadwell, Eben^r Shelley, Nath^{ll} Allis Jonathan Lee, Eli Grave, Joseph Doud, Capt Elias Grave Jehiel Willcox, Nath^{ll} Lee, Simeon Chittenden Ju^r Sam^{ll} Fitch Willm Rosseter, Timothy Eliot Jonathan Fowler, Josiah Fowler, Nath^{ll} Steevens & Eben^r Field, were Chosen Inspectors of Provisions	303
Voted that Capt Nath^{ll} Nortons Wife may have Liberty to draw Money out of the Town Treasury as her Necessitys may Require… on this Condition… that the S^d Norton Shall be Responsible to the Town for the Same	304

10 Apr 1780

Liu^t Thos Power was Chosen Grandjuror	304
Voted John Heburts Town Rate 20/ be abated out of Collector Benjn Nortons Rate Book	304
Voted that the Town Rates of Catling Griffing 2/3 & Benjn Stone Meigs 2/3 be abated out of Collt^r Eber Dudleys Rate Book	304
Voted that the Town Rates of James Hall £4.. 0.. [ ] Bela Stone £4..5..0 & Wid^o Mary Norton £1..0..9.. be abated out of Collector Ambrose Leets Rate Book	304
Selah Murray was chosen Grandjuror in the Room of Elias Meigs Excused from Serving	304
Voted, That Capt Dan Collens be an Agent for this Town to prepare.. a Suitable [*Lock*] to the	305

Guilford

Town House Dore and to Commence & prosecute.. any Person.. who Shall be guilty of any abuse to the Town House by Breaking or attempting to Break open the Dore or Windows or by breaking the Glass of the House or by any other Insult or abuse
23 Jun 1780

Gen^{ll} Andrew Ward was chosen Moderator	*305*
Elon Lee Junr was Chosen Collector to Collect the Town Rates.. within the Limits of the 1st & 4th Societies	*306*
Levi Ward was chosen Collector to collect the Town Rates.. within the Limits of East Guilford Society	*306*
Timothy Eliot was chosen Collector to collect the Town Rates.. within the Limits of North Guilford Society	*306*
Didymus French was Chosen Collector to collect the Town Rate.. within the limits of North Bristol Society	*306*

13 Nov 1780

John Burgis Esqr was Chosen Moderator	*306*
Liu^t Eben^r Hopson Mr Abra^m Chittenden Liu^t Timothy Field & Mr Sam^{ll} Fitch were Chosen Inspectors & Packers of Provisions	*307*
Abra^m Chittenden Junr was chosen Collector & Excused from Serving	*307*
Voted that Mes^{rs} Eben^r Hopson, Abra^m Chittenden Tim^o Field & Sam^{ll} Fitch be a Com^{tee} to Purchase the Several Articles of Provisions, as is required by a late Act of the Genl Assembly of this State upon the Towns Credit	*307*
Nathan Cramton was chosen collector, to gather the Town Rate.. in the Room of Didymus French who refused to serve	*307*
Abel Norton was chosen collector to gather the Town Rate.. within the Limits of North Guilford Society	*307*
Eben^r Wakely was chosen collector to gather the Town Rate.. within the limits of North Bristol Society	*308*
Timothy Seaward was Chosen collector to gather the Town Rate.. within the limits of the 1st & 4th Societies	*308*
Julius Willard was chosen Collector to gather the Town Rate.. within the limits of East Guilford Society	*308*
Voted, That Capt Noah Fowler, Capt Dan Collens, Capt Gilbert Dudley, Capt Augustus Collens, & Capt Timothy Munger, be a Com^{tee} to procure or Hire this Towns Quota of abel Bodyed & Effective Men to Inlist into the Continental Army for the Term of three Years or dureing the War	*308*

12 Dec 1780

John Burgis Esqr was Chosen Moderator	*308*
Thos Burgis Junr was Chosen Town Clerk	*308*
Mr Joel Tuttle, Lieu^t Ambrose Evarts, Dea^n Caleb Munger, Liu^t Wm Rosseter, & Mr John Hotchkiss were Chosen Select Men	*309*
Mr Nath^{ll} Cruttenden was chosen a Select Man & Refused to Serve	*309*
David Seaward Junr was Chosen Constable to Collect the Country Rate	*309*
Lieu^t Timothy Field, Jared Chittenden Aaron Stone, & John Starr were Chosen Constables	*309*
Benjn Teal, David Parks, & Philemon French were Chosen Grandjurors	*309*
Capt Elias Grave, Eli Grave, Abra^m Grave, Abra^m Kimberly Junr Nath^{ll} Steevens Junr Eliakim	*309*

Guilford

Steevens Elias Cadwell & Joseph Chittenden Junr wre chosen Tythingmen	
Capt David Seaward, Sam^ll Chittenden Junr Sam^ll Robinson Liu^t Nath^ll Stone, Capt Gilbert Dudley Jonathan Todd Junr Ambrose Dudley, Luther Dudley, Lieu^t David Dudley, & Phineas Johnson were Chosen Listers	309

19 Dec 1780

Nath^ll Ruggles Esqr was Chosen Moderator Pro Tempr^[ ]	310
Mr Reuben Stone & Mr Thos Hart } were Chosen Select Men	310
Mr Wm Starr was Chosen Town Treasurer	310
Nathan Chittendon, Eber Parmele, Reuben Leete, Joseph Weld, Jared Benton, Elon Lee Junr Joseph Bartlet, Jabez Benton, Simeon Grave Ambrose Grave Jehiel Willcox, Amaziah Evarts Tim^o Benton, Eben^r Hall Medad Dudley, Nathan Fowler, Abra^m Grave, Didymus French, Tim^o Scranton Zechariah Field, Nathan Dudley Capt Noah Fowler, Aaron Evarts, & George Kimberly were chosen Surveyors of Highways	310
Eber Dudley & Asael Murray were chosen Tythingmen	310
Thos Hart, Eben^r Hopson, Josiah Scrantom, James Munger Junr Benjn Norton, Silas Fowler, Deac^n Caleb Munger, & Capt John Hopson, were Chosen Fence Viewers	310
Joel Tuttle, John Hotchkiss & Reuben Stone were Chosen Mill Com^tee	310
Nath^ll Hall, Benjn Hart, John Hill, Thomas Fitch, Joshua Blatchley, Sam^ll Chittenden Reuben Parmele, & John Burgis Esqr were Chosen Pound Keepers	310
Nath^ll Hall, Tim^o Hill Esqr Thos Fitch & Joshua Blatchley were chosen Branders of Horses	310
Capt Sam^ll Parmele was Chosen Sealer of Troy Weights	310
Thelus Ward was chosen Sealer of Averdupois Weights	311
Joseph Chittenden, Simeon Munger, & Philemon French were chosen Sealers of Measures	311
Thos Burgis & Joseph Doud { were chosen Sealers of Leather	311
Sam^ll Brown Esqr was chosen Gauger of Cask	311
Nath^ll Hall, Joseph Weld Nath^ll Allis, & Joseph Chittenden, were chosen Cullers of Staves and Surveyors of Timber	311
Nathan Johnson, Sam^ll Benton, John Norton Junr Nath^ll Dudley 2^d Sam^ll Evarts 3rd Capt Noah Fowler Peletiah Leete Junr Nathan Chidsey, Simeon Chittenden Junr Isaac Johnson, Capt John Hopson, Jonathan Judd, Benjn Hart & Selah Murray were Chosen Com^tee of Supplies	311

26 Dec 1780

Increase Pendleton & Timothy Bartlet were chosen Grandjurors & refused to Serve	311
Absalom Minor was chosen Surveyor of Highways	311
Thos Burgis & Eben^r Hopson were chosen Grandjurymen	311
Sam^ll Loper and Eben^r Bishop 2nd were Chosen Tythingmen	311
Voted, that the Town Rates of James Hall 3/ Meria Hotchkiss 1/8½ Jane Kirkum 1/3½, Hannah Leete [ ] Mary Norton 8¼ Sibble Stone 1/5 Bela Stone 2/[ ] & Thos Wheeler [1]/2 be abated out of Collector Elon Lee Jun^rs Rate Book	312

Guilford

29 Dec 1780

Tim° Cruttenden was chosen Collector to Collect the Town Rate within the Limits of the 1st & 4th Societys	313
John Scranton was chosen Collector to Collect the Town Rate within the Limits of East Guilford Society	313
Tim° Rosseter was chosen Collector to Collect the Town Rate within the Limits of North Guilford Society	313
Tim° Munger 3rd was Chosen collector to Collect the Town Rate within the Limits of North Bristol Society	313
Voted that the Town Rates of Daniel Bishop £1..1..5 ½ Abra^m Bishop 7/6 Noah Cruttenden £5..1..9 John Cruttenden £5..5..5 Joseph Lee £2..2..3 be abated from Collect^r Jehiel Willcox Rate Book	313
Reuben Stone, Ambrose Evarts, Wm Rosseter & Caleb Munger were chosen chosen Receivers of the Provisions & other Articles that Shall be paid in for Town Rate	313
Voted, That the Cowyard of Eben^r Wakely Shall be deemed… a lawful Town Pound for impounding Creatures liable to be taken and pounded by Law	313
Eben^r Wakely was Chosen Pound Keeper	314

8 Jan 1781

Sam^{ll} Robinson, Nath^{ll} Allis, Liu^t Robert Griffing & Capt John Hopson, were Chosen Receivers and Packers of the Flour	314
Eber Norton was Chosen Collector to Collect the Town Rate within the Limits of the 1st & 4th Societys	314
Timothy Hill Junr was chosen Collector to Collect theTown Rate within the Limits of East Guilford Society	314
Josiah Fowler Junr was chosen Collector to collect the Town Rate within the Limits of North Guilford Society	314
Noadiah Norton was Chosen Collector to Collect the Town Rate within the Limits of North Bristol Society	314
Joel Tuttle was chosen Receiver of the Town Rate.. in the Room of Reuben Stone Excused from Serving	314
Ens^n Daniel Chittenden was Chose Collector to Collect the Town Rate in the Room of Tim° Rosseter who was Excused from Serving	315
Capt Dan Collens, Capt Gilbert Dudley, Capt Augustus Collens & Capt Tim° Munger were Chosen a Com^{tee} to Inlist 11 State Soldiers	315
Voted, That the Town Rates of Chapman £1..0..0 James Cook 10/ Jedidah Cook 15/ be abated out of Collet^r Benjn Nortons Rate Book	315

15 Feb 1781

Elias Cadwell was Chosen Collector of the Town Rate in the Room of Eber Norton who Refused toServe	316
Nath^{ll} Allis Junr was chosen Collector of the Town Rate in the Room of Tim° Hill Excused from Serving	316
Augustus Collens Esqr was Chosen Collector of the Town Rate in the Room of Josiah Fowler Junr Excused from Serving	316
Tim° Seaward was Chosen Collector of the Town Rate.. within the Limits of the 1st & 4th Societys	316
Tim° Hall was Chosen Collector of the Town Rate.. within the Limits of East Guilford Society	316
Joseph Fyler was Chosen Collector of the Town Rate.. within the Limits of N Guilford	316

Guilford

Society

Eben^r Wakely was Chosen Collector of the Town Rate.. within the Limits of North Bristol Society	316
Simeon Saxton was chosen Collector of the Town Rate in the Room of Tim^o Cruttenden who refused to Serve	316

16 Feb 1781

Capt Noah Fowler, Capt Augustus Collens, Capt Dan Collens, Capt Gilbert Dudley, Mr Benjn Hart & Capt Timothy Munger be a Committee to procure or Hire this Towns Quota of Able Bodyed & Effective Men to Inlist in to the Continental Army	317
Richard Bristol was chosen Collector of the Town Rate.. in the Room of Eben^r Wakely who refused to Serve	317
Eli Grave was chosen Collector of the Town Rate, in the Room of Nath^{ll} Allis Junr Excused from Serving	317
Timothy Todd was chosen Collector of the Town Rate in the Room of John Scranton who refused to Serve	317
Voted, That the Guard that Shall be Set by Gen^{ll} Wards Orders, .. Shall be paid out of the town Treasury	317

13 Mar 1781

Elias Willard was Chosen Collector of the Town Rate in the Room of Eli Grave Excused from Serving	318
John Hill Junr was Chosen Collector of the Town Rate.. within the Limits of E Guilford Society	318
Tim^o Rosseter was chosen Collector of the Town Rate..within the Limits of North Guilford Society	318
Beriah Norton was chosen Collector of the Town Rate.. within the Limits of the 1st & 4th Societies	318
Elias Munger was chosen Collector of the Town Rate.. within the Limits of North Bristol Society	318
Saul Foster was chosen Collector of a Town Rate in the Room of Tim^o Todd, Excused from Serving	318
Voted, That the Town Rates of John Cruttenden 3/6¼ Noah Cruttenden 5/7¾, Joseph Lee 1/5 Reuben Norton Junr 3/6, Abra^m Bishop 0/3 Jane Maltbey 0/4¾ Tim^o Willcox 3/6½ & Zacheriah Doud 3/1¾ be abated out of Levi Wards Rate Book	318

22 Mar 1781

Voted, That the Inhabitants.. be Devided into Eleven Classes, in Order to raise this Towns Quota of Soldiers for the State Battallion for the Term of One Year, and That Capt Noah Fowler, Capt Dan Collens Mr Sam^{ll} Robinson, Genl Andrew Ward, Mr Wm Starr Capt Gilbert Dudley, Mr Benjn Hart, Capt Augustus Collens, Mr Sam^{ll} Fitch, Capt Timothy Munger & Capt John Hopson, be a Com^{tee} for that purpose	319

22 Mar 1781

Capt Noah Fowler, Capt Dan Collens, Capt Gilbert Dudley, Capt Augustus Collens, & Capt Timothy Munger, were Chosen a Com^{tee} to Assertain the Number of Soldiers from this Town in the Continental Army	319
Darius Collens was chosen Collector of a Town Rate (in the Room of Beriah Norton Excused from Serving) & refused to Serve	319
Isaac Stone was Chosen Collector of a Town Rate in the Room of Elias Munger Excused from Serving	319

Guilford

Liu{t} David Hull was chosen Collector of a Town Rate in the Room of Darius Collens who refused to Serve	319
Daniel Hill was chosen Collector of a Town Rate in the Room of Saul Foster Excused from Serving	319

9 Apr 1781

Timothy Hill was chosen Brander of Horses	320
The following Persons were chosen Class Collectors (viz) George Kimberly Collector for the 1st Class Nathll Hall D{o} for 2nd D{o}, John Scranton D{o} 3rd D{o} Pitman Collens D{o} 5th D{o} Ezra Griswould D{o} 4th D{o} Stephen Fowler Collector 1st Class North Guilford Simeon Chittenden Junr D{o} 2nd D{o} Ebenr Field D{o} for the Class in North Bristol Noah Stone Collector 1st Class in East Guilford, Elijah Crane D{o} 2nd D{o} And Aaron Jones Collector for the Class to which he belongs	320
Jedediah Coe was chosen Collector of a Town Rate in the room of Danll Hill who refused to Serve	320
Nathll Allis Junr was chosen Collector of the Town Rate.. within the Limits of East Guilford Society	321
John Hopson Junr was chosen Collector of the Town Rate.. within the Limits of N Bristol Society	321
Elihu Benton was chosen Collector of the Town Rate.. within the Limits of N Guilford Society	321
John Parmele Junr was chosen Collector of the Town Rate.. within the Limits of the 1st & 4th Societys	321
Timothy Field was chosen Collector of a Town Rate in the Room of Jedadiah Coe excused from Serving	321
Capt Peter Vaill & Ens{n} Jonathan Todd were chosen Receivers of the Town Rate	321

26 Jun 1781

John Burgis Esqr was chosen Moderator	321
David Seaward Junr was Chosen Collector of the Town Rate granted this Day	322
Samll Lee Junr was chosen Collector of a Town Rate. granted last April in the Room of John Parmele Junr who refused to Serve	322

18 Sep 1781

Voted, That the Town Treasurer pay Doctr Phineas Clark the one half of his Acct.. for Doctering Aaron Hill[erd] in his last Sickness	322
Saul Foster was chosen Collector of the Town Rate.. within the Limits of E Guilford Society	322
Elihu Benton was chosen Collector of the Town Rate.. within the Limits of N Guilford Society	322
Noah Benton was chosen Collector of the Town Rate.. within the Limits of North Bristol Society	323
Benjn Chittenden was chosen Collector of the Town Rate.. within the Limits of the 1st & 4th Societys	323
Luman Grave was chosen Collector of a Town Rate.. in the Room of Nathll Allis Junr who refused to Serve	323
Jared Chittenden was chosen Collector of a Town Rate.. in the Room of Elihu Benton who refused to Serve	323
Capt Peter Vaill & Jonathan Todd Junr were chosen to Receive the Provisions that Shall be paid for the Town Rate	323

Guilford

Capt Peter Vaill & Liu^t Timothy Field were chosen Purchasers of Provisions for the Guard	323
5 Nov 1781	
Mr Eben^r Hopson, Mr Levi Ward, Capt John Hopson and Mr Lot Benton were chosen procurers of Cask & Receivers & Packers of Beef, Pork &c	323
11 Dec 1781	
Genl Andrew Ward was chosen Moderator	324
Thos Burgis Junr was chosen Town Clerk	324
Messrs Increase Pendleton, Abra^m Chittenden Nath^{ll} Hall, Nath^{ll} Allis, Sam^{ll} Fitch, Deac^n Caleb Munger, & Miles Hotchkiss were Chosen Select Men	324
John Starr was chosen Constable to gather the Country Rate	324
Sam^{ll} Scranton Junr.. Jared Chittenden.. Aaron Stone & Daniel Miegs { were Chosen Constables	324
Sam^{ll} Lee.. Noah Stone.. Joshua Rockwell.. Zachariah Field, & Capt David Seaward { were chosen Grandjurors	324
Ambrose Leete, Edmund Willcox, The^o Scrantom, Benjn Norton, Eben^r Fowler Ju^r Zebulon Hail, Joshua Field, Felix Norton, Seth Benton, and John Cramton Junr were Chosen Tythingmen	324
Increase Pendleton was chosen Town Treasurer	324
Increase Pendleton, Abra^m Chittenden & Miles Hotchkiss, were chosen Mill Com^{tee}	325
Liu^t Thos Power, Ambrose Chittenden Ens^n Abra^m Fowler, Liu^t Sam^{ll} Lee Levi Ward, Julius Willard, Jairus Chittenden Jared Dudley Junr Miles Munger, & Elias Munger were chosen Listers	325
Capt Noah Fowler Sam^{ll} Benton Nathan Chittenden, Tim^o Bartlet, Eben^r Hodgkin John Parmele Junr Nathan Chidsey Abra^m Grave, Sam^{ll} Field Junr Joseph Doud Elihu Meigs, & Josiah Scrantom were chosen Com^{tee} of Supplies	325
Daniel Stone, Jonth^n Evarts, Elon Lee Ju^r Sam^{ll} Scrantom, Simeon Grave, Jehiel Willcox, John Scrantom, Hull Cramton Joel Rose, Daniel Chittenden, Simeon Chittenden Ju^r Abra^m Kimberley Junr Joseph Chittenden Junr Aaron Jones Silas Benton, Gideon Hopson, Didymus French, Joshua Blatchley, James Willcox & Sam^{ll} Parmele, were chosen.. Surveyors of Highways	325
Voted, That Phineas Peltons Town Rate 4/4 in Collector Richard Bristols Rate Book be abated	325
Voted, that the Town Rates of Abra^m Bi[shop] 0/1½ John Cruttenden 2/6 2/4 The^o Cruttenden 2/4 Zechariah Doud 3/3 Joseph Lee 1/10 1/[ ] Reuben Norton Ju^r 3/6 Mehetable Scrantom 2/4½ & Tim^o Willcox 6/3½ be abated out of Colct^r Tim^o Fields Rate Book	326
Voted, That Enos Bishops Town Rates in Colet^{rs} Tim^o Munger Junr Isaac Stone, John Hopson Junr & Noah Bentons Rate Books be abated	326
18 Dec 1781	
Eber Norton & Nath^{ll} Stone { were Chosen Surveyors of Highways	326
Thos Hart, Eben^r Hopson, Josiah Scrantom Tim^o Meigs, Benjn Norton, Silas Fowler Capt John Hopson, & Dec^n Caleb Munger were chosen Fence Viewers	326
Nath^{ll} Hall, Benjn Hart, John Hill, Thos Fitch, Joshua Blatchley, Jared Benton, Reuben Parmale, Sam^{ll} Chittenden & Eben^r Wakely were chosen Pound keepers	326
Nath^{ll} Hall, Tim^o Hill, Thos Fitch & Joshua Blatchley, were Chosen Branders of Horses	327
Thelus Ward was chosen Sealer of Troy & Averdupois Weights	327

Guilford

Joseph Chittenden, Simeon Munger, Philemon French, & Thos Fitch were chosen Sealers of Measures	327
Thos Burgis & Joseph Doud { were Chosen Sealers of Leather	327
Sam^{ll} Brown Esqr was chosen Gauger	327
Joseph Weld, Nath^{ll} Allis & Joseph Chittenden Ju^r were chosen Cullers of Staves & Surveyors of Timber	327
John Leete, Miles Hall, David Bishop Eber Dudley & Eben^r Wakely, were chosen to be joined with the Com^{tee} of Supplies	327
Voted Tim^o Scrantoms Town Rate 19/ in Miles Mungers Rate Book be abated	327
Voted That the Town Rates of Abra^m Bishop 0/1½ John Cruttenden 3/2 Noah Cruttenden 6/9 Thos Cruttenden 3/1 Joseph Lee 2/4 Reuben Norton Ju^r 4/4½ & Mehetable Scrantom 2/11½ be abated out of Colct^r John Hill Junr Rate Book	327
Voted, That the Town Rates of John Hebard of John Hill 3/4 & Stephen Whedon 3/9 be abated out of Colct^r Augustus Collens Rate Book	328
Voted, That the Town Rates of Stephen Whedon of 6½ George Coan of 11½ Joshua Cook 1/4 Jedida Cook 0/6 John Heberd 0/8 Abra^m Kimberly 0/6 3/4 be abated out of Colct^r Tim^o Eliots Rate Book	328
Voted, That the Town Rates of Barnabas M Kein 3/2, Mercy Leete 1/5¾ Miles Stone 3/2 be abated out of Colct^r Elon Lee Junr Rate Book	328
Voted, That the Town Rates of Mary Forsdick of 0/[5] ½ Meriam Hotchkiss 1/0 Wid Sarah Stone 1/5 James Parmele 1/0 Anne Parmele 0/3¼ & Miles Stone 5/5 be abated out of Simeon Saxtons Rate Book	328

25 Dec 1781

Voted, That there be Auditors appointed to audite & Settle the Town accounts and that Messrs Wm Starr, Eben^r Hopson & Capt David Seaward were chosen a Com^{tee} for that purpose	328
Voted, that Mr Joel Tuttle be an Agent for this Town to prepare & fix a Suitable Lock to the Town House Dore, &.. prosecute.. any Person.. guilty of any abuse to the Town House by breaking or attempting to break open the dore or Windows, or by breaking the Glass of the House, or by any other insult or abuse of what kind or Sort Soever	329
Voted, that the Town Rates of John Brewster 1/ Wid^o Mary Forsdick 0/5 Wid Meriam Hotchkiss 0/8 Wid^o Jane Kirkum 1/2 Wid^o Mercy Leete 1/1½ Wid^o Mary Norton 0/8½ James Parmele 0/8 Anne Parmele 0/2¼ Wid^o Sarah Stone 0/10 and Miles Stone 3/7½ be abated out of Sam^{ll} Lee Ju^r Rate Book	329

12 Feb 1782

John Burgis Esqr was chosen Moderator	330
John Burgis Esqr was chosen Agent for this Town	330

26 Feb 1782

Augustus Collens Esqr was Chosen to Assertain the Number of Soldiers from this Town that were in the Continental & State Service the last Year, and also this Towns Quota of Soldiers for the Continental Army for the present Year, before the Com^{tee}.. to Set at New Haven this Week	331

Guilford

7 Mar 1782

David Bishop was chosen Surveyor of Highways	331
Voted, To Choose a Com[tee] to procure this Towns Quota of able Bodyed & Effective Men for the Continental Army.. And Cap[t] Noah Fowler, Cap[t] Augustus Collens Lieu[t] Sam[ll] Lee, Liu[t] Tho[s] Power, Deac[n] Benj[n] Hart, Capt Tim[o] Munger, & Elias Grave Esq[r] were chosen a Com[tee] for that purpose	332
Tim[o] Meigs was chosen Collector of the Town Rate.. within the limits of East Guilford Society	332
Josiah Cramton was chosen Collector of the Town Rate.. within the Limits of North Bristol Society	332
Tim[o] Benton was chosen Colct[r] of the Town Rate.. within the limits of North Guilford Society	332
Reuben Parmele was Chosen Colct[r] of the Town Rate.. within the limits of the 1st & 4th Society's	332

8 Apr 1782

Elias Meigs was chosen Town Collector in the Room of Tim[o] Meigs who refused to Serve	333
Eliakim Steevens was chosen Town Colct[r] in the Room of Josiah Cramton who was Excused from Serving	333
Voted, That the Town Rates of Eber Hall 3/9¾.. Wid[o] Rebecca Leete 2/2, Philip Man 4/10¾ & Wid[o] Mary Norton 0/1¾ be abated out of Simeon Saxtons Rate Book	333

17 Sep 1780

Nathan Chittenden Jun[r] was chosen Colct[r] of the Town Rate in the Room of Tim[o] Benton Released from Serving	333
Joseph Dudley was chosen Colct[r] of a Town Rate in the Room of Elias Meigs who refused to Serve	333
Tim[o] Benton was chosen Grandjuror	333
Voted, That the Town Rates of Eber Hall 9/2 Jane Kirkum 1/[11]½ Wid[o] Rebecca Leete 1/0 1/2 Wid[o] Mary Norton 0/10½ Miles Stone 4/6¾ & Shubal Shelley 7/7 be abated out of Colct[r] David Halls Rate Book	333
Voted, That the town Rates of Enos Bishop 7/9½ John Pelton 7/3 Phineas Pelton 5/10 Tho[s] Doud 5/2 1/2 & Mary Cramton 0/10½ be abated out of John Hopson Ju[r] Rate Book	334
Voted, That the Town Rates of Enos Bishop 7/9½ Phineas Pelton 5/10 John Pelton 7/2 & Asher Seaward 0/6 be abated out of Tim[o] Munger 3[d] Rate Book	334
[*Voted, That the*] Town Rates of John Cruttenden.. [ ]den 5/5 & Tho[s] Cruttenden [ ] be abated out of Colct[r] Luman Grave Rate Book	334

10 Dec 1782

John Burgis Esq[r] was Chosen Moderator	334
Tho[s] Burgis Jun[r] was chosen Town Clerk	334
M[r] David Bishop, M[r] Nath[ll] Stone M[r] Abra[m] Chittenden M[r] Nath[ll] Allis, M[r] Lot Benton, & Cap[t] Tim[o] Munger were chosen Select Men	334
Increase Pendleton was chosen Town Treasurer	334
John Starr was chosen Constable to gather the Country Rate	335
Hooker Bartlet, Daniel Meigs, Jared Chittenden, Aaron Stone, & Timothy Cruttenden were chosen Constables	335
Cap[t] David Seward, Elias Cadwell, Nath[ll] Allis Jun[r] Zachariah Field, & Lieu[t] Robert Griffing	335

Guilford

were chosen Grandjurymen

Joseph Weld, Elias Meigs, John Shelley, Selah Dudley Jun[r] John Stone 2nd Benj[n] Cramton Jun[r] Eben[r] Wakeley, Aaron Jones & Felix Norton, were chosen Tythingmen — *335*

Sam[ll] Chittenden Jun[r] Noah Hotchkin Jun[r] Miles Hall, Lieu[t] Abra[m] Fowler, Tim[o] Meigs Josiah Scrantom, Jared Dudley Jun[r] The[o] Fowler Miles Munger & Lieu[t] Joshua Blatchly were Chosen Listers — *335*

Joseph Chittenden Jun[r] Philemon Hall, Nath[ll] Parmele, Eber Norton Joseph Stone Joseph Cruttenden Jun[r] Nath[ll] Hall Jonathan Evarts, John Leete, The[o] Scrantom Tim[o] Doud Ezra Willcox, Jesse Munger Medad Dudley Eben[r] Fowler Jun[r] Sam[ll] Loper, John Bartlet Simeon Chittenden Jun[r] Josiah Fowler, Benj[n] Cramton Jun[r] Zebulon Hail, Nathan Cramton Benj[n] Johnson & John Hotchkiss, were chosen Surveyors of Highways — *335*

Abraham Chittenden & David Bishop } were Chose Mill Committee — *336*

Voted, That the Town Rate of Oliver Collens 13/5 be abated out of Reuben Parmeles Rate Book — *336*

17 Dec 1782

Tho[s] Hart, Eben[r] Hopson, Cap[t] James Munger Cap[t] Gilbert Dudley, Silas Fowler, Caleb Fowler, Deac[n] Caleb Munger, & Cap[t] John Hopson, were chosen Fence Viewers — *336*

Simeon Grave, John Hill Jun[r] Tho[s] Fitch Joshua Blatchley, Reuben Parmele, Jared Benton, Nath[ll] Hall, Benj[n] Chittenden & Eben[r] Wakeley were Chosen pound keepers — *336*

Nath[ll] Hall, Tim[o] Hill, Tho[s] Fitch, & Joshua Blatchley, were chosen Branders of Horses — *336*

Thelus Ward ws Chosen Sealer of Troy & Averdupois Weights — *336*

Joseph Chittenden, Simeon Munger, Tho[s] Fitch, & Philemon French, were Chosen Sealers of Measures — *336*

Tho[s] Burgis & Joseph Doud { were Chosen Sealers of Leather — *337*

Eli foot was Chosen Gauger of Cask — *337*

Joseph Weld.. Tho[s] Hotchkin & Joseph Chittenden Ju[r] { were Chosen Cullers of Staves & Surveyors of Timber — *337*

Tho[s] Griswould Jun[r] was chosen Tythingman — *337*

Increase Pendleton was chosen Select Man — *337*

Elihu Meigs was chosen Collector of a Town Rate in the Room of Joseph Dudley who refused to Serve — *337*

24 Feb 1783

Voted, That the Town Rates of Wid[o] Mercy Leete 1/10 & W[m] Barker 1/8 be abated out of Elias Cadwells Rate Book — *337*

Timothy Baldwin was chosen Constable to gather the Country Rate — *337*

Nathan Chittenden, John Hotchkiss, Col Noah Fowler, Eben[r] Hotchkin Jared Benton Eber Dudley, Darius Collens, Noah Benton & Joel Rose were chosen Com[tee] of Supplies — *338*

Voted That the Select Men are directed to Sell the Dwelling House that formerly belonged to Jonathan hatch, but now to this Town — *338*

Abraham Dudley was chosen Collector of the Town Rate — *338*

Will[m] Dudley was chosen Collector of the Town Rate — *338*

Sam[ll] Field Jun[r] was chosen Collector of the Town Rate — *338*

Elisha Basset was chosen Collector of the Town Rate — *338*

Gilead Bradley was chosen Collector of the Town Rate in the Room of Elihu Meigs who — *338*

Guilford

refused to Serve	
Voted That the Town Treasurer pay those People that Supplied Capt Vaills Guard with Beef	338
Voted that the Select Men are desired to Settle the account between Mr Joel Tuttle & this Town by Arbitration	339
Voted that John Norton Junr hath Liberty to Erect a fulling Mill on his own Land a little below Mr Elon Lees Dwelling House provided S^d Norton Shall agree with the People that own the Land adjoining and Answer all Damages that Shall arise by Erecting S^d Mill	339
Voted that we will choose a Com^{tee} to Settle the preliminaries & agree upon Articles Respecting the Parish of East Guilford being made a seperate Town.. and that William Starr Esqr Dec^n Benjn Hart Capt David Seaward, Capt James Munger & Deac^n Simeon Chittenden be a Com^{tee} for that purpose	339
Voted, That the Town Rate of Levi Spinning 12/7 State Money be abated out of Levi Wards Rate Book	340
Voted, That the Town Rates of Miles Stone 3/7½ Wid^o Mercy Leete 1/1½ Wid^o Jane Kirkum 1/2 Wid^o Mary Forsdick 0/4¾ Wid^o Sar[a]h Stone 0/10 & Shubal Shelley 12/1½ be abated out of Benjn Chitendens Rate Book	340
Voted, That the Town Rates of Eben^r Stone 1/9 & Shubal Shelley 12/3½ be abated out of Sam^{ll} Lee Junr Rate Book	340
Voted, That the town Rates of Eben^r Bragg 8/3½ John Pelton 7/2¼ & Asher Seaward 5/6 be abated out of Noah Bentons Rate Book	340
7 Apr 1783	
Luther Dudley was chosen Tythingman	340
Voted, that this Town will lend Mr Thos Caldwell so much Money as to Settle his State Taxes, with the following Collectors viz, Capt David Seaward, Doct^r Jonathan Todd, Mr Hooker Bartlet, & Mr David Seaward Junr & that the Town Treasurer take S^d Caldwells Security for the Same	340
Voted, That the Town Rate of Levi Spinning in Julius Willards Rate Book be abated	341
22 Apr 1783	
The Articles hereafter mentioned are agreed upon by the Committee chosen by the Town of Guilford upon the Memorial of a Number of the Inhabitants of the Parish of East Guilford requesting that the s^d Parish may be set off from the s^d Town.. for a Separate Town.. it is agreed.. that the Boundaries of s^d Society Shall be.. begining at North East Corner of s^d Society where the Brook Enters into Hamanasset River a little below Fosters Mill, .. Runing Westerly to the Ivy Swamp .. & from thence to the Foot of the Hill called the Opening Hill & from thence to the Dam in the Nack River called the Seaward Mill dam, & from s^d dam with the s^d River down to Tail of Reuben Nortons Mill, & from s^d Mill down to the foot of the Hill East of David Cruttenden Dec^d.. David Seaward.. Simeon Chittenden.. Benjamin Hart.. James Munger.. William Starr } Committee	341
David Bishop Junr was chosen Collector of the Town Rate in the Room of Reuben Parmele who is Removed out of the State	344
Capt Thos Power was chosen to keep the Key & take the care of the Town House	344
Voted, That this Town gives Lemuel Barns One half of his Town Rates that are due on the Several Collectors Books	344
1 Sep 1783	
John Burgis Esqr was Chosen Moderator	344
Voted, To choose two Committee Men to Represent this Town at the proposed Convention to	344

Guilford

be held at Middletown.. to Consider what ought to be done upon the Subject of Commutation, in order to some Constitutional mode of Redress, & Doct[r] John Redfield, and Cap[t] John Hopson were Chosen a Committee for that purpose

Haddam

Town Records
Vol. 2

Located at the Town Clerk's Office

Haddam

12 Dec 1775

Lieu^t Corneliu Higins Chosen Moderator	109
this meeting is adjourn^d to the houe of Capt James Hazelton	109
Put to vote wheither this meeting will allow a Certain bill brought in against this town.. by Doc^t Brainerd for Doctring Mehetibel Clark	109
Capt Joseph Seldin Lieu^t Daniel Ventrus Nehe Brainerd were Chosen Select Men	109
Voted the Select men shall give Giles Porter a Certificate or the Select Men of.. Farmington Predicated upon the law	109

13 Dec 1775

Gideon Brainerd & Doc^t Brainerd were Chosen Select Men	109
Nehe Brainers Chosen Town Clerk	109
Capt James Hazelton Chosen Treasurer	109
Charles Smith & Samuel Scovil were Chosen Constables	109
Samuel Scovil is Chosen Collector of the Colony Tax	109
John Willcock Prosper Brainerd & Bezaleel Shailer were Chosen Grandjurors	109
Lieu^t Ebenezer Thomas & Josiah Scovil were Chosen Tything Men	109
Aaron Smith Sam. Arnold Ju^r Sam. Arnold Stephen Clark Saml Lewis Nathan Tyler Oliver Wells Shailer Hubbard Saml Scovil Capt Saml Hubbard Abijah Brainerd Ju^r Lt James Clark Solomon Wackly Jonathan Boardman Richard Johnson were Chosen Surveyor	109
Lieu^t John Ventrus Ens James Arnold Capt Charles Sears James Hubbard Dec^n Ezra Brainerd Lieu^t James Clark Phinehas Brainerd Ju^r Saml Clark were Chosen Listers	109
Heber Brainerd Lt Hazelton were Chosen fence Viewers	109
Lieu^t Hazelton & Ens Gideon Brainerd were Chosen leather Sealers	109
Capt Hazelton Esqr Brainerd & Jonathan Brainerd were Chosen Branders of horses	109
Lieu^t Charles Hazelton was Chosen sealer of weights & measures	109
Capt Hazelton Abram Tyler Abijah Brainerd & Ens Richard Johnson were Chosen key keepers	109
upon the Request of Ens John Ventrus & others at the lower End of the Town this Meeting granted them Liberty to Erect a Pound at their own Charge	109
Meeting granted a tax of One Penny Lawfull Money to be levied upon the Poles [*and*] Rateable Estate of this Town sent into the General Assembly in October Last.. Jedediah Brainerd Ju^r Aaron Hubbard & ~~Ezra Shailer~~ [ ] Seldin Ju^r were Chosen Collectors	109
this Meeting granted Liberty to Jeremiah Baley to Erect a house on the highway in the upper meadow for the Conveniency of ferrying	109
Lt Phinehas Brainerd & Serg Saml Brooks were appointed a Committe to affix the Place for building Jere^{ah} Baileys House	109
Elisha Brainerd Simon Tyler Capt Abra^m Brooks Richard Knowles James Pelton James Young Esqr Wells Daniel Brainerd Joseph Tyler Ens Gideon Brainerd Josiah Brainerd Lt Cornelius Higgins were Chosen Hayward	109

6 Feb 1776

Joseph Brooks Esqr Chosen Moderator	109
Meeting is adjourn^d to Capt Hazeltons Dwelling House	109

Haddam

Esqr Brooks Lieu^t Higgins Capt Stephen Smith Doc^t Brainerd Ens Jeremiah Hubbard Capt Hazelton Serg Sam. Scovil Nathan Tyler Dea^{cn} Ezra Brainerd Esq Wells Lieu^t Phin^{has} Brainerd were Chosen a Com^{tte} of Inspection | 110

Lieu^t Cornelius Higgins chosen Agent to Represent the Town at our General Assembly Respecting the Case.. between us & the west Quarter People | 110

Voted we will will allow Esq Wells for his Services Past as Treasurer £1:2.6 | 110

10 Dec 1776

Joseph Brook Esqr Chosen Moderator | 110

Capt Joseph Seldin Lieu^t Daniel Ventrus Nehemiah Brainerd Hezekiah Brainerd & Gideon Brainerd were Chosen Select Men | 110

Meeting is adjourned to the Dwelling house of Capt Hazelton | 110

Capt James Hazelton Chosen Town Treasurer | 110

Samuel Scovil & David Brainerd were Chosen Constables | 110

David Brainerd is Chosen Collector of the Colony Tax | 110

Esq Joseph Brooks Abner Tibbels Ju^r Dec^n Ezra Brainerd Lieu^t John Smith Shailer Hubbard Gideon Bailey Asa Shailer Samuel Tyler Jonathan Boardman Elihu Bates William Scovil Phinehas Done Richard Knowles William Smith & Jeremiah Brainerd were Chosen Surveyors of Highways | 110

Joel Hubbard Zecheriah Brainerd & Thomas Shailer Ju^r were chosen Grandjurors | 110

Elisha Brainerd & Joshua Brook were Chosen fence Viewers | 110

Prosper Brainerd ~~Jabez Brooks Ju~~^{r} Samuel Tyler Solomon Wackly John Seward were Chosen Listers | 110

12 Dec 1776

Phinehas Brainerd Ju^r Dec^n Ezra Brainerd James Clark Lieu^t James Clark Lt John Ventrus & Reuben Smith wre Chosen Listers | 110

Cephas Seldin is appointed a Collector to Collect the Rate that Joseph Seldin was appointed to Collect | 110

~~James Hubbard~~ Thos Hubbard Ju^r is appointed Collector in the Room of ~~his Brother~~ Aaron Hubbard | 110

Lt Charles Hazelton & Ens Gideon Brainerd were Chosen Leather Sealers | 110

Elijah Brainerd and Joshua Brooks were Chosen Tything Men | 110

Jabez Brainerd Jonathan Brainerd & Lieu^t Charles Hazelton were Chosen Branders of horses | 110

Lt Charles Hazelton is appointed sealer of weights & measures | 110

James Hazelton Abijah Brainerd Elijah Brainerd Ezra Tyler were Chosen key Keepers | 110

It was Put to vote whither this meeting will Excuse Thos Shailer Ju^r from Serving as grandjuriman.. Voted in the negative | 110

Lieu^t Charles Hazelton Chosen a Grandjuryman | 110

7 Jan 1777

Joseph Brooks Esqr Chosen Moderator | 110

Joseph Brooks Esqr Hez. Brainerd Nehe Brainerd Charles Smith Joseh Wells Esqr were Chosen a Com^{tte} of Inspection | 110

this Meeting granted a Rate or Tax of two Pence halfpenny on the Pound.. Eber Tibbals Thomas Church & John Brainerd were appointed Collectors | 110

Haddam

27 Mar 1777

Jabez Brainerd Esq[r] Chosen Moderator	111
Cap[t] Tyler L[t] Phinehas Brainerd & Esq[r] Brooks were chosen a Com[tee] to treat with.. the Governor respecting our Quota of men & the sudden rise of Cattle occasioned by under Commisaries	111

31 Mar 1777

Voted.. that the families of such Soldiers who have already or Shall Enlist.. to fill up the Batalions to be raised in this State be supplied with Nessesaries in their absence by a Com[tee] appointed for that Purpose at the Prices affixed by Law on his or their Lodging or Remiting money to s[d] Com[tee] for that Purpose the additional Cost if any their be to be born by s[d] Town.. Voted that Nehe Brainerd Cap[t] Abraham Tyler Ens Jeremiah Hubbard Elijah Brainerd Ezra Brainerd Cap[t] John Ventrus & Charles Smith be a Com[tee].. to Execute the same	111

22 Apr 1777

Cap[t] Higgins Chosen Moderator	111
Voted that a Com[tee] be appointed to Provide money to Pay of the Soldiers that have or Shall Enlist.. Jabez Brainerd Esq[r] Cap[t] Eliakim Brainerd & Cap[t] James Hazelton are a Com[tee].. to Execute the same	111

2 May 1777

Voted by this Meeting that Will[m] Glading Seth Spencer & John Nicols Be Paid their Bounty.. by the Com[tee] appointed for that Purpose	111
Voted.. that a Premium or Bounty of four Pounds Money be given to Every able Bodied ~~Man~~ Soldier of this Town who shall Enlist into the Continental Army till our Quto be Compleated.. until the first of January Next.. Voted that Esq Jabez Brainerd Cap[t] Eliakim Brainerd & Cap[t] Hazelton be a Com[tee] to Procure money & Pay the.. Bounty to those that Shall Enlist	112

22 May 1777

Voted by the Meeting that Abner Porter & Aaron Porter be Paid their Bounty	112
the Meeting granted a Rate or Tax of six Pence on the Pound.. Hezekiah Clark Richard Knowles & Ebenezer Smith are Chosen Collectors of the aforesaid Tax	112

24 Sep 1777

Lieu[t] Daniel Ventru Chosen Moderator	112
Stephen Brainerd Chosen Collector in the room of his Brother John Brainerd to Collect the Last December Rate	112
Richard Wackly appointed a Collector in the room of Hezekiah Clark	112
Samuel Stanard Chosen Collector in the room of M[r] Richard Knowles	112
Voted.. that a Committee be appointed of assessors.. Cap[t] James Hazelton Doc[t] Brainerd & Cap[t] Cornelius Higgins Josiah Brainerd Ju[r] & Major Abr[m] Tyler be a Committee	112
Voted that the.. Salt when Come Shall be Equally Distributed amongst the Inhabitants.. William Smith Asa Shailer & Cap[t] Eliakim Brainerd be a Comm[tte] to Destribute the afores[d] Salt	112

9 Dec 1777

Cap[t] Cornelius Higgins Chosen Moderator	112
Lieu[t] Phinehas Brainerd Doc[t] Brainerd Major Abraham Tyler Lieu[t] Daniel Ventrus & Serg[t]	112

Haddam

Charles Smith were Chosen Select Men
Nehe. Brainerd Chosen Town Clerk   112

10 Dec 1777

Capt James Hazelton Chosen Town Treasurer	113
Samuel Scovil & David Brainerd were Chosen Constables	113
Samuel Scovil was Chosen Collector of the State Taxes	113
Samuel Arnold Aron Thomas Dudley Brainerd Nathan Harden John Brainerd J^r William Knowles Ezra Shailer Richard Wackly Thos Shailer J^r James Clark Ju^r Ezra Tyler Nathl Brainerd Eber Tibbals Aaron Smith were Chosen Surveyors	113
Capt James Hazelton & Capt Charles Sears were appointed fence Viewers	113
Jonathan Brainerd Samuel Clark Ens Oliver Wells Edmund Porter Lt Samuel Brooks Serg^t Asa Shailer Jeremiah Hubbard Ju^r Prosper Brainerd & Samuel Tyler were Chosen listers	113
Ens Gideon Brainerd & Lt Charles Hazelton Chosen leather Sealers	113
Capt Eliakim Brainerd Lt Elijah Brainerd & Serg^t Abner Spencer Lt Arnold Hazelton were Chosen Grandjurors	113
Daniel Brainerd & Serg^t Asa Shailer were Chosen Tything Men	113
Francis Lewis Caleb Bailer Bezeleel Shailer James Merwin Wakeman Brooks John Willcox were Chosen hayards	113
Lt Charles Hazelton Jonathan Brainerd & John Brainerd J^r were Chosen Branders of horses	113
Lt Charles Hazelton Chosen sealer of weights & measures	113
Capt James Hazelton Lt Elijah Brainerd Abijah Brainerd Ezra Tyler were Chosen keykeepers	113
Voted that Mr John Willcox Lieu^t Saml Brooks & Timothy Tyler be were Chosen a Com^{tte} to Procure Cloathing for the non Commissioned Officers & Soldiers in the Continental Army	113
Gideon Brainerd David Brainerd Aaron Capt Sears Smith [ ] are Chosen a Committe to Provide for the families of the non Commissioned Officers & Soldiers.. in the Continental Army	113
Lieu^t Charles Hazelton Capt Saml Clark & Ens Oliever Wells Chosen a Com^{ee} of Inspection	113
Major Abr^m Tyler Capt Cornelius Higgins & Deacon Ezra Brainerd were Chosen Assessors	113
Voted that a tax be levied.. of six Pence upon the Pound.. David Hubbard John Brainerd Phinehas Brainerd J^r are Chosen Collectors	113
Voted by this Meeting that the Town Treasurer Pay unto Ens Saml Scovil Collector of the Colony Tax £1-13-4 money on abatement of William Bailey Ju^r Rate	113
Voted that the Town Treasurer Pay unto Mr David Brainerd Collector of the Collony Tax on abatement of Joseph Bates J^r Rate £3-15-2^d and on Abatement to Wm Baily J^r £2-14 on abatement to the w^d Abigail Spencer £0-15-8-2	113

6 Jan 1778

Doc^t Brainerd Chosen Moderator	113
Voted.. that the Old Meeting House be lowered One Story & Repaired out of what Remains of the lower Part.. Voted that a Com^{tte} be appointed to lower & Repair the Old Meeting House.. Ser^t Asa Shailer Capt Abr^m Brooks Joseph Tyler Ens Saml Scovil David Brainerd Elihu Bates & Wm Clark Capt John Smith & Capt Charles Sears were appointed a Com^{tte}	113

6 Apr 1778

Voted.. that we will appoint an agent to Sue for & Collect the fine of Ebenezer Smith Town	114

Haddam

Collector for his Delinquency in Collecting a Town Rate	
David Brainerd whas Chosen Agent for the Town agreable to the above Vote	114
Jabez Arnold is Chosen Collector of a Town Rate.. in the Room of Ebenezer Smith who Refused or Neglected	114
Voted that we will further Repair our Town House by making four windows & Repairing otherways as far as the nails & board will go.. Capt Saml Hubbard & Capt James Hazelton & Doc^t Brainerd were appointed a Com^{tte} to Execute the above vote	114
Voted we will add to the number of Assessors.. Capt Eliakim Brainerd & Charles Smith were chosen	114

8 Dec 1778

Capt Cornelius Higgins Chosen Moderator	114
Lt Phinehas Brainerd Hezekiah Brainerd Esqr Lt Daniel Ventrus Serg^t Charles Smith and Capt Charles Sears were Chosen Select Men	114
Nehemiah Brainerd was Chosen Town Clerk	114
Capt James Hazelton Chosen Town Treasurer	114
En^s Samuel Scovil & David Brainerd were Chosen Constables	114
David Brainerd was Chosen Collector of the State Taxes	114
Lieu^t William Smith was Chosen Constable in the Place of David Brainerd who hath Declin^d Serving	114

9 Dec 1778

Lieu^t Willm Smith Chosen Collector of the State tax	114
Jepthah Brainerd John Spencer Isaac Augur Jesse Brainerd Nathaniel Tyler Heman Brainerd Jonathan Brooks Asa Wackley Nathl Burr Ju^r David Hubbard Daniel Brainerd Willm Scovil J^r Eber Tibbals Jeremiah Brainerd Oliver Bailey & Jonathan Cook were Chosen Surveyors	114
Samuel Clark & Samuel Arnold were Chosen fence Viewers	114
Capt Eliakim Brainerd Capt James Hazelton Lieu^t Elijah Brainerd Dee^n Ezra Brainerd Ebenezer Smith & Edmund Porter were Chosen Listers	114
Lieu^t Charles Hazelton & En^s Gideon Brainerd were Chosen Leather sealers	114
John Brainerd Ju^r & Willm Brainerd were Chosen Tything Men	114
Serg^t Nathan Smith Solomon Wackley and David Brainerd & En^s Aaron Smith were Chosen Grandjurors	115
Lieu^t Charles Hazelton Chosen sealer of weights & measures	115
Capt James Hazelton Lt Elijah Brainerd Ezra Tyler & Abijah Brainerd were Chosen key keepers	115
David Brainerd & Lieu^t Elijah Brainerd were appointed a Com^{tte} to Provide for the Soldiers families	115
Voted that a Com^{tee} be appointed to view & affix a Place where to Erect a Hospital for the small Pox & also to Purchase the ground if Necessary - Josep Brooks Esqr Lt Phinehas Brainerd & Doc^t Brainerd were appointed a Committe agreable to the above vote	115
granted a rate or tax of nine Pence on the Pound.. on the Present List.. James Clark Ju^r Luther Beardman & Ebenezer Smith were appointed Collectors of the aforesaid tax	115
Serg^t Charles Smith was appointed a Collector to Collect a Part of a tax to which Ebenezer Smith was sometime Since appointed & refused	115

Haddam

21 Dec 1778

Capt Samuel Clark Ens Oliver Wells & Capt Samuel Hubbard were Chosen a Com^{tte} of Inspection — 115

Voted.. that any number of Inhabitants of this Town have Liberty to Erect a Pre[ ] House.. at their own Cost.. where people taken with the small Pox may be Remov^d to the Place prefix^d in about one hundred Rods Back of the Dwelling House of Jos Brooks Esq — 115

5 May 1779

Capt Cornelius Higgins Chosen Moderator — 115

Meeting granted a tax of nine Pence on the Pound.. Abner Spencer Haus Higgins & Cornelius Brainerd were Chosen Collectors — 115

Voted.. that we will make Choice of.. Agents to Prefer a memorial to the next Genaral Assembly.. Seting forth our grievances respecting our Present mode of taxation & Praying for redress - Capt ~~Capt~~ Cornelius Higgins & Doc^t Brainerd were made Choice of agents — 115

21 Jun 1779

Joseph Brooks Esqr Chosen Moderator — 116

Voted that a Com^{tee} be appointed to Purchase Clothing for the Army in the Connecticut line.. Serg^t John Willcox Ezra Tyler Lt Arnold Hazelton John Brainerd Ju^r Dec^n Ezra Brainerd Abner Spencer Nathan Tyler & Nathan Smith were appointed a Com^{te} agreable to the above vote — 116

John Seward is appointed a Com^{tte} man in the room of Abner Spencer Releas^d — 116

14 Dec 1779

Capt Cornelius Higgins Chosen Moderator — 116

Lieu^t Phinehas Brainerd Chosen Select man — 116

15 Dec 1779

Capt Eliakim Brainerd Chosen Select man in the room of Lieu^t Phinehas Brainerd Resigned — 116

Capt Cornelius Higgins Edmund Porter Lieu^t Charles Hazelton were Chosen Select men — 116

28 Dec 1779

Nehe Brainerd Chosen Town Clerk — 116

Capt James Hazelton Chosen Town Treasurer — 116

Samuel Scovil & William Smith Chosen Constables — 116

Ens Samuel Scovil Chosen Collector of the State Tax — 116

Samuel Arnold Serg^t Jeremiah Hubbard William Scovil Ju^r & Haus Higgins were Chosen Granjurors — 116

Serg^t Stephen Dickerson David Brainerd Lieu^t James Arnold Ens Oliver Wells Jacob Arnold Capt James Hazelton Capt Charles Sears Capt Samuel Hubbard Capt Samuel Brooks Samuel Stanard Lieu^t James Hubbard Lieu^t Gideon Baley Ambrose Arnold John Seward William Bailey Ju^r Samuel Lewis Jeremiah Brainerd & Nathaniel Tyler were Chosen Surveyors of highway — 116

Capt Samuel Clark & Lieu^t William Smith were Chosen fence Viewers — 116

Thomas Hubbard Ju^r Ebenezer Smith John Willcox Lieu^t James Clark & David Brainerd were Chosen Listers — 116

Timoth Tyler & Lieu^t Ebenezer Thomas were appointed Tything men — 116

Haddam

Lieu^t Charles Hazelton & Capt Eliakim Brainerd were appointed Leather Sealers	116
Lieu^t Charles Hazelton John Brainerd Ju^r & Jonathan Brainerd were Chosen Branders of horses	116
Lieu^t Charles Hazelton Chosen saler of weights & measures	116
Capt James Hazelton Lieu^t Elijah Brainerd Ezra Tyler & Abijah Brainerd were Chosen key keepers	116
En^s Josiah Brainerd Chosen Select Man	116
Doc^t Brainerd Lieu^t Phinehas Brainerd & Capt Saml Hubbard were Chosen a Com^{te} of Inspection	116
Ser^t Asa Shailer & Lieu^t Elijah Brainerd were Chosen a Com^{tte} to Supply the Soldiers families with Necessaries	116
Serg^t Thomas Shailor is chosen a Committe man to assist in providing necessary Provisions for the families of such Soldiers as are now from this town in the Continental Army	117
Upo[n] a memorial of Lieu^t Ebenezer Thomas & others.. praying for Reliefe.. of the badness of their Road from Richard Knowles^{es} to James Thomasas that Some better road may be had	117
This meeting on hearing of the foregoing memorial granted the Petitioner a Committe to go & view their Circumstances.. Esqr Joseph Brooks John Willcox & Capt Higgins were Chosen a Committee for the Purpose	117

14 Feb 1780

Voted.. that a Com^{tte} be appointed to Examine into the Case Respecting our soldiers families how they were furnished with neessaries beore the 1st of Novr 1777.. Mr David Brainerd Lt Elijah Brainerd & En^s Samuel Scovil were Chosen a Com^{tee}	117
Voted.. that the Present Committe for Supplying the Soldiers families be Directed to Supply Such families beginning where Mr David Brainerd Left Supplying them	117
Lieu^t William Smith is chosen a Lister	117
Samuel Scovil is appointed a Comm^{tte} man to assist in furnishing the Soldiers families	117
Isaac Ray William Scovil Ju^r & Elias Selden were Chosen Collectors	117

21 Mar 1780

Capt Cornelius Higgins was Chosen Moderator	117

21 Mar 1780

This Meeting made Choice of the following Gentlemen as a Com^{tee} of Inspection of Provisions (viz) Capt Saml Brooks Capt James Hazelton Ens Nathan Tyler Lieu^t Willm Smith Capt Charles Sears Dec^n Ezra Brainerd Serg^t Jeremiah Hubbard Mr Jonah Rutly Capt John Smith Mr John Willcox Mr Ezra Tyler Lieu^t Phineas Brainerd & Mr David Brainerd	117

21 Mar 1780

The Question was Put.. whether we will do anything Respecting making the soldiers families good that have not had their money Laid out in full in the Year 1777 voted in the affirmative - Voted that a Com^{tee} be appointed to find what is Equtably Due to those families & award them accordingly - Ens Saml Scovil Mr David Brainerd & Lieu^t Elijah Brainerd are Chosen	117
Upon the Request of Capt Abraham Brooks.. that he may have some highway from his house to the House of Public worship.. Meeting Desir^d that the Select men.. view the Circumstances..	117
Upon the Request of Ens Jeremiah Hubbard & others desireing that their may be an open highway to begin between Doc^t Woodruffs home & the bridge & Empty into the road a little northward of the School by Mr Richd Knowles^s.. Meeting desired that the Select men.. view	118

Haddam

Circumstances..

upon the Report of Esq[r] Brooks & the Rest of the Com[tte] appointed to view the Road from Rich[d] Knowles[s] to to James Thomas[s] - & finding something necessary to be done.. The Select men.. to view the Circumstances   *118*

10 Apr 1780

granted a Tax of four Shillings on the Pound.. on the List 1779.. Aaron Hubbard Samuel Tyler & Lamberton Stocking were Chosen Collectors   *118*

The Question was put.. whether they will Except.. the highway Laid by them near Doc[t] Woodruffs house & order the Survey thereof.. voted in the negative.. the Question was Put for a Reconsideraiton of the Last vote voted it be reconsidered   *118*

voted.. that the Select men be directed to to Convey a highway to John Willcox   *118*

26 Jun 1780

Cap[t] Cornelius Higgins Chosen moderator   *118*

Voted that a Com[tte] be appointed to Consult the means & method for raising our Quota of the Continential Army.. Cap[t] Tho[s] Seldin L[t] Phineas Brainerd Esq[r] Brooks Cap[t] James Hazelton & Cap[t] Abr[m] Brooks were chosen   *118*

27 Jun 1780

Voted that a Com[tte] be appointed to.. Report make what they Judge will be Just & Reasonable.. to do.. to to raise our Proportion of Twenty five Hundred men order[d] to be rais[d] in this State for 3 months.. Esq[r] Brooks Ens Josiah Brainerd Ens Jeremiah Hubbrd Doc[t] Brainerd & Col. Tyler were chosen   *118*

Ens Josiah Brainerd Dec[n] Smith Doct Brainerd Col. Tyler & Cap[t] Sears were appointed a Com[tee] to form a Resolve.. to support the Present State money   *119*

granted a Tax of Seven pence on the Pound.. on the List 1779.. Serg[t] James Stephen Cephas Seldin & Silas Cone were Chosen Collectors of the above Tax   *119*

7 Jul 1780

Cap[t] Eliakim Brainerd Chosen moderator   *119*

Voted.. that 25 shilling p[r] month be given to Every able Bodied Effective soldier who shall voluntarily Inlist himself into the Continental Army till the last Day of December next in addition to his wages to be Quarterly paid in wheat at 5 shillings p[r] bushel or other Provision.. While in actuel service.. voted that Provided there is a demand of a man from this Town from Cap[t] Arnold Hazelton Company & he shall inlist for the term afores[d] & by the time prefix[d] he shall be intitled to the above reward   *119*

meeting desir[d] Col. Tyler to Collect the Continental Soldiers Enlisted from this Town or that shall inlist to Compleat this Towns Quota & deliver them to the Officer appointed to take the Charge of them &.. have an adequate Reward for his services   *119*

13 Nov 1780

Cap[t] Joseph Brainerd Chosen moderator   *120*

Cap[t] James Hazelton and John Brainerd were Chosen Receivers of Provisions   *120*

Voted by this meeting that a Tax.. be levied on the.. List 1779.. Lieu[t] Cornelius Higgins Elisha Day and Lieu[t] Gideon Bailey were Chosen Collectors   *120*

20 Nov 1780

Voted.. that a Committe be appointed [*to devide the*] Inhabitants into [ ] Classes.. Ens[n] Josiah Brainerd Cap[t] Higgins Lieu[t] Charles Hazelton Cap[t] Edmund Porter Ens Samuel Scovil Serg[t] Thomas Shailer & Lieu[t] Phineas Brainerd were Chosen   *120*

Haddam

4 Dec 1780

Voted.. that a Committee be appointed to affix upon some Standard.. what Shall be given to Every.. Recruit who shall Enlist.. into the Continental Army to Compleat this Towns Quota.. Capt Higgins David Brainerd Capt Sears Lt Phinehas Brainerd & Esqr Brooks were Chosen	121

12 Dec 1780

Hez^h Brainerd Esqr Chosen moderator	121
Capt Edmund Porter Capt Eliakim Brainerd & Capt Joseph Brooks were Chosen Select Men	121
Nehe Brainerd Chosen Town Clerk	121
Capt James Hazelton Chosen Town Treasurer	121
Lieu^t Wm Smith & Mr David Brainerd were Chosen Constables	121
Serg^t Reuben Smith Josiah Scovil [ ] Brainerd and Gideon Brainerd were Chosen Granjurors	121
Richard Knowles & James Pelton were Chosen Tything men	121
Capt Arnold Hazelton Lamberton Stocking David Clark Joel Hubbard Evan Thomas Daniel Spencer Joel Arnold Elij^h Brainerd Capt Saml Brooks Job Hubbard John Brainerd J^r Serg^t Cornelius Higgins Wakeman Brooks William Willcox Hez^h Shailer Reuben Shailer & John [Su]tlief were Chosen Surveyors of highways	121
Lieu^t James Clark & Capt Samuel Brooks were Chosen fence Viewers	121
Jacob Arnold Capt John Smith Lt Ebnezer Thomas & Ezra Tyler were Chosen Listers	121

13 Dec 1780

Ens Oliver Wells & Serg^t Wakeman Brooks were Chosen Constables	121
Serg^t Wakeman Brooks Chosen Collector of the State Taxes	121
Serg^t Thos Shailer & Serg^t Challenge Smith were Chosen Listers	121
Lieu^t Charles Hazelton & Capt Eliakim Brainerd were Chosen Leather Sealers	121
meeting was adjourned to the house of Capt James Hazelton	121
John Brainerd Lt Jonathan Brainerd & Lt Charles Hazelton were Chosen branders of horses	121
Lt Charles Hazelton was Chosen sealer of weigts & measures	121
Capt James Hazelton Abijah Brainerd Ezra Tyler [&] Elijah Brainerd were Chosen keykeepers	121
Capt Arnold Hazelton Mr David Brainerd John Willcox James Child Isaac Ray Ezra Shailer Capt Saml Brooks John Willcox Ephraim Sawyer Saml Clark Nathan Tyler Dec^n Brainerd & Stephen Bailey were Chosen a Com^{tte} of Inspection of Provisions	121
John Brainerd Ju^r & Cephas Seldin were Chosen a Com^{tee} of Supply to furnish the Soldiers familys	121

1[8] Dec 1780

Voted that a Committe be appointed to Procure our Quota of Continental men.. Col^o Tyler Mr David Brainerd Lieu^t Gid^n Bailey Lt James Hubbard & Ens Josiah Brainerd were Chosen	122
Capt Arnold Hazelton was made Choice of as one of the afores^d Committe	122

15 Jan 1781

David Hubbard & Heman Brainerd were Chosen Constables	122
Heman Brainerd Chosen Collector of the State Taxes	122

377

Haddam

Luther Boardman Chosen Grandjuryman	122

17 Jan 1781

Voted.. we will appoint an agent.. to take some sutiable measures to have Saml B Whitmore suspended from being Conservator over John Thos for which he was appointed by the County Court.. Capt Higgins & Ens Saml Scovil were appointed agents	122
Voted that a Comte be appointed to Report to the meeting what they shall Judge Just & reasonable for the Town to do in order to raise our Quota of men for horseneck.. Doct^r Brainerd Lt Gid^n Bailey & Capt Higgins were Chosen	122
meeting is adjourn^d to the house of Capt James Hazelton	123

29 Jan 1781

Voted.. that a Tax of six pence on the pound be levied.. to be paid in this States Bills Emitted since January 1780 or new Continental money or old Continental Bills at the rate of forty for one of the former.. Serg^t Nathan Smith James Thomas & En^s Jedediah Brainerd were Chosen Collectors	123
Doct Brainerd & Capt Samuel Clark were chosen a Comtte to view the house that was Eliphalet Smiths & report.. what Damages they shall Judge hath been done the house by the small pox being there	123
Voted.. that Capt James Hazelton Lay out the money that he shall Receive by the way of the provision Tax for fish & put them up in good order procureing salt & Barrels as he did for the meat.. furthermore that Capt Hazelton Indent with the fishermen for 40 Barrels of fish upon the Credit of the Town	123
Voted.. that the Bill brought in by Capt Ventrus for a Journey to Lebanon be paid which bill is Eighteen Shilings & 2^d State money 18^s 2^d	123

26 Mar 1781

Joseph Brooks Esqr Chosen Moderator	123
Voted.. that the Inhabitants of this Town be Clased in order to Raise our Quota of State Soldiers for the Defence of horse neck.. Ens Joseph Brainerd David Brainerd Saml Scovil Nehe Brainerd Daniel Ventrus Jeremiah Hubbard Ju^r Capt Edmund Porter Co^l Tyler Lt Wm Smith were mad Choice of a Comtt^e for the purpose	123
Capt Sears appointed a a Comt: man in [*the*] Room of David Brainerd	123
Capt James Smith Chosen a Com^{tee} man in the Room of Col Tyler	123
Capt Higgins Capt Sears Ens Josiah Brainerd Capt Abraham Brooks were appointed a Com^{tee} to.. Consult what.. to do in order to raise our Quota of Continential men	123

29 Mar 1781

Voted that one man of Each Class be appointed to warn the Several Clases.. To Choose a Class Master &c - Capt Arnold Hazelton Ens Gideon Brainerd Ens Aaron Smith Lt James Hubbard Capt Saml Brooks Capt John Smith Lt Ebenezer Thomas Serg^t Thomas Shailer & Jonathan Brainerd were appointed	124
Voted that a Committe be appointed to State our grievances Respecting Taxation.. that it may be laid Before the General Assembly.. Deac^n Ezra Brainerd Capt Higgins & Doct Hez Brainerd were appointed a Com^{tte} to Execute the above Vote	124
Lieu^t Charles Hazelton is appointed to Collect the Rearage of Thos Church^s Rate Bill	124

9 Apr 1781

Voted.. that the memorial & Remonstrance drawn up by the Com^{tte} Respecting the mode of Taxation be laid Before the General Assembly in their Session in may next.. Capt Higgins &	124

Haddam

Jos Brooks Esqr were Chosen Agents to Prefer the memorial	
22 Jun 1781	
Joseph Brooks Esqr Chosen Moderator	*124*
Voted.. that we adopt some measures to procure a number of Beef Cattle for the use of the Continental Army -- Voted we will appoint two Contractors of Beef for the Continental Army -- Ens Josiah Brainerd & Capt James Hazelton were Chosen	*125*
Nehe Brainerd Appointed Agent to appoint apprizers of s^d Beef Cattle	*125*
Voted.. that a Tax of four pence Lawful money on the Pound be levied.. on the List 1780.. Payable in good merchantable Beef Cattle agreeable to the prices affixed by the general Assembly.. or one penny on the pound in Silver & gold.. Capt James Hazelton & Ens Josiah Brainerd were Chosen Collectors	*125*
Capt James Hazelton John Brainerd & Lt Phin^{as} Brainerd were Chosen to procure Barrels Recive & Salt Beef & Pork that Shall be Brought in by way of Tax	*125*
27 Sep 1781	
Lieu^t Phinehas Brainerd Chosen moderator	*125*
11 Dec 1781	
Hez Brainerd Esqr Chosen Moderator	*125*
Joseph Brook Esqr Capt Eliakim Brainerd and Capt Edmund Porter were Chosen Select men	*125*
Nehe Brainerd Chosen Town Clark	*125*
Capt James Hazelton Chosen Town Treasurer	*125*
Capt Oliver Wells & Mr Heman Brainerd were Chosen Constables	*125*
Capt Wells appointed Collecttor of the State taxes	*125*
Lieu^t Elijah Brainerd John Willcox John Brainerd and Capt Arnold Hazelton were Chosen grandjurors	*125*
John Dickerson Solomon Wackly John Smith 3^d Luther Boardman Richard Knowles John Scovil Challenge Smith Oliver Brainerd Eber Tibbals Joshua Smith Ju^r Eleazer Bates James Hubbard Samuel Brooks Jeremiah Brainerd Gideon Bailey Jacob Arnold and Cornelius Higgins were Chosen Surveyors of Highways	*125*
Capt Samuel Clark & Ens Gideon Brainerd were Chosen fence viewers	*125*
Hezekiah Smith Cornelius Higgins Thomas Shailer Ju^r Abner Spencer David Brainerd & Jabez Arnold were Chosen listers	*125*
Lieu^t Charles Hazelton & Ens Gideon Brainerd were Chosen leather Sealers	*125*
Jonathan Smith & Capt John Smith were Chosen Tithing Men	*125*
John Brainerd Ju^r Lt Charles Hazelton & Jonathan Brainerd were Chosen Branders of horses	*125*
Lt Charles Hazelton Chosen sealer of weights & measures	*125*
Capt James Hazelton Elijah Brainerd Ezra Tyler & Abijah Brainerd Chosen keykeepers	*125*
20 Dec 1781	
Capt Samuel Clark Capt Samuel Brooks Ens Nathan Tyler Capt Arnold Hazelton Isaac Ray Lieu^t Phinehas Brainerd David Brainerd & Ens Aaron Smith were appointed a Committe of Inspection	*126*
Voted.. that Joseph Brooks Esqr be allowed forty three Shillings money for his Services as a Select man the year past	*126*

Haddam

Voted that Capt Eliakim Brainerd be allowed fifty Shillings for the like Service	126
Voted that Capt Porter be allowed forty three Shillings for his Services as Selectman the year past	126
Voted that Inhabitants have liberty to discharge their several Taxes.. in articles of Produce at the following prices, viz, wheat at six Shillings p^r Bushel Rye at 4 Shillings, Indian Corn at three Shillings, good merchantable beaf a 25 Shillings p^r Hundred w^t flax at 8 pence p^r lb: & other articles of produce in like proportion.. Jonathan Brainerd Abr^m Spencer & Hez Shailer were Chosen Collectors of the afores^d Tax	126
Upon the petition of a number of the Inhabitants at athe Lower End of the Town Requesting.. some Sutiable place for Burying their dead.. This meeting granted the petitioners their request whereupon Mes^{rs} Saml Clark & William Smith were appointed to view their Circumstances & Lay out a Burying yard & to make Exchange of highways for that purpose if necessary	126
Voted.. that we will appoint an agent to prefer a memorial to the General Assembly for forbearance of payment of penny halfpenny Tax.. Capt James Hazelton was Chosen agent	126

25 Feb 1782

Capt Cornelius Higgins Chosen Moderator	126
Nathaniel Burr Ju^r is Chosen Collector in the Place of Abraham Spencer to Collect part of a two penny Tax granted by the town last December	126
Voted an abatement to w^d Ruth Arnold of twenty one Shillings State money as is Set down in Mr Elisha Days Rate Bill	126
Voted that a Committe be appointed to to devise means for raising our Quota of men for horseneck.. Dec^n Era Brainerd Nehe Brainerd Lt Phinehas Brainerd & Capt Porter were Chosen	126
Voted.. that Messrs Oliver Wells David Brainerd Edmund Porter & Ezra Brainerd be a Com^{tee} to Engage Six men for the Defence of the Post at horseneck or western frontiers	126
Provision deliver^d in.. payment of the Two penny Tax granted Last December & the penny Tax granted at this meeting to Joseph Brooks Esqr Capt Eliakim Brainerd & Capt Edmund Porter & Jonathan Brainerd the East side the River	126
Deac^n Ezra Brainerd David Dickerson & Lewis Smith are Chosen Collectors of the penny Tax	127
Capt Cornelius Higgins is appointed Agent.. to meet with the Com^{tee} Appointed by the Assembly to ascertain the Deficiences of the several Town Respecting their Quota of Soldiers	127

18 Mar 1782

Giles Brainerd Chosen Collector of Part of a peny Tax in the Room & Stead of Lewis Smith	127
Doct Hez Brainerd Chosen Agent to manage & Settle the peny halfpeny tax which was granted by the General Assembly payable in flower	127

1 Apr 1782

upon a motion made in Behalf of Ephraim Sawyer by Mr David Brainerd that he may have liberty to Erect a Dwelling house on the highway at Heganumps Landing	127
Mesr^s David Brainerd Jeremiah Hubbard and James Child are Chosen a Com^{tte} to view the Circumstances of the highway & affix a Place where the s^d Sawyer may build a house	127
Voted that Capt James Hazelton be desired to Lay Before the next adjourn^d meeting the arrearages Due on the Provision Rate	127

8 Apr 1782

Voted we will form the 9 Classes in the Town into three Classes & Each Class to raise 2 men	127

for State Service.. Ens Saml Smith Dec^n Brainerd & Capt Arnold Hazelton were appointed a Com^{te} for the purpose	
Cap^n Cornelius Higgins & Dec^n Ezra Brainerd were Chosen Agents to prefer a memorial to the General Assembly.. respecting the unjust mode of Taxation	127
The Committee appointed to affix a place for Ephraim Sawyer to Erect a house on are desired to Review the place & act as they Shall Judge it may be lest prejudicial to publick & private	127

8 Aug 1782

Ens Jeremiah Hubbard was Chosen moderator	128
Voted that Capt Cornelius Higgins & Dec^n Ezra Brainerd they or Either of them attend the County Convention	128

20 Aug 1782

Voted.. we will raise our Quota of State Soldiers by a Committe.. Col Abraham Tyler James Pelton & Joel Arnold were chosen a Committe in addition to the Committe appointed at a Town meeting Last April	128

10 Dec 1782

Capt Cornelius Higgins was chosen moderator	128
Nehemiah Brainerd Hez^h Brainerd Esqr and Capt Oliver Wells were Chosen Select men	128
Nehe Brainerd Esqr chosen Register	128
Capt James Hazelton Chosen Town Treasurer	128

11 Dec 1782

Hezekiah Smith & Daniel Smith Ju^r were Chosen Constables	128
Capt Samuel Clark Mr David Brainerd Lt Cornelius Higgins Capt Edmund Porter and Lieu^t Josiah Brainerd Chosen Listers	129
Phinehas Brainerd Joshua Smith Ju^r & Joshua Brook were Chosen grandjurors	129
Lieu^t James Hubbard & Elias Smith Elisha Brainerd were chosen Tything men	129
Daniel Smith Ju^r Chosen Collector of the State Taxes	129
Capt James Hazelton was Chosen a Com^{tee} to take Care & Shingle the west side the Town house & provide two lights at the Cost of this Town	129
Samuel Arnold Nathan Harden Elisha Day John Dickerson Wakeman Brooks Francis Lewis Elisha Brainerd Wm Bailey Joel Arnold Isaac Ray Elihu Bates Giles Brainerd William Brainerd Timothy Towner Thos Hubbard Ju^r Stephen Clark & James Thomas & Capt Sears Chosen Surveyors	129
Gideon Brainerd & Charles Hazelton Chosen Leather Sealers	129
Lt Charles Hazelton Chosen sealer of w^{ts} & measures	129
John Brainerd & Jonathan Brainerd were Chosen branders of horses	129
Capt James Hazelton Elijah Brainerd Abijah Brainerd & Ezra Tyler chosen Keykeepers	129
Capt James Hazelton Jonah Rutly David Ventrus & Ephraim Sawyer were Chosen Kullers of Lumber	129
Mr Saml Clark & David Brainerd were appointed a Com^{te} to Enquire into the State of our ferries	129

Haddam

23 Dec 1782

Mesr^s Samuel Clark David Brainerd Willm Smith Jonathan Smith Samuel Brooks Luther Boardman Jeremiah Hubbard Ju^r Joel Arnold Cornelius Higgins Ju^r Nathan Tyler Ezra Brainerd Samuel Northam & James Knowles Richd Thomas & Wm Brainerd were appointed a Com^{te} of Inspection	129
Voted we will appoint a Collector in the room of Lt Gid^n Bailey to Collect the rerage of s^d Bailys Rate bill	129
Ens Samuel Scovil Chosen a grandjuror	129
Richard Wackly chosen a Collector to Collect the Rearrages of Gid^n Baily Ju^r Rate bill	129
Voted that a Committee be appointed to make out on a statement of the [ ]h & flower Tax & also adjust accounts with the Town Treasurer.. Capt Edmund Porter David Brainerd and Samuel Clark were chosen a Com^{te}	129
Joseph Brook Doct^r Brainerd were Chosen a Com^{te} to Confer with Joseph Arnold respecting a highway through his Land leading to the great River	129

2 Jan 1783

Voted that a Committe be appointed to Confer with Capt James Hazelton & Capt Eliakim Brainerd with Respect to the money they paid out for the Town before the S[ ]ale took place	129
Daniel Brainerd Chosen Collector to the Rearage of Gid^n Baily Ju^r Rate Bill in the Place of Richd Wackly	129
Voted that we will appoint an agent or agents to.. the General Assembly.. to oppose Mr Jonah Rutlys Petition Respecting the ferry	130
Capt Higgins & Josiah Brainerd were Chosen agents to.. the General Assembly agreable to the last vote	130
Hez Brainerd Col Tyler & David Brainerd were appointed a Com^{tte} to Confer with Capt James Hazelton & Eliakim Brainerd with regard to the moneys the Town had of them	130

13 Jan 1783

Joseph Brook Esq Chosen Moderator	130
Voted that the dispute Between the town & Capt Eliakim Brainerd respecting a debt due from the Town to s^d Brainerd be Refered to men for the Desicion viz Dea^n Elish Cone Daniel Ventrus & Saml Brook	130
Voted we will appoint a Committe to Settle with Capt James Hazelton.. Relative to the £5 Bounties &c he paid to the Soldiers	130
David Brainerd Nehe^h Brainerd & Oliver Wells were appointed a Com^{te} for the purpose mentioned in the Last vote	130
Voted that David Brainerd be an agent for this Town in the Case of this Town & Capt Eliakim Brainerd	130
Voted that a Tax of four pence on the pound be levied.. Nathan Harden Nathaniel Cook & Shailer Hubbard were Chosen Collector of the foregoing Tax	130

7 Sep 1783

Capt Cornelius Higgins Chosen moderator	130

7 Sep 1783

Voted that we will take some Spirited measures.. for the Spedy Collection of the arrearages of the Taxes in the hands of Mr Saml Scovil	130

7 Sep 1783

Voted that Ens Scovil proceed with vigour & Resolution to a Speedy Collection of the arrearages of the Taxes in his hands	130

Haddam

7 Sep 1783

Voted that the Selectmen be Impower^d to to hire a Sum of money.. Sufficient to settle an Execution now in the hands of the Sheriff against the Selectmen together with the arrearages Ens Scovil shall Collect   *130*

Voted that Hez^h Brainerd Esqr & Lt Phinehas Brainerd be a Committe to Confer with Mr Jonah Rutly Respecting the ferry   *130*

Voted that Capt Cornelius Higgins be Agent.. at the next General Assembly Respecting a highway petitioned for from Middletown through part of the Town to blackrock   *130*

9 Dec 1777

Names of those Persons who took the Oath of fidelity.. Samuel Clark.. Willm Scovil Ju^r.. Elisha Spencer.. Nathan Smith.. Abr^m Williams.. Isaac Ray.. Jeremiah Hubbard J^r.. Zache^{ah} Brainerd.. Jeremiah Brainerd.. Timothy Tyler.. Charles Brainerd.. David Clark.. Saml Stanard.. James Thomas.. Henry Thomas.. Jonathan Burr.. Nathl Hazelton.. Saml Ray Ju^r.. Haus Higgins.. Heman Brainerd..   *148*

9 Dec 1777

..Nathan Hardin.. Gideon Bailey.. Elihu Bates.. Aaron Brainerd.. Nathl Burr J^r.. Solomon Bates.. James Child.. Richd Wackly.. Ebenezer Smith.. Cephas Selden.. Nathl Burr.. Heber Brainerd.. Willm Ely.. Stephen Clark.. David Arnold.. Challenge Smith.. Daniel Brainerd.. Nathl Stocking.. Saml Tyler.. Willm Clark.. Job Hubbard.. Ezra Tyler.. Lt Charles Hazelton.. Thos Hubbard Ju^r.. Saml Smith.. Roger Thomas.. Oliver Wells.. Obadiah Dickerson.. John Brainerd.. Jesse Brainerd.. John Spencer.. James Merwin.. William Bailey.. Solomon Wackly.. John Scovil.. Amos Bates.. Paul Brooks.. Mr John Kelly.. Ezra Porter.. Joshua Simmons.. Amsa Johnson.. Daniel Smith J^r.. Joseph Arnold.. Oliver Baily.. Aaron Isaacs..   *148*

..Ashbel Stilman.. Saml Arnold.. Jon^{thn} Boardman.. Ezra Shailer.. Nehe Dickerson.. David Leach.. Timothy Towner.. Abraham Spencer.. Aaron Hubbard.. Jacob Ely.. Josiah Brainerd 3^d.. Jonathan Cook.. Jacob Arnold.. John Brainerd.. Stephen Smith Ju^r.. Cornelius Brainerd.. Bushnel Brainerd.. David Dickerson.. John Dickerson.. John Hubbard.. B[ ]ton Smith.. Elias Smith.. John Scovil [ ].. [ ] Thomas J^r.. John Arnold.. Silas Cone.. Joseph Scovil.. Giles Brainerd.. Jonathan Brainerd.. Saml [ ].. Joshua Smith J^r.. Barzillai Dudley.. Calvin Brooks.. Aaron Smith   *148*

Hartford

Town Votes
Copy 2
1717 – 1796

Located at City and Town Clerk's Office

Hartford

20 Dec 1774

John Pitkin Esqr Moderator	250
Resolved.. That we do appoint for our Comittee of Corrispondence & Observation the following Gentlemen: (they or the major Part of them) Viz. Samuel Wadsworth, George Smith, Samuel Talcott, Benjamin Payne, Thomas Seymour, John Pitkin, George Pitkin, David Mills, Isaac Sheldon, Aaron Bull, Samuel Wyllys, Timothy Cheeney, Richard Pitkin, Abijah Colton, Noah Webster, Ebenezer Wells and John Cook	250

10 Apr 1775

John Pitkin Esqr Moderator	251
Voted that Messrs John Skinner, Zebulon Seymour and Daniel Goodwin be Surveyors of Highways	251
Upon the Memorial of Mathew Webster, praying to have a small Piece of Land lying in rocky=Hill belonging to the Town, leased to him &c, Voted that Joseph Church, Abijah Cotton, Jonathan Bigelow, and Jonathan Wells, be.. a Comittee to view the Place prayed for and lease to the said Mathew Webster.. such Piece of Land.. provided they shall judge the same can be done without incommoding the Highways, or any Injury to private Property	251(2)
Whereas.. Difficulty is likely to arise..in a Deed, given by.. Pantry Jones.. of a Highway leading from the Road by Capt Keith's, to the landing Place, to Samuel Kilborn's.. Voted, that Messrs Benjamin Payne Jonathan Seymour Samuel Smith Joseph Meakens John Lawrence & Samuel Cadwell.. be a Comittee to repair to said Highway.. view the same, and the horse=House.. and all Circumstances relating to said Highway and Buildings.. And make Report.. whether any such Alterations may reasonably and equitably be made.. for the Use of the Public, and not prejudice the private Property of the said Pantry Jones	251(2)

6 Sep 1775

Voted that Benjamin Payne Esqr, Be Moderator	251(2)
Voted that Mr John Dod, one of the present Constables.. shall collect the Country Rate.. in the Room and Stead of Mr Theophilus Steel, a Constable.. now deceased	251(2)
Voted that the Report of a Committee appointed.. relative to a certain Highway (some time since conveyed to this Town by Mr Pantry Jones) leading from the Street by Capt Keith's, down to the landing Place by the Great River now exhibited by Said Comittee.. be referred to the annual Meeting.. for Consideration	251(2)
Voted that John Pitkin Esqr be Moderator	253
Voted that George Wyllys be Clerk or Register	253
Voted that Messrs Joseph Church, Zachariah Pratt, Jonathan Bigelow, Jonathan Wells Timothy Cowle, David Hills, and Abijah Colton, be the Selectmen	253
Voted that Messrs John Cook, John Dod, Job Norton, Seth Collins, and Stephen Cone ----, be Constables	253
Voted that, John Cook, now chosen Constable, do, and shall collect the Country Rate.. and account with the Colony Treasurer	253
Voted that Messrs Samuel Burr, Jonathan Huntington, Joseph Meakins Junr, James Porter Junr, John Whitman Junr, Gideon Butler Junr and Solomon Gilman. be Grandjurymen	253
Voted that Messrs William Lawrence, Ebenezer Barnerd Junr Lemuel Steel, Samuel Webster Junr Daniel Bidwell Junr, Epaphras Olmsted, Moses Gaylord, Elisha Hosmer, Robert M^{c}kee and Josiah Olcott Junr be Tythingmen	253
Voted that Messrs Peletiah Pierce, Barnabas Hinsdale, Daniel Pitkin, Solomon Williams Ward Woodbridge and Ebenezer Wells be Listers	253

Hartford

Voted that Mess[rs] James Church, John Cook, Daniel Seymour, William Andruss, Aaron Bull, Selah Norton, Elias Gilman, Zebulon Bidwell, Nehemiah Abbee, Moses Forbes, Elias Roberts, Thomas Slade, John Mckee, Joseph Steadman, Jabez Darte Jun[r], Gideon Merrels, and Isaac Webster be Surveyors of Highways	253
Voted that Mess[rs] John Burket, Jonathan Easton Jonathan Stanly Jun[r] Peleg Heath be Sealers of Leather	253
Voted that Mess[rs] Moses Burr, Richard Skinner, Timothy Steel, Joseph Meakins, Samuel Smith Jun[r] Moses Seymour, Noah Butler, John Steel, and Richard Pitkin be fence Viewers	253
Voted that Mess[rs] John Shepard & Jonathan Olmsted, be Sealers of Measures	253
Voted that M[r] Thomas Sloan, be Sealer of Weights	253
Voted that Mess[rs] Isaac Bunce, John Hurlburt, David Hills, Daniel Semour, and Amos Bidwell, be Surveyors and Packers of Tobacco	253
Voted that Mess[rs] Timothy Shepard and Isaac Bunce be Gaugers & Packers of Beef and Pork	*252(2)*
Voted that, M[r] Gideon Morrels chosen a Surveyor of Highways.. now excused from serving	*252(2)*
Voted that, M[r] Ashbell Wells be a Surveyor of Highways	*252(2)*
20 Dec 1775	
Voted that Jesse Root Esq[r] be Moderator	*252(2)*
Voted that M[r] John Palsgrave Wyylys be Clerk of this Meeting	*252(2)*
Voted that the Excuse offered by Solomon Gilman to be freed from the Office of Grandjuryman.. is not sufficient	*252(2)*
Voted that Silas Birnham be a Grandjuryman	*252(2)*
Upon the Memorial of Tim[o] Skinner Ashbel Wells &c.. shewing that the Memorialists are much distressed in the Summer.. on account of water for their Creatures, and praying for leave to turn the Spring in M[r] Sam[l] Merrel's Lot into the highway.. Voted that the Memorialists have Liberty to turn said Spring into the highway.. to accommodate the public with a common watering place	*252(2)*
Voted that M[r] John Cook be Collector of the Town rate.. on the West side of the great River	255
Voted that M[r] Stephen Cone be a Collector of the Town rate	255
2 Jan 1776	
Jesse Root Esq[r] Moderator	255
Voted that the present Selectmen take into their Consideration, a certain Account exhibited by Doct[rs] Smith and Coit of Medicines supplied the Widow Wilson, a poor Woman.. from March 1772 to March 1774.. £4.5.3	255
We the Subscribers, being appointed a Comittee.. viewed the Highway.. And the Horse:House and all Circumstances, relating to said Highway, and Buildings.. Report, That it appears to us, That considering the.. almost constant Use of Said Lane for the passing and repassing of Carts and Carriages.. That said Lane is too Narrow.. especially at the South:West Corner of M[ ] Bull's Lott where the Fence makes a Jogg by projecting into said Highway, Wee are therefore of Opinion that if the said Jones would therefore agree to Streighten the south Line.. by removing his Fence, into a streight Line.. from.. the northwest Corner of said Jones's Garden Fence.. at the Street, by Cap[t] Keith's to the North:West Corner of the Cooper Shop, now in the Occupation of Noah Washburn.. And that the Town.. would allow said Jones to improve the Gound whereon said Horse:House is erected.. John Lawrence.. Samuel Cadwell.. Joseph Maken.. Benj[a] Payne.. Samuel Smith } Comittee	255

Hartford

On Reconsideration of a Vote.. granting Liberty to certain Persons to turn a Spring in Mr Samuel Merrels's Lott, into the Highway for a watering Place.. It is now, voted that the said former Vote..be.. made to be null, and void	255

8 Apr 1776

Jesse Root Esqr Moderator	255
Voted that Messrs Zebulon Seymour and Eleazer Burnham be Surveyors of Highways	255
Voted that Jesse Root Esqr, be added to.. the present Committee who are appointed to.. take the Care, Oversight and Regulation of the Grammar School	255
Voted that Messrs Nathaniel Goodwin, Joseph Talcott Junr, John Skinner John Cook, William Wadsworth Richard Skinner, Ashbel Steel, Levi Robbins, Jonathan Bigelow, Daniel Seymour Eliphalet Roberts, Henry Arnold Benjamin Gilman Nehemiah Abbee, Joseph Goodwin, Silas Easton Elias Roberts, Ebenezer Wells, Seth Collins, Rosseter Belden, Amos Bidwell Zacheus Butler, Charles Seymour, John Whitman Junr, Abraham Morrells Junr, Daniel Phelps Austin Ledyard, Gideon Merrells and Joseph Wadsworth Junr be Haywards	255A
Voted that Mr Samuel Mattocks be a Grandjuryman	255A

11 Dec 1776

Voted that John Pitkin Esqr be Moderator	255A
Voted that George Wyllys be Clerk or Register of the Town	255A
Voted that Messrs Joseph Church, Zachariah Pratt, Jonathan Bigelow, Jonathan Wells, Timothy Cowle, David Hills, and Abijah Colton, be the Selectmen	255A
Voted that Messrs John Cook, John Dod, Job Norton, Seth Collins, and Stephen Cone be Constables	255A
Voted that Messrs Caleb Bull Hugh Ledlie, Ezra Hide, Elisha Pitkins, Joseph Goodwin Timothy Cheeney, Henry Brace Junr, and Samuel Stanly be Grandjurymen	255A
Voted that Messrs Joseph Talcott Junr Nathaniel Skinner Timothy Steel, Samuel Benton Jacob Williams, Russel Woodbridge Junr Mathew Cadwell Nathan Steadman Jonathan Sedgwick and Aaron Butler, be Tythingmen	255A
Voted that Messrs Peletiah Pierce Barnabas Hinsdale, Daniel Pitkin, Solomon Williams, Ward Woodbridge and Ebenezer Wells, be Listers	255A
Voted that Messrs James Church John Cook, William Andruss, Aaron Bull, Daniel Seymour, Israel Seymour, Elisha Benton, Benjamin Gilman, Timothy Burnham Junr, David Little, Jonathan Hills, Timothy Forbes, John Mackee, Asa Brown, William Buckland, Amos Bidwell, Rosseter Belden, and Daniel Hosmer be Surveyors of Highways	255A
Voted that Messrs John Burket, Jonathan Easton, Nehemiah Abbee, Pelegg Heath, and Nathaniel Omstead, be Sealers of Leather	256
Voted that Messrs Moses Burr, Richard Skinner, Timothy Steel Joseph Meakins, Samuel Smith Junr Moses Seymour Noah Butler, John Steel and Richard Pitkin be fence:Viewers	256
Voted that Messrs John Shepard & Jonathan Olmstead be Sealers of Measures	256
Voted that Mr Sealer of Weights	256
Voted that Messrs Isaac Bunce John Hurlburt, David Hills Daniel Seymour and Amos Bidwell be Surveyors and Packers of Tobacco	256
Voted that Messrs Timothy Shepard, and Isaac Bunce be Gaugers and Packers of Beef and Pork	256

23 Dec 1776

Voted that Benj^a Payne Esqr be Moderator	256

Hartford

Voted that Mr Hez. Wyllys be Clerk of this Meeting	256
Voted that the Select Men.. make.. a Deed of release of a certain small Peice of Ground on which the Town Pound formerly was erected Situate a little South of the Dwelling House of Samuel Burr to him the said Burr on his procuring a good.. Deed to this Town of the same Quantity of Land as.. where the Pound is Lately erected a little North of the dwelling House of John Sheldon, on his said Burr paying to said Select Men.. the expence of removing the Timber from.. where said Pound Lately stood, to said Place, and the expence of erecting said Pound	257

30 Dec 1776

Benjamin Payne Esqr Moderator	257
Voted that Stephen Cone be Collector of the Country Rate	257
Voted that John Dodd be Collector of the.. Town Rate.. on the West Side of the Great River	257

22 Jan 1777

Voted that John Pitkin Esqr be Moderator	258
Voted that Mr John Dod chosen .. to collect the Town Rate.. on the west Side of Connecticut River be now released from that Service	258
Voted that Mr Seth Collins be Colector of the Town Rate.. on the Persons living on the west Side of Connecticut River in the Room and Stead of Mr John Dod who was.. Chosen to that Office and now released	258
Voted that Mr Ward Woodbridge chosen a Lister.. be released from serving	258
Voted that Mr Timothy Cheeny be a Lister.. in Stead of Mr Ward Woodbridge	258
Voted that Mr Joseph Meakins be a Surveyor of Highways	258
Voted that Messrs Samuel Talcott, Benjamin Payne Thomas Seymour Oliver Elsworth, Aaron Bull Hezekiah Wyllys John Wels, John Pitkin, George Pitkin, Richard Pitkin Timothy Cheeney, Abijah Colton, Noah Webster, Ashbel Wells, James Church and Solomon Gilman (they or the major Part, or any five of them) be the Comittee of Correspondence, Observation and Inspection	258
Whereas one of the eight Battalions ordered to be raised in ths State.. for the continental Service, comanded by Col^o Samuel Wyllys, is ordered to rendezvouse in this Town, the Winter for.. filling up said Battalion & attending military Exercises, for the better furnishing the Officers, and soldiery for actual Service, And said Col^o Wyllys moving to be furnished with some sutable Acomodations for.. said Regiment, and necessary Utensils for dressing their Food.. Voted that the Selectmen.. assist.. Col^o Wyllys in procuring sutable Barrack Room for.. said Regiment.. and also in procuring necessary Utensils for the cooking their Victuals	259

7 Apr 1777

John Pitkin Esqr Moderator	259
Voted that Messrs Joseph Church, Zachariah Pratt, Jonathan Bigelow, Jonathan Wells, Timothy Cowle, David Hills, and Abijah Colton be.. appointed a Comittee to.. provide Necessaries for the Families of such Soldiers, belonging to this Town, who, have engaged or shall engage and actually go into any of the continental Battalions, now raising in this State, And deliver such Necessaries.. at the Prices, affixed by Law.. on his or their remitting Money to said Comittee	259

Hartford

9 Apr 1777

John Pitkin Esqr Moderator — 259

14 Apr 1777

John Pitkin Esqr Moderator — 260

Granted a Tax, of so many Pence on the Pound.. on the List given in to the General Asembly in october Last.. as will raise the Sum of Twenty Pounds money to be paid Each Soldier, who shall inlist himself, (for a Time, not less than three Years) into either of the eight continental Battalions, ordered to be raised in this State..Voted that Messrs William Olmstead Junr, and John Dod be the Collectors of the Tax or the Town Rate granted at this Meeting, viz, the said William Olmstead.. on the East side of Connecticut River, And the said John Dod.. on the west Side of Connecticut River — 260

16 Sep 1777

Voted that John Pitkin Esqr, be Moderator — 260

Voted that Messrs John Cook, John Dod, Job Norton, Stephen Cone and Seth Collins, be Collectors of the Town Rate — 260

Whereas.. the Governor and Council of Safety have recomended.. to procure imediately, one Shirt, or more (if they see fitt) Linnen or Woolen, one hunting Shirt or Frock, one Pair of woolen Overhalls, one or two Pair of Stockins, and a Pair of good Shoes, for each Non-Comision Officer or Soldier in the continental Army..and deliver the same to Messrs Elijah Hubbard, or Royal Flint, superintending Comessaries for this State.. Voted that the Selectmen.. deliver the same to the said Elijah Hubbard of Midletown — 261

22 Dec 1777

Voted that John Pitkin Esqr be Moderator — 261a

Voted that George Wyllys be Clerk or Register of the Town — 261a

Voted that, Mr Joseph Church, Capt Joseph Talcott, Mr Moses Butler Capt Jonathan Bull, Mr Ashbel Pitkin, Col^o Jonathan Wells, and Mr John Whitman Junr be the Selectmen — 261a

Votd that Messrs Ebenezer Barnerd Junr John Dodd Job Norton Abraham Webster, and Stephen Cone, be Constables — 261a

Voted that Messrs Ashbel Steel, Jonathan Butler, Samuel Talcott Junr Joseph Coit, Peletiah Pierce Daniel Goodwin George Pitkin Joseph Goodwin, Benjamin Porter, Richard Pitkin, John Seymour, and Amos Lee be Grandjurymen — 261a

Voted that Messrs Ebenezer Barnerd Nathaniel Skinner Jonathan Steel James Bunce, Selah Norton, Russel Kilborn, Benjamin Brown, Elijah Peck, Francis Smith, and Ebenezer Steel, be Tythingmen — 261a

Voted that Messrs John Cook, Barnabas Hinsdale, Daniel Pitkin, Samuel Smith, Timothy Cheeney, Ebenezer Wells and Charles Seymour, be Listers — 261a

23 Dec 1777

John Pitkin Esqr Moderator — 263

Voted that Joseph Flagg, Ashbel Spencer, Peletiah Pierce William Andruss Jonathan Burr, Elisha Cole Stephen Hills, Daniel Warren, David Hills, John Spencer Timothy Steadman, Josiah Olcott Junr Henry Treat Junr Nathaniel Brayman, George Kellogg, and Joseph Lyman, be Surveyors of Highways — 263

Voted that, Messrs John Burket, Jonathan Stanly Junr Nehemiah Abbee, and Elisha Seymour be Sealers of Leather — 263

Voted that Messrs Moses Burr Richard Skinner Timothy Steel, Joseph Meakins, Roswell — 263

Hartford

Judson Moses Seymour Noah Butler John Steel and Richard Pitkin, be Fence:Viewers	
Voted that Messrs John Shepard and Jonathan Olmstead be Sealers of Measures	263
Voted that Mr Thomas Sloan be Sealer of Weights	263
Voted that Messrs Isaac Bunce, John Hurlburt David Hills Daniel Seymour and Amos Bidwell be Surveyors and Packers of Tobacco	263
Voted that Messrs Timothy Shepard and Isaac Bunce be Gaugers and Packers of Beef and Pork	263
Voted that Messrs John Dod, and Stephen Cone two of the Constables.. be Collectors of the Town Rate granted at this Meeting	263
Voted that Mr Abraham Webster, one of the Constables.. shall collect the Country Rate.. and Account with the Colony Treasurer	263
Voted that Mr John Seymour chosen a Grandjuryman.. be released from Serving in that Office	263
Voted that Mr Benjamin Gilbert, be a Grandjuryman	263
Upon the Motion.. of Colonel Jonathan Wells and others, Voted that the Selectmen.. impowered to purchase.. a sutable Piece of land.. south of Hoccanum River on the East side of the great River, for the Purpose of a decent burying Ground	263

30 Dec 1777

John Pitkin Esqr Moderator	263
Voted that Mr George Kellogg chosen one of the Surveyors of Highways.. be released from serving	263
Voted that Mr Jonathan Skinner be a Surveyor of Highways	263
Voted that Mr Moses Butler, chosen one of the Selectmen.. be released from serving	263
Voted that Mr Joseph Sheldon be a Selectman	263A
Voted that William Pitkin, George Wyllys, Benjamin Payne, Thomas Seymour Jesse Root, John Pitkin and Benjamin Colton Esqr be.. appointed.. to take into Consideration the Articles of Confederation.. proposed by Congress.. to be adopted and come into by the United States of America, consider and examine the same, And make.. Observations.. And what may be proper for this Town to do relative to said Articles	263A

6 Jan 1778

Voted that John Pitkin Esqr be Moderator	263A
Voted that Messrs Daniel Skinner Junr and Thomas Steel be Grandjurymen	263A
Voted that Mr Thomas Sloan be a Surveyor of Highways	263A

15 Jan 1778

John Pitkin Esqr Moderator	263A

15 Jan 1778

Upon the Motion of Mr John Goodwin.. for Satisfaction.. for the Use of his Land, on which the Pest House stands, whilst the same was improved by this Town, and also for Damages, done by cutting his Wood &c Voted that the Selectmen.. state an Account of what the said John Goodwin is entituled to..vfor the use of said Lane, or for Damages done him	265

13 Apr 1778

John Pitkin Esqr Moderator	265

Hartford

Voted that Mr William Goodwin, 2^d be a Surveyor of Highways	265
Voted that Messrs Oliver Ellsworth, Hez^h Wyllys, Elisha Pitkin, David Hills, Noah Webster and Richard Pitkin, be Assessors.. with the Listers, to assess all Traders Tradesmen &c	265
Voted that Messrs Joseph Church, Joseph Talcott Junr, Joseph Sheldon, Jonathan Bull Jonathan Wells Ashbel Pitkin and John Whitman Ju^r the present Selectmen, be appointed a Comittee.. to provide Necessaries, for the Families of Such Officers and Soldiers, belonging to this Town who have engaged, or shall engage, and actually go into Service in any of the continental Battalions, now raising in this State.. at the Prices affixed by Law, without any additional Expence to such Officers or Soldiers, on his or their remitting Money to said Comittee for that Purpose	265
Upon the Motion of Caleb Turner.. shewing.. that his dwelling House, was impressed in .. December 1776, at the Request of the Selectmen.. and used as an Hospital for.. such Persons as were vilified with the small Pox.. and used for several Months.. And.. sustained considerable Damages by the Loss of a Quanatity of Hay and other Articles.. for which he hath not been compensated.. Voted that Messrs Joseph Church, William Ellery, Zachariah Pratt, John Olcott the 1st and Daniel Butler the 3^d, be.. a Comittee.. to enquire into the Matter	265
Voted that Mr John Benton.. be allowed to have and receive out of the Towns Monies .. £2.6.10½ .. the Ballance of his certain Account of Beef, supplied sundry Persons by Order of the Selectmen in.. 1760 and 1761	265

10 Dec 1778

Voted that Benjamin Payne Esqr be Moderator	266
Voted that George Wyllys be Clerk or Register of the Town	266

16 Dec 1778

Benjamin Payne Esqr Moderator	266
Voted that Messrs Joseph Church, John Cook, Joseph Sheldon, Jonathan Bull Ashbel Pitkin, Col^o Jonathan Wells, and Mr John Whitman Junr, be the Selectmen	266
Voted that Messrs Daniel Skinner Junr, John Dod, Selah Nortonn and Abraham Webster and Stephen Cone be Constables	266
Voted that Messrs Caleb Bull Junr, William Burr, Peletiah Pierce, Ashbel Steel Elisha Stanly Eleazer Burnham Samuel Roberts Robert Mackee, Jacob Bidwell and Timothy Cadwell be Grandjurymen	266
Voted that Messrs James Goodwin, Nathaniel Skinner, George Butler, Daniel Seymour, Theodore Stanly, Elisha Hills, John Kempfield, Daniel Swetland Joseph Steadman Eliphaz Steel, and Daniel Hosmer be Tythingmen	266
Voted that Messrs Aaron Cook, Barnabas Hindsdale, Daniel Pitkin, David Little, Timothy Cheeney, Ebenezer Wells and Charles Seymour, be Listers	266
Voted that Messrs Thomas Sandford, Israel Seymour, Medad Webster, Benjamin Gilman, William Goodwin Junr, William Hills Junr, William Wadsworth, Samuel Kenedy, Thomas Slate Simon Gaines Zacheus Butler, Elijah Tryon, and George Roberts, be, Surveyors of Highways	266
Voted that Messrs John Burket, Thomas Warren, Jonathan Stanly Junr Nehemiah Abbee & Elisha Seymour be Sealers of Leather	267
Voted that Messrs Moses Burr Richard Skinner Timothy Steel Joseph Goodwin Roswell Judson, George Kellogg Noah Butler, John Steel Richard Pitkin, be Fenceviewers	267
Voted that Messrs Joshua Shepard and Jonathan Olmsted be Sealers of Measures	267
Voted that Mr Thomas Sloan be Sealer of Weights	267

Hartford

Voted that Mess[rs] Isaac Bunce, John Hurlburt, David Hills, Daniel Seymour, Amos Bidwell, be Surveyors, and Packers of Tobacco	267
Voted that Mess[rs] Timothy Shepard and Isaac Bunce be Gaugers and Packers of Beef & Pork	267
Voted that M[r] John Hurlburt, be a Brander of Horses	267

24 Dec 1778

Benjamin Payne Esq[r] Moderator	267

28 Dec 1778

Benjamin Payne Esq[r] Moderator	267
Voted that Mess[rs] Oliver Ellsworth Hezekiah Wyllys, Elisha Pitkin, David Hills Noah Webser and Richard Pitkin, be Assessors.. with the Listers to assess all Traders Tradesmen &c	267
Voted that Mess[rs] Joseph Church, Jonathan Bull, John Pitkin Jun[r], David Hills, Noah Webster and Richard Pitkin, be.. a Comittee.. to provide Necessaries, for the Families of such Officers and Soldiers belonging to this Town, who have engaged or shall engage and actually go into Service, in any of the continental Battalions, raised or raising in this State	268
Voted that M[r] Uriah Burket, be a Surveyor of Highways	268
Voted that M[r] Elisha Stanly, chosen a grandjuryman.. be released from serving	268
Voted that Mess[rs] Ashbel Olmstead, and Elisha Eaglestone be grandjurymen	268
Voted tha[t] M[r] Timothy Cheeney, chosen a Lister.. be released from serving	268
Voted that Josiah Ocott Jun[r] be a Lister	268
Voted that Mess[rs] Daniel Skinner Jun[r] and Selah Norton, two of the Constables.. be the Collectors of the Town Rate	268

31 Dec 1778

Benjamin Payne Esq[r] Moderator	269
Voted that M[r] Selah Norton one of the Constables.. shall collect the Country Rate.. and account with the State Treasurer for the same	269
Voted that Cap[t] Jonathan Bull, be added to.. the Committee.. to make out, an Account of the Expences incurred by the small Pox.. in 1776 and 1777, and to apportion the said Expences to the several Persons legally chargeable therewith	269
Voted that M[r] Ashbel Olmstead, chosen a Grandjuryman.. be released from serving	269
Voted that M[r] Daniel Call, be a Grandjuryman	269
Voted that M[r] John Dod, Constable, and Collector of the certain Town Rate granted.. April 1777, be allowed.. Twenty Pounds Money as a Recompence	269

12 Apr 1779

Voted that M[r] Joseph Church be Moderator	270
Voted that Hez[h] Wllys be Clerk of this Meeting	270
Whereas Thomas Seymour hath requested Liberty to build a Grist Mill and Saw Mill in and upon the Little River and the Banks adjacent somewhere between the Town Bridge and opposite the Front of his own Home Lot.. It is therefore Voted and Granted.. so as not to obstruct the Highways.. and prevent the Use of the other Mills.. reserving Liberty for the Inhabitants.. to dig and carry away the Gravel above such Dam and to Let out the Water at any Time.. to repair the Bridge.. Doc[t] Solomon Smith, Col[o] Samuel Talcott, Col[o] Jonathan Wells, Cap[t] John Cook and Col[o] Hez[h] Wyllys.. are.. appointed a Committee.. to.. lay out said	270

Hartford

granted place
20 Apr 1779

Mr Joseph Church Moderator	270
Voted that Col^o Hez Wyllys Capt Richard Pitkin and Capt Noah Webster be a Committee.. to prefer a Memorial to the General Assembly.. that the Highways.. might be mended and repaired by a Rate	270

9 Sep 1779

Voted that Benjamin Payne Esqr be Moderator	271
Voted that a Rate or Tax of two Shillings on the Pound, be levied on the Polls and rateable Estate of the Inhabitants.. According to their Lists.. for the Purpose of procuring and supplying Cloathing for the Soldiers, raised in this Town, as their Quota and inlisted into the continental Army, either for three Years or during the War.. Voted that Messrs Daniel Skinner Junr and Stephen Cone be Collectors	271

21 Sep 1779

Benjamin Payne Esqr Moderator	271
Voted that Mr Daniel Skinner Junr Collector of the Town Rate.. be allowed.. ten Pounds in Addition to the Sum of fifty Pound, granted to him.. as a Reward for his Service in collecting	271
Voted that Mr Stephen Cone chosen a Collector of the Town Rate.. be released from serving	272
Voted that Mr Theodore Stanley be a Collector of the Town Rate.. and paid.. sixty Pounds as a Reward	272
Voted that Col^o Samuel Talcott, Capt Elisha Pitkin, Oliver Ellsworth Esqr and Col^o Thomas Seymour be.. appointed to meet and confer at Hartford.. with.. Delegates, from the other Towns in this State on the late Recommendation of Congress.. for preventing further Depreciation of the paper Currency, and for facilitating, public Loans	272

16 Dec 1779

Voted that Benjamin Payne, Esqr, be Moderator	272
Voted that George Wyllys, be Clerk or Register of the Town	272
Voted that Messrs Joseph Church, John Skinner, Joseph Sheldon, Jonathan Bull Ashbel Pitkin, Solomon Williams, and Seth Collins, be Selectmen	272
Voted that Messrs Daniel Skinner Junr, John Dod, Selah Norton, Abraham Webser, and Stephen Cone, be Constables	272
Voted that Messrs Caleb Bull Junr, Elihu Eaglestone Peletiah Pierce, Ashbel Steel, Elisha Stanly, Silas Burnham, Thomas Wadsworth Junr Joseph Lyman, Jacob Bidwell, and Timothy Cadwell be Grandjurymen	272
Voted that Messrs Timothy Pratt, John Sheldon Junr, Joseph Bunce Lemuel Steel Theodore Stanly, Elisha Hills, Russel Kilborne Daniel Swetland Thomas Spencer, Gideon Webster and Simeon Merrels, be Tythingmen	272
Voted that Messrs Aaron Cook, Barnabas Hinsdale, Daniel Pitkin David Little Josiah Olcott Junr, Ebenezer Wells and Charles Seymour, be Listers	272
Voted that Mr Selah Norton, chosen a Constable.. be released from serving	272
Voted that Mr Theodore Stanly be a Constable	272
Voted that Mr Abraham Webster chosen a Constable.. be released from serving	272
Voted that Mr Moses Goodman, be a Constable	272
Voted that Mr Stephen Cone, chosen a Constable.. be released from serving	273

Hartford

Voted that Mr Josiah Olcott, Junr, be a Constable	273
Voted that Messrs Joseph Talcott Junr, George Butler, John Williams Jonathan Roberts Timothy Forbes, Alexander Steadman Simeon Keeney, Asa Goodman, and Ebenezer Crosby, be Surveyors of Highways	273
Voted that Messrs John Burket, Thomas Warren, Jonathan Stanly Junr Nehemiah Abbe, and Elisha Seymour be Sealers of Leather	273
Voted that Col^o Hez^h Wyllys Capt Richard Pitkin and Capt Noah Webster, be a Committee.. to preferr a Memorial to the General Assembly.. that the Highways.. might be mended and repaired by a Rate	273
Voted that Messrs Nathaniel Goodwin, William Goodwin Richard Skinner Timothy Steel, Joseph Goodwin Roswell Judson George Kellogg Noah Butler, John Steel Richd Pitkin & Robt Makee be Fence Viewers	273
Voted that Messrs John Shepard & Jonathan Olmstead be Sealers of Measures	273
Voted that Mr Robert Sloan be Sealer of Weights	273
Voted that Messrs Isaac Bunce John Hurlburt, David Hills Daniel Seymour & Amos Bidwell be Surveyors and Packers of Tobacco	273
Voted that Messrs Timothy Shepard and Isaac Bunce be Gaugers and Packers of Beef & Pork	273

23 Dec 1779

Benjamin Payne Esqr Moderator	273
Voted that Messrs Joseph Church, Jonathan Bull, William Olmstead Junr, John Wells, Henry Brace Junr and John Cadwell, be.. a Committee.. to provide Necessarys, for the Families of such Officers and Soldiers belonging to this Town, who have engaged or shall engage, and actually go into Service, in any of the continental Battalions, or Corps of Artillary or light Dragoons, raised or raising in this State	273

27 Dec 1779

Benjamin Payne Esqr Moderator	274
Voted that Mr John Stanly, be a Surveyor of Highways	274
Voted that Mr Theodore Stanly chosen a Constable.. be released from serving	274
Voted that Mr John Cowle be a Constable	274
Voted that Mr Joseph Lyman chosen a Grandjuryman.. be released from serving	274
Voted that Mr Jabez Dart, be a Grandjuryman	274
Voted that Mr John Dod, one of the Constables.. shall collect the Country Rates or Taxes.. and account with the State Treasurer	274
Voted that Messrs John Dod, and John Cowle, two of the Constables.. be the Collectors of the Town Rate granted at this Meeting.. And that they shall severally receive.. the Value of five Pounds.. Provided they.. pay and satisfy the Sums of the Rates that shall be assigned them	274
Voted that Mr Selah Norton the Constable appointed to collect the several State Taxes.. be allowed.. three hundred Pounds Money, as a Recompence for his extraordinary Service & Labour in making the proper Rate Bills and collecting the said several Taxes	275

28 Feb 1780

Voted that Benjamin Payne Esqr be Moderator	275
Voted that Capt John Skinner, Mr Joseph Church, Capt John Cook, Capt Samuel Mattox Capt Medad Webster, Capt Jonathan Bull, Lieu^t Barnabas Hinsdale, Capt John Kentfield, Mr Jonathan Bigelow, Mr Daniel Pitkin, Mr Samuel Colton, Lieu^t David Little, Mr John Hurlburt,	275

Hartford

Mr Timothy Cowle, Lieu^t David Hills, Capt Daniel Marsh, Mr Samuel Roberts Mr Stephen Cone Mr Solomon Gilman, Mr Ebenezer Faxon, Mr Joseph Skinner, Mr Seth Collins, Lieu^t John Seymour, Mr Timothy Cadwell, Mr Timothy Seymour Junr, Capt Abraham Sedgwick Mr William Goodwin, Mr Stephen Abbee and Capt George Butler.. are hereby appointed Inspectors of Provisions.. to stop, detain and Secure any embargoed Provisions which they shall suspect are driving carrying or Transporting through the Town.. with an Intent to carry or drive the same out of this State, contrary to Law

Voted that the Selectmen.. pay.. Capt Abraham Sedgwick.. to reimburse him for what he advanced as Premium to one Ebenezer Bibbins, a Soldier, he inlisted in April 1777, as one of the Quota of this Town, and now in continental Service   275

Voted that Col^o Thomas Seymour Col^o Hez^h Wyllys, Col^o Jeremiah Wadsworth and Mr Barzillai Hudson, be.. a Comittee to estimate the Cost of a stone Bridge   275

10 Apr 1780

Benjamin Payne Esqr Moderator   276

Whereas a Stone : Bridge across the Rivulet, will be of great Use and Security to this Town and the public Travailing Voted that Col^o Thomas Seymour, Col^o Jeremiah Wadsworth Col^o Hez^h Wyllys, and Mr Barzillai Hudson, be.. Agents, to apply to the Honble General Assembly.. for Liberty of a Lottery, for.. erecting a stone Bridge, over the Rivulet, that crosseth the main Street or Road, through this Town, at or near the Place, where the Town Bridge now stands   276

26 Jun 1780

Voted that Benjamin Payne Esqr be Moderator   276

Voted That Capt Caleb Bull Ju^r be.. appointed Muster Master to those Soldiers belonging to this Town who shall inlist themselves to Serve in the Continental Army..   277

3 Jul 1780

Benjamin Payne Esqr Moderator   277

13 Jul 1780

Benjamin Payne Esqr Moderator   278

For the better Encouragement of the Militia to undertake, their respective Tours of Duty - Voted that every Militia Man, and non-Comissioned Officer belonging to this Town, that shall be called upon & do, a Tour of Duty.. before the first Day of November next, shall be paid.. in Grain or Bills of the new Emission in Addition to the Wages granted by this State such Sum or Sums as shall make their Wages equivalent to fourty Shillings per Month, for a Private.. for every Month they shall serve.. they producing a Certificate from the comanding Officer of the Company under whom they shall serve.. Voted that Capt Caleb Bull, Col^o Jonathan Wells, and Capt Seth Collins, be a Comittee to receive said Certificates, and make up the pay Rolls   278

Voted that a Rate or Tax of two Pence half Penny, in Bills of the late Emission of this State be levied.. for the Purpose of paying the Bounties or Premiums.. to such able bodied effective Men, as have or shall voluntarily inlist into the continental Army, to compleat the Quota.. or Melitia.. Voted that Messrs William Bull, Joseph Skinner, John Cowle, and Josiah Olcott Junr be Collectors   279

5 Oct 1780

Voted that Benjamin Payne Esqr be Moderator   279

Voted that Mr Josiah Olcott Junr, chosen one of the Collectors of the Town Rate.. for payments of certain Bounties and Premiums, to Soldiers, for enlisting in the Army &c be   279

Hartford

released from serving

Voted that Mr Aaron Buckland, be Collector of a certain Town Rate, of which Josiah Olcott Junr was appointed Collector and at this Meeting excused from serving. But upon further Consideration Voted that the said Aaron Buckland, be also now released from that Office	279
Voted that Mr Nathan Steadman, be a Collector of the Town Rate.. for Encouragement of Soldiers, to inlist, into the Army & in the room and Stead of Mr Josiah Olcott Junr	279
Voted that Col^o Jeremiah Wadsworth, Col^o Thomas Seymour, and Benjamin Payne be Agents, to appear .. before the General Assembly.. to shew.. Reasons.. against the dividing of this Town, as prayed for, by a Memorial preferred for that Purpose	279

15 Nov 1780

Voted that John Pitkin Esqr be Moderator	280
Voted that Capt Jonathan Bull on the west, and Mr Daniel Pitkin on the East Side of Connecticut River, be appointed to receive the Salt, procure Cask, to put up Provisions, to receive and inspect the same	280
Voted, that Capt Seth Collins, and Lieu^t David Hills, John Pitkin Junr, and Capt John Skinner, be.. a Committee to purchase the several Articles of Provisions required of this Town	280
Voted, that Mr Moses Goodman be appointed to collect that Part of the Rate or Tax granted this Meeting.. on the west Side of Connecticut River	280
Voted that Mr John Cowle, Constable, be appointed to collect that part of said Tax.. on the East Side of Connecticut River	280

21 Dec 1780

Col^o Jonathan Wells was chosen Moderator	280
Upon the Request.. of Col^o Jonathan Wells, Voted that he be excused from serving in the Office of Moderator	280
Voted that John Pitkin Esqr be Moderator	280
Voted that Messrs Joseph Church, John Skinner, Jonathan Bull, Ashbel Pitkin, Solomon Williams, Richard Pitkin and Seth Collins, be Selectmen	281
Voted that Messrs Daniel Skinner Junr John Dod, John Cowle, Moses Goodman, and Alexander Steadman be Constables	281
Voted that Capt Caleb Bull, Messrs Elihu Eaglestone, Ashbel Steel, Jonathan Huntington Epaphras Olmstead, George Burnham, Thomas Wadsworth Junr Jabez Dart, Francis Smith & Timothy Seymour Junr be Grandjurymen	281
Voted that Capt Joseph Talcott, Mr Nathaniel Goodwin, Capt Daniel Seymour, Messrs William Adams Elisha Cowle, Joseph Arnold, George Bidwell, Timothy Steadman, David Demmau, Thomas Goodman, and Moses Steel Junr, be Tythingmen	281
Voted that Messrs Aaron Cook Barnabas Hinsdale, Daniel Pitkin, David Little, Josiah Olcott Junr, Ebenezer Wells, and Charles Seymour, be Listers	281
Voted that Capt John Cook, Mr Barzillai Hudson, Capt Elisha Pitkin, Messrs Elisha Stanly Elisha Bidwell, Ephraim Webster, David Buckland, Samuel Merrels, Amaziah Stanly, Samuel Kilbourne. Samuel Stanly Elisha Hills, and Ozias Bissell Junr be Surveyors of Highways	281
Voted that Messrs John Burket, Thomas Warren, Jonathan Stanly Junr Nehemiah Abbee and Elisha Seymour be Sealers of Leather	281

25 Dec 1780

John Pitkin Esqr Moderator	281
Voted that George Wyllys, be Clerk of Register of the Town	281

Hartford

Voted that Mess.rs Ezra Coming and Ezra Hide be Sealers of Leather	281
Voted that Mess.rs Nathaniel Goodwin, William Goodwin, Richard Skinner Timothy Steel Joseph Goodwin, Roswell Judson, George Kellogg Noah Butler, John Steel, Stephen Cone & Nathaniel M.ckee be fence:Viewers	281
Voted that John Shepard and Jonathan Olmstead be Sealers of Measures	281
Voted that Thomas Sloan be Sealer of Weights	281
Voted that Isaac Bunce John Hurlburt, David Hills, Daniel Seymour and Amos Bidwell be Surveyors and Packers of Tobacco	281
Voted that Timothy Shepard, Isaac Bunce, Timothy Shepard Jun.r and John Nevins be Gaugers, and Packers of Beef, and Pork	281

28 Dec 1780

John Pitkin Esq.r Moderator	281

2 Jan 1781

John Pitkin Esq.r Moderator	281
Voted that Mess.rs Daniel Skinner Jun.r, and Alexander Steadman two of the Constables.. be Collectors of the Town Rate granted at this Meeting.. And.. shall receive.. the Value of five Pounds, .. provided they shall pay and satisfie the.. Rates that shall be assigned	281
Voted that M.r Daniel Skinner Jun.r one of the Constables.. shall collect the Country Rates or Taxes.. and account with the Treasurer of the State for the same	281
Voted that M.r Charles Caldwell Daniel Olcott Nehemiah Hubbard Medad Webster, Ashbel Olmstead, Cap.t John Wells, Stephen Bidwell, and Timothy Seymour Jun.r be.. a Comittee.. to provide Necessaries, for the Families of such Officers and Soldiers belonging to this Town, who have engaged or shall engage, and actually go into Service in any of the continental Battalions or Corps of Artillery or light Dragoons.. without any Additional Expence	283
Voted that Cap.t Jonathan Bull and M.r Daniel Pitkin.. to procure Cask, for.. Flour, and receive and inspect the same, and.. indian Corn, and see that the same is good and merchantable, and.. Flour be well packed.. and cause the same to be branded, and stored in some safe Place	283
Voted that Mess.rs Moses Goodman and John Cowle, be appointed Collectors, to collect said Tax of one Penny half Penny on the Pound in Flour and Corn and.. warn all the Persons named in their.. Rate Bills, viz those on the west Side of Connecticut River to carry their Flour and Corn.. to Cap.t Jonathan Bull, and those on the East Side.. to M.r Daniel Pitkin	283

9 Jan 1781

Voted that Benjamin Payne Esq.r be Moderator	283

5 Feb 1781

Voted that George Wyllys Esq.r be Moderator	282
Whereas this Town are ordered by the General Assembly to furnish fifteen Men to join in compleating a Regiment to be stationed at Hors Neck until the first Day of March 1782 ~ Voted that Mess.rs William Bull, Daniel Marsh Jun.r Barnabas Hinsdale, Cap.t Abraham Sedgwick, Cap.t Moses Forbes, be.. a Comittee to hire and engage the said fifteen	282
Voted that Mess.rs Daniel Skinner Jun.r, and Alexander Steadman be the Collectors of Rate or Tax granted at this Meeting	285
Voted that Mess.rs John Cadwell, and William Wadsworth, be of, and added to the Comittee.. to take Care of, and supply with Provisions &c The Families of the Officers and Soldiers, belonging to this Town, in Service, in the continental Army	285

Hartford

15 Feb 1781

Voted that Benjamin Payne Esqr, be Moderator — 285

26 Feb 1781

Benj^a Payne Esqr Moderator — 285

Voted that Messrs Thomas Sloan, Amasai Jones James Jepson, James Marsh, William Hooker Elisha Babcock, George Pitkin Junr Elisha Hills, Thos Slade Alex^r Steadman David Little Saml Flagg Rosseter Belding Joseph Skinner and Saml Merrels be.. appointed.. to collect in the respective Classes, to which they belong the Tax.. for procuring an able bodied effective Man, to serve for said Classes, in a Battalion.. for the Defence of the Post at Horsneck, the western Frontiers and the Sea Coasts of this State — 285

9 Apr 1781

Benjamin Payne Esqr Moderator — 284

Upon the Memorial of Capt John Cook.. praying to have leased to him a certain Piece of Land or Part of a Highway lying at a Place called the Neck of Land, where he has now Erected some Works.. for the making of Ropes &c being in Length about forty Rods and in Breadth about twelve Feet. Voted that the Selectmen.. repair to said Place.. and provided .. that said Piece of Land, can be taken out of said Highway without any Detriment to the Public or Prejudice to any private Person.. lease to him.. the Piece of Land aforesaid for.. twenty Years.. for the Purpose of making Cordage only — 284

30 Apr 1781

Benjamin Payne Esqr Moderator — 284

Voted that Messrs Daniel Skinner Junr, and Alexander Steadman two of the Constables.. be collectors of the Town Rate granted at this Meeting.. And.. receive.. the Value of five Pounds, Money as it passed in the Year 1774 in current Bills.. provided they shall pay and satisfie, the Sums of the Rates — 285A

Upon the Motion of Benjamin Payne Esqr, representing.. that there is a certain Highway.. lying about half a Mile west of the Highway leading to Wethersfield, which runs to Weathersfield Line, that there hath never been, any Highway laid out in Weathersfield to comunicate with said Highway, and that said Highway is not needed to travail in, except for a Few Individuals who have Land adjoining to said Highway,.. that the Town would lease to him that Part of said Highway which adjoins to his Land, lying East of his Pasture.. Voted that the Selectmen.. lease that Part of said Highway which lieth East of the said Benj^a Payne's lane, and South of said Barret's Line, to Weathersfield Line for the Term of Ten Years — 285A

25 Jun 1781

Voted that Benjamin Payne Esqr be Moderator — 285A

Voted that a Rate or Tax of four Pence on the Pound, be levied.. on the Polls and rateable Estate of the Inhabitants.. According to their Lists bro^t.. in October last.. to be paid in good merchantable Beef Cattle.. for the use of the State, and the continental Army.. or in Silver and Gold Coin.. for the Purpose of supplying this Towns Quota of Beef Cattle, for the Use of the continental Army.. Voted that Messrs Daniel Skinner Junr John Cowle, Alexander Steadman and Moses Goodman be Collectors — 286

10 Jul 1781

Voted that Benjamin Payne Esqr be Moderator — 286

Hartford

20 Dec 1781

Voted that Col° George Wyllys be Moderator	*287*
Voted that George Wyllys be Clerk or Register of the Town	*287*

24 Dec 1781

Upon the Request and Desire of Col° George Wyllys, to be excused from further serving in the Office of Moderator.. Voted that John Pitkin Esqr be now Moderator of this Meeting	*287*
Voted that Messrs John Skinner Joseph Church, Jonathan Bull, Ashbel Pitkin, Solomon Williams, Richard Pitkin and Seth Collins, be Selectmen	*287*
Voted that Messrs Daniel Skinner Junr John Dod, John Cowle, Moses Goodman, and Alexander Steadman, be Constables	*287*
Voted that Messrs Charles Merrels, John Spencer Junr Elijah Spencer, William Adams, Samuel Webster, Daniel Call, Stephen Abbee Junr Mathias Treat Alexander Keeney Junr, Andrew M^{c}kee, Isaac Olmstead, David Butler, Aaron Cadwell Junr and Isaac Webster Junr be Tythingmen	*287*
Voted that Messrs Aaron Cook, Barnabas Hinsdale, Daniel Pitkin David Little, Nathan Steadman, Ebenezer Wells and Charles Seymour, be Listers	*287*
Voted that Messrs Samuel Kilbourne, John Olcott 2^d, Elisha Babcock, Jonathan Bigelow Jonathan Stanly Junr Nathaniel Olmstead Junr Elisha Hills, John Cadwell Junr, Aaron Buckland Alexander Keeney Junr Thomas Olmstead, Simeon Hosmer, and Isaac Webster, be Surveyors of Highways	*287*
Voted that Messrs Thomas Steel Jonathan Stanly Junr and Elisha Seymour be Sealers of Leather	*287*
Voted that Messrs Thomas Sandford, William Goodwin, Richard Skinner, Timothy Steel, Joseph Goodwin Roswell Judson George Kellogg, Gideon Deming, Stephen Cone and Nathaniel M^{c}kee, be fence Viewers	*288*
Voted that John Shepard and Jonathan Olmstead, be Sealers of Measures	*288*
Voted that Mr Thomas Sloan, be Sealer of Weights	*288*
Voted that Messrs Isaac Bunce John Hurlburt, David Hills, Daniel Seymour & Aaron Bidwell be Surveyors and Packers of Tobaccoe	*288*
Voted that Messrs Isaac Bunce Timothy Shepard Junr and John Nevins, be Gaugers and Packers of Beef and Pork	*288*

27 Dec 1781

John Pitkin Esqr Moderator	*288*
Voted that Capt Caleb Bull Messrs Elihu Eaglestone, Ashbel Steel, Jonathan Huntington, Epaphras Olmstead Benjamin Gilman, James Porter Daniel Swetland Jonathan Skinner, and Timothy Seymour Junr be Grandjurymen	*288*
Votd, that Mr Pelegg Heath, be a Sealer of Leather	*288*
Voted that Mr Daniel Skinner Junr, one of the Constables.. shall collect the State Rates or Taxes.. and account with the Treasurer of the State	*288*
Voted Mr Solomon Smith, and Capt Elisha Pitkin, be a Comittee to make the Country or State Rates or Taxes	*289*
Voted that Messrs Daniel Skinner Junr, John Cowle, and Alexander Steadman Constables.. be Collectors of the Town Rate.. And.. shall severally receive from this Town viz, the said Daniel Skinner Junr the Sum of five Pounds.. John Cowle the Sum of two Pounds, ten Shillings, and.. Alexander Steadman the Sum of two Pounds ten Shillings.. for their Service	*289*
Voted that Mr Moses Goodman chosen a Constable.. be released from serving	*289*

Hartford

Voted that Mr Samuel Whitman be a Constable	289
Voted that Capt Daniel Marsh be a Surveyor of Highways	289
Voted that Mr Samuel Kilborne, chosen a Surveyor of Highways.. released from serving	289
Voted that Capt Frederick Bull be a Surveyor of Highways	289
Voted that Benjamin Payne Esqr, be.. appointed, an Agent.. to.. defend against a Petition, preferred to the Honble superior Court, by Caleb Turner	289
On hearing the.. Request of.. John Dod, a Constable and Collector of certain Rates.. granted that.. the said Dodd, have.. six Pounds in State Bills, in Lieu of three fourty Shilling Bills, returned upon his Hands which appear to be false and counterfeit, to reimburse him.. for the Loss	289
granted to Capt John Cook the Sum of twenty Shillings.. for his Service as a Lister chosen in the Year 1778, in Lieu of.. any former Grants made him for the Service aforesaid	289

31 Dec 1781

John Pitkin Esqr Moderator	289
Voted that Capt Medad Webster Capt Daniel Skinner, Messrs Charles Caldwell and Daniel Olcott be.. a Comittee.. to provide Necessaries for the Families of.. Officers and Soldiers belonging to this Town, who have engaged or shall engage, and actually go into Service into any of the continental Battalions, or Corps of Artillery or light Dragoons, raised or raising in this State, and deliver such Necessaries.. without any additional Expence	289
Voted that Mr Solomon Smith, and Capt Elisha Pitkin, appointed.. to make the State Rates or Taxes.. be released from that Service	290
Voted, that Mr Barnabas Hinsdale, do make the Country or State Taxes.. and seasonably deliver the proper Rate Bills to the Constable appointed to collect the said Taxes	290

25 Feb 1782

Voted that Col^o John Pitkin, be Moderator	290

8 Apr 1782

Col^o John Pitkin, be Moderator	290
Voted that Capt John Skinner, be a Collector of the Town Rate.. in the Room and Stead of Mr Daniel Skinner Junr.. who declined to officiate in that Office and that he.. receive. five Pounds lawfull Money for his Service	290
Voted that Col^o Thomas Seymour be.. an Agent.. to appear and defend against a Petition preferred to the Honble superior Court.. by Caleb Turner	291
Voted that Capt Selah Norton be one of the Committee.. to provide for the Soldiers Families	291
Voted that Capt Jonathan Bull, be.. appointed, a Comittee in the Place of Benjamin Payne Esqr and Mr Daniel Sheldon now deceased, to carry into Execution the Vote and Order of this Town passed on the 9th Day of April 1770.. respecting a Grant made to Zebulon Mygat	291
Voted that the Selectmen.. sett out a small Piece of Land, to build a small House on for the Use of Neel McLean, the old Soldier) as long as he lives, between the Gaol, and the town Mills, on the Bank of the River, to remain to the Town for a Poor House	291

4 Jul 1782

Voted that Col^o Thomas Seymour be Moderator	291
Voted that Samuel Talcott, George Pitkin, and Noah Webster Esqr, be appointed, to represent this Town, in the County Convention	291

Hartford

5 Dec 1782

Voted that John Pitkin Esqr be Moderator	291
Capt Jonathan Bull, by the Votes or Ballots, brought in by the Inhabitants present and counted, .. was declared to be chosen Register	291

6 Dec 1782

John Pitkin Esqr Moderator	292
On the Motion and Request of Capt Jonathan Bull, chosen Register.. on the 5th Instant, to be released &c - Voted that the said Captain Jonathan Bull be excused and released from serving	292
George Wyllys by the unaminous Votes.. was now chosen Clerk or Register of the Town	292
Messrs George Smith, Jonathan Bull John Pitkin Junr Seth Collins and Richard Pitkin.. chosen Selectmen	292
Messrs Daniel Skinner Junr John Dod John Cole Daniel Hosmer and Richard Pitkin Junr.. chosen Constables	292
Voted that Mr Daniel Hosmer one of the Constables.. shall collect the States Rates or Taxes.. and account with the Treasurer of the State	292
Voted that Capt Caleb Bull, Messrs Elihu Eaglestone, Ashbel Steel, Eli Warner Epaphras Olmstead Benjamin Gilman, James Porter, Daniel Swetland, Jonathan Skinner Timothy Seymour Junr Henry Brace Junr, James Church, Jonathan Steel, Thomas Steel and Barzillai Hudson be Grandjurymen	292
Voted that Messrs Samuel Goodwin, Asa Corning, George Pratt William Adams 2^d Joseph Webster, George Bidwell Richard Goodman, Jonathan Belding Balch Daniel Kellogg Jabez Dart, and Calvin Gilman, be Tythingmen	292
Voted that Messrs Aaron Cook Barnabas Hinsdale, Daniel Pitkin, John Whitman Junr, and Nathan Steadman, be Listers	292
Voted that Messrs Daniel Goodwin Hez^h Wyllys, George Pitkin Junr Nathaniel Pratt, William Cowle Junr, Joseph Lyman, Stephen Bidwell Thomas Spencer, Aaron Buckland, Timothy Cadwell, and John Seymour, be Surveyors of Highways	292

9 Dec 1782

John Pitkin Esqr Moderator	293
Voted that Messrs Thomas Steel, Jonathan Stanly Junr, and Elisha Seymour be Sealers of Leather	293
Voted that Messrs Thomas Sandford, William Goodwin Richard Skinner, Timothy Steel, Joseph Goodwin Roswell Judson George Kellogg Gideon Deming Stephen Cone and Nathaniel Mackee, be Fence Viewers	293
Voted that Messrs John Shepard and Jonathan Olmstead be Sealers of Measures	293
Voted that Mr Thomas Sloan be Sealer of Weights	293
Voted that Messrs Isaac Bunce John Hurlburt David Hills, Daniel Seymour and Aaron Bidwill, be Surveyors and Packers of Tobacco	293
Voted that Messrs Isaac Bunce Timothy Shepard Junr, and John Nevins, be Gaugers and Packers of Beef and Pork	293

10 Dec 1782

John Pitkin Esqr Moderator	293
Voted, that Mr Caleb Bull, be added to, and joined with the Survivors of a certain Committee appointed.. 10th Day of April 1769 for.. Selling and Disposing of the Lands on the Banks on either Side of the little River between the lower Mill Dam.. and the East Ends of the Streets.	293

Hartford

adjacent to said Banks

On the Motion of Mr John Pitkin Junr, chosen one of the Selectmen.. Voted that the said Mr John Pitkin Junr be now excused and released from serving *293*

Mr Ashbel Pitkin.. was unamimously chosen a Selectman *294*

Voted that Mr James Church, be added to, and joined with the Survivors of the Comitttee.. to have the Care Management and Oversight, of the free Gramar School *294*

Whereas large Quantities of Wood and Lumber, are from Time to Time bro^t down Connecticut River, to market, and landed in this Town, at the comon landing Places, But no Rules or Regulations are made for the Surveying or ascertaining, the Quantities or Quality of the same whereby great Injustice may, and is often done, to the People of this Town & State Voted that Col^o Thomas Seymour and Mr Samuel Lyman, be.. Agents to represent the Difficulties and Inconveniencies, attending the afores^d Matter.. and to obtain by some proper public Act, a Redress of the same at the next General Assembly *294*

Whereas it is represented, that there is some Hinderance or incumbrance, attending the comon landing Place, at the Ferry, on the west Side Connecticut River, in the free Use and Improvement of it, as has been usual, which ought to be enquired into and removed, for Remedy whereof, Messrs James Church Thomas Seymour, John Chenward, Daniel Pitkin and Elisha Pitkin.. be.. a Comittee to.. enquire into the Difficulties or Embarrasments suggested to attend the free use of the landing Place or Places.. on either Side the River *294*

24 Dec 1782

John Pitkin Esqr chosen Moderator at the opening of this Meeting being absent, It is now Voted that Col^o Thomas Seymour be Moderator *295*

Voted that Mr Ashbel Pitkin, chosen to be a Selectman.. be excused and released from serving *295*

Mr Daniel Pitkin.. chosen a Selectman *295*

Voted that Mr Eli Wadsworth, be a Surveyor of Highways *295*

Voted that Mr Benjamin Brown, be a Sealer of Leather *295*

We your Comittee appointed.. to view the public landing Places, on each Side of the great River, and to find what.. Obstructions now attend the same, And what.. Improvements may be made.. for the Advancement of Trade and Commerce.. report.. upon Enquiry and Examination of the ancient Records, that when the original owners of said Lotts sold or transferred their said Lotts, they did not bound the Grantee.. Therefore your Comittee conclude.. that notwithstanding the Banks of the River or landing Places may in some Places have varied.. the Town and all Others have Right, to use and improve the landing Places on each Side the River.. further give it as their Opinion, that it would be of very great public and comercial Advantage if proper.. Highways, were opened upon the high Banks of said River, from the Creek.. North of Col^o Talcott's Store.. *295*

..south of Capt Knox's.. southward to the Lott now owned by John Pantry Goodwin.. And your Comittee further report it as their Opinion, that it will be necessary to extend the landing Places, from the Road leading to the River, on the north side of Jones's Land, to the south Side of Olmstead's Islands.. and that a Road be laid open from the lower Road leading to the Ferry, on the north Side of Williams's House to the River.. Thos Seymour.. Elisha Pitkin.. John Chenward.. James Church.. Daniel Pitkin } Com^{tee} *295*

The Town do now.. appoint, Messrs Thomas Seymour Elisha Pitkin John Chenward James Church, and Daniel Pitkin be a Comittee to treat with & purchase of the Proprietors and Owners of the Lands reported necessary for public Highways & landing Places *296*

Voted that Capt Elisha Pitkin and Col^o Thomas Seymour be.. Agents.. to preferr a Memorial *297* to the general Assembly, praying.. that the State Bills, and other public Securities in the Hands of the Town Treasurer be received in Payment of the Execution in the Sheriff's Hands, against.. this Town

Voted there be allowed.. to Mr Elihu Eaglestone.. Twenty Shillings.. on his Account.. for keeping Rachel Turner and Family, when supposed to be visited with the Small Pox 297

30 Dec 1782

Col^o Thomas Seymour Moderator	297
resolved that Col^o Jonathan Wells Mr Caleb Bull, Capt Jonathan Bull, Capt John Chenward, and Capt Elisha Pitkin.. be.. a Comittee.. to call upon all Collectors, and all Others, who, owe, or have been appointed, to, or have received any of the Monies, or other Thing, granted, due or any manner of Way coming to this Town and not yet accounted for, and to liquidate finally settle and adjust the Same, with them	297

7 Jan 1783

Col^o Thomas Seymour Moderator	298
Voted that, Messrs Daniel Hosmer, John Cowle and Stephen Hills, be Collectors of the Town Rate granted at this Meeting.. Daniel Hosmer .. on the west Side of Connecticut River.. John Cowle.. on the east Side of said River, belonging to the 3^d Society.. Stephen Hills.. of the Society of Orford..	298
Voted that Mr Richard Pitkin Junr chosen one of the Constables.. be released from serving	298
Voted that Mr Stephen Hills, be a Constable	298

29 Jan 1783

Voted that Col^o Jonathan Hills be Moderator	299
Voted that Col^o Hez^h Wyllys be Clerk of this Meeting	299
Voted that Col^o George Pitkin Samuel Lyman Esqr Mr John Trumbull Mr Caleb Bull & Mr Jeremiah Platt, be appointed a Committee to represent.. to the.. General Assembly.. the Minds of the Inhabitants.. in regards to a Certain Act .. Respecting the Admission of Mr Richard Smith as a Member of this State together with his Effects	299

7 Apr 1783

Col^o Thomas Seymour Moderator	299
Voted, that Mr Stephen Hills chosen a Constable.. be released from serving	299
Voted, that Mr Stephen Hills, chosen a Collector of the Town Rate.. be released from serving	299
Voted, that Mr Timothy Bryant, be a Collector of the Town Rate.. in the Room of Stephen Hills, now released from serving	299
Voted that Mr Ashbel Stanly be a Tythingman	299
Voted, that Mr Henry Brace Junr chosen a Grandjuryman.. be released from serving	299
Voted, that Mr David Butler, be a Grandjuryman	299
Voted, that Mr Eli Warner, chosen a Grandjuryman.. be released from serving	299
Whereas, this Town.. on the 15th Day of December 1749 appointed Messrs Daniel Edwards, James Church and Thomas Seymour, all now deceased a Comittee, to disperse of certain small Parcels of Land, belonging to the Town.. And Whereas said Comittee did not fully compleat the Business.. And some of the said Parcels of Land, are wanted by the Owners of the Lotts adjoining thereto in Front &c — It is.. voted that Messrs Samuel Wadsworth Caleb Bull and Joseph Sheldon, be.. a Comittee, in the Place and Stead of the said former Comittee	299

Hartford

21 Aug 1783

Voted that Col° Thomas Seymour be Moderator　　　　　　　　　　　　　　　*300*

Voted, That Capt Hugh Ledlie Capt Seth Collins, Capt George Smith Col° Thomas Seymour,　*300*
and Mr Daniel Pitkin, Be.. a Comittee to make a Draft.. devising the most candid and
constitutional Method of Address to be laid before the Legislature, for some Releif, and Ease,
from the public Burthens viz, Commutation &c And.. be a Comittee, to conferr, and
corrispond with any other Town on the same Subject

16 Sep 1783

Col° Thomas Seymour Moderator　　　　　　　　　　　　　　　　　　　*300*

The Town.. now agreed, upon a certain Address and Instructions to their Representatives, iin　*300*
the next General Assembly of this State.. viz - To Col° Thomas Seymour and Col° George
Pitkin Representatives for the Town of Hartford in the next General Assembly.. [*ed: a letter
of instructions follows*]

Hartland

Town Meeting Records
Vol. 1
1761- 1993
Annual Meeting of December 1782 is missing.

Located at the Town Clerk's Office

Hartland

1 Mar 1775

Voted that Neh^m Andrews Esqr Should be Moderator	41
Voted that Neh^m Andrews Esqr Capt Brace Mr John Wilder Do^{tr} Assa Smith and Mr Isaac Burnham Should Bee a Com^{ee} Inspection or Correspondence	41

19 Sep 1775

a Town Meeting Legally warned and Holden att the Dwelling House of Mr Daniel Ensign	42
then Was Leiu^t Thos Beman Chosen moderator	42
Voted to Raise three pence on the pound to pay the Reven^d Mr Church Sallary the Year past	42
Voted to Chuse a Com^{ee} to Reckon with the Select men & Town treasury.. Chose.. Alex^r Bushnell.. Leit Thos Beman.. D^n Thos Giddings.. Eldad Shepherd	42
Voted that Mr Uriah Hide be A Choristor to Assist In Tuining the Psalm	42
Test Phin^{as} Kingsbery Reg^r	42

9 Oct 1775

a Legal Town Meeting Holden att the House of Mr Daniel Ensign	42
Voted.. that Leiu^t Eleazer Ensign Should Be Moderator	42
Chose a Com^{ee} for Scholling (Viz) Mr Joshua Giddings.. Dr Jeremiah Emons.. Mr Oliver Bates.. Mr Eldad Shepherd.. Mr Phinehas Bates.. Mr Joseph Wilder	42
Voted to allow Ensign Uriel Holms accoumpts Bording the Revnd Mr Church Before Ordination and Mr Forward and Mr Roots while they Preached In town	42
Voted to Chuse a Committee to Build the above S^d Bridg (Viz) Ensign Uriel Holmes Mr Oliver Bates Mr Saml Phelps	42

4 Dec 1775

an Annuel Town Meeting Legally Warned and Holden att the Dwelling House of Mr Daniel Ensign	43
Chose Capt Benjn Hutchens Moderator	43
Phinehas Kingsbery { Town Clark	43
Engisn Uriel Holms.. Israel Williams { Constables	43
Alexander Bushnel.. Ephraim Wilder { Collector of Rates	43
Asahel Brainerd.. Nathl Butler.. Asher Benjamin..Gam^l Wilder.. Leiu^{nt} E Ensign.. Joseph Brace { Tything men	43
Jeremiah Emons.. Thos Beman jur.. Capt A Brace.. John Bates.. Phin^{as} Kingsbery { Listers	43
Saml Benjamin { Sealer of Weights and measures	43
N Andrews Esqr .. Daniel Dreggs { Kee Keeper	43
Thomas Beman ju^r.. Eldad Shephard { Leather Seallers	43
Voted that Dec^n Thos Gidding Ensign Uriel Holms & Phin^{as} Kingsbery Town Com^{ee} to Lay out and Exchang Highways	43
Phinehas Kingsbery.. Capt Abel Brace.. Capt Benjn Hutchens { Select Men	43
Isaac Burnham.. Gamaliel Wilder.. Dr Assa Smith.. Leiu^{nt} E Ensign.. Saml Benjamin.. Joseph Wilder.. Oliver Bates { Granjurers	43
Wm Chapman.. Paul Simons..John Kingsbery.. Samuel Banning.. Joseph Wilder..Hezekiah Adkins.. Samuel Borden.. Rubin Burnham.. Samuel Phelps.. Asher Benjamin { Surveyors of highway	43

Hartland

Joel Miner.. Uriah Hide Miner { Brander of horses	43
David Gidding.. Thos Beman ju^r.. John Treek.. Prince Talor ju^r { Fence Vewers	43
Joel Meacham { Packer of meat &c	43
Voted to Chuse an Agant to Go to the.. Assembly to pray the assembly Not to Lay a tax on the town Voted that Neh^m Andrews Esqr Should be an a Gent..	43
Voted that the Town Will Chuse a Gentleman to assist Esqr Andrews.. and Go if Esqr Should fail (Viz) Capt Benjamin Hutchens	43
Voted that the Town Will Chuse a Com^{ee} to take Care of that Estate that Leu^{nt} David Day Decsed has Given to the Town for the Support of the Gospel Ministry.. Voted that Alex^r Bushnel Joseph Wilder & Neh^m Andrews Esqr Should Be the Com^{ee}	43
Voted that the Town Will Seat the meetinghouse Voted and Chose Seators as followeth (Viz) D^n Thos Gidding.. Phin^{as} Kingsbery.. N Andrews Esqr.. Capt A Brace.. John Wilder.. Alex^r Bushnell.. Joseph Wilder	43

1 Jan 1776

An Adjurned Meeting Held att the meetinghouse.. Adjourned to Capt Benjamin Hutchens Dwelling House	43
Chouse a Com^{ee} to Seet the meetinghouse (Viz) Mr Isaac Burnham.. Mr Jeremiah Emons.. Mr Israel Williams.. Mr OliverBates.. Mr Enos Lane	43

31 Jan 1776

Voted that Leiu^t Eleazer Ensign & Mr Joseph Wilder Should assist In Reading the Psalm on the West Mountain on the Lords Day and other publick Meetings	44
Voted to Chuse a Committee to Lease out the Land that Leiu^t David Day Gave to the Town.. for the Support of the Gospel Ministry for Nine Hundred and Ninety Nine Years.. the Names of the Com^{ee} Chosen Viz Leiu^t Oliver Bates.. Neh^m Andrews Esqr.. Ensign Uriel Holms.. Mr Joseph Wilder.. Mr Alexander Bushnel { Towns Com^{ee}	44
the Grand Levy for the Year 1775.. Neh^m Andrews Esqr.. Addams Daniel.. Andrews Ely.. Andrews Neh^m ju^r.. Andrews Samuel.. Beman Thos Leiu^t..Benjamin Samuel.. Banning Samuel.. Borden John.. Bill Jonathan.. Beman Thos ju^r.. Banning Abner.. Bill Bennajah.. Burnham Isaac.. Bush Aaron.. Butler Nathl.. Brainaird Asahel.. Benjamin Asher.. Butler Jonathan.. Bushnel Alexander.. Bigalow Jabez.. Coudry Moses..Chapman William..	44
..Church Uriah.. Colton Eleazer.. Clemons William.. Chapel Noah.. Clark Thos.. Clark George.. Cadwell Moses.. Daniel Peletiah..Daniel John.. Dimmiz Ebenezer.. Emons Jonathan.. Emons Jeremiah.. Frazier Daniel.. D^n Giddings Thos.. Giddings Joshua.. Gates Jesse.. Giddings David.. Giddings Dan.. Scovel Micha.. Thos Giddings ju^r.. Giddings Elisha.. Holms Uriah Ensign.. Hodgkins John.. Capt Hutchens Benjamin.. Hays Micha.. Hutchens Joseph.. Jones John.. Jones Thomas.. Kingsbery John.. Kellogg Ezekiel..	44
.. Jones John.. Jones Thomas.. Kingsbery John.. Kellogg Ezekiel.. Kingsbery Phinehas.. Lane Enos.. Moses Abel.. Mack Jonathan.. Meacham Isaac.. Meacham Joel.. Phelps Charles.. Pirkins Eliphaz.. Pirkins Phinehas.. Phelps Samuel.. Parker Benjamin.. Parker Eliphelet.. Pirkins Phinehas ju^r.. ..Reed Benjamin.. Roberts Seth.. Remmington Elihu.. Simons Paul..	44
..Sandors Ephraim.. Selby William.. Warner Aaron.. Worter Abner.. William Williams.. Couch Timothy.. Joel Ackley.. Joel miner.. Benjamin Giddings.. Ebenezer Hall.. Shipman Fradrick.. Phelps Samuel ju^r.. Zachariah Pratt.. Golard Abel..	44
.. Hezekiah Adkins.. Jabez Adkins.. Titus Allen.. Titus Allin ju^r.. Cephas Beech.. Thomas Beach.. Martin Bushnell.. Capt Ael Brace.. Daniel Bushnel.. Samuel Beech.. Rubin Burnham.. Phinehas Bates.. Jededaz Bushnell.. Joseph Brace.. Bennoni Beech.. Stephen Bushnell.. Samuel ~~Bushnell~~ Borden.. Samuel ~~Bushnell~~ Banning ju^r.. Ezekiel Beech.. John	45

Hartland

Bates.. Oliver Bates..

.. Jonathan Cough.. David Couch.. Samuel Crosby.. Simeon Crosby.. John Cowls.. Jacob Coudry.. Obed Crosby.. Daniel Dreggs.. Daniel Ensign.. Leiu^t Eleazer Ensign.. Elkanah Fox.. Jeams Foster..Ephraim Fox.. Joseph Gilbert.. David Gilbert.. James Hungerford.. Uriah Hide.. Jabez Harger.. Rubin Hale.. 45

.. Cornelus Merry.. Josiah Meeker.. Samuel Miller.. Samuel Miller ju^r.. Francis Porter.. Isaac Penfield.. Elishama Porter.. John Porter.. Thomas Rube.. Joel Robenson.. Eldad Shephard.. Daniel Suard.. Remembrance Sheldin.. Dr Asa Smith.. Thomas Sill.. [ ] Stephens.. Prince Taylor.. Prince Taylor ju^r.. Samuel Tiffany.. Consider Tiffany.. John Treet.. Timothy Tiffany.. Jonas Wilder.. Joseph Wilder.. John Wilder.. Gamaliel Wilder.. Israel Williams.. Ephraim Wilder.. Elijah Wilder.. Leu^t Theodore Woodbrige.. Jonth Wilder.. *[ed: signed by]* John Borden.. Alexander Bushnel { Listers for the Year 1775 45

Capt Abel Brace & Leiu^t E Ensigns Were In the Levy 29=10-0 more then their Lists and I took It out of the Levy by order of a Lister P^r me Phin^{as} Kingsbery Reg^r 45
22 Apr 1776

Att a Town meeting Legally Worned and Holden att the Dwelling House of Mr Daniel Ensigns 45

Chose Leiu^t Thomas Beman Moderator 45

Voted to Seat the Meetinghouse again Voted to Dignify the Pews In the Meetinghouse A Com^{ee} Chosen to Dignify the Pews and Seet the Meetinghouse as followeth (Viz) Neh^m Andrews Esqr Capt Abel Brace.. Mr John Borden 45

Voted to Releas Noah Chappel In his Rate In the Grand Levy for the Year 1774 for that part that he was over Charged 45

Voted that Ensign Uriel Holms and Phinehas Kingsbery Go and take Advise In What methot the Town Should proceed.. to obtain a Land tax 45

Voted that the Town will Chuse a Com^{ee} to Sue all Debts of the Town and Recon With all the Select men... from the time of the Rever^d Mr Sterling Graves De^d to this time and.. give Discharges as they find they have paid.. a Com^{ee} Chosen for the above purpose (Viz) { Mr Wm Selby.. Mr Joseph Wilder.. Mr AlexanderBushnel 45
10 May 1776

Voted to apply to the Honble Assembly for a Land tax of three pence on the a[ ]re Voted that Phin^{as} Kingsbery Should be a Surveyer of highways Voted that Ensign Uriel Holmes Should be a Collector to Gather Said tax If it Please the Honble Assembly to Grant it 45
17 Sep 1776

a Town Meeting Legally Worned and holden att the Dwelling House of Mr Daniel Ensigns 46

Chose Neh^m Andrews Esqr Moderator 46

Chose Mr Joshua Giddings & Mr Eldad Shepherd Select men In addition to act With the other Select men the Remainder of this Year 46

Chose Mr Enos Lane Constable to Gather the Contry Rate 46

Chose Mr Jonathan Emons & Mr Daniel Kingsbery to Assist In Tuning the Psalm In Publick Worship 46
12 Dec 1776

Att a Town Meeting.. holden att the Dwelling House of Mr Daniel Ensigns.. then Was Mr Joshua Giddings Chosen Moderator 46

Phinehas Kingsbery Chosen Town Clark 46

Voted to Chuse the Select men by Nomination.. Phinehas Kingsbery Refused to Serve as Select man then Was D^n Thos Giddings Chosen	46
Neh^m Andrews Esqr Was Chosen Town Treasury	46
Phinehas Kingsbery.. Leiu^{nt} Eleaz^r Ensign.. Alexander Bushnel.. Capt Abel Brace.. Mr Joshua Giddings..D$^{[ ]}$ Thos Giddings { Select Men	46
Voted that Mr Israel Williams Should be the first Constable to Gather the Contry Rate.. and Mr Enos Lane to be the 2nd Constable	46
Mr Isaac Penfield.. Mr Ebenez^r Hall.. Mr Eldad Shepherd.. Mr Wm Selby { Grand Jurors	46
Mr Thos Beman ju^r.. Mr John Treet { Collectors of rates	46
Mr Israel Williams.. Mr Nath^{ll} Butler.. Mr Sam^{ll} Miller ju^r.. Mr Joel Meacham.. Mr Micha Scovel.. D^n Thos Giddings.. Mr Alex^r Bushnel.. Mr Joseph Wilder.. Mr Cornelius Merry { Surveyors of Highways	46
Mr Urial Hide.. Mr Wm Selby.. Mr John Borden.. Mr Asher Benamin.. Mr Ely Andrews { Listers	46
Mr Joel Miner.. Mr Sam^{ll} Andrew.. Mr Joel Robinson.. Mr Phin^{as} Bates { Fence Vewers	46
Mr Jonathan Emons.. Mr Elishama Porter.. Mr Rubin Burnham.. Mr Wm Chapman.. Mr Ephraim Wilder { Tythingmen	46
Mr Thos B[ ] { Leather Sealer	46
Mr Joel miner.. Mr Uriah Hide { Branders of Horses	46
Mr Ely Andrews.. Mr Prince Taylor { Kee Keepers	46
Chose Mr Charles Phelps Saxton	46
Mr John Borden.. Mr Benjamin Reed.. Mr Israel Williams.. Mr Joel Meacham.. Mr Consider Tiffany.. Mr Saml Borden.. Mr John Bates.. Mr Isaac Penfield { School Com^{ee}	46
Voted that Mr Benjamin Reed Should Be a Collector to Collect a School Rate.. in the North East Corner of the Town Where the S^d Reed Lives.. and Lay out the Money in the Districts for Schoolling	46
Voted to Releas Mr Israel Williams from Being School Com^e	46
Capt Abel Brace Chosen School Com^{ee} In the Room of Mr Israel Williams	46
Voted to Chuse a Com^{ee} to Divide Distrects.. on the West Side of the River (Viz) D^n Thos Giddings Mr Alex^r Bushnel Mr Joshua Giddings	46
Voted that Liu^t Eleaz^r Ensign Should Be tax Gatherer In the Room of Lieu^t Uriel Holms	46
Voted that Leiu^t Thos Beman & Israel Williams Should Secure the Bridge this Winter and have pay out of the tax	46
21 Mar 1777	
a Town Meeting Legally Worned and holden att the Dwelling House of Mr Daniel Ensigns	46
Voted that Dec^n Thos Giddings Should be moderator	46
31 Dec 1776	
[illegible] of the West Mountain Since October.. Miller Samuel.. Miller Samuel Ju^r.. Borden Samuel.. Woodbridge Theodore.. Daniel Adkins.. Foster James.. Cephas Beech	47
The grand Levy for the West Mountain of the Tiown of Hartland for the year 1776.. [*ed: signed by*] Jeremiah Emmons.. Thomas Bemas Ju^r.. Phinehas Kingsbery { Listers	47
[*Grand Levy list for the West Mountain*] Andrews [ ] Esqr.. Ackley Joel.. Andrews Samuel.. Andrews Nehemiah Ju^r.. Andrews Ely.. Adams Daniel.. Bille Jonathan.. Benjamin Samuel.. Butler Jonathan.. Bush Aaron.. Beman Thomas Lis^t.. Beman Thomas Ju^r.. Butler Nathaniel..	47

Hartland

Burnham Isaac.. Bushnell Alexander..

Daniel John.. Ensign Caroline Widow.. Emons Jonathan.. Emons Jeremiah Do^r.. [ ]ns Thomas Decon.. [*Gid*]dings David.. [*G*]iddings Thomas Ju^r.. [*G*]iddings Dan.. [*G*]iddeon Joshua.. [*G*]iddeons Benjamin.. [*G*]iddings Joshua Ju^r.. ..Holm Uriel Lieu^t.. [*Hit*]chcock Oliver.. [ ]hine Benjamin Capt.. [*H*]all Ebenezer.. Hayes Seth.. Kingsbery Phinehas Dec^n.. Kingsbery Daniel.. Kellogg Ezekiel.. Lane Enos.. *M*]oses Abel Ju^r.. Meecham Joel.. Mack Sarah Widow.. Meecham Isaac.. Charles Phelps.. Praat Zachariah.. Parker Eliphalet.. Parker Benjamin.. Phelps Samuel Ju^r.. Phelps Joab.. Roberts Jonathan.. Roberts Seth.. Remmenton Elihu.. Reed Benjamin.. ..Scovil Micha.. Selby William.. Spencer Thomas..Williams William.. Borden John.. Borden Asahel.. Moses Abel.. Hodgkins John.. Frazier Daniel.. Daniels peletiah.. Phelps Samuel.. Pirkins Phinehas.. Pirkins Eliphaz.. Pirkins Phinehas Ju^r.. Pirkins Gideon   47

[ ]ick Ebenezer.. Jones Thomas.. Miner Joab.. Baning Abner.. Baning David.. Chapman William.. Branerd Asahel.. Colten Eleazer.. Cowdry Moses.. Church Uriah Lieu^t.. Gates Jesse.. Bills Benajah.. Chappel Noah.. Cadwell Moses.. Waters Abner.. Jones John.. Warner Aaron.. Simon Paul.. Waters Lydia.. Clark Thomas.. Clark George.. Spencer.. S[ ] Caleb.. Dimmick Ebenezer.. Spencer Caleb.. Borden John.. The Grand Levy of the East Mountain.. for the year 1776.. Tes^t Jeremiah Emmons.. Thomas Beman Ju^r.. Phinehas Kingsbery { Listers   48

[*ed: Grand Levy list for the East Mountain district*] [*A*]dkins Hezekiah.. Atkins Jabez.. Allen Titus Ju^r.. Allin Nathaniel.. Brace Abel Capt.. Bates John.. Bushnell Stephen.. .. Bates Phinehas.. Bush Ezekiel.. Baning Samuel Ju^r.. Bush Benoni.. Bates Oliver Lieu^t.. Beech Thomas.. Bushnell Daniel.. Benjamin Asher.. Brace Joseph.. [B]ates James.. [Be]nham Reuben.. [Bu]shnell Martin.. [C]rosby Simeon.. Crosby Samuel.. Couch David.. Caudry Jacob.. Driggs Daniel.. Ensign Daniel.. Ensign Eleazer Lieu^t.. Fox David Ju^r.. Fox David.. Fox Harrie.. Fox Ephraim.. Fox Nathan.. Gilbert Joseph.. Gilbert David.. Jedediah Bushnell.. P[ ] Rubin.. [ ] Uriah.. Hungerford James.. Herger Jabish.. Meeker Josiah.. Merry Cornelius.. Munroe Dan.. Penfield Isaac.. Porter Elishama.. Porter John.. Robenson Joel.. Kirby Thomas.. Suerd Daniel.. Shepherd Eldad.. Smith Asa D^r..Sill Thomas Lieu^t.. Treet John.. Tiffany Samuel.. Taylor Prince Ju^r.. Taylor Prince.. Taylor Job.. Wilder Jonas.. Wilder Joseph.. .. Wilder John.. Wilder Gamaliel.. Wilder Ephraim.. Wilder Jonathan.. Williams Israel.. Woodbridge Theodore Capt.. Beech Samuel.. Couch Jonathan.. Tiffany Consider.. Test Phin^{a}s Kingsbery Reg^r 48

7 Apr 1777

an Adjourned Meeting.. Held att the Dwelling House of Mr Daniel Ensigns   49

Voted to Chuse a man to Go to his Ho^n the Governor & Com^{ee} of Safety.. Respecting men that are Ordered to be Drafted or Detached to for the Supply of the army Voted that Capt Benjamin Hutchens Should Be the man   49

Voted that Mr Stephen Bushnel Should have Liberty to Set up a Grist Mill   49

Voted to Chuse a Com^{ee} to See what is Due to the Revnd Mr Aaron Church for Preaching Since he has Been In Town Before & Since his Ordination and Setle with the Treasuryes and Collectors of Rates.. Chose John Borden Israel Williams & Phienhas Kingsbery   49

14 Apr 1777

an Adjoun^d Meeting.. Held by Adjurment att the house of Mr Daniels Ensigns   49

Voted to Chuse a Com^{ee} of Safty.. Chose Neh^m Andrews Esqr.. Capt Thos Gidding.. Dr Asa Smith.. Capt Abel Brace.. Mr John Borden.. Mr Samuel Benjamin.. Mr Samuel Borden.. Mr Phinehas Bates.. Capt Benjn Hutchens   49

Hartland

Voted to Chuse a Com^{ee} to Lease out that Land that Leu^t David Day Decs^d Gave… for the Suppord of the Gospel Ministry.. Voted & Chouse Neh^m Andrews Esqr.. Leiu^t Oliver Bates.. Leiu^t Joseph Wilder.. Mr Alex^r Bushnel.. Leiu^t Uriel Holms { Com^{ee}	49
Chose Mr Hez^{ah} Adkins Surveyor of highways	49
Chose Capt Thomas Giddings & Phinehas Kingsbery to Make a tax bill to mend high Ways &c	49
Leiu^t Oliver Bates Chosen a Com^{ee} With others.. to finsh the Bridge In the Hollow	49

10 Sep 1777

Meeting.. Holden att the Dwelling House of Mr Daniel Ensigns	49
Voted that Capt Benjamin Hutchens Should be moderator	49
Voted to Give the Revnd Mr Aaron Church Sixty Seven pounds ten Shilling.. for his Salary for the Year past	49
Voted to Chuse a Com^{ee} Consult With Mr Church with to his Sallary.. & Chose.. Capt Benjn Hutchens.. Phinehas Kingsbery.. Capt Thos Giddings.. Capt Abel Brace.. Mr Rubin Burnham.. Leiu^t Eleazer Ensign.. Mr Joshua Gidding.. Leiu^t Thos Beman..Neh^m Andrews Esqr.. Mr Eldad Shepherd.. Leiu^t Uriel Holmes	49
Chose a Com^{ee} to Lay out & Exchange highways West of the River or west Mountain.. (Viz) Leiu^t Oliver Bates.. Mr Abraham Bishop.. Mr John Wilder	49
Voted to Sell or Lease out the Personage Land on the west Mountain if the Inhabitants of S^d Mountain think Best to Lease out S^d Land.. Viz / Capt Abel Brace.. Leu^t Eleazer Ensign.. Mr John Wilder	49
Voted that Ephraim Wilder Should Be Surveyor of Highways	49

1 Dec 1777

a Town Meeting Meeting.. Holden att the Dwelling House of Mr Daniel Ensign	49
Chose Neh^m Andrews Esqr Moderator	49
Phin^{as} Kingsbery Was chosen Town Clarke	49
Capt Benjamin Hutchens.. Dc^{tr} Asa Smith.. Leiu^t Uriel Holms { Select men	49
Ensign Daniel Kingsbery.. Mr John Treet Constabels	49
Phin^{as} Kingsbery Town Treasury	49
Dct^r Jeremiah Emons.. Mr Daniel Dreegs { Grandjurors	49
[ ] [C]hurch [ ].. Brainard.. [ ] [ ]ley.. M^r [ ] Shepherd.. M^r A[br]aham Bishop.. Mr James Markham.. Mr Cornelius Merry.. Mr Samuel Benjamin.. Mr Isaac Penfield.. Mr Thos Ruby { Surveyors of Highways	50
Mr Joel Miner.. Mr Sam^{ll} Andrews.. Mr Aaron Bates.. Mr Mirten Bushnel.. { Fence Vewers	50
Mr Elihu Remonton.. Mr Eldad Shepherd { Leather Sealers	50
Mr Aaron Bush.. Mr Joel Ackley.. Mr Rubin Hale.. Mr Phin^{as} Bates { Tything men	50
Mr Joel Meachan Packer	50
Mr Joel Miner.. Mr Uriah Hide { Branders of Horses	50
Mr Samuel Benjamin Sealer of Weights & measures	50
Mr Joel Miner.. Mr Saml Crosby.. Mr Elishama Porter { Kee keepers	50
Mr Isaac Burnhan.. Mr Rubin Burnham.. Mr Saml Miller ju^r { Listers	50

Hartland

Mr Joel Robenson and Mr Ely Andrews Collectors of Rates	50
Mr Joel Ackley.. Mr Joel Meacham.. M^r [R]ubin Burnham.. M^r [M]oses Coudry.. Mr Abraham Bishop.. Leiu^t Oliver Bates / School Com^{ee} and Colectors	50
Voted to Divide the Town Salt that is att Neh^m Andrews Esqr House	50

26 Jan 1778

[*Town Meeting held*] att the Dwelling House of Mr Daniel Ensign	50
Chose Leiu^t Uriel Holms Moderator	50
Leiu^t Thos Beman.. Ensign Israel Williams.. Mr Alexander Bushnel { Com^{ee} to Provid for the Families of the Soldiers	50
Voted to Chuse a Com^{ee} to provid Tents (Viz) Mr Samuel Bordin.. Leiu^t Uriel Holms.. Mr Eldad Shepherd.. Leiu^t Uriel Church.. Mr Alex^r Bushnel.. Mr John Bates	50
Voted to Except the doings of the Select men In Laying out a Highway from the meetinghouse on the west mountain to Samuel Bordin Dwelling house Where he Now Lives	50
Voted to Chuse a Com^{ee} to Divid preaching (Viz) Leiu^t Uriel Holms.. Ensign Israel Williams	50
Voted.. To abate Remembrance Sheldin Decs^d and Rubin Hadlock Rates the one on Ensign Israel Williams Rate Bill and the other on Mr Eldad Shepherds Rate Bill	50

22 Aug 1777

The Names of those that have taken the oath of Fidelity & freemans oath In the Year 1777.. The oath of Fidelity Administered.. Nehemiah Andrews Esqr..	51

4 Sep 1777

..Oath of Fidelity Was Administered.. Phinehas Kingsbery.. Daniel Kingsbery..	51

8 Sep 1777

..the oath of Fidelity was Administered.. Enos Lane & Saml Andrews	51

16 Sep 1777

The Oath of Fidelity Administred to Cap Benjamin Hutchens.. Mr Joshua Giddings.. Capt Giddings.. Leun^t Thos Beman.. Leu^{nt} Uriel Holms.. Ensign Samuel Baning.. Leiu^t Eleazer Ensign.. Dc^{tr} Asa Smith..Thos Beman ju^r.. Uriah Hide.. Oliver Hitchcock.. Eldad Shephard.. Capt Abel Brace.. Leiu^t Oliver Bates.. Jedediah Bushnel.. Ely Andrews.. Rubin Hale.. James Hungerford.. Samuel Borden.. John Treet.. Samuel Sutlief.. Phinehas Bates.. Aaron Bates.. Cornelius Merry.. Ephraim Wilder.. Abraham Bishop.. Elishama Porter.. Daniel Ensign	51
Fremens Oath Administred In open freemens Meeting.. Nehm Andrews Esqr	51

25 Jan 1780

Ephram Tiffany has Taken the Oath of Fidelity	51

Sep 1783

the Freemans Oath was Administred to Childs Taylor & Samuel Benjamins	51

16 Sep 1777

Oath of Fidility.. Mr Miner & all under have not taken the Freemens Oath.. James Markham.. Alexander Bushnell.. Ephraim Wright.. Joel Robinson.. Aaron Bush.. Rubin Burnham.. John Bates.. Ezekiel Kellogg.. John Borden.. Samuel Andrews.. Joel Miner.. Jacob Coudry.. Thos Spencer.. Neh^m Andrews ju^r.. Martin Bushnel.. Abner Bushnel..	51
.. Doct^r Jeremiah Emmons.. Phinehas Pirkins.. Joel Meacham.. Samuel Miller Ju^r.. William Chapman.. Gamaliel Wilder.. Phinehas Coe.. Phinehas Kingsbery J^r.. Samuel Phelps Ju^r.. Noah Chappel.. Asahel Brainerd.. Thomas Reuby.. David Gilbert.. Joel Ackley.. Ezekiel	51

Hartland

Bush.. Lieu^t Uriah Church

Fremans Oath.. Moses Cowdry.. Daniel Driggs.. Titus Allen.. Phinehas Pirkins.. Jonathan Bill.. Epafras Gilman.. Daniel Suyuard.. Nathl Butlor.. Jonathan Robards   51

15 Sep 1778

Fremans Oath.. Nathl Butlor.. Jonathan Robards   51

14 Oct 1778

Mr Consider Tiffany By way of afformation had the oath of Fidelity administred to him Before Asel Hocomb Esqr   51

the oath of fidelity.. Daniel Fraisor.. Daniel Beeman.. George Treet.. Samuel Crosby.. Nathn^l Allyn.. Abither Nuton.. Samuel Benjamens.. Nathan Hatch   51

[ ] Dec 1778

the oath of fidelity.. was administred to Mr Samuel Phelps   51

27 Nov 1778

Dan Gidding Took the Oath of Fidelity   51

[ ] Apr 1779

Eliphas Pirkins has this Day Taken the Oath of Fidelity   51

[Dec] 1777

The grand Levy for the East Mountain.. 1777.. Andrews Nehemiah.. Andrews Nehem^{ah} Ju^r.. Andrews Eli.. Andrews Sam^{ll}.. Ackly Joel.. Adams Daniel.. Benjamin Sam^{ll}.. Butler Nath^{ll}.. Borden Jno.. Borden Asael.. Bill Jothⁿ.. B[e]nham Isaac.. Beaman thomas.. Beaman Daniel.. Beaman tho^s Ju^r.. Brockway Edward.. Brainard Asael.. Baning Abner.. Bushnell Alexan^d.. Bush Aron.. Bill Banaijah.. Cowdry Moses.. Church Uriah.. Cotton Eleazer.. Chapman Willm.. Coe Elijah.. Clark thomas.. Couch timothy.. Chundly J[ ]^[ ].. Coe Phinehas.. Chapell Noah.. Daniels Peletiah.. Daniels Jno.. Emmons Jothⁿ.. Emmons Jeremiah.. Fraser Daniel.. Giddins Thomas.. Giddins Joshua.. Giddins Dan.. Giddins thomas Ju^r.. Gates Jesse..   52

.. Hayes Seth.. Hull Phebe.. Hitchcock Oliver.. Hatch Nathan.. Hodgkin Jno.. Holmes Uriel.. Hutchens Ben^m.. Harger Jobish.. Jones Jno.. Jones thomas.. Kingsbury Daniel.. Kingsbury Phinehas.. Kingsbury Phinehas Ju^r.. Kellogg Ezekiel.. Lane Enos.. Meacham Joel.. Meacham Isaac.. Minor Joel.. Ma[ ]ly timothy.. Mack Zebulon.. Moses Abel Ju^r.. Morin Abel.. Perkins Phinenhas.. Perkins Phinehas Ju^r.. Perkins Eliphas.. Perkins Gidion.. Parker Benjamin.. Parker Eliphalet.. Phelps Sam^{ll}.. Phelps Charles.. Phelps Sam^{ll} Ju^r.. Phelps Joab.. Zaciheviah Pratt.. ..Roberts Jothⁿ.. Roberts Seth.. Remington Elihu.. Selby William.. Scovil Micah.. Sawer Jacob.. Spencer thomas.. Shipman Jothan.. Waters Abner.. Williams Williams.. Wright Ephraim.. Wa[ ] Aron   52

[*Grand Levy*] for the West Mountain.. Alin Nath^{ll}.. Adkins Hezekiah.. Alin Titus.. Alin Titus Ju^r.. Bates Oliver.. Bates Phinehas.. Bates Jno.. Bates Aron.. Borden Sam^{ll}.. Brace Abel.. Beach Sam^{ll}.. Beach Benoni.. Beach Cephas.. Beach thomas.. Beach Ezekiel.. Burnham Reuben.. Bushnell Stephen.. Bushnell Daniel.. Bushnell Abner.. Bushnell Jede^{ah}.. Bushnell Murtin.. Bishop Abraham.. Baning Samuel.. Burington Eb[ ].. Benjamins Elizabth..   53

.. Couch Jothaⁿ.. Couch David.. Crosby Simeon.. Crosby Sam^{ll}.. Coudry Jacob.. Drigs Daniel.. Ensign Daniel.. Ensign Eleazer.. Fox David.. Fox David Ju^r.. Fox Ephraim.. Gilbert David.. Gilburt Eunice.. Gilman Eph^m.. Hyde Uriah.. Hail Reubin.. Huyes Jno.. Hayes titus.. Hungerford James.. Mathew Reubin.. Marcham James.. Murry Cornelius.. Miller Sam^{ll}.. Miller Sam^{ll} Ju^r.. Porter Elishama.. Penfield Isaac.. Ruby thomas.. Robinson Joel.. Smith   53

Hartland

Asa.. Sutlief Sam^{ll}.. Sill thomas.. Shepard Eldad.. Seward Daniel.. Taylor Prince.. Taylor Childs.. Treet Jno.. Tifany Consider.. Tiffany Sam^{ll}.. Williams Jeavail.. Wilder James.. Wilder Jno.. Wilder Gamaliel.. Wilder Ephraim.. Wilder Joth^n.. Atested by Uriah Hyde.. Ely Andrews { Listers
24 Mar 1778

a Meeting Legally Worned [and] Holden.. Att the Dwellin[g *House*] of Mr Daniel Ensigns	54
Voted that Capt Benjamin Hutchens Should be Moderator	54
Phineas Kingsbery Being about to Remove out of Town Resigned [*from the O*]ffice of Town Clark and.. Town Treasury	54
Voted that Dec^n Jeremiah Should Be Town Treasury	54
[*Vo*]ted that Leu^t Eleazer Ensign Should Be Town Clark	54
Voted to Chuse a Committee to Recken.. what is Due to the Town.. Voted and Chose as Committee (Viz) Sergant Elez^r Bushnel.. Sergat John Borden.. Leu^t Eliazer Ensign	54
Voted that the Select men Should Draw an order on the Treasury [*w*]hat is Due from the Town to Leiu^t Uriel Holms	54
Names that Have Taken the oath of Fidelity (Viz) Benjamin Parker.. Wm Williams.. Jesse Gates.. Elehu Remington.. Isaac Burnham.. Josiah [ ] Adkins.. Abner Banning.. Chiles Taylor.. Prince Taylor ju^r.. Jacob Sawyer	54

13 Apr 1778

a Town Meeting held by Adjurnment.. att the Dwelling House of Mr Daniel Ensign	55
Neh^m Andrews Esqr and Capt Benjamin Hutchens and Lieu^t Thos Beeman and Eleaz^r Ensign and Mr Alexander Bushnell and Mr Israel Williams ~ ware Chosen a Committee to Settle with Dec^n Phinehas Kingbury ~ Conserning Som Money that he has which Belongs to this Townd [*sic*]	55
Voted that the Selectmen Should abate Mr Enos Lane Coletor what they think is Just of the Bad Rates on his Rate Bill	55
Voted that the South Destrect on the west Mountain Should have the School Rate that was voted in.. 1775 ~ and that Mr Jeams Markham Should be the Committee and Coletor for the Same	55
the Oath of Fidelity was administred.. To Misters Prince Taylor and William Selby and Bennoney Bush and Rufus Hall Titus Allyn Junr and Josiah Adkins	55
the freemans Oath was Administred.. To Misters Israel Williams.. and Prince Taylor and Phinehas Perkins and John Baits and Titus Allyn Junr and Joel Miner and Jesse Gaits and Daniel Drigs and Wm Selby and Elihu Remington and Wi^m Williams and Bennoney Beach and Rufus Hall and Simeon Crosbey and David Fox and Reuben Hayl	55

[ ] Apr 1779

the Gentlemen whose Naims are as follows Have this Day Taken the Freemans Oath viz Isaac Meecham.. ~~Eliphlet Parker~~.. Gideon Perkins.. Asael Borden.. Timothy Morley.. David Banning.. Zebulon Mack.. Samuel Phelps.. Moses Cowdrey.. Neh^m Andrews Junr.. Noah Chappel.. Elihu Hall.. David Gidding of Barkhamton.. Dan Gidding.. Daniel Fraisor.. Titus Hays	55

15 Sep 1778

a Meeting.. Holden att the Dwelling House of Mr Daniel Ensign	55
Colonel Benjn Hutchens Chosen Moderator	55
Voted to adjorn this Meeting to Mr John Bateses on weddings Day the 23^d Day of this Instant	55

414

Hartland

September

23 Sep 1778

an Adjornd Meeting Holden att the Dwelling House of Mr John Baitses	55

30 Sep 1778

Voted that Eleaz^r Ensign Should be the agent to Git a Memorial and Persent it to the General Assembley for a Committee to Devide this Tound	55
Voted.. that Daniel Humphrey Esqr of Simsbury and Coln^l Seth Smith Esqr of [N] Hartford and Colon^l Nathan^l Terrey Esqr of Endfield Should be a Committee to Devid this Tound into two Parishes	55
Voted to the Revernd Mr Aaron Church one Hundred and forty Pounds Salery the Presant Year	55

19 Nov 1778

a Meeting.. Legally warnd att the Dwelling House of Mr Daniel Ensign	56
Colonel Benj^a Hutchens Chosen Moderator	56
Mr John Wilder Chosen to go after a Committee to Make Parish Lines a ppointed by the Honorable General Assembly	56
Colonel Benjaⁿ Hutchens and ~ ~ Eleaz^r Ensign and Capt Urial Holms and John wileder and Capt Thos Gidding and Doctor Asa Smith and Neh^m Andrews Esqr and the Revrnd Mr Sam^{ll} Woodbridge and Lieu^t Thos Beeman and Abra^m Bishop and Samuel Benjamen and Eldad Shepard and Ensgⁿ Alexander Bushnell and Gamaliel Wilder ~ ~ were Chosen to wait on the Committee appointed by the.. General Assembley to Inform them of the Curcumstanses of this Town.. Capt Urial Holms and Mr Gamaliel Wileder ware Chosen to See that the Committee be Paid	56

[ ] Dec 1778

a Lawful Town Meeting.. Conveand att the Dwelling House of Mr Daniel Ensigns	56
voted.. that Neh^m Andrews Esqr Should be the Moderator	56
Voted.. that Eleaz^r Ensign Should be the Rigester	56
Voted.. that Colonel Benjaⁿ Hutchens and Capt Urial Holms and Lieu^t Thos Beeman and Ensign Israel Williams and Eleaz^r Ensign Should Be the Select Men	56
Voted.. that Doctor Jeremiah Emmons Should be the Townd Treasurer	56
Voted.. that Ensign Daniel Kingsbury and Ensign Israel Williams Should be Constables	56
Voted.. that Mr William Selby and Mr Samuel Sutliff Should be the Grandjurys	56
Voted that Mr John Borden and Mr Samuel Crosby and Mr Eli Andrews and Mr Cornelius Mury Should be the Tithing Men	56
Voted.. that Mr Samuel Benjamen and Mr Samuel Crosbey and Mr Edward Brockway and Mr Abner Banning and Mr Nathaniel Clark Junr and Lieut Uriah Church and Mr Isaac Burnham and Colo^l Benj Hutchens and Mr David Gilbert and Mr Reuben Hayl and Mr Aaron Baits and Mr Josiah Adkins and Mr Elisheme Porter and Mr Phinehas Coe and Mr Dan Gidding Should be Survayers of Heighways	56
Voted.. that Lieu^t Thos Beeman and Ensign Israel Williams and Capt Urial Holms and Lieu^t Urial Church and Ensign Alexander Bushnell and Mr John Baits and Eleaz^r Ensign should be the Listers	56
Voted.. that Mr Joel Miner and Mr Samuel Andrews and Mr Phnehas Baits and Mr Aaron Baits Should be the fence Vewers	56

Hartland

Voted.. Mr Elihu Rimington and Mr Eldad Shepard Should be Leather Sealors	56
Voted.. Mr Joel Mner and Mr Uriah Hide [s]hould be Branders of Horses	56
Voted.. Mr Dan Gidding and Mr Marten Bushnell Should be Colectors of Rates	56
Voted.. Mr Samuel Benjamen Should be Sealor of waits and Measurs	56
Voted.. Mr Joel Miner and Mr Samuel Crosbey and Mr Elisheme Porter Should be Keekeepers	56
Voted.. Mr Joel Mecham Should Gager and Packer of Meat	56
Voted.. Capt Urial Holms and Mr John Baits and Lieut Uriah Church and Ensign Israel williams Should be a Committee to take Care the families of those Men that have Inlisted in to the American Armey for three Years or Deuring the War	56

15 Feb 1779

a Lawful Townd [sic] Meeting.. Conveand att the Dwelling House of Mr Daniel Ensign	57
Colonel Benja^n Hutchens Chosen Moderator	57
Voted to Raise Money to Pay the Revrnd Mr Church untill this Townd was Devided into two Parishes ~ Mr Simeon Crosby and Capt Thos Gidding and Capt Urial Holms and Mr John Treete and and Doctor Jer^m Emmans Chosen a Committee to See what is Just to Give the Revrnd Mr Church	57
Mr John Borden & Capt Abel Bracc and Mr Wm Selby & Mr John Wileder } Chosen a Committee to Recken and Settle with the Treasurer and Colectors and Committees for Cloathing	57
Voted that Mr John Borden and Mr Reuben Burnham and Lieu^t Uriah Church and Mr John Treete Should Committee men to Provid Cloathing for the Solgers in the Contenential Armey	57

22 Feb 1779

Voted.. to Raise a Rate of four Pence Half peny on the Pound on the List of.. 1778 to Pay the Revrnd Mr Church for the three Last months Preaching while the Townd was one Society	57

[ ] 1779

Made Choise of Colonel Benja^n Hutchens to the Moderator	57
Made Choise of Capt Urial Holms to be Constable and Colector to Colect the Countery Rate	57
Con^l Benj^a Hutchens.. Mr William Selby.. Mr Jonathan Roberts.. Mr John Baits { were chosen Committee men to Settle with.. Benj^a Reede.. Titus Hays.. Cherls Phelps	57

16 Sep 1779

the Gentlemen whose Naims are as follows have this Day Taken the freemans Oath (Viz) the Revarnd Mr Saml Woodbridge Mr Prince Taylor Junr Mr Elijah Coe Mr Simeon Crosbey Mr John Wileder Mr Jacob Sawyer Mr Saml Banning Ju^r Mr Abner Bushnell Mr Saml Miller Junr	57

5 Nov 1779

Colon^l Benja^n Hutchens Chosen Moderator	57
Voted to Chuse a Committee to Settle with the Old Committees and Colectors.. the Committee Chosen Ware { Mr Wil^m Selbey.. Mr Jonathan Roberts.. Mr John Wileder.. Mr Abra^m Bishop.. Col^n Benja Hutchens	57

Hartland

6 Dec 1779

Lieu^t Oliver Baits was Chosen Moderator	58
Saml Andrews.. Phinehas Baits } Town Coletors	58
Joel Miner.. Saml Andrews.. Ephram wileder.. Uriah Hide } Fence Vewers	58
Jacob Sawyer Leather Sealor	58
Joel Meecham Packer of Meete	58
Saml Benjam^n Sealor of Measurs and weights	58
Joel Miner.. Saml Crusbey } Keekepers	58
Thos Beeman.. John Borden.. Samuel Sutliff.. Alexander Bushnell.. John Baits { Select Men	58
Eleazar Ensign Rigester	58
Doct Jeremiah Emmans Tresuer	58
Israel Williams and Capt Urial Holms { Constables	58
Enos Lane.. Abraham Bishop { Granjury Men	58
Thos Beman Junr.. Moses Cowdrey.. Prince Taylor Ju^r.. Epham Wileder } Tithing Men	58
William Selbey.. Elihu Hall.. Titus Hays.. Prince Taylor.. Doc^t Asa Smith } Listers	58
Isack Mecham.. Aaron Bush.. Benaj^h Bill.. William Chapman.. Danl Fraisor.. Aaron warner.. John Treette.. Phinehas Baits.. Joel Roberson.. Bennony Beach.. Saml Miller.. John Baits } Survarers of Heighways	58

20 Jun 1780

Made Choise of Lieu^t John Borden to be the Moderator	58
Voted.. to Chuse a Committee to Recken with the Selectmen & Committeese that have Handlied the Townds Money ~ the Committee Chosen are } Ensign Israel Williams.. Mr John Wileder.. Mr Wm Selbey.. Mr Isaac Burnham.. Mr Thos Beeman Junr	58

24 Nov 1780

a Meeting.. Convened at the Dwelling House of Mr Daniel Ensign	58
Lieu^t Thos Beeman Chosen Moderator	58
Voted that Capt Urial Holms Should be the Purcheser and Receiver of Provision and Colector of the Rate	58

4 Dec 1780

Capt Uriel Holmes Chosen Moderator	59
Capt Uriel Holmes Chosen Rigester	59
Capt Thomas Giddings Mr John Bates Capt Abel Brace Col^o Benjamen Hutchens Capt Uriel Holmes ware Chosen Selectmen	59
Mr William Selby Chosen Town Treasurer	59
Ens Israel Williams Chosen Constable and Collector to Colect the Countery Rates	59
Mr Elihu Hall Chosen Constable	59
Mr Benjaman Read Mr Isaac Burnham Mr Ruben Burnham Mr Cornelus Mury Chosen Granjury Men	59
Mr Titus Hays Mr William Selby Mr Prince Taylor J^r Mr Elihu Hall Doc^t Asa Smith Chosen Listers	59

Hartland

Mr Jonathan Emmons Mr Joel Meecham Mr Thomas Beeman Junr Mr Titus Hays Mr Samuel Crosby Mr Gamaliel Wilder Mr Joel Roberson Chosen Tithing men	59
Ens Alexander Bushnel Mr Enos Lane Mr Benjaman Read Mr Dani[el] Fraisor Mr Samuel Crosby Mr Ephrm Gilman Mr Nathan Hatch Mr Jedediah Bushnel Mr Aashel Borden Mr Josiah Adkins Mr Jonah [ ] Chosen Survaers of Highways	59
Mr Thomas Beeman Jr Mr Benjaman Gidding Mr Prince Taylor Mr Ephraim Wilder Chosen Fence Vewers	59
Mr Elihu Hall Mr ~~Prince~~ Phinehas Bates Chosen Colectors of Town Rates	59
Mr Jacob Sawyer Chosen Leather Sealor Mr Titus Hays Chosen Sealor of mea[t]	59
Mr Joel Mecham Mr John Treat ~~Packers of m~~ Chosen Packers of m[eat]	59
Mr Joel Miner Mr Samuel Crosby Mr Elishama Porter Chosen Ke[e] Keepers	59
Mr Joel Miner Brander and Recorder of Horses	59
Voted that the Votes that was Past the Last Town meeting held att The Dwelling House of Mr Daniel Ensigns Should be nul and Void	59
Mr Isaac Burnham Capt Uriel Holmes Mr John Treet Mr Eph[ ] Gelman Chosen a Committee and Rceivers of the meet and Flower.. collected for the Continental Army	59
Voted to Take up the matter About Running the Line between Granvell[ ] and this town o[r] the Coloney Line.. Mr Abraham Bishop Colo Benjaman Hutchens Mr Samuel Sutleff Mr John Bates Capt Uriel Holmes Chosen A Committee for the Purpose of Running the above menshened Line	59
Mr Eldad Shepard Chosen a Committee to Provide for the Soldiers Familyes	59

18 Dec 1780

Voted to Chuse A Committee to make A return to.. the Governor of the Number of the Soldiers that Belong to Said Town and if Sd Commi[ttee] find that there are men wanting to make up the whole Quoto.. then Sd Committee are Directed to proceed and hier Sd men that are wanting.. Colo Benjaman Hutchens Dor Jeremiah Emmons Ens Israel Will[ ] Lieut Uriah Church Capt Abel Brace Chosen A Towns Committee for the Purpus	59
Voted to Chuse A Committe to Devide the nonresidents Proprieters List between the Parishes Chosen William Selby Titus Hays Elihu Hall Asa Smith Prince Taylor Jr Decn Thomas Gidding A Committee for the Above purpus	59

[ ] Dec 1780

meeting.. Ajurned to the house of Mr Isaac Miller	59
Voted to make an addition to the Committee that was appointed to Make Returns to.. the Governor of the Soldiers in the Army and Chose Capt Uriel Holmes Isaac Burnham for a Commit[tee] for that purpus	59

8 Jan 1781

Chose of Nehemiah Andrews Esqr for there moderator	59
Voted to Adjourn.. to Capt Uriel Holmes Hou[se]	59
Voted to Chuse A Committee to Recken and Settle With all the Collectors and if they Refuse to Settle Said Committee hath full power To Bring them to A Just Settlement.. Isaac Burnham William Selby Thomas Beeman Jr Chosen	60
Voted to Raise A rate of three penc on the pound on the List that was Given in the year 1779 for purchising provition for this State Capt Uriel Holmes Mr Isaac Burnham Mr Titus Hays Mr John Brace Mr Epaprus Gilman Chosen A Committee to receive Said provition	60
Ens Israel Williams Chosen A Committee to purches Cloathing for our Soldiers.. in the	60

Hartland

Continental Army

9 Apr 1781

Capt Thomas Gidding Was Chosen moderator	60
Voted to Chuse a Committee.. Col^o Benjaman Hutchens Leu^t Alexander Bushnel Capt Abel Br[ace] Leu^t John Borden Es[ ] Elezer Ensign was Chosen a Commit[ee] for the parpus above mentioned [*ed: purpose/name of committee was not written*]	60
Voted to Chuse a Committe to go Litchfield to make returns of the men that we have in Continental Service to the County Committee.. Col^o Benj Hutchens Capt Abel Brace was Chosen for the Said purpos	60
Voted to give all the Soldiers that Capt Sill Listed that Count For the Coto of this towns Continental men ten pounds State m[*oney*] pr man	60
Voted to Chuse A Comitte man to agree with Capt Rockwell Conserning this men that Capt Sill inlisted.. Capt Uriel Holmes was Chosen for that porpus	60

25 Jun 1781

Col^o Benjaman Hutchens was Chosen moderator	60

28 Jun 1781

Vote that Benjaman Giddings Should be a Committee to hier Continental Soldiers	60
Voted to Comply with the Late resolve of the.. Assembly to raise four pence on the pound on the List 1780 in Silver money or in beaf.. Voted that Ens Joel Ackly Should be Colletor to Collect Said money or beaf Ephraim Wilder Chosen Collector for the same porpus	60

17 Sep 1781

Leiu^t John Borden Chosen moderator	60
Voted to Chuse an Agent or two to go to Hartford in october next and git a memorial.. to See if the Assembley would grant.. Sum Releas as to our buplic Taxes Capt Abel Brace and Lieu^t Isaac Burnham Chosen Agents	60

3 Dec 1781

Capt Thomas Giddings Chosen moderator	61
Uriel Holmes Chosen Town Clark	61
Mr Isaac Burnham Mr John Wilder.. Mr Uriah Church.. Elezer Ensign Esq.. Mr Thomas Beman J^r Chosen Selectmen	61
Mr Israel Williams Mr Elihu Hall.. Chosen Constables Mr Williams is To Collet the State Tax	61
Uriel Holmes Chosen Town Trasurer	61
Granjuary Was Chosen Mr Titus Hays.. Mr Isaac Mecham.. Mr Urial Hide	61
Chosen Listers.. Mr William Selby.. Mr Joel Miner.. Mr Elihu Hall.. Mr Prince Tailor J^r.. Mr Titus Hays.. Mr John Treat	61
Chosen tithingmen Mr Benjaman Giddings.. Mr Joel Mecham.. Mr Samuel Crosby.. Mr Ashel Branard.. Mr Nathan Hatch	61
Chosen Town Collectors Mr Elihu Hall.. Mr Chiles Tailer	61
Chosen Servairs of highway Joel Miner.. Eliphas Purkens.. Capt Alexander Bushnel.. Benjamen Giddings.. Phenihas Coe.. Hezekiah Adkins.. Uriah Hide.. Eldad Shepard.. John Wilder.. Aaron Bates.. Nehemiah Andrews J^r	61
Chosen pakers of meat Leu^t Joel Meacham.. Ephraim Wilder	61
Chosen receivers of the State provison - Joel Meacham.. Isaac Meacham.. Ephraim Wilder	61

Hartland

Chosen fence vewers Asa Andrewes.. Benjaman Gidding.. Ephraim Wilder.. Uriah Hide	61

19 Dec 1781

a town meeting.. at the Dweling house of Capt Oliver Bates	61
Nehemiah Andrewes Esq Chosen Moderator	61
Voted to Keep the Continental Army full Mr Edward Brockway Mr John Treat Mr Benjaman Gidding Mr Nathan Hatch Chosen A Committe for to hire all the men that this Town is Wanting in the Continental Army	61
Mr Titus Hays chosen a Committe to receive the flour that this Town is to put up for the use of this State	61

1 Mar 1782

a town meeting.. at the Dwelling house of Capt Oliver Bates	61
Eleazer Ensign Esq Chosen Moderator	61
Voted that they would.. rais three State men Uriel Holms Chosen a committee to hier Said men and to give his note as Town Treasurer Eleazer Ensign Esq Chosen Agent or to go To Litchfield to meet the State Committe	61

8 Apr 1782

Capt Thomas Giddings Chosen moderator	61
Voted that the Selectmen Should have a Wright to warn A town meeting in four days on any Suden acassion and Set three Warnings one at East meeting and one at the West meething House and one on Mr Nathan Hatches house	61

1 Jul 1782

Capt Thomas Gidding Chosen moderator	61
Voted to Chuse a committe to Recon With the old Colletors and all others that have Handled the Towns money Jeremiah Emmons William Selby Nathaniel Clark Uriah Hide Ruben Burnham Chosen a committe for the above purpus	61

17 Sep 1782

Capt Thomas Giddings Chosen moderator	61
David Banning and Ephraim Wilder Chosen Commite to provide Barrels for the Town	61

3 Feb 1783

Maj^r Urial Holms Chosen Moderator	62
Voted to adgorn this Meeting to the Dwelling of Mr Isaac Millers	62
Voted that Doct^r Emmons ~~Might~~ Liberty to Buld a House.. on the Highway West of Mr Aaron Bushes for to have the Small [Pox] in	62

7 Apr 1783

Lt Thos Beeman Chosen Moderator	62
Voted to Chuse a Committee to Enquier.. of Springfield and Suffield and Simsbury and Colebroock to See if it be Best to have a Publick Road through those Town and this Town ~ Voted that Maj^r Urial Holms and Mr John Wileder Should be the Committee	62

16 Sep 1783

Col^o Benamin Hutchens Chosen Moderator	62
Voted that Lieu^t Thos Beeman & Col^o Benjn Hutchens & Mr John Wileder Shall be the agents to Go to the Convention at Middletown	62

Hartland

Voted that Capt Thos Giddings and Capt Israel Williams Should be our agents to Present a   *62*
Memorial.. to the Honarable General Assembly for an abatement of our State Taxes

Harwinton

Town Records
Vol. 2
Pages 523, 534 – 535

Land Records
Vol. 3, Part 2
Pages 2 – 26

Located at the Town Clerk's Office

Harwinton

10 Apr 1775

Abijah Catlin Moderator	534
Voted that David Curtis be Collector & Treasurer of the School Money.. in the Place of Joseph Woodin who was Chosen a Treasurer & Collector of S^d Money in Decr 1774 but afterward wholy Refusing to Collect or pay out any of s^d Money	534
Voted that Ezeziel Scovil Asa Preston John Preston Thomas Philips John Barbur Aaron Bristol Aaron Bristol Ju^r Reuben Bristol Nathan Brunson Samuel Lambert James Olcott James Olcot Ju^r White Griswold Jhon [sic] Alford George Scott Reuben Scott Jabez Frisbee Benoni Olcott & Benjamin Barbur Shall be a District by themselves. S^d District to begin South Takeing in Ezekiel Scovil East by the highway that Runs North by Saml Phelpses	534

19 Sep 1775

John Willson Chosen Moderator	534
Voted to fence the Burying Lot with pine Boards.. Voted that Joseph Cook Jesse Woodruff & John Watkins be a Committee to See the above fence be made	534

[ ] Dec 1775

John Willson is Moderator	533
Nath^{ll} Bull is Town Clerk	533
Voted Ashbil Skinner Joseph Cook Reuben Barbur Cyprian Webster & Eli Willson be Select Men	533
Voted Eli Willson be the first Constable to geather the Countery Tax	533
Voted Uriah Hopkins be the Second Constable	533
Voted Joseph Heydon Ju^r & David Curtiss be Grand Juriors	533
Voted George Catlin be town Treasurer	533
Voted John Mathews Azariah Kellogg Gideon Peck Reuben Bristol Jacob Catlin Aaron Foot Jacob Hinsdell Joel Catlin Saml Bull William Heydon Elijah Heydon be a Committee to have the Ordering of Repairing highways	533
Voted Reuben Barthol^w & Elijah Bills be fence Viewers	533
Voted George Catlin Jacob Tyler Bennajah Heydon Abijah Catlin Ju^r & Amos Rosseter be Listers and Rate Makers	533
Voted Elijah Heydon & Ebenezer Sperry be Collectors of Rates	533
Voted Wm Cook be Leather Sealer	533
Voted Jacob Tyler & Stephen Preston be Tythingmen	533
Voted Azariah Kellogg be Brander of Horses	533
Voted Reuben Bartholomew be Sealer of Measures	533
Voted Andrew Bartholomew Ju^r be Key keeper	523
Voted Ashbil Skinner John Willson Abijah Catlin John Watkins Aaron Foot Elija Heydon Asahel Hodge Joel Catlin & Jacob Hinsdell be a Committee of Inspection	523
Voted ~~Joseph Cook~~ William Abernethy be a School Committee Collector & Treasurer & Joseph Cook & George Catlin be a School Committee	523
Voted Jacob Hinsdell be a School Committee Collector and Treasurer & Uriah Hopkins & Josiah Phelps be a School Committee	523
Voted Joel Catlin be a School Committee Man Collector & Treasurer & David Androus & David C[ ] be Committee men for Schooling	523

423

Harwinton

Voted Cyprian Webster be a School Committeeman Collector & Treasurer & Jacob Benton Medad Hall be Committeed Men for Schooling	523
Voted Hezekiah Rogers be a school Committee Collector & Treasurer & Aaron Foot & Benoni Hough be a School Committee	523
Voted that Benjn Butler be a School Committee Collector and Treasurer & Abraham Norton & Reuben Blakesly be a School Committee	523
Voted Thomas Judd be a School Committee Collector & Treasurer & Elijah Heydon & Alexander Alford be a School Committee	523
Voted Reuben Barbur be a School Committee Collector & Treasurer & Abner Willson & Gideon Peck be a School Committee	523
Voted Samuel Cook be a School Committee Collector & Treasurer & John Watkins & Asahel Hodge be a School Committee	523
Voted Reuben Bristol be a School Committee Collector & Treasurer & White Griswold & John Alford be a School Committee	523

13 Aug 1778

[*This ma*]y Certefy.. that this Day I Administered the Oath of Fidelity to [ ]on Allin - Test Phinehas Royce Justis of peace   2

14 Aug 1778

Abel Way personly appear^d and took the Oath of Fidelity Before me -- Daniel Catlin Just^s Peace   2

17 Aug 1778

Benoni Hough personly appear^d and took the Oath of Fidelity before me Daniel Catlin Justis peace   2

[ ] Aug 1778

Benjamin Graves Abraham Norton Stephen Graves and Joseph Gaylord.. Personly appear^d, and took [the] Oath of Fidelity Before me Daniel Catlin Justis Peace   2

[ ]

Isaac Beacher personly appear^d and took the Oath of Fidelity Before me Daniel Catlin Justis Peace   2

William Alford George Griswold John Preston and Sebe Thompson Took the Oath of Fidelity before me Daniel Catlin Justis peace   2

18 Aug 1778

The following persons whose Names are under Written have Taken the Freemans Oath before Daniel Catlin Justis peace - Mark Prindle John Preston Isaac Beecher Thomas Judd David Curtiss Medad Hall Sebe Thompson Eliphalet Alford Eliphalet Bristol Benjamin Butler Jesse Potter & Reuben Bristol   2

21 Sep 1779

[*The*] following persons whose Names are Under Written [*have*] Taken the freemans Oath and the Oath of Fidelity [*before me*] Daniel Catlin Esqr [ ]ge Loomis.. [ ] Catlin.. [ ]ge Griswold.. [ ]d Griswold.. [ ] Brace.. [ ] Willson.. [ ]hael Bull.. [ ] Alford.. the Revd Samuel Mills.. the Revd David Perry   2

The following persons have taken the oath of Fidelity and Freemans Oath - Jabez Frisbey.. J[ ] Meacham.. [ ]vens 2^d.. [ ] Bartholomew.. [ ] [ ]stle.. [ ] Hungerford.. Levi Castle.. John Kimball.. Daniel Sherman.. Benjn Judd.. Hez^h Hopkins.. Charles Bartholo^w .. Samuel Weston Ju^r.. Charles Prindle.. Abner Barbur.. Joshua Stephens.. Zeba Meach[ ]   2

The following persons whose Names are under Written Have taken the Oath of Fidelity and Freemans [*Oath*] April 15th 1778 - and at other times - Viz Deacon Daniel Phelps.. Deac^n 3

Harwinton

John Willson.. Esq[r] Daniel Catlin.. Lieu[t] W[m] Heydon..Cap[t] Joel Catlin..Azariah Kellogg.. W[m] Cook.. John Matthews.. Reuben Barbur.. Doct[r] W[m] Abernethy.. Cap[t] George Catlin.. Lieu[t] Joseph Cook.. Cap[t] Nath[ll] Copley.. Eli Dewey.. Jacob Benton.. Nathan Daviss Ju[r].. Andrew Bartho[w].. Hezekiah Bell.. Job Cook.. Jacob Hinsdale.. Asahel Hodge.. Christop[r] Johnson.. Ashbil Skinner Ju[r].. Lieu[t] Eli Willson.. John Barbur Ju[r].. Amos Webster.. Eben[r] Butler Ju[r].. W[m] Stone.. Lieu[t] Samuel Cook.. Simeon Catlin.. Jacob Barthol[w].. Ens[n] Nath[ll] Bull.. Joseph Haydon Ju[r].. Thomas Skinner.. Havilah Thompson.. Josiah Butler.. Samuel Bull.. Abraham Catlin.. Cap[t] Joel Gillet.. David Mansfield.. Doct[r] Isaac Cowles.. Ens[n] Abner Willson.. Stephen Preston.. Ens[n] Cyprian Webster.. Reuben Barthol[w].. Jonathan Catlin Ju[r].. Joseph Huntington.. Ezra Hinsdale.. Elizur Brace.. Uriah Hopkins.. Samuel Phelps.. Oliver Phelps.. John Daviss.. Jacob Tyler.. Isaac Butler.. Amos Rosseter..Ebenez[r] Sperry.. Moses Webster.. Abijah Catlin Ju[r].. Dan Catlin.. Justis Stedman.. Hezeki[h] Rogers.. Benoni Hough.. Jacob Catlin 2[d].. Solomon Peck.. Samuel Cook Ju[r].. Seth Meacham.. Thomas Moody.. Josiah Butler Ju[r].. Timothy Barbur.. Jonathan Cook Ju[r].. Joseph Woodin.. Benj[n] Griswold.. Sam[l] S. Butler.. Nehemiah Meacham
2 Aug 1778

At a Town Meeting.. The following person[s] took the Oath of Fid[elity] Before Dan[l] Catlin Just pea[ce].. Jonathan Cook.. John Frisbie.. James Olcott.. Joseph Woodin.. Jabez Gilbert.. Jonathan Tyler.. Asa Smith.. Joseph Scovil.. Benj[n] Barb[ ].. Eliphalet Alford.. Josiah Butler Ju[r].. Sam[l] Cook Ju[r].. Benj[n] Butler.. Jacob Catlin 2[d].. Tho[s] Bull.. Charles Webster.. Jacob Catlin.. Joel Castle.. Hez[h] Rogers.. Levi Austin.. Ezekiel Scovil.. Solomon Peck.. Elijah Bills.. Reuben Barbur Ju[r].. Aaron Bristol Ju[r].. Tho[s] Judd *17 Sep 1782*	3
Freemans Oath.. Daniel Catlin Ju[r].. Azariah Kellogg Ju[r].. Asa Phelps Ju[r].. John Willson Ju[r].. Oliver Loomis.. Joseph Holsted.. John Bull.. George Catlin.. L[ ] Catlin.. Joel [ ] *[ ] Dec 1776*	3
Voted Daniel Catling be Moderator	4
Voted Nath[ll] Bull be Town Clerk	4
Voted Uriah Hopkins Joel Catlin Samuel Cook Jacob Hinsdale & Elijah Heydon be Select Men	4
Voted Joseph Heydon Ju[r] be the first Constable and to Collect the Country Rate	4
Voted Andrew Bartholomew be Second Constable	4
Voted Thomas Skinner and Ezra Hinsdale be Grand Juriors	4
Voted Daniel Catlin Esq[r] Stephen Butler Stephen Preston Joel Catlin John Frisbie Gideon Peck Samuel Heydon and Aaron Foot - be Surveyors of Highways	4
Voted Jacob Tyler Abijah Catlin Ju[r] and Amos Rossetter be Listers & Rate Makers	4
Voted W[m] Stone and Joseph Huntington be Collectors of Rates	4
Voted W[m] Cook be Sealer of Leather	4
Voted Reuben Barthol[w] be Sealer of Measures	4
Voted Azariah Kellogg be Brander of Horses	4
Voted Andrew Bartholomew be key keeper	4
Voted Nathan Daviss and Jesse Woodruff & Oliver Phelps be Tything Men	4
Voted George Catlin be Town Treasurer	4

Harwinton

Voted Jesse Woodruff be Sealer of Wates	4
Voted Saml Phelps Azariah Kellogg & Jacob Bartholomew be fence Viewers	4
Voted to Raise a penny Rate for Schooling - [ ]ph Cook Jacob Catlin and Doct^r Wm Abernethy [*be a School*] Committee	4
[ ]riah Kellogg Saml Cravath and Nathan Davis be a [*Com*]mittee for [ ]	4
Voted Stephen Preston Josiah Phelps and Moses Willcoks be a School Committee	5
Voted Isaac Miner Amos Webster & Abel Gridley Be a School Committee	5
Voted Jonathan Tyler Joel Catlin and Ebenezer Johnson & Capt Cook be a School Committee	5
Voted Eli Dewey Eli Willson & John Frisbie be a School Committee	5
Voted Joseph Heydon Havilah Thompson & David Mansfield be a School Committee	5
Voted John Preston John Allin & Benjn Butler be a School Committee	5
Voted Reuben Bristol Aaron Bristol Ju^r & White Griswold be a School Committee	5

10 Mar 1777

Voted Capt John Willson be Moderator	5
Voted Wm Abernethy be Clerk of S^d meeting	5
Voted Samuel Meacham Cyprian Webster Samuel Bull Eli Wilson Josiah Phelps Wm Abernethy Reuben Barbur Nath^{ll} Copley John Willson Ashbil Skinner And Aaron Foot be a Committee of Inspection	5
Voted that Isaac Minor Wm Cook Wm Abernethy Abner Willson and Gideon Peck Be a Committee...to prevent persons from Spreading and Exposing People to the Small Pox	5

31 Mar 1777

Made Choice of Capt Joel Catlin Moderator	5
Voted Wm Heydon Daniel Catlin and John Willson be a Committee to see that the families of Each person Enlisting.. be provided for so that they do not suffer while s^d Soldiers are in the Service - S^d Families are to be provided for at their own Cost	5

7 Apr 1777

Daniel Catlin Moderator	6
Voted the Town Treasurer have it in his power to lend Job Cook £10-0-0 out of the Town Treasury and take S^d Cooks Note for S^d Money - That is to say when S^d Cooks fine is brought into S^d Treasury the fine laid on him for not going when Call^d to go in the Melitia In August 1776	6

[ ] Sep 1777

Daniel Catlin Moderator	6
Voted to chuse a Committee to hear the Grievencies of those persons Fined for Not going in the Melitia when call^d in August 1776 - Voted Joseph Cook Reuben Barbur Joel Catlin Uriah Hopkins David Mansfield William Heydon John Watkins Joel Gillet George Catlin Nathan Daviss Andrew Bartholomew & Cyprian Webster be a Committee as afore S^d	6

29 Sep 1777

Voted Deacon John Willson be Moderator	6

20 Oct 1777

Made Choice of Joel Catlin Moderator	6

Harwinton

Voted Samuel Bull Isaac Miner George Catlin Reuben Barbur Azariah Kellogg Ebenezer Sperry Joseph Heydon Ju^r & Josiah Butler be A Comittee to provide Shoes Stockings Shirts &c for our proportion for the Continential Army	6

[ ] Dec 1777

Voted Joel Catlin be Moderator	7
Voted Nath^{ll} Bull be Town Clerk	7
Voted George Catlin be Town Treasurer	7
Voted Joel Catlin Samuel Cook Joseph Cook George Catlin and Reuben Barbur be Select Men	7
Voted Abijah Catlin Ju^r be Constable to Collect Countery Rates	7
Voted Joseph Haydon Ju^r be Second Constable	7
Voted Stephen Butler & Azariah Kellogg be Grand Juriors	7
Voted Eli Willson Samuel Phelps David Mansfield Thos Skinner John Preston Elizur Brace Stephen Preston Isaac Miner Joseph Woodin Jonathan Tyler Benoni Hough Samuel Cook Ebenezer Butler & Havilah Thompson be Surveyors of Highways	7
Voted Josiah Phelps & Uriah Hopkins be fence Viewers	7
Voted Jacob Tyler Abijah Catlin Ju^r Amos Rosseter Allyn Haydon and Thomas Skinner be Listers and Rate Makers	7
Voted William Cook be Leather Sealer	7
Voted William Cook and Eli Willson be Tything Men	7
Voted Azariah Kellogg be Brander of Horses	7
Voted Reuben Bartholomew be Sealer of Measur^s	7
Voted Jacob Bartholomew be Key keeper	7
Voted Oliver Phelps and Charles Webster be Collectors of Rates	7
Voted Ashbil Skinner Wm Abernethy Samuel Meacham Elijah Heydon & John Watkins be a Committee of Inspectors	7
The following persons are School Committees & Collector for the Different Disricts the first Mentioned person in Each District is a Committee Man and Collecter - of the School Money - Voted Ezra Hinsdale Josiah Phelps and Stephen Preston Be a School Committee as afore S^d	7
..Stephen Butler George Catlin & Jesse Woodruff be a School Committee..	8
..Voted Cyprian Webster Samuel Bull & Amos Webster be a School Committee..	8
..Voted Ebenez^r Johnson Joseph Woodin & Jonath^n Tyler be a School Committ[ee]..	8
..Voted Hezekiah Rogers be a School Committee & Collector..	8
..Voted John Watkins Daniel Catlin & Saml Cook be a School Committee..	8
..Voted Thomas Skinner Abner Willson & Abner Perkins be a School Committ[ee]..	8
..Voted Elijah Heydon Havilah Thompson & Samuel Heydon be S:C..	8
..Voted Sebe Thompson Israel Merriman & John Preston be a School Comm[ittee]..	8
..Voted Reuben Bristol Luther Evens & Hezekiah Bell be a School Committee	8
Voted Samuel Cook and Ebenezer Butler have power and Liberty to Draw out of the Town Treasury Ten Pounds Each for the Service of their Sons in the Service in.. 1777	8

Harwinton

13 Apr 1778

Joel Catlin Moderator at an ajourn^d Town Meeting	8

20 Aug 1778

Voted Deacon John Willson be Moderator	8
Voted to Raise a Rate of Six pence on the pound to Defray Town Charges.. Voted Levi Austin and Josiah Butler be Collectors to geather S^d Rate	8
Vote Daniel Catlin Esqr and Deacon John Willson be a Committee to meet a Committee at Litchfield.. to Consult what new mode of Taxation will be proper	9

15 Sep 1778

Joel Catlin Moderator	9
Voted Deacon John Willson William Heydon Daniel Catlin Eli Duey Nathan Daviss Dan Catlin & Joel Catlin be a Committee.. to provide for the Families of those persons who are in the Continential Army	9

19 Mar 1778

Voted Deac^n John Willson Moderator George Catlin Clerk	9
Voted Josiah Butler Azariah Kellogg Joseph Heydon Ju^r Samuel Bull Reuben Barber William Abernethy Ebenezer Sperry Eli Willson & Joel Gillit be a Committee to provide Cloathing for the Continential Soldiers	9

[ ] Dec 1778

Voted Josiah Phelps Moderator	9
Voted Nath^{ll} Bull be Town Clerk	9
Voted Joseph Cook Ashbil Skinner Reuben Barbur Josiah Phelps and Ezra Hinsdale be Select Men	9
Voted Abijah Catlin be the first Constable to geather the Countery Tax	9
Voted Joseph Heydon Ju^r be Second Constable	9
Voted George Catlin Jacob Hinsdale Eli Willson Elijah Heydon and Josiah Butler be Listers and Rate makers	9
Voted Josiah Butler Samuel Phelps Stephen Preston Ebenezer Sperry John Frisbie Allyn Heydon Azariah Kellogg Jacob Catlin Eli Dewey Abel Gridley and Israel Merriman be Surveyors of Highways	10
Voted Isaac Miner Joseph Huntington be Grand Juriors	10
Voted Azariah Kellogg and Daniel Catlin be fence Viewers	10
Voted Azariah Kellogg be Brander of Horses	10
Voted William Cook be Sealer of Leather	10
Voted Solomon Peck and Amos Rosseter be Tything Men	10
Voted Reuben Bartholomew be Sealer of Measures	10
Voted Jesse Woodruff be Sealer of Wates	10
Voted Andrew Bartholomew be key keeper	10
Voted The following persons are School Committees and Collecters (Viz) the first Mentioned person in Each District is Committee and Collector the Other two are Committee Men - Voted Jesse Woodruff Ebenezer Butler and George Catlin be a School Committee..	10

Harwinton

..Voted Jacob Catlin the Second Moses Willcox and Uriah Hopkins be a School Committee..	10
..Voted Asa Smith Joseph Woodin and Jabez Gilbert be a School Committee..	10
..Voted Samuel Bull & Cyprian Webster be a School Committee..	10
..Voted Benoni Hought be a School Committee & Treasurer..	10
..Voted ~~Nathan Daviss~~ Samuel Phelps Nathan Daviss and Azariah Kellogg be a School Committee..	10
..Voted Allyn Heydon Benjamin Butler and Samuel Heydon be a School Committee..	10
..Voted Abner Willson John Frisbie and Reuben Barbur Ju^r be a School Committee	10
..Voted James Olcott Ju^r Aaron Bristol and Elijah Bill be a School Committee..	10
..Voted Eliphalet Bristol Israel Merriman and Sebe Thompson be a School Committee..	11
Voted Hezekiah Hopkins Levi Austin and Martha Yale have Liberty to Joine part of a District in Torringford and have their own School Money as long as they lay S^d Money out for Schooling	11
Voted Medad Hall and Daniel Willson be Collectors	11
Voted William Abernethy John Watkins and Cyprian Webster be a Committee of Inspection	11

12 Apr 1779

Capt Josiah Phelps Moderator	11
Voted that Jacob Tyler be not released from paying a Certain fine laid on him for not going with the Melita to New York when Call^d on in August 1776	11

4 May 1779

Voted Daniel Catlin Esqr be Moderator	11
Voted David Andruss be Surveyor of Highways	11

[ ] Aug 1779

Voted Josiah Phelps Be Moderator	12
Voted Jacob Tyler be Clerk of S^d Meeting	12
Voted to Raise a Rate of three Shillings on the pound to Defray present Town Charges and to purchase Cloathing for the Army.. Voted Charles Prindle and George Merrman be Collectors of S^d Rate	12
Voted that Capt Josiah Butler Lieu^t Eli Willson Joseph Heydon Ju^r And Doct^r William Abernethy be a Committee to procure and purchase Cloathing for the Army	12

21 Sep 1779

Capt Josiah Phelps Moderator	12
Voted Daniel Catlin Esqr Joel Catlin and Eli Duey be A Committee to provide for Soldiers Families	12
Voted Noah Loomis Ju^r and Oliver Loomis be freed from paying a Certain fine Inflickted on them for Not going to New York in.. 1776 provided they pay the Cost Arisen on S^d Fine	12

[ ] Dec 1779

made choice of Capt Josiah Phelps to be Moderator	13
Voted Ashbil Skinner Reuben Barbur Joseph Cook Ezra Hinsdale And William Abernethy be Select Men	13
Voted Nath^{ll} Bull be Town Clerk	13

Harwinton

Voted George Catlin be Town Treasurer	13
Voted ~~George~~ Thomas Skinner be first Constable	13
Voted Abijah Catlin be Second Constable	13
Voted Capt Josiah Butler Uriah Hopkins Joseph Heydon Ju^r Eli Willson And Abijah Catlin be Listers and Rate Makers	13
Voted William Cook Zadoc Johnson John Bristol Abner Willson John Preston Thomas Lankton Jonathan Tyler Charles Prindle Job Alford Samuel W. Baldwin and Abraham Norton be Surveyors of Highways	13
Voted Amos Webster & Elijah Heydon be Grand Juriors	13

28 Dec 1779

Josiah Phelps Moderator	13
Voted to Chuse two more Select Men.. Voted Jacob Catlin & Eli Willson be Select Men	13
Voted Benjamin Judd & Andrew Bartholomew be Tything Men	13
Voted William Cook be leather sealer	13
Voted Azariah Kellogg be Brander of Horses	13
Voted Reuben Bartholomew be Sealer of Measures	13
Voted Andrew Bartholomew be Key keeper	14
Voted Oliver Phelps Jesse Woodruff and Samuel Phelps Ju^r be fence Viewers	14
Voted Reuben Barbur Ju^r Abner Willson & John Frisbie School Committee	14
Voted Jonathan Catlin Ju^r John Bristol and John Watkins School Committee	14
Voted Reuben Bristol John Barbur Ju^r and Thos Judd a School Committee	14
Voted Alex^r Alford Exekiel Scovil & Havilah Thompson a School Committee	14
Voted Abel Bristol Eliphalet Bristol & Joel Castle a School Committee	14
Voted Medad Hall Joseph Cook & Jesse Woodruff a School Committee	14
Voted Ebenezer Sperry Jabez Gilbert & Joshua Stephens a School Committee	14
Voted Isaac Miner and Abel Gridley A School Committee	14
Voted Hezekiah Rogers Aaron Foot & Benoni Hough a School Committee	14
Voted Jacob Hinsdale Joel Gillet & Uriah Hopkins A School Committee.. The first mentioned persons in Each of the above Districts are Chosen Treasurer^s and Collecters for S^d Districts	14
Voted to Chuse a Committee to lay out a highway Near Saml Baldwins - Voted Joseph Cook John Watkins & Elijah Heydon be a Committee as Afore S^d	14

10 Apr 1780

Capt Josiah ~~Butler~~ Phelps Moderator	14
Voted George Griswold be Clerk of S^d Meeting	14
Voted Eli Willson Lieu^t Joseph Cook Messrs Uriah Hopkins Azariah Kellogg and Abijah Catlin be Inspectors of provisions	14
Voted Cyprian Webster Esqr Doct^r Wm Abernethy Lieu^t Joseph Cook and Mr Jacob Catlin be a Committee to Enquire and see if it be for the publick Benefit to have a highway laid out from the public highway that goes North & South by Mr Jacob Catlins to go by or near the	15

Harwinton

House of Hez^h Hopkins Mr Levi Austins &c

23 Jun 1780

Voted Deac^n John Willson be Moderator	15
Voted Abijah Catlin be Clerk pro tempore	15

19 Sep 1780

Voted Ashbil Skinner be Moderator	15
Voted to Raise a Rate of two pence on the pound to Defray town Charges to be paid in State Money - Voted John Daviss & Isaac Catlin be Collectors of S^d Rate	15

20 Nov 1780

Voted Deac^n John Willson be Moderator	16
Voted to Comply with the Requisition of the Assembly.. with regard to raising Provision for the Continental Army &c.. Voted Eli Willson and George Catlin is Appointed to Receive the provision	16
Voted Solomon Peck and John Frisbie be Collectors to Collect the above Rate of provision which is six pence on the pound	16

5 Dec 1780

Voted Capt John Watkins be Moderator	16
Voted Ashbil Skinner Reuben Barbur Joseph Cook William Abernethy Jacob Catlin Ezra Hinsdale and Eli Willson be Select Men	16
Voted Nath^{ll} Bull be Town Clerk	16
Voted George Catlin be Town Treasurer	16
Voted Elizur Brace be the first Constable & to Collect the Countery Rate	16
Voted Thomas Skinner be Second Constable	16
Voted Levi Austin & David Mansfield be Grand Juriors	16
Voted Oliver Phelps Ashbil Skinner Ju^r Reuben Bartholomew Joseph Heydon Ju^r Jonathan Catlin Ju^r Matthew Hungerford Jesse Woodruff Zadoc Johnson Jabez Gilbert Jonathan H: Coult Isaac Catlin and Abraham Norton be Surveyors of Highways	16
Voted Aaron Foot Josiah Butler Ju^r & Hezek^h Rogers be fence Viewers	16
Voted Jacob Tyler Josiah Butler Abijah Catlin Joseph Heydon Ju^r and Eli Willson be Listers & Rate Makers	16
Voted William Cook be Leather Sealer	17
Voted Hezekiah Hopkins Ashbil Skinner Ju^r & Allin Heydon be Tything Men	17
Voted Azariah Kellogg be Brander of Horses	17
Voted Jesse Woodruff be Sealer of Wates	17
Voted Reuben Bartholomew be Sealers of Measures	17
Voted Andrew Bartholomew be Key keeper	17
Voted the first Mentioned person in the following Districts is School Committee Collecter and Treasurer.. Voted Azariah Kellogg Josiah Butler & Joseph Huntington be a School Committee..	17
..Voted George Merriman Joseph Heydon Ju^r Ezekiel Schovil Havilah Thompson and Isaiah Loomis be A School Committee..	17

Harwinton

..Voted Matthew Hungerford John Preston & Israel Merriman be a School Committee..	17
..Voted Reuben Bristol Samuel Phelps and Cotton Marther be a School Committee..	17
..Voted Reuben Barbur Ju^r Eli Dewey and Abner Willson be a School Committee..	17
..Voted Jacob Catlin Jesse Woodruff & William Abernethy be a School Committee..	17
..Voted Josiah Phelps Jacob Hinsdale and Stephen Preston be a School Committee..	17
..Voted Amos Webster Jonathan Higley Coult And Abel Gridley be a School Committee..	17
..Voted Jonathan Tyler Ebenezer Sperry and Asa Smith be a School Committee..	17
..Voted Aaron Foot Benoni Hough and Hezekiah Rogers be a School Committee..	17

13 Dec 1780

Voted Thomas Skinner be Clerk of S^d Meeting	18
Voted to Chuse a Committee to hire Soldiers for the Continental Army..Voted George Catlin Abner Willson and Josiah Butler & Jesse Potter be a Committee as above	18
Voted a Rate of Six pence on the pound Hard Money for the above Use.. Voted Benjamin Griswold and Abijah Catlin be Collector of the above Money	18

16 Jan 1781

Voted William Abernethy be Moderator	18
Voted to Chuse a Committee to procure 4 Men to Guard the Sea Coast at Horse Neck one Year.. and.. to procure S^d 4 Men On As reasonable terms as may be.. Voted the following persons be a Committee.. to sit in Comfort with the Committee before Chosen to procure Men for the Continental Army.. Voted Abijah Catlin and Samuel Phelps be a Committee	19
Voted Joel Gillit be a Collector (in the room of Abijah Catlin who has Resigned) to Collect the one Shilling on the pound Granted to raise Soldiers	19

13 Feb 1781

Made Choice of George Catlin Moderator	19
Voted Abijah Catlin be Clerk of S^d Meeting, pro tempore	19
Voted A Rate of three pence on the Pound State Money to Raise Men to go to Horse Neck for the Defence of this State - Voted Benjamin Griswold and Joel Gillet Collect the Above Rate	19
Voted Eli Willson and George Catlin be purchasers of provisions for a Sixpenny Rate Before Granted	19

2 Apr 1781

Voted William Abernethy be Moderator	19
Voted Abijah Catlin be Clerk of S^d Meeting	19
Voted Abner Willson Cyprian Webster Josiah Butler Joel Gillet John Watkins Joseph Heydon Joseph Cook Joel Catlin Levi Austin & Samuel Phelps be A Committee to Class the Town	20
Voted Hezekiah Catlin be paid by the Town for his serving in the Continental Service as he was Agreed with for Calves &c	20
Voted an Addition of one Class more and one Committee Man More.. Voted Havilah Thompson be A Committee Man as Afore S^d	20
Voted there be but one Committee Man to Each Class - Voted the above S^d Committee Man Cast lots to know which Class Thomas Green shall fall to	20

Harwinton

Voted to Raise A Rate of two pence on the pound in Addition to the three pence on the pound.. Voted Joel Gillet be a Collector to Collect the five penny Rate 9 Apr 1781	20
Voted John Watkins be Moderator and Abijah Catlin Clerk	20
Voted Jacob Hinsdale Ju[r] be Collector to Collect the penny half penny Rate paid in provisions or three pence State Money 6 Jul 1781	20
Voted Deacon John Willson Moderator	20
Voted to Class into five Classes in Order to hire Soldiers.. Voted Eli Willson Samuel Phelps Cyprian Webster Josiah Phelps an[d] Tho[s] Judd be a Committee to Class the Town into five Classes.. [ed: and] Collectors for their Classes	21
Voted to Class into four Classes in the Town in Order to procure the Beef agreeable to a Requisition of Assembly in May 1781.. Voted Tho[s] Skinner William Abernethy Cap[t] Josiah Butler and Joseph Heydon be a Committee to Class the Town into four Classes 15 Aug 1781	21
Voted Ashbil be Moderator	21
Voted to Raise a Rate of four pence on the pound to procure Beef for the Continental Army.. Voted Joseph Haydon be Collector for his Class	21
Voted Levi Austin be Collector for Doct[r] Abernethy[s] Class	21
Voted Thomas Skinner be Collector for his Class	21
Voted Azariah Kellog be Collector for Cap[t] Josiah Butlers Class	21
Voted Ashbil Porter and Oliver Phelps provide for Soldiers Families	21
18 Sep 1781	
Cap[t] John Watkins Moderator	22
Voted to Rais a Rate of four pence on the pound to Defray Town [C]harges to be paid in hard Money or in produce.. [V]oted Oliver Phelps & Jeremiah Meacham be Collectors	22
[V]oted Eli Dewey and Christopher Johnson be A Committee to provide [for] Soldiers Families [ ] Dec 1781	22
Voted W[m] Abernethy Moderator	22
Voted Nath[ll] Bull Town Clerk	22
Voted Reuben Barbur Joseph Cook Mark Prindle Josiah Phelps [an]d Eli Willson be Select Men.. N.B. Josiah Phelps and Eli Willson were Chosen Select Men After This Meeting was Ajourn[d], on the Next Day	22
Voted to Rais a Rate of two farthings on the pound for the Benefit of Hezekiah Leech and Family	22
Voted Andrew Bartholomew be Collector of the above Happeny Rate	22
Voted Joseph Heydon be first Constable to Collect Countery Rate	22
Voted Elizur Brace Second Constable	22
Voted Sebe Thompson and Joel Gillit be Grand Juriors	22
Voted George Catlin be Town Treasurer	22
Voted Jacob Hinsdale W[m] Cook Jonathan H Coult W[m] Merriam Nathan Daviss Abner Barbur	22

Harwinton

Wm Alford Joseph Huntington Saml Phelps & Daniel Sherman be Surveyors of Highways	
Voted Andrew Miner and Samuel Phelps be fence Viewers	23
Voted Solomon Peck Thomas Skinner and Abijah Catlin be Listers & Rate Makers	23
Voted William Cook be Leather Sealer	23
Voted Azariah Kellogg Ju^r & Isaac Catlin be tything Men	23
Voted Azariah Kellogg be Brander of Horses	23
Voted Reuben Bartholomew be Sealer of Measurs	23
Voted Andrew Bartholomew be Key keeper	23
Voted to Raise a Rate of three pence on the pound for the benefit of Schooling.. N.B. the first Mentioned School Committee is also Collector & Treasurer.. Voted Nath^ll Copley and Elijah Heydon be a School Committee	23
Voted Joel Castle and John Preston be a School Committee	23
Voted Joseph Scovil and Reuben Barbur Ju^r be a School Committee	23
Voted Oliver Phelps and Joseph Huntington be a School Committee	23
Voted Samuel Phelps and Reuben Bristol be a School Committee	23
Voted Abijah Catlin and Wm Abernethy be a School Committee	23
Voted Benoni Hough be a School Committee	23
Voted Corbun Woodin and Jabez Gilbert be a School Committee	23
Voted Cyprian Webster and Jonath^n H H Coult be a School Committee	23
Voted Josiah Phelps and Ezra Hinsdale be a School Committee	23
Voted Elizur Brace Andrew Bartholomew and John Frisbie be a Committee to provide for Soldiers Families	23
Voted to Give all the Soldiers that went from this Town the Year 1780 ten Shillings p^r Month the time they were in Service.. Voted to Raise a Rate of one penny half penny on the pound.. to pay the Above S^d Soldiers.. Voted Ashbil Porter be Collector	23
27 May 1782	
Reuben Barbur Moderator	24
Voted to Raise a Rate of one halfpenny on the pound hard Money To pay the Dooming of one Man in the Continental Army of which we were Deficient.. Voted Daniel Catlin Ju^r and Nath^ll Brace be Collectors	24
17 Sep 1782	
Voted Wm Abernethy Moderator	24
7 Oct 1782	
Doct^r William Abernethy Moderator	24
24 Oct 1782	
Voted Cyprian Webster be Moderator	24
Voted William Abernethy be Clerk P T	24
Voted to Tax themselves two pence on the pound for the Use of the Town.. Voted Ashbil Porter be Collector	24

Harwinton

[ ] Dec 1782

Voted William Abernethy be Moderator	24
Voted Nathll Bull be Town Clerk	24
Voted Thomas Skinner Mark Prindle Eli Willson Abijah Catlin and Joseph Heydon be Select Men	24
Voted Nathll Bull be Town Treasurer	24
Voted Joseph Heydon be Constable and Collector of State Tax	24
Voted Elizur Brace be Second Constable	24
Voted Havilah Thompson and Moses Willcox be Grand Juriors for Town and County	24
Voted Solomon Peck Charles Prindle and Thomas Judd be Listers and Rate Makers	25
Voted Zadock Johnson James Brace Amos Webster Hezekiah Rogers Jonathan Tyler James Lankton Abner Willson Samuel Phelps Dan Catlin Timothy Barbur Levi Munson And Abner Barbur be Surveyors of Highway	25
Voted John Watkins Oliver Phelps and Azariah Kellogg be fence Viewers	25
Voted Grove Catlin and Daniel Catlin Ju^r be Collectors	25
Voted William Cook be Sealer of Leather	25
Voted James Brace and Jannah Griswold Ju^r be Tything Men	25
Voted Azariah Kellogg be Brander of Horses	25
Voted Christopher Johnson be Sealor of Wates	25
Voted Reuben Bartholomew be Sealer of Measurs	25
Voted Andrew Bartholomew be Key keeper	25
Voted A Rate of one Penny on the pound for the benefit of Schooling.. N.B. The first Mentioned Committee is Chosen Collecter & Treasurer.. Voted Elizur Brace and Abijah Catlin be School Committee	25
Voted Eli Willson and Eli Dewey be School Committee	25
Voted Jacob Bartholomew and John Bristol be School Committee	25
Voted Amos Webster and Michael Bull be School Committee	25
Voted William Merriam and David Curtiss be School Committee	25
Voted Elijah Heydon and Ezekiel Scovil be School Committee Collector & Treasurer	25
Voted Cotton Marther and Thomas Judd be School Committee	25
Voted Joel Castle and Thomas Hungerford be a School Committee	25
Voted Benoni Hough and Aaron Foot be School Committee	25

7 Apr 1783

William Abernethy Moderator	25
Voted to Give Gad Ely given ten pounds for his service in the United States	25
Voted to raise a Rate of one penny on the pound to Defray Town Charges.. Voted Joseph Heydon be Collector	25
Voted Daniel Catlin Ju^r Doct^r William Abernethy and Doct^r Isaac Cowles be manigers of a Lottery which the Town has petitioned for (if Granted)	25

Harwinton

1 Sep 1783

Deacon John Willson Moderator 26

Voted that George Catlin be Appointed to represent this Town at a Convention..at Middle Town.. to Consult.. on the Most prudent and Effectual Measures to prevent the Act of Commutation lately Granted by Congress in favour of the Officers of the Continental Line takeing Effect or any Other Greivencies Inconsistant with the Liberties of the free Citizens of America 26

16 Sep 1783

Joseph Heydon Moderator 26

Voted Capt Abner Willson be Appointed ~~to~~ in Addition to George Catlin Esqr to Represent the Town at an Ajourn^d Convention to be holden at Middle Town 26

Hebron

Town Meetings
Volumes 1 – 4
1708 - 1799

Many pages are torn or illegible.
Pages 233 & 234 are a hand-written transcript,
not the original pages.

Entries for the annual meetings of
December 1778 and December 1781 were not found.

Located at the Town Clerk's Office

Hebron

10 Apr 1775

At a Freemans Meeting.. Alexander White John Buel Adonijah White Wm Dube Obadiah Barbur Stephen Barbur Ju^r Benj^a Pepoon Thomas Dewey John Norton Frances Norton & Bethuel Phelps took the oath of Freemen	216

25 Jul 1775

D^n William Buel was Chosen Moderator	216
the following Gentlemen was Chosen Com^{tee} of Inspection according to the Direction of the Continental Congress viz: Capt Obadiah Horsford Capt Joel Jones Doct^r Neziah Bliss John Phelps Esqr Lt Solomon Saml Gilbert Esqr Capt Josiah Mack William Talcott Timothy Wales Capt Benjamin Buel Capt Worthy Waters Daniel Horsford Capt Adam Waters	216

19 Sep 1775

At a Freemans Meeting.. Joseph Pepoon Joseph White Wm Polly James Post David Post John Stewart Daniel White Jonth Hall Abel Bissel David Skinner Nathan Baxter Ezekiel Phelps Took the oath of Freemen	216

12 Dec 1775

Deacon William Buel was Chosen Moderator	216
Doct^r Neziah Bliss was Chosen Town Clerk & Town Treasurer	216
Capt Obadiah Horsford Capt Edmund Wells Col John Peters Elijah Kellog & Doct^r Neziah Bliss was Chosen Selectmen	216
Capt Joel Jones Head Constable & Col^r Asahel Phelps & Malachi Lovland Constables & Col^r of Town Rates	216
Capt John Phelps Lt Sol: Tarbox En^s Elisha Beach Asa White John Mack Asaph Trumbull Joel Man David Townsend & Simeon Edgerton Grandjurors	216
Sol Huntington Ez: Gillit Saml Palmer Wm Rollo Saml Wells Jonathan Ju^r Joseph Nieland & Tim^o Wales Tythingmen	216
Eben^r Fuller Caleb Root Increce Porter Ju^r Joel Swetland William Tallcott & David Nieland Listers	216
Sol [ ]ton David Strong Asa White James Bliss John Gilbert Saml Wright Joshua Pratt Ez: Gillit John Northom Thos Burk Gad Talcott Jo[ ] Wells Nathan Rowlee John Ellis Ju^r Jonth Peters Zeb[ ] Phelps Ju^r Barret Phelps Timothy Wales John Til[ ] Capt Joel Jones Silvenas Phelps Eliphaz Lovland [ ] Phelps Nathan Man Daniel Kellog Ju^r Elizur Ti[ ] Dudley Horsford Zeph: Reede Jonth Chappel Ju^r Ch[ ] Crouch Ju^r Surveyors of Highways	217
Capt Horsford Capt Peters & Amos owen Fence Viewers	217
Capt Peters Saml Dewey & Capt Abij: Rowlee Branders & Recorders of Horses - & Ezra Chapman	217
Abner Brown Wm Rollo & Stephen Palmer Lether Sealers	217
Capt Abij: Rowlee & Elihu Marven Sealers of Wates & measures	217
John Fuller & Jos: Waters Pound keepers	217
Ruben Phelps Packer of Beef & Pork	217
John Phelps Esqr was Chosen Agent for the Town	217

19 Dec 1775

Lt John Skinner was Chosen Constabel & Collector	217
Lt John Skinner Benajah Jones & Oliver Phelps Grandjurors	217

Hebron

David Owen Ezekiel Jones Tythingmen	217
Elihu Marven Joseph White & Nehemiah Porters Surveyors	217
Jesse Townsend Daniel Bushnel Saml Kellog Az: Beach Ju^r Jonth Peters Stephen Horton Gad Tallcott Daniel Gott David Strong David Owen Barret Phelps Az: Swetland Hez: Bissell Ez: Gillit Ab^m Fox Thos Crouch Hawyard	217

7 Jan 1776

Col John Peters was Chosen Moderator	218

Apr 1776

[*at a*] Freemans Meeting.. Eleazer Porter [ ] Bolles Daniel Chapman & Joseph Tuttle was made freemen	218

11 [ ] 1776

[*several names illegible*] Nathl Dube Ju^r & John Ford Ju^r was admitted freemen	218

10 Dec 1776

Deacon Wm Buel was Chosen Moderator	218
Neziah Bliss Esqr was Chosen Town Clerk & Treasurer	218
Col Jno Peters Capt Edmund Wells Elijah Kellog Neziah Bliss & Jno Phelps Esqr Selectmen	218
Major Joel Jones Head Constable & Collector Malachi Loveland Jno Skinner & Capt Joshua Phelps was Chosen Constables & Col^{rs}	218
Roger Phelps Benj^a Jones D^n Isaac Ford Jno Mack Elihu Marvin Lt Asaph Trumbull Abij: Phelps Ezekiel Gillit & Oliver Phelps Grandjurors	218
Amos Phelps Slvester Gilbert Capt Jno Wells Nathl Phelps Ju^r Azariah Swetland Levi Swetland Elizur Tillitson Simeon Edgerton & Samuel Wright Tythingmen	218
Eben^r Fuller Sylvester Gilbert Sol: Perring David Kneeland Absolum Peters David Townsend & Jos: Pepoon Listers	218
Sol: Hunton Aaron Barbur Increce Porter Lt Samuel Jones Jeh^d Buel Elisha Beach Peter Post Benj^a Taylor Ju^r Gideon Jones Hez: Bissel Jno Kellog Sol: Tarbox Joseph Kneeland Samuel Kellog Ashbel Phelps Isaac Waters Wm Buel Ju^r Eben^r Gilbert [L]uben Sumner Jno Curtis Jonth Root Jonth Hutchinson Samuel Gilbert Esqr Capt Mack Jonth Chappel Ju^r Dickinson Kingsbury Zaph: Davis Surveyors	218
Elihu Marven Sealer of wates & Measures	218
Eph: Chapman Wm Rollo & Abner Brown Leather Sealers	218
Eben^r Fuller Jos: Waters Pound keepers	218
Amos Owen Col Peters Col Horsford fence viewers	218
[ ] Dewey Ezra Chapman Branders & Recorders of Horses	218
[ ] Phelps Packer of meat	218
John Phelps Esqr Agent with Power of Subscription	218

12 Feb 1777

Col Jno Peters was Chosen Moderator	219
Neziah Bliss Esqr was appointed Agent for the [ ] to give Deeds & to make Exchanges of Lands belonging to [ ] Town…	219

Hebron

31 Mar 1777

Deacon William Buel was Chosen Moderator 219

Voted that a Com^tee [*be*] Chosen..[*to*] Take Care of & Provide the Necessarys of Life for the Famalies of Such Soldiers in their absence as Shall Inlist into any of the Battallions.. at the Prices by Law Established without any aditional Expence for Trouble on Condition Such Soldiers Shall Lodge with or from Time to Time Transmit money to Such Com^tee ..Samuel filer Lt Sol: La[*nk*]on D^n Isaac Ford Elihu [ ] Eben^r Gilbert Capt Jed: Post Capt Danl Ingham Saml Gilbert Esqr Capt Josiah Mack Wm Buel Ju^r Lt Solomon Phelps Doct^r Bingham Joel Swetland & Gideon Jones be a Com^tee for the Purpose 219

7 Apr 1777

At a Freemans Meeting.. John Little Jon^th Tarbox Sylvester Gilbert Solomon Severy Adonijah Strong Ezra Chapman & Samuel Jones Ju^r was admitted to the oath of Freeman 219

24 Sep 1777

Elijah Kellog was Chosen Moderator 219

Capt David Tarbox Elihu Marven Wm Rolo [ ] Horsford & Timothy Wales were Chosen a Com^tee to Chuse a Cloathing for the Soldiers 219

Voted that Elij: Kellog be a Com^tee to Exchange the [ ] with D^n Isaac ford & Give a Deed 219

8 Dec 1777

Wm Buel was Chosen Moderator 220

Neziah Bliss Esqr was Chosen Town Clerk & Town Treasurer 220

Col Obadiah Horsford Col Jno Peters Elijah Kellog Capt Benj^a Buel & Capt Samuel filer Selectmen 220

Col Joel Jones Head Constable & Col^r Capt John Skinner Capt Joshua Phelps & Malachi Lovland Constables & Col^rs 220

D^n Isaac ford Ez: Gillit John Mack Elihu Marven Lt Asaph Trumbull Nathl Phelps Ju^r Roger Phelps Slvester Gilbert Benaj Jones Jon^th Jones Grand [*jurors*] 220

Anstem Anable Timothy Porter Josaph Pepoon Gad Talcott Ruben Sumner Wm Blackman Abijah ~~White~~ Strong Gideon Jones & Timothy Wales Tythingmen 220

11 Dec 1777

Saml Palmer & Wm Bird Ju^r Chose Grandj^r 220

John Gilbert Ju^r Joseph Pepoon Joseph Water Ju^r Levi Swetland Joseph Kneeland & Daniel Chapman Listers 220

Sol: Hunton David Carver Ju^r Silas Pepoon Jehiel Wil[ ] Zach: Perrin Asa White Capt John Wells Jonah Porter Jo[ ] White 2^d Ellis Bliss Capt Adam Waters Increce Porter Barret Phelps Nehemiah Porter Joel Swetland Nathan Ma[ ] Tim^o Wales Dudley Horsford Bissel Phelps Isaac Waters Roger Phelps Wm Root Surveyers of Highways 220

Elihu Marven Sealer of wates & measures 220

Simeon Dunham Benj^a Taylor Ju^r Leather Sealers 220

Amos Owen Col Horsford & Col Peters fence Vewers 220

Col Horsford Elihu Marven Jos: Waters Ju^r Pound keepers 220

Col [ ] Ichabod Buel Branders & Recorders of Horses 220

5 May 1778

D^n Wm Buel was Chosen Moderator 231

Hebron

Col John Peters Elihu Marven & John Phelps Esqr was Chose a Com^{tee} to view & agree with all Parties for the Exchange of a Highway by Jonth Chappels *5 Jan 1779*	*231*
Neziah Bliss Esqr was Chose a Com^{ttee} to give & Receive Deeds in Exchange for Highway from Cornelas Phelps by Chappells & So on to new Boston Road & also with Esqr Gillet near his Dwelling House	*231*
Col Joel Jones & Capt Joshua Phelps was Chose [*illegible*] of Continental Soldiers *28 Jun 1780*	*231*
Dn. Wm. Buel ws Chosen Moderator	*233*
voted that we will Raise a Certain sum to hire Soldiers.. and voted to give Each Recriut £36.. as a Premium to Inlist for 3 years or During the War.. Col Joel Jones Esqr En^s Wm Buel Daniel Horsford Col Horsford Lt Trumbull Timothy Wales Elisha Beach Capt Palmer Asa White Daniel Brown Capt Roger Phelps David Townsend Sol: Huntington Jordan Post Ju^r & Joel Sweetland be appointed as a committee to Hire s^d men *30 Oct 1780*	*233*
Capt Samuel filer was Chosen Moderator *15 Nov 1780*	*233*
Capt Samuel filer was Chosen Moderator	*233*
Voted to Raise a Tax.. to Procure a Quantity of Provision Pursuant to act of Assembly and that Roger fuller Daniel Brown Daniel Horsford & Capt Buel are appointed to Purchase Receive & Put up S^d Provisions and also to Collect the money &c	*233*
Neziah Bliss, Esqr Col Jones Saml Gilbert Timothy Dutton Elijah Kellog Esqr Capt David Tarbox -- Daniel Brown & Wm Buel Ju^r were [ ] to act [ ] *[ ] Dec 1779*	*233*
Capt Samuel filer was Chosen Moderator	*234*
Neziah Bliss Esqr was Chosen Town Clerk & Town Treasurer	*234*
Neziah Bliss Esqr Col John Peters Elijah [ ] & John Phelps Esqr & Capt Benj: Buel Selectmen	*234*
Col Jones Head Constable Col^r Capt Joshua Phelps Capt John Skinner & Wm Buell Ju^r Constables & Col^r	*234*
Amos Phelps Sol: Hunton Anslem Anable Beth^l Phelps Ruben Sumner Simeon Dunham Elijah Graves Malachi Loveland Ezekiel Jones Stephen Bingham Grandjurors	*234*
Joseph Pepoon David Strong Gaylord Porter Simeon House Jonah [ ] Sol: Perrin B[ ] Willes & Daniel Kellog Ju^r Tythingmen	*234*
Elihu Marven Samuel Filer Ju^r Capt John H Wells Listers	*234*
[ ] Gilbert Neziah Bliss Elijah Kellog & John Phelps [ ] Phelps Phinehas Srong Samuel Jones [*Ju^r*] [ ] Birge Capt Buel Azariah Swetland Wm Blackman [ ] Norton Capt John Skinner Abijah Man Thos Post Ju^r [ ] Hutchinson Ju^r Samuel Wright Daniel Chapman [ ] Phelps Ju^r Amos Hall Jonth Dunham John Curtise Dudley Horsford Ab^m Fox Ju^r Timothy Phelps Eliphaz Love[ ] Amos Fuller Surveyors of Highways *24 Dec 1779*	*234*
[ ] Horsford Amos Owen Col Peters fence viewers	*234*
[ ] Jones Col Horsford Capt Waters Pound keepers	*234*
Elihu Marven John H Wells Sealer of Weights & Measures	*234*

Hebron

Simon Dunham Benj Taylor Ju^r Leather Sealers	234
[ ] [ ] Ruben Phelps Packers	234
[ ] Gilbert Ju^r Elijah Kellog Esqr Wm Talcott Comm^{tee} for Cont^l Soldiers [*families*]	234
[ ] Phelps Esqr Agent for Town	234
[ ] Jan 1781	
Made Choice of Capt Daniel Ingham Moderator & [ ] Gilbert Esqr Clark Pro Tempore	235
Voted to appt a Com^{tee} to Procure Recruits.. & app^t Capt Stephen [ ] Asa White Roger fuller Capt Skinner Daniel B[ ] E[ ] [ ] Doct^r Joseph Parker	235
Voted to Raise a Rate.. to Procure flower & Corn.. app^t Joel Post Eben^r Gilbert Lt Malachi [ ] Benj^a Skinner A Com^{tee} to Collect & Receive S^d flower & Corn	235
Voted to Chose a Com^{tee} to adjust & Settle with those Soldiers [ ] in the Continental Service Last Sumer or those who Procurd [ ].. app^t Samuel Gilbert Wm Buel Ju^r & Tim^o Dutton	235
[*Voted*] Joseph [ ] may Set his Sheep on the Highway [ ] near the Dwelling House of Dea^n Benja[ ]	235
12 Dec 1780	
Samuel filer was Chosen Moderator	236
[ ] Bliss Esqr was Chosen Town Clerk & Treasurer	236
[ ] Bliss John Phelps Esqr Wm Buel Ju^r Samuel Gilbert Capt Timothy Dutton were Chosen Selectmen	236
[ ] Jones Head Constable & Coll^r Capt Joshua Phelps & Capt John [ ] Constables & Coll^{rs}	236
[ ] Phelps anslem anable Silas Pepoon Silv^s Gilbert Saml [ ] Ruben Sumner Danl Brown Joseph Kneeland Stephen [ ] Benj: Taylor Ju^r was Chosen Grandjurors	236
[ ] Brown Beth^l Phelps Joseph Pepoon Joel Swetland and [ ] Waters Listers	236
[ ] Jones Ju^r Nehemiah Porter Abel Bissel Jehiel Wil[ ] [ ] Hutchinson Aaron Swetland Dudly Horsford Robt Loveland Tythingmen	236
[ ] Phelps Increas Porter John Kellog Elihu Pomery Elihu [ ] Joshua Phelps Ju^r Aaron Stiles Capt Stephen Barbur Asa [ ] John Taylor John Jonth Dunham Timothy Porter Aaron [ ] Eben^r Root Elizur Tillotson John Ackeley Adonijah Strong [ ] Chappel Adonij White Benaj Jones Elijah Webster [ ] Ellis Ju^r Israel Hutchinson Sol Perrin Asaph Trumbull [ ] Gilbert Peter Post & Amos Hall Surveyor Highways	236
[ ]ord Eliphaz Loveland Eekiel Jones Jeh^d Phelps Ju^r [*Ch*]ose Com^{tee} Supplies	236
[ ] Marven Capt John H Wells Sealer Wates & measures	236
[ ]ford Amos Owen Col Peters fence Viewers	236
[ ]n Waters Col Horsford Pound keepers	236
[ ] Dunham Benj Taylor Ju^r Lether Sealers	236
[ ] [ ]helps Esqr Agent	236
11 Mar 1782	
Saml Gilbert was Chosen Moderator	245
Silvanas Phelps Capt John Skinner Joseph Waters Ju^r Elizur Tillotson Joel Swetland & Gideon Jones was Chosen Classing Com^{tee} in adition to the Last Com^{tee}	245
22 Apr 1782	
Capt Samuel filer Moderator	245

Hebron

2 May 1782

Capt John Skinner & Capt Roger Phelps was Chosen a Comttee to Hire the 2 Continental Soldier at Large	245

11 Dec 1782

John Phelps Esqr Moderator	245
Neziah Bliss Town Clerk & Treas^r	245
Neziah Bliss John Phelps Saml Gilbert Esqr Capt Timothy Dutton & Wm Buel Ju^r Selectmen	245
Col Joel Jones Head Constable & Col^r Capt Joshua Phelps Malachi Loveland & Danl Brown Constables & Col^{rs}	245
John Gilbert Ju^r Capt Saml Jones Caleb Root John Ellis Ju^r Elijah Webster Jordan Post Ju^r Hez: Bissel Benajah Jones Zach: Cone Grandjurors	245
Elihu Marven Silvester Gilbert Danl Brown Gideon Jones Doct^r Joseph Parker Listers	246
Phinehas Strong Daniel Pepoon Timothy Porter Increce Porter Ju^r Zach Perrin James Brown Alex^r White Jonah Root & Solomon Phelps Ju^r Tythingmen	246
Ezekiel Gillet Obadiah Barbur Sol Hunton John Waters David Strong Ezekiel Jones Abel Bissel Jonah Porter Thos F Crouch fraderick Phelps Wm Talcott John H Welles Elihu Welles Saml Peters Danl Bushnal Ralph Mack Saml Geer Thos Post Ju^r Dudly Horsford Bissel Phelps Isaac Waters Joel Porter Nathan Niles & Neh$^{[]}$ Porter Stephen Bingham Aaron Swetland & James White Ju^r Sury^s Highways	246

18 Dec 1782

Adonijah Strong was Chosen Grandjuror	246
Joseph White Sealer of Wates & Measures	246
Joseph White & Col Peters Branders & Recorders of Horses	246
Eph^m Chapman Simeon Dunham & Benj$^{[]}$ Taylor Lether Sealers	246
Col Peters Col Horsford & Capt Stephen Barbur fence [*viewers*]	247
Capt Adam Waters Col Jones & Roger Fuller Pound keepers	247
Voted that Col Jones & Roger fullers Barn yard be Improved for Pounds	247
Capt Timothy Dutton Eben^r Gilbert Thos F Crouch & Thos Post be a Com^{ttee} for the Supply of Soldiers Famalys	247
Voted to Prefer a Memorial to the General Assembly..for Liberty.. to Tax Them Selves for the Purpose of mending & Repairing their Highways.. & that Col Joel Jones & Capt Daniel [ ].. be appointed a Com^{ttee} for the Purpose	247

9 Jan 1783

John Phelps Esqr was Chosen Moderator	247
Capt Timothy Dutton & Saml Gilbert Esqr was Chosen a Com^{ttee} to view the Highway from Zachariah Cones Southward & See what Exchanges are Necessary	247
Daniel Brown Col Jones and Silvanas Phelps was Chosen a Com^{ttee} to audit Acc^{ts} with the Selectmen & Treasurer	247

21 Apr 1783

John Phelps Esqr Moderator	248
Gad Talcott Lt Loveland & Samuel Geer was Chosen a Com^{ttee} to Exchange Highway &c with Alex^r White	248

443

Hebron

29 Apr 1783

Voted that the Method for Mending Highways by Tax Shall be one Year & Shall be Divided in to 13 Districts & that Ezekiel Gillit Jonathan Tarbox Joseph Pepoon Fraderick Phelps Joseph Waters Elihu Wells Gad Talcott John H Wells Gardner Gilbert Aaron Swetland & Jonathan Chappel be Sy^s of Highways & Collectors & Nathan Niles & Elizur Tillotson   248

19 Aug 1783

Neziah Bliss Esqr Mod^r 249

D^n Isaac Ford Capt Joshua Phelps Capt Daniel Ingham Messrs Daniel Horsford & David Townsend be a Com^{ttee} to Divide the Districts & make alterations &c & to Divide the Tax & Make the Bills   249

Kent

Land Records, Volume 3
here labeled "A"

Vital Records, Volume 6
here labeled "B"
Unpaginated

Land Records, Volume 6
here labeled "C"
Unpaginated

Town Records, 1780 – 1834
Here labeled "D"
Unpaginated

Tax Lists 1771 – 86
Oath of Fidelity
Role of the Freemen - Town of Kent 1777 – 1818
Here labeled "E"

Located at the Town Clerk's Office

Kent

26 Oct 1774

Made Choise of Capt Nathaniel Swift Moderator	*[A26]*
..taking into Consideration the Distressing Circomstances of the Poor in Boston have appointed Capt Jedidiah Hubbel Capt Joseph Pratt Mr Peter Pratt Mr Eleazer Curtis Ju^r Capt Joseph Carter Nathan Eliot Esqr and Mr Joseph Guthrie as a Comittee of Corrispondence to Receive the generous Donations of the Inhabitants of the Town.. and to Transmit the Same to the Comittee of Corrispondence or Selectmen.. of Boston for the Releif of the Poor in Boston and to Keep a free Corrispond and Consult all Matters Relitive to American affairs with other Comittees in the Neighbouring Towns and Colonies	*[A26]*

29 Nov 1774

Made Choise of Nathaniel Berr Moderator	*[A27]*
Made Choise of Doc^t Oliver Fuller Peter Mills Nathaniel Berry Ruben Murry Jirai Swift Israel Noble Capt Justus Sacket Doc^t Ebenezer Man Samuel Averil Ju^r Jonathan Sacket Samuel Carter and Isaac Camp be a Comittee of Inspection agreeable to the Eleventh Article of Association	*[A27]*

12 Dec 1775

Made Choise of Ephraim Hubbel Ju^r Esqr Moderator	*[A28]*
Made Choise of Jedidiah Hubbel Town Clerk & Register	*[A28]*
Made Choise of Ephraim Hubbel Ju^r Thomas Hatch Nath^n Berry Reuben Sacket and Joseph Guthrie to be Select men	*[A28]*
Made Choise of Noah Pratt to be Town treasurer	*[A28]*
Made Choise of Lewis Mills first Constable and Collector of Colny Rates and John Bliss and Moses Averil Constables	*[A28]*
Made Choise of Jedidiah Hubbel Joseph Pratt Ju^r Peter Pratt Joseph Carter Eleazer Curtis Ju^r Nathan Eliot and Joseph Guthrie to be a Comitee of Corrispondence	*[A28]*
Made Choise of Oliver Fuller Peter Mills Nath^n Berry Reuben Murry Jairah Swift Israel Noble Justus Sacket Ebenezer Man Jonathan Sacket Saml Carter Isaac Camp Moses Averill David Whittlesey Josiah Raymond Nathan Sloson Thomas Hatch Peleg Sturdevent to be a Comitee of Inspection	*[A28]*
Made Choise of Josiah Raymond Abijah Comstock John Ransom Ju^r Thomas Hatch David Lewis Abijah Hubbel Daniel Beebe Jehiel Barnum Eleazer Chamberlin Eliezer Thomson Daniel Payne Peter Pratt Gideon Root Perry Averil Noah Murry Joel Tirril Eph^m Guthrie Martin Whittlesey Israel Holmes John Wedge Butler Mallery Joseph Hopkins John Taylor Benj^a Bentley John Bliss Abel Comstock Ezra Gilbert to be Surveyors of Highways	*[A28]*
Made Choise of Nathaniel Gray Abijah Hubbel Jered Basset Eleazer Carter to be Grand Juriors	*[A28]*
Made Choise of Elijah Palmer Benony Carter Philip Judd Ju^r Ebenezer Comstock and Asa Hall to be Tything men	*[A28]*
Made Choise of Noah Pratt John Ransom Ju^r Justus Sacket and Joseph Peters to be fence Vewers	*[A28]*
Made Choise of Nathaniel Hatch Robert Ransom Josiah Raymond Abijah Hubbel Daniel Payne Stephen Skiff Joseph Peters Moses Case Ju^r Nathan Sloson Eleazer Finey Isaac Daton & John Whittlesey to be Listers	*[A28]*
Made Choise of Abijah Comstock Israel Holmes & Henry Deans to be Leather Sealers	*[A28]*
Made Choise of Thomas Stephens Benony Carter Eph^m Guthrie to be Key keepers & Branders of Horses and Joseph Guthrie to be Key keeper	*[A28]*

Kent

made Choise of Noah Pratt to be Sealer of Measures	[A28]
Made Choise of Thomas Stephens to be Sealer of Weights	[A28]
Made Choise of John Ransom Ju^r and Nathaniel Grey to be Packers	[A28]
Voted that the following Town Rates in the Hands of Wil^m Guthrie to Collect be abated (Viz) .. Thomas Fairweather £0-1-7.. Ben Adam Gallop 0-7-0.. Beszaliel Gurney 0-5-2.. Ezra Murry 0-5-6	[A24]
Voted that the following Town Rates in the hands of Barzilai Swift to Collect be abated (Viz) .. John Hardin 0-4-2.. Luke Stuart 0-6-2-.. Joseph Troop 0-7-2.. George Thomson 0-3-10.. Eben^r Hoit 0-3-0.. Salmon Cridenton 0-3-6	[A24]

15 Jan 1776

Made Choise of John Ransom Esqr Moderator	[A24]
Voted that the Selectmen Inspect Perez Surdevants Rate Bill and Make Such abatements thereon as they Shall Judge proper	[A24]

7 Oct 1776

Made Choise of Ephraim Hubbel Ju^r Esqr Moderator	[B1]

15 Oct 1776

Voted that we will Prefer a Memorial to the General Assembly to have Liberty and Have it passed in to a Law.. to Mend and Maintain the Highways.. by a Town Rate for the futer.. Voted that Capt Jethro Hatch and Capt Justus Sacket be agents for the Town to Prefere Said Memorial	[B1]

10 Dec 1776

Made Choise of Ephraim Hubbel Ju^r Esqr Moderator	[B1]
Made Choise of Jedidiah Hubbel Town Clerk	[B1]
Made Choise of Ephraim Hubbel Ju^r Esqr Jeremiah Fuller Lewis Mills Samuel Carter and John Whittlesey to be Selectmen	[B1]
Made Choise of Noah Pratt to be Town Treasurer	[B1]
Made Choise of John Ransom Ju^r first Constable and Collector of Collony Rates and of John Bliss and Israel Noble to be Constables	[B1]
Made Choise of Nathaniel Berry Noah Pratt Capt Abraham Fuller Nathaniel Hatch Ephraim Bardsley Daniel Payne Jehiel Barnam Jacob Stanton Perry Averil Israel Noble Elijah Waller Silas Stuart Peleg Sturdevant Eleazer Carter and Joseph Peters to be Surveyors of Highways	[B1]
Made Choise of Noah Pratt John Ransom Ju^r Justus Sacket Joseph Peters Ephraim Guthrie and Caleb Hitchcock to be fence vewers	[B1]
Made Choise of Eliphalet Comstock Philip Judd Ju^r Nathaniel Gray Nathaniel Hatch Eleazer Carter Joseph Peters Eleazer Finney David Whittlesey Joseph Guthrie and Isaac Daton to be Listers	[B1]
Made Choise of Abijah Comstock Benony Carter and Isaac Camp to be Collectors	[B1]
Made Choise of Abijah Comstock Israel Holmes and Jared Basset to be Leather Seallers	[B2]
Made Choise of Joseph Judd Ephraim Bardsley Nathaniel Palmer and Peter Waller to be Grand Juriors	[B2]
Made Choise of Timothy St John Comfort Judd John Barns and Hezekiah Gray to be Tything Men	[B2]
Made Choise of Nathaniel Gray John Ransom Ju^r and Joseph Peters to be Packers	[B2]
Made Choise of Thomas Stevens Benony Carter and Ephraim Guthrie to be Branders of	[B2]

Kent

Horses	
Made Choise of Thomas Stevens to be Sealer of Weights	[B2]
Made Choise of Noah Pratt to be Sealer of Measures	[B2]
Made Choise of Thomas Stevens and Benony Carter to be Keykeepers	[B2]
Made Choise of Eleazer Thomson Jedidiah Hubbel Abraham Fuller Nathaniel Gray Justus Sacket Peleg Sturdevant Philip Strong David Whittlesey and Israel Noble to be Comittee of Inspection	[B2]
Voted that the following Rates in the hands of Nathaniel Hatch Collector be abated Viz Silas Gears Rate of £0-2-1-½.. Amasa Gears Rate of 0-2-3.. Silvanus Hatchs Rate of 0-6-0.. Luke Stuarts Rate of 0-1-6	[B2]

7 Mar 1777

Made Choise of Ephraim Hubbel Ju^r Esqr Moderator	[B3]
Voted that Mes^{rs} Robert Ransom Peter Pratt and Capt Peter Mills be a Commitee to Examin into the State of the List.. for 1775	[B3]
Voted that Nathaniel Swift Ju^r be Surveyor of Highways	[B3]
Voted that Nathaniel Swift Ju^r be Lister	[B3]
Voted that Ephraim Hubbel Ju^r Esqr Mr Eliphalet Comstock Jehoshaphet Eldrid Reuben Sackett Capt Eliphalet Whittlesey & Mr John Benidict be a Committee to Take Care of the Soldiers families in their absence	[B3]

7 Apr 1777

Voted that Ephraim Hubbel Ju^r Esqr and Capt Justus Sacket be a Committee to See the List.. for.. 1775 Rectified with the State Treasurer	[B3]

11 Apr 1777

Made Choise of Nathan Eliot Esqr Moderator	[B3]

15 Sep 1775

Charltown Janu^y 20th 1775 We the Subscribers.. Do Engage that if Jacob Comins Who has Lately Resided in our Town Shall through Sickness or Extream Povery be Disabled to Suport Him Self We are willing to Receive Him again Per us.. Jacob Davis.. Nehemiah Stone { Select Men of Chaltown [sic]	[B6]

31 May 1776

These Certify where as Edward Cogswell an Inhabitant of New Milford has Moved himself and family Into.. Kent and haveing not Gained a Residence.. and.. Being poor and Judging that he Can Better Support his family if Suffered to Reside in Said Town than in.. New Milford.. the Subscribers are of oppinion that it May be Best for.. Cogswell to Reside in.. Kent.. if the Said Cogswell Should Not be able to Support himself and famely without the assstance of the Select men of.. Kent that the Select men of Kent will.. Notify the Select men of New Milford.. Certified by us New Milford May 9th 1776.. Sam^{ll} Canfield.. Abel Hine.. Sherman Boardman.. Willm Cogswell { Select Men	[B6]

9 Dec 1777

Made Choise of Ephraim Hubbel Ju^r Esqr Moderator	[C555]
Made Choise of Ephraim Hubbel Ju^r Esqr Lewis Mills Jeremiah Fuller Samuel Carter and Joseph Guthrie Select men	[C555]
Made Choise of Jedidiah Hubel be Town Clerk	[C555]

Kent

Made Choise of Noah Pratt Town treasurer	[C555]
Made Choise of Joseph Pratt Ju^r first Constable and Collector of the State Tax and of John Bliss and Isac Camp Constables	[C555]
Made Choise of Joseph Berry Nathl Hatch Abijah Hubbel Abraham Fuller John Ransom Ju^r John Payne Stephen Skiff Eleazer Thomson Daniel Payne Stephen Dodge Peleg Sturtevant Reuben Sacket John Hitchcock Eben^r Nye Nathan Tibbals Perry Averil Peter Waller and Israel Noble be Surveyors of Highways	[C555]
Made Choise of Noah Pratt John Ransom Ju^r Justus Sacket Joseph Peters Ephraim Guthrie Nathan Tibbals fence vewers	[C555]
Made Choise of Nathaniel Gray Eliphalit Comstock Nathl Hatch Philip Judd Ju^r Stephen Skiff third Eldrid Joseph Peters Gershom Holmes Eph^m Guthrie Peter Waller David Whittlesey be Listers	[C555]
Voted that the following Rates be abated to Joseph Wheaton Collector Viz Seth Rows Rate of £0-3-0.. William Murches Rate of 0:9-2.. Jonas Barns Rate of 0=3=6.. Tho^{ms} Carter Deceas^d Rate of 0=2=3	[C555]
Voted that the following be abated to William Guthrie Collector Viz Oliver Thares Rate of £0-0-0	[C555]
Made Choise of Timothy St John Joseph Peters and William Parks be Collectors	[C555]
Made Choise of Abijah Comstock Israel Holmes and William Parks Leather Sealers	[C555]
Made Choise of Timothy St John Philip Judd Ju^r Justus Sacket Joseph Carter Eph^m Guthrie Israel Noble and Abraham Fuller be Grand Juriors	[C555]
Voted Nathaniel Gray Barnabas Hatch Ju^r Eph^m Tanner Ebenezer Nye be Tythingmen	[C554]
Voted Nathl Gray John Ransom Ju^r Philip Strong be Packers	[C554]
Voted Thomas Stevens Benony Carter Peter Waller Eph^m Guthrie be Branders of Horses and Keykeepers	[C554]
Made Choise of Thomas Stevens Sealer of Weights	[C554]
Made Choise of Noah Pratt Sealler of Measures	[C554]
Made Choise of Capt Abraham Fuller Israel Noble Benony Carter Nathl Swift Ju^r John Whittlesey and Jedidiah Hubbel to be Committee of Inspection	[C554]
Made Choise of Nathaniel Berry Reuben Murry Eliphalet Comstock Jonah Camp Jehoshaphat Eldrid Reuben Sacket be a Comitee to Provide Provisions for Soldiers famelyes	[C554]
Voted that the following Rates be abated to Benony Carter Collector.. Viz Thomas Carter Deceas^d £0-5-7.. Eleazer Stockwells Rate 0-3-0-.. Oliver Thare Rate 0-0-10	[C554]
Voted that the following Rates be abated in the hands of John Brownson Collector.. Viz Mathias Beman Rate £0-3-6.. Thomas Carter Decas^d Rate 0-1-4½.. Oliver Thare Rate 0-6-3	[C554]
Voted that the following highway Rates in Nathl Berry Surveyor Hands be abated Viz Josiah Raymonds £0-15-1.. Benjamin Eatons 0-16-1	[C554]
Voted Samuel Halls Highway Rate in the Hands of Ephraim Bardsley Surveyor be abated	[C554]
Meeting is ajourned for 10 Minits to Mr Azariah Pratts House	[C554]
Voted that the following Rates be abated to Barzaila Swift Collecor.. Viz Aaron Cooks Rate £0-4-8	[C554]
Voted that the following Rates be abated to Nathaniel Hatch Collector.. Viz Gideon Barnums Rate £0-2-7½.. Semor Cridenton Rate of 0-2-7-½.. Charles Dudleys Rate of 0-4-7½.. Ebenezer Merry Rate of 0-3-4-½.. Daniel Murry 0-2-3.. Simeon Leach 0-0-10.. Martain Finey 0-2-3	[C554]
Made Choise of Ephraim Hubbel Ju^r Esqr Moderator	[C553]

Kent

Voted that Isaac Williams Town Rate in Abijah Comstocks hands to Collect of 1/1 is abated	[C553]

7 Dec 1778

Made Choise of Eph^m Hubbel Ju^r Esqr Moderator	[C552]
Made Choise of Eph^m Hubbel Ju^r Esqr Nathaniel Berry Nathan Sloson Samuel Carter Joseph Guthrie to be Select men	[C552]
Made Choise of Jedidiah Hubbel to be Town Clerk	[C552]
Made Choise of Noah Pratt to be Town Treasurer	[C552]
Made Choise of Peter Mills first Constable and Collector of State Taxes	[C552]
Made Choise of John Bliss and John Whittlesey to be Constables	[C552]
Made Choise of Barnabas Hatch Ju^r John Payne Eleazer Chamberlin Eliphalet Comstock Ebenezer Berry Jehiel Barnum Daniel Beebe Leavit How Nathaniel Gear Israel Carter Justus Sackett Moses Knap Benony Carter Joseph Hopkins William Spooner Peabody Smith Samuel Gregory Perry Averil Isaac Camp Ephraim Guthrie to be Surveyors of Highways	[C552]
Made Choise of Noah Pratt John Ransom Ju^r Justus Sackett Joseph Peters Jonah Camp Isaac Camp to be fence vewers	[C552]
Made Choise of James Stuart Abraham Fuller Peter Pratt Peleg Sturtevant Jeremiah Fuller Ephraim Bardsley Nath^{ll} Swift Ju^r Israel Noble John Brownson Martain Whittlesey Isaac Camp to be Listers	[C552]
Made Choise of Thomas Stevens Nathaniel Swift Ju^r Israel Camp to be Collectors of Rates	[C552]
Made Choise of Abijah Comstock John Bliss Jered Basset to be Leather Sealers	[C552]
Made Choise of Isaiah Gibson Joseph Skiff Benony Carter Eleazer Chamberlin Nathaniel Swift Ju^r Samuel Gregory and Jonah Camp to be Grand Juriors	[C552]
Made Choise of Israel Carter Nathan Skiff Martain Curtis and Joseph Hopkins to be Tythingmen	[C552]
Made Choise of Thomas Stevens Benony Carter Ephraim Guthrie to be Keykeepers and Branders of Horses	[C552]
Made Choise of Noah Pratt to be Sealers of Measures	[C552]
Made Choise of Joseph Berry Timothy St John Joseph Peters Peabody Smith and Isaac Camp to be a Comitee to Provide for Soldiers famelies	[C552]
Made Choise of Barnabas Hatch Ju^r John Odle Comstock John Bliss Eph^m Turner Peter Waller and Perry Averill be a Comitee to provid Cloathing for the Soldiers	[C551]
Voted that the following Rates in the Hands of John Brownson to Collect be abated Viz Blackman Nath^{ll} Cade £2-9.. Beman Matthias 0-6.. Thomas Carter Decas^d 0-1-4-2.. Church Ezra 0-5-1.. Lyon Mathew 0-0-4-2.. Thare Oliver 0-6-8	[C551]
Voted that the following State Rates in the hands of Capt Joseph Pratt to Collect be abated.. Viz Benjamin Eatons £2-12-9.. Benjamin Merry 0-17-8.. George Curtis 0-11-0.. John Main Ju^r 1-8-0.. George Mills 0-15-0.. Daniel Die 2-13-6	[C551]

20 Apr 1779

Made Choise of Eliphalet Comstock Moderator	[C551]
Voted that Maj^r Jethro Hatch is.. Chosen an agent.. to Joyn the agent of the Town of Litchfield to Prefer a Joynt Petition to the General Assembly in May next that the North East Corner Bound of SaidTown of Washington May be affixed twenty Rods above Shipogue Bridge So Called according to the original Intent aned Meaning of Each party	[C551]
Voted that Joseph Berry and Nathaniel Berry have Liberty to fence a Cross the Road on the West Side of ousatunac River from the Corner of Mr Jeremiah Fullers Land by Jacksons Land	[C550]

Kent

and on the East Side of Said River in the Lane in the Most Convenient Place from the first Day of May Next to the first Day of November Next they Keeping up Convenient Gates
Voted that Uriel Lee and Asahel Lees Town Rates.. be abated [C550]

Made Choise of Moses Knap Comitee in adition to the Comitee of Supplys for Soldiers famelies [C550]

26 Apr 1779

Made Choise of Ephraim Hubbel Ju^r Esqr Moderator [C550]

Voted that the Highway from Nathaniel Berrys across the River to Skiff Mountain Shall be an open ~~Highway~~ Road Not withstanding the vote passed the last town Meeting [C550]

Made Choise of John Benidict to be a Collector [C550]

30 Sep 1779

Made Choise of Nathan Eliot Esqr Moderator [C550]

Voted we will Chose a Comitee to attend the State Convention at Hartford.. and Made Choise of Nathan Slosson to be Comitee for Said Purpose [C550]

Voted that for the futer the Warnings for Town Meetings in the Parrish of New Preston be Set up at or Near Nathan Eliot Esqr [C550]

19 Aug 1779

Made Choise of Nathan Slosson Moderator [C550]

Voted that we will appoint a Comittee to Bring a Bill.. in alteration of the present Mode of Taxation.. Voted that Nathaniel Gray Nathan Slosson Capt Joseph Carter Dot^r Ebenezer Man & Jedidiah Hubbel be a Committee for the purpose [C550]

Made Choise of Nathaniel Berry Peleg Sturtevant Capt Joseph Pratt be a Comitee to attend a County Convention if Called to Come into Some Measures to Regulate Commerce [C550]

14 Dec 1779

Made Choise of Nathan Slosson Moderator [C548]

Made Choise of Nathaniel Berry Nathan Slosson Joseph Pratt Ju^r Reuben Sackett and Eleazer Curtis Ju^r to be Selectmen [C548]

Made Choise of Jedidiah Hubbel Town Clerk [C548]

Made Choise of Noah Pratt Town Treasurer [C548]

Made Choise of Peter Pratt first Constable and Collecttor of the State Taxes and of Timothy St John John Bliss to be Constables [C548]

Made Choise of Eliphalet Comstock Eben^r Berry Barnabas Hatch Ju^r Abraham Fuller Eliz^r Thomson Daniel Beebe Peleg Chamberlin Jehiel Barnum John Payne Leavit How Samuel Beacher Pebody Smith Israel Noble Eleazer Curtis William Stone John Bliss Adonijah Carter and Benajah Dunning to be Surveyors of Highways [C548]

Made Choise of John Ransom Ju^r Noah Pratt Benony Carter Joseph Peters Fence Vewers [C548]

Made Choise of Abraham Fuller Ephraim Bardsley Jeremiah Fuller James Stuart John Ransom Ju^r Peleg Sturdevant ~~Jeremiah Fuller~~ Nath^{ll} Swift Ju^r John Brownson Israel Noble to be Listers [C548]

Made Choise of Joseph Judd Martain Curtis and Peter Waller Collectors of the Town Rate [C548]

Made Choise of Abijah Comstock and John Bliss to be Leather Sealers [C548]

Made Choise of Joseph Bates Barnabas Hatch Ju^r Nathan Chamberlin Ward Eldrid John Benidict to be Grand Juriors [C548]

Made Choise of Eleazer Chamberlin Ebenezer Comstock Joel Finney Judah Hopkins [C548]

Kent

Peabody Smith to be Tythingmen

Made Choise of Thomas Stevens Benony Carter to be Branders of Horses and Key Keepers and also of Peter Waller to be Keykeeper [C548]

Made Choise of Noah Pratt and Benony Carter to be Sealer of Measures [C548]

Mde Choise of Joseph Judd and Martain Curtis to be Comitee to Provide Cloathing for the Contenental army [C548]

Made Choise of Joseph Berry Nathan Avery and Israel Noble to be a Comitee to provide for Soldiers famelies [C548]

Voted that we will Release one Half of the fine that was against Moses Knap for Not going out in a Draught which is £120 one Half £60 [C548]

Voted that the following Rates in the Hands of Nathl Swift Ju^r to Collect be abated.. (Viz) Nath^{ll} Browns £2-6-1.. Benj^a Lamkins 1-11-0.. Elnathan Bordmans 0-11-0 [C548]

Voted that the following Rates in the hands of Timothy St John to Collect be abated (viz).. Daniel Dye 0-1-4.. Paltiah Hunt 0-9-0 [C548]

14 Feb 1780

Made Choise of Justus Sackett Esqr Moderator [C547]

Made Choise of Abijah Comstock to be Comitee of Cloathing to Provide Cloathing for Soldiers in the Contenental army [C547]

Made Choise of Asahel Hitchcock to be Lister [C547]

10 Apr 1780

Made Choise of Nathan Eliot Esqr Moderator [C547]

Made Choise of Peter Pratt Joseph Carter Eliphalet Comstock to be Auditors to audit with the Selectmen and Treasurer and Lay the acounts before the Town [C547]

2 May 1780

Made Choise of Maj^r Jethro Hatch Moderator [C547]

Voted that we will Chose a Comitee to Settle and ajust the whole of the Town acounts with full powers to Call upon the Treasurer and Selectmen and all persons that have any acounts for or against the Town.. Voted that Lewis Mills Benjamin Akley and David Waterman be a Comitee for the porpuse [C547]

Voted that the Town Treasurer pay Back to Isaac Haws Ju^r the fine of five pounds which he paid to the Treasurer in July [C547]

19 Jun 1780

Made Choise of Nathan Eliot Esqr Moderator [C546]

Comitees Report is as follows.. in Reconing with the Selectmen find a Balance in favour of the Town of £671-8-6.. [*signed*] Lewis Mills.. Benjamin Akley.. David Waterman [C546]

Voted that we will Alow to Nathaniel Berry the Extraordinary Costs over what he obtained Judgment for in the Windham Suit [C546]

13 Mar 1780

Made Choise of Maj^r Jethro Hatch Moderator [C546]

Made Choise of Capt Abraham Fuller Barnabas Hatch Ju^r Nathaniel Gray John Payne Samuel Gregory Leiu^t Nath^{ll} Swift Joseph Peters and Gershom Holms be Inspectors of Imbargoed articals [C546]

28 Jun 1780

Made Choise of Justus Sackett Esqr Moderator [C545]

Kent

Voted that there Shall be Paid out of the Treasury.. unto Capt Peter Mills Capt Abraham Fuller Capt Peleg Sturtevant Capt Joseph Carter Provided they Shall Procure five ablebodied affective Men or any Number under five to Inlist into Either of the Connecticut Batallions in the Continental army for three years or Dureing the war Such.. Sums.. as Shall be Necessary to Make good Each Soldiers Wages Equal to forty Shillings per Month Estimated at the Prise of Wheat at four Shillings per Bushel to be paid the first Day of July annualy	[C545]
Voted that the Select Men Give orders to the Sheriff to Desist from Collecting John Bull and Aaron Chappels fines *31 Jul 1780*	[C545]
Made Choise of Jethro Hatch Esqr Moderator	[C545]
31 Jul 1780	
Voted that John Barlow and Jedidiah Hubbel administrator on the Estate of Eph^m Hubbel Esqr Dece^d to have Each of their Lost Blanketts paid for by this Town *19 Sep 1780*	[C545]
Made Choise of Mr Benjamin Ackley Moderator	[C544]
20 Nov 1780	
Made Choise of Maj^r Eleazer Curtis Moderator	[C544]
Made Choise of Doc^t Eben^r Man Clerk for the present Meeting	[C544]
Voted that Eliphalet Comstock be a person to Receive the Salt Provisions and Collect and put up Said Provisions &c	[C544]
Voted that M^{rssers} Justus Sackett and Eli Thomson be persons to Collect and Receive and put up &c Said Provisions	[C544]
Voted that Me^{ssers} Capt Abraham Fuller Capt Peter Mills Leiu^t Stephen Dodge Leiu^t Israel Carter Joseph Skiff Leiu^t Israel Noble John Payne Capt Joseph Carter Capt Peleg Sturtevant Maj^r Eleazer Curtis Ju^r Leiu^t Sam^{ll} Carter Leiu^t John Bliss Nathan Eliot Esqr and Nathaniel Berry be a Comitee to Class the people of the Town acording to their Lists to obtain Recrutes to fill up the Connecticut Line in the Contental army	[C543]
Comittee appointed to Recon and ajust the acounts with the Selectmen.. Report.. we.. Met att the House of Mr Stevens.. Rectiifed the apparent Mistakes.. and find Due in favour of the Town the Sum of £152=14=2 Contenental Corency.. and as to the State of the Treasurery we Called upon him but he Not being ready .. Could not give us the Exact State of the Town Therefore Must Refer your Honours to our former Report.. Signed per order.. Lewis Mills.. Benjn Ackley.. David Waterman { Towns Comit[*ee*].. Voted that the Said Report afore Said is Not Excepted.. Per Ebenezer Man Clerk Pro temp[ ] *20 Nov 1780*	[C543]
Personally appeared Doc^t Eben^r Man and Made oath to the foregoing vote before me Jedidiah Hubbel Jus^t of [ ] *12 Dec 1780*	[C543]
Made Choise of Nathan Eliot Esqr Moderator	D1
Made Choise of Jedidiah Hubbel Town Clerk	D1
Made Choise of Capt Joseph Pratt Nath^{ll} Berry Lewis Mills Eleazer Curtis Ju^r Reuben Sackett and Isaac Noble to be Sellectmen	D1
Made Choise of Noah Pratt to be Town Treasurer	D1
Made Choise of Peter Pratt to be first Constable and Collector of State Taxes	D1

Kent

Made Choise of Timothy S[t] John and John Bliss to be Constables	D1
Made Choise of Eliphalet Comstock Abraham Full[er] Ebenezer Berry Peleg Chamberlin Elieazer Thomson John Payne Barnabas Hatch Ju[r] Samuel Beacher Jehiel Barnum Daniel Bebee William Stone Alexander Sackett Adonijah Carter Asahel Hitchcock John Bliss Josiah Caswell and Peabody Smith to be Surveyors of Highways	D1
Made Choise of John Ransom Ju[r] Noah Pratt Benony Carter Nath[ll] Swift Ju[r] to be fence Vewers	D1
Made Choise of Doc[t] Oliver Fuller John Ransom Jeremiah Fuller Nath[ll] Gray Peter Comstock Eph[ ] Bardsley William Hillhouse Peleg Sturtevant Ebene[ ] Man Asahel Hitchcock John Brownson to be Listers	D1
Made Choise of Samuel Barnum John Bliss Le[ather] Sealers	D1
Made Choise of Noah Smith Adijah fuller Sam[ ] Beacher and John Payne to be Grand Jurors	D1
Made Choise of Hendrick Winegar Joseph [ ] Isaac Haws Ju[r] and Joseph Foster to be Tythingm[en]	D1
Made Choise of Eliphalet Comstock Justus Sack[ ] and Eleazer Thomson to be Packers	D1
Made Choise of Noah Pratt and Benony Carter to be Sealers of Measures	D1
Made Choise of Thomas Stevens Benony Carter and Isaac Daton to be Key keepers	D1
Made Choise of Thomas Stevens and Benony Carter to be Branders of Horses	D1
Made Choise of Ephraim Fuller and Gershom Holms and Peter Waller to be Collectors of the Town Rate *2 Jan 1781*	D2
Made Choise of Nathan Eliot Esq[r] Moderator	D2
Made Choise of Ephraim Fuller Gershom Holms and Peter Waller to be a Commitee to Procure Cloathing for the Soldiersin the Contenental army *17 Jan 1781*	D2
Made Choise of Maj[r] Jethro Hatch Moderator	D2
14 Feb 1781	
Made Choise of Peter Pratt Clerk Pro tempr[e]	D3
Made Choise of Maj Eleazer Curtis Moderator	D3
Voted that Philip Strong be an agent for the Town to go to Winsor to Treat with Col[n] Roger Eno Relitive to the Case of Ann Cheeney one of the Towns poor *20 Mar 1781*	D3
Made Choise of Robert Ransom Moderator	D3
Made Choise of Cap[t] Abraham Fuller Cap[t] Joseph Pratt & Leiu[t] John Ransom Ju[r] to be a Commitee to Veiw the Great Bridge	D3
Voted that Maj[r] Eleazer Curtis.. represent the State of the Town before the Commitee appoint[ed] by the General Assembly to ascertain the Coto of Each Town for Soldiers *25 Jun 1781*	D3
Made Choise of Nathan Eliot Esq[r] Moderator	D5
Made Choise Benjamin Ackley Maj[r] Jethro Hatch Nathaniel Hatch John Ransom Ju[r] Nath[ll] Berry Joseph Carter Ju[r] and John Brownson to be a Commitee to Divide the Town into Two Classes and to Hire a Recruit for Each Class into the Connecticut Line in the Contenental army and Make a Rate on the Inhabitants to Defray the Charge and Collect the Money and	D5

Kent

pay the men

Made Choise of Maj^r Eleazer Curtis as a Committee Man to Procure the proper Evedence for the Claims.. to the Three Men usualy acounted for this Town Now Excluded by the Assembly	D5
Made Choise of Peter Pratt Collector of the 4^d Rate	D5
Made Choise of Nathaniel Berry and Philip Strong to be Receivers of the 4^d Tax in Live Cattle	D5
Made Choise of Eliphalet Comstock Justus Sackett Esqr and Elieazer Thomson to be Reeceivers and Packers of the 2/6 Rate	D5
Voted that the Select abate what Rates they find Reasonable in the hands of Joseph Judd to Collect	D5
Voted that Peter Pratt Benony Carter and Eph^m Baradsley be Receiers of the 2/6 Tax paid in Beaf	D5

18 Sep 1781

Made Choise of Nathan Sloson Moderator	D5
Voted that we will appoint to assest Mr Peter Pratt in Collecting four Rates of one peney on the Pound each	D5
Made Choise of Benoni Carter and Eph^m Bardsley to be Collectors for the purpose above mentioned	D5
Voted that we will Prosecute the Suit Commenced against Col^n Eno	D5

8 Oct 1781

Made Choise of Maj^r Eleazer Curtis Moderator	D6
Made Choise of Capt Joseph Pratt and Justus Sackett Esqr agents to.. Prosecute the Memorial.. Now lying before the General assembly or to withdraw Said Memorial and agree with the agents of Washington for a Settlement of the Lines and the Bridge over Shipouge River	D6
Voted that the Select men.. abate Such Rates as they Shall Judge Reasonable in the Hands osf Nath^{ll} Swift Ju^r to Collect	D6

12 Nov 1781

Made Choise of Justus Sackett Esqr Moderator	D6

11 Dec 1781

Made Choise of Nathan Eliot Esqr Moderator	D7
Made Choise of Jedidiah Hubbel Town Clerk	D7
Made Choise of Capt Joseph Pratt Nath^{ll} Berry John Ransom Ju^r Reuben Sackett Benjamin Ackley Israel Noble to be Select men	D7
Made Choise of Noah Pratt to be Town Treasurer	D7
Made Choise of Peter Pratt Timothy St John and Ward Eldrid to be Constables	D7
Made Choise of Ebenezer Berry Ebenezer Spooner Ju^r Eliphalet Comstock Abraham Fuller Nath^{ll} Gear Thomas Stevens Daniel Beebe Nathan Chamberlin Stephen Skiff Joseph Carter Ju^r Amos Swan Daniel Fuller Josiah Webb Sam^{ll} Morris Ju^r Elijah Benidict Peter Waller Stephen Dodge Zacha^s Fuller to be Surveyors of Highways	D7
Made Choise of John Ransom Ju^r Noah Pratt Benoni Carter and John Bliss to be fence vewers	D7
Made Choise of Oliver Fuller Peter Comstock Nath^{ll} Gray Timothy Hatch Ebenezer Man	D7

Kent

Asahel Hitchcock Wil^m Sackett Wil^m Hilhouse to be Listers	
Made Choise of James Grayham Levi Rust Martain Curtis to be Grand Juriors	D7
Made Choise of Nath^ll Gray Peleg Sturtevant Eleazer Curtis and Gershom Comstock to be Tything men	D7
Made Choise of Sam^ll Barnum Joseph Carter to be Leather Sealers	D7
Made Choise of Benoni Carter & Asa Parrish Elijah Waller to be Branders of Horses	D7
Made Choise of Noah Pratt & Benoni Carter to be Sealers of Measures	D7
Made Choise of Eliphalet Comstock and Benony Carter Isaac Daton Keykeepers	D7
Made Choise of Nathan Skiff Ju^r Ephraim Tanner and Julious Caswell to be Collectors	D7
Voted that Reuben Sackett Dispose of the Horse Sadle and Bridle Holsters and Pisteels and Sword belonging to the Town	D7
Made Choise of Sam^ll Barnum and Julious Caswell to be a Commitee to Provide for the Soldiers Famelies	D8

20 Feb 1782

Made Choise of Nathan Eliot Esqr Moderator	D8
Voted that Nathan Slosson Nath^ll Hatch Peleg Chamberlin John Bliss John Brownson Elijah Benidict Jehiel Barnum Capt Abraham Fuller Leiu^t Israel Carter Martain Curtis Joseph Carter Ju^r Peter Waller be a Commitee to Raise Six Men	D8

17 Sep 1782

Made Choise of Nathan Eliot Esqr Moderator	D9

10 Dec 1782

Made Choise of Mr Nathaniel Berry Moderator	D10
Made Choise of Jedidiah Hubbel Town Clerk	D10
Made Choise of Nath^ll Berry Joseph Pratt John Ranson Ju^r Benjamin Ackley Reuben Sackett and Israel Noble to be Select men	D10
Made Choise of Noah Pratt to be Town Treasurer	D10
Made Choise of Timothy St John first Constable and Collector of the State Rate	D10
Made Choise of Ward Eldrid to be Constable	D10
Made Choise of Eliphalet Comstock Lemuel Berry Ebenezer Spooner Ju^r Nathl Gear Thomas Stevens Abraham Fuller Abraham Beecher Peleg Chamberlin William Spooner Israel Noble Benony Carter Sam^ll Carter Ephraim Tanner Silas Curtis Samuel Littlefield Philo Bardsley Stephen Fairchild Samuel Grigory to be Surveyors of Highways	D10
Made Choise of Noah Pratt John Ransom Ju^r Benony Carter Joseph Peters to be fence Vewers	D10
Made Choise of Capt Abraham Fuller Joseph Bates Peter Comstock John Bliss Samuel Carter and Julias Caswell to be Listers	D10
Made Choise of Eliphalet Comstock Capt Joseph Carter to be Leather Sealers	D10
Made Choise of Ebeneer Peck Ju^r and Benony Carter to Branders of Horses	D10
Made Choise of Noah Pratt and Benoni Carter to be Sealers of Measures	D10
Made Choise of Benoni Carter Isaac Daton and Noah Pratt to be Key Keepers	D10
Made Choise of Silvanus Dileno Jeremiah Fuller Joseph Peters to be Grand Juriors	D11

Kent

Made Choise of Jethiel Carter Nathan Slosson and Adonijah Carter and ~~John Brownson~~ Eleazer Finny and Asa Hall to be Tythingmen	D11
Made Choise of David Bradley Joseph Finney and Philo Bardsley to be Collectors of the Town Rate	D11
Made Choise of Capt Abraham Fuller be a Commitee to take Care of the Great Bridge	D11

5 Feb 1783

Made Choise of Maj^r Jethro Hatch Moderator	D12
Made Choise of Doct^r Oliver Fuller Clerk	D12
Voted that this Meeting Chuse a Comitee to Vew the ground from the Town Street Near Nathaniel Grays to Litchfield Line through East Grinwich as the Most Suitable and Beneficial for a Public Road	D12
Voted Maj^r Methro Hatch Capt Joseph Carter Capt Abraham Fuller Wil^m Spooner Noah Pratt Capt John Bliss be a Comitee to for the above Purpose	D12
Personally appeared Doct^r Oliver Fuller and Made oath to the foregoing Votes before me.. Jedediah Hubbel Justice of peace	D12

7 Apr 1783

Voted to Prefer a Memorial to the General assembly.. to Grant a Lotery for.. Building a Bridge over ousatunac River.. Voted that Capt Joseph Pratt and Capt Joseph Carter to be a Comitee to Perfer Said Memorial	D12

25 Feb 1783

Made Choise of Maj^r Eleazer Curtis Moderator	D13

6 May 1783

Made Choise of Nathan Eliot Esqr Moderator	D13

21 Jun 1783

Made Choise of Nathan Eliot Esqr Moderator	D13

21 Jun 1783

Voted that this Town Accept the Bill.. from the last General assembly for a Lotry to Build a Bridge over ousatunac River.. Made Choise of Capt Joseph Pratt Capt Abraham Fuller Capt Joseph Carter to be a Comitee to Lay out the money.. that Shall be Raised by Said Lotry or So much of it as Shall be Necessary to Compleat Said Bridge	D13

16 Sep 1783

Made Choise of Nathaniel Berry Moderator	D14
Voted that we will Defend the Suit Commenced against the Town.. Made Choise of Nathaniel Berry to be agent to defend the above Suit	D14
Voted to Send an agent to Middletown to atend the Convention.. and Made Choise of John Ransom Ju^r to be agent at Middletown	D14
Voted that the following Rates in [the] hands of Nathan Skiff Jur to Collect be abated viz.. Barshuba Coracker £0-0-10.. Thomas Dixson 0-0-7	D14

16 Sep 1777

the persons whose Names are underwritten Took the oath of Fidelity to the State of Connecticut.. Revd Joel Bardwell.. Revd Peter Starr.. John Ransom Esq.. Eph^m Hubbel Ju^r Esq.. Jethro Hatch Esq.. Capt Justus Sacket.. Capt Joseph Pratt Ju^r.. Capt Jedidiah Hubbel.. Capt Jehiel Benton.. Capt Abraham Fuller.. Capt Peter Mills.. Capt Joseph Carter.. Capt Eliphalet Whittlesey.. .. Sam^{ll} Bates.. Joseph Berry.. Stephen Skiff.. Abijah Hubbell..	E58

Kent

.. Timothy St John.. Mathew Judd.. Isaac Haws Ju^r.. Ward Eldrid.. Sam^{ll} Beacher.. Moses Case.. Wil^m Roose.. Jacob Stanton.. Nathl Swift Ju^r.. Perry Avery.. Nathl Hatch.. Barnabas Hatch Ju^r.. Ebenezer Comstock.. Thomas Beman.. Eliphalet Comstock.. Eph^m Bardsley.. Joseph Judd.. Philip Judd.. Lewis Mills.. John Idle Comstock.. Benjamin Chase.. Peleg Chamberlin.. Thomas Avery.. Eliezer Thomson.. Daniel Payne.. Abner Kelsey.. Nathan Murry.. Israel Noble.. Ebenezer Hills.. David Phelps.. Benony Carter.. Eleazer Chamberlin.. Reuben Sacket.. John Whittlesey.. Nathl Gray.. Robt Ransom.. Peleg Sturtevant.. William Stone.. Nathl Berry.. James Stuart.. Perez Sturtevant.. Joel Finney.. Abijah Comstock.. Jeremiah Fuller.. Noah Pratt.. Peter Pratt.. Joseph Guthrie.. Eleazer Curtis Ju^r.. Reuben Murry.. Prince Bryant.. John Bliss.. Saml Whitlock Ju^r.. Eleazer Finey.. Sam^{ll} Haws.. Gershom Holms.. Joseph Peters.. David Whittlesey.. David Taylor.. Wil^m Sacket.. Judah Hopkins.. Josiah Finney.. Eph^m Fanner.. Peabody Smith.. Zachariah Fuller.. Philip Strong.. Joseph Hopkins.. Martin Curtis.. Ebenezer Neigh.. John Ransom Ju^r.. Ebenezer Mann.. *E58*

20 Oct 1777

.. Daniel Lee Esq.. Benjn Bentley.. *E59*

4 Nov 1777

..Cyrenus Clark.. *E59*

9 Dec 1777

.. Moses Averil.. Jonah Camp.. Nathan Tibbals.. Joshahop Eldrid.. Israel Holmes.. Isaac Camp.. Wil^m Guthrie.. Stephen Starkweather.. Wil^m Park.. Lemuel Berry.. Eph^m Guthrie.. Saml Carter.. Ward Eldrid.. Nathan Eliot Esq.. Abel Comstock.. Amos Swan.. Peter Waller.. Eleazer Curtis.. Wil^m Spooner.. Stephen Dodge.. Joseph Rockwell.. Asa Barnes.. Elijah Barns.. Asa Parrish.. Israel Carter.. Simeon Rust.. Thomas Stevens.. Leavit How.. Timothy Pearl.. Jehiel Barnum.. Azariah Pratt.. *E59*

11 Dec 1777

..Sam^{ll} Mott.. John Finney Ju^r.. John Barns.. Nathaniel Fuller.. Saml Whitlock.. Eben^r Spooner.. Howard Fuller.. Asahel Brownson.. Prince Hopkins.. Daniel Fuller.. Daniel Hitchcock.. Nathaniel Swift.. Peleg Holms.. Asher Ross.. Abijah Fuller.. Moses Billins.. Benjamin Ackley.. Benjamin Saunders.. Ezra Gilbert.. Silas Curtis.. Ebenezer Beman.. Park Beman.. Nathan Averil.. John Brownson.. Samuel Littlefield.. Green Bentley.. Wil^m Spooner Ju^r.. Elijah Palmer.. Asahel Lee.. Saml Palmer.. Obediah Judd.. *E59*

15 Dec 1777

..Isaiah Gibson.. Wil^m Parrish.. *E59*

2 Feb 1778

..Malichi Merry.. *E59*

12 Mar 1778

..James Sprage.. *E59*

8 Apr 1778

..Nathan Skiff.. *E59*

13 Apr 1778

..Nathl Swift..Nathan Skiff Ju^r.. *E59*

Kent

21 Jun 1778
..Martain Whittlesey.. *E59*
3 Dec 1777
..Butler Mallery.. *E59*
13 Apr 1778
..Saml Averil.. John Silleman.. ~~Isaiah Gibson~~.. *E59*
[ ] Apr 1778
..Stephen Fairchild.. *E59*
17 Jun 1778
..Ezra Gear Ju^r.. *E59*
18 Jun 1778
..Asahel Wedge.. *E59*
27 Jul 1778
..Silas Paten.. *E59*
28 Jul 1778
..Nathan Chamberlin.. *E59*
6 Aug 1778
..Isaac Swift.. Ichabod Bates.. *E59*
18 Aug 1778
..Eli Daton.. *E60*
29 Aug 1778
..Isachar Rowley.. *E60*
2 Sep 1778
..Levi Fairchield.. *E60*
14 Sep 1778
..John Lamphier.. *E60*
15 Sep 1778
..Josiah Raymond.. *E60*
6 May 1778
..David Olmsted.. Hendrick Winegar.. *E60*
15 Apr 1779
..Solomon Chase.. *E60*
27 Dec 1779
..Samuel Miller.. Samuel Carter Ju^r.. Benjamin Carter.. *E60*
10 Apr 1780
..Josiah Webb.. Daniel Thomson.. Abel Rust.. *E60*

Kent

12 Dec 1780
..Daniel Beebe..   *E60*

12 Jul 1781
..Abel Comstock Jur.. Benjamin Sackett.. William Tanner.. Truman Beman..   *E60*

10 Dec 1781
..Joseph Eaton Ju^r..   *E60*

16 Dec 1781
..Barnabas Berry..   *E60*

9 Feb 1782
..Joseph Phepaney..   *E60*

25 Feb 1782
..Demon Read Convess..   *E60*

28 Aug 1782
..Aaron Coleman.. Ozias Hatch.. Daniel Mason   *E60*

2 Dec 1782
..Noah Smith Ju^r..   *E60*

14 Feb 1783
..Jonathan Main.. Caleb Main..   *E60*

27 Mar 1783
..Benajah Fuller..   *E60*

18 Dec 1782
..Saml Hall..   *E60*

30 Jan 1783
..Aaron Case..   *E60*

2 Nov 1783
..Abijah Beach..   *E60*

18 Feb 1779
..John Convess.. Elijah Convess.. John Bull.. Joel Whitlock.. Benjamin Eaton.. Daniel Roots.. Theopilous Fitch.. Jacob Bull..   *E60*

22 Mar 1781
..Stephen Rockwell.. Manaseth Martain.. Eleazer Curtis 3^d.. Philip Strong Ju^r..   *E60*

8 Apr 1782
..Julious Caswell.. John Gorham Ju^r.. Samuel Hubbel..   *E60*

26 Aug 1782
..Zahariah Blackman.. Stephen Eaton.. Robert Brownen.. Ezbon Fuller.. David Comstock..   *E60*

Kent

27 Aug 1782	
..Jabez Bardsley..	E60
4 Sep 1782	
..Gideon Roots..	E60
5 Sep 1782	
..Ebenezer Peck Ju^r..	E60
17 Sep 1782	
..Phineous Peck.. Nath^{ll} Spooner..	E60
7 Apr 1783	
..Salmon Hurlbut.. Clark Hatch.. Stephen Barnum..	E60
16 Sep 1783	
..Abel Fuller	E60
9 May 1782	
These may Certify.. that Robert Squire a free Negro Man Personally appeared Before me.. And Voluntaryly took the oath of fidelity to this State.. Hezekiah Hubbel Justice of pe[ace]	E61
16 Sep 1777	
A Role of the Freeman of the Town of Kent Sworn in open Meeting.. Revd Joel Bordwell.. Revd Peter Starr.. Maj^r Jethro Hatch Esq.. Eph^m Hubbel Ju^r Esq.. Capt Justus Sacket.. Capt Jehiel Benton.. Capt Joseph Pratt Ju^r.. Capt Jedidiah Hubbel.. Capt Abraham Fuller.. Capt Peter Mills.. Capt Joseph Carter.. Capt Eliphalet Whittlesey.. Sam^{ll} Bates.. Joseph Berry..	E62
..Stephen Skiff.. Abijah Hubbel.. Timothy St John.. Mathew Judd.. Isaac Haws Ju^r.. Ward Eldrid.. Saml Beacher.. Moses Case.. William Rose.. Jacob Stanton.. Nathaniel Swift Ju^r.. Perry Avery.. Nathaniel Hatch.. Barnabas Hatch Ju^r.. Ebenezer Comstock.. Thomas Beeman.. Eliphalet Comstock.. Eph^m Bardsley.. Joseph Judd.. Philip Judd Ju^r.. Lewis Mills.. John Odle Comstock.. Benjamin Chase.. Peleg Chamberlin.. Thomas Avery.. Eliezer Thomson.. Israel Noble.. Ebenezer Hills.. David Phelps.. Benony Carter.. Eleazer Chamberlin.. Reuben Sacket.. John Whittlesey.. Nathaniel Gray.. Robert Ransom.. Peleg Sturtevant.. William Stone.. Nathaniel Berry.. James Stuart.. Perez Sturtevant.. Joel Finney.. Abijah Comstock..	E62
..Jeremiah Fuller.. Noah Pratt.. Peter Pratt.. Joseph Guthrie.. ..Eleazer Curtis Ju^r.. Reuben Murry.. Prince Bryant.. John Bliss.. Saml Whitlock Ju^r.. Eleazer Finney.. Saml Haws.. Gershom Holms.. Joseph Peters.. David Whittlesey.. David Taylor.. William Sacket.. Judah Hopkins.. Josiah Finney..	E62
..Ephraim Tanner.. Peabody Smith.. Zachariah Fuller.. Philip Strong.. Joseph Hopkins.. Martain Curtis.. Ebenezer Neigh.. John Ransom Ju^r.. Ebenezer Man.. Adijah Fuller.. Nathan Sloson.. Samuel Mott.. Benjamin Ackley.. Joseph Bates.. Martain Whittlesey.. Ebenezer Beman.. Daniel Lee Esq.. Cp^t Nathl Swift.. Azariah Pratt.. Nathan Skiff.. Nathan Skiff Ju^r..	E63
..Isaac Camp.. Samuel Averil.. Abel Comstock.. Butler Mallery.. Isaiah Gibson.. John Brownson.. Thomas Stevens.. Howard Fuller.. Peter Waller.. Thomas Dixson.. Daniel Roots.. Nathan Chamberlin.. Alixander Sackett.. Theophilous Fitch.. David Bradley.. Oliver Fuller.. Hendrick Winegar.. Malechi Merry.. Josiah Webb.. Lemuel Berry.. John Berry.. Daniel Thomson.. Abraham Raymond Ju^r.. Abel Rust..	E63
9 Apr 1782	
..Sam^{ll} Carter Ju^r.. William Trappe.. John Hendricks.. John Payne.. Benjamin Lamkin.. Joseph Eaton Ju^r.. Nath^{ll} Spooner.. Silas Curtis.. Phineous Peck.. Salmon Hurlburt.. Stephen	E63

Kent

Dodge.. Bardock Carter.. Abel Comstock Ju^r.. William Spooner Ju^r.. Barnabas Berry.. Ebenezer Peck Ju^r.. Clark Hatch.. Stephen Barnum.. Moses Eaton.. Benjamin Sackett.. Abel Fuller.. Isaac Daton.. Nathaniel Johnson.. Slvester Finney. Philo Bardsley.. Salmon Sackett.. Eben Strong.. John Eliot.. Silas Norton..
..Nath^{ll} Palmer.. Silas Leanard.. Ezekiel Beman.. Eben^r Tanner.. Jesse Benidict.. Sam^{ll} Fairchield.. John Fuller.. Augustis Curtis.. Asahel Fuller.. M$^{[ ]t}$ Luther Comstock.. Samuel Morgan.. David Morgan.. Aaron Coleman.. Daniel Beebe Ju^r.. Ichabud Bates.. Mathew Eliot.. John Eliot.. Lucious Cook.. Noah Hopkins

E64

Killingly

Town Meetings
1728 – 1781
[pages 82a – 98]

Town Meetings
1780 – 1818
[pages 4 – 43]

Located at the Town Clerk's Office

Killingly

6 Dec 1774

Chose Briant Brown Moderator	85
Chose Mr Deac^n Amos Larned Sam^{ll} Watson Dac James Dike Daniel Davas Ju^r Decon Jason Pheps Dac Ebenezer Larned Dac Benj^a Leavins Benj^a Joy Parly Howe Wm Danelson Esqr James Day Capt Eleaz^r Warren Capt Ezekiel Little Wyman Huchens Committe of Enspection	85a

[ ] Dec 1775

Chose Esqr Brown Moderator	86
Chose Mis^s Jonathan Ellis Benjn Leavins Capt Warren Wyman Huchans Hez^a Green Selectmen	86
Chose Thos Moffitt Town Clerk & Town Treasurer	86
Chose Joseph Torrey Stephen Crosby James Day Costables [*sic*] & Town Collectors	86a
Chose.. Nath^{ll} Teller Edward Joslin Wm Dwight Winthrop Chandler John Bates Joseph Joslin Jesse Larned Isaac Whitmore Ebenez^r Lee Luke Upham Nath^{ll} Mills Junr Capt Keth Francies Elliot Surveyors Highways	86a
John Adams David Perry oliver Richmond D Benj^a Leavens John fuller Jared Tolbut Eleaz^r Meghill Capt felsham James Paul Bazilla Fisher Zadock Spaulding Comfort Day John Barrit Nath^{ll} Spaulding Isaac Cady Josiah Hulit Dudley Wade for highwaymen	86a
John Mason fence Vewer	86a
Thomas Dike Alphius Convars John Whitmore Joseph Torry Parly howe David Cady Barsilla Fisher Listers	86a
Nath^{ll} Mi[ ]d Jur Michall Adams Wymon Hutchens be Sealers of Leather	86a
Benjn Meriam David Buck Bresilla Fisher Jacob Spaulding be Granjury Men	86a
[ ] Bates Obed Clow Ebenezer Star Samson Howe Joseph Cady Sen^{er} James Paul Tithingmen	86a
Jacob Convers Resolved Johnson Ezra Browen Branders of horses	86a
Simon Davis Sealer of Wates and Mesures	86a
Sam^{ll} Watson John Felshaw J^r Simon Spaulding Kee Keepers	86a
John Leavon & Elijah Childs hog Constables	86a

[ ] Jan 1776

Granted to Jonathan Ellis 3.6.0	87
Granted to Sam^{ll} Danielson Jr 4.5.6.	87
Granted to James Dike 10.7.9	87
Granted to Hanah Fuller 1.0.0	87
Granted to Joseph Town 0.7.10-1	87
Granted to Israel Joslin 9.7.9	87
Granted to Luke Upham 4.2.6	87
Granted to Simon Davis 0.16.0	87
Granted to Joseph Torry 0.12.8	87
Granted to Comfort Eaton 14.17.6	87
Granted to John Green 0.8.0	87

Killingly

Granted to James Day 3.14.10	87
Granted to Joel Convers 0.6.6	87

[ ] Dec 1776

Chose Jacob Dresser .. Moderator	87
Chose Hezekiah Green Jo[s] Torry James Day Davis Spaulding and Amos Carvil Selectmen	87
Chose John Mason Town Clark and Town Treasury	87
Chose James Day Jo[s] Torry and Daniel Davis Constables and Town Collectors	87
Chose Peter Keth Samson Howe Daniel Waters and John Eaton Ju[r] Grand Jurors	87a
Chose Dea James Dike Nathaniel Sheffield Cap[t] James Fuller Ebenezer Howard Dea Jason Phips David Burrit Jacob Convers Josiah Convers Dea Lusher Gay Hez Cutter Dea Larned Dea Benjamin Leavins Josiah Brown John Brooks Ens[n] Benj[n] Cady Cap[t] David Cady Dea Sam[ll] Knight Oliver Hulet Cap[t] Warrin Jo[s] Hutchens Dea John Eaton James Day Ephraim Gile -- Survawers of Highways	87a
Chose Enouch Lennard & James Larned fence Vewers	87a
Chose Tho[s] Dike Alpheus Convers Dea Jason Phips Joseph Torry Perrly Howe Sam[ll] Danielson Davis Spaulding Listors	87a
Chose Jo[s] Cady Nathaniel Mills Ju[r] Sealers of Leather	87a
Chose James Dike Benj[n] Convers Tho[s] Dike Will[m] Pierce Cap[t] Ephraim Warren & John Sprauge tythingmen	87a
Chose Jacob Convers & Resolved Thonson Branders of horses	87a
Chose Simon Davis Sealers of Weights & Measures	87a
Chose John Felshaw & Sam[ll] Watson Kee Keepers	87a

[ ] Jan 1777

Chose Bria[ ] Esq[r] Moderator	88
Granted to Isreal Joslen £11.10.1	88
Granted to Dec[n] Jeams Dike 11.15.4	88
Granted to John Mason --.10.6	88
Granted to Joseph Adams -- 5.----	88
Granted to Isaac Whitmore -- 14.12.6	88
Granted to Luke Upsom 5.1.-	88
Granted to Wiman Huchens -- 4 --	88
Granted to Doct[r] Goyate -- 2.11.4	88
Granted to James Day --6--	88
Chose Thom[s] Moffit.. and Jacob Dresser.. and.. Perly How a Comitty to Settel The line between Killingly and Volentown	88

3 Feb 1777

Chose Jacob Dresser Esq[r] Moderator	88a
Granted To Nathaniel Walker for Keeping Simon Kee Three Pounds p[r] year from.. 1774 To This Present Time Likewise Granted.. for The Further Suport of.. Kee During his Naturel Life Eighteen Pounds	88a

Killingly

Granted Dec[n] Jeams Dike.. for Keeping Rhoady utters Boy.. £ 0.13.0	88a

7 Apr 1777

Chose Briant Brown Esq[r] Moderator	89
Voted that any Soldiers that Shall Enlist into The Contanantel Service for Three years or During The Present war who fills up Part of The Quota for this Town that their Familyes in Their absence upon Their Reasonable Request Shall be Provided for the Necessaryes of life at The Price Stated by Law in this State on Such Soldier laying or Remiting mony from Time to Time for that Purpose.. Chose a Comity for Suplying The Familys..(Viz) Daniel Davis Ju[r].. Dec[n] Luther Gay.. Ephrom Gile. Benj[n] Meroam.. Dec[n] Ebenezer Larned.. Cap[t] Elizer Warin.. Sam[ll] Danielson } Wimon Hutchens. Cap[t] Ezekil Little.. Josiah Brown.. Dec[n] Sam[ll] Knight.. Theophilus Chandler.. Ezekil Smith } Comitty	89

14 Apr 1777

Chose Briant Esq[r] Moderator	89a

12 May 1777

Chose Briant Brown Esq[r] Moderator	90

19 May 1777

Chose Cap[t] Pain Convers.. Leu[t] Obidiah Clough.. Is[n] Daniel Larned.. Cap[t] Jeams Dike.. Leu[t] Jason Phips.. Is[n] John Whitmore.. Cap Joseph Cady } Leu[t] David Buck.. Leu[t] Jonathan Cady.. Cap[t] David Cady.. Cap[t] Luther Hawkens.. Cap[t] Ephrom Warrin.. Is[n] Elias Starns.. Cap[t] John Eaton.. Is[n] Esaker Beats } a Comity To Procure Soldiers To Inlist To fill up the Quota.. for the Contanantal Service	90

9 Sep 1777

Chose Briant Brown Esq[r] Modrator	91

10 Nov 1777

Chose Cap[t] Simon Larned Moderator	91
Chose a Com[t] To Procure.. Clothing [*for the Continental Soldiers*].. Cap[t] Simon Larned.. Cap[t] Pain Convers.. Leu[t] Obedah Clough.. Dec[n] Jason Phips.. Cap[t] James Dike.. Is[n] Nath[l] Brown.. Eleazer Meghels.. John Mason.. Is[n] Jered Talbut.. Samson How.. Leu[t] Daniel Walters.. Cap[t] Ephrom Warrin.. Leu[t] Sam[ll] Danilson.. Zadock Spaulding.. Leu[t] Comfort Day.. Jeams Day	91

[ ] Dec 1777

Chose Briant Brown Esq[r] Moderator	91a
Chose Hezekiah Green Joseph Torry Barziler Fisher Zadock Spoulding Leu[t] Obediah Clough Selectmen	91a
Chose John Mason Town Clerk & Town Treasurer	91a
Chose Daniel Davis Ju[r] Samson How Zadock Spoulding Constables & Town Collectors S[d] Davis to Colect the State Tax	91a
Chose Jesse Brown Comfort Eaton Edward Holton Winthrop Chadler William Richards Joseph Joslin Ebenezer Howard Cap[t] John Green Simon Davis Sam[ll] Fay Daniel Perrin Alpheus Convers Leu[t] Jonathan Cady Charles Leavens Cap[t] Joseph Cady Cap[t] Joseph Cutler Phillip Whita[ ]or David Russel Ens[n] Elias Stearns Cap[t] Luther Hawkens Cap[t] John Eaton David Day Ezra Hutchens Nath[l] Spaulding Dec[n] Sam[ll] Knight Servaers of Highways	91a
Chose Cap[t] John Falshaw Jeames Larned Fence Viewers	92

Killingly

Thomas Dike Is[n] John Whitmore Tho[s] Ormbe Joseph Torry Samson How Barziler Fisher Isaac Hutchens Listers	92
Chose Cap[t] Pain Convers Joseph Cady Wimon Hutchins Sealers of Leather	92
Chose Cap[t] Pain Convers Eleazer Moffat Cap[t] Luther Hawkins Daniel Sprauge Grand Jurers	92
Chose Ebenezer Blanchard Nathan Bigby Dec[n] Jeams Dike Eleazer Mighels Jeams Day Cap[t] David Cady Tithing men	92
Jacob Convers Resolved Johnson Branders of Horses	92
Chose Sam[ll] Watson John Falshaw Keepers	92
Chose Sam[ll] Watson Cp[t] John Green Theophelus Chandler John Jacobs Cap[t] Joseph Cady Eleazer Moffet Leu[t] Daniel Walters Cap[t] Ephrom Warrin Davis Spaulding Com[te] to Suply the Solder Familys	92
Chose Leu[t] Obediah Clough Sam[ll] Watson Amos Carril Cap[t] John Green Leu[t] Jason Phips Ebenezer Coper Dec[n] Ebenezer Larned Joseph Torry Benj[n] Joy Is[n] Barziler Fisher Leu[t] Daniel Walters Zadock Spaulding Leu[t] Josiah Robins Com[te] of Enspection	92
Granted To Israel Joslen -- £17.10.4	92
[ ] Jan 1778	
Granted To Luke upham -- £8.00-	92
Granted To Amos Carril -- £--16.6	92
Granted To Uriah Thonson -- £1.5.6	92
Granted To Nathan Green -- £1.10-	92
Granted To Rachel Burril -- £1.16-	92
Granted To Daniel Russel -- £18.4-	92
Granted To David Barrit -- £15.9-	92
Granted To Benj[n] Fay -- £3.4-	92a
Granted To Dec[n] Jeames Dike -- £19.10-	92a
Granted To Doc[r] Tho[s] Wever -- £1.16-	92a
Granted To Jacob Dresser -- £-8-	92a
Granted To Tho[s] Moffit -- £--11--	92a
Granted To Cap[t] Perly How -- £--9-	92a
Granted To Cap[t] Benoni Cutler & Benj[n] Cady Ju[r] £3.12	92a
Granted To Cap[t] Benoni Cutler & Benj[n] Cady Ju[r] £3.12	92a
12 Jan 1778	
Granted To Hezekiah Green-- £2-	92a
12 Jan 1778	
Granted To Cap[t] David Cady -- £--6-	92a
Granted To Cap[t] Jeams Dike in adition To [ ] Grant mad in Last meting { £3.18	92a
Settled with John Mason Town Treasurer all the Mony That had bin Paid in as Fines by Draughted men and all the Rate Bills Maid uppon the List Taken in.. 1775.. and Found Due to the Town from S[d] Treasurer Sixty Pounds Nine Shillings & Ten Pence.. witness our hands - Hezekiah Green.. Jos: torrey.. Obe[d] Clough { Select men	92a

Killingly

2 Apr 1778

Chose Briant Brown Esqr Moderator	93
Voted a Com^{tt} To Colect Cloathing.. Chose Cp^t John Green Sam^{ll} Watson Ebenezer Coper Is^n John Whitmore Ebenezer Bunday John Jacobs Ju^r Is^n Elihu Lorrence Capt Jo^s Cady Dea Ebenezer Larned Benjn Joy Cp^t Eph^m Warrin Dea Robart Baxter Cp^t Luther Hawkins Cp^t David Cady John Sprauge	93
Voted That The Selectmen be Impowerd to dispose of The Child born of Hannah Trip Now living with Olive Buck	93
Voted That Dea Simon Larned be Impower^d To Hire The Farm that Jedediah Cady Now lives on For the use of The Famely Now under his Care	93

[ ] Sep 1778

Maid Choise of.. Sam^{ll} Watson Moderator	93a

8 Dec 1778

Maid Choise of Briant Brown Esqr Moderator	94
Chose } Briant Brown.. Benjn Joy Zadock Spaulding Dea: Jonathan Day & Capt Benjn Meriam Selectmen	94
Chose } John Maon Town Clark & Town Treasurer	94
Chose Samson How Daniel Davis Zadock Spaulding Constables	94
Chose.. William Richards Nathaniel Mills Daniel Hendrick James Paul Theophilus Chandler Chester Cono[ ] Robart Plank Capt Steven Keth John Plumer John Falshaw Ju:^{r} Samson How Jacob Whitmore Ebenezer Wilson Capt Jo:^{s} Cady Benjn Fearbanks Samuel Brooks Isaah Cady James Day Phillip Richmond Jonathan Herrenden John Jacobs Dea Robart Baxter Andrew Wilson Isaac Hutchens Comfort Walker Capt John Eaton Benjn Seamons Nathaniel Spaulding Samuel Fay Eleazer Mighells Ebenezer Bunday Servaors of Highways	94
Chose } John Mason & Robart Plank fence Viuers	94
Chose } Thos Dike Simon Davis Dea Jason Phips Dea Jo:^{s} Torry Samson How Capt Ephrom Warrin Dea Robart Baxter Capt David Cady & Zadock Spaulding Listors	94
Chose Capt Pain Convers .. Joseph Cady & Wimon Hutchins Leather Sealers	94
Chose Ebenezer Coper Elihu Larrence Dea Jacob Spaulding & James Day Grand Jurors	94
Chose Briant Brown Ju^r Nathaniel Dike John Jacobs Leu^t Jonathan Cady Isaac C How Josiah Robins Leu^t Comfort Day Ins^n Elias Stearns Tything men	94a
Chose Leu^t Jacob Convers Resolved Johnson James Day Branders of Hor[ses]	94a
Chose Simon Davis Sealer of waits & Measurs	94a
Chose.. Sam^{ll} Watson John Falshaw Kee Kepers of Pounds	94a
Chose Mes^{rs} Sam:^{ll} Walson Capt Simon Learned Leu^t Obediah Clough Dea Jason Phips Ebenezer Coper Capt John Green Dea Jo^s Torry Dea Ebenezer Learned Benjn Joy Dea Robart Baxter Capt Ephrom Warrin Leu^t John Sprauge Barziler Fisher Capt David Cady Elias Stearns Com:^{tt} of Inspection	94a
Chose John Whitmore Samuel Watson Dea Ebenezer Green Leu^t Jacob Dresser Capt Peter Keth Eleazer Moffitt Capt Jo:^{s} Cady Davis Spaulding Leu^t Sam:^{ll} Danielson.. Comi:^{tt} of Supply	94a

[ ] Jan 1779

Granted To Edward Joslin for Keeping Sam:^{ll} Convers - 73.4	94a

Killingly

Granted To Dea James Dike for Keeping Jediah utter -- 87.5	94a
Granted To Izrael Joslin for Keeping Tho:ˢ Buffinton - 78.17	94a
Granted To Izrael Joslin for Keeping Tho:ˢ Buffinton - 78.17	94a
Granted To Jo:ˢ Torry -- 18	94a
Granted To Eleazer Mighlls for Minding Cargils bridge - 31--	94a
Granted To Eleazer Dº for Minding Cargils bridge - 3	94a
Granted To David Barritt for Keeping Mʳ Lane - 67.12.6	94a
Granted To David Barritt for Keeping Mʳ Lane - 67.12.6	94a
Granted To Sam:ˡˡ H Torry ---- -18-	94a
Granted To Benj:ⁿ Joy Ju:ʳ for Keeping Mary Phillips - 66.16	94a
Granted to Isaac Cutter --- 1.4	94a
Granted to Daniel Russel for Keeping Mʳ Norrimor & wife.. 62.8	94a
Granted to Luke Uppon for Keepping Mʳ Barton & wife - 77.2	94a
Granted to Leuᵗ Jonathan Cady ---- 1.4	94a

[ ] Jan 1779

Granted to Daniel Davis Ju:ʳ ----- 1.4	94a
Voted that Dea Jo:ˢ Torry Dea Ebenezer Learned & John Mason be a Comᵗᵗ: .. to Setil with Phillip Richmond for Keeping Mary Burch	95
Granted to John Sprauge ---- [£] 3-	95
Granted to John Sprague & Zadock Spaulding for Service [£] 2-	95

10 Jun 1779

Settled with John Mason Town Treasurer for all the Money that had bin Paid in by the Collʳˢ up to the Presant Date.. Witness.. Briant Brown.. Zadok Spalding.. Benjⁿ Joy.. Benjⁿ Merian }Selectmen	95

12 Apr 1779

Maid Choise of Brant Esqʳ Moderator	95a
Granted to Joseph Joslin for the use of the Schoolhouse in Stors District	95a

29 Apr 1779

Maid Choise of Briant Brown Esqʳ Moderator	95a

14 Jul 1779

Maid Choise of Leuᵗ Obidiah Clough Moderator	95a
Voted to Raise Two Shillings on the Pound upon all the Poles & Ratable Estate in this Town uppon the List 1778 for the Purpose of Hireing Men to fill up the Deficeancy of the Quots of this Town for the Continantil army.. Chose Capᵗ John Green Capᵗ Pain Convers Capᵗ Isachar Ba[ ] Capᵗ Peter Keith Leuᵗ Jason Phips Capᵗ Jonathan Cady Capᵗ Joseph Cuter Capᵗ Ephraim Warrin Leuᵗ Samˡˡ Danielson Capᵗ David Cady Capᵗ John Eaton Capᵗ Samˡˡ Chandler be a Comitty to Enlist Sᵈ Men	96
Chose Dea Jonathan Day Capᵗ Simon Larned Dea Joseph Torry Insⁿ Barziller Fisher Dea Jason Phips To be a Comᵗᵗ to Consider whether any and who Shall be abated from the afor Sᵈ Tax	96

Killingly

Granted To Leu^t David Buck & Samson How for Repairing Cargils Bridge -- [£] 74.5	96
Voted.. the Selectmen Pay Thomas Davis for a gun Lost in the Service- [£]3.12	96

31 Aug 1779

maid Choise of Briant Brown Esqr Moderator	96
Chose Capt Simon Learned & Mr Amasa Learned & John Mason } a Comitty to atend a County Convention	96

[ ] Sep 1779

Chose John Mason & Mr Daniel Learned a Com:^{ee} to atend the State Convention..	96a

[ ] Dec 1779

Maid Choise of Briant Brown Esqr Moderator	96a
Chose Capt John Green Mr Benjn Joy Capt Ephraim Warrin Capt John Eaton & Leu^t Obediah Clough Selectmen	96a
Chose Capt Simon Learned Town Clark & Town Treasurer	96a
Chose Zadock Spaulding Leu^t Daniel Davis & Isaac C Howe Constables & Town Colectors	96a
Chose Nathan Bixby Roger Elliot John Jacobs Ju^r Elijah Robartson Capt Pain Convers Elijah Child Daniel Perrin Davis Flint Daniel Larned Capt John Green James Hosmer Jacob Whitmore Capt Jonathan Cady .. Benj$^{[ ]}$ Joy Dea Jo:^{s} Torry Daniel Whitmore John Farrow Barnabus Davis Richard Whitemore Barzala Fisher Capt Ephraim Warrin Andrew Brown Silas Hutchins Davis Spaulding Peter Cooper Isreal Day Servaers of Highways	96a
Chose James Learned and Capt John Falshaw fence Vewers	96a
Chose Alpheus Convers Thomas Dike Capt Jonathan Cady Willm Gevins Ins^n Samuel Stearns Isaac Hutchens Isreal Day and Mark Eames Grand Jurors	97
Chose Comfort Eaton Leu^t Jacob Dresser Peleg Corbin Capt Jonathan Cady John Mason David Danielson Leu^t John Sprauge Dec^n Jacob Spaulding & James Westcock Listors	97
Chose Capt Pain Convers Joseph Cady and Capt John Eaton Leather Sealers	97
Chose Dea Ebenezer Green Capt Peter Keth Jess Brown Natha^{ll} Dike John Jacobs Ju^r Eleazer Mighels Benj$^{[ ]}$ Joy Ju^r Benj$^{[ ]}$ Bateman Capt Ephraim Warrin and Capt David Cady Tythingmen	97
Chose Simon Davis Sealer of wieghts & Measures	97
Chose Jacob Convers Oliver Williams and James Day Branders of Horses	97
Chose.. Sam^{ll} Watson and .. John Falshaw Kee Keepers of the Pounds	97
Chose Natha:^{ll} Mills Ju:^{r} Leu^t Jacob Convers John Falshaw Ju^r Leu^t David Buck James Day and Davis Spaulding Com:^{ee} of Suply	97

1 Jan 1780

Setteled with John Mason as Town Treasurer all State Orders that had bin Deliver^d To him and all.. Orders.. from the Several Colectors of this Town [*signed*] Benjamin Joy.. John Green.. Obadiah Clough.. Ephraim Warren } Selectmen	97

31 Jan 1780

Made Choise of Briant Brown Esqr Moderator and John Mason Clerk for Said Day	97a

[ ] Feb 1780

Voted.. the Present Selectmen Together with Ensign Daniel Learned and Capt Peter Keith be a Com:^{ee} To allow Town Debts	97a

Killingly

Dea:[n] Jason Phips.. Sam[ll] Watson Ens[n] Daniel Learned Cap[t] John Green Dea[n] Joseph Torrey Ens[n] Elias Stearns and Cap[t] Davis Cady be a Com[tee] to Inspect into provision and to Prevent any Imbargoed Articals from being Drove out of State	97a
Voted that Daniel Eams.. Eleazer Cooper.. Benj[n] Joy and Zadok Spalding be a Com:[tee] to Purches Cloathing	97a

14 Apr 1780

Voted to have a work house for the poor Choose M[r] David Barrit and Cap[t] Ephraim Warrin Masters of the work houses	97a
Choose Maj Joseph Cady Com[tte] of Suplies of familys	97a
Choose Ebenezer Prince Surveyor of high way	97a
Voted to give Isaac Cady Howe for Servis Done.. £6.0.0	97a
Voted.. to allow Town Debts.. as followeth.. to Bryant Brown for keeping Rhoda Utter 270.0.0	97a
to Cap[t] Benj[m] Meriam for keeping s[d] Rhoda and for Cloathing.. 180.0	97a
Allowed to Edward Joslen for Keeping Samuel Convers and Cloathing.. £506.12.6	98
to Israel Joslen for keeping Thomas Bofinton and funeral Charges.. 253.10.0	98
to Zadock Spalding for provisions for Straits family.. 010.0.0	98
to Jonathan Harndon house Rent for Straits family.. 012.0.0	98
to Zadock Spalding Carring a woman out of Town 042.16.0	98
to Silas Huchens for boarding Straits family.. 012.0.0	98
to David Barritt keeping Benj[m] Lane.. 390.0.0	98
to Israel Day for keeping a Child and Cloathing.. 207.15.0	98
to Jonathan Day for board and Cloathing Straits Child.. 205.7.6	98
to Doc[r] Thomas Weaver for Doctring the poor.. 136.10.9	98
to Cap[t] James Dike for keeping Jedidiah Utter.. 413.12.6	98
to Luke Upham for bording Sam[ll] Barton and wife.. 457.10.0	98
to Doct[r] Joseph Coit Doctring poor.. 009.12.6	98
to Daniel Russel for bording Samuel Narrowmore.. 679.10.0	98
to Eleazer Moffit for going to Hartford.. 045.0.0	98
to the Widow Johnson for keeping widow Marshs Child.. 018.0.0	98
to Cap[t] David Cady for keeping Sam[ll] Whitmore & Cloathing.. 347.17.6	98
to Ensig Daniel Learned for keeping Rhoda Utter.. 030.0.0	98
to Benj[m] Joy Jur for keeping Widow Phillip and Cloathing.. 447.0.0	98
to Benj[m] Joy for keeping Samuel Whitmore 2 weeks.. 13.0.0	98
to Cap[t] Eleazer Warren for keeping Mary Burch.. 405.0.0	98
to John Mason going to Windham and Hartford.. 030.0.0	98
to Capt Ephraim Warren going to Windham &c.. 018.0.0	98
to Leiut Obadiah Clough for keeping one of the Widow Marsh Children.. 033.0.0	98

Killingly

to.. Amasa Learned for going to Windham &c.. 007.10.	98
to Robert Baxter for String piece for Cargils bridge.. 004.10.	98
to Phillip Richmond for keeping Mary Birch.. 042.0.0	98
to Perley Cady for bullets &c.. 14.0.0	98
to Capt Stephen Keith mending Stoney River bridge.. 020.0.0	98
to Simon Learned for going to Windham &c.. 007.10.0	98
to Leiu^t Daniel Davis Transporting a woman out of Town.. 009.0.0	98

31 Jan 1781

Setteled with Simon Larned Late Town Treasurer all State Orders that had bin Delivered to him and all Moneys and orders Rec^d by him from the Collectors of this Town.. Davis Converss.. Eleazar Moffitt.. David Cady.. Samuel Watson } Select-Men	98

[1780-Apr 1783]

Isaiah Cady & Ro[bar] Leavens took [*the Oath of*] Fidelity before Benjn Leavens Esqr a Justice [*of the peace*]	4
Jesse Bixby Took oath of Fidility and the New fre[*mens*] oath .. Sepr 11 1[ ] [*ed: between 1780, beginning of the book, and April 1783, next entry*]	4

7 Apr 1783

Asahel Taft Took the Oath of Fidellity	4
Peleg Corbin Lister Sworn [*ed: with oath of fidelity*]	4
Jesse Joslin.. Joseph Deamon.. Elijah Bates.. Mosses Corbin.. Elijah Converse.. Willm Coopland.. Joseph Prince.. Daniel Barritt.. John Jacobs Ju^r.. Mical Tur[ ]lott.. Willm Smith.. appeared and took the Oath of fre[*emen*]	4

26 Jun 1780

Made Choice of Briant Brown.. Moderator	5
Voted to Choose a Com^{tee} to hire Men to fill up the Quota of this Town for the Continental army for three years or During the War or untill the Last Day of December Next.. Chose Capt Isacher Bates Capt Pain Convers Capt Peter Keith Capt John Green Leu^t Jason Phips Capt Jonathan Cady Capt Joseph Cutler Capt Hope Smith Leu^t Samuel Danielson Capt David Cady Capt Samuel Chandler Capt John Eaton Leu^t Davis Flint	5

5 Jul 1780

Chose Mr David Barritt to Repair the Bridge over Quinabouge River near Capt Peter Keith	6

1 Aug 1780

the Moderator not there they Chose Mr Benjn Joy Moderator	6

[ ] Sep 1780

Voted that the Town was Desierous that the.. County Court Should Send a Com^{tee} to.. Lay out a Road from Mr Daniel Larneds or there a bouts by Mr Leavens and Leu^t Cloughs & Mr Dikes to the Coutry Road that Leads to Boston Near Mr Martons	6
Chose Mr Daniel Larned and Mr John Mason a Com^{te} to Examin the Soldiers and See what is their just Due	6

5 Dec 1780

Chose Thaddeus Larned Clerk for the Day	7

Killingly

Chose Briant Brown Esqr Moderator	7
Chose Capt Pain Convers Mr Eleazer Moffitt Mr Andrew Brown Capt David Cady Mr Samuel Watson Select Men	7
Chose Samson Howe Town Clerk	7
Chose Samson Howe Town Tteasurer	7
Chose Lieu^t Daniel Larned Mr Isaac Cady Howe & Mr Zadock Spalding Constables.. & also Town Collectors	7
Chose Thomas Holbrook Elijah Convers Ivory Upham Asa Corbin Lieu^t Jacob Convers Henry Larned John Whitmore Thomas Dike John Plummer Capt Peter Keith Jesse Brown John Elliot Mr John Jacobs Eleaz[er] Mighells Jacob Whitmore Capt Job Olney Maj^r Joseph Cady Mr Oliver Wilson Squier Miller Caleb All[ ] Pelitiah Mason John Day David Russell Sam^{ll} Den[ ] Dea^n Jonathan Day Comfort Walker John Hutchen Davis Spalding Ens^n Elias Stearns &.. Andrew Wilson Surveyors of High Ways	7
Chose Capt John Felshaw & Mr John Mason Fence Vewers	7
Chose William Dwight Samuel Corbin Ju^r Mr Edward Joslin Capt Jonathan Cady Capt Ephraim Fisk Capt James Westcut Leiu^t John Fisher Silas Hutchens Siloam Short Listers	7
Chose Capt Pain Convers Capt John Eaton Capt Jonathan Cady Leather Sealers	8
Chose Capt John Green Simon Davis Ozariah Cutler David Copp James Day Benjn Bateman Comfort Walker Ezra Huhins Junr Grandjurors	8
Chose Lieu^t Obediah Clough Robart Plank John Mason Joseph Adams Ebenez^r Leach Noah Day John Carder William Pearce Tythin Men	8
Chose Simon Davis Sealer of weights & Measuer	8
Chose Mr Samuel Watson & Capt John Felshaw Kee Keepers	8
Chose Lieu^t Jacob Conver & Mr James Day Branders of Horses	8

[ ] Jan 1781

Chose William Danielson Esqr a Selectman in the Rome & Stead of Mr Andrew Brown	8
Chose the Select Men together with Capt Simon Larned & Lieu^t Obediah Clough as a Com^{tee} to Examin the Town Debts & to Give.. Judgments.. what they Shall think is Due to Each Man from this Town Then Voted that Said Com^{tee} Look into the afairs of this Town as to Debt and Credit	8

20 Nov 1780

Made Choice of Briant Brown Esqr Moderator	9
Chose Dea^n Jason Phips Ens^n Daniel Larned Mr Samson Howe Ens^n Berzilla Fisher & Capt John Eaton to Rece[ive] the Salt and Provision and put up the Same	9
Chose Sa[ ] Jason Phips Daniel Larned Samson Howe Berzilla Fishe[ ] & John Eaton Collectors to Collect Said provisions	9
Chose Mr Daniel Larned Thomas Dike Capt John Green Luie^t Jason Phips Capt Pain Convers Mr John Mason Samson Howe Maj^r Joseph Cady and Eleazer Moffitt Capt Ephraim Warren Mr Andrew Brown Leu^t Samuel Danielson Capt John Eaton Leu^t John Sprague & Zadock Spalding a Com^{tee} to Class all the Inhabitants into as Many Classes as the Town is Deficiant in their Quota in the Continental army	9
Select Men and Mr Daniel Larned be a Com^{tee} to Say what will be a Reasonable Reward for the Melitia that was Called out Last Summer	10

Killingly

18 Dec 1780

Voted to Reconsider the Choice of Mr Zadock Spalding as Constable & Collector	10
Chose Capt David Cady Constable & Collector	10

10 Jan 1781

We the Subscribers.. Conven^d at the House of Capt John Felshaw.. to Examin and Adjust accompts Brought in against Said Town.. — 11

..David Barritts accompt for Keeping Benjamin Lane from January.. 1780 to Jan^y ..1781.. Articles of Cloathing.. To Mending the Bridge.. Total £16-14-2½ — 11

..Edward Joslin accompt for Keeping Samuel Convers from Jan^y .. 1780 to Jan^y .. 1781.. Articles of Cloathing.. Total.. £16-7-3 — 11

..Timothy Eatons accompt for Keeping Samuel Whitmore from March.. 1780 to Jan^y .. 1781.. Articles of Cloathing.. .. Total.. £14-16-[ ] — 11

..Daniel Russells accompt for Keeping Samuel Naramore and his wife from.. March 1780 to.. Jany 1781.. articles of Cloathing & one Bushell of Corn.. Total £19-9 — 11

..Jonathan Days accompt for Keeping Willm Strait from March.. 1780 to Jan^y .. 1781.. Articles of Cloathing.. Total £6-3-8 — 11

..Capt James Dikes accompt Keeping Jedediah Utter from.. Jany 1780 To D^o 1781.. Articles of Cloathing Total £15-13-9 — 12

..Capt Eleazer Warrins accompt for Keeping Mary Burch from.. March 1780 to Jany 1781.. Articles of Cloathing.. Total £12-12-0 — 12

..Capt John Green accompt for Keeping Hannah Marshs Child nine weeks.. articles of Cloathing.. £1.2.0 — 12

..John Plank accompt for Keeping Hannah Mashs Child fromDecember.. 1779 to December.. 1780.. Articles of Clothing.. Total £5-12-0 — 12

..Briant Brown.. Accompt for Keeping Rhoda Utter from March.. 1780 to Jan^y.. 1781.. Articles of Clothing.. Total £21-[8]-0 — 12

..Benjn Joy Ju^r accompt for Keeping the Widow Mary Phillips from March.. 1780 to Jan^y .. 1781.. Articles of Clothing.. Total £12-4-6 — 12

..Joseph Coits accompt for Doctorin Mrs Ruth Burton.. Doctring W^d Hannah Wilkey.. Total £5.15.0.. — 12

..Luke Upham accompt for Keeping Samuel Barton & wife from.. March 1780 To Jan^y .. 1781.. £12.2.0 — 12

..Doct^r Jeremiah Rounds To Doctring Widdow Hannah Wilkey at Capt Greens.. £13.10.0 — 13

..Doct^r Albigene Waldo for Doctering w^d Hannah Wilkey and Med^s.. £2-6-0 — 13

..Capt John Green for Keeping Hannah Wilkey.. when under Salavation.. To 3 Gallon of Rum.. Total.. .. £6-18-0 — 13

..Ens^n Daniel Larned accompt for Transporting Anne Comes and 3 Children 14 Miles.. £1-6-0 — 13

..Capt Simon Larned accompt.. £0-8-0 — 13

the above accompts was allow^d in Silver or other Mony Equavilent David Cady Clerk of S^d Com^{tee} — 13

Voted to allow the following accompts.. To Isaac Cady Howe for Boarding a woman & three Children one Day.. £0-3-0.. To Doc^r Carril for Doctring Mr Lain.. £0-7-7.. To Daniel Olney for a String Peace for Cargill Bridge .. £0-3-0 — 13

Chose Dea^n Jason Phips Ens^n Daniel Larned Samson Howe Ens^n Berzila Fisher & Capt John Eaton Receivers to Recive the flowe[r] & Corn & Collectors to Collect the Same and put it up in Casks — 13

Killingly

15 Feb 1781

Chose Lt Jacob Convers Ebenezer Prince Capt John Felshaw Ens^n Jarid Talbut Mr James Day Dea^n Jacob Spalding a Com^{tee} to Supply the Soldiers Familys	14
Chose Ebenezer Cooper Daniel Davis Ju^r Maj^r Joseph Cady Lt Elihu Lawrence Capt Ephraim Warren John Day Lt John Sprague a Com^{tee} to Supply Clothing for the Soldiers in the Continental Army	14
Chose Ens^n Daniel Larned Maj^r Joseph Cady Capt Ephraim Warren & Capt David Cady a Com^{tee} to Procuer the Quota of Men which S^d Town are Called upon.. to Serve in the Western frontears for one year	14

19 Mar 1781

Made Choice of Capt Simon Larned Moderator	15
Voted that the Com^{tee}.. to Class the Men to Procure Recruits for the Continental army Shall Break Mr Bundays Class (So Called) and add them to other Clases	15
Voted to Reconsider a Vote.. Chooseing Samson Howe as a Receaver to Receive the flower & Grain to be Collected.. Chose Mr Benjn Joy to Receive S^d flower & Grane	15
Chose Capt David Cady a Receiver & Collector to Collect the flower & Grain as afore s^d in the Rome of Capt John Eaton	15

[ ] Apr 1781

Chose Mr Daniel Larned as an agent to Go to Windham.. to Represent to a Com^{tee} appointed by the General assembly to Settle the Claims of the Soldiers in Each Town in the County of Windham	16

28 Jun 1781

Made Choice of Briant Brown Esqr Moderator	16
Voted to Raise four pence on the Pound.. to Procuer a Quantity of Beef for the State.. Chose Leu^t Daniel Larned & Capt Ephraim Warren as a Com^{tee} to Purchase a Quantity of Beef afores^d	16
Chose Dea^n Lusher Gay & Co[l][^{l}] William Danielson to aprise the Said Beef Cattle when Delivered to the Comisssary	16
Chose Leu^t Daniel Larned Mr Berzilla Fisher Capt David Cady Samson Howe & Leu^t Jason Phips to Receive the Provisions & articels of Clothing & put them up	17
Chose Leu^t Daniel Larned as a Com^{tee} to hire a Recruit to Serve in the Continental army for one year	17
Chose Maj^r Joseph Cady as a Com^{tee} to Supply those Families of those Persons that are in the Continental army	17

11 Sep 1781

Made Choice of Briant Brown Esqr Moderator	17

4 Dec 1781

Made Choice of Capt Simon Larned Moderator	18
Made Choice of Capt Simon Larned, Capt David Buck Col^o William Danielson, Mr John Mason & Capt Stephen Keeth Selectmen	18
Samson Howe Town Clerk & Town Treasurer	18
Dea^n Joseph Torrey Constable to Collect the Colony Tax	19
Daniel Larned, &.. Silas Hutchens Constables	19
Dea^n Joseph Torrey Mr Daniel Larned & Mr Silas Hutchens Town Collectors	19

Killingly

Chose Mr Thomas Holbrook, Mr Ebenezer Prince Mr Daniel Mansfield, Mr John Jacobs, Mr Eben^r Howard Junr, Mr Nathan Bixbey, Capt Peter Keeth, Mr Eben^r Bunday, Mr John Younglove, Mr Barnu Tur[]alot, Mr Wm Read Capt Obediah Clough, Capt Pain Convers, Capt John Felshaw, Mr Azariah Cutler, Mr James Larned, Mr Squire Miller Mr David Law Capt Job Olney, Mr Joseph Adams, Mr Richard Tucker, Mr Caleb Allen, Ens^n Berzillai Fisher, Mr David Danielson, Mr Perley Whitmore, Mr Ishmael Davis, Capt Ephraim Warren, Mr Amasa Hutchens, Mr Davis Spalding, Capt John Eaton.. Mr Comfort Walker, Mr Siloam Short, Surveyors of High ways	19
Chose Capt John Felshaw, Mr James Larned, fence Viewers	19
chose Leu^t Jacob Convers, Mr Hezekiah Bellows, Mr Samuel Corbin Ju^r Mr David Copp, Capt David Buck, Mr Andrew Brown, Ens^n Elias Sterns, Mr Timothy Eaton, & Mr Ezra Hutchens Ju^r Listers	19
Chose.Mr John Wilson, Capt Jonathan Cady Mr William Corder, & Mr Wiman Hutchens Leather Sealers	19
Chose Mr Jesse Brown, Mr Jacob Leavens, Mr John Corder, Mr Peter Cooper, Grandjurors	19
Chose Mr Edward Holton, Leu^t Davis Flint, Mr John Mason, Jonathan Herrington Ju^r, Samson Howe Mr Pellatiah Mason, Leu^t Elihu Lawrence, & Leu^t Comfort Day Tything Men	19
Chose Leu^t Jacob Convers, Mr Oliver Williams & Mr John Day Branders of Horses	19
Chose Samson Howe Sealers of Wates & Measures	20
Chose Mr Read Watson, Capt John Felshaw, & Dea^n Jacob Spaulding Kee Keepers	20
Voted that the Present Selectmen together with Capt Pain Convers & Capt David Cady be a Com^{tee} to Look into the Town Debts	20

[ ] Jan 1782

Chose Leu^t Daniel Larned & Samson Howe agents to prefer a Memorial to the General Assembly for Liberty.. to Tax themselves for.. Mending the High Ways	20
Chose Mr Eleazer Moffitt agent.. in a Case to be Depending at Windham.. whereas S^d Town are Cited by Dea^n Ebenezer Green	20
Voted to allow.. accounts.. as follows (Viz) To Edward Joslin for Keeping Samuel Convers From.. January 1781 to.. Jany 1782.. [and] For Cloathing S^d Converse.. £16-3-3	20
Voted to allow.. Luke Upham for Keeping Samuel Barton & Wife from .. January 1781 to January.. 1782.. [and] articles of Cloathing.. £14-12-0	21
Voted to allow David Barrit for Keeping Benjn Lane from January.. 1781 to January.. 1782.. [and] articles of Cloathing.. £15-17-4½	21
..Briant Brown.. for Keeping Rhoda Utter 14 weeks [and] mending her Cloaths.. £16-9-0	21
..Jacob Converse for Keeping Samuel Narramore.. March 1781.. January 1782.. £8-26-	21
..Israel Richards for Making a Coffin for Sam^{ll} Narramore wife.. £0-7-0	21
..Wid^w Watson for Keeping Hannah Wilkey.. [and] Shoes £3-0-6	21
..Capt James Dike for Keeping Jedediah Utter from.. January 1781 to.. Janu^y 1782 [and] for Articles of Cloathing.. [£]15-8-0	21
..Thomas Dike for Keeping Hannah Wilkey.. £2-14-0	21
..Wid^w Elizabeth Gay for Keeping Rhoda Utter.. [and] Articles of Cloathing.. £17-1-6	21
..Benjn Joy Junr for Keeping the Widow Mary Phillips.. January.. 1781.. [to] Sept^r.. While Sick [and] Articles of Cloathing.. £10-4-10	22
..Doct Jos Coit for Doctering Sundry Persons of the poor.. £9-14-9	22

Killingly

..Capt David Bucks account for Service done in repareing at Publick Bridge Called Cargills Bridge.. £4-19-0	22
..Capt Buck.. To 27½ Days work of Common Labourers.. £6-19-5	22
..David Copp for Service Done on.. Cargills Bridge.. £4-13-8	22
..Capt Ephraim Warrens for Collecting Beef &c.. £2-6-0	22
..Capt John Felshaw for apprising Cattle .. £1-10-2	22
..Dea^n Lusher Gays for Apprising Cattle.. £0-10-6	22
..Col^o Wm Danielson for apprising Cattle.. £0-3-0	22
..Leu^t Daniel Larned for Service done.. in Sundry Journeys & Other Service	23
..Capt Eleazer Warrin for Keeping Mary Burch from.. January 1781 to.. January 1782 [and] one pair of shoes.. £14-5-6	23
..David Nickols for Opening a Grave for Mrs Narramore.. £0-3-0	23
..Daniel Russel for Keeping Sam^{ll} Narramore and wife three Days.. & Nursing the Woman.. [and] rum Malasses &c While Sick.. £4-14-6	23
..Timothy Eaton for Keeping Sam^{ll} Whitmore from.. Janu^y 1781 to D^o 1782 [and] Articles of Cloathing.. £15-14-0	23
..Jacob Brown for Keeping the W^w Mary Phillips.. [and] one pair of Shoes.. £4-3-0	23
..Sam^{ll} Anderson for Keeping Thomas Allyn 33 weeks.. [and] one pair of shoes.. One pair Stockens.. £10-12-6	23
..Col^o Wm Danielson for Repairing the Bridge Called Danielsons Bridge.. £17-8-0	23
..Wid^w Mary Graves fro Keeping Thomas Allyn Nine weeks.. and Cloathing.. £3-0-0	24
..Capt John Green in addition to what the Town allow^d in Jany 1781 for Keeping Hannah Wilkey.. £2-2-0	24
..Ephraim Ellingwood for Keeping the w^d Mash^s Child.. fifty five weeks.. [and] Articles of Cloathing.. £6-0-0	24
Voted to allow to an Account Singnd by Benjn Joy Obediah Clough & Eph^m Warren as Select Men in.. 1780 in adition to What the State had allow^d them for Procuring and Sending Provision with the Melitia Called out on the 30th Day of July AD 1780 to Due a Tower of Duty at East Greenwich	24
5 Mar 1782	
Made Chocie of Briant Brown Esqr Moderator	25
Voted to Choose a Com^{tee} to hire the Quota of Men.. for the State Service; ..Chose Maj^r Joseph Cady Capt Ephraim Warren & Mr Ebenezer Bunday	25
Chose Leu^t Daniel Larned agent to represent.. Town before the Com^{tee} appointed by.. the General Assembly	25
Chose Mr Ebenezer Bunday as a Com^{tee} to hire Twenty Seven pounds of hard Money for the Town & Deliver the Same to the Com^{tee} Chose to hire the Towns Quota of Soldiers for the State Service for one year to be paid to S^d Soldiers as a Bounty	25
[ ] Mar 1782	
Chose Leu^t Daniel Larned & Capt Ephraim Warren as a Com^{te} to Settle with the Soldiers that went to Horse nect the year past	26
Chose Mr Elezer Mofitt an agent.. to Settle with Joseph Robbins by an arbitration.. Selectmen to gather with Mr Moffitt be a Com^{tee} to appoint the Arbitrators	26
Chose David Alton James Day Capt John Felshaw & Capt Isacher Bates a Com^{te} to Supply	26

Killingly

the Soldiers Families
[ ] Apr 1782
the Moderator being absent .. Chose Capt Simon Larned Moderator for the Day in his Room   27
Chose Mr Ebenezer Bunday to Go & Make Demand of the State of Rhodiesland of all those   27
Persons who have Inlisted themselvesinto S^d Rhodiesland Service who are Legal Inhabitants
of this Town; and also to procure a Coppy of their Inlistments or of their being Mustered
Select Men Shall allow to Obediah Robinson what they Shall Judge proper if he.. Shall Join   27
the Continental Army and Shall Count as a Soldier for this Town
Voted to Releas Mr James Day from providing for the Soldiers Families & Chose Mr John   27
Fuller in his Rome
18 Apr 1782
Chose Maj^r Joseph Cady Mr Ebenezer Bunday & Capt Ephraim Warren a Com^{tee} to Equipt   28
the State Soldiers Called for to Join the State Service at Horse Neck
Chose Leu^t Jonathan Nickels as a Com^{tee} to repair the Bridge over Quinabougg River Called   28
Dwights Bridge
Chose Capt Stephen Keeth a Com^{tee} to repair the Bridge over Stoney River   28
[ ] Jun 1782
Chose Maj^r Joseph Cady Mr Ebenezer Bunday & Capt Ephraim Warren a Com^{tee} to Hire three   28
Men to Serve in the Continentall Army
Voted to allow the following accompts to the following Gentlemen (Viz) to Mr Nathan Day   28
for Keeping Thomas Allen fifty Two weeks & Some Clothing which account in Cludes an
accompt S^d Day carried in to Mr Benjn Joy being Conservator to the Estate of S^d Allen.. £18-
8-0 D^o to an other account.. to Said Day for Keeping S^d Allen by order of Capt Ephraim
Warren & others as Selectmen.. £5-17-0
allow^d to Sam^{ll} Danielson Junr for Keeping Mehatible Adams fifty weeks.. & one pair of   29
Shoes.. £5-5-0
1 May 1782
Made Choice of Capt Simon Larned Moderator   29

Chose Co^{ll} Wm Danielson & Mr Daniel Larned agents to prefer a Memorial to the General   29
Assembly.. for the purpose of haveing Said Town Devided & praying that To have
Thompson Parish in Coperated into a Destrict Town by itself
26 Dec 1782
Setteled with Samson Howe Late Town Treasurer all orders Delivered to him & all Moneys   30
& orders Rec^d by him from Town Collectors.. Jonathan Ellis.. Jonathan Nichols Ju^r.. Eleazer
Bunday∕Selectmen
9 Dec 1782
Chose Dea^n Simon Larned Moderator   31
Chose Jonath^n Ellis Leu^t Jonath^n Nichols Co^{ll} William Danielson Mr Zadock Spalding and M^r 31
Ebenez^r Bundy Select Men
Chose Alpheus Converse Town Clerk   31
Chose Alpheus Converse Town Treasurer   31
Chose William Dwight first Constable to Collect The Colony Tax   31
Chose Dea^n Joseph Torry and Capt Ephraim Warrin and Silas Hutchens Constables   31
Chose Wm Dwight Dea^n Joseph Torrey Capt Ephraim Warrin and Silas Hutchens Collectors   31

Killingly

Chose Mr Joseph Joslen, Nathll Mills Ju{r} Wm Coopland Ju{r} Mr Luke Upham Elijah Crosbey Peleg Corbin, Samll W[ ]all, Simon Davis John Alton Capt Peter Keeth, Henry Larned, Edward Joslen Capt David Buck, Dea{n} Joseph Torrey, Samll Brooks Mr Eleaz{r} Moffitt, Zadock Hutchens, John Carder Mr Pelatiah Mason Mr Nathan Day, Mr Amasa Hutchens Mr Davis Spalding, Timothy Eaton, Abner Day Survayors of high Ways	31
Chose Mr James Larned & Mr John Mason fence Vewers	32
Chose Mr Elijah Nichols, Mr Peleg Corben.. Benj[ ] Larned, Capt David Buck Mr David Coopp, Mr Andrew Brown Ensign Elias Stearns Samll Anderson and John Hutchens Listers	32
Chose John Wilson Mr Joseph Cady and William Carder Leather Sealers	32
Chose Hezekiah Bellows Mr Asa Lawrance James Dixen, James Day Ju{r} Grand Juriors	32
Chose Mr Samll Spalding Mr Ivory Upham John Jacobs Capt Jonathan Cady Leu{t} Samll Danilson and Noah Day Tythenmen	32
Chose Mr Jacob Converse Mr Oliver Williams and John Day Branders of Horses	32
Chose Mr Samson Howe Sealer of Weights & measures	32
Chose.. I{n} Read Watson and Capt John Felshaw Kee Keepers	32
Chose Capt Stephen Keith Mr Eleazer Mofitt as a Committee to Examine Town Debts together With The Select Men	32
Voted to Mr Ebenez{r} Prince for a gun Which Was Lost in the Service	32

6 Jan 1783

Allowed to Mr David Barritt for Keeping Benja Lane and Funeral Charges.. £18=7=2=2	33
To.. Doc{t} James Gleason for Doctering.. Samll Converse.. £1=10=6=0	33
Allowed to Mr Edward Joslen for Keeping Samll Converse and Funeral Charges £16=7=0=0	33
Allowed to Mr Jacob Brown for Keeping the Widow Mary Fillips.. & One Pare of Shoes £13=6=9=0	33
Allowed to Capt James Dike for Keeping of Jedediah Utter and Clotheing.. £17=10=6=0	33
Allowed to Mr Samll Anderson for Keeping Thos Allyn and Clotheing.. £17=19=0=0	33
Allowed to Capt Eleazer Warrin for Keeping Mary Burch and Clotheing.. £16=15=3=[ ]	34
Allowed to the Widow Elisabeth Gay for Keeping Rhoda Utter and Clotheing.. £22=1=0=0	34
Allowed to Mr Luke Upham for Keeping Samll Barton & His Wife and Clotheing.. £15=15=6=0	34
Allowed to Doctr Joseph Coit for Doctering the Widdo Hannah Wilke and Benja Lar[ ].. £2=10=7=0	34
Allowed to Samll Spalding for Keeping Samll Narramore.. £4=8=0=0	34
Allowed to Leu{t} Jonth{n} Nichols for Building Quonibog Bridge.. £22-9-9	34

14 Feb 1783

Allowed to Mr Eleazer Moffitt for Doing Business for the Town.. £8=14=0=0	34
Allowed to Mr Ebenezer Bundy for Costs and troble of hireing mony and Enlisting Sogers for hors Neck and Equipting of them.. £31=18=0=0	34
Allowed to Mr Eleazer Miles for Providing Timber for Cargils Bridge.. £1=2=2=0	35
Allowed to Mr Joy for Triming Casks.. £0=6=0=0	35
Allowed to Dea{n} Simon Larned for Providing Clothes for Benja Baxter a Soldier for hors Neck and a Jorney to Labanon to Cary the Returns of the Inhabiti[ ].. £1=13=6=0	35

Killingly

Allowed to Mr Gulener Leonard for Keeping the Widow Marshes Child.. Fifty two Weeks [*and*] articles of Clotheing.. £5=16=0	35
Voted to Mr Silas Huchens for Careing one Martha Mott a Transiant Person to Foster in the State of Rodiland..£0=12/0	35
Allowed Mr Daniel Larned Bills.. £8=4=8=0	35
Chose Capt John Mason Leu^t Silvanus Perry a Committee to Exammin affairs of the Sogers That Did a Tower of Duty at Horse Neck in the Militia in.. 1781	35

6 May 1783

Made Choice of Capt Dan^{ll} Larned for Moderator	36
Voted to Chuse a Committee for Dividing the Town Into Districks.. for Working at the High Ways.. Chose Capt Simon Larned Capt Jason Phips Capt Pain Converse Deaⁿ Joseph Torrey Capt Ephraim Warrin Mr Zadock Spalding	36
Voted that Maj^r Cady Mr Bundy and Capt Eph^m Warrin Be a Committee to Settle With the Hors Neck Sogers that Was Out In the Summer 1782 In the Militia	37

Killingworth

Town Meeting Book
Volume II
1740

Located at the Town Clerk's Office

Killingworth

13 Sep 1774

Martain Lord Aaron Eliot Capt Saml Crane Caleb Baldwin Capt William Griswold to be a Committy of Corespondence   *42*

Voted that Doc^r Saml Gale Benony Hillard George Eliot Martain Lord Caleb Baldwin Elisha Crane and Aaron Steevens be a Committee of Corespondence and Inspection and they are hereby requested to Use all proper Measures to See thatt the Resolves of S^d Congress be Faithfully Observed and that they Publish the Names of any who Shall Presume to Violate the Same   *43*

10 Apr 1775

Mes^s Daniel Redfield Hiel Buell and Nathan Griswold be Desired to to Assist the Town Clerk in Examining the Old Town Book of Records   *43*

22 Jun 1775

Mr Stephen Willcok was Chosen Moderator   *43*

Mr Daniel Redfield John Willcok Capt Stephen Lane Sam^ll [ ]ther was Chosen in Adition to the former Committee of Corespondents   *43*

12 Dec 1775

made Choise of Mr Stephen Willcok for their Moderator   *44*

Daniel Redfield George Eliot Nath$^{[ ]}$ Griswold Hezek^h Lane Abel Willcok { was Chosen Selectmen   *44*

Co^{ll} Aaron Eliot was Chosen Town Regest[er]   *44*

Capt Saml Crane was Chosen Constable And to Colect the County Rate   *44*

John Person also Chosen Constable   *44*

Mes:^{s} Nathl Kelcey Amos Kelcy Bezeelel Bristol Daniel Parmele { were Chosen Grandjurors   *44*

Capt Hiel Buell was Chosen Keper   *44*

Mess^s Benoni Hillard Daniel Redfield Stephen Lane John Willcoks Saml [ ]ther Saml Crane Elisha Crane Hez$^{[ ]}$ Lane Aaron Kelcey { was Chosen a Com^y of Inspection & Corespondence   *44*

19 Dec 1775

Leu^t Noah Lane.. Jonth Buell.. Caleb L Hurd.. Dan Kelcey.. Elna^n Hurd.. Saml Kelcy 2^d.. Amos Carter.. Israel Steevens 2^d.. Elip^t Steevens.. John Lane.. Jeramiah Nettelton.. Nathan Steevens.. Elisha Kelcey.. James Nettelton.. George Nettelton { Surveyors of Highways Josiah Rosseter.. Cornelius Holms.. Saml Persons.. Jehiel { Fencevers   *44*

Ambros Ward.. Capt Aaron Steevens { Leather Sealers   *44*

Leu^t Job Wright.. Benj$^{[ ]}$ Carter.. Selvester Redfield.. Lt Martin Lord.. Josiah Redfield.. Elisha Lane.. Aaron Kelcey { Listers   *44*

Cornelius Holms.. Abra^m Hurd.. Enos French.. Jonathan Kelcey { Thying men   *44*

John Willcocks 2^d.. Amos Parmele { Town Colectors   *44*

Daniel Redfield.. Jeremiah Parmele { Sealers of waits & M[*easures*]   *44*

Willm Griffen.. Jehiel Everts { Kee Keepers   *44*

Joseph Hillard Josiah Kelcy George Nettelton Cornelus Parmele Josiah Baldwin 2^d Roger Rose Jerem^h Nettelton Abr^m Hurd Danl Clark Peter Hull was Chosen Hawards   *45*

Voted the the County Rate of Abel Hull Should be paid out of the Town Tresurer.. Like wise Elez$^{[ ]}$ Wright.. Christopher Steevens   *45*

Killingworth

Leu^t John Crane Cornelius Holms Joseph Hillard was Chosen Inspectors of the oyster Acct	45
Capt John Person was Chosen Surveyors of Highways	45
24 Dec 1775	
Noah Lane Enos Hull Isaac Kelcey was Chosen Haywards - Jeremiah Parmele	46
[ ] Dec 1775	
Capt Elnath Steevens Capt Buel [J]ehel Kelcey John Rosseter George [ ] Capt Lane be a Commity.. to Exchange & Lay out to Saml Redfield and Others.. Some of the Proprietors Land on the west side of the Lower and Northerly of S^d Redfields House	46
Voted that Mr Abner Farnam be joined to the Proprietors Comttee	46
24 Dec 1775	
John Lewes Gager & Packer & Culler of Lumber	47
Voted that Saml [ ]lds Town Rate be paid out of the Town Tressur.. to Ezrah Nettelton also to Saml Palmele	47
Gideon Allen.. Stephen Willcoks.. Benj$^{[\ ]}$ Turner Ju^r Josiah Nettelton { Town Haywards	47
Voted to D[ ] Ruben Buell [ ] Cruttendens Cuntry Rate.. test Hiel Buell Clerk Protempore	47
8 Apr 1776	
Voted that Benjn Chatfield Rate be Granted out of the Treasuer to Nehemiah Higgens	47
10 Sep 1776	
Stephen Lane was Chosen Constable	47
12 Dec 1776	
Mr Stephen Willcoks was Chosen Moderator	47
Co^{ll} Aaron Eliot was Chosen Regester	47
Capt Hiel Buell was chosen Tresurer	47
Capt Saml Crane.. Aaron Kelcey.. Jared Eliot.. Jehiel Everts Elish Crane { Selectmen	47
Abner Farnum.. Jonathan Buell.. Eliph^t Steevens.. Roswell Parmele { Tithyingmen	47
Elisha Lane was Chosen Constable to Colect the Cunty Rate	47
Saml Redfield Constable	47
Mes^s David Dible.. David Buell.. Livi Rutty.. Ebenezer Willcoks.. Bile Buell.. Stephen Willcoks 2^d James Hull Chosen { Listers	47
Mes^s Amos Kelcey Josiah Kelcey Benoni Hillard Jedediah Buell 2^d Daniel Griswold Elihu Parmele Ad[ ] Willcoks Jed^h Harris Joel Hull Nathan Hull Nathl Kelcey Nehemiah Parmele Saml Person 2^d Simeon Wilcoks Natha^l Griswold 2^d Leu^t Martin Lord Jehel [ ]ins was Chosen Surveyors of Highways	47
16 Dec 1776	
Josiah Rossetor.. Cornelius Holms.. Saml Person.. Jehiel Everts { fence vewers	48
Abner Farnam.. Jonathan Buell.. Eliphett Steevins.. Roswel Parmele { Tythingmen	48
Ambros Ward.. Maj^r Silvanus Graves { Sealers of Leather	48
Daniel Redfield.. Jeremiah Parmele { Sealer of weights & Measures	48
Elnathan Steevens.. Elisha Crane { Branders of Horses	48

Killingworth

Mr John Lewes was Chosen Gauger Culler & Packer	48
Willia^m Griffen.. Jehiel Everts { Kee keepers	48
Voted that Two pence on the Pound be Granted in a Tax to pay the Charges of S^d Town - Abel Nettelton.. Lt Noah Lane { Colectors of S^d Rate	48
Benony Hillard Steeven Wilcoks Daniel Redfield Nathan Griswold Abel Wilcoks { were Chosen a Comitty of Enspection and Corespondence	48

27 Mar 1777

Doct^r Benj$^{[ ]}$ Gale was Chosen Moderator	48
Voted that the Town would Abide by the.. Request of the Goernour and Committee of Safety - and that the Town will Supply the Soldiers that are or Shall be Inlisted into the Continental Service.. Voted Likewis that Mes^s John Person Esq Dec^n Abel Willcoks Capt Stephen Lane Mr George Elliot Lt Noah Lane Lt Martain Lord be a Committy for the Service above	48
Voted that 40/ Should be given to Each Soldier that have or Shall Inlist into Service over and above what is already given for the Encoragement of Soldiers in this Town - and that two pence on the pound be Granted for raising of S^d Sum.. Jonathan Kelcey.. Elisha Kelcey was Chosen Collectors to Co^{ll} S^d Rate	48

17 Dec 1777

John Person Esqr was Chosen Moderator	49
Co^{ll} Aaron Eliot was Chosen town Regester	49
Capt Saml Crane.. Jared Eliot.. Aaron Kelcey.. Elisha Crane.. Lt Martain Lord { was Chosen Selectmen	49
Abr^m Person.. Saml Redfield { Constables	49
Mes^s John Lewes.. John Spencer.. Saml Person.. Jeremia^h 2^d Nettelton { Grandjurers	49
Votted that the Rates of the Widow Hannah Ward Should be Paid out of the Town Treasury	49
Mes^s Jared Eliot.. Noah Lane.. Elisha Kelcey.. Abner Farnam.. Saml Kelcey 2^d.. Daniel Willcoks.. George Nettelton.. Bili Buell.. Abel Clark.. Josiah Pelton.. Nathl Kelcey.. Isack Kelcey.. Eliphelet Steevens.. Gideon Buell.. Eliab Parmele.. Reuben Steevens.. was Chosen Surveyors of Highways	49
Joseph Rosseter.. Cornelius Holms.. Jehiel Everts.. Saml Person { Fence Viewers	49
Jonathan Buell.. Roswel Parmele.. James Hull.. Jared Baldwin { Tityingmen	49
Ruben Steevens.. Ambros Ward { Leather Sealers	49
Mes^s Stephen Willcoks 2^d David Buell Bili Buell Israel Steevens 2^d Ebenezer Wilcoks Roswel Hull Benj$^{[ ]}$ Rosseter ~ Listers	49
Mes^s Daniel Redfield.. Capt Job Wright.. Josiah Redfield.. Abel Willoks 2^d.. Capt Bezalel Bristol.. Benoni Hillard.. Hez$^{[ ]}$ Lane Esq$^{r\{}$ Assessers	49
Livi Kelsey.. John Rutty { Colectors	49
Capt Stephen Lane.. Lt Noah Lane.. Ruben Steevens.. Dodo Person.. Capt Nathan Griswold.. Capt Job Right -- a Comitty to Provide for the Soldiers Fameleys	49
Robert Wilkensons Rate of 32/.. Joshua Glading Rate 12/.. Was Voted to be paid out of the Town Rate	49
Barber Griffen.. Jehiel Everts Kee Keepers	49

19 Mar 1778

George Eliot Esqr was Chosen Moderator	50

Killingworth

Mr Josiah Redfield was Chosen Selectman	50
Capt Stephen Lane Benoni Hillard Elisha Lane Livi Hull Daniel Towner John Spencer Daniel Parmele was Chosen a Committy to Procure Cloathing for the Soldiers [ ] Dec 1778	50
George Eliot Esqr was Chosen Moderator	50
Co^{ll} Aaron Eliot was Chosen Town Regester	50
Capt Willm Morgan Mr John Spencer Mr Daniel Parmele Mr Josiah Redfield and Mr John Lane was Chosen a Comy^t of Supplys	50
Mr Abraham Person was Chosen Constable and to Collecter of y^e Cuntry Tax.. Capt Wi^{ll} Morgan - Dito	50
Saml Person Ebenezer Willcoks John Willcoks & Le^t Jed$^{[\ ]}$ Buell 2^d was Chosen Granjurors	50
Josiah Griswold Capt Job Wright Ambros Ward Johnthan Buell George Nettelton Israel Steevens 2^d Saml Nettelton John Nettelton Thomas Francis Martain Kelcey Elisha Lane Abel Nettelton Elisha Kelcey - was Chosen Surveyors of the Highway	50
Ben$^{[\ ]}$ Carter Willm Morgan John Spencer Daniel Parmele Josiah Redfield John Lane Daniel Towner Capt Josiah Baldwin Ezra Nettelton Chosen a Comy^t of Suplys 22 [ ] 1779	50
George Eliot was Chosen Moderator	50
A Com^y to Ro[ ]d Cloathing for the Soldiers in the Continental Armey & John Willcox Capt Silas Kelcy Stephen Wilcox Simeon Wilcox Jonathan Kelcy Cornelius Parmele Gurdon Buell Saml Redfield 14 Dec 1779	50
Esqr George Eliot was Chosen Moderator	51
Co^{ll} Aaron Eliot was Chosen Town Regester	51
Mes^s Capt Stephen Lane Daniel Redfield Abel Willcox 2^d Leu^t Martain Lord & Capt Aaron Kelcey was Chosen Selectmen	51
Saml [ ]ther & Abr^m Person was Chosen Constables to Colect the Rate	51
Daniel Peck Barber Grinnel George Nettelton Caleb L Hurd Benj$^{[\ ]}$ Willcok Nathan Willcox Jared Eliot Josisah Buell Abner Hull Benj$^{[\ ]}$ Gale Daniel Griswold Israel Steevens Ruben Steevens David Everts Ozias Parmele Noah Hill Josiah Pelton Daniel Parmele John Spencer was Chosen Surveyors of Highwais	51
Jehiel Everts Saml Person Cornelius Holms & Josisah Rosseter Chosen fence Viewers	51
Capt Job Wright Capt William Morgan Elishsa Lane John Willcox Simeon Willcox Levi Rutty Capt Bezalel Bristol & James Hull was Chosen Listers	51
Ambros Ward and Dan Kelcey Grandjurors	51
James Nettelton Levi Redfield Stephen Willcox Jared Eliot chosen Tything men	51
Amos Kelcey Elisha Kelcey Josiah Buell Jonathan Kelcey Israel Steevens John Purson Esqr was Chosen a Committy to Supply Soldiers Families	51
John Lewes Culler	51
Hiel Steevens Elisha Crane Branders	51
Daniel Redfield Josiah Parmele Sealers	51
Willm Griffen Hiel Everts Kee Keepers	51

Killingworth

Peter Kelcey & Moses Griswold was Chosen town Collectors	51
Ambros Ward & Ruben Steevens was Chosen Leather Sealers	51
Eliphelet Steevens Amos Parmele Cornelius Parmele Ezra Kelcey Abra^m Hurd to Supply Cloathing ~~Daniel~~ Griswold	51
14 Mar 1780	
George Eliott Esqr in the Chair Daniel Redfield in the Absence of the Town Clerk to take to the Votes and transmit them to him	51
Voted that Mes^s Capt Saml Crane Capt Stephen Lane Cornelius Holms John Lewes Abram Hurd John Spencer Capt Beezalel Bristol Dec^n Abel Willcox Capt Aaron Kelcey & George Nettelton be a Committy of Inspectors	51
9 Apr 1780	
Saml Purson ye 2^d Noah Hill Ebenezer Willcox was Chosen Listers	51
[ ] 1779	
Whereas George Eliot Esqr has represented to this Meeting that one principle reason of the great decreas of the Oysters in this town he Supposes is Oweing to the removing two great a Proportion of Shels from the Oysters Grown Desiring that he may have Liberty to place a Quantity of Shels and Oysters in the [ ]ion River Adjoining to his Meadow.. Voted that the s^d George Eliot have Liberty to to [ ]uller Shels & Oysters in S^d River	51
8 Sep 1780	
George Eliot Esqr Chosen [*Moderator*]	52
10 Nov 1780	
George Eliot Esqr was Chosen Moderator	52
Voted that Six pence on the Pound be Granted.. to be paid in Provisions According to the Stipulated Prices in an Act of Assembly.. or Eight pence on the Pound to be made on the List of ye Year 1779 and to be Paid in States Money or Old Continental Money in Proportion or in New Continentel Money.. and Seth Redfield and Ens^n Ab^m Hurd was Chosen Colector of S^d Rate	52
Capt Martain Lord was Appointed Purchaser and Receiver of the above Artickles of Provisions	52
16 Nov 1780	
John Purson Esqr Moderator	52
In Order to fill up and Compleat the States Quota of the Continental Army ~ it was Voted that they would Adobt the Rule, or Law, made by the General Assembly.. and the Committy Chosen to Class the People.. to Procure the men is Capt Saml Gale Capt Saml Crane George Eliot Esqr Capt Aaron Kelcey Capt Beazeelel Bristol Hez^h Lane Esqr and Dec^n Abel Willox	52
12 Dec 1780	
Esqr George Eliot was Chosen Moderator	52
Co^{ll} Aaron Eliot was Chosen Town Clerck	52
Capt Stephen Lane Daniel Redfield Dec^n Abel Willcox Capt Aaron Kelcey & Capt Martain Lord was Chosen Selectmen	52
Elisha Lane was Chosen Constable to Colect the Cuntry Rate	52
Selvister Redfield Constable	52
Jonathan Buel Caleb L Hurd Levi Redfield Bili Buell was chosen Grandjurers	52

Killingworth

Joseph Willcox Abner Farnam Benj[l.] Rossetor Na[ll] Griswold was Chosen Tythingmen	52
Abram[ll] Purson Job Seaward Leu[t] Sam[l] Purson 2[d] Leu[t] Noah Lane was Chosen Tythingmen	52
Jared Eliot Doc[t] Gale Abner Farnam Daniel Willcoks Amos Kelcey Cornelus Holms Abner Parmele James Hull John Lane George Griswold John Franklin Aaron Norton Cap[t] Josiah Baldwin Sam[l] Davis 2[d] James Nettelton Simon Willcoks Leu[t] George Nettelton was Chosen Surveyers of Highways	53
Jonathan Williams Cornelus Holms Elihu Parmele Jehiel Everts was Chosen fence Veiwers	53
Co[ll] Graves & Ambros Ward Sealers of Leather	53
Daniel Redfield & Jeremiah Parmele Sealers of weights and Mesures	53
John Lewes Gauger [ ]er and Culler of Lumber	53
Elnathan Steevens & Elisha Crane Brandors & Tollers of Horses	53
Will[m] Griffen & Jehiel Everts Kee Keeers	53
four Pence on the Pound States money was Granted for the Town[s] Use - Sam[l] Buell & Es[n] Ab[m] Hurd was Chosen Collectors	53
Levi Hull Elihu Parmele Israel Steevens John Person Daniel Griswold Ambros Ward Benoni Hillard John Lane Nathan Kelcey was Chosen a Committy of Supply	53
Mes[s] Daniel Parmele Cornelius Parmele Simeon Willcox Caleb Hurd Benj[n] Merrel Ezra Kelcey was Chosen a Com[y] to Provide Cloathing for the Soldiers	53

[ ] Dec 1780

Elisha Lane Cap[t] Nathan Griswold Cap[t] Job Wright Cap[t] Josiah Baldwin Cap[t] Noah Lane Benoni Hillard was Chosen a Committ[y] to Class the Town to rais Soldiers	53
John Lewes Cap[t] Bazalel Bristol Daniel Parmele Cap[t] Sam[l] Crane Cap[t] Joseph Chatfield Cap[t] Job Wright Jonathan Kelcey was Chosen a Comm[ty] of Inspection of Provisions	53
Sam[l] Redfield was Chosen Lister	53
Stephen Willcox 2[d] Levi Rutty was Chosen in Adition to the Committy for Providing Provision for the Soldiers	53
Voted that one penne half pene on the Pound on the List 1779 to Purchus Flower rye Indian Corn at the Stipulated prices - Sam[l] Redfield & Joseph Wheler was Chosen to Collect[rs] Receivers and Packer[s]	53
Martain Kelcey was Chosen to Collect the money from the Delinquent Classes and Ab[m] Hurd was Chosen to the Same Service	53

12 Sep 1781

Voted that one pence on the Pound be Granted to Defray the Incident Charges of S[d] town in Silver in wheat at the Rate of Six Shillings p[r] bushel or Other Articles of Provisions in Equal Proportion - Likewise M[r] Abr[m] Purson was Appointed Receiver of the Severil Articles above Mentioned in Order to Supply y[e] soldiers in Provision	54

11 Dec 1781

George Eliot Esq[r] was Chosen Moderator	54
Co[l] Aaron Eliott was Chosen Regester	54

Killingworth

[ ] Dec 1781

Capt Stephen Lane.. Mr Abner Farnam Capt Beezel Bristol.. Mr Abram Purson and James Hill { Selectmen	54
Elisha Lane.. Peter Kelcey { Constables	54
Mes^s Barber Grenell.. David Buell.. Levi Rutty.. Job Seaward.. [ ] Franklin { Listers	54
Levi Kelcey.. Dea^n Carter.. Julius Everts 2^d.. Levi Hull { Grandjurors	54
Ambros Ward & Co^{ll} Graves { Chosen Leather Sealers	54
Leu^t Saml Purson.. Jehiel Everts.. Cornelius Holms.. Josiah Rossetor { Fence Veiwers	54
Gurden Hull.. Jeremiah Redfield.. Saml Towner.. Job Parmele.. John Spencer.. George Nettelton.. Elisha Kelcey.. Moses Kelcey.. Josiah Carter.. Cornelius Holms.. Josiah Hull.. Elias Parmele.. Levi Hull.. Elisha Crane and Phillip Steevens { Surveyor of Highway	54
Mes^s Moses Griswold.. Thomas Steevens 2^d.. Job Buell 2^d { Chosen Tythingmen	54
Mr$^{[s]}$ John Lewes Gauger & Packer	54
Mr$^{[s]}$ Daniel Redfield.. Josiah Parmele Sealer^s of waights & Mesures	54
Mes^s Elnath^n Steevens.. Elisha Crane { Branders	54
Jehiel Everts.. Willm Griffen { Keepers	54
Voted that two pence on the Pound be Granted for the Incident Charges of S^d Town to be Paid in Silver or in wheat at y^e Rate of Six Shillings ye bushel or Other Provision at in ye Same Proportion.. and James Hill 2^d Benj^{l} ^{l} Merrils was Chosen Collectors	54
John Purson Esqr Jonathan Kelcy Stephen Willcox Ambros Ward Caleb L Hurd was Chosen a Committy for the Supplying the Soldiers Famalies	55
George Eliot Esqr Job Wright & Stephen Willcox be a Committy to Settle all Matters Subsisting between Mr Amos Steevens and the Town	55

7 Apr 1782

Ebenezer Wilcoks was Chosen Lister	55

11 Sep 1782

Voted that John Purson Esqr & Theop$^{[ ]}$ Morgan be a Committee… to Petition the.. General Assembly that the twentieth Part of the State Taxes.. to be Abated to Individuals in Each Town Respectively Shall be Colected and Paid into the Town Treasury.. to be Disposed of as the Town by their Vote Shall Think Proper	55

10 Dec 1782

George Eliot Esqr was Chosen Moderator	55
Co^{ll} Aaron Eliot was Chosen Cleark	55
Daniel Redfield George Eliot Esqr Capt Nathan Griswold Capt Martain Lord De^c Abel Wilcox was Chosen Selectmen	55
Capt Aaron Steevens was Chosen Constable To Colect the State Taxes	55
Leu^t John Crane.. Mr Jared Eliot.. Abner Parmele.. Jeremiah Buell { Grandjurors	55
Leu^t Noah Lane.. Mr Saml Redfield.. Capt Willm Morgan.. Capt Josiah Baldwin.. Mr John Lane.. D[ ]$^{[ ]}$ Joseph Cone Leu George Nettelton { Listers	55
Simion Willcox.. David Dible.. Nath^n Willcox.. Ruben Steevens.. Amos Kelcey.. Noah Hill.. Nathan Griswold.. Daniel Willcox.. Elnathan Hurd.. Co^l Silvanus Graves.. Elihu Parmele.. James Hill 2^d.. Israel Stevens.. Levi Kelcy.. Thomas Francis.. George Nettelton { Surveyors	55

Killingworth

of Highways
[ ] Jan 1782

Phillip Stevens.. Saml Griswold.. Silvester Redfield.. Ebenez^r Willcox { Tythingmen	55
Jehiel Everts.. Josiah Rossetor.. Cornelius Holms.. Saml Purson { Fence Viewers	55
Daniel Parmele.. Ambros Ward { Leather Sealers	55
Mr John Lewes -- Culler Gager & Packer	55
Capt Josiah Baldwin.. Mr Elnat^n Stevens { Horse Brandors & Tooler^s	55
Mr Saml Davis.. Josiah Carter { Colect^s of Rate or Rates	55
Hez Land Esq.. Capt Job Wright.. [ ] Purson.. [ ] Morgan.. D[ ]$^{[ ]}$ Gale was Chosen a Committy to Examine y^e Classes	55

21 Aug 1783

George Eliot Esqr was Chosen Moderator	56
Voted that D[ ][ ] Gale with the Selectmen Should be a Committy to take into Consideration the Commutation or half Pay Granted to the Continentel officers by Congress	56
Voted that Co^{ll} Aaron Eliot Capt Saml Gale & Capt Aaron Kelcey be a Committy of Correspondence	56

7 Dec 1777

The Names of those that are Qualified Acording to Law to Vote in Town Meetings.. Doc^t Benjn Gale.. Co^{ll} A^n Eliot.. Lt Aaron Kelcy.. Enos Hull.. Josiah Watrous.. John Nickles.. George Eliot.. Marten Kelcy.. Roswel Parmele.. Bili Buell.. Tim$^{[ ]}$ Rutty.. Nathl Williams 2^d.. Dea^n Woodruff.. Amos Parmele.. Daniel Chittenden.. Saml Purson 2^d.. Joel Hull.. Josiah Hull.. John Rutty.. Jerimiah Buell 2^d.. Eliphelet Steevens.. Nathl Griswold 2^d..	145
..Abner [ ]on.. Joel Parmele.. Nathan Steevens.. Saml H[ ]on.. Caleb L Hurd.. Constant Redfield.. Cornelus Holms.. Capt Lemuel Hull.. Josiah Rosseter.. Samuel Buell.. Saml Smith.. Eliakim Redfield.. Gideon [ ].. Capt Seth Griffen.. Simion Redfield.. Orsbon Steevens.. Capt Willm Morgan.. Joseph Hillard.. Jared Baldwin.. Daniel Towner.. Nehemiah H[ ].. Daniel Kelcey.. David Jones.. Orsborn Steevens.. Joseph Chatfield.. Nathan Graves..	145
..Ruben Buell.. John Rosseter 2^d.. Uriah Kelcey.. Ezra Kelcy.. Jonathan Kelcey.. Josiah Baldwin 2^d.. Ambros Ward.. James Hill 2^d.. Saml Nettelton.. Ezekel Hull.. Ezra Palmele.. Ezra Nettelton.. Capt Silas Kelcy.. Leu^t Noah Lane.. Theop$^{[ ]}$ Morgan.. Philip Steevens.. Theoplus Crane.. Nathan Kelcy.. Josiah Griswold.. Hiel Steevens.. Daniel Crane.. John Chatfield.. Oulon Button.. John Nettleton.. David Lebaron.. Esrael Steevens 2^d.. Saml Kelcey..	145
..Abner Hull.. Saml Hull.. Dudly White.. Thomas Wilkiinson.. John Rossetor.. Nathl Lewiss.. Ruben Towner.. Hubble Steevens.. Co^l Sylvanus Graves.. Daniel Merrels.. Josiah Parmele.. Oliver Hull.. [ ] Lane.. Dan Kelcy.. Saml [ ]ther.. Josiah Hull.. Daniel Towner 2^d.. Sylvester Redfield.. Martin Redfield.. [ ] Steevens.. James Ward.. Enos Smith.. Mr Abij[ ] Willcox.. Theop[ ] Morgan 2^d.. Barnabas Hillard.. John Carter.. Joseph Farnam 2^d	145

[4] Sep 1777

The Names of the Fremen of the Town of Killingworth who hath taken the Oath of fidelity and the Fremans Oath - Dec^n David Buell.. Mr Stephen Willcok.. Capt Stephen Lane.. Mr Josiah Chatfield.. Mr Cornelus Parmele.. Mr John Lewes.. Mr John Norton.. Mr Joseph Lane.. Mr Isiah Franklin.. Capt Lemuel Hull.. Mr James Hull.. Mr Ezra Nettelton.. Mr Josiah Relton.. Mr Saml Rogers.. Mr Elijah Willcok.. Mr Saml Nettelton. Dec^n Abel Willcoks..	146
..Mr James Steevens.. Mr Elisha Lane.. En^s Daniel Steevens.. Capt Elisha White.. Capt Saml Gale.. John Purson Esq.. Mr Josiah Rosssetor.. Mr Israel Steevens.. Mr Job Buell.. Mr Benona	146

Killingworth

Hillard.. Mr Nehemiah Parmele.. Mr Daniel Redfield.. Mr Abra^m Willcoks.. Mr Abner Farnam.. Dec^n Dodo Purson.. Mr Joseph Nettelton.. Capt Bazalel Bristol.. Mr Josiah Redfield.. ..Mr Zadock Welman.. Mr Eliab Parmele.. Le^t John Crane.. Mr John Lane.. Ebenezer Willcoks.. Co^{ll} Aaron Eliot.. Revd Mr Toun[ ].. D^n Nathl Steevens.. Joseph Kelcy.. ~~Josiah Redfield~~.. George Eliot.. Aaron Kelcey.. Giels Griswold.. Ambros Ward.. Oliver Parmele.. Nehemiah Huggins.. Jonathan Kelcy.. Uriah Kelcy.. Roswel Parmele.. Elezor Woodruff.. ..Josiah Waterous.. Daniel Towner.. Hubbel Steevens.. Enos Hull.. Cornelius Holms.. Saml Purson 2^d.. Levi Rutty.. Ezra Kelcey.. Ruben Towner.. Silvanus Graves.. Theophiles Morgan.. Capt Josiah Baldwin.. Orsborn Steevens.. Capt John Chatfield.. Josiah Buel.. Josiah Parmele.. Daniel Merrels.. John Nickels.. Daniel Chittenden.. Capt [ ] Redfield.. ~~[ ] Smith~~.. Samuel Smith.. Elias Parmele.. Amos Parmele.. [ ] Parmele.. Joseph Hillard.. Nath^n Willcox.. Benj[ ] Carter.. Peter Kelcy.. Amos Kelcy.. Martin Kelcey.. James Nettelton.. Jonathan Franklin.. Mickel Merrett.. Roswel Hull.. Willm Wright.. Wil^{lm} Eliott

146

146

Lebanon

Town Meetings
Volume 1

1689-1802

Located at the Town Clerk's Office

Lebanon

12 Dec 1774

made Choice of his Honor Govr Trumbull, Moderator	290
We Do.. Appoint Wm Williams, Joshua West John Clark Benajah Bill Esq^{rs} Mr Jon^a Trumbull Ju^r Mr Pel^a Marsh, Mr James Pinneo Ju^r Cap Beach Williams Cap Elij Hide Ju^r Mr Nathan Cheever, Mr Sam^{ll} Hide Ju^r & Mr Noah Colman.. a Committee of Inspection or Com^{te} of Safety, Whose Business it Shall be attentively to observe the Conduct of all Persons in this Town... Wm Williams T Clerk	294

10 Apr 1775

Govr Trumbull, Moderator as before	296
a Highway.. from North Pond Highway.. thro Land late belonging to Mr Cutting Dec^d now Dorothy Hills.. to Land of Lt Wm Wattles & Capt Jno Wattles now Dec^d to the Mile Line.. to the Bridge near ye House of Cap James Fitch, now Cap Jer Mason's or inhabited by Him &c Was proposed & .. after some Objection by Eb^r Bacon &c.. is accepted	296
a highway.. from ye House of Cap Israel Williams thro his land, & Land of Dan^{ll} Abel & Sol^o Abel to Exeter Meeting House, was.. approved	296
a Highway.. from near the House of Lt Danl Clark, thro his, to Sol^o Abels Land & corner of And^w Fitch, to ye Highway called ye North Pond Way year ye House of s^d Fitch & Joel Chamberlin to accommodate the Traval to Colchester &c was.. approved	296
a Highway from ye back side of Exeter Meeting House thro Land of Elip^t Abels Heirs, Elihu Thomass lands chiefly, to Jos Lomis to Danl Strongs Land to ye Highway leading from Benjn Brewsters to Silas Clarks &c.. is also accepted	296
a Deed of a Highway by Mes^{rs} Josiah Bartlet, Amos Thomas, & Cyprian Lothrop.. is accepted	296

11 Dec 1775

Joshua West Esqr was chosen, Moderator	297
Wm Williams was chosen Town Clerk & also Town Treasurer	297
Wm Williams.. Jon^a Trumbull Ju^r.. Elijah Hyde Ju^r.. James Pinneo Ju^r.. Veach Williams.. Pelatiah Marsh } Select Men	297
Chose the following Persons to the following officers.. Viz Constables.. Ammi Fitch$^{\wedge excused}$ Lebbeus Woodworth, And^w Metcalf & Ozias Colman & said Coleman to collect the next Colony Rate & afterwards on s^d Fitch's Declining & consistly requesting to be excused, They released him & Chose Mr Caleb Abel again, a Constable	297
Surveyors, viz Dav^d Trumbull, Daniel Brewster, Saml Hide Ju^r, Allen Wightman Josiah Webster, Elip^t Barker, Step^n Bingham Elijah Hide Senr, Jos. Leach, Roland Swift Rhodolphus Thatcher, Bezaleel Fuller, Thos Bingham, Eb^r Gillet Ju^r, Saml Bliss, Eldad Hunt, Jos. Hill, Benj^a Lyman, Eleaz^r Richardson, Azariah Brown, Elias Bliss, Joel Wright, Jacob Eliot, Bezaleel Badger, Aaron Thorp Wm Frink, Saml Wattles, Amos Bliss, Peleg Thomas Thos Perkins, James Hutchinson Oliver Bill, Eb^r Cole Ju^r Hubbard McKall & Jacob Clark	297
Fence Viewers.. Israel Loomis.. Josiah Rockwell.. Beriah Southworth	298
Listers.. David Trumbull.. Rhodol^s Thacher.. Benjn Lyman.. Consid^r Little.. Aaron Peabody.. Zach^s Tracy.. Levi Jones	298
Grand Jurors.. Enoch White.. Comfort Brewster.. James Crocker.. Nathl Bartlet.. Malachi Thomas.. John Doggett	298
Collectors of Rates.. Elip^t Metcalfe.. Bez^a Fuller.. Nathl Hide Ju^r.. Joel Loomis.. Daniel Yeomans.. Simon Williams.. Azariah Bill	298
Leather Sealers.. John Lyman.. Simeon Gray.. Aaron Bunce.. Eben^r Hinckley.. Stephen Powells	298

Lebanon

Tything Men.. James Tickner.. Isaac Gillet.. Josiah Buell.. John Lomis.. John Henry.. Consid^r Little.. James Woodworth.. Jesse Brown.. Isaiah Loomis.. Aaron B[ ].. Amos Clark.. Zacheus Loomis	298
Haywards.. Jos. Blackman.. Stephen Payn.. Wm White.. Joshua Chappel	298
Chimney Viewer.. John Huntington	298
Gager.. S[ ]h^a Robinson	298
Packers.. Jed^h Strong Ju^r.. James Wright	298
Branders.. Wm Huntington.. Biri: Southworth.. Moses Clark.. Hinch^n Bennet	298
Sealer of Weights.. Eben^r Tisdale	298
of Measures.. Wm Beamont.. Isr^l Dewey.. Ben$^{[\ ]}$ Wood	298
Key Keepers.. And^w Alden Senr.. Saml Clark Ju^r.. Cap Dijah Fowler.. Pelatiah Marsh	298

9 Dec 1776

Chose Joshua West Esqr Moderator	299
Then Chose Wm Williams Town Clerk & also s^d Mr Williams Town Treasur^r	299
Wm Williams.. Elij. Hide Ju^r.. Silus Phelps.. James Penneo Ju^r.. Veach Williams & Danl Abel Ju^r } Select Men	299
The following Persons to ye following offices Viz, Constables.. Caleb Abel, Lebbeus Woodworth, Andrew Metcalf & Ozias Colman s^d Woodworth to Collect ye Colony Rate	299
Surveyors of Highways.. Dav^d Trumbull.. Caleb Abel Ju^r.. Saml Hide, Son of ye late Dec^d.. Allen Wightman.. Josiah Webster.. Elkanah Tisdale.. Elip^t Barker.. Stephen Bingham.. Elijah Hide Senr.. Jos Leech.. Roland Swift.. Rhodol^s Thacher.. Bez^a Fuller.. Thos Bingham.. Eben^r Gillet.. Saml Bliss.. David Treadway.. Saml Woodward Ju^r.. Nathl Hide Ju^r.. Dav^d Cole.. Nathl Fitch.. Consid^r Little.. Beza^l Badger.. Abijah Thomas.. Oliver Buell.. Jos Loomis.. Leb^s Metcalfe.. Israel Lee.. Peleg Thomas.. Ozias Colman.. Jos. Bissell.. Amos Clark.. Simon Williams & Paul Hutchinson	299
Fence Viewers.. Israel Loomis.. Josiah Rockwell.. Beriah Southworth	299
Listers.. Dav^d Trumbull.. Rhodol^s Thacher.. Consid^r Little.. Saml Guild.. Aaron Peabody.. Abel Webster & Benj$^{[\ ]}$ Sprague	299
Grand Jurors.. Enoch White.. Wm Hall.. Saml Allen.. Nathl Bartlet.. Reuben Metcalfe.. Eleaz^r Hutchinson	299
Collectors of the Rate.. Caleb Hayward.. Joseph Post. Nath$^{[\ ]}$ Fitch.. Azariah Brown.. Mason Brown.. Jacob Clark.. Richd English	299
Leather Sealers.. D^n Jno Lyman.. Sim^n Gray.. Aaron Bunce.. Eben^r Hinckley.. Stephen Powell	299
Tything Men.. Jno Loomis.. Elip^t Metcalfe.. James Bayley.. James Turner.. Isaac Gillet.. James Wright.. Gershom Clark.. Joel Loomis.. Elk^a Parker.. Patric Butler.. Jno Willliams.. Jno Clark Ju^r.. Jacob Clark	299
Haywards.. Stephen Payn.. Wm Hall.. Wm White.. Joshua Chappel	299
Chimney Viewer.. Zeb^n Lathrop	299
Gager.. Ich^a Robinson	299
Packers.. Jed^h Strong Ju^r.. James Crocker.. Oliver Buell	299
Branders.. Wm Huntington.. Beri: Southworth.. Moses Clark.. Hinch^n Bennet	299
Sealer of Weights.. Eb^r Tisdale	299

Lebanon

Pound Keepers.. wid Lyd^a Alden.. Saml Clark Ju^r.. Dijah Fowler	299
Benj^{l l} Wood.. Seal^r Measurs	299
on Request of Caleb Hayward, vote Him Liberty to Set up a Weavers Shop.. in the Road near his House, by the Discretion & Inspection of Dⁿ Jno Lyman & Jos Hitcherson to Stand During the Towns Pleasure	300

11 Feb 1777

Chose Dⁿ Jno Lyman, Moderator	300
Chose Allen Wrightman a Collector of ye Town Rate, instead of Jos Post, refused	300

5 Mar 1777

a Warning to Chose a Collector in ye room of Caleb Hayward who was chose & refuses & also another in stead of Richd English , then Chosen & since Dec^d	301
Chose Dⁿ Jno Lyman, Moderator	301
Chose John Loomis a Collector of Town Rate in stead of s^d Hayward	301
Chose Paul Hutchinson, Col^r instead of s^d English	301

31 Mar 1777

Chose His Honor Govr Trumbull, Moderator	301
the Familyes of [*Soldiers*].. Shall be furnished & Supplied During their Service with such necessaries as they may want at prices not exceeidng the Sums Stated & limited by law..This Town Do appoint Mes^{rs} Jon^a Lyman, Oliv^r Huntington, Tim^o Holbrook Eleaz^r Richardson, John House Jer^h Mason Ichabod Bartlet & Ephraim Carpenter.. for that purpose	302
Chose Malachi Thomas a Lister... in Stead of Abel Webster lately Dec^d	303

24 Sep 1777

Made Choise of Joshua West Esqr Moderator: and Thos Williams clerk pro Temp:	303
the Question was put, Whether the Town will appoint a Com^{tee} to procure immediately the various Articles of Cloathing, specified in the Resolve & Requisition of the ~~State~~ Governor & Council of this State.. for Each non Commissioned Officer & Soldier in the Continental Army, belonging to this Town.. as Cheap as may be.. Pass'd in the Affirmative.. chose John Clark Esqr Capt William Huntington, Capt Samuel Fuller, Lieu^t Joseph Hill, Messrs John Williams, Elijah House, Dr Andrew Metcalf, Jared Hinckley, Capt Carpenter, Malichi Thomas, Elkanah Tisdale & Eleazer Richardson to be A Com^{tee} for the above s^d Purpose	304

8 Dec 1777

Governor Trumbull, was Chosen Moderator	304
Thos Williams, was chosen Clerk pro Tempore	304
Colo. William Willliams, was chosen Town Clerk.. also chosen Town Treasurer	304
then Chose William Williams.. Elijah Hide Junr.. Silas Phelps.. James Pinneo Junr.. Nehe^h Williams & Danl Abel Junr } Select Men	305
And the following Persons to the following Offices, Viz Constables.. Elisha Hutchinson.. Lebbeus Woodworth.. Andrew Metcalfe & Ozias Colman s^d Hutchinson to Collect the Colony Rate	305
Surveyors of Highways.. Aaron Bushnell, Saml Hide, Josiah Buel, Abraham Fitch, Benjamin Throope, Benjamin Payn, Dan Terry, Jno Vaughan, Jno Dewey, Charles Swift, Abijah Smith, Daniel Smalley Junr, Eleazar Bingham, Israel Dewey, Joseph Loomise, Eliphalet Bill, Joseph Sullard Junr, Peter Newcomb, Danl Dunham, Saml West, Eldad Hunt, Denison Wattles, Danl	305

Lebanon

Emmons, Aaron Thorpe, Levi Jones, Patrick Butler, Jacob Eliot, Daniel Strong, Jonathan Webster.. Darius Hills.. Silas Clark.. Isaiah Williams Junr and Elijah House Grandjurors.. Josiah Rockwell Junr, Ammi Fitch, John Williams, Peleg Thomas, ~~Samuel Hutchinson~~, Ephraim Carpenter, Samuel Hutchinson	305
Listers.. Eliphalet Metcalfe.. Rhodolphus Thacher.. Samuel Guild.. Eldad Hunt.. Amos Thomas Junr.. Malichi Thomas.. Benjamin Sprague	305
Fence Viewers.. Israel Loomis.. Josiah Rockwell.. Beriah Southworth	305
Tything Men.. John Loomiss, Eliphalet Metcalfe.. Isaac Gillet - Eleazar Hutchinson.. Samuel Gay, Jeriah Wright, Benoni Loomis Ju^r.. Rufus Collins Junr.. Samuel Brewster.. Patrick Butler.. Andrew Wattles.. Jacob Clark.. Charles Williams	305
Chimney Viewer.. Zebulon Lothrop	305
Gager.. Ichabod Robinson	305
Branders.. William Huntington.. Beriah Southworth.. Moses Clark.. Hinchman Bennet	305
Sealer of Weights.. Ebenezer Tisdale	305
Sealer of Measures.. Benjamin Wood	305
Leather Sealers.. Dan Throope.. Deac^n John Lyman.. Aaron Bunce.. Ebenezer Hinckley.. Ozias Colman	305
Collectors of Town Rates.. Benjamin Throope, Ebenezer Gillet - Samuel Brewster.. Zerubbabel Collins.. Isaiah Loomise.. John Webster Junr.. Simon Jones	305
Haywards.. John Johnson.. Caleb Hayward.. Peter Newcomb.. William White.. Joshua Chappel.. Stephen Payn	305
Key Keepers.. William Waterman.. Samuel Clark Junr.. Dijah Fowler.. Charles Williams	305
voted, that the Select Men..take Care that the Highway lately laid out, near the house of Capt Daniel Clark, leading to Colchester, be opened & made fit for public use	306
Voted, That the folllowing Persons be a Com^{tee} to provide for the Support of the Families of poor Soldiers ..., belonging to the continental Army; and to procure Cloathing that Shall be wanted for the Continental Soldiers.. Viz.. Messrs Daniel Dewey, Josiah Rockwell, Israel Loomise, Nathan Cheever, Jabez Mecalfe, Capt Dijah Fowler, Jared Hinckley, Archippus McCall, Joseph Hill, John House, Silas Clark & Ephraim Carpenter	306
Voted that a Sign Post for the warning of public Meetings, be erected & kept up near the house of William Frink at the lower end of Goshen	306

1 Jan 1778

Chose Joshua West Esqr, Moderator	306

28 Sep 1778

Joshua West Esqr Moderator	309
Voted That Jno Shapleys Fine of £5 w^h he has paid for not joining ye Continental Army he having after ward hired a Man for three years, be abated & repaid	309

7 Dec 1778

Chose His Excellency Gover^r Trumbull, Moderator	310
Chose Wm Williams, Town Clerk.. & T. Treas^r	310
then Chose & appointed in Sucession Viz.. Wm Williams.. Maj^r Elijah Hyde.. Mr Silas Phelps.. Cap James Pinneo.. Cap Nehe^h Williams & Cap Danl Abel } to be Select Men	310
Then They Chose the folowing Persons to the following Ofices.. Viz.. Constables.. Elisha Hutchinson.. Lebbeus Woodworth.. Andrew Metcalfe.. Oliver Bill.. Metcalf, chosen also to	310

495

Lebanon

Collect the Colony Rate..s^d Bill also took ye Oath of Fidelity

Surveyors of Highways..Jos. Robinson.. Danl Hide.. Danl Bissell.. Allen Whitman.. Jos. Throope.. Jed^h Phelps.. Wm Torrey Ju^r.. Saml Gay.. Jno Arnold.. Sexton Bailey.. Ammi Fitch.. Jed^h Strong.. Jon^a Strong.. Israel Dewey.. Danl Franklin.. Ab^m Bliss.. Robt Bennet.. Thos Buckingham.. Elip^t Woodworth.. Azariah Brown.. Elias Bliss. Sluman Wattles.. Joshua West Ju^r.. And^w Metcalf.. Jesse Brown.. Peleg Thomas.. Israel Lee Ju^r.. Isaiah Loomis.. Simon House.. Simon Williams.. Nathan Spafford.. Gershom West & Asael Clark of Exeter *310*

Fence Viewers.. Israel Loomis.. Josiah Rockwell.. Beri: Southworth *311*

Listers.. Elip^t Metcalfe.. Jon^a Goodwin Ju^r.. Eldad Hunt.. James Crocker.. Amos Thomas Ju^r.. Jos. Payne.. Eph^m Carpenter *311*

Grand Jurors.. Elip^t Metcalfe.. Jon^a Goodwin Ju^r.. Hinch^n Bennet.. And^w Waterman.. Saml Hutchinson.. Darius Hill *311*

Collectors.. Enoch White.. Jacob Loomis.. Dav^d Treadway.. Elip^t Bill.. Dennison Wattles.. Levi Metcalfe.. Azar^h Bill *311*

Leather Sealers.. John Lyman.. Dan Throope.. Simon Clark.. Eben^r Hinckley.. Ozias Colman *311*

Tytheing Men.. Jno Alden.. Danl Hide.. Wm Torrey Ju^r.. Eben^r Hide.. Pelatiah Holbrook.. Jon^a Strong.. Ja^s Woodworth.. Elip^t Bill.. Jno Williams Ju^r.. Joel Loomis.. Amos Thomas Ju^r.. Denis^n Wattles.. Jon^a Clark Exet^r.. Isa. Williams Ju^r *311*

Haywards.. Jno Johnson.. Caleb Hayward.. Wm White.. Joshua Chappel.. Stephen Payn *311*

Chimney Viewer.. Zebulon Lothrop *311*

Gager.. Ich^a Robinson *311*

Packers.. Jed^h Strong.. Robt Patrick.. Phil: Harris.. James Wright *311*

Branders.. Wm Huntington.. Beri: Southworth.. Moses Clark.. Hinch^n Bennet *311*

Sealer of Weights.. Eben^r Tisdale *311*

of Measures.. Benj$^{[ ]}$ Wood, Wm Beamont, Isr^l Dewey *311*

Pound Keepers.. Wm Waterman.. Saml Clark Ju^r.. Dijah Fowler.. Thos Williams *311*

Chose a Com^{tee} to provide necessary Provision for Soldiers Familys.. & to procuer Such Cloathing as Shall be wanted.. Viz Wm Lyman, Josiah Rockwell, Capt Isaac Loomis, Nathan Cheever, Jabez Metcalfe, Dijah Fowler (he excused & Amos Thomas Ju^r instead, Peleg Thomas, Archips McKall, Jos. Hill, Eleaz^r Richardson, Jno House, Silus Clark, & Ep^m Carpenter *311*

on Motion of Eben^r Hide (Son of Elijah Hide) for Liberty to Set his Black smith Shop in y^e highway nearly opposite his new House, Voted That He may have Liberty to do so *312*

on Motion of D$^{[ ]}$ Jno Clark, that y^e Town wod pay him for Doctering Pel^a Webster a poor young Fellow &c *312*

on Motion of Mr Jos. Rockwell, Voted that the Select Men pay him £3-1-0 for Some Cloathing Some time Since D^d young Richd Lyman, a Soldier *312*

3 Sep 1779

made Choice of Co^l Wm Williams Moderator *313*

appointed Wm Williams John Clark James Pinneo [ ] Esq^{rs} Messrs Elkanah Tisdale, Cap Ep^m Carpenter & Capt Vetch Williams a Com^{tee} to meet Com^{tee} of the Sev^l Towns in this County.. to take into Consideration what.. measures may be taken.. to prevent the further Rise of the Prices of Provisions *313*

Lebanon

14 Sep 1779

Chose Wm Williams & Joshua West Esqr Delegates..to attend a Meeting or Convention of Delegates from the other Towns in this State at Hartford	*314*

13 Dec 1779

Chose Joshua West Esqr Moderator	*315*
Chose Wm Williams, Town Clerk.. Then Chose s^d W Williams, T Treas^r	*315*
They then chose & appointed.. Wm Williams.. Elijah Hyde Ju^r.. Silas Phelps.. Asael Clark Ju^r.. Peleg Thomas & Danl Abel Ju^r } Select Men but NB. Cap Ja^s Penneo & Capt Vetch Williams, were chosen Select Men.. Declined Serving any longer & thereupon they were excused & s^d Clark & Thomas were chosen in their room	*315*
They then chose the following Persons to the following offices.. Viz..Constables.. Elisha Hutchinson.. Joel Loomis.. And^w Metcalfe & Oliver Bill, & s^d Loomis was chosen to collect ye State Tax	*315*
Surveyors of Highways..Elijah Hide Senr.. Jos. Robinson.. Caleb Abel Senr.. Benjn Hyde.. And^w Huntington.. Seth Payn.. Eleaz^r Hutchinson.. George Williams.. Saml Bailey.. John Dewey.. Oliv^r Seabury.. Abijah Smith.. Eleaz^r Manning.. Jon^a Strong.. Seth Wright.. Gam^l Little.. J[ ] Rude.. Henry Bliss.. Tim^o Allen.. Wadwth Brewster.. Ab^m Porter.. Jos Loomis.. Stephen Lee Ju^r.. Simon Abel.. Oliv^r Wattles.. Peleg Thomas.. Aaron Miller.. Asa Bolles.. Jon^a Webster.. Sol^o Abel Ju^r.. Jon^a Webster Ju^r.. Amos Clark & Thos Perkins	*315*
Fence Viewers.. Cap Israel Lomis.. Josiah Rockwell.. Beriah Southworth	*315*
Listers.. Elip^t Metcalfe.. Jon^a Goodwin Ju^r.. Eldad Hunt.. Jos Loomis.. Patrick Butler.. Ep^m Carpenter.. Jos Payn	*316*
Grand Jurors.. Jon^a Strong.. Seth Payn.. Nath[ ] Hyde Ju^r.. Danl Yeomans.. Danl Clark.. Jno Doggett	*316*
Collectors.. Jos Robinson.. Saxton Bailey.. Seth Wright.. Jonah Swetland.. John Williams.. Ep^m Wilcox.. Benjn Sprague	*316*
Leather Sealers.. Jno Lyman.. Dan Throop.. Simon Clark.. Eben^r Hinckley.. [ ] Williams	*316*
Tything Men.. Jacob Loomis.. John Alden.. George Sims.. Wm Lyman.. Isaac Bailey Ju^r.. Rhodol^s Thacher.. Jos Loomis.. Dav^d Treadway.. Rufus Colins Ju^r.. Jon^a Williams.. Step: Lee Ju^r.. Col Jed[ ] Mason.. Jon^a Clark Exe^r & Billy Williams	*316*
Haywards.. John Johnson.. Caleb Hayward.. Wm White	*316*
Chimney Viewer.. Zebulon Lothrop	*316*
Gager.. Ich^a Robinson	*316*
Packers.. Jed^h Strong.. Wm Torry Ju^r.. Philip Harris.. James Wright	*316*
Branders.. Wm Huntington.. Beri:^{h} Southworth.. Hinch^n Bennet.. Jesse Brown	*316*
Sealer of Weights.. Eben^r Tisdale	*316*
Sealer of Measures.. Wm Beamont.. Isr^l Dewey.. Benjn Wood.. Aaron Walter	*316*
Key Keepers.. Walker Alden.. Saml Clark Ju^r.. Cap Dij^h Fowler	*316*
Chose a Com^{te} to provide for Continental Soldiers Familys & also to procure Cloathing… for Soldiers &c viz Wm Lyman.. Josiah Rockwell, Israel Loomis, Nathan Chever, Jabez Metcalfe, Amos Thoms Ju^r Elihu Thomas, Joseph Hill, Elijah House & Ephraim Carpenter	*316*
Select Men proposed to ye Town whether.. to give a certificate to Danl Bissells Negro.. in Case he Shod soon to want upon manumitting him.. upon considerable discourse Voted That They will not do anything about it	*317*

Lebanon

Voed to accept of ye Doings of ye Select Men laying out a highway.. and of ye heirs of Capt Seth Wright Dec^d & Lebbeus Woodworth	317
Voted that the Select Men be authorized to exchange .. land with James Woodworth, by ye mouth of ye lane leading from near late Revd Mr Wheelocks tow^d Coventry allowing him to take up a [ ] Shop on ye highway	317
Voted to allow Dan Payn to Set up a Small Dwelling house on the highway in Goshen	317
Voted That the Select Men may receive & liquidate.. Dav^d Strongs [ ] vs Saml Thomas to allow him what they Shall judge ocasonable & proper	317

23 Mar 1780

Joshua West Esqr Moderator	318
Chose Mes^{rs} John Alden, Elijah Hyde Ju^r, Nathl Williams Israel Loomis Ju^r, Jno Vaughan, Jon^a Goodwin, Silas Phelps, Asael Clark Ju^r, Jos. Hill, Thos Perkins, James Crocker, John House, Elias Bliss, Danl Strong, Col Jer. Mason, Jared Hinckley, Zebulon Metcalf, Danl Clark, Isr^l Williams & Joel Chamberlin ~ to be Inspectors of Provisions	318

9 May 1780

Made Choice of Wm Williams Esq Moderator	318
Granted That this Town for & as a Bounty to each able bodied Recruit, who Shall inlist in to ye Continental Army.. Granted a Tax.. to raise the money for the.. Bountys & any surplus.. to be applied to the common use of ye Town.. appointed Elisha Hutchinson (a Constable) to Collect the whole of s^d Tax	319

27 Aug 1780

Chose Jno Clark Esqr Moderator & Jon^a Trumbull Ju^r Esq Clerk of ye Day (being my Self absent at ye County court..)	319
Voted that a Com^{te} conisting of 47 persons be Chosen for the purpose of engaging & procuring 47 able bodied effective men.. as Recruits to fill up this Towns quota of Men to Serve in the Continental Army for the term of three years or during ye War.. Voted That Col Jer. Mason Maj Ja^s Clark Jno Trumbull Ju^r Cap W Huntington, Cap Danl Tilden, Cap Jno Vaughan, Cap Danl Dewey, Cap Jos Bill, Cap Elias Bliss, Lt Danl Dunham, Lt Thos Bill, Cap And Waterman, Lt Elihu Thomas, Cap Danl Clark, Lt Jacob Eliot, Cap Ab^m Fitch, Lt Amos Thos Ju^r, Lt Jos Leech, Lt And. Huntington, Lt Jno Alden, Lt Simon Crocker, Lt Is^l Williams, Cap Saml Fuller, Cap Ep^m Carpenter, Ens Simon Abel, Lt Jos Loomis, Cor: Gam^l Little, Dav^d Trumbull, Ens Josiah Buell, Chas Swift, Lt Joel Chamberlin, Ens Malichi Thomas, Jos Payn, Isr^l Loomis Ju^r, Abr^m Bliss, Ja^s Pinneo Esq, Denison Wattles, J[ ] Crocker, D^n Thos Williams, Step. Payn Ju^r, Dav^d Lothrop, Danl Hyde, Oliv^r Kingsley, ... Elkanah Tisdale, Josiah Rockwell Ju^r & Jared Hinckley, be a Com^{tee} for.. Recruits	320
Voted That Elisha Hutchinson, Andrew Metcalf, Oliver Bill & Joel Loomis be Collectors to receive & collect the Tax	321
Voted That Maj^r Elijah Hyde Jared Hinckley Cap Asael Clark & Cap Danl Clark be Receivers of Grain that Shall be.. Paid on the Tax	321

[ ] Jul 1780

Joshua West Esqr Chosen, Moderator	322
Jon^a Trumbull Ju^r Clerk for ye Day T Cler[k] being absent	322
Voted That So much of the Tax voted.. on ye 27th of June as Shall be necessary, shall be appropriated to the purpos of paying the Bounties engaged to the Recruits who shall inlist for 8 months or untill 31 Decr next.. Voted that Joel Loomis be excused from being a Collector of the above mentioned Tax, & That Mr Hinchman Bennet be appointed in his room	323

Lebanon

17 Nov 1780

John Clark Esq was chosen Moderator	*323*
Elkanah Tisdale was chosen Clerk of this Meeting.. (NB That Clerk absent)	*323*
Maj Elijah Hyde was.. appointed to receive & put up the Towns Quota of the Provisions	*323*
voted That a Tax of one Shilling State's money on ye pound.. on ye List of Aug 1779 to be collected & paid to Maj Elijah Hyde.. (who is chosen.. to receive the Sev^l articles of provisions..)	*324*

17 Nov 1780

Voted That the Select Men.. & Mr Elkanah Tisdale be a Com^{te}.. to Contract with s^d Hyde for his procuring s^d provisions…	*324*
Mr Wm Torrey, Mr Jon^a Goodwin Ju^r, Mr Simon Clark, Mr Oliver Buell, Mr Benj Sprague & Mr Joel Chamberlin were Chosen Collectors to Collect the above granted Tax	*325*
Meeting proceeded to chuse a Com^{te} to form the Inhabitants of this Town into Classes.. & Cap Danl Tilden, Maj James Clark, Cap Danl Dewey, Cap Ab^m Fitch, Cap Wm Huntington, Ja^s Pinneo Ju^r Esq, Cap Elias Bliss, Cap Jos Hill, Mr Danl Dunham, Mr Gam^l Little, Cap Saml Fuller, Col Jer Mason, Cap Isaac Williams, Mr Peleg Thomas, Cap And^w Waterman, Jacob Eliot Esq, Ep^m Carpenter Esq, Cap Danl Abel Ju^r, Mr Jos Pan, Mr Saml Hutchinson, Col^o Wm Williams, Cap Danl Clark, Mr Elk^a Tisdale, Jno Clark Esq & Mr Isr^l Williams were chosen a Com^{te} for that purpose	*325*

11 Dec 1780

They Chose Joshua West Esq Moderator	*326*
They then chose Wm Williams Esq T. Clerk	*326*
They then Chose Wm Williams Esq T. Treas^r	*326*
They then Chose ye following Persons to ye following offices.. Viz Wm Williams.. Elij Hyde Ju^r Excused.. Silas Phelps.. Asael Clark Ju^r.. Peleg Thomas.. Danl Abel Ju^r.. } Select Men.. s^d Hyd declined & Cap Wm Huntington was chosen in his Stead & s^d Hyde excused	*326*
Constables.. Elisha Hutchinson.. Joel Loomis.. And^w Metcalfe.. Oliver Bill & s^d Bill Collector of State Taxes	*326*
Surveyors of H. Ways.. Lina Hide, Josiah Rockwell Ju^r, Comf^t Brewster, Jos. Hyde, Ab^m Fitch, Saml Fitch, Benj Seabury Ju^r, Benj Throop, Tim^o Holbrook, Jacob Loomis, Simon Crocker, Richd Lyman Ju^r, Nathl Hyde 3^d, Danl Tilden, Thos Bell, Jon^a Abel, Paul Bascomb, Saml Bliss Ju^r, Saml Allen Ju^r, Dav^d Treadway, Asa Basker, Chandl^r Bartlet, Sol^o Lee, Eldad Sabin, Jos. Loomis, Eb^r Hinckley, Mason Brown, Danl Wattles, Jon^a Webster, Simon Williams, Ira Hinckley, Jacob Clark, Jno House & Elisha Bill	*326*
Fence Viewers.. Israel Lomis.. Josiah Rockwell &Beri. Southworth	*326*
Listers.. Jon^a Goodwin.. Comf^t Brewster.. Jos. Loomis.. Sol^o Wright.. Patrick Butler.. Ich^a Brewster Ju^r & Elij. House	*326*
Grand Jurors.. Wm Torrey, Jos Robinson, Saml Fish, Tim^o Allen, Jon^a Williams & Sol^o Abel Ju^r	*326*
Collectors.. Simion Waterman.. Jonah Gross.. Wm Sprague Ju^r.. Jos. Rude.. Joel Hinckley.. James Webster & Alex^r House	*326*
Tything Men.. Wm Lyman, Danl Hyde, Jed. Strong.. Jos. Robinson.. Wm Goodwin, Joel Wright.. Eleaz^r Woodward.. Thos Buckingham.. Peleg Thomas.. Step. Lee Ju^r.. Veach Williams.. Benij^n Wattles.. Saml Hunt Ju^r & Elij. Abel	*326*
Leather Sealers.. Aaron Bushnel.. Saml Fuller.. Simeon Clark.. Eben^r Hinckley & Isr^l Williams	*326*

Lebanon

Haywards.. Step^n Payn.. Joshua Chappel & Wm White	*326*
Chimney Viewer.. Zebulon Lothrop	*327*
Gager.. Ich^a Robinson	*327*
Packers.. Wm Torrey, Jed^h Strong & J[ ]$^{[~]}$ Crocker	*327*
Branders.. Bire. South. Wm Huntington, Hinch Bennet & Danl Wattles	*327*
Sealer of Weights.. Eb^r Tisdale	*327*
D^o of Measures.. Wm Beamont.. Benj. Wood.. Aaron Walker	*327*
Pound Keepers.. Walker Alden.. Saml Clark Ju^r.. Dijah Fowler	*327*
They Then Chose as a Com^{te} to provide for Soldiers Familys viz Capt Wm Huntington, Danl Alden, Eleaz^r Richardson, Saml Hutchinson, And^w Waterman & Silas Clark	*327*
Com^{te} to provide or purchase Cloathing, which may be needed for Soldiers viz Cap Israel Loomis & Capt Ep^m Carpenter	*327*
Voted that Col Wm Williams be.. appointed Agent.. to appear act transact & defend.. to a Case.. commenced by Thos Perkins Esq & y^e [*illegible*] Inhabitants.. of Somers agst ye Inhabitants.. of Lebanon of &.. the Support of one Rebecca Mills a Pauper	*327*
Voted to excuse Joel Chamberlin from collecting the 2^d Tax.. for procuring Provisions & Chose Sol^o Abel Ju^r in his room	*328*

2 Jan 1781

Chose Joshua West Esq Moderator	*328*
Granted a Tax of one penny half penny on ye pound of ye List of Aug Last.. to be paid by in Silver or Gold.. for.. procuring.. Flour or Grain, with.. Condition that every Person assesd shall hve Liberty to pay his quota .. in wheat flour.. Rye Flour.. or Ind^n Corn.. the first Society proportion to be delivered to Maj Elijah Hyde, that y^e 2^d Society.. to Cap Asael Clark, that in Goshen to D$^{[~]}$ And^w Metcalf, that in Exeter to Capt Ep^m Carpenter	*329*
Chose Wm Torrey, Jon^a Goodwin, Simon Clark, Oliv^r Buell, Sol^o Abel Ju^r, Benj$^{[~]}$ Sprague Collectors of s^d Tax	*329*
Chose a Com^{te} to Divide or Class the Inhabitants into 12 Classes.. Cap Danl Tilden, Maj^r Ja^s Clark, Cap Saml Fuller, Cap Jos. Hide, Cap Elias Bliss, Corn^t Saml Little, Cap Isaac Williams, Cap And^w Waterman, Cap Ep^m Carpenter, Cap Danl Clark & D[ ] Saml Hutchinson	*330*
excused Wm Torrey of Serv^g as a Grand Juror, chosen in Decemb^r & Chose James Bailey in his room	*330*

[9] Apr 1781

Wm Williams Chosen Moderator	*330*

25 Jun 1781

Chose Joshua West Esqr Moderator	*331*
Maj^r Elijah Hide, for ye 1st Society & Goshen, & James Penneo Esq for ye C[ ] Andover part, & Exeter &c are appointed to procure provide & receive all such beef Cattle as Shall be Delivered.. &.. deliver [ ] over to Such Recievers &c so that the Supplies of the Army do not fall	*331*
Voted also That s^d Hyde & Pinneo be a Com^{te} to procure barrels, receive & Salt Pack & Secure the Beef & Pork that Shall be brot.. &.. Such other Articles as Shall be d^d	*332*

10 Dec 1781

Wm Williams was Chosen Moderator	*333*

Lebanon

Wm Williams, was Chosen Town Clerk.. & was also Chosen Town Treasurer	333
The following Officers were, in ye following Order chosen to ye following Offices.. Viz Wm Williams.. Silas Phelps, on his Request excused.. Wm Huntington.. Beriah Southworth.. Asael Clark Ju^r.. Peleg Thomas.. Danl Abel Ju^r } Select Men	333
Constables.. Elisha Hutchinson.. Joel Loomis.. And^w Metcalf.. Oliver Bill.. Hutchinson chosen to Collect ye State Taxes & on his Request escus^d &.. Metcalf chosen for ye purpose in his Room	333
Surveyors of Highways.. Jabez West.. Aaron Bushnell.. Dav^d Trumbull.. Simon Fitch.. James Pettis.. Salmon Champion.. Abijah Badcock.. Seth Payne.. Saml Bailey.. Danl Dewey Ju^r.. Lathrop Davis.. Jed^h Strong.. Oliver Hyde.. Rowl^d Swift.. Isaac Ticker.. Consid^r Little.. Nathl Fitch.. Dav^d Clark.. Asa Aspinwall.. Jonah Swetland.. John Holbrook.. Eldad Sabin.. Amos Thomas Ju^r.. Wm Bissell.. Peleg Thomas.. Danl Yeomans.. Capt Thos Loomis.. Charles Wattles.. Jon^a Webster.. Billy Williams.. Amos Clark.. Jos. Payne & Danl Reed Ju^r	333
Fence Viewers.. Cap Isr^l Loomis.. Josiah Rockwell.. Beriah Southworth	334
Listers.. Comfort Brewster.. Elisha Hutchinson.. Solomon Wright.. Walter Walker.. Abijah Thomas.. Ich^a Brewster Ju^r.. Elijah House	334
Grand Jurors.. Lina Hyde.. Wm Goodwin.. Saml Guild.. Paul Newcomb, excused.. Eleaz^r Richardson.. Chandler Bartlet.. Amos Clark	334
Collectors of T Rates.. Dav^d Lothrop.. Cap Danl Tilden.. Jos. Sullard.. Isaac Tickner.. Wm Bissell.. Billy Williams.. Eleaz Hutchinson ye younger	334
Leather Sealers.. Aaron Bushnel.. Cap Saml Fuller.. Simeon Clark.. Eben^r Hinckley & Israel Williams	334
Tything Men.. Richard Lyman.. Dav^d Metcalf.. Jesse Doubleday.. Abner Gardner.. Jos. Hutchinson.. Jos. Rude.. Saml Bliss Ju^r.. Saml Brewster.. Eldad Hunt.. Simon Abel.. Jon^a Williams.. Dennison Wattles.. Jacob Clark.. William Gay	334
Haywards.. James Huntington.. Wm White.. Capt Isaac Williams	334
Chimney Viewer.. Stephen Lee	334
Gager.. Ichabod Robinson	334
Packers.. Simeon Waterman.. Jed^h Strong.. James Crocker	334
Horse Branders.. Beriah Southworth.. Wm Huntington.. John Holbrook.. Danl Wattles	334
Sealer of Weights.. Eben^r Tisdale	334
D^o of Measures.. Wm Beamont.. Benj^a Wood.. Aaron Walker	334
Pound Keepers.. Walter Alden.. Saml Clark Ju^r.. Cap Dijah Fowler	334
Com^{te} to provide for Soldiers Familys.. Wm Huntington.. Danl Tilden.. Eleaz^r Richardson.. Isaac Williams & Silas Clark..	334
Com^{te} to procure Soldiers Cloath^g, if called for.. Cap Isa^l Loomis.. Cap Ep^m Carpenter	334

8 Mar 1782

Wm Williams was chosen Moderator	336
Voted.. That the Deficient Quota of this Town for s^d Army.. be raised by Classing the Inhabitants &c. ... also Voted That Maj James Clark, Cap Danl Dewey, Cap Danl Tilden, Capt Elias Bliss, Cap Jos. Hill, Capt And^w Waterman Capt Isaac Williams, Cap Ep^m Carpenter, Cap Danl Clark & Mr Saml Hutchinson be.. a Com^{te}, for the purposes	337
Voted That Col Jer. Mason & Cap Danl Tilden are appointed a Com^{te} to appear in behalf of s^d Town as occasion Shall require before ye Com^{te} of the Assembly	338

Lebanon

8 Apr 1782

Chose Wm Williams, Moderator

Granted a Tax of one penny on ye pound on ye List of Augt 1781 for ye purpose of procuring the number of Soldiers.. to be procured by the Town.. Chose Constables, Hutchinson, Loomis, Metcalf & Bill to collect ye Same

Ques^t was put whether they will procure another in ye room of Sam Rice who was procured last year by a Class & was enlisted & afterward was.. objected by ye Army [ ] & was [*negatived*]

Ques^t whether they will find a man in room of [ ] Fish also procured by a Class.. &c.. ye Clas took much.. to find him & negatived

Chose Col Jos. Mason to be added to ye Com^{te}.. to procure ye Soldier to be found.. for ye Con^t Army

[ ] Hutchinson moved to be excused from collecting.. & neg^d

22 Apr 1782

Chose Wm Williams Moderator

22 Apr 1782

Chose Cap Saml Fuller a Surveyor of Highways, in his District

22 Apr 1782

D^n Metcalf moved & also Mr Hutchinson to be excused from Collect^g ye Rate granted last Meeting, &.. were not Excused

9 Dec 1782

Made Choice of Col W Williams Moderator

They Then Chose Wm Williams, Town Clerk & also, Chose s^d W Willliams, Town Treas^r

They Then Chose the following Persons in order, as follows to ye Several offices Viz Col^o Wm Williams.. Capt Wm Hutington.. Capt Saml Fuller.. Mr Eleaz^r Ricardson.. Lt Peleg Thomas.. Cap Danl Abel Ju^r } Select Men.. NB Mr Beri. Southworth & Cap Asael Clark were chosen, & declined & Cap Fuller & Mr Richardson were then chosen in their Stead

Constable.. Elisha Hutchinson & Col^r of State Taxes.. Joel Loomis.. And^w Metcalf.. Oliver Bill

Surveyors of Highways.. Lena Hide.. Eb^r Bushnel Ju^r.. Jno Clark Esq.. Benj$^{[\ ]}$ Hyde.. And^w Huntington.. And^w Fitch.. Dan Terry.. Jno Johnson Ju^r.. Elip^t Barker.. Eben^r Gillet.. Jno Dewey.. Rhodol^s Thacher.. Jos. Leech.. Ezekiel Loomis.. Ammi Fitch.. Sol^o Dewey.. John Williams Ju^r.. Joel Loomis.. James Barker Ju^r.. Elijah Hunt.. Saml Woodward.. Joseph Rude.. Elkanah Porter.. Jon^a Williams.. Phillip Harris.. Asa Bolles.. Ich^a Bartlet.. Amos Bliss.. Israel Lee.. Ich^a Brewster Ju^r.. Jehiel Williams.. Charles Williams.. Hubbard McCall & Thos Lavory

Fence Viewers.. Israel Loomis.. Beri. Southworth.. Josiah Rockwell

Listers.. Danl Tilden.. And. Huntington.. Walter Sabin.. Saml West.. Abijah Thomas.. Danl Clark & Edward Sims

Grand Jurors.. James Bailey.. Oliv^r Hunting.. Asa Aspinwall.. Amos Bliss & Eph^m McCall

Collectors of Rates.. Joseph Throope.. John Newcomb.. Ab^m Dewey Ju^r.. Jno Williams Ju^r.. Enos Fowler.. Ambrose Williams.. Jos. Payne

Leather Sealers.. Saml Fuller.. Joseph Leech.. Simon Clark.. Eben^r Hinckley.. Dyer Sprague

Tything Men.. Wm Swift.. Jon^a Goodwin Ju^r.. Rhodol^s Thacher.. Jon^a Strong.. Darius Dewey.. Israel Dewey.. Jon^a Abel.. Solomon Wright.. Dav^d Huntington.. Charles Wright.. Simon

Lebanon

Abel.. Denison Wattles.. Peleg Thomas	
Haywards.. James Huntington.. Wm White.. Leonard Hill	342
Chimney Viewer.. Lee Stephen Ju^r	342
Gager.. Ich^a Robinson	342
Packers.. Simeon Waterman.. Jed^h Strong.. James Crocker	342
Branders.. Wm Huntington.. Beriah Southworth.. Hinch^n Bennet.. Dan Wattles	342
Sealer of Weights.. Eben^r Tisdale	342
Sealers of Measures.. Wm Beamont.. Benj^a Wood.. Aaron Walker	342
Key Keepers.. Walker Alden.. Saml Clark Ju^r.. Cap Dijah Fowler.. Hobart McCall	342
Com^{te} to provide for Soldiers Famalys.. And^w Huntington.. John Dewey.. Simon Clark.. Elihu Thomas.. Israel Williams	342
Com^{te} to provide Cloathing if wanted.. Is^{rl} Loomis.. Ep^m Carpenter	342
Voted That Hobart McCalls yard, may be a Town pound	342
Appointed Saml Barstow & Nathan Loomis, Collectors of ye one penny Tax granted in April last, to pay Soldiers Bountys.. in ye room of Joel Loomis, who refused to Serve	342
17 Feb 1783	
Chose Wm Williams, Moderator	343
appointed Samuel Beamont, a Collector in y^e room of Jos. Throop, who refused	343
appointed Caleb Abel Ju^r & Joseph Phelps, Grand Jurors in y^e room of Oliv^r Huntington & Jos Baley	343
granted Liberty to Maj^r James Clark, Cap Huntington & others.. to erect a Dam for a Saw Mill, at or near the land of D$^{[\ ]}$ Thos Williams	343

Litchfield

Town Records
1775 – 1808

Located at the Town Clerk's Office

Litchfield

6 Dec 1774

The Hon. Oliver Wolcott Esqr was Chosen Moderator	127
Voted That the Honorable Oliver Wolcott Esqr & Messrs Jedidiah Strong, John Marsh, Jacob Woodruff, John Coburn, Jehiel Pamerly, Abraham Bradley, Seth Bird, Abraham Kilborn, Archibald McNeile, Nathan Garnsey James Morris & Ebenezer Benton be a Committee for the Purposes mentioned in the Eleventh Article of the Association Agreement of the Grand Continental Congress in Philadelphia 5th September Last	128

5 Dec 1775

The Hon. Oliver Wolcott Esqr Chosen Moderator	128
Messeurs Abraham Bradley, Jedidiah Strong, Seth Bird, John Osborn & Archibald McNeile were chosen Select Men	128
The Hon. Oliver Wolcott, Seth Bird, Jedidiah Strong, Reuben Smith, Andrew Adams, Lynde Lord, Jacob Woodruff, William Stanton, James Morris, Ebenezer Benton, Abraham Bradley, John Osborn, Jehiel Palmerly & Jonathan Mason were Chosen Committee of Inspection	128
Jedidiah Strong Chosen Town Clerk & Abraham Bradley Chosen Town Treasurer	128
William Stanton, Jonathan Mason, Briant Stoddard and David Stoddard Chosen Constables. The said Stanton Chosen Collector of the Country Rates	129
Seth Bird, Jacob Woodruff Junr, Jonah Sanford, Samuel Sheldon, Charles Smith, Ozias Goodwin, Ephraim Smedley Junr, Noah Bartholomew, Isaac Kilborn, David Beach, Philo Peck, Abel Camp, Charles Grant, Jonah Stone, Nathaniel Goodwin, Reuben Lewis, Jonathan Wright, Edward Phelps Junr, William Fancher, Benjamin Stone, Elijah Marsh, Roswel Kilborn, Eliphaz Parsons, Nathaniel Benton, Dan Throope and Thomas Coe Chosen Surveyors of Highways	129
Ozias Goodwin, William Marsh Junr and Nathaniel Woodruff Chosen Fence Viewers	129
Abraham Bradley, Jedidiah Strong, Seth Bird, Amos Moss, Calvin Comstock, Laban Beach, Nathaniel Goodwin, Seth Landon, Reuben Stone, Zebulon Taylor, Moses Barns, Peter Buell Junr Chosen Listers	129
Jonathan Smith and Thomas Goodwin chosen Leather Sealers	129
John Pierce, Arthur Emons, Elihu Harrison, Edward Linsley, Moses Sanford and Reuben Dickenson Chosen Grand Jurors	129
William Marsh Junr, Joseph Sanford, Levi Moss, Alexander Waugh, Sylvanus Bishop, Leaming Bradley, Archibald McNeile Junr & Seth Landon Chosen Tythingmen	129
Miles Beach & Lemuel Harrison Chosen Gagers	129
Miles Beach was Chosen Packer	129
Elijah Wadsworth, Obed Stoddard, Calvin Comstock, Samuel Ensign, Samuel Barnard, Leaming Bradley, Joseph Cole & Timothy Woodruff Chosen Branders of Horses	129
Abraham Bradley Chosen Sealer of Weights & Measures	129
Ozias Goodwin Chosen Key Keeper	129
Capt Moses Seymour, Brainerd Cleeveland Reuben Stone, Jonathan Mason & Amos Barns chosen Collectors and Receivers	129

16 Dec 1776

Reuben Smith Esqr was Chosen Moderator	130
Jedidah Strong, Reuben Smith, Capt John Marsh, Capt Archibald McNeile & Capt John Osborn were chosen Select Men	130

Litchfield

Jedidiah Strong was Chosen Town Clerk	130
Caleb Gibbs, Lynde Lord, Seth Bird, Nathaniel Goodwin, Moses Sanford, Archibald McNiele Junr, Nathaniel Woodruff, Tapping Reeve and William Stanton were Chosen Committee of Inspection	130
Voted that the Select Men be impowered to buy of Mr Thomas Waugh Half an Acre of Land about Twenty Rods South of Joseph Waughs Dwelling House for the Sum of thirty Shillings for the purpose of a publick Burying Place	130
William Stanton was chosen Treasurer	130
Jonathan Mason, Briant Stoddard, David Stoddard & Alexander Catlin were Chosen Constables; The said David Stoddard to collect the Country Rates	130
Voted that Jedidiah Strong be.. authorized to make proper Application to the. General Assembly.. for Liberty to repair their highways by a Town Rate or Tax	131
Alexander Catlin, Benjamin Hall, Jonathan Johnson, Clark Royce, Solomon Kilborn, George Baldwin, Timothy Skinner, Amos Moss, Ebenezer Plumbe, Archibald McNeile Junr, Thomas Waugh, Philemon Murray, Jonathan Wright, John Stoddard, Reuben Stone, Charles Smith Junr and Joseph Agard were chosen Surveyors of Highways	131

30 Dec 1776

Ozias Goodwin, Timothy Skinner and Nathaniel Woodruff Chosen Fence Viewers	131
Jedidiah Strong, Lynde Lord, Edward Linly, Arthur Emons, Nathaniel Goodwin, Joseph Wetmore, Archibald McNiele Junr, Levi Moss, Phineas Baldwin the 2nd Seth Landon and Reuben Stone were Chosen Listers	131
Thomas Goodwin & Jesse Kilborn were Chosen Leather Sealers	131
Timothy Skinner, Jeremiah Riggs, Calvin Comstock, Benjamin Peck, Seth Bishop, Reuben Stone and Lemuel Harrison were chosen Grand Jurors	131
Eli Smith, Lemuel Gibbs, William Hall, Joel Frost, Abner Cone & Asa Bull were Chosen Tything Men	131
Miles Beach Chosen Gager	131
Miles Beach chosen Packer	131
Elijah Wadsworth, Obed Stoddard, Timothy Woodruff, Samuel Ensign, Calvin Comstock, Leaming Bradley, William Preston and Joseph Cole were Chosen Branders of Horses	131
Miles Beach was Chosen Sealer of Weights & Measures	132
Ozias Goodwin Chosen Key Keeper	132
Abel Barns, James Harrison and Amos Barns were chosen addition to the Committee of Inspection	132
Moses Seymour, Oliver Sanford, Edward Phelps Junr Reuben Stone and Amos Barns were Chosen Collectors and Receivers of the Town Rates and Stores	132
Voted That John Clemons Junr have Liberty to set his Blacksmiths Shop on the Highway near the Iron Works the Place to be affixed by Messeurs Nathaniel Benton, Reuben Stone and David Stoddard	132

27 Mar 1777

Capt John Marsh chosen Moderator	133
Voted That the Families of such Soldiers belonging to this Town who shall undertake in the Continental Army in the Connecticut Battallions & have not Time & Opportunity to lay out their Money & make proper Provision for their s^d Families in their Absence: be supplied with Necessaries at the Prices stated by Law on reasonable Request & lodging Money therefor	133

Litchfield

And the Messrs Caleb Gibbs, Lynde Lord, Seth Bird, Nathaniel Goodwin, Moses Sanford, Archibald McNiele Junr, Nathaniel Woodruff, Tapping Reeve, William Stanton, Abel Barns, James Morris and Amos Barns be a Committee to transact the Matter
15 Apr 1777

Reuben Smith Esqr Chosen Moderator	133
Voted to pay on the first Day of January annually.. to each & every Non Commissioned Officer and Private Soldier who already hath or hereafter Shall inlist into either of the Eight Continental Battallions now raising in this State for Three Years or during the War.. Voted that the Select Men make a Rate or Rates for that Purpose.. Miles Beach, Leman Stone, Moses Barns & Stephen Bidwell Chosen Collectors	133

16 Sep 1777

Andrew Adams Esqr Moderator	134
Samuel Lyman Esqr was Chosen Chosen Town Treasurer in the Room of William Stanton Resigned	134

7 Oct 1777

Jacob Woodruff Esqr Chosen Moderator	134
Voted That Messrs Lynde Lord, Thomas Catlin, Caleb Gibbs, David Welch and Alexander Catlin be a Committee to purchase & provide Shirts, Frocks, Overhalls, Stockings & Shoes for the non-commissioned Officers and Soldiers in the Continental Army	134

10 Dec 1777

General Oliver Wolcott was chosen Moderator	134
Jedidiah Strong, Capt Archelos Buell, Jacob Woodruff Esqr Capt John Osborn & Miles Beach were chosen Select Men	134
Jedidiah Strong was chosen Town Clerk	134
Reuben Smith Esqr was Chosen Treasurer	134
David Stoddard, Solomon Goodwin, Levi Moss & Timothy Skinner were Chosen Constables The said Timothy Skinner to collect the State Taxes	134
John Stoddard, Ozias Goodwin, Wright Woodruff, Samuel Woodruff Junr, Thomas Palmerly Junr, Timothy Webster Junr, Isaac McNiele, Seth Farnam, Benjamin Throop, George Bull, Nathaniel Benton, John Humaston Junr, Moses Stoddard, John Marsh 2nd, Seth Bishop & Moses Barns were chosen Surveyors of Highways	134
Ozias Goodwin, Nathaniel Woodruff & Timothy Skinner were chosen Fence Viewers	134
Jedidiah Strong, Seth Bird, Solomon Goodwin, James Burgis Junr, John Osborn Junr, Phineas Baldwin 2nd, Levi Moss, Amos Barns & Abraham Bradley were chosen Listers	135
Timothy Skinner was chosen Collector of Town Rates	135
Thomas Goodwin, Jesse Kilborn & Capt Peter Buell were Chosen Leather Sealers	135
John Marsh Junr, John Pierce, Benjamin Webster, Asahel Strong, Roger N Whittlesey & Cornelius Allen were chosen Grand Jurors	135
Philo Peck, Elihu Hotchkiss, David Gibbs, Solomon Buell Junr Seth Bishop, Nathan Stewart, John Webster and Seth Landon were Chosen Tything Men	135
Miles Beach & Lemuel Harrison were chosen Gagers	135
John Pierce was chosen Packer	135
Levi Stone, Moses Barns, Joseph Heath, Timothy Woodruff, Silas Dibble, Samuel Ensign, Joseph Cole, Calvin Comsock Epaphras Wadsworth and Abel Darling were chosen Branders	135

Litchfield

of Horses	
Capt Abraham Bradley was chosen Sealer of Weights and Measures	135
Ozias Goodwin was chosen Key keeper	135

15 Dec 1777

D[ ] Seth Bird ws chosen Moderator instead of Genl Wolcott detained at Home by Sickness	135
Jeremiah Riggs and Eli Smith were Chosen Surveyors of Highways	135
David Welch, Nathaniel Woodruff, Archibald McNeile Junr Ebenezer Benton & Thomas Waugh were chosen Committee to provide for the Families of Soldiers	135
On Motion & Request of Jedidiah Strong & Select Men Tapping Reeve, Seth Bird, Andrew Adams, Samuel Lyman & Lynde Lord were chosen a Committee to prepare state and present for Recovery sundry Matters & Accounts.. due to the Town	135

6 Jan 1778

Andrew Adams Esqr being previously Chosen Moderator	137

23 Mar 1778

Jacob Woodruff Esqr Moderator	137
David Welch, Caleb Gibbs, Alexand^r Catlin, Thomas Catlin & Joseph Vail were Chosen a Committee to provide Clothing for the Continental Soldiers	137

27 Apr 1778

Capt Lynde Lord chosen Moderator	137
Capt Amos Barns Chosen Committee to buy Clothing for the Soldiery	137
Voted to oppose the Petition of the Inhabitants of the Southwest Part of Litchfield Praying in Conjunction with the Society of Judea.. to be incorporated into a distinct Township and Major Andrew Adams Chosen Agent for that Purpose	137

10 Aug 1778

Reuben Smith Esqr Chosen Moderator	138
On Petition of Ebenezer & John Marsh 3rd to Remove the East Mill & Bridge &c.. Philemon Murray, Caleb Gibbs & Amos Parmele chosen Com^{tee} to view and report	138
on Petition of Messrs Ebenezer & John Marsh Granted That the Bridge be removed up Stream & the Mill & Dam down Stream so that the Bridge be built near where the Mill now stands and the Mill & Dam where the Bridge now stands	138
A Vote of.. Norfolk being presented by their Committee Mr Daniel Mack & read Voted that Capt Abraham Bradley &.. Erastus Bradley, Reynold Marvin & Abel Barns be a Committee to join the Committees of the other Towns in the County to prepare.. a Petition to the next General Assembly for some Amendments of the Mode of Taxation	138

15 Sep 1778

Upon the Memorial of Ebenezer Kellogg of Goshen Clothier Praying for Liberty to make a Canal or Water course across the Highway leading to Goshen East Street near the Bridge on the West Branch of Bantam River for the Convenience of a Fulling Mill.. Granted only so long as he or his Heirs &c shall maintain & keep in good Repair a firm & well made Bridge across such Canal so as not in anywise to discommode the Travelling or Transportation on that Road	138

28 Dec 1778

the Honble Oliver Wolcott Esqr Chosen Moderator	139

Litchfield

Capt Abraham Bailey Capt Archibald McNeile Junr Maj^r Bezaleel Bebe Capt Briant Stoddard & Major David Welch were chosen Select Men	139
Jedidiah Strong chosen Town Clerk	139
Reuben Smith Esqr Chosen Treasurer	139
Levi Moss, Timothy Skinner, Solomon Goodwin & Asahel Strong Chosen Constables.. & the said Asahel Strong Collector of the State Taxes	139
John Stoddard, Ebenezer Plumbe, Thomas Goodwin, Jacob Baker, Ozias Goodwin, Abel Atwater, William Horsford, Joshua Mason, George Bull, Amos Parmele, Robert Lemmon Junr, Thomas Coe, Nathan Farnum, Noah Stone, Judson Gitteau, Epaphras Wadsworth, Charles Smith Junr, Seth Bishop, David Stoddard & Daniel Lord Chosen Surveyors of Highways	139
William Marsh Junr, Ozias Goodwin and Timothy Skinner Chosen Fence Viewers	139
Ebenezer Plumbe, Ebenezer Benton, Seth Landon, Seth Farnum, Peter Buell Junr, Abraham Dudley, Timothy Skinner, John Horsford, Theodore Catlin, Thomas Parmele Junr, James Morris & David Stoddard Chosen Listers	139
Thomas Goodwin and Jesse Kilborn chosen Leather Sealers	139
Stephen Bidwell, Laban Beach, Seth Landon, Lemuel Gibbs & Gad Farnum Chosen Grand Jurors	139
Samuel Woodruff, William Marsh Junr, Isaac Bissell, James Woodruff, Stephen Plant, Eli Smith and Moses Stoddard were Chosen Tything Men	139
Capt Miles Beach Chosen Gauger	139
Capt Miles Beach chosen Packer	139
Epaphras Wadsworth, Abner Baldwin, Levi Stone, Samuel Ensign, Calvin Comstock & Joseph Cole were chosen Branders of Horses	139
Capt Abraham Bradley Sealer of Weights & Measures	139
Ozias Goodwin Chosen Key keeper	139

31 Dec 1778

Jedidiah Strong Chosen Select Man in the Room of Abraham Bradley resigned	140
Arthur Emons, Phineas Baldwin 2nd, Capt Solomon Marsh, Lt David Stoddard and Moses Stoddard were Chosen a Committee to provide necessary Supplies for the Families of Continental Soldiers	140
Voted to raise a Tax of one Shilling & Six Pence on the Pound on the List of the Inhabitants.. for the Year 1778.. Capt Zebulon Taylor Chosen Collector of said Tax and Voted to give him Sixteen Pounds Money therefore	140

12 Apr 1779

Reuben Smith Esqr Moderator	140
Voted to raise a Tax of Eighteen Pence on the Pound on the List of 1778.. to Discharge Town Debts. Capt Zebulon Taylor chosen Collector of said Tax & also of the one Shilling Tax for Payment of Soldiery & allowed £5 therefore	140
Chose Major Andrew Adams Agent, To Prepare & prefer a Petition to Assembly & cite the Town of Washington, to regulate the Line of the Town	140
Voted to excuse Zachariah Long from his military Fine	140
On Request of Capt John Marsh Consented.. he might have the exclusive Pickerel Fishery in the Loon Pond.. for Twenty Years	140

Litchfield

20 Dec 1779

General Oliver Wolcott Chosen Moderator	141

27 Dec 1779

Jedidiah Strong, David Welch Esq^{rs} Capt Archibald McNeile Junr Major Bezaleel Beebe & Capt Briant Stoddard were chosen Select Men	141
Jedidiah Strong Chosen Town Clerk	141
Reuben Smith Esqr Chosen Town Treasurer	141
Asahel Strong Chosen Constable and Collector of State Taxes.. Levi Moss, Roger Newton Whittlesey, Samuel Sheldon & Capt Reuben Stone were chosen Constables	141
Stephen Webster, Samuel Sheldon, Abner Baldwin Junr, Remembrance Gibbs, Enos Barns, Seth Farnum, Jonathan Griswold, Noah Garnsey, Isaac Bissell, Jehiel Kilborn, Elijah Peck, William Baldwin, Stephen Plant, Benjamin Gibbs Junr, George Bull, Nathan Stewart, Reuben Stone & Charles Grant were Chosen Surveyors of Highways	141
Ozias Goodwin, William Marsh Junr & Nathaniel Woodruff were Chosen Fence Viewers	141
Miles Beach, Lemuel Gibbs, Ephraim Smedley Junr, Benjamin Webster, Isaac McNeile, Timothy Skinner, David Stoddard, Heben Stone, Michael Dickenson, Jonathan Wright & Solomon Sanford were Chosen Listers	141
Jesse Kilborn, Ebenezer Benton & Timothy Webster Chosen Leather Sealers	142
Ephraim Kirby, Samuel Barnard, Abel Camp Junr, Abel [ ]ler, Phineas Baldwin J^r & Benjamin Gibbs J^r were Chosen Grand Jurors	142
Ezra Plumbe Junr, Levi Peck, Calvin Comstock, Timothy Webster Junr, Samuel Bard & Seth Bishop were chosen Tything Men	142
Capt Miles Beach was Chosen Gauger	142
James Hallocks was Chosen Packer	142
Levi Stone, Epaphras Wadsworth, Abner Baldwin, Samuel Ensign, Jacob Peck, Moses Barns, Joseph Cole & William Preston were Chosen Branders of Horses	142
Capt Abraham Bradley was Chosen Sealer of Weights and Measures	142
Ozias Goodwin was chosen Key Keeper	142
Judson Gitteau, Jonathan Wright and Phineas Baldwin Junr Chosen a Committee to supply the Families of Soldiers	142
Judson Gitteau, Thomas Catlin, Jonathan Wright & Timothy Skinner chosen a Committee to procure Clothing for the Army	142
Granted a Tax of Three Shillings on the pound on the List of 1778.. Judson Gitteau, Thomas Catlin, Jonathan Wright & Timothy Skinner Chosen Collector of said Taxes	142

1 Mar 1780

Honble Oliver Wolcott Esqr was chosen Moderator	143
Mr Asahel Strong, Capt Miles Beach, Capt Reuben Stone, Lt Thomas Catlin, Capt Archibald McNeile Junr, Ensign Jonathan Wright, Abel Capt Junr, Lt Lemuel Harrison, Capt Zebulon Taylor, Capt Alexander Waugh, Mr Edward Linsley & Mr Levi Stone were Chosen Inspectors of Provisions	143

10 Apr 1780

The Hon. Oliver Wolcott Esqr Chosen Moderator	143
Granted a Tax of four Shillings on the Pound on the List of 1779.. Timothy Skinner, Thomas Catlin, Jonathan Wright & Judson Gitteau appointed Collectors thereof	143

510

Litchfield

8 Jul 1780

Hon. Oliver Wolcott chosen Moderator	143
Voted that whereas the Militia of this Town are required by an Order of Col. Andrew Adams.. to furnish fourteen able effective Men to serve in the Connecticut Line.. plight themselves to pay to every such Recruit or his Assigns as shall voluntarily inlist Himself.. such Sum in Money as shall be sufficient, including the Wages which he shall receive from this State or the United States, to procure as much good merchantable Wheat as might be obtained by the monthly Wages of forty Shillings in.. 1774	144
Voted that a Rate or Tax of Six Pence on the Pound on the List of 1779.. is hereby laid and made payable in Gold or Silver Coin or Bills of Credit of this State.. Judson Gitteau, Timothy Skinner Jonathan Wright and Ozias Lewis appointed & chosen to collect the Same.. And the Same Ozias Lewis appointed to collect the Taxes lately granted of which Lt Thomas Catlin was chosen Collector and refused to accept	145

15 Nov 1780

Major David Welch was Chosen Moderator	145
Voted that a Tax of One Shilling upon the Pound be laid.. for Purchasing Provisions and requisite Supplies for the Army & to defray other necessary Expences of the Town ~ .. Voted That Messrs Timothy Skinner, Seth Farnam, Theodore Catlin & Harris Hopkins be Collectors	145
Voted That Timothy Skinner, Seth Farnam, Theodore Catlin & Harris Hopkins be a Committee to purchase Provisions	146
Voted that.. Miles Beach & Leman Stone be appointed to receive the Salt procure Casks to contain said Provisions, to receive & inspect the same, & Store the Casks.. also.. to purchase any of such Provisions as Occasion may offer	146
Voted that the said Timothy Skinner, Seth Farnam, Theodore Catlin, Harris Hopkins, Miles Beach & Leman Stone be also appointed to purchase the Clothing required for the Army	146

26 Dec 1780

Reuben Smith Esqr was Chosen Moderator	146
Jedidiah Strong, Archibald McNeile Junr, David Welch, Jonah Sanford & John Stoddard were chosen Select Men	146
Jedidiah Strong was Chosen Town Clerk	146

28 Dec 1780

Reuben Smith Esqr was chosen Town Treasurer	146
Asahel Strong was chosen Constable & Collector of State Taxes.. Roger Newton Whittlesey, Uriah Tracey, Levi Moss & Reuben Stone were Chosen	146
Capt Miles Beach, Russel Emons, Daniel Lord, Eli Smith, Calvin Comstock, Noah Stone, Seth Farnam, Gideon Smedley, Ozias Lewis, Leaming Bradley, Stephen Russell, Noah Ryard, Stephen Plant, Abel Darling, Harris Hopkins, William Baldwin, Philo Peck, Williams Graves, James Woodin Ju^r, Thomas Coe, Asa Bull and John Marsh the 2nd were chosen Surveyors of Highways	146
Nathaniel Woodard J^r, Ozias Goodwin and William Marsh Junr chosen Fence Viewers	147
Abraham Bradley, Amos Barns, Gad Farnam, Philemon Murray, Edward Phelps Junr, Isaac Baldwin Junr, Timothy Skinner, Heber Stone, Reuben Stone, Ebenezer Benton, Judson Gitteau, Eli Smith, Calvin Comstock, Ozias Lewis & John Humaston Junr were chosen Listers	147

Litchfield

Jesse Kilborn, Timothy Webster and James Stoddard were chosen Leather Sealers	147
Jesse Judd, Samuel Ensign, Lawrence Wessells, Caleb Gibbs, Nathaniel Benton, Stephen Baldwin, Titus Turner and David King were Chosen Grand Jurors	147
Levi Stone, James Goodwin, Richard Wallace, Leaman Bishop, Asa Bull, Moses Stoddard and Oliver Landon were chosen Tything Men	147
Miles Beach & Leman Stone Chosen Gaugers	147
Miles Beach & Leman Stone Chosen Packers	147
Levi Stone, Epaphras Wadsworth, Abel Darling, Joseph Heath, Jacob Peck, Joseph Cole, Samuel Ensign & Calvin Comstock Chosen Branders of Horses	147
Capt Abraham Bradley was chosen Sealer of Weights and Measures	147
Ozias Goodwin chosen Key Keeper	147
Gad Farnam, Benjamin Webster and John Smith were chosen a Committee to supply Soldiers Families	147
Voted that.. Timothy Skinner, Heber Stone, James Stoddard, Reuben Stone, David Welch and Zebulon Taylor be a Committee to hire...the requisite Number of Recruits to complete the Quota of this Town in the Connecticut Line of the Army of the United States	147
Granted a Rate or Tax of One Shilling on the Pound on the List.. for the Year 1779.. Voted That Asahel Strong be Collector of said Tax	147

9 Jan 1781

Chose Col Andrew Adams Moderator	148
Lieu^t Thomas Catlin added to the Committee for hiring Recruits for the Army	148
Calvin Comstock having been appointed a Lister, on his Desire is excused	148

16 Jan 1781

Granted a Tax of Three Pence on the Pound on the List of 1779.. with Liberty for the Inhabitants to discharge the same by paying Half the Sum in Wheat Flour.. Rye Flour.. or Indian Corn.. Timothy Skinner, Harris Hopkins, Seth Farnam & Theodore Catlin Chosen Collectors	148
Capt Abraham Bradley & Leman Stone are appointed Receivers of the Flour & Corn which may be brought in thereon	148
Major Welch & Lieu^t Skinner on Motion are excused of the Committee for hiring Recruits for the Army	149
Benjamin Webster chosen Surveyor of Highways	149

18 Jan 1781

On Motion & Request of Jedidiah Strong in Behalf of Himself & the other Select Men & the Town Capt Abraham Bradley Reuben Smith Esqr & D$^{[\ ]}$ Seth Bird were appointed to audit the Towns Accounts	149
Voted that the Select Men together with Capt Abraham Bradley, Capt John Osborn Ens. Edward Phelps & D$^{[\ ]}$ Seth Bird be a Committee to divide the Town into Classes for raising Recruits for the Army	149
Capt Abraham Bradley & Leman Stone appointed to receive.. Produces	149

26 Mar 1781

Reuben Smith Esqr was chosen Moderator of a Town Meeting	150
Voted that whereas nine Foot Soldiers & two Horsemen are required to be forthwith raised in this Town for the Service of the State.. That the two Horsemen be hired at large by the Select	150

Litchfield

Men or a Committee of the Town.. Heber Stone is appointed a Committee to hire said two Horsemen
9 Apr 1781

Granted a Tax of one Shilling on the Pound on the List of 1780.. to defray the Expences of the Town.. Asahel Strong Chosen Collector of said Tax | 150
9 Jul 1781

The Honble Oliver Wolcott Esqr Moderator | 151

Granted a Tax of one Penny in the Pound on the List of 1780 payable in Silver Money.. & three other Taxes each of one Penny on the Pound.. payable in Silver Money severally.. provided never the less that any or all of said Taxes may be paid in good Beef Cattle at four Pence per Pound.. for the use of this State & the Continental Army.. Asahel Strong Chosen Collector | 151

Voted that the Men belonging to this Town lately detached for a Tour of Three Months by special Order of the Captain General.. granted on the earnest Requisition of his Excellency General Washington for 300 men &.. receive out of the Town Treasury.. each the Sum of Twenty Shillings in Silver or other equivalent for each Month he shall be in actual Service | 151
18 Sep 1781

The Moderator being absent Lynde Lord Esqr was chosen Moderator | 152

Miles Beach, Philemon Murray & Zina Bradley chosen a Committee to meet a Committee of Harwinton at the Bridge on Waterbury River.. to determine whether to Build the Abutments of Stone or Wood | 152

Capt Miles Beach was Chosen Receiver of Clothing & Provisions &c on the 2/6^d tax.. Lemon Stone also Chosen Receiver of such Part of said Tax as shall be delivered to him | 152
7 Dec 1781

Abraham Bradley Esqr Chosen Moderator | 152

Jedidiah Strong, Abraham Bradley, Archibald McNeile Junr, David Welch and Jonah Sanford were chosen Select Men | 152

Jedidiah Strong was chosen Town Clerk | 152

Reuben Smith was chosen Town Treasurer | 152

Asahel Strong, Nathaniel Smith 2nd Timothy Skinner Roger N. Whittlesay and Levi Moss were Chosen Constables.. & the said Asahel Strong appointed to collect the State Taxes | 152

Jonathan Page, Stephen Webster, Russell Emons, Daniel Lord, Levi Stone, Zina Bradley, Abner Baldwin Junr, David Beach, Benjamin Landon, Amos Parmely 2nd, John Shelhar, David Stoddard, Stephen Bidwell, Jacob Woodruff Junr, Gideon Smedley, Calvin Comstock, Titus Turner, Alexander Catlin, Isaac McNeile and John Marsh were Chosen Surveyors of Highways | 152

Nathaniel Woodruff, Ozias Goodwin and William Marsh Junr Chosen Fence Viewers | 153

Samuel Sheldon, Caleb Gibbs, Seth Landon, Fredrick Stanley, Solomon Goodwoin, Phineas Baldwin 2nd, Jesse Kilborn, Harris Hopkins, Calvin Comstock, Noah Garnsey and Tapping Reeve were Chosen Listers | 153

Jesse Kilborn, Ebenezer Benton & Oliver Bordman were Chosen Leather Sealers | 153

Capt Miles Beach, David Kilborn, Russel Emons, Phineas Baldwin 2nd, Eli Smith, Joseph Thomas, Seth Farnam & Amos Moss were Chosen Grand Jury Men | 153

James Goodwin, John Osborn Junr, John Webster, Epaphras Wadsworth, Nathan Smedley, Joshua Smith, Noah Agard & Asahel Griswold were chosen Tything Men | 153

Litchfield

Capt Miles Beach was chosen Gauger & Packer	153
Capt Abner Baldwin, Samuel Ensign, Calvin Comstock, Jacob Peck, Theodore Bidwel, Levi Stone, James Stone & Zophas Beach were Chosen Branders of Horses	153
Capt Abraham Bradley was chosen Sealer of Weights & Measures	153
Ozias Goodwin was chosen a Key Keeper	153

31 Dec 1781

Ebenezer Plumbe & John Marsh Chosen Committee to supply Soldiers Families	153
David Kilborn & Capt Miles Beach excused from serving as Grand Jurors	153
Ebenezer Benton excused serving as Leather Sealer	153
Amos Galpin Chosen Leather Sealer	153
Jedidiah Strong, Abraham Bradley & Lynde Lord appointed a Committee.. to settle the Controversy with the Town of Washington set forth in the Petition of this Town now depending in the General Assembly	153
Asahel Strong excused as Collector, his Desire	153
Timothy Skinner Chosen Collector of State Taxes	153

3 Jan 1782

Voted that Jedidiah Strong be.. appointed Agent to oppose a Petition of Inhabitants of Bethlem praying for a new Township to include one Mile of this Town adjoining to s^d Bethlem	154
Levi Moss was chosen Collector of Town Taxes	154
Capt Archibald McNiele Junr on his Desire is Excused & Isaac Baldwin Esqr appointed a Select Man	154
Granted Liberty to the 10th School District to build a School House on the Highway near Doctor Little's Dwelling House	154
Eliphalet Hotchkiss, Thomas Catlin & Stephen Webster appointed a Committee to remove Encroachments & Nuisances on the Highways	154
Upon the Memorial of Daniel Landon Solomon Kilborn & David Kilborn Praying Liberty to set a Fulling Mill on the Highway which crosses the River.. Granted they may build & improve such Mill on said Highway during the Pleasure of the Town	154

25 Feb 1782

Lynde Lord Esqr Chosen Moderator	155
Abraham Bradley Esqr chosen Clerk pro Tempore	155
Voted to raise Ten Men for State Service or the Regiment of Guards for Horsenecks as required.. And chose Capt Abraham Bradley, Col. Bezaleel Beebe & Capt Lynde Lord a Committee to divide the Town into 10 Classes accordingly	155
Voted that Ten Men be added to the above Committee.. to proceed in raising Recruits.. Viz for the First Class Ens. Edward Phelps.. For the 2nd D^o Ozias Lewis, For the 3rd D^o Benjamin Peck Junr.. For the 4th D^o Elihu Harrison.. For the 5th D^o Ephraim Smedley Junr.. For the 6th D^o Leaming Bradley.. For the 7th D^o Ens Jonathan Wright.. For the 8th D^o Lt David Stoddard.. For the 9th D^o Capt Alexander Catlin.. For the 10th D^o Lt Timothy Skinner	155

25 Mar 1782

The Hon. Andrew Adams Esqr Chosen Moderator	156

Litchfield

25 Mar 1782

Stephen Stone, Elijah Griswold & Benjamin Kilborn having lately been assessed on Examination & by the Civil Authority & Select Men.. for Each a Son gone to the Enemy &c & having requested a Hearing in Town Meeting.. The Question was proposed relative said Stone in particular & the Town by Vote did not discharge the said Assessments	156
Col Adams being absent Reuben Smith Esqr was Chosen Moderator	156
on Motion of Stephen Stone, Voted to reconsider the Votes of last Monday respecting his Assessment & adjourned	156

2 Apr 1782

On the Question whether Stephen Stone shall be acquitted from his assessment &c Voted in affirmative	156
Whereupon Elijah Griswold & Benjamin Kilborn requesting the Town to release them from the assessment	156
Voted.. and that Messrs Timothy Skinner, Moses Seymour & Abraham Bradley be a Committee to make Inquiry whether any of the Deserters from the Army & belonging to this Town & not accounted as part of the Quota.. are joined or likely to join the Army	157

8 Apr 1782

Voted that the Select Men grant Assistance & Relief to Saml Woodwock in his present Sickness	157
Granted a Tax of Two Pence on the Pound on the List of 1781 payable.. in specie or in Wheat at 4/0 p^r Bushel ~ or Rye at 3/0 p^r Bushel ~ or Indian Corn at 2/0 p^r Bushel or Flax at /6^d p^r lb - Ebenezer Plumbe, Gad Farnam & Benjamin Peck Chosen Receivers of said Tax.. Paid in Provision &c	157

8 Apr 1782

Gad Farnam was chosen Committee to supply Soldiers Families	157
D[ ] Seth Bird, Capt Moses Seymour & Lynde Lord Esqr were appointed Auditors of the Town Accounts	157

23 Dec 1782

Capt Moses Seymour Chosen Moderator	158
Isaac Baldwin, Ebenezer Marsh, Jesse Kilborn & James Morris Junr Chosen Select Men	158

26 Dec 1782

Chose Abraham Bradley Esqr to be a Select Man	158
Chose Jedidiah Strong to be Town Clerke	158
Chose Reuben Smith Esqr to be Treasurer	158
Timothy Skinner Chosen Constable & Collector of State Taxes	158
Nathaniel Smith 2nd Roger N. Whittlesey, Heber Stone Jesse Grant & John Phelps Chosen Constables	158
John Shethar, James Webster, Samuel McNeile, David King, Calvin Bissell, Alexander Catlin, Timothy Barns, Roger Marsh, Nathaniel Goodwin, Benjamin Gibbs Junr, Charles Smith Junr, Abner Baldwin Junr, Solomon Buell Junr, Jesse Grant, Leaming Bradley, Noah Stone, Hezekiah Agard, Abel Camp Junr, Seth Bishop [J^r], Thomas Catlin, Theophilus Allen & Noah Humaston were chosen Surveyors	158
Nathaniel Woodruff, Ozias Goodwin. Caleb Gillet & William Marsh Junr were Chosen Fence Viewers	158

Litchfield

John Shethar, Uriah Tracy, Heber Stone, Timothy Barns, Luman Bishop, Jesse Grant, Alexander Catlin, Solomon Goodwin, Edward Linsley & Eliphaz Parsons were Chosen Listers	158
Amos Galpin, Alex^r McNeile, Eaton Jones, James Stoddard & Benamin Landon were Chosen Leather Sealers	158
Isaac Baldwin Junr, David Buell, David Kilborn, Bezaleel Beebe, Philemon Murray, Julius Deming, Gideon Smedley & Joseph Wetmore were chosen Grand Jurors	158
Abijah Warren, George Dare, Jonathan Johnson, David Parmely, David King, Silas Dibbal, Ozias Lewis & Amos Parmely 2nd were chosen Tything Men	158
Capt Miles Beach Chosen Gauger & Packer	158
Levi Stone, Theodore Bidwel, Epaphras Wadsworth, Jonathan Smith J^r, Silas Dibbol & Joseph Cole Chosen Branders of Horses	158
Capt Abraham Bradley Chosen Sealer of Weights & Measures	158
Ozias Goodwin Choen Key Keeper	158

31 Dec 1782

Epaphras Wadsworth Chosen appointed a Grand Juror	159
Jedidiah Strong is.. appointed with the Assistance of the Select Men to prepare & State the Town Accounts	159
Capt Lynde Lord, Reuben Smith Esqr & Dr Seth Bird appointed Auditors of the Town Accounts	159
Timothy Skinner, Eli Smith & Abel Camp Junr appointed to view the lower Part of the Court House & report whether the same may be made convenient for holding Town Meetings & estimate the Cost	159
David Gibbs appointed Surveyor instead of Timothy Barns Excused	159
Capt Abraham Bradley & Capt Moses Seymour appointed a Committee to examine into the Matters.. in a Memorial of Capt Miles Beach & Capt Briant Stoddard Receivers of Provisions &c on the Half Crown Tax praying for Allowance of Wages & Wastage &c in Addition to what is allowed at the Pay Table	159

20 Jan 1783

Timothy Skinner, Ozias Goodwin, Jedidiah Strong, James Morris Junr & Bezaleel Beebe were Chosen a Committee to Exchange Highways where convenient & needful for the Publick	159
Col B Beebe Excused serving as Grand Juror	159
Capt Zebulon Gibbs, Capt Reuben Stone, Capt Solomon Marsh, Capt Eli Catlin, Capt John Osborn, Arthur Emons & Amos Moss Chosen a Committee to remove Nuisances & Encroachments on the Highways	159
Granted a Tax of Three Pence in the Pound.. Heber Stone Chosen Collector thereof & to be allowed Three Pence in the Pound	160

11 Mar 1783

Abraham Bradley Esqr Chosen Moderator	160
Granted Permision for the Small Pox to be communicated & carried on by Innoculation in Gillets Folly so called, it being a Peninsula or Neck of Land belonging to Stephen Baldwin in the Northern Part of the Great Pond	160

7 Apr 1783

Voted that no Hogs be suffered to go at large on the Highways or elsewhere in this Town..	160

Litchfield

without being well ringed in the Nose or Snout on Penalty or forfeiture of Two Shillings L Money and Poundage for each Hog.. in Order to prevent Mischief by such Hogs Voted that Capt Solomon Marsh, Capt Lynde Lord, Ens Ozias Goodwin, Ozias Lewis, Jonathan Page. Charles Smith, Nathan Farnam, Asher Thorp. John Moss & John Horsford be a Committee to carry this Vote into effectual Execution
12 May 1783

Capt Moses Seymour chosen Moderator	*161*
Voted that the Inhabitants living in the District near Capt Reuben Smith be permitted to erect a Pound in said District *1 Sep 1783*	*161*
Capt Abraham Bradley Moderator	*161*
D[ ] Seth Bird was chosen to attend the Convention.. at Middletown next Wednesday.. & D[ ] Seth Bird, Capt Abraham Bradley & I Baldwin Junr appointed to prepare Instructions for the Deputies soon to be chosen *10 Oct 1783*	*161*
Capt Moses Seymour Moderator	*161*

Mansfield

Town Meetings
1710 – 1803
Miscellaneous Records

Located at the Town Clerk's Office

Mansfield

10 Apr 1775

In Open Freemans Meeting.. the following persons.. were Admitted Freemen.. John Conant, Philip Turner, Amos Field, Stephen Brigham, Joshua Bassett, Willm Hovey, Seth Dunham, Timothy Bibbens & Isaac Royse	233

12 Sep 1775

And in freemans Meeting.. The following persons.. were Admitted.. Enoch Hovey, Peter Aspenwall Junr, Jacob Waters Junr, James Calkings, Enoch Pierce Junr & Walter Trumbull	233

8 Apr 1776

And in freemans Meeting.. the following persons.. were Admitted.. Joseph Ames, Samuel Campbell, Seth Fletcher, Benit Field, Samuel Dimock, Jonathan Hovey, Amos Hovey, Joseph Bennit, Jonathan Dexter & Solomon Royse	233

7 Apr 1777

In Open Freemans Meeting.. Elnathan Bassett, Lemuel Eldredge & James Bennit.. were Admitted Freemen	233

13 Sep 1774

John Salter Esqr was Chosen Moderator	255
Made Choise of John Salter Esqr Dean Cons^t Southworth Maj^r Joseph Storrs, Dea^n Edmund Freeman & Capt Exp^r Storrs to be a Comittee of Correspondence	255

10 Oct 1774

Chose John Salter Esqr Dea^n Constant Southworth Maj^r Joseph Storrs Dea^n Edmund Freeman & Capt Exp^r Storrs be a Comittee of Correspondence	258

25 Apr 1775

John Salter Esqr was chosen Moderator	262

25 Apr 1775

made Choice of Col^o Expe^r Storrs and Mr Nathl Attwood Agents.. at the General Assembly.. relating to Mr Uriah Brighams Memorial	262

25 Apr 1775

granted Liberty for Messrs Phineas Allen, Benjamin Chaplin: Hez: Allen, James Leavens & James Lane to Erect a hors Shed in the Town Street.. Southerly of the meeting house	262

12 Sep 1775

Dea^n Benj^a Chaplin was Chosen Moderator	262

12 Sep 1775

The Question was put.. whether Ebenezer Slate should receive any reward for removing out of Town, his Sister Sarah Slate a poor person, now under the Care of the Town	262

5 Oct 1775

John Salter Esqr was Chosen Moderator	263
Voted.. the Representitives of S^d Town viz Messrs Benj^a Chaplin & Amariah Williams To move in the General Assembly, that the Lands belonging to those persons who are inimical to the Common cause of Liberty, lying within this Government might be disposed of or regulated by some General Law of the Colony	263
made Choice of Mr Elijah Mackcall to be One of the Comittee of Correspondence & Observation	263

Mansfield

17 Oct 1775

To the.. General Assembly of the Colony of Connecticut now Sitting at New haven.. We complain that Mr Hez:^h Bissell a Commissary appointed.. in April last has given.. Occasion.. to Suspect, that he has Misused the public money this Suspicion.. grounded on the Information of Messrs Edmund Badger, Shubael Abbe and Henry DeWitt.. Gentlemen of undoubted veracity & of each.. Mr Bissell purchased goods or Merchandize for the Use of the Troops.. and at the time of payment.. required a receipt of each of the.. Gentlemen, for a Sum Exceeding that.. agreed for, & by him.. paid.. And in the presence.. of.. Joseph Barrows.. Mr Bissell Ordered his Servant Jeremiah Williams to mark the.. Sundry Barrels, below, or less than their true weight, which Barrels were to Contain Flour.. which.. has Created a belief.. that he had a latent design to defraud the public — 265

the Question was put whether the Same Should be considered as the Memorial.. & Complaint of said Inhabitants ~ Resolved.. in the Affirmative.. & Order^d the Same or a duplicate thereof be transmitted to Mr Benj^a Chaplin & Capt Amariah Williams now at New haven, to be.. laid before the Honourable General Assembly — 266

4 Dec 1775

John Salter Esqr was Chosen Moderator	267
Con: Southworth was Chosen Town Clerk	267
Mr Jacob Sargeant was Chosen Town Treasurer	267
Mr Cornelius Storrs was Chosen Constable & Collector of the Colony Tax	267
Messrs James Leavens, & Josiah Badcock Chosen Constables	267
Messrs Nathaniel Cary, John Conant, Jacob Waters, Samuel Stetson, Nathan Hall, Nathaniel Hall, Thomas Swift Junr, Samuel Jacobs, Moses Phelps, Jonathan Nichols, Cornelius Storrs, Joseph Whittemore, Abraham Spafford, Joseph Hovey Junr, Seth Peirce Junr, John Badcock, Richard White Hanks, Asa Carpenter, Hez Crane Junr, Jesse Waldo, Peter Cross, Jonathan Strickland, Zechariah Parker Junr, Matthew Warner, Jabez Goodell, Josiah Storrs, & Phineas Allen, Surveyors of highways	267
Col^o Exp^r Storrs, Mr Enoch Pierce, Capt Amazriah Williams Capt James Hall & Con: Southworth were Chosen Select Men	267
Messrs Samuel Sargeant, Phineas Allen Hovey & Josiah Taylor Fence Viewers	268
Messrs David Eldredge & Isaac Barrows Junr Collectors	268
Messrs Elnathan Brigham, Nathl Bennit & Benajah Conant Leather Sealers	268
Messrs Shubael Conant, Elijah Mackcall, Nathaniel Hall, Oliver Dimmock, Aaron Hovey, Grandjurors	268
Messrs Thomas Swift Junr, Prince Aspenwall, Jabez Cary, Jonathan Davis, Josiah Taylor, Jacob B Gurley, James Allen Junr, William Johnson & Eleazar Wright Tything Men	268
Mr Shubael Gager of Cask	268
Messrs Skiff Freeman, Edward Dimock, Benj^a Hutchens Peter Cross, Lemuel Clark Listers	268
Mr Benajah Conant Packer	268
Capt Jonathan Nichols & Mr Aaron Hovey Branders of horses	268
Mr Jacob Sargeant Sealer of Weights & Measures	268
Mr Samuel Sargeant Key keeper	268

Mansfield

18 Dec 1775

Maj^r Joseph Storrs ws chosen Moderator	269
27 Feb 1776	
John Salter Esqr was Chosen moderator	270
Mr Silas Hanks was chosen Collector of Rates in the Room of Mr Eldredge who refuses to Serve & has paid his fine	270
8 Apr 1776	
Dea^n Edmund Freeman was chosen Moderator	270
2 Dec 1776	
John Salter Esqr was Chosen Moderator	271
Con. Southworth Esqr was Chosen Town Clerk	271
Cons^t Southworth Esqr Capt James Hall, Mr Enoch Pierce Chosen Select men	271
Mr Shubael Conant was Chosen Town Treasurer	271
Mr Cornelius Storrs, was chosen Constable, and Collector of the Colony, or State Tax	271
Mr Aaron Hovey ws Chosen Constable	271
Messrs Elijah Mackcall, Jonathan Nichols, Skeff Freeman, Daniel Baldwin, Lemuel Barrows, Jabez Barrows Junr, Benja^n Hutchens, Josiah Southworth, James Lane, Josiah Storrs, Nathaniel Hall, Timothy Clark, John Read, Isaac Farwell, Richard Fletcher, James Royse Junr, Joseph Hovey Junr, Jon^a Gurley Junr, Moses Bicknell & Stephen Brigham were Chosen Surveyors of highways	271
Messrs Phineas Allen, Samuel Sargeant, Aaron Hovey Josiah Taylor were Chosen Fence Viewers	271
Messrs Thomas Storrs, Joseph Balcam, Barzillai Swift, Jonathan Fuller & Jesse Williams were Chosen Listers	271
Messrs Joseph Turner & Joseph Dimmock were chosen Collectors of rates	271
Messrs Elnathan Brigham & Benajah Conant were Chosen Leather Sealers	271
Messrs Isaac Barrows, Phinehas Allen, Jonathan Nichols Jacob B Gurley, & Calvin Topliff, were Chosen Granjurors	271
Messrs Thos Swift, Prince Aspenwall, Ebenezer Cary, Nathl Hunt Junr, Samuel Slater, Seth Peirce Junr, David Royse Junr & Samuel Southworth were Chosen Tything men	271
Mr Shubael Conant was Chosen Gager	271
Mr Benajah Conant was Chosen Packer	272
Messrs Jonathan Nichols, Nathl Hall & Aaron Hovey were Chosen Branders of Horses	272
Mr Samuel Sargeant Sealer of Weights and Measures	272
Mr Samuel Sargeant Keykeeper	272
Messrs Elijah Mackcall & Joseph Hovey Junr Haywards	272
Voted to Choose a Comittee to Divide the highway Districts.. & carry into Execution the resolve of the General Assembly.. granting Liberty to said Inhabitants to Tax themselves for the purpose of repairing highways.. and made Choise of Messrs Saml Sargeant, Thomas Barrows. Oliver Clark. Samuel Stetson. Nathaniel Attwood. Josiah Badcock & Josiah Taylor	272

Mansfield

18 Feb 1777

John Salter Esqr was Chosen Moderator	273
Mr Jonathan Hovey was chosen Collec^r of Rates in the room of Mr Joseph Turner	273
Capt Eleazar Huntington was Chosen Grandjuror in the room of.. Mr Phinehas Allen	273
Capt Nathl Hall Capt Abraham Spafford Capt Lemuel Barrows, Capt Jonathan Nichols and Mr Josiah Badcock were by vote.. added to the .. Comittee of Inspection	273

10 Mar 1777

Maj^r Joseph Storrs was Chosen Moderator	274
Made Choice of Messrs Thomas Davis, James Leavons, Thos Storrs, Benj^a Chaplin, Nathl Hall, Aaron Whittmore, Oliver Clark, Saml Jacobs, Josiah Badcock, Saml Stetson Daniel Dunham & Peter Cross to assist the Select Men in procuring Camp Equipage (if any can be obtained)	274

1 Apr 1777

Joseph Storrs Esqr was Chosen Moderator	275
Voted.. That a Com^{tee} .. to Consider the Circumstances of each Inhabitant, their past Services, Losses and Expences in the War, and make an Assessment.. which Tax Shall be made Annually so as to pay the Soldiers in s^d Service & that have been in Service... said Addition to their wages every Six Months, the first Six Months wages to be advanced at their Enlistment.. and that said Com^{tee} Shall provide for the families of the Soldiers.. Made Choice of John Salter Esqr, Messrs Jonathan Nichols, Timothy Clark, Amariah Williams, Nathl Attwood, John Swift, Nathl Hall & Josiah Badcock a Com^{tee} for the above purpose	275

6 May 1777

John Salter Esqr was Chosen Moderator	276

9 Sep 1777

John Salter Esqr was Chosen Moderator	276
the Several Persons hereafter named took the Oath prescribed for Freemen.. Eleaz^r Huntington.. Mulford Eldredge, Saml Thompson.. Benj^a Chaplin.. Ens^n Saml Stetson.. Thos Barrows.. [ ] Jabez Barrows.. Capt James Hall.. Enoch Peirce.. Skeff Freeman.. Josiah Taylor.. Moses Bicknell.. John Salter Esqr.. Edm^d Freeman.. Danl Hovey.. James Leavens.. Capt Lem^l Barrows.. Jon^a Davis.. Hez Allen.. Wm Johnson.. Stephen Turner.. John Martin.. .. James Parker.. Neh^h Peirce.. Asa Edgerton.. Isaac Farwell.. Joseph Balcam.. Seth Peirce..	277
Capt Aaron Whittmore.. Joseph Grow.. Nathl Attwood.. Lt Richd Fletcher.. Matt Warner.. Ens^n Zech$^{[\ ]}$ Parker.. Robt Barrows Junr.. Saml Campbell.. Isaac Barrows Junr.. Seth Peirce Junr.. Philip Turner.. Rich^d W$^{[\ ]}$ Hanks.. David Royse Junr.. Enoch Hovey.. Jon^a Dexer.. Aaron Hovey.. Ens^n Corn^s Storrs.. Eben^r Storrs.. Solomon Barrows.. Elip^t Dimmock.. .. Skeff Freeman Junr.. Josiah Storrs.. Lt Lem$_l$ Clark.. Israel Clark.. Nathl Southworth.. Judah Storrs.. Capt Jonath^n Nichols.. Capt Am^r Williams.. John Swift.. Capt Nathl Hall.. John Read.. Heman Attwood.. Barz^a Swift.. Capt Amaz^h Wright..Archp^s Parrish.. Solomon Royse.. Nathl Eaton.. Oliver Smith.. Thos Attwood.. Capt Gershom Barrows.. Eph^m Parker.. Doc^r Jesse Williams.. Isaac Dexter.. Jacob Waters Junr.. Ens^n Joseph Hovey Junr.. Peter Cross..	277
..Saml Sargeant.. Elisha Barrows.. Roswell Fenton.. D^n Jon^a Gurley.. Thos Barrows Junr.. Joseph Fenton.. Ens^n Prince Aspenwell.. Jon^a Hovey.. Mr Jed^h Huntington.. Capt Isaac Barrows.. Thos Swift.. Wm Trumbull.. Josiah Conant.. Shub^l Conant.. Sololom Lamphear.. Jacob Hovey.. David Dexter.. Con Southworth Esqr.. Bradford Newcomb.. Dr Jon^a Fuller.. Enoch Peirce Junr.. Levy Allen.. Benj^a Hutchens.. Nathl Cary.. Saml Jacobs.. James Lane..	278

Mansfield

Jacob Waters.

The Several persons Mentioned in the foregoing List, / Excepting Con: Southworth, Edmund Freeman, John Salter, Aaron Hovey, Cornelius Storrs & William Johnson, who had before taken the Oath / Took the Oath of Fidelity to this State.. Sworn p^r Con Southworth Just Pac^s
22 Aug 1777 — 278

These Certify That Messrs Edmund Freeman & Con South.. have taken the Oath of Fidelity.. before me Titus Holmes Just Pac^s
5 Sep 1777 — 279

John Salter.. These Certify That John Salter Esqr has taken the Oath of Fidelity to this State.. before me Con Southworth Just Pac^s
9 Sep 1777 — 279

These Certify That Messrs William Johnson, Aaron Hovey and Cornelius Storrs have taken the Oath of Fidelity to this State.. Sworn before Me.. Con Southworth Just Pac^s
1 Dec 1777 — 279

These Certify, That Col^o Exp^r Storrs, Judah Agard, Ephraim Hodges, Jonathan Gurley Junr, John Gilbert, Joel Starkweather, Lt Joseph Whittemore, Nathl Hunt Junr, Jon^a Brown, Jabez Cary, Eben^r Martin, Jabez Barrows Junr, Silas Hanks, Gershom Hall, John Conant, Isaac Turner, Tim^o Bibbens, Thos Storrs, John Hammond Daniel Baldwin Elijah Mackall Saml Bosworth Thos Davis Saml Turner, have taken the Oath of Fidelity to this State.. Sworn p^r Con Southworth Just Pacis
15 Dec 1777 — 279

These Certify that Joseph Storrs Esqr has taken the Oath of Fidelity to this State.. before me Con Southworth Just Pacis
5 Jan 1778 — 280

These Certify That Stephen Brigham has taken the Oath of Fidelity to this State.. Before Me Con Southworth Just Pacis
12 Jan 1778 — 280

These Certify That Messrs Moses Phelps, Isaac Sargeant Nathl Phelps, Ebenezer Baldwin, Josiah Southworth Abijah Harris, Nathan Hall William Hovey Amos Hovey, Elnathan Brigham, Elnathan Bassett, Oliver Bassett, Asa Southworth, Benjamin Nichols Junr Israel Waters Timothy Fuller Junr Robert Martin & Uriah Hanks have taken the Oath of Fidelity to this State.. Before Me Con Southworth Just Pacis
31 Aug 1778 — 280

These Certify, That Mr Dan Storrs and.. Messrs Ebenezer Allen Phinehas Turner Timothy Turner, Calvin Topliff, Oliver Dimock, Phinehas Gurley, Hezekiah Dimock, Stephen Barrows, Jonathan Balch Eben^r Cary, Nathl Nichols, Ebenez^r Snow, James Dana, Joshua Morgan, Dan Dunham & James Bicknell, have taken the Oath of fidelity to this State.. Excepting Dan Dunham who took a Solemn Affirmation ~ before Me Con Southworth Justice Pacis
13 Apr 1778 — 280

In open Freeman Meeting.. The following persons.. were made Free of this State.. #Messrs Ebenezer Allen Ebenez^r Martin, #Phinehas Turner #Timothy Turner #Calvin Topliff #Oliver Dimmock Nathaniel Mosely, #Phinehas Gurley Amos Hovey Silas Hanks, Hez Dimock, Josiah Badcock William Hovey, Israel Waters #Stephen Barrows Thos Davis #Jonathan Balch Moses Phelps John Badcock #Eben^r Cary Jacob B. Gurley #Nathl Nichols Joseph Storrs Esqr Tim^o Bibbens Gershom Hall Jabez Barrows Junr Saml Turner, #Eben^r Snow, Isaac — 281

Mansfield

Turner ~~James Bicknall~~ #James Dana Col⁰ Exp^r Storrs #Joshua Morgan Lt Joseph Whitteman Saml Bosworth #Dan Dunham took an Affirmation ~ #James Bicknall Thos Storrs Lt Danl Dunham Phin^s Clark Jonath^n Gurley Junr Robt Martin #Nathl Southworth Junr #Jon^a Church #Moses Webster.. N.B. Those whose names are mark^d this (#) took the oath of fidelity, as Enter^d on the Left hand
8 Sep 1778

In Open Freemans Meeting.. The following persons.. were Addmitted Freemen.. Verney Fellows Jabez Barrows John Hammond Ephraim Hodges John Royse Daniel Howe *7 Dec 1778*	281
This is to Certify that Messrs James Roys Junr Seth Conant Peter Aspenwall James Royse, Timothy Stetson Azariah Freeman Ephraim Campbell, this Day took the oath of Fidelity to this State.. Before Me Con Southworth Just Pacis *2 Dec 1778*	281
Prince Turner took the Oath of Fidelity to this State before John Salter Just Pacis	281
29 Sep 1777	
Col⁰ Exp^r Storrs was Chosen Moderator	282
To Choose a Committee to Supply the Soldiers in the Continental Army with Necessary Articles of Cloathing, agreeable to Request of his Excellency the Govr.. made Choice of Messrs Jonathan Nichols Nathl Hall, Aaron Hovey, Elijah Mackcall & Amariah Williams a Committee for the purpose of of Supplying Cloathing as above Said *1 Dec 1777*	282
Col⁰ Exp^r Storrs Chosen Moderator	282
Con Southworth Esqr was Chosen Town Clerk	282
Con Southworth Esqr Col⁰ Expe^r Storrs, Capt Azariah Williams Capt James Hall & Mr Nathl Attwood Chosen Select Men	282
Mr Shubael Conant Chosen Town Treasurer	282
Mr Cornelius Storrs Chosen Constable and Collector of the State Tax	283
Mr Aaron Hovey Chosen Constable	283
Capt Nathl Hall Lt Thos Barrows, Lt Joseph Whittemore Messrs Asa Edgerton, Robert Barrows Junr John Conant Elijah Mackcall Joel Starkweather Saml Jacobs, James Leavens Judah Storrs, Timothy Clark Saml Thompson Aaron Whittmore, Archippus Parrish John Dunham Jonathan Brown John Royse Dan Dunham & Jesse Waldo Chosen Surveyors of highways	283
Messrs Saml Sargeant & Aaron Hovey Chosen Fence Viewers	283
Messrs Heman Attwood Gerhsom Barrows, John Badcock Nathl Eaton Matthew Warner Jacob B. Gurley, Elijah Mackcall, Thos Barrows, Zach^h Parker Junr Chosen Grandjurors	283
Messrs Ebenezer Storrs Ephraim Parker, Prince Aspenwall, Daniel Barrows, Josiah Taylor Silas Hanks Seth Dunham & Calvin Topliff, Tything men	283
Messrs Shubael Conant & Edmund Freeman Chosen Gager of Casks	283
Mr Benajah Conant Chosen Packer	283
Messrs Nathl Hall Jonathan Nichols & Aaron Hovey Chosen Branders of Horses	283
Mr Jacob Sargeant Sealer of Weights & Measures	283
Mr Samuel Sargeant Chosen Key keeper	283

Mansfield

Mess[rs] Jonathan Nichols Lem[l] Barrows Dan Storrs Daniel Dunham & Richard Fletcher Chosen Listers	283
M[r] Ephraim Robbins & Dea[n] Benj[a] Chaplin Chosen Collectors of Rates	283
Mess[rs] Benajah Conant and Elnathan Brigham Chosen Leather Sealers	283
Mess[rs] Sam[l] Sargeant, Thomas Barrows, Samuel Stetson, Nath[l] Attwood, Josiah Badcock, Josiah Taylor & Lemuel Clark Chosen to Make up the Surveyors highway Rate Bills	284
M[r] Nath[l] Hall Jonathan Nichols, Elijah Mackcall Aaron Hovey Cap[t] Amariah Williams Eleazar Huntington Daniel Dunham Aaron Whittmore Nath[l] Moseley Samuel Thompson, Joseph Hovey Jun[r] Thomas Swift Lemuel Barrows & Peter Cross Chosen a Comittee to procure Cloathing and to Provide for the families of persons in the Continental Army	284
12 Jan 1778	
Col[o] Exper Storrs was Chosen Moderator	284
Voted That This Town Will Assist in Supporting the Widow of M[r] Barnabas Hall for the present Year	285
9 Feb 1778	
John Salter Esq[r] Chosen Moderator	285
Voted to release M[r] Benjamin Chaplin from being Collector & Also M[r] Ephraim Robbins on.. Robbins' promise of paying the Fine of 26/ & Made Choice of Matthew Warner, and Peter Aspenwall Jun[r] & Eleazar Slafter Collectors of rates	285
12 Mar 1778	
John Salter Esq[r] Chosen Moderator	324
M[r] Cady Allen was Chosen Collector of Rates.. in the room of.. M[r] Peter Aspenwall Jun[r]	324
19 Mar 1778	
Col[o] Exper Storrs was Chosen Moderator	325
25 Jun 1778	
Col[o] Exper Storrs was Chosen Moderator	326
M[r] Timothy Bibbens was Chosen Surveyor of highways in the room of M[r] John Conant	326
released Cap[t] Jonathan Nichols (at his Desire) from his Trust as a Com[tee] Man for procuring Cloathing	326
7 Dec 1778	
John Salter Esq[r] Chosen Moderator	328
Const Southworth Esq[r] wasChosen Town Clerk	328
Col[o] Experience Storrs Con Southworth Esq[r] Cap[t] Amariah Williams M[r] Nath[l] Attwood & Cap[t] James Hall were Chosen Select Men	328
M[r] Shubael Conant was Chosen Town Treasurer	328
M[r] Aaron Hovey was chosen Constable & Collector of the State Tax	328
M[r] Cornelius Storrs Was Chosen Constable	328
Mess[rs] Daniel Baldwin, Cap[t] Isaac Sargeant, Silas Hanks Simeon Robes, Gershom Hall, Nathaniel Hunt Jun[r], Seth Allen, Aaron Goodell, Hez[h] Allen Nathan Palmer Moses Phelps Peter Aspenwall Jun[r] Ebenezer Storrs, Cap[t] Eleazar Huntington, Seth Peirce Isaac Barrows Jun[r], Joseph Fenton James Royse, William Johnson Oliver Dimock & Hezekiah Crane were all Chosen Surveyors of highways	328

Mansfield

Messrs Saml Sargeant and Josiah Taylor were Chosen Fence Viewers	328
Messrs Elijah Mackcall Capt James Dana, Capt Gershom Barrows Nathaniel Eaton & Josiah Badcock were Chosen Listers	328
Capt Lemuel Barrows Lieu^t Thomas Barrows Josiah Southworth Ebenezer Allen, Thomas Barrows Junr Zebulon Gurley and Ebenezer Storrs were Chosen Grandjurors	328
Messrs Skeff Freeman Junr & Bradford Newcomb Collectors	328
Capt Joseph Whittemore & Lt Elnathan Brigham Leather Sealers	328
Messrs Thomas Hutchens Lt Josiah Stoel Eph^m Campbell Jonathan Brown & Samuel Slafter were Chosen Tythingmen	328
Mr Benajah Conant was chosen Packer	328
Capt Jonathan Nichols & Mr Aaron Hovey Branders of Horses	328
Mr Samuel Sargeant Sealer of Weights and Measures & Also Key keeper	328
Accepted of an highway laid out lately near the Dwelling house of Mr Nathl Bennit	329
Voted to Pay Jacob Waters & Nathaniel Bennit.. 18 Dollars for.. a Com^{tee} to View a proposed highway	329
Voted to Assist in the Support of the Widow of Mr Barnabas Hall	329
Voted to rebuild the Bridge Across Fentons river near John Royses Dwelling house.. Peter Cross and John Royse Chosen a Com^{tee} for.. Rebuilding S^d Bridge	329

14 Jan 1779

Col^o Exp^r Storrs Chosen Moderator	333
Capt Jonathan Nichols Clark Pro Tempore	333

25 Mar 1779

John Salter Esqr Chosen Moderator	333

1 Apr 1779

Chose a Com^{tee} to Draft Instructions for the Representatives in May next viz Col^o Exp^r Storrs Capt Eleazar Huntington Con Southworth Esqr Capt James Dana, Capt Amariah Williams Mr James Leavins & John Salter Esqr	333
Dismissed Thomas Swift from being One of the Com^{tee} of Supplies for Soldiers Families, and made Choice of Mr Ebenezer Storrs in his room	334

3 Sep 1779

Maj^r Joseph Storrs Chosen Moderator	335

6 Dec 1779

John Salter Esqr was Chosen Moderator	335
Con Southworth Esqr Town Clerk	335
Col^o Expe^r Storrs, Con Southworth Esqr Capt James Hall Capt Amariah Williams & Mr Nathl Attwood Select men	335
Mr Shubael Conant Town Treasurer	335
Constable and Collector of the State Taxes	335
Mr Aaron Hovey Constable	335
Messrs Joseph Hovey Junr Capt Eleazar Huntington Ens^n Elijah Mackall Com^{tee} for Supplying Cloathing for the Continental Soldiers	336

Mansfield

Mess[rs] Moses Webster, Joseph Balcam Mathew Warner Jacob B. Gurley & Eben[r] Baldwin Com[tee] Supplying Soldiers Families	336
Mess[rs] Dan Storrs James Leavens John Russ Jun[r] Cap[t] Nath[l] Hall Nath[l] Bennit, Timothy Stetson Joshua Parker Elisha Barrows Joshua Morgan, Josiah Storrs, Jabez Goodell, Benjamin Hutchens James Lane Jacob Hoven John Royse, Joseph Dimock Lot Dimock Bennit Field, Verney Fellows Cap[t] Sam[l] Thompson Samuel Millington John Badcock & Eleazer Slafter Surveyors of Highways	336
Mess[rs] Sam[l] Sargeant & Josiah Taylor Fence Viewers	336
Mess[rs] Eleazar Conant Zechariah Parker Jun[r], Seth Dunham, Josiah Stoel Nath[l] Bennit Jun[r], Listers	336
Messrs Nath[l] Storrs & Enoch Pierce Jun[r] Collectors of Rates	336
Mess[rs] Elnathan Brigham, Benajah Conant Leather Sealers	336
M[r] Benjamin Hutchens Cap[t] Lemuel Barrows M[r] Nath[l] Mosely, M[r] Eben[r] Storrs, Cap[t] Jonathan Nichols Cap[t] Nath[l] Hall, Ens[n] Peter Cross Dea[n] Oliver Dimock & Calvin Topliff Grandjurors	336
Mess[rs] Ephraim Parker Nathan Hall, Zurick Campbell, Nath[l] Hunt Jun[r] Sam[l] Turner, James Royse Jun[r] Sam[l] Southworth & Archippus Parish Tythingmen	336
M[r] Shubael Conant Gager of Casks	336
M[r] Benajah Conant Packer	336
Cap[t] Jonathan Nichols Cap[t] Nath[l] Hall & M[r] Aaron Hovey Branders of Horses	337
M[r] Sam[l] Sargeant Sealer of Weights & Measures & Key keeper	337
Voted to Accept the highways lately laid out near Cap[t] Danas	337
Voted to Choose a Com[tee] to Sette Acc[ts] with the Select Men ~ and made Choice of Cap[t] Jonathan Nichols John Salter Esq[r] & M[r] Joseph Balcam	337
Made Choice of the same Com[tee] as in 1777 with Addition of Col[o] Exp[r] Storrs to make up the highway rate Bills	337
12 Apr 1779	
In Open Fremans Meeting.. the following Persons.. were made free of the State of Connecticut and Sworn p[r] John Salter Just Pacis viz Mess[rs] Boaz Stearns Gideon Abbe, William Abbe, Elijah Abbe, Samuel Southworth, Isaac Sarg[t] Palmer, Gideon Arnold Cap[t] Sam[l] Storrs, Sam[l] Upham Amariah Storrs, Rev[d] Richard Salter, Eleazar Conant Enoch Freeman, Peter Aspenwall, Jabez Cary James Clark, & Isaac Royse ~ The above persons being Previously admitted to the Oath of Fidelity to this State and took the Same, antecedent to their taking the Freemans Oath	338
14 Sep 1779	
In open Freemans Meeting.. the Following Persons Took the Oath of Fidelity to this State, and.. were Admitted Freeman.. p[r] Con Southworth Just Pacis viz Mess[rs] Josiah Stoel William Basset, Asa Moulton & Bennit Field	338
10 Apr 1780	
In open Fremans Meeting.. Nathan Simonds Malachi Conant Nath[l] Hopkins #Seth Conant Theophilus Hall Silvanus Conant, Frederic Freeman, Benjamin Upham, Samuel Wood #Samuel Slafter, Timothy Stetson, #Seth Fletcher #Hezekiah Crane #John Russ Jun[r] #Joseph Upham James Royse Jun[r], #Asa Royce #Jesse Bennit #Isaac Davis & #Zebulon Gurley were Admitted Freemen.. those mark[d] thus /#/ having previously taken the Oath of Fidelity to this State. Sworn p[r] Con Southworth Just Pacis	338

Mansfield

9 Apr 1781

In open Freemans Meeting.. The following Persons.. were Admitted Freemen.. and also were previously Admitted to the Oath of Fidelity Except Oliver Clark who has before taken said Oath of fidelity viz Jesse Waldo James Fletcher Elijah Freeman, Thomas Farwell Calvin Topliff Junr David Brown, Oliver Clark Jonathan Stoel Daniel Barrows & Jonathan Lane ~ Sworn p^r Con Southworth Just Pacis *339*

3 Dec 1781

Decr 3^d 1781 Messrs Thomas Welch & Elijah Turner & Decr 31st 1781 Messrs Moses Cook Welch & Samuel Thompson Junr, Took the Oath of Fidelity to this State.. Sworn p^r Con Southworth Just Peace *339*

8 Apr 1782

In Open Freeman's Meeting.. The following persons.. were Admitted freemen.. and those marked thus /#/ also took previously the Oath of Fidelity to this State viz Messrs Moses Cook Welch, Thomas Welch #Joseph Storrs Junr #Benjamin Storrs Nathl Phelps #Edward Dimock #Tiras Preston #Daniel Harris Elijah Turner #Nathl Nichols Junr & Shubael Dimock Junr *339*

7 Apr 1783

In open Freemans Meeting.. Messrs John Arnold & Benjamin Chaplin Junr took the oath of Fidelity to this State, and were Admitted Freemen of the Corporation.. *339*

9 Sep 1783

In open Freemans Meeting.. Mr Asher Allen took the Oath of fidelity to this State and was Admitted a freeman of the Corporation *340*

24 Mar 1783

Messrs Arad Simonds Philip Perkins Rufus Spaulding, Charles Starkweather & Eliphalet Simonds took the Oath of Fidelity, *340*

5 Apr 1782

And.. Levi Bumpos took the said Oath of Fidelity *340*

16 Mar 1780

John Salter Esqr was Chosen Moderator *341*

granted Liberty to Mr Nathl Moseley to Erect a Damm Across Natcharige river below the Saw Mill & above the New bridge near to the said Moseleys Dwelling house *341*

made Choice of Mr Saml Stetson Com^{tee} for Supplying Soldiers Families *341*

10 Apr 1780

Made Choice of Mr Seth Peirce Junr Collector in the room of Enoch Peirce Junr *341*

Capt James Dana & Lt Thomas Barrows were chosen Surveyors of highways *341*

Capt Isaac Sargeant was Chosen Lister *341*

27 Mar 1780

Joseph Storrs Esqr was Chosen Moderator *341*

27 Mar 1780

Voted to Choose a Com^{tee} to Correspond with Com^{tees} of other Towns or Counties, on.. removing the Embargo Act.. and that the rate of Discount may be fixed on the present Currency, and that the £10 State Notes may be paid in such manner as that Justice may be Done ~ Dea^n Benjamin Chaplin, Capt Eleazar Huntington, Capt Nathl Hall, Capt Amaziah Wright & Doct Jesse Williams were Chosen *342*

Mansfield

10 Apr 1780

John Salter Esqr was Chosen Moderator in the room of Maj^r Storrs Absent	342

23 Jun 1780

Maj^r Joseph Storrs Was Chosen Moderator	342
Voted to give.. fifty pounds.. to Each able Bodied recruit who shall inlist for this Town to Serve in the Army of the United States for the Term of three years or During the War.. ~ And that the Commission^d Officers of the several Military Companies in this Town, together with Dea^n Benjamin Chaplin Capt James Dana Capt John Shumway & Capt Amariah Williams be a Com^{tee} to Engage.. Soldiers on the lowest Terms.. & in Case.. Soldiers Cannot be Obtained.. That s^d Com^{tee} Endeavour to Engage a Sufficient number of men for s^d Service for the term of six months.. on the best Terms, not Exceeding Six pounds to Each one in Silver money or produce	342

9 Oct 1780

Dea^n Benjamin Chaplin was Chosen Moderator	345
Capt Joseph Whittemore and & Mr Enoch Peirce Junr were Chosen Collectors of rates	345

16 Nov 1780

Maj^r Joseph Storrs was Chosen Moderator	345
Voted to Class the Inhabitants.. for the purpose of filling in this Town's Quota of the Continental Army.. Made Choice of Constant Southworth Esqr Col^o Exp^r Storrs, Capt Nathl Hall, Capt Saml Thompson Capt Eleazar Huntington, Capt Jesse Waldo, Capt Joseph Whittemore, Capt Aaron Whittmore, John Salter Esqr Capt Isaac Sargeant, Capt James Dana Mr Nathl Attwood, Capt Amariah Williams, Capt Tim^o Clark & Capt Jonathan Nichols a Com^{tee} for the purpose	346
Voted to raise 6^d on the pound Lawful money on the List.. for 1779, to be paid in provision.. in Beef Pork or Flour.. Col^o Experience Storrs, and Mr Josiah Taylor were Chosen Receivers and packers of.. provisions and Collectors of s^d provisions and Collectors of the S^d Tax	346

4 Dec 1780

Col^o Experience Storrs was Chosen Moderator	347
Con Southworth Esqr Town Clerke	347
Mr Shubael Conant Town Treasurer	347
Con Southworth Esqr, Col^o Expe^r Storrs, Mr Nathaniel Attwood, Capt Amariah Williams & Capt James Hall Select Men	347
Mr Cornelius Storrs Constable & Collector of the State Tax	347
Mr Jacob Barker Gurley Constable	347
Messrs Jabez Barrows Junr, Daniel Howe, Lieu^t Thos Barrows, Timothy Stetson, Joshua Morgan, James Leavens, Saml Sargeant, Nathan Hall, Samuel Jacobs, Elijah Mackcall, Jabez Goodell, Josiah Storrs, Daniel Baldwin, Richard White Hanks, Samuel Millington, Joseph Chamberlain, Seth Peirce, Peter Cross, Zechariah Parker Junr, Phinehas Gurley, & Skeff Freeman Junr - Surveyors of Highways	347
Messrs Samuel Sargeant and Josiah Taylor Fence Viewers	347
Messrs Shubael Conant James Dana Lemuel Barrows Hezekiah Dimock & Enoch Peirce Junr Listers	347
Messrs Benjamin Chaplin & Jesse Bennit Collectors of rates	348

Mansfield

Messrs Elnathan Brighham and Joseph Whittemore ~ Leather Sealers	348
Leiu^t Thomas Barrows Capt Nathaniel Hall, Lieu^t Elijah Mackall Mr Thos Swift Capt Aaron Whittmore & Jonathan Gurley, Grandjurors	348
Messrs Nathl Southworth Junr Timothy Bibbens Daniel Barrows, Elnathan Basset Jonathan Hovey John Royse, Samuel Slaster & Bradford Newcomb Tythingmen	348
Mr Shubael Conant Gager of Cask	348
Mr Heman Attwood Packer	348
Capt Jonathan Nichols Brander of Horses	348
Mr Samuel Sargeant Sealer of Weights and Measures and Key Keeper	348
Voted to Exchange the old highway by John Read's for the new highway leading from Samuel Turners By Joseph Chamberlains Dwelling house	348
Voted that in Case Mr Daniel Hovey becomes Chargeable to the Town, That the Select men apply to the County Court.. to Enforce a maintenance from such of his Children as are able to support him	348
Made Choice of Capt Samuel Thompson, Capt Eleazar Huntington, Capt Jesse Waldo, & Capt Joseph Whittemore, a Committee to Settle.. what is Due.. to the 6 months Continental Soldiers and 3 months Militia Soldiers, for their Services the last Campaign	349

9 Jan 1781

John Salter Esqr was Chosen Moderator	349
released Jesse Bennit from being Collector of rates.. And Made Choice of Lot Dimock.. in his room	349
Voted, that One peny half peny on the pound on the S^d Town's List of AD 1779, be raised in Merchantable wheat flour at 24/ p^r hundred weight gross; Or Rye flour at 16/ p^r hund^d weight gross; or Indian Corn at 4/ p^r bushel.. Made Choice of Col^o Exper Storrs, and Mr Josiah Taylor Receivers, and Storers of the aforesaid Flour and Corn	350
Cap^{ts} James Dana & Gershom Barrows be a Com^{tee} to Engage this Town's Quota viz Eight Men, to Serve for.. One year in the State Regiment.. for the Defence of this State at Horseneck &c	350

12 Feb 1781

Col^o Exp^r Storrs and Mr Josiah Taylor be Collec^{rs} of the Flour and grain Tax	350
Voted to Excuse Dea^n Benj^a Chaplin from being Collec^r of rates, on Condition of his paying his Forfieture	350
Chose Capt Jonathan Nichols Collec^r of the Town Taxes.. & that he receive the Forfieture that shall be paid.. by Dea^n Benj^a Chaplin	350
Made Choice of Mr Jonathan Brown Collec^r of rate in the room of Lot Dimock, and that if any forfieture is Collected of s^d Dimock the s^d Brown receive the same	350
Lieu^t Elijah Mackcall, Capt Nathl Hall Moses Webster & Daniel Gurley Com^{tee} for Supplying Soldiers Families	350
Hez Allen and Mr Joseph Hovey Junr Com^{tee} for Supplying Cloathing for the Soldiers	350
John Salter Esqr was Chosen Moderator	351
Met.. to Se if said Town will give Directions for laying out a highway from Mr Ephraim Parkers to Windham Line.. Voted that the Select Men View the Circumstances and Consider of the Necessity of the proposed highway from Mr Parkers to Windham Line	351

19 Mar 1781

John Salter Esqr was Chosen Moderator	351

Mansfield

Made Choice of the same Committee, with addition of Lieu^t Josiah Stoel, to Class the Inhabitants	351
9 Apr 1781	
John Salter Esqr was Chosen Moderator	352
Voted to Support Daniel Hovey at the Cost of the Town for the Term of three Months	352
Voted to release Mr Joseph Hovey Junr from being One of the Cloathing Committee ~ and Chose Mr Enoch Peirce Junr in his room	352
26 Jun 1781	
John Salter Esqr was Chosen Moderator	352
Voted to raise 4^d L^l money on the Pound on the List of Said Town for 1780, to be paid in Beef Cattle.. made Choice of Capt Isaac Barrows and Capt Amaziah Wright Collectors of s^d Tax, and purchasers of s^d Beef Cattle	352
Made Choice of Col^o Expe^r Storrs and Mr Josiah Taylor receivers and packers of provisions &c on the 2/6^d Tax	352
Mr Ebenezer Baldwin Chosen Lister in the room of Capt Dana in the public Service	352
3 Dec 1781	
John Salter Esqr was Chosen Moderator	353
Con Southworth Town Clerk	353
Messrs Shubael Conant Con Southworth Barzillai Swift Aaron Hovey and Zech^r Parker Junr Select Men	353
Mr Shubael Conant Town Treasurer	353
Mr Jacob B. Gurley Constable & Collector of the State Tax	353
Mr Eleazar Conant Constable	353
Messrs John Conant Thos Storrs, Joseph Mosely, Robert Martin, Joel Starkweather Ebenezer Storrs, Silas Hanks Gershom Hall James Leavens, James Bennit, Saml Jacobs John Russ Junr Frederick Freeman, Daniel Crane, Timothy Turner, Hez^h Crane Junr, Seth Conant John Badcock, Thomas Barrows Junr ~~Seth Conant~~ & Hez^h Dimmock: Surveyors of highways	353
Messrs Saml Sargeant & Josiah Taylor Saml Sergeant & Josiah Taylor Fence Viewers	353
Messrs Jonathan Hovey Amariah Storrs, Eliph^t Dimmock Frederick Freeman & Joseph Whittemore Listers	353
Dea^n Benjamin Chaplin & Jacob B. Gurley Collectors	353
Capt Joseph Whittemore & Lieu^t Elnathan Brigham Leather Sealers	353
Messrs Jonathan Hovey Samuel Campbell Eleazar Huntington Isaac Barrows Peter Cross Jesse Williams David Royse Junr Granjurors	353
Messrs Daniel Barrows Ephraim Parker Asa Southworth Joseph Fenton Nathl Eaton Elijah Freeman & Edward Dimock Tything Men	353
Mr Shubael Conant Gager of Cask	353
Mr Benajah Conant Packer	353
Capt Jonathan Nichols Brander of horses	353
Mr Saml Sargeant Sealer of Weights & measures	353
Mr Benajah Conant Key keeper	353
Messrs Jacob Waters & Daniel Baldwin Howards	353

Mansfield

Voted To Accept the highway.. from Mr Ephraim Parkers to the Town Line near Capt Linkons	354
Mr Barzillai Swift to manage the Cause at the County Court against John Scripture	354
Made Choice of John Salter Esqr Messrs Samuel Sargeant & Daniel Dunham a Committee to Settle Acc^{ts} with Capt Amariah Williams and Mr Joseph Hovey Junr in regard to the Extra prices of Cloathing	354
Voted That the Select Men withdraw the Action now pending in the County Court against Enoch Hovey for his Fathers Support	354
Voted That Cap^{ts} Eleazar Huntington Joseph Whittemore Samuel Thompson & Jesse Waldo be a Committee to make.. Settlement with the Six Months Soldiers and three months Soldiers.. and Determine what is Due.. to said Soldiers	354

31 Dec 1781

John Salter Esqr was chosen Moderator	355
Mes^{srs} Cornelius Storrs & Enoch Peirce Junr were Chosen Constables	355
released Mr Benj^a Chaplin from being Collector of rates	355
made Choice of Messrs Mathew Warner and Daniel Barrows Edward Dimmock & Moses Webster Collectors of the Town rate	355
released Mr Jacob B Gurley from being Constable, Collector of the State Tax and Town Tax	355
Made Choice of Mr Eleazar Conant heretofore Chosen Constable, The Collector of the State Tax	355
released Mr Hez^h Dimock from being Surveyor of highways & Chose Mr Jonathan Brown Surveyor in his room	355
Accepted the report of the Committee appointed to Settle with Capt Am^r Williams and Joseph Hovey Junr & ordered payment viz to Capt Williams £13..1..3 & To Mr Hovey.. 4..2..11	355
released Capt Eleaz^r Huntington from being ~~Surveyor~~ Grandjuror, and Chose Mr Gideon Arnold Grandjuror in his room	355

11 Mar 1782

John Salter Esqr Chosen Moderator	356
Voted to raise Eight men, Soldiers for the Defence of this State at Horseneck.. Voted to Class the Inhabitants.. for the purpose of raising said Men - Made Choice of John Salter Esqr, Capt Nathl Hall Capt Eleazar Huntington Capt Joseph Whittemore Capt Aaron Whittmore, Capt Richard Fletcher Capt Jesse Waldo Capt Elijah Mackall Capt Amariah Williams Capt Samuel Thompson Capt Josiah Stoel & Capt James Dana, a Committee to Class said Inhabitants, and Superintend the procuring the said Eight Soldiers	356

8 Apr 1782

John Salter Esqr was Chosen Moderator	356
Made Choice of Messrs Dan Storrs, Samuel Storrs Junr, Enoch Peirce Junr Jonathan Hovey, Josiah Badcock Jacob Hovey James Clark & Elijah Mackall Collectors of Rates in the respective Classes to which they belong	356
Messrs Elijah Mackall Judah Storrs & Thomas Swift were Chosen a Committee immediately to rebuild Upham Bridge	356

15 Jul 782

Capt Jonathan Nichols was chosen Moderator	357

Mansfield

2 Dec 1782

John Salter Esqr was Chosen Moderator	357
Con Southworth Esqr was chosen Town Clerk	357
Con Southworth Esqr John Salter Esqr Messrs Shubael Conant Nathaniel Attwood & Capt Amariah Williams, Chosen Select men	357
Mr Shubael Conant Town Treasurer	357
Mr Enoch Peirce Junr Constable & Collector of the State Tax	357
Mr Eleazar Conant Constable	357
Messrs Eleazar Huntington Elijah Mackall, Benjamin Storrs Jonathan Nichols, Nathaniel Southworth Junr William Trumbull William Clark, John Russ Junr, Gershom Hall, Benjamin Hutchens, Stephen Barrows, Nathan Hall ~ Prince Turner, Nathl Eaton Enoch Hovey, Eliphalet Dimock, Moses Webster, Aaron Hovey, Jonas Huntington & Zebulon Gurley ~ Surveyors of highways	357
Messrs Samuel Sergeant & Josiah Taylor Fence Viewers	357
Messrs Zephaniah Swift Daniel Dunham, Samuel Thompson Benjamin Chaplin Junr & Andrew Hall Listers	357
Messrs Benjamin Storrs, Peter Aspenwal Junr Timothy Turner & Aaron Whittmore ~ Collectors	357
Messrs Elnathan Brigham & Jabez Barrows Junr Leather Sealers	357
Capt Nathl Hall, Capt Lemuel Barrows Mr Timothy Bibbens Doc^t Jonathan Fuller, Messrs Jacob B. Gurley & Seth Dunham Grandjurors	357
Messrs David Allen, Elnathan Bassett, Asher Allen Seth Conant, Moses Bicknall & Jonathan Brown Tythingmen	358
Mr Shubael Conant Gager of Cask	358
Col^o Exp^r Storrs Packer	358
Capt Jonathan Nichols Brander of Horses	358
Mr Samuel Sargeant Sealer of Weights & Measures	358
Mr Benajah Conant Key Keeper	358
Made Choice of the Same Com^{tee} as Serv^d the last year to make up the highway rate Bills for the several Surveyors of highways, Capt Josiah Stoel being appointed in the room of Mr Samuel Stetson Dec^d ~ viz Messrs Samuel Sargeant, Thomas Barrows, Josiah Stoel, Col^o Exp^r Storrs, Lemuel Clark, Nathaniel Attwood Josiah Badcock and Josiah Taylor	358
Chose Mr Jacob B. Gurley, Joshua Parker & Joshua Millington a Com^{tee} to Supply Soldiers Families	358

28 Jan 1783

John Salter Esqr was Chosen Moderator	359
Question was put whether said Town would appoint an agent to appear at the adjourn County Court in Feb^{ry} next.. to oppose the Memorial of Stephen Turner &c.. for a highway across Capt Jesse Waldo^s Land - Resolved in the Negative	359

7 Apr 1783

Col^o Expe^r Storrs was Chosen Moderator	359
The Question was put whether said Town will Accept of the highway as laid out across the farm of Capt Jesse Waldo.. ~ Resolved in the Negative	359

Mansfield

released Mr Peter Aspenwall Junr from being Collector	359
Question, was put whether said Town Will release Capt Aaron Whittmore from being Collector of rates - Resolved in ye negative Whereupon.. Capt Whittmore refused to Serve and promised to pay the Fine.. Whereupon said Town Chose Mr Enoch Hovey Collector of rates	359
made Choice of Mr John Russ Junr Collector in the room of Mr Aspenwall released	359

27 May 1783

Capt Nathaniel Hall chosen Moderator	360
Constant Southworth Esqr Chosen Agent to Defend in any action brought, or pending before the County Court against said Town	360
Voted to accept the highway across Capt Jesse Waldo's Land	360

9 Sep 1783

Samuel Thompson Esqr was chosen Moderator	360
Capt Zeph^h Swift Col^o Exp^r Storrs and Samuel Thompson Esqr were Chosen a Com^{tee} to draw.. Instructions for the Representitives.. in General Assembly in October next	360

Middletown

Town Votes and Proprietors Records
Volume 2
1735 – 1798

Located at the Town Clerk's Office

Middletown

5 Dec 1774

Voted That Titus Hosmer Esq[r] be Moderator	*342*
Voted That Major Matthew Tallcott, Cap[t] Phillip Mortimer, Tit[ ] Hosmer Esq[r] Major Jehosphephat Starr, M[r] George Phillips Cap[t] Solomon Sage, Joseph Frany, Cap[t] Roger Riley. Cap[t] Nathaniel Gilbert, Cap[t] Isaac Miller, Daniel Whitmore Cap[t] Stephen Hubbard, Francis Clark. Cap[t] Ebenezer Johnson Joel Adkins Lieu[t] David Tryon & Elijah Hubbard Ju[r] [be] a Committee.. to inspect the Conduct of the Inhabitants of this Town	*342*

19 Sep 1775

These may Certify That Andrew Bacon, Stephen Miller Jun[r] Zebulon Stow, Samuel Johnson, Daniel Southmayd Josiah S[ ] Jabez Brainard, Samuel Chamberlain, Isaac Hedges, D[ ] Brainard Miller, George Phillips Jun[r] Samuel Hubbard Jun[r] [ ] Plum & William Syzer.. are attained to the age of Twenty One Years, and person of an honest Conversation and Quallify[d].. to be made Freemen.. Then the Oath.. was Administered in open Freemens Meeting.. By me Titus Hosmer Jus[t] Pac[s] { Seth Wetmore.. P: Mortimer.. Matthew Tallcott. Titus Hosmer.. Solomon Sage.. Benjamin Galpin} Select Men	*344*

[ ] Oct 1775

Voted that Coln[l] Matthew Tallcott be the Moderator	*344*

4 Dec 1775

Voted, That Coln[l] Jabez Hamlin be Moderator	*345*
Select Men { Cap[t] Phillip Mortimer, Titus Hosmer Esq[r] Cap[t] Solomon Sage, M[r] Benjamin Galpin	*345*

13 Dec 1775

upon the absence of the Moderator, Seth Wetmore Esq[r] be the Moderator of the Meeting pro Tempore	*345*
Select Men { Joseph Bacon, Cap[t] Isaac Miller, M[r] George Phillips	*345*
Constables { Lieu[t] Jonathan Johnson, M[r] Joel Adkins M[r] Samuel Porter and Chosen to Collect y[e] Colony Tax	*345*
Granjurors { Cap[t] Nathaniel Brown, Cap[t] John Cotton, David Lyman, Amos Churchil, Elijah Loveland, Hugh White Ju[r], Daniel Alvord, Nehemiah Hubbard, George Hubbard, Sylvanus Young	*345*
Listers { Winslow Hobbey, Joel Adkins, Hezekiah Hale, John Rogers Cap[t] Stephen Hubbard Cap[t] Roger Riley Joseph Johnson Cap[t] Sam[l] Savage Joseph Clark Ju[r]	*345*
Tything Men { Elijah Hubbard, Sam[l] Word 3[d] Adino Pomroy Jabez Hamlin Ju[r] Nathan Lewis Amos Sage Daniel Savage Daniel Wetmore William Miller Ju[r] Hezekiah Willcox Aaron Plum, Amos Hosford William Hall Abner Mitchel Timothy Clark	*345*
Sealer of Weights { Thomas Danforth	*345*
Sealer of [ ] Measur[s t] John Rogers	*345*
Fence Viewers { M[r] Return Meigs, M[r] Daniel Sumner	*345*
Guagers { Cap[t] Samuel Willis, Coln[l] Comfort Sage, M[r] Daniel Stocking Wenslow Hobbey	*345*
[Sea]lers of [Lea]ther.. Richard Hamlin Eleazer Gaylord William White Francis Whitmore	*345*
[Br]anders of Horses.. Ebenezer Rockwell, Cap[t] John Hinsdale, Elisha Stocking Richard Doud, John Roberts Jun[r] Jonathan Hubbard Ju[r]	*345*
Packers of Meat { Joseph Warner, Elijah Tuel, Lamberton Cooper Jonathan Stow	*346*
Treasurer { M[r] George Phillips Jun[r]	*346*

Middletown

Committee To liquidate the Towns Accomps with the Town Treasurer and Select Men.. Mr John Stocker, Capt Samuel Russel & Mr Benjamin Henshaw *26 Dec 1775*	346
Seth Wetmore Moderator pro Tempore	346
Surveyors of Highways { Capt Phillip Mortimer, Colon^l Comfort Sage, Lieu^t Return Meigs, Elijah Hubbard Ju^r Benjamin Henshaw, Capt Samuel Russel Joseph Driggs, Lieu^t David Tryon Collins Saml Robbards Deac^n John Earl Hubbard Jabez Brooks Junr Samuel Carrier David Starr, Samuel Adkins Junr William White, Comfort Butler Aaron White, Capt Solomon Sage Capt Nathaniel Gilbert Stephen Bacon Josiah Savage Elijah Loveland Elihu Stow, Jonathan Turner Capt Isaac Miller, Nathan Coe Capt David Miller Hezekiah Hale William Willcox Josiah Bacon Patridge Southmayd Thomas Allin William Hamlin Nehemiah Hubbard Solomon Adkins Stephen Johnson Capt Ebenezer Johnson John Sears	346
Commi^{tte} of Inspection { Matthew Tallcott Esqr Capt Phillip Mortimer Titus Hosmer Maj^r Jehosphephat Storr Mr George Phillips, Capt Solomon Sage Mr Joseph Frany, Capt Roger Riley, Capt Nathl Gilbert Deac^n Giles Miller, Mr Daniel Whitmore, Capt Stephen Hubbard, Mr Francis Clark, Capt Ebenezer Johnson, Mr Joel Adkins, Lieu^t David Tryon Mr Elijah Hubbard Junr Mr Benjamin Henshaw Mr Zacheus Higbe, Mr Amos Miller	346
Voted That the Select Men.. with the addition of the Constables, Mr Joel Adkins & Lieu^t Jonathan Johnson be a a Committee to abate.. the Rates of the Collecors of the Town Rates as they shall think necessary *22 Jan 1776*	347
Voted, That Constable Samuel Porter be the Collector to Collect the Colony Tax	347
Hog Hawyard { Thomas Hulbert, Samuel Bull, Timothy Boardman Elihu Starr, Capt Timothy Starr William Harris Ju^r John Birdsey Amos Wetmore Hezekiah Hale Joseph Clark Ju^r Jabez Hall, Jeremiah Willcox David Higbe Allin Gilbert Daniel Plum Daniel Hall, William Hamlin, Jonathan Hubbard Ju^r Abner Lucas, Hezekiah Tallcott, Jabez Barns, Willliam Prout Ju^r Josiah Ward, Daniel Tryon Amos Hosford, Daniel Willcox, Jonathan Hubbard Daniel Kirbey, Daniel Edwards Thomas Ranney Joshua Plum Joseph Hubbard Junr	347
Collectors { Ephraim Fenno, George Butler, Jedediah Sage Joseph Higbe, Daniel Miller Middlefield John Crowell Samuel Word Son to Capt Word William Johnson John Cone	347
Voted that if Doct^r Eliot Rawson^s Fine Is paid... for not taking the Rate Bill provid for him to Collect.. Then the Said Select Men Impowered to apoint Mr Ephraim Fenno or some other Person to take Said Bill and Collect the same	348
Voted that the Petition of Higbe^s School Destrict for the Grant of Three Pounds Money, to help them Build a Bridge.. near Widow Lois Warners Be Granted *17 Sep 1777*	348
The Select Men.. Certify that: - Joshua Plum & Andrus Campbell.. Are Persons of the Age of Twenty One Years of a quiet & peaceable Behaviour & Civil Conversation and have Each of them Such an Estate as Quallifys them by Law be made free of this Colony: Certifyed in Freemans Meeting.. Then the Oath provided by Law for Freemen was Administered.. By me Titus Hosmer Jus^{ts} Pac^s *4 Dec 1776*	348
Voted, That Titus Hosmer Esqr be the Moderator	349
Select Men { Capt Phillip Mortimer, Titus Hosmer Esqr Coln^l Matthew Tallcott Mr George Phillips, Deac^n Solomon Sage, Mr Benjamin Galpin, Deac^n Giles Miller	349
Mr George Phillips Junr Chosen Treasurer	349

Middletown

Collectors { Wenslow Hobby Joel Adkins Hezekiah Hale John Rogers Capt Stephen Hubbard Capt Roger Riley Joseph Johnson Capt Saml Savage Joseph Clark Ju^r	349
Sealer of Weights { Thomas Danforth	349
Sealer of Measures { John Rogers	349
Fence Viewers { Lieu^t Samuel Johnson, Elijah Hubbard Junr	349
Guagers { Capt Samuel Willis, Coln^l Comfort Sage, Wenslow Hobbey Daniel Stocking	349
Leather Sealers { Ephraim Stone, Eleazer Gaylord, Richard Hamlin, William White	349
Branders of Horses { Ebenezer Rockwell.. Capt John Hinsdale.. Elisha Stocking.. Richard Doud, John Robbards Ju^r.. Jonathan Hubbard Ju^r.. Cornwell Doud	349
Pound and Key Keepers { Elijah Blackman.. Capt John Hinsadale.. Amos Savage.. Capt William Ward.. William Cotton.. Jonathan Robbards	349
Packers of Meat { Capt Joseph Warner, Elijah Tuel, Lamberton Cooper Jonathan Stow	349
Voted that, Capt Samuel Russel Elihu Starr & Chauncey Whittlesey be a Committee to Liquidate Town Acc^{ts} with the Select Men and Treasurer	349
Surveyors of Highways.. Capt Philip Mortimer.. Lieu^t Return Meigs.. Joseph Driggs.. Deac^n Hubbard.. Jacob Hall.. Comfort Butler.. Capt Nath^{ll} Gilbert.. Ensign John Heart.. Capt Isaac Miller.. Hezekiah Hale, Seth Wetmore.. Nehemiah Hubbard.. Jeptha Brainard.. Chauncey Whittelsey.. Elijah Hubbard Ju^r.. Lieu^t David Tryon.. Jabez Brooks Junr.. Capt Stephen Hubbard.. Aaron White.. Stephen Bacon.. Elihu Stow.. Nathan Coe.. Amos Churchel.. Thomas Allin.. Solomon Adkins.. Joseph Johnson.. Benjn Henshaw.. Andrew Campbel.. Collins Robbards.. Sam^{ll} Carrier.. William White..Deac^n Solomon Sage.. Sam^{ll} Hubbard Ju^r.. Jonathan Turner.. Capt David Miller.. Josiah Bacon.. Capt William Hamlin.. Stephen Johnson 9 Dec 1776	349
Tything Men { Giles Meigs Eliphalet Hubbard Timothy Butler Jeremiah Willcox Stephen Parsons Nathaniel Miller Hezekiah Hulbert Junr William White Charles Hamlin Ju^r Peet Galpin Stephen Miller Ju^r Micha Hubbard Timothy Gipson Joseph Clark Ju^r Asael Johnson Caleb Hubbard Ju^r	350
Constables { Elijah Hubbard Ju^r Joel Adkins Sam^{ll} Porter Daniel Stocking Hezekiah Hale Capt Samuel Russel Joseph King Joseph King appointed by the Town to Collect the Tax	350
Granjurors { Capt Thomas Goodwin Bezaleel Fisk Josiah Bacon Samuel Parsons Hugh White Junr Allin Gilbert Timothy Cornwell Farmer.. Stephen Tryon Simeon Roberts Ebenezer Whitmore Daniel Miller of Middlefield Excused & Ethe Wetmore Chosen	350
Committee of Inspection { Major Jehosphephat Starr Wensley Hobbey Coln^l Comfort Sage, Capt Thomas Goodwin Deacon Ebenezer Bacon, Capt Jared Shepard Amos Miller, since Dead & Capt Isaac Miller [ ] Capt Roger Riley Maj^r Nathl Brown Capt Ebenezer Johnson Elijah Hubbard	350
Voted That the Select Men make what Provision they think needful ... for Eleazer Vescy in his Distress^d Circumstances	350
Hogg Hayards Chosen { Joseph Bacon Timothy Borardman Benjn Henshaw Resigned Elihu Starr Timothy Starr William Harris Ju^r Capt Isaac Miller Amos Wetmore John Roberts Joseph Clark Ju^r Jeremiah Willcox David Higbe Edward Higbe Allin Gilbert Daniel Plum Daniel Hall Wm Hamlin Jonathan Hubbard Ju^r [Ab]ner Lucas Hezekiah Tallcott Jabez Barns Josiah Word Daniel [ ] Amos Hosford Daniel Willcox Jonathan [ ] Daniel Kirbey, Daniel Edwards Thomas Ranney Joshua Plum, Joseph Hubbard Ju^r Joshua Rockwell Capt Abner Smith	350
Voted. That the Constabels, Capt Sam^{ll} Russel & Mr Elijah, with the Select Men, be a Committee to make the necessary Abatements to the Town Rates	351

Middletown

Voted, That Mr Chauncey Whittelsey & Mr Elihu Starr be a Committee to make an Estimate of What the Assembly ordered to be provided for the Soldiers *7 Jan 1777*	*351*
Voted, that Coln^l Matthew Tallcott be Moderator	*351*
upon a Motion made.. for a Committee to Remove Governor Franklin out of this Town, Capt Samuel Russel, Coln^l Comfort Sage & Seth Wetmore Junr be a Committee to prefer a Petition to his Honour Governor Trumble to remove Said Governor Franklin from this for Safety of this Town & State *21 Jan 1777*	*351*
Voted, That Coln^l Jabez Hamlin be Moderator	*351*
Voted, That Colonel Matthew Tallcott, Joseph Clark Esqr Deacⁿ Solomon Sage Mr Daniel Willcox Mr Josiah Bacon Mr Elihu Stow, Mr Stephen Johnson, Mr Francis Clark & Mr Nehemiah Hubbard.. be a Committee.. to Enter into a Submission with Mr Joseph King.. to agree upon Some Suitable Person in any of the Neighbouring Towns, To Determin whether the Town or.. King Shall bear the Loss of about £69:10:0 which the s^d King Received for the Benefit of the Schools.. and which he allows was Clandestinely taken from him in March last *10 Feb 1777*	*351*
an adjourned Town Meeting.. opened by Coln^l Hamlim the Moderator	*351*
Collectors of the Town Rate { Joseph King William White, Jonathan Hubbard William Hall, Capt Isaac Miller, Micha Hubbard Collins Robbards Ju^r Mr John Cande Daniel Clark	*351*
Resolved by this Meeting that the Treasurer pay.. to Joseph King.. £69:10:0.. agreable to the Judgment of Arbitration.. for that Sum felloniusly taken from him and not by [*his*] Negligence.. School Money he received of the Colony Treasurer for the Use.. of the Several Schools in this Town *10 Feb 1777*	*352*
Upon the Petition of Eleazer Vescy & Wife to take.. a Note that of Right belons to her Due from Capt John Barns of Sixteen Pouns now in the Hands of George Hubbard and help her to some Cloaths out of the Avails there.. Voted that the Select Men Recieve the Contents of above s^d Note and Apply the Same to the Support & Comfort of.. Vescy and Wife *14 Apr 1777*	*352*
Voted, That Coln^l Jabez Hamlin be Moderator	*353*
Voted, That this Town will.. to.. the Inhabitants.. having Familys who have Inlisted or shall Inlist into any of the Continentiol Battallions of Infantry Raising in this State For the Term of Three Years or Dureing the War; That they will take Care that their Families in their Absence shall be Supplied with all such Necessarys of Life as they may Stand in Need of at the Prices limited by Law They leaving or Remitting Monies to a Committee of Supply.. And Chauncey Whittelsey, Elihu Starr, Thomas Allin, Seth Wetmore Junr Capt Stephen Hubbard, Stephen Johnson, Capt Ebenezer Johnson, Daniel Whitmore, Lieu^t David Tryon Deacⁿ John Earl Hubbard, Fracis Clark, Cumfort Butler, Joshua Plum, Timothy Gipson, Israel Kelsey, Danel Willc[ox] John Kirbey, John Willcox, John Higbe, Deacⁿ Ebenezer Bacon & Capt David Coe are appointed a Committee..	*353*
Resolved that a Committee be appointed.. To obtain an exact Account of the Numbers of noncommissioned Officers [*and*] private Soldiers .. of this Town who have Inlisted into any of the Continental Battallions of Infantry and [ ]educting the same from 158 our Quota ascertain the Number yet to be raised.. [*Secon*]dly, To obtain.. an Exact Account of all Male Persons of the Age of Sixteen years or upwards.. Thirdly, that they ascertain the Proportion	*354*

Middletown

of our Quota yet to be raised to each of the.. Destricts.. Fourthly.. that they divide the Males of Sixteen Years and upwards in Each Destrict into as many Distinct & Equal Clases as the Number of Soldiers to be raised.. Fifthly That it shall be the Duty of .. Said Classes.. to procure one Soldier to Inlist into some one of the Continental Battallians.. and that Capt Phillip Mortimer, Titus Hosmer Esqr Joseph Clark Capt Thomas Goodwin, Lieu^t Hugh White, Capt Samuel Savage Ozias Willcox, Thomas Kirbey, Capt Roger Riley, Sam^{ll} Porter, Joseph Graves, Zacheus Higbe, Josiah Bacon Joel Adkins, Daniel Hall, Nehemiah Hubbard Hezekiah Hale, Capt David Miller, Capt Jabez Brooks, Elijah Johnson Ens^n John Rogers, Lieu^t David Tryon Ens^n Oliver Hubbard & Joseph Johnson be said Committee

Upon, Mr Joseph Kings Publishing to this Meeting that he Does Relinquish his Claim.. for.. £73.. for the School Money taken from him.. Voted that this Meeting.. Acknowledg the same as a free Gift   354

25 Sep 1777

Voted, That Coln^l Jabez Hamlin be Moderator   355

Voted, That a Committee Man be appointed in each School District to provide the Cloathing for the Soldiersas Ordered by the Gov[*ernour*] and Counsil of Safety.. And, Samuel Bull, Joseph King Lieu^t Jeremiah Bacon, Seth Wetmore Junr, Capt Stephen Hubbard, Capt Jabez Brooks Mr Daniel Whitmore, Elijah Johnson, Lieu^t David Tryon, Francis Clark, Deac^n John E. Hubbard Lieu^t Hugh White, Capt Solomon Sage, Mr Ozias Willcox, Mr Samuel Shephard Lieu^t Abraham Wright, Jonathan Hubbard of Worthington, Joseph Graves, Deac^n Ebenezer Bacon, Mr Elisha Schovel Capt Isaac Miller & Hezekiah Hale, were Chose   355

Voted, that the part of Newfield Street that belongs to Westfield, be annexed to Lieu^t Jeremiah Bacons District   355

Voted, that Lieu^t Thomas Ward be a Committee Man in the [*place*] of Mr Thomas Allin Deceas^d To Supply the Soldiers Familys   355

[ ] Dec 1777

Voted That Coln^l Jabez Hamlin be Moderator.. he not being able to attend Voted Titus Hosmer be Moderator   356

Voted that Joshua Plum Harris Prout & Lieu^t Jacob Whitmore be a Committee, to inquire of the Inhabitants who hath taken the Oath of Fidelity and Desire those that have not, to offer themselves and take the same   356

Voted { That Timothy Boardman Thomas Goodwin, Chauncey [ ] Deac^n Giles Miller, John Kirby Elijah Tredway, Abijah [ ] be Select Men   356

upon Capt George Phillips^s Refusing to be Town Treasurer Maj^r Nathaniel Brown was Chosen Town Treasurer   356

Listers { Wensley Hobbey Joel Adkins Hezekiah Hale John Rogers Capt Stephen Hubbard Capt Roger Riley Joseph Johnson Capt Samuel Savage Joseph Clark Junr 356

Voted { that Coln^l Sage, Capt Russel & Mr Elihu Starr be a Committee to settel with the Town Treasurer & Liquidate the Town's Accounts   356

Sealer of Weights & Liquid Measures { Thomas Danforth   356

Sealer of Dry Measure { John Rogers   356

Fence Viewers Mr Elijah Tredway & Capt Samuel Russel   356

Guagers { Coln^l Sage Wensloy Hobbey Daniel Stocking   356

Leather Sealers { Ephraim Stone Eleazer Gaylord Richard Hamlin William White Capt Isaac Miller   356

Branders of Horses { Ebenezer Rockwell John Hinsdale Elisha Stocking Richard Doud John Roberts Junr Cornwell Doud Jonathan Hubbard   356

Middletown

Key & Pound Keepers { Capt Samuel Russel Capt John Hinsdale Amos Savage Capt William Ward William Cotton Jonathan Roberts	356
Packers { Elijah Tuel Lamberton Cooper Jonathan Stow	356
Constables { Capt Samuel Russel Joseph King & Chose Collector of Colony Rate, Hezekiah Hale Sam^{ll} Porter, Sam^{ll} Sage Chose & Excused, Nathaniel Eells Chose	356
Granjurors { Elihu Starr Excus^d Lamburton Cooper paid his fine Joshua Plum Ebenezer Elton Josiah Word Nathan Sears Samuel Carrier Jonathan Hubbard Excus^d & Sam^{ll} Hall Chose Joseph Spaulding Doct^r John Dickinson paid his Fine Doct^r Rawson	356

8 Dec 1777

[On] the Representation of Mary Vescy: That She has been obliged to spend a Considerable Sum of Money.. given to her for her private Use, to help Support her Husband, praying that it may be refunded to her.. and that the Town Grant him a Sufficient Supply for his Support	357
[On] Mr John Abbot of Norwalks Motion to take his Sister Widow of Ebenezer Bishop lat of Middletown Deceas^d, and her Two youngest Children to.. Norwalk.. Voted that the Select Men be Impowered to agree with Said Abbot for the Transportation of Said Family.. and Do what is Necessary for the Security of this Town in the Cause	357
Joseph King Chose Collector of Colony Rate	357
Tything Men { Elijah Hubbard Sam^{ll} Bull paid his Fine, Sam^{ll} Chamberlain, Daniel Southmayd Patridge Southmayd Abel Willc[ox] Timothy Johnson Capt Ichabod Wetmore, Seth Doolittle Joseph Driggs Ju^r Peter Goodrich William Sage Elisha Willcox Capt Amos Wetmore James Tappin Ward Abisha Doolittle Aaron Norton Elihu Cotton Elijah Loveland	357
Surveyors of Highways.. Capt Mortimer Chauncey Whittelsey Andrew Campbel Adino Pomroy, Elihu Starr, Capt John Wetmore Deac^n Jno E Hubbard Capt Jabez Brooks, Sam^{ll} Carrier, Cumfort Butler, Sam^{ll} Shephard Deac^n Solomon Sage, Joseph Driggs, John Word 3^d Capt Amos Tryon, Jacob Hall, Capt Stephen Hubbard William White, Joseph Clark Junr, Stephen Bacon Ephraim Croofoot, Ens^n John Heart, Capt David Coe, Jonathan Turner, David Lyman, Nathan Coe, Capt David Miller, Capt William Ward Amos Churchill, Phin[eas] Bacon, Giles Southmayd, Lieu^t Jeremiah Bacon, Capt Wm Hamlin, [ ] Hubbard, Solomon Adkins	357

15 Dec 1777

Committee of Inspection { Voted That Maj^r Jehoshephat Starr, Wenslow Hobbey Coln^l Comfort Sage, Maj^r Nathaniel Brown, Doct^r John Dickinson, Elijah Hubbard, Capt Jared Shepherd Lieu^t Hugh White Ju^r Capt Roger Riley David Adkins Deac^n Ebenezer Bacon, Capt Amos Wetmore, Capt Da[ ] Miller, Lieu^t Elisha Savage, Capt Ebenezer Johnson Capt Amos Tryon, Francis Clark, be said Committee	358
Voted that Mr Chauncey Whittelsey be to Supply the Officers and Soldiers Familys that are to be Supplyed with the proportionable part of West India Goods	358
The following Persons having Engaged to Supply the Familys of the following persons that are set against their Names.. Viz Seth Witmore to Supply the Family of Capt Blackman..	358
..Deac^n Allin - Gideon Cruttenden..	358
..Coln^l Tallcott - John Harris..	358
..Thos Goodwin - John Foster..	358
..Ichabod Miller Ju^r - Mrs Hull..	358
..Ebenezer Bacon - Comfort Marks..	358
..Chauncey Whittelsey - Wm Graves..	358

Middletown

..Capt Wm Word - Moses Boardman..	*358*
..Daniel Hall - Capt Robt Warner..	*358*
..Giles Miller - Joseph Lung..	*358*
..Nehem^h Hubbard - Davis Johnson..	*358*
..Capt Nath^{ll} Gilbert - Butler Gilbert..	*358*
..Joseph Cornwell - Joseph Harris..	*358*
..Wm White - { Capt Eells.. Capt Abij$^{[\ ]}$ Savage.. Jno Robinson.. Joseph Bower..	*358*
.. Capt Ebenez^r Johnson - Wm Brown..	*358*
..Elisha Savage - Thos Powers..	*358*
..Sam^{ll} Hubbard - Ariel Peck..	*358*
..Jedediah Sage - Roswell Hubbard..	*358*
..Zac & Joseph Higbe - Jo^s & Danl Cone..	*358*
..Lieu^t David Tryon - Wm Henshaw..	*358*
..Daniel Whitmore - Lieu^t Hez^h Hubbard..	*358*
..Solomon Adkins - Thos Barnes..	*358*
..Capt David Miller - Ens^n Oth^l Clark..	*358*
..Steph^n & Eb^r Johnson - Ozias Cone..	*358*
..Francis Clark - Lieu^t Jon^n Hubbard	*358*
Haywards { Joseph Bacon Amos Tredway, Elihu Starr, Timothy Starr, William Harris Ju^r Capt Isaac Miller Capt Amos Wetmore, John Roberts, Joseph Clark Junr Jeremiah Willcox, David Higbe, Daniel Alvord Daniel Plum, Daniel Hall, William Hamlin Junr Hinksman Robbards, Abner Lucas, Hezekiah Tallcott Jabez Barns, Josiah Ward, Daniel Pryor, Amos Hosford, Daniel Willcox, Jonathan Hubbard Daniel Kirbey Daniel Edwards, Thomas Ranney, Joshua Stark Joshua Rockwell, Capt Abner Smith, David Adkins William Prout Ju^r Collectors of the Town Rate { Joseph King, Amos Savage, Samuel Porter Phinehas Bacon, Ichabod Miller Junr Daniel Crowel Oliver Hubbard, Timothy Johnson, Oliver Wetmore *29 Dec 1777*	*359* *359*
Voted that this Meeting choose a Committee to.. Consider the Articles of Confederacy.. Col^l Talcott, Col^o Hamlin, Deac^n Bacon, Doc^t Dickenson, Doc^t Rawson, Mr Henshaw, John Kirby, [ ] Sage, Deac^n Giles Miller, Capt David Miller, Capt Jared Shepard, Joseph Graves, Capt Eben^r Johnson be the Committee *6 Jan 1778*	*360*
Voted - That Jabez Hamlin Esqr be Moderator	*360*
That Lieu^t Thos Ward, Lieu^t [ ]^h & Capt David Miller be a Committee to fix the Spott where the Hay Machine lately Standing in the Town Street Shall be Erected and to Determine at whose Cost *9 Mar 1778*	*361*
Voted - That Jabez Hamlin Esqr be Moderator	*361*
Voted that Messrs Francis Clark, Hezekiah Hulbert Junr Joseph Hall, Aaron White, Abijah Ranney, Capt Sol^o Sage Hugh White Junr, Samuel Porter, Peet Galpin, Joseph Graves, Joseph Higbe, Joseph Clark Junr, Ebenezer Gilbert, Capt William Hamlin, Daniel Hall Nehemiah	*361*

Middletown

Hubbard Capt David Miller, Capt Isaac Miller, Nathan Coe, Timothy Cornwell, John Crowell, Lieu^t Jere^h Hubbard Jesse Coe, Eben^r Arnold, Lieu^t David Tryon & Phi Bacon ~ be a Committee to Provide the Articles of Cloathing for the Soldiers ordered by the Assembly
1 Dec 1777

The Following Persons took the Oath of Fidelity to the State.. Joseph Wetmore.. Elihu Stow.. Capt Saml Savage.. Daniel Higbe.. Deac^n Eben^r Bacon.. John Cande.. Jepthae Brainerd.. Elisha Clark.. Henry Hedges.. Jeremiah Arnold.. Stephen Dolewolf.. Stephen Sears.. Capt Jno Wetmore.. Nathan Coe.. Lieu^t John Bacon.. Harriss Prout.. Josiah Savage.. Joseph Clark 2^d.. Jabez Barnes.. Jonathan Kirby.. Joseph Graves.. Andrew Campbell.. Phineas Bacon.. Giles Clark.. Samuel Ward 3^d.. Timothy Johnson.. Danl Stocking.. Stephen Bacon.. Cornelius Cornwell.. James Adkins.. Richd Hamlin.. Danl Wetmore.. David Adkins.. Ephraim Higbe.. Bill [Smith].. Joel Adkins.. Jehiel Williams.. John Rogers.. Abijah Peck Junr.. Daniel Plum.. Joseph Bacon.. Abel Sizer.. Maj^r Nathl Brown.. John Higbe.. David Edwards.. Jabez Hubbard.. Abner Mitchel.. John Ward 3^d.. Isaac Cornwell J^r.. Joseph Higbe.. John Sage.. Joseph Driggs.. Capt Wm Hamlin.. Eben^r Robards.. David Doud.. Wm Southmayd.. James Tappen Ward.. Peter Goodrich.. Lieu^t Thos Ward.. Beriah Higgins.. Zach^s Higbe.. Thomas Bridgen.. Seth Johnson.. William Warner.. Capt Geo. Phillips.. Joseph Cornwell.. Oliver Hubbard.. Prosper Hubbard.. Jesse Coe.. Oliver [ ]ing Warner.. Giles Meigs.. Seth Doolittle.. Elijah Willcox.. Timothy Powe[ ].. Oliver Clark.. John Crowell.. Edward Crowell.. Eben^r Allen.. Doc^t Jehiel Hoadley.. Ichabod Miller Ju^r.. Eben^r Markham   *362*

15 Dec 1777

The Following Took ye Afors^d Oath.. William White.. Richard Miller.. Samuel Hubbard.. Nathl Cornwell.. Elisha Croofoot.. John Gipson.. John Ward 4th.. Joseph Doolittle.. Isaac Andrews.. Noah Robards.. Ashbel Cornw[ell].. Ethimar Adkins.. David Stow.. Joseph Driggs.. Eben^r Griffen.. Amos Barnes..Noadiah Hubb[ard].. Jedidiah John[son].. Jonathan Gilbert.. Joseph Hubbard [ ] Partridge Southma[yd].. Caleb Fuller..   *362*

..Giles Sage.. Abraham Plum.. Graves Hosmer.. Seth Kirby.. Roland Richardson.. Aaron Plum.. Ethe Wetmore.. Nathl Bordman.. Nathan Bordman.. Daniel Southmayd.. Isaac Cornwell.. Josiah Bordman.. Elisha Willcox.. Ely Willcox.. Stephen Treat.. Nathan Sears   *363*

29 Dec 1777

[The] Following Persons took [the afo]res^d oath.. John Willcox.. Stephen Pierce.. Julius Riley.. Benjamin Babbet.. Seth Coe.. Robert Rand.. Elisha Scovel.. Wm Prout Junr.. [ ] Markham.. John Willcox Junr.. John Hall Junr.. John Robards.. William Lee.. Danl Kirby.. David Heart.. Samuel Markham.. [ ]niel Hall.. [ ]ard Rockwell.. [ ]on Savage.. [ ] Cande.. Asahel Dudley.. Jonathan Pratt.. Abisha Doolittle.. Nathl Eells.. Amos Savage.. Amos Tryon.. Jonathan Southmayd.. Solomon Stow Junr.. Solomon Stow.. Joseph Willis Junr.. Benjamin Tarbox.. Jonathan Stow.. Bradley Elton.. Joseph Ranney J^r.. Nathl Ranney.. Henry Rockwell.. Wm Keith.. Joseph Smith   *363*

Jan 1778

The Following [Persons] took ye Afors^d Oath.. Capt Saml Heart.. Peet Galpen.. Eben^r Hough.. Elijah Teulls.. Abijah Ranney.. Giles Sage (Farmer).. Danl Savage.. Dec^n Joseph Kirby.. David Strickland.. Saml Simmons.. Timothy Gipson.. Stephen Miller Junr.. Samuel Carrier.. William Hubbard.. Israel Carrier.. Aaron Robards J^r.. William Savage.. John Bacon Junr.. Abraham Doolittle.. Obadiah Brainard.. Samuel Pousley.. Anthony Ames.. Ichabod Brookes.. Wm Tryon.. Comfort Butler.. Manoah Hubbard.. Caleb Tryon.. Daniel Adkins..   *363*

..John Rockwell Junr.. Samuel Plum.. William Babbet.. Capt Eli Butler.. Eben^r Sage.. Jeduthun Higbe.. Doc^t Francis Gitto.. Giles Hall Junr.. Doc^t Reuben Garlick.. Doc^t John Osborn.. Phinehas M^{c}key.. Samuel Torrey.. Nathl Stow.. Noyce Robards.. Lamberton Clark..   *363*

Middletown

Danl Hulbert.. Eben^r Rockwell.. John Goodwin.. Nehemiah Hubbard.. Hinksman Robards.. George Spooner.. Jacob Goodwin.. Giles Willcox.. Seth Higbe.. Samuel Griffen.. Josiah Ward.. George Hubbard.. Jesse Robards

8 Apr 1778

Oath Administred ye 8th Ap^r 1778 by N Chauncey Jus^t Peace.. J[ ] Stocking.. William Strickland.. Churchil Edwards.. Nathl Sage.. John Savage.. Jonathan Savage.. Elias White.. Saml Frara.. Zeb Stow.. Amos Sage.. Joseph Stow.. Danl Edwards.. James Smith.. Zebulon Stocking.. Geor[ge] Butler.. Eb^r Ranney Junr.. Doc^t Robards.. Francis Willcox   *364*

13 Apr 1778

..Ap^r 13th by T Hosmer Esqr - Giles Sage.. Thompson Phillips.. Daniel Higbe.. William Warner.. Prosper Hubbard.. Levi Dudley.. Henry Hedges Junr.. Isaac Andrews.. Hugh Brown.. Nathl [ ] Miller.. Nathl Robards.. Ephraim Stone.. Joshua Miller.. Darcy Prout.. William Sizer.. Elisha Miller.. Levy Dudley.. George Adkins.. Moses Lucass   *364*

[ ] 1778

Oath Adm^d by T Hosmer.. Joseph Coe Junr.. Joshua Rockwell.. William Johnson Junr.. Giles Barnes..   *364*

27 Apr 1778

..before N Chauncey Esqr .. John White.. Hosea Miller.. Elisha Sage.. Thos Ranney.. Nathl Smith..   *364*

22 May 1778

..Gershom Birdseye..   *364*

27 Nov 1778

.. Asahel Johnson.. Ich^d Wetmore..   *364*

3 Dec 1778

.. John Alsop Esqr.. Wm Joyce.. John Stocker..   *364*

21 Dec 1778

..John Adkins.. Caleb Hubbarde..   *364*

7 Dec 1778

.. Nathaniel Sage.. Ebenezer Bevin.. Jonathan Gilbert.. Jedidiah Hubba[rd].. William Sizer..   *364*

17 Dec 1778

.. Arthur Magill..   *364*

25 Sep 1777

..before Jo^s Clark Esqr.. Jabez Brookes.. Saml Chamberlain.. Elijah Johnson..   *364*

2 Jan 1779

..Stephen Ranney..   *364*

13 Jan 1779

.. Jabez Hall..   *364*

Middletown

15 Jan 1779	
.. Eben[r] Coe..	*364*
15 Jan 1779	
..Sam[l] Tuells..	*364*
25 Jan 1779	
..Benjamin Birds[*eye*]..	*364*
22 Jan 1779	
..Oath Adm[d] by M Wait, N London.. Sanford Thompson.. Tim[o] Sage.. Nath[l] Savage.. Sam[l] Waterman of Cha[ ].. Francis Weeks of Massachus[*etts*]	*364*
1 Feb 1779	
.. Stephen Treat Jun[r]..	*364*
8 Feb 1779	
.. Newton Whittelsey..	*364*
8 Feb 1779	
..Amasa Jones..	*364*
9 Feb 1779	
..Jesse Wetmore..	*364*
1 Mar 1779	
..Josiah Bacon.. Sam[l] Johnson Ju[*n*[r]].. Joseph Hall..	*364*
10 Mar 1779	
..Daniel Russel..	*364*
15 Mar 1779	
..Sam[l] Plum Ju[*n*[r]]..	*364*
5 Dec 1777	
Town Treas[r] [*listed current accounts*]	*365*
By Am[l] of y[e] Balance of Several Rate Bills now in y[e] Collectors hands & not yet Accounted with y[e] Treasurer } [£]403..15..9.. By 14 Notes Rec[d] of Men belonging to Militia for fines } [£]70.. By a Ball[ce] due from y[e] Treasurer to the Town } 328..16..10 .. £802..12..[ ].. Examin'd By us Sam[l] Russel.. Elihu Starr } Auditers	*365*
27 Dec 1777	
Rec[d] of Cap[t] George Phillips form[*er*] Town Treasurer the Ballance due to the Town as above Stated.. Nath[l] Brown Town Treasurer	*365*
13 Apr 1778	
We the Subscribers Select-Men of said Town do Certify, that Oliver Ring Warner, Giles Sage, Zebulon Stocking, Thompson Phillips, Daniel Higbe, William Warner, Ebenezer Sage, Prosper Hubbard, Levi Dudley, Henry Hedges Jun[r], Isaac Andrews.. have Severally Attained to the Age of Twenty One Years, are Persons of a Quiet and Peacable Behaviour & Civil Conversation & Quallified.. to be made free of this State ~ Certified by us Elijah Treadway.. Timothy Bordman.. Thomas Goodwin.. John Kirby } Select-Men	*365*
At the Same Meeting the Freemans Oath By Law Enjoined was Administred to (Oliver Ring	*365*

Middletown

Warner, Giles Sage, Zebulon Stocking, Thompson Phillips, Daniel Higbe, William Warner, Ebenezer Sage, Prosper Hubbard, Levi Dudley, Henry Hedges Junr, Isaac Andrews,) Joseph Smith, Thomas Ward, Ephraim Fenno, Josiah Savage, Abraham Plum, Solomon Stow Junr, Caleb Fuller, Hugh Br[ ] Nathaniel Miller, Harriss Prout, Samuel Chamberlain, Adino Pomroy, William Prout, Aaron Plum, David Adkins, Jehiel Hoadly, Stephen Pierce, Samuel Carrier, Nathl Robards, Samuel Frara, Ephraim Stone, Joseph Bacon, Jeremiah Markham, Joseph Driggs, Joshua Miller, Darcy Prout, Elijah Johnson, William Southmayd, Obadiah Brainard, Elisha Clark..

..Jonathan Kirby, William Sizer, Giles Clark, Nathaniel Brown, John Gipson, Jesse Coe, John Wetmore, Samuel Savage, William Hamlin, Elihu Stow, Ebenezer Bacon, Elisha Miller, Caleb Tryon, Amos Barnes, Abner Smith, George Adkins, Amos Tryon, Joseph Kirby, Ichabod Miller Junr Ebenezer Robards, - By me Titus Hosmer Justis Pac^s 366

The Freemans Oath was Administred to Giles Meigs, Eli Butler, John Rogers, Richard Hamlin, Jabez Barnes, Capt David Sage, David Tryon, James Adkins, Amos Horsford, Asahel Dudley, Israel Fuller, By me Jabez Hamlin Assistant ~ NB ~ ye foregoing Persons Included in a Crotchet were made freeman ye following beginning w^h Joseph Smith were freemen before ~   366

5 May 1778

Jabez Hamlin Esqr was Chosen Moderator   366

Bezaleel Fisk was .. Chosen Town Clerk   366

Voted That Mr Joseph King, One of the Constables.. be appointed to Collect the Remainder of the Country Rate which Maj^r Jonathan Johnson was formerly Entrusted to Collect, and from finishing which he is Released   366

Voted That Capt Abraham Plum, be Appointed Surveyor of Highways.. untill the Next Annual Meeting   366

Voted That Capt Sol^o Sage, Capt Jared Shepherd, & Capt John Kirby be a Committee to View the State of a Bridge Near Mr Danl Willcox's Saw Mill   366

Sep 1778

The Subscribers.. do hereby Certify that the Persons hereafter Named have Accomplished the Age of Twenty One Years are Possessed of Estate Sufficient .. to be made free of this Corporation, and are Persons of a Quiet and Peaceable Behaviour, and Civil Conversation, and also have taken the Oath Required by Law .. Viz ~ Eliphalet Hubbard.. Ch Whittelsey.. Timothy Bordman Thos Goodwin.. Giles Miller } Select Men   367

The Freemans Oath was Administred to Eliphalet Hubbard Nathan Coe, Peleg Bow, Elijah Burr, Nathan Strong, Abijah Hubbard, Joseph Hale, John Elsworth, Joshua Rockwell, Jo[ ] Bacon Junr & Stephen Bacon - By Elijah Treadway Esqr 367

16 Sep 1777

The oaths.. One Entitled ".. An Oath of Fidelity to the State," the other.. ".. An Oath to be taken by ye Freemen of this State.. was Administred .. to the Persons hereafter named.. - to wit - Jabez Hamlin Esqr.. Seth Wetmore Esqr.. Matthew Tallcott Esqr.. Nathl Chauncey Esqr.. Joseph Clark Esqr.. Philip Mortimer.. George Phillips.. Solomon Sage.. Giles Miller.. Benj^a Galpin.. Hugh White.. Thos Adkins.. Joseph Hubbard.. Henry Hedges.. Eliot Rawson.. Amos Wetmore.. Icha^d Starr.. Tim^o Cornwell.. Simeon Robards.. Francis Clark.. Giles Hall.. Elisha Brewster.. Saml Starr.. Enoch Huntington.. Thos Miner.. Abner Benedict.. Joseph Starr.. Jon^a Allen.. Robt Hubbard.. John Dickinson.. John Eliot.. John Sumner.. John Russel.. Benjamin Henshaw.. Chauncey Whittelsey.. Elijah Hubbard.. Samuel Adkins.. Return Meigs.. Tim^o Bordman.. Eben^r Sumner.. Jacob Whitman.. Stephen Hubbard..   367

Middletown

..Hezekiah Hale.. Elihu Starr.. Stephen Johnson.. Moses Lucass.. Comf^t Sage.. David Coe.. Thos Goodwin.. Aaron Parsons.. Wensley Hobby.. Isaac Miller.. Bezaleel Fisk.. William Sage.. Thomas Tryon.. Jonathan Turner.. Edward Rockwell J^r.. Eben^r Gilbert.. John Cotton.. Israel Kelsey.. Elijah Treadway.. Solomon Hubbard.. Oliver Wetmore.. Wm Miller Junr.. Nathl Gilbert.. Oliver Johnson.. Allen Gilbert.. Danl Prior.. Saml Lucass.. Saml Russel.. Thomas Danforth.. Jedidiah Johnson.. Jer^h Bacon.. Andrew Bacon.. Eben^r Elton.. Josiah Bacon.. .. Giles Southmayd.. Danl Alvard.. Richd Doud.. David Lyman.. John Ward.. Silvanus Young.. Elihu Cotton.. Hez^h Hulbert Junr.. Lamberton Cooper.. Josiah Starr.. Bennet Eaglestone J^r.. Danl Willson.. Roger Riley.. Elisha Savage.. Jedediah Sage.. Danl Clark.. Danl Starr.. Abraham Wright.. Isaac Hedges.. Jonathan Hubbard.. Jno Earl Hubbard.. Nehemiah Hubbard.. Saml Johnson.. Eben^r Johnson.. Adino Pomroy.. Jared Shepard.. Saml Porter.. William Starr. Saml Gleason.. Danl Whitman.. Stephen Parsons.. Tim^o Starr.. John Cotton.. Jonah Fletcher.. William Ward.. Samuel Bull.. Joshua Plum.. Hugh White Junr.. Saml Shepard.. Aaron White.. Elijah Hubbard.. David Brainerd Miller.. Jeremiah Hubbard.. David Miller.. Nathl Starr.. Danl Sumner.. Eben^r Arnold.. Tim^o Cornwell (Farmer).. Jacob Hall.. Prince Winbon.. Zachariah Paddock.. Asahel Camp.. Moses Pain.. Seth Wetmore Junr.. Amos Treadway.. John Kirby.. Jedediah White.. Joseph King.. Wm Ward Junr.. George Starr.. Jonathan Otis ~ Sworn.. Before me ~ Titus Hosmer Jus^{ts} Pac^s 368

At the Same Meeting the Oath.. for ye Freeman was Administred to Titus Hosmer Esqr by me Matthew Tallcott Just^s Pac^s 368

7 Dec 1778

Jabez Hamlin Esqr was Chosen Moderator   369

Select Men { Messrs Capt Thomas Goodwin, Deac^n Ch^s Whittelsey, Capt Isaac Miller, Mr John Kirby, Elijah Treadway Esqr Lieu^t Hugh White and Mr Elijah Hubbard   369

Maj^r Nathl Brown Town Treasurer   369

Listers { Messrs Wensley Hobby.. John Rogers.. Joseph Johnson.. Joel Atkins.. Mica Hubbard.. Capt Saml Savage.. Hez^h Hale.. Jedidiah Sage.. & Joseph Clark   369

Voted That Messrs Elihu Starr, Benjamin Henshaw & George Phillips be a Committee to Settle the Town Acc^{ts} with the Treasurer

Constables { Capt Saml Russel.. Joseph King.. Hez^h Hale.. Saml Porter & William White   369

21 Dec 1778

Col^o Comfort Sage was Chosen Moderator   369

Sealers of Measures { Thomas Danforth for Liquid Measure, John Rogers for Drye Measure   369

Fence Viewers Capt Saml Russel, Ephraim Stone   369

Gagers.. Col^o Comf^t Sage Wensley Hobby & Danl Stocking   369

Leath^r Sealers { Hezekiah Hubbert Junr.. Richd Hamlin.. Eleazer Gaylord.. Wm White.. Capt Isaac Miller   369

Branders of Horses { Ebenezer Rockwell John Hensdale Timothy White Richd Dowd John Robards Junr Cornel Dowd & Jedidiah Johnson Junr 370

Key & Pound Keepers { Capt John Hensdale, Amos Savage, Capt Wm Ward, Wm Cotton, Benj^a Bevin & Ephraim Stone   370

Packer of Meat &c { Elijah Tuells, Lamberton Cooper, Jonathan Stow   370

Grand Jurors { Joseph Hall.. Capt Jacob Whitmore..Zebulon Stocking Paid his fine Joseph Ward, Elijah Johnson.. John Ward 3^d Silvanus Young.. Bela Strong, Aaron Plum.. John Robards Junr.. & Lt Noadiah Hubbard   370

Middletown

Mr Joseph King was Chosen to Collect the State Tax.. Voted that Mr Joseph King be Allow'd One & a Quarter PC^s Cent as an an Additional fee for Collecting the State Tax.. Voted That Mr Joseph King (Constable) Collect ye Town Rate 370

Tything-men { Daniel Starr William Starr Oliver Wetmore Capt Eben^r Sumner.. Simeon Robards.. Henry Hedges Junr.. Capt Geo Phillips Asahel Johnson Ephraim Higbe.. Saml Doolittle Nathl Eells.. Danl Edwards.. Richd Miller.. Eben^r Coe.. Joseph Higbe.. Stephen Treat Junr.. George Hubbard 370

Committee of Inspection { Maj^r Jeh^h Starr, Wensley Hobby, Col^o Sage, Maj^r N Brown Benj^a Henshaw, Jacob Whitmore Jared Shepard Col^o Sage, Benj^a Galpin, David Adkins, Dec^n Eb^r Bacon David Lyman, C^t David Miller, Elisha Savage Capt Eb^r Johnson, Amos Tryon, Francis Clark Seth Wetmore 370

Surveyors of Highways { Messrs Philip Mortimer Esqr, Thompson Phillips, Andrew Campbell, Adino Pomroy.. John Dickenson Esqr, Capt John Wetmore.. Dec^n Jno E Hubbard, Capt Jabez Brooks Capt Eb^r Johnson, Capt Oliver Johnson Stephen Whitmore, Seth Johnson Junr, Abijah Ranney Thos Kirby, Deac^n Jo^s Kirby, Danl Stocking Joseph Hubbard Junr, Capt Amos Tryon.. Jacob Hall, Lt Noadiah Hubbard.. Joseph Clark Jeduthan Higbe.. Saml Porter, Josiah Edwards, Wm Ward Junr Lt David Wetmore.. David Lyman.. Joshua Rockwell David B Miller.. Capt Wm Ward, Amos Churchell, Phin^s Bacon.. Fenno Arnold John Cotton Capt Wm Hamlin, Nehemiah Hubbard, Amos Barns.. Joseph Johnson Capt Eben^r Sumner.. Solomon Adkins 371

Hog Hayards { David Stow, Giles Meigs.. James Jones.. Richd Hamlin.. Edward Rockwell J^r Wm Harriss J^r Capt Isaac Miller Capt Amos Wetmore, John Robards Joseph Clark, Ju$^{[l]}$ Willcox, David Higbe Danl Alvard Danl Plum.. Danl Hall Wm Hamlin J^r John Robards 3^d Abner Lucass, Beriah Cone, Moses Lucass, Josiah Ward, Danl Prior Amos Hosford Danl Willcox, Jon^a Hubbard Danl Kirby Danl Edwards, Thos Ranney, Joshua Plum, Jedidiah White, Elihu Stow, Lt David Atkins Wm Prout Ju^r Darius Weston 371

Voted That this Town will Except of Mr Benjamin Henshaw Offer, Viz That this Town may Erect a Pound, on the West Corner of his Lott (Near ye Meet^g-house, which he lately bough[t] of Saml Frara & Wife) 371

Voted That Messrs Nehemiah Hubbard, Col^o Matthew Tallcott, be addded to ye Committee to Exchange Highways 372

Whereas by Several Acts of the Genl Assembly of this State, it is Enjoined and upon the.. Towns .. to Provide for the Familys of the Officers and Soldiers.. Serving in the Continental Army in Proportion Following.. for the Family of a Field Officer necessarys to the Am^t of Twenty four Pounds, for the Family of a Captain or a Sabaltarn.. Eighteen Pounds, for the Family of a Non Commissioned Officer or Soldier.. Twelve Pounds.. to be Computed .. at ye Rate and Prices at which they were.. limitted by an Act of the Genl Assembly.. & the Cost of Such Supplys & Necessaries to be Reimbursed by the State ~ This Town do now appoint the undermentioned Persons Committee to Provide Such necessaries.. for y^e Familys of y^e Respective Officers & Soldiers to their names Severally annexed.. Joseph Hall for Capt E Blackman.. 372

..L^t Ju$^{[l]}$ Bacon - Gideon Cruttenton.. 372

..Thompson Phillips - John Harriss.. 372

..Benj^a Henshaw - Wm Bacon.. 372

..Elijah Hubbard - John Foster 3^d & Ozias Cone.. 372

..D^n Eb^r Bacon - Comf^t Marks.. 372

..Capt Jabez Brooks - Wm Graves.. 372

Middletown

..Capt Wm Ward - Moses Bordman..	*372*
..Giles Southmayd - Capt R Warner..	*372*
..Capt Giles Miller - Joseph Lung..	*372*
..Giles Sage - Capt Edwd Eells..	*372*
..Ozias Willcox - Capt A Savage..	*372*
..Saml Sage - John Robinson..	*372*
..Capt O Johnson - Wm Bacon..	*372*
..Amos Horsford - Thos Powers..	*372*
..Joseph Galpin - Ariel Peck..	*372*
..David Ha[ll] - R[*oswe*]ll Hubbard..	*372*
..James Ward - Danl Cone..	*372*
..Nathan Coe - Joseph Cone..	*372*
..Jesse Coe - Wm Henshaw..	*372*
..Prosper Hubbard - Lt Hez^h Hubbard..	*372*
..Sol^o Adkins - Thos Barnes..	*372*
..Mica Hubbard - Lt Oth^l Clark..	*372*
..John Ward - Lt David Stow..	*372*
..Deac^n C Whittelsey - Christ^r Fisher..	*372*
..Capt Isaac Miller - Saml A Bordman..	*372*
Capt Jno Witmore - Geo Anger..	*372*
Saml Plum - Jon^a Sizer..	*372*
Maj^r Nathl Brown - Eb^r Willis..	*372*
..Lt Ich^d Miller - Jacob Gilson..	*372*
..Stephen Miller - James Francis	*372*
Town of Middletown in Acc^{ts} Current w^h Nathl Brown Town Treasurer..	*373*
..Exam'd by us.. Benjn Henshaw.. Elihu Starr.. George Phillips } Auditors	*373*

28 Dec 1778

Voted.. That Messrs John Cone, Benjamin Henshaw, Deac^n Joseph Kirby, Amos Savage, Timothy Gipson, Sam[ ] Frara, Danl Willcox, Asahel Dudley, David Higbe, Amos Horsford, Richd Dowd, Joseph Ward, John M^{c}kye, George Atkins, Capt Tim^o Clark, Jonathan Gilbert, Elisha Miller, Saml Adkins, Elihu Stow, Jonathan Turner, Wm Lee, Harriss Prout, Elias Sears, Collins Saml Robards, Lieu^t David Tryon, Richd Hamlin, be a Committee to Provide.. Cloathing for ye Soldiers *373*

Voted That Mr Wensley Hobby Provide and Supply ye Officers and Soldiers Familys, with their Propertionable part of West India Goods to wit Sugar, Coffe & Salt *374*

Voted { That Amos Churchill be Excused from being a Surveyor of Highways &.. Nathl Bordman is Chosen in his Room *374*

Voted { That Capt Isaac Miller be not Excus'd from Paying his fine to this Town for Coming out of the Small Pox Contrary to ye Regulations *374*

Middletown

Voted { That this Town will not Choose a Committee to inquire into ye affair of David B Miller Concerning his Note payable to this Town for Going Contrary to ye Regulations of ye Small Pox	374
Voted { That Col^o Tallcott Deac^n Bacon & Mr Benjamin Henshaw be a Committee to Consider the Petition of Mr Abel Sizer, & Examine into the Circumstances of the Bridge where it is Said Mr Jonathan Mitchel got the wound whereof he Died, and also all Bills Presented for Said Mitchels Care..	374
Voted That any Three of ye Select-men be a Committee to Enquire into ye Memorial of Phinehas M^{c}kye	374
Upon Request of Mr Giles Sage Junr That the Town would Regrant to him and his Heirs forever a Mill] Place in the North Society.. which they Granted to his Father Mr John Sage Junr on ye 5th of Feby 1732/33.. with further Liberty to Dam across the Highway where the Crossway is now Provided the Dam be never Raised so high as to Prevent Travaling.. Voted that this Bill be Pass^d	375

15 Mar 1779

Jabez Hamlin Esqr was Chosen Moderator	375

15 Mar 1779

Voted ~ That a Tax of Three Shillings on the Pound be laid.. & That Joseph King be appointed to Collect the Same	375
Voted ~ That Titus Hosmer Esqr, Matthew Tallcott Esqr, Mr Benjamin Henshaw & Mr Joel Adkins Be a Committee to Settle all Acc^{ts} Matters & Thing Relating to Mr Stephen Blake late Collect^r…of this Town Dec^d.. of the Country or Town Rates and in order to make a final and Copleat Settlement of said Matters they are to Settle with the Heirs of Seth Wetmore Esqr Dec^d as Administrator on said Blakes Estate..	375

2 Apr 1779

Oath of Fidelity ~ brought From Page 364.. Nathaniel Bacon.. Noah Bacon.. Joel Bacon..	376

9 Apr 1779

..Edward Hamlin Junr..	376

12 Apr 1779

..in Freeman Meeting { Return Jon^a Meigs.. Elijah Blackman.. Stephen Tryon.. David Starr.. William Miller.. Joseph Johnson..	376
..Asher Ward.. Edward Camp.. Asher Miller.. Ezekiel Gilbert..	376

15 June 1779

.. James Keith.. Charles Milling.. George Collic } Oath Administred by E Treadway Esqr..	376

2 Jul 1779

..Elihu Lyman.. Seth Turner } D^o	376

8 Jul 1779

..Isaac Bow..	376

11 Jul 1779

..Benj^a Tuells..	376

12 Jul 1779

..Wm Marks..	376

Middletown

28 Aug 1779

..Eb.r Doolittle.. 376

21 [ ] 1779

..Josiah Prior.. Jonathan Miller.. John Hubbard..Stephen Whitmore.. Fenno Arnold.. Samuel Bow.. Abraham Sage.. James Hopkins.. Rev.d Gershom Buckley.. Recompence Robards.. Sam.l Adkins Jun.r.. 376

12 Nov [ ]

..Josiah Willcox.. 376

6 Dec [ ]

..Gilbert Butler.. Edward Johnson.. Sam.l Canfield.. Daniel Crowel.. 376

..Cap.t Tim.o Clark.. Sam.l Hall } before Esq.r Gilb.t.. 376

..Eleazer Gaylord.. Jeremiah Willcox.. Joseph Willcox.. James Plum.. Jn.o Bacon 3.d.. Jn.o Warner.. Asahel Dudly Jun.r.. [ ] [Spencer].. Joseph Starr.. Nath.n Starr.. 376

27 Aug 1781

..Jon.a Thayre - Administ.d by E T Esq.r.. 376

..Micah Hubbard - by E T.. 376

7 Jan 1782

..Joseph Danforth.. 376

8 Apr 1782

..Elisha Adkins.. W.m Clever } at F Meet.g.. 376

17 Sep 1782

..Zenas Hubbard.. Sam.l Galpin } at T.n Meet.g.. 376

7 Apr 1783

..Thomas Barns.. Abel Willcox.. James Cotton.. Dan.l Kelley } at Freemens Meeting.. 376

22 May 1781

..Prosper Auger before J Miller Esq.r.. 376

..Caleb Wetmore.. Jon.a Gilbert Jun.r.. W.m Hamlin Jun.r.. Jesse Wetmore.. Ich.d Spencer.. David Hubbard.. Stephen Turner.. Eben.r Markham } at Freemens Meeting 376

12 Apr 1779

This may Certify that Col.o Return Jon.a Meigs, Cap.t Elijah Blackman, Stephen Tryon, William White, Joseph Hall, Amos Churchill, Dan.l Adkins, Joseph Hubbard Jun.r, Amos Sage, Samuel Hubbard, Joseph Clark, John Willcox, Mica Hubbard, Joseph Coe Jun.r, John Robards, Micajah Tuells, David Starr, Joseph Higbe Joseph Graves, Sam.l Markham, Giles Barnes, Dan.l Plum, Robert Warner, W.m Joyce, Jonathan Gilbert, W.m Wa[rd] Jun.r James Tappen Ward, Hezekiah Ranney, John Crowel George Spooner, William Miller, Josiah Ward, .. are Persons of an Honest Conversation & Quallify'd in Point of Estate to be made Freemen of this State.. [signed] Chauncey Whittelsey.. Elijah Hubbard.. Tho.s Goodwin.. Hugh White } Select-Men 377

The Freeman's Oath.. was Administrred to Return Jon.a Meigs, Elijah Blackman, Stephen Tryon, William White, Amos Churchill, Dan.l Adkins, Joseph Hubbard Jun.r Amos Sage, Sam.l Hubbard, Joseph Clark, John Willcox, Mica Hubbard, Joseph Coe Jun.r, John Robards, 377

Middletown

Micajah Tuells, David Starr, Joseph Higbe, Joseph Graves, Saml Markham, Giles Barnes, Danl Plum, Robert Warner, Wm Joyce, Jonathan Gilbert, William Ward Junr, James Tappen Ward, John Crowel, George Spooner, William Miller, Josiah Ward, Amos Barns, Joseph Johnson & Joel Adkins by me Matthew Tallcott Jus^t Peace

The Freemans Oath.. was Administred to Joseph Hall & Hezekiah Ranney .. by me Elijah Treadway Justice of P[*eace*]   377
21 Sep 1779

The Persons whose Names are under Written we hereby Certify are Qualified According to Law, to be made Freemen.. Ashbel Burnham, Manoah Hubbard, Elnathan Norton, Peet Galpin, Ephraim Crawfoot, Revd Gershom Buckley, James Hopkins, Fenno Arnold, Abraham Sage, Recompence Robards, Stephen Whitmore, John Hubbard, Jonathan Miller, Josiah Prior, Samuel Adkins Junr, Jacob Saber, Phinehas Bacon, George Hubbard & John Ward 4th.. [*signed*] Elijah Hubbard.. John Kirby.. Hugh White.. Chauncey Whittelsey } Select-Men   378

Then in Freemens Meeting.. was the Freemens oath Prescrib'd by Law Duly Administered to the Persons above Named.. P^r me Elijah Treadway Justice of Peace   378

The Honble Jabez Hamlin Esqr was Chosen Moderator   378

Voted that Messrs Matthew Tallcott Esqr Deacon Ebenezer Bacon & Mr Timothy Bordman.. are appointed a Committee.. to meet the Committees from the other Towns in this State in Convention at Hartford   378
6 Dec 1779

Titus Hosmer Esqr was Chosen Moderator   379

Select-Men { Capt Thomas Goodwin, Dec^n Chauncey Whittelsey, Isaac Miller Esqr, Mr Amos Horford, Mr Lambert[on] Cooper, Lieu^t Hugh White & Mr Elijah Hubbard   379

Town-Treasurer - Mjor Nathaniel Brown   379

Listers { Messrs Wensley Hobby.. John Rogers.. Joseph Johnson.. Joel Adkins.. Mica Hubbard.. Amos Sage.. Hezekiah Hale.. Jedidiah Sage.. & Joseph Clark   379

[Committee to Settle with the Treasurer] } Messrs Elihu Starr, Benj$^{[l]}$ Henshaw & Col^o Comfort Sage   380

Constables { Capt Samuel Russel.. Bezaleel Fisk.. Mr Hezekiah Hale.. Mr Samuel Porter & Mr William White   380

Voted - That Bezaleel Fisk be a Collector of the State Tax.. Voted - That Bezaleel Fisk.. be Allowed One & a Quarter Pr Cent by this Town as an an Additional fee for Collecting S^d Tax   380

Sealer of Liquid Measures - Thomas Danforth   380

Ditto of Drye - D^o - John Rogers   380

Fence Viewers - Capt Samuel Russel Mr Ephraim Stone   380

Gaugers - Col^o Comf^t Sage Wensley Hobby & Danl Stocking   380

Leath^r Sealers - Hezekiah Hulbert Junr, Richd Hamlin, Eleazer Gaylord, Wm White.. & Isaac Miller Esqr 380

Branders of Horses } Thomas Hulbert, John Hensdale Timothy White.. Richard Dowd, John Robards Junr Cornwell Dowd.. Jedidiah Johnson Junr 380

Key & Pound Keepers } Ephraim Stone John Hensdale Amos Savage Wm Ward Wm Cotton Jonathan Robards   380

Packers - Lamberton Cooper Jonathan Stow   380

Grand-Jurors - Micajah Tuells.. Andrew Campbell.. Elisha Willcox.. John Cande Excus'd by E Treadway as far as he had power.. Tim^o Johnson Saml Ward Stephen Sears Joseph Galpin Samuel Hall James Tappin Ward Lieu^t Noadiah Hubbard   380

Middletown

Tything-Men - Daniel Southmayd, Giles Meigs.. Isaac Bow.. Thomas Hulbert.. Nathan Starr Simeon Robards Rowland Allen Phinehas Bacon Hinchman Robards Gideon Savage.. Timothy White.. Asahel Camp Seth Coe 10 Dec 1779	381
Tything-Men - Joseph Spaulding Giles Willcox Aaron Norton	381
Committee of Inspection } Messrs Majr Jeh[ ] Starr, Mr Wensley Hobby, Col^o Comfort Sage, Maj^r Nathl Brown, Mr Benjamin Henshaw Capt Jared Shepherd, Mr Abijah Ranney Mr Benjamin Galpin, Mr David Adkins, Mr Joseph Higbe, Mr David Lyman, Mr Elihu Stow Capt Ebenezer Johnson, Mr Amos Tryon Mr Fran[cis] Clark, & Mr Seth Wetmore	381
Surveyors of Highways } Philip Mortimer Esqr, Thompson Phillips Exc[used] Andrew Campbel Adino Pomroy John Dickinson Esqr, Dec^n Jno Earl Hubard Samuel Chamberlain Capt Eben^r Johnson Capt Oliver Johnson Stephen Whitmore Seth Johnson Junr Abijah Ranney Thomas Kirby Dec^n Joseph Kirby Danl Stocking.. Joseph Hubbard Junr Capt Amos Tryon Josiah Ward, Lieu^t Noadiah Hubbard Capt Tim^o Clark Jeduthan Higbe Saml Porter Joseph Peck Wm Ward Junr, Daniel Wetmore David Coe Junr Joshua Rockwell, David B Miller, John Robards Saml Willcox Aaron Plum Oliver Wetmore John Cande.. Capt Wm Hamlin Nehemiah Hubbard Amos Barns Joseph Johnson Hinksman Robards Solomon Adkins	381
Hog Howards { Rowland Richardson, Giles Meigs, John Paddock, Rowland Allin Edward Rockwell J^r Wm Harriss Junr Joseph Coe Junr Elisha Miller John Robards Junr Seth Doolittle Jer[ ] Willcox Danl Hulbert, Danl Alvard, Danl Plum Danl Hall, Saml Savage John Robards 3^d Abner Lucas Moses Lucas Josiah Ward Danl Prior Bela Strong Danl Willcox Jonathan Hubbard, Danl Kirby David Edwards Junr.. Thomas Ranney, James Smith.. Jedidiah White, Eli Coe, John Bacon 3^d Charles Tryon, John Ward 4th Jonathan Gilbert Junr, Jonathan Robards Junr	382
Voted that Lieu^t Noadiah Hubbard be Excusd from being Grand-Juror - Samuel Adkins Junr Chosen in his Room	382
Committee to Provide for Soldiers Familys } Lieu^t Ju[ ] Bacon to Provide for Gideon Crittentons Family..	382
..Mr Elijah Hubbard - John Harriss ~ D^o -- D^o - Ozias Cone..	382
..Mr Seth Coe - William Bacon..	382
..Capt Thompson Phllips - John Foster 3^d..	382
..Capt Jabez Brookes - Wm Graves ..	382
..Capt Wm Ward - Moses Boardman..	382
..Mr Wm Miller Junr - Capt Robt Warner..	382
..Mr Gershom Birdseye - Joseph Lung..	382
..Mr David Edwards Junr - Capt Edwd Eells..	382
..Mr Jesse Willcox - Capt Abijah Savage..	382
..Mr Oliver Johnson - Wm Brown..	382
..Lieu^t Elisha Savage - Thomas Powers..	382
..Mr Israel Fuller - Ariel Peck..	382
..Mr Josiah Edwards - Roswell Hubbard..	382
..Mr James T Ward - Danl Cone..	382

Middletown

..Mr Nathan Coe - Joseph Cone..	382
..Mr Elijah Johnson - Lieu^t Wm Henshaw..	382
..Capt Amos Tryon - Lieu^t Hez^h Hubbard..	382
..Mr Solomon Adkins - Thomas Barns..	382
..Mr Ithamar Adkins - Lieu^t Othniel Clark..	382
..Mr John Ward - Capt David Starr..	382
..Dec^n Chancey Whittelsey - Christ^o Fisher ..	382
..Isaac Miller Esqr - Saml Allen Bordman..	382
..Mr Elisha Miller - George Anger..	382
..Saml & James Plum - Jonathan Sizer..	382
..Jonathan Gilbert - Eben^r Willis..	382
..Capt John Wetmore - Jacob Gilson..	382
..Mr Stephen Miller Junr - James Francis..	382
..Mr John Willcox - Col^o Ret^n Meigs ..	382
..Mr Daniel Whitmore - Col^o John Sumner..	382
..Dec^n Jonathan Allen - Col^o Jon^a Johnson..	382
..Mr Benj^a Birdseye - Mr David Hull..	382
..Mr Wm Ward Junr - Mr Ab^m Tyler Kimball..	382
..Mr Elijah Burr - Joseph Will[ ]	382
Voted that a Tax of Six Shillings on the £ on List 1778 be Collected.. Voted That Mr Joseph King be appointed to Collect ye Afores^d Six Shilling Rate	383
We your Committee appointed to Adjust the Accounts of the Town and Country Rates which were in the Hands of Stephen Blake Dec^d to Collect with the Heirs of Seth Wetmore Esqr who was Administrator of of the Estate.. and with the Town of Chatham, and to cause the Ballance due.. beg leave to Report.. Submitted by your obedient humble Servants ~ Mathew Tallcott.. Titus Hosmer.. Benjamin Henshaw } Com^{tee}	383

27 Dec 1779

Surveyors { Capt Giles Hall & Mr Joseph Bacon } for the.. Cross Way	384
Thompson Phillips Excusd from being a Surveyor of Highways & Ich^d Wetmore Chosen in his Room	384
Grand Jurors { Tim^o Johnson Excus'd Harriss Prout Chosin in his Room.. Saml Ward D^o Joseph Hubbard Junr D^o in D[ ]	384
Voted That the Select-Men pay Maj^r Nathl Brown an Equivalent to Fifty Shillings Pr Year.. for Each of the Two Years that he has Serv'd as Town Treasurer	385
Voted That Bezaleel Fisk Collect ye Town Rate of 4/ on the Pound	385
Voted That a Committee be appointed on the Memorial of John Kirby & Elias Squire	385
Voted That Col^o Comfort Sage, Col^o Matthew Tallcott & Mr Benjamin Henshaw be a Committee to View the Premises Set forth in the Memorials of John Kirby & Elias Squire	385
Voted Unanimously that this Town do highly approve of the Conduct of the Committee of Inspection in Prosecuting ye affair against Capt George Phillips - The Memorial in Mr Henshaws Hands	385

Middletown

Voted That Titus Hosmer Esqr be Added to a Former Committee, to view The Flowing of Hop-Swamps, &c	385
Tything-Man Edward Rockwell Senior	385
Com^{tee} Inspection { En^s Oliver Hubbard.. En^s And^r Campbell.. Mr Adino Pomroy.. Lieu^t Saml Bull.. Amos Tryon - Excus'd.. Wensley Hobby D^o.. Col^o Sage D^o	385
Committee to Liquidate your Accounts with your Treasurer, and to consider his Services in said office.. report that.. they have been kept with great care.. we also find that Mr Joseph King late Collector is in Advance for the Town.. we are of opinion that his care and Vigilence in said Office merits as much as any of his predecissors.. Benjamin Henshaw.. Comfort Sage.. Elihu Starr } Auditors	386

1 Mar 1780

Col^o Comf^t Sage was chosen Moderator	386
Voted That the Select-Men Set a Suitable Guard, to Guard the Magaxene of Powder Deposited in Mr Danforths Barn till it can be Conveniently Remov'd	386
Voted That Capt Thos Goodwin, Mr Joseph King, Leiu^t Wm Starr Mr Thos Danforth, Col^o Comfort Sage, Mr Richard Hamlin, Capt Jared Shepherd, Lt Hugh White, Abijah Ranney, Benj^a Galpin, Israel Fuller, Jedidiah Sage, Zacheus Higbe, Phinehas Bacon, Joseph Clark, Seth Wetmore, Capt Giles Miller, Elihu Stow Mr David Lyman, Lt Noadiah Hubbard, Capt George Hubbard, Mr Joseph Johnson, Capt Danl Clark, Stephen Whitmore, Saml Ward 3^d, Lieu^t Jer^h Bacon, Stephen Tryon, Lieu^t Saml Bull & Elijah Johnson, be a Committee to Inspect provision	387
Voted That Messrs Elijah Hubbard, Isaac Miller Esqr Stephen Bacon, Capt Jared Shepherd & Mr Daniel Willcox be Added to ye former Committee to Lay out & Alter Highways	387
..Petition of Wm Bigland.. to Erect a Work-Shop by the Bridge Highway Near Capt David Starrs or by Mis^s Miller'es.. for the Use of his Business	387

10 Apr 1780

The following Persons were admitted, to take the Freemens Oath.. Viz ~ John Gilbert, Seth Coe, Wm Keith, Isaac Bow, Timothy Gipson, Joseph Stow, Henry Rockwell.. Test - Elijah Hubbard.. Chy Whittelsey.. Thom^s Goodwin.. Hugh White } Select-Men	388
Saml Plum, Solomon Barns, Elijah Tuells, Oliver Clark, Wm Redfield, Capt Edwd Eells - had new oath Administred.. before me.. Test Isaac Miller Jus^t Peace	388

22 May 1780

Matthew Tallcott Esqr was Chosen Moderator	388
Voted That Messrs Hez^h Hale, Dec^n Giles Miller & Mr Seth Wetmore be a Committee to Examine the Memorial of John Birdseye, Thomas Lyman & Abel Lyman ~ Concerning shutting up a Highway near the Mountain	388
Voted That Mr Elijah Hubbard, John Dickerson Esqr & Mr Seth Wetmore be a Committee to Repair to the Burying Yard of Middlefield and Ascertain the Bounds	388
Voted That a Tax of Six Shillings on the Pound, on all the Polls Rateable Estate of List 1779 - be Collected.. and that Bezaleel Fisk be.. appointed to Collect the Same	388
Voted That Capt Eli Butler Provide for Stephen Savage, Family - Tim^o Gipson.. D^o.. John Swift.. D^o - John Dickinson Esqr D^o.. Capt Wm Sizer.. D^o	389
Voted That the Honble Titus Hosmer Esqr, Matthew Tallcott Esqr & Col^o Comfort Sage be appointed as Agents.. to oppose.. the Inhabitants of Worthington praying with the Inhabitants of New Britain & Kensington to be Sett of a New and Distinct Township	389
Voted That nothing be done on Ep^m Stones Petition Concerning his Supplying Hay &c for the Light Horse	389

Middletown

26 Jun 1780

The Honble Jabez Hamlin Esqr was Chosen Moderator 389

Voted That Chauncey Whittelsey, Elijah Hubbard, Lamber[ton] Cooper, John Dickerson 389
Esqr, Hugh White, Eli Butler, Isaac Miller, Elihu Stow, Israel ~~Porter, Samuel~~ Fuller, Samuel
Porter, Ebenezer Bacon, Oliver Wetmore, Oliver Hubbard, Samuel Chamberlain, & Francis
Clark or any of them, be a Committee.. to hire the Seven Men to Compleat our Quota of the
Continental Army

Voted That a Tax of Four pence on the Pound.. on the List of 1779 be Granted.. to pay the 390
Bounties and Committee Shall agree to pay to the Soldiers who shall inlist into the
Continental Army, or Militia Regiments.. Bezaleel Fisk chosen collecter of s^d Rate

Fence Viewer } Nehemiah Hubbard 390

19 Sep 1780

This may Certify that Messrs Seth Miller & Josiah Bacon, have Attained to the Age of 390
Twenty One Years, are Persons of an Honest conversation & Qualify'd in point of Estate to
be made Freemen of this State - in Freeman's Meeting.. Elijah Hubbard.. Chy Whittelsey..
Lam^t Cooper } Select-Men

The Fremans Oath.. was Administred to Each of the Persons, Mentioned in the foregoing 390
Certificate, By me - Matthew Tallcott Jus^t Pac^s

30 Jun 1780

Eliot Rawson.. being truly Desirous.. to Relieve all those that are Suffering for their Country 391
for Liberty, or for Righteousness.. Determine that all my five Africans, or Negroes - Shall be
free, if they behave Well, upon the Select-Men Giving a Certificate According to Law, that
Phillip Rawson Shall be free in Six Months from the first Day of Next June, that Dutchess
Rawson, Francis Rawson, Lettice Rawson and Eve Rawson Shall be made free at Twenty
four Years of Age

In Presence of ~ Giles Miller.. Isaac Miller.. Hezekiah Hale.. } Eliot Rawson personally 391
appeared and Acknowledged the within Instrument to be his free Act.. Isaac Miller Jus^t Pacis

13 Nov 1780

Matthew Tallcott Esqr was Chosen Moderator 391

Voted That Col^o Comfort Sage, all the Captains (or Commanding Officers of the Several 391
Militia companys & Lt Horse belonging to this Town & John Dickinson Esqr.. be a
Committee to Enquire.. the Number of Men we have Enlisted & now Serve During the War
& all those whose Times are not out till after the 1st of March Next

Voted That a Tax.. of One Shilling on the Pound on all the Polls & Rateable Estate.. on the 392
List 1779 be Collected.. also Voted that Bezaleel Fisk Collect the Same

Voted that Messrs Isaac Miller Esqr, Elijah Hubbard and Amos Horsford be a Committee to 392
Purchase.. Provisions

Voted That Mr Lamberton Cooper, be Packer & Overseer of the Same 392

4 Dec 1780

Matthew Tallcott Esqr was Chosen Moderator 392

Select Men - Capt Thomas Goodwin Dec^n Chauncey Whittelsey Isaac Miller Esqr Mr Amos 392
Horsford Mr Lamberton Cooper Mr Hugh White & Mr Elijah Hubbard

Listers - Messrs Wensley Hobby.. John Rogers Joseph Johnson Joel Adkins Micah Hubbard.. 393
Amos Sage Hez^h Hale.. Jedediah Sage.. & J[ ]^[ ] Clark

Committee to Settle w^h Treas^r] Mr Elihu Starr, Mr Benjamin Henshaw & Col^o Comfort Sage 393

Middletown

Voted That Bezaleel Fisk Collector of the State Tax.. Voted That Bezaleel Fisk be allow'd.. an Additional fee for Collect[g] Said State Tax	393
Sealer of Liquid Measures Thomas Danforth	393
D[o].. drye.. Ditto John Rogers	393
Fence Viewers Cap[t] Sam[l] Russel M[r] Nehemiah Hubbard Cap[t] John Wetmore M[r] Saml Hubbard M[r] Joseph Clark	393
Gaugers - Col[o] Comfort Sage M[r] Wensley Hobby M[r] Daniel Stocking	393
Leath[r] Seal[rs] Mess[rs] Seth Paddock Eleazer Gaylord W[m] White Isaac Miller Esq[r]	393
Branders of Horses } Thomas Hulbert John Hensdale Tim[o] White Cornwell Dowd John Robards Jun[r] & Jed[h] Johnson Jun[r]	393
Pound & Key Keepers } Mess[rs] Ephraim Stone John Hensdale Amos Savage Cap[t] W[m] Ward, W[m] Cotton, Benj[a] Bevin	394
Packers of Meat } Lamberton Cooper Jonathan Stow	394
Grand Jurors - Thomas Hulbert Hezekiah Hulbert Excus'd.. Solomon Savage, Sam[l] Hall.. Harriss Prout Cap[t] Joseph Hubbard.. Stephen Sears Peat Galpin Joseph Coe Jun[r].. John Cande	394
Tything Men Cap[t] W[m] Starr.. Willard Wright, John Paddock, Edward Rockwell.. Simon Robards Amos Tryon Rowland Allin Ithamar Adkins, W[m] Sage Asher Riley Elijah Willcox Jeremiah Willcox.. Ich[l] Spence,.. Ethe Wetmore.. Ephraim Crofoot	394
Com[t] Inspection Maj[r] Starr, Maj[r] Brown, M[r] Benj[a] Henshaw Cap[t] Jared Shepherd M[r] Abijah Ranney, M[r] Benjamin Galpin M[r] David Adkins M[r] David Lyman M[r] Elihu Stow, Cap[t] Eben[r] Johnson M[r] Francis Clark, M[r] Seth Wetmore M[r] Oliver Hubbard, M[r] W[m] Starr, M[r] Adino Pomroy M[r] Sam[l] Bull & M[r] Elisha Savage	394
Surveyors ~ Philip Mortimer Esq[r] Cap[t] Ich[d] Wetmore, Adino Pomroy.. John Dickinson Esq[r] Dec[n] John Earl Hubbard, Sam[l] Chamberlain.. Elijah Johnson Cap[t] Oliver Johnson.. Stephen Wetmore, Seth Johnson Jun[r] Amos Savage, Thomas Kirby Dec[n] Joseph Kirby, Sam[l] Frara, Josiah Prior.. Cap[t] Amos Tryon Josiah Ward Noadiah Hubbard, Tim[o] Clark.., Stephen Bacon.., Abijah Hubbard Abraham Wright Ichabod Miller Jun[r] Amos Wetmore.. Lem[l] Camp.. Nathan Coe,... Sam[l] Willcox Aaron Plum.. Oliver Wetmore Dan[l] Plum.. Ebenezer Gilbert ~~Noadiah~~ Manoah Hubbard, Abner Lucas Hinksman Robards George Adkins.. Stephen Parsons ~ sworn (Quaker fashion) John Robards	394
Hog Hayards David Stow.. Giles Meigs John Paddock.. Edw[d] Rockwell Jun[r].. James Jones W[m] Harriss Gershom Birdseye,... Beriah Cone.. Stephen Turner Seth Doolittle J[ ][l] Willcox Joseph Higbe Dan[l] Alvard Dan[l] Plum.. Eleazer Gaylord Dan[l] Hall John Robards 3[d] Josiah Ward Joseph Ward Dan[l] Prior Bela Strong Abner Lucas W[m] Hubbard Dan[l] Kirby W[m] Savage Julius Riley Dan[l] Eells James Tap[n] Ward Eli Coe Charles Tryon Timothy Hall.. Sam[l] Markham Jonathan Gilbert Jun[r] Jonathan Robards Jun[r]	395
Elihu Stow, Benjamin Henshaw, Doc[t] Rauson Col[o] Tallcott & Col[o] Sage - be a Committee to draw Instruction for our Representatives	395

18 Dec 1780

Elijah Treadway Esq[r] was Chosen Moderator	395
Grand Jurors.. Hez[h] Hulbert Excus'd - John Paddock & Dan[l] Crowel Chosen	395
Committee to Supply Soldiers familys } Hezekiah for L[t] Othn[l] Clark..	395
..Elijah Hubbard D[o] Ozias Cone ..	395
..Giles Meigs D[o] W[m] Bacon..	395

Middletown

..Jabez Brooks D⁰ Wᵐ Graves..   *395*

..Jehᵈ Stow Shelden Spencer D⁰ Moses Boardman..   *395*

..Oliver Wetmore D⁰ Capᵗ Robᵗ Warner..   *395*

..Gershom Birdseye D⁰ Joseph Lung..   *395*

..Cornelius Cornwell D⁰ Jn⁰ Foster 3ᵈ..   *395*

..Capᵗ Sol⁰ Sage D⁰ Capᵗ Edwᵈ Eells..   *395*

..Deaⁿ Whittelsey D⁰ Lᵗ Wᵐ Henshaw..   *395*

..Jesse Coe D⁰ Lᵗ Hezʰ Hubbard..   *395*

..Jn⁰ Ward D⁰ Capᵗ David Starr..   *395*

..Joseph Driggs D⁰ George Anger..   *395*

..Capᵗ John Wetmore D⁰ for Jacob Gilson..   *395*

..Joseph King D⁰ Joseph Willis..   *395*

..Decⁿ Allin D⁰ for Col⁰ Johnson..   *395*

..Jonathan Turner D⁰ David Hull..   *395*

..David Lyman D⁰ Abrᵐ Tyler Kimbal..   *395*

..Joseph Coe Junʳ D⁰ David Robards Junʳ..   *395*

..Elisha Savage D⁰ Stephen Savage..   *395*

..Elisha Willco D⁰ Capᵗ Wᵐ Sizer..   *395*

Upon a Motion to Reconsider the Fees Granted to Mʳ Fisk Collectʳ of the State Tax.. it was unanimously Voted to make no Alteration   *396*

Voted That Messʳˢ Amos Churchill, Isaac Miller Esqʳ, Elijah Hubbard, Seth Wetmore & Elihu Stow, be a Committee to Lay out the Highway Reported to be necessary - Through the Land of Mary Alsop, Seth Higbe David Higbe & the Wᵈ of Isaac Higbe Decᵈ   *396*

Voted That Messʳˢ Capᵗ Jared Shepherd, Capᵗ John Wetmore, Messʳˢ Stephen Bacon & Mʳ Seth Wetmore, be a Committee to Lay out the Highway.. (Proposed by Lᵗ Cornwell & others) through the Land of Mary Alsop & others & Through the Notch   *396*

The Petition of David Adkins and others humbly Sheweth.. a Great Saving might be made to the Publick Travels in altering the Road to Meridon, to turn in by the Widow Higbe Lott or the Widow Alsops.. [*signed*] David Adkins.. Benjᵃ Henshaw.. Giles Meigs   *396*

Voted That Messʳˢ Seth Wetmore, Phinehas Bacon & Elijah Hubbard, be a Committee on the Afore Said Petition   *397*

Upon the Memorial of Cornelius Cornwell & others Praying that the Highway that runs by Sᵈ Cornwells House may be opened through Wrights Farm &c - Voted that Messʳˢ Stephen Bacon Capᵗ John Wetmore & Capᵗ Jared Shepherd be a Committee to View & Examine the same & Report   *397*

27 Dec 1780

Decⁿ Joˢ Kirby Released from being Surveyor of Highways & Capᵗ Jared Shepherd Chosen in his Room   *397*

Capᵗ John Wetmore Released from being Fence Viewer & Joseph Bacon chosen in his Room   *397*

Voted that a Committee be appointed to Hire the Twelve Men & One Light Horse-Man to Serve a Twelve Months Tower at Horse Neck.. Voted That Majʳ Brown Mʳ Benjᵃ Henshaw, Lᵗ Samˡ Bull Mʳ Abijah Ranney, Lieuᵗ David Lyman, Lᵗ David Adkins, Mʳ Jedidiah Sage, Mʳ   *398*

Middletown

Elijah Johnson & Mr Elijah Hubbard - be a Com^t to Hire ye 13 Men	
Voted That a Tax of One Shilling on the £ in the Late Emitted Bills of this State be laid on all the Polls & Rateable Estate of this Town According to the List Return'd to the Genl Assembly in Augt 1780.. & that Bezaleel Fisk be a Collector of the Same	398
Voted That Messrs Lieu^t Saml Bull, Capt Amos Wetmore Mr Nathaniel Eells, Mr Joseph Clark & Mr Jonathan Hubbard (of Worthington) be a Committee to Purchase this Towns Quota of Flower &c.. & that Mr Saml Bull Receive, Inspect, & make Return of the Same	398
Voted that Capt Jacob Whitmore be Excus'd providing for John Foster 3^d Family &.. Mr Cornelius Cornwell Chosen..	398
..also that Capt Wm Ward be Excus'd Provid^g for Moses Boardmans Family & Ich^d Stow Sheldin Spencer chosen	398
Voted That the Select Men be a Committee to do every thing that is Ncessary for the Highway that Runs from Tim^o Mccoughs W[ ]t to Durham	398
Tything Men Samuel Canfield	399
Grand-Juror - John Paddock Excus^d - & Nathan Strong chosen.. and Solomon Stow J^r Chosen	399
Leath^r Sealer Seth Paddock Excus'd, & Bennit Eagleston Chosen	399
The Auditors Report of the State of ye Town Acc^{ts} with the Treasurer was Accepted.. N.B. this Rep^d not Ent^d in the Proper place being Lent to Maj^r Brown	399
I.. Petitioneth.. for the Priviledge of Setting up a Saw Mill in the Publick Highway near my Dwelling House (to Say) on the South Side of my Present Mill-pond, for the use of the Publick as for my Private Business.. Giles Sage Junr The Memorial Petition is Granted	399
We the Subscribers being appointed a Committee on the Memorial of Lieu^t Cornelius Cornwell and others.. Whether it is Necessary to Lay a Highway from the Highway that Lieu^t Cornwell lives on to the Highway that Mr Treat Lives on.. and are of opinion that it is Necessary.. One through the Notch (so called and the other Through Land belonging to Mr Joseph Wrights Heirs.. Jared Shepard.. John Wetmore.. Stephen Bacon	399
9 Apr 1781	
Select-Men.. do hereby Certify that the Persons whose names are hereafter written are Duly qualify'd for Freemen.. Viz ~ Hezekiah Tallcott, Jedidiah Johnson Junr, Samuel Canfield, Eliakim Rich, Cornelius Cornwell & Jonathan Pratt..	400
The Freemens oath.. was Administred to the foregoing Persons in Freemans Meeting.. by me - Isaac Miller Jus^t Peace	400
16 Apr 1781	
John Dickinson Esqr was Chosen Moderator	400
Voted That a Tax of 12^d on the £ in the late Emitted Bills of this State (be laid on all the Polls & Rateable Estate of the Inhabitants of this Town) be Collected.. & Voted that Bezaleel Fisk be a Collector of the Same	400
Voted That Mr Elijah Hubbard be a Com^{te} to Provide the Cloathing for the Soldiers	401
Voted that Messrs Benj^a Henshaw, Jo^s King, Jn$^{[o]}$ Gibson, Jared Shepard, Seth Wetmore, Nathl Gilbert Esqr & Jno Wetmore be a Com^{te} for to Provide for the Genl Assembly, See the Vote on file ~	401
29 Sep 1781	
The Honble Jabez Hamlin Esqr was Chosen Moderator	402
Voted That a Tax of 4^d on the Pound in Beef Cattle be Granted on all the Polls & Rateable Estate.. Agreeable to a late Act of the Genl Assembly be Collected.. Voted That Bezaleel Fisk be Collector	402

559

Middletown

Voted that Isaac Miller Esqr, Mr Elijah Hubbard, Lieu^t Hugh White & Lieu^t Amos Hosford, be a Committee to Purchase the Beef Cattle	402
Voted That this Town will Hire the Men, we are now call'd upon to Serve Three Months (which has lately been ordered to be Draughted) ~ ..Doc^t John Dickinson, Mr Amos Savage, Capt David Miller, Mr Amos Hosford, Dec^n Eben^r Bacon, Capt Eben^r Johnson & Mr Francis Clark be a Committee to Hire the Soldiers	402
upon the Memorial of Capt John Wetmore, Ephraim Stone & Others — the Select Men are Desired to Collect the Acc^{ts} of the Several Inhabitants.. that Supplyd Col^o Moylands Lt Horse with Provision &c & have Received no pay	402
This may Certify that Jeremiah Arnold, Daniel Russel, Elisha Brewster Junr, Isaac Hubbard & Eli Coe have Attained to the Age of Twenty One Years, are Persons of an honest Conversation and Qualify'd in Point of Estate to be made Freemen of this State.	402
the Freemens Oath.. was Administred to each of the Persons mentioned in the foregoing Certificate, by me, J Hamlin Assist^t	402

3 Dec 1781

John Dickinson Esqr was chosen Moderator	403
Select-Men - Capt Thomas Goodwin, Isaac Miller Esqr Mr Amos Hosford Mr Lamberton Cooper, Lieu^t Hugh White, Mr Elijah Hubbard & Mr Seth Wetmore	403
Town Treas^r Colo^l Nathl Brown	403
Listers.. Messrs Wensley Hobby John Rogers Joseph Johnson Joel Adkins Micah Hubbard Nathl Eells, Jedidiah Sage, Joseph Clark & Joseph Coe Junr..	403
Com^t to Audit Town Acc^{ts} w^h Treas^r } Doc^t Rawson, Dec^n Bacon & Col^o Sage	403
Constables - Messrs Hezekiah Hale.. Saml Porter.. William White.. Ashbel Cornwell.. (Doc^t Eliot Rawson X Soon after voted out)	404
Voted That Mr Hezekiah Hale Collect ye State Taxes	404

17 Dec 1781

Sealers of Weights & Liquid Measures } Thomas Danforth	404
D^o of Drye D^o John Rogers	404
Fence Viewers.. Capt Saml Russel Nehemiah Hubbard, Joseph Bacon Samuel Hubbard, & Joseph Clark	404
Guagers - Col^o Comfort Sage Wensley Hobby & Daniel Stocking	404
Leather Sealers Bennit Eaglestone Eleazer Gaylord Wm White & Isaac Miller Esqr	404
Brander of Horses } Thomas Hulbert Samuel Willcox Junr Israel Fuller, Timothy White Cornwell Dowd, John Robards Junr Jedidiah Johnson Junr	404
Pound & Key Keepers } Ephraim Stone, Israel Fuller, Amos Savage John Robards Wm Cotton & Benjamin Bevin	404
Packers of Meat Lamberton Cooper & Jonathan Stow	404
Grand Jurers ~ (Sol^o Stow J^r) Hez^h Hulbert.. Capt Giles Meigs.. Wm Hamlin Junr.. Harriss Prout, Amos Tryon John Cone Abraham Wright.. Seth Coe John Cande & Abijah Ranney	404
Tything Men.. Edward Rockwell Wm Paddock Prosper Hubbard Wm Cone.. Joseph Danforth.. Ichabod Wetmore Gideon Savage Justus Willcox Nathan Coe.. Edward Johnson.. Ebenezer Hale Seth Hawley Eli Willcox Josiah Bacon Ephraim Crofoot Junr Reuben Cook	405
Com^{tee} Inspection } Maj^r Jeh$^{[]}$ Starr, Doc^t Eliot Rawson, Mr Benjamin Hunshaw, Capt Jared Shepherd, Mr Abijah Ranney Mr Benj^a Galpin, Mr David Adkins Mr David Lyman Mr Elihu Stow, Capt Ebenezer Johnson Mr Francis Clark Mr Oliver Hubbard, Capt Wm Starr Mr Adino	405

Middletown

Pomroy, Mr Samuel Bull, Mr Elisha Savage Capt Saml Russel, Col^o Return Jon^a Meigs, Capt David Miller, Mr Noadiah Hubbard & Mr Joseph Higbe	
Constables Mr Nathan Strong.. Capt Saml Russel	405
Voted That - the Vote of Mr Hale being Collector of State Taxes.. be Reconsidered & is Contested	405
Com^{tee} to Provide for Soldies familys } Seth Wetmore for Lieu^t Othniel Clark..	405
..Elijah Hubbard for Ozias Cone & John Foster..	405
.. Giles Meigs - Wm Bacon..	405
..Jabez Brooks J^r - Wm Graves..	405
..David Lyman - Moses Boardman..	405
..Oliver Wetmore - Capt Warner..	405
..Wm Ward Junr - Joseph Lung..	405
..Abijah Ranney - Capt Eells..	405
..Chauncey Whittelsey - Lt Wm Henshaw..	405
..Daniel Whitmore - Lt Hezekiah Hubbard..	405
..John Ward - David Starr..	405
..Jacob Whitmore - George Anger..	405
..Joseph Bacon - Jacob Gilson..	405
..Joseph King - Joseph Willis..	405
..Hezekiah Tallcott - David Hull..	405
..Joseph Coe Junr - David Robards Junr..	405
..Elisha Savage - Stephen Savage	405
Com^{tee} to Audit Town Acco^{ts} } Mr Benjamin Henshaw, Col^o Tallcott & Mr Elihu Starr are appointed in addition to those that Was chose the [ ] meeting	406

24 Dec 1781

Surveyors.. P Mortimer Esqr Ich^d Wetmore Excused.. Adino Pomroy Hezekiah Hulbut John Dickinson Esqr Sol^o Hubbard Saml Chamberlain Elijah Johnson.. Oliver Johnson Stephen Whitmore Seth Johnson, Amos Savage Thomas Kirby Dec^n Joseph Kirby, Saml Frara, Noad^ah Hubbard James Cotton Joseph Higbe, Israel Fuller, Seth Kirby Ich^d Miller Junr, Amos Wetmore.. Isaac Miller Esqr.. Nathan Coe, Jeremiah Willcox David Adkins, Daniel Plum Ebenezer Gilbert, Manoah Hubbard, Abner Lucas, Hinchman Robards, George Adkins, Beriah Cone Nehemiah Hubbard, Hezekiah Hale, Seth Wetmore	406
Hog Howards ~ David Stow John Paddock, Edward Rockwell Junr Capt Tim^o Starr Wm Harriss Lem^l Camp Elisha Miller, Stephen ~~Miller~~ Turner, Seth Doolittle Joseph Graves Ep^m Higbe, Daniel Alvard Danl Plum Eleazer Gaylord Danl Hall John Robards 3^d Josiah Ward, Joseph Ward Daniel Prior Abijah Peck Junr Abner Lucas Saml Hubbard, Daniel Kirby, Wm Savage Julius Riley Daniel Eells, James T Ward, Eli Coe Charles Tryon Tim^o Hall Saml Markham Jon^a Gilbert Junr Jon^a Robards Ju^r Stephen Treat Junr	406
Constables.. Bezaleel Fisk Chosen	406

31 Dec 1781

Voted That Mr Cornelius Cornwell be Surveyor of Highways	407

Middletown

Upon the Memorial of Doc^t Dickinson & Doc^t Ward for Granting Liberty to Enoculate for the Small Pox.. Voted That the Small Pox Shall not be Introduc'd into this Town the Year Ensuing by Innoculation	407
Voted That Isaac Miller Esqr Mr Elijah Hubbard & Mr Lamberton Cooper be Desir'd to Reaassume the Characters of Select-Men	407
Com^{tee} to Remove Nusances of the Highway } Capt Amos Wetmore, Ozias Willcox, Capt Jeremiah Bacon, Elijah Johnson, Nehemiah Hubbard, Daniel Willcox, Stephen Bacon, & Francis Clark	407
Com^{tee} to Lay & alter Highways } Capt Jared Shepherd, Seth Wetmore Hez^h Hale, Col^o Sage, Amos Tryon, Elijah Hubbard, & John Dickenson Esqr	407
Surveyors -- Ich[ ] Wetmore Excus'd, Ashbel Burnham chosen & Saml Ward Excus'd	407
[Committee to] Provide for Soldiers family } Abijah Ranney Excus'd Providing for Capt Eells Family & Capt Eli Butler Chosen	407
Upon the Memorial of Capt Thomas Goodwin to Erect a Cooper Shop, near his Still, House Voted that John Dickinson Esqr Mr Elijah Hubbard & Col^o Comfort Sage be a Com^t Impowered to give Capt Goodwin Liberty to Erect a Building	408
Upon the Memorial of Capt Jno Smith for Liberty to Erect a Store at the foot of his Wharf near Capt Stockings Store Voted that he have Liberty to Bring in his Bill.. Voted that his Bill be Passed	408

25 Feb 1782

Matthew Tallcott Esqr was Chosen Moderator	409
Voted That Mr Joseph King, Doc^t Eliot Rawson, Mr Benjamin Henshaw, Capt Jared Shepherd, Mr Benjamin Galpin Mr Joseph Graves, Mr Joseph Coe Junr, Mr Noadiah Hubbard, Mr Elijah Johnson, Capt Amos Tryon, Capt Eli Butler, Mr Elihu Stow, Mr Joseph Johnson, Mr Phinehas Bacon, Mr Daniel Alvard & Capt John Smith, be a Com^{tee} to hire Fifteen Men for State Guards	409
Voted That Col^o Sage be appointed to ascertain the Number of Non Commis^n Officers & Soldiers in the Continent^l Army	409

9 Sep 1782

The Honble Jabez Hamlin Esqr was Chosen Moderator	410
Voted That a Tax be Granted to Defray the Town Expences.. Voted That Mr Nathan Strong be the Collector of said Tax	410
Voted That Mr Benjamin Henshaw, Doc^t Dickinson Mr Asher Miller, Col^o Tallcot & Mr Elijah Hubbard be a Committee to draw Instructions for the Representatives	410
To the Inhabitants of Middletown.. ~ .. The Education of Children we look upon a matter of Great Importance & which in ma[ny] places too very much neglected and in order that our Children may no longer Share in the Common Calamity we the Subscribers have Enterd into a written Agreement to Sett up Support & Maintain at our own private Expence a School.. Nathl Eells.. Wm Sage.. Tim^o Gibson } Com^{tee} in behalf of the whole ~ .. Voted that the Memorillists have liberty to Errect a School House as mentioned above during the Towns Pleasure ~	410

17 Sep 1782

This may Certify that the following persons whose names are hereunder written are Qualifyd.. to be made Freemen of this State Viz ~ Jesse Peck, Zenas Hubbard, Samuel Galpin, Eli Willcox, Elisha Willcox, & Julias Riley	411
At the afores^d Freemans Meeting, The Freemans Oath.. was administred.. by me Isaac Miller Jus^t peace	411

Middletown

At the afores^d Meeting the Freemens Oath was administered to John Bacon, Giles Sage & Elijah Willcox, ~ by me, Jabez Hamlin Assist^t	411
2 Dec 1782	
Matthew Tallcott Esqr was Chosen Moderator	412
Select-Men Capt Thomas Goodwin, Isaac Miller Esqr Mr Amos Hosford, (Mr Lamberton Cooper) Lieu^t Hugh White, Mr Elijah Hubbard & Mr Seth Wetmore (Mr Cooper is Excus'd) & Col^o Comfort Sage is Chosen in his Room	412
Town Treas^r Colo Nathaniel Brown	412
Listers ~ Messrs Wensley Hobby, John Rogers, Joseph Johnson, Joel Adkins, Nathl Eells Jedidiah Sage, Joseph Clark Joseph Coe Junr & Danl Crowel	412
Constables Hezekiah Hale,.. Saml Porter,.. Wm White,... Ashbel Cornwell.. Capt Saml Russel,.. Nathan Strong,... & Willard Wright	412
Joseph Danforth.. to Seal Liquid W^{ts} & Measures	412
John Rogers.. to Seal dry.. Ditto	412
Fence Viewers, Capt Saml Russel Nehemiah Hubbard,.. Joseph Bacon Saml Hubbard.. & Joseph Clark	413
Gaugers ~ Col^o Comf^t Sage, Wensley Hobby, & Danl Stocking	413
Leath^r Sealers Bennit Eaglestone.. Eleazer Gaylord, William White.. Isaac Miller Esqr Benj^a Galpin	413
Branders ~ Thos Hulbert Saml Willcox J^r.. Israel Fuller.. Tim^o White, Cornel Doud John Robards Junr, and Jedidiah Johnson Junr	
Pound & Key Keepers } Capt Tim^o Starr.. Israel Fuller, John Gibson, John Robards Junr, Wm Cotton & Benj^a Bevin	413
Packers of Meat } Lamberton Cooper & Jonathan Stow	413
Grand Jurors (Capt Ich^d Wetmore) excused Amos Treadway.. Giles Willcox.. Harriss Prout.. Amos Tryon.. (Jno Cone excus'd) Seth Kirby.. Joseph Ward, Abijah Ranney.. Seth Coe	413
Voted ~ That the Collector of the State Taxes.. be allow'd the Same fee as Mr Strong was the last year.. Voted That Mr Willard Wright Collect the State Taxes	413
Tything-Men Edward Rockwell.. Wm Paddock.. Prosper Hubbard.. Wm Cone, Noadiah Rockwell Jeh^d Wetmore, Nathan Coe.. Edwd Johnson, Eben^r Hale, Stephen Turner John Warner.. Joseph Doolittle.. George Hubbard.. Reuben Cook Joseph Ranney J^r.. Joz[ ] Stocking	413
Com^{tee} to Supply Soldiers Familys } Benjamin Henshaw for Lt John Meigs Family ~ ..	413
..Seth Wetmore D^o Ozias Cone Ditto ~ ..	413
..Elijah Hubbard D^o John Foster Ditto ~ ..	413
..John Dickinson D^o Wm Bacon Ditto..	413
..Seth Miller d^o Moses Boardman Ditto..	413
..Wm Ward Junr D^o Joseph Lung Ditto..	413
..Oliver Wetmore D^o Maj^r Warner Ditto..	413
..Thos Kirby D^o Capt Eells Ditto..	413
..Chauncey Whittelsey D^o Jacob Gilson Ditto..	413
..Joseph Bacon D^o George Anger Ditto..	413
..Joseph King D^o Joseph Willis Ditto..	413

Middletown

..Capt David Miller D^o David Hull Ditto..	413
..Jacob Miller D^o David Robards J^r Ditto	413
..Elisha Savage D^o Stephen Savage..	413
..John Cotton 3^d D^o for En^s Geo Cotton Ditto	413
Com^{tee} to Audit Town Acct^s } Messrs Elihu Starr, Ch^y Whitteley & Bezaleel Fisk	414

Surveyor of Highways } P Mortimer Esqr (Excus'd) Thompson Phillips Capt Giles Meigs Hezekiah Hulbert.. Capt Danl Clark.. Saml Chamberlain.. Eben^r Robards.. John Gilbert.. Stephen Whitmore Seth Johnson Junr.. Jehiel Williams Capt Eli Butler Wm Sage.. Abijah Savage John Hall Junr.. James Cotton.. Joseph Higbe.. Israel Fuller Asahel Dudley Junr.. Ich^d Miller Junr Amos Wetmore David Lyman, Dec^n Giles Miller, Joel Bacon.. Dec^n Eben^r Bacon Jer$^{[l]}$ Bacon.. Elisha Ward,.. Manoah Hubbard.. Abner Lucas Hinksman Robards.. Col^o R Meigs.. Hez^h Tallcott, Isaac Hubbard.. John Robards Junr Giles Southmayd 414

Voted That Mr Seth Wetmore & Hezekiah Hale be a Com^{tee} to Examine Highway near James Bartlits 414

16 Dec 1782

Col^o Comfort Sage was chosen Moderator 414

24 Dec 1782

John Dickinson Esqr was chosen Moderator 415

Voted That David Adkins & others ~~Petition~~ Memorial for Liberty to Erect a School House near the Dwelling House of Mr Samuel Plum Granted 415

Voted that Luther Savage have Liberty to Errect a Shop on the Bank near Capt Smiths Ware House... Lieu^t Hugh White, Mr Elijah Hubbard & Capt Thomas Goodwin to agree 415

Voted That Isaac Miller Esqr & Col^o Sage be Excused Serving.. in the Office of Select-Men.. & Bezaleel Fisk & Capt Amos Wetmore are Chosen in their room 415

Voted That a Tax of Eight pence.. on the Pound on all the polls & Rateable Estate of the Inhabitants.. on the List of 1782 be Collected.. &.. That Col^o Nathl Brown, Saml Porter, Phinehas Bacon Hezekiah Hale, Capt Jared Shepherd, Seth Wetmore William Warner Silvanus Young & Ithamar Adkins be Collectors 415

Com^{tee} Inspect^n Maj^r Starr, Doc^t Rawson Mr Henshaw, Capt Shepherd, Abijah Ranney, Benj^a Galpin, Dec^n Bacon, David Lyman, Elihu Stow, Eben^r Johnson, Francis Clark, Oliver Hubbard Wm Starr, Adino Pomroy Saml Bull Elisha Savage Capt Russel Col^o Miegs Capt D Miller & Noad^h Hubbard & Joseph Higbe ~ 415

Haywards Doc^t Rawson, Elijah Hubbard, Elisha Miller, Stephen Turner, Seth Doolittle, Isaac Miller Esqr Joseph Graves, Ep^m Higbe, Danl Alvard, Danl Plum Eleazer Gaylord Danl Hall John Robard 3^d Josiah Ward Joseph Ward, Danl Prior Abijah Peck Junr, Abner Lucas Saml Hubbard Daniel Kirby.. Wm Savage.. Julius Riley.. Tim^o Starr Danl Eells James Ward Elihu Sto[w] Capt Jabez Brooks, Benj^a Henshaw, Saml Markham, Jon^a Gilbert Junr Jon^a Robards Stephen Treat Junr Nathan Starr Capt Amos Wetmore Jon^a Tryon John Robards Joseph Driggs 416

30 Dec 1782

Grand-Jurors } Voted That John Cone & Ich^d Wetmore be Excus'd Service.. & Silvanus Young.. & Nath^n Starr who is Chosen in thire Room} 416

Tything Men Voted that Edward Johnson be Excusd & Edward Powers, Thos Hall.. Micah Hubbard & Jacob Hall Chosen 416

Surveyors ~ P Mertimer Capt Amos Wetmore & Thompson Phillips Excusd & Capt John Wetmore & Decon Whittelsey Chosen ~ Lieu^t Danl Wetmore & Abijah Hubbard also Chosen 416

Middletown

Collectors 8^d Town Tax } Capt Jared Shepherd & Col^o Brown Excused & Saml Sage & Saml Canfield are Chosen in thire Room	416
Com^{tee} to Remove Nusances of ye Highways } Isaac Miller Esqr. Ozias Willcox Jeremiah Bacon Elijah Johnson, Nehemiah Hubbard, Danl Willcox Stephen Bacon & Capt Daniel Clark	417
Com^{tee} to Lay out & alter Highways } Jared Shepard, Seth Wetmore Hezek^h Hale Col^o Sage Amos Tryon Elijah Hubbard & John Dickinson Esqr	417
On the Memorial of Col^o Sumner, Joseph Drigs & Others.. for Libberty to Errect & keep up a fence to the Buttments of the New Bridge by Col^o Sumners.. Voted that the Memorialists have liberty to Build a fence to S^d Butments	417
Upon the Petition of Chauncey Whittelsey.. for a Grant.. of a Store Lott on the Bank of the River South next adjoining The House.. where Capt Saml Bement now Lives and the Priviledge of Building a Wharf adjoining s^d Store.. Voted That Col^o Nathaniel Brown, Phillip Mertimer Esqr & Mr Saml Bull be a.. Committee to View the premises and Sett a price.. to give a Quit Claim of the Towns Right thereof	417

9 Jan 1783

Voted That the Select Men be appointed to take a Bond from Mr Seth Wetmore of £10,000 to Endemnifie the Town of Mr Willard Wright Collecting the State Taxes	417
Collect of 8^d Tax Silvanus Young Excus'd & ~~Samuel Car~~ Israel Carrier Chosen in his Room	417
Com^{tee} to provide for Sold^s Familys Voted That Nathl Gilbert Esqr provide for Allin Gilbert Junr..	417
..David Tryon -- for Abijah Hubbard	417
Voted That an agent be appointed to present a Memorial to the Genl Assembly for Liberty to mend the Highway, by tax & Mr Benjamin Henshaw & Mr Seth Wetmore is appointed to prepare & present the same	418
Voted That Mr Benj^a Henshaw, John Dickinson Esqr M Tallcott Esqr Asher Miller Esqr Elijah Hubbard Esqr Mr Elihu Stow & Genl Parsons - be a Com^{tee} to draw Instructions for our Representatives	418
Voted That an addition be made to a former Com^{tee} for Looking up Town Moneys.. Voted that Mr Asher Miller be added to Said Committee	418

8 Feb 1783

At a General Assembly.. at Hartford.. 8th day of Jan^y.. 1783 ~ Upon the Memoral of the Town of Middletown by their agents Benjamin Henshaw and Seth Wetmore,.. That said Town are Desirous of Liberty to Repair their Highways by a Tax.. Resolved by this assembly that the said Town.. be Impowered.. to repair all their Highways, by a Tax or Rate	418

7 Apr 1783

This may Certify that the following persons whose names are hereunder written, are Qualifyd.. to be made freemen of This State Viz ~ Abel Willcox Junr, Abraham Doolittle Daniel Kelley, Abner Michel, John Willcox Junr, Thomas Barns, John Paddock, John Hall Junr, James Jones, Jeremiah Willcox, Nathaniel Boardman, Nathan Boardman, James Cotton, Giles Willcox, William Cone, Nathan Coe & Amos Higbe..	419
The freemens Oath.. was administered to each of the Persons mentioned in the foregoing Certificate by me, J Hamlin Assistant	419

28 May 1783

John Dickinson Esqr was Chosen Moderator	420

2 Sep 1783

The Honble Jabez Hamlin Esqr was Chosen Moderator	420

Middletown

Voted That a Committee be appointed to Collect what Evidence they can for and against the Commutation Act.. Voted That Col° Tallcott, John Dickinson Esqr, Mr Elihu Stow, Col° Sage, Genl Parsons, Dec^n Bacon, Dec^n Whittelsey, Roger Riley Esqr, Mr Hobby Capt Geo Hubbard, The Honble Jabez Hamlin Esqr & Capt Jared Shepherd be the Committee *420*
8 Sep 1783

Voted That the Representatives.. to represent this Town at the Genl Assembly in October next use their upmost endeavours.. to obtain a Redress of the General and almost universal Grievance on acc^t of the half pay to the Officers and the Commutation therefor ~ Voted That Mr Elihu Stow & Dec^n Eben^r Bacon be a Com^{tee} to meet with ye Convention *421*
16 Sep 1783

This may Certify that the Following persons whose names are hereunder Written are Qulify'd.. to be made freemen of this State Viz ~ Capt Caleb Wetmore, Stephen Ranney, Cornwell Doud, Jonathan Gilbert Junr Wm Hamlin Junr, Jesse Wetmore, Ichabod Spencer, David Hubbard, Stephen Turner, Wm Johnson, Nathl Cornwell & Ebenezer Markham *421*
The freemens Oath.. was administered to each of the Persons mentioned in the foregoing Certificate ~ p^r me, J Hamlin Assist^t *422*

Milford

Town Records
Volume 2
1751 – 1827

Located at the Town Clerk's Office

Milford

post Sep 1774

Resolved.. That we highly approve of and will.. abide by the Association and every particular thereof as formed by.. the delegates in general continental Congress held at Philadelphia in September last past.. Resolved That the following Person be a Committee for the Purposes.. in the afores^d eleventh Article Viz: For the first Society, Col. Edward Allen, Mr Jonas Wooster, Capt Isaac Smith, Lieu^t Samuel Treat, D^n Elias Carrington, Mr Gideon Buckingham..	78
For the Second Society, Mr Joseph Treat, Capt Benjamin Fenn, Capt Arnold Tibbals, Mr Jeremiah Baldwin..	78
..For the Episcopal Society, Messrs John Herpin, Lewis Mallet Ju^r..	78
..For the Parish of Amity, Messrs Phineas Peck, John Dibble..	78
..For the Parish of Parish of Bethany, Mr Jonathan Andrew..	78
Resolved, That Ephraim Strong Esqr, Capt Isaac Miles, Messrs John Harpin, Garrit Van Horn D^c Hill, Gideon Buckingham, John Dibble and Samuel Whittelsey be a committee of Correspondence	78

1 May 1775

Deac^n Nathaniel Buckingham chose Moderator	80
Samuel Whittelsey Clerk	80
Voted that the Select Men be a Committee to take Care & provide for the mounting the Gunns.. provide powder &c & everything needful respecting the great Gunns.. provide Guns, Bayonets & provisions for such as are called forth for the defence of the liberty of America & are unable to provide for themselves [*ed: at a town meeting on Decr 17, 1774, Isaac Miles, Nathan Baldwin, Benjamin Hine, Garrit V H DeWitt, John Dibble and Isaac Clark elected Selectmen for the year ensuing*]	80
Voted that a Minute Post be supported in this Town.. untill next Monday under the direction of C^t Isaac Miles	81

8 May 1775

Nathaniel Buckingham Moderator	81
Samuel Whittelsey Clerk	81
Voted that the Minute Post continued under the direction of C^t Isaac Miles.. untill the first Monday in June	81
Voted that John Fowler Esqr & Ephraim Strong Esqr represent the Town to the Generall Assembly, & Petition for liberty to have a Company enlisted & Commissioned, to be stationed in town for its defence & at the expence of the Colony	81
Voted that Some gratuity be allowed those that have formed themselves into a Company under the Command of John Fowler Ju^r & have spent voluntarily much time in acquainting themselves with the military Arts	81
Petition of Elisha Johnson praying to be admitted as an Inhabitant of this Town.. Voted that the Petition be granted	81

5 Jun 1775

Nathaniel Buckingham Moderator	81
Samuel Whittelsey Clerk	81

12 Dec 1775

John Fowler Esqr Chose Moderator	81

Milford

Samuel Whittelsey Clerk	81
Selectmen } Isaac Miles, Nathan Baldwin Benjamin Hine Garrit V H D^{e}Witt, John Dible & Isaac Clark	82
Constables } Michael Peck, Enoch Baldwin Stephen Baldwin who is also Chose to Collect the County Rate	82
Surveyor of Highways } Elias Carrington, Jonas Green, Michael Peck, David Lambert Richard Platt, Elihu Baldwin, Ab^m Tomlinson, Charles Hine Ramond Sanford Moses Thomas	82
Listers } Elnathan Baldwin, Nathan Fowler, Samuel Fenn, William Battle, Fisk Peck, Jonathan Andrew, Isaac Botsford	82
Sealer of Weights } John Colebreath	82
Sealer of Measures Jonathan Marshall	82
Grand Jurors } Nehemiah Clark, Isaac Stone, Samuel Prudden Isaac Gunn, Ephraim Buckingham, Joel Smith Richard Baldwin	82
Tything Men } Ashbel Baldwin, Jonathan Marshall, Samuel Durand, David Baldwin Junr	82
Leather Sealers } Peter Perit, John Arnold	82
Fence Viewers } Joseph Prudden, Isaac Smith, Joseph Platt Junr	82
Sexton { Moses Mallery is chosen..., who is to Ring the Bell on all published Occasions, for Funerals and at 9 O Clock at Night, and to Sweep the Meeting Houses as often as necessary, also to take Care of the Clock that it keeps proper time for which Service he is to receave Four Pounds Lawful Money	82
Packers { James Goldsmith, Job Marchant, Jonathan Marshall Laurence Clinton	82
Gauger { James Goldsmith	82
granted a Rate of one Penney halfpenney.. on the Pound to be levied.. on the List for the Year 1775 for defraying the necessary Charges of the Town.. Mr Jonathan Prudden is chosen Collector.. and is also chosen Treasurer for said Town, for which Services he is to receave Three Pounds Lawful Money	83

9 Jan 1776

Ephraim Strong Esqr Chose Moderator	83
Gideon Buckingham chose Clerk	83
Lazarous Northop is chosen Collector to Collect the Town Rate in the Room of Jonathan Prudden who refused also is chosen Town Treasurer	83
Voted that the Town is willing that the Revd Josiah Sherman should to Improve the Towns Meadow that the Revd Job Prudden Deceased formerly Improved dureing his work of the Ministry in the second Society	83

22 Feb 1776

Mr Jonas Wooster chose Moderator	83

27 Mar 1776

Ephraim Strong Esqr Chose Moderator	84
Voted that Messrs Isaac Miles, John Herpin John Arnold Samuel Peck & Ephraim Strong Esqr shall be a Committee to.. agree upon a place sutable to erect a Battery or Fortification	84
Voted that Capt Isaac Miles be added to Committee of Inspection	84

25 Apr 1776

Ephraim Strong Esqr Chose Moderator	84

Milford

Voted that the Town will proceed to Build a Battery at West Point.. Voted that Lieu^t Benjamin Hine, Capt Benjamin Fenn, Capt Arnold Tibbles, Lieu^t Samuel Peck and Mr John Herpin be a Committee to build the same	84
Voted that the Committee be Impowered to treat Mr John Arnold for Lane to erect the Battery upon	84

9 May 1776

Capt Isaac Miles is chose Moderator	85
Select Men } Capt Isaac Miles, Nathan Baldwin, John Dibble, Isaac Clark Lewis Mallit and Gideon Buckingham	85
Constables & Collector } Amos Baldwin, Stephen Baldwin and Fletcher Prudden who is also chose to Collect the County Rate	85
Surveyors of Highways } Aaron Fenn Junr Capt Arnold Tibbells, Ephraim Smith Junr David Lambert, Aaron Hine, Fletcher Prudden, Capt Isaac Smith Jonas Platt, Nathan Platt Junr, Daniel Tolls, Archibald McNeal & Jo^s Plumb	85
Listers } Samuel Fenn, William Battle, Solomon Baldwin Jeremiah Rogers, Nathan Clark, Jacob Hotchkiss	85
Sealer of Weights } John Colebreath	85
Sealer of Measures } Jonathan Marshall	85
Grand Jurymen } Lieu^t Samuel Peck, John Peck, Col. Edward Allin, David Merwin Capt Richard Bristoll, Lazarous Clark, & Oliver Buckingham	85
Tything Men } John Clark Junr, James Fenn, John Churchill Joshua Baldwin, and Landu Beech	85
Leather Sealers } Peter Perrit, John Arnold, and Capt Isaac Smith	85
Fence Viewers } Joseph Prudden, Samuel Prudden, and Thos Clark Junr	85
Packers } James Goldsmith, Job Marchant, Jonathan Marshall, and Levi Clinton	85
Guager } Mr John Herpin	85
Sexton { Moses Mallery is chosen.. who is to Ring the Bell on all public Occasions, for Funerals and at 9 O Clock at Night, and to Sweep the Meeting Houses as often as necessary, Also to take Care of the Clock that it keep proper time, for which Service he is to receive four Pounds lawful Money	86
Committee of Inspection } Col. Edward Allen, Mr Jonas Wooster, Capt Isaac Smith, Capt Saml Treat Doc^r Elias Carrington, Gideon Buckingham Esqr Deacon Jo^s Treat Co^l Benjamin Fenn, Capt Arnold Tibballs, Mr Jeremiah Baldwin, Mr John Herpin, Mr Lewis Mallit Junr Deacon Phineas Peck, Mr Jno Dibble, and Mr Jonathan Andrew	86

20 Jan 1777

Voted that James Thomson be a Tything Man	86
Vited That Mr Landu Beech be one of the Committee of Inspection	86

17 Feb 1777

granted a Rate of three Pence.. on the Pound to be levied.. on all the Poles & Reatable Estates of the Inhabitants.. on the List for the Year 1776 for defraying the necessary Charges of the Town.. Mr Samuel Peck is chosen Collector to geather the aforesaid Rate & also Treasurer	86
Voted that Nathaniel Cary Clark be a Grand Jury Man	86

22 Sep 1777

Capt Isaac Miles chose Moderator	87

Milford

8 Dec 1777

John Dibble Esqr have Moderator	87
Select Men { Capt Isaac Miles, Mr Nathan Baldwin, John Dibble Esqr, Capt Isaac Clark, Gideon Buckingham Esqr and Capt Lewis Mallet Junr	87
Constables { Fletcher Prudden, Nathan Fowler and Enoch Baldwin and Fletcher Prudden is also chose Collector to gather the Country Rates	88
Surveyors of Highways { Amos Baldwin Capt Arnold Tibballs, Bend^t Arnold Law, Samuel Fenn William Nott, Robert Treat, Joseph Plumb the 3^d, Fisk Peck, Jacob Hotchkiss and Archibald McNeal	88
Listers } Samuel Fenn, Isaac Botsford, Solomon Baldwin, Joseph Marshall Caleb Smith, Nathan Clark and Daniel Tolls	88
Sealer of Weights } Benjamin Bears	88
Sealer of Measures } Jonathan Marshall	88
Grand Jurymen } Jonathan Marshall, Capt Samuel Peck, John Miles, Hezekiah Smith Nathan Platt Junr and John Gibb	88
Tything Men } Barzillai Benjamins, Clement Northrop, Ashbell Baldwin David Barn and Jonathan Rogers	88
Leather Sealers } Peter Perrit, Capt Isaac Smith, and John Buckingham Junr	88
Packers } Jonathan Marshall, James Goldsmith, Job Marchant Lawrence Clinton and Isaac E Marshall	88
Guager } Mr John Herpin	88
Sexton } Moses Mallery is chosen.. to Ring the Bell on all Public Occasions for Funerals and at 9 O Clock at Night and to Sweep the Meeting Houses as often as necessary, Also to take care of the Clock that it keep Proper time for which Service he is to receave a reasonable reward	88
Committee of Inspection } Mr Jonas Wooster, Capt Samuel Treat, Doct^r Elias Carrington, Capt Arnold Tibballs, Mr Jeremiah Baldwin, Mr John Herpin & Capt Isaac Smith	88
Fence Viewers } Lieu^t John Fowler, Philo Treat Daniel Lawrence	88
Committee to Provide for Soldiers families } Mr Jonas Wooster, Mr John Herpin, Capt Jonas Green Lieu^t Saml Peck Mr Elihu Baldwin, Lieu^t Nathan Clark, Jno Merwin & Capt Saml Treat	88
Voted that George Clark and Elijah Clark be each of them entitled to ten Pounds as a gratuity for their enlisting into the Continental Service	89
Granted a Rate of Five Pence lawful Money on the Pound to be levied.. on the List for the Year 1777 for defraying the necessary Charages of the Town.. Mr Samuel Peck is Chosen Collector to gather said Rate and also Treasurer	89
Voted that Capt Benjamin Hine, Stephen Gunn and Lieu^t Benj. Fenn be a Committee to take Care of the Indians Land at Turkey Hill	89
Voted that Mr Stephen Gunn Lieu^t Nathan Clark and Mr John Herpin be a Committee to take care of the Schools & School Moneys	89

22 Dec 1777

John Dibble Esqr Moderator	89
Voted that the Town will refund the several five Pounds or.. Sums paid by the Classes last Spring to raise Men by a Tax.. Voted that Capt Lewis Mallet Junr, Gideon Buckingham, Capt Benj. Hine and Capt Arnold Tibballs be a Committee to review the accounts of the Sums paid out	89

Milford

2 Jan 1778

John Dibble Esqr chose Moderator	90

9 Feb 1778

At a Meeting warned and held.. to adjournment John Dibble Esqr in the Chair	90
Voted that Joel Northrop be a Committee Man to take care of the Soldiers Familys in Amity	90

19 Mar 1778

Ephraim Strong Esqr Chose Moderator	90
Voted That Capt Samuel Treat and Mr John Smith be a Committee to.. view the Land belonging to the School lying in Norfolke and Guilford and make Report	91

27 Apr 1778

John Dibble Esqr Moderator	91

14 Dec 1778

John Dibble Esqr chose Moderator	91
Select Men } Isaac Miles Esqr Mr Nathan Baldwin, John Dibble Esqr, Gideon Buckingham Esqr and Capt Lewis Mallett & Nathan Clark	91
Constables } Enoch Baldwin, Michael Peck, and Samuel Clark who is also chose Collector	91
Surveyors } Jeremiah Baldwin, Joseph Peck, David Bryan, Samuel Prudden Aaron Hine, Jared Burwell, Solomon Hotchkiss, Oliver Buckingham George Clark, and Thaddeus Nettleton	91

13 May 1779

John Dibble Esqr chosen Moderator	92
Select Men } Isaac Miles Esqr, Nathan Baldwin, Gideon Buckingham Lewis Mallet, Nathan Clark and Joel Northrop	92
Constables } John Smith, Michael Peck, Capt Jehiel Bryan, & Capt Enoch Baldwin	92
Surveyors } Newton Prudden, Joseph Peck, David Bryan, Samuel Stone Samuel Burwell, Moses Hine, George Clark, Thaddeus Nettleton Phin^s Tirrel, and John Newton Junr	92
Listers } Benjamen Fenn, John Herpin, Arnold Tibbells, James Cebra Enoch Woodruff, ~~Enoch Woodruff~~ and Zenos Peck	92
Sealer of Weights } Asa Gilbert	92
Sealer of Measures } Jonathan Marshall	92
Grand Jurymen } Hiel Baldwin, Nathan Bristoll, Samuel Nettlebon John Buckingham Junr William Attwater & Fisk Peck	92
Tything Men } Samuel Terrell, Arnold Tibballs, Joel Hine and Dan Fenn	92
Leather Sealers } Peter Perrit, Capt Isaac Smith, John Buckingham Ju^r	92
Packers } James Goldsmith, Job Marchant Jonathan Marshall, Isaac Eliot Marshall and Lawrence [Clin]ton	92
Gauger } Mr John Herpin	92
Sexton } Moses Mallery is chosen.. to Ring the Bell on all Public Occasions, for Funerals and at 9 O Clock at Night and to Sweep the Meeting Houses as often as necessary also to take care of the Clock that it keep proper Time	92
Fence Viewers } Fitch Weltch, John Down Junr and William Davidson	93

Milford

Committee for Soldiers Families } Joseph Platt, Stephen Gunn, Ebenezer Platt, Joshua Baldwin, Moses Northrop, George Clark, Samuel Burwell, Capt Isaac Clark Elnathan Baldwin, Thos Clark Junr Nehemiah Clark, Dea Phin[eas] Peck, Enoch Clark, David Camp. Stephen Treat, James Goldsmith and Capt Benjamin Peck	93
granted a Rate of three Shillings lawful Money on the Pound.. on the List for the Year 1779 for defraying the necessary Charges of the Town.. Mr Samuel Peck is chosen Collector to gather said Rate and also Treasurer for said Town, for which Service he is to receive three Pounds as in 1774 or an equivalent in Continential Money *28 Feb 1780*	93
Samuel Treat Esqr chosen Moderator	93
Michael Peck chose Collector in Stead of Lieu^t John Smith chose at the annuel Town meeting in Decr last and since refused to serve *6 Jan 1780*	93
Voted that Jno Powel, [ ] [ ] David Prince, Arnold Tibballs Wm Gillitt, Dani[ ] [ ], Peter Hipburn, Saml Clark, [ ] Baldwin, Enoch Northrop, [ ] Newton, Stephen Gunn, Doct^r Elias Carrington, [ ] [ ] Junr, Andrew Baldwin, Abijah Buckingham, Joel Northrup, Jacob Hotchkiss, Benjn Fenn, and Elias Clark, be inspectors of Provisions *11 May 1780*	93
Isaac Miles Esqr chose Moderator	94
the Memorial.. of the Parish of Amity and Bethany being read.. It was thereupon Voted that the Town disaproves of their being Incorporated into a Town.. and that, Isaac Miles Esqr and Capt Charles Pond be their Agents to oppose the.. said Memorial before the.. Genl Assembly *11 Jul 1780*	94
John Dibble Esqr chose Moderator *12 Jul 1780*	94
Sam^{ll} Treat Esqr chose Moderator *17 Jul 1780*	95
granted a Tax of one Penny half Penny on the Pound.. on the List for the Year 1779, for the Exigencies of the Town, Mes^{rs} John Churchill and Jehiel Bristoll chose Collectors to Collect said Tax with the encouragement of thirty shillings Lawful Money each	95
Voted That Capt Jehiel Bryan, Capt Lewis Mallet, Capt Saml Peck Capt Jonah Newton, Gideon Buckingham Esqr & Capt Charles Pond be a Committee to.. Pay six Pounds to those that have engaged for six Months and three Pounds to each Person that have engaged for three Months *12 Oct 1780*	95
Mr John Herpin chose Moderator	96
Voted That Gideon Buckingham Esqr and Capt Isaac Clark be Agents to oppose the Parishes of Amity and Bethany being Incorporated into a Town at the Genl Assembly *20 Nov 1780*	96
John Dibble Esqr chose Moderator	96
granted a Tax of six Pence halfpenny on the Pound.. on the List for the Year 1779 payable in Provisions.. said Provisions to be put up for the Use of the State.. Voted That Capt Lan^r Lawrence and John Dibble Esqr be Collectors.. and put up said Provisions	96
Voted the Select Men for the Time being, Capt Samuel Peck Capt Jehiel Bryan, Capt Samuel	97

Milford

Peck, Capt Charles Pond, Capt Samuel Sanford, Capt Enoch Woodruff, Samuel Treat Esqr, Captain Peter Perrit, and Daniel Tolls be a Committee to ascertain the Towns deficiency of the Troops in the Continental Army
11 Dec 1780

John Dible Esqr Moderator	97
Select Men } Gideon Buckingham, Lewis Mallet Junr Lieu^t Nathan Clark Capt Joel Northrup, Nathan Fowler and Fletcher Prudden	97
Constables } Michael Peck Jehiel Bryan, Capt Enoch Baldwin and Solomon Baldwin, who is also chosen Collector of the State Taxes	97
Surveyors } Lieu^t John Prudden, David Tomson Tibbals Aaron Fenn John Ford William Clark, John Bryan, Thos Beach, Josiah Perdee, Jehiel Baldwin, Judah Andruss, Zadock Sanford, and Benj Hine	97
Listers } James Cebra, Capt Enoch Woodruff, Zenos Peck John Powel Nathan Bristoll, Capt Jonah Newton, Capt Raymond Sanford	97
Sealer of Weights } Moses Mallery, Junr	97
Sealer of Measures } Jonathan Marshall	97
Grand Jurymen } Samuel Turril Junr, Arnold Tibballs Junr, Joel Hine Dan Fenn and Isaac Eliot Marshall	98
Tything Men } Joseph Pardee Joseph Platt Junr and Abel Summers	98
Leather Sealers } Peter Perrit, Capt Isaac Smith, and John Buckingham Junr	98
Packers } James Goldsmith, Job Marchant, Jonathan Marshall Isaac E Marshall and Lawrence Clinton	98
Gauger } John Herpin	98
Sexton } Samuel Plumb is chosen.. to Ring the Bell upon all public Occasions for funerals and at 9 O Clock at Night and to sweep the Meeting Houses as often as necessary also to take care of the Clock that it keep proper Time for which Service he is to receave four Pounds in Spanish Milled Dollars a^d six Shillings each or in other current Money equivalent	98
Fence Viewers } John Churchill Lieu^t John Prudden, and Nath^{ll} Cary Clark	98
Committee for Soldiers Families } Samuel Andrew, Capt Enoch Baldwin, Barzillia Benjamins Hez^h Smith, Isaac Botsford Dea^n Joseph Treat, Capt Isaac Treat, Joseph Rogers, Capt Enoch Woodruff, Lieu^t John Smith Jonathan Rogers Elias Clark, Aaron Hine William Andrew, John Ford Sam^{ll} Platt and Thos Baldwin	98

15 Dec 1780

John Dibble Esqr Moderator	98
Voted that Lieu^t John Fowler, Lieu^t John Smith Lieu^t John Smith and Capt Enoch Woodruff be a Committee to procure the Towns deficiency of Continental Troops	98

25 Dec 1780

Samuel Treat Esqr chose Moderator	99
granted a Tax of four Pence on the Pound in hard Money.. on the List for the Year 1780, for the purpose of raising the Towns deficiency of Troops in the continental Armey ~ Capt William Nott is chosen Collector	99
granted a Tax of six Pence upon the Pound in Bills of this State.. on the List for the Year 1780, for defraying incident Charges of the Town.. Lieu^t Samuel Peck is chosen Collector to gather said Rate and also Treasurer for s^d Town	99
Voted That Joseph Peck Amos Baldwin, and Capt Raymond Sanford be added to the	100

Milford

Committee for supplying the Soldiers Families

15 Jan 1781

John Dibble Esqr chosen Moderator	100
Capt Jonas Green is chosen Collector to gather the Tax of four Pence hard Money upon the Pound in the roome of Capt William Nott	100
granted a Tax of one penny halfpenny on the Pound.. on the List for the Year 1779 to be paid in Flower and Indian Corn at the Prices affixed by the Gen^{ll} Assembly.. said Indian Corn and Flower to be Collected and put up for the Use of the State.. Voted that Capt Daniel Lawrence and Solomon Hotchkiss be Collectors to Collect receive and put up said Indian Corn and Flour as the Law directs	100

5 Feb 1781

Samuel Treat Esqr Moderator	100
Voted That Lieu^t John Fowler Capt Enoch Baldwin & M^r Wm Attwater be a Committee to Inspect the Accounts of the Select Men	101

19 Feb 1781

Samuel Treat Esqr Moderator	101

10 Dec 1781

Samuel Treat Esqr chose Moderator	102
Select Men } Messrs Gideon Buckingham, Nathan Clark Nathan Fowler, Fletcher Prudden, William Attwater, & Jacob Hotchkiss	102
Constables } Michael Peck, Jehiel Bryan, Enoch Baldwin & Jeremiah Baldwin who is also chosen Collector of State Taxes	102
Surveyors } Capt John Smith, Aaron Fenn, Ephraim Buckingham Sam^{ll} Ford, Jonathan Clark, Nathan Bristoll, Benjamin Platt, Iaac Platt, Benjamin Clark, Thaddeus Nettleton, James Goldsmith Richard Baldwin, & Joel Hine of Bethany	102
Listers } Nathan Bristoll, Capt Jonah Newton, Raymond Sanford Moses Hine, William Davidson, Newton Prudden, Elias Clark & David Botsford	102
Sealer of Weights } Moses Mallery Junr	102
Sealer of Measures } Jonathan Marshall	102
Grand Jurymen } Joseph Perdee, Joseph Platt Junr Abel Summers, Moses Northrop and George Clark	102

24 Dec 1781

Samuel Treat Esqr Moderator	102
Tything Men } Andrew Beard, Zachariah Pond, Jeremiah Bull, & Dan^{ll} Munson	102
Leather Sealers } Capt Isaac Smith, John Buckingham Junr & John Churchill	103
Packers } James Goldsmith, Job Marchant, Jonath^n Marshall & Lawrence Clinton	103
Gauger } John Herpin	103
Sexton } Samuel Plumb is chosen.. to Ring the Bell upon all public Occasions, for funerals and at 9 O Clock at Night, and to sweep the meeting Houses, as often as necessary, also to take care of the Clock. that it keep proper Time for which service he is to receive four Pounds	103
Committee for Soldiers Families } Benjamin Clark, David Botsford Theophilus Miles, Capt Enoch Wodruff, Stephen Gunn, Samuel Buckingham Clark Aaron Fenn, John Hine Junr, Jeremiah Baldwin, Donald Treat, Joseph Plumb Junr Jared Clark Miles Merwin, Sam^{ll} Clark.	103

Milford

John Newton William Clark, Isaac Platt, Hezekiah Smith, Jonathan Fowler, Sam[ll] Stone, and John Fenn	
Newton Prudden chose Collector of State Taxes in stead of Jeremiah Baldwin excused	103
Treasurer } Lieu[t] Samuel Peck	103

8 Apr 1782

Samuel Treat Esq[r] chosen Moderator	103
Voted that the Towns deficiences of Troops be raised by a Tax for one Year -- granted a Tax of one Penney lawful Money upon the Pound upo the List for the Year 1781.. for the Purporse of raising Men.. Lieu[t] James Thomson chosen Collector	104

9 Dec 1782

Stephen Gunn Esq[r] chosen Moderator	104
Select Men } Gideon Buckingham Esq[r] Cap[t] Nathan Clark, Mess[rs] Fletcher Prudden William Attwater, Nathan Fowler and Jacob Hotchkiss	104
Constables } Michael Peck, Jehiel Bryan & Collector of State Taxes Enoch Baldwin and Daniel Tolls	104
Surveyors } Daniel Munson, Aaron Fenn, Joseph Platt Sam[ll] Ford David Miles Moses Mallery Jun[r] Sam[ll] Clark Benjamin Clark, Nathaniel Smith Jun[r] Nathan Prince & Lamberton Smith	104
Listers } Moses Hine, William Davaidson, Newton Prudden Elias Clark, David Botsford Jun[r] Jeremiah Bull & James Wheeler	104
Sealer of Weights } Moses Mallery Jun[r]	104
Sealer of Measures } Jonathan Marshall	104
Grand Jurymen } William Smith, Thaddeus Nettleton John Buckingham Jun[r] Landee Beech, Enoch Clark John Powel, Enoch Clark the 2[d] and Solomon Hotchkiss	104
Tything Men } Edward Baldwin, Ephraim Strong Jun[r] and Newton John Morris	104
Leather Sealers } Cap[t] Isaac Smith, John Buckingham Jun[r] & Jn[o] Churchill	105
Packers } James Goldsmith, Job Marchant Jonathan Marshall and Rich[d] Sperry	105
Gauger } John Herpin	105
Fence Viewers } Joseph Platt Jun[r] Aaron Fenn and Richard Platt	105
Sexton Samuel Plumb is chosen.. to ring the Bell upon all public occasions for funerals & at 9 O clock at Night to Sweep the Meeting Houses as often as necessary, Also to take care of the Clock that it keep proper time, for which service he is to receive four Pounds lawful Money	105
Granted that the Parish of Bethany have liberty to.. set up a Pound.. at their own expence and that Cap[t] Raymond Sanford be key keeper of the same	105

13 Jan 1783

Stephen Gunn Esq[r] Moderator	105
M[r] Fletcher Prudden chose Clerk	105
Voted to pay some part of the Debt of Isaac Miles Esq[r] Decsd.. granted a Tax of two pence on the pound upon the List for the Year 1782.. for that purpose	105
M[r] Joseph Peck chose Collector to Collect said Rate	105
Voted That.. the Rate to be Collected by Lieu[t] James Thomson is to Collect be appropriated for the expences & charge of the Town	106

Milford

10 Feb 1783

Stephen Gunn Esq[r] Moderator	106
Gideon Buckingham chose Clerk	106
The following Persons chose a Committee to supply the Soldiers Families.. (viz) Joseph Platt Jun[r] Matthew Woodruff, Samuel Clark, Sam[ll] Stone Elias Camp, Hezekiah Smith Andrew Clark W[m] Clark, Joseph Buckingham, Israel Nettleton, Benedict Law Jn[o] Fenn, Nathaniel Camp, Josiah Camp, Newton J[ ] Morris, Joseph Treat, Joel Smith, Samuel Nettleton	106
Voted That the Select Men pay Samuel W[ ] the sum of five Pounds.. as a Bounty for inlisting in to the Continental Army	106
Voted That the Monies that shall.. arise for the rent of the Ferry shall be appropriated for the payment of the Debts due to the Estate of Isaac Miles Esq[r] Decsd untill the Debts with the addition of two penney Tax already appropriated.. shall be paid	106

10 Mar 1782

Stephen Gunn Esq[r] Moderator	106

17 Mar 1783

Samuel Treat Esq[r] Moderator	106
Lieu[t] James Thomson chose Collector to gather the Tax of 2[d] on the pound.. In Sted of Joseph Peck excused	106
Voted That Thaddeus Nettleton, Lieu[t] Samuel Peck, Abel Northrup and James Goldsmith to take proper measures for the Preservation of the Clams & Oysters in s[d] Town	106
William Attwater chosen Treasurer	106

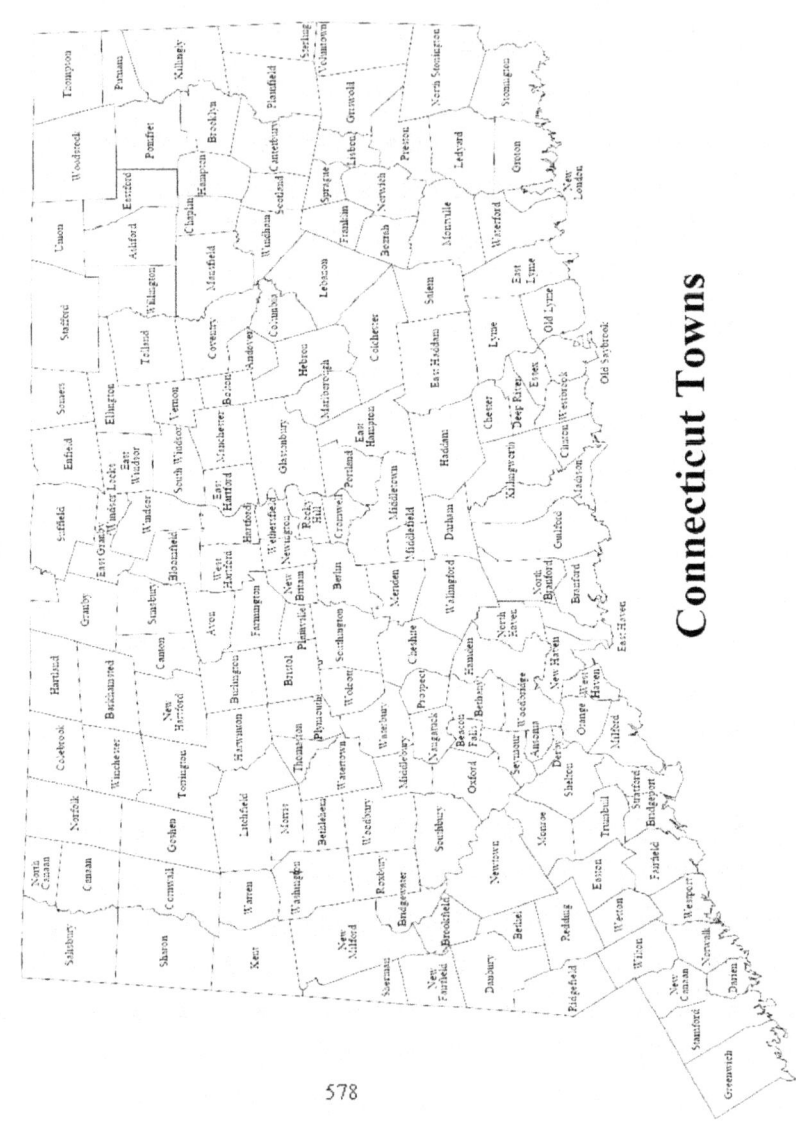

Parent Towns

Town	County	Est.	Parent Town(s)
Andover	Tolland	1848	Coventry, Hebron
Ansonia	New Haven	1889	Derby
Ashford	Windham	1714	
Avon	Hartford	1830	Farmington
Barkhamsted	Litchfield	1779	
Beacon Falls	New Haven	1871	Bethany, Naugatuck, Oxford, Seymour
Berlin	Hartford	1785	Farmington, Middletown, Wethersfield
Bethany	New Haven	1832	Woodbridge
Bethel	Fairfield	1855	Danbury
Bethlehem	Litchfield	1787	Woodbury
Bloomfield	Hartford	1835	Farmington, Simsbury, Windsor
Bolton	Tolland	1720	
Bozrah	New London	1786	Norwich
Branford	New Haven	1685	
Bridgeport	Fairfield	1821	Fairfield, Stratford
Bridgewater	Litchfield	1856	New Milford
Bristol	Hartford	1785	Farmington
Brookfield	Fairfield	1788	Danbury, New Milford, Newtown
Brooklyn	Windham	1786	Canterbury, Pomfret
Burlington	Hartford	1806	Bristol
Canaan	Litchfield	1739	
Canterbury	Windham	1703	
Canton	Hartford	1806	Simsbury
Chaplin	Windham	1822	Hampton, Mansfield, Windham
Chatham	Middlesex	1767	Middletown renamed "East Hampton" in 1915
Cheshire	New Haven	1780	Wallingford
Chester	Middlesex	1836	Saybrook
Clinton	Middlesex	1838	Killingworth
Colchester	New London	1698	
Colebrook	Litchfield	1779	
Columbia	Tolland	1804	Lebanon
Cornwall	Litchfield	1740	
Coventry	Tolland	1712	
Cromwell	Middlesex	1851	Middletown
Danbury	Fairfield	1687	
Darien	Fairfield	1820	Stamford
Deep River	Middlesex	1635	*See Saybrook.*
Derby	New Haven	1675	

Durham	Middlesex	1708	
East Granby	Hartford	1858	Granby, Windsor Locks
East Haddam	Middlesex	1734	
East Hampton	Middlesex	1767	*See Chatham.*
East Hartford	Hartford	1783	Hartford
East Haven	New Haven	1785	New Haven
East Lyme	New London	1839	Lyme, Waterford
East Windsor	Hartford	1768	Windsor
Eastford	Windham	1847	Ashford
Easton	Fairfield	1845	Weston
Ellington	Tolland	1786	East Windsor
Enfield	Hartford	1683	
Essex	Middlesex	1852	Saybrook
Fairfield	Fairfield	1639	
Farmington	Hartford	1645	
Franklin	New London	1786	Norwich
Glastonbury	Hartford	1690	
Goshen	Litchfield	1739	
Granby	Hartford	1786	Simsbury
Greenwich	Fairfield	1665	
Griswold	New London	1815	Preston
Groton	New London	1705	
Guilford	New Haven	1643	
Haddam	Middlesex	1668	
Hamden	New Haven	1786	New Haven
Hampton	Windham	1786	Brooklyn, Canterbury, Pomfret, Windham
Hartford	Hartford	1635	
Hartland	Hartford	1761	
Harwinton	Litchfield	1737	
Hebron	Tolland	1708	
Kent	Litchfield	1739	
Killingly	Windham	1708	
Killingworth	Middlesex	1667	
Lebanon	New London	1700	
Ledyard	New London	1836	Groton
Lisbon	New London	1786	Norwich
Litchfield	Litchfield	1719	
Lyme	New London	1667	
Madison	New Haven	1826	Guilford
Manchester	Hartford	1823	East Hartford
Mansfield	Tolland	1702	
Marlborough	Hartford	1803	Colchester, Glastonbury, Hebron
Meriden	New Haven	1806	Wallingford

Middlebury	New Haven	1807	Waterbury, Woodbury, Southbury
Middlefield	Middlesex	1866	Middletown
Middletown	Middlesex	1651	
Milford	New Haven	1639	
Monroe	Fairfield	1823	Stratford
Montville	New London	1786	New London
Morris	Litchfield	1859	Litchfield
Naugatuck	New Haven	1844	Bethany, Oxford, Waterbury
New Britain	Hartford	1850	Berlin
New Canaan	Fairfield	1801	Norwalk, Stamford
New Fairfield	Fairfield	1740	
New Hartford	Litchfield	1738	
New Haven	New Haven	1638	
New London	New London	1646	
New Milford	Litchfield	1712	
Newington	Hartford	1871	Wethersfield
Newtown	Fairfield	1711	
Norwalk	Litchfield	1758	
North Branford	New Haven	1831	Branford
North Canaan	Litchfield	1858	Canaan
North Haven	New Haven	1786	New Haven
North Stonington	New London	1807	Stonington
Norwalk	Fairfield	1651	
Norwich	New London	1662	
Old Lyme	New London	1855	Saybrook
Old Saybrook	Middlesex	1854	Saybrook
Orange	New Haven	1822	Milford, New Haven
Oxford	New Haven	1798	Derby, Southbury
Plainfield	Windham	1699	
Plainville	Hartford	1869	Farmington
Plymouth	Litchfield	1795	Watertown
Pomfret	Windham	1713	
Portland	Middlesex	1841	Chatham
Preston	New London	1687	
Prospect	New Haven	1827	Cheshire, Waterbury
Putnam	Windham	1855	Killingly, Pomfret, Thompson
Redding	Fairfield	1767	
Ridgefield	Fairfield	1709	
Rocky Hill	Hartford	1843	Wethersfield
Roxbury	Litchfield	1796	Woodbury
Salem	New London	1819	Colchester, Lyme, Montville
Salisbury	Litchfield	1741	
Saybrook	Middlesex	1635	remained "Deep River" in 1947
Scotland	Windham	1857	Windham

Seymour	New Haven	1850	Derby
Sharon	Litchfield	1739	
Shelton	Fairfield	1789	Stratford
Sherman	Fairfield	1802	New Fairfield
Simsbury	Hartford	1670	
Somers	Tolland	1734	
South Windsor	Hartford	1845	East Windsor
Southbury	New Haven	1787	Woodbury
Southington	Hartford	1779	Farmington
Sprague	New London	1861	Franklin, Lisbon
Stafford	Tolland	1719	
Stamford	Fairfield	1641	
Sterling	Windham	1794	Voluntown
Stonington	New London	1662	
Stratford	Fairfield	1639	
Suffield	Hartford	1674	
Thomaston	Litchfield	1875	Plymouth
Thompson	Windham	1785	Killingly
Tolland	Tolland	1715	
Torrington	Litchfield	1740	
Trumbull	Fairfield	1797	Stratford
Union	Tolland	1734	
Vernon	Tolland	1808	Bolton
Voluntown	New London	1721	
Wallingford	New Haven	1670	
Warren	Litchfield	1786	Kent
Washington	Litchfield	1779	Kent, Litchfield, New Milford, Woodbury
Waterbury	New Haven	1686	
Waterford	New London	1801	New London
Watertown	Litchfield	1780	Waterbury
West Hartford	Hartford	1854	Hartford
West Haven	New Haven	1921	Orange
Westbrook	Middlesex	1840	Saybrook
Weston	Fairfield	1787	Fairfield
Westport	Fairfield	1835	Fairfield, Norwalk, Weston
Wethersfield	Hartford	1634	
Willington	Tolland	1727	
Wilton	Fairfield	1802	Norwalk
Winchester	Litchfield	1771	
Windham	Windham	1692	
Windsor	Hartford	1633	
Windsor Locks	Hartford	1854	Windsor
Wolcott	New Haven	1796	Southington, Waterbury

Woodbridge	New Haven	1784	Milford, New Haven
Woodbury	Litchfield	1673	
Woodstock	Windham	1690	

INDEX

Name	Index Page	Name	Index Page
[ ], Ebenezr Junr	GROT ([4])	[ ], Uriah	HARL (48)
[ ]nor, John	EWIN (10)	[ ], Wait	GOSH (112)
[ ]ry, Benjamin N	EWIN (8)	[ ], William	CANA (64, 28)
[ ], Aaron	CANA (64), HADD (113), HEBR (236)	[ ], Willm Ensn	FARM (8)
		[ ]d, Jeremiah	CHES (14)
[ ], Abell	FARM (9)	[ ]ford, [ ]	HEBR (236)
[ ], Abijah	FARM (455), MIDD (356)	[ ]helps, [ ]	HEBR (236)
		[ ]hine, Benjamin Capt	HARL (47)
[ ], Asa	HEBR (235, 236)	[ ]ins, Jehel	KILH (47)
[ ], August	CANA (64)	[ ]lds, Saml	KILH (47)
[ ], Bartholomew	CANA (64)	[ ]ler, Abel	LITC (142)
[ ], Benajah	CANA (64)	[ ]man, Elisha	CANA (77)
[ ], Benja[ ]	HEBR (235)	[ ]ns, Thomas	HARL (47)
[ ], Benjamin	DERB (167)	[ ]on, Abner	KILH (145)
[ ], Brant	KILY (95a)	[ ]rns, Aaron	CANA (12)
[ ], Bria[ ]	KILY (88)	[ ]stle, [ ]	HARW (2)
[ ], Briant	KILY (89a)	[ ]ther, Saml	KILH (51, 43, 145)
[ ], Chauncey	MIDD (356)	[ ]tlief, John	HADD (121)
[ ], Daniel	CANA (77), ENFD (35), MIDD (350)	[ ]ton, Sol	HEBR (217)
		[ ]ugg, William	CANA (12)
[ ], Daniel Capt	HEBR (247)	[ ]vens, [ ] 2d	HARW (2)
[ ], Ebenezer	GLAS (98), HARL (48)	[ ]eil[ ], Amos Junr	CANA (64)
[ ], Edwar	DERB (168)	[Smith], Bill	MIDD (362)
[ ], Edward	FARM (449)	Abbe, John Junr	ENFD (34)
[ ], Elihu	HEBR (219, 236)	Abbe, Daniel	ENFD (26, 35)
[ ], Elijah	FARM (456), HEBR (234), MIDD (351)	Abbe, Elijah	MANS (338)
		Abbe, Gideon	MANS (338)
[ ], Eliphalet	GLAS (99)	Abbe, John 2d	ENFD (30, 32)
[ ], Gaven	ASHF (232)	Abbe, Jonathan	ASHF (310)
[ ], George	KILH (46)	Abbe, Liut	ENFD (26)
[ ], Gideon	FARM (444), KILH (145)	Abbe, Nehemiah	HARF (273)
[ ], Gilbert	HEBR (235)	Abbe, Richard	ENFD (26)
[ ], James	FARM (9)	Abbe, Richard Capt	ENFD (30)
[ ], Jerediah	CANA (64)	Abbe, Shubael	MANS (265)
[ ], Jeremiah	HARL (54)	Abbe, William	MANS (338)
[ ], Joel	HARW (3)	Abbee, Nehemiah	HARF (253, 255A, 256, 263, 267, 281),
[ ], John	ASHF (231)		
[ ], John [ ]	CANA (77)	Abbee, Stephen	HARF (275)
[ ], John Capt	HEBR (236)	Abbee, Stephen Junr	HARF (287)
[ ], Jonah	HARL (59), HEBR (234)	Abbot, Abel	CORN (17, 23, 87, 91)
[ ], Jonathan	MIDD (351)	Abbot, Daniel	CORN (16, 87)
[ ], Jonathan Jur	HEBR (216)	Abbot, Jno	ASHF (213)
[ ], Joseph	HEBR (235), KENT (D1)	Abbot, John	MIDD (357)
[ ], Juday	FARM (449)	Abbot, Wm	ASHF (214)
[ ], Junr	ENFD (28)	Abbott, Abel	CORN (10)
[ ], Lazarus	GOSH (184)	Abbott, Abiel	EWIN (1315, 85, 88)
[ ], Lemmuel	CANA (64)	Abbott, Daniel	CORN (9, 10, 12, 86)
[ ], Malachi Lt	HEBR (235)	Abbott, John	ASHF (310, 311)
[ ], Phinehas	CANA (12)	Abbott, Nathan	CORN (89, 90)
[ ], Reuben	FARM (436)	Abbott, Saml	ASHF (310)
[ ], Saml	FARM (456), HADD (148), HEBR (236)	Abbott, Sele	CORN (9, 12, 86)
		Abbott, Wm	ASHF (308, 311)
[ ], Samuel Jur	CHES (14)	Abby, Benjamin	CHAT (51, 55)
[ ], Seth	GOSH (121)	Abby, Saml	CHAT (32)
[ ], Silas	DANB (39)	Abby, Saml Ensn	CHAT (45, 50, 58, 64, 68
[ ], Solomon Lt	HEBR (216)	Abby, Thos	CHAT (55)
[ ], Stephen	FARM (445), HEBR (236)	Abel, Caleb	LEBA (297, 299)
		Abel, Caleb Jur	LEBA (299, 343)
[ ], Stephen Capt	HEBR (235)	Abel, Caleb Senr	LEBA (315)
[ ], Timothy	FARM (8)	Abel, Danl	LEBA (296)

INDEX

Name	Index Page
Abel, Danl Cap	LEBA (310)
Abel, Danl Jur	LEBA (299, 315, 326, 333)
Abel, Danl Jur Cap	LEBA (325, 341)
Abel, Elij	LEBA (326)
Abel, Elijah	CHAT (33), FAIR (253, 257, 258, 260, 269)
Abel, Elijah Colo	FAIR (253)
Abel, Elijah Major	FAIR (254, 255, 256, 257, 258, 259, 260, 263, 264)
Abel, Elipt	LEBA (296)
Abel, Jona	LEBA (326, 342)
Abel, Simon	LEBA (315, 334, 342)
Abel, Simon Ens	LEBA (320)
Abel, Solo	LEBA (296)
Abel, Solo Jur	LEBA (315, 326, 328, 329)
Abell, Abijah	FAIR (267)
Abell, Elijah	FAIR (262, 267)
Abell, Elijah Capt	FAIR (266, 267)
Abell, Elijah Major	FAIR (261)
Abernatha, Samuel	CHES (11, 14)
Abernethy, Doctr	HARW (21)
Abernethy, William	HARW (9, 11, 13, 16, 17, 18, 19, 21, 24, 25, 523)
Abernethy, William Doctr	HARW (12, 24, 25)
Abernethy, Wm	HARW (5, 7, 22, 23)
Abernethy, Wm Doctr	HARW (3, 4, 15)
Acerly, Nathaniel	GREE (123)
Ackeley, John	HEBR (236)
Ackley, Abraham	EHAD (59, 84)
Ackley, Amasa	EHAD (54, 64)
Ackley, Benjamin	KENT C544, C546,D5, D7, D10, E59, E63)
Ackley, Benjn	KENT (C543)
Ackley, Elijah	EHAD (80)
Ackley, Elijah 2d	EHAD (79)
Ackley, Elijah 2nd	EHAD (64)
Ackley, Ephraim	EHAD (54, 65, 86)
Ackley, Ezra	CHAT (54, 58)
Ackley, Isaac	EHAD (65, 69, 80, 87)
Ackley, Isaac C	EHAD (87)
Ackley, Joel	HARL (44, 47, 50, 51, 52)
Ackley, Joseph	EHAD (69)
Ackley, Nathaniel 3d	EHAD (64, 69)
Ackley, Saml	CHAT (59, 39)
Ackley, Samuel	CHAT (40)
Ackley, Simeon	EHAD (69)
Ackley, Simeon 2d	EHAD (65)
Ackley, Stephen	CHAT (54)
Ackley, Thomas	CHAT (42)
Ackly, Ephraim	EHAD (46)
Ackly, Joel Ens	HARL (60)
Acly, James	CHAT (40, 50)
Acley, James Jur	CHAT (37)
Acley, Saml	CHAT (51)
Acley, Samuel	CHAT (30, 50)
Acley, Thomas	CHAT (45, 51)

Name	Index Page
Acly, Oliver	CHAT (62)
Acly, Thomas	CHAT (66, 67)
Adams, [ ]	CANT (160)
Adams, Andrew	LITC (128, 134, 135, 137, 156)
Adams, Andrew Col	LITC (144, 148)
Adams, Andrew Major	LITC (137, 140)
Adams, Benjamin	COLC (243)
Adams, Col[ ][ ]	CANT (150)
Adams, Col	LITC (156)
Adams, Cornelius	CANT (171, 178)
Adams, Daniel	HARL (47, 52)
Adams, David	FAIR (256, 265, 267)
Adams, Ebenr	CANT (180)
Adams, Eliashib	CANT (138, 139, 146, 147, 154, 155, 158, 160, 162, 164), 165, 172, 176, 177, 180)
Adams, Elis	CANT (150)
Adams, James	CANT (146)
Adams, Jno Bradford	CANT (180)
Adams, John	CANT (146, 151, 163, 166, 168, 179, 180, 182), KILY (86a)
Adams, John B	CANT (156)
Adams, John Jr	CANT (144, 147)
Adams, John Jur	CANT (156, 160)
Adams, John Lieut	CANT (150, 151)
Adams, Jos Jr	CANT (144, 146)
Adams, Jos Lieut	CANT (150)
Adams, Joseph	CANT (181), KILY (8, 19, 88)
Adams, Joshua	FAIR (255)
Adams, Levi	CANT (161, 168)
Adams, Mehatible	KILY (29)
Adams, Michall	KILY (86a)
Adams, Nathan	CANT (178), FAIR (253, 256, 258)
Adams, Nathan Jur	FAIR (259, 262)
Adams, Nehem	CANT (144)
Adams, Nehemiah	CANT (160, 168)
Adams, Saml	CANT (178, 181), FARM (449, 455)
Adams, Saml 4th	CANT (153)
Adams, Saml Jr	CANT (168, 176, 177, 180)
Adams, Solomon	CANT (176, 180)
Adams, Squier	FAIR (253, 255)
Adams, Thomas	CANT (140, 143, 144, 156, 161, 162)
Adams, Thos	CANT (148)
Adams, Timo	CANT (146)
Adams, William	HARF (281, 287)
Adams, William 2d	HARF (292)
Addams, Daniel	HARL (44)
Addams, Darius	CHAT (37, 45)
Adkins, Daniel	HARL (47), MIDD (363)
Adkins, Danl	MIDD (377)

INDEX

Name	Index Page	Name	Index Page
Adkins, David	MIDD (358, 359, 362, 365, 370, 381, 394, 396, 405, 406, 415)	Alford, Wm	HARW (22)
		Algar, Ashbel	GLAS (94)
		Alger, Simeon	GLAS (114)
Adkins, David Lt	MIDD (398)	Algor, Ashbel	GLAS (66, 70)
Adkins, Elisha	MIDD (376)	Alin, Nathl	HARL (53)
Adkins, Ethimar	MIDD (362)	Alin, Titus	HARL (53)
Adkins, George	MIDD (364, 366, 394, 406)	Alin, Titus Jur	HARL (53)
		Allcox, Jesse	FARM (455)
Adkins, Hezah	HARL (49)	Allen, Asher	MANS (340, 358)
Adkins, Hezekiah	HARL (43, 45, 48, 53, 61)	Allen, Barnabas	CANT (156)
		Allen, Cady	MANS (324)
Adkins, Ithamar	MIDD (382, 394, 415)	Allen, Caleb	KILY (7, 19)
Adkins, Jabez	HARL (45)	Allen, Capt	ASHF (229)
Adkins, James	MIDD (362, 366)	Allen, Cary	MANS (278)
Adkins, Joel	MIDD (342, 345, 346, 347, 349, 350, 354, 356, 362, 375, 377, 379, 393, 403, 412)	Allen, Cornelius	LITC (135)
		Allen, Daniel	ASHF (203)
		Allen, Daniel Capt	ASHF (227)
		Allen, Danl	FARM (443)
Adkins, John	MIDD (364)	Allen, Danl Capt	ASHF (238)
Adkins, Josiah	HARL (55, 56, 59)	Allen, Danl Jur	ASHF (209)
Adkins, Josiah [ ]	HARL (54)	Allen, David	ASHF (232, 308, 310, 312), CHAT (59), EWIN (13), FAIR (252, 253, 254, 255, 256, 257, 258, 259, 262, 263, 267, 358)
Adkins, Saml	MIDD (373)		
Adkins, Saml Junr	MIDD (376)		
Adkins, Samuel	MIDD (367)		
Adkins, Samuel Junr	MIDD (346, 378, 382)		
Adkins, Solo	MIDD (372)	Allen, David Jur	FAIR (265, 265)
Adkins, Solomon	MIDD (346, 349, 357, 358, 371, 381, 382)	Allen, Ebenezer	MANS (280, 281, 328)
		Allen, Ebenr	MIDD (362)
Adkins, Thos	MIDD (367)	Allen, Edward	CORN (26)
Adkins, Thos Junr	GUIL (270, 274, 288)	Allen, Edward Col	MILF (78, 85, 86)
Agard, Hezekiah	LITC (158)	Allen, Elijah	CORN (12, 18, 24, 25)
Agard, Joseph	LITC (131)	Allen, Gideon	KILH (47)
Agard, Judah	MANS (279)	Allen, Hez	MANS (277, 350, 262)
Agard, Noah	LITC (153)	Allen, Hezh	MANS (328)
Ainsworth, Ebenezer	COVE (314)	Allen, Hezi	EWIN (13)
Ainsworth, John	COVE (168, 314)	Allen, James Junr	MANS (268)
Aken, Saml Ensn	CHAT (42)	Allen, Joel	FARM (444)
Aken, Saml Lt	CHAT (60)	Allen, John	FAIR (269)
Aken, Thomas Jur	CHAT (59)	Allen, John Doctr	FAIR (262, 264, 266, 267)
Akins, Andw	DANB (63)		
Akley, Benjamin	KENT (C547)	Allen, John Jur	FAIR (267)
Albertson, John [P]	EHAD (79)	Allen, Jona	MIDD (367)
Alcox, Jesse	FARM (433, 438, 444, 449)	Allen, Jonathan	MIDD (382)
		Allen, Moses	ENFD (25, 26 28, 29, 30, 32, 34, 35)
Alden, Amos	ENFD (28, 32, 34)		
Alden, Andw Senr	LEBA (298)	Allen, Noah	EWIN (13)
Alden, Danl	LEBA (327)	Allen, Phineas	MANS (262, 267, 268, 271)
Alden, Jno	LEBA (311)		
Alden, Jno Lt	LEBA (320)	Allen, Phinehas	MANS (273)
Alden, John	LEBA (316, 318)	Allen, Rowland	MIDD (381)
Alden, Lyda	LEBA (299)	Allen, Saml	ASHF (206, 308, 310), DERB (122), LEBA (299)
Alden, Walker	LEBA (316, 342)		
Alden, Walter	LEBA (327, 334)		
Alford, [ ]	HARW (2)	Allen, Saml Jur	LEBA (326)
Alford, Alexander	HARW (523)	Allen, Samuel	ASHF (204), DERB (120)
Alford, Alexdr	HARW (14)	Allen, Seth	MANS (328)
Alford, Eliphalet	HARW (2, 3)	Allen, Silas	CANT (150)
Alford, Job	HARW (13)	Allen, Silas Doct	CANT (177)
Alford, John	HARW (534, 523)	Allen, Theophilus	LITC (158)
Alford, William	HARW (2)	Allen, Thomas	KILY (28)

INDEX

Name	Index Page
Allen, Timo	LEBA (315, 326)
Allen, Titus	HARL (45, 51)
Allen, Titus Jur	HARL (48)
Allen, Zach	EWIN (13)
Alley, Amous	GROT ([15])
Allin, [ ]	MIDD (358, 395)
Allin, [ ]on	HARW (2)
Allin, A	GLAS (99)
Allin, Danl	FARM (447, 456)
Allin, David	EWIN (12, 15, 85, 89)
Allin, Ebenezar	CANA (27)
Allin, Ebenezer	EWIN (85, 88)
Allin, Ebenr	CANA (17, 64), FARM (456)
Allin, Hez	EWIN (89)
Allin, Hezekiah	EWIN (10, 12, 13, 85)
Allin, John	HARW (5)
Allin, Joseph	EWIN (10, 12, 14, 15, 17, 85, 88)
Allin, Joseph Jur	EWIN (8, 9)
Allin, Nathaniel	EWIN (85, 89), HARL (48)
Allin, Noah	EWIN (12, 15, 17, 85, 88)
Allin, Rowland	MIDD (382, 394)
Allin, Samuel	COVE (170), EWIN (8, 12, 15, 85, 89)
Allin, Thomas	MIDD (346, 349, 353, 355)
Allin, Titus jur	HARL (45)
Allin, Zach	EWIN (14)
Allin, Zachariah	EWIN (11, 12, 13, 85, 88)
Allis, David	BOLT (146, 148, 149, 151, 152, 153, 154, 155, 156, 157, 158, 159, 160, 163, 165, 166, 167, 168, 180, 182)
Allis, Nathl	GUIL (271, 275, 277, 286, 287, 288, 295, 300, 301, 304, 311, 314, 324, 327, 334)
Allis, Nathl Junr	GUIL (316, 317, 321, 323, 335)
Ally, James Junr	GROT [6]
Allyn, Amos	GROT ([4], [6], [9], [12], [18], [19])
Allyn, Barnabas	CANT (157)
Allyn, Chris	GROT ([4])
Allyn, Ephraim	GROT ([23])
Allyn, Epraim	GROT ([23])
Allyn, James	GROT ([25])
Allyn, John	FARM (6, 8, 430, 442, 446)
Allyn, John Capt	FARM (23, 442, 450, 452, 454)
Allyn, John Ct	FARM (445)
Allyn, Jos	GROT ([25])
Allyn, Joseph	GROT ([4], [12], [13], [18], [23])
Allyn, Nathan 2d	GROT ([6], [12], [18], [25])
Allyn, Nathnl	HARL (51)

Name	Index Page
Allyn, Robert	GROT ([4], [24])
Allyn, Robert Lieut	GROT ([11], [14], [17], [18], [22], [23], [24])
Allyn, Rufus	GROT ([4])
Allyn, Samuel	GROT ([6], [8], [9], [12])
Allyn, Samuel Leut	GROT ([15])
Allyn, Simeon	GROT ([9], [16])
Allyn, Simeon Capt	GROT ([15])
Allyn, Thomas	GROT ([25]), KILY (23, 24)
Allyn, Thos	GROT ([15]), KILY (33)
Allyn, Titus	GOSH (183)
Allyn, Titus Junr	HARL (55)
Allyn, Tryal	GROT ([9])
Alsop, [ ]	MIDD (397)
Alsop, John	MIDD (364)
Alsop, Mary	MIDD (396)
Alton, David	KILY (26)
Alton, John	KILY (31)
Alvard, Daniel	MIDD (406)
Alvard, Danl	MIDD (368, 371, 416)
Alverd, Asahel	CORN (90)
Alvord Seth	CHAT (44)
Alvord, [ ]	GOSH (112)
Alvord, Asahel	CORN (9, 12)
Alvord, Daniel	MIDD (345, 359, 409)
Alvord, Danl	MIDD (382, 395)
Alvord, Oren	CHAT (43, 44, 45)
Alvord, Ruel	CHAT (54)
Alvord, Saul	BOLT (146, 148, 149, 151, 152, 153, 154, 155, 156, 157, 158, 160, 163, 164, 165, 167, 180, 182)
Alvord, Saul Jur	BOLT (155, 157, 160, 161, 164, 165, 166, 167, 181, 182)
Amadown, Joseph	ASHF (218)
Ames, Anthony	MIDD (363)
Ames, Benjn	DURH (19)
Ames, Daniel	FARM (5)
Ames, James	FARM (17)
Ames, Joseph	MANS (233)
Ames, Nicholas	CHAT (34, 38, 39, 40, 43, 44, 51, 59), 62, 67)
Amidown, Joseph	ASHF (310)
Ammedown, Harring	ASHF (204)
Anable, Anslem	HEBR (234, 236)
Anable, Anstem	HEBR (220)
Anderson, Isaac	GREE (128)
Anderson, Saml	KILY (23, 32, 33)
Anderson, Serjt	GLAS (69)
Andrew, Jonathan	MILF (78, 82, 86)
Andrew, Saml	HARL (46)
Andrew, Samuel	MILF (98)
Andrew, William	MILF (98)
Andrewes, Asa	HARL (61)
Andrewes, Asael	EHAD (59, 65, 86)
Andrewes, Joseph	EHAD (59, 80, 84, 85)
Andrews, John Jur	DANB (51)
Andrews, [ ]	HARL (47)

INDEX

Name	Index Page	Name	Index Page
Andrews, Abraham	FAIR (261)	Andrus, Josiah	FARM (449, 443)
Andrews, Asael	EHAD (44)	Andrus, Josiah 2d	FARM (456)
Andrews, Asahel	CHES (11)	Andrus, Josiah Jur	FARM (433, 438, 444)
Andrews, Benja	FARM (28)	Andrus, Leml	FARM (456)
Andrews, Benjamin	GLAS (78, 80), 94)	Andrus, Lemuel	FARM (2, 9, 16, 18, 29, 438)
Andrews, Charles	GLAS (94)		
Andrews, Charles Jur	GLAS (78, 83, 94, 104)	Andrus, Levi	FARM (2, 9, 17, 29, 443, 444)
Andrews, Daniel	FAIR (264, 267, 269), GLAS (93)	Andrus, Livi	FARM (449)
Andrews, Daniel Jur	FAIR (252, 253)	Andrus, Miles	FARM (455)
Andrews, Danl	FAIR (265, 259)	Andrus, Moses	FARM (434, 442, 445, 446)
Andrews, Danl Jur	FAIR (254), 255, 262)		
Andrews, Eli	HARL (52, 56)	Andrus, Noah	FARM (441, 455, 456)
Andrews, Ely	HARL (44, 46, 47, 50, 51, 53)	Andrus, Obad Capt	FARM (433)
		Andrus, Obadiah	FARM (28, 436, 442, 449
Andrews, Isaac	MIDD (362, 364, 365)	Andrus, Obadiah Capt	FARM (433, 447)
Andrews, John	DANB (45, 58), EHAD (49), FAIR (267)	Andrus, Ozias	FARM (444, 456)
		Andrus, Samuel	FARM (9)
Andrews, John Capt	FAIR (264)	Andrus, Thos	FARM (443)
Andrews, John Jur	DANB (61)	Andrus, Timo	FARM (449)
Andrews, John Silliman	FAIR (254, 257, 258), 262)	Andrus, Timothy	FARM (435, 456)
		Andruss, David	HARW (11)
Andrews, N	HARL (43)	Andruss, Hezekiah	CANA (15, (16, 17, 64)
Andrews, Nehemah Jur	HARL (52)	Andruss, Hezh	CANA (20, 23)
Andrews, Nehemiah	HARL (51, 52, 59, 61)	Andruss, Jeremiah	CANA (16, 17, 19, 24, 64
Andrews, Nehemiah Jr	HARL (47, 61)	Andruss, Judah	MILF (97)
Andrews, Nehm	HARL (41, 43, 44, 45, 46, 49, 50, 55, 56)	Andruss, William	HARF (253, 263, 255A)
		Anger, Geo	MIDD (372)
Andrews, Nehm Junr	HARL (55)	Anger, George	MIDD (382, 395, 413)
Andrews, Nehm jur	HARL (44, 51, 55)	Angur, George	MIDD (405)
Andrews, Noah	FARM (28)	Annabel, John	EHAD (44)
Andrews, Saml	HARL (50, 52, 58)	Annabel, Joseph	EHAD (49)
Andrews, Samuel	HARL (44, 47, 51, 56)	Annable, John	EHAD (64, 80)
Andrews, Thomas	CHES (12, 14)	Annable, Joseph	EHAD (69, 73)
Androus, David	HARW (523)	Applegate, [ ]	FAIR (254, 259)
Androus, Saml	GROT ([18], [25])	Archer, Joseph	FARM (13)
Androus, Samuel	GROT ([6], [12], [23])	Arnold, Ambrose	HADD (116)
Androws, Charles Junr	GLAS (66)	Arnold, Colo	DURH (14, 17)
Androws, Saml	GROT ([4])	Arnold, David	HADD (148)
Androws, Samuel	GROT ([23])	Arnold, Ebenr	MIDD (361, 368)
Andrus, [ ]	FARM (456)	Arnold, Enoch	EHAD (66)
Andrus, Benajah	CANA (77)	Arnold, Ephraim	EHAD (59, 69)
Andrus, Benja	FARM (12, 442, 456)	Arnold, Fenno	MIDD (371, 376, 378)
Andrus, Charles Jur	GLAS (99, 105)	Arnold, Gideon	CHAT (30, 33, 37, 39, 40, 50, 51, 52, 56, 63, 64, 68), MANS (338, 355)
Andrus, Eli	FARM (434, 444)		
Andrus, Elijah	FARM (32, 443, 448)		
Andrus, Elisha	GOSH (183)	Arnold, Henry	HARF (255A)
Andrus, Elizur	FARM (5, 17)	Arnold, Jabez	HADD (114, 125)
Andrus, Ezekl	FARM (456)	Arnold, Jacob	HADD (116, 121, 125, 148)
Andrus, Gideon	FARM (29, 434, 436, 438, 444, 449, 455, 456)	Arnold, James Capt	DURH (11)
Andrus, Hezekiah	CANA (15)	Arnold, James Col	DURH (13, 16)
Andrus, Hezh	FARM (9)	Arnold, James Ens	HADD (109)
Andrus, Ichabod	FARM (2, 3, 9, 28, 455)	Arnold, James Lieut	HADD (116)
Andrus, Jeremiah	CANA (77)	Arnold, Jeremiah	MIDD (362, 402)
Andrus, John Jur	DANB (63)	Arnold, Jno	LEBA (310)
Andrus, Jona	FARM (442, 443)	Arnold, Joel	HADD (121, 128, 129)
Andrus, Jona Leut	FARM (452)	Arnold, John	COVE (171), HADD (148), MANS (339), MILF (82, 84, 85)
Andrus, Jos	FARM (18)		
Andrus, Joseph	FARM (433)		

588

INDEX

Name	Index Page
Arnold, John 2nd	EHAD (54)
Arnold, John Capt	COVE (178)
Arnold, John Ens	EHAD (79, 81)
Arnold, Joseph	EHAD (3, 54, 55, 59, 61, 64, 69, 80, 82, 83, 85, 87, 89), HADD (129, 148, 281)
Arnold, Joseph 2d	EHAD (49, 50)
Arnold, Ruth	HADD (126)
Arnold, Sam	HADD (109)
Arnold, Sam Jur	HADD (109)
Arnold, Saml	EHAD (45, 148)
Arnold, Samuel	HADD (113, 114, 116, 129)
Arthur, Richard	GROT ([9])
Ashbell, Phebe	FARM (19)
Ashman, Lt	GOSH (103)
Aspenwall, [ ]	MANS (359)
Aspenwall, Peter	MANS (338), 281)
Aspenwall, Peter Junr	MANS (233, 285, 324, 328, 357, 359)
Aspenwall, Prince	MANS (268, 271, 283)
Aspenwall, William	CANT (168)
Aspenwall, Wm	CANT (156)
Aspenwel, Asa	CANT (150)
Aspenwell, Asa	CANT (146)
Aspenwell, Prince Ensn	MANS (278)
Aspinwall, Asa	LEBA (333, 341)
Atkin, Joel	FARM (443)
Atkins, Benoni	FARM (436)
Atkins, Benony	FARM (443)
Atkins, David Lt	MIDD (371)
Atkins, George	MIDD (373)
Atkins, Jabez	HARL (48)
Atkins, Joel	MIDD (369)
Atkins, Luther	FARM (433, 438)
Atkins, Zealous	FARM (442)
Attwater, Moses	CHES (5)
Attwater, William	MILF (92, 101, 102, 104, 106)
Attwood, Elijah Capt	EHAD (49)
Attwood, Heman	MANS (277, 283, 348)
Attwood, Nathaniel	MANS (272, 347, 357, 358)
Attwood, Nathl	MANS (262, 275, 277, 282, 284, 328, 335, 346)
Attwood, Thos	MANS (278)
Atwater, Abel	LITC (139)
Atwater, Amos	CHES (15)
Atwater, Benjamin	CHES (11, 14)
Atwater, Enos Capt	CHES (5, 12, 16)
Atwater, John	CHES (17)
Atwater, Moses Jur	CHES (4)
Atwater, Reuben	CHES (14, 16)
Atwater, Reuben Major	CHES (4, 5, 6, 7, 8, 9, 10, 11, 12, 15, 17)
Atwater, Samuel	CHES (12)
Atwater, Samuel Jur	CHES (15)
Atwood, Elijah	EHAD (59, 66)

Name	Index Page
Atwood, Elijah Capt	EHAD (45)
Aucly, Nat	GREE (128)
Auger, Isaac	HADD (114)
Auger, Prosper	MIDD (376)
Augur, John Junr	BRAN (171, 172)
Augur, Joseph	BRAN (170)
Augur, Peter	BRAN (164, 173)
Austin, Jess	DURH (11, 17)
Austin, Levi	HARW (3, 8, 11, 15, 16, 20, 21)
Avary, Amos	COVE (170, 172)
Averil, Moses	KENT (A28, E59)
Averil, Nathan	KENT (E59)
Averil, Perry	KENT (A28, B1, C552, C555)
Averil, Saml	KENT (E59)
Averil, Samuel	KENT (E63)
Averil, Samuel Jur	KENT (A27)
Averill, Moses	KENT (A28)
Averill, Perry	KENT (C551)
Avery Elijah	GROT ([7])
Avery, Thephilus Lieut	GROT ([19])
Avery, Amos	COVE (314)
Avery, Asa	GROT ([9])
Avery, Asa Capt	GROT ([17])
Avery, Benajah	GROT ([4], [9])
Avery, Chrisr Junr	GROT ([9])
Avery, Daniel	GROT [4], [6], [9], [12], [15], [18]
Avery, Daniel Ensn	GROT ([15])
Avery, David	GROT ([3], [4], [6], [7], [8], [9], [10], [17])
Avery, Ebenezer	GROT ([23], [14])
Avery, Ebenezer 2nd	GROT ([12])
Avery, Ebenezer Col	GROT ([4], [5], [8], [13])
Avery, Ebenezer Lieut	GROT ([15], [21])
Avery, Ebenezr 2d	GROT ([3])
Avery, Ebenezr 3d	GROT ([4]), GROT ([9])
Avery, Elijah	GROT ([4], [6], [9], [16])
Avery, Elijah Capt	GROT ([12], [14], [19], [20])
Avery, Elisha Capt	GROT ([7], [16])
Avery, Isaac	GROT ([4], [6], [9], [13], [18])
Avery, James	GROT ([11], [12], [14])
Avery, James 2d	GROT ([4], [6])
Avery, James 3d	GROT ([15])
Avery, Jasper	GROT ([15])
Avery, Jesse	GROT ([6])
Avery, John	GROT ([12], [23], [24])
Avery, John 2nd	GROT ([9], [12])
Avery, John Lieut	GROT ([14], [17], [18])
Avery, Jonas	GROT ([4])
Avery, Jonath	ASHF (313)
Avery, Jonathan	ASHF (313)
Avery, Nathan	KENT (C548)
Avery, Park Junr	GROT ([12])
Avery, Park Junr Lieut	GROT ([21])
Avery, Park Leut	GROT ([15])

INDEX

Name	Index Page	Name	Index Page
Avery, Park Lieut	GROT ([14], [21])	Bacon, Andw	CANA (15, 16, 17, 20, 23, 27, 64, 77)
Avery, Parke	GROT ([4], [6], [8], [13], [15], [17], [20], [25])	Bacon, Asa	CANT (179)
Avery, Parke Junr	GROT ([4], [9], [13], [23], [24])	Bacon, Asa Capt	CANT (143, 144, 146, 150, 153, 154, 155, 158, 159, 165, 166, 170, 172, 174, 175, 176, 179, 180, 183)
Avery, Parke Junr Lieut	GROT ([6], [18])		
Avery, Parke Lieut	GROT ([18], [23])		
Avery, Perry	KENT (E58, E62)	Bacon, Benj Capt	CANT (146)
Avery, Peter	GROT ([11], [12], [18], [19], [23], [24], [25])	Bacon, Benja Capt	CANT (149, 158, 165, 166, 171, 177, 178, 181)
Avery, Peter Doct	GROT ([14])	Bacon, Benja Jr	CANT (180)
Avery, Simeon	GROT ([4], [6], [9], [15], [18], [23])	Bacon, Benjamin	CANT (154)
		Bacon, Benjamin Capt	CANT (154, 155, 162, 167, 179)
Avery, Theophilus	GROT ([9], [12], [18], [25])	Bacon, Beriah	CHAT (34, 41)
Avery, Theophilus Lieut	GROT ([10], [23], [25])	Bacon, Ebenezer	CORN (87), CORN (90), MIDD (350, 353, 355, 358, 366, 378, 390)
Avery, Thomas	KENT (E58, E62)		
Avery, Thomas Capt	GROT ([23])	Bacon, Ebenr	MIDD (402, 414, 421, 362)
Avery, Thomas Lieut	GROT ([15])		
Avery, William	GROT ([3], [4], [6], [7], [9], [11], [14], [15], [17], [18], [19], [23], [24], [25],	Bacon, Ebr	LEBA (296), MIDD (370, 372)
		Bacon, Jacob	CANT (146, 155, 176)
B[ ], Aaron	LEBA (298)	Bacon, Jer[ ]	MIDD (414)
B[ ], Daniel	FARM (9), HEBR (235)	Bacon, Jeremiah	MIDD (417)
B[ ], Joseph	FARM (456)	Bacon, Jeremiah Lieut	MIDD (355, 357)
B[ ], Thos	HARL (46)	Bacon, Jerh	MIDD (368)
B[ ]sh, James	GREE (128)	Bacon, Jerh Lieut	MIDD (387)
Ba[ ], Saml	CANA (64)	Bacon, Jno 3d	MIDD (376)
Babbet, Benjamin	MIDD (363)	Bacon, Jo[ ] Junr	MIDD (367)
Babbet, William	MIDD (363)	Bacon, Joel	MIDD (376, 414)
Babbits, Jacob	COLC (11)	Bacon, John	MIDD (411)
Babcock, [ ]	ASHF (219, 233), COLC (244)	Bacon, John 3d	MIDD (382)
		Bacon, John Junr	MIDD (363)
Babcock, Amos	ASHF (308)	Bacon, John Lieut	MIDD (362)
Babcock, Capt	ASHF (224)	Bacon, Jos	CANT (144, 151), FARM (17)
Babcock, Elijah	CANA (64)		
Babcock, Elijah Capt	ASHF (223,, 311)	Bacon, Joseph	CANT (163), FARM (444, 445, 449), MIDD (350, 359, 362, 365, 384, 397, 404, 405, 413),
Babcock, Eliph Capt	ASHF (308)		
Babcock, Elisha	HARF (285, 287)		
Baber, Noah Capt	EWIN (14)		
Babock, Amos	ASHF (194)	Bacon, Joseph Capt	FARM (15)
Backus, Elisha	CANT (146, 156, 161, 168)	Bacon, Joseph Jur	FARM (8, 433, 436, 438, 444)
Backus, Isaac	CANT (156, 174, 175, 177, 181)	Bacon, Josh	FARM (442)
		Bacon, Josh Capt	FARM (17)
Backus, Timo	CANT (144, 145, 147)	Bacon, Josiah	MIDD (345, 346, 349, 350, 351, 354, 364, 368, 390, 405)
Backus, Timo Capt	CANT (151, 176, 177)		
Backus, Timo Junr	CANT (160)		
Backus, Timothy Capt	CANT (181)	Bacon, Ju[ ] Lieut	MIDD (372, 382)
Backus, Timothy Junr	CANT (170, 183)	Bacon, Moses	FARM (2, 449)
Bacon, Jeremiah Capt	MIDD (407)	Bacon, Nathaniel	MIDD (376)
Bacon, [ ]	MIDD (374, 403, 415, 420, 360)	Bacon, Noah	MIDD (376)
		Bacon, Phi	MIDD (361)
Bacon, [ ]h Lieut	MIDD (361)	Bacon, Phineas	MIDD (357)
Bacon, Abner	CANT (144, 146, 147)	Bacon, Phinehas	MIDD (359, 362, 378, 381, 387, 397, 409, 415)
Bacon, Abner Capt	CANT (166, 180)		
Bacon, Andrew	MIDD (344, 368)	Bacon, Phins	MIDD (371)

INDEX

Name	Index Page
Bacon, Pierpont	COLC (8, 11, 242, 243, 250, 254, 255)
Bacon, Saml	CANT (159, 168, 175, 176, 177, 155, 156)
Bacon, Samuel	CANT (169)
Bacon, Stephen	MIDD (346, 349, 357, 362, 367, 387, 394, 396, 397, 399, 407, 417)
Bacon, William	CANT (177), MIDD (382)
Bacon, Wm	MIDD (372, 395, 405, 413)
Badcock, Abijah	LEBA (333)
Badcock, Daniel	BOLT (183)
Badcock, John	COVE (165, 167, 170, 172, 175, 178, 180, 314, 267, 281, 283, 336, 353)
Badcock, Josiah	MANS (267, 272, 273, 274, 275, 281, 284, 328, 356, 358)
Badcock, Robert	COVE (165, 174)
Badcock, William	COVE (314)
Badger, Abner	COVE (177, 180)
Badger, Abraham	COVE (174)
Badger, Bezal	LEBA (299)
Badger, Bezaleel	LEBA (297)
Badger, Daniel Jur	COVE (174)
Badger, David	CHES (14, 15)
Badger, Edmund	MANS (265)
Badger, Enoch	COVE (179)
Badger, Enoch Jur	COVE (168, 179)
Badger, Ezek	ASHF (311)
Badger, John	CHES (A)
Badley, Abraham	LITC (129)
Badwin, David Junr	CORN (87)
Bailey, Caleb	HADD (113)
Bailey, Gideon	EHAD (86, 110, 125, 148
Bailey, Gideon Lieut	HADD (116, 120)
Bailey, Gidn Lieut	HADD (122, 129)
Bailey, Isaac Jur	LEBA (316)
Bailey, James	LEBA (298, 330, 341)
Bailey, Oliver	HADD (114)
Bailey, Saml	LEBA (315, 333)
Bailey, Saxton	LEBA (316)
Bailey, Sexton	LEBA (310)
Bailey, Stephen	HADD (121)
Bailey, William	HADD (148)
Bailey, William Jur	HADD (113, 116)
Bailey, Wm	HADD (129)
Baily, Andrew	GOSH (115, 183)
Baily, Gidn Jur	HADD (129)
Baily, Jos	GOSH (138)
Baily, Oliver	HADD (148)
Baily, Wm Jr	HADD (114)
Baits, Aaron	HARL (56)
Baits, John	HARL (55, 56, 57, 58)
Baits, Oliver Lieut	HARL (58)
Baits, Phinehas	HARL (56, 58)
Baker, Avery	FAIR (262)
Baker, Constant	GLAS (105, 109)
Baker, Elisha	CANA (11, 14, 20, 24)
Baker, Enice	BOLT (146)
Baker, Jacob	LITC (139)
Baker, Nathaniel	EHAD (84)
Baker, Saml	FAIR (266, 267)
Baker, Samuel Junr	CORN (90)
Baker, William	EHAD (44)
Bakley, Joseph Jur	CANA (11)
Balcam, Joseph	MANS (271, 277, 337)
Balch, Jonathan	MANS (280, 281)
Balch, Jonathan Belding	HARF (292)
Balcom, Joseph	MANS (336)
Balden, David	CANT (150)
Baldwein, Dudley	FAIR (252)
Baldwin, [ ]	MILF (93)
Baldwin, Aaron	BRAN (162, 163, 164, 170, 175, 176, 178, 179, 180)
Baldwin, Abial	DURH (10, 11, 12, 14, 16, 18, 19, 21, 23, 25, 26)
Baldwin, Abner	LITC (139, 142)
Baldwin, Abner Capt	LITC (153)
Baldwin, Abner Junr	LITC (141, 152, 158)
Baldwin, Amos	MILF (85, 88, 100)
Baldwin, Andrew	MILF (93)
Baldwin, Ashbel	MILF (82)
Baldwin, Ashbull	MILF (88)
Baldwin, Benjamin Capt	BRAN (173)
Baldwin, Benjamin Lieut	BRAN (179)
Baldwin, Benjn Capt	BRAN (170, 174)
Baldwin, Brewen	GOSH (138, 183, 186)
Baldwin, Caleb	DANB (48, 69), KILH (42, 43)
Baldwin, Caleb Jur	DANB (39)
Baldwin, Cornt	DURH (20)
Baldwin, Daniel	BRAN (174, 178), MANS (271, 279, 328, 347, 353)
Baldwin, Danl	GOSH (112, 115, 120, 130, 131, 138, 184, 185)
Baldwin, David	CANT (144, 146, 147, 150, 159, 160, 162, 165, 167, 175, 176, 179, 180), CORN (3, 13, 87)
Baldwin, David Junr	CORN (16), MILF (82)
Baldwin, Dudley	FAIR (252)
Baldwin, Ebenezer	MANS (280, 352)
Baldwin, Ebenr	CANT (160, 161, 168), MANS (336)
Baldwin, Edward	MILF (104)
Baldwin, Elihu	BRAN (163, 166, 174, 178, , 179), MILF (82, 88)
Baldwin, Elihu Ensign	BRAN (170)
Baldwin, Elijah	DERB (140)
Baldwin, Elijah Doctor	DERB (121, 134)
Baldwin, Elisha	GOSH (186)

INDEX

Name	Index Page
Baldwin, Elnathan	MILF (82, 93)
Baldwin, Enoch	MILF (82, 88, 91, 102, 104)
Baldwin, Enoch Capt	MILF (92, 97, 98, 101)
Baldwin, Ephraim	BRAN (165, 178)
Baldwin, Ezra	DURH (22)
Baldwin, George	LITC (131)
Baldwin, Hiel	MILF (92)
Baldwin, I Junr	LITC (161)
Baldwin, Isaac	LITC (158, 154)
Baldwin, Isaac Junr	LITC (147, 158)
Baldwin, Israel	BRAN (163, 173, 179)
Baldwin, Jacob	CANT (160, 161, 168, , 169, 176, 177, 181)
Baldwin, Jared	KILH (49, 145)
Baldwin, Jehiel	MILF (97)
Baldwin, Jeremiah	MILF (78, 86, 88, 91, 102, 103)
Baldwin, John	CANT (144)
Baldwin, John Jur	BRAN (163, 165, 173)
Baldwin, Joseph	BRAN (163)
Baldwin, Joshua	MILF (85, 93)
Baldwin, Josiah 2d	KILH (45, 145)
Baldwin, Josiah Capt	KILH (50, 53, 55, 146)
Baldwin, Moses	BRAN (173)
Baldwin, Nathan	MILF (80, 82, 85, 87, 91, 92)
Baldwin, Nathaniel	MILF (81)
Baldwin, Nathl	GOSH (110, 117, 137, 184)
Baldwin, Nicodemas	BRAN (164)
Baldwin, Noah	BRAN (175, 12, 18)
Baldwin, Noah Junr	BRAN (179)
Baldwin, Phineas 2nd	LITC (131, 135, 140, 153
Baldwin, Phineas Junr	LITC (142)
Baldwin, Phinehas	BRAN (164, 167, 168, 172, 174, 175, 180)
Baldwin, Richard	BRAN (178), MILF (82, 102)
Baldwin, Ruben	DERB (106, 120, 122, 124, 125, 131, 135, 141, 147, 168)
Baldwin, Saml	GOSH (102, 104, 110, 121, 184) ,HARW (14)
Baldwin, Saml Jur	GOSH (186)
Baldwin, Samuel	CORN (88), BRAN (179)
Baldwin, Samuel 2d	BRAN (175)
Baldwin, Samuel Lieut	BRAN (170, 174, 179)
Baldwin, Samuel W	HARW (13)
Baldwin, Silas	DERB (122)
Baldwin, Silas Doctr	DERB (120)
Baldwin, Solomon	MILF (85, 88, 97)
Baldwin, Stephen	CORN (88), LITC (147, 160), MILF (82, 85)
Baldwin, Thaddeus	DERB (120)
Baldwin, Thaddus	DERB (124)
Baldwin, Thadeus	DERB (126, 127, 141, 145)
Baldwin, Thads	DERB (167)
Baldwin, Thos	MILF (98)

Name	Index Page
Baldwin, Timo	GUIL (303)
Baldwin, Timo Jnr	DERB (122)
Baldwin, Timothy	GUIL (274, 295, 337)
Baldwin, Timothy Capt	DERB (107, 120, 122, 127, 132)
Baldwin, Timothy Jur	DERB (120, 124, 134,)
Baldwin, Will	CANT (151)
Baldwin, William	CANT (147, 168), LITC (141, 146)
Baldwin, Wm	CANT (144, 146, 181)
Baldwin, Zacheus	BRAN (166, 170)
Baley, Abraham	CHAT (40)
Baley, Bethuwel	GROT ([4])
Baley, Bethuwil	GROT ([6])
Baley, James	GROT ([23])
Baley, Jeremiah	HADD (109)
Baley, John	GROT ([25])
Baley, Jonath	GROT ([12])
Baley, Jos	LEBA (343)
Baley, Joshua	CHAT (58)
Baley, Noah	GROT ([15])
Baley, Obadiah	GROT ([4], [17], [22], [24], [25])
Baley, Obadiah Junr	GROT ([9])
Baley, Recompence	CHAT (55, 65)
Baly, Jos	GOSH (184)
Baly, Obadiah	GROT ([15])
Bancroft, John	EWIN (8, 10, 12, 85, 89)
Bancroft, Saml	EWIN (13)
Bancroft, Samuel	EWIN (10)
Bancroft, Thomas Jur	EWIN (8)
Baning, Abner	HARL (48, 52)
Baning, David	HARL (48)
Baning, Samuel	HARL (53)
Baning, Samuel Jur	HARL (48)
Banks, Benja Jur	FAIR (257, 259, 260)
Banks, Benjamin Jur	FAIR (253)
Banks, Daniel	FAIR (253, 256, 267)
Banks, Danl	FAIR (255, 257, 258, 262, 265, 267)
Banks, David	FAIR (266)
Banks, David Capt	FAIR (264)
Banks, Ebenezer	FAIR (252)
Banks, Ebenr	FAIR (253, 254, 255, 258, 259, 260, 264, 266, 267)
Banks, James	GREE (121, 124)
Banks, John	FAIR (260, 262, 263, 266
Banks, Joseph	GREE (128)
Banks, Nehemiah	FAIR (252, 253, 254, 256, 258)
Banks, Nehemiah Jur	FAIR (253, 256)
Banks, Obadiah	GREE (119)
Banks, Thomas	FAIR (252)
Banks, Thos	FAIR (258, 263, 267)
Banning, Abner	HARL (44, 54, 56)
Banning, David	HARL (55, 61)
Banning, Saml Jur	HARL (57)
Banning, Samuel	HARL (43, 44)

INDEX

Name	Index Page
Banning, Samuel Ensign	HARL (51)
Banning, Samuel jur	HARL (45)
Bar[ ], Ephm	DANB (39)
Barb[ ], Benjn	HARW (3)
Barber, Ashbel	EWIN (85, 88)
Barber, Benjamin	HARW (534)
Barber, Benjn	DANB (51)
Barber, James	CANA (24)
Barber, John	GROT ([9], [15], [18])
Barber, Jonathan	EWIN (85, 88)
Barber, Noah	EWIN (8, 12, 85)
Barber, Noah Capt	EWIN (14)
Barber, Oliver	EWIN (13, 85, 88)
Barber, Shadrach	EWIN (85, 88)
Barber, Simeon	EWIN (85, 88)
Barbour, Jabez Junr	MANS (281)
Barbur, Aaron	HEBR (218)
Barbur, Abner	HARW (2, 22, 25)
Barbur, John	HARW (534)
Barbur, John Jur	HARW (3, 14)
Barbur, Obadiah	HEBR (216, 246)
Barbur, Reuben	HARW (3, 5, 6, 7, 9, 13, 16, 22, 24, 523, 533)
Barbur, Reuben Jur	HARW (3, 10, 14, 17, 23)
Barbur, Stephen Capt	HEBR (236, 247)
Barbur, Stephen Jur	HEBR (216)
Barbur, Timothy	HARW (3, 25)
Barce, Isaiah	CORN (89, 90)
Barce, James	CORN (6, 28)
Barce, Joseph	CORN (2, 3, 4, 5, 8, 10, 12, 13, 19, 20, 22, 23, 24, 25, 27)
Barce, Joseph Capt	CORN (29)
Barce, Joseph Ensign	CORN (1)
Bard, Samuel	LITC (142)
Bardsley, Ephm	KENT (D5, E58, E62)
Bardsley, Ephraim	KENT (B1, B2, C548, C552, C554, D1)
Bardsley, Jabez	KENT (E60)
Bardsley, Philo	KENT (D10, D11, E63)
Bardsly, Nehemiah	CORN (12)
Barington, Ebenr	FARM (17)
Barker, [ ]	GOSH (112)
Barker, Daniel Jur	BRAN (167, 168, 173)
Barker, Ebenezer	BRAN (176)
Barker, Ebenezer Capt	BRAN (171, 172)
Barker, Edward	BRAN (164, 169, 173, 174, 175, 179)
Barker, Edwd	BRAN (170)
Barker, Elipt	LEBA (297, 299, 341)
Barker, Jacob	BRAN (164, 165, 179)
Barker, James	BRAN (163, 175, 176, 178, 179, 180)
Barker, James Capt	BRAN (170, 176)
Barker, James Jur	LEBA (341)
Barker, Jams Capt	BRAN (166)
Barker, John	BRAN (165, 178)
Barker, Joseph	BRAN (164, 165, 167, 169, 170, 172, 173, 174, 178, 179)
Barker, Papillon	BRAN (165, 168)
Barker, Saml	BRAN (167)
Barker, Saml Ct	BRAN (163, 164)
Barker, Samuel	BRAN (168, 169, 170, 172, 173, 175, 176, 177, 178, 179, 180)
Barker, Samuel Capt	BRAN (170, 172)
Barker, Samuel Jur	BRAN (169, 180)
Barker, Timothy	BRAN (175)
Barker, Wm	GUIL (337)
Barlow, John	KENT (C545)
Barn, David	MILF (88)
Barn, Stephen	FARM (446)
Barn, Stepn	FARM (442)
Barn, Thos	FARM (434)
Barnam, Jehiel	KENT (B1)
Barnard, Samuel	LITC (129, 142)
Barnerd, Ebenezer	HARF (261a)
Barnerd, Ebenezer Junr	HARF (253, 261a)
Barnes, Amos	MIDD (362, 366)
Barnes, Asa	KENT (E59)
Barnes, Benjn	CANA (77)
Barnes, Gideon Jur	CANA (64, 77)
Barnes, Giles	MIDD (364, 377)
Barnes, Jabez	MIDD (362, 366)
Barnes, Thomas	CANA (64)
Barnes, Thos	FARM (444, 358, 372)
Barnham, Joseph	ASHF (311)
Barns, Aaron	CANA (11)
Barns, Abel	LITC (132, 133, 138)
Barns, Amos	FARM (2, 6, 430, 435, 436, 442, 449, 450), LITC (129, 132, 133, 135, 147), MIDD (371, 377, 381)
Barns, Amos Capt	FARM (9, 433, 441), LITC (137)
Barns, Asa	FARM (443, 446, 450, 440)
Barns, Asahel	FARM (433, 435, 436, 440)
Barns, Asal	FARM (431)
Barns, Daniel	FARM (17, 28)
Barns, Danl	FARM (8, 9)
Barns, David Capt	FARM (433)
Barns, Dimon	CHES (4, 9, 12)
Barns, Ebenr	FARM (443)
Barns, Ebenr 2d	FARM (456)
Barns, Elijah	KENT (E59)
Barns, Enos	LITC (141)
Barns, Ester	FARM (19)
Barns, Gideon	CANA (26)
Barns, Gideon Junr	CANA (12)
Barns, Jabez	MIDD (347, 350, 359)
Barns, Jesse	GROT ([12])
Barns, John	KENT (B2, E59)
Barns, John Capt	MIDD (352)
Barns, John Jur	FARM (456)

INDEX

Name	Index Page	Name	Index Page
Barns, Jona	FARM (434, 438, 443, 444, 445)	Barritt, Daniel	KILY (4)
Barns, Jonas	KENT (C555)	Barritt, David	KILY (6, 11, 33, 98, 94a)
Barns, Jonthn	FARM (433)	Barrows, Daniel	MANS (283, 339, 348, 353, 355)
Barns, Judah	FARM (2, 9, 28, 449)	Barrows, Elisha	MANS (278, 336)
Barns, Lemuel	GUIL (344)	Barrows, Gershom	MANS (283)
Barns, Moses	FARM (24), LITC (129, 133, 134, 135, 142)	Barrows, Gershom Capt	MANS (278, 328, 350)
Barns, Nathan	FARM (436, 456)	Barrows, Isaac	MANS (271, 353)
Barns, Nathan Jur	FARM (443)	Barrows, Isaac Capt	MANS (278, 352)
Barns, Nathl	FARM (433)	Barrows, Isaac Junr	MANS (268, 277, 328)
Barns, Noah	FARM (441)	Barrows, Jabez	MANS (277, 281)
Barns, Reuben	FARM (9)	Barrows, Jabez Junr	MANS (271, 279, 347, 357)
Barns, Rufus	FARM (12)		
Barns, Solomon	MIDD (388)	Barrows, Joseph	MANS (265)
Barns, Stephen	FARM (430, 434, 441, 444, 445, 446, 449, 451)	Barrows, Leml	MANS (283)
		Barrows, Leml Capt	MANS (277)
Barns, Stephen Ensn	FARM (452)	Barrows, Lemuel	MANS (271, 284, 347)
Barns, Stephen Jur	FARM (433, 436, 438, 440)	Barrows, Lemuel Capt	MANS (273, 328, 336, 357)
Barns, Stepn	FARM (446)	Barrows, Robert Junr	MANS (283)
Barns, Thomas	FARM (438, 376, 382, 419)	Barrows, Robt Junr	MANS (277)
		Barrows, Solomon	MANS (277)
Barns, Thos	FARM (2, 17, 443)	Barrows, Stephen	MANS (280, 281, 357)
Barns, Timothy	LITC (158, 159)	Barrows, Thomas	MANS (272, 284, 358)
Barns, William	FARM (433)	Barrows, Thomas Junr	MANS (328, 353)
Barns, Wm	FARM (443)	Barrows, Thomas Lt	MANS (328, 341, 348)
Barns, Zac	FARM (443)	Barrows, Thos	MANS (275, 283, 277)
Barnum, Abijah	DANB (53, 198)	Barrows, Thos Junr	MANS (278)
Barnum, Benja	DANB (63)	Barrows, Thos Lieut	MANS (283, 347)
Barnum, Benjn	DANB (60)	Barstow, Jno Jr	CANT (182)
Barnum, Ebenezer	KENT (E63)	Barstow, John	CANT (144, 146, 147, 182)
Barnum, Eliphalet	DANB (40, 43, 51, 58, 61)		
Barnum, Ephm	DANB (39, 51)	Barstow, John Jr	CANT (168)
Barnum, Ephm Capt	DANB (45, 55)	Barstow, Saml	CANT (147, 161, 168, 177, 182, 154), LEBA (342)
Barnum, Gideon	KENT (C554)		
Barnum, Jehiel	KENT (A28, C548, C552, D1, D8, E59)		
		Barthol, Saml	GOSH (184)
Barnum, John 3d	DANB (63)	Bartholeme, Glad	DERB (141)
Barnum, John Jur	DANB (47)	Bartholemeu, Glad	DERB (122)
Barnum, Joseph	DANB (39, 49, 69, 70)	Barthollomew, Moses	GOSH (138)
Barnum, Judah Jur	DANB (59)	Barthollomew, Saml	GOSH (102, 120)
Barnum, Justus	DANB (39, 40, 47, 51, 52, 55, 58, 63, 64)	Bartholomew, [ ]	HARW (2)
		Bartholomew, Andrew	HARW (4, 6, 10, 13, 14, 17, 22, 23, 25)
Barnum, Matthew	DANB (49)		
Barnum, Mattw	DANB (40, 47)	Bartholomew, Andrew Jur	HARW (523)
Barnum, Nathl	DANB (49)		
Barnum, Nathl Jur	DANB (51)	Bartholomew, Gideon	BRAN (166, 169)
Barnum, Richard	DANB (39)	Bartholomew, Glad	DERB (140)
Barnum, Richd	DANB (40)	Bartholomew, Ira	CORN (25)
Barnum, Saml	KENT (D7, D8, E63)	Bartholomew, Jacob	FARM (9, 28, 433, 436, 444), HARW (4, 7, 25)
Barnum, Samuel	KENT (D1)		
Barnum, Stephen	KENT (E60, E63)	Bartholomew, Jonathan	BRAN (166, 170, 175, 179)
Barnum, Thads	DANB (40)		
Barnum, Thadus	DANB (47, 59)	Bartholomew, Jonth	BRAN (163)
Barny, Joseph	ASHF (311)	Bartholomew, Joseph	BRAN (163, 164, 166, 173), CORN (18, 23, 25)
Barret, John	FARM (443, 444)		
Barret, Robert	FARM (28)	Bartholomew, Josh	BRAN (165)
Barrit, David	KILY (21, 92, 97a)	Bartholomew, Josiah	CORN (88, 89)
Barrit, John	KILY (86a)	Bartholomew, Noah	LITC (129)

INDEX

Name	Index Page
Bartholomew, Reuben	HARW (7, 10, 13, 16, 17, 23, 25, 533)
Bartholomew, Saml Jur	BRAN (166, 170)
Bartholomew, Timothy	BRAN (167)
Bartholow, Andrew	HARW (3)
Bartholow, Charles	HARW (2)
Bartholw, Jacob	HARW (3)
Bartholw, Reuben	HARW (3, 4)
Bartholw, Saml	GOSH (103)
Barthow, Jacob	FARM (456)
Bartlet, [ ]	GLAS (81)
Bartlet, Abraham	DURH (10, 12, 14, 19, 21)
Bartlet, Benjn	GUIL (287)
Bartlet, Chandler	LEBA (334)
Bartlet, Chandlr	LEBA (326)
Bartlet, Daniel	ASHF (203)
Bartlet, Elihu	GUIL (269, 274)
Bartlet, Henry	GUIL (303)
Bartlet, Hooker	GUIL (335, 296, 299, 340)
Bartlet, Icabud	GUIL (296)
Bartlet, Icha	LEBA (341)
Bartlet, Ichabod	LEBA (302)
Bartlet, John	GUIL (280, 335)
Bartlet, Joseph	GUIL (286, 301, 310)
Bartlet, Josiah	LEBA (296)
Bartlet, Nathl	LEBA (298, 299)
Bartlet, Reuben	GUIL (286)
Bartlet, Saml	DURH (25)
Bartlet, Samuel	DURH (18)
Bartlet, Timo	GUIL (325)
Bartlet, Timothy	GUIL (287, 303, 311)
Bartlett, Abrm	DURH (11, 25)
Bartlett, Edmond	EWIN (12)
Bartlett, Eliphalet	EWIN (85, 88)
Bartlett, Hooker	GUIL (300)
Bartlett, John	EWIN (12)
Bartlett, Jonathan Capt	EWIN (8, (89)
Bartlett, Jonathn Capt	EWIN (85)
Bartlett, Saml	EWIN (13, 17, 85)
Bartlett, Samuel	EWIN (8, 11, 88)
Bartlett, Widw	GLAS (108)
Bartlit, Fisk	CHAT (29, 39)
Bartlit, James	MIDD (414)
Bartlit, John	CHAT (30)
Bartlit, Moses	CHAT (35, 36, 39, 47, 52, 55, 61, 66)
Bartlit, Moses Doct	CHAT (33, 40, 41, 42, 45, 50, 58, 64)
Bartlit, William	CHAT (43, 58)
Bartlitt, Moses Doctr	CHAT (30)
Bartoleme, Glad	DERB (120)
Barton, [ ]	KILY (94a)
Barton, Saml	KILY (34, 98)
Barton, Samuel	KILY (12, 21)
Bartram, Ebenezer	FAIR (269)
Bartram, Ebenr	FAIR (259)
Bartram, Job	FAIR (262, 265, 266, 267, 269)
Bartram, Job Capt	FAIR (261, 262, 263, 264)

Name	Index Page
Bascomb, Paul	LEBA (326)
Basit, Abraham	DERB (122, 131, 132)
Basit, Abraham Capt	DERB (145, 168)
Basit, Amos	DERB (132, 139, 142, 144)
Basit, Benjamin	DERB (120)
Basit, Benjn	DERB (141)
Basit, David	DERB (122, 131)
Basit, Ebenezer	DERB (120, 122)
Basit, James	DERB (121, 122)
Basit, John	DERB (113, 126, 140, 141, 145)
Basit, John Lieut	DERB (114, 135)
Basit, Joseph	DERB (122, 145)
Basit, Saml	DERB (132)
Basit, Samuel	DERB (135, 140, 145)
Basker, Asa	LEBA (326)
Basset, Elisha	GUIL (338)
Basset, Elnathan	MANS (348)
Basset, Jared	KENT (B2)
Basset, Jered	KENT (A28, C552)
Basset, Samuel	CORN (16)
Basset, William	MANS (338)
Bassett, Elnathan	MANS (233, 280, 358)
Bassett, Joshua	MANS (233)
Bassett, Oliver	MANS (280)
Bassett, Samuel	CORN (86)
Bassit, Abraham	DERB (120, 133, 167)
Bassit, Abraham Capt	DERB (147)
Bassit, Abram Jnr	DERB (131)
Bassit, Amos	DERB (120, 122)
Bassit, Benjamin	DERB (132)
Bassit, Benjn	DERB (106, 122, 124)
Bassit, David	DERB (106, 126)
Bassit, John Lieut	DERB (107, 139)
Bassit, Saml	DERB (127)
Bassitt, John	DERB (125)
Bateman, Benj[ ]	KILY (97)
Batemen, Benjn	KILY (8)
Bates, [ ]	KILY (86a)
Bates, Aaron	HARL (50, 51, 61)
Bates, Abner	CHAT (65, 68)
Bates, Amos	HADD (148)
Bates, Aron	HARL (53)
Bates, Curtis	DURH (18, 19)
Bates, David	CHAT (42, 45, 46, 51, 52, 58, 64, 65, 67, 68)
Bates, Eleazer	HADD (125)
Bates, Elihu	HADD (110, 113, 129, 148)
Bates, Elijah	KILY (4)
Bates, Ichabod	KENT (E59, E64)
Bates, Isachar Capt	KILY (96)
Bates, Isacher Capt	KILY (5, 26)
Bates, James	DURH (14, 16, 19, 25), HARL (48)
Bates, Jno	HARL (53)
Bates, Job	CHAT (40, 41)

595

INDEX

Name	Index Page	Name	Index Page
Bates, John	CHAT (33, 38, 40, 45, 65), HARL (43, 45, 46, 48, 50, 51, 55, 59, 86a)	Beach, Miles	LITC (129, 131, 132, 133, 134, 135, 141, 146, 147, 152)
Bates, Joseph	KENT (C548, D10, E63)	Beach, Miles Capt	LITC (139, 142, 143, 146, 152, 153, 158, 159)
Bates, Joseph Jr	HADD (113)		
Bates, Moses	DURH (12, 18, 21)	Beach, Saml	HARL (53)
Bates, Oliver	COLC (243), HARL (42, 43, 45, 53)	Beach, Samuel	CHES (4, 16)
		Beach, Thomas	HARL (45, 53)
Bates, Oliver Capt	HARL (61)	Beach, Thos	MILF (97)
Bates, Oliver Lieut	HARL (44, 48, 49, 50, 51)	Beach, Zophar	LITC (153)
		Beacher, Abell	FARM (443)
Bates, Phinas	HARL (46, 50)	Beacher, Abraham	DERB (106, 113, 120, 122, 124, 126)
Bates, Phinehas	HARL (42, 45, 48, 49, 51, 53, 59)		
		Beacher, Amos	FARM (443, 449)
Bates, Saml	DURH (10, 12, 17, 23, 26), KENT (E58, E62)	Beacher, Isaac	DERB (106, 126), HARW (2)
Bates, Samuel	DURH (14, 16, 25)	Beacher, John	FARM (443)
Bates, Solomon	HADD (148)	Beacher, Joseph	FARM (430, 435, 442, 452)
Bates, Thomas	KENT (E63)		
Battle, William	MILF (82, 85)	Beacher, Joseph Capt	FARM (454)
Bauldwin, David	CANT (156)	Beacher, Joseph Leut	FARM (452)
Bauldwin, Wm	CANT (156)	Beacher, Saml	KENT (E62, E58)
Baxter, Benja	KILY (35)	Beacher, Samuel	KENT (C548, D1)
Baxter, Nathan	HEBR (216)	Beaman, Daniel	HARL (52)
Baxter, Robart	KILY (93, 94, 94a)	Beaman, Thomas	HARL (52)
Baxter, Robert	KILY (98)	Beaman, Thos Jur	HARL (52)
Baxter, Thomas	COVE (315)	Beamont, Samuel	LEBA (343)
Bayley, Aron	GLAS (64)	Beamont, Wm	LEBA (298, 311, 316, 327, ,334, 342)
Bayley, James	LEBA (299)		
Bayley, Nathn	FARM (2)	Bearce, Joseph	CORN (22)
Bazell, David	CHAT (42)	Bearce, Austin	CORN (87)
Beace, Joseph	FARM (436)	Bearce, Joseph	CORN (15, 16, 18, 20, 22, 23)
Beach, Abijah	KENT (E60)		
Beach, Andrew	BRAN (164, 166, 174, 175, 179)	Beard, Andrew	MILF (102)
		Beard, George	DERB (148, 167, 168)
Beach, Az Jur	HEBR (217)	Beard, James	DERB (107, 113, 120, 122, 124, 126, 131, 132, 135, 140, 141, ,145, 170)
Beach, Bennoney	HARL (55)		
Beach, Bennony	HARL (58)		
Beach, Benoni	HARL (53)	Beardslee, Nehemiah	CORN (2, 10, 22, 88, 91)
Beach, Cephas	HARL (53)	Beardsley, Hezh	FARM (442)
Beach, David	LITC (129, 152)	Beardsley, Nehemiah	DANB (39)
Beach, E	BRAN (173, 178)	Bears, Benjamin	MILF (88)
Beach, Ebenezr	BRAN (163)	Bearse, Joseph	CORN (10, 13, 16, 86)
Beach, Edmond	CORN (86)	Beats, Esaker Isn	KILY (90)
Beach, Elisha	HEBR (218, 233)	Bebee, Daniel	CANA (11), KENT (D1)
Beach, Elisha Ens	HEBR (216)	Bebee, Elisha	CANA (11, 27)
Beach, Elnathan	BRAN (164, 165, 166), 167, 170, 173, 174, 175, 176, 178, 179, 180)	Bebee, Isaac	CANA (27, 28)
		Becher, Abraham	DERB (127)
		Beckley, Elijah	CANA (64)
Beach, Ephraim	BRAN (164, 169, 173)	Beckley, Joseph	CANA (64)
Beach, Ezekiel	HARL (53)	Beckley, Joseph Jur	CANA (64)
Beach, John	CHES (16)	Beckley, Saml	CANA (64)
Beach, John Harrington	BRAN (167)	Beckley, Samuel	CANA (77)
		Becknal, Saml	ASHF (311)
Beach, Josiah	CORN (16, 86)	Becknal, Wm	ASHF (311)
Beach, Laban	LITC (129, 139)	Becknal, Zecheh	ASHF (214)
Beach, Linus	CORN (22, 88)	Beckwith, Barzillai	EHAD (44, 54, 66, 68)
Beach, Mathew	CORN (1)	Beckwith, Eliot	EHAD (84, 86)
Beach, Matthew	CORN (10, 22, 86)	Beckwith, Ezekiel B	EHAD (50, 55, 69, 79)

INDEX

Name	Index Page
Beckwith, Ezekiel Brockway	EHAD (48)
Beckwith, James	FARM (28)
Beckwith, James Jur	FARM (443)
Beckwith, Job	EHAD (86)
Beckwith, Joseph	EHAD (54)
Beckwith, Joseph 2d	EHAD (50, 69)
Beckwith, Joseph 3d	EHAD (65, 81, 87)
Beckwith, Joseph jur	EHAD (59)
Beckwith, Nathaniel	EHAD (60)
Beckwith, Saml	FARM (456)
Beckwith, Stephen	EHAD (69)
Beckwith, Thomas	EHAD (59, 65)
Beckwith, Thos	FARM (17)
Beeb, Robert	COLC (251)
Beebe, [ ]	DANB (71)
Beebe, Abner Doctr	EHAD (43)
Beebe, Asa	COLC (9, 243, 244, 245, 251)
Beebe, Asahel	CANA (9, 11, 12, 13, 20, 23, 24, 64, 77)
Beebe, B Col	LITC (159)
Beebe, Benjn	COLC (7)
Beebe, Bezaleel	LITC (158, 159)
Beebe, Bezaleel Col	LITC (155)
Beebe, Bezaleel Major r	LITC (139, 141)
Beebe, Caleb	EHAD (80)
Beebe, Capt	DANB (71)
Beebe, Da[ ]	CANA (16)
Beebe, Daniel	CANA (20, 28, 64), KENT (A28, C548, C552, D7, E60)
Beebe, Daniel Jur	KENT (E64)
Beebe, David	DANB (63)
Beebe, Elihu	EHAD (60)
Beebe, Elisha	CANA (12, 15, 17, ,19, 26, 28, 64)
Beebe, Isaac	CANA (18, 23, 77)
Beebe, James	CANA (11)
Beebe, John	EHAD (49, 80)
Beebe, John 2nd	CANA (14)
Beebe, John Capt	CANA (11)
Beebe, Joseph	DANB (39, 40, 41, 49, 45
Beebe, Joseph Jur	DANB (47, 54)
Beebe, Levi	EHAD (69, 86)
Beebe, Reuben	EHAD (61)
Beebe, Robert	COLC (10)
Beebe, Silas	EHAD (79)
Beebee, Reuben	EHAD (44)
Beebee, Robart	BOLT (180)
Beech, Adna	GOSH (102, 104, 112, 125, 120, 184)
Beech, Adna Jur	GOSH (115, 130, 138, 185)
Beech, Amos	GOSH (122, 184)
Beech, Amos Jur	GOSH (185)
Beech, Bennoney	HARL (55)
Beech, Benoni	HARL (45)

Name	Index Page
Beech, Capt	GOSH (102, 104, 105, 109, 110, 112, 113, ,116, 120, 126, 132, 133, 136, ,138, 184)
Beech, Cephas	HARL (45, 47)
Beech, Chauncy	GOSH (110, 112, 120. 122, 130, 138, 184)
Beech, E Capt	GOSH (133, 140)
Beech, Edmund Capt	GOSH (112, 116, 118, 120, 125, 134, 137, 138)
Beech, Elnathan	CHES (A)
Beech, Ezekiel	HARL (45)
Beech, Fisk	GOSH (102, 104, 109, 110, 112, 115, 119, 120, 122, 123, 124, 126, 128, 129, 130, 134, 138, 139, 184)
Beech, Jacob	GOSH (102, 120, 184)
Beech, John	CHES (4, 11, 16, 14, A)
Beech, Landee	MILF (104)
Beech, Lander	MILF (85, 86)
Beech, Linus	GOSH (102, 184)
Beech, Minius	GOSH (184)
Beech, Moses	GOSH (186)
Beech, Munson	GOSH (183)
Beech, Oliver	GOSH (115)
Beech, Olliver	GOSH (183)
Beech, Samuel	CHES (7, 8, 11, 14), HARL (45, 48)
Beech, Thomas	HARL (48)
Beech, William	GOSH (120, 127, 185)
Beech, Wm	GOSH (183)
Beech. Edmund Capt	GOSH (115)
Beeche, John	CHES (8)
Beecher, Abraham	DERB (131, 133, 140, 145, 148) ,KENT (D10)
Beecher, Hezekiah	CHES (9, 11, 14)
Beecher, Isaac	DERB (131, 132, 133, 140, 141, 145), HARW (2)
Beecher, Josh	FARM (442)
Beedbe, Benjn	COLC (9)
Beeman, Daniel	HARL (51)
Beeman, Thomas	KENT (E62)
Beeman, Thomas Jr	HARL (59, 60)
Beeman, Thos	HARL (58)
Beeman, Thos Lieut	HARL (55, 56, 58, 62)
Beemis, Jonathan	ASHF (311)
Beemis, Jonth	ASHF (313)
Beers, David	FAIR (267)
Beers, Eber	BRAN (173)
Beers, Nathan	FAIR (255, 258)
Beers, Nehemh	FAIR (262, 263)
Beers, Nehemiah	FAIR (254, 257, 260, 262)
Beers, Reuben	FAIR (267)
Beers, Saml Jur	FAIR (259, 263)
Beers, Wheeler	BRAN (176)
Begles, En	ASHF (202)
Belcher, Jonathan	CHAT (47)
Belcher, Jonth Enn	CHAT (45)

INDEX

Name	Index Page	Name	Index Page
Belden, Rosseter	HARF (255A)	Benedict, [ ]	DANB (65)
Belding, Bartholomew	CANA (77)	Benedict, Abner	MIDD (367)
Belding, Benja	FARM (9, 17, 28, 455)	Benedict, Benjn	DANB (39)
Belding, Charles	CANA (12, 15, 17, 19, 27, 64, 77)	Benedict, Caleb	DANB (47, 51, 68, 70)
		Benedict, Ebenr 3d	DANB (55)
Belding, Charles Jur	CANA (64)	Benedict, Ebenr Jur	DANB (45, 64)
Belding, Ezra	FARM (443)	Benedict, Eleazer	DANB (63)
Belding, Ezra Jur	FARM (456)	Benedict, Eliakim	DANB (56, 59)
Belding, Gideon	FARM (2, 438, 455)	Benedict, Ezra	DANB (70)
Belding, John [ ]	FARM (28)	Benedict, Isaac	DANB (39, 60)
Belding, Jona	FARM (2, 6, 18, 23, 27, 435, 438, 443, 446, 447, 449, 452)	Benedict, Jakin	DANB (59, 68, 71)
		Benedict, John	DANB (39), KENT (D3)
		Benedict, John Lut	DANB (47)
Belding, Jonathan	CANA (11, 12, 15, 16, 64) ,FARM (29)	Benedict, Jonah	DANB (50, 51, 58, 63)
		Benedict, Jonas	DANB (49, 40, 43, 47)
Belding, Jonathn	FARM (433)	Benedict, Jonth	DANB (51, 58)
Belding, Leonard	FARM (28, 443)	Benedict, Joseph	DANB (40, 43, 47, 51, 55, 56, 58, 63)
Belding, Rosseter	HARF (285)		
Belding, Sarah	CANA (26, 64)	Benedict, Joshua	DANB (43, 51, 58, 63)
Beldling, John	FARM (456)	Benedict, Leml	DANB (47, 56)
Belknap, Job	EWIN (8)	Benedict, Lemuel	DANB (39)
Belknap, Simeon	EWIN (8, 85, 89)	Benedict, Levi	DANB (47)
Bell, Elisha	FARM (443, 449)	Benedict, Nathl	DANB (39), DANB (43)
Bell, Elizur	GLAS (94)	Benedict, Noble	DANB (49, 51, 54, 58, 60, 61, 64)
Bell, Hezekiah	HARW (3, 8)		
Bell, Ketchel	CORN (1, 2, 9, 10, 20, 22, 23, 86)	Benedict, Noble Capt	DANB (47, 50, 53, 65)
		Benedict, Oliver	DANB (47, 56)
Bell, Ketchel Junr	CORN (89, 90)	Benedict, Robert	DANB (43, 51, 58, 63)
Bell, Ketchell	CORN (14)	Benedict, Saml	DANB (39)
Bell, Kitchel	CORN (15, 18)	Benedict, Saml 4th	DANB (51, 58, 63)
Bell, Soln	FARM (436)	Benedict, Samuel 3d	DANB (63)
Bell, Thos	LEBA (326)	Benedict, Thads	DANB (41)
Bellamey, Aaron	CHES (5)	Benedict, Theophs Jur	DANB (59)
Bellamey, Mathew	CHES (4)	Benedict, Thos	DANB (39, 43, 49)
Bellamy, Aaron	CHES (9, 12)	Benedict, Timo	DANB (40)
Bellamy, Amos	CHES (8)	Benedict, Zadock	DANB (41)
Bellamy, Henry	CHES (12)	Benedict, Zadok	DANB (40)
Bellamy, Justus	CHES (11)	Benedt, Elear	DANB (40)
Bellows, Hezekiah	KILY (19, 32)	Benedt, Eliakim Jur	DANB (63)
Bellows, John	GROT [4], [15], [25]	Benedt, Jonth	DANB (63)
Bellows, John Leut	GROT ([15])	Benedt, Joseph	DANB (40)
Bellows, John Lieut	GROT ([18])	Benedt, Leml	DANB (41)
Belton, Jonas Capt	GROT ([10], [12])	Benedt, Noble	DANB (50)
Beman, Ebenezer	KENT (E59, E63)	Benedt, Oliver	DANB (40)
Beman, Ezekiel	KENT (E64)	Benedt, Saml 4th	DANB (40)
Beman, Mathias	KENT (C554)	Benedt, Thos	DANB (40, 41)
Beman, Matthias	KENT (C551)	Benham, Isaac	HARL (52)
Beman, Park	KENT (E59)	Benham, James	FARM (455)
Beman, Thomas	HARL (47), KENT (E58)	Benham, Jeames Jur	FARM (455)
Beman, Thomas Jr	HARL (43, 47, 48, 61)	Benham, Joel	FARM (455)
Beman, Thomas Leiut	HARL (45)	Benham, Joseph	FARM (443, 455)
Beman, Thos Junr	HARL (43, 44, 46, 51, 58)	Benham, Reuben	HARL (48)
Beman, Thos Leiut	HARL (42, 44, 46, 49, 50, 51)	Benham, Uri	CHES (12)
		Benhame, John	CHES (9)
Beman, Truman	KENT (E60, E63)	Benidict, Elijah	KENT (D7, D8)
Bemas, Jonathan	ASHF (232)	Benidict, Jesse	KENT (E64)
Bement, Denis	ENFD (27, 35)	Benidict, John	KENT (B3, C548, C550)
Bement, Denis Jur	ENFD (26, 30, 34)	Benidict, Noble	DANB (46)
Bement, Saml Capt	MIDD (417)	Benitt, Deliverance	FAIR (255)
Bemis, Jonathan	ASHF (236)	Benjaman, Samuel	BOLT (183)

INDEX

Name	Index Page
Benjamen, Samuel	HARL (56)
Benjamens, Samuel	HARL (51)
Benjamin, Asher	HARL (43, 44, 46, 48)
Benjamin, Saml	HARL (43, 52, 58)
Benjamin, Samuel	HARL (44, 47, 49, 50)
Benjamins, Barzillia	MILF (88, 98)
Benjamins, Elizabth	HARL (53)
Benjamins, Samuel	HARL (51)
Benjamins, Simeon	CANT (146)
Bennedict, John	CORN (87)
Bennet, Christopher	COVE (314)
Bennet, Henchman	LEBA (305)
Bennet, Hinch	LEBA (327)
Bennet, Hinchn	LEBA (298, 299, 311, 316, 342)
Bennet, Hinchson	LEBA (323)
Bennet, Robt	LEBA (310)
Bennit, Christopher	COVE (172, 180)
Bennit, James	FAIR (259, 233, 353)
Bennit, Jesse	MANS (338, 348, 349)
Bennit, Joseph	MANS (233)
Bennit, Nathaniel	MANS (329)
Bennit, Nathl	MANS (268, 336)
Bennit, Nathl Junr	MANS (336)
Bennitt, Daniel Capt	FAIR (255, 259)
Bennitt, Danl	FAIR (255, 257, 259, 260, 262, 263, 266)
Bennitt, Danl Capt	FAIR (254, 255)
Bennitt, Deliv	FAIR (263)
Bennitt, Delive	FAIR (262)
Bennitt, Deliverance	FAIR (252, 253, 254, 255, 257, 259, 267)
Bennitt, Isaac	FAIR (255, 261, 262, 263
Bennitt, James	FAIR (256, 257, 258, 259, 260, 261, 262)
Bennitt, Joseph	FAIR (255, 258, 259, 262, 265, 266)
Bennitt, Joseph Capt	FAIR (252, 253, 254)
Bennitt, Joseph Lieut	FAIR (261)
Bennitt, Najah	FAIR (253, 263)
Bennitt, Nathan Jur	FAIR (265, 267)
Bennitt, Saml 3d	FAIR (254)
Bennitt, Samuel 3d	FAIR (252)
Bennitt, Thads	FAIR (267)
Bennitt, William	FAIR (259)
Bennitt, Wm	FAIR (257)
Bennnit, Del	FAIR (261)
Bentley, Benja	KENT (A28)
Bentley, Benjamin	KENT (E63)
Bentley, Benjn	KENT (E59)
Bentley, Green	KENT (E59)
Benton, Caleb	GUIL (270, 277)
Benton, Caleb Junr	GUIL (279)
Benton, Ebenezer	LITC (128, 135, 139, 142, 147, 153)
Benton, Ebenr	GLAS (93)
Benton, Eber	GUIL (274)
Benton, Edward	GLAS (70, 84, 93, 104)
Benton, Elihu	GUIL (285, 286, 288, 321, 322, 323)

Name	Index Page
Benton, Elisha	HARF (255A)
Benton, Jabez	GUIL (296, 310)
Benton, Jacob	HARW (3, 523)
Benton, Jared	GUIL (296, 310, 326, 336, 338)
Benton, Jehiel Capt	KENT (E58, E62)
Benton, John	HARF (265)
Benton, Josiah	GLAS (93, 110, 120, 184)
Benton, Josiah Jr	GLAS (96)
Benton, Josiah Jur	GLAS (89, 106, 108)
Benton, Levy	CANA (77)
Benton, Lot	GUIL (270, 301, 323, 334
Benton, Nathaniel	LITC (129, 132, 134, 147
Benton, Noah	GUIL (274, 323, 326, 338, 340)
Benton, Saml	GUIL (269, 287, 300, 311, 325)
Benton, Samuel	HARF (255A)
Benton, Seth	GUIL (324)
Benton, Silas	GUIL (296, 325)
Benton, Timo	GUIL (310, 332, 333)
Benton, Timothy	GUIL (278, 286)
Berry, Barnabas	KENT (E60, E63)
Berry, Ebenezer	KENT (C552, D1, D7)
Berry, Ebenr	KENT (C548)
Berry, John	KENT (E63)
Berry, Joseph	KENT (C548, C550, C552, C555, E58, E62, E63)
Berry, Lemuel	KENT (D10, E59, E63)
Berry, Nathaniel	KENT (A27, B1, C543, C546, C548, C550, C552, C554, D5, D10, D14, E62)
Berry, Nathl	KENT (D1, D7, E58)
Berry, Nathn	KENT (A28)
Berstow, John	CANT (150)
Bestow, Saml	CANT (150)
Betts, Silas	GREE (119, 124, 126, 127)
Beul, Capt	GOSH (105, 109, 110, 114, 117, 139, 141)
Beul, Jonath Jur	GOSH (112)
Beul, Linus	GOSH (110)
Beul, Timoth	GOSH (183)
Bevin, Benja	MIDD (370, 394, 413)
Bevin, Benjamin	MIDD (404)
Bevin, Ebenezer	MIDD (364)
Bevin, Ezra	CHAT (33, 37, 43, 50)
Bevin, Isaac	CHAT (44, 58, 59, 68)
Bevin, William	CHAT (43)
Bevins, Ezra	CHAT (39)
Bevins, William Jur	CHAT (43)
Bewel, Elijah	COLC (246)
Bewel, Joseph	GLAS (94)
Bewell, Jesse	CORN (16)
Bibbens, Timo	MANS (279, 281)
Bibbens, Timothy	MANS (233, 326, 348, 357)
Bibbins, Ebenezer	HARF (275)

INDEX

Name	Index Page	Name	Index Page
Bibbins, Israel	FAIR (251, 256)	Biglow, Jonathn	COLC (8)
Bibbins, Isreal	FAIR (253)	Bill, Elijah	HARW (10)
Bicknell, James	MANS (280, 281)	Bill, [ ]	LEBA (339)
Bicknell, John	ASHF (310)	Bill, Azarh	LEBA (311)
Bicknell, Moses	MANS (271, 277, 358)	Bill, Azariah	LEBA (298)
Bicknell, Saml	ASHF (202, 209)	Bill, Banaijah	HARL (52)
Bicknell, Willm	ASHF (236)	Bill, Benajah	LEBA (294)
Bicknell, Zachariah	ASHF (210, 310)	Bill, Benajh	HARL (58)
Bicknil, Zecheh	ASHF (308)	Bill, Benjn	GROT ([4], [9])
Bidwel, Capt	FARM (445)	Bill, Bennajah	HARL (44)
Bidwel, Isaac Capt	FARM (450)	Bill, Eliphalet	LEBA (305)
Bidwel, Theodore	LITC (153, 158)	Bill, Elipt	LEBA (311)
Bidwell, Aaron	HARF (288, 293)	Bill, Elisha	LEBA (326)
Bidwell, Amos	HARF (253, 255A, 256, 263, 267, 273, 281)	Bill, James	CHAT (30, 36, 37, 41, 43, 45, 50, 58), 60, 67, 69)
Bidwell, Benjamin	CHAT (40)	Bill, James Lt	CHAT (59, 64, 66)
Bidwell, Benjamin En	CHAT (39)	Bill, Jonathan	HARL (44, 51)
Bidwell, Capt	FARM (23, 25, 32, 450)	Bill, Jos Cap	LEBA (320)
Bidwell, Daniel	CHAT (42)	Bill, Jothn	HARL (52)
Bidwell, Daniel Junr	HARF (253)	Bill, Oliver	LEBA (297, 310, 315, 321, 326,, 333, 341)
Bidwell, Eleazer	COLE (2, 5, 7, 9, 10, 11, 13, 113, 115)	Bill, Thos Lt	LEBA (320)
Bidwell, Elisha	HARF (281)	Bille, Jonathan	HARL (47)
Bidwell, George	HARF (281, 292)	Billings, Jesse	COLC (255)
Bidwell, Hezekiah	GLAS (93)	Billings, Stephen	GROT [4], [6], [7], [8], [9], [16]
Bidwell, Hezh	GLAS (105)		
Bidwell, Isaac	FARM (5, 27, 449, 451, 443, 444, 446)	Billings, Stephen Capt	GROT [7], [15], [20], [21], [22], 25]
Bidwell, Isaac Capt	FARM (2, 3, 8, 17, 29, 434, 436, 438, 447, 454)	Billins, Jesse	COLC (249)
Bidwell, Jacob	HARF (266, 272)	Billins, Moses	KENT (E59)
Bidwell, John	CHAT (29, 32, 34, 37, 40, 46, 51, 56, 58, 61, 63, 64, 68)	Bills, Benajah	HARL (48)
		Bills, Elijah	HARW (3, 533)
		Bingham, Asa	BOLT (157, 180, 182)
Bidwell, Jonathan	GLAS (94)	Bingham, Doctr	HEBR (219)
Bidwell, Joseph	COLE (4, 5, 113), GLAS (66, 70, 75, 78, 83, 85, 94, 98, 108),	Bingham, Eleazar	LEBA (305)
		Bingham, Stephen	HEBR (234, 246), LEBA (299)
Bidwell, Saml	GLAS (106)	Bingham, Stepn	LEBA (297)
Bidwell, Saml [ ]	GLAS (114)	Bingham, Thos	LEBA (297, 299)
Bidwell, Samuel	GLAS (66, 70, 74, 79, 83, 92, 94, 95, 98)	Bingham, Will	CANT (150, 151)
		Bingham, William	CANT (144, 145, 147, 165)
Bidwell, Stephen	HARF (283, 292), LITC (133, 139, 152)	Bingham, Wm	CANT (155, 156, 180)
Bidwell, Thomas	GLAS (111)	Birch, Mary	KILY (98)
Bidwell, Zebulon	HARF (253)	Birchard, Phinehas	ASHF (209, 227, 310)
Bigby, Nathan	KILY (92)	Bird, Jona Doctr	FARM (12)
Bigelow, Asa	COLC (11)	Bird, Saml	FARM (5, 24)
Bigelow, Bond	COLC (10, 248)	Bird, Seth	LITC (128, 129, 130, 133, 135, 149, 159, 161)
Bigelow, Daniel	COLC (243)		
Bigelow, David	GLAS (78, 80, 111)	Bird, Seth D	LITC (149)
Bigelow, Elisha	COLC (11)	Bird, Wm Jur	HEBR (220)
Bigelow, Jabez	HARL (44)	Birdsey, [ ]	CORN (11, 28)
Bigelow, John Junr	COLC (249)	Birdsey, Ebenezer	CORN (90)
Bigelow, Jonathan	COLC (249), HARF (251(2), 255A, 253, 259, 275, 287, 251(2), 255A)	Birdsey, John	MIDD (347)
		Birdseye, Benja	MIDD (382)
		Birdseye, Benjamin	MIDD (364)
Bigland, Wm	MIDD (387)	Birdseye, Gershom	MIDD (364, 382, 395, 395)
Biglow, Azariah	COLC (255)		
Biglow, David	GLAS (93)	Birdseye, John	MIDD (388)

600

INDEX

Name	Index Page	Name	Index Page
Birge, [ ]	HEBR (234)	Bissell, Hezh	MANS (265)
Birge, Jonathan Capt	BOLT (146)	Bissell, Isaac	LITC (139, 141)
Birnham, Silas	HARF (252(2))	Bissell, Jerijah	EWIN (85)
Bishop, Abraham	DURH (12), HARL (59, 49, 50, 51, 53, 58, 59)	Bissell, John	BOLT (181)
		Bissell, Jonathan Jur	EWIN (89)
Bishop, Abram	GUIL (326, 318, 327), HARL (56, 57)	Bissell, Jonathn Jur	EWIN (85)
		Bissell, Jos	LEBA (299)
Bishop, Benja	FARM (28)	Bissell, Mat[ ]	EWIN (8)
Bishop, Benjn	FARM (443)	Bissell, Mathew	EWIN (13)
Bishop, Charles	DURH (17)	Bissell, Matthew	EWIN (8, 10, 11, 12, 15, 85, 88)
Bishop, Daniel	GUIL (313)		
Bishop, David	GUIL (280, 286, 287, 293, 294, 299, 302, 327, 331, 334, 336)	Bissell, Noah	EWIN (8, 10, 11, 85, 88)
		Bissell, Ozias Junr	HARF (281)
		Bissell, Timothy	EWIN (13, 17, 85, 89)
Bishop, David Junr	GUIL (344)	Bissell, William	EWIN (9)
Bishop, Ebenezer	MIDD (357)	Bissell, Wm	LEBA (333, 334)
Bishop, Ebenr 2nd	GUIL (311)	Bixbey, Nathan	KILY (19)
Bishop, Enos	GUIL (326, 334)	Bixby, Ebenr	FAIR (258, 260, 263, 266, 267)
Bishop, James	FARM (9), GUIL (279, 299)		
		Bixby, Jesse	KILY (4)
Bishop, James 2d	GUIL (293)	Bixby, Nathan	KILY (96a)
Bishop, Jesse	CANA (64), GUIL (269)	Blackman, Aaron	COVE (174)
Bishop, John	BOLT (18, 182), GUIL (269)	Blackman, Aron	COVE (166)
		Blackman, Capt	MIDD (358)
Bishop, John Jur	BOLT (167, 180)	Blackman, David	COVE (174)
Bishop, Joseph	FARM (433)	Blackman, E Capt	MIDD (372)
Bishop, Josiah	GUIL (270)	Blackman, Elijah	MIDD (346, 349, 376, 377)
Bishop, Leaman	LITC (147)		
Bishop, Luman	LITC (158)	Blackman, Elijah Capt	MIDD (377)
Bishop, Nathl 2nd	GUIL (274)	Blackman, Jos	LEBA (298)
Bishop, Saml	GOSH (110, 115, 121, 184), GUIL (270, 277)	Blackman, Nathl Cade	KENT (C551)
		Blackman, Wm	HEBR (220, 234)
Bishop, Seth	LITC (131, 134, 135, 139, 142, 158)	Blackman, Zahariah	KENT (E60)
		Blague, Joseph	CHAT (69)
Bishop, Sylvanus	LITC (129)	Blague, Joseph Capt	CHAT (31, 51, 53)
Bishop, Timo	DURH (17, 21, 24, 25)	Blague, Joseph Majr	CHAT (64, 67)
Bishop, Widow	MIDD (357)	Blake, Stephen	CHAT (48), MIDD (375, 383)
Bishop, Willm	DURH (25)		
Bissel, Abel	HEBR (216, 236, 246)	Blakesley, Asa	CHES (14, 15)
Bissel, Hez	HEBR (217, 218, 245)	Blakesley, Ithamer	CANA (15, 24, 64)
Bissell, [ ]	EWIN (13)	Blakesley, Moses	CHES (4)
Bissell, Aaron	EWIN (8, 9), 10, 12, 13, 15, 17, 85, 88)	Blakesly, Reuben	HARW (523)
		Blakeston, John Junr	BRAN (178)
Bissell, Aaron Capt	EWIN (14, 16)	Blakeston, Stephen	BRAN (169)
Bissell, Aaron Jur	EWIN (17, 85, 89)	Blakiston, John Junr	BRAN (169)
Bissell, Calvin	LITC (158)	Blakiston, Stephen	BRAN (170, 176)
Bissell, Charles	EWIN (8, 17, 85, 89)	Blakslee, Ithamar	CANA (27)
Bissell, Dan	EWIN (85, 88)	Blaksly, Samuel	COLE (13)
Bissell, Danl	EWIN (85), LEBA (310, 317)	Blanchard, Ebenezer	KILY (92)
		Blatchley, Aaron	GUIL (300)
Bissell, David	EWIN (7, 85, 88)	Blatchley, Joshua	GUIL (310, 325, 326, 327, 336)
Bissell, Ebenezer	EWIN (85)		
Bissell, Ebenr	EWIN (88)	Blatchley, Joshua Lieut	GUIL (277, 287)
Bissell, Eli	EWIN (12, 13, 14, 15, 16. 85, 89)	Blatchley, Joshuah Lieut	GUIL (288, 295)
Bissell, Elisha	EWIN (11, 12, 16)	Blatchly, Joshua	GUIL (300)
Bissell, Hez Capt	EWIN (88)	Blatchly, Joshua Lieut	GUIL (270, 300, 301, 335)
Bissell, Hezekiah	EWIN (8, 10)		
Bissell, Hezekiah Capt	EWIN (12, 13, 14, 15, 16, 17, 85)	Blatchly, Joshuah Lieut	GUIL (277)

INDEX

Name	Index Page	Name	Index Page
Blatchly, Moses Junr	GUIL (272)	Bolles, Asa	LEBA (315, 341)
Blatchly, Moses Liut	GUIL (301)	Bolles, David	ASHF (201)
Blin, Bille	CANA (11, 12, 16, 17, 19, 23, 64, 77)	Bolls, [ ]	ASHF (237)
		Bolls, David	ASHF (228)
Blish, Benjamin	BOLT (181)	Bolls, David Capt	ASHF (226, 235, 236)
Blish, David	GLAS (98)	Boman, Joseph	CANA (27)
Blish, John	COLC (5, 6, 8, 12, 248, 251, 254, 255, 256)	Bond, Will	CANT (150, 151)
		Bond, William	CANT (145, 161, 168, 182)
Blish, Joseph	BOLT (146, 148, 180, 182)	Bond, Wm	CANT (146, 147, 156, 177)
Blish, Silvanus	COLC (4, 8, 242, 246, 247, 248, 249)	Bonney, Jethro	CORN (12)
Bliss, [ ]	HEBR (236)	Bonney, Levi	CORN (2, 9, 10, 22, 23, 25)
Bliss, Abm	LEBA (310)		
Bliss, Abm Jur	LEBA (320)	Bonney, Perez	CORN (87, 90)
Bliss, Amos	LEBA (297, 341)	Bonney, Titus	CORN (18, 23, 25, 87)
Bliss, Elias	LEBA (297, 310, 318)	Bonni, Asa	GOSH (185)
Bliss, Elias Capt	LEBA (320, 325, 330, 337)	Bonny, [ ]	GOSH (127)
		Bonny, Asa	GOSH (130, 135)
Bliss, Ellis	HEBR (220)	Bonny, Perez	GOSH (135)
Bliss, Henry	LEBA (315)	Bonny, Titus	CORN (16, 22)
Bliss, James	HEBR (217)	Booge, Amos	EHAD (45, 50)
Bliss, John	KENT (A28, B1, C548, C551, C552, C555, D1, D7, D8, D10, E58, E62), LEBA (296)	Booge, James	EHAD (50, 87)
		Booge, Jeffery	FARM (13)
		Booge, Jonathan	EHAD (44, 45, 50, 55, 86
		Booge, Oliver	FARM (13)
Bliss, John Capt	KENT (D12)	Booge, Saml	FARM (13, 18)
Bliss, John Leiut	KENT (C543)	Booge, Saml C	FARM (444)
Bliss, Neziah	HEBR (218, 219, 220, 231, 233, 234, 245, 249, 234)	Booge, Saml Cook	FARM (3)
		Booge, Samuel	EHAD (88, 18)
		Booge, Timothy	EHAD (49, 55)
Bliss, Neziah Doctr	HEBR (216, 216)	Booles, Capt	ASHF (233)
Bliss, Saml	LEBA (297, 299)	Booles, David Capt	ASHF (202)
Bliss, Saml Jur	LEBA (326, 334)	Bools, Capt	ASHF (229, 232, 238)
Bliss, Thomas	CHAT (45, 58, 65)	Bools, David Capt	ASHF (232)
Blodgett, Abner	EWIN (85, 88)	Booth, Joseph Capt	ENFD (27)
Blush, David	GLAS (63, 66, 70, 74, 82)	Booth, Caleb	EWIN (17)
		Booth, Caleb Jur	EWIN (11, 17, 85, 88)
Blush, David Jur	GLAS (78, 91)	Booth, Capt	ENFD (26, 28, 29, 32, 33, 34, 35)
Bluss, David	GLAS (93)		
Blyn, Billa	CANA (27, 28)	Booth, Daniel	ENFD (18, 24, 30, 34)
Boardman, Ephm	FARM (17)	Booth, Elisha	FARM (442)
Boardman, Ephraim	FARM (455)	Booth, Elisha Jur	FARM (9, 455)
Boardman, Ephrm	FARM (436)	Booth, James	FARM (2, 3, 9, 17, 18, 29, 433, 434, 438, 444, 445, 449, 455)
Boardman, Epm	FARM (17)		
Boardman, Jonathan	HADD (109, 110)		
Boardman, Jonthn	HADD (148)	Booth, John	ENFD (28, 30, 32, 33, 34, 35)
Boardman, Luther	HADD (115, 122, 125, 129)		
		Booth, John Junr	ENFD (19, 24, 25)
Boardman, Moses	MIDD (358, 382, 395, 398, 405, 413)	Booth, John Liut	ENFD (26)
		Booth, Joseph	FARM (9, 29, 441, 450)
		Booth, Joseph Capt	ENFD (26, 27, 28, 29, 30, 32)
Boardman, Nathan	MIDD (419)		
Boardman, Nathaniel	MIDD (419)	Booth, Joseph Jur	ENFD (18, 19, 24, 34)
Boardman, Ozias	CANA (28)	Booth, Leut	FARM (8)
Boardman, Sherman	KENT (B6)	Booth, Levi	EWIN (85, 88)
Boardman, Timothy	MIDD (347, 356)	Booth, Nathan	FARM (5, 443)
Bofinton, Thomas	KILY (98)	Booth, Nathan Jur	FARM (436)
Bohan, [ ]	COLC (256)	Booth, Nathl	FARM (455)
Boles, David Capt	ASHF (218)	Booth, Robert	FARM (24), 29)
Bolles, [ ]	HEBR (218)		

INDEX

Name	Index Page
Booth, Zachariah	ENFD (28)
Boradman, Timothy	MIDD (350)
Borden, Aashel	HARL (59)
Borden, Asael	HARL (52, 55)
Borden, Asahel	HARL (47)
Borden, Jno	HARL (52)
Borden, John	HARL (44, 45, 46, 47, 48, 49, 51, 57, 58)
Borden, John Lieut	HARL (58, 60)
Borden, John Sergat	HARL (54)
Borden, Saml	HARL (46, 53)
Borden, Samuel	HARL (43, 45, 47, 49, 51
Bordin, John	HARL (56)
Bordin, John Lieut	HARL (60)
Bordin, Samuel	HARL (50)
Bordman, Elnathan	KENT (C548)
Bordman, Ephm	FARM (444)
Bordman, Josiah	MIDD (363)
Bordman, Moses	MIDD (372)
Bordman, Nathan	MIDD (363)
Bordman, Nathanl	MIDD (363)
Bordman, Nathl	MIDD (374)
Bordman, Oliver	LITC (153)
Bordman, Ozias	CANA (12, 14, 19, 21, 64, 77)
Bordman, Saml	CHAT (42, 51)
Bordman, Saml A	MIDD (372)
Bordman, Saml Allen	MIDD (382)
Bordman, Timo	MIDD (367)
Bordman, Timothy	MIDD (365,367, 378)
Bordwell, Joel Revd	KENT (E58, E62)
Bortun, Saml	CHAT (41, 52)
Bosworth, Aaron	ASHF (232)
Bosworth, Allen	ASHF (236)
Bosworth, Benja	ASHF (308)
Bosworth, Ebenezer	ASHF (227, 232)
Bosworth, Ebenr	ASHF (218, 232)
Bosworth, Eber	ASHF (209)
Bosworth, Ebnr	ASHF (236, 237)
Bosworth, John	ASHF (232, 310)
Bosworth, Saml	MANS (279, 281)
Botchford, John	DERB (120, 122, 134)
Botchford, Nehemiah	DERB (106, 113, 120, 122, 134, 140)
Botchford, Samuel Jur	DERB (120)
Botsford, David	MILF (102, 103)
Botsford, David Junr	MILF (104)
Botsford, Isaac	MILF (82, 88, 98)
Bouge, Jeffery	FARM (13)
Bouge, Oliver	FARM (13)
Bouge, Saml	FARM (9, 434)
Bouge, Saml B	FARM (29)
Bouge, Saml C	FARM (29, 445)
Bouge, Saml Cook	FARM (438, 455)
Bouge, Samuel	FARM (434)
Bouge, Samuel C	FARM (449)
Boughton, Benja	DANB (61)
Boughton, Benja Jur	DANB (69)
Boughton, Benjn Jur	DANB (39, 41, 51, 60)
Boughton, Benjn Lut	DANB (55)

Name	Index Page
Boughton, Daniel	DANB (51, 54)
Boughton, David	DANB (39, 40, 45, 51)
Boughton, David Jur	DANB (40, 47, 49, 51)
Boughton, Eli	DANB (54)
Boughton, Mattw	DANB (51)
Bougton, Daniel	DANB (50)
Boutwell, [ ]	ASHF (206)
Bow, Isaac	MIDD (376, 381, 388)
Bow, Peleg	MIDD (367)
Bow, Samuel	MIDD (376)
Bowe[ ], Joseph	MIDD (358)
Bowen, [ ]	ASHF (217)
Bowen, Christor	ASHF (311, 313)
Bowers, Azel	EWIN (17)
Bowers, Benjamin	CHAT (30)
Bowers, Jonathan	CHAT (58)
Bowers, Jonathn	CHAT (51)
Bowman, Elisha	CANT (180)
Bowman, Joseph	CANA (23)
Boyles, [ ]	ASHF (213)
Boyls, Deborah	BRAN (171)
Boynton, Oliver	COVE (177)
Bozworth, Ebenr	ASHF (220, 226, 308)
Bozworth, Ebenr	ASHF (311)
Br[ ], Hugh	MIDD (365)
Br[ ], Isaac	FARM (17)
Br[ ], Luke	FARM (17)
Brace, [ ]	HARW (2)
Brace, A Capt	HARL (43)
Brace, Abel	HARL (53)
Brace, Abel Capt	HARL (41, 43, 45, 46, 48, 49, 51, 57, 59, 60, 45)
Brace, Elizur	HARW (3, 7, 16, 22, 23, 24, 25)
Brace, Henry Junr	HARF (255A, 273, 292, 299)
Brace, James	HARW (25)
Brace, John	HARL (60)
Brace, Jonath	GLAS (83)
Brace, Jonathan	GLAS (92)
Brace, Joseph	HARL (43, 45, 48)
Brace, Nathl	HARW (24)
Bradford, Doct	CHAT (35)
Bradford, Jer Doctr	CHAT (62)
Bradford, Jeremiah	CHAT (60)
Bradford, Jeremiah Doctr	CHAT (43, 44, 45, 56, 58)
Bradford, Jerh	CHAT (29)
Bradford, Jerh Doctr	CHAT (29, 46, 54, 59, 67, 68)
Bradford, John	CANT (180)
Bradford, Saml	CANT (178)
Bradford, William	CANT (147, 160)
Bradford, Willm	CHAT (45)
Bradley, Abel	FAIR (263, 266)
Bradley, Abraham	LITC (128, 129, 135, 14, 147, 152, 153, 155, 157, 158, 160)

603

INDEX

Name	Index Page	Name	Index Page
Bradley, Abraham Capt	LITC (135, 138, 139, 142, 147, 148, 149, 153, 155, 158, 159, 161)	Brainard, John	HADD (120)
		Brainard, Obadiah	MIDD (363)
		Brainard, Stephen Capt	COLC (255)
Bradley, David	FAIR (255, 258, 260, 262, 263, 267), KENT (D11, E63)	Brainard, Timth	GLAS (106)
		Brainard, William	COLC (247, 251, 252)
		Brainard, Wm Ensign	COLC (255)
Bradley, David 2d	FAIR (253)	Brainerd, Doct	HADD (123)
Bradley, David Jur	FAIR (254, 262)	Brainerd, Josiah Ens	HADD (125)
Bradley, Elisha	FAIR (253, 255, 259, 263, 265)	Brainerd, [ ]	HADD (121, 127, 109)
		Brainerd, Aaron	HADD (148)
Bradley, Elnath	FAIR (262)	Brainerd, Abijah	HADD (109, 110, 113, 115, 116, 121, 125, 129)
Bradley, Elnathan	FAIR (260)		
Bradley, Enos	FAIR (253, 260)	Brainerd, Abijah Jur	HADD (109)
Bradley, Erastus	LITC (138)	Brainerd, Abner	CHAT (67)
Bradley, Francis Jur	FAIR (266)	Brainerd, Amasa	EHAD (45, 50, 64, 69)
Bradley, Gershom	FAIR (258, 266)	Brainerd, Amasa Lt	EHAD (80)
Bradley, Gilead	GUIL (338)	Brainerd, Asahel	HARL (51)
Bradley, Hez	FAIR (253, 255, 256, 258, 259, 262, 263, 265, 267)	Brainerd, Bezaleel	EHAD (54, 69, 89)
		Brainerd, Bushnel	HADD (148)
		Brainerd, Charles	HADD (148)
Bradley, Hezekiah	FAIR (254, 255, 260, 269	Brainerd, Cornelius	HADD (115, 148)
Bradley, Increase	FAIR (259, 261, 262, 269	Brainerd, Daniel	EHAD (44, 49, 109, 113, 114, 129)
Bradley, Isaac	FAIR (256)		
Bradley, James	FARM (443, 444)	Brainerd, Daniel Capt	CHAT (31, 33, 34, 37, 43, 45, 56, 61, 68)
Bradley, John	FAIR (258, 262, 263)		
Bradley, John 2d	FAIR (267)	Brainerd, Danll	EHAD (48)
Bradley, John Jur	FAIR (266)	Brainerd, David	EHAD (69), HADD (110, 113, 114, 115, 116, 117, 121, 122, 123, 125, 126, 127, 129, 130)
Bradley, Joseph	FAIR (267, 269)		
Bradley, Justice	FAIR (263)		
Bradley, Leaming	LITC (129, 131, 146, 155, 158)	Brainerd, Doct	HADD (109, 110, 112, 113, 114, 115, 116, 119, 122, 129)
Bradley, Miles	CANA (64)		
Bradley, Moses	FAIR (260)	Brainerd, Dudley	HADD (113)
Bradley, Nathan Jur	FAIR (258)	Brainerd, Eleazer	EHAD (55, 60, 69, 80, 87
Bradley, Oliver	CHES (14, 15)	Brainerd, Eleazer Lt	EHAD (50)
Bradley, Peter	FAIR (255)	Brainerd, Eliakim	HADD (130)
Bradley, Philemon	FARM (5, 443)	Brainerd, Eliakim Capt	HADD (111, 112, 113, 114, 116, 119, 121, 125, 126, 129, 130)
Bradley, Seth	FAIR (253, 263)		
Bradley, Simri	GUIL (278)		
Bradley, Timothy	BRAN (165, 166)	Brainerd, Elijah	HADD (110, 111, 121, 125, 129)
Bradley, Timy	FARM (443)		
Bradley, Zalmon	FAIR (265, 269)	Brainerd, Elijah Lieut	HADD (113, 114, 115, 116, 117, 125)
Bradley, Zina	LITC (152)		
Bradly, Abraham Cap	LITC (161)	Brainerd, Elijh	HADD (121)
Bradly, Capt	GOSH (119)	Brainerd, Elisha	HADD (109, 110, 129)
Bradly, Enos	DERB (106, 113, 120, 122, 124, 126, 127, 132, 141, 145, 168)	Brainerd, Enoch	EHAD (49, 54, 59)
		Brainerd, Enoch Capt	EHAD (67, 87)
		Brainerd, Ezra	HADD (109, 110, 111, 113, 114, 116, 117, 124, 126, 127, 128, 129)
Bradly, Simri	GUIL (295)		
Bradly, Timothy	BRAN (165)	Brainerd, Gideon	HADD (109, 110, 113, 121, 129)
Bragg, Ebenr	GUIL (294, 340)		
Brague, Joseph Capt	CHAT (56)	Brainerd, Gideon Ens	HADD (109, 110, 113, 114, 124, 125)
Brainaird, Asahel	HARL (44)		
Brainard, [ ]	HARL (50)	Brainerd, Giles	HADD (127, 129, 148)
Brainard, Asael	HARL (52)	Brainerd, Heber	HADD (109, 148)
Brainard, Asahel	HARL (43)	Brainerd, Heman	HADD (114, 122, 125, 148)
Brainard, Ashel	HARL (61)		
Brainard, Eleazer	EHAD (45)	Brainerd, Hez	HADD (125)
Brainard, Jabez	MIDD (344)	Brainerd, Hez Doct	HADD (124, 127)
Brainard, Jeptha	MIDD (349)		

604

INDEX

Name	Index Page
Brainerd, Hezekiah	HADD (110, 114)
Brainerd, Hezh	HADD (121, 128, 130)
Brainerd, Jabez	HADD (110, 111, 112)
Brainerd, James	CHAT (58)
Brainerd, Jared	EHAD (44)
Brainerd, Jedediah Ens	HADD (123)
Brainerd, Jedediah Jur	HADD (109)
Brainerd, Jepthae	MIDD (362)
Brainerd, Jepthah	HADD (114)
Brainerd, Jeremiah	HADD (110, 114, 116, 125, 148)
Brainerd, Jesse	HADD (114, 148)
Brainerd, John	EHAD (86, 110, 112, 113, 115, 121, 125, 129, 148)
Brainerd, John Jur	HADD (113, 114, 116, 121, 125)
Brainerd, Jonah	EHAD (54)
Brainerd, Jonathan	HADD (109, 110, 113, 115, 116, 124, 125, 126, 129, 148)
Brainerd, Jonathan Lt	HADD (121)
Brainerd, Joseph Capt	HADD (120)
Brainerd, Joseph Ens	HADD (123)
Brainerd, Josiah	HADD (109, 130)
Brainerd, Josiah 3d	HADD (148)
Brainerd, Josiah Ens	HADD (116, 119, 120, 122, 123, 125)
Brainerd, Josiah Jur	HADD (112)
Brainerd, Josiah Lieut	HADD (129)
Brainerd, Nathan	CHAT (29, 39, 40, 58, 64)
Brainerd, Nathl	HADD (113)
Brainerd, Nehe	HADD (109, 110, 111, 112, 116, 121, 123, 125, 126)
Brainerd, Neheh	HADD (130)
Brainerd, Nehemiah	HADD (110, 114, 128)
Brainerd, Obadiah	MIDD (365)
Brainerd, Oliver	HADD (125)
Brainerd, Othnail	CHAT (30)
Brainerd, Othniel	CHAT (33, 40, 46, 54)
Brainerd, Ozias	CHAT (31)
Brainerd, Phineas Lieut	HADD (120)
Brainerd, Phinehas	HADD (129)
Brainerd, Phinehas Jur	HADD (109, 113)
Brainerd, Phinehas Lieut	HADD (109, 110, 111, 112, 114, 115, 116, 117, 118, 121, 125, 126, 130)
Brainerd, Phinhehas Jur	HADD (110)
Brainerd, Prosper	HADD (109, 110, 113)
Brainerd, Simon	CHAT (31, 45, 54)
Brainerd, Stephen	CHAT (31, 38, 39), HADD (112)
Brainerd, Stephen Capt	CHAT (45, 56, 59, 64, 68)
Brainerd, William	HADD (129)
Brainerd, Willm	HADD (114)
Brainerd, Wm	HADD (129)
Brainerd, Zacheah	HADD (148)
Brainerd, Zecheriah	HADD (110)

Name	Index Page
Brainers, Eleazer	EHAD (65)
Brainsmaide, Josiah	FAIR (258, 260)
Brandon, [ ]	ASHF (217)
Branerd, Asahel	HARL (48)
Branierd, Daniel	HADD (148)
Bray, Asa	FARM (430, 442, 445)
Bray, Asa Major	FARM (19)
Bray, Capt	FARM (445)
Brayman, Nathaniel	HARF (263)
Braynard, Timothy	EHAR (3)
Bread, John	COLC (251)
Brewer, Israel	GLAS (70, 93, 106)
Brewster Jedidiah	CANT (151)
Brewster, Benj n	LEBA (296)
Brewster, Comfort	LEBA (298, 334)
Brewster, Comft	LEBA (326)
Brewster, Daniel	LEBA (297)
Brewster, Elisha	MIDD (367)
Brewster, Elisha Junr	MIDD (402)
Brewster, Icha Jur	LEBA (326, 334, 341)
Brewster, Jedh	CANT (177, 182)
Brewster, Jesse	COVE (314)
Brewster, John	GUIL (329)
Brewster, Peleg	CANT (144)
Brewster, Prince	COLC (245)
Brewster, Saml	LEBA (334)
Brewster, Samuel	LEBA (305)
Brewster, Wadwth	LEBA (315)
Briant, Brown	KILY (95)
Bridgen, Thomas	MIDD (362)
Bridges, Samuel	COLC (249)
Brigg, Thos	ASHF (311)
Brigham, Elnathan	MANS (268, 271, 280, 283, 336, 357)
Brigham, Elnathan Lt	MANS (328, 353)
Brigham, Gershom	COVE (314)
Brigham, Paul	COVE (167)
Brigham, Paul Capt	COVE (178, 179)
Brigham, Stephen	MANS (233, 271, 280)
Brigham, Thomas	COVE (165, 167)
Brigham, Uriah	MANS (262)
Brighham, Elnathan	MANS (348)
Brinsmaide, Jonah	FAIR (253)
Brinsmaide, Josiah	FAIR (257, 258, 262, 263, 265, 267)
Bristall, David	FARM (433)
Bristol, Aaron	HARW (10, 534)
Bristol, Aaron Jur	HARW (3, 5, 534)
Bristol, Abel	HARW (14)
Bristol, Bazalel Capt	KILH (53, 146)
Bristol, Beazeelel Capt	KILH (52)
Bristol, Beezel Capt	KILH (54)
Bristol, Bezalel Capt	KILH (49, 51)
Bristol, Bezeelel	KILH (44)
Bristol, Eliphalet	HARW (2, 11, 14)
Bristol, John	HARW (13, 14, 25)
Bristol, Nathan	MILF (102)
Bristol, Nathan Junr	CORN (10, 23, 25)
Bristol, Nathn Junr	CORN (17)

INDEX

Name	Index Page	Name	Index Page
Bristol, Reuben	CHES (A), HARW (2, 5, 8, 14, 17, 23, 523, 533, 534)	Brooks, Josiah	GLAS (95)
		Brooks, Paul	HADD (148)
Bristol, Richard	GUIL (299, 317, 325)	Brooks, Saml	FARM (9), GLAS (113), KILY (31)
Bristol, Thomas	CHES (14)	Brooks, Saml Capt	HADD (117, 124)
Bristoll, David	FARM (2)	Brooks, Saml Lieut	HADD (113)
Bristoll, Jehiel	MILF (95)	Brooks, Saml Serg	HADD (109)
Bristoll, Nathan	MILF (92, 97, 102)	Brooks, Samuel	GLAS (67, 83, 92, 94, 125, 129), KILY (94)
Bristoll, Richard Capt	MILF (85)		
Brockway, Edward	BRAN (178), HARL (52, 56, 61)	Brooks, Samuel Capt	HADD (116, 121, 126)
		Brooks, Samuel Lt	HADD (113)
Brockway, Isaiah	EHAD (60)	Brooks, Thomas	GLAS (102)
Brockway, Saml	FARM (438, 444, 456)	Brooks, Thos	FARM (9)
Brockway, Saml Jur	FARM (456)	Brooks, Wakeman	HADD (113, 121, 129)
Bronson, David Revd	DERB (120, 122)	Brooks, Wakeman Sergt	HADD (121)
Bronson, Stephen	FARM (17)		
Brook, Abram	FARM (455)	Brooks, Wm B	DANB (69)
Brook, Joel	GLAS (94)	Brounson, [ ]	FARM (456)
Brook, John	GLAS (93)	Brounson, Achsa	FARM (454)
Brook, Joseph	HADD (110, 125, 130)	Brounson, Anne	FARM (19)
Brook, Joshua	HADD (110, 129)	Brounson, Bennoni	FARM (449)
Brook, Saml	HADD (130)	Brounson, Benoni	FARM (17, 455)
Brook, Samuel	GLAS (84)	Brounson, Chreles	FARM (443)
Brookes, Ichabod	MIDD (363)	Brounson, Ebenr A	FARM (444)
Brookes, Jabez	MIDD (364)	Brounson, Ebenr Allyn	FARM (14)
Brookes, Jabez Capt	MIDD (382)	Brounson, Eldad	FARM (449)
Brooks Thomas Jur	GLAS (95)	Brounson, Elijah	FARM (455)
Brooks, [ ]	HADD (110, 111, 118, 119, 121)	Brounson, Elijah Jur	FARM (455)
		Brounson, Jesse	FARM (18, 28)
Brooks, Abih	ASHF (308)	Brounson, Job	FARM (456)
Brooks, Abijah	ASHF (218, 222, 225, 311)	Brounson, John	FARM (12, 28, 434, 436, 438, 445, 449, 450)
Brooks, Abraham	FARM (28)	Brounson, Jona	FARM (436, 443, 456)
Brooks, Abraham Capt	HADD (117, 123)	Brounson, Luke	FARM (436, 443)
Brooks, Abram Capt	HADD (109)	Brounson, Nathl	FARM (2, 443)
Brooks, Abrm Capt	HADD (113, 118)	Brounson, Saml	FARM (5)
Brooks, Calvin	HADD (148)	Brounson, Samuel	FARM (455)
Brooks, Daniel	CHES (5)	Brounson, Seth	FARM (2, 438)
Brooks, David	CHES (8, 9, 10, 12)	Brounson, Silas	FARM (9)
Brooks, Henry	CHES (11, 12, 14)	Brounson, Simeon	FARM (455)
Brooks, Henry Jur	CHES (A)	Brounson, Stephen	FARM (32, 438, 455)
Brooks, Isaac Junr	CHES (4)	Brounson, Thads	DANB (40)
Brooks, Jabez	MIDD (395)	Brounson, Titus	FARM (443, 444)
Brooks, Jabez Capt	MIDD (354, 355, 357, 371, 372, 416)	Brounson, Zadock	FARM (449, 455)
		Browen, Ezra	KILY (86a)
Brooks, Jabez Junr	MIDD (346, 349, 405)	Brown, [ ]	ASHF (219), HEBR (236), KILY (86)
Brooks, Jabez Jur	HADD (110)		
Brooks, Jere	CHES (15)	Brown, Aaron	CANA (77)
Brooks, Jno	ASHF (311)	Brown, Abner	HEBR (217, 218)
Brooks, Joel	GLAS (66, 95, 98)	Brown, Amasa	GLAS (112)
Brooks, John	KILY (87a)	Brown, Andrew	KILY (7, 8, 10, 19, 32, 96a)
Brooks, John Jur	GLAS (114)		
Brooks, Jonathan	HADD (114)	Brown, Asa	HARF (255A)
Brooks, Jos	GOSH (139), HADD (115, 124)	Brown, Azariah	LEBA (297, 299, 310)
		Brown, Benj	CANT (51)
Brooks, Joseph	HADD (109, 110, 115, 116, 117, 123, 124, 126, 129)	Brown, Benja	CANT (168, 178)
		Brown, Benja Jr	CANT (178, 181)
		Brown, Benjamin	GROT ([23]), HARF (295, 261a)
Brooks, Joseph Capt	HADD (121)		
Brooks, Joshua	HADD (110)	Brown, Benjn	GROT ([4])

606

INDEX

Name	Index Page
Brown, Bezaleel	GREE (118, 119, 120, 121, 123, 124, 125, 126, 127, 128)
Brown, Bezaleel Lieut	GREE (119, 121, 124)
Brown, Briant	KILY (5, 7, 9, 12, 16, 17, 21, 25, 90, 84a, 89, 91, 91a, 93, 94, 95a, 96, 96a, 97a)
Brown, Briant Jur	KILY (94a)
Brown, Cirel	ASHF (213)
Brown, Colo	MIDD (416)
Brown, Comfort	GROT ([9])
Brown, Conl	COVE (176)
Brown, Cyrel	ASHF (206, 218, 219, 220, 222, 310)
Brown, Daniel	HEBR (233, 233, 247)
Brown, Danl	HEBR (236, 245, 246)
Brown, David	ASHF (226, 232, 236, 237), GREE (119, 126, 127), GROT ([9]), MANS (339)
Brown, Ebenezer	CANT (178), GROT ([9])
Brown, Ebenr	CANT (146), EWIN (17)
Brown, Edmond	GREE (121)
Brown, Edmund	GREE (127)
Brown, Elijah	COVE (167, 314), GROT ([25])
Brown, Francis	CORN (20)
Brown, Hugh	MIDD (364)
Brown, Jacob	CANA (19, 64), KILY (23, 33)
Brown, James	ASHF (219), GREE (119), HEBR (246)
Brown, Jerediah	CANA (11, 12)
Brown, Jess	KILY (97)
Brown, Jesse	GROT ([25]), KILY (7, 19, 91a), LEBA (298, 310, 316)
Brown, John	CANT (160, 177)
Brown, Jona	MANS (279)
Brown, Jonathan	CHAT (29), EWIN (8, 88), MANS (283, 328, 350, 355, 358)
Brown, Jonathn	CHAT (50, 64)
Brown, Jonth	CHAT (33, 39)
Brown, Josiah	COVE (180, 181), KILY (87a, 89)
Brown, Lovil	ASHF (204)
Brown, Majr	MIDD (394, 398, 399)
Brown, Mason	LEBA (299, 326)
Brown, N Majr	MIDD (370)
Brown, Nathaniel	CHAT (33, 366)
Brown, Nathaniel Capt	MIDD (345)
Brown, Nathaniel Colo	MIDD (412, 417)
Brown, Nathaniel Majr	MIDD (356, 358, 379, 393)
Brown, Nathl	CHAT (31, 37, 39), KENT (C548, 365, 373)
Brown, Nathl Colo	MIDD (403, 415)
Brown, Nathl Isn	KILY (91)
Brown, Nathl Majr	MIDD (350, 362, 369, 372, 381, 385)
Brown, Obediah Dr	ASHF (311)
Brown, Robert	CHES (9)
Brown, Roger	GREE (120, 123, 126, 127)
Brown, Saml	CHAT (40), CHAT (45), GUIL (271, 273, 282, 275, 288, 295, 301, 311, 327)
Brown, Samuel	CHAT (39, 43, 260)
Brown, Sarah	GROT ([3])
Brown, Thomas	COVE (166, 169, 171, 176, 180)
Brown, Thomas Chononal	COVE (176, 177179)
Brown, Thomas Choronal	COVE (174)
Brown, Thomas Colo	COVE (173, 178, 315)
Brown, Thomas Maj	COVE (169)
Brown, William	GROT ([6])
Brown, Wm	GOSH (115, 140, 183), MIDD (358, 382)
Brownell, Aaron	CANA (28)
Brownell, Edward	CANA (11, 12, 17, 19, 20, 28, 64, 77)
Brownell, Ichabod	CANA (18, 28, 77)
Brownen, Robert	KENT (E60)
Brownson, Asahel	KENT (E59)
Brownson, Jacob	CORN (86, 87)
Brownson, Jacob Junr	CORN (9, 10, 18, 23)
Brownson, Jesse	FARM (9)
Brownson, John	FARM (435, C548, C551, C552, C554, D1, D5, D8, E59, (E63)
Brownson, Saml	CORN (17)
Brownson, Samuel	CORN (10, 88, 91)
Brownson, Thads	DANB (40)
Brownson, Thadus	DANB (39, 43, 47, 51)
Brownson, Timothy	CORN (12, 13, 16, 17, 87, 90)
Brownson, Titus	FARM (433)
Brownson, Zadock	FARM (436)
Bruisters, Jonathan	GROT ([21])
Brundage, Charles	GREE (128)
Brundige, Willm	GREE (119)
Brunson, Asa	CHES (4, 8, 9, 12)
Brunson, Isaac	BOLT (180)
Brunson, Jesse	FARM (29)
Brunson, Nathan	HARW (534)
Brush, Marvin	FAIR (255)
Bruster, Israel	COVE (172, 178)
Bruster, Jacob	COVE (173, 180, 314)
Bruster, Jessa	COVE (172)
Bruster, Prince	BOLT (181, 182)
Bryan, David	MILF (91, 92)
Bryan, Jehiel	MILF (102, 104, 97)
Bryan, Jehiel Capt	MILF (92, 95, 96)
Bryan, John	CHES (4, 8, 12, 14), MILF (97)
Bryant, Prince	KENT (E58, E62)

INDEX

Name	Index Page	Name	Index Page
Bryant, Timothy	EHAR (3, 299)	Buel, Jonath Jur	GOSH (120, 130, 138, 139, 183, 184)
Bubbe, Josiah Junr	ASHF (308)		
Buck, Capt	KILY (22)	Buel, Joseph	GLAS (92)
Buck, David	KILY (86a)	Buel, Josiah	LEBA (305)
Buck, David Capt	KILY (18, 19, 22, 31, 32, 18, 19, 22, 31, 32)	Buel, Oliver	LEBA (305)
		Buel, William	HEBR (219, 216)
Buck, David Leut	KILY (90, 96, 97, 90, 96, 97)	Buel, Wm	HEBR (218, 233, 220, 231)
Buck, Eunice	FARM (19)	Buel, Wm Ens	HEBR (233)
Buck, Isaac	FARM (436, 438, 442)	Buel, Wm Jur	HEBR (218, 219, 233, 235, 236, 245)
Buck, Jacob	FARM (456)		
Buck, Olive	KILY (93, 93)	Buell, [ ]	COVE (168)
Buck, Phyllis	FARM (19)	Buell, Archelos Capt	LITC (134)
Buckingham, Abijah	MILF (94)	Buell, Benj Capt	HEBR (234)
Buckingham, Andrew	COLE (2, 11, 115)	Buell, Benjaman	COVE (166, 167)
Buckingham, Ebenezer	DERB (126)	Buell, Bile	KILH (47)
Buckingham, Ebenezer Capt	DERB (107)	Buell, Bili	KILH (49, 52, 145)
		Buell, Capt	GOSH (184)
Buckingham, Ebenr Capt	DERB (142)	Buell, Daniel	KILH (146)
		Buell, David	KILH (47, 49, 54), LITC (158)
Buckingham, Ephraim	MILF (82, 102)		
Buckingham, Gideon	MILF (78, 83, 85, 86, 87, 89, 91, 92, 95, 96, 97, 102, 104, 106)	Buell, Elas Capt	COVE (161)
		Buell, Elias	COVE (172, 178, 166, 167)
Buckingham, John Junr	MILF (88, 92, 98, 103, 104, 105)	Buell, Elias Capt	COVE (163)
Buckingham, Joseph	MILF (106)	Buell, Elias Majr	COVE (177, 179)
Buckingham, Nathan	DERB (113, 120, 122, 127, 131, 132)	Buell, Gideon	KILH (49)
		Buell, Gurden	KILH (50)
Buckingham, Nathaniel	MILF (80, 81)	Buell, Hiel	KILH (43, 47)
		Buell, Hiel Capt	KILH (44, 47)
Buckingham, Oliver	MILF (85, 91)	Buell, Jed[ ] 2d Let	KILH (50)
Buckingham, Thos	LEBA (310, 326)	Buell, Jedediah 2d	KILH (47)
Buckland, Aaron	HARF (279, 287, 292)	Buell, Jeremiah	KILH (55)
Buckland, David	HARF (281)	Buell, Jerimiah 2d	KILH (145)
Buckland, Elisha	EHAR (3)	Buell, Jesse	CORN (9, 10, 11, 16, 23, 25, 27, 88)
Buckland, William	HARF (255A)		
Buckley, Gershom Revd	MIDD (376, 378)	Buell, Jesse Lieut	CORN (3, 9, 11, 14, 25)
		Buell, Job	KILH (146)
Buddington, Walter	GROT [4], [9], [19], [25]	Buell, Job 2d	KILH (54)
Buddington, Walter Junr	GROT [9], [25]	Buell, Johnthan	KILH (50)
		Buell, Jonath Capt	GOSH (112)
Budington, Walter	FAIR (264)	Buell, Jonathan	KILH (47, 48, 49, 52)
Buel, Benja Capt	HEBR (220)	Buell, Jonth	KILH (44)
Buel, Benjamin Capt	HEBR (216)	Buell, Josiah	KILH (47, 51, 146), LEBA (298)
Buel, Capt	GOSH (104, 109, 110, 113, 117, 120, 122, 125, 127, 128, 137, 138), HEBR (233, 234), KILH (46)		
		Buell, Josiah Ens	LEBA (320)
		Buell, Mager	COVE (176)
		Buell, Oliver	LEBA (299, 325)
Buel, Elias	COVE (177)	Buell, Olivr	LEBA (329)
Buel, Elijah	COLC (243, 249, 251, 255)	Buell, Peter Capt	LITC (135)
		Buell, Peter Junr	LITC (129, 139)
Buel, Elijah Jur	COLC (254)	Buell, Ruben	KILH (47, 145)
Buel, Ichabod	HEBR (220)	Buell, Saml	KILH (53)
Buel, Jehd	HEBR (218)	Buell, Samuel	KILH (145)
Buel, Jesse	CORN (91)	Buell, Solomon Junr	LITC (135, 158)
Buel, John	HEBR (216)	Buell, Timoth	GOSH (138)
Buel, Jonath	GOSH (115)	Buell, Wm Jur	HEBR (234)
Buel, Jonath Capt	GOSH (111, 113, 114, 130)	Buffinton, Thos	KILY (94a)
		Bugbe, [ ]	ENFD (18, 28)

608

INDEX

Name	Index Page
Bugbe, Amos	ASHF (308)
Bugbee, Abial	ASHF (228)
Bugbee, Amos	ASHF (311)
Bugbee, Isaiah	ASHF (312)
Bugbee, Josiah	ASHF (226, 308)
Bugbee, Saml	ASHF (311, 308)
Bugbee. Josiah	ASHF (311)
Bukby, Joseph Jur	CANA (19)
Bukley, Joseph Jur	CANA (23)
Bukley, Saml	CANA (17)
Bulkley, Capt	COLC (244)
Bulkley, Chancey	CHAT (36, 37, 38, 39, 41, 43, 50, 52, 58, 61, 64, 66, 67, 69)
Bulkley, Charles	COLC (8, 10, 242, 248, 249, 256)
Bulkley, Coll	COLC (256)
Bulkley, Danl	COLC (7)
Bulkley, Ebenr	FAIR (253, 258, 263, 265
Bulkley, Eliph	COLC (252)
Bulkley, Eliphalet Capt	COLC (251, 252)
Bulkley, Eliphalet Col	COLC (254)
Bulkley, Elipht	COLC (255)
Bulkley, Gershom	COLC (248)
Bulkley, Gershom 3d	FAIR (253)
Bulkley, James	FAIR (259)
Bulkley, John	COLC (12)
Bulkley, Jonathan	FAIR (269)
Bulkley, Jonth	FAIR (259, 267)
Bulkley, Joseph	COLC (11, 245, 249, 255)
Bulkley, Joseph 3d	FAIR (253)
Bulkley, Joshua	COLC (11, 246)
Bulkley, Nathan	FAIR (253, 256, 258, 259, 260, 262, 264, 266 267)
Bulkley, Peter	COLC (11, 242, 243, 251, 252)
Bulkley, Peter Capt	COLC (244, 252, 255)
Bulkley, Roger	COLC (243)
Bulkley, Talcott	FAIR (258)
Bulkley, William	COLC (11, 245, 249)
Bulkley, Willm	FAIR (266)
Bulkly, Charles	COLC (254)
Bulkly, Danl	COLC (255)
Bull, [ ]	HARF (255)
Bull, [ ]hael	HARW (2)
Bull, Aaron	HARF (250, 253, 255A, 258)
Bull, Asa	LITC (131, 146, 147)
Bull, Caleb	HARF (255A, 293, 297, 299, 300)
Bull, Caleb Capt	HARF (278, 281, 288, 292)
Bull, Caleb Junr	HARF (266, 272)
Bull, Caleb Jur Capt	HARF (277)
Bull, Frederick Capt	HARF (289)
Bull, George	LITC (134, 139, 141)
Bull, Hennry Ens	MILF (100)
Bull, Jacob	KENT (E60)
Bull, Jeremiah	MILF (102, 104)
Bull, John	HARW (3), KENT (C545, E60)
Bull, Jona	FARM (443, 456, 442)
Bull, Jona Leut	FARM (2)
Bull, Jonathan	FARM (441), HARF (265, 266, 268, 272, 273, 281, 287, 292)
Bull, Jonathan Capt	HARF (261a, 269, 275, 280, 283, 291, 292, 297)
Bull, Martan	FARM (440)
Bull, Martin	FARM (3, 5, 8, 9, 23, 27, 31, 431, 433, 434, 441, 442, 443, 444, 445, 450, 454)
Bull, Michael	HARW (25)
Bull, Nathl	FARM (9), HARW (4, 7, 9, 13, 16, 22, 24, 533)
Bull, Nathl Ensn	HARW (3)
Bull, Noah	CORN (86)
Bull, Saml	HARW (533), MIDD (357, 394, 415, 417)
Bull, Saml Lieut	MIDD (385, 387, 398)
Bull, Samuel	HARW (3, 5, 6, 8, 9, 10), MIDD (347, 355, 368, 405)
Bull, Thos	HARW (3)
Bull, William	HARF (279, 282)
Bullard, Willm	ASHF (308)
Bullen, David	ENFD (32)
Bullin, David	ENFD (26)
Bumpos, Levi	MANS (340)
Bunce, Aaron	LEBA (298, 299, 305)
Bunce, Isaac	HARF (252(2), 253, 256, 263, 267, 273, 281, 288, 293)
Bunce, Joseph	HARF (272)
Bunch, James	HARF (261a)
Bunday, [ ]	KILY (15)
Bunday, Ebenezer	KILY (25, 27, 28, 93, 94)
Bunday, Ebenr	KILY (19)
Bunday, Eleazer	KILY (30)
Bundy, [ ]	KILY (37)
Bundy, Ebenezer	KILY (34)
Bundy, Ebenezr	KILY (31)
Bunel, Isaac	DERB (106)
Bunell, Joseph Jur	FARM (456)
Bunnel, Abner Jur	CHES (15)
Bunnel, Amos	FARM (13)
Bunnel, Capt	FARM (23)
Bunnel, Daniel	FARM (2)
Bunnel, Danl	FARM (9, 18, 29, 442, 445, 450)
Bunnel, Enos	CHES (8)
Bunnel, Isaac	DERB (106)
Bunnel, Israel	CHES (4, 5, 7, 8, 9, 11, 12, 13, (A)
Bunnel, Jacob	BRAN (164, 165, 166, 179)
Bunnel, Jacob Lt	BRAN (166)
Bunnel, Jairus	BRAN (175)
Bunnel, Jairus Lieut	BRAN (170)

609

INDEX

Name	Index Page	Name	Index Page
Bunnel, Nathaniel	CHES (6, 7, 14)	Burnham, Isaac	ASHF (310), HARL (41, 43, 44, 47, 50, 54, 56, 58, 59, 60, 61)
Bunnel, Nathaniel Capt	CHES (5)		
Bunnel, Nathaniel Major	CHES (13)	Burnham, Isaac Leut	HARL (60)
Bunnel, Samuel	CHES (11)	Burnham, James	EWIN (85, 89)
Bunnel, Titus	FARM (2, 3, 6, 8, 9, 12, 17, 435, 445, 449, 442)	Burnham, Joseph	ASHF (222, 226, 308)
		Burnham, Joseph Ensn	ASHF (218)
Bunnel, Titus Capt	FARM (14)	Burnham, Joshua	EHAD (54)
Bunnel, Titus Ensn	FARM (442)	Burnham, Josiah	FARM (444)
Bunnel, Tonuel	CHES (14)	Burnham, Nathan	ASHF (313), EHAD (45, 50, 86)
Bunnell, Daniel	FARM (433)		
Bunnell, Danl	FARM (438)	Burnham, Reuben	HARL (53, 57)
Bunnell, Joseph	DANB (55)	Burnham, Ruben	HARL (59, 61)
Bunnell, Ruth	DERB (133)	Burnham, Rubin	HARL (50, 43, 45, 46, 49, 50, 51)
Bunnell, Titus	FARM (8, 430, 433, 434, 435)		
		Burnham, Silas	HARF (272)
Bunnıl, Jacob	BRAN (163, 164)	Burnham, Timothy Junr	HARF (255A)
Bur[ ], Aaron	CANA (64)		
Bural, [ ]	CANA (28)	Burnhm, Eleazer	HARF (255)
Burbank, Daniel	ENFD (28, 29, 34)	Burns, Dimon	CHES (11)
Burbank, Elias	ASHF (308)	Burr, [ ]	FAIR (266)
Burch, Mary	KILY (12, 23, 34, 95, 98)	Burr, Danl	FAIR (259, 260)
Burchard, Phinehas	ASHF (214), 226)	Burr, Danl Jur	FAIR (265)
Burdick, Ebenr	FARM (433)	Burr, David	FAIR (266)
Burges, Joseph	CANT (168)	Burr, David Jur	FAIR (255, 256)
Burges, Stephen	ASHF (311)	Burr, Ebenr	FAIR (258, 260, 263, 266)
Burges, Stephen Junr	ASHF (311)	Burr, Ebenr 2d	FAIR (252, 253, 255, 256, 257)
Burgess, Jos	CANT (140)		
Burgess, Joseph	CANT (160)	Burr, Ebenr Jur	FAIR (258)
Burgis, James Junr	LITC (135)	Burr, Elijah	MIDD (367, 382)
Burgis, John	GUIL (275, 286, 287, 293, 295, 299, 300, 303, 306, 308, 310, 321, 330, 334, 344)	Burr, Ephm	FAIR (267)
		Burr, Eunice	FARM (24)
		Burr, George	FAIR (251, 254, 255, 256, 257, 258, 261, 262, 265, 266, 267, 269)
Burgis, Thos	GUIL (271, 280, 282, 285, 286, 288, 295, 301, 311, 327, 337, 274, 277, 279)	Burr, George Capt	FAIR (254, 263)
		Burr, Gershom	FAIR (266)
		Burr, Increase	FAIR (256)
Burgis, Thos Junr	GUIL (269, 272, 273, 274, 285, 288, 293, 299, 308, 324, 334)	Burr, John	FAIR (255)
		Burr, Jonathan	HADD (148), HARF (263)
Burham, Joseph	ASHF (218)	Burr, Moses	FAIR (253), FAIR (257), HARF (253, 256, 263, 267)
Burington, Eb[ ]	HARL (53)		
Burit, William	DERB (113)		
Burk, Thos	HEBR (217)		
Burket, John	HARF (253, 256, 263, 267, 273, 281)	Burr, Nathaniel	COLE (1, 4, 5, 6, 7, 8, 11, 12)
Burket, Uriah	HARF (268)	Burr, Nathaniel Jur	HADD (126)
Burnap, Abraham	COVE (168, 169, 173, 178, 179)	Burr, Natheniel	COLE (8)
		Burr, Nathl	COLE (113, 115), HADD (148)
Burnap, Abraham Jur	COVE (168, 170, 171, 179)	Burr, Nathl Jr	HADD (114, 148)
		Burr, Noadiah	FARM (450)
Burnap, Jerejah	COVE (180)	Burr, Saml	FAIR (259, 267, 434, 438, 443, 444, 449)
Burnap, Jeriah	COVE (314)		
Burnham, [ ]	FARM (22)	Burr, Saml Jur	FARM (3)
Burnham, Ashbel	EWIN (88), MIDD (378, 407)	Burr, Samuel	FARM (13), HARF (253, 257)
Burnham, David	EHAD (44, 80)	Burr, Talcott	FAIR (252, 256)
Burnham, Eleazer	HARF (266)	Burr, Thaddeus	FAIR (269)
Burnham, George	EWIN (85, 88, 281)		

INDEX

Name	Index Page
Burr, Thads	FAIR (253, 254, 255, 256, 257, 258, 259, 260, 261, 262, 264, 265, 266, 267, 269)
Burr, Timy	FAIR (256)
Burr, Titus	FARM (4)
Burr, Wakeman	FAIR (262)
Burr, William	HARF (266)
Burral, Charles Col	CANA (28)
Burral, Charles Jur	CANA (28)
Burrall, Charles Junr	CANA (18)
Burrall, Capt	CANA (14, 20, 21)
Burrall, Charles	CANA (23)
Burrall, Charles Col	CANA (11, 14, 16, 17, 22), 23, 27, 28, 29, 64, 77
Burrall, Charles Jur	CANA (11, 12, 14, 15, 17, 19, 20, 22, 23, 24 , 26, 28, 64, 77)
Burrall, Col	CANA (11, 19, 24)
Burrall, Jonathan	CANA (77)
Burrall, Ovid	CANA (77)
Burrall, William	CANA (28)
Burrall, William Capt	CANA (12, 14, 17, 19, 20, 24, 25, 27, 29, 64, 77)
Burrall, Wm Capt	CANA (16)
Burrell, Charles Junr	CANA (25)
Burril, Rachel	KILY (92)
Burrit, Charles	DURH (21, 23, 24, 26)
Burrit, David	KILY (87a)
Burrit, Israel	DURH (20, 21)
Burrit, William	DERB (120, 126, 140, 145), DURH (16)
Burrit, Willm	DERB (131)
Burritt, Charles	DURH (24)
Burritt, Israel	DURH (12, 19, 25)
Burrous, Hubbard	GROT ([16])
Burrows, Hubbard	GROT ([10], [12], [16])
Burrows, Hubbard Junr	GROT ([7], ([9])
Burrows, Hubbard Junr Capt	GROT ([7])
Burrows, John	GROT ([6])
Burrows, Jonathan	GROT ([14])
Burrr, Moses Jur	FAIR (265)
Burrull, Charles Junr	CANA (25)
Burt, Richard	CANT (183)
Burton, Ruth	KILY (12)
Burton, Solomon	FAIR (267)
Burwell, Jared	MILF (91)
Burwell, Samuel	MILF (92, 93)
Busect, John	ASHF (218)
Bush, Aaron	ENFD (18, 26),HARL (44, 47, 50, 51, 58, 62)
Bush, Aron	HARL (52)
Bush, Benoni	HARL (48)
Bush, Capt	ENFD (32, 33, 34)
Bush, Eli	ENFD (26, 32, 33, 34, 35
Bush, Ezekiel	HARL (48, 51)
Bush, George	CHAT (46)
Bush, Jonathan	CHAT (39), ENFD (26)
Bush, Jonathan Capt	ENFD (30)

Name	Index Page
Bush, Jonathn	CHAT (52)
Bush, Jonth	CHAT (37)
Bush, Moses	CHAT (39)
Bush, Moses Capt	CHAT (29, 37)
Bush, Oliver	ENFD (18, 24, 26, 32, 34)
Bush, Rufus	ENFD (30)
Bush, William	GREE (129)
Bush, William Doctor	GREE (128)
Bushnal, Abraham	CANA (27)
Bushnal, Danl	HEBR (246)
Bushnall, Abraham	CANA (11, 12, 17, 19, 23, 24, 64)
Bushnel, Aaron	LEBA (326, 334)
Bushnel, Abner	HARL (51)
Bushnel, Abraham	CANA (28)
Bushnel, Alexander	HARL (43, 44, 45, 46, 50
Bushnel, Alexander Capt	HARL (61)
Bushnel, Alexander Ens	HARL (59)
Bushnel, Alexander Leut	HARL (60)
Bushnel, Alexr	HARL (49)
Bushnel, Daniel	HARL (45), HEBR (217)
Bushnel, Ebr Jur	LEBA (341)
Bushnel, Elezr Sergant	HARL (54)
Bushnel, Jedediah	HARL (51, 59)
Bushnel, Martin	HARL (51)
Bushnel, Mirten	HARL (50)
Bushnel, Stephen	FARM (444), HARL (49)
Bushnell, Aaron	LEBA (305, 333)
Bushnell, Abner	HARL (53, 57)
Bushnell, Abraham	CANA (16, 28)
Bushnell, Alexand	HARL (52)
Bushnell, Alexander	HARL (47, 51, 55, 58)
Bushnell, Alexander Ensign	HARL (56)
Bushnell, Alexr	HARL (42, 43)
Bushnell, Daniel	HARL (48, 53)
Bushnell, Jedeah	HARL (53)
Bushnell, Jedediaz	HARL (45)
Bushnell, Jedediah	HARL (48)
Bushnell, Marten	HARL (56)
Bushnell, Martin	HARL (45, 48)
Bushnell, Murtin	HARL (53)
Bushnell, Stephen	FARM (28), HARL (45, 48, 53)
Bushwell, Abraham	CANA (77)
Buswel, Thoms Jr	CANT (150)
Buswell, Thomas Jr	CANT (144, 147, 160, 161, 168)
Buswell, Thos Jur	CANT (156), 157)
Butlar, Thomas	ASHF (213, 214)
Butlar, Thos	ASHF (213, 308)
Butler, Josiah Capt	HARW (21)
Butler, Aaron	HARF (255A)
Butler, Abel	CORN (90, 102, 104, 110, 120, 183)
Butler, Abel Jur	GOSH (183)
Butler, Abell	GOSH (115, 184)

611

INDEX

Name	Index Page
Butler, Benjamin	HARW (2, 10)
Butler, Benjn	HARW (3, 5, 523)
Butler, Comfort	MIDD (346, 349, 363)
Butler, Cumfort	MIDD (353, 357)
Butler, Daniel 3d	HARF (265)
Butler, David	HARF (287, 299)
Butler, Ebener Jur	HARW (3)
Butler, Ebenezer	HARW (7, 8, 10)
Butler, Eli	MIDD (366, 389)
Butler, Eli Capt	MIDD (363, 389, 407, 409, 414)
Butler, George	HARF (266, 273), MIDD (347, 364)
Butler, George Capt	HARF (275)
Butler, Gideon Junr	HARF (253)
Butler, Isaac	HARW (3)
Butler, Jared	FARM (436, 442, 449)
Butler, Jeremiah	DURH (14, 16, 19, 21, 24
Butler, Jeremiah Lieut	DURH (24)
Butler, John	BRAN (164)
Butler, John Junr	BRAN (170)
Butler, Jonathan	HARF (261a), HARL (44, 47)
Butler, Jos	GOSH (102, 103, 186)
Butler, Josiah	HARW (3, 6, 8, 9, 10, 16, 17, 18, 20)
Butler, Josiah Capt	HARW (12, 13, 21)
Butler, Josiah Jur	HARW (3)
Butler, Lt	DURH (20)
Butler, Moses	HARF (261a, 263)
Butler, Nathaniel	HARL (47)
Butler, Nathl	HARL (43, 44, 46, 52)
Butler, Noah	HARF (253, 256, 263, 267, 273, 281)
Butler, Patric	LEBA (299)
Butler, Patrick	LEBA (305, 316, 326)
Butler, Saml S	HARW (3)
Butler, Samuel	CORN (86)
Butler, Samuel Junr	CORN (89)
Butler, Stephen	HARW (4, 7, 8)
Butler, Thomas	ASHF (226, 232, 236)
Butler, Thos	ASHF (202, 209, 210, 214, 218, 222, 226, 310)
Butler, Timothy	MIDD (350)
Butler, Zacheus	HARF (255A, 266),
Butlor, Nathl	HARL (51)
Butt, Ebenr	CANT (155, 180)
Butt, Saml 3rd	CANT (156)
Butt, Sherebiah Capt	CANT (175, 176, 180, 182)
Butt, Stephen	CANT (150, 147, 151, 156, 159, 160, 167, 176, 180, 181)
Butten, Capt	CANT (151)
Butten, Jonathan	EWIN (85, 89)
Buttles, Elijah	CANA (28)
Buttolph, William	GROT ([5])
Button, Asa	GROT ([23])
Button, Jos	CANT (150)
Button, Matthias	ASHF (311)

Name	Index Page
Button, Matthias Capt	CANT (144, 156)
Button, Oulon	KILH (145, 145)
Byington, Danl	FARM (443)
Byington, Jacob	FARM (6)
Byington, Joseph	FARM (6, 23, 28, 430, 452)
Byington, Joseph Ensn	FARM (443)
Byington, Josh	FARM (17)
Byington, Leut	FARM (7, 8)
Byington, Samuel	FARM (445)
Byinton, Jonathan	BRAN (166)
Byinton, Joseph	FARM (444)
Byinton, Mary	FARM (19)
Byinton, Saml	FARM (443)
Byles, [ ]	ASHF (212, 217)
Byles, E[ ]	ASHF (208, 209, 212)
Byles, Eben	ASHF (217)
Byles, Ebenr	ASHF (217)
Byles, Josiah	ASHF (226)
Byles, Josias	ASHF (232, 236)
Byrnham, Joseph	ASHF (227)
C[ ], David	HARW (523)
Cable, [ ]	FAIR (266)
Cable, Elijah	CANA (12)
Cable, James	GLAS (105)
Cable, John	GLAS (67)
Cable, Saml	FAIR (255)
Cable, Thomas	FAIR (269)
Cable, Thos	FAIR (256, 258, 260)
Cadwell, Aaron Junr	HARF (287)
Cadwell, Elias	GUIL (272, 294, 304, 309, 316, 335, 337)
Cadwell, James	FARM (9)
Cadwell, John	EHAR (3, 273, 285)
Cadwell, John Junr	HARF (287)
Cadwell, Mathew	FARM (2, 8, 433, 443, 450, 255A)
Cadwell, Mathw	FARM (28, 455)
Cadwell, Moses	HARL (44, 48)
Cadwell, Rhoderick	FARM (5, 7, 18, 436, 444)
Cadwell, Rhodrick	FARM (443)
Cadwell, Samuel	HARF (251(2), 255)
Cadwell, Timothy	HARF (266, 272, 275, 292)
Cady, Benjn Ensn	KILY (87a)
Cady, Benjn Jur	KILY (92a)
Cady, Danl	CANT (146)
Cady, David	KILY (13, 86a, 98)
Cady, David Capt	KILY (5, 7, 10, 14, 15,17, 20, 87a, 90, 92, 92a, 93a, 94, 94a, 96, 97, 97a, 98)
Cady, Isaac	KILY (86a)
Cady, Isaah	KILY (94)
Cady, Isaiah	KILY (4)
Cady, Jedidiah	KILY (93)
Cady, Jonathan Capt	KILY (5, 8, 19, 32, 96, 96a, 97)
Cady, Jonathan Leut	KILY (90, 91a, 94a)
Cady, Jos	KILY (87a)

INDEX

Name	Index Page	Name	Index Page
Cady, Jos Capt	KILY (94, 94, 94a)	Campbell, Saml	MANS (277)
Cady, Joseph	KILY (7, 32, 92, 94, 97, 97a)	Campbell, Samuel	MANS (233, 353)
		Campbell, Zurick	MANS (336)
Cady, Joseph Capt	KILY (90, 91a, 92)	Cande, [ ]	MIDD (363)
Cady, Joseph Majr	KILY (10, 14, 17, 25, 28)	Cande, Caleb Jnr	DERB (106)
Cady, Joseph Sener	KILY (86a)	Cande, Gideon	DERB (140)
Cady, Majr	KILY (37)	Cande, John	MIDD (351, 362, 380, 381, 394, 404)
Cady, Perley	KILY (98)		
Cady, Uriah Jr	CANT (144, 147, 159, 161)	Cande, Medad	DERB (138)
		Candee, Caleb	DERB (124, 168)
Caldwell, Charles	HARF (283, 289)	Candee, Justice	DERB (167)
Caldwell, Nathl	GUIL (275)	Candee, Naboth	DERB (141)
Caldwell, Thos	GUIL (340)	Candee, Neheah	DERB (121)
Calkings, James	MANS (233)	Candee, Nehemiah	DERB (122)
Call, Daniel	HARF (269, 287)	Candee, Saml	DERB (145)
Cambel, Thomas	KENT (E63)	Candee, Samuel	DERB (131)
Cambridge	DERB (146)	Canfield, Abial	DERB (131)
Camp, Abel	LITC (129)	Canfield, Ashur	DURH (22, 23)
Camp, Abel Junr	LITC (142, 143, 158, 159	Canfield, David	DERB (145)
Camp, Abiathur	GLAS (94)	Canfield, Gideon	DURH (16)
Camp, Asahel	MIDD (368, 381)	Canfield, John	DURH (11, 12, 14, 16, 19, 22, 25)
Camp, Capt	DURH (11)		
Camp, David	MILF (93)	Canfield, Joseph	DERB (120, 122, 134)
Camp, Edward	MIDD (376)	Canfield, Phinehas	DURH (12)
Camp, Elah	DURH (14, 22)	Canfield, Phins	DURH (10, 19, 25)
Camp, Elias	DURH (8, 11, 14, 18, 23, 25), MILF (106)	Canfield, Saml	KENT (B6), MIDD (376, 416)
Camp, Elnathan	DURH (8, 10, 12, 14, 15, 18, 19, 20, 21, 22, 23, 24, 26)	Canfield, Samuel	MIDD (399, 400)
		Capron, Giles	GROT ([6])
		Capron, Simeon	GROT [12], [25]
Camp, Heth	DURH (14, 17, 19, 25)	Car[ ], Jacob	FARM (433)
Camp, Hezekiah	DURH (24)	Carder, John	KILY (8, 31)
Camp, Hezh	DURH (25)	Carder, William	KILY (32)
Camp, Isaac	KENT (A27, A28, B1, C552, C555, E59, E63)	Carew, William	CANT (168)
		Carew, Wm	CANT (156)
Camp, Isaac Doctr	FARM (12)	Carington, John	GOSH (104, 112, 115, 121, 137, 184)
Camp, Israel	DURH (11), KENT (C552)		
		Carpener, Josiah	COVE (173)
Camp, Israel Capt	DURH (8, 12, 14)	Carpenter, Asa	MANS (267)
Camp, Job	DURH (21, 23)	Carpenter, Benja Junr	COVE (314)
Camp, Job Capt	DURH (12, 14, 18, 19, 21)	Carpenter, Benjn	DERB (120)
		Carpenter, Capt	LEBA (304)
Camp, Jonah	KENT (C552, C554, E59)	Carpenter, Daniel	EWIN (85, 89)
Camp, Joseph	DURH (21, 25, 24)	Carpenter, Elijah	COVE (315)
Camp, Josiah	MILF (106)	Carpenter, Eliphalet	COVE (166)
Camp, Leml	MIDD (394, 406)	Carpenter, Eliphalet Capt	COVE (167)
Camp, Nathaniel	MILF (106)		
Camp, Phinehas	DURH (16, 18, 19, 21)	Carpenter, Eliphalet Junr	COVE (314)
Camp, Phins	DURH (14, 17, 25)		
Camp, Saml	DURH (11, 23)	Carpenter, Ephraim	LEBA (302, 305, 306, 316)
Camp, Saml Capt	DURH (14, 20, 26)		
Camp, Samuel	DURH (8, 10)	Carpenter, Epm	LEBA (311, 325, 342)
Camp, Samuel Capt	DURH (12, 16, 18, 19, 21, 24)	Carpenter, Epm Capt	LEBA (313, 320, 327, 329, 330, 334, 337)
Campbel, Andrew	MIDD (349, 357, 381)	Carpenter, Hezekiah	ASHF (232, 312)
Campbell, Andr Enn	MIDD (385)	Carpenter, James	COVE (168)
Campbell, Andrew	MIDD (348, 362, 371, 380)	Carpenter, Jonah	ASHF (227, 232, 236, 310)
Campbell, Ephm	MANS (328)	Carpenter, Jonth	ASHF (310)
Campbell, Ephraim	MANS (281)	Carpenter, Josiah	COVE (174, 180)

INDEX

Name	Index Page	Name	Index Page
Carpenter, Ruben	BOLT (167)	Carter, Jacob Jur	FARM (438, 442, 443)
Carpenter, William	COVE (177)	Carter, Jehiel	KENT (D11)
Carr, Caleb	GOSH (183)	Carter, John	CORN (19, 87), FARM (443, 145)
Carr, John	GOSH (183)		
Carr, Levi	GOSH (183)	Carter, John Jr	CANT (144)
Carrier, Andrew	CHAT (37, 43, 59)	Carter, Jona	FARM (443)
Carrier, Ebenezer	COLC (243)	Carter, Joseph	KENT (C547, C555, A28, D7)
Carrier, Isaac	COLC (8, 245, 248, 249, 251)		
		Carter, Joseph Capt	KENT (A26, C543, C545, C550, D10, D12, D13, E58, E62)
Carrier, Israel	MIDD (363, 417)		
Carrier, John	COLC (7, 245, 249)		
Carrier, Joseph	COLC (252)	Carter, Joseph Jur	KENT (D5, D7, D8, E63)
Carrier, S[ ]	COLC (10)	Carter, Josiah	KILH (54, 55)
Carrier, Saml	COLC (255), MIDD (349, 357)	Carter, Nathan	GOSH (185)
		Carter, Saml	KENT (A28, E59)
Carrier, Samuel	MIDD (346, 356, 363, 365)	Carter, Saml Jur	KENT (E63)
		Carter, Saml Leiut	KENT (C543)
Carrier, Thomas	COLC (11, ,249)	Carter, Samuel	KENT (A27, B1, C552, C555, D10)
Carrier, Thos	COLC (8)		
Carrier, Thos Jur	COLC (8)	Carter, Samuel Jur	KENT (E60)
Carrier, Titus	CHAT (30, 44, 45)	Carter, Thomas	KENT (C551, C554)
Carrier, Uriah	COLC (11, 254)	Carter, Thoms	KENT (C555)
Carril, Amos	KILY (92, 92)	Cartey, Clark	COLC (10)
Carrill, Docr	KILY (13)	Cartey, John	COLC (10, 247, 249, 252)
Carrington, [ ]	FARM (28)	Cartey, John Lieut	COLC (245)
Carrington, Aaron	FARM (433)	Cartor, Elizer	COLC (243)
Carrington, David	FARM (5)	Carty, John	COLC (8, 255)
Carrington, Elias	MILF (82, 78)	Carver, Benjamin	EWIN (85, 89)
Carrington, Elias Doctr	MILF (86, 88, 93)	Carver, Benjn	CANA (64)
Carrington, John	FARM (444)	Carver, David Jur	HEBR (220)
Carrington, Jona	FARM (444)	Carver, Ebenezer	BOLT (151, 155, 167, 180, 182)
Carrington, Jonathan	FARM (438, 443)		
Carrington, Lemuel	FARM (17)	Carver, Gideon	CANT (147, 168, 180)
Carrington, Nathl	FARM (436, 449, 456)	Carver, John	BOLT (151, 155, 157, 181, 183)
Carrington, Saml	FARM (28)		
Carter, [ ]	CORN (14), KILH (54)	Carver, Joseph	BOLT (158, 180, 182)
Carter, Abell	FARM (443)	Carver, Joseph Ensign	BOLT (151, 161, 165)
Carter, Abell Jur	FARM (436, 443)	Carver, Nathl	CANT (160)
Carter, Adonijah	KENT (C548, D1), KENT (D11)	Carver, Samuel	BOLT (168, 181, 182)
		Carver, Samuel 3d	BOLT (180)
Carter, Amos	KILH (44, 44)	Carver, Samuel Jur	BOLT (139, 145, 146, 164, 183)
Carter, Bardock	KENT (E63)		
Carter, Benj[ ]	KILH (44, 50, 44, 50, 146)	Carver, Samuel Jur Lieut	BOLT (157)
		Carver, Samuel Lieut	BOLT (159, 180, 182)
Carter, Benj[ ]	KILH (146)	Carvil, Amos	KILY (87)
Carter, Benjamin	KENT (E60)	Cary, Ebenezer	MANS (271)
Carter, Benoni	KENT (D5, D10, D7)	Cary, Ebenr	MANS (280, 281)
Carter, Benony	KENT (A28, B1, B2, C548, C552, C554, D1, D5, D10, E58, E62)	Cary, Jabez	MANS (268, 279, 338)
		Cary, Nathaniel	MANS (267)
Carter, Danl	FARM (456)	Cary, Nathl	MANS (278)
Carter, Eleazer	COLC (8), KENT (A28, B1)	Cary, Waitl	CHAT (41)
		Case, Aaron	KENT (E60)
Carter, Eliezer	COLC (245)	Case, Alexander	CHAT (34)
Carter, Elizer	COLC (251)	Case, Benjaman Jur	COVE (165, 172)
Carter, Ezra	COLC (243, 245, 249)	Case, John	FARM (456)
Carter, Hezekiah	CORN (3, 16, 87)	Case, Jonah	GOSH (121, 183)
Carter, Hezh	CORN (9)	Case, Moses	KENT (E58, E62)
Carter, Israel	KENT (C552, E59)	Case, Moses Jur	KENT (A28)
Carter, Israel Leiut	KENT (C543, D8)	Case, Reuben	FARM (443)

INDEX

Name	Index Page
Cases, Reuben	FARM (433)
Casey, Hugh	GLAS (99)
Cassell, Saml	CHAT (55)
Casswel, John	CHAT (42)
Casswell, Julious	KENT (E60)
Castle, Joel	HARW (3, 14, 25)
Castle, Levi	HARW (2)
Castle, Peter	DANB (69)
Caswell, Josiah	KENT (D1)
Caswell, Julias	KENT (D10)
Caswell, Julious	KENT (D3, D7, D8, E63)
Cate	DERB (146)
Catlin, [ ]	HARW (2)
Catlin, Abijah	HARW (9, 13, 14, 15, 16, 18, 19, 20, 23, 24, 25, 523, 534)
Catlin, Abijah Jur	HARW (3, 4, 7, 533)
Catlin, Abraham	HARW (3)
Catlin, Alexander	LITC (130, 131, 134, 137, 152, 158)
Catlin, Alexander Capt	LITC (155)
Catlin, Dan	HARW (3, 9, 25)
Catlin, Daniel	HARW (2, 3, 4, 5, 6, 8, 9, 10, 11, 12)
Catlin, Daniel Jur	HARW (3, 24, 25)
Catlin, Eli	FARM (9)
Catlin, Eli Capt	LITC (159)
Catlin, George	HARW (3, 4, 6, 7, 8, 9, 10, 13, 16, 18, 19, 22, 26, 523, 533)
Catlin, George Capt	HARW (3)
Catlin, Grove	HARW (25)
Catlin, Hezekiah	HARW (20)
Catlin, Isaac	HARW (15, 16, 23)
Catlin, Jacob	HARW (3, 4, 10, 13, 15, 16, 17, 533)
Catlin, Jacob 2d	HARW (3, 10)
Catlin, Joel	HARW (4, 5, 6, 7, 8, 9, 12, 20, 23, 523, 533)
Catlin, Joel Capt	HARW (3, 5)
Catlin, Jonathan Jur	HARW (3, 14, 16, 14, 16)
Catlin, L[ ]	HARW (3)
Catlin, Roger	CORN (10, 11, 23, 25, 88
Catlin, Simeon	HARW (3)
Catlin, Theodore	LITC (139, 145, 146, 148
Catlin, Thomas	LITC (134, 137, 142, 143, 154, 158)
Catlin, Thomas Lieut	LITC (143, 145, 148)
Catling, Daniel	HARW (4)
Caudry, Jacob	HARL (48)
Caverley, John	COLC (249)
Caverly, John	COLC (9)
Cebra, James	MILF (92, 97)
Chadler, Winthrop	KILY (91a)
Chafee, Jos	ASHF (308)
Chafee, Josiah	ASHF (310)
Chaffe, David Jur	ASHF (310)
Chaffe, Francis	ASHF (310)
Chaffe, Jonth Jur	ASHF (310)
Chaffee, David	ASHF (204, 213, 230, 311)
Chaffee, David Jur	ASHF (218, 230, 308)
Chaffee, Frances	ASHF (222, 308)
Chaffee, Francis	ASHF (232)
Chaffee, Francis G	ASHF (223)
Chaffee, Francis Green	ASHF (209)
Chaffee, Jonath Junr	ASHF (218)
Chaffee, Jonathan	ASHF (236)
Chaffee, Jonth	ASHF (308)
Chaffee, Joseph	ASHF (311)
Chaffee, Josiah	ASHF (205, 209)
Chafy, Ebenr	CANT (156)
Chalker, Jabez	DURH (16, 19, 25)
Chamberlain, Joseph	MANS (347, 348)
Chamberlain, Richard	GLAS (106)
Chamberlain, Saml	MIDD (357, 364, 394, 406, 414)
Chamberlain, Samuel	MIDD (344, 381, 365, 390)
Chamberlain, Wm	GLAS (105, 111, 112, 114)
Chamberlin, Nathl	COLC (245)
Chamberlin, Abner	CANA (64, 77)
Chamberlin, Benjamin	GLAS (92)
Chamberlin, Benjn	GLAS (94)
Chamberlin, Capt	COLC (12)
Chamberlin, Eleazer	KENT (A28, C548, C552, E58, E62)
Chamberlin, Eliph	COLC (243, 251)
Chamberlin, Eliphalet	COLC (248)
Chamberlin, Freedom	COLC (255)
Chamberlin, James Capt	EWIN (13, 14, 15, 16, 17)
Chamberlin, Job	COLC (254, 256)
Chamberlin, Joel	LEBA (296, 318, 325, 328)
Chamberlin, Joel Lt	LEBA (320)
Chamberlin, John	COLC (7, 8, 10)
Chamberlin, John Capt	COLC (6, 246)
Chamberlin, Nathan	KENT (C548, D7, E59, E63)
Chamberlin, Nathaniel	COLC (249)
Chamberlin, Nathl	COLC (8, 243)
Chamberlin, Peleg	KENT (C548, D1, D8, D10, E58, E62)
Chamberlin, Richard	GLAS (95)
Chamberlin, Rosel	COLC (252)
Chamberlin, William	COLC (246)
Chamberlin, Wm	COLC (242), GLAS (78, 79, 83, 98, 100)
Champin, Epaphs	COLC (254)
Champion, Col	COLC (13)
Champion, Epaphrodilus	COLC (244)
Champion, Henry	COLC (7, 47)
Champion, Henry Capt	COLC (254)
Champion, Henry Coll	COLC (4)
Champion, Henry Junr	COLC (244)
Champion, Israel	EHAD (43, 44, 49, 51, 52, 54, 56, 57, 58)

INDEX

Name	Index Page
Champion, Reuben	EHAD (86)
Champion, Salmon	LEBA (333)
Chandler, [ ]	ASHF (237)
Chandler, Benjamin	CORN (9, 10)
Chandler, David	ENFD (26, 28, 29, 32, 34)
Chandler, Isaac	ENFD (28)
Chandler, John	HARL (47)
Chandler, Miah	ENFD (19)
Chandler, Nehemiah	ENFD (19, 24, 28, 30, 32)
Chandler, Saml Capt	KILY (96)
Chandler, Samuel Capt	KILY (5)
Chandler, Solomon	ENFD (32)
Chandler, Stephen	ENFD (19, 30)
Chandler, Theophelus	KILY (92)
Chandler, Theophilus	KILY (89, 94)
Chandler, Winthop	KILY (86a)
Chandlor, Nehemiah	ENFD (18)
Chapel, Joshua	EHAD (69)
Chapel, Noah	HARL (44)
Chapell, Noah	HARL (52)
Chapen, Ebenezar	ENFD (28, 29, 32, 34)
Chapen, Ebenezer	ENFD (26)
Chapen, Eliphalet	ENFD (18, 28, 34)
Chapen, Nathl	ENFD (25, 26)
Chapin, Aaron	EWIN (85, 89)
Chapin, Eliphalet	EWIN (8, 85, 88)
Chapin, Gideon	EWIN (85, 89)
Chapin, Joseph	EWIN (85, 88)
Chaplin, Benja	MANS (262, 263), 266, 274, 283, 350, 355)
Chaplin, Benja Ln	MANS (277)
Chaplin, Benjamin	MANS (262, 285, 342, 345, 348, 353)
Chaplin, Benjamin Junr	MANS (339, 357)
Chapman, [ ]	ASHF (311), GUIL (315)
Chapman, Aaron	EHAD (59)
Chapman, Abner	COLC (8)
Chapman, Albert Major	FAIR (254)
Chapman, Benja	ASHF (311), FARM (456)
Chapman, Daniel	HEBR (218, 220, 234)
Chapman, David	GROT ([6])
Chapman, Edward	EHAD (73, 74), GLAS (64)
Chapman, Elias	ASHF (230, 311, 313)
Chapman, Elisha	COLC (10, 248)
Chapman, Elizur	CHAT (69)
Chapman, Eph	HEBR (218)
Chapman, Ephm	HEBR (246)
Chapman, Ezra	HEBR (217, 218, 219)
Chapman, Francis	EHAD (64)
Chapman, Hosea	EWIN (15)
Chapman, Isaac	EHAD (60, 79)
Chapman, Jabez	EHAD (48, 49), EWIN (8, 9, 10, 12, 13, 14, 17)
Chapman, Jabez Colo	EHAD (67, 71)
Chapman, Jacob	ASHF (204, 222, 308, 311)

Name	Index Page
Chapman, James	FAIR (253)
Chapman, Jeremiah	BOLT (157, 181, 182), GREE (128)
Chapman, John	BOLT (183), EHAD (44), EHAD (46), FAIR (254)
Chapman, Jona	ASHF (213)
Chapman, Jonah	GLAS (66, 70, 93)
Chapman, Jonath	ASHF (213, 214, 222)
Chapman, Jonath Jur	ASHF (202)
Chapman, Jonathan	ASHF (308), EWIN (12, 85, 88), ASHF (208, 210, 211, 213, 217, 218, 226, 232)
Chapman, Jonathan Jur	ASHF (236)
Chapman, Jonth	ASHF (209, 210, 210, 310)
Chapman, Jonth Jur	ASHF (310)
Chapman, Joseph	ASHF (218, 230, 232, 310), GROT ([24])
Chapman, Joseph Junr	GROT ([24])
Chapman, Joshua	GROT ([6], [9], [12], [15], [23], [25])
Chapman, Lemuel	BOLT (164, 167, 183)
Chapman, Noah	COLC (8, 10, 246, 247, 251)
Chapman, Oliver	EWIN (12, 15, 85, 89)
Chapman, Ozias	EHAD (44, 59, 69, 88)
Chapman, Phenehas	BOLT (146, 180, 182)
Chapman, Phenihas	BOLT (151)
Chapman, Simeon	EHAD (59, 79)
Chapman, Thomas	BOLT (181)
Chapman, Thomas Juner	BOLT (165)
Chapman, Thomas Jur	BOLT (157, 181)
Chapman, Thos	ASHF (213, 311)
Chapman, Thos Jur	ASHF (213, 308)
Chapman, Timothy	EHAD (46, 54, 60, 64, 65, 69)
Chapman, William	HARL (44, 48, 51, 58)
Chapman, Willm	HARL (52)
Chapman, Wm	HARL (43, 46)
Chapman, Zachariah	EHAD (85)
Chapman, Zachariah Doct	EHAD (73, 83)
Chapmon, Elisha	COLC (253)
Chapmon, Nath	COLC (243)
Chapmon, Noah	COLC (243)
Chappel, [ ]	HEBR (236)
Chappel, Aaron	KENT (C545)
Chappel, Jonathan	HEBR (248)
Chappel, Jonth	HEBR (231)
Chappel, Jonth Jur	HEBR (217, 218)
Chappel, Joshua	LEBA (298, 299, 305, 311, 326)
Chappel, Noah	HARL (45, 48, 51, 55)
Chappell, [ ]	HEBR (231)
Charmberlin, [ ]	GLAS (68)
Charmberlin, Daniel	GLAS (93)
Charmberlin, William	GLAS (66, 70)
Charmberlin, Wm	GLAS (93)
Chase, Benjamin	KENT (E58, E62)

616

INDEX

Name	Index Page
Chase, Solomon	KENT (E60)
Chatfield, Benjn	KILH (47)
Chatfield, Daniel	DERB (120, 122, 124, 125, 127)
Chatfield, Daniel Capt	DERB (135)
Chatfield, Daniel Leiut	DERB (114)
Chatfield, John	KILH (145)
Chatfield, John Capt	KILH (146)
Chatfield, Joseph	DERB (120, 122, 127, 131, 132, 145), KILH (145)
Chatfield, Joseph Capt	KILH (53)
Chatfield, Josiah	KILH (146)
Chauncey, Capt	DURH (16)
Chauncey, Colo	DURH (10, 12)
Chauncey, Elihu Colo	DURH (8, 10, 11)
Chauncey, N	MIDD (364)
Chauncey, Nathl	MIDD (367)
Cheeney, Ann	KENT (D3)
Cheeney, Benja	ASHF (311)
Cheeney, Timothy	HARF (250, 255, 258, 261a, 266, 268)
Cheeny, Timothy	HARF (258)
Cheever, Nathan	LEBA (294, 306, 311)
Chenward, John	HARF (294, 296)
Chenward, John Capt	HARF (297)
Chester, Benajah	GROT ([4], [12], [13])
Chester, Benjn	GROT ([14])
Chester, Starr	GROT ([23])
Chester, Thomas Capt	GROT ([13])
Chestor, Starr	GROT ([24])
Chettenden, Daniel	KILH (146)
Chever, Nathan	LEBA (316)
Chidsey, Joseph	DURH (10, 12, 14, 15, 19, 21, 23), GUIL (300)
Chidsey, Josh	FARM (28)
Chidsey, Nathan	GUIL (311, 325)
Child, Elijah	KILY (96a)
Child, James	HADD (121, 127, 148)
Childs, Elijah	KILY (86a)
Chipman, Capt	COLE (3)
Chipman, Ebenr	CHAT (58)
Chitssy, Joseph	BRAN (179)
Chittenden, Abraham	GUIL (269, 272, 336)
Chittenden, Abram	GUIL (289, 294, 307, 324, 325, 334)
Chittenden, Abram Junr	GUIL (286, 307)
Chittenden, Abrm Junr	GUIL (274)
Chittenden, Ambrose	GUIL (296, 302, 325)
Chittenden, Benjn	GUIL (323, 336, 340)
Chittenden, Daniel	KILH (145, 146), GUIL (325)
Chittenden, Daniel Ensn	GUIL (300, 315)
Chittenden, Jairus	GUIL (274), 275, 325)
Chittenden, Jared	GUIL (269, 274, 290, 301, 309, 323, 324, 335)
Chittenden, Joseph	GUIL (270, 277, 290, 295, 301, 311, 327, 336)
Chittenden, Joseph Jur	GUIL (294, 309, 325, 327, 335, 337)
Chittenden, Nathan	GUIL (286, 287, 293, 294, 302, 310, 325, 338)
Chittenden, Nathan Junr	GUIL (333)
Chittenden, Saml	GUIL (272, 277, 280, 287, 295, 300, 304, 310, 326)
Chittenden, Saml Junr	GUIL (288, 294, 309, 335)
Chittenden, Simeon	GUIL (277, 291, 294, 299, 300, 339, 343)
Chittenden, Simeon Jur	GUIL (271, 289, 291, 294, 304, 311, 320, 325, 335)
Chittenden, Wm	GUIL (275, 282, 287, 291)
Chub, William	ASHF (218)
Chub, Wm	ASHF (308, 310)
Chubb, Joseph	GLAS (99, 108)
Chubb, Wm	ASHF (202)
Chubbuck, Ebenr	EWIN (85, 89)
Chundly, J[ ][ ]	HARL (52)
Church, [ ]	EHAD (50), HARL (50)
Church, Aaron Revnd	HARL (49)
Church, Aaron Revrnd	HARL (55)
Church, Caleb	DANB (40)
Church, Caleb Lut	DANB (47)
Church, Daniel	DANB (58, 60, 63)
Church, Danl	DANB (40)
Church, Ezra	KENT (C551)
Church, Ira	EHAD (45, 55, 60)
Church, James	HARF (253, 255A, 258, 292, 294, 296, 299)
Church, John	DERB (133, 167)
Church, Jona	MANS (281)
Church, Joseph	EHAD (45, 55, 60, 65, 66, 69, 79, 80, 82, 86, 87, 89), HARF (251(2), 253, 255, 259, 261a, 265, 266, 268, 270, 272, 273, 275, 281, 287)
Church, Revnd	HARL (42)
Church, Revrnd	HARL (57)
Church, Richard	EHAD (59)
Church, Saml	COLC (255)
Church, Thomas	DANB (43), HADD (111)
Church, Thos	HADD (124)
Church, Uriah	HARL (44, 52, 61)
Church, Uriah Lieut	HARL (48, 51, 56, 57, 59)
Church, Uriel Leiut	HARL (50)
Church, William 2d	EHAD (49)
Church, William jur	EHAD (59)
Churchel, Amos	MIDD (349)
Churchel, Benja	FARM (17, 449)
Churchel, John	DERB (122)
Churchel, Jos Capt	CHAT (67)
Churchel, Joseph	GLAS (66, 83, 84, 98)
Churchel, Joseph Capt	CHAT (39, 40, 43, 45, 46, 58)

INDEX

Name	Index Page	Name	Index Page
Churchel, Joseph Leut	CHAT (31, 38)	Clark, Darius	COLC (8)
Churchel, Nathl	FARM (433, 441)	Clark, Davd	LEBA (333)
Churchel, Nathl Capt	FARM (28)	Clark, David	CORN (1, 6, 9, 10, 12, 25, 86), HADD (121, 148)
Churchell, Amos	MIDD (371)		
Churchell, Benja	FARM (446)	Clark, Edman	DERB (122)
Churchell, Daniel	CHAT (43)	Clark, Edmond	DERB (121)
Churchell, Joseph	GLAS (95)	Clark, Elias	MILF (94, 98, 102, 104)
Churchell, Joseph Lieut	GLAS (108, 109)	Clark, Elihu	COLC (8, 9, 10, 242, 243, 244, 245, 246, 247, 249, 251, 254)
Churchell, Nathl	FARM (9)		
Churchell, Nathl Leut	FARM (456)	Clark, Elijah	EHAD (85), MILF (89)
Churchil, Amos	MIDD (345)	Clark, Elisha	CANT (156), MIDD (362, 365)
Churchill, Amos	MIDD (357, 374, 377, 396)		
		Clark, Enoch	MILF (93, 104)
Churchill, Jno	MILF (105)	Clark, Enoch 2d	MILF (104)
Churchill, John	MILF (85, 95, 98, 103)	Clark, Enos	FARM (456)
Churchill, Joseph	GLAS (108)	Clark, Enos Jur	FARM (455)
Churchol, John	DERB (121)	Clark, Ephm	FARM (455)
Clapp, Thos	GREE (128)	Clark, Fracis	MIDD (353)
Clark, [ ]	ASHF (231, 235), COLC (4)	Clark, Francis	MIDD (342, 346, 351, 355, 358, 361, 367, 370, 381, 390, 394, 402, 405, 407, 415)
Clark, Aaron	CHAT (44)		
Clark, Abel	FARM (433), KILH (49)		
Clark, Abell	FARM (8, 12, 27, 29, 444)	Clark, George	HARL (44, 48), MILF (89, 91, 92, 93, 102)
Clark, Able	FARM (442)	Clark, Gershom	LEBA (299)
Clark, Amos	CHAT (50, 58, 69), FARM (33, 436, 447, 455, 456), LEBA (298, 299, 315, 333, 334)	Clark, Giles	MIDD (362, 366)
		Clark, Hezekiah	CORN (10), HADD (112)
		Clark, Hezh	CORN (86)
Clark, Andrew	MILF (106)	Clark, Isaac	MILF (80, 82, 85)
Clark, Andrew Jur	CHES (8)	Clark, Isaac Capt	MILF (87, 93, 96)
Clark, Asael	LEBA (296, 311)	Clark, Israel	FARM (443), MANS (277)
Clark, Asael Cap	LEBA (321, 329, 341)		
Clark, Asael Jur	LEBA (315, 318, 326, 333)	Clark, J[ ][ ]	MIDD (393)
		Clark, Jabez	CHAT (34, 37, 64)
Clark, Benj Majr	ASHF (214)	Clark, Jacob	DURH (12, 17, 19, 24), LEBA (297, 299, 305, 326, 334)
Clark, Benja	ASHF (217, 229, 310, 313)		
Clark, Benja Majr	ASHF (211, 214, 216, 217, 218, 220, 221, 226, 229, 308)	Clark, James	DANB (49, 57, 58, 63), MANS (338, 356)
		Clark, James Capt	DANB (57, 60, 61, 66)
Clark, Benjamin	ASHF (206, 229), MILF (102, 103, 104)	Clark, James Jur	HADD (113, 115)
		Clark, James Lieut	HADD (109, 110, 116, 121)
Clark, Benjamin Majr	ASHF (216, 230)		
Clark, Benjn Capt	ASHF (199, 208)	Clark, James Maj	LEBA (325, 337, 343)
Clark, Benjn Majr	ASHF (212, 234, 238)	Clark, Jared	MILF (103)
Clark, Capt	ASHF (204, 205, 206, 207, 237), DANB (61, 66)	Clark, Jas Maj	LEBA (320)
		Clark, Jas Majr	LEBA (330)
Clark, Cyrenus	KENT (E59)	Clark, Jno	LEBA (319, 341, 325)
Clark, Dan	FARM (2, 17, 443)	Clark, Jno D[ ]	LEBA (312)
Clark, Daniel	CHAT (46, 52, 64), MIDD (351)	Clark, Jno Jur	LEBA (299)
		Clark, John	BOLT (158), CHAT (31, 35, 40, 42, 47), COLC (244), FARM (433, 443), LEBA (294, 304, 313, 323)
Clark, Daniel Capt	LEBA (306), MIDD (417)		
Clark, Danl	KILH (45), LEBA (316, 318, 341), MIDD (368)		
		Clark, John Jur	CHAT (38, 43, 58, 64), MILF (85)
Clark, Danl Cap	LEBA (320, 321, 325, 330)	Clark, Jona	LEBA (311, 316)
Clark, Danl Capt	LEBA (337), MIDD (387, 414)		
Clark, Danl Lt	LEBA (296)		

618

INDEX

Name	Index Page
Clark, Jonah	BRAN (163, 164, 171, 172, 173, 174, 176), CHES (14)
Clark, Jonan Jur	CHAT (68)
Clark, Jonathan	MILF (102), CHAT (64)
Clark, Jonathan Jur	CHAT (30, 41, 42)
Clark, Jonth	CHAT (37)
Clark, Jonth Jur	CHAT (43)
Clark, Jos	CANT (144), MIDD (364)
Clark, Joseph	CANT (168), MIDD (354, 367, 369, 371, 377, 379, 387, 393, 398, 403, 404, 412, 413, 351)
Clark, Joseph 2d	MIDD (362)
Clark, Joseph Jur	MIDD (345, 347, 349, 350, 356, 357, 359, 361)
Clark, Jude	FARM (2, 9, 449, 455)
Clark, Lamberton	MIDD (363)
Clark, Lazarous	MILF (85)
Clark, Leml Lt	MANS (277)
Clark, Lemuel	MANS (268, 284, 358)
Clark, Lieut Othniel	MIDD (405)
Clark, Ma[ ]en	FARM (444)
Clark, Major	ASHF (212, 222, 224, 225, 232, 233, 234, 238)
Clark, Martin	FARM (5)
Clark, Marvin	FARM (6, 9, 22, 433)
Clark, Mathew	FARM (2, 9, 18, 29, 433, 438, 445)
Clark, Mathw	FARM (442, 450)
Clark, Mehetibel	HADD (109)
Clark, Michal	DERB (132)
Clark, Moses	DERB (120, 145), LEBA (298, 299, 305, 311)
Clark, Nath	COLC (243, 248)
Clark, Nathan	MILF (85, 88, 91, 92, 102)
Clark, Nathan Capt	MILF (104)
Clark, Nathan Lieut	MILF (88, 89, 97)
Clark, Nathaniel	CHAT (33), HARL (61)
Clark, Nathaniel Cary	MILF (86)
Clark, Nathaniel Junr	HARL (56)
Clark, Nathl	CANT (144, 148, 154, 156, 162, 171, 182), CHAT (31, 51, 52, 67), COLC (245, 249)
Clark, Nathll Cary	MILF (98)
Clark, Nehemiah	MILF (82, 93)
Clark, Obed	FARM (456)
Clark, Oliver	MANS (272, 274, 339, 362, 388)
Clark, Othl Ensn	MIDD (358)
Clark, Othl Lt	MIDD (372)
Clark, Othniel Lieut	MIDD (382)
Clark, Othnl Lt	MIDD (395)
Clark, Phineas Doctr	GUIL (322)
Clark, Phins	MANS (281)
Clark, Saml	CANA (64, 77),FARM (455), HADD (109, 121, 126), MILF (93, 104)
Clark, Saml Capt	HADD (113)

Name	Index Page
Clark, Saml Jur	LEBA (298, 299, 311, 316, 327, 334, 342)
Clark, Samuel	CANA (16, 18, 19), EHAD (81, 87), HADD (113, 114, 129, 148), MILF (91, 106)
Clark, Samuel Buckingham	MILF (103)
Clark, Samuel Capt	HADD (115, 116, 123, 125, 126, 129)
Clark, Samuel Junr	LEBA (305)
Clark, Shelden	DERB (106, 107)
Clark, Silas	CORN (1, 9, 10, 15, 16, 17, 22, 23, 25), FARM (436), LEBA (296, 305, 306, 327, 334, 311), FARM (456)
Clark, Silas Jur	FARM (445, 456)
Clark, Simon	FARM (433), LEBA (311, 316, 325, 326, 329, 334, 342)
Clark, Stephen	CHAT (48), HADD (109, 129, 148)
Clark, Thomas	HARL (48, 52), DERB (114, 120, 122, 126, 127, 141, 142, 144)
Clark, Thomas Capt	DERB (107, 124, 168)
Clark, Thos	HARL (44)
Clark, Thos Capt	DERB (139)
Clark, Thos Junr	MILF (85, 93)
Clark, Timo	FARM (442), MIDD (394)
Clark, Timo Capt	FARM (452), MANS (346), MIDD (373, 376,381)
Clark, Timothy	FARM (430, 440, 444), MANS (271, 275, 283, 345)
Clark, Timothy Capt	FARM (442)
Clark, Uzziel Capt	CANA (20)
Clark, William	CHAT (33, 36, 39, 54), CHES (A), MANS (357), MILF (97, 103)
Clark, William Capt	DERB (120, 122)
Clark, Willm	HADD (148)
Clark, Wm	HADD (113), MILF (106)
Clarke, Aaron	CHAT (30)
Clarke, Benja Majr	ASHF (213, 222)
Cleark, Jos	CANT (150)
Cleark, Nathl	CANT (150)
Cleaveland, Aaron Col	CANT (150, 154, 183)
Cleaveland, Aaron Jr	CANT (150)
Cleaveland, John	CANT (166)
Cleaveland, Jos Capt	CANT (140, 151)
Cleaveland, Josiah Jur	CANT (156)
Cleaveland, Saml	CANT (156)
Cleaveland, Samuel	CANT (150)
Cleavland, Aaron Capt	EHAD (45)

INDEX

Name	Index Page	Name	Index Page
Cleavland, Aaron Colo	CANT (148, 150, 158, 160, 162, 163, 167, 173, 175)	Coe, Ebenr	MIDD (364, 370)
		Coe, Eli	MIDD (382, 395, 402, 406)
Cleavland, Asa	CANT (146, 160)	Coe, Elijah	HARL (47, 52, 57)
Cleavland, Curtis	CANT (173, 178, 179, 181)	Coe, Ephraim	DURH (12)
		Coe, Jedadiah	GUIL (321)
Cleavland, Jno Ensn	CANT (178, 181, 182)	Coe, Jedediah	GUIL (287, 320)
Cleavland, John	CANT (147)	Coe, Jesse	MIDD (361, 362, 366, 372, 395)
Cleavland, Josiah Capt	CANT (168, 177, 181)		
Cleavland, Josiah Junr	CANT (171, 172)	Coe, John	DERB (107, 113, 120, 122, 124, 131, 132, 147), DURH (11, 12, 23, 25)
Cleavland, Saml	CANT (146)		
Cleavland, Shubael	CANT (168, 177)		
Cleavland, Silas	CANT (145), 147, 168)	Coe, John Jur	DURH (10)
Cleavland, Timo Jr	CANT (168)	Coe, Jonathan	GREE (121, 126, 127, 128, 129)
Cleavld, Jos Capt	CANT (160)		
Cleavld, Josiah Jr	CANT (160)	Coe, Joseph Junr	MIDD (364, 377, 382, 394, 395, 403, 405, 409, 412)
Cleavld, Silas	CANT (148)		
Cleeveland, Brainerd	LITC (129)		
Clemens, Joel	GOSH (185)	Coe, Josiah	DURH (19)
Clemins, Joel	GOSH (183)	Coe, Nathan	MIDD (346, 349, 357, 361, 362, 367, 372, 382, 394, 405, 406, 413)
Clemons, [ ]	GOSH (184)		
Clemons, John Junr	LITC (132)		
Clemons, William	HARL (44)	Coe, Phenihas	HARL (61)
Clerk, Sheldon	DERB (106)	Coe, Phinehas	HARL (47, 51, 52, 56)
Clerk, Silas	CORN (86)	Coe, Seth	MIDD (363, 381, 382, 388, 404, 413)
Clever, Wm	MIDD (376)		
Clinton, Laurence	MILF (82)	Coe, Simeon Jur	DURH (17, 19)
Clinton, Lawrence	MILF (88, 92, 98, 103)	Coe, Thomas	LITC (129, 139, 146)
Clinton, Levi	MILF (85)	Coe, Timo	DURH (23, 25)
Close, Odel	GREE (126)	Coe, Timo Jur	DURH (23)
Close, Odell	GREE (120)	Coe, Timothy	DURH (10, 21)
Close, Odle	GREE (125)	Cogswell, David	FARM (442, 450)
Close, Odle Capt	GREE (127)	Cogswell, David Jur	FARM (456)
Clother, John	CORN (10, 13)	Cogswell, Edward	KENT (B6)
Clough, Leut	KILY (6)	Cogswell, Moses	FARM (436)
Clough, Obadiah	KILY (97)	Cogswell, Robert	FARM (454, 456)
Clough, Obadiah Leiut	KILY (98)	Cogswell, Willm	KENT (B6)
Clough, Obed	KILY (92a)	Cogwell, Nathl	CANT (168)
Clough, Obediah	KILY (24)	Coit, Doctr	HARF (255)
Clough, Obediah Capt	KILY (19)	Coit, Jos Doct	KILY (22)
Clough, Obediah Leut	KILY (8, 91, 91a, 92, 91a, 94a), KILY (96a)	Coit, Joseph	HARF (261a), KILY (12)
		Coit, Joseph Doctr	KILY (34, 98)
Clough, Obidiah Leut	KILY (90, 95a)	Cole, Davd	LEBA (299)
Clouth, Obediah Lieut	KILY (8)	Cole, Ebr Jur	LEBA (297)
Clow, Obed	KILY (86a)	Cole, Elijah	FARM (433, 443)
Co[ ], Isaac	FARM (9)	Cole, Elisha	FARM (443), HARF (263)
Coan, George	GUIL (328)		
Coan, Mulford	GUIL (278, 294)	Cole, Ezra	CORN (22, 23, 87, 90)
Coats, Benja	ASHF (311)	Cole, Gideon	FARM (442)
Cobb, Elijah	CANA (11, 16, 17, 19, 23, 28, 64)	Cole, Job	FARM (442)
		Cole, John	FARM (2), HARF (292)
Cobb, Elkanah Capt	CANT (144, 148, 154)	Cole, Joseph	LITC (129, 131, 135, 139, 142, 147, 158)
Cobb, James	CANT (151, 156)		
Coborn, John	LITC (128)	Cole, Marcus Lt	CHAT (45)
Cobs, Wm	DANB (70)	Cole, Mathew	FARM (430)
Coe, Abel	DURH (14)	Cole, Mathew Capt	FARM (442, 449, 451, 454)
Coe, Daniel	DURH (17)		
Coe, David	MIDD (368)	Cole, Moses	CHAT (31, 34, 40, 43, 67
Coe, David Capt	MIDD (353, 357)	Cole, Nathl	FARM (443)
Coe, David Junr	MIDD (381)	Cole, Nathn	FARM (8)

620

INDEX

Name	Index Page	Name	Index Page
Cole, Selah	FARM (10, 13, 456)	Colten, Eleazer	HARL (48)
Cole, Stephen	FARM (2, 6, 9, 14, 23, 442)	Colton, Abijah	HARF (250, 253, 255A, 258, 259)
Cole, Stephen Jur	FARM (438)	Colton, Benjamin	HARF (263A)
Cole, Timothy	COVE (172, 177)	Colton, Eleazer	HARL (44)
Cole, Zebn	FARM (2, 28)	Colton, George Revd	BOLT (181)
Cole, Zebulen	FARM (3)	Colton, Samuel	HARF (275)
Cole, Zebulon	FARM (9, 17, 456)	Combs, Wm	DANB (69)
Cole, Zebulun	FARM (18)	Comes, Anne	KILY (13)
Colebreath, John	MILF (82, 85)	Coming, Ezra	HARF (281)
Coleman, Aaron	KENT (E60, E64)	Comins, Jacob	KENT (B6)
Coleman, Asaph	GLAS (93)	Comstock, Abel	KENT (A28, E59, E63)
Coleman, Asaph Dr	GLAS (103, 112)	Comstock, Abel Jur	KENT (E60, E63)
Coleman, Daniel	COLC (248)	Comstock, Abijah	KENT (A28, B1, B2, C547, C548, C552, C553, C555, E58, E62)
Coleman, John	CANA (12, 64, 77)		
Coleman, Samuel	COVE (177)		
Coles, Timothy	COVE (174, 180)	Comstock, Andrew	DANB (39, 40, 41)
Coley, Ebenr Capt	FAIR (255)	Comstock, Andw	DANB (47, 58)
Coley, Elipt	FAIR (266)	Comstock, Calvin	LITC (129, 131, 135, 139, 142, 146, 147, 148, 152, 153)
Coley, Hez	FAIR (260, 267)		
Colins, Rufus Jur	LEBA (316)		
Collens, Agt Capt	GUIL (273)	Comstock, Cristopher	CHAT (52)
Collens, Agustus Capt	GUIL (270)	Comstock, Daniel	DANB (47, 48, 57, 69)
Collens, Augustus	GUIL (316, 331, 328)	Comstock, Danl	DANB (40)
Collens, Augustus Capt	GUIL (275, 308, 315, 317, 319, 332)	Comstock, David	KENT (E60)
		Comstock, Ebenezer	KENT (A28, C548, E58, E62)
Collens, Cyprian	GOSH (104)		
Collens, Dan	GUIL (269)	Comstock, Eliphalet	KENT (B1, B3, C544, C547, C548, C551, C552, C554, C555, D1, D10, D5, D7, E58, E62)
Collens, Dan Capt	GUIL (304, 305, 308, 315, 317, 319)		
Collens, Darius	GUIL (297, 302, 319, 338		
Collens, Oliver	GUIL (302, 336)	Comstock, Gershom	KENT (D7)
Collens, Pitman	GUIL (320)	Comstock, Israel	EHAD (64)
Collic, George	MIDD (376)	Comstock, Jabez	EHAD (44, 49, 54, 66, 68, 83, 85)
Collins, Ambrose	GOSH (115, 183)		
Collins, Cyprian	GOSH (105, 110)	Comstock, Jabez 2d	EHAD (85)
Collins, Dan Capt	GUIL (296)	Comstock, John Odle	KENT (C551, E58, E62)
Collins, Edward	ENFD (17, 18, 19, 24, 25, 26, 27, 28, 29, 32, 34, 35)	Comstock, Joseph	EHAD (64)
		Comstock, Luther	KENT (E64)
Collins, Eliphalet	ENFD (28, 30, 34, 35)	Comstock, Peter	KENT (D1, D7, D10)
Collins, Ens	GOSH (109, 115, 121, 124, 126, 127, 184)	Conant, Benajah	MANS (268, 271, 272, 283, 328, 336, 353, 358)
Collins, Howard	ENFD (29)	Conant, Eleazar	MANS (336, 338, 353, 355, 357)
Collins, Lt	GOSH (130, 134)		
Collins, Rufus Junr	LEBA (305)	Conant, John	MANS (233, 267, 279, 283, 326, 353)
Collins, Seth	HARF (253, 255A, 258, 260, 272, 275, 281, 287, 292)		
		Conant, Josiah	MANS (278)
		Conant, Malachi	MANS (338)
Collins, Seth Capt	HARF (278, 280, 300)	Conant, Seth	MANS (281, 338, 353, 358)
Collins, Zerubbabel	LEBA (305)		
Collit, Widdow	COLC (249)	Conant, Shubael	MANS (268, 271, 282, 283, 328, 335, 336, 347, 348, 353, 357, 358)
Colman, Asaph	GLAS (101)		
Colman, Asaph Dot	GLAS (102)		
Colman, Eleazer	COVE (168)	Conant, Shubl	MANS (278)
Colman, Ephraim	COVE (165, 168, 169, 177, 314)	Conant, Silvanus	MANS (338)
		Condly, John	GLAS (65)
Colman, Gershom	COVE (172, 314)	Cone, Silvanus 2d	EHAD (68)
Colman, Noah	LEBA (294)	Cone, Abner	LITC (131)
Colman, Ozias	LEBA (297, 299, 305, 311)	Cone, Beriah	MIDD (371, 395, 406)
		Cone, Cephas	COLC (10, 255)
		Cone, Daniel	EHAD (45)

621

INDEX

Name	Index Page
Cone, Daniel Capt	EHAD (50, 52, 55, 56, 59, 60, 62, 63, 65, 66)
Cone, Daniel Majr	EHAD 68, 69, 73, 75, 79, 80, 82, 87)
Cone, Danl	MIDD (358, 372, 382)
Cone, Ebenezer 2nd	EHAD (63, 66, 67, 68, 74
Cone, Ebenezer jur	EHAD (59)
Cone, Elijah Lt	EHAD (50, 60)
Cone, Elish	HADD (130)
Cone, Elisha	EHAD (64)
Cone, George [ ]	EHAD (49)
Cone, George 2nd	EHAD (57, 73, 84)
Cone, George jur	EHAD (53)
Cone, George Lt	EHAD (79)
Cone, James	EHAD (49, 69)
Cone, Jared Capt	BOLT (161, 165, 168, 180, 182)
Cone, Jared Liut	BOLT (146)
Cone, Jeremiah	EHAD (48, 49, 55, 69)
Cone, Jeremiah 2d	EHAD (50)
Cone, Jno	MIDD (413)
Cone, Joel	EHAD (44, 54, 64, 80, 83
Cone, John	MIDD (347, 373, 404, 416)
Cone, Jonah Capt	EHAD (51, 55, 64)
Cone, Jos	MIDD (358)
Cone, Joseph	KILH (55), MIDD (372, 382)
Cone, Judah	EHAD (64, 72, 87)
Cone, Nathanael	EHAD (44)
Cone, Nathaniel	EHAD (54)
Cone, Nathl	CHAT (55, 58, 61, 64, 67
Cone, Nehemiah	EHAD (71)
Cone, Noadiah	EHAD (59, 80)
Cone, Ozias	MIDD (358, 372, 382, 395, 405, 413)
Cone, Roswell	EHAD (64, 86)
Cone, Saml 2d	EHAD (50)
Cone, Samuel	EHAD (50)
Cone, Silas	HADD (119, 148)
Cone, Silvanus	EHAD (60, 65)
Cone, Silvanus 2nd	EHAD (44, 82)
Cone, Solomon	EHAD (54, 59, 69)
Cone, Stephen	HARF (253, 255, 255A, 257, 260, 261a, 263, 266, 271, 272, 273, 275, 281, 288, 293)
Cone, Sylvanus 2d	EHAD (84)
Cone, Timothy	EHAD (49, 73, 86)
Cone, William	MIDD (419)
Cone, William 2nd	EHAD (45, 80)
Cone, William Capt	EHAD (44, 48, 49, 53, 57
Cone, William jur	EHAD (59)
Cone, Willm Capt	EHAD (82)
Cone, Wm	MIDD (405, 413)
Cone, Zacariah	BOLT (180, 182)
Cone, Zach	HEBR (245)
Cone, Zachariah	BOLT (148), EHAD (45, 46, 49, 79) ,HEBR (247)
Cono[ ], Chester	KILY (94)

Name	Index Page
Convars, Alphius	KILY (86a)
Conver, Jacob Lieut	KILY (8)
Convers, Alpheus	KILY (87a, 91a, 97)
Convers, Benjn	KILY (87a)
Convers, Elijah	KILY (7)
Convers, Jacob	KILY (86a, 87a, 92, 97)
Convers, Jacob Lieut	KILY (7, 14, 19, 94a, 97)
Convers, Joel	KILY (87)
Convers, Josiah	KILY (87a)
Convers, Pain Capt	KILY (5, 7, 8, 10, 19, 20, 90, 91, 92, 94, 96, 96a, 97
Convers, Saml	KILY (94a)
Convers, Samuel	KILY (20, 98)
Converse, Alpheus	KILY (31)
Converse, Capt	GOSH (116)
Converse, Elijah	KILY (4, 31)
Converse, Jacob	KILY (21, 32)
Converse, Pain Capt	KILY (36)
Converse, Saml	KILY (33)
Converse, Samuel	KILY (11)
Converse, Thomas	GOSH (102)
Convess, Demon Read	KENT (E60)
Convess, Elijah	KENT (E60)
Convess, John	KENT (E60)
Cook, Ephraim Capt	CHES (4)
Cook, [ ]ph	HARW (4)
Cook, Aaron	ASHF (209, 218, 232, 236), HARF (266, 272, 281, 287, 292), KENT (C554)
Cook, Amasa	GOSH (102, 104, 115, 120, 184)
Cook, Benjamin	EWIN (85, 89)
Cook, Capt	GOSH (184)
Cook, Elam	CHES (12)
Cook, Elijah Capt	CHAT (56, 64)
Cook, Elijah Lt	CHAT (44)
Cook, Ephraim	CHES (8)
Cook, Gideon	EHAD (80, 86, 87)
Cook, Isaac	BRAN (175)
Cook, James	GUIL (315)
Cook, Jedida	GUIL (328)
Cook, Jedidah	GUIL (302, 315)
Cook, Jesse	COVE (177, 180), DURH (15, 17)
Cook, Job	HARW (3, 6)
Cook, John	FARM (455), HARF (250, 253, 255, 255A, 260, 261a, 266)
Cook, John Capt	HARF (270, 275, 281, 284, 289)
Cook, Jonathan	HADD (114, 148), HARW (3)
Cook, Jonathan Jur	HARW (3)
Cook, Joseph	HARW (6, 7, 9, 13, 14, 16, 20, 22, 523, 533, 534)
Cook, Joseph Lieut	HARW (3, 14, 15)
Cook, Joshua	CHAT (44, 52, 58), GUIL (302, 328)
Cook, Josiah Jur	CHAT (29)

622

INDEX

Name	Index Page
Cook, Lucious	KENT (E64)
Cook, Moses	CHAT (30, 40, 41, 43, 46, 50, 58, 64, 67)
Cook, Nathaniel	HADD (130)
Cook, Philip	GOSH (110, 184)
Cook, Reuben	MIDD (405, 413)
Cook, Richard	CHAT (31, 34, 41, 51, 68, 69)
Cook, Richd	CHAT (46, 54, 64)
Cook, Robert	FARM (443)
Cook, Roswel	COLE (10)
Cook, Saml	FARM (443)
Cook, Samuel	HARW (4, 7, 8, 523)
Cook, Samuel Jur	HARW (3)
Cook, Samuel Lieut	HARW (3)
Cook, Shobel	COVE (166, 180)
Cook, Stephen	FARM (2, 443)
Cook, Stepn	FARM (6)
Cook, Thos	DURH (10, 23)
Cook, Uzziel	BRAN (175)
Cook, William	HARW (7, 10, 13, 17, 23, 25)
Cook, Wm	HARW (3, 4, 5, 22, 533)
Cook, Zacheus	CHAT (54)
Cooke, Aaron	ASHF (213, 222, 226)
Cooke, Col	DANB (43, 56, 58, 63)
Cooke, Joseph Col	DANB (65)
Cooke, Joseph P	DANB (41, 46)
Cooke, Joseph P Col	DANB (46, 57)
Cooke, Joseph P Jur	DANB (59)
Cooke, Joseph Platt	DANB (51)
Cooke, Joseph Platt Coln	DANB (62)
Cooke, Saml	DANB (51, 61)
Cooke, Stephen	FARM (449)
Cooley, Samuel	BOLT (181, 183)
Cooper, Ebenezer	KILY (14)
Cooper, John	CHAT (29, 31, 36)
Cooper, John Capt	CHAT (37, 39, 41)
Cooper, Lamberton	MIDD (346, 349, 356, 368, 370, 379, 380, 389, 392, 394, 403, 404, 407, 412, 413)
Cooper, Lamburton	MIDD (392)
Cooper, Lamt	MIDD (390)
Cooper, Peter	KILY (19, 96a, 97a)
Cooper, Thomas	CHAT (33, 37, 38, 43, 44, 46, 50, 67, 68)
Cooper, William	CANT (183)
Coopland, Willm	KILY (4)
Coopland, Wm Jur	KILY (31)
Coopp, David	KILY (32)
Coper, Ebenezer	KILY (92, 93, 94, 94a)
Copley, Nathl	HARW (5, 23)
Copley, Nathl Capt	HARW (3)
Copp, David	KILY (8, 19, 22)
Coracker, Barshuba	KENT (D14)
Corben, Peleg	KILY (32)
Corbin, [ ]	ASHF (220)
Corbin, Asa	KILY (7)

Name	Index Page
Corbin, Mosses	KILY (4)
Corbin, Peleg	KILY (4, 31, 97)
Corbin, Samuel Jur	KILY (7, 19)
Corder, John	KILY (19)
Corder, Wiliam	KILY (19)
Corning, Asa	HARF (292)
Cornwall, Elisha	CHAT (29)
Cornwell, [ ]	CORN (18, 21)
Cornwell, Abijah	CHES (11)
Cornwell, Ashbel	MIDD (362, 393, 404, 412)
Cornwell, Cornelius	FARM (29), MIDD (362, 395, 397, 398, 400, 407)
Cornwell, Cornelius Lieut	MIDD (399)
Cornwell, Elisha	CHAT (42)
Cornwell, Isaac	MIDD (363)
Cornwell, Isaac Jr	MIDD (362)
Cornwell, Joseph	MIDD (358, 362)
Cornwell, Lt	MIDD (396)
Cornwell, Nathl	CHAT (31, 37, 41, 362, 421)
Cornwell, Saml	CHAT (51, 61, 67)
Cornwell, Thomas	CHAT (30)
Cornwell, Thos	CHAT (43)
Cornwell, Timo	MIDD (368, 367)
Cornwell, Timothy	CHAT (29), MIDD (350, 361)
Cornwill, Moses	CHAT (30)
Cotton, Abijah	HARF (251(2))
Cotton, Eleazer	HARL (52)
Cotton, Elihu	MIDD (357, 368)
Cotton, Geo Ens	MIDD (413)
Cotton, George Reverd	BOLT (182)
Cotton, James	MIDD (376, 406, 414, 419)
Cotton, John	MIDD (368, 371)
Cotton, John 3d	MIDD (413)
Cotton, John Capt	MIDD (345)
Cotton, William	MIDD (346, 349, 356)
Cotton, Wm	MIDD (370, 380, 394, 404, 413)
Couch, David	HARL (45, 48, 53)
Couch, Eliz	FAIR (262)
Couch, Jonathan	HARL (45, 48)
Couch, Jothan	HARL (53)
Couch, Simon	FAIR (254)
Couch, Simon Jur	FAIR (255, 265, 267)
Couch, Thos	FAIR (263)
Couch, Timothy	HARL (44, 47, 52)
Coudry, Jacob	HARL (45, 51, 53)
Coudry, Moses	HARL (50, 44)
Coult, Jonathan H	HARW (16, 22)
Coult, Jonathan Higley	HARW (17)
Coult, Jonathn H	HARW (23)
Covel, Elijah	GLAS (92, 94, 106)
Covel, John	GLAS (95)
Covel, Philip	GLAS (92, 94, 111)
Covel, Samuel	GLAS (83, 94, 95)
Covell, Saml Capt	GLAS (112)

623

INDEX

Name	Index Page	Name	Index Page
Covey, Elisha	FARM (9, 17, 27)	Cowles, Thos	FARM (18, 29, 442, 445, 451)
Covey, Nathan	FARM (13)		
Cowdery, Thomas	CHAT (31, 37, 38, 39, 41, 50, 58, 65, 66)	Cowls, John	HARL (45)
		Cowls, Timothy	CANA (64)
Cowdery, Thos	CHAT (36, 67)	Cox, Isaiah	DURH (19)
Cowdrey, Moses	HARL (55, 58)	Cox, Nathan	MIDD (419)
Cowdry, Moses	HARL (48, 51, 52)	Cox, Simeon	DURH (25)
Cowle, Elisha	HARF (281)	Coyt, Abel	ASHF (313)
Cowle, John	HARF (274, 279, 280, 281, 283, 286, 287, 289, 298)	Crampton, Benj	GUIL (269)
		Crampton, Benjn	GUIL (277)
		Crampton, Jona	FARM (456)
Cowle, Timothy	HARF (253, 255A, 259, 275)	Cramton, Benjn	GUIL (294)
		Cramton, Benjn Junr	GUIL (335)
Cowle, William Junr	HARF (292)	Cramton, Hull	GUIL (325)
Cowles, Amos	FARM (5, 6, 9, 12, 441, 443, 444, 445, 449, 450, 451, 456)	Cramton, John Junr	GUIL (324)
		Cramton, Josiah	GUIL (297, 332, 333)
		Cramton, Josiah Junr	GUIL (272)
Cowles, Asahel	FARM (434, 443, 446, 450)	Cramton, Mary	GUIL (334)
		Cramton, Miles	FARM (17, 438, 455)
Cowles, Ashbel	FARM (445)	Cramton, Nathan	GUIL (307, 335)
Cowles, Ashbell	FARM (443, 450)	Crane, Daniel	KILH (145), MANS (353)
Cowles, Calvin	FARM (436, 442, 449)		
Cowles, Capt	FARM (11, 19)	Crane, Eli	DURH (10, 17)
Cowles, Danl Jur	FARM (443)	Crane, Elihu	DURH (11, 12, 14, 20, 26)
Cowles, Elijah	FARM (28, 446, 450, 455)	Crane, Elijah	GUIL (299, 320)
Cowles, Elijah Jur	FARM (29, 31)	Crane, Elish	KILH (47)
Cowles, Eneas	FARM (444)	Crane, Elisha	KILH (44, 48, 49, 51, 53, 54)
Cowles, Ezekiel	FARM (4, 31)		
Cowles, Ezekiel Jur	FARM (31)	Crane, Ely	DURH (12)
Cowles, Ezekl	FARM (433, 442, 450)	Crane, Frederick	DURH (22)
Cowles, Gamaliall	FARM (438)	Crane, Fredrick	DURH (25)
Cowles, Gamaliel	FARM (433, 442, 444)	Crane, Henry	DURH (10, 14, 18)
Cowles, Gideon	FARM (2, 5, 8, 9, 17, 433	Crane, Hez Junr	MANS (267)
Cowles, Isaac	FARM (2, 3, 8, 17, 23, 28, 32, 449, 456)	Crane, Hezekiah	EWIN (85, 88), MANS (328, 338)
Cowles, Isaac Doctr	HARW (3, 25)	Crane, Hezh Junr	MANS (353)
Cowles, Jabez	FARM (9)	Crane, Jesse	DURH (11, 14, 18, 19, 21, 24, 25, 26)
Cowles, James	FARM (2, 31, 454, 456)		
Cowles, John	FARM (28, 443)	Crane, John	DURH (10, 14, 25)
Cowles, Jona	FARM (5)	Crane, John Leut	KILH (45, 55, 146)
Cowles, Josiah	FARM (21, 30, 440, 442, 446, 449, 453)	Crane, Saml	KILH (44)
		Crane, Saml Capt	KILH (42, 44, 47, 49, 51, 52, 53)
Cowles, Josiah Capt	FARM (19, 430, 445, 451		
Cowles, Matthew	FARM (442)	Crane, Theoplus	KILH (145)
Cowles, Noah	FARM (14, 17, 29, 433, 434, 435, 440, 442, 443, 445, 450, 452)	Crary, Nathan	GROT ([15])
		Crary, Richard	GLAS (88, 99, 114)
		Cravath, Saml	HARW (4)
Cowles, Phineas	FARM (451)	Craw, John Jur	EWIN (85, 88)
Cowles, Phinehas	FARM (28)	Crawfoot, Ephraim	MIDD (378)
Cowles, Saml	FARM (442, 444)	Crawford, John	DERB (120, 122, 167)
Cowles, Saml Jur	FARM (433, 438)	Crery, Isaac	GROT ([12], [23])
Cowles, Selah	FARM (2)	Crery, Nathan	GROT [4], [6], [17], [25]
Cowles, Soln	FARM (5, 445)	Crery, Nathan Junr	GROT ([4], [9])
Cowles, Soln Capt	FARM (17, 434, 438, 444, 445, 452, 456)	Cridendon, Josiah	COLC (248)
		Cridendon, Nathl	FARM (455)
Cowles, Solomon	FARM (21, 444, 450)	Cridenton, Salmon	KENT (A24)
Cowles, Solomon Capt	FARM (2, 3, 5, 8, 19, 433, 436, 441, 449)	Cridenton, Semor	KENT (C554)
		Crisey, Solomon	COLE (5, 11, 113, 115)
Cowles, Solomon Jur	FARM (2, 3)	Crittenden, Jairus	GUIL (299)
Cowles, Thomas	FARM (3, 5, 433, 434, 438, 449, 450)		

624

INDEX

Name	Index Page
Crittenden, Joseph Ensn	GUIL (287)
Crittenden, Josiah	COLC (251)
Crittenden, Nathl	GUIL (274)
Crittenden, Saml Junr	GUIL (299)
Crittendon, Daniel	CHAT (40, 42)
Crittendon, Josiah	COLC (7)
Crittenten, Nathaniel	FARM (443)
Crittenton, Gideon	MIDD (382)
Crocker, Andrew	COVE (177)
Crocker, J[ ]	LEBA (320)
Crocker, J[ ][ ]	LEBA (327)
Crocker, James	LEBA (298, 299, 311, 318, 334, 342)
Crocker, John Dr	COVE (161, 163)
Crocker, Jonathan	CORN (87)
Crocker, Simeon	COLC (8, 249)
Crocker, Simon	LEBA (326)
Crocker, Simon Lt	LEBA (320)
Crofoot, Ephraim	MIDD (394)
Crofoot, Ephraim Junr	MIDD (405)
Croft, Edward Doct	DERB (120, 122)
Crofut, Danl	DANB (59)
Crofut, Joseph	DANB (51)
Crofut, Matthew Jur	DANB (68, 70)
Cromwell, Thomas	GREE (121)
Cromwell, Thos	GREE (119)
Croofoot, Elisha	MIDD (362)
Croofoot, Ephraim	MIDD (357)
Crosbe, John	CHAT (67)
Crosbee, Levy	EHAD (50)
Crosbey, Elijah	KILY (31)
Crosbey, Saml	HARL (58)
Crosbey, Samuel	HARL (56)
Crosbey, Simeon	HARL (55, 57)
Crosby, Ebenezer	HARF (273)
Crosby, Increase	EHAD (49, 54, 64, 70, 86)
Crosby, Increase Ens	EHAD (53, 57)
Crosby, John	CHAT (34)
Crosby, Levi	EHAD (44, 54)
Crosby, Levi 2d	EHAD (80)
Crosby, Obed	HARL (45)
Crosby, Saml	HARL (50, 53)
Crosby, Samuel	HARL (45, 48, 51, 56, 59, 61)
Crosby, Simeon	HARL (45, 48, 53, 57)
Crosby, Stephen	KILY (86a)
Crosman, John	FAIR (263, 264)
Cross, John	GLAS (94)
Cross, Peter	MANS (267, 268, 274, 278, 284, 329, 347, 353)
Cross, Peter Ensn	MANS (336)
Crouch, Ch[ ] Jur	HEBR (217)
Crouch, Thos	HEBR (217)
Crouch, Thos F	HEBR (246, 247)
Crowel, Daniel	MIDD (376)
Crowel, Danl	MIDD (395, 412)
Crowel, John	MIDD (377)
Crowell, Daniel	MIDD (359)
Crowell, Edward	MIDD (362)
Crowell, John	MIDD (347, 361, 362, 377)
Crowfoot, James	FAIR (260)
Cruttenden, Nathl	GUIL (309)
Cruttenden, [ ]	KILH (47)
Cruttenden, David	GUIL (341)
Cruttenden, Gideon	MIDD (358)
Cruttenden, Hull	GUIL (277)
Cruttenden, John	GUIL (313, 318, 326, 327, 334)
Cruttenden, Joseph	GUIL (303)
Cruttenden, Joseph Junr	GUIL (299, 335)
Cruttenden, Nathl	GUIL (294)
Cruttenden, Noah	GUIL (313, 318, 327)
Cruttenden, Theo	GUIL (326)
Cruttenden, Thos	GUIL (296), 327, 334)
Cruttenden, Timo	GUIL (313, 316)
Cruttenden, Timothy	GUIL (303, 335)
Cruttendon, Daniel	CHAT (58)
Cruttenton, Gideon	MIDD (372)
Crutttenden, Joseph Junr	GUIL (270)
Culver, Saml	FARM (9, 433, 444)
Culver, Samuel	FARM (441)
Cummings, George	EWIN (85, 88)
Cuningham, Dennis	GLAS (114)
Curtice, Saml	CANA (64, 77)
Curtis, Abijah	DURH (26)
Curtis, Abner	FARM (436, 442, 449)
Curtis, Abner Jur	FARM (28)
Curtis, Augustus	KENT (E64)
Curtis, Benjamin	COLC (243)
Curtis, Danl	FARM (442)
Curtis, David	HARW (534)
Curtis, Eleazer	KENT (D7, E59, C548)
Curtis, Eleazer 3d	KENT (E60, E63)
Curtis, Eleazer Jur	KENT (A26, A28, C548, D1, E58, E62)
Curtis, Eleazer Jur Majr	KENT (C543)
Curtis, Eleazer Majr	KENT (C544, D3, D5, D6, D13)
Curtis, George	KENT (C551)
Curtis, Henry	COVE (170, 174, 177, 314)
Curtis, Jesse	FARM (442)
Curtis, Jno	HEBR (218)
Curtis, John	FARM (443)
Curtis, John Jnr	CANT (182)
Curtis, Martain	KENT (C548, C552, D7, D8, E63)
Curtis, Martin	KENT (E58)
Curtis, Oliver	DERB (113)
Curtis, Oliver Lieut	DERB (120)
Curtis, Peter	FARM (430, 449, 438, 442)
Curtis, Peter Capt	FARM (17, 447)
Curtis, Peter Leut	FARM (433, 435)

INDEX

Name	Index Page	Name	Index Page
Curtis, Ransom	ASHF (232)	Dana, Joshua	MANS (280)
Curtis, Saml	FARM (442, 443)	Daneals, Thomas	EHAD (45)
Curtis, Silas	KENT (D10, E59, E63)	Danelson, Wm	KILY (85a)
Curtis, Soln	FARM (443, 444)	Danforth, [ ]	MIDD (386)
Curtise, John	HEBR (234)	Danforth, Joseph	MIDD (376, 405, 412)
Curtiss, Abijah	DURH (16, 18, 19, 23, 25	Danforth, Thomas	MIDD (345, 349, 356, 368, 369, 380, 393, 404)
Curtiss, Abner	FARM (450)		
Curtiss, Abner Jur	FARM (10, 23, 456)	Danforth, Thos Lieut	MIDD (387)
Curtiss, Allin Capt	CANA (64)	Daniel, John	HARL (44, 47)
Curtiss, Capt	DURH (10, 14, 15, 16, 17, 18)	Daniel, Peletiah	HARL (44)
		Daniels, Amasa	CHAT (33, 43, 51, 55, 65, 66, 67)
Curtiss, Danl	FARM (32, 436)		
Curtiss, David	CHES (A), HARW (2, 25, 533)	Daniels, Asa	COLC (8, 243, 249, 251, 254)
Curtiss, Eleazer	FARM (17)	Daniels, Daniel	BOLT (181)
Curtiss, Gabriel	FARM (4, 28)	Daniels, David	GLAS (94)
Curtiss, James	DURH (12, 22)	Daniels, Jno	HARL (52)
Curtiss, Jeremiah	FARM (456)	Daniels, John	BOLT (146, 148, 160, 181, 183)
Curtiss, Jesse	FARM (2, 456)		
Curtiss, John	DURH (10, 16, 21), FARM (435, 440, 443, 445, 446, 449, 451, 452, 454, 455, 456)	Daniels, John Junr	BOLT (183)
		Daniels, Nehemiah	COLC (245)
		Daniels, Nehh	COLC (8)
		Daniels, Peletiah	HARL (47, 52)
Curtiss, John Jur	DURH (23)	Danielson, David	KILY (19, 97)
Curtiss, Nathan	DURH (11)	Danielson, Saml	KILY (87a, 89)
Curtiss, Oliver	DERB (113)	Danielson, Saml Junr	KILY (29, 87)
Curtiss, Peter	FARM (2)	Danielson, Saml Leut	KILY (94a, 96)
Curtiss, Peter Capt	FARM (14, 23, 27, 28, 31	Danielson, Samuel Leut	KILY (5, 10)
Curtiss, Saml	FARM (436)		
Curtiss, Stephen	DANB (51)	Danielson, William	KILY (8)
Cushman, Alerton Jur	COVE (166)	Danielson, William Col	KILY (16, 18, 31)
Cushman, Allerton	COVE (172)		
Cushman, Danl	CANT (153, 178, 181)	Danielson, Wm Col	KILY (22, 23, 29)
Cushman, Ephram	COVE (165)	Danilson, Saml Leut	KILY (32, 91)
Cutler, Azariah	KILY (19)	Dare, George	LITC (158)
Cutler, Benoni Capt	KILY (92a)	Darke, Jonathan	BOLT (155)
Cutler, Joseph Capt	KILY (5, 91a, 96)	Darling, [ ]	FARM (20)
Cutler, Ozariah	KILY (8)	Darling, Abel	LITC (135, 146, 147)
Cutter, Hez	KILY (87a)	Darren, Daniel	FARM (436)
Cutter, Isaac	KILY (94a)	Darren, Stephen	FARM (9)
Cutting, [ ]	LEBA (296)	Dart, Jabez	HARF (274, 281, 292)
D[ ], George	GOSH (184)	Dart, Jonathan	BOLT (148)
Daboll, John	GROT ([23])	Dart, Jos Capt	CHAT (43)
Daboll, John Junr	GROT ([15])	Dart, Joseph	CHAT (31, 36, 47, 52, 58, 61, 62, 64, 66, 67, 68, 69)
Dabool, John Junr	GROT ([24])		
Dagget, Samll	COVE (314)	Dart, Joseph Capt	CHAT (38, 40, 41, 42, 45, 50)
Dakeson, Saml	FARM (9)		
Daley, Joseph	CHAT (43)	Darte, Daniel	BOLT (155, 180, 182)
Damon, Jonathan	EWIN (89)	Darte, Jabez Junr	HARF (253)
Dana, Capt	MANS (337, 352)	Darte, John	BOLT (180, 182)
Dana, Jacob	ASHF (211, 308, 310)	Darte, Jonathan	BOLT (146, 151, 180, 182)
Dana, James	MANS (281, 347)		
Dana, James Capt	MANS (328, 333, 341, 342, 346, 350, 356)	Darte, Saml	BOLT (156)
		Darte, Samuel	BOLT (181)
Dana, Jed. Junr	ASHF (308)	Darte, Timothy	BOLT (180)
Dana, Jeda	ASHF (308)	Darte, William	BOLT (180)
Dana, Jedadh Jur	ASHF (213)	Daten, Henry	COLC (242)
Dana, Jedh	ASHF (310)	Daton, Eli	KENT (E60)
Dana, Jedh Jur	ASHF (310)	Daton, Henry	COLC (249, 251)
Dana, Jedidiah Jur	ASHF (209)		

INDEX

Name	Index Page
Daton, Isaac	KENT (A28, B1, D1, D7, D10, E63)
Davas, Daniel Jur	KILY (85a)
Davenpor, Ephraim	COVE (180)
Davenport, Ephraim	COVE (314)
Davenport, Paul	CANT (161)
Davenport, Saml	CANT (180)
Davidson, William	MILF (93, 102, 104)
Davinson, Asa	ASHF (204)
Davinson, Zeph	ASHF (310)
Davis, Ruben	DERB (138)
Davis, [ ]	DERB (168)
Davis, Barnabas	KILY (96a)
Davis, Benjn	DERB (134, 167)
Davis, Charles	CHAT (47)
Davis, Daniel	DERB (106, 120, 126, 134), KILY (87, 94)
Davis, Daniel Jur	KILY (14, 89, 91a, 94a)
Davis, Daniel Leut	KILY (96a, 98)
Davis, Elijah	DERB (122, 131, 134, 140)
Davis, Isaac	MANS (339)
Davis, Ishmael	KILY (19)
Davis, Jacob	KENT (B6)
Davis, John	DERB (106, 107, 113, 114, 120, 122, 124, 126, 131, 133, 140, 145, 167)
Davis, Jona	MANS (277)
Davis, Jonathan	CANT (145, 156), MANS (268)
Davis, Jos Jur	DERB (168)
Davis, Joseph	BOLT (183), DERB (133)
Davis, Joseph Capt	DERB (133)
Davis, Joseph Junr	DERB (120, 122)
Davis, Lathrop	LEBA (333)
Davis, Nathan	HARW (4)
Davis, Nathan Junr	DERB (120, 131)
Davis, Saml	KILH (55)
Davis, Saml 2d	KILH (53)
Davis, Simon	KILY (8, 31, 86a, 87, 87a, 91a, 94, 94a, 97)
Davis, Stephen	GREE (121, 127)
Davis, Thomas	KILY (96), MANS (274)
Davis, Thos	MANS (279, 281)
Davis, Zeph	HEBR (218)
Davise, Jonathan	CANT (151)
Davison, Asa	ASHF (311)
Davison, Zeph	ASHF (308)
Davison, Zepheniah	ASHF (218)
Daviss, John	HARW (3, 15)
Daviss, Nathan	HARW (6, 9, 10, 22)
Daviss, Nathan Jur	HARW (3)
Daw, Abel	ASHF (236)
Dawis, Naomi	FARM (13)
Dawset, Amos	ASHF (233)
Day, Aaron	FARM (442, 445)
Day, Abner	KILY (32)
Day, Adonijah	EWIN (12)
Day, Amasa	COLC (8, 246, 247, 249, 251, 254)
Day, Comfort	KILY (86a)
Day, Comfort Leut	KILY (19, 91, 94a)
Day, David	COLC (242), COLC (245), KILY (91a)
Day, David Lieut	COLC (243, 251) HARL (43, 49)
Day, Elijah	COLC (248)
Day, Elisha	COLC (249), HADD (120, 126, 129)
Day, Israel	KILY (96a, 97, 98)
Day, James	KILY (8,14, 26, 27, 85a, 86a, 87, 87a, 88, 94, 94a, 97)
Day, James Jur	KILY (32)
Day, Jeams	KILY (91, 92)
Day, Jesse	COLC (242, 251, 255)
Day, John	KILY (7, 14, 19, 32)
Day, Jonathan	KILY (7, 11, 94, 96, 98)
Day, Joseph Junr	COLC (10, 243, 245)
Day, Justus	EWIN (11, 12, 15)
Day, Nathan	EWIN (85, 88), KILY (28, 32)
Day, Noah	COLC (6, 245, 246), KILY (8, 32)
Day, Oliver	EWIN (11, 12, 13, 15, 17, 85, 89)
Day, Russel	COLC (4)
Day, Stephen	COLC (249, 251, 252)
Day, Stephen Capt	COLC (251, 254)
Day, Wm	FARM (443, 444)
Deains, Saml	CANT (155)
Deamon, Joseph	KILY (4)
Dean, [ ]	CORN (14)
Dean, Abner	COLC (243, 246, 249)
Dean, Benja	FAIR (252, 256, 258, 260, 262, 263, 266, 267)
Dean, Benja Capt	FAIR (252, 254, 255, 258, 262)
Dean, Benjamin	CORN (86), FAIR (264, 266)
Dean, Benjamin Capt	FAIR (253, 260)
Dean, Ebenr Jr	CANT (178)
Dean, Elijah	CHAT (42)
Dean, John	FARM (433)
Dean, Phinehas	CHAT (44)
Dean, Roswell	CANA (12, 15, 26, 77)
Dean, Simeon	ASHF (210, 311)
Dean, Thomas	CORN (3, 9, 16, 22, 23, 25, 86)
Deane, Roswell	CANA (64)
Deans, Ebenr Jr	CANT (180)
Deans, Henry	KENT (A28)
Deans, Saml	CANT (168)
Dearing, Theday	ASHF (236)
Deavenport, Ephraim	COVE (165, 166)
Deavenport, Thomas	COVE (174)
Deckerson, Seth	FARM (29)
Deen, John 2nd	CANA (27)
Deer, George	GOSH (183)

INDEX

Name	Index Page	Name	Index Page
Deforest, Capt	DANB (57)	Dewey, Josiah	CANT (145, 147, 148, 150), FARM (9, 28, 441)
Deforest, David	DERB (106, 113, 114, 120, 122, 124, 127, 131, 140, 145, 169)	Dewey, Saml	HEBR (217)
Delino, Silvanus	BOLT (181)	Dewey, Silas	COLC (12)
Delop, James	CANT (144, 146, 169, 176)	Dewey, Solo	LEBA (341)
		Dewey, Soloman	BOLT (148)
Deming, Chauncy	FARM (5)	Dewey, Solomon	BOLT (167, 180, 182)
Deming, Daniel	CANA (64)	Dewey, Thomas	HEBR (216)
Deming, Dr	GOSH (183)	Dewitt, Garrit V H	MILF (80, 82)
Deming, Eliakim	FARM (435, 441, 442)	DeWitt, Henry	MANS (265)
Deming, Elias Dr	GOSH (104)	Dexter, David	MANS (278)
Deming, Elisha	FARM (450)	Dexter, Isaac	MANS (278)
Deming, Gideon	HARF (288, 293)	Dexter, Jona	MANS (277)
Deming, Henry	COLC (9, 247, 248, 249, 252, 254)	Dexter, Jonathan	MANS (233)
		Dibbal, Silas	LITC (158)
Deming, Hezekiah	CANA (12, 15)	Dibble, Benja Doctr	CORN (13)
Deming, James	CANA (64, 77)	Dibble, Benjamin	CORN (12, 16, 87, 91)
Deming, John	FARM (14, 444)	Dibble, David	CORN (6, 16, 88, 91)
Deming, Jonath	COLC (243, 249, 251), GOSH (185, 186)	Dibble, Ebenezer	CORN (6)
		Dibble, Ebenezer Lieut	CORN (22)
Deming, Jonath Capt	COLC (13)	Dibble, Ebenr	CORN (86)
Deming, Jonathan	COLC (244, 247, 248), GLAS (64)	Dibble, Elisha	DANB (39, 47, 58)
		Dibble, Ezra	DANB (40)
Deming, Jonathan Capt	COLC (254)	Dibble, Ezra Capt	DANB (65)
Deming, Jonathan Lieut	COLC (245, 247)	Dibble, Ezra Jur	DANB (40, 43, 47, 49, 51, 54, 58, 63)
		Dibble, Ezra Lieut	DANB (45, 51)
Deming, Jonn	COLC (8, 254)	Dibble, Israel	CORN (12)
Deming, Julius	LITC (158)	Dibble, Jno	MILF (86)
Deming, Moses	FARM (2, 440, 441, 456)	Dibble, John	MILF (78, 80, 85, 87, 89, 90, 91, 92, 94, 96, 98, 100)
Deming, Roswell	CANA (64, 77)		
Deming, Saml	FARM (9, 23, 456)		
Deming, Seth	FARM (5, 8, 438, 441, 449, 456)	Dibble, John 2nd	CORN (16, 22, 88)
		Dibble, John 3rd	CORN (13, 14, 16, 87, 91)
Deming, Seth Capt	FARM (9)	Dibble, Joseph Jur	DANB (59)
Demmau, David	HARF (281)	Dibble, Nathan	DANB (68, 71)
Demming, Daniel	CANA (77)	Dibble, Saml	DANB (47)
Demming, Joel	CANA (64, 77)	Dibble, Silas	CORN (17, 87), LITC (135)
Demming, Lemmuel	CANA (77)		
Den[ ], Saml	KILY (7)	Dibbol, Silas	LITC (158)
Denton, Humphrey	GREE (127)	Dible, David	KILH (47, 55)
Deuty, Matthew	COVE (170), COVE (177)	Dible, John	MILF (82, 97)
		Dickenson, Doct	MIDD (360)
Devenport, Joseph	CANT (155)	Dickenson, John	MIDD (371, 407)
Dewey, [ ]	HEBR (218)	Dickenson, Michael	LITC (141)
Dewey, Abm Jur	LEBA (342)	Dickenson, Reuben	LITC (129)
Dewey, Bithiah	FARM (24)	Dickenson, Thomas	GLAS (95)
Dewey, Daniel	LEBA (306)	Dickenson, Thos	GOSH (110, 183, 184)
Dewey, Danl Cap	LEBA (320, 325, 337)	Dickerson, David	HADD (127, 148)
Dewey, Danl Jur	LEBA (333)	Dickerson, David Junr	GLAS (83)
Dewey, Darius	LEBA (342)	Dickerson, George	FARM (455)
Dewey, David	FARM (28, 450, 455)	Dickerson, John	HADD (125, 129, 148), MIDD (388, 389)
Dewey, Eli	HARW (3, 5, 10, 17, 22, 25)		
		Dickerson, Moses	FARM (3, 9, 433, 449)
Dewey, Israel	LEBA (305, 310, 342)	Dickerson, Nathan	GLAS (77, 83, 85, 89, 90, 98, 99, 102)
Dewey, Isrl	LEBA (298, 311, 316)		
Dewey, Jno	LEBA (305, 341)	Dickerson, Nathan Jur	GLAS (79)
Dewey, John	GLAS (105), LEBA (315, 342)	Dickerson, Nehe	HADD (148)
		Dickerson, Obadiah	EWIN (89), HADD (148)
		Dickerson, Saml	FARM (443, 450)

INDEX

Name	Index Page	Name	Index Page
Dickerson, Stephen Sergt	HADD (116)	Dimock, Oliver	MANS (280, 328, 336)
Dickerson, Thomas	GLAS (83, 89, 90)	Dimock, Samuel	MANS (233)
Dickinson, David	GLAS (93)	Dimock, Shubael Junr	MANS (339)
Dickinson, David Jur	GLAS (94)	Dimock, Thos	CANT (157)
Dickinson, Doct	MIDD (407, 410)	Dimock, Tim	ASHF (308)
Dickinson, Elisha	CORN (88)	Dimock, Timo	ASHF (226)
Dickinson, John	MIDD (367, 381, 389, 391, 394, 400, 403, 406, 408, 413, 415, 417, 418, 420)	Dimock, Timothy	ASHF (222, 226)
		Dimock, Timothy Capt	COVE (179)
		Dimon, [ ]	FAIR (266)
		Dimon, David	FAIR (269)
		Dimon, Jonathan	FAIR (269)
Dickinson, John Doctr	MIDD (356, 358, 402)	Dimon, Jonathan Colo	FAIR (252)
Dickinson, Moses	FARM (442)	Dimon, Jonth	FAIR (267)
Dickinson, Nathan	GLAS (69, 74, 93, 104, 105, 108)	Dimon, Jonth Colo	FAIR (256, 259, 261)
		Dimon, Jonth Capt	FAIR (266)
Dickinson, Obadiah	EWIN (8, 85)	Dimon, Moses	FAIR (265)
Dickinson, Thomas	GLAS (66, 71, 94)	Dimon, Wm.	FAIR (263)
Dickinson, Wm	FARM (443, 444)	Dimuck, Benja Lieut	ASHF (308)
Dickson, James	EHAD (58, 60)	Dimuck, Daniel	ASHF (232, 237)
Die, Daniel	KENT (C551)	Dimuck, Timothy	ASHF (227, 232, 237, 310)
Diggens, Joseph Ens	EWIN (88)		
Diggers, Joseph Ens	EWIN (85)	Disbrow, Asa	FAIR (265)
Diggins, [ ]	ENFD (27)	Dishon, Richard	GLAS (107)
Diggins, Agustus	ENFD (24, 32)	Dixen, James	KILY (32)
Diggins, Augustus	ENFD (26, 29, 34, 35)	Dixon, James	EHAD (44)
Dike, [ ]	KILY (6)	Dixon, John	GROT ([9], [12], [18])
Dike, James	KILY (85a, 87, 87a, 94a)	Dixon, William	CHAT (33, 38, 41, 43, 45, 46, 50, 51, 58, 59, 65)
Dike, James Capt	KILY (12, 21, 33, 91, 98)		
Dike, Jeames	KILY (92a)	Dixson, Edward	EHAD (69, 86)
Dike, Jeams	KILY (88, 88a, 92)	Dixson, James	EHAD (45, 50, 55, 64)
Dike, Jeams Capt	KILY (90, 92a)	Dixson, Thomas	KENT (D14, E63)
Dike, Nathal	KILY (97)	Dixson, William	CHAT (64)
Dike, Nathaniel	KILY (94a)	Doane, Seth	CHAT (33, 37, 43, 58, 64, 67)
Dike, Thomas	KILY (7, 10, 21, 86a, 92, 97)		
		Doane, Seth Capt	CHAT (59)
Dike, Thos	KILY 87a, 94)	Dobson, John	CANA (64)
Dikeman, Thadus	DANB (55, 63)	Dochister, David	BOLT (148)
Dileno, Silvanus	KENT (D11)	Dod, John	HARF (251(2), 253, 255A, 258, 260, 263, 266, 269, 272, 274, 281, 287, 289, 292)
Dileno, Sylvanus	KENT (E63)		
Dimmick, Ebenezer	HARL (48)		
Dimmiz, Ebenezer	HARL (44)		
Dimmock, Danl	DURH (23)	Dodd, John	HARF (257, 261a)
Dimmock, Edward	MANS (355)	Dodge, Daniel	COLC (252)
Dimmock, Elipht	MANS (353)	Dodge, Jonath	COLC (245)
Dimmock, Elipt	MANS (277)	Dodge, Jonath Junr	COLC (249)
Dimmock, Hezh	MANS (353)	Dodge, Oliver	COLC (245)
Dimmock, Joseph	MANS (271)	Dodge, Stephen	KENT (C555, D7, E59, E63)
Dimmock, Oliver	MANS (268, 281)		
Dimmock, Thomas	CANT (159, 161, 169)	Dodge, Stephen Leiut	KENT (C543)
Dimmock, Thos	CANT (144, 160, 168, 176)	Dogget, John	LEBA (298)
		Doggett, Jno	LEBA (316)
Dimock, Daniel	ASHF (218)	Doggit, Samuel	COVE (166, 169, 180)
Dimock, Danl	DURH (21)	Dolbear, Samuel	COLC (243, 245, 248)
Dimock, Edward	MANS (268, 339, 353)	Dolewolf, Stephen	MIDD (362)
Dimock, Eliphalet	MANS (357)	Done, Phinehas	HADD (110)
Dimock, Hez	MANS (281)	Doolittle, Abisha	MIDD (357, 363)
Dimock, Hezekiah	MANS (280, 347)	Doolittle, Abraham	MIDD (363, 419)
Dimock, Hezh	MANS (355)	Doolittle, Ambrose Jur	CHES (8)
Dimock, Joseph	MANS (336)	Doolittle, Amos	CHES (9)
Dimock, Lot	MANS (336, 349, 350)	Doolittle, Benjamin	CHES (11)

629

INDEX

Name	Index Page
Doolittle, Benjamin Leut	CHES (4)
Doolittle, Ebenezer	CHES (4, 9, 14)
Doolittle, Ebr	MIDD (376)
Doolittle, Ephraim	CHES (14)
Doolittle, Ezra	CHES (8, 14)
Doolittle, Jonathan	CANA (64, 77)
Doolittle, Joseph	CHES (14), MIDD (362, 413)
Doolittle, Obed	CHES (A)
Doolittle, Saml	MIDD (370)
Doolittle, Samuel	CHES (A)
Doolittle, Seth	MIDD (357, 362, 382, 395, 406, 416)
Dor[ ], Dudley	COVE (166)
Dorchester, David	EWIN (8, 10), BOLT (151)
Dorchester, Reuben	CHES (8)
Dorchester, Stephen	FARM (430, 449)
Dorchester, Stepn	FARM (442)
Dorman, Amos	COVE (170)
Dorman, Dudley	COVE (180)
Dorman, Ezra	FARM (9)
Dorson, John	FARM (456)
Dotchester, David	BOLT (146, 151, 152, 155, 180)
Doubleday, Jesse	LEBA (334)
Doubleday, Joseph	COVE (167)
Doud, Cornel	MIDD (413)
Doud, Cornwell	MIDD (349, 356, 404, 421)
Doud, David	MIDD (362)
Doud, Ebenr Junr	GUIL (303)
Doud, Ens	GOSH (138)
Doud, Jno	GOSH (184)
Doud, John	GOSH (112)
Doud, John Ens	GOSH (114)
Doud, Joseph	GUIL (274, 280, 282, 288, 289, 295, 301, 304, 311, 325, 337)
Doud, Moses	GUIL (274)
Doud, Richard	MIDD (345, 349, 356)
Doud, Richd	MIDD (368)
Doud, Thos	GUIL (334)
Doud, Timo	GUIL (335)
Doud, Zacheriah	GUIL (318)
Doud, Zechariah	GUIL (326)
Douglas, Benajah	CANA (12, 27, 28, 64)
Douglas, David	GOSH (186)
Douglas, James M	CORN (91)
Douglas, John	COLC (10)
Douglas, Wm Capt	BRAN (180)
Douglass, Benajah	CANA (11, 12, 15, 17, 19, 23, 25, 77)
Douglass, Benjah	CANA (24)
Douglass, James	CORN (25)
Douglass, James M	CORN (17)
Douglass, James Marsh	CORN (87)
Doulbear, Samuel	COLC (249)

Name	Index Page
Dow, Abel	ASHF (230), 36)
Dow, Abell	ASHF (313)
Dow, Ephraim	COVE (165)
Dow, Humphrey	COVE (167)
Dow, Levi	COVE (172)
Dowd, Amos	FARM (444, 455)
Dowd, Cornel	MIDD (370)
Dowd, Cornwell	MIDD (380, 393)
Dowd, Ezra	FARM (2, 444, 455)
Dowd, Richard	MIDD (380)
Dowd, Richd	MIDD (370, 373)
Dowe, Ephraim	COVE (167)
Dowe, Humphrey	COVE (166, 172)
Down, Chauncey	FAIR (253, 262, 263)
Down, John Junr	MILF (93)
Down, Joseph	FAIR (262)
Down, Seth	FAIR (264, 266, 267)
Downing, Levi	CANT (146, 179)
Downs, Abraham	DERB (113, 120, 122, 141)
Drake, Joel	EWIN (85)
Drake, Silas	EWIN (8, 10, 14, 16)
Drake, Simeon	EWIN (12, 13, 15, 89)
Drake, Simeon Lt	EWIN (13, 15, 16, 17)
Drake, Thomas	EWIN (85, 88)
Dreegs, Daniel	HARL (49)
Dreggs, Daniel	HARL (43, 45)
Dresser, Jacob	KILY (87, 88, 88a, 92a)
Dresser, Jacob Leut	KILY (94a, 97)
Drigg, Bartholomew	FARM (449)
Driggs, B[ ]	FARM (9)
Driggs, Bartholemew	FARM (442)
Driggs, Bartholomew	FARM (16, 438)
Driggs, Barthow	FARM (17, 452)
Driggs, Barthw	FARM (7, 8)
Driggs, Daniel	HARL (48, 51)
Driggs, John	EHAD (44, 54, 80)
Driggs, Joseph	MIDD (346, 349, 357, 362, 365, 395, 416)
Driggs, Joseph Jur	MIDD (357)
Drigs, Daniel	HARL (53, 55)
Drigs, Joseph	MIDD (417)
Dubbeldy, Joseph	COVE (174)
Dube, Nathl Jur	HEBR (218)
Dube, Wm	HEBR (216)
Dudley, Abial	CORN (11, 14)
Dudley, Abraham	GUIL (338), LITC (139)
Dudley, Abrm	GUIL (274)
Dudley, Ambrose	GUIL (297, 302, 309)
Dudley, Amos	GUIL (272)
Dudley, Asahel	MIDD (363, 366, 373)
Dudley, Asahel Junr	MIDD (414)
Dudley, Barzillai	HADD (148)
Dudley, Charles	KENT (C554)
Dudley, David 2nd	GUIL (269, 277, 280, 289)
Dudley, David 3rd	GUIL (286, 294, 299)
Dudley, David Lieut	GUIL (309)
Dudley, Ebenr Ensign	GUIL (277)

INDEX

Name	Index Page	Name	Index Page
Dudley, Eber	GUIL (299, 304, 310, 327, 338)	Dunham, Simeon	HEBR (220, 234, 246)
		Dunham, Simon	HEBR (234)
Dudley, Gilbert	GUIL (280)	Duning, [ ]	DANB (71)
Dudley, Gilbert Capt	GUIL (308, 309, 315, 317, 319, 336)	Duning, John	DANB (39, 65, 68)
		Duning, Moses	FARM (433)
Dudley, Gilbert Lieut	GUIL (289)	Duning, Seth	FARM (433)
Dudley, Jared Capt	GUIL (294)	Dunn, Timo	DURH (25)
Dudley, Jared Junr	GUIL (325, 335)	Dunn, Timo Jur	DURH (26)
Dudley, Joseph	GUIL (333, 337)	Dunning, Benajah	KENT (C548)
Dudley, Levi	MIDD (364, 365)	Dunning, Nathn	DANB (64)
Dudley, Luther	GUIL (278, 309, 340)	Durand, Ebenezer	DERB (106, 120, 124, 140)
Dudley, Medad	GUIL (280, 289, 310, 335		
Dudley, Nathan	GUIL (299, 310)	Durand, Ebenr	DERB (113, 126, 131, 145, 168)
Dudley, Nathl 2d	GUIL (311)		
Dudley, Oliver	GUIL (287)	Durand, Elezer	DERB (167)
Dudley, Paul	GUIL (287, 289)	Durand, Isaac	DERB (120, 122, 131)
Dudley, Selah	GUIL (270, 277)	Durand, Jeremiah	DERB (124)
Dudley, Selah Junr	GUIL (274, 286, 335)	Durand, Joseph	DERB (120, 122)
Dudley, Willm	GUIL (338)	Durand, Noah	DERB (121)
Dudly, [ ]	GUIL (271)	Durand, Noah 2d	DERB (113)
Dudly, Asahel Junr	MIDD (376)	Durand, Noah 3d	DERB (121)
Dudly, Caleb Junr	GUIL (269)	Durand, Noah Junr	DERB (120, 126)
Dudly, Ebenr Ensn	GUIL (294)	Durand, Samuel	MILF (82)
Dudly, Ebenr Junr	GUIL (296)	Durfee, Benja	CANT (178, 181)
Dudly, Gilbert Lieut	GUIL (270)	Durfy, James	CANT (155)
Dudly, Oliver	GUIL (260, 275)	Dutcher, [ ]	CANA (20)
Duey, Eli	HARW (9, 12)	Dutcher, Capt	CANA (24)
Duggan, James	CANT (181)	Dutcher, Ruluff	CANA (11)
Duggen, James	CANT (178)	Dutcher, Ruluff Capt	CANA (18, 20, 28, 77)
Dunawon, John	DURH (17)	Dutchester, Susannah	BOLT (181)
Duncan, Daniel	FAIR (258, 260)	Dutton, Amasa	EHAD (54, 59, 60, 64, 79, 83, 85)
Duncan, Daniel Capt	FAIR (253, 254, 256)		
Duncan, Danl	FAIR (256, 257, 259, 261, 262, 263, 264, 265, 266, 267)	Dutton, Ambrose	EHAD (85)
		Dutton, Benja	FARM (442)
		Dutton, Benja Jur	FARM (443)
Duncan, Danl Capt	FAIR (255)	Dutton, Ebenezer Capt	EHAD (54, 60, 62, 65, 68, 74, 78, 88)
Dunham, [ ]	HEBR (236)		
Dunham, Barnabas	FARM (2, 9, 18, 29, 433, 438, 445, 450)	Dutton, John	FARM (443)
		Dutton, Joseph	EHAD (87), FARM (443, 449)
Dunham, Cornelious	FARM (20)		
Dunham, Cornelius	FARM (456)	Dutton, Timo	HEBR (235)
Dunham, Daniel	MANS (274, 280, 281, 283, 284, 354, 357)	Dutton, Timothy	HEBR (233), COLC (249)
Dunham, Danl	LEBA (305, 325)	Dutton, Timothy Capt	COLC (247), HEBR (236, 245, 247)
Dunham, Danl Lt	LEBA (320), MANS (281)		
		Dutton, Wm	GLAS (95)
Dunham, Eleazer	COLC (7)	Duty, Matthew	COVE (168, 172, 177, 180, 314)
Dunham, James	CANA (64)		
Dunham, John	MANS (283)	Dwight, William	KILY (7, 31)
Dunham, Jonath	COLC (10, 245)	Dwight, Wm	KILY (86a)
Dunham, Jonn	COLC (8)	Dwolf, Benoni	GLAS (80)
Dunham, Jonth	HEBR (234, 236)	Dyar, Elij Capt	CANT (150)
Dunham, Joseph	FARM (449)	Dyar, Elijah Capt	CANT (144, 147, 156, 159)
Dunham, Seth	MANS (233, 283, 336, 357)		
		Dyar, Eliphalet	DURH (18)
Dunham, Silas	CHAT (29), 30, 52, 55, 61)	Dyar, John Jur	CANT (147, 151, 155, 157)
Dunham, Silas Capt	CHAT (29, 39, 45, 50, 53, 54, 58)	Dye, Daniel	KENT (C548)
		Dyer, James Capt	CANT (163, 176)
Dunham, Silvanus	FARM (20, 449, 456)	E[ ]ton, Ebenr	FARM (443)

631

INDEX

Name	Index Page
Eagleston, Bennit	MIDD (399)
Eaglestone, Bennet Jr	MIDD (368)
Eaglestone, Bennit	MIDD (404, 413)
Eaglestone, Elihu	HARF (272, 281, 288, 292, 297)
Eaglestone, Elisha	HARF (268)
Eames, Mark	KILY (97)
Eams, Daniel	KILY (97a)
Eansworth, John	COVE (166, 177, 180)
Eastabrook, Hobart	EHAD (79, 86)
Eastman, Ebenr	ASHF (310)
Eastman, Peter	ASHF (218, 308, 311)
Eastman, Timothy	ASHF (311)
Easton, Calvin	ASHF (222)
Easton, Jonathan	HARF (253, 256)
Easton, Silas	HARF (255A)
Easton, Timothy	GLAS (67, 70, 71)
Eaton, Asa	ASHF (209, 218, 226, 236, 310)
Eaton, Asa Ensn	ASHF (218)
Eaton, Benjamin	KENT (C551, C554, E60)
Eaton, Calvin	ASHF (202, 205, 212, 214, 218, 222, 226, 232, 236, 308, 310)
Eaton, Comfort	KILY (87, 91a, 97)
Eaton, Ebenr	ASHF (209, 236, 313)
Eaton, John	KILY (9, 87a)
Eaton, John Capt	KILY (5, 8, 9, 10, 13, 15, 19, 90, 91a, 94, 96, 96a, 97)
Eaton, John Jur	KILY (87a)
Eaton, Joseph	ASHF (202)
Eaton, Joseph Jur	KENT (E60, E63)
Eaton, Joshua	ASHF (204)
Eaton, Moses	KENT (E63)
Eaton, Nathaniel	MANS (328)
Eaton, Nathl	MANS (278, 283, 353, 357)
Eaton, Sam	ASHF (308)
Eaton, Saml	ASHF (222, 226, 209, 311), ENFD (18)
Eaton, Saml Junr	ENFD (18)
Eaton, Samuel	ASHF (228)
Eaton, Stephen	KENT (E60)
Eaton, Sylvanus	CHAT (54)
Eaton, Timothy	KILY (11, 19, 23, 32)
Eddy, John Jur	CHAT (41, 42, 43, 58, 62, 64)
Eddy, Thomas	CHAT (61), GLAS (86)
Eddy, Tisdale	GROT ([12])
Edee, John	DERB (120, 122, 124)
Edgecomb, Saml	GROT ([10], [14])
Edgecomb, Samuel	GROT ([12])
Edgerton, Asa	MANS (277, 283)
Edgerton, Jabez	COVE (169, 172, 174, 175)
Edgerton, Simeon	HEBR (216, 218)
Edridge, Daniel	ASHF (205)
Edward, Jona	FARM (435)
Edwards, Benajah	COVE (165)

Name	Index Page
Edwards, Churchil	MIDD (364)
Edwards, Daniel	HARF (299), MIDD (347, 351, 359)
Edwards, Danl	MIDD (364, 370, 371)
Edwards, David	MIDD (362)
Edwards, David Junr	MIDD (382)
Edwards, Joshua	COVE (172, 174, 177, 314)
Edwards, Josiah	MIDD (371, 382)
Edy, Charles	FARM (449, 450, 455)
Edy, Constant	GROT ([12])
Eells, Capt	MIDD (358, 405, 407, 413)
Eells, Daniel	MIDD (406)
Eells, Danl	MIDD (395, 416)
Eells, Edwd Capt	MIDD (372, 382, 388, 395)
Eells, Nathaniel	COVE (174, 177), MIDD (356, 398)
Eells, Nathl	MIDD (363, 370, 403, 410, 412)
Eels, John	COLC (254)
Eising, [ ]	ASHF (206)
Elderkin, John	GROT ([3], [4], [6], [9], [10], [15])
Elderkin, Joshua	GROT ([4])
Eldredge, Charels Junr	GROT ([13])
Eldredge, Charles	GROT ([6])
Eldredge, Charles Junr	GROT [1], [4], [6], [10], [12], [15], [17]
Eldredge, Daniel	GROT ([12], [15], [18], [20], [23], [24]
Eldredge, David	MANS (268, 270)
Eldredge, Lemuel	MANS (233)
Eldredge, Mulford	MANS (277)
Eldredge, Saml	GROT ([25])
Eldrid, Jehoshaphet	KENT (B3, C554)
Eldrid, Joshahop	KENT (E59)
Eldrid, Ward	KENT (C548, D7, D10, E58, E59, E62)
Eldridge, Charles	GROT ([6], [9])
Eldridge, Hez	ASHF (308)
Eldridge, Hezh	ASHF (213, 311)
Eliot, George	KILH (52)
Eliot, Aaron	KILH (42)
Eliot, Aaron Col	KILH (44, 47, 49, 50, 51, 52, 55, 56, 146)
Eliot, An Col	KILH (145)
Eliot, George	KILH (43, 44, 48, 50, 51, 52, 54, 55, 145, 146)
Eliot, Jacob	LEBA (297, 305, 325)
Eliot, Jacob Lt	LEBA (320)
Eliot, Jared	KILH (47, 49, 51, 52, 53, 55)
Eliot, John	KENT (E63, E64), MIDD (367)
Eliot, John Col	GUIL (275, 279, 285, 294, 301)
Eliot, Mathew	KENT (E64)

632

INDEX

Name	Index Page
Eliot, Nathan	KENT (A26, A28, B3, C543, C546, C547, C550, D1, D2, D5, D7, D8, D9, D13, E59)
Eliot, Nathl	GUIL (269, 270, 272, 277)
Eliot, Timo	GUIL (328)
Eliot, Timothy	GUIL (304, 306)
Eliott, Aaron Col	KILH (54)
Eliott, George	KILH (51, 52, 56)
Eliott, Willm	KILH (146)
Ellery, William	HARF (265)
Ellingwood, Ephraim	KILY (24)
Elliot, Francies	KILY (86a)
Elliot, Roger	KILY (96a)
Elliott, John	KILY (7)
Ellis, [ ] Jur	HEBR (236)
Ellis, Elisha	ASHF (202, 209, 213, 214, 218, 219, 308, 310)
Ellis, John Jur	HEBR (217, 245)
Ellis, Jonathan	KILY (30, 86, 87)
Ellis, Jonathn	KILY (31)
Ellsworth, Oliver	HARF (258, 265, 272)
Elmer, Alexr	EWIN (85, 88, 89)
Elmer, Daniel	EWIN (88)
Elmer, Danl	EWIN (85)
Elmer, Jacob	EWIN (85, 88)
Elmer, Joseph	DANB (63)
Elmer, Roswell	EWIN (8)
Elmer, Timothy	EWIN (85, 88)
Elmoni, Joseph	DANB (40)
Elsworth, John	MIDD (367)
Elsworth, Charles Jur	EWIN (7)
Elsworth, Daniel	EWIN (8)
Elsworth, Daniel 3rd	EWIN (12)
Elsworth, Daniel Jur	EWIN (7, 8, 10, 12, 15, 16, 85, 88, 89)
Elsworth, Danl	EWIN (10, 14)
Elsworth, Danl 3d	EWIN (13, 15)
Elsworth, Danl Jur	EWIN (9, 11, 13)
Elsworth, Fred	EWIN (13)
Elsworth, Frederick	EWIN (10, 11, 12)
Elsworth, Fredric	EWIN (8, 9)
Elsworth, Fredric Ens	EWIN (85, 88)
Elsworth, Gurdon	EWIN (8, 10, 12, 13)
Elsworth, Oliver	HARF (267)
Elsworth, Solomon	EWIN (8, 89)
Elsworth, Solomon Lt	EWIN (85)
Elton, Bradley	MIDD (363)
Elton, Ebenezer	MIDD (356)
Elton, Ebenr	MIDD (368)
Elton, Wm	FARM (444, 456)
Elwood, Richard	FAIR (267)
Ely, Gabriel	EHAD (59)
Ely, Gad	HARW (25)
Ely, Jacob	HADD (148)
Ely, Willm	HADD (148)
Emerson, Andrew	BOLT (181, 182)
Emerson, Jabez	BOLT (181)
Emerson, Jabez Juner	BOLT (181)

Name	Index Page
Emmans, Jeremiah Doct	HARL (58)
Emmans, Jerm Doctor	HARL (57)
Emmon, Solomon	CORN (23)
Emmons Asa	CORN (10)
Emmons, Arthur	LITC (159)
Emmons, Asa	CORN (89, 90)
Emmons, Daniel	EHAD (79, 86)
Emmons, Danl	LEBA (305)
Emmons, Doctr	HARL (62)
Emmons, Ebenezer	EHAD (44, 51)
Emmons, Ebenezer Capt	EHAD (79, 86)
Emmons, Jeremiah	HARL (47, 48, 52, 61)
Emmons, Jeremiah Doctr	HARL (51, 56, 59)
Emmons, Jonathan	HARL (59)
Emmons, Joseph	EHAD (78, 79, 86)
Emmons, Jothn	HARL (52)
Emmons, Noadiah	EHAD (86)
Emmons, Salmon	CORN (10, 16, 17, 23, 25, 87, 91)
Emmons, Samuel	EHAD (86)
Emmons, Simeon	CORN (17, 87)
Emmons, Solomon	CORN (1, 10, 17, 22, 23, 24, 25, 87, 90)
Emmons, Woodruff	CORN (3, 6, 10, 12, 25, 84, 87)
Emons, Arthur	LITC (129, 131, 140)
Emons, Daniel	EHAD (54, 64, 69, 73)
Emons, Ebenezer	EHAD (49, 54, 59, 63)
Emons, Ebenezer Capt	EHAD (68)
Emons, Jeremiah	HARL (42, 43, 44)
Emons, Jeremiah Dctr	HARL (47, 49)
Emons, Jonathan	HARL (44, 46, 47)
Emons, Joseph	EHAD (65, 73, 74)
Emons, Russel	LITC (146)
Emons, Russell	LITC (152)
Emons, Salmon	CORN (10, 11, 91)
Emons, Saml	EHAD (60)
Emons, Samuel	CORN (10), EHAD (49, 54, 65, 66, 68)
Emons, Thomas	EHAD (50)
Emons, Woodruff	CORN (12)
English, Richd	LEBA (299, 301)
Eno, Coln	KENT (D5)
Eno, Roger Coln	KENT (D3)
Enos, David	CANT (170)
Enos, Joab	ASHF (311)
Ensign, Capt	CANA (11, 19, 24)
Ensign, Caroline	HARL (47)
Ensign, Daniel	HARL (59, 42, 43, 45, 46, 48, 49, 50, 51, 53, 54, 55, 56, 57, 58)
Ensign, E Leiunt	HARL (43)
Ensign, Eleazar	HARL (58)
Ensign, Eleazer	HARL (53, 61)
Ensign, Eleazer Leut	HARL (42, 44, 45, 48, 49), HARL (51, 54)

633

INDEX

Name	Index Page	Name	Index Page
Ensign, Eleazer Lieut		Fairchild, Abiel	DERB (106, 113, 147, 148, 167)
Ensign, Eleazr	HARL (55, 56)		
Ensign, Eleazr Liut	HARL (46)	Fairchild, Abiel Jnr	DERB (132, 135, 141)
Ensign, Elezer	HARL (60)	Fairchild, Joseph	DERB (121, 167)
Ensign, John	CANA (12, 20, 29)	Fairchild, Nathan	DERB (131, 140)
Ensign, John Capt	CANA (11, 15, 16, 20, 27, 28, 64)	Fairchild, Stephen	KENT (D10, E59)
		Fairchild, Zachariah	DERB (122, 126, 140, 168)
Ensign, John Jur	CANA (13, 15, 17, 23, 64		
Ensign, Samuel	LITC (129, 131, 135, 139, 142, 147, 153)	Fairweather, Thomas	KENT (A24)
		Falshaw, John	KILY (94a, 97)
Ensigns, E Leiut	HARL (45)	Falshaw, John Capt	KILY (92, 96a)
Ensworth, Gid	CANT (151)	Falshaw, John Jur	KILY (94, 97)
Ensworth, Giden	CANT (150)	Fancher, William	LITC (129)
Ensworth, Gideon	CANT (144, 160, 168, 172, 182)	Faning, James	CANA (11, 12, 15, 19, 23
		Faning, Jonathan	GROT ([4])
Ensworth, Jabez	CANT (155, 159)	Fanning, David	GROT ([9], [12], [15])
Ensworth, Jabez Capt	CANT (167, 178, 182, 183)	Fanning, James	CANA (28)
		Fanning, Jonathan	GROT ([6])
Ensworth, Jes	CANT (151)	Fanning, Thomas	GROT ([8], [11])
Ensworth, Jesse	CANT (168, 176)	Fanning, Thomas Capt	GROT ([4], [6])
Ensworth, Jz Capt	CANT (179)	Fanning, Thos	GROT ([7])
Ensworth, Nathl	CANT (180)	Fanton, Hez	FAIR (267)
Ensworth, Saml	CANT (143, 144, 145, 146, 147, 150, 154, 157, 161, 162, 163, 166, 168, 175, 177, 179)	Fanton, John Jur	FAIR (253)
		Fanton, Zebulon	FAIR (258)
		Fanton, Zubulon	FAIR (252)
		Farmer, Thomas	DERB (168)
Ensworth, Will	CANT (150)	Farnam, Abial	CANT (181)
Ensworth, Wm Jur	CANT (155)	Farnam, Abner	KILH (46, 48, 49, 52, 53, 54, 146)
Erklins, Gosuirus	CHAT (66)		
Evans, Mary	FARM (19)	Farnam, Gad	LITC (147, 157)
Evarts, Aaron	GUIL (275, 279, 282, 285, 288, 298, 310)	Farnam, Jos	CANT (180)
		Farnam, Jos Jr	CANT (146)
Evarts, Amaziah	GUIL (310)	Farnam, Joseph	KILH (146)
Evarts, Ambrose	GUIL (286, 313)	Farnam, Joseph 2d	KILH (145)
Evarts, Ambrose Ensn	GUIL (294)	Farnam, Manassah	ASHF (308, 311)
Evarts, Ambrose Lieut	GUIL (309)	Farnam, Nathan	LITC (160)
Evarts, Daniel	GUIL (302)	Farnam, Seth	LITC (134, 146, 148, 153)
Evarts, Eleazer	GUIL (287, 300)		
Evarts, Eleazer Junr	GUIL (302)	Farnham, Asa	ASHF (222)
Evarts, Jehiel	KILH (44)	Farnsworth, Philip	FARM (443)
Evarts, Jonathan	GUIL (303, 335)	Farnum, Abner	KILH (47)
Evarts, Jonathan Junr	GUIL (270, 286)	Farnum, Asa	ASHF (209, 223, 226, 236, 310)
Evarts, Jonth Junr	GUIL (287)		
Evarts, Jonthn	GUIL (325)	Farnum, Gad	LITC (139, 157)
Evarts, Joseph	GUIL (274)	Farnum, Man[ ]	ASHF (226)
Evarts, Saml	GUIL (274)	Farnum, Nathan	LITC (139)
Evarts, Saml 3rd	GUIL (311)	Farnum, Seth	LITC (139, 141, 145)
Evarts, Timo	GUIL (300)	Farrand, Daniel Revd	CANA (77)
Evens, Luther	HARW (8)	Farrington, James	ENFD (19, 28, 30, 32, 35)
Everest, Daniel	CORN (6, 10, 16, 22, 87, 91)	Farrow, John	KILY (96a)
		Farwell, Isaac	MANS (271, 277)
Everts, David	KILH (51)	Farwell, Thomas	MANS (339)
Everts, Hiel	KILH (51)	Faxon, Ebenezer	HARF (275)
Everts, Jehiel	KILH (44, 47, 48, 49, 51, 53, 54, 55)	Fay, Benjn	KILY (92a)
		Fay, Capt	ASHF (213, 217, 225)
Everts, Julius 2d	KILH (54)	Fay, Jedediah	ASHF (217, 310)
Ewing, Thomas	ASHF (313)	Fay, Jedidiah Capt	ASHF (194, 211)
F[ ], Daniel Junr	COLC (251)	Fay, Saml	KILY (91a)
Fairchield, Levi	KENT (E60)	Fay, Samuel	KILY (94)
Fairchield, Saml	KENT (E64)	Fayerweather, Benja	FAIR (255, 262)

634

INDEX

Name	Index Page
Fearbanks, Benjn	KILY (94)
Felch, [ ]	CANT (160)
Felch, John	CANT (139, 144, 146, 148, 149, 150, 151, 153, 154, 155, 156, 157, 158, 159, 162, 163, 167, 168, 176, 177, 180, 181)
Felch, Saml	CANT (176)
Felch, Samuel	CANT (166)
Fellow, Abiel	CANA (16)
Fellowes, Isaac	BOLT (139)
Fellows, [ ]	CANA (64)
Fellows, Abial	CANA (19)
Fellows, Abiel	CANA (11, 12, 15, 16, 17, 20, 21, 23, 25, 27, 28, 29, 77)
Fellows, Abil	CANA (64)
Fellows, Isaac	BOLT (145)
Fellows, Isaac Lieut	BOLT (146, 147, 149)
Fellows, Joseph	CANA (11, 12, 15, 19, 24, 28, 64, 77)
Fellows, Libies	CANA (64)
Fellows, Roswel	CANA (27)
Fellows, Roswell	CANA (19, 23, 77)
Fellows, Thomas	CANA (11, 12, 15, 19, 24, 64)
Fellows, Thos	CANA (27, 77)
Fellows, Verney	MANS (281, 336)
Felsham, Capt	KILY (86a)
Felshaw, John	KILY (87a)
Felshaw, John Capt	KILY (7, 8, 11, 14, 19, 20, 22, 26, 32)
Felshaw, John Jr	KILY (86a)
Fenn, Aaron	MILF (97, 102, 103, 104, 105)
Fenn, Aaron Junr	MILF (85)
Fenn, Benj Lieut	MILF (89)
Fenn, Benjamen	MILF (92)
Fenn, Benjamin Capt	MILF (78, 84)
Fenn, Benjamin Col	MILF (86)
Fenn, Benjn	MILF (94)
Fenn, Dan	MILF (92, 98)
Fenn, James	MILF (85)
Fenn, Jno	MILF (106)
Fenn, John	MILF (103)
Fenn, Samuel	MILF (82, 85, 88)
Fenno, Ephraim	MIDD (347, 348, 365)
Fenton, Joseph	MANS (278, 328, 353)
Fenton, Roswell	MANS (278)
Ferri, Josiah Capt	GREE (126)
Ferris, Isaac	GREE (126, 128)
Ferris, Jabez	GREE (119)
Ferris, James	GREE (119, 120, 124, 126, 127, 128)
Ferris, Jeduthan	GREE (119, 126, 128)
Ferris, Joshua	GREE (119)
Ferris, Josiah	GREE (121, 124, 125, 127)
Ferris, Josiah Capt	GREE (121, 125, 126, 127, 128)
Ferris, Nathaniel	GREE (119)
Ferris, Oliver	GREE (127, 128)
Ferris, Silvanus	GREE (123, 124)
Ferris, Stephen	GREE (124)
Ferris, Timo	GREE (119)
Ferry, Elip[ ]	DANB (58)
Ferry, Elipht	DANB (60)
Field, Ambrose	DURH (10, 17)
Field, Ambrous	DURH (12)
Field, Amos	MANS (233)
Field, Bennit	MANS (233, 336, 338)
Field, David	GUIL (269, 270)
Field, Docr	ENFD (31)
Field, Doctor	ENFD (27)
Field, Ebenr	GUIL (274, 304, 320)
Field, Isaac	EWIN (8)
Field, Joarib	GUIL (287, 294)
Field, Joshua	GUIL (324)
Field, Joshuah	GUIL (289)
Field, Saml Junr	GUIL (288, 325, 338)
Field, Samuel Junr	GUIL (294)
Field, Timo	GUIL (307)
Field, Timo Lt	GUIL (294)
Field, Timothy	GUIL (270, 274, 286, 291, 321)
Field, Timothy Lieut	GUIL (299, 307, 309, 323)
Field, Zachariah	GUIL (324, 335)
Field, Zechariah	GUIL (310)
Fields, Timo	GUIL (326)
Fiendly, John	GLAS (78)
Fildin, Joshua	COVE (174)
Filer, Samuel	HEBR (219, 236)
Filer, Samuel Capt	HEBR (220, 233, 234, 245)
Filer, Samuel Jur	HEBR (234)
Fillips, Mary	KILY (33)
Filmore, Henry	CORN (10, 87, 91)
Fince, Daniel	FARM (433)
Fince, Eleazer	FARM (443)
Fince, Gideon	FARM (443)
Finch, Caleb	GREE (124, 126, 127)
Finch, Ebenezer	BRAN (179)
Finch, Jonathan Junr	GREE (121)
Findley, John	GLAS (66, 83, 86, 106, 70)
Findley, Samuel	GLAS (70)
Findley, Wm	GLAS (111)
Findly, John	GLAS (72, 74, 93)
Finey, Eleazer	KENT (A28, E58)
Finey, Martain	KENT (C554)
Finley, Saml	COLC (8)
Finley, Samuel	COLC (11)
Finney, Eleazer	KENT (B1, D11, E62)
Finney, Joel	KENT (C548, E58, E62)
Finney, John Jur	KENT (E59)
Finney, Joshua	FARM (32)
Finney, Josiah	KENT (D11, E58, E62)
Finney, Solomon	GREE (124, 128)
Finney, Sylvester	KENT (E63)

INDEX

Name	Index Page	Name	Index Page
Firman, James	ENFD (19)	Fitch, Jeremiah	COVE (314), EWIN (8, 9, 10, 11, 12)
Fish, [ ]	LEBA (339)		
Fish, Darias	CANT (155)	Fitch, John	COVE (314)
Fish, Darius	CANT (144, 147, 161)	Fitch, Jz Jr	CANT (140, 147)
Fish, Ebenr	FARM (442)	Fitch, Medina	EWIN (10)
Fish, John	GROT ([25])	Fitch, Medinah	EWIN (12)
Fish, John Capt	GROT ([19], [23])	Fitch, Nath[ ]	LEBA (299)
Fish, Jonathan	GROT ([4], [7])	Fitch, Nathl	LEBA (299, 333)
Fish, Levi	EWIN (12, 13, 15)	Fitch, Saml	GUIL (286, 287, 294, 300, 304, 307, 319, 324, 293), LEBA (326)
Fish, Nathan	CANT (151, 156, 160, 168, 177, 180)		
Fish, Nathan Junr	GROT ([15])	Fitch, Simon	LEBA (333)
Fish, Nathn	CANT (150)	Fitch, Theopilous	KENT (E60, E63)
Fish, Rufus	GROT ([15])	Fitch, Thomas	GUIL (310)
Fish, Saml	LEBA (326)	Fitch, Thos	GUIL (270, 277, 287, 288, 291, 295, 300, 326, 327, 336)
Fish, Thomas	GROT ([4], [19])		
Fisher, Barsilla	KILY (86a)		
Fisher, Barzala	KILY (96a)	Flagg, Joseph	HARF (263)
Fisher, Barzeler	KILY (92, 94a)	Flagg, Saml	HARF (285)
Fisher, Barziler Isn	KILY (92)	Flagg, Sary	FARM (434)
Fisher, Barziller	KILY (91a)	Fletcher, James	MANS (339)
Fisher, Barziller Insn	KILY (96)	Fletcher, Jonah	MIDD (368)
Fisher, Berzila Ensn	KILY (13)	Fletcher, Richard	MANS (271, 283)
Fisher, Berzilla	KILY (9, 17)	Fletcher, Richard Capt	MANS (356)
Fisher, Berzilla Ensn	KILY (9)	Fletcher, Richd Lt	MANS (277)
Fisher, Berzillai Ensn	KILY (19)	Fletcher, Seth	MANS (233, 338)
Fisher, Christo	MIDD (382)	Flint, Davis	KILY (96a)
Fisher, Christr	MIDD (372)	Flint, Davis Leut	KILY (5, 19)
Fisher, Eleazer	FARM (24)	Flint, Royal	HARF (261)
Fisher, John Leiut	KILY (8)	Flynt, Archelus	EWIN (85, 88)
Fisher, Olcutt	ASHF (312)	Fobes, Simeon	MANS (328)
Fisk, [ ]	MIDD (396)	Follet, William	COLC (10, 248, 251)
Fisk, Bezaleel	MIDD (350, 366, 368, 380, 385, 388, 390, 392, 393, 398, 400, 402, 406, 414, 415)	Follet, Wm	COLC (8)
		Follon, John	GLAS (94)
		Foord, Hezh	CORN (9)
		Foord, Oliver	CORN (23, 25)
Fisk, Ephraim Capt	KILY (8)	Foot Adonijah	COLC (250)
Fitch, Abm	LEBA (326)	Foot, Aaron	COLC (7, 243, 245), HARW (4, 5, 14, 16, 17, 25, 523, 533)
Fitch, Abm Cap	LEBA (320, 325)		
Fitch, Abner	COVE (314)		
Fitch, Abner Jur	COVE (168, 180)	Foot, Abraham Captain	BRAN (170)
Fitch, Abraham	LEBA (305)	Foot, Adonijah	COLC (12), 243, 246, 251
Fitch, Ammi	LEBA (297, 310, 341, 305)	Foot, Asa	COLC (7, 8, 11, 242, 244, 250, 255, 256)
Fitch, Andw	LEBA (296, 341)	Foot, Asa Capt	COLC (4, 8, 9, 11, 242, 243, 245, 247, 250, 254)
Fitch, Augustus	EWIN (85)		
Fitch, Hezekiah	COLE (9)	Foot, Benjn	COLC (7)
Fitch, Jabez	GREE (120, 124, 126, 127, 128, 129)	Foot, Capt	HARW (5)
		Foot, Charles	COLC (9, 242, 243, 244, 246, 247, 248, 251, 254)
Fitch, Jabez Captain	GREE (128)		
Fitch, Jabez Doct	CANT (150, 156, 165, 173, 174)	Foot, Daniel	BRAN (173), COLC (11, 244, 247, 248, 250, 251, 252, 253, 254)
Fitch, Jabez Jr	CANT (145, 146)		
Fitch, James 2nd	EWIN (8)	Foot, Danl	COLC (5, 7, 255)
Fitch, James Cap	LEBA (296)	Foot, Doctr	GUIL (302)
Fitch, Jeptha	COVE (172, 177)	Foot, Eli	GUIL (269, 337)

636

INDEX

Name	Index Page
Foot, Ephraim	BRAN (165, 170, 175, 178)
Foot, Hab	COLC (11, 242, 248, 251)
Foot, Habak	COLC (249)
Foot, Habakkuk	COLC (247)
Foot, Habb	COLC (245, 246)
Foot, Habk	COLC (8, 254)
Foot, Hels	BRAN (170)
Foot, Hosea	COLC (254)
Foot, Ichabod	BRAN (166)
Foot, Isaac	BRAN (164, 166, 167, 169, 170, 173, 174, 175, 176, 178, 179)
Foot, Israel	COLC (254)
Foot, Jacob	FARM (2, 6, 8, 23, 440, 445, 453)
Foot, Jared	BRAN (166, 250)
Foot, Jared Docr	BRAN (163, 164)
Foot, Jeremiah	COLC (243, 248, 251)
Foot, John	BRAN (173)
Foot, Jonathan	BRAN (164, 166, 170, 174, 178)
Foot, Jonathn	BRAN (165)
Foot, Jonth	BRAN (168, 172)
Foot, Jos	COLC (7)
Foot, Joseph	COLC (10)
Foot, Nath Junr	COLC (10, 247)
Foot, Nathaniel Junr	COLC (249)
Foot, Nathl Junr	COLC (243, 251)
Foot, Nathl Jur	COLC (7, 254)
Foot, Robert	FARM (456)
Foot, Samuel	BRAN (170, 172, 176, 178)
Foot, Steph	BRAN (179)
Foot, Stephen	BRAN (170, 173, 176)
Foot, Stephen Lieut	BRAN (174, 179)
Foot, Timothy	FARM (441)
Forbes, Capt	CANA (24)
Forbes, Moses	HARF (253)
Forbes, Moses Capt	HARF (282)
Forbes, Samuel	CANA (29)
Forbes, Timothy	HARF (255A, 273)
Forbs, Moses Capt	EHAR (3)
Forbs, Saml	CANA (23)
Forbs, Saml Capt	CANA (14, 77)
Forbs, Samuel Capt	CANA (11, 12, 16, 17, 18, 19, 20, 64)
Ford, Charles	BRAN (165)
Ford, Hezekiah	CORN (87)
Ford, Isaac	HEBR (218, 219, 220, 249)
Ford, John	BRAN (164, 174, 176, 178, 179, 180), MILF (97, 98)
Ford, John Jur	HEBR (218)
Ford, Saml	BRAN (164, 165, 167), MILF (102, 104)
Ford, Samuel	BRAN (170, 173, 176, 179)
Ford, William	FARM (4, 35)

Name	Index Page
Ford, Willm	FARM (8)
Ford, Wm	FARM (6, 7, 9, 11, 13, 17, 27, 453)
Fordick, Mary	GUIL (329)
Forrest, Vieto	GLAS (98)
Forsdick, Mary	GUIL (328, 340)
Forward, [ ]	HARL (42)
Foster, [ ]	GUIL (341)
Foster, Abraham	EWIN (88)
Foster, Abrahm	EWIN (85)
Foster, Asa Jur	CHAT (54)
Foster, Daniel	CANT (156, 166)
Foster, Danl	CANT (165)
Foster, Danl Capt	CANT (179)
Foster, James	HARL (47)
Foster, Jeams	HARL (45)
Foster, Jno 3d	MIDD (395)
Foster, John	MIDD (358, 405, 413)
Foster, John 3d	MIDD (372, 382, 398)
Foster, Joseph	KENT (D1)
Foster, Pelatiah	EWIN (8, 10, 11, 12, 15, 17)
Foster, Pelh	EWIN (13)
Foster, Saul	GUIL (318, 319, 322)
Foster, Stephen	ASHF (311)
Foster, Thomas	EWIN (13, 15, 17, 85)
Foster, Wareham	EWIN (17)
Foster, William	CANT (144, 145)
Foster, William Jnr	CANT (165)
Foster, William Junr	CANT (160, 162, 166, 167, 169, 181, 182)
Foster, Willm Junr	CANT (172)
Foster, Wm	CANT (154)
Foster, Wm Jur	CANT (157, 159, 172)
Fowler, Abraham	GUIL (260, 270)
Fowler, Abraham Ensn	GUIL (275, 294)
Fowler, Abram	GUIL (299)
Fowler, Abram Ensn	GUIL (325)
Fowler, Abram Junr	GUIL (288)
Fowler, Abram Lieut	GUIL (335)
Fowler, Abrm	GUIL (278)
Fowler, Abrm Ensgn	GUIL (273)
Fowler, Amos	DURH (16)
Fowler, Asher	GUIL (277)
Fowler, Caleb	DURH (11, 13, 16, 19), GUIL (336)
Fowler, Daniel	BOLT (151, 160, 165, 180, 182)
Fowler, David	GUIL (270, 277)
Fowler, Dijah	LEBA (299, 305, 311, 327, 342)
Fowler, Dijah Capt	LEBA (298, 306, 334)
Fowler, Dijh Cap	LEBA (316)
Fowler, Ebenr	GUIL (260, 273, 275, 301)
Fowler, Ebenr Jur	GUIL (295, 324, 335)
Fowler, Enos	LEBA (342)
Fowler, Ichabod	COVE (169)
Fowler, James	BOLT (180, 182)
Fowler, John	GUIL (270), MILF (81)
Fowler, John Jur	MILF (81)

637

INDEX

Name	Index Page
Fowler, John Lieut	MILF (88, 98, 101)
Fowler, Jonah Jur	BRAN (164)
Fowler, Jonathan	GUIL (304), MILF (103)
Fowler, Joseph	EHAD (44, 49, 54, 59, 61, 63, 68, 79, 83, 85, 86, 88)
Fowler, Josiah	GUIL (304, 335), BRAN (176)
Fowler, Josiah Capt	BRAN (164, 170, 173, 175, 176, 178, 179, 180)
Fowler, Josiah Jur	BRAN (165), GUIL (314, 316)
Fowler, Nathan	GUIL (301, 310), MILF (81, 82, 88, 97, 102, 104)
Fowler, Noah Capt	GUIL (288, 293, 300, 304, 308, 310, 311, 317, 319, 325, 332)
Fowler, Noah Col	GUIL (338)
Fowler, Phineas	GUIL (287, 294)
Fowler, Silas	GUIL (310, 326, 336)
Fowler, Stephen	GUIL (269, 286, 295, 320
Fowler, Temperance	BOLT (181)
Fowler, Theo	GUIL (299, 335)
Fowler, Timothy	GUIL (274)
Fox, Abm	HEBR (217)
Fox, Abm Jur	HEBR (234)
Fox, Amos	GLAS (92)
Fox, Daniel	EHAD (48, 50, 55, 60)
Fox, David	GLAS (95, 99), HARL (48, 53, 55)
Fox, David Jur	HARL (48, 53)
Fox, Ebenr	GLAS (94)
Fox, Eliphalet	GLAS (86, 99)
Fox, Elisha	FARM (28)
Fox, Elkanah	HARL (45)
Fox, Ephraim	HARL (45, 48, 53)
Fox, Ezekiel	EHAD (69)
Fox, Harrie	HARL (48)
Fox, Hosea	GLAS (85, 93, 103)
Fox, Isaac	GLAS (70, 75, 93, 98, 106)
Fox, Israel	GLAS (95)
Fox, Jabez	EWIN (85, 89)
Fox, John	CHAT (42)
Fox, Jonah	GLAS (94, 101, 104)
Fox, Joseph	GLAS (70)
Fox, Josiah	GLAS (98)
Fox, Martha	GLAS (80, 100)
Fox, Martha Wo	GLAS (102)
Fox, Nathan	HARL (48)
Fox, Reuben	CORN (19, 87, 90)
Fox, Richard	GLAS (93)
Fox, Roswell	GLAS (105)
Fox, Stephen	GLAS (94)
Fox, Timothy William	EHAD (45)
Fox, Wm	GLAS (94)
Fraisor, Daniel	HARL (51, 55, 59)
Fraisor, Danl	HARL (58)
Frances, Capt	GOSH (121)
Frances, Elias	FARM (1, 13)

Name	Index Page
Frances, Elijah	FARM (2, 442, 444)
Frances, Elijah Ensn	FARM (433)
Frances, James	FARM (9, 17)
Francess, James	FARM (29)
Francis, Asa Capt	GOSH (115)
Francis, Capt	GOSH (110, 120, 124, 127, 134, 141, 184)
Francis, Elijah	FARM (448)
Francis, James	MIDD (372, 382)
Francis, Saml	GOSH (102, 103)
Francis, Saml 2d	GOSH (184)
Francis, Thomas	KILH (50, 55)
Frank, Andrew	CANA (28)
Frank, Andw	CANA (15, 64)
Frank, Jeremiah	FARM (456)
Franklen, John	KILH (53)
Franklin, [ ]	KILH (54)
Franklin, Danl	LEBA (310)
Franklin, Governor	MIDD (351)
Franklin, Isiah	KILH (146)
Franklin, John	CANA (64)
Franklin, Jonathan	KILH (146)
Franses, Daniel	DURH (25)
Franses, Thos	DURH (25)
Frany, Joseph	MIDD (342, 346)
Frara, Sam[ ]	MIDD (373)
Frara, Saml	MIDD (364, 371, 394, 406)
Frara, Samuel	MIDD (365)
Fraser, Daniel	HARL (52)
Frazier, Daniel	HARL (44, 47)
Freeman, Elijah	MANS (353)
Freeman, Azariah	MANS (281)
Freeman, Edmd	MANS (277)
Freeman, Edmund	MANS (255, 258, 270, 275, 278, 279, 283)
Freeman, Elijah	MANS (339)
Freeman, Enoch	MANS (338)
Freeman, Frederic	MANS (338)
Freeman, Frederick	MANS (353)
Freeman, Natha	CHAT (37)
Freeman, Skeff	MANS (271, 277)
Freeman, Skeff Junr	MANS (277, 328, 347)
Freeman, Skiff	MANS (268)
Freeman, Sylvanus	CHAT (39)
Freeman, Thankful	GLAS (108)
Freman, Otes	COVE (170)
French, Charles	DERB (106, 107, 113, 120, 122, 124, 126, 131, 140, 141, 142, 145, 167)
French, Didymus	GUIL (272, 306, 307, 310, 325)
French, Enos	KILH (44)
French, Francis	DERB (120)
French, Isrel Junr	DERB (120)
French, John	BOLT (181), ENFD (26, 30)
French, Nathan	DERB (120, 145)
French, Nathaniel	DERB (106, 120, 122, 125, 127, 132, 141)

638

INDEX

Name	Index Page
French, Nathl	DERB (113)
French, Noah	DERB (120, 122)
French, Philemon	GUIL (270, 274, 275, 276, 277, 279, 282, 286, 288, 295, 299, 300, 301, 309, 311, 327, 336)
French, Saml	DERB (122)
French, Samuel	DERB (120)
Frinck, Jno	ASHF (213)
Frink, Jno	ASHF (311)
Frink, Jno Ens	ASHF (308)
Frink, John	ASHF (202, 209)
Frink, Nathan	ASHF (311)
Frink, William	LEBA (306)
Frink, Wm	LEBA (297)
Frisbee Zebulon Jur	FARM (29)
Frisbee, Jabez	HARW (534)
Frisbee, Zebn	FARM (27)
Frisbee, Zebn Jur	FARM (28)
Frisbee, Zebulin Jur	FARM (6)
Frisbee, Zebulon	FARM (455)
Frisbee, Zebulun	FARM (7, 17, 28, 433, 455)
Frisbee, Zebulun Jur	FARM (15)
Frisbey, Jabez	HARW (2)
Frisbie, Benjamin	BRAN (175)
Frisbie, Caleb	BRAN (171)
Frisbie, Hooker	BRAN (174, 178)
Frisbie, Jacob	BRAN (164, 165, 173, 179)
Frisbie, John	HARW (3, 4, 5, 10, 14, 16, 23)
Frisbie, Saml	BRAN (164, 165, 166)
Frisbie, Samuel	BRAN (170, 173, 179)
Frisbie, Thomas	BRAN (166)
Frisbie, Timothy	BRAN (179, 180)
Frisbie, Timothy Lieut	BRAN (179)
Frisbie, Titus	BRAN (179)
Frisbie, William	BRAN (178)
Frisbie, Willm	BRAN (164)
Frisby, Job	FARM (455)
Frisby, Zebulon	FARM (449)
Frost, Aaron	EWIN (10, (89)
Frost, Daniel	CANT (150, 151, 156, 159, 177, 179, 183)
Frost, Danl	CANT (144, 146, 147, 158, 160, 168, 172, 174, 178, 181)
Frost, Henry	CANT (144)
Frost, Joel	LITC (131)
Frost, Jos	FAIR (262)
Frost, Joseph	FAIR (263, 266)
Fullar, Aaron Capt	CANT (150)
Fullar, Jeremiah	EWIN (85)
Fuller, Aaron Capt	CANT (162, 174, 181)
Fuller, Abel	KENT (E60, E63)
Fuller, Abijah	CHAT (54), KENT (E59, E63)

Name	Index Page
Fuller, Abraham	KENT (C548, C552, C555, D1, D10, B2, C555, D7)
Fuller, Abraham Capt	KENT (B1, C543, C545, C546), C554, D3, D8, D10, D11, D12, D13, E58, E62)
Fuller, Adijah	KENT (D1)
Fuller, Amos	HEBR (234)
Fuller, Asahel	KENT (E64)
Fuller, Barnabas	GLAS (92)
Fuller, Benajah	KENT (E60)
Fuller, Benjamin	EHAD (44, 60, 88, 89)
Fuller, Beza	LEBA (298, 299)
Fuller, Bezaleel	LEBA (297)
Fuller, Caleb	MIDD (362, 365)
Fuller, Daniel	EHAD (50, 87), KENT (D7, E59)
Fuller, Ebenr	ASHF (308), HEBR (216, 217, 218)
Fuller, Eliphalet	EHAD (55, 59)
Fuller, Eliphelet	EHAD (49)
Fuller, Elkanah	CHAT (44)
Fuller, Ephm	KENT (E63)
Fuller, Ephraim	EHAD (59), KENT (D2)
Fuller, Ezbon	KENT (E60)
Fuller, Hanah	KILY (87)
Fuller, Howard	KENT (E59, E63)
Fuller, Israel	MIDD (366, 382, 387, 390, 404, 406, 413, 414)
Fuller, Ithamer	EHAD (87)
Fuller, Jacob	CANT (146, 176), COLC (247)
Fuller, James Capt	KILY (87a)
Fuller, Jehel	EHAD (81)
Fuller, Jehiel	EHAD (48, 50, 54, 55, 60, 61, 65, 66, 68, 69, 83, 87)
Fuller, Jeremiah	KENT (B1, C548, C550, C552, C555, D1, D11, E58, E62)
Fuller, Jesse	FARM (28, 455)
Fuller, John	FARM (455, 456), KENT (E64), KILY (27, 86a)
Fuller, Jona	MANS (278)
Fuller, Jonathan	MANS (271)
Fuller, Jonathan Doct	MANS (357)
Fuller, Josiah	COVE (174)
Fuller, Matthias	EHAD (51, 55, 60, 66, 89)
Fuller, Nathaniel	KENT (E59)
Fuller, Noadiah	EHAD (80)
Fuller, Noadiah 2d	EHAD (87)
Fuller, Oliver	KENT (A28, D7, E63)
Fuller, Oliver Doct	KENT (A27, D1, D12)
Fuller, Roger	HEBR (233, 235, 247)
Fuller, Saml	CHAT (40, 55, 58, 64), LEBA (342, 326)
Fuller, Saml Capt	LEBA (320, 325, 330, 334, 340, 341)
Fuller, Samuel	CHAT (33), CORN (22), EHAD (64)

INDEX

Name	Index Page	Name	Index Page
Fuller, Samuel Capt	LEBA (304)	Galpin, Benjn	MIDD (415)
Fuller, Thomas	EHAD (45, 45, 49, 50, 53, 54, 57, 59, 60, 62, 64, 65, 70, 81, 82, 83, 84, 85)	Galpin, Joseph	MIDD (372, 380)
		Galpin, Peat	MIDD (394)
		Galpin, Peet	MIDD (350, 361, 378)
Fuller, Timothy Junr	MANS (280)	Galpin, Saml	MIDD (376)
Fuller, William W	EHAD (79)	Galpin, Samuel	MIDD (411)
Fuller, Zachar	KENT (D7)	Gardiner, John	GROT ([4], [9], [12]
Fuller, Zachariah	KENT (E58, E63)	Gardner, Abner	LEBA (334)
Furrand, Daniel Revd	CANA (64)	Gardner, Daniel	COLC (252, 253)
Fyler, Joseph	GUIL (269, 316)	Gardner, James	COLC (252)
G[ ]tson, William	EHAD (86)	Gardner, Jonath	COLC (252)
Gailord, Giles	GOSH (130)	Gardner, William	COLC (247)
Gailord, Titus	GOSH (115, 184)	Gardnor, Daniel	COLC (252)
Gaines, Simon	HARF (266)	Garlick, Reuben Doct	MIDD (363)
Gains, John	CHAT (39, 64), GLAS (78)	Garnsey, Capt	DURH (10, 14, 15, 16, 17, 18, 21, 23, 25)
Gains, John Junr	ENFD (30)	Garnsey, Ebenezer Capt	DURH (10, 12)
Gains, Jono	GLAS (95)		
Gains, Nathal	GLAS (95)	Garnsey, Lemuel	DURH (10, 11, 13, 14, 16, 19, 20, 21, 23, 25)
Gaits, Jesse	HARL (55)		
Gale, [ ]	KILH 55, 56)	Garnsey, Nathan	LITC (128)
Gale, Benj[ ]	KILH (51)	Garnsey, Noah	LITC (141, 153)
Gale, Benj[ ] Doctr	KILH (48)	Gate, Joseph 3d	EHAD (50)
Gale, Benjn Doct	KILH (145)	Gate, Joseph Lt	EHAD (50)
Gale, Doct	KILH (53)	Gates, Bezaleel	EHAD (44, 54, 59, 60, 69, 87)
Gale, Saml Capt	KILH (52, 56, 146)	Gates, Caleb	EHAD (44, 53, 64, 69)
Gale, Saml Docr	KILH (43)	Gates, Dan[]	EHAD (54)
Gallop, Ben Adam	KENT (A24)	Gates, Ephraim	EHAD (59, 69)
Gallup Nathan Lieut	GROT [5]	Gates, Gen	GOSH (109)
Gallup, Thomas Prentice	GROT [23]	Gates, Jesse	HARL (44, 48, 52, 54)
Gallup, [ ]	GROT [6]	Gates, John	GROT ([12], 15]
Gallup, Adam Junr	GROT [23]	Gates, Joseph	EHAD (48, 55, 60, 65, 69, 81, 87)
Gallup, Benadam	GROT [1], [3], [4], [6], [19]		
		Gates, Joseph 2d	EHAD (64, 79, 86)
Gallup, Benadam Col	GROT [6], [7], [10], [11], [12], [13], [14], [15], [16], [17], [18], [19], [21], [22], [23], [25]	Gates, Joseph 3d	EHAD (53, 59)
		Gates, Joshua 2nd	EHAD (59, 64, 69, 73)
		Gates, Joshua Junr	EHAD (44)
		Gates, Josiah Lieut	COLC (255)
Gallup, Benadam Junr	GROT ([4], [6], 12], [25]	Gates, Matthias	EHAD (87)
Gallup, Benadm	GROT ([12])	Gates, Nathan	EHAD (53, 57, 64, 66, 83, 85)
Gallup, Henry	GROT ([15])		
Gallup, Isaac	GROT ([18])	Gates, Nathaniel	EHAD (65, 81, 84, 87)
Gallup, Jesse	GROT ([4], [6], [9], [12], [15], [18], [19], [25]	Gates, Nathl	CANT (173, 178, 181, 182)
Gallup, Jessee	GROT ([23]	Gates, Nehemiah	CHAT (54, 61), COLC (250)
Gallup, Joseph	GROT ([7		
Gallup, Joseph Capt	GROT ([7]	Gates, Noadiah	EHAD (44, 46, 54, 72, 74, 78), 83, 87, 88)
Gallup, Nathan	GROT ([3], [4], [16]		
Gallup, Nathan Col	GROT ([8], [9], [13], [15], [16], [17]	Gates, Obadiah	EHAD (59)
		Gates, Phineas	EHAD (54, 86)
Gallup, Nathan Majr	GROT ([6])	Gates, Samuel	COLC (10)
Gallup, Thomas P	GROT ([15])	Gates, Samuel Capt	EHAD (48, 51, 53, 56, 57, 60, 62, 67, 71)
Gallup, Thos P	GROT ([4], [9], [12]		
Galpen, Peet	MIDD (363)	Gates, Thomas	COLC (12)
Galpin, Amos	LITC (153, 158)	Gates, Timothy	EHAD (44, 48, 51, 54, 58, 61, 63, 68, 79, 86)
Galpin, Benja	MIDD (367, 370, 387, 405, 413)		
		Gates, Zachariah	EHAD (65, 69)
Galpin, Benjamin	MIDD (344, 345, 349, 381, 394, 409)	Gates, Zechariah	EHAD (60, 66)
		Gay, Elizabeth	KILY (21, 34)

INDEX

Name	Index Page
Gay, Fisher	FARM (427)
Gay, Fisher Colo	FARM (435)
Gay, Ichabod	BOLT (183)
Gay, John	BOLT (182)
Gay, John Doct	BOLT (181)
Gay, Lusher	KILY (16, 22, 87a, 89)
Gay, Saml	LEBA (310)
Gay, Samuel	LEBA (305)
Gay, William	LEBA (334)
Gaylord, Abiel	EWIN (85, 88)
Gaylord, Eleazer	MIDD (345, 349, 356, 369, 376, 380, 393, 395, 404, 406, 413, 416)
Gaylord, Elijah	FARM (29)
Gaylord, Jason	FARM (8)
Gaylord, Jesse	FARM (2, 433, 436, 444, 449, 456)
Gaylord, John	FARM (17)
Gaylord, John Jr	FARM (456)
Gaylord, Joseph	FARM (2, 9), HARW (2)
Gaylord, Moses	HARF (253)
Gaylord, Nathan	CHES (5)
Gaylord, Thomas	CHES (9)
Gear, Amasa	KENT (B2)
Gear, Ezra Jur	KENT (E59)
Gear, Nathaniel	KENT (C552)
Gear, Nathl	KENT (D7, D10)
Gear, Silas	KENT (B2)
Geer, Amos	GROT [1], [3], [4], [6], [9], [15], [21]
Geer, George	GROT [9], [14], [15]
Geer, Isaac	GROT [4], [9]
Geer, Isaac Lieut	GROT [14], [18]
Geer, Israel	CANT (176)
Geer, James	GROT [10], [18], [23]
Geer, Robert	GROT [5], [7], [15], [18]
Geer, Robert 2d	GROT [23
Geer, Robert Junr	GROT [19], [23]
Geer, Saml	HEBR (246)
Geer, Samuel	HEBR (248)
Gelbert, Seth	FARM (438)
Gelman, Epha[ ]	HARL (59)
Gere, David	GROT [24]
Gere, George	GROT [11]
Gere, Isaac	GROT [25]
Gere, Isaac Lieut	GROT [11]
Gere, James	GROT [12], [24], [25]
Gere, Jesse Capt	GROT [25]
Gere, Robert	GROT [25]
Gere, Robert 2nd	GROT ([12], [24]
Gershom, Jennings	FAIR (267)
Gevins, Willm	KILY (97)
Gibb, John	MILF (88)
Gibbs, Benjamin Junr	LITC (141, 142, 158)
Gibbs, Caleb	LITC (130, 133, 134, 137, 138, 147, 153, ,158)
Gibbs, David	LITC (135, 159)
Gibbs, Lemuel	LITC (131, 139, 141)
Gibbs, Levi	EWIN (85, 89)
Gibbs, Remembrance	LITC (141)
Gibbs, Zebulon Capt	LITC (159)
Gibson, Isaiah	KENT (C552, E59, E63)
Gibson, Jacob	MIDD (395)
Gibson, Jno	MIDD (401)
Gibson, John	MIDD (413)
Gibson, Samuel	GLAS (70, 93)
Gibson, Timo	MIDD (410)
Giddeon, Joshua	HARL (47)
Giddeons, Benjamin	HARL (47)
Gidding, Benjaman	HARL (59, 61)
Gidding, Dan	HARL (51, 55 56)
Gidding, David	HARL (43, 55)
Gidding, Joshua	HARL (46, 49)
Gidding, Thomas	HARL (59)
Gidding, Thomas Capt	HARL (60, 61)
Gidding, Thos	HARL (43, 46)
Gidding, Thos Capt	HARL (57)
Giddings, Benjaman	HARL (60, 61)
Giddings, Benjamin	HARL (44)
Giddings, Capt	HARL (51)
Giddings, Dan	HARL (44, 47)
Giddings, David	HARL (44, 47)
Giddings, Elisha	HARL (44)
Giddings, John	CHAT (30, 33, 37, 38, 39, 40, 43)
Giddings, Joshua	HARL (42, 44, 46, (51)
Giddings, Joshua Jur	HARL (47)
Giddings, Thomas Capt	HARL (49, 59, 61)
Giddings, Thomas Jur	HARL (47)
Giddings, Thos	HARL (42, 44, 46)
Giddings, Thos Capt	HARL (56, 62)
Giddings, Thos jur	HARL (44)
Giddins, Dan	HARL (52)
Giddins, John	CHAT (33, 36, 41, 45, 50
Giddins, Joshua	HARL (52)
Giddins, Thomas	HARL (52)
Giddins, Thomas Jur	HARL (52)
Gilbart, Ezra	KENT (E59)
Gilbert, [ ]	HEBR (234, 236)
Gilbert, [ ] Jur	HEBR (234)
Gilbert, Allen	MIDD (368)
Gilbert, Allin	MIDD (347, 350)
Gilbert, Allin Junr	MIDD (417)
Gilbert, Asa	MILF (92)
Gilbert, Benjamin	HARF (263)
Gilbert, Butler	MIDD (358, 376)
Gilbert, David	HARL (45, 48, 51, 56)
Gilbert, Ebenezer	MIDD (361, 394, 406)
Gilbert, Ebenr	HEBR (218, 219, 235, 247), MIDD (368)
Gilbert, Ezekiel	MIDD (376)
Gilbert, Ezra	KENT (A28)
Gilbert, Gardner	HEBR (248)
Gilbert, Hooker	FARM (2)
Gilbert, Jabez	HARW (3, 10, 14, 16, 23)
Gilbert, John	FAIR (255), FARM (444), HEBR (217), MANS (279), MIDD (388, 414)

INDEX

Name	Index Page	Name	Index Page
Gilbert, John Jur	HEBR (220, 245)	Gilman, Solomon	HARF (252(2), 253, 258, 275)
Gilbert, Jona Junr	MIDD (376, 406, 416)		
Gilbert, Jonathan	MIDD (362, 364, 373, 377, 382)	Gilson, Jacob	MIDD (372, 382, 405, 413)
Gilbert, Jonathan Junr	MIDD (382, 395, 421)	Gipson, John	MIDD (362, 366)
Gilbert, Joseph	EHAD (64), FARM (2, 17), HARL (45, 48)	Gipson, Samuel	CORN (84)
		Gipson, Timo	MIDD (389)
Gilbert, Nathaniel Capt	MIDD (342, 346)	Gipson, Timothy	MIDD (350, 353, 363, 373, 388)
Gilbert, Nathl	MIDD (368, 401, 417)		
Gilbert, Nathl Capt	MIDD (346, 349, 358)	Gitteau, Judson	LITC (139, 142, 143, 145, 147)
Gilbert, Saml	HEBR (216, 219, 233, 245, 247)		
		Gitto, Francis Doct	MIDD (363)
Gilbert, Samuel	HEBR (218, 235, 236)	Glading, Joshua	KILH (49)
Gilbert, Seth	FARM (17, 449, 456)	Glading, Willm	HADD (111)
Gilbert, Silvester	HEBR (246)	Glass, James	GOSH (183)
Gilbert, Silvs	HEBR (236)	Glass, Silas	CANT (173, 178, 181)
Gilbert, Sylvester	HEBR (218, 219, 220)	Gleason, David	FARM (2, 9, 12, 16, 17, 28, 29, 433, 438, 442, 444, 449)
Gilbert, Zacheus	FARM (445)		
Gilburt, David	HARL (53)		
Gile, Ephraim	KILY (89, 87a)	Gleason, Isaac	ENFD (34), FARM (2, 4, 9, 433, 436, 443)
Gillet, [ ]	HEBR (231)		
Gillet, Aaron	COLC (242)	Gleason, James Doct	KILY (33)
Gillet, Abijah	FARM (455)	Gleason, Joseph	ENFD (19, 25, 30)
Gillet, Abraham	FARM (455)	Gleason, Peter B	FARM (451)
Gillet, Alexander Revd	FARM (442)	Gleason, Saml	FARM (13, 17), MIDD (368)
Gillet, Ebenezer	LEBA (305)		
Gillet, Ebenr	LEBA (299, 341)	Glenson, Asel	CANA (64)
Gillet, Ebr Jur	LEBA (297)	Godfrey, Daniel	FAIR (262)
Gillet, Eliphalet	COLC (10)	Godfrey, Daniel Capt	FAIR (255)
Gillet, Ezekiel	HEBR (246)	Godfrey, Danl	FAIR (258)
Gillet, Isaac	LEBA (298, 299, 305)	Godfrey, David	FAIR (260, 262, 263, 266, 267)
Gillet, Joel	HARW (9, 14, 19, 20, 22)		
Gillet, Joel Capt	HARW (3)	Godfrey, Ebenr	FAIR (264, 266)
Gillet, Joseph	COLC (12)	Godfrey, Isaac	FAIR (253)
Gillet, Josiah	FARM (17)	Godfrey, Nathan	FAIR (264)
Gillet, Noah	FARM (436)	Godfrey, Silliman	FAIR (255, 258)
Gillet, Zach	FARM (442)	Godfrey, Stephen	FAIR (253, 260, 262)
Gillet, Zacheous Jur	FARM (443)	Godowdy, Saml	ENFD (30)
Gillet, Zacheus	FARM (449)	Goff, Benjamin	CHAT (37, 41, 43, 51, 58, 67)
Gillet, Zacheus Capt	FARM (19, 454)		
Gillett, Aaron	COLC (255)	Goff, Benjn	CHAT (38, 46, 64)
Gillett, Benjamin	EWIN (16)	Goff, Comfort	COLC (255)
Gillit, Aaron	COLC (245)	Goff, Elisha	GLAS (114)
Gillit, Ez	HEBR (216, 217, 220)	Goff, Ezekiel	CHAT (51, 58)
Gillit, Ezekiel	HEBR (218, 248)	Goff, John	CHAT (41, 65)
Gillit, Jeremiah	DERB (167)	Golard, Abel	HARL (44)
Gillit, Joel	HARW (6, 19, 20)	Gold, [ ]	CORN (6, 11, 14, 24, 29)
Gillit, Josiah	FARM (28)	Gold, Abel	FAIR (253, 255, 258, 259, 260, 262, 263, 265, 267)
Gillit, Noah	FARM (32)		
Gillitt, Jeremiah Capt	DERB (120)	Gold, Abel Jur	FAIR (262)
Gillitt, Wm	MILF (93)	Gold, Abram Capt	FAIR (266)
Gilman, Benjamin	HARF (255A, 266, 288, 292)	Gold, Abram Colo	FAIR (265)
		Gold, David	FAIR (256, 263)
Gilman, Calvin	HARF (292)	Gold, Hezekiah Revd	CORN (3, 13, 21, 25, 26, 28, 30)
Gilman, Elias	HARF (253)		
Gilman, Epafras	HARL (51)	Gold, Hezh	CORN (86)
Gilman, Epafrus	HARL (60)	Gold, Nathan	FAIR (263)
Gilman, Ephm	HARL (59)		
Gilman, Gorge	EHAR (3)		

642

INDEX

Name	Index Page
Gold, Revd	CORN (2, 3, 4), CORN (5), CORN (6, 7, 12, 13, 14, 15,18, 21, 24, 25, 26, 27, 28, 29, 30, 84)
Goldsmith, James	MILF (82, 85, 88, 92, 93, 98, 102, 103, 105, 106)
Goodale, Asa	GLAS (74, 78, 94)
Goodale, Ebenezer	GLAS (92)
Goodale, Ebenr	GLAS (94, 111)
Goodale, Isaac	GLAS (94, 95)
Goodale, Joseph	GLAS (69, 75, 77, 79, 93, 98, 112)
Goodale, Joseph Jur	GLAS (78, 93, 109)
Goodale, Moses	CANT (150)
Goodell, Aaron	MANS (328)
Goodell, Jabez	MANS (267, 336, 347)
Goodell, Moses	CANT (172, 175, 182)
Goodman, Asa	HARF (273)
Goodman, Moses	HARF (272, 280, 281, 283, 286, 287, 289)
Goodman, Richard	HARF (292)
Goodman, Thomas	FARM (33), HARF (281)
Goodrich, [ ]	DURH (21, 24, 26)
Goodrich, Asa	FARM (442, 449)
Goodrich, Asahel	FARM (456)
Goodrich, Bartholomew	BRAN (164, 166, 179)
Goodrich, Bartw	BRAN (170, 173)
Goodrich, Benjamin	CHAT (61)
Goodrich, Benjn	CHAT (62)
Goodrich, Capt	GLAS (85)
Goodrich, Charles	CHAT (29, 36, 43, 68)
Goodrich, Crafts	BOLT (180, 182)
Goodrich, David	BRAN (178), GLAS (93, 95, 98, 106)
Goodrich, Elijah H	GLAS (106, 109)
Goodrich, Elijah Hubbard	GLAS (101)
Goodrich, Elisha	GLAS (66, 77, 94, 98, 106, 111)
Goodrich, Elizur	GLAS (96)
Goodrich, Elizur Revd	DURH (10, 13, 15, 17, 19, 21, 24, 25)
Goodrich, Gehiel	GLAS (94)
Goodrich, George	GLAS (95)
Goodrich, Hezekiah	CHAT (30, 33, 37, 38, 39, 45, 56, 58, 67)
Goodrich, Hezh	CHAT (31, 34, 51, 65)
Goodrich, Isaac	GLAS (66, 70, 72, 73, 77, 95, 101)
Goodrich, Isaac Capt	GLAS (87, 90, 99, 102, 103, 105)
Goodrich, Jedh	FARM (442)
Goodrich, Jehiel	GLAS (71, 75, 106, 113)
Goodrich, Jeremiah	CHAT (38)
Goodrich, Jeremiah Capt	CHAT (37, 39)
Goodrich, Jeremiah Jur	CHAT (33, 37, 39, 40, 43, 45, 51, 52, 64)
Goodrich, Jerh Jur	CHAT (30, 50, 58, 59)

Name	Index Page
Goodrich, John	FARM (2, 8, 9, 17, 28, 29, 31, 433, 436, 442, 444), 449, 454), GLAS (93)
Goodrich, Joshua	CHAT (38)
Goodrich, Moses	BOLT (181, 182)
Goodrich, Peter	MIDD (357, 362)
Goodrich, Revd	DURH (18, 19)
Goodrich, Roswell	GLAS (106)
Goodrich, Saml	FARM (2, 443)
Goodrich, Solomon	CHAT (30, 41, 46, 59, 65, 68)
Goodrich, Stephen	GLAS (74, 78, 89, 94, 100)
Goodrich, Stephen Capt	GLAS (89, 90, 98, 102, 105, 108)
Goodrich, Stephen Lieut	GLAS (86)
Goodrich, Thomas	CHAT (33, 41, 42)
Goodrich, Timothy	BRAN (173, 174, 175, 176)
Goodrich, Wait	GLAS (68, 70, 75, 80, 93, 100, 111)
Goodrich, Wait Capt	GLAS (81, 82, 83, 86, 89, 90, 99, 101, 103, 104, 109, 110, 111, 113, 114, 115)
Goodrich, Wm	GLAS (98)
Goodrich, Wm Jur	GLAS (113)
Goodsell, Lewis	FAIR (255, 256)
Goodsell, Thos	FAIR (258)
Goodshall, John	DERB (124)
Goodsped, Nathan	EHAD (80)
Goodspeed, Nath[ ]	EHAD (84)
Goodspeed, Nathan	EHAD (49, 70, 85)
Goodwell, Moses	CANT (176)
Goodwin, Capt	GOSH (110, 113, 115, 117, 120, 124, 127, 131, 139, 140, 141, 184)
Goodwin, Daniel	HARF (251, 261a, 292)
Goodwin, Jacob	MIDD (363)
Goodwin, James	HARF (266), LITC (147, 153)
Goodwin, John	HARF (265), MIDD (363)
Goodwin, John Pantry	HARF (296)
Goodwin, Jona	LEBA (318, 326, 329)
Goodwin, Jona Jur	LEBA (311, 316, 325, 342)
Goodwin, Joseph	HARF (255A, 261a, 267, 273, 281, 288, 293)
Goodwin, Morgain	FARM (436)
Goodwin, Morgan	FARM (9)
Goodwin, Nathaniel	HARF (255A, 273, 281), LITC (129, 130, 131, 133, 158)
Goodwin, Ozias	LITC (129, 131, 132, 134, 135, 139, 141, 142, 147, 153, 158, 159)
Goodwin, Ozias Ens	LITC (160)
Goodwin, Samuel	HARF (292)

643

INDEX

Name	Index Page
Goodwin, Solomon	LITC (134, 135, 139, 153, 158)
Goodwin, Step Capt	GOSH (112)
Goodwin, Thomas	GLAS (65), LITC (129, 131, 135, 139), MIDD (356, 365)
Goodwin, Thomas Capt	MIDD (350, 354, 369, 379, 392, 403, 408, 412, 415)
Goodwin, Thoms	MIDD (388)
Goodwin, Thos	MIDD (367, 368, 377, 358)
Goodwin, Thos Capt	MIDD (387)
Goodwin, William	GOSH (126), HARF (273, 275, 281, 288, 293)
Goodwin, William 2d	HARF (265)
Goodwin, William Junr	HARF (266)
Goodwin, Wm	GOSH (183, 185), LEBA (326, 334)
Gool, Aaron	GLAS (94, 98)
Gordan, Elex	CANT (150)
Gordin, Wm	DERB (134)
Gordon, Alaxr	CANT (150)
Gordon, Alex	CANT (151)
Gordon, Alexander	BRAN (172), CANT (183)
Gordon, Alexanr	CANT (144)
Gordon, Alexr	CANT (155, 156, 160, 167, 176)
Gordon, John	BRAN (163, 179)
Gorham, Benjn	DANB (47, 59)
Gorham, Ebenr	FAIR (253)
Gorham, John	KENT (E63)
Gorham, John Jur	KENT (E60, E63)
Gorham, Lockwood	DANB (69)
Gorham, Stephen	FAIR (267, 269)
Gorum, Lockwood	DANB (69)
Gott, Daniel	HEBR (217)
Gould, Willm Docr	BRAN (164)
Gould, Cole W	BRAN (180)
Gould, John	GOSH (111)
Gould, Thomas	BRAN (173, 178)
Gould, William	CANA (64, 77)
Gould, William Coll	BRAN (179)
Gould, Willm Doctr	BRAN (171)
Gove, John	COVE (181)
Goway, Saml	ENFD (19)
Gowdy, Saml	ENFD (24, 26, 28, 32, 34, 35)
Goyate, Doctr	KILY (88)
Graccey, Ebenezer Capt	DERB (107)
Gracey, Ebenezer	DERB (122)
Gracey, Ebenezer Capt	DERB (126, 146)
Gracy, Ebenezer	DERB (120)
Gracy, Ebenr	DERB (127)
Graidy, Edmon	CANA (18, 23)
Grandy, Edmon	CANA (64)
Granger, Capt	GLAS (110)
Graniss, Joel	FARM (449, 455)

Name	Index Page
Graniss, Rusell	FARM (455)
Graniss, Stephen	FARM (455)
Grannis, Joel	FARM (444)
Granniss, Stephen Jur	FARM (455)
Grant, Aaron	EWIN (10, 11, 12, 13, 15, 17, 85, 88)
Grant, Azariah	EWIN (8, 10, 11, 12, 15, 17, 85, 89)
Grant, Azh	EWIN (13)
Grant, Chap Ens	EWIN (12)
Grant, Charles	LITC (129, 141)
Grant, Ebenezer	GLAS (64), EWIN (10)
Grant, Ebenezer Capt	EWIN (7, 8, 9, 10, 12, 85)
Grant, Ebenr Capt	EWIN (13, 88)
Grant, Edward Chap	EWIN (12)
Grant, Edward Chapman	EWIN (7, 8, 9, 10)
Grant, Edward Chapman Lt	EWIN (9)
Grant, Edwd Chap	EWIN (11, 13, 15, 88)
Grant, Edwd Chap Ens	EWIN (85)
Grant, Ephraim Jur	COVE (171)
Grant, Gideon	EWIN (15)
Grant, Jesse	LITC (158)
Grant, Justus	EWIN (85, 89)
Grant, Matthew Capt	EWIN (85, 88)
Grant, Noah	COVE (172)
Grant, Ozias	BOLT (158, 180)
Grant, Peter	BRAN (179)
Grant, Roswell Capt	EWIN (14, 16)
Grant, Roswell Ens	EWIN (85, 88)
Grant, Saml Rockwell	EWIN (8)
Grant, William	EWIN (10, 12, 15)
Grant, Wm	EWIN (13, 17)
Grave, Abram	GUIL (299, 300, 309, 310, 325)
Grave, Ambrose	GUIL (310)
Grave, Ebenr Junr	GUIL (286)
Grave, Eli	GUIL (297, 304, 309, 317, 318)
Grave, Elias	GUIL (269, 273, 291, 332)
Grave, Elias Capt	GUIL (299, 304, 309)
Grave, John	GUIL (282)
Grave, Luman	GUIL (323, 334)
Grave, Simeon	GUIL (274, 310, 325, 336)
Grave, Sterling Reverd	HARL (45)
Graves, Benja	GUIL (272)
Graves, Benjamin	HARW (2)
Graves, Benjn	GUIL (275)
Graves, Col	KILH (53, 54)
Graves, Elijah	HEBR (234)
Graves, Joseph	MIDD (354, 355, 360, 361, 362, 377, 406, 409, 416)
Graves, Mary	KILY (24)
Graves, Nathan	KILH (145)
Graves, Silvanus	KILH (146)
Graves, Silvanus Col	KILH (55)
Graves, Silvanus Majr	KILH (48)
Graves, Stephen	HARW (2)

INDEX

Name	Index Page
Graves, Sylvanus Col	KILH (145)
Graves, William	LITC (146)
Graves, Wm	MIDD (358, 372, 382, 395, 405)
Gray, Amos	FAIR (258)
Gray, Elijah	FAIR (253)
Gray, Hezekiah	KENT (B2)
Gray, Hezh	DANB (63)
Gray, Isaac	DANB (51)
Gray, John	FAIR (258, 259)
Gray, Nathan Jur	FAIR (253)
Gray, Nathaniel	KENT (A28, B1, B2, C546, C550, C554, C555, D12, E62)
Gray, Nathl	KENT (D1, D7, E58)
Gray, Simeon	LEBA (298)
Gray, Simn	LEBA (299)
Gray, Solomon	FAIR (266)
Grayham, Doctr	FARM (4)
Grayham, James	KENT (D7)
Green, Barzilla	EWIN (85)
Green, Barzillia	EWIN (89)
Green, Benjamin	GREE (126)
Green, Capt	KILY (13)
Green, Ebenezer	KILY (20, 94a, 97)
Green, Heza	KILY (86)
Green, Hezekiah	KILY (87, 91a, 92a)
Green, Jacob	CORN (88)
Green, James Capt	EHAD (44, 49, 54, 58, 66, 71, 82, 86)
Green, John	KILY (87, 97)
Green, John Capt	KILY (5, 8, 10, 12, 13, 24, 91a, 92, 94a, 96, 96a, 97a)
Green, John Junr	CANA (64)
Green, Jonas	MILF (82)
Green, Jonas Capt	MILF (88, 100)
Green, Nathan	KILY (92)
Green, Thomas	HARW (20)
Green, Warren	CHAT (31, 34, 37, 38, 39, 40, 45)
Green, Warren Jur	CHAT (29, 33, 42, 43)
Green, Willard	CANA (64)
Gregory, [ ]	DANB (69, 70)
Gregory, Abijah	FAIR (258, 259)
Gregory, Daniel	DANB (68)
Gregory, Ebenr	DANB (45, 63, 69, 70)
Gregory, Elnathan	DANB (63)
Gregory, Esther Wo	DANB (70)
Gregory, John	DANB (39, 69, 70)
Gregory, John Sergt	DANB (68, 71)
Gregory, Mattw	DANB (43, 51, 63)
Gregory, Nathan	DANB (39, 47, 59, 198)
Gregory, Nathan Ens	DANB (55)
Gregory, Nathl	DANB (39, 45, 59)
Gregory, Nathn	DANB (40)
Gregory, Samuel	KENT (C546, C552)
Gregory, Wo	DANB (69)
Grenell, Barber	KILH (54)
Grey, Nathaniel	CORN (24), KENT (A28)

Name	Index Page
Gridley, Abel	HARW (5, 10, 14, 17)
Gridley, Abraham	FARM (17)
Gridley, Abram	FARM (443)
Gridley, Abrm	FARM (9)
Gridley, Amos	FARM (17, 442)
Gridley, Amos Dr	FARM (444, 445)
Gridley, Capt	FARM (8, 23)
Gridley, Clement	FARM (2, 18, 432)
Gridley, Daniel	FARM (5, 23)
Gridley, Danl	FARM (5, 442)
Gridley, Danl Jur	FARM (9)
Gridley, Ebenr	FARM (442)
Gridley, Elijah Jur	FARM (28)
Gridley, Elnathan	FARM (6, 433, 442, 449, 450)
Gridley, Hez Capt	FARM (9, 445)
Gridley, Hezakiah	FARM (7)
Gridley, Hezekiah	FARM (9)
Gridley, Hezh	FARM (8, 17, 436, 438, 442, 446, 449, 452)
Gridley, Hezh C[ ]	FARM (12)
Gridley, Hezh Capt	FARM (3, 11, 29, 442, 454)
Gridley, Hezh Jur	FARM (430, 435)
Gridley, Isaac	FARM (4, 9, 449, 455)
Gridley, James	FARM (455)
Gridley, Job	FARM (2, 7, 10, 17, 29, 443, 444)
Gridley, John	FARM (442, 444)
Gridley, Jonathan	FARM (13)
Gridley, Joseph	FARM (443)
Gridley, L[ ]	FARM (9)
Gridley, Luke	FARM (2, 9, 18, 29, 31, 433, 438, 442, 450)
Gridley, Noah	FARM (436)
Gridley, Oliver	FARM (2, 434)
Gridley, Rezen	FARM (445, 450)
Gridley, Rezin	FARM (431, 442)
Gridley, Roger	FARM (443, 444)
Gridley, Saml	FARM (449)
Gridley, Stephen	FARM (23)
Gridley, Thomas	FARM (456)
Gridley, Thos	FARM (2, 9, 436)
Gridley, Timo	FARM (8, 442)
Grifeth, Joshua	CHAT (32)
Griffen, Barber	KILH (49)
Griffen, Ebenr	MIDD (362)
Griffen, Samuel	MIDD (363)
Griffen, Seth Capt	KILH (145)
Griffen, William	KILH (48)
Griffen, Willm	KILH (44, 51, 53, 54)
Griffeth, Joshua	CHAT (44)
Griffin, Elisha	DERB (120, 124)
Griffing Lemuel 2d	EHAD (69)
Griffing, Catling	GUIL (304)
Griffing, George	EHAD (60, 65, 70, 83, 85, 86)
Griffing, Jasper Capt	GUIL (275)
Griffing, Lemuel 2d	EHAD (79, 85)
Griffing, Lemuel jur	EHAD (60)

INDEX

Name	Index Page	Name	Index Page
Griffing, Robert	GUIL (260)	Griswold, Simeon	BOLT (160, 181, 182)
Griffing, Robert Lieut	GUIL (287, 335)	Griswold, Thomas	CANA (64)
		Griswold, White	HARW (5, 523, 534)
Griffing, Robert Lt	GUIL (294, 300, 314)	Griswold, William	KILH (42)
Griffing, Robt Lieut	GUIL (270, 275)	Capt	
Griffings, Catling	GUIL (292)	Griswold, Zach Jur	GOSH (183)
Griffis, James	CORN (87)	Griswould, Ashbell	FARM (16)
Grigg, John Capt	GREE (120, 121, 126)	Griswould, Ezra	GUIL (320)
Griggs, Icabod	ASHF (311)	Griswould, Jereh	FARM (17, 455)
Griggs, Joseph	ASHF (209, 226, 311, 313)	Griswould, Jeremiah	FARM (2, 3, 9, 23, 28, 436)
Griggs, Nathan	ASHF (226, 311)	Griswould, Jonah	FARM (455)
Grigory, Samuel	KENT (D10)	Griswould, Miles	GUIL (286, 301)
Grigory, Stephen	KENT (E63)	Griswould, Roger	ENFD (34)
Grimes, Abraham	CORN (89)	Griswould, Rogor Junr	ENFD (32)
Grimes, Christopher	CORN (86)	Griswould, Shubael	ENFD (32)
Grinnel, Barber	KILH (51)	Griswould, Thos Junr	GUIL (287, 337)
Grinnel, Wm	DERB (122)	Groevenor, Caleb	ASHF (218)
Grinnil, Wm	DERB (121)	Grosbenor, Caleb	ASHF (218)
Griswd, Zach Jur	GOSH (110)	Gross, Jonah	LEBA (326)
Griswold, [ ]d	HARW (2)	Grosvenor, Caleb	ASHF (310)
Griswold, [ ]ge	HARW (2)	Grover, John Jur	COVE (172, 174)
Griswold, Aaron	COLE (4, 7, 8, 13, 113)	Grover, Pheneas	GLAS (94)
Griswold, Asahel	LITC (153)	Grover, Phineas	GLAS (95)
Griswold, Benjamin	HARW (18, 19)	Grow, Joseph	MANS (277)
Griswold, Benjn	CANA (64), HARW (3)	Guild, Saml	LEBA (299, 334)
Griswold, Daniel	BOLT (180, 182), KILH (47, 51, 53)	Guild, Samuel	LEBA (305)
		Gunn, Abigail	DERB (133)
Griswold, Darias	GOSH (186)	Gunn, Isaac	MILF (82)
Griswold, Elijah	LITC (156)	Gunn, Stephen	MILF (89, 93, 103, 104, 105, 106)
Griswold, Elizur	CANA (64)		
Griswold, Frances	COLE (115)	Gurley, Daniel	MANS (350)
Griswold, Francis	COLE (113)	Gurley, Jacob B	MANS (268, 271, 281, 283, 336, 353, 355, 357, 358)
Griswold, George	BOLT (148, 151, 157, 160, 164, 167, 180, 182), HARW (2, 14), KILH (53)		
		Gurley, Jacob Barker	MANS (347)
		Gurley, Jona	MANS (278)
Griswold, George Ensign	BOLT (155)	Gurley, Jona Junr	MANS (271)
		Gurley, Jonathan	MANS (348)
Griswold, Giels	KILH (146)	Gurley, Jonathan Junr	MANS (279)
Griswold, Giles	GOSH (102, 112, 114, 115, 116, 130, 138, 183)	Gurley, Jonathn Junr	MANS (281)
		Gurley, Phineas	MANS (280)
Griswold, Giles Leut	GOSH (111)	Gurley, Phinehas	MANS (281, 347)
Griswold, Jannah Jur	HARW (25)	Gurley, Zebulon	MANS (328, 339, 357)
Griswold, Jereh	FARM (8)	Gurney, Beszaliel	KENT (A24)
Griswold, Jonathan	LITC (141)	Gustin, Edward	COLC (7, 251, 254)
Griswold, Josiah	KILH (50, 145)	Guthrie, Joseph	KENT (A26)
Griswold, Manass	CANA (12)	Guthrie, Ephm	KENT (A28, C554, E59)
Griswold, Manus	CANA (11, 12, 15, 16, 64	Guthrie, Ephraim	KENT (B1, B2, C552, C555)
Griswold, Mathew	DURH (18)		
Griswold, Moses	KILH (51, 54)	Guthrie, Joseph	KENT (A28, B1, C552, C555, E58, E62)
Griswold, Nal	KILH (52)	Guthrie, William	KENT (C555)
Griswold, Nath[ ]	KILH (44)	Guthrie, Wilm	KENT (A24, E59)
Griswold, Nathal 2d	KILH (47)	Guy, John	BRAN (171)
Griswold, Nathan	KILH (43, 48, 55)	Guy, Mary Mrs	BRAN (171)
Griswold, Nathan Capt	KILH (49, 53, 55)	Guy, Willm	BRAN (163)
Griswold, Nathl 2d	KILH (145)	Gwier, Stephen	FAIR (254, 258, 264)
Griswold, Nehemiah	GUIL (260, 271)	H[ ], Judah	FARM (449)
Griswold, Saml	KILH (55)	H[ ], Nehemiah	KILH (145)

646

INDEX

Name	Index Page
H[ ]on, Saml	KILH (145)
Hadlock, Rubin	HARL (50)
Hadsdell, James	FARM (2)
Hadsell, James	FARM (452)
Hagaboom, Jeremiah	CANA (77)
Hail, Daniel	CANA (64)
Hail, Nathan	CANA (77)
Hail, Zebulon	GUIL (294, 324, 335)
Haines, Silas	FAIR (267)
Hakins, Aaron	BOLT (180)
Hale, [ ]	CANA (24), MIDD (405)
Hale, Adino	GOSH (116, 138, 139, 183, 185)
Hale, Beman	DERB (120, 122)
Hale, Benj[ ]	GLAS (81)
Hale, Benjamin	CHAT (68, 93)
Hale, Benjamin Jur	GLAS (106)
Hale, Benjn	CHAT (54)
Hale, Benjn Jur	GLAS (96)
Hale, Daniel	GLAS (70, 75, 93, 113)
Hale, David	CHAT (42, 66, 70, 75, 78, 66, 70, 75, 78, 83, 93, 98, 106, 108, 112)
Hale, David Jur	CHAT (42, 81, 113)
Hale, Ebenezer	MIDD (405)
Hale, Ebenr	MIDD (413)
Hale, Eli	ENFD (30)
Hale, Elisha	GLAS (74, 75, 78, 79, 81, 82, 83, 93, 98, 106, 113, 114)
Hale, Elizur	GLAS (94)
Hale, Elizur Capt	GLAS (83, 86, 88, 89, 90, 102, 104)
Hale, Elizur Doctr	GLAS (86102, 112)
Hale, Elizur Junr	GLAS (92, 100, 101)
Hale, Elizur Jur Capt	GLAS (82)
Hale, Gideon	GLAS (66, 70, 74, 78, 82, 88, 89, 93, 98, 100, 105, 106, 111, 114)
Hale, Hezakiah	MIDD (412)
Hale, Hezekh	MIDD (417)
Hale, Hezekiah	MIDD (345, 346, 347, 349, 350, 354, 355, 356, 368, 379, 380, 391, 393, 404, 406, 414, 415)
Hale, Hezh	MIDD (369, 388, 407)
Hale, Isaac	GLAS (71)
Hale, John	BOLT (180), COVE (165, 167, 170, 175), GLAS (83, 89, 99, 102, 105)
Hale, Jonathan Junr	GLAS (92)
Hale, Jonathn	CHAT (54)
Hale, Joseph	COVE (314), GLAS (90, 112), MIDD (367)
Hale, Josiah	GLAS (60, 63, 65, 66, 67, 70, 71, 72, 74, 78, 82, 93, 98, 103, 105, 106, 111, 113)
Hale, Nathan	CANA (17, 20, 25, 26, 27, 28, 29, 64)

Name	Index Page
Hale, Richard	COVE (165, 166, 167, 168, 169, 170, 171, 172, 173, 177, 181, 315)
Hale, Richd	COVE (314)
Hale, Ritchard	COVE (169)
Hale, Rubin	HARL (45, 50, 51)
Hale, Saml	FARM (456)
Hale, Theodore	GLAS (66, 77, 86, 94, 108, 109, 110)
Hale, Timothy	GLAS (81, 93, 108, 109)
Hale, Timothy Capt	GLAS (89, 90, 102, 109, 110, 114)
Hale, Timothy Junr	GLAS (66, 70, 74, 78, 82, 93)
Hale, Timothy Lieut	GLAS (87)
Hale, Wm	GLAS (92)
Haley, Caleb	GROT ([4], [12], [19])
Hall, A Capt	GOSH (138)
Hall, Abijah	CHAT (4, 32, 37)
Hall, Abijah 3d	CHAT (46, 47)
Hall, Abijah Capt	CHAT (29, 30, 31, 33, 34, 35, 36, 37, 39, 40, 41, 45, 46, 50, 51, 53, 59, 64, 68)
Hall, Abner	EHAD (44, 60, 64, 66, 80
Hall, Amasa	CHES (4, 8, 9, 11, 14)
Hall, Amos	FARM (443), HEBR (234, 236)
Hall, Andrew	CHES (8, 11, 14), MANS (357)
Hall, Andrew Jur	CHES (A, 5, 6)
Hall, Asa	KENT (A28, D11)
Hall, Asaph	GOSH (102)
Hall, Asaph Capt	GOSH (105, 112, 113, 114, 115, 118, 140)
Hall, Barnabas	MANS (285, 329)
Hall, Benjamin	LITC (131)
Hall, Benjn	GUIL (286)
Hall, Benjn Junr	GUIL (294)
Hall, Capt	GOSH (110, 111, 112, 113, 115, 117, 119, 120, 124, 125, 126, 127, 130, 134, 139, 184)
Hall, Chales	FARM (443)
Hall, Chancey	CHES (A)
Hall, Charles	FARM (443)
Hall, Daniel	COLE (113, 115), DURH (8, 13, 14, 15, 16, 17, 18, 19, 20, 21, 26, 347, 350, 354, 358, 359, 361, 363)
Hall, Daniel Jur	DURH (12, 16, 21)
Hall, Danl	DURH (23, 24, 27), MIDD (371, 382, 395, 406, 416)
Hall, Danl 3d	DURH (10)
Hall, Danl Ensn	DURH (12)
Hall, Danl Jur	DURH (14, 18, 19, 23, 25
Hall, Danll	EHAD (69)
Hall, David	CHAT (55), GUIL (334), MIDD (372)
Hall, David Junr	ENFD (35)

647

INDEX

Name	Index Page	Name	Index Page
Hall, Dewey	CHAT (31, 33, 39, 51, 62, 65)	Hall, Nathl	GUIL (271, 277, 286, 288, 300, 303, 310, 311, 320, 324, 326, 327, 335), GUIL (336), MANS (272, 274, 275, 282, 283, 284, 350)
Hall, Ebenezer	CHAT (33), GUIL (270), HARL (44, 47)		
Hall, Ebenezr	CHAT (37), HARL (46)		
Hall, Ebenr	CHAT (29, 61), GUIL (287, 299, 310)	Hall, Nathl Capt	MANS (273, 277, 283, 336, 337, 342, 346, 356, 357)
Hall, Eber	GUIL (272, 333)		
Hall, Elihu	HARL (55, 58, 59, 61)		
Hall, Eliphalet Jur	GUIL (278, 292)	Hall, Nathl Ensn	GUIL (295, 298, 301)
Hall, Ephraim Timothy Jur	CHES (14)	Hall, Philemon	GUIL (274, 335)
		Hall, Richard Dr	COVE (165)
Hall, Esbon	FAIR (267)	Hall, Rufus	HARL (55)
Hall, Ezbun	FAIR (266)	Hall, Saml	CHAT (31), FARM (28), KENT (E60), MIDD (356, 376, 394)
Hall, Gershom	MANS (279, 281, 328, 353, 357)		
Hall, Gideon	CHAT (31, 39, 51, 61, 62, 64, 65)	Hall, Saml Capt	CHAT (30, 31, 34, 35, 37, 39, 40, 41, 45, 46, 48, 49, 58, 64, 65, 68)
Hall, Giles	MIDD (367)		
Hall, Giles Capt	MIDD (384)	Hall, Samuel	CHES (9), MIDD (380)
Hall, Giles Junr	MIDD (363)	Hall, Samuel Capt	CHAT (11, 51)
Hall, Heman	FARM (433, 442, 449)	Hall, Samuel Jur	CHES (11, 14, 16)
Hall, Isaac	FARM (9, 433, 438, 445, 456)	Hall, Theophilus	MANS (338)
		Hall, Thomas 2d	EHAD (65, 87)
Hall, Isaac Jur	CHAT (42)	Hall, Thos	MIDD (416)
Hall, Isaiah	CHES (A)	Hall, Timo	DURH (21, 23, 25), GUIL (316), MIDD (406)
Hall, Jabez	CHAT (29, 42, 46, 51, 58, 65, 68), MIDD (347, 364)	Hall, Timothy	CHES (4, 8, 11, 12), DURH (22) ,MIDD (395)
Hall, Jacob	MIDD (349, 357, 368, 371, 416)	Hall, Vashni	ENFD (32)
Hall, James	FAIR (267), GUIL (304, 312)	Hall, William	CHES (8), LITC (131), MIDD (345, 351)
Hall, James Capt	MANS (267, 271, 277, 282, 328, 335, 347)	Hall, Wm	LEBA (299)
		Hallarn, Edward	GLAS (65)
Hall, Jared	CHES (4, 15)	Hallemback, John	CANA (11, 25)
Hall, Jedediah	CHES (4)	Hallock, Jesse	GREE (119, 120)
Hall, Jedidiah	CHES (11)	Hallocks, James	LITC (142)
Hall, Joel	CHAT (29, 42, 51, 64)	Halls, Samuel	KENT (C554)
Hall, John	CANA (64), EWIN (11), ENFD (27), GUIL (269, 299)	Hamblin, Ebenezer	FARM (438, 455)
		Hamblin, Ebenr	FARM (2, 3, 8, 431)
		Hamblin, Ensign	FARM (444)
Hall, John Junr	MIDD (363, 414, 419)	Hamblin, Jno	FARM (2)
Hall, Jonathan	CHES (4, 5, 8)	Hamblin, John	FARM (4, 28)
Hall, Jonathan Jur	CHES (A, 4, 5, 8, 11, 14)	Hamilton, James	COLC (243)
Hall, Jonth	HEBR (216)	Hamilton, Paul	DANB (40, 47, 63)
Hall, Joseph	DURH (14), MIDD (361, 364, 370, 377, 372)	Hamilton, Silas	DANB (56)
		Hamilton, Silas Jur	DANB (69)
Hall, Medad	HARW (2, 11, 14, 523)	Hamlen, Giles	CANA (27, 28)
Hall, Miles	CHES (6, 7, 8, 16), GUIL (270, 289, 293, 296, 303, 327, 335)	Hamlin, Charles Jur	MIDD (350)
		Hamlin, Colnl	MIDD (351, 360)
		Hamlin, Ebenr	FARM (13)
Hall, Miles Capt	CHES (5, 10, 13)	Hamlin, Edward Junr	MIDD (376)
Hall, Nath Ensn	GUIL (301)	Hamlin, Giles	CANA (11, 12, 23, 64, 77)
Hall, Nathan	MANS (267, 280, 336, 347, 357)	Hamlin, J	MIDD (402, 419)
		Hamlin, Jabez	MIDD (361, 366, 367, 369, 375, 378, 389, 402, 410, 411, 420, 422, 360)
Hall, Nathaniel	MANS (267, 268, 271)		
Hall, Nathaniel Capt	MANS (348, 360)		
		Hamlin, Jabez Colnl	MIDD (345, 351, 353, 355, 356)
		Hamlin, Jabez Jur	MIDD (345)

648

INDEX

Name	Index Page
Hamlin, Richard	MIDD (345, 349, 356, 387)
Hamlin, Richd	MIDD (362, 369, 371, 373, 380)
Hamlin, William	MIDD (346, 347, 366)
Hamlin, William Capt	MIDD (349, 361)
Hamlin, William Junr	MIDD (359)
Hamlin, Wm	MIDD (350)
Hamlin, Wm Capt	MIDD (357, 362, 371, 381)
Hamlin, Wm Junr	MIDD (371, 376, 404, 421)
Hammod, Nathaniel	BOLT (182)
Hammond, Elijah	BOLT (146, 148, 149, 151, (155,157, 180, 182)
Hammond, John	MANS (279, 281)
Hammond, Nathaniel	BOLT (155, 158, 164, 181)
Hammond, Nathl	BOLT (157, 167)
Hand, Abraham	CORN (12, 17)
Hand, Daniel Capt	GUIL (294)
Hand, Darius	CORN (88)
Hand, Lemuel	CORN (1, 9, 10, 87, 91)
Handy, Danll	GUIL (274)
Handy, Jairus	GUIL (303)
Hanfield, William	ASHF (228)
Hanford, Joseph	FAIR (269)
Hanford, Noah T	FAIR (264)
Hanford, Noah Taylor	FAIR (255, 258, 264), 265, 266, 267)
Hanks, John	ASHF (232)
Hanks, Richard White	MANS (267, 347)
Hanks, Richd W[ ]	MANS (277)
Hanks, Silas	MANS (270, 279, 281, 283, 328, 353)
Hanks, Uriah	MANS (280)
Hansdell, Abel	CANA (15, 77)
Hansdell, Abell	CANA (12)
Hanshaw, James	CANA (64)
Hanson, John	CANA (77)
Harden, Nathan	HADD (113, 129, 130, 148)
Hardin, John	KENT (A24)
Harding, Ebenezer	CHAT (51)
Harding, Ebenr	CHAT (54)
Harding, Ephraim	CHAT (34, 59)
Harding, Thos	GLAS (65)
Harger, Edward	DERB (134)
Harger, Ephraim	DERB (106)
Harger, Jabez	HARL (45)
Harger, Jobesh	HARL (52)
Harndon, Jonathan	KILY (98)
Harper, James Capt	EWIN (12, 85, 88)
Harpin, John	MILF (78)
Harris, Abijah	MANS (280)
Harris, Daniel	GLAS (65, 105), MANS (339)
Harris, Ebenr	CANA (64)
Harris, James	LITC (132)
Harris, Jedh	KILH (47)

Name	Index Page
Harris, John	MIDD (358)
Harris, Joseph	MIDD (358)
Harris, Nathl	COLC (6)
Harris, Nathl Capt	COLC (254)
Harris, Peter Capt	GLAS (107)
Harris, Phil	LEBA (311)
Harris, Philip	LEBA (316)
Harris, Phillip	LEBA (341)
Harris, Reuben	CANT (146, 176)
Harris, William Jur	MIDD (347, 350, 359)
Harrison, Aaron	FARM (430, 434, 438, 443, 446, 449)
Harrison, Aaron Dr	FARM (444)
Harrison, Abraham	BRAN (175)
Harrison, Amos	BRAN (163, 164, 173, 175)
Harrison, Asahel	BRAN (170, 171, 175, 176)
Harrison, Asahel Ct	BRAN (164)
Harrison, Asahel Ensign	BRAN (170)
Harrison, Daniel	CORN (13, 23, 86)
Harrison, Daniel Junr	CORN (10, 16, 18, 87, 90)
Harrison, Danl Foot	BRAN (164, 165)
Harrison, Danl F	BRAN (163, 166)
Harrison, Edward	BRAN (169, 178)
Harrison, Elihu	LITC (129, 155)
Harrison, Farrington	BRAN (164, 166, 173, 174, 175, 176, 178, 180)
Harrison, Farrington Ens	BRAN (170)
Harrison, Farrinton	BRAN (165)
Harrison, Jacob	BRAN (163, 164, 166, 170)
Harrison, James	BRAN (164, 170, 175, 178, 179)
Harrison, Jared	BRAN (165, 173, 179), FARM (433, 442, 444)
Harrison, Joel	CORN (88, 91)
Harrison, Josiah Capt	BRAN (176, 178)
Harrison, Justus	BRAN (166)
Harrison, Lemuel	LITC (129, 131, 135)
Harrison, Lemuel Lt	LITC (143)
Harrison, Mark	FARM (442, 444, 449)
Harrison, Noah	CORN (18)
Harrison, Peter	BRAN (175, 176, 178, 179)
Harrison, Saml	BRAN (163, 164), FARM (443)
Harrison, Samuel	BRAN (172, 173, 174, 178, 179)
Harrison, Timothy	BRAN (173, 176)
Harrison, Timothy Jur	BRAN (164, 166)
Harrison, Timy Jur	BRAN (165)
Harrison, Wooster	BRAN (163)
Harrison. Saml	FARM (433)
Harriss, Daniel	CANA (17, 64)
Harriss, Ebenr	CANA (23, 24)
Harriss, John	MIDD (372, 382)
Harriss, Wm	MIDD (395, 406)

INDEX

Name	Index Page	Name	Index Page
Harriss, Wm Junr	MIDD (371, 382)	Hart, Stepn	FARM (17)
Hart, [ ]	FARM (22)	Hart, Thomas	CORN (1, 6, 22, 88, 91), FARM (28, 456), GUIL (271)
Hart, Amasa	FARM (9, 445)		
Hart, Ambros	FARM (444)		
Hart, Amos	FARM (449, 456)	Hart, Thoms	CORN (22)
Hart, Amos Jur	FARM (456)	Hart, Thos	FARM (17, 18, 434, 438, 445, 449), GUIL (269, 270, 274, 277, 287, 290, 291, 294, 300, 310, 326, 336)
Hart, Anthony	FARM (28)		
Hart, Asa	FARM (5, 11, 18, 29)		
Hart, Benjamin	GUIL (270, 343)		
Hart, Benjn	GUIL (277, 287, 294, 295, 300, 302, 303, 310, 311, 317, 319, 326, 332, 339)	Hart, Titus	CORN (17, 23, 25, 87, 89, 90)
		Hart, Willm	FARM (454)
Hart, Charles	COLC (254)	Hart, Wm Jur	FARM (5, 433)
Hart, David	GOSH (186)	Hart, Zachariah	FARM (441)
Hart, Eldad	FARM (433)	Harvey, Asa	EHAD (6, 86, 89)
Hart, Elias	CORN (23, 25, 89)	Harvey, Ithamer Capt	EHAD (82, 89)
Hart, Elihu	FARM (17)	Harvy, Asa	EHAD (59, 66)
Hart, Elizur	FARM (31, 442)	Harvy, Ithamer Capt	EHAD (63, 68)
Hart, Elnathan	FARM (9, 13, 17, 434, 436, 453)	Harvy, Robert	EHAD (64)
		Harvy, Zachariah	EHAD (64)
Hart, Gideon	FARM (2, 17, 438, 445, 450, 454)	Hasington, Ebenr	FARM (5)
		Hasington, Elisha	FARM (9)
Hart, Hawkins	FARM (433, 443)	Hasington, James	FARM (433, 436, 456)
Hart, Isaac	FARM (433)	Haskin, Aaron	BOLT (157)
Hart, Joel	FARM (5, 13)	Haskins, Aaron	BOLT (146, 165, 167)
Hart, John	CORN (10), FARM (433)	Haskins, William	BOLT (180, 181, 182)
Hart, Jona	FARM (28, 443)	Hatch, Barnabas Jur	KENT (C546, C548, C551, C552, C554, D1, E58, E62)
Hart, Jos	FARM (443)		
Hart, Joseph	FARM (434, 438)		
Hart, Joseph Jur	FARM (433, 435)	Hatch, Benjamin	COLC (11)
Hart, Josh	FARM (17)	Hatch, Clark	KENT (E60, E63)
Hart, Josiah	FARM (443)	Hatch, Jethro	KENT (C545, E58)
Hart, Judah	FARM (434, 443)	Hatch, Jethro Capt	KENT (B1)
Hart, Judah Jur	FARM (442, 449)	Hatch, Jethro Majr	KENT (C546, C547, C551, D2, D12, D5, E62)
Hart, Lot	CORN (11, 16, 89, 90)		
Hart, Luke	FARM (455)	Hatch, Jonathan	GUIL (338)
Hart, Medad	FARM (436)	Hatch, Nathan	HARL (51, 52, 59, 61)
Hart, Munson	FARM (28)	Hatch, Nathaniel	KENT (A28, B1, B2, C554, D5, E62)
Hart, Noadh Leut	FARM (435)		
Hart, Noadiah	FARM (17, 455)	Hatch, Nathl	KENT (C555, D8, E58)
Hart, Noah	FARM (430)	Hatch, Ozias	KENT (E60)
Hart, Oliver	FARM (435, 440, 446)	Hatch, Silvanus	KENT (B2)
Hart, Phinehas	CORN (89)	Hatch, Thomas	KENT (A28)
Hart, Reuben	FARM (27, 436)	Hatch, Timothy	KENT (D7)
Hart, Reuben Capt	FARM (456)	Hawkens, Luther Capt	KILY (90, 91a)
Hart, Saml Capt	MIDD (401)	Hawkins, Abraham	DERB (113, 114, 120, 122, 124, 126, 131, 135, 137, 140, 145)
Hart, Samuel	DURH (18)		
Hart, Sealah	FARM (450)		
Hart, Selah	FARM (30, 435)	Hawkins, Eleazer	DERB (107, 120, 122, 167)
Hart, Selah Genl	FARM (17, 28)		
Hart, Seth	FARM (12, 17)	Hawkins, Elezer	DERB (122, 124)
Hart, Simeon	FARM (8, 29, 430, 434, 435, 440, 442, 445, 446, 449, 454)	Hawkins, Eli	DERB (122, 132, 140, 168)
		Hawkins, Freegift	DERB (113, 120, 122, 126, 131, 140, 145)
Hart, Simeon Capt	FARM (442)	Hawkins, Joseph	COVE (172, 180), DERB (120, 140, 167)
Hart, Simion	FARM (438)		
Hart, Simon	FARM (434, 435)	Hawkins, Luther Capt	KILY (92, 93)
Hart, Solomon	CORN (23, 88, 91)	Hawkins, Ozias	COVE (177)
Hart, Stephen	FARM (5, 443)	Hawkins, Zachariah	DERB (106)

650

INDEX

Name	Index Page
Hawkins, Zachh Capt	DERB (168)
Hawkins, Zackah	DERB (106)
Hawkins, Zackariah Capt	DERB (107)
Hawkins, Zecheriah Capt	DERB (169)
Hawley Abell	FARM (444)
Hawley Reuben	FARM (444)
Hawley, Abel	FARM (456)
Hawley, Abell	FARM (5)
Hawley, Amos	FARM (9, 17, 442, 444)
Hawley, Ebenr	FARM (2, 436)
Hawley, Reuben	FARM (9), 436)
Hawley, Rufus Revn	FARM (442)
Hawley, Seth	MIDD (405)
Haws, Isaac Jur	KENT (C547, D1, E58, E62)
Haws, Saml	KENT (E58, E62)
Hay, John	GOSH (184)
Hay[ ], Isaac	CANA (64)
Hayden, Joseph Jur	HARW (6, 9)
Hayden, William	HARW (6)
Haydon, Allyn	HARW (7)
Haydon, Joseph	HARW (25, 21)
Haydon, Joseph Jur	HARW (3, 7)
Haydon, Wm	HARW (5)
Hayes, J[ ]	DANB (41)
Hayes, James	DANB (59)
Hayes, Jonth	DANB (55, 69)
Hayes, Peter	DANB (63)
Hayes, Seth	HARL (47, 52)
Hayford, John	FARM (5)
Hayford, Joseph	FARM (444)
Hayford, Josh	FARM (17)
Hayl, Reuben	HARL (56)
Hayl, Ruben	HARL (55)
Hays, Abraham	GREE (121)
Hays, Abrm	GREE (127)
Hays, Ezekiel	BRAN (173, 174, 175)
Hays, Ezekiel Capt	BRAN (166, 170, 71)
Hays, Ezl Ct	BRAN (164)
Hays, Micha	HARL (44)
Hays, Titus	HARL (55, 57, 58, 59, 60, 61)
Hayward, Caleb	LEBA (299, 300, 301, 305, 311, 316)
Hayward, Jonathan	ASHF (311)
Hazard, Robert	FARM (449)
Hazard, Saml	FAIR (254)
Hazelton, Arnold Capt	HADD (119, 121, 122, 124, 125, 126, 127)
Hazelton, Arnold Lt	HADD (113, 116)
Hazelton, Capt	HADD (109, 110, 112)
Hazelton, Charles	HADD (129)
Hazelton, Charles Lieut	HADD (109, 110, 113, 114, 115, 116, 120, 121, 124, 125, 129, 148)
Hazelton, James	HADD (110)

Name	Index Page
Hazelton, James Capt	HADD (109, 110, 111, 112, 113, 114, 115, 116, 117, 118, 120, 121, 123, 125, 126, 127, 128, 129, 130)
Hazelton, Lieut	HADD (109)
Hazelton, Nathl	HADD (148)
Hazzard, Robert	FARM (456)
He[ ], Allyn Capt	FARM (7)
Heacox, Saml	FARM (28)
Heard, Genl	FARM (8)
Heart, Amos	FARM (2, 13)
Heart, Antony	FARM (13)
Heart, Benja	FARM (2, 17, 455)
Heart, Cal	FARM (451)
Heart, Col	FARM (450, 451)
Heart, David	FARM (456), MIDD (363)
Heart, Ebenr	FARM (441)
Heart, Eleazer	FARM (436, 449)
Heart, Elihu	FARM (13, 443)
Heart, Elijah	FARM (11, 442, 444, 450)
Heart, Elijah Jur	FARM (28)
Heart, Elizer	FARM (2)
Heart, Elizur	FARM (6, 28, 444)
Heart, Generall	FARM (5, 7, 11)
Heart, Gideon	FARM (15)
Heart, J[ ]	FARM (9)
Heart, Jehuda	FARM (443)
Heart, Jehudah	FARM (2)
Heart, John Ensign	MIDD (349, 357)
Heart, Joseph	FARM (2, 433)
Heart, Judah Jur	FARM (28)
Heart, Mathew	FARM (2, 449)
Heart, Mathw	FARM (6)
Heart, Mattw	FARM (443)
Heart, Noadiah	FARM (2, 9, 449, 452)
Heart, Oliver	FARM (9, 433, 436, 443, 450)
Heart, Saml Capt	MIDD (363)
Heart, Selah	FARM (13, 427, 452, 453, 454)
Heart, Selah Col	FARM (450, 455, 456)
Heart, Selah Genl	FARM (2, 3, 8, 12, 14, 16, 18, 23, 25, 26, 29, 32, 33, , 454)
Heart, Seth	FARM (12, 13)
Heart, Simeon	FARM (3, 5, 12, 15, 18, 440, 455)
Heart, Simeon Capt	FARM (451, 452)
Heart, Thomas	FARM (3, 16, 29)
Heart, Thos	FARM (9, 443, 449)
Heart, Wm Jur	FARM (2)
Heart, Zach	FARM (444)
Heart, Zachariah	FARM (2, 9, 28, 449)
Heart, Zachh	FARM (455)
Heath, Ebenr	ASHF (311)
Heath, Joseph	LITC (135, 147)
Heath, Peleg	HARF (253)
Heath, Pelegg	HARF (256, 288)

651

INDEX

Name	Index Page	Name	Index Page
Heatin, [ ]	GOSH (134)	Herger, Jabish	HARL (48)
Heaton, Revd	GOSH (183)	Herpin, John	MILF (78, 84, 85, 86, 88, 89, 92, 96, 98, 103, 105)
Heaton, Wm	GOSH (184)		
Hebard, John	GUIL (328)	Herrek, John Jr	CANT (150)
Hebbard, Andrew	CANT (181)	Herrenden, Jonathan	KILY (94)
Hebbard, William Capt	CANT (165, 172, 178)	Herrick, John	CANT (139, 140, 146, 154, 168, 178, 181)
Hebbard, Wm Capt	CANT (157, 181, 182)		
Hebbard, Wm Jur	CANT (155)	Herrick, John Jr	CANT (160)
Heberd, John	GUIL (328)	Herrick, Robert	CANT (181)
Heburt, John	GUIL (304)	Herrick, Robt	CANT (178)
Hedges, David	ASHF (311)	Herrington, Clark	CANT (156)
Hedges, Henry	MIDD (362, 367)	Herrington, Jonathan Jur	KILY (19)
Hedges, Henry Junr	MIDD (364, 365, 370)		
Hedges, Isaac	MIDD (344, 368)	Heusted, Abraham	GREE (124, 127)
Hegy, William	CANA (64)	Heusted, Joseph	GREE (127, 128)
Heldreth, Wm	GLAS (89, 94)	Heusted, Moses junr	GREE (126, 128)
Hemsted, John	GLAS (65)	Hewet, Benjn	CANA (64)
Hende, Caleb	ASHF (310)	Hewet, Gersham	CANA (15)
Hende, Caleb Capt	ASHF (201, 202, 209, 212)	Hewet, Increase	CANT (155)
		Hewett, Increase	CANT (144)
Hende, Calib Capt	ASHF (199)	Hewett, Stephen	CANT (184)
Hende, Capt	ASHF (206)	Hewit, Benjn	CANA (77)
Hendee, Asa	BOLT (157)	Hewit, Gershom	CANA (77)
Hendee, Caleb Capt	ASHF (213, 214, 218, 220, 308)	Hewit, Gershum	CANA (12)
		Hewlett, John	FARM (454)
Hendee, Capt	ASHF (206, 222, 224, 225, 226, 232)	Heydon, Allin	HARW (17)
		Heydon, Allyn	HARW (10)
Hendee, Eiphalit	COVE (180)	Heydon, Bennajah	HARW (533)
Hendee, Eliphalet	BOLT (155, 181, 182), COVE (177)	Heydon, Elija	HARW (523)
		Heydon, Elijah	HARW (4, 7, 8, 9, 11, 13, 14, 23, 25, 523, 533)
Hendey, Asa	BOLT (180, 182)		
Hendrick, Daniel	KILY (94)	Heydon, Joseph	HARW (5, 20, 21, 22, 24, 26)
Hendricks, John	KENT (E63)		
Hendy, Eliphalit	COVE (167)	Heydon, Joseph Jur	HARW (4, 9, 12, 13, 16, 533)
Henfield, Benja	ASHF (311)		
Henfield, Wm	ASHF (311)	Heydon, Samuel	HARW (4, 8, 10)
Henman, Eben	DERB (131)	Heydon, William	HARW (9, 533)
Henman, Joseph	CANA (12, 24)	Heydon, Wm Lieut	HARW (3)
Henry, John	COLC (10, 245, 252, 254), LEBA (298)	Heyford, Jas	FARM (443)
		Heyford, John	FARM (14)
Henry, Saml	CANT (146, 168, 169)	Heyford, Joseph	FARM (433)
Hensale, John	MIDD (393)	Hibbard, Dan	EWIN (13)
Hensdale, Elijah	FARM (2)	Hickcox, James	DURH (21, 23, 24, 25, 26)
Hensdale, John	MIDD (370, 380, 394)	Hickcox, Nathl	DURH (22)
Hensdale, John Capt	MIDD (370)	Hickok, Benja	DANB (62, 63, 61)
Hensdale, William	CANA (28)	Hickok, Benja Capt	DANB (65)
Hensdell, Abel	CANA (15)	Hickok, Benjamin	DANB (47, 51, 58)
Henshaw, [ ]	MIDD (360, 385)	Hickok, Benjn	DANB (40, 60)
Henshaw, Benj[ ]	MIDD (380)	Hickok, Benjn Capt	DANB (48, 49)
Henshaw, Benja	MIDD (372, 397, 398, 401, 416, 394, 418)	Hickok, Daniel	DANB (40, 41, 64)
		Hickok, Daniel Capt	DANB (50)
Henshaw, Benjamin	MIDD (346, 367, 369, 370, 371, 373, 374, 375, 381, 384, 385, 386, 393, 395, 406, 409, 410, 413, 418)	Hickok, Danl	DANB (51, 63)
		Hickok, Ebenr	DANB (40, 46, 63)
		Hickok, Saml	DANB (39)
		Hickox, Saml	FARM (2)
		Hide, Abijah	DERB (106)
Henshaw, Benjn	MIDD (349, 350)	Hide, Benja	CANT (146)
Henshaw, Doct	MIDD (415)	Hide, Benjamin	CANT (161)
Henshaw, Wm	MIDD (358, 372)	Hide, Comfort	CANT (159, 168, 181)
Henshaw, Wm Lieut	MIDD (382, 395, 405)	Hide, Danl	LEBA (310, 311)

INDEX

Name	Index Page
Hide, Ebenr	LEBA (311, 312)
Hide, Elij Jur	LEBA (299)
Hide, Elijah	LEBA (312)
Hide, Elijah Junr	LEBA (305)
Hide, Elijah Senr	LEBA (297, 299, 315)
Hide, Ezra	HARF (255A, 281)
Hide, Isaac	CANT (147, 157, 180)
Hide, Isaac Jr	CANT (144)
Hide, John	FAIR (253, 257, 259, 260, 261, 262)
Hide, John Jur	FAIR (253)
Hide, Jos	FAIR (252, 267)
Hide, Jos Cap	LEBA (330)
Hide, Joseph	FAIR (251, 253, 255, 257, 258, 260, 261, 262, 263, 264, 265, 266, 269)
Hide, Lena	LEBA (341)
Hide, Lina	LEBA (326)
Hide, Nathan	CANT (168)
Hide, Nathl Jur	LEBA (298, 299)
Hide, Saml	CANA (23, 27, 77), LEBA (305, 299)
Hide, Saml Jur	LEBA (294, 297)
Hide, Samuel	CANA (17)
Hide, Thomas L	COLC (11)
Hide, Uriah	HARL (42, 45, 46, 50, 51, 56, 58, 61)
Hide, Urial	HARL (46)
Higbe, [ ]	MIDD (397)
Higbe, Amos	MIDD (419)
Higbe, Daniel	MIDD (362, 364, 365)
Higbe, David	MIDD (347, 350, 359, 362, 371, 373, 396)
Higbe, Edward	MIDD (350)
Higbe, Ephraim	MIDD (362, 370)
Higbe, Epm	MIDD (406, 416)
Higbe, Isaac	MIDD (396)
Higbe, Jeduthan	MIDD (371, 381)
Higbe, Jeduthun	MIDD (363)
Higbe, John	MIDD (353, 362)
Higbe, Joseph	MIDD (347, 358, 361, 362, 370, 377, 381, 395, 405, 406, 414, 415)
Higbe, Seth	MIDD (363, 396)
Higbe, Widow	MIDD (396)
Higbe, Zac	MIDD (358)
Higbe, Zacheus	MIDD (346, 354, 387)
Higbe, Zachs	MIDD (362)
Higgens, Nehemiah	KILH (47)
Higgins, Beriah	MIDD (362)
Higgins, Capt	HADD (111, 117, 120, 121, 122, 123, 124, 130)
Higgins, Cornelius	HADD (125)
Higgins, Cornelius Capt	HADD (112, 113, 114, 115, 116, 117, 118, 126, 127, 128, 130)
Higgins, Cornelius Jur	HADD (129)
Higgins, Cornelius Lieut	HADD (109, 110, 120, 129)

Name	Index Page
Higgins, Cornelius Sergt	HADD (121)
Higgins, Elkanah	EHAD (49, 59)
Higgins, Haus	HADD (115, 116, 148)
Higgins, Israel	CHAT (43)
Higgins, Israel Jur	CHAT (33)
Higgins, Jedadiah	EHAD (74, 79)
Higgins, Leml	CHAT (46)
Higgins, Lemuel	CHAT (38, 58, 65)
Higgins, Lieut	HADD (110)
Higgins, Moses	CHAT (29, 40, 50, (67)
Hilhouse, Wilm	KENT (D7)
Hill, [ ]	MILF (78)
Hill, Augustus	FAIR (267), GOSH (113)
Hill, Capt	ASHF (224), 225, 229, 232)
Hill, Col	GOSH (113, 120, 184)
Hill, Dan	FARM (430, 433, 444, 446, 456)
Hill, Daniel	GUIL (319)
Hill, Danl	GUIL (320)
Hill, Darius	LEBA (311)
Hill, David	FARM 17, 456)
Hill, Ebenr	FAIR (253, 258, 259, 260, 262, 265, 266, 267)
Hill, Ebenr Capt	FAIR (253, 254, 263, 264
Hill, Elijah	GLAS (95)
Hill, Henry	GUIL (299)
Hill, Jabez	FAIR (267, 269)
Hill, Jabez Capt	FAIR (265, 266)
Hill, Jabez Major	FAIR (264)
Hill, James	KILH (54)
Hill, James 2d	KILH (54, 55, 145)
Hill, John	GUIL (270, 277, 287, 295, 300, 310, 326, 328)
Hill, John Junr	GUIL (318, 327, 336)
Hill, Jona	FARM (456)
Hill, Jonas	CHES (12, 15)
Hill, Jos	LEBA (297, 311, 318)
Hill, Jos Capt	LEBA (325, 337)
Hill, Joseph	LEBA (306, 316)
Hill, Joseph Jur	FAIR (253, 258)
Hill, Joseph Lieut	LEBA (304)
Hill, Lemuel	GOSH (186)
Hill, Leonard	LEBA (342)
Hill, Luke	FARM (455)
Hill, Medad	GOSH (115)
Hill, Noah	KILH (51, 55)
Hill, Rebecca	GUIL (302)
Hill, Saml	CHAT (44, 50, 59)
Hill, Saml Jur	GLAS (112)
Hill, Samuel	CHAT (61)
Hill, Seth	CORN (18, 23, 25, 89, 90), GOSH (130, 183, 185)
Hill, Squire	ASHF (222, 223, 310)
Hill, Squire Capt	ASHF (214, 226, 226, 308)
Hill, Timo	GUIL (273, 310, 316, 327, 336)

INDEX

Name	Index Page	Name	Index Page
Hill, Timothy	GUIL (275, 295, 300, 320)	Hine, Moses	MILF (92, 102, 104)
Hill, Timothy Capt	GUIL (260, 270, 277, 288)	Hine, Thadeus	DERB (122)
Hill, Timothy Junr	GUIL (269, 274, 299, 314)	Hine, William	DERB (122)
Hillard, Barnabas	KILH (145)	Hines, James	ASHF (308)
Hillard, Benona	KILH (146)	Hinkley, Joel	COLC (11)
Hillard, Benoni	KILH (44, 47, 49, 50, 53)	Hinkley, John	CHAT (37, 38, 51)
Hillard, Benony	KILH (43, 48)	Hinman, Amos	FARM (5)
Hillard, Joseph	KILH (45, 145, 146)	Hinman, Capt	GOSH (183)
Hillerd, Aaron	GUIL (322)	Hinman, Eben	DERB (106, 122, 126)
Hillhouse, William	KENT (D1, E63)	Hinman, Elihu	DURH (17, 25, 26)
Hills, Azell	FARM (449)	Hinman, James	DURH (11)
Hills, Da[ ]	FARM (435)	Hinman, Nevil	GOSH (184)
Hills, Dan	FARM (450)	Hinman, Phinehas	GOSH (104)
Hills, Darius	LEBA (305)	Hinman, Wait	GOSH (109, 130, 138)
Hills, David	HARF (253, 255A, 256, 259, 263, 265, 267, 268, 273, 281, 288, 293)	Hinsdale, Barnabas	HARF (253, 255A, 261a, 272, 281, 282, 287, 290, 292)
Hills, David Lieut	HARF (275, 280)	Hinsdale, Barnabas Lieut	HARF (275)
Hills, Dorothy	LEBA (296)		
Hills, Ebenezer	KENT (E58), E62)	Hinsdale, Ezra	HARW (3, 4, 7, 9, 13, 16, 23)
Hills, Ebenezer Jur	KENT (E63)		
Hills, Elijah	EWIN (85, 88)	Hinsdale, Jacob	HARW (3, 4, 9, 14, 17, 22)
Hills, Elisha	GLAS (94), HARF (266, 272, 281, 285, 287)	Hinsdale, Jacob Jur	HARW (20)
Hills, Jacob	ENFD (18)	Hinsdale, John	MIDD (356)
Hills, Jonathan	HARF (255A)	Hinsdale, John Capt	MIDD (345, 346, 349, 356)
Hills, Jonathan Colo	HARF (299)		
Hills, Lebbeus	COLC (255)	Hinsdale, William	CANA (77)
Hills, Libbeus	COLC (249)	Hinsdell, Abel	CANA (26)
Hills, Moses Capt	FARM (435)	Hinsdell, Jacob	HARW (523, 533)
Hills, Oliver	EWIN (8, 85)	Hinsman, Joel	GOSH (184)
Hills, Saml	GLAS (106, 108, 113, 114)	Hinsman, Phinehas	GOSH (185)
		Hinsman, Saml	GOSH (186)
Hills, Samuel	GLAS (66, 70, 71, 72, 78, 83, 98, 100, 103)	Hipburn, Peter	MILF (93)
		Hitchcock, Amasa	CHES (12)
Hills, Samuel Jur	GLAS (78, 92)	Hitchcock, Amos	FARM (456)
Hills, Stephen	HARF (263, 298, 299)	Hitchcock, Asahel	CHES (4, 13), KENT C547, D1, D7)
Hills, William Junr	HARF (266)		
Himock, Timo	ASHF (222)	Hitchcock, Caleb	KENT (B1)
Hinchen, Oliver	ASHF (222)	Hitchcock, Dan	CHES (4, 8, 11)
Hinckley, Ebenezer	LEBA (305)	Hitchcock, Daniel	CHES (9, 14), KENT (E59)
Hinckley, Ebenr	LEBA (298, 299, 311, 316, 334, 342)	Hitchcock, David	CHES (6, 10, 13), DERB (120, 122, 141, 145, 146, 167), FARM (443)
Hinckley, Ebr	LEBA (326)		
Hinckley, Ira	LEBA (326)		
Hinckley, Jared	LEBA (304, 306, 318, 321)	Hitchcock, David Capt	CHES (6)
		Hitchcock, Ebener	DERB (120)
Hinckley, Joel	LEBA (326)	Hitchcock, Eliakim	CHES (12), EWIN (85, 88)
Hinckley, John	CHAT (39, 43, 44, 68)		
Hindman, [ ]	CORN (22)	Hitchcock, Joel	FARM (28)
Hindsdale, Barnabas	HARF (266)	Hitchcock, John	KENT (C555)
Hine, Aaron	MILF (85, 91, 98)	Hitchcock, Jonathan	DERB (120, 122, 124)
Hine, Abel	KENT (B6)	Hitchcock, Matthias	CHES (8)
Hine, Benj	MILF (97)	Hitchcock, Nathl	FARM (433, 438, 443, 445, 450)
Hine, Benjamin	MILF (80, 82)		
Hine, Benjamin Capt	MILF (89)	Hitchcock, Oliver	HARL (47, 51, 52)
Hine, Benjamin Lieut	MILF (84)	Hitchcock, Robert	CHES (10)
Hine, Charles	MILF (82)	Hitchcock, Saml	FARM (442)
Hine, Joel	MILF (92, 98, 102)	Hitchcock, Stephen	FARM (438, 444)
Hine, John Junr	MILF (103)	Hitchcock, Stepn	FARM (443)

INDEX

Name	Index Page
Hitchcock, Titus	CHES (4)
Hitchcock, Voluntine	CHES (7)
Hitchcoct, Jonathan	DERB (139)
Hitchcok, David	CHES (7)
Hitchcok, Eliakim	EWIN (17)
Hitchcox, Joel	FARM (456)
Hix, John	GROT ([4])
Hoadley, Daniel	BRAN (168)
Hoadley, Ebenezer	BRAN (179)
Hoadley, Isaac	BRAN (173)
Hoadley, James	BRAN (164, 72)
Hoadley, Jehiel Doct	MIDD (362)
Hoadley, Jonan	BRAN (165)
Hoadley, Saml	BRAN (166)
Hoadley, Samuel	BRAN (169, 172, 173, 175)
Hoadley, Samuel Lt	BRAN (170)
Hoadley, Timothy	BRAN (174, 176, 179)
Hoadley, Timothy Capt	BRAN (170, 171, 172, 173)
Hoadley, Timothy Ct	BRAN (165)
Hoadly, Danl	BRAN (179)
Hoadly, Ebenezer	BRAN (175, 179)
Hoadly, James	BRAN (165)
Hoadly, Jehiel	MIDD (365)
Hoadly, Rufus	BRAN (176, 178, 180)
Hoadly, Saml	BRAN (165, 166)
Hoadly, Saml Lieut	BRAN (174)
Hoadly, Samuel	BRAN (176, 178, 180)
Hoadly, Timothy	BRAN (176)
Hobart, Abijah	BRAN (175)
Hobart, Justin	FAIR (259)
Hobart, Mason	BRAN (166)
Hobart, Moses	BRAN (172)
Hobbey, Wensley	MIDD (350, 356)
Hobbey, Wenslow	MIDD (345, 349, 358)
Hobbey, Winslow	MIDD (345)
Hobbey, Winsloy	MIDD (356)
Hobby, [ ]	MIDD (420)
Hobby, Benjamin	GREE (124)
Hobby, John	GREE (119, 120, 121, 126, 128)
Hobby, Jonathan	GREE (119)
Hobby, Joseph Junr	GREE (119, 128, 129)
Hobby, Thomas Col	GREE (121)
Hobby, Thomas Majr	GREE (119)
Hobby, Thos	GREE (128)
Hobby, Thos Col	GREE (126, 127, 128)
Hobby, Thos Majr	GREE (120)
Hobby, Wensley	MIDD (368, 369, 370, 374, 380, 381, 385, 393, 403, 404, 412, 413)
Hochkin, Abraham	CORN (89)
Hochkin, Beriah	CORN (23, 29)
Hocomb, Asel	HARL (51)
Hodge, Asahel	HARW (3, 523)
Hodge, Benjamin	GLAS (66, 74, 93, 106)
Hodge, Benjamin Junr	GLAS (83)
Hodge, Benjn	GLAS (69, 70, 83, 98)

Name	Index Page
Hodge, Benjn Jur	GLAS (92, 95, 98, 105, 112)
Hodge, Elijah	GLAS (85, 87, 93)
Hodge, John	GLAS (74, 83, 93, 98, 106)
Hodge, John Jur	GLAS (93)
Hodge, Saml	CHAT (42)
Hodges, Ephraim	MANS (279, 281)
Hodgkin, Ebenr	GUIL (274, 289, 325)
Hodgkin, Jno	HARL (52)
Hodgkin, Noah Junr	GUIL (274)
Hodgkins, Abraham	CORN (12, 90, 91)
Hodgkins, John	HARL (44, 47)
Hogaboom, Jeremiah	CANA (12)
Hogeboom, Jeremiah	CANA (28)
Hogkins, Abraham	CORN (12)
Hogoboom, Jeremiah	CANA (64)
Hoit, David	GUIL (286)
Hoit, David Ensn	GUIL (293)
Hoit, Ebenr	KENT (A24)
Holbrok, John Capt	DERB (122)
Holbrook, Daniel	DERB (106, 107, 141, 145, 120)
Holbrook, Daniel Capt	DERB (131, 132, 135, 137, 140, 142, 148, 167, 168, 169)
Holbrook, Daniel Junr	DERB (106, 113, 122, 124, 126)
Holbrook, Danl	DERB (138)
Holbrook, Danl Jnr	DERB (127)
Holbrook, John	LEBA (333, 334)
Holbrook, John Capt	DERB (107, 120, 125, 126, 127, 132)
Holbrook, John Jnr	DERB (167)
Holbrook, Pelatiah	LEBA (311)
Holbrook, Philo	DERB (122, 145, 167, 168, 169)
Holbrook, Thomas	KILY (7, 19)
Holbrook, Timo	LEBA (302, 326)
Holcomb, Abraham	CANA (11, 16, 28, 64)
Holcomb, Amasa	CANA (23, 28)
Holcomb, David	CANA (15, 17, 23, 25, 27, 28, 64)
Holcomb, Elijah	CANA (10, 11, 12, 17, 19, 27, 28, 64, 77)
Holcomb, Isaac	CANA (77)
Holcomb, Noah	CANA (18, 19, 64)
Holcomb, Timothy	CANA (11)
Holden, John Jur	GLAS (109)
Holding, John Junr	GLAS (102)
Holdridge, Israel	COLC (12)
Holemback, John	CANA (28)
Holembeck, John	CANA (77)
Holembeck, Saml	CANA (77)
Holembeck, Samuel	CANA (11)
Holkins, Elijah	ENFD (26, 30)
Hollemback, Abraham	CANA (77)
Hollemback, John	CANA (23)
Hollembak, John	CANA (24)
Hollembeck, Abraham	CANA (64)

655

INDEX

Name	Index Page
Hollembeck, John	CANA (23)
Hollembeck, Lieut	CANA (19)
Hollenbeck, John	CANA (11)
Hollenbeck, Saml	CANA (16)
Hollester, Ephm	FARM (438)
Hollester, Ephraim	FARM (2)
Hollester, Gideon	FARM (444)
Hollester, James	FARM (17)
Hollester, Salmon	FARM (9, 17)
Hollester, Stephen	FARM (9, 452)
Hollester, Stepn	FARM (442)
Holliser, Abraham Junr	GLAS (93)
Hollister, Aaron	GLAS (92)
Hollister, Amos	GLAS (93)
Hollister, Ashbel	GLAS (104, 105)
Hollister, David	GLAS (74, 98, 99)
Hollister, Elijah	GLAS (63, 67, 69, 71, 75, 79, 80, 84, 85, 89, 93, 100, 108, 113)
Hollister, Elisha	GLAS (60, 63, 66, 67, 70, 71, 75, 77, 78, 80, 93)
Hollister, Elisha Capt	GLAS (68, 77, 80, 81, 82, 98, 105, 108)
Hollister, Elizur	GLAS (111)
Hollister, George	GLAS (83, 94, 95, 98, 111)
Hollister, Gideon	FARM (456), GLAS (94)
Hollister, Gideon Junr	GLAS (75, 93)
Hollister, Israel	GLAS (78, 100)
Hollister, John	GLAS (74, 112)
Hollister, Jonathan	GLAS (87, 93)
Hollister, Joseph	GLAS (83, 94, 95)
Hollister, Joseph Junr	GLAS (98)
Hollister, Nathaniel	GLAS (81, 93)
Hollister, Nehemiah	GLAS (79, 92, 112)
Hollister, Plenny	GLAS (92)
Hollister, Stephen	GLAS (70, 74, 79, 83, 93, 98, 106, 112)
Hollister, Stepn	FARM (442)
Hollister, Theodore	GLAS (94)
Hollister, Thomas	GLAS (77, 92, 94)
Hollister, Thomas Jur	GLAS (66, 73, 94, 113)
Hollister, Thomas Lieut	GLAS (86)
Hollombeck, John	CANA (27)
Hollombeck, Saml	CANA (64)
Holm, Uriel Lieut	HARL (47)
Holman, Ebenr	EWIN (16, 85, 89)
Holmes, Eliphalet Capt	EHAD (83)
Holmes, Christopher	EHAD (48)
Holmes, Christopher Capt	EHAD (45, 50, 53, 55, 57)
Holmes, Ebenezer	EHAD (55, 80, 87, 121)
Holmes, Eliphalet Capt	EHAD (53, 67, 68, 73, 74, 78), 79, 82, 84, 85, 86, 88, 89)
Holmes, Eliphelet 2nd Capt	EHAD (45)
Holmes, George	COLC (242)

Name	Index Page
Holmes, Gershom	KENT (C555)
Holmes, Isaac Junr	GREE (120)
Holmes, Israel	KENT (A28, B2, C555, E59)
Holmes, John	COLC (251)
Holmes, John Ens	ASHF (202)
Holmes, John Jur	ASHF (202, 206, 210)
Holmes, Joseph	ASHF (207)
Holmes, Reuben	GREE (119, 125, 126, 128)
Holmes, Saml	ASHF (311, 217)
Holmes, Samuel	COLC (243, 249, 251)
Holmes, Titus	MANS (279)
Holmes, Uriel	HARL (52, 61)
Holmes, Uriel Capt	HARL (59, 60)
Holmes, Uriel Ensign	HARL (45)
Holmes, Uriel Leiut	HARL (49)
Holmes, Wm	GLAS (92)
Holms, Appleton	GLAS (94)
Holms, Cornelius	KILH (44, 45, 48, 49, 51, 54, 55, 146)
Holms, Cornelus	KILH (53, 145)
Holms, George	COLC (7)
Holms, Gershom	KENT (C546, D2, E58, E62)
Holms, Libeus	GOSH (185)
Holms, Peleg	KENT (E59)
Holms, Saml	COLC (7)
Holms, Uriah Ensign	HARL (44)
Holms, Urial Capt	HARL (56, 57, 58)
Holms, Urial Majr	HARL (62)
Holms, Uriel	HARL (61)
Holms, Uriel Ensign	HARL (42, 43, 44, 45)
Holms, Uriel Lieut	HARL (46, 49, 50, 51, 54)
Holms, Wm	GLAS (95)
Holsted, Joseph	HARW (3)
Holt, Ezekiel	ASHF (202, 308)
Holt, Ezekl	ASHF (310)
Holt, Josiah	FARM (6, 456)
Holten, Timothy	ENFD (26)
Holton, Edward	KILY (19, 91a)
Holton, Timothy	EWIN (12, 13, 17)
Homes, Appleton	GLAS (106)
Homes, Urial Capt	COLE (4)
Hooker Roger	FARM (450)
Hooker, Asahel	FARM (10, 28, 433, 443, 445)
Hooker, Col	FARM (7, 8, 10, 12, 15, 23, 24, 31, 445, 450, 451, 454)
Hooker, Elijah	FARM (6, 8, 17, 23, 27, 28, 430, 433, 436, 440, 442, 445, 446, 449, 452)
Hooker, Elnathan	FARM (31, 433, 438, 443, 444, 445, 455, 456)
Hooker, Gilbert	FARM (433)
Hooker, J[ ]s	FARM (442)
Hooker, Joseph	FARM (6, 17, 28, 449)

INDEX

Name	Index Page
Hooker, Noadiah	FARM (27, 28, 427, 430, 432, 452, 453)
Hooker, Noadiah Col	FARM (3, 4, 5, 12, 16, 17, 23, 27, 29, 31, 32, 34, 446, 449)
Hooker, Roger	FARM (2, 6, 9, 24, 31, 450)
Hooker, Roger Majr	FARM (27, 446)
Hooker, Rogor Majr	FARM (443)
Hooker, Rowlen	FARM (456)
Hooker, Saml Jur	FARM (442)
Hooker, Thomas	FARM (433)
Hooker, Thos	FARM (17, 442)
Hooker, William	HARF (285)
Hoolbrook, Daniel Jnr	DERB (113)
Hopkins, Benja	FARM (17, 449)
Hopkins, Benjn	FARM (443)
Hopkins, Caleb	FARM (9, 433, 444)
Hopkins, Elijah	CORN (19, 87)
Hopkins, Harris	LITC (145, 146, 148, 153
Hopkins, Hezekiah	HARW (11, 17)
Hopkins, Hezh	HARW (2, 15)
Hopkins, James	MIDD (376, 378)
Hopkins, Joseph	KENT (A28, C552, E58, E63)
Hopkins, Josiah	CORN (89, 90)
Hopkins, Judah	KENT (C548, E58, E62)
Hopkins, Nathl	MANS (338)
Hopkins, Noah	KENT (E64)
Hopkins, Prince	KENT (E59)
Hopkins, Saml	GOSH (102, 110, 117, 119, 120, 123, 130, 131, 136, 138, 140, 184)
Hopkins, Samuel	GOSH (115)
Hopkins, Uriah	HARW (3, 4, 6, 7, 10, 13, 14, 523, 533)
Hoppin, Gideon	GUIL (299)
Hopson, [ ]	COLC (244, 245)
Hopson, Capt	GUIL (283)
Hopson, Ebenezer Lieut	GUIL (286)
Hopson, Ebenr	GUIL (278, 290, 300, 307, 310, 311, 323, 326, 328, 336)
Hopson, Ebenr Lieut	GUIL (273, 274, 275, 287, 294, 307)
Hopson, Gideon	GUIL (325)
Hopson, John	COLC (247, 270)
Hopson, John Capt	GUIL (273, 277, 286, 287, 291, 293, 294, 300, 310, 311, 314, 319, 323, 326, 336, 344)
Hopson, John Jur	GUIL (301, 321, 326, 334)
Hopson, John Lieut	GUIL (260, 270, 275)
Horford, Amos	MIDD (379)
Horlburt, Timo	CANA (29)
Horlbut, Timothy	CANA (27)
Horsdell, Abel	CANA (64)
Horsdell, Joseph	CANA (64)
Horsey, Thomas	DERB (122, 124)

Name	Index Page
Horsey, Thomas Capt	DERB (167, 169)
Horsford, [ ]	HEBR (219, 234)
Horsford, Aaron	CHAT (37)
Horsford, Amos	MIDD (366, 372, 373)
Horsford, Capt	HEBR (217)
Horsford, Col	HEBR (218, 220, 233, 234, 236, 247)
Horsford, Daniel	CANA (15), HEBR (216, 233, 249)
Horsford, Daniel Capt	CANA (11, 19, 23, 27, 64, 77)
Horsford, Dudley	HEBR (234)
Horsford, Dudly	HEBR (217, 220, 236, 246)
Horsford, Jeremiah	CANA (11, 12, 19, 23, 64, 77)
Horsford, John	FARM (443), LITC (139, 160)
Horsford, Obadiah Capt	HEBR (216)
Horsford, Obadiah Col	HEBR (220)
Horsford, Roger	CANA (19, 28, 64, 77)
Horsford, William	LITC (139)
Horsington, Ebenr	FARM (5)
Horton, Benjn	COLE (113)
Horton, Elisha	FARM (443)
Horton, Stephen	HEBR (217)
Hosford, Amos	MIDD (345, 347, 350, 359, 371, 392, 402, 403, 412)
Hosford, Amos Lieut	MIDD (402)
Hosford, Daniel	CANA (15)
Hosford, Daniel Capt	CANA (16)
Hosford, Jeremiah	CANA (12)
Hoskens, Daniel	CORN (17)
Hoskins, Elijah	COLE (113, 115)
Hosmar, Thos Capt	CANA (27)
Hosmer, Daniel	HARF (255A, 266, 292, 298)
Hosmer, Elisha	HARF (253)
Hosmer, Graves	MIDD (363)
Hosmer, James	KILY (96a)
Hosmer, Simeon	HARF (287)
Hosmer, Stephen	CHAT (29, 52)
Hosmer, T	MIDD (364)
Hosmer, Thomas	CANA (11, 12, 19, 23, 77
Hosmer, Thos	CANA (15, 24)
Hosmer, Thos Capt	CANA (27)
Hosmer, Timothy	FARM (431, 443)
Hosmer, Timothy Docr	FARM (27)
Hosmer, Titus	BOLT (180), CORN (86), MIDD (342, 344, 345, 346, 348, 349, 354, 356, 366, 368, 375, 379, 384, 385, 389)
Hotchkin, Abraham	CORN (17)
Hotchkin, Beniah	CORN (17)
Hotchkin, Ebenr	GUIL (338)
Hotchkin, Noah Junr	GUIL (272, 303, 335)
Hotchkin, Thos	GUIL (269, 299, 337)
Hotchkis, Levi	DERB (169)

657

INDEX

Name	Index Page	Name	Index Page
Hotchkis, Stephen	FARM (2)	House, Eleazer	GLAS (98, 112)
Hotchkiss, [ ]	DERB (131, 140), FARM (438)	House, Elezarus	GLAS (95)
		House, Elij	LEBA (326)
Hotchkiss, Amos	CHES (7)	House, Elijah	GLAS (78), LEBA (304, 305, 316, 334)
Hotchkiss, Amos Capt	CHES (4, 5, 10)		
Hotchkiss, Benjamin Jur	CHES (4)	House, Jno	LEBA (311, 326)
		House, John	LEBA (302, 306, 318)
Hotchkiss, Bennoni	CHES (4)	House, Jonathan	GLAS (66, 93)
Hotchkiss, Benoni	CHES (9, 11)	House, Nathl	GLAS (64)
Hotchkiss, Capt	FARM (8, 435)	House, Nathl Capt	EWIN (8, 9, 10, 85, 88)
Hotchkiss, David	CHES (8, 15, 17)	House, Samuel	GLAS (109)
Hotchkiss, Elihu	LITC (135)	House, Simon	HEBR (234), LEBA (311)
Hotchkiss, Elijah	DERB (113, 120, 122)		
Hotchkiss, Eliphalet	LITC (154)	House, William	GLAS (66, 93)
Hotchkiss, Eliphelet	DERB (107, 120, 122, 124, 126, 135, 139, 147)	Hovey, Aaron	MANS (268, 271, 272, 277, 278, 279, 282, 283, 284, 328, 335, 337, 353, 357)
Hotchkiss, Eliphet	DERB (167)		
Hotchkiss, Elipt	DERB (127, 142)		
Hotchkiss, Ensn	FARM (453)	Hovey, Amos	MANS (233, 280, 281)
Hotchkiss, Jacob	MILF (85, 88, 94, 102, 104)	Hovey, Daniel	MANS (348, 352)
		Hovey, Danl	MANS (277)
Hotchkiss, Jason	CHES (A)	Hovey, Enoch	MANS (233, 277, 354, 357, 359)
Hotchkiss, John	GLAS (95), GUIL (270, 286, 309, 310, 335, 338)	Hovey, Jacob	MANS (278, 336, 356)
Hotchkiss, Jonah	CHES (5, 8, 14, 15)	Hovey, Jona	MANS (278)
Hotchkiss, Josiah	CHES (4, 8, 11), FARM (17)	Hovey, Jonathan	MANS (233, 273, 348, 353, 356)
Hotchkiss, Lamuel	FARM (433)	Hovey, Joseph Junr	MANS (267, 271, 272, 284, 336, 350, 352, 354, 355)
Hotchkiss, Lemuel	FARM (6, 442)		
Hotchkiss, Lemuel Ensn	FARM (442)	Hovey, Joseph Junr Ensn	MANS (278)
Hotchkiss, Leut	CHES (9)	Hovey, William	MANS (280, 281)
Hotchkiss, Levi	DERB (106, 122, 131, 140, 141, 145, 168)	Hovey, Willm	MANS (233)
Hotchkiss, Levi Leiut	DERB (135)	How, [ ]	CANA (64), GOSH (110)
Hotchkiss, Lieut	CHES (8)	How, Dr	ASHF (210, 212, 224, 229, 233, 240)
Hotchkiss, Lodwick	FARM (8, 430, 434, 436, 441)	How, Elisha	GLAS (83, 89, 90, 94, 100, 102, 109, 112, 113)
Hotchkiss, Meria	GUIL (312)	How, Isaac	CANA (64)
Hotchkiss, Meriam	GUIL (328, 329)	How, Isaac C	KILY (94a)
Hotchkiss, Miles	GUIL (274, 289, 295, 303, 324, 325)	How, Jacob	CANA (28, 64, 77)
Hotchkiss, Saml	FARM (28)	How, Jere	GOSH (185)
Hotchkiss, Samuel Ensn	FARM (446)	How, Jeremiah	CANA (11)
		How, John	CORN (87), GLAS (70, 93)
Hotchkiss, Solomon	MILF (91, 100, 104)		
Hotchkiss, Stephen	FARM (27, 427, 440, 441, 455, 456)	How, John Jur	GLAS (81, 94)
		How, Jos	GOSH (110, 184)
Hotchkiss, Stepn	FARM (8, 442)	How, Joseph	COVE (178), GOSH (115)
Hotchkiss, Timo	FARM (456)		
Hotchkiss, Waitstil	CHES (14)	How, Leavit	KENT (C548, C552, E59)
Hough, Andrew	CHES (5)	How, Nathl	CANA (64)
Hough, Benoni	HARW (2, 3, 7, 14, 17, 23, 25, 523)	How, Nathl Jur	CANA (27, 64, 77)
		How, Neh Dr	ASHF (308)
Hough, Ebenr	MIDD (363)	How, Nehemiah	ASHF (211, 227, 311)
Hough, John	CANT (144, 154, 167, 170, 172, 177)	How, Nehemiah Dr	ASHF (225, 228, 229)
		How, Perly	KILY (88)
Hought, Benoni	HARW (10)	How, Perly Capt	KILY (92a)
House, Alexr	LEBA (326)	How, Philip	CANA (64)
House, Benjamin	GLAS (66, 93)	How, Saml	BRAN (174)
House, Benoni	GLAS (93)	How, Saml 2d	CANA (17, 64)

658

INDEX

Name	Index Page
How, Samson	KILY (91, 91a, 92, 94, 96)
How, Samuel	BRAN (178)
How, Stephen	CANA (64), COVE (180)
How, Zadock Lieut	BOLT (164, 183)
Howard, Benjamin	BOLT (181)
Howard, Ebenezer	KILY (87a, 91a)
Howard, Ebenr Junr	KILY (19)
Howard, John	BOLT (146, 147, 148, 155, 156, 167, 180, 182)
Howd, Edward	DERB (106, 113, 122, 124, 127, 141, 145)
Howd, Edward Leut	DERB (121)
Howd, Joel	BRAN (175)
Howd, John	DERB (107, 120, 122, 126, 127, 139, 141, 144, 145, 167, 168)
Howd, Josiah	BRAN (173, 175, 176)
Howd, Judah	BRAN (163, 172)
Howd, Pennock	BRAN (165, 169, 172, 176, 178)
Howd, Whitehead	FARM (433, 444, 445)
Howd, Whithead	FARM (438)
Howe, Daniel	MANS (281, 347)
Howe, Dr	ASHF (232, 233, 234, 234)
Howe, Isaac C	KILY (96a)
Howe, Isaac Cady	KILY (7, 13, 97a)
Howe, Isaac junr	GREE (124, 125)
Howe, James	ASHF (308)
Howe, James Jur	ASHF (232)
Howe, Joseph	COVE (180)
Howe, Nemiah Dr	ASHF (234)
Howe, Parly	KILY (85a, 86a)
Howe, Perrly	KILY (87a)
Howe, Samson	KILY (7, 9, 10, 13, 15, 17, 18, 19, 20, 21, 30, 32, 86a, 87a)
Howell, Edmond	COLE (7, 8, 9, 10, 11, 113, 115)
Howell, Edmund	COLE (14)
Hows, James	ASHF (236)
Hoyt, Amos	DANB (63)
Hoyt, Comfort	DANB (39, 41, 49, 63, 198)
Hoyt, Comfort Capt	DANB (40, 45, 50)
Hoyt, Comfort Jur	DANB (40, 41, 46, 51, 58, 64, 66)
Hoyt, Daniel	DANB (40, 47, 51)
Hoyt, David	DANB (47)
Hoyt, David Jur	DANB (39)
Hoyt, Drake Jur	DANB (43)
Hoyt, Elijah	DANB (40, 47, 51, 57, 58, 64)
Hoyt, Enos	DANB (51)
Hoyt, Jonth	DANB (51)
Hoyt, Justus	DANB (47)
Hoyt, Nathan	DANB (58, 60)
Hoyt, Nathl	DANB (39, 40, 47)
Hoyt, Noah	DANB (39, 43, 47, 49, 55, 64)
Hoyt, Starr	DANB (52)

Name	Index Page
Hubbard, [ ]	ENFD (27) GLAS (80, 108), MIDD 357, 349)
Hubbard, Aaron	GLAS (74, 76, 78, 80, 82, 83, 93, 101, 111), HADD (109, 110, 118, 148)
Hubbard, Abijah	MIDD (367, 394, 416, 417)
Hubbard, Abraham	GUIL (272)
Hubbard, Aron	GLAS (63, 66, 67, 70, 71)
Hubbard, Caleb Jur	MIDD (350)
Hubbard, David	HADD (113, 114, 122), MIDD (376, 421)
Hubbard, Eleazer	GLAS (94)
Hubbard, Eleazer Junr	GLAS (70)
Hubbard, Eleazur	GLAS (87)
Hubbard, Elijah	GLAS (92), HARF (261), MIDD (345, 350, 355, 357, 358, 367, 390, 369, 372, 377, 378, 379, 382, 387, 388, 389, 390, 392, 395, 396, 397, 398, 401, 402, 403, 405, 407, 408, 410, 412, 413, 415, 416, 417, 418)
Hubbard, Elijah Jur	MIDD (342, 346, 349, 350)
Hubbard, Eliphalet	MIDD (350, 367)
Hubbard, Elizur	GLAS (75, 78, 79, 84, 87, 93)
Hubbard, Elizur Capt	GLAS (83, 89, 90, 99, 102, 108)
Hubbard, Elnathan	FARM (456)
Hubbard, Ephm Junr	GLAS (93)
Hubbard, Ephraim	GLAS (93)
Hubbard, Ephraim Jur	GLAS (84)
Hubbard, Geo Capt	MIDD (420)
Hubbard, George	MIDD (345, 352, 363, 370, 378, 413)
Hubbard, George Capt	MIDD (387)
Hubbard, George Lt	CHAT (44)
Hubbard, Hezekiah Junr	GLAS (92)
Hubbard, Hezekiah Lt	MIDD (405)
Hubbard, Hezh	GLAS (68)
Hubbard, Hezh Lieut	MIDD (358, 372, 382, 395)
Hubbard, Isaac	MIDD (402, 414)
Hubbard, Jabez	MIDD (362)
Hubbard, James	HADD (109, 110, 125)
Hubbard, James Lieut	HADD (116, 122, 124, 129)
Hubbard, Jedediah	CHAT (31, 43, 45, 54, 59, 64, 67)
Hubbard, Jedidiah	MIDD (364)
Hubbard, Jereh Lieut	MIDD (361)
Hubbard, Jeremiah	HADD (127), MIDD (368)
Hubbard, Jeremiah Ens	HADD (110, 111, 118, 119, 128)
Hubbard, Jeremiah Jur	HADD (113, 123, 129, 148)

INDEX

Name	Index Page	Name	Index Page
Hubbard, Jeremiah Sergt	HADD (116, 117)	Hubbard, Solomon	MIDD (368)
Hubbard, Jno E	MIDD (357, 371)	Hubbard, Stephen	MIDD (367)
Hubbard, Jno Earl	MIDD (368, 381)	Hubbard, Stephen Capt	MIDD (342, 345, 346, 349, 353, 355, 356, 357)
Hubbard, Job	HADD (121, 148)	Hubbard, Thomas	CHAT (31, 34, 41, 47, 51
Hubbard, Joel	HADD (110, 121)	Hubbard, Thomas Jur	HADD (116)
Hubbard, John	HADD (148), MIDD (376, 378), GUIL (280)	Hubbard, Thos Jur	HADD (110, 129, 148)
		Hubbard, William	GREE (124, 128), MIDD (363)
Hubbard, John E	MIDD (355)		
Hubbard, John Earl	MIDD (346, 353, 394)	Hubbard, Wm	MIDD (395)
Hubbard, John Ensn	GUIL (277)	Hubbard, Zenas	MIDD (376, 411)
Hubbard, John Jur	CHAT (34, 41, 44, 65, 68	Hubbarde, Caleb	MIDD (364)
Hubbard, John Lieut	GUIL (286, 293, 294)	Hubbel, Abijah	KENT (A28, C555, E58, E62)
Hubbard, Jona	MIDD (371)		
Hubbard, Jonathan	GLAS (66, 93), MIDD (347, 351, 355, 356, 359, 368, 382, 398)	Hubbel, Ephm	KENT (C545)
		Hubbel, Ephm Jur	KENT (E58, E62)
		Hubbel, Ephraim Jur	KENT (A28, B1, B3, C550, C555)
Hubbard, Jonathan Jur	MIDD (345, 347, 349, 350)		
		Hubbel, Ephrm Jur	KENT (C552)
Hubbard, Jonn Lieut	MIDD (358)	Hubbel, Ezra	DANB (63)
Hubbard, Joseph	MIDD (362, 367)	Hubbel, Hezekiah	KENT (E61)
Hubbard, Joseph Capt	MIDD (394)	Hubbel, Jedadiah	KENT (D12)
Hubbard, Joseph Junr	MIDD (347, 351, 371, 377, 381, 384)	Hubbel, Jedidiah	KENT (A28, B1, B2, C543, C545, C548, C550, C552, C554, C555, D1, D7, D10)
Hubbard, Manoah	MIDD (363, 378, 394, 406, 414)		
Hubbard, Mica	MIDD (369, 372, 377, 379)	Hubbel, Jedidiah Capt	KENT (A26, E58)
		Hubbel, Lewis	DERB (121, 122)
Hubbard, Micah	MIDD (376, 393, 403, 416)	Hubbel, Saml	KENT (E63)
		Hubbel, Samuel	KENT (E60)
Hubbard, Micha	MIDD (350, 351)	Hubbell, Amos	FAIR (256, 258, 259, 263
Hubbard, Nehemh	MIDD (358)	Hubbell, Benja	FAIR (262, 266)
Hubbard, Nehemiah	HARF (283), MIDD (345, 346, 349, 351, 354, 361, 363, 368, 371, 372, 381, 390, 393, 404, 406, 407, 413, 417)	Hubbell, Benjamin	FAIR (267)
		Hubbell, David	FAIR (253, 257, 258, 262, 265, 267, 269)
		Hubbell, David Capt	FAIR (261, 264, 266)
		Hubbell, Ephraim Jur	KENT (C553)
Hubbard, Nezh	GLAS (93)	Hubbell, Gershom	FAIR (253, 255, 260, 261, 262, 264, 267)
Hubbard, Noadah	MIDD (406)		
Hubbard, Noadh	MIDD (415)	Hubbell, Gideon	FAIR (253, 259, 262)
Hubbard, Noadiah	MIDD (362, 394, 405, 409)	Hubbell, Hez	FAIR (254, 257, 258, 259, 262, 264, 265, 267)
Hubbard, Noadiah Lieut	MIDD (370, 371, 380, 381, 382, 387)	Hubbell, Hez Capt	FAIR (263, 264)
		Hubbell, Hezekiah	FAIR (252, 253, 255, 256, 260, 266, 269)
Hubbard, Oliver	MIDD (359, 362, 390, 394, 405, 415)		
		Hubbell, Hezekiah Capt	FAIR (262)
Hubbard, Oliver Ensn	MIDD (354, 385)		
Hubbard, Prosper	DURH (11), MIDD (362, 364, 365, 372, 405, 413)	Hubbell, Jedidiah Capt	KENT (E62)
		Hubbell, John	FAIR (269)
Hubbard, Robt	MIDD (367)	Hubbell, Nathl	FAIR (258, 266)
Hubbard, Roswell	MIDD (358, 372, 382)	Hubbell, Richard Jur	FAIR (266, 251, 253, 256, 257, 258, 259, 260, 261, 262, 263, 264, 265, 266, 267)
Hubbard, Saml	MIDD (358, 393, 406, 413, 416)		
Hubbard, Saml Capt	HADD (109, 114)		
Hubbard, Saml Jur	MIDD (349)	Hubbell, Walter	FAIR (253, 255, 258)
Hubbard, Samuel	MIDD (362, 377, 404)	Hubbert, Hezekiah Junr	MIDD (369)
Hubbard, Samuel Capt	HADD (115, 116)		
Hubbard, Samuel Junr	MIDD (344)	Hubby, Joseph junr	GREE (124, 128)
Hubbard, Seth	CHAT (30, 31, 50, 54)	Huchans, Wyman	KILY (86)
Hubbard, Shailer	HADD (109, 110, 130)	Huchens, Benm	HARL (52)
Hubbard, Solo	MIDD (406)	Huchens, Silas	KILY (35, 98)

INDEX

Name	Index Page	Name	Index Page
Huchens, Wiman	KILY (88)	Hull, Samuel Jnr	DERB (131)
Huchens, Wyman	KILY (85a)	Humaston, John Junr	LITC (134, 147)
Hudson, Barzillai	HARF (275, 276, 281, 292)	Humaston, Noah	LITC (158)
Hudson, David	GOSH (102, 104)	Humphrey, Abel	ASHF (308)
Hudson, George	COLE (7)	Humphrey, Daniel	HARL (55)
Hudson, Step	GOSH (112)	Humphrey, Ebnr	ASHF (238)
Hudson, Timoth	GOSH (183)	Humphries, Oliver	FARM (13)
Hugg, William	CANA (77)	Humphry, Abell	FARM (9, 436)
Huggins, Nehemiah	KILH (146)	Humphry, Abill	FARM (438)
Hulbert, Danl	MIDD (363, 382)	Humphry, Daniel	COLE (9)
Hulbert, Hezekiah	MIDD (394, 395, 414)	Humphry, Daniel Revd	DERB (120, 122, 146)
Hulbert, Hezekiah Junr	MIDD (350, 361, 380)	Humphry, Danl	GOSH (185)
Hulbert, Hezh	MIDD (404)	Humphry, David	GOSH (102, 183)
Hulbert, Hezh Junr	MIDD (368)	Humphry, David Jur	GOSH (186)
Hulbert, Thomas	MIDD (347, 380, 381, 393, 394, 404)	Humphry, Frederick	FARM (2, 456)
		Humphry, Isaac	GOSH (102, 104)
Hulbert, Thos	MIDD (413)	Humphry, James	DERB (121, 122, 132)
Hulburt, Calvin	FARM (9)	Humphry, John	DERB (106, 107, 122, 124, 135, 140, 144, 167)
Hulburt, Timothy	CANA (15)	Humphry, John Ensign	DERB (120, 124, 126, 127)
Hulbut, Hezekiah	MIDD (406)		
Hulbut, Timothy	CANA (12, 16, 19, 20, 23, 26)	Humphry, Noah	GOSH (185, 186)
		Humphry, Simeon	GOSH (186)
Hulet, Oliver	KILY (87a)	Humphry, Thos	GOSH (185)
Hulit, Josiah	KILY (86a)	Humphrys, John	DERB (131, 145, 170)
Hull, Abel	DERB (167), KILH (45)	Humprey, Abell	FARM (455)
Hull, Abijah	DERB (106, 113, 121, 122)	Hungarford, Green	EHAD (49, 50)
		Hungarford, Robart	EHAD (44)
Hull, Abner	KILH (51, 145)	Hungarford, Samuel	EHAD (49)
Hull, Danl	FAIR (263, 267)	Hungerfor, Robert 2d	EHAD (83)
Hull, David	MIDD (382, 395, 405, 413)	Hungerford, [ ]	HARW (2)
		Hungerford, Elijah	EHAD (64, 87)
Hull, David Liut	GUIL (319)	Hungerford, Green	EHAD (48, 55, 60, 65, 69, 79)
Hull, Elipt	FAIR (262)		
Hull, Enos	KILH (46, 145, 146)	Hungerford, Jacob	FARM (2, 436, 456)
Hull, Ezekel	KILH (145)	Hungerford, James	HARL (45, 48, 51)
Hull, Ezekiel	FAIR (258, 260, 262)	Hungerford, John	FARM (442)
Hull, Ezekiel Capt	FAIR (253, 255, 256)	Hungerford, Mathew	FARM (436, 449), HARW (16, 17)
Hull, Gurden	KILH (54)		
Hull, Gurdon	DURH (12)	Hungerford, Mathw	FARM (433, 456)
Hull, James	KILH (47, 49, 51, 53, 146	Hungerford, Nathan	EHAD (46)
Hull, Joel	KILH (47, 145)	Hungerford, Nathaniel	EHAD (69, 79, 81, 87)
Hull, John	FAIR (258, 262, 263)	Hungerford, Reuben	FARM (9)
Hull, Joseph	DURH (10, 18, 12)	Hungerford, Robart	EHAD (49)
Hull, Josiah	DURH (26), KILH (54, 145)	Hungerford, Robert	EHAD (54, 59, 61)
		Hungerford, Robert 2nd	EHAD (54, 59, 63, 68, 79, 86, 87)
Hull, Lemuel Capt	KILH (145, 146)		
Hull, Levi	KILH (53, 54)	Hungerford, Stephen	FARM (5, 436)
Hull, Livi	KILH (50)	Hungerford, Stepn	FARM (17, 456)
Hull, Mrs	MIDD (358)	Hungerford, Thomas	FARM (2, 436), HARW (25)
Hull, Nathan	KILH (47)		
Hull, Oliver	KILH (145)	Hungerford, Thos	FARM (6, 8, 17, 28, 433, 442, 444)
Hull, Peter	KILH (45)		
Hull, Phebe	HARL (52)	Hungerford, Timy	FARM (456)
Hull, Roswel	KILH (49, 146)	Hungerford, Zachariah Capt	EHAD (58, 60, 62, 69, 79)
Hull, Saml	DERB (127, 145), KILH (145)		
		Hungerford, Zechariah Capt	EHAD (66)
Hull, Saml Jnr	DERB (113, 122)	Hunshaw, Benjamin	MIDD (401, 405)
Hull, Samuel	DERB (114, 132, 146, 167, 169)	Hunt, Benjamin	CHAT (46)

661

INDEX

Name	Index Page	Name	Index Page
Hunt, Benjn	CHAT (58)	Huntington, Wm Capt	LEBA (325, 327, 341)
Hunt, Eldad	LEBA (297, 305, 311, 316, 334)	Huntley, Rich H	COLC (247)
		Huntley, Richard H	COLC (246)
Hunt, Elijah	LEBA (341)	Huntley, Richd H	COLC (243)
Hunt, Elipas	COVE (174, 177, 180)	Huntly, Richd H	COLC (249, 251)
Hunt, Elipaz	COVE (165, 166)	Hunton, Sol	HEBR (218. 220, 234, 246)
Hunt, Eliphas	COVE (167, 168, 170, 178, 314)		
		Hurbut, John	GROT ([6])
Hunt, Gad	COVE (314, 177, 180)	Hurd, Abm	KILH (53)
Hunt, Gold	COVE (170)	Hurd, Abm Ensn	KILH (52, 53)
Hunt, Nathaniel Junr	MANS (328)	Hurd, Abram	KILH (44, 51)
Hunt, Nathl Junr	MANS (271, 279, 336)	Hurd, Abrm	KILH (45)
Hunt, Paltiah	KENT (C548)	Hurd, Caleb	KILH (53)
Hunt, Russel	CANA (27, 28)	Hurd, Caleb L	KILH (44, 51, 52, 55, 145)
Hunt, Russell	CANA (11, 17, 64, 77)	Hurd, Crippen	EHAD (86)
Hunt, Russell 2d	CANA (64, 77)	Hurd, Elisha	GROT ([25])
Hunt, Saml Jur	LEBA (326)	Hurd, Elnan	KILH (44)
Hunt, Thomas	GLAS (69, 70, 74, 77, 79, 83, 93, 98, 113)	Hurd, Elnathan	KILH (55)
		Hurd, Jacob	CHAT (43, 45, 50, 54)
Hunt, Thos	GLAS (80, 106, 113)	Hurd, Joseph	CHAT (41)
Hunt, William	BOLT (159, 182)	Hurd, Robart Jr	EHAD (49)
Hunter, Benjn	GLAS (94)	Hurlbert, Ozias	CORN (a)
Huntington, And	LEBA (341)	Hurlburt, Calvin	FARM (2, 443)
Huntington, And Lt	LEBA (320)	Hurlburt, Isaac	FARM (443)
Huntington, Andw	LEBA (315, 342)	Hurlburt, John	HARF (253, 256, 263, 267, 273, 275, 281, 288, 293)
Huntington, Cap	LEBA (343)		
Huntington, Davd	LEBA (342)		
Huntington, Dr	ASHF (222, 226, 232, 235, 233, 311)	Hurlburt, Salmon	KENT (E63)
		Hurlburt, Timothy	CANA (10, 28, 64, 29)
Huntington, Eleazar	MANS (275, 284, 353, 357)	Hurlbut, Calvin	FARM (17, 436)
Huntington, Eleazar Capt	MANS (273, 336, 346, 349, 354, 356)	Hurlbut, Elisha	CHAT (38, 43, 45, 67), GOSH (102, 110, 111, 184)
Huntington, Eleazer Capt	MANS (328, 333, 342)	Hurlbut, Gid	GOSH (185)
		Hurlbut, Gideon	CHAT (43, 45, 50, 58), GOSH (103, 111)
Huntington, Eleazr	MANS (277)		
Huntington, Eleazr Capt	MANS (355)	Hurlbut, John	GROT ([1], [3], [4], [6], [7], [8])
Huntington, Enoch	MIDD (367)	Hurlbut, John Colo	EHAD (79)
Huntington, Enoch Revd	GOSH (123)	Hurlbut, Josiah	CANA (64)
		Hurlbut, Leut	GOSH (102, 104, 106), GOSH (110, 112, 113, 121, 133, 184)
Huntington, James	LEBA (334, 342)		
Huntington, Jedh	MANS (278)	Hurlbut, Ozias	CORN (25)
Huntington, John	LEBA (298)	Hurlbut, Rufus	GROT [6], [12], [18]
Huntington, Jonas	MANS (357)	Hurlbut, Rusul	GROT [15]
Huntington, Jonathan	HARF (253, 281, 288)	Hurlbut, Salmon	KENT (E60)
Huntington, Joseph	HARW (3, 4, 10, 17, 22, 23)	Hurlbut, Stephen	CHAT (43, 51)
Huntington, Olivr	LEBA (302, 341, 343)	Hurlbut, Timothy	CANA (16)
Huntington, Samuel	EHAD (51, 53, 55, 57)	Hurlbut, William	CHAT (46)
Huntington, Sol	HEBR (216, 233)	Hurlbutt, Elisha	GOSH (104, 112, 115)
Huntington, Thomas Dr	ASHF (231, 233, 239)	Hurtwell, Oliver	CANA (64)
		Husted, Moses Jur	GREE (119)
Huntington, Thos Dr	ASHF (240)	Hutchen, John Jur	BOLT (157, 180)
Huntington, W Cap	LEBA (320)	Hutchens, Amasa	KILY (19, 32)
Huntington, William	LEBA (305)	Hutchens, Benja	MANS (268, 278)
Huntington, William Capt	LEBA (304)	Hutchens, Benja Colonel	HARL (56)
Huntington, Wm	LEBA (298, 299, 311, 316, 326, 327, 333, 334, 342)	Hutchens, Benjamen Colo	HARL (59, 60)

662

INDEX

Name	Index Page
Hutchens, Benjamin	MANS (336, 357)
Hutchens, Benjamin Colo	HARL (62)
Hutchens, Benjamin Capt	HARL (43, 44, 49, 51, 54, 55)
Hutchens, Benjan	MANS (271)
Hutchens, Benjan Colonel	HARL (57)
Hutchens, Benjn Capt	HARL (43)
Hutchens, Ezra	KILY (91a)
Hutchens, Ezra Jur	KILY (19)
Hutchens, Isaac	KILY (92, 94, 97)
Hutchens, John	KILY (7, 32)
Hutchens, John Church	BOLT (157, 180, 183)
Hutchens, John Jur	BOLT (146, 160, 182)
Hutchens, Jos	KILY (87a)
Hutchens, Joseph	HARL (44)
Hutchens, Silas	KILY (8, 19, 31)
Hutchens, Thomas	MANS (328)
Hutchens, Wimon	KILY (19, 89)
Hutchens, Wymon	KILY (86a)
Hutchens, Zadock	KILY (31)
Hutchenson, James	COVE (170)
Hutchings, Abner	GREE (128)
Hutchins, Silas	KILY (96a)
Hutchins, Wimon	KILY (92, 94)
Hutchinson, [ ]	LEBA (339, 340), HEBR (236)
Hutchinson, [ ] Jur	HEBR (234)
Hutchinson, Eleaz	LEBA (334)
Hutchinson, Eleazar	LEBA (305)
Hutchinson, Eleazr	LEBA (299, 315)
Hutchinson, Elisha	LEBA (305, 310, 315, 319, 321, 326, 333, 334, 341)
Hutchinson, Israel	HEBR (236)
Hutchinson, James	LEBA (297)
Hutchinson, Jonth	HEBR (218)
Hutchinson, Jos	LEBA (300, 334)
Hutchinson, Paul	LEBA (299, 301)
Hutchinson, Saml	LEBA (311, 325, 327, 330, 337)
Hutchinson, Samuel	LEBA (305)
Huthins, Ezra Junr	KILY (8)
Huxford, Henry	GLAS (68, 94, 100)
Huxford, Peter	GLAS (67, 93, 113)
Hyde, Benj[ ]	LEBA (341)
Hyde, Benjn	LEBA (315)
Hyde, Danl	LEBA (320, 326)
Hyde, Elij Jur	LEBA (326)
Hyde, Elij Jur Cap	LEBA (294)
Hyde, Elij Maj	LEBA (324)
Hyde, Elijah Jur	LEBA (297, 315, 318)
Hyde, Elijah Major	LEBA (310, 321, 329, 331, 332, 323)
Hyde, Enock	BOLT (181)
Hyde, Jos	LEBA (326)
Hyde, Lina	LEBA (334)
Hyde, Nath[ ] Jur	LEBA (316)
Hyde, Nathl 3d	LEBA (326)

Name	Index Page
Hyde, Oliver	LEBA (333)
Hyde, Uriah	HARL (53)
Ingersol, Simon	GREE (119)
Ingham, Daniel Capt	HEBR (235, 249)
Ingham, Danl Capt	HEBR (219)
Ingham, Jona	FARM (456)
Ingolsbe, [ ]	ASHF (194)
Ingraham, Isaac	BRAN (163, 164)
Ingraham, Isaac Junr	BRAN (176, 178)
Ingraham, Jacob	COLC (251)
Isaacs, [ ]	BRAN (172)
Isaacs, Aaron	HADD (148)
Isaacs, Ralph	BRAN (168)
Isham, Capt	COLC (256)
Isham, Daniel	COLC (10, 249)
Isham, John	COLC (243)
Isham, John 2nd	COLC (6, 7, 251, 252)
Isham, John 3rd	COLC (11)
Isham, John Capt	COLC (247, 251, 252, 254)
Isham, John Lieut	COLC (243)
Isham, Jos Capt	COLC (4, 6, 254, 255)
Isham, Jos Jr Capt	COLC (7, 9, 13)
Isham, Jos Jur	COLC (6, 7)
Isham, Joseph	COLC (246)
Isham, Joseph Junr	COLC (11, 244, 245, 246, 247, 248) ,GLAS (64)
Isham, Joseph Junr Capt	COLC (11, 250, 254)
Isham, Saml	COLC (7, 254)
Isham, Samuel	COLC (249, 251)
Isham, Timothy	BOLT (181, 182)
Ives, Benja	FARM (14)
Ives, Enos	FARM (28)
Ives, Joel	BRAN (170)
Ives, Josiah	FARM (17, 433, 444, 456
Ives, Jotham	CHES (14)
Ives, Reuben	FARM (17, 449)
Ives, Zachariah	CHES (A)
J[ ], Thomas	COVE (180)
Jackson, [ ]	KENT (C550)
Jackson, Ebenezer	CORN (15, 25, 26, 88, 91)
Jackson, Francis	FAIR (259, 266)
Jackson, Jno Jur	LEBA (341)
Jackson, Selah	CHAT (55)
Jackways, Ebenr	CANA (64, 77)
Jacobs, John	KILY (7, 19, 32, 92, 94, 94a)
Jacobs, John Jur	KILY (4, 93, 96a, 97)
Jacobs, Saml	MANS (274, 278, 283, 353)
Jacobs, Samuel	MANS (267, 347)
James, Col	HEBR (247)
Jeffery, Edward	GROT ([18])
Jennings, Aaron	FAIR (258, 260, 262, 269
Jennings, Andw	FAIR (267)
Jennings, Benja	FAIR (263)
Jennings, Benjaman	CORN (87)
Jennings, David	FAIR (253)

663

INDEX

Name	Index Page	Name	Index Page
Jennings, David 2d	FAIR (257)	Johnson, Benjn	CHAT (58), GUIL (294, 300, 335)
Jennings, David 3d	FAIR (253)		
Jennings, Ephm	FAIR (256, 257, 258, 259, 260, 262)	Johnson, Bristow	COLC (256)
		Johnson, Capt	DURH (26)
Jennings, Ezra	FAIR (258)	Johnson, Christopher	HARW (22, 25)
Jennings, Gershom	FAIR (253, 258, 260, 266	Johnson, Christopr	HARW (3)
Jennings, Hezekiah	FAIR (256)	Johnson, Colo	MIDD (395)
Jennings, Isaac	FAIR (253, 255, 257, 259, 260, 262, 264, 267)	Johnson, Daniel	FARM (456)
		Johnson, Danl	FARM (28, 434, 435, 436, 438, 445, 449, 456)
Jennings, Jeremh Jur	FAIR (265)		
Jennings, Jeremiah	FAIR (258)	Johnson, David	CANA (15, 64), DERB (120, 122, 124), EWIN (11, 12, 13)
Jennings, Justin	FAIR (260, 262)		
Jennings, Lemuel	CORN (9, 10, 12, 13, 17, 87)		
		Johnson, David Capt	EWIN (14)
Jennings, Lyman	FAIR (259)	Johnson, Davis	MIDD (358)
Jennings, Matthew	FAIR (256)	Johnson, Ebenezer	DERB (122, 131, 141), HARW (5)
Jennings, Moses	FAIR (257, 265, 267)		
Jennings, Peter	FAIR (253, 258)	Johnson, Ebenezer Capt	MIDD (342, 346, 350, 353, 358, 381, 405)
Jennings, Zac Jur	FAIR (255)		
Jepson, James	HARF (285)	Johnson, Ebenezr	HARW (8)
Jerom, Robert	FARM (455)	Johnson, Ebenezr Capt	MIDD (358)
Jerome, Wm	FARM (456)	Johnson, Ebenr	DERB (120), FARM (443), MIDD (368, 415)
Jeroms, Zerubable	FARM (455)		
Jesup, Ebenr	FAIR (253, 255, 259, 263, 264, 267)	Johnson, Ebenr Capt	MIDD (360, 394, 402)
		Johnson, Ebr	MIDD (358)
Jesup, Ebenr Doctr	FAIR (261)	Johnson, Ebr Capt	MIDD (370, 371)
Jesup, Jonathan	GREE (127, 128)	Johnson, Edward	MIDD (376, 405, 416)
Jesup, Nathaniel	GREE (121)	Johnson, Edwd	MIDD (413)
Jesup, Silvanus	GREE (121)	Johnson, Elijah	CHAT (65), MIDD (355, 364, 365, 370, 382, 387, 394, 398, 406, 407, 409, 417)
Jewet, Benja Jur	CANT (155)		
Jewet, Gibbon Doctor	EHAD (48)		
Jewet, Ichabod	COVE (169, 314)		
Jewett, David	EHAD (59, 64)	Johnson, Eliphalet	MIDD (354)
Jewett, Ebenr	CANT (180)	Johnson, Elisha	MILF (81)
Jewett, Gibbin Doctr	EHAD (51)	Johnson, Enoch	FARM (433, 455)
Jewett, Gibbon	EHAD (54)	Johnson, Ensn	DURH (20)
Jewett, Gibbon Doctr	EHAD (48, 53, 56, 57, 59, 83, 84)	Johnson, Gideon	DERB (113, 120, 122, 126, 135, 141, 169)
Jewett, Gibbons	EHAD (85)	Johnson, Hezekiah	DERB (120, 140)
Jewett, Gibbons Doct	EHAD (67, 73)	Johnson, Isaac	DERB (106, 120, 124, 126, 132) ,GUIL (311)
Jewett, Ichabod	COVE (165, 170, 174, 177, 180)		
		Johnson, Jedediah	MIDD (368)
Jewett, Nathan	EHAD (54)	Johnson, Jedh Junr	MIDD (393)
Jewett, Nathan Capt	EHAD (58, 59, 63)	Johnson, Jedidiah	MIDD (362)
Jewett, Nathan Lieut	EHAD (53, 57)	Johnson, Jedidiah Junr	MIDD (370, 380, 400, 404, 413)
Jewitt, David	EHAD (49)		
Jezup, Sylvanus	GREE (119)	Johnson, Jening	FARM (443)
Johns, Abijah	BOLT (155, 164, 181)	Johnson, Jeremiah	DERB (106, 120, 122, 145)
Johnson, Nathl	DERB (122)		
Johnson, Amos	CORN (23, 86)	Johnson, Jese	CHAT (31)
Johnson, Amos Capt	CORN (9, 17, 18, 23, 25)	Johnson, Jesse	CHAT (38, 41, 42, 43, 51, 66, 67)
Johnson, Amos Junr	CORN (17)		
Johnson, Amsa	HADD (148)	Johnson, Jno	LEBA (311)
Johnson, Artimious	BRAN (179)	Johnson, John	CANT (144), CHAT (44), COLC (8, 10, 243, 246, 247, 249, 251, 254), DURH (11, 14, 16, 19, 21, 22, 23, 25), LEBA (305, 316)
Johnson, Asa	FARM (442)		
Johnson, Asael	MIDD (350)		
Johnson, Asahel	DERB (120, 122), MIDD (364, 370)		
Johnson, Benjamin	CHAT (44, 64)		

INDEX

Name	Index Page
Johnson, John Capt	CANT (157, 160, 161, 165, 178, 179), DURH (24)
Johnson, John Ensn	DURH (24)
Johnson, John Jur	CHAT (34, 50, 68), DURH (10, 14, 18, 21, 24)
Johnson, John Lt	CHAT (64)
Johnson, Jona Colo	MIDD (382)
Johnson, Jonathan	LITC (131, 158)
Johnson, Jonathan Lieut	MIDD (345, 347)
Johnson, Jonathan Majr	MIDD (366)
Johnson, Jos	COLC (8, 255)
Johnson, Joseph	CHAT (51), DERB (120), MIDD (345, 349, 354, 356, 369, 371, 376, 377, 379, 381, 387, 393, 403, 412, 409)
Johnson, Lemuel	DURH (15, 16, 19, 24, 25
Johnson, Miles	GUIL (299)
Johnson, Nathan	GUIL (294, 301, 311)
Johnson, Nathaniel	KENT (E63, 121)
Johnson, Nathaniel Capt	DERB (106, 120, 122, 132, 167)
Johnson, Nathl Capt	DERB (107, 127)
Johnson, Nathl 3d	GUIL (272)
Johnson, Nethaniel	DERB (147)
Johnson, Nethaniel Capt	DERB (148)
Johnson, O Capt	MIDD (372)
Johnson, Obadiah Capt	CANT (140)
Johnson, Obadiah Colo	CANT (174, 177)
Johnson, Oliver	MIDD (368, 382, 406)
Johnson, Oliver Capt	MIDD (371, 381, 394)
Johnson, Peter	DERB (106, 120, 122, 140, 141)
Johnson, Philo	DERB (113, 120, 122, 124, 168)
Johnson, Phineas	GUIL (279, 296, 303, 309
Johnson, Phinehas	GUIL (287)
Johnson, Resolved	KILY (86a, 92, 94a)
Johnson, Reuben	ASHF (311)
Johnson, Richard	HADD (109)
Johnson, Richard Ens	HADD (109)
Johnson, Saml	GUIL (269), MIDD (368)
Johnson, Saml Junr	DERB (120), MIDD (364)
Johnson, Samuel	ASHF (226), MIDD (344)
Johnson, Samuel Jnr	DERB (122)
Johnson, Samuel Lieut	MIDD (349)
Johnson, Seth	CHES (4), MIDD (362, 406)
Johnson, Seth Junr	MIDD (371, 381, 394, 414)
Johnson, Stephen	ASHF (202, 209, 213, 218, 222, 226, 232, 310), FARM (456), MIDD (346, 349, 351, 353, 368)
Johnson, Stephn	MIDD (358)

Name	Index Page
Johnson, Thomas	CHAT (29, 37, 39, 45)
Johnson, Thos	GREE (126)
Johnson, Thos Capt	CORN (11)
Johnson, Timo	MIDD (380, 384)
Johnson, Timothy	MIDD (357, 359, 362)
Johnson, Wellford	BRAN (174)
Johnson, Widow	KILY (98)
Johnson, Willford	BRAN (165, 166, 173, 175)
Johnson, William	MANS (268, 278, 279, 328, 347)
Johnson, William Junr	MIDD (364)
Johnson, Wm	CANT (147), DURH (25), GUIL (296), MANS (277), MIDD (421)
Johnson, Zadoc	HARW (13, 16)
Johnson, Zadok	HARW (25)
Johnston, Samuel	ASHF (232)
Johnston, Stephen	ASHF (236)
Jones, Samuel Lt	HEBR (218)
Jones, [ ]	HARF (255, 296, 234, 236)
Jones, [ ] Jur	HEBR (236)
Jones, Aaron	GUIL (303, 320, 325, 335
Jones, Abijah	EWIN (85, 89)
Jones, Abner	COLC (245)
Jones, Amasa	MIDD (364)
Jones, Amasai	HARF (285)
Jones, Amos	COLC (246, 249, 251)
Jones, Amos Capt	COLC (9, 246)
Jones, Arial	COLC (247)
Jones, Ariol	COLC (255)
Jones, Asel	COVE (170, 177)
Jones, Bejaman	COVE (180)
Jones, Benaj	HEBR (220, 236)
Jones, Benajah	HEBR (217, 245)
Jones, Benja	HEBR (218)
Jones, Benjaman	COVE (168, 172, 177, 178)
Jones, Benjamen	COVE (165)
Jones, Benjamin	COVE (314)
Jones, Caleb	CORN (28, 86)
Jones, Col	HEBR (233, 234, 247)
Jones, David	KILH (145)
Jones, Eaton	LITC (158)
Jones, Elisha	COVE (174, 178, 314)
Jones, Elisha Jur	COVE (165)
Jones, Ezekiel	HEBR (217, 234, 236, 246)
Jones, Gideon	HEBR (218, 219, 220, 245, 246)
Jones, Jabez	COLC (8, 10, 243, 247, 249, 251, 255)
Jones, Jabez Junr	COLC (248)
Jones, James	MIDD (371, 395, 419)
Jones, Jared	GOSH (184)
Jones, Jno	HARL (52)
Jones, Joel Capt	HEBR (216, 217, 247)
Jones, Joel Col	HEBR (220, 231, 233, 245)

665

INDEX

Name	Index Page	Name	Index Page
Jones, Joel Major	HEBR (218)	Judd, Heman	FARM (6, 443, 450)
Jones, John	CORN (1, 17, 89), DURH (10, 16), FAIR (258), HARL (44, 48)	Judd, Hez	FARM (443, 452)
		Judd, Hezh	FARM (436, 445, 449)
		Judd, Himan	FARM (449)
Jones, Jonth	HEBR (220)	Judd, Immer	FARM (456)
Jones, Lemuel	GLAS (94, 102, 106)	Judd, Jacob	DANB (54, 58, 3)
Jones, Levi	LEBA (298, 305)	Judd, James	FARM (2, 8, 435, 441, 442, 450)
Jones, Nathan	BOLT (151, 180, 182)		
Jones, Noah	COVE (165)	Judd, James Jur	FARM (12, 28)
Jones, Pantry	HARF (251(2), 251(2)	Judd, James Lt	FARM (447)
Jones, Saml	ENFD (18, 24, 26, 27), GOSH (183)	Judd, Jesse	LITC (147)
		Judd, John	FARM (18, 443)
Jones, Saml Capt	HEBR (245)	Judd, John Jur	FARM (2, 9, 433, 435, 443, 444)
Jones, Samuel	CORN (10)		
Jones, Samuel Jur	HEBR (219, 234)	Judd, Jonathan	GUIL (311)
Jones, Simon	LEBA (305)	Judd, Joseph	KENT (B2, C548, D5, E58, E62)
Jones, Thomas	HARL (44, 48, 52)		
Jones, Zachariah H	CORN (23)	Judd, Levi	FARM (2, 445, 450)
Jones, Zachariah How	CORN (25)	Judd, Levy	FARM (443)
Jones, Zechariah H	CORN (6, 91)	Judd, Mathew	KENT (E58, E62)
Jones, Zechariah How	CORN (16, 18, 87)	Judd, Nathn	FARM (455)
Jopp, John	GLAS (92, 93)	Judd, Obediah	KENT (E59)
Joselin, Amaziah	GUIL (271)	Judd, Philip	KENT (E58)
Joslen, Edward	KILY (31, 33, 98)	Judd, Philip Jur	KENT (A28, B1, C555, E62)
Joslen, Israel	KILY (92, 98)		
Joslen, Isreal	KILY (88)	Judd, Phisns	FARM (442)
Joslen, Joseph	KILY (31)	Judd, Thomas	COVE (166, 177, 180, 314), HARW (2, 25, 523)
Joslin, Edward	KILY (8, 11, 20, 86a, 94a)		
Joslin, Israel	KILY (87)	Judd, Thos	HARW (3, 14, 21)
Joslin, Izrael	KILY (94a)	Judd, Thos Jur	DANB (63)
Joslin, Jesse	KILY (4)	Judd, William	FARM (27, 29)
Joslin, Joseph	KILY (86a, 91a, 95a)	Judd, William Capt	FARM (28)
Joy, [ ]	KILY (35)	Judd, Willm	FARM (430, 432)
Joy, Benj[ ]	KILY (96a)	Judd, Wm	FARM (427, 446)
Joy, Benj[ ] Jur	KILY (97)	Judd, Wm Capt	FARM (26)
Joy, Benja	KILY (85a)	Judson, Abel	CORN (23, 25, 86)
Joy, Benjamin	KILY (97)	Judson, Roswell	HARF (263, 267, 273, 281, 288, 293)
Joy, Benjm	KILY (98)		
Joy, Benjm Jur	KILY (98)	Justin, Charles	CANT (171)
Joy, Benjn	KILY (6, 15, 24, 28, 92, 93, 94, 95, 94a, 96a, 97a)	K[ ]lberis, Apleton	GOSH (183)
		Katell, Ens	GOSH (120)
Joy, Benjn Jur	KILY (12, 22, 94a)	Kee, Simon	KILY (88a)
Joyce, Wm	MIDD (364, 377)	Keeney, Alexander Junr	HARF (287)
Jud, Immer Jur	FARM (456)		
Jud, Jesse	GOSH (104)	Keeney, Ebenezer	DERB (107, 120, 125, 132, 135)
Judd James	FARM (445)		
Judd, [ ]	FARM (446)	Keeney, Ebenr	DERB (114, 134)
Judd, Antony	FARM (9, 455)	Keeney, Simeon	HARF (273)
Judd, Benjamin	HARW (13)	Keeney, Wm	DERB (134)
Judd, Benjn	HARW (2)	Keeth, Peter Capt	KILY (19, 31)
Judd, Calvin	FARM (28)	Keeth, Stephen Capt	KILY (18, 28)
Judd, Comfort	KENT (B2)	Kein, Barnabas M	GUIL (328)
Judd, Daniel	DANB (55), COLC (251)	Keith, Capt	HARF (255, 251(2)
Judd, Daniel Junr	COLC (243, 245)	Keith, James	MIDD (376)
Judd, Daniel Lieut	COLC (252)	Keith, Peter Capt	KILY (5, 6, 7, 96, 97a)
Judd, Danl	COLC (8, 256)	Keith, Stephen Capt	KILY (32, 98)
Judd, David	DANB (40, 50, 51, 52, 56, 58)	Keith, Wm	MIDD (363, 388)
		Keiyes, John	ASHF (231)
Judd, Elnathan	FARM (444)	Keiyes, John Majr	ASHF (230)
Judd, Gideon	FARM (436, 443)	Keiyes, Majr	ASHF (233)

INDEX

Name	Index Page
Kelcey, Ezra	KILH (53)
Kelcey, [ ]ehel	KILH (46)
Kelcey, Aaron	KILH (44, 47, 49, 146)
Kelcey, Aaron Capt	KILH (51, 52, 56)
Kelcey, Amos	KILH (47, 51, 53, 55)
Kelcey, Asa	KILH (146)
Kelcey, Dan	KILH (44, 51)
Kelcey, Daniel	KILH (145)
Kelcey, Elisha	KILH (44, 48, 49, 50, 51, 54)
Kelcey, Ezra	KILH (51)
Kelcey, Isaac	KILH (46)
Kelcey, Isack	KILH (49)
Kelcey, Jonathan	KILH (44, 48, 51, 53, 145
Kelcey, Josiah	KILH (47)
Kelcey, Levi	KILH (54)
Kelcey, Livi	KILH (49)
Kelcey, Martain	KILH (50, 53)
Kelcey, Martin	KILH (146)
Kelcey, Moses	KILH (54)
Kelcey, Nath[ ]	KILH (44)
Kelcey, Nathan	KILH (53)
Kelcey, Nathl	KILH (47, 49)
Kelcey, Peter	KILH (51, 54)
Kelcey, Saml 2d	KILH (49)
Kelcey, Uriah	KILH (145)
Kelcy, Aaron Lt	KILH (145)
Kelcy, Amos	KILH (44, 146)
Kelcy, Dan	KILH (145)
Kelcy, Ezra	KILH (145, 146)
Kelcy, Jonathan	KILH (50, 55, 146)
Kelcy, Joseph	KILH (146)
Kelcy, Josiah	KILH (45)
Kelcy, Levi	KILH (55)
Kelcy, Marten	KILH (145)
Kelcy, Nathan	KILH (145)
Kelcy, Peter	KILH (146)
Kelcy, Saml	KILH (145)
Kelcy, Saml 2d	KILH (44)
Kelcy, Silas Capt	KILH (50, 145)
Kelcy, Uriah	KILH (146)
Kelleg, Jonath	GOSH (111)
Kelleg, Saml	GOSH (139)
Kellel, Jonath Ens	GOSH (120)
Kelley, Daniel	MIDD (419)
Kelley, Danl	MIDD (376)
Kellog, Abner	COLC (246)
Kellog, Daniel Jur	HEBR (217, 234)
Kellog, Eliasaph	DANB (51, 58)
Kellog, Elijah	HEBR (216, 218, 219, 220, 233, 234)
Kellog, Ens	GOSH (138)
Kellog, Ezekiel	HARL (52)
Kellog, Israel 2nd	COLC (10)
Kellog, Jno	HEBR (218)
Kellog, John	HEBR (236)
Kellog, Jonath Ens	GOSH (112)
Kellog, Saml	GOSH (110), HEBR (217)
Kellog, Samuel	HEBR (218)

Name	Index Page
Kellogg, Aaron	COLC (11, 243, 249, 251, 252, 255)
Kellogg, Abner	COLC (10, 249, 251)
Kellogg, Amos	COLC (11)
Kellogg, Asa	CANA (77, 64)
Kellogg, Asahel	CANA (18, 19, 28)
Kellogg, Azariah	HARW (3, 4, 6, 7, 9, 10, 13, 14, 17, 21, 23, 25, 533)
Kellogg, Azariah Jur	HARW (3, 23)
Kellogg, Daniel	COLC (10, (249), HARF (292)
Kellogg, Ebenezer	LITC (138)
Kellogg, Ebenezer Reverd	BOLT (180, 182)
Kellogg, Eliaph Jur	DANB (61)
Kellogg, Eliasaph	DANB (58)
Kellogg, Elijah	CANA (17, 27, 64, 77)
Kellogg, Ezekiel	HARL (44, 47, 51)
Kellogg, George	HARF (263, 267, 273, 281, 288, 293)
Kellogg, Israel	COLC (249)
Kellogg, Israel Jur	COLC (254)
Kellogg, John	COLC (245)
Kellogg, Joseph	CANA (64, 77),CHAT (37, 39, 43, 47, 52, 61)
Kellogg, Joseph Capt	CHAT (45, 50, 53, 58, 64, 66)
Kellogg, Joseph Jur	CANA (11, 15, 18, 77)
Kellogg, Judah	CORN (a, 1, 2, 4, 5, 9, 10, 11, 12, 15, 17, 20, 22, 23, 24, 25, 26, 27, 28, 29, 84, 86, 89)
Kellogg, Judh	CORN (88)
Kellogg, Russel	COLC (11)
Kellogg, Saml	GOSH (105, 109, 129, 184)
Kellogg, Saml Jur	COLC (4), GOSH (185)
Kellogg, Samuel Junr	COLC (243, 245, 248)
Kelly, John	HADD (148)
Kelsey, Abner	KENT (E58)
Kelsey, Israel	MIDD (353, 368)
Kempfield, John	HARF (266)
Kenady, John	GROT ([25])
Kendal, Amos	ASHF (204)
Kendal, Isaac	ASHF (206)
Kendal, Joseph	ASHF (202, 209)
Kendall, Amos	ASHF (227, 313)
Kendall, Ens	ASHF (225)
Kendall, Joseph	ASHF (218, 222, 226, 239)
Kendall, Peter	CANT (177)
Kendall, Phins	CANT (168)
Kendel, Joseph	ASHF (213)
Kendel, Joseph Junr	ASHF (218)
Kendell, Joseph	ASHF (213, 311)
Kenedey, Samuel	HARF (266)
Kenedy, Benja	FARM (449)
Kennady, John	GROT ([9])
Kennedy, John	GROT ([23])

INDEX

Name	Index Page	Name	Index Page
Kent, Moss	FAIR (253, 260, 267, 269	Kimbal, Timothy	COVE (172)
Kentfield, John Capt	HARF (275)	Kimball, Abm Tyler	MIDD (382)
Ketchum, John	GLAS (114)	Kimball, John	HARW (2)
Keth, Capt	KILY (86a)	Kimberley, Abram Junr	GUIL (325)
Keth, Peter	KILY (87a)		
Keth, Peter Capt	KILY (94a, 97)	Kimberley, Wido	GLAS (86)
Keth, Steven Capt	KILY (94)	Kimberly, Abram	GUIL (328)
Kettel, Ens	GOSH (124, 138)	Kimberly, Abram Junr	GUIL (309)
Kettel, Jonath	GOSH (134)	Kimberly, George	GUIL (310, 320)
Kettell, Ens	GOSH (130, 138)	Kimberly, Mary	GLAS (68)
Kettil, Ens	GOSH (126)	Kimberly, Thomas	GLAS (60, 63, 66, 67, 69, 70, 71, 72, 73)
Kettle, Jonath	GOSH (184)		
Keyes, Jno Majr	ASHF (220, 308, 311)	Kimbull, Jesse	CANA (77)
Keyes, John Majr	ASHF (228, 229)	Kimbull, Jesse Capt	CANA (17, 64)
Keyes, Sampn	ASHF (308)	Kindal, [ ]	ASHF (238)
Keyes, Sampson	ASHF (224, 228)	Kindal, Joseph	ASHF (232, 236)
Keyes, Samson	ASHF (199, 206, 212, 310)	Kindall, Joseph	ASHF (233)
		Kindell, Amos	ASHF (313)
Keyes, Soln	ASHF (308)	King, Hezekiah Capt	BOLT (150)
Keyes, Solomon	ASHF (203, 213, 228, 310)	King, Alexander	EWIN (10)
		King, Alexr Ens	EWIN (16)
Keyes, Solon	ASHF (214)	King, Benjn	ENFD (18, 28, 32)
Keys, Jno Majr	ASHF (221, 225)	King, Capt	BOLT (146)
Keys, John Majr	ASHF (218, 228)	King, Charles	BOLT (146, 148, 151, 180, 182)
Keys, Majr	ASHF (224, 225)		
Keys, Samson	ASHF (222)	King, Charles Jur	BOLT (181)
Ki[ ]um, Eben	GUIL (271)	King, David	BOLT (181, 183), LITC (147, 158)
Kibbe, Elisha	ENFD (30, 33, 34, 35)		
Kibbe, Isaac	ENFD (16, 17, 18, 19, 25, 26, 27, 28, 29, 30)	King, Gideon	BOLT (147, 154, 155, 156, 160, 165, 180, 182)
Kies, Nathl	CHAT (42, 52)	King, Hezekiah Capt	BOLT (145, 149)
Kilborn, Abraham	LITC (128)	King, Joel	BOLT (183)
Kilborn, Benjamin	LITC (156)	King, Jos	MIDD (401)
Kilborn, David	COLC (7, 8, 245, 247, 251, 254, 256), LITC (153, 154, 158)	King, Joseph	MIDD (350, 351, 352, 355, 356, 357, 359, 366, 368, 369, 370, 375, 383, 386, 387, 395, 405, 409, 413)
Kilborn, Isaac	LITC (129)		
Kilborn, Jehiel	LITC (141)		
Kilborn, Jesse	LITC (131, 135, 139, 142, 147, 153, 158)	King, Oliver	BOLT (148, 151, 155, 157, 160, 180, 182)
Kilborn, John	FARM (443)	King, Ruben	BOLT (160, 180)
Kilborn, Jonathan Capt	EHAD (64, 67)	King, Saml Lt	EWIN (16)
Kilborn, Joseph	GLAS (93)	King, Samuel	BOLT (167, 181), EWIN (8, 17)
Kilborn, Josiah	FARM (2, 29, 433, 440, 443)	King, Seth	BOLT (145, 146, 149, 152, 167, 180, 182)
Kilborn, Martha	GLAS (75)		
Kilborn, P[ ]	FARM (4)	King, Seth Jur	BOLT (181, 183)
Kilborn, Roswel	LITC (129)	King, Stephen	BOLT (146, 147, 180, 182)
Kilborn, Russel	HARF (261a)		
Kilborn, Samuel	HARF (251(2))	King, Titus	EWIN (85, 89)
Kilborn, Solomon	LITC (131, 154)	King, Zebulon	EWIN (85, 88)
Kilborne, Russel	HARF (272)	Kingbery, Ephraim	COVE (168)
Kilborne, Samuel	HARF (287, 289)	Kingbury, Phinehas	HARL (55)
Kilbourn, Martha Wo	GLAS (102)	Kingman, Joseph	CANA (17, 18, 27, 28, 77)
Kilbourn, Russell	EHAR (3)	Kingman, Mitchel	CANA (64)
Kilbourne, Samuel	HARF (281)	Kings, Joseph	MIDD (354)
Kilburn, Saml	CHAT (43)	Kingsberry, John	ENFD (32, 28)
Killam, Eliphalet	ENFD (33, 34, 35)	Kingsberry, John Junr	ENFD (24, 26)
Killborn, Samuel	CHAT (34)	Kingsberry, Joseph	ENFD (29, 35, 19, 28, 33)
Kimbal, Abrm Tyler	MIDD (395)	Kingsberry, Lemuel	ENFD (24, 28, 35)

668

INDEX

Name	Index Page
Kingsbery, Daniel	HARL (46, 47, 51)
Kingsbery, Daniel Ensign	HARL (49)
Kingsbery, Ebenezer	COVE (170, 169)
Kingsbery, Ebenezer Capt	COVE (161, 163, 164, 165, 167, 177, 180)
Kingsbery, Ephraim	COVE (165, 166, 172, 173, 177, 178)
Kingsbery, Ephraim Capt	COVE (178)
Kingsbery, Ephraim Leut	COVE (169)
Kingsbery, John	HARL (43, 44)
Kingsbery, Joseph	COVE (174)
Kingsbery, Nathaniel	COVE (170, 172, 174)
Kingsbery, Phinehas	HARL (43, 44, 45, 46, 47, 48, 49, 51, 54)
Kingsbery, Phinehas Jr	HARL (51)
Kingsbery, Samuel	COVE (172)
Kingsbury, Andw	CANA (17, 20)
Kingsbury, Andw Capt	CANA (24)
Kingsbury, Daniel	HARL (52)
Kingsbury, Daniel Ensign	HARL (56)
Kingsbury, Dickinson	HEBR (218)
Kingsbury, Ephraim	COVE (315)
Kingsbury, Joseph	COVE (314), ENFD (19)
Kingsbury, Joseph Jur	COVE (314)
Kingsbury, Leml Capt	CANA (25, 28, 29, 64)
Kingsbury, Lemuel	CANA (10, 11, 12, 18, 77
Kingsbury, Lemuel Capt	CANA (23)
Kingsbury, Phinehas	HARL (52)
Kingsbury, Phinehas Jur	HARL (52)
Kingsbury, Willard	CANA (64, 77)
Kingsley, Olivr	LEBA (320)
Kingsman, Joseph	CANA (64)
Kingsman, Mitchel	CANA (77)
Kinkead, Andrew	FARM (19, 456)
Kinkead, Robert	FARM (456)
Kirbey, Daniel	MIDD (347, 351, 359)
Kirbey, John	MIDD (353)
Kirbey, Thomas	MIDD (354)
Kirby, Daniel	MIDD (406, 416)
Kirby, Danl	MIDD (363, 371, 382, 395)
Kirby, Ephraim	LITC (142)
Kirby, John	MIDD (356, 360, 365, 368, 369, 378, 385)
Kirby, John Capt	MIDD (366)
Kirby, Jonathan	MIDD (362, 366)
Kirby, Jos	MIDD (371, 397)
Kirby, Joseph	MIDD (363, 366, 373, 381, 394, 406)
Kirby, Seth	MIDD (363, 406, 413)
Kirby, Thomas	HARL (48), MIDD (381, 394, 406)
Kirby, Thos	MIDD (371, 413)
Kirk, Thos	FARM (455)
Kirkum, Jane	GUIL (312, 329, 333, 340

Name	Index Page
Kirtland, Gilbert	DURH (26)
Kitborn, Joseph	GLAS (114)
Kitt	FARM (24)
Knap, Benjamin	DANB (198)
Knap, Bracy	DANB (40, 45, 49, 51)
Knap, Elnathan	DANB (45)
Knap, James	FAIR (252, 255)
Knap, Joshua	DANB (40)
Knap, Justus	DANB (41)
Knap, Luke	CANA (64, 77)
Knap, Moses	CORN (87), KENT (C548, C550, C552)
Knapp, Charles	GREE (128)
Knapp, Eben	GREE (119, 123, 124, 126, 128)
Knapp, Enos	GREE (126)
Knapp, Israel Junr	GREE (119, 120, 129)
Knapp, John	GREE (125, 126, 127, 128)
Knapp, John Junr	GREE (119, 123)
Knapp, Jonah	GREE (124, 128)
Knapp, Joseph	GREE (126)
Knapp, Joshua	GREE (121, 127, 128)
Knapp, Sylvanus	GREE (119)
Knapp, Uriah	GREE (119, 125)
Kneeland, David	CHAT (54, 64), HEBR (218)
Kneeland, Edward	EWIN (12, 85, 88)
Kneeland, Edwd	EWIN (10, 11)
Kneeland, Isaac	CHAT (33, 38, 39, 52, 68
Kneeland, Joseph	EWIN (85, 88), HEBR (220, 236)
Knight, Isaac	GUIL (260)
Knight, Joseph	ENFD (24, 25, 28, 31, 32, 33, 35)
Knight, Saml	KILY (87a, 89, 91a)
Knot, Stephen	ASHF (310)
Knowels, Lucy	CHAT (35)
Knowles, Daniel	GROT ([22], [24], [25]
Knowles, James	HADD (129)
Knowles, Richard	HADD (109, 110, 112, 117, 121, 125)
Knowles, Richd	HADD (118)
Knowles, William	HADD (113)
Knowleton, Thos Majr	ASHF (212)
Knowlton, Abrm	ASHF (312)
Knowlton, Capt	ASHF (205, 206)
Knowlton, Daniel	ASHF (205, 311)
Knowlton, Elizabeth	ASHF (216)
Knowlton, Joseph	COLC (249)
Knowlton, Stephen	CHAT (41, 64)
Knowlton, Stephen Jur	CHAT (41)
Knowlton, Thomas	EHAD (44)
Knowlton, Thomas Capt	ASHF (204)
Knowlton, Thomas 2nd	EHAD (54)
Knowlton, Thos Liut	ASHF (201)
Knowlton, Willm	ASHF (200)
Knox, [ ]	ASHF (238, 239)

INDEX

Name	Index Page	Name	Index Page
Knox, Adam	ASHF (311)	Lane, Ashbil	CANA (27)
Knox, Capt	HARF (295)	Lane, Benja	KILY (33)
Knox, Jno	ASHF (311)	Lane, Benjamin	KILY (11)
Knox, John	ASHF (202)	Lane, Benjm	KILY (98)
Knox, Saml	ASHF (308, 311)	Lane, Benjn	KILY (21)
Knox, Samuel	ASHF (204)	Lane, Capt	KILH (46)
Knox, Willm	ASHF (236)	Lane, Elisha	KILH (44, 47, 50, 51, 52, 53, 54, 146)
Knox, Wm	ASHF (308, 311)		
Kollet, Jonath	GOSH (102)	Lane, Enos	HARL (43, 44, 46, 47, 51, 52, 55, 58, 59)
L[ ]s, John	CHES (9)		
Lanken, Sol Lt	HEBR (219)	Lane, Hez	KILH (55)
Lacy, Benja	FAIR (252, 261, 266)	Lane, Hez[ ]	KILH (44, 49)
Lacy, Benjamin	FAIR (269)	Lane, Hezh	KILH (52)
Lacy, Daniel	FAIR (252, 262)	Lane, James	MANS (262, 271, 278, 336)
Lacy, Daniel Capt	FAIR (254)		
Lacy, Danl	FAIR (253, 258, 259, 260, 263, 264, 266, 267)	Lane, John	KILH (44, 50, 53, 55, 146)
		Lane, Jonathan	MANS (339)
Lacy, Danl Capt	FAIR (254)	Lane, Joseph	KILH (146)
Lacy, Josiah	FAIR (253)	Lane, Noah	KILH (46, 49)
Lacy, Josiah Capt	FAIR (254)	Lane, Noah Capt	KILH (53)
Lacy, Zachariah	FAIR (253)	Lane, Noah Leut	KILH (44, 48, 49, 52, 55, 145)
Lad, Nathaniel	COVE (166)		
Ladd, Daniel	BOLT (146, 157, 180, 182)	Lane, Stephen	KILH (44)
		Lane, Stephen Capt	KILH (43, 48, 49, 50, 51, 52, 54, 146)
Ladd, David	EWIN (85, 89)		
Ladd, Elisha	EWIN (85)	Lank, Daniel	FARM (453)
Ladd, Ephraim	EWIN (13, 15, 85)	Lankton, [ ]	FARM (435)
Ladd, Ezekiel	EWIN (85, 88)	Lankton, Daniel	FARM (21, 30, 434)
Ladd, Ezekiel Jur	EWIN (85, 89)	Lankton, Daniel Capt	FARM (19)
Ladd, Nathaniel	COVE (167)	Lankton, Danl	FARM (430, 433, 438, 442, 444, 445, 446, 449, 450, 451, 452)
Ladd, Samuel	COVE (166)		
Ladd, Samuel Jur	COVE (168)		
Ladd, Thomas	EWIN (10)	Lankton, Danl Capt	FARM (449)
Ladd, Thomas Jur	EWIN (17)	Lankton, Ebenr	FARM (2)
Ladd, Thomas Lt	EWIN (85)	Lankton, Isaac	FARM (444, 456)
Ladd, Thos Jur	EWIN (13, 14)	Lankton, James	HARW (25)
Lain, [ ]	KILY (13)	Lankton, John	FARM (430, 442)
Lain, Ashbill	CANA (12)	Lankton, John Capt	FARM (9)
Lain, Elijah	FARM (443)	Lankton, John Leut	FARM (433)
Lamb, Abial	GROT [25]	Lankton, Jona	FARM (434, 438, 443, 444)
Lamb, Benjamin	COVE (172)		
Lamb, James	GROT [4], [12]	Lankton, Jonathan	FARM (2, 436)
Lamb, Joseph	GLAS (114)	Lankton, Joseph	FARM (14, 28, 433, 435, 438, 444, 449, 456)
Lamb, Saml	GLAS (114, [15])		
Lamb, Samuel	GROT [9], [18], [23]	Lankton, Levi	FARM (5, 456)
Lamb, Thos	GLAS (109)	Lankton, Seth	FARM (456)
Lambert, David	MILF (82, 85)	Lankton, Solomon	FARM (13, 28)
Lambert, Samuel	HARW (534)	Lankton, Thomas	FARM (434), HARW (13)
Lamkin, Benjamin	KENT (E63)		
Lamkins, Benj	KENT (C548)	Lanton, Joseph	FARM (449)
Lamphear, Solomon	MANS (278)	Lar[ ], Benja	KILY (34)
Lamphier, John	KENT (E60)	Larcom, J[ ]	FARM (455)
Landon, Benjamin	LITC (152, 158)	Larned, [ ]	KILY (87a)
Landon, Daniel	LITC (154)	Larned, Amos	KILY (85a)
Landon, David	GUIL (260, 271, 277)	Larned, Benj[ ]	KILY (32)
Landon, David Capt	GUIL (275)	Larned, Daniel	KILY (6, 9, 10, 16, 19, 29, 35, 96a)
Landon, Oliver	LITC (147)		
Landon, Seth	LITC (129, 131, 135, 139, 153)	Larned, Daniel Ensn	KILY (9, 13, 14)
		Larned, Daniel Isn	KILY (90)
Lane, [ ]	KILY (94a, 145)		

670

INDEX

Name	Index Page
Larned, Daniel Leut	KILY (7, 16, 17, 20, 23, 25, 26)
Larned, Danl Capt	KILY (36)
Larned, Ebenezer	KILY (85a, 89, 92, 93)
Larned, Henry	KILY (7, 31)
Larned, James	KILY (19, 32, 87a)
Larned, Jeames	KILY (92)
Larned, Jesse	KILY (86a)
Larned, Simon	KILY (31, 35, 93, 98)
Larned, Simon Capt	KILY (8, 13, 15, 18, 27, 29, 36, 91, 96)
Larned, Thaddeus	KILY (7)
Larrabe, Enoch	COVE (314)
Larrence, Elihu	KILY (94)
Larribee, Enoch	COVE (168)
Latham, Jasper Capt	GROT [4], [19], [23]
Latham, Jasper Junr	GROT [12], [19], [23], 25]
Latham, Joseph	GROT [18], [20], [21], [22], [23], [25]
Latham, Joseph Junr	GROT [12]
Lathrop, Zebn	LEBA (299)
Lathrop, Zebulon	LEBA (327)
Lavory, Thos	LEBA (341)
Law, Bendt Arnold	MILF (88)
Law, Benedict	MILF (106)
Law, David	KILY (19)
Law, William	CHES (11)
Lawrance, David	CANA (64)
Lawrance, Isaac Capt	CANA (9, 24), 25, 26, 27, 28)
Lawrance, Jonas	CANA (27, 64)
Lawrance, Jonathan	CANA (77)
Lawrance, Nathaniel	CANA (64)
Lawrance, Nathl	CANA (27)
Lawrance, Nehm Capt	CANA (28)
Lawrence, Asa	KILY (32)
Lawrence, Daniel	MILF (88)
Lawrence, Daniel Capt	MILF (100)
Lawrence, Danl Capt	MILF (96)
Lawrence, David	CANA (15, 18, 19, 77)
Lawrence, Elihu Leut	KILY (14, 19)
Lawrence, Isaac	CANA (23)
Lawrence, Isaac Capt	CANA (10, 12, 22, 23, 26, 28, 29, 64)
Lawrence, Jeremiah	CANA (64, 77)
Lawrence, John	CANA (64, 77), HARF (255, 251(2)
Lawrence, Jonas	CANA (11, 16, 20, 23, 28, 77)
Lawrence, Nathaniel	CANA (12, 20)
Lawrence, Nathl	CANA (77)
Lawrence, Nehemiah	CANA (10, 11, 12, 15, 23, 64, 77)
Lawrence, Nehemiah Capt	CANA (17, 18, 20, 26, 28)
Lawrence, Nehemiah jur	CANA (77)
Lawrence, Nehh	CANA (24)
Lawrence, Nehh Capt	CANA (25)
Lawrence, Oliver	DANB (63)
Lawrence, Solm	CANA (28)
Lawrence, William	CANA (77), HARF (253)
Leach, David	HADD (148)
Leach, Ebenezr	KILY (8)
Leach, Elisha	CANT (146, 156, 160)
Leach, Jos	CANT (144), LEBA (297)
Leach, Robert	ASHF (213, 236, 311)
Leach, Simeon	KENT (C554)
Leaming, David	FARM (438)
Leanard, Silas	KENT (E64)
Learned, [ ]	GROT [11], [17], [21], [22], [24]
Learned, Amasa	KILY (96, 98)
Learned, Daniel	KILY (96a)
Learned, Daniel Ensig	KILY (97a, 98)
Learned, Ebenezer	KILY (94a, 95)
Learned, James	KILY (96a)
Learned, Simon	KILY (98)
Learned, Simon Capt	KILY (94a, 96, 96a)
Leaven, [ ]	KILY (6)
Leaven, John	KILY (86a)
Leavens, Benja	KILY (86a)
Leavens, Benjn	KILY (4)
Leavens, Charles	KILY (91a)
Leavens, Jacob	KILY (19)
Leavens, James	MANS (262, 267, 277, 283, 336, 347, 353)
Leavens, Ro[bar]	KILY (4)
Leavins, Benjamin	KILY (87a)
Leavins, Benjn	KILY (86)
Leavins, James	MANS (333)
Leavitt, Josiah G	FAIR (253)
Leavitt, Josiah Gold	FAIR (258, 260, 262)
Leavons, James	MANS (274)
Lebaron, David	KILH (145)
Ledlie, Hugh	HARF (255A)
Ledlie, Hugh Capt	HARF (300)
Ledyard, Austin	HARF (255A)
Ledyard, Ebenezer	GROT [4], [9], [11]
Ledyard, Ebenezer Junr	GROT [25]
Ledyard, Ebenezer	GROT [3], [13], [14]
Ledyard, William	GROT [4], [6], [10], [14]
Ledyard, William Capt	GROT [1]
Ledyard, William Col	GROT [16]
Lee, [ ]	FARM (442)
Lee, Abijah	CANA (64, 77)
Lee, Amos	HARF (261a)
Lee, Asahel	KENT (C550, E59)
Lee, Col	FARM 8, 12, (440)
Lee, Daniel	CHAT (30, 34, 46, 65), KENT (E59, E63)
Lee, Ebenezr	KILY (86a)
Lee, Ebenr	CANA (64)
Lee, Elon	GUIL (270, 339)
Lee, Elon Junr	GUIL (306, 310, 312, 325, 328)
Lee, Henery	ASHF (202, 209, 213)

671

INDEX

Name	Index Page	Name	Index Page
Lee, Henry	ASHF (218, 308, 311)	Leete, Hannah	GUIL (312)
Lee, Isaac	FARM (449)	Leete, John	GUIL (270, 280, 286, 292, 327, 335)
Lee, Isaac 3d	FARM (2, 438, 442, 444, 445, 449, 453)	Leete, Mercy	GUIL (328, 329, 337, 340)
Lee, Isaac Col	FARM (5, 6, 7, 29, 33, 34, 435, 442, 444, 449, 454)	Leete, Pelatiah Junr	GUIL (304)
		Leete, Peletiah	GUIL (297, 291)
Lee, Isaac Jur	FARM (29, 442, 443, 448, 455, 456)	Leete, Peletiah Junr	GUIL (286, 294, 311)
		Leete, Rebecca	GUIL (302, 333)
Lee, Israel	LEBA (299, 341)	Leete, Reuben	GUIL (310)
Lee, Israel Jur	LEBA (310)	Leete, Solomon	GUIL (260, 273, 275, 291, 298, 303)
Lee, James	FARM (3,6, 8, 12, 17, 18, 27, 29, 434, 436, 438, 444, 445, 450, 456)	Leete, Solomon Junr	GUIL (300)
		Leete, Timothy	GUIL (272)
		Lemmon, Robert Junr	LITC (139)
Lee, James Leut	FARM (28)	Lennord, Enouch	KILY (87a)
Lee, Jared	FARM (443, 456)	Leonard, Gulever	KILY (35)
Lee, Jeames	FARM (9, 29)	Lester, Amos	GROT [9], [12], [14], [23]
Lee, John	FARM (430, 444, 445)		
Lee, Jona	FARM (436, 449, 456)	Lester, Benajah	GROT [23]
Lee, Jonathan	GUIL (304)	Lester, John	GROT ([6], [9], [12], [15], [21]
Lee, Joseph	FARM (442), GROT ([12]), GUIL (313, 318, 326, 327)	Lester, John Ensn	GROT [18]
		Lester, Nathan	GROT [9], [15], [19], [23], [25]
Lee, Josiah Capt	FARM (434)		
Lee, Nathl	GUIL (295, 300, 304)	Lester, Saml Jur	GROT [19], [25]
Lee, Oren	FARM (18)	Lester, Samuel	GROT [12]
Lee, Saml	GUIL (269, 272, 273, 278	Lester, Samuel Junr	GROT [12], [23]
Lee, Saml Junr	GUIL (269, 273, 275, 285, 322, 324, 329, 340)	Lester, Thomas	GROT [4], [6], [9], [12], [15], [19], [23]
Lee, Saml Lieut	GUIL (325, 332)	Lester, Wd	GROT [22]
Lee, Samuel	FARM (2, 7)	Lesters, Thomas	GROT [25]
Lee, Seth	FARM (2, 4, 432, 435, 442)	Levins, Benja	KILY (85a)
		Lewcas, Saml	CHAT (42)
Lee, Solo	LEBA (326)	Lewcas, Samuel	CHAT (30)
Lee, Squire	GROT ([23])	Lewcus, Samuel	CHAT (52)
Lee, Step	GOSH (185)	Lewes, Benja	FARM (28)
Lee, Step Jur	LEBA (326, 316)	Lewes, John	KILH (47, 48, 49, 51, 53, 54, 55, 146)
Lee, Stephen	EWIN (85, 88), GOSH (183), LEBA (334)		
		Lewis, Abel	FARM (456)
Lee, Stephen Jur	LEBA (315, 342)	Lewis, Abell	FARM (2, 445)
Lee, Thedon	CANA (64)	Lewis, Abraham	GOSH (185)
Lee, Thomas	FARM (5)	Lewis, Asahel	FARM (443, 449)
Lee, Timo	FARM (435, 442)	Lewis, Barnabus	CHES (A)
Lee, Timothy	FARM (433, 434, 438, 445, 449, 450)	Lewis, Danl	ASHF (202)
		Lewis, David	FARM (5, 456), KENT (A28)
Lee, Uriel	CORN (10, 89), KENT (C550)	Lewis, Ebenr	FAIR (263)
Lee, William	FARM (15, 29), MIDD (363)	Lewis, Eldad	FARM (430, 442)
		Lewis, Eleazer	DERB (113, 120, 125, 145)
Lee, Willm	FARM (3, 438, 449)		
Lee, Wm	FARM (9, 18, 434, 444, 456), MIDD (373)	Lewis, Elezer	DERB (122, 126, 168)
		Lewis, Eli	FARM (6, 9, 12, 16, 444, 447, 456)
Leech, Hezekiah	HARW (22)		
Leech, Jos	LEBA (299, 341)	Lewis, Elihu	GOSH (185, 186)
Leech, Jos Lt	LEBA (320)	Lewis, Elijah	FARM (9, 17, 28, 31)
Leech, Joseph	LEBA (342)	Lewis, Ens	GOSH (121, 183)
Leeds, Jedediah Junr	GROT ([19])	Lewis, Francis	HADD (113, 129)
Leet, Ambrose	GUIL (304)	Lewis, George	CHAT (42)
Leete, Ambrose	GUIL (286, 302, 324)	Lewis, George Jur	CHAT (43, 52)
Leete, Daniel	GUIL (290, 295, 303)	Lewis, Isaac	CANA (64)
Leete, Danl	GUIL (269)		

INDEX

Name	Index Page
Lewis, Jabez	GLAS (86)
Lewis, Jacob	CHES (9)
Lewis, Job	FARM (435, 443, 444, 449)
Lewis, John	FARM (12, 19, 443, 442)
Lewis, John Jur	FARM (24, 455)
Lewis, Jona	FARM (442)
Lewis, Jonath	FAIR (265)
Lewis, Jonathan	FAIR (258, 260, 262, 266, 269)
Lewis, Jonth	FAIR (261, 264)
Lewis, Joseph	GROT [4], [6], [12]
Lewis, Josiah	FARM (17, 442, 451, 452
Lewis, Josiah Jur	FARM (9, 433, 444, 456)
Lewis, Judah	COLC (251)
Lewis, Lemuel	FARM (436, 442)
Lewis, Moses	CHAT (59)
Lewis, Nathan	CHAT (31, 33, 37, 43, 45, 67, 68), FARM (456), MIDD (345)
Lewis, Nathl	FARM (436, 442)
Lewis, Nathn Jur	FARM (442)
Lewis, Nehe	GOSH (115, 130, 138)
Lewis, Nehe Jur	GOSH (102, 183, 184)
Lewis, Nehe Leut	GOSH (104)
Lewis, Nehemiah	GOSH (120)
Lewis, Ozias	LITC (145, 146, 147, 155, 158, 160)
Lewis, Phenihas	FARM (12)
Lewis, Phineas	FARM (442, 444)
Lewis, Re[ ]	FARM (442)
Lewis, Reuben	LITC (129)
Lewis, Riyce	FARM (9)
Lewis, Roice	FARM (9)
Lewis, Royce	FARM (2, 3, 18, 27, 29, 431, 434, 438, 442, 445, 446, 449, 450)
Lewis, Saml	FARM (436, 442), HADD (109)
Lewis, Samuel	FARM (7, 20), HADD (116)
Lewis, Sturges	FAIR (257, 262)
Lewis, Thomas	FARM (6, 7, 8, 14, 15, 16, 28, 438, 442, 446, 450), GREE (119)
Lewis, Thos	FARM (11, 23, 27, 431, 432, 433, 434, 435, 445), GOSH (112)
Lewis, Timothy	FARM (433, 443, 450)
Lewis, William	CHES (A), EWIN (89), FARM (433, 436, 438)
Lewis, Wm	EWIN (85), FARM (2, 442)
Lewiss, Nathl	KILH (145)
Leyard, Wm	GROT ([16])
Lilley, Samuel	COVE (179, 180)
Lilley, Samuel Jur	COVE (180)
Lincoln, Simon	FARM (24)
Lindley, Samuel	CORN (1)
Lindly, Samuel	CORN (17, 23, 25)
Lindsey, Felix	GLAS (92)
Lindsley, Benj[ ]	FARM (456)
Lindsley, Benja	FARM (433)
Lindsley, Felix	GLAS (86)
Lindsley, Jona	FARM (9)
Lindsley, Samuel	CORN (2, 87, 91)
Lindsly, Aaron	FARM (456)
Lindsly, Benja	FARM (444)
Lindsly, Benjn	FARM (438)
Lindsly, Ebenezer Capt	BRAN (172)
Lindsly, Jona	FARM (456)
Lines, Erastus	CHES (4, 8, 14, 16)
Lines, Rufus	CHES (A)
Linkon, Capt	MANS (354)
Linley, [ ]	DANB (69)
Linley, Leml	DANB (69)
Linley, Mattw	DANB (39, 41, 51)
Linly, Edward	LITC (131)
Linly, Leml	DANB (40)
Linn, Alexander	DURH (25)
Linsley, Abraham	BRAN (179)
Linsley, Abrahm	BRAN (164)
Linsley, Daniel	BRAN (179)
Linsley, Danl	BRAN (164, 165)
Linsley, Ebenezer Capt	BRAN (170, 173, 174)
Linsley, Ebenezer Junr	BRAN (179)
Linsley, Ebenezr Ct	BRAN (164)
Linsley, Edward	LITC (129, 143, 158)
Linsley, Israel	BRAN (164, 165)
Linsley, John Jur	BRAN (166)
Linsley, Josiah	BRAN (164, 179)
Linsley, Mattw	DANB (45)
Linsley, Rufus	BRAN (164)
Linsly, Abraham	BRAN (169)
Linsly, Daniel	BRAN (166, 170, 173, 174, 175, 176, 178)
Linsly, Ebenezer	BRAN (170)
Linsly, Ebenezer Capt	BRAN (170)
Linsly, Ebenezer Junr	BRAN (175)
Linsly, Mattw	DANB (43)
Linsly, Solomon	BRAN (169, 170)
Litchfield, Israel	CANT (150)
Little, Barzillai	BOLT (164, 165)
Little, Bezaleel	BOLT (181)
Little, Considr	LEBA (298, 299, 333)
Little, David	HARF (255A, 266, 272, 281, 285, 287)
Little, David Lieut	HARF (275)
Little, Doctor	LITC (154)
Little, Ephm Junr	COLC (247), GLAS (64)
Little, Ephraim Junr	COLC (248, 250, 251)
Little, Ephraim Jur Capt	COLC (12, 253)
Little, Epm Jur	COLC (4, 254, 256)
Little, Epm Jur Capt	COLC (5)
Little, Ezekiel Capt	KILY (85a)
Little, Ezekil Capt	KILY (89)
Little, Gaml	LEBA (315, 325)
Little, Gaml Cor	LEBA (320)
Little, John	HEBR (219)
Little, Saml Cornt	LEBA (330)

673

INDEX

Name	Index Page
Little, William	BOLT (167, 181)
Little, William Jur	BOLT (183)
Littlefield, Samuel	KENT (D10, E59)
Loas, John	DURH (17, 24, 25, 26)
Lockwood, Abraham	GREE (119, 121, 128)
Lockwood, Albert	FAIR (253)
Lockwood, Daniel	GREE (128)
Lockwood, Enos	GREE (128)
Lockwood, George	GREE (127, 128)
Lockwood, Gershm	GREE (119)
Lockwood, Gershom	GREE (121, 128)
Lockwood, Gershom 3d	GREE (119, 125)
Lockwood, Gershom Junr	GREE (121, 123, 124, 126, 127, 128)
Lockwood, Jacob	GREE (120, 121, 128)
Lockwood, Jeremiah	GREE (119)
Lockwood, John Jur	FAIR (253)
Lockwood, Jonathan 3d	GREE (121)
Lockwood, Mat	GOSH (185)
Lockwood, Philip	GREE (126)
Lockwood, Saml	GREE (125)
Lockwood, Saml Capt	GREE (127)
Lockwood, Saml junr	GREE (126, 127)
Lockwood, Samuel Capt	GREE (124)
Lockwood, Seth	GOSH (183)
Lockwood, Thaddeus	GREE (126)
Logan, Saml	GOSH (139)
Logon, Saml	GOSH (184, 130)
Lomis, Elijah	EWIN (12)
Lomis, Solomon	COLC (243)
Lomis, Abner Capt	BOLT (166)
Lomis, Abner Ens	BOLT (148)
Lomis, Amasa	EWIN (13, 17)
Lomis, Amasa Capt	EWIN (11, 12, 13, 14, 15, 16, 17, 85, 88)
Lomis, Benajah	EWIN (17, 85, 89)
Lomis, Elijah	EWIN (13, 15, 85)
Lomis, Ezekiel	EWIN (12)
Lomis, Gideon	EWIN (10, 85, 88)
Lomis, Israel	COLC (248, 251)
Lomis, Israel Cap	LEBA (315)
Lomis, Jacob	COLC (245)
Lomis, Joel	EWIN (8, 11, 12, 13)
Lomis, Joel Capt	EWIN (8, 9, 10, 11, 12, 13, 15, 17, 85, 88)
Lomis, John	COLC (242, 314), EWIN (85, 88)
Lomis, John Jur	EWIN (85)
Lomis, Jos	LEBA (296)
Lomis, Luke	EWIN (8)
Lomis, Nathaniel	EWIN (85)
Lomis, Nathl	EWIN (89)
Lomis, Roger	EWIN (8, 12), GOSH (115)
Lomis, Samuel	COLC (242, 245, 251)
Lomis, Solomon	COLC (249, 255)
Lomis, Zachariah	COVE (177)

Name	Index Page
Long, Lemuel	COVE (177, 180)
Long, Zechariah	LITC (140)
Looming, Matthas	FARM (430)
Loomis, [ ]	ASHF (233, 222), LEBA (339)
Loomis, [ ]ge	HARW (2)
Loomis, Abner	BOLT (158, 166, 180)
Loomis, Abner Capt	BOLT (164)
Loomis, Abner Lieut	BOLT (153, 154, 155, 157)
Loomis, Charles Jur	BOLT (146, 180)
Loomis, Daniel	COVE (170, 172, 177)
Loomis, Ezekiel	LEBA (341)
Loomis, Ezra	BOLT (164, 165, 168, 180, 182)
Loomis, Hezekiah	BOLT (157, 160, 165, 180)
Loomis, Isaac Capt	LEBA (311)
Loomis, Isaiah	HARW (17), LEBA (298, 310)
Loomis, Israel	LEBA (298, 299, 311, 316, 326, 341)
Loomis, Israel Cap	LEBA (327)
Loomis, Israel Jur	LEBA (318)
Loomis, Isrl	LEBA (342)
Loomis, Isrl Cap	LEBA (334)
Loomis, Isrl Jur	LEBA (320)
Loomis, Jabez	COVE (174)
Loomis, Jacob	LEBA (311, 316, 326)
Loomis, Jerijah Jur	BOLT (151, 157, 160, 180, 181, 182)
Loomis, Jno	LEBA (299)
Loomis, Joel	LEBA (298, 299, 311, 315, 321, 323, 326, 333, 341, 342)
Loomis, John	COVE (178, 180, 298, 301)
Loomis, Jos	LEBA (299, 315, 316, 326)
Loomis, Jos Lt	LEBA (320)
Loomis, Joseph	BOLT (181)
Loomis, Levi	BOLT (154, 155, 157, 180, 182)
Loomis, Liet	BOLT (160)
Loomis, Matthew Capt	BOLT (180, 182)
Loomis, Nat	ASHF (214, 226, 308)
Loomis, Nathan	LEBA (342)
Loomis, Nathaniel	ASHF (223, 232)
Loomis, Nathl	ASHF (201, 202, 209, 210, 212, 236, 310)
Loomis, Natl	ASHF (213)
Loomis, Noah Jur	HARW (12)
Loomis, Oliver	HARW (3, 12)
Loomis, Rachel	BOLT (181)
Loomis, Rachel Juner	BOLT (181)
Loomis, Roger	EWIN (17)
Loomis, Roger Juner	BOLT (181)
Loomis, Roger Leut	BOLT (181, 183)
Loomis, Thomas	BOLT (146, 160, 162, 164, 180, 182)
Loomis, Thos Cap	LEBA (333)

INDEX

Name	Index Page
Loomis, Zachariah	COVE (166, 314)
Loomis, Zacheus	LEBA (298)
Loomise, Benoni Jur	LEBA (305)
Loomise, Hezekiah	BOLT (167)
Loomise, Isaiah	LEBA (305)
Loomise, Israel	LEBA (305, 306)
Loomise, Joseph	LEBA (305)
Loomiss, Ezra	BOLT (168)
Loomiss, John	LEBA (305)
Loper, Saml	GUIL (311, 335)
Lord, Daniel	EHAD (49, 65), LITC (139, 146, 152)
Lord, Daniel 2d	EHAD (70)
Lord, Daniel jur	EHAD (78)
Lord, Elisha	COLC (10, 245, 246, 248)
Lord, Epaphras Junr	COLC (248)
Lord, Eps Jur	COLC (255, 256)
Lord, John	COLC (255)
Lord, Lynde	LITC (128, 130, 131, 133, 134, 135, 152, 153, 155, 157)
Lord, Lynde Capt	LITC (137, 155, 159, 160
Lord, Martain	KILH (42, 43)
Lord, Martain Capt	KILH (52, 55)
Lord, Martain Leut	KILH (48, 49, 51)
Lord, Martin Leut	KILH (44, 47)
Lord, Nathaniel	EHAD (79, 85)
Lord, Nehemiah	CHAT (67)
Lord, Saml [P]	EHAD (49)
Lord, Samuel [P]	EHAD (60, 65, 68)
Lord, Theodor	COLC (251)
Lord, Theodore	COLC (7, 10, 248, 254)
Lorey, Nathl	CANA (19, 24, 64)
Loroy, Nathl	CANA (77)
Lorrence, Elihu Isn	KILY (93)
Lothrop, Cyprian	LEBA (296)
Lothrop, Davd	LEBA (320, 334)
Lothrop, Dyer	COLC (251)
Lothrop, Jedediah	COLC (249, 252)
Lothrop, Thatcher	EWIN (8, 17, 85, 89)
Lothrop, Zebulon	LEBA (305, 311, 316)
Lothrup, Jedediah	COLC (254)
Lott, Moses	GLAS (79)
Lounsbury, John	FARM (9)
Lounsbury, Saml	FARM (28)
Love Land, Ashbel	DERB (120)
Lovejoy, Phinehas	ENFD (18)
Loveland, Ashbel	DERB (122, 124, 126, 140, 145, 169)
Loveland, Ashbell	DERB (113)
Loveland, Daniel	GLAS (109)
Loveland, David	GLAS (66, 70, 94, 95)
Loveland, David Jur	GLAS (70, 95)
Loveland, Elijah	MIDD (345, 346, 357)
Loveland, Eliphaz	HEBR (234, 236)
Loveland, Elisha Jur	GLAS (68, 102)
Loveland, Elizur	GLAS (74, 80, 92, 94, 112)
Loveland, Joseph	DERB (122, 126)
Loveland, Joseph Capt	DERB (131, 145, 168)
Loveland, Lazarus	GLAS (96)
Loveland, Levi	GLAS (78, 87, 92, 94, 106, 113)
Loveland, Lot	GLAS (102, 109)
Loveland, Lt	HEBR (248)
Loveland, Malachi	HEBR (218, 234, 245)
Loveland, Peletiah	GLAS (94)
Loveland, Pelitiah	GLAS (66)
Loveland, Robt	HEBR (236)
Loveland, Solomon	GLAS (74, 79, 83, 93, 98, 106, 112)
Loveland, Solon	GLAS (70)
Loveland, Thomas	GLAS (66, 70, 75, 78)
Loveland, Thomas Jur	GLAS (83, 94)
Loveland, Titus	DURH (21)
Lovland, Elephaz	HEBR (217)
Lovland, Malachi	HEBR (216, 220)
Loweridge, Abner	COLC (251)
Loweridge, David	COLC (7)
Lowree, Danl	FARM (2)
Lowree, Saml	FARM (438, 444)
Lowrey, Danl	FARM (28)
Lowrey, John	FARM (28)
Lowrey, Samuel	FARM (28)
Lucas, [ ]	GOSH (104)
Lucas, Abner	MIDD (347, 350, 359, 382, 394, 395, 406, 414, 416)
Lucas, Allyn	GOSH (119, 183, 185)
Lucas, David	CANA (28, 64)
Lucas, Moses	MIDD (382)
Lucas, Thos	GOSH (102, 110, 184)
Lucass, Abner	MIDD (371)
Lucass, David	CANA (77)
Lucass, Moses	MIDD (364, 368, 371)
Lucass, Saml	MIDD (368)
Luciss, David	CANA (19)
Lucus, David	CANA (11, 12)
Lucuss, David	CANA (16, 20, 23)
Luddington, Collens	FARM (456)
Ludington, Col	BRAN (163)
Ludington, Collens	FARM (18)
Lum, Jonathan Jnr	DERB (106, 139, 141)
Lum, Lemuel	DERB (120)
Lumm, Jonathan	DERB (106, 120)
Lumm, Jonathan Jur	DERB (120, 122, 124, 126, 132, 145)
Lumm, Joseph Capt	DERB (120, 122)
Lumm, Lemuel	DERB (122)
Lumm, Ruben	DERB (113, 131)
Lummis, John	ASHF (308, 313)
Lung, Joseph	MIDD (358, 372, 382, 395, 405, 413)
Lusk, James	FARM (5, 6, 8, 17, 27, 444)
Lusk, James Capt	FARM (9)
Lusk, John	FARM (444)
Lyman, Abel	DURH (16, 23), MIDD (388)
Lyman, Benj[ ]	LEBA (297, 298)

INDEX

Name	Index Page	Name	Index Page
Lyman, David	MIDD (345, 357, 368, 370, 371, 381, 387, 394, 395, 405, 414, 415)	Lyon, Ephra	ASHF (225)
		Lyon, Ephraim	ASHF (202, 218, 222, 225, 226, 227, 228, 238), CANT (147, 148, 159, 160), FAIR (269)
Lyman, David Lieut	MIDD (398)		
Lyman, Elihu	MIDD (376)		
Lyman, Ens	GOSH (184)	Lyon, Ephraim Capt	CANT (166, 172, 174, 179), FAIR (252)
Lyman, Jacob	BOLT (146, 148, 151, 161, 165, 180, 182), COVE (165, 167, 169, 171)		
		Lyon, Ephram	ASHF (311)
		Lyon, Ephriam	ASHF (313)
		Lyon, Ephriam Insgn	ASHF (239)
Lyman, James	BOLT (157, 165, 180)	Lyon, Gershom	FAIR (255, 258)
Lyman, Jno	LEBA (299, 300, 301, 316)	Lyon, Humphry	EHAD (48, 51, 60)
		Lyon, Humphry Lieut	EHAD (56)
Lyman, John	LEBA (298, 305, 311)	Lyon, Insgn	ASHF (229, 231, 233, 235)
Lyman, Jona	LEBA (302)		
Lyman, Jonathan	DERB (121)	Lyon, James	GREE (119)
Lyman, Jonn	DERB (122)	Lyon, John	FAIR (255, 257)
Lyman, Joseph	HARF (263, 272, 274, 292)	Lyon, Jonathan	FAIR (253)
		Lyon, Joseph	FAIR (253, 265)
Lyman, Lt	GOSH (120)	Lyon, Josiah Lieut	ASHF (219)
Lyman, Moses	GOSH (102, 104, 110, 122)	Lyon, Mathew	KENT (C551)
		Lyon, Saml	GOSH (115)
Lyman, Moses Ens	GOSH (110)	Lyon, Seth	FAIR (266)
Lyman, Moses Leut	GOSH (112, 115, 119, 12, 138)	Ma[ ], Nathan	HEBR (220)
		Ma[ ]y, Timothy	HARL (52)
Lyman, Noah	DURH (15, 23, 24)	MacCall, Jacob	COLC (246)
Lyman, Noah Russel	DERB (113)	Mack, Capt	HEBR (218)
Lyman, Noah Russell	DERB (106, 124, 145, 167)	Mack, Daniel	LITC (138)
		Mack, Hezekiah	EHAD (86)
Lyman, Richard	LEBA (334)	Mack, Jno	HEBR (218)
Lyman, Richd	LEBA (312)	Mack, John	HEBR (216, 220)
Lyman, Richd Jur	LEBA (326)	Mack, Jonathan	HARL (44)
Lyman, Saml	GLAS (114)	Mack, Josiah Capt	HEBR (216, 219)
Lyman, Samuel	GLAS (102, 108, 109), HARF (294, 299), LITC (134, 135)	Mack, Ralph	HEBR (246)
		Mack, Sarah	HARL (47)
Lyman, Sarah	GLAS (81)	Mack, Zebulon	HARL (52)
Lyman, Sarah Bartlet	GLAS (81)	Mackall, Daniel	CHAT (44)
Lyman, Thomas	DURH (12, 14, 18, 19, 20, 23), MIDD (388)	MacKall, Ebenezer	COLC (249, 251)
		Mackall, Elijah	MANS (279, 356, 357)
Lyman, Thos	DURH (10, 16, 17, 21, 24, 25, 26)	Mackall, Elijah Capt	MANS (356)
		Mackall, Elijah Ensn	MANS (336)
Lyman, Wm	LEBA (311, 316, 326)	Mackall, Elijah Lieut	MANS (348)
Lymmons, Abel	ASHF (311)	Mackaul, Jacob	COLC (4, 255)
Lynch, Noah	DURH (21)	Mackay, Jno	GREE (118)
Lynd, [ ]	GOSH (119)	Mackay, John	GREE (119, 120, 124, 126, 127, 128)
Lyon, Abel	CANT (156)		
Lyon, Caleb	EWIN (8)	Mackcall, Elijah	MANS (263, 268, 271, 272, 282, 283, 284, 328, 347)
Lyon, Caleb Junr	GREE (119, 124, 125, 127)		
Lyon, Daniel Junr	GREE (119, 121, 123, 124, 125, 128)	Mackcall, Elijah Lieut	MANS (350)
		Mackee, Robert	HARF (266)
Lyon, David	FAIR (266)	Mackee, John	HARF (253, 255A)
Lyon, Elipt	FAIR (260)	Mackee, Nathaniel	HARF (293)
Lyon, Ensn	ASHF (224)	Mackey, John	GREE (119)
Lyon, Ephm	CANT (156, 157, 165), FAIR (259, 260, 262, 265, 267)	Magill, Arthur	MIDD (364)
		Main, Caleb	KENT (E60)
		Main, John Jur	KENT (C551)
Lyon, Ephm Capt	CANT (167, 176), FAIR (254, 255)	Main, Jonathan	KENT (E60)
		Makee, Robt	HARF (273)
Lyon, Ephm Lieut	CANT (150)	Maken, Joseph	HARF (255)

INDEX

Name	Index Page
Makham, Joseph	CHAT (34)
Malbie, Noah	GOSH (183)
Mallery, Butler	KENT (A28, E59, E63)
Mallery, Moses	MILF (82, 86, 88, 92)
Mallery, Moses Junr	MILF (97, 102, 104)
Mallet, Lewis	MILF (92)
Mallet, Lewis Capt	MILF (91, 95)
Mallet, Lewis Junr	MILF (78, 97)
Mallet, Lewis Junr Capt	MILF (87, 89)
Mallison, Joseph	GROT [3]
Mallison, Samuel	GROT [4], [6], [18]
Mallit, Lewis	MILF (85)
Mallit, Lewis Junr	MILF (86)
Maltbey, Jane	GUIL (318)
Maltbey, John	GUIL (296)
Maltbie, Benjamin	BRAN (176)
Maltbie, Benjamin 3d	BRAN (173)
Maltbie, Benjamin Capt	BRAN (178)
Maltbie, Benjn Jur	BRAN (163, 164, 166)
Maltbie, Daniel Capt	BRAN (180)
Maltbie, James	BRAN (175)
Maltbie, Lt	GOSH (104)
Man of Color, Cambridge	DERB (146)
Man of Color, Kitt	FARM (24)
Man of Color, Prince	GLAS (82)
Man of Color, Sawney	GLAS (107)
Man of Color, Sharper	GROT [17], [24]
Man of Color, Sonny	GLAS (86)
Man, Abijah	HEBR (234)
Man, Abitha	BOLT (180)
Man, Ebene[ ]	KENT (D1)
Man, Ebenezer	KENT (A28, C543, D7, E63)
Man, Ebenezer Doctr	KENT (A27, C550)
Man, Ebenr Doct	KENT (C543, C544)
Man, Joel	HEBR (216)
Man, Nathan	HEBR (217)
Man, Philip	GUIL (333)
Manley, Asa	COVE (170, 174)
Mann, Ebenezer	KENT (E58)
Mann, Mathw	FARM (456)
Manning, Calvin	COVE (177, 180)
Manning, Eleazr	LEBA (315)
Manross, Elisha	FARM (5), 444, 449, 450)
Mansfield, Daniel	KILY (19)
Mansfield, David	HARW (3, 5, 6, 7, 16)
Mansfield, Nathan	DERB (120, 122)
Mansfield, William	DERB (138)
Marble, Benjamin	CORN (13)
Marchant, Job	MILF (82, 85, 88, 92, 98, 103, 105)
Marcy, Benjn	ASHF (237, 240)
Marcy, Capt	ASHF (224, 226, 228, 229, 231, 232, 238)
Marcy, Leut	ASHF (202, 206)
Marcy, Mathew	ASHF (239)
Marcy, Reuben	ASHF (206, 310)

Name	Index Page
Marcy, Reuben Capt	ASHF (213, 222, 223, 225, 226, 236)
Marcy, Reuben Leut	ASHF (202)
Marcy, Reun Capt	ASHF (308)
Marcy, Ruben Capt	ASHF (239)
Marcy, Rubin Capt	ASHF (232)
Marcy, Zebadiah	ASHF (312)
Mark, Zebulon	HARL (55)
Markas, David	FARM (28)
Markham, [ ]	MIDD (363)
Markham, Barzillah	ENFD (26)
Markham, Darias	ENFD (28, 32)
Markham, Ebenezer	MIDD (421)
Markham, Ebenr	MIDD (362, 376)
Markham, Gustus	ENFD (32)
Markham, James	HARL (50, 51)
Markham, Jeams	HARL (55)
Markham, Jehial	ENFD (18)
Markham, Jehiel	ENFD (30, 32, 33)
Markham, Jeremiah	MIDD (365)
Markham, John	CHAT (44, 61)
Markham, John Jur	CHAT (65, 67)
Markham, Joseph	ENFD (28, 30)
Markham, Justus	ENFD (19, 24, 30, 32)
Markham, Nathan	ENFD (32)
Markham, Nathaniel	CHAT (41)
Markham, Nathl	CHAT (44, 58, 69)
Markham, Saml	MIDD (377, 395, 406, 416)
Markham, Samuel	MIDD (363)
Marks, Comfort	MIDD (358)
Marks, Comft	MIDD (372)
Marks, Miles	FARM (456)
Marks, Wm	MIDD (376)
Marriner, Asa	COLC (246)
Marsh, Daniel Capt	HARF (275, 289)
Marsh, Daniel Junr	HARF (282)
Marsh, Ebenezer	LITC (138, 158)
Marsh, Edmund	EHAD (59)
Marsh, Elijah	LITC (129)
Marsh, Hannah	KILY (12)
Marsh, James	CANA (12), HARF (285)
Marsh, John	CANA (64), LITC (128, 138, 152, 153)
Marsh, John 2nd	LITC (134, 146)
Marsh, John 3rd	LITC (138)
Marsh, John Capt	LITC (130, 133, 140)
Marsh, John Junr	LITC (135)
Marsh, Jonas	CANA (64, 77)
Marsh, Jonath Revd	GOSH (123)
Marsh, Lemuel	EHAD (64)
Marsh, Moses	CANA (17, 20, 64, 77)
Marsh, Nathaniel	CANA (28)
Marsh, Nathl	CANA (64)
Marsh, Nehemiah	CANA (64, 77)
Marsh, Pela	LEBA (294)
Marsh, Pelatiah	LEBA (297, 298)
Marsh, Roger	LITC (158)
Marsh, Rufus	CANA (17)
Marsh, Samuel	EHAD (44)

INDEX

Name	Index Page	Name	Index Page
Marsh, Solomon Capt	LITC (140, 159, 160)	Mason, Jerh	LEBA (302)
Marsh, Widow	KILY (35, 98)	Mason, John	ASHF (204, 206), KILY (6, 7, 8, 10, 18, 19, 32, 87, 88, 91, 94, 95, 96, 97, 86a, 91a, 92a, 96a, 97a, 98)
Marsh, William Junr	LITC (129, 139, 141, 147, 153, 158)		
Marshal, Jeremiah	COLC (10, 249, 255)		
Marshal, Jonathan	MILF (98)		
Marshall, Andrew	GREE (126, 127, 128)	Mason, John Capt	KILY (35)
Marshall, Eliakim	FARM (456)	Mason, Jonathan	LITC (128, 129, 130)
Marshall, Ezra	GREE (124, 126, 128)	Mason, Joshua	LITC (139)
Marshall, Ichabod	BOLT (151, 155, 157, 163, 164, 166, 180, 182)	Mason, Pelatiah	KILY (32)
		Mason, Pelitiah	KILY (7)
Marshall, Isaac E	MILF (88, 98)	Mason, Pellatiah	KILY (19)
Marshall, Isaac Eliot	MILF (92, 98)	Materson, Thomas Jur	GLAS (83)
Marshall, Jonathan	MILF (82, 85, 88, 92, 97, 102, 104, 105)	Mather, Augustus Doct	EHAD (65)
		Mather, Benjamin	COLC (13)
Marshall, Jonathn	MILF (103)	Mather, Charles Doctr	EWIN (85, 88)
Marshall, Joseph	MILF (88)	Mather, David	FARM (5, 7, 8, 15, 435, 436, 442, 446, 453, 454)
Marshall, Oliver	FARM (5)		
Marshall, Seth	FARM (5)	Mathew, Caleb [ ]	FARM (28)
Marshall, Simeon	FARM (5)	Mathew, Nath[ ]	FARM (17)
Marshall, Thomas	EHAD (49)	Mathews, Asahell	FARM (455)
Marshel, Ichabod	BOLT (167)	Mathews, Caleb	FARM (455)
Marshell, Eliakim	FARM (28)	Mathews, Caleb Jur	FARM (455)
Marshell, Isaac Elott	DERB (168)	Mathews, Jesse	FARM (456)
Marshell, Seth	FARM (28)	Mathews, John	HARW (533)
Martain, Manaseth	KENT (E60, E63)	Mathews, Moses	FARM (456)
Marther, Cotton	HARW (17, 25)	Mathews, Nathl	FARM (9)
Marther, David	FARM (434)	Matson, Amos	GLAS (93, 94)
Martin, David	CHAT (33)	Matson, Joseph	GLAS (92)
Martin, Ebenezr	MANS (281)	Matson, Thomas	GLAS (95)
Martin, Ebenr	MANS (279)	Matson, Thomas Junr	GLAS (67)
Martin, Enos	COLE (113)	Matterson, Amos	GLAS (84)
Martin, John	MANS (277)	Matterson, Thomas	GLAS (84)
Martin, Robert	CHES (6, 7, 8, 16), MANS (280, 353,	Matthews, John	HARW (3)
Martin, Robert Capt	CHES (5, 13)	Mattocks, Samuel	HARF (255A)
Martin, Robt	MANS (281)	Mattox, Samuel Capt	HARF (275)
Marton, [ ]	KILY (6)	May, Edward	CORN (87, 91)
Marven, [ ]	HEBR (236)	Mayo, Elisha	GOSH (130, 138)
Marven, Elihu	HEBR (217, 218, 219, 220, 231, 234, 246)	Mayo, Elisha Jur	GOSH (185)
		Mayo, Jonath	GOSH (183, 184)
		Mayo, Richard	CHAT (31, 37, 40, 42, 46
Marven, Elihue	HEBR (217)	Mc Lane, Allixander	BOLT (155, 167)
Marvin, Elihu	COLC (245), HEBR (218)	Mc Lane, Elaxander	BOLT (148)
		McCall, Archippus	LEBA (306)
Marvin, Nehemiah Junr	CORN (88)	McCall, Daniel	CHAT (64)
		McCall, Ebenezer	COLC (245)
Marvin, Reynold	LITC (138)	McCall, Ephm	LEBA (341)
Mash, Hannah	KILY (12)	McCall, Hobart	LEBA (342)
Mason, Daniel	KENT (E60)	McCall, Hubbard	LEBA (341)
Mason, Eben Junr	ASHF (226)	McCartee, John	CANT (178)
Mason, Ebenezer	ASHF (237)	McClean, James	GLAS (110)
Mason, Ebenezer Junr	ASHF (218, 234)	Mccough, Timo	MIDD (398)
Mason, Ebenr	ASHF (310)	McCray, William	EWIN (85, 89)
Mason, Ebenr Jur	ASHF (202, 213, 222, 225, 231, 232, 311)	McDowel, Allexr	GLAS (64)
		McKall, Archips	LEBA (311)
Mason, Ebnr Jur	ASHF (236)	McKall, Ebenezer	COLC (243, 248)
Mason, Jed[ ] Col	LEBA (316)	McKall, Hubbard	LEBA (297)
Mason, Jer Cap	LEBA (296)	Mckee, Andrew	HARF (287)
Mason, Jer Col	LEBA (325, 338, 339, 318, 320)	Mckee, Nathaniel	HARF (281, 288)
		Mckee, Robert	HARF (253)

INDEX

Name	Index Page
Mckey, Phinehas	MIDD (363)
McKinney, Alexr Capt	EWIN (14)
McKinney, Andrew	EWIN (8, 9, 10, 15, 17, 85, 88)
McKinney, James 3d	EWIN (11)
McKinney, James Jur	EWIN (8, 11, 12)
McKinney, William	EWIN (9)
McKinney, Wm	EWIN (8, 10, 13, 17)
McKinstry, Ezekiel	EWIN (8, 10, 12)
McKinstry, Paul	EWIN (8)
Mckye, John	MIDD (373)
Mckye, Phinehas	MIDD (374)
McLane, Alexand	BOLT (180)
McLane, Allixander	BOLT (182)
McLane, James	GLAS (106)
McLean, John	DANB (40, 43, 49, 65)
McLean, Neel	HARF (291)
McNeal, Archibald	MILF (85, 88)
McNeile, Alexr	LITC (158)
McNeile, Archibald	LITC (128)
McNeile, Archibald Capt	LITC (130)
McNeile, Archibald Junr	LITC (129, 130, 131, 135, 146, 152)
McNeile, Archibald Junr Capt	LITC (139, 141, 143, 154
McNeile, Isaac	LITC (134, 141, 152)
McNeile, Samuel	LITC (158)
McNiele, Archibald Junr	LITC (133)
Me[ ]ton, John	ENFD (29)
Meach, Amos	CANT (176)
Meacham, Abner	ENFD (35)
Meacham, David	ENFD (18, 24, 26, 28, 29, 33)
Meacham, Isaac	HARL (44, 52, 61)
Meacham, J[ ]	HARW (2)
Meacham, Jeremiah	HARW (22)
Meacham, Joel	HARL (43, 44, 46, 50, 51, 56, 61)
Meacham, Joel Leut	HARL (61)
Meacham, Samuel	HARW (5, 7)
Meacham, Seth	HARW (3)
Meacham, Zeba	HARW (2)
Meachan, Joel	HARL (50, 52)
Mead, Abraham	GREE (125)
Mead, Abraham Capt	GREE (124)
Mead, Abrm	GREE (119)
Mead, Amos	GREE (118, 120)
Mead, Amos Docr	GREE (121, 119)
Mead, Andrew	GREE (126)
Mead, Benjamin	GREE (120)
Mead, Benjamin Junr	GREE (119, 120, 121, 124, 126, 127, 129)
Mead, Caleb Junr	GREE (121)
Mead, Col	GREE (126)
Mead, David	GREE (124, 128)
Mead, Ebenezer	GREE (124)
Mead, Edmond	GREE (121)
Mead, Edmund	GREE (123, 125, 126, 127)
Mead, Eli	GREE (125)
Mead, Elijah	GREE (119)
Mead, Eliphalet junr	GREE (124, 126, 128)
Mead, Elkanah	GREE (126, 128)
Mead, Jared	GREE (125, 126, 127)
Mead, Jehial	GREE (124, 127, 128)
Mead, Jehiel	GREE (119)
Mead, Jered	GREE (123, 124, 125)
Mead, Jeremiah	GREE (128)
Mead, Jeremiah junr	GREE (128)
Mead, John	GREE (119, 123, 124)
Mead, John 3d	GREE (126)
Mead, John Brigadier Genl	GREE (129)
Mead, John Col	GREE (119, 120, 121, 123, 124, 126)
Mead, John General	GREE (127)
Mead, John Genl	GREE (128)
Mead, Mathew	GREE (119)
Mead, Matthew	GREE (125, 126, 128, 121)
Mead, Matthew Capt	GREE (121, 127)
Mead, Nathaniel 3d	GREE (121)
Mead, Nathaniel Junr	GREE (121, 123, 124)
Mead, Nathl	GREE (127, 128)
Mead, Nathl 3d	GREE (126)
Mead, Nathl 4th	GREE (124)
Mead, Nathl junr	GREE (127, 120, 126, 128)
Mead, Nehemiah	GREE (118, 119, 120, 121, 123, 125, 126, 128)
Mead, Nehemiah junr	GREE (127)
Mead, Peter	GREE (119, 120, 124, 128)
Mead, Peter junr	GREE (124, 126, 127)
Mead, Silas Junr	GREE (121, 127)
Mead, Silvanus	GREE (125)
Mead, Silvanus Capt	GREE (125)
Mead, Stephen junr	GREE (125)
Mead, Thaddeus	GREE (121, 123, 126)
Mead, Titus	GREE (118, 123, 124, 126, 127, 128)
Mead, Zacheus	GREE (127)
Meaham, Nehemiah	HARW (3)
Meakens, Joseph	HARF 251(2)
Meaker, Daniel	FAIR (253)
Meaker, Danl	FAIR (254), 258, 266)
Meaker, Danl 2d	FAIR (267)
Meaker, Seth	FAIR (266)
Meakins, Joseph	HARF (253, 256, 258, 263)
Meakins, Joseph Junr	HARF (253)
Mecham, Isaac	HARL (61)
Mecham, Isack	HARL (58)
Mecham, Joel	HARL (59, 61)
Medcalf, Elijah	EHAD (55, 64, 65, 66, 70, 80, 87)

INDEX

Name	Index Page	Name	Index Page
Medcalf, John	GOSH (111, 120, 130, 131, 184)	Merrils, Benj[ ]	KILH (54)
		Merriman, Chauncy	FARM (444)
Meecham, Isaac	HARL (47, 55)	Merriman, Eber	FARM (446, 449)
Meecham, Joel	HARL (47, 58, 59)	Merriman, George	HARW (17)
Meeker, Josiah	HARL (45, 48)	Merriman, Israel	HARW (8, 10, 11, 17)
Meghels, Eleazer	KILY (91)	Merrit, Daniel	GREE (121, 124, 126, 128)
Meghill, Eleaz	KILY (86a)		
Meigs, Benjn Stone	GUIL (304)	Merrit, Nathan	GREE (119)
Meigs, Daniel	GUIL (295, 335)	Merrit, Reuben	GREE (123)
Meigs, Elias	GUIL (303, 304, 333, 335)	Merrit, Thomas	CANT (160)
		Merrman, George	HARW (12)
Meigs, Elihu	GUIL (272, 274, 297, 300, 325, 337, 338)	Merry, Benjamin	KENT (C551)
		Merry, Cornelius	HARL (46, 48, 50, 51)
Meigs, Giles	MIDD (350, 362, 366, 371, 381, 382, 395, 397, 405)	Merry, Cornelius	HARL (45)
		Merry, Ebenezer	KENT (C554)
		Merry, John	KENT (C554)
Meigs, Giles Capt	MIDD (404, 414)	Merry, Malichi	KENT (E59, E63)
Meigs, Jehiel Lieut	GUIL (269, 270)	Mertimer, P	MIDD (416)
Meigs, Jno Lt	MIDD (401)	Mertimer, Phillip	MIDD (417)
Meigs, John Lt	MIDD (413)	Mervin, Merlain	CANA (64)
Meigs, Phins	DURH (26)	Merwin, Danl	DURH (11)
Meigs, R Colo	MIDD (414)	Merwin, David	MILF (85)
Meigs, Retn J Colo	MIDD (382)	Merwin, Fowler	GOSH (109, 112, 115)
Meigs, Return	MIDD (345, 367)	Merwin, James	HADD (113, 148)
Meigs, Return Jona	MIDD (376)	Merwin, Jno	MILF (88)
Meigs, Return Jona Colo	MIDD (377, 405)	Merwin, Miles	MILF (103)
		Messenger, Nathl	FARM (434)
Meigs, Return Lieut	MIDD (346, 349)	Metcalf, [ ]	LEBA (339, 340)
Meigs, Timo	GUIL (326, 332, 333, 335	Metcalf, Andrew	LEBA (299, 321)
Meigs, Timothy	GUIL (274, 289, 298)	Metcalf, Andrew Dr	LEBA (304)
Meklewain, Timothy	EWIN (8)	Metcalf, Andw	LEBA (297, 328, 333, 341)
Meloy, Edward	BRAN (175)		
Meriam, Benjm Capt	KILY (97a)	Metcalf, Davd	LEBA (334)
Meriam, Benjn Capt	KILY (94)	Metcalf, Elijah	EHAD (45)
Meriam, Ebenr	FARM (443)	Metcalf, Elipt	LEBA (316)
Merian, Benjn	KILY (86a, 95)	Metcalf, Zebulon	LEBA (318)
Meroam, Benjn	KILY (89)	Metcalfe, Andrew	LEBA (305, 310)
Merrel, Benjn	KILH (53)	Metcalfe, Andw	LEBA (315, 326)
Merrell, Ebenr	CANA (77)	Metcalfe, Eliphalet	LEBA (305)
Merrell, Saml	HARF (252(2))	Metcalfe, Elipt	LEBA (298, 299, 311)
Merrells, Abraham Junr	HARF (255A)	Metcalfe, Jabez	LEBA (306, 311, 316)
		Metcalfe, Lebs	LEBA (299)
Merrells, Benj	KILH (146)	Metcalfe, Levi	LEBA (311)
Merrells, Gideon	HARF (255A)	Metcalfe, Reuben	LEBA (299)
Merrels, Charles	HARF (287)	Michel, Abner	MIDD (419)
Merrels, Daniel	KILH (145, 146)	Michel, Azariah	COLC (247)
Merrels, Gideon	HARF 253, 252(2)	Middlebrook, Oliver	FAIR (258, 267)
Merrels, Saml	HARF (285)	Middlebrook, Silvenus	FAIR (253, 262)
Merrels, Samuel	HARF (255, 281)	Middlebrook, Silvs	FAIR (255, 257, 258)
Merrels, Simeon	HARF (272)	Miegs, Colo	MIDD (415)
Merrett, Mickel	KILH (146)	Miegs, Daniel	GUIL (274, 324)
Merriam, Munson	CHES (12)	Miegs, Return Jona	MIDD (377)
Merriam, William	HARW (25)	Mighells, Eleazer	KILY (7, 94)
Merriam, Wm	HARW (22)	Mighells, John	CHAT (30, 31, 34)
Merrill, James	FARM (456)	Mighels, Eleazer	KILY (92, 97)
Merrill, Moses	FARM (1, 13)	Mighlls, Eleazer	KILY (94a)
Merrills, Elisha	CANA (64)	Miles Stephen	CORN (87)
Merrills, James	FARM (449)	Miles, [ ]	DERB (133)
Merrills, Moses Jur	FARM (433)	Miles, Caleb	GOSH (127)
Merrills, Timothy	FARM (438, 444)	Miles, Charls	GOSH (104, 110, 183)

680

INDEX

Name	Index Page
Miles, Daniel	GOSH (113, 129, 130)
Miles, Daniel Junr	GLAS (83)
Miles, Danl	GOSH (102, 104, 109, 110, 111, 112, 117, 121, 123, 125, 126, 127, 128, 131, 133, 134, 137, 138, 139, 184)
Miles, Danl Ens	GOSH (133, 134)
Miles, Danl Lt	GOSH (112)
Miles, David	MILF (104)
Miles, Eleazer	KILY (35)
Miles, Ens	GOSH (138)
Miles, Isaac	GOSH (185, 186), MILF (80, 81, 82, 84, 91, 92, 94, 105, 106)
Miles, Isaac Capt	MILF (78, 84, 85, 87)
Miles, Isaac Ct	MILF (81)
Miles, John	CHES (14), MILF (88)
Miles, Jonan	DERB (134)
Miles, Lewis	KENT (C546, C547)
Miles, Saml	GOSH (119, 128, 131)
Miles, Stephen	CORN (91)
Miles, Theophiles	DERB (167)
Miles, Theophilus	MILF (103)
Miles, Theous	DERB (134)
Millard, David	ASHF (231)
Millard, Isaac	HARL (59)
Millard, John	CORN (86)
Millard, John Ensign	CORN (11)
Millard, John Jur	CORN (10, 13, 16, 20, 23, 25, 86)
Millard, Nathan	CORN (1, 13, 18, 23, 25, 86)
Miller, David Capt	MIDD (405)
Miller, [ ]	MIDD (376, 387)
Miller, Abijah	GLAS (93)
Miller, Amos	MIDD (346, 350)
Miller, Andrew	GREE (121)
Miller, Asher	MIDD (376, 410, 418)
Miller, Benjamin	CANA (11, 18, 24)
Miller, Benjn	CANA (64, 77)
Miller, Brainard	MIDD (344)
Miller, D Capt	MIDD (415)
Miller, Da[ ] Capt	MIDD (358)
Miller, Daniel	CHAT (65), MIDD (347, 350)
Miller, David	COLC (8, 242, 243, 245), MIDD (368)
Miller, David B	MIDD (371, 374, 381)
Miller, David Brainerd	MIDD (368)
Miller, David Capt	COLC (247), MIDD (346, 349, 354, 357, 358, 360, 361, 402, 413)
Miller, David Ct	MIDD (370)
Miller, Elisha	FARM (6, 8, 9, 433, 441, 442, 450, 452, 454), MIDD (364, 366, 373, 382, 406, 416)
Miller, Elizur	GLAS (83, 89)
Miller, Giles	MIDD (346, 349, 356, 358, 360, 367, 388, 414)
Miller, Giles Capt	MIDD (372, 387, 391)
Miller, Hosea	MIDD (364)
Miller, Ichabod Jur	MIDD (358, 359, 362, 366, 394)
Miller, Ichd Junr	MIDD (406, 414)
Miller, Ichd Lt	MIDD (372)
Miller, Isaac	GLAS (65), HARL (62), MIDD (368, 379, 380, 382, 387, 388, 390, 391, 392, 393, 396, 400, 402, 403, 404, 406, 407, 411, 412, 413, 415, 416, 417)
Miller, Isaac Capt	MIDD (342, 345, 346, 349, 350, 351, 355, 356, 359, 361, 369, 371, 372, 374)
Miller, Jacob	MIDD (413)
Miller, Job	FARM (9, 31, 433, 438, 444)
Miller, John	GLAS (87, 94, 106)
Miller, Jona	FARM (444)
Miller, Jona Jur	FARM (9, 449)
Miller, Jonathan	MIDD (376, 378)
Miller, Jos[ ]	FARM (430)
Miller, Joshua	MIDD (364, 365)
Miller, Marthew	GLAS (93)
Miller, Mathew	GLAS (70)
Miller, Matthew	GLAS (81, 113)
Miller, Nathaniel	MIDD (350, 365)
Miller, Nathl [ ]	MIDD (364)
Miller, Reuben	FARM (3, 9, 18, 29, 438, 444, 445, 449, 456)
Miller, Richard	MIDD (362)
Miller, Richd	MIDD (370)
Miller, Ruben	FARM (434)
Miller, Saml	HARL (58)
Miller, Saml Junr	HARL (46, 50, 57)
Miller, Samuel	HARL (45, 47, E60)
Miller, Samuel jur	HARL (45, 47, 51)
Miller, Seth	MIDD (390, 413)
Miller, Squier	KILY (7)
Miller, Squire	KILY (19)
Miller, Stephen	MIDD (372)
Miller, Stephen Jur	MIDD (344, 350, 363, 382)
Miller, William	GLAS (93), MIDD (376, 377)
Miller, William Jur	MIDD (345)
Miller, William Lieut	GLAS (102)
Miller, Wm Junr	MIDD (368, 382)
Miller, Wm Liut	GLAS (83)
Milles, Revd	COLE (7)
Milling, Charles	MIDD (376)
Millington, Samuel	MANS (336, 347, 358)
Millor, Thomas	COLC (245)
Mills, David	HARF (250)
Mills, George	KENT (C551)
Mills, Joseph	FAIR (256)
Mills, Leut	COLE (1)

INDEX

Name	Index Page	Name	Index Page
Mills, Lewis	KENT (A28, B1, C543, C555, D1, E58, E62)	Moore, Eli	EWIN (15)
		Moore, Jos	CANT (182)
Mills, Nathal Jur	KILY (97)	Morce, Asa	CORN (88)
Mills, Nathaniel	KILY (94)	Mordoc, Anw Capt	CANT (150)
Mills, Nathaniel Jur	KILY (87a)	Mordock, Andrew Capt	CANT (154)
Mills, Nathl Jur	KILY (31, 86a)		
Mills, Peletiah	COLE (1, 115)	Mordock, Andw Capt	CANT (150)
Mills, Peter	KENT (A27, A28, C552)	More, Roswell	FARM (20, 449)
Mills, Peter Capt	KENT (B3, C543, C545, E58, E62)	Morehouse, Abijah	FAIR (258, 259)
		Morehouse, David	FAIR (257, 258, 263)
Mills, Rebecca	LEBA (327)	Morehouse, Eben	FAIR (252)
Mills, Saml	COLE (10)	Morehouse, Ebenr	FAIR (253, 255, 258, 259, 260, 262, 266)
Mills, Samuel	COLE (1, 2, 4, 5, 7, 8), 9, 11, 14, 113, 115)	Morehouse, John Jur	FAIR (261)
Mills, Samuel Revd	HARW (2)	Morehouse, Seth	FAIR (252, 256, 259, 262, 264, 266, 267)
Miner, Anderson	BOLT (157, 165)		
Miner, Andrew	HARW (23)	Morehouse, Silvenus	FAIR (258, 263, 267)
Miner, Isaac	HARW (6, 7, 10, 14)	Morehouse, Thadus	DANB (51)
Miner, Joel	HARL (43, 44, 46, 48, 50, 51, 55, 56, 58, 59, 61)	Morgain, Amos	CHAT (40, 41, 50)
		Morgan, [ ]	KILH (55)
Miner, Thos	MIDD (367)	Morgan, Amos	CHAT (69)
Miner, Uriah Hide	HARL (43)	Morgan, Benjamin	COLC (248)
Minor, Absalom	GUIL (311)	Morgan, Chrisr	GROT [4], [12], [13], [12], [18]
Minor, Anderson	BOLT (161, 181, 182)		
Minor, Andrus	BOLT (155)	Morgan, Christopher	GROT [9], [15], [23]
Minor, Isaac	HARW (5)	Morgan, David	KENT (E64)
Minor, Joel	HARL (52)	Morgan, Ezrael	GROT ([25])
Minor, Wm	FARM (435)	Morgan, Isaac	GROT ([12])
Mitchel, Abner	MIDD (345, 362)	Morgan, Israel	GROT ([15], [23])
Mitchel, Azariah	COLC (249)	Morgan, James	GROT ([6])
Mitchel, Jonathan	MIDD (374)	Morgan, John	ASHF (308), CANA (64),GROT ([7], [9], [15], [16], [19], [25])
Mitchels, Micall	FARM (434)		
Mix, Theoph	GOSH (130)		
Mix, Theophilus	GOSH (115, 183, 184)	Morgan, John 2d	GROT [6], [23]
Mix, Timothy	FARM (17)	Morgan, John Capt	GROT [7], [11], [13], [14], [18], [21]
Mixer, John Jur	FARM (433)		
Mnning, Calvin	COVE (176)	Morgan, Jonn	COLC (4, 255)
Mobs, Pierce	EHAD (85)	Morgan, Joseph Capt	GROT [9], [10], [11], [19]
Moffat, Eleazer	KILY (92)		
Moffatt, Lemuel	DURH (19)	Morgan, Joshua	COLC (12), MANS (280, 281, 336, 347)
Moffet, Eleazer	KILY (92)		
Moffit, Eleazer	KILY (98)	Morgan, Nathan	GROT [12], [14], [22], [23], [24]
Moffit, Thos	KILY (92a)		
Moffitt, Eleazar	KILY (98)	Morgan, Saml	COLC (254)
Moffitt, Eleazer	KILY (7, 10, 20, 32, 34, 94a)	Morgan, Samuel	KENT (E64)
		Morgan, Shapley	GROT [4], [9], [12], [18], [19], [23], [25]
Moffitt, Eleazr	KILY (31)		
Moffitt, Elezer	KILY (26)	Morgan, Stephen	FAIR (267)
Moffitt, Lemuel	DURH (14)	Morgan, Theop[ ]	KILH (55, 145)
Moffitt, Thoms	KILY (88)	Morgan, Theop[ ] 2d	KILH (145)
Moffitt, Thos	KILY (86)	Morgan, Theophiles	KILH (146)
Monro, John	BRAN (173, 178)	Morgan, Thomas	GROT ([6])
Monro, William	BRAN (179)	Morgan, William	GROT [3], [4], [6], [14], [23], [25]
Monross, Elisha	FARM (442)		
Moody, Thomas	HARW (3)	Morgan, William A	GROT [23]
Moor, Eli	EWIN (8, 89)	Morgan, William Avery	GROT [13], [14]
Moor, Eli Lt	EWIN (16, 17)		
Moor, Roswell	FARM (456)	Morgan, William Capt	KILH (51)
Moor, Wareham	EWIN (11, 13, 15, 85, 88)	Morgan, William N	GROT [18]
Moor, Warham	EWIN (8, 10)	Morgan, Willm	KILH (50)
		Morgan, Willm Capt	KILH (55)

682

INDEX

Name	Index Page	Name	Index Page
Morgan, Youngs	GROT ([6], [19])	Moss, Amos	LITC (129, 131, 153, 159
Morgen, Willm Capt	KILH (50, 145)	Moss, Elihu	FARM (433)
Morin, Abel	HARL (52)	Moss, Isaac Bowers	CHES (A)
Morley, Demick	GLAS (95)	Moss, Jesse	CHES (11, 12)
Morley, Dimock	GLAS (96)	Moss, John	LITC (160)
Morley, Timothy	GLAS (93, 95), HARL (55)	Moss, Joseph	DERB (121)
Morrells, Elisha	CANA (77)	Moss, Levi	LITC (129, 131, 134, 135, 139, 141, 146, 152, 154)
Morris, [ ]	DURH ()	Moss, Moses	FARM (456)
Morris, James	LITC (128, 133, 139)	Moss, Nathaniel	CHES (12)
Morris, James Junr	LITC (158, 159)	Moss, Sollomon	GOSH (185)
Morris, Josiah	GROT ([15])	Moss, Solomon	GOSH (114, 185)
Morris, Newton J[ ]	MILF (106)	Moss, Theophilous	CHES (4)
Morris, Newton John	MILF (104)	Moss, Theophilus	CHES (9, 11)
Morris, Saml Jur	KENT (D7)	Moss, Thomas	CHES (9, 11)
Morrish, John	FARM (456)	Moss, Titus	CHES (4, 11, 14)
Morrison, John	ENFD (24, 30, 32)	Mott, Col	GROT ([8])
Morriss, Thomas	FARM (13)	Mott, Martha	KILY (35)
Mors, Nathan	ASHF (312)	Mott, Nathaniel	CHAT (34)
Morse, Anthony	CANT (155, 182)	Mott, Nathl	CHAT (31, 65, 68)
Morse, Benja	CANT (160)	Mott, Saml	KENT (E59)
Morse, Ely	ASHF (313)	Mott, Samuel	KENT (E63)
Mortimer, Capt	MIDD (357)	Moulton, Asa	MANS (338)
Mortimer, P	MIDD (344, 406, 414, 406)	Moyland, Colo	MIDD (402)
Mortimer, Philip	MIDD (367, 371, 381, 394)	Mulford, Barnabas	BRAN (162, 178, 179)
		Mulford, Barnaby	BRAN (180)
		Mulford, Edw	BRAN (163, 165, 166)
Mortimer, Phillip Capt	MIDD (342, 345, 346, 349, 354)	Mulford, Edw Lt	BRAN (166)
		Mulford, Edward	BRAN (164, 170, 173, 174, 175, 178, 179)
Morton, John	EWIN (15)		
Moseley, Isaac	GLAS (60, 71, 95, 109)	Mulford, Edward Ensign	BRAN (170)
Moseley, Isaac Doct	GLAS (83, 84, 85, 102, 104, 109)	Mumford, [ ]	GROT [20]
Moseley, Joseph	GLAS (68, 69, 70, 75, 84, 100, 103, 105, 108)	Mumford, Capt	EHAD (48)
		Mumford, Thomas	GROT [1], [3], [4], [6], [9], [10], [11], [12], [17], [19], [21]
Moseley, Joseph Capt	GLAS (82, 83, 108, 112, 114)		
Moseley, Nathl	MANS (284, 341)	Mumford, Thos	GROT [5], [7], [13]
Moseley, Thos	GLAS (107)	Mun, Isaiah	COLC (8)
Moseley, William	GLAS (75, 93)	Mungar, Caleb	GUIL (260, 270, 275)
Moseley, Wm	GLAS (113)	Mungar, Timothy	GUIL (270)
Moseley, William	GLAS (108)	Munger, Caleb	GUIL (277, 280, 285, 287, 288, 289, 294, 299, 300, 309, 310, 313, 324, 326, 336)
Mosely, Increase	DANB (39)		
Mosely, Isaac	GLAS (94, 101)		
Mosely, Joseph	GLAS (78, 79, 80, 81, 93), MANS (353)	Munger, Ebenr	GUIL (294, 301)
Mosely, Nathaniel	MANS (281)	Munger, Elias	GUIL (302, 318, 319, 325)
Mosely, Nathl	MANS (336)		
Moses, Abel	HARL (44, 47)	Munger, James	GUIL (343)
Moses, Abel Jur	HARL (47, 52)	Munger, James Capt	GUIL (336, 339)
Moses, Othniel	FARM (2, 444, 455)	Munger, James Junr	GUIL (277, 287, 294, 300, 310)
Moses, Thomas	MILF (82)		
Moses, Timo Jur	CANA (28)	Munger, James Liut	GUIL (299)
Moses, Timothy	CANA (9, 15, 23)	Munger, Jesse	GUIL (335)
Moses, Timothy Capt	CANA (11, 12, 15, 17, 19, 20, 26, 27, 77)	Munger, Miles	GUIL (269, 274, 280, 286, 293, 294, 299, 325, 327, 335)
Moses, Timothy Jur	CANA (28, 64)		
Moses, Timy Capt	CANA (16)	Munger, Simeon	GUIL (270, 277, 291, 295, 301, 311, 327, 336)
Mosley, Thomas Doct	EHAD (65)		
Moss, [ ]	CHES (14)	Munger, Timo 3rd	GUIL (313, 334)

INDEX

Name	Index Page
Munger, Timo Capt	GUIL (315, 332, 334)
Munger, Timo Junr	GUIL (326)
Munger, Timothy	GUIL (274, 296, 299)
Munger, Timothy Capt	GUIL (308, 317, 319)
Munro, Willm	BRAN (164, 165)
Munroe, Dan	HARL (48)
Munsell, Elisha	EWIN (85, 89)
Munsell, Hezekiah	EWIN (85, 88)
Munsell, Jacob	EWIN (85, 88)
Munsell, Jonathan	EWIN (8)
Munsell, Zaccheus	EWIN (12)
Munsell, Zacheus	EWIN (10)
Munson, [ ] Ens	GOSH (184)
Munson, Abijah	GOSH (183)
Munson, Caleb	GOSH (183)
Munson, Daniel	MILF (102, 104)
Munson, Ebenr	DANB (60)
Munson, Fowler	GOSH (184)
Munson, John	GOSH (102, 110, 115, 135, 183)
Munson, Levi	HARW (25)
Munson, Peter	CHES (8)
Munson, Reuben	FARM (456)
Munson, Solomon	FARM (20)
Munson, Thos Ens	GOSH (115, 131, 183, 184)
Murch, William	KENT (C555)
Murdock, And Capt	CANT (160)
Murdock, Andrew	CANT (148)
Murray, Asael	GUIL (310)
Murray, Philemon	LITC (131, 138, 147, 152, 158)
Murray, Sealah	GUIL (272)
Murray, Selah	GUIL (276, 304, 311)
Murrell, Ebenr	CANA (64)
Murry, Daniel	KENT (C554)
Murry, Ezra	KENT (A24)
Murry, Nathan	KENT (E58)
Murry, Noah	KENT (A28)
Murry, Reuben	KENT (A28, C554, E58, E62)
Murry, Ruben	KENT (A27)
Murvin, Fowler	GOSH (120)
Murwin, Seth	FAIR (255, 258), 262, 263, 266)
Mury, Cornelius	HARL (56)
Mury, Cornelius	HARL (59)
Mygat, Col	DANB (53)
Mygat, Zebulon	HARF (291)
Mygatt, Col	DANB (66)
Mygatt, Eli	DANB (41, 46, 51, 64)
Mygatt, Eli Col	DANB (54)
Mygatt, Eli Major	DANB (198)
Naramore, Samuel	KILY (11)
Narramore, Mrs	KILY (23)
Narramore, Saml	KILY (23, 34)
Narramore, Samuel	KILY (21)
Nash, Capt	GOSH (104)
Nash, Ebenezer	EWIN (12, 15, 17, 85)
Nash, Frances	GREE (128)

Name	Index Page
Nash, Josiah	GOSH (103, 104, 120, 183)
Nash, S	GOSH (120, 183, 185, 186)
Nash, Saml	GOSH (102, 104, 105, 109, 110, 112, 115, 116, 120, 122, 125, 128, 130, 131, 134, 137, 138, 184)
Nash, Seth	GOSH (183)
Nash, Thomas Capt	FAIR (252, 260)
Nash, Thos	FAIR (258, 259, 260, 262, 265, 266, 267)
Nash, Thos Capt	FAIR (253, 254, 255, 256, 262, 263, 264)
Nash, Wm	GOSH (115, 183, 185)
Neal, Aaron	FARM (440)
Neal, David	FARM (433)
Neal, Moses	DANB (63)
Neal, Noah	FARM (438, 443)
Neckolson, Ambrs	GLAS (74)
Neigh, Ebenezer	KENT (E58, E63)
Nerton, Ebenez Jur	GOSH (130)
Nettelton John	KILH (145)
Nettelton, Abel	KILH (48, 50)
Nettelton, Ezra	KILH (50, 145, 146)
Nettelton, Ezrah	KILH (47)
Nettelton, George	KILH (44, 45, 49, 50, 51, 54, 55)
Nettelton, George Leut	KILH (53, 55)
Nettelton, James	KILH (44, 51, 53, 146)
Nettelton, Jeramiah	KILH (44)
Nettelton, Jeremh	KILH (45)
Nettelton, Jeremiah 2d	KILH (49)
Nettelton, John	KILH (50)
Nettelton, Joseph	KILH (146)
Nettelton, Josiah	KILH (47)
Nettelton, Saml	KILH (145, 50, 146)
Nettleton, Isaac	MILF (106)
Nettleton, Samuel	MILF (92, 106)
Nettleton, Thaddeus	MILF (91, 92, 102, 104, 106)
Nevel, Revd	GOSH (119)
Nevel, [ ]	GOSH (116, 117, 120, 122, 123, 126, 139)
Nevel, Abel Revd	GOSH (110, 113, 114, 116, 117, 119, 125)
Nevel, Revd	GOSH (103, 114, 104), 110, 113, 114, 115, 116, 122)
Nevil, [ ]	GOSH (139)
Nevil, Revd	GOSH (102, 184)
Nevins, John	HARF (281, 288, 293)
Newberry, [ ]	FARM (22)
Newberry, Amasa	EWIN (85, 89)
Newberry, Benjamin	EWIN (8, 85)
Newberry, Benjn	EWIN (88)
Newberry, Chauncey	EWIN (16, 17)
Newberry, Chaunsey	EWIN (85, 89)
Newcomb, Bradford	MANS (278, 328, 348)
Newcomb, John	LEBA (342)

INDEX

Name	Index Page
Newcomb, Paul	LEBA (334)
Newcomb, Peter	LEBA (305)
Newel, [ ]	FARM (8)
Newel, David	FARM (28, 436, 442, 449
Newel, Elisha	FARM (456)
Newel, Isaac	FARM (435, 442)
Newel, John	FARM (442, 444, 445, 455, 456)
Newel, John Jur	FARM (433, 436)
Newel, Josiah	FARM (442)
Newel, Josiah J[ ]	FARM (433)
Newel, Josiah Jur	FARM (435)
Newel, Medad	CANA (11, 13, 19, 64)
Newel, Nathan	CANA (77)
Newel, Nathan junr	CANA (64)
Newel, Pomroy	FARM (443, 444)
Newel, Saml Revd	FARM (440, 442)
Newel, Simeon	FARM (2, 9, 12, 24, 442, 443, 456)
Newel, Simeon Leut	FARM (452)
Newel, Soln	FARM (442)
Newel, Solomon	FARM (436)
Newel, Thomas Sert	FARM (436)
Newel, Thos Jur	FARM (17, 436)
Newel, William	CANA (19)
Newell, Josiah	FARM (444)
Newell, Medad	CANA (17)
Newell, Nathan	CANA (12, 17)
Newell, Nathan Jur	CANA (15)
Newell, William	CANA (77)
Newhall, Nathl	EWIN (11, 12)
Newill, Nath[ ]	GOSH (115)
Newill, Natha	GOSH (104)
Newton, [ ]	MILF (93)
Newton, Abel	GROT (6], [9], [12], [15], [18], [25]
Newton, Abel Leiut	GROT ([23])
Newton, Agrippa	GROT ([4], [23])
Newton, Gold Gift	CHES (10)
Newton, Isaac	EWIN (85, 89)
Newton, Israel	COLC (245)
Newton, Israel 3rd	COLC (249)
Newton, John	DURH (8, 11, 13), MILF (103)
Newton, John 3rd	COLC (10)
Newton, John Junr	MILF (92)
Newton, Jonah Capt	MILF (95, 97, 102)
Newton, Joseph	CHES (12, 13)
Newton, Marke	GROT ([18])
Newton, Thomas	CHES (A)
Newton, Thomas Jur	CHES (9)
Nicholas, Nathl	MANS (280)
Nicholds, Saml	DANB (40, 45, 47, 198)
Nichols, Benjamin Junr	MANS (280)
Nichols, Elijah	KILY (32)
Nichols, Hez	FAIR (256, 262, 265, 267
Nichols, Hezekiah	FAIR (263)
Nichols, John Jur	FAIR (259, 260, 264, 266, 267)
Nichols, Jonathan	MANS (267, 271, 272, 275, 282, 283, 284, 357)
Nichols, Jonathan Capt	MANS (268, 273, 326, 328, 333, 336, 337, 346, 348, 350, 353, 357, 358)
Nichols, Jonathan Jur	KILY (30)
Nichols, Jonathn Capt	MANS (277)
Nichols, Jonathn Leut	KILY (31, 34)
Nichols, Moses	FAIR (259)
Nichols, Nathl	MANS (281)
Nichols, Nathl Junr	MANS (339)
Nichols, Paul	FAIR (263)
Nichols, Peter	FAIR (265)
Nichols, Saml	DANB (48)
Nicholson, Ambrose	GLAS (106, 110, 112)
Nickels, John	KILH (146)
Nickels, Jonathan Leut	KILY (28)
Nickles, John	KILH (145)
Nickleson, Ambrose	GLAS (83, 84)
Nickols, David	KILY (23)
Nickolson, Ambrose	GLAS (79)
Nickolson, Ambrous	GLAS (93)
Nicols, John	HADD (111)
Nieland, David	HEBR (216)
Nieland, Joseph	HEBR (216)
Niles, [ ]	GROT ([24])
Niles, Ambros	COLC (245)
Niles, Ambrose	COLC (8)
Niles, Elisha	GROT [12], [13], [14], [22]
Niles, Nathan	GROT ([15]), HEBR (246, 248)
Niles, Nathan[ ]	GROT [23]
Niles, Nathaniel	GROT[12], [18], [19], [23]
Niles, Nathanl	GROT [25]
Niles, Thomas N P	GROT [15]), 17]
Niles, Thomas Np	GROT [7]
Niles, Thos N	GROT [12]
Niles, Thos N P	GROT [9], [19]
Niles, Thos Np	GROT [9]
Nivel, [ ]	GOSH (105)
Noble, Israel	KENT (A27, A28, B1, B2, C548, C552, C554, C555, D7, D10, E58, E62
Noble, Israel Leiut	KENT (C543)
Nooney, James	BOLT (180)
Nor[ ], Thomas	CANA (64)
Norcott, William	CHAT (42)
Norrimor, [ ]	KILY (94a)
Norrowmore, Samuel	KILY (98)
North, [ ]	FARM (436)
North, Asa	CANA (18, 20, 26, 28), FARM (2, 436, 456)
North, Asher	FARM (19, 434)
North, Daniel Jur	FARM (450)
North, Danl Jur	FARM (9, 28, 443, 445)
North, David	FARM (433, 436, 438, 449, 455)
North, Ebenz Jur	GOSH (184)

INDEX

Name	Index Page	Name	Index Page
North, Eli	FARM (9, 28, 433, 434, 444, 456)	Norton, Eben	GOSH (185)
		Norton, Eben Jur	GOSH (120)
North, Ezekiel	GOSH (138, 184)	Norton, Ebenez	GOSH (141)
North, James	FARM (2, 3, 9, 17, 18, 23, 29, 434, 438, 442, 444, 445, 447, 449)	Norton, Ebenez Jur	GOSH (102, 24)
		Norton, Ebenezer Col	GOSH (184)
		Norton, Ebenz	GOSH (185, 183, 185)
North, James Leut	FARM (28)	Norton, Ebenz Col	GOSH (112)
North, John	CANA (64), FARM (5, 9, 28, 449)	Norton, Ebenz Jur	GOSH (104, 112, 115, 131, 138)
North, Josiah	FARM (445)	Norton, Eber	GUIL (287, 294, 314, 316, 326, 335)
North, Josiah Jur	FARM (436)		
North, Reuben	FARM (17, 449)	Norton, Ebez	GOSH (185)
North, Saml	FARM (433, 442, 454)	Norton, Ebz	GOSH (185)
North, Saml Jur	FARM (23, 433, 435, 436, 455)	Norton, Elias	CHES (A)
		Norton, Elihu	GOSH (184)
North, Stephen	GOSH (185)	Norton, Elijah	FARM (454)
North, Thos	FARM (456)	Norton, Elnathan	MIDD (378)
Northam, Elijah	COLC (255)	Norton, Ens	GOSH (130)
Northam, Elijah	COLC (249, 251, 253)	Norton, Felix	GUIL (324, 335)
Northam, Jonn	COLC (255)	Norton, Frances	HEBR (216)
Northam, Saml	COLC (255)	Norton, G Gift	CHES (A)
Northam, Samuel	HADD (129)	Norton, Gold Gift Dotr	CHES (4)
Northom, John	HEBR (217)	Norton, Hooker	GUIL (298)
Northop, Lazarous	MILF (83)	Norton, Ichabod	FARM (2, 3, 5, 13, 18, 21, 27, 30, 427, 435, 440, 442, 446, 452, 453)
Northrop, Clement	MILF (88)		
Northrop, David	DANB (47)		
Northrop, Joel	MILF (90, 92)	Norton, Ichabod Capt	FARM (433, 435, 442)
Northrop, Moses	MILF (93, 102)	Norton, Ichabod Major	FARM (12, 29, 34, 454)
Northrup, Abel	MILF (106)	Norton, Isaac	FARM (449, 456)
Northrup, Enoch	MILF (93)	Norton, J[ ]n	FARM (456)
Northrup, Joel	MILF (94)	Norton, Jabez	GOSH (102)
Northrup, Joel Capt	MILF (97)	Norton, Jedediah	FARM (433, 449)
Northway, James	FARM (455)	Norton, Jedediah Jur	FARM (3, 8)
Norton John	KILH (53)	Norton, Jedidiah	FARM (456)
Norton, [ ]	FARM (7), GOSH (112), HEBR (234)	Norton, Jedidiah Jur	FARM (435)
		Norton, Job	HARF (253, 255A, 260, 261a)
Norton, A	GOSH (138)		
Norton, Aaron	GOSH (102, 104, 110, 112, 130, 137, 184), KILH (53), MIDD (357, 381)	Norton, John	CHAT (45, 46, 50, 68), GOSH (185), HEBR (216)
		Norton, John Jur	CHAT (30, 31, 32, 33, 34, 40), DURH (26), GUIL (294, 311, 339)
Norton, Aaron Ens	GOSH (115)		
Norton, Abel	GUIL (272, 307)		
Norton, Abraham	HARW (2, 13, 16, 523)	Norton, John Revd	CHAT (37)
Norton, Aren	GOSH (120)	Norton, Jos	GOSH (183, 185)
Norton, Ashbil	GUIL (270)	Norton, Joseph Leut	CHES (5)
Norton, Ashbill	GUIL (277)	Norton, Josiah	FARM (28)
Norton, Benjn	GUIL (301, 302, 304, 310, 315, 324, 326)	Norton, Major	FARM (8, 10, 12, 14, 15, 23, 32)
Norton, Beriah	GUIL (294, 318, 319)	Norton, Mary	GUIL (302, 304, 312, 329, 333)
Norton, Capt	FARM (430, 449, 450, 451)	Norton, Miles	GOSH (102, 110, 116, 121, 137, 138)
Norton, Charles	DURH (10, 21, 23, 25)		
Norton, Charles Capt	DURH (14, 16, 18, 19, 20, 21, 24, 26)	Norton, Miles Ens	GOSH (104)
		Norton, Miles Lt	GOSH (126, 127, 184)
Norton, Chars Capt	DURH (25)	Norton, Nathl	GOSH (120)
Norton, Col	GOSH (102, 104, 105, 110, 111, 112, 115, 116, 120, 125, 128, 130, 131, 138)	Norton, Nathll Capt	GUIL (304)
		Norton, Noadiah	GUIL (272, 286, 287, 294, 314)
Norton, Daniel Ensn	GUIL (301)	Norton, Noah	DURH (14, 16, 21)

INDEX

Name	Index Page
Norton, Reuben	GUIL (341)
Norton, Reuben Jur	GUIL (318, 326, 327)
Norton, Roger	FARM (2, 443, 450, 452)
Norton, Roger Jur	FARM (5, 17, 28, 435, 442, 443, 444, 449)
Norton, Sam Jur	GOSH (184)
Norton, Saml	GOSH (184)
Norton, Saml Jur	GOSH (110, 115, 130, 183)
Norton, Samuel	FARM (28)
Norton, Samuel Jur	GOSH (116)
Norton, Sarah	CANA (64)
Norton, Selah	HARF (253, 261a, 266, 268, 269, 272, 275)
Norton, Selah Capt	HARF (291)
Norton, Silas	KENT (E63)
Norton, Simeon	GUIL (271)
Norton, Stephen	FARM (3, 5, 8, 9, 12, 17, 430, 434, 438, 442, 444, 449, 454)
Norton, Stephen Capt	DURH (12, 14, 16, 18, 19, 20, 21, 22, 23, 24)
Norton, Stephen Jur	DURH (23)
Norton, Stepn	FARM (6)
Norton, Thomas	BRAN (166, 174, 178)
Norton, Timo	GUIL (269)
Nortton, Stephen Capt	FARM (28)
Nott, William	MILF (88)
Nott, William Capt	MILF (99, 100)
Nouland, Samuel	GLAS (95)
Noys, William	CANA (11, 64)
Nuton, Abither	HARL (51)
Nuton, Israel 3d	COLC (7)
Nye, David	GLAS (110, 111)
Nye, Ebenezer	KENT (C554)
Nye, Ebenr	KENT (C555)
Nye, Malatia	GLAS (93)
Nye, Malatiah	GLAS (75)
Nye, Maletiah	GLAS (78)
Nye, Melatiah	GLAS (106)
Nye, Melitiah	GLAS (83, 84)
Oakley, Jere	FAIR (262)
Oakly, Jeremiah	FAIR (266)
Odell, Azariah	FAIR (264, 265, 266, 267, 269)
Odell, John	FAIR (252, 253, 256, 260
Odell, Saml	FAIR (255, 257, 259, 260, 261, 263)
Offiria, Asa	GOSH (183)
Ogden, Humy	FAIR (267)
Ogden, [ ]	COLE (11)
Ogden, Ebenr	FAIR (252, 253, 255, 259, 262, 263, 264, 265, 267)
Ogden, Hez	FAIR (258, 263)
Ogden, Humphrey	FAIR (257, 265, 266)
Ogden, Humy	FAIR (263)
Ogden, Jacob	COLE (1, 2, 4, 5, 7, 8, 11, 13, 115)
Ogden, John	GREE (121)

Name	Index Page
Ogden, Moses	FAIR (253, 255, 259, 267)
Olcot, James Jur	HARW (534)
Olcott, Asahel	EWIN (12)
Olcott, Benoni	EWIN (7, 8, 9, 10, 13, 17, 85, 88), GLAS (64), HARW (534)
Olcott, Daniel	HARF (283, 289)
Olcott, Dorcas	BOLT (181)
Olcott, Ezekiel Capt	BOLT (146, 147, 148, 150, 151, 155, 164, 165, 166, 168, 180, 182)
Olcott, James	HARW (3, 534)
Olcott, James Jur	HARW (10)
Olcott, John	BOLT (181, 183)
Olcott, John 1st	HARF (265)
Olcott, John 2d	HARF (287)
Olcott, Josiah Junr	HARF (253, 263, 268, 272, 273, 279, 281)
Olcott, Thomas	EHAD (69)
Olcott, William Jur	EWIN (9)
Olcutt, Joseph	ASHF (231)
Olds, [ ]	ASHF (233)
Olds, Daniel	BRAN (176)
Olds, Daniel Capt	BRAN (170, 174, 178)
Olds, Robert	BRAN (173)
Ole, Oliver	ASHF (311)
Oles, Ebenr	ASHF (311)
Oliver, Capt	GROT ([20])
Olmstead, [ ]	HARF (296)
Olmstead, Ashbel	HARF (268, 269, 283)
Olmstead, Elijah	BOLT (180, 182)
Olmstead, Epaphas	HARF (288)
Olmstead, Epaphras	HARF (253, 281, 292)
Olmstead, Isaac	HARF (287)
Olmstead, John	COLC (243, 244, 246)
Olmstead, John Jur	COLC (8, 248, 249, 250)
Olmstead, Jonathan	HARF (253, 256, 263, 267, 273, 281, 288, 293)
Olmstead, Nathaniel	HARF (256)
Olmstead, Nathaniel Junr	HARF (287)
Olmstead, Thomas	HARF (287)
Olmstead, William Junr	HARF (260, 273)
Olmsted, Joseph	ENFD (35)
Olmsted, Asa	ENFD (26, 30)
Olmsted, Ashbel	EHAD (44)
Olmsted, Daniel 2d	EHAD (80)
Olmsted, Danl 2d	EHAD (50)
Olmsted, David	KENT (E60)
Olmsted, Elijah	BOLT (148)
Olmsted, Elijah Liut	BOLT (167)
Olmsted, Ichabod Capt	EHAD (50, 51, 53, 57, 82, 88, 89)
Olmsted, James	EHAD (60, 61, 69)
Olmsted, John	FAIR (253, 259, 265, 255, 267)
Olmsted, John 2d	FAIR (253)
Olmsted, John Jur	FAIR (255, 258, 265, 267)

INDEX

Name	Index Page	Name	Index Page
Olmsted, Jonathan Capt	EHAD (49, 60, 65, 80)	Packer, Danl	GROT [14]
		Packer, Edward Ensn	GROT [18]
Olmsted, Joseph	ENFD (18, 19, 24, 26, 28, 30, 32, 34, 35)	Packer, Eisha	GROT [24]
		Packer, Elisha	GROT [4], [19], [23]
Olmsted, Samuel	EHAD (86)	Packer, Jos	GROT [25]
Olmsted, Simeon	ENFD (18, 28, 32, 35)	Packer, Joseph	GROT [3], [4], [6], [8], [9], [11], [15]
Olmsted, Stephen	CHAT (32)		
Olmsted, Stephen Capt	CHAT (29, 30, 31, 33, 37, 39, 40)	Packer, Joseph Ensn	GROT [4]
		Packer, Joseph Junr	GROT [12], [19], [25]
Olney, Daniel	KILY (13)	Padden, Robert	FARM (4)
Olney, Job Capt	KILY (7, 19)	Paddock, John	MIDD (382, 394, 395, 399, 406, 419)
Ormbe, Thos	KILY (92)		
Orsborn, Zebedee	EWIN (85)	Paddock, Seth	MIDD (393, 399)
Orvese, Roger	COLE (11)	Paddock, Wm	MIDD (405, 413)
Orvile, Dr	ASHF (232)	Paddock, Zachariah	MIDD (368)
Orvis, Mary	FARM (19)	Page Daniel	BRAN (179)
Orvis, Zadock	FARM (9, 450)	Page, Abiel	BRAN (175)
Osbon, Naboth	DERB (140)	Page, Able	BRAN (179)
Osborn, Abner	DANB (63)	Page, Daniel	BRAN (176, 178, 179, 180)
Osborn, Daniel	EWIN (8, 14, 16, 88), FAIR (252, 259)		
		Page, Ephraim	BRAN (164, 178, 179)
Osborn, Danl	EWIN (85), FAIR (258, 263)	Page, John	BRAN (168, 175)
		Page, Jonathan	LITC (152, 160)
Osborn, David	DANB (62), FAIR (255, 262, 263, 267)	Page, Nathl Junr	BRAN (175)
		Page, Saml	BRAN (165)
Osborn, Ezekiel	EWIN (85, 88)	Page, Thomas	COVE (167, 177)
Osborn, Howes	FAIR (253, 256, 258)	Pain, Moses	MIDD (368)
Osborn, John	LITC (128)	Paine, Abraham	CORN (12, 89)
Osborn, John Capt	LITC (130, 134, 149, 159	Paine, David	CANT (139, 140, 144, 145, 146, 147, 148, 149, 150, 154, 165, 173)
Osborn, John Doct	MIDD (363)		
Osborn, John Junr	LITC (135, 153)		
Osborn, Joseph Junr	DERB (106)	Paine, Edward	BOLT (182)
Osborn, Naboth	DERB (145, 168)	Paine, Edward Capt	BOLT (155, 157)
Osborn, Peter	FAIR (253, 255, 258, 260, 262, 263)	Paine, Edward Ensign	BOLT (146)
		Paine, Edward Lieut	BOLT (151, 181)
Osborn, Samuel Jr	EWIN (15)	Paine, Noah	ASHF (311)
Osborn, Thomas	BRAN (170)	Paine, Rosel	BOLT (180)
Osborn, Zebedee	EWIN (88)	Paine, Roswell	EWIN (89)
Osgood, Jereh H	FARM (17)	Paine, Rufus	CORN (86)
Otis, John	COLC (245)	Paine, Seth	CANT (147, 151, 157, 176, 180)
Otis, Jonathan	MIDD (368)		
Otis, Nathl	COLC (251, 254)	Paine, Seth Jr	CANT (144)
Otis, Stephen	COLC (10, 242, 243)	Paine, Solomon	CANT (139, 146, 148, 163, 173, 178, 180)
Oulds, James	ASHF (310)		
Ovit, [ ]	GOSH (127, 138)	Paine, Solon	CANT (150)
Ovit, Saml	GOSH (115, 183)	Paine, Stephen	EWIN (85, 88)
Ovitt, [ ]	GOSH (129, 131)	Paine, Thomas	CANA (64)
Ovitt, Benj	GOSH (131, 183)	Palmele, Saml	KILH (47)
Ovitt, Saml	GOSH (112, 185)	Palmele, Ezra	KILH (145)
Owen, Amos	HEBR (217, 218, 220, 234, 236)	Palmer, Asahel	BRAN (165, 173, 175, 176, 179)
Owen, David	HEBR (217)	Palmer, Benja Dr	ASHF (308, 311)
Oysterbanks, Isaac	FAIR (264)	Palmer, Benjn	BRAN (170)
Oysterbanks, Joshua	FAIR (253)	Palmer, Capt	HEBR (233)
Ozgood, Jere H	FARM (443)	Palmer, David	GROT [6], [9], [19]
P[ ], Rubin	HARL (48)	Palmer, Denham	GREE (119, 126)
Pa[ ], Jona	FARM (431)	Palmer, Dr	ASHF (232)
Pack, Benoni	CORN (10, 12)	Palmer, Ebenezer	BRAN (170, 176, 178), CORN (87)
Packer, Daniel	GROT [11], [12]		
Packer, Daniel Captain	GROT [4], [11]	Palmer, Ebenezr	BRAN (165)

688

INDEX

Name	Index Page
Palmer, Elias	COLC (243, 249, 174, 314)
Palmer, Elihu	CANT (145, 147, 148, 150, 151, 154, 156, 161, 162, 168, 169, 177)
Palmer, Elijah	KENT (A28, E59)
Palmer, Elijah Junr	BRAN (179)
Palmer, Isaac	BRAN (165)
Palmer, Isaac Sargt	MANS (338)
Palmer, Jabez	BRAN (175)
Palmer, Jabish	BRAN (179)
Palmer, Jeremiah	GREE (125, 127, 128)
Palmer, Jno Capt	ASHF (308)
Palmer, John	BRAN (173, 178), GREE (125, 127)
Palmer, John Junr	GREE (119, 120, 121)
Palmer, John Wd	GREE (126)
Palmer, John Wood	GREE (124, 126, 127, 128)
Palmer, Joseph	GREE (124)
Palmer, Joseph Dr	ASHF (232)
Palmer, Levi	EHAD (53, 57, 64, 70, 80)
Palmer, Messenger	GREE (120, 126, 127)
Palmer, Nathan	MANS (328)
Palmer, Nathaniel	COVE (174), KENT (B2)
Palmer, Nathl	KENT (E64)
Palmer, Saml	BRAN (166), HEBR (216, 220), KENT (E59), GREE (119)
Palmer, Saml Junr	GREE (119, 123)
Palmer, Samuel	GREE (121, 128), BRAN (170)
Palmer, Samuel Junr	BRAN (176, 179)
Palmer, Seth	GREE (119, 124, 126, 127, 128)
Palmer, Seth Lieut	GREE (121)
Palmer, Stephen	BRAN (173, 175, 176, 178), 179) ,HEBR (217)
Palmer, Stephen Junr	BRAN (173, 174, 175, 176, 179)
Palmer, Titus	GREE (121)
Palmerly, Jehiel	LITC (128)
Palmerly, Phineas	EHAD (44)
Palmerly, Thomas Junr	LITC (134)
Pamerlee, Bryan	CHAT (30, 32, 37, 39, 40, 41, 42, 45, 50)
Pamerlee, Bryan Capt	CHAT (56)
Pamerlee, Jared	CHAT (43)
Pamerlee, Jonathn Jur	CHAT (40)
Pamerlee, Jonth	CHAT (37)
Pamerlee, Jonth Jur	CHAT (41)
Pamerly, Jehiel	LITC (128)
Pane, Edward	BOLT (148)
Pardee, Joseph	MILF (98, 102)
Pardy, David	FARM (449)
Parish, Archeppus	MANS (336)
Parish, Leml	CANT (157)
Parish, Saml	CANT (177)
Park, John	CANT (150)
Park, John Jr	CANT (146, 181)

Name	Index Page
Park, John Junr	CANT (160)
Park, Joseph	GROT ([11])
Park, Simeon	CANT (144)
Park, Wilm	KENT (E59)
Parke, Joseph	CHAT (52), GROT ([11])
Parker, Amos	CHES (12)
Parker, Benjamin	HARL (44, 47, 52, 54)
Parker, Ebenezer	CHES (4, 12)
Parker, Eliphalet	HARL (47, 52)
Parker, Eliphelet	HARL (44)
Parker, Eliphlet	HARL (55)
Parker, Elka	LEBA (299)
Parker, Elkanah	LEBA (341)
Parker, Ephm	MANS (278)
Parker, Ephraim	EWIN (85, 89), MANS (283, 336, 351, 353, 354)
Parker, James	COVE (165, 168, 172, 174), MANS (277)
Parker, Job	CHES (14)
Parker, John	EHAD (59, 79)
Parker, Joseph Doctr	HEBR (235, 246)
Parker, Joshua	MANS (336, 358)
Parker, Samuel	COVE (174)
Parker, William	CHES (8)
Parker, Zachariah Junr	MANS (267)
Parker, Zech[ ] Ensn	MANS (277)
Parker, Zechariah Junr	MANS (336, 347)
Parker, Zechh Junr	MANS (283)
Parker, Zechs Junr	MANS (353)
Parkes, Job	FARM (455)
Parks, David	GUIL (309)
Parks, Elijah	CANT (180)
Parks, John	CANT (150)
Parks, John Jr	CANT (168)
Parks, Reuben	CANT (160)
Parks, William	KENT (C555)
Parmale, Reuben	GUIL (326)
Parmalee, Abraham	GOSH (116)
Parmalee, Bryan	CHAT (69)
Parmalee, Bryan Capt	CHAT (66)
Parmalee, Lt	GOSH (104, 112, 115, 116)
Parmalee, Lt Senr	GOSH (183)
Parmalee, Theod Lt	GOSH (115)
Parmalee, Theodore	GOSH (125, 184)
Parmel, Capt	BRAN (178)
Parmele, [ ]	KILH (146)
Parmele, Abner	KILH (53, 55)
Parmele, Amos	KILH (44, 51, 145, 146), LITC (138, 139)
Parmele, Anne	GUIL (328, 329)
Parmele, Archelus	GUIL (292)
Parmele, Cornelius	KILH (50, 51, 53)
Parmele, Cornelus	KILH (45, 146)
Parmele, Dan	DURH (12, 14, 16, 18, 19, 21, 23, 25)
Parmele, Daniel	KILH (44, 50, 51, 53, 55)
Parmele, Ebenr Junr	GUIL (259, 269)
Parmele, Eber	GUIL (272, 310)
Parmele, Eliab	KILH (49, 146)

INDEX

Name	Index Page
Parmele, Elias	KILH (54, 146)
Parmele, Elihu	KILH (47, 53, 55)
Parmele, Eliphas	DURH (12)
Parmele, Eliphaz	DURH (14, 16, 17, 18, 19)
Parmele, James	GUIL (328, 329)
Parmele, Jeremiah	KILH (44, 46, 48, 53)
Parmele, Jno	GUIL (300)
Parmele, Job	KILH (54)
Parmele, Joel	KILH (145)
Parmele, John Junr	GUIL (321, 322, 325)
Parmele, Joseph	BRAN (163, 164, 170, 172, 173, 174, 175, 176, 178, 179, 269)
Parmele, Joshua	CORN (87)
Parmele, Josiah	KILH (51, 54, 145, 146)
Parmele, Levi	DURH (10, 16, 21, 23)
Parmele, Nathl	GUIL (335)
Parmele, Nehemiah	KILH (47, 146)
Parmele, Oliver	KILH (146)
Parmele, Ozias	KILH (51)
Parmele, Phinehas	DURH (16)
Parmele, Reuben	GUIL (271, 277, 287, 295), 300, 310, 332, 336, 344)
Parmele, Roswel	KILH (47, 48, 49), 145, 146)
Parmele, Saml	GUIL (325)
Parmele, Saml Capt	GUIL (270, 277, 288, 295, 301, 310)
Parmele, Thomas Junr	LITC (139)
Parmelee, Bryan	CHAT (33, 34, 36, 58, 67)
Parmelee, Bryan Capt	CHAT (64, 59, 64, 67)
Parmelee, Jared	CHAT (58, 64, 67)
Parmelee, Theody	GOSH (183)
Parmely, Amos 2nd	LITC (152, 158)
Parmely, David	LITC (158)
Parmerlee, Bryan	CHAT (60)
Parmerlee, Jared	CHAT (61)
Parmerley, Phineas	EHAD (70)
Parmerly, Phineas	EHAD (59, 65, 80)
Parrish, Archippus	MANS (283)
Parrish, Archps	MANS (278)
Parrish, Asa	KENT (D7, E59)
Parrish, Epharim	BRAN (179)
Parrish, Ephraim	BRAN (165, 166, 167, 170, 173, 175, 176, 178)
Parrish, Ephraim Capt	BRAN (172)
Parrish, Leml	CANT (144)
Parrish, Saml	CANT (144)
Parrish, Wilm	KENT (E59)
Parrit, John	FAIR (262, 265, 258, 259
Parry, Robert	ASHF (310)
Parsivel, John 2nd	EHAD (54)
Parson, Thos	FARM (20)
Parson, William	FARM (20)
Parsons, Aaron	DURH (25), MIDD (368)
Parsons, Amos	FARM (19)

Name	Index Page
Parsons, Asahel	ENFD (26, 30, 32, 34)
Parsons, Ben	ENFD (35)
Parsons, Benjn	ENFD (24, 28, 30, 32, 34)
Parsons, Caleb	EWIN (15, 17)
Parsons, Capt	DURH (20, 26)
Parsons, Christopher Junr	ENFD (18, 34)
Parsons, Ebenezar	ENFD (28)
Parsons, Edward	ENFD (19, 24, 28)
Parsons, Eldad	ENFD (18, 26, 35)
Parsons, Eli	ENFD (32)
Parsons, Elijah	ENFD (19, 24, 26, 32, 35)
Parsons, Eliphaz	LITC (129, 158)
Parsons, Genl	MIDD (418, 420)
Parsons, Hezekiah	ENFD (34, 35)
Parsons, Hezekiah Capt	ENFD (27)
Parsons, Ithamar	DURH (16)
Parsons, Ithamar Jur	DURH (10, 12, 16, 17, 20, 22, 25)
Parsons, Ithamer Jur	DURH (19)
Parsons, Ithar	DURH (15)
Parsons, Jesse	GREE (118, 119, 120)
Parsons, John	ENFD (19, 28, 29, 32, 35)
Parsons, Jonathan	ENFD (27)
Parsons, Joseph	DURH (14, 16, 18, 21, 23, 35)
Parsons, Josiah	DURH (12)
Parsons, Mathew	FARM (19)
Parsons, Peter	ENFD (18, 24, 28, 30)
Parsons, Rachel	FARM (19)
Parsons, Saml Fenn	DURH (24)
Parsons, Saml Lieut	DURH (11)
Parsons, Samuel	DURH (13, 17), MIDD (350)
Parsons, Samuel Jur	DURH (19)
Parsons, Simeon	DURH (24)
Parsons, Simeon Capt	DURH (21, 22, 23, 24, 26, 27)
Parsons, Simeon Jur	DURH (10, 11, 17, 19)
Parsons, Simeon Jur Lieut	DURH (14, 16, 18)
Parsons, Simeon Leut	DURH (12)
Parsons, Stephen	MIDD (350, 368, 394)
Parsons, Thomas	ENFD (17, 18, 19, 24), 34
Parsons, Timo	DURH (14, 23)
Parsons, Wareham	ENFD (34)
Parsons, William	FARM (19)
Partredge, Stephen	CANA (64)
Partridge, James	CANA (23)
Patchen, Jared	DANB (40, 43)
Patchin, David	FAIR (257, 262, 263)
Patchin, Jared	DANB (47, 53, 59)
Paten, Silas	KENT (E59)
Paterson, Matthew Lieut	CORN (16, 17, 19)
Patrick, Robt	LEBA (311)
Patten, Daniel	COVE (174)
Patterson, Elnathan	CORN (6, 87)

INDEX

Name	Index Pages	Name	Index Pages
Patterson, James	GLAS (64)	Pease, Edward	ENFD (28, 30, 32)
Patterson, Josiah	CORN (1, 6, 10, 15, 22, 23, 26, 86)	Pease, Elias	ENFD (32)
		Pease, Ephraim	ENFD (17)
Patterson, Lieut	CORN (24)	Pease, Ephraim Capt	ENFD (28)
Patterson, Mathew	CORN (25)	Pease, Ephrm Capt	ENFD (30)
Patterson, Mathew Lieut	CORN (3, 14, 15)	Pease, Ezekiel	ENFD (27, 29)
		Pease, Ezekil	ENFD (24)
Patterson, Matthew	CORN (4, 5, 7, 9, 17, 21, 22, 23, 24, 27)	Pease, Heman	ENFD (35)
		Pease, Isaac	ENFD (24, 25, 26, 32, 34, 35)
Patterson, Matthew Lieut	CORN (7, 9, 10, 11, 12, 20, 22, 24, 26, 27, 28, 88)	Pease, Isaac 2d	ENFD (18, 28)
Patterson, Sherman	CORN (12, 88, 91)	Pease, Isaac Capt	ENFD (32)
Pattin, David	COVE (170, 176)	Pease, James	ENFD (34)
Paul, James	KILY (94, 86a, 94)	Pease, Joel	EWIN (8, 10, 11, 12, 13)
Payn, Benjamin	LEBA (305)	Pease, John 3d	ENFD (30, 35)
Payn, Dan	LEBA (317)	Pease, Joseph	ENFD (27)
Payn, Jos	LEBA (316), 320, 325)	Pease, Moses	ENFD (18)
Payn, Seth	LEBA (315, 316)	Pease, Nathan 2d	ENFD (28, 30, 32, 34)
Payn, Step Jur	LEBA (320)	Pease, Nathl	GOSH (186)
Payn, Stephen	LEBA (298, 299, 305, 311)	Pease, Noadiah	ENFD (28)
		Pease, Saml	ENFD (18, 19, 24, 28)
Payn, Stepn	LEBA (326)	Pease, Saml 2d	ENFD (18, 24, 26, 28, 30, 35)
Payne, Abraham	CORN (9, 20, 21, 23, 87, 91)		
		Pease, Sharon	ENFD (28)
Payne, Benja	HARF (255, 256)	Pease, Thomas	ENFD (32, 34)
Payne, Daniel	KENT (A28, B1, C555, E58)	Pease, Timothy Junr	ENFD (19, 26, 34)
		Pecivil, Rowland	CHAT (31)
Payne, Edward Capt	BOLT (158, 159, 160, 164)	Peck, Abel	FARM (456)
		Peck, Abell	FARM (449)
Payne, Elisha	CANT (182, 183)	Peck, Abijah Junr	MIDD (362, 406, 416)
Payne, John	BOLT (158), KENT (C543, C546, C548), C552, C555, D1, E63)	Peck, Amos	FARM (456)
		Peck, Amos Jur	FARM (9)
		Peck, Ariel	MIDD (358, 372, 382)
Payne, Jos	LEBA (311, 333, 342)	Peck, Benjamin	GREE (121, 126, 127, 128), LITC (131, 157)
Payne, Noah	ASHF (222)		
Payne, Rufus	CORN (1, 16, 18, 23, 84)	Peck, Benjamin Capt	MILF (93)
Payne, Seth	LEBA (333)	Peck, Benjamin Junr	LITC (155)
Peabody, Aaron	LEBA (298, 299)	Peck, Benoni	CORN (13, 88, 91)
Peabody, Ephraim	ASHF (203)	Peck, Daniel	KILH (51)
Peace, Isaac 3d	ENFD (35)	Peck, Danl Jur	FARM (443)
Peace, John 2d	ENFD (35)	Peck, David	FARM (434, 438, 442, 444, 449)
Peacom, Moses	FARM (455)		
Pearce, William	KILY (8)	Peck, Ebenezer	GREE (123, 126, 128)
Pearl, Joshua	BOLT (151, 157, 158, 168, 180, 182)	Peck, Ebenezer Jur	KENT (D10, E60, E63)
		Peck, Eldad	FARM (5, 444, 456)
Pearl, Timothy	KENT (E59)	Peck, Eleazer	FARM (443, 447, 451)
Pearsall, Saml	FAIR (256)	Peck, Eliakim	FARM (430, 443)
Pearsall, Samuel	FAIR (259)	Peck, Elias	COLC (242)
Peas, Isaac	ENFD (34)	Peck, Eliazer	FARM (433)
Peas, James	ENFD (19)	Peck, Elijah	HARF (261a), LITC (141)
Peas, Jonathan	GLAS (94, 95)		
Peas, Lemuel	GLAS (94)	Peck, Fisk	MILF (82, 88, 92)
Peas, Peter	GLAS (76)	Peck, Gideon	HARW (4, 5, 523, 533)
Peas, Samuel	GLAS (93)	Peck, Jacob	LITC (142, 147, 153)
Peas, Thomas	ENFD (19)	Peck, Jas	FARM (444)
Pease, Saml Junr	ENFD (19)	Peck, Jesse	MIDD (411)
Pease, Aaron	ENFD (19, 28)	Peck, Jno	ASHF (311)
Pease, Asa	ENFD (30, 32, 34)	Peck, John	ASHF (308), CHES (4, 8, 11, 14, 16), MILF (85)
Pease, Benjn	ENFD (18, 34)		
Pease, Capt	ENFD (25, 33, 34, 35)	Peck, John 2d	CANA (19, 23, 64, 77)
Pease, Cumins Junr	ENFD (30)	Peck, John Jur	CHES (A)
Pease, Cummis Junr	ENFD (30)		

INDEX

Name	Index Pages	Name	Index Pages
Peck, Joseph	ASHF (236, 313), FARM (2, 9, 29, 433), GREE (119, 128), MIDD (381), MILF (91, 92, 100, 105, 106)	Peirce, Nehemiah	CANT (144)
		Peirce, Nehh	MANS (277)
		Peirce, Phinehas	CANA (64)
		Peirce, Samuel	CANA (77)
		Peirce, Seth	CORN (23), MANS (277, 328, 347)
Peck, Josh	FARM (18, 443)		
Peck, Josiah	FARM (17, 28, 456)	Peirce, Seth Capt	CORN (20, 25)
Peck, Justice	FARM (436, 443)	Peirce, Seth Ensgn	CORN (18)
Peck, Justus	FARM (449)	Peirce, Seth Junr	MANS (267, 271, 277, 341)
Peck, Lament	FARM (449)		
Peck, Lamont	FARM (17)	Pell, Saler	DANB (64)
Peck, Lemuel	FARM (456)	Pell, Saller	DANB (62)
Peck, Levi	LITC (142)	Pell, Saller Doctr	DANB (65, 65)
Peck, Mary	GREE (128)	Pellet, Jos Jr	CANT (180)
Peck, Michael	MILF (82, 82, 91, 92, 93, 97, 102, 104)	Pellet, Joseph Jr	CANT (160)
		Pelton, Abner	CHAT (51, 55)
Peck, Oliver	FARM (3, 442, 449)	Pelton, Ethemar	EWIN (85, 88)
Peck, Philo	LITC (129, 135, 146)	Pelton, Ithamer	CHAT (31, 47, 52, 58, 59, 60, 65, 66, 67, 69)
Peck, Phineas	MILF (78, 86, 93)		
Peck, Phineous	KENT (E60, E63)	Pelton, Ithamer Capt	CHAT (61, 63, 65)
Peck, Reuben	CANT (144, 147, 159, 167, 177, 178, 180, 183)	Pelton, Ithemer	CHAT (64)
		Pelton, James	HADD (109, 121, 128)
Peck, Robert	GREE (121, 124, 126, 127, 128)	Pelton, John	CHAT (30), GUIL (334, 340)
Peck, Ruben	CANT (150)	Pelton, Johnson	CHAT (51)
Peck, Saml	FARM (17, 28), GREE (119, 120, 123, 128)	Pelton, Joseph	CHAT (68, 39, 61)
		Pelton, Joseph Jr	CHAT (30, 55, 67)
Peck, Saml Capt	MILF (95)	Pelton, Josiah	CHAT (40, 43, 50), KILH (49, 51, 146)
Peck, Saml Jur	FARM (9, 18), GREE (119, 127, 128)		
		Pelton, Nathan	EWIN (12, 85, 88)
Peck, Saml Lieut	MILF (88)	Pelton, Phineas	GUIL (325, 334)
Peck, Samuel	FARM (456), GREE (121, 125, 126), MILF (84, 86, 89, 93)	Pelton, Thomas	GROT [4], [12]
		Pember, Elijah	EWIN (17)
		Pendleton, Increase	GUIL (271, 274, 290, 300, 311, 324, 325, 334, 337)
Peck, Samuel Capt	MILF (88, 96)		
Peck, Samuel Junr	GREE (121)		
Peck, Samuel Lieut	MILF (84, 85, 99, 103, 106)	Penfield, Isaac	HARL (45, 46, 48, 50)
		Penfield, James	FAIR (253, 256, 258, 259)
Peck, Seth	FARM (9, 16, 28)		
Peck, Solomon	HARW (3, 10, 16, 23, 25)	Penfield, John	CHAT (29, 30, 43, 44, 47, 52)
Peck, Thomas	FARM (436), GREE (124)		
		Penfield, John Capt	CHAT (29)
Peck, Thos	FARM (443)	Penfield, John Coll	CHAT (37, 39, 45, 50, 53, 54, 56, 66, 67)
Peck, Zeb	GOSH (111)		
Peck, Zebn	FARM (442)	Penfield, John Majr	CHAT (30, 33)
Peck, Zebn Jur	FARM (2, 23, 443)	Penfield, Jonan	CHAT (61, 66)
Peck, Zebulon Jur	FARM (29, 438)	Penfield, Jonathan	CHAT (32, 35, 37, 39, 43, 48, 58, 67)
Peck, Zebulun Jur	FARM (433)		
Peck, Zenos	MILF (92, 97)	Penfield, Jonathn	CHAT (33, 51, 64, 68, 69
Pecks, John	FARM (455)	Penfield, Jonth	CHAT (30, 42)
Peek, John	EHAD (59)	Penfield, Phenias	FARM (12)
Pees, Joseph	DERB (131)	Penfield, Phinehas	FARM (18)
Peese, Ezekiel	ENFD (18)	Penfield, Saml	FAIR (253, 255, 258, 262)
Peet, Abirem	CANA (64)		
Peet, William	CANA (64)	Penfield, Samuel	FAIR (263)
Peirce, Amos Jur	CANA (77)	Penfield, Simeon	CHAT (29)
Peirce, Delceno	CANT (155)	Penfield, Stephen	CHAT (31)
Peirce, Enoch	MANS (277)	Penneo, James	LEBA (331, 332)
Peirce, Enoch Junr	MANS (278, 341, 345, 347, 352, 355, 356, 357)	Penneo, James Jur	LEBA (299)
		Pepoon, Benja	HEBR (216)
Peirce, John Lieut	CORN (17, 18)	Pepoon, Daniel	HEBR (246)
Peirce, Joshua Capt	CORN (18)	Pepoon, Jos	HEBR (218)

692

INDEX

Name	Index Pages
Pepoon, Joseph	HEBR (216, 220, 234, 236, 248)
Pepoon, Silas	HEBR (220, 236)
Perce, Philip	GLAS (92)
Perce, David	DANB (39, 47, 49, 50, 54, 58)
Percevall, James	FARM (443)
Percival, James	FARM (451)
Percival, John	EHAD (44)
Percival, John 2nd	EHAD (59)
Percival, John 3d	EHAD (87)
Percival, John Junr	EHAD (50, 58, 60)
Percivall, [ ]	FARM (7)
Percivall, James	FARM (7, 11, 18, 27, 449)
Percivel, John Junr	EHAD (45, 49)
Percivel, Timothy Capt	CHAT (45)
Percivil, Rowland	CHAT (43, 45, 67)
Percivil, Timo	CHAT (61)
Percivil, Timo Capt	CHAT (44)
Percivil, Timothy	CHAT (47, 52, 55)
Percivil, Timothy Capt	CHAT (50, 58)
Perdee, Josiah	MILF (97)
Perit, Peter	MILF (82)
Perkins, [ ]	ASHF (221, 228, 233)
Perkins, Abner	HARW (8)
Perkins, Daniel Capt	ENFD (18)
Perkins, Eliphas	HARL (52)
Perkins, Eliphaz	CANT (177, 180)
Perkins, Elisha	GROT [19]
Perkins, Ethiel	DERB (113, 120, 124, 126, 131, 135)
Perkins, Gideon	HARL (55)
Perkins, Gidion	HARL (52)
Perkins, Isaac	ASHF (202, 209, 213, 214, 216, 218, 219, 222, 224, 226, 229, 238, 239, 240, 308, 310)
Perkins, Isaac Ensn	ASHF (232)
Perkins, Isaack	ASHF (209)
Perkins, John	GROT [4], [6]
Perkins, Land	ASHF (222)
Perkins, Landd	ASHF (213, 219)
Perkins, Obadiah	GROT [4], [12]
Perkins, Philip	MANS (340)
Perkins, Phinehas	HARL (52, 55)
Perkins, Phinehas Jur	HARL (52)
Perkins, Ruben	DERB (120, 122, 124, 131, 134, 140)
Perkins, Solomon Capt	GROT [3], [4], [6], [15]
Perkins, Thos	LEBA (297, 315, 318, 327)
Perkins, William	CANT (171)
Perkins, Wm	CANT (180)
Perl, Joshua	BOLT (148)
Perler, Seth	GOSH (186)
Perrin, Daniel	KILY (91a, 96a)
Perrin, Sol	HEBR (234, 236)
Perrin, Zach	HEBR (220, 246)
Perring, Sol	HEBR (218)
Perrit, Peter	MILF (85, 88, 92, 98)
Perrit, Peter Captain	MILF (97)

Name	Index Pages
Perry, David	KILY (86a)
Perry, David Revd	HARW (2)
Perry, Jabez	FAIR (253)
Perry, James	DERB (106, 167)
Perry, Jos Revd	EWIN (88)
Perry, Joseph Revd	EWIN (85)
Perry, Obediah	ASHF (311)
Perry, Peter	FAIR (252, 253, 254, 257, 260, 262)
Perry, Saml	ASHF (311)
Perry, Silvanus Leut	KILY (35)
Persevall, James	FARM (6)
Persival, John 2d	EHAD (64)
Persivall, James	FARM (3)
Person, David	DERB (131)
Person, [ ]	KILH (55)
Person, Abel	DERB (120)
Person, Abraham	DERB (106, 126), KILH (50)
Person, Abrm	KILH (49, 51, 54)
Person, David	DERB (120, 122, 124, 132, 133, 140, 145, 167)
Person, Davis	DERB (126)
Person, Dodo	KILH (49)
Person, John	KILH (44, 48, 49, 53)
Person, John Capt	KILH (45)
Person, Joseph	DERB (120, 122, 124, 145)
Person, Nathan	DERB (106, 113, 126, 140)
Person, Nathan Capt	DERB (120, 122, 135)
Person, Saml	DERB (121, 122), KILH (48, 49, 50, 51, 55)
Person, Saml 2d	KILH (47, 145, 146)
Persons, Lemwill Revd	CHAT (61)
Persons, Moses	FARM (455)
Persons, Saml	KILH (44)
Persson, Abraham	FARM (455)
Peters, Asbolum	HEBR (218)
Peters, Capt	HEBR (217)
Peters, Col	HEBR (218, 220, 234, 236, 246, 247)
Peters, Eldrid Joseph	KENT (C555)
Peters, Jno Col	HEBR (219, 220)
Peters, John Col	HEBR (216, 218, 231, 234)
Peters, Jonth	HEBR (217)
Peters, Joseph	KENT (A28, B1, B2, C546, C548, C552, C555, D10, D11, E58, E62)
Peters, Saml	HEBR (246)
Pettebone, Giles Majr	COLE (4)
Pettibone, Abram	FARM (17)
Pettibone, Capt	GOSH (184)
Pettin, David	COVE (172)
Pettis, James	LEBA (333)
Phelps, Ashbel	HEBR (218)
Phelps, [ ]	HEBR (217, 218, 234, 236)
Phelps, [ ] Jur	HEBR (234)
Phelps, Abel Jur	GOSH (102, 104, 105, 183, 184)

INDEX

Name	Index Pages	Name	Index Pages
Phelps, Abij	HEBR (218)	Phelps, Solomon Lt	HEBR (219)
Phelps, Amos	HEBR (218, 234)	Phelps, Timothy	HEBR (234)
Phelps, Asa Jur	HARW (3)	Phelps, Zeb[ ] Jur	HEBR (217)
Phelps, Asahel	HEBR (216)	Phepaney, Joseph	KENT (E60)
Phelps, Barret	HEBR (217, 220)	Pheps, Jason	KILY (85a)
Phelps, Benjn Jur	CANA (28, 64)	Philips, John	FAIR (253, 262, 265)
Phelps, Bethl	HEBR (234, 236)	Philips, Thomas	HARW (534)
Phelps, Bethuel	HEBR (216)	Phillip, Widow	KILY (98)
Phelps, Bissel	HEBR (220, 246)	Phillips, Mary	KILY (23)
Phelps, Charles	HARL (44, 46, 47, 52)	Phillips, Geo Capt	MIDD (362, 370)
Phelps, Cherls	HARL (57)	Phillips, Geo Jur	MIDD (365)
Phelps, Cornelas	HEBR (231)	Phillips, George	MIDD (342, 346, 349, 369, 373, 345, 367)
Phelps, Daniel	HARF (255A), HARW (3)		
		Phillips, George Capt	MIDD (356, 365, 385)
Phelps, David	KENT (E58, E62)	Phillips, George Junr	MIDD (344, 346, 349)
Phelps, Edward	COLE (113, 115)	Phillips, Mary	KILY (12, 22, 94a)
Phelps, Edward Ens	LITC (149, 155)	Phillips, Samuel	COLE (113)
Phelps, Edward Junr	LITC (129, 132, 147)	Phillips, Thompson	MIDD (364, 365, 371, 372, 381, 384, 414, 416)
Phelps, Eldad	ENFD (26, 30, 34)		
Phelps, Ezekiel	HEBR (216)	Phillips, Thompson Capt	MIDD (382)
Phelps, Fraderick	HEBR (246, 248)		
Phelps, Friend	CANA (11, 12, 16, 17, 64	Phiney, Oliver	FARM (442)
Phelps, Isaac	EWIN (85, 88)	Phiney, Solomon	GREE (121)
Phelps, Jedh	LEBA (310)	Phips, Jason	KILY (9, 13, 87a, 91, 94, 94a, 96)
Phelps, Jehd Jur	HEBR (236)		
Phelps, Joab	HARL (47, 52)	Phips, Jason Capt	KILY (36)
Phelps, John	HEBR (216, 217, 218, 231, 234, 236, 245, 247, 248), LITC (158)	Phips, Jason Leut	KILY (5, 10, 17, 90, 92, 96)
		Picket, Benjamin	DURH (10, 23)
Phelps, John Capt	HEBR (216)	Picket, Benjn	DURH (11, 19, 26)
Phelps, Joseph	LEBA (343)	Picket, David	DANB (45, 63, 69)
Phelps, Joshua	FARM (9, 442, 454)	Picket, Ebenr Jur	DANB (40, 49)
Phelps, Joshua Capt	HEBR (249, 218, 220, 231, 234, 236, 245)	Picket, Joseph	DERB (107, 113, 114, 122, 125)
Phelps, Joshua Jur	HEBR (236)	Picket, Timo	DANB (45)
Phelps, Josiah	HARW (5, 7, 9, 11, 12, 13, 17, 21, 22, 23, 523)	Pickett, Benjn	DURH (11, 16, 17, 21)
		Pickett, Timothy	KENT (D11)
Phelps, Josiah Capt	HARW (12, 13, 14)	Pickit, Joseph	DERB (120, 141)
Phelps, Moses	MANS (267, 280, 281, 328)	Pickitt, Benjamin	DURH (12)
		Pierc, Joshua Junr	CORN (27)
Phelps, Nathl	MANS (280, 339)	Pierce, Seth Capt	CORN (9)
Phelps, Nathl Jur	HEBR (218, 220)	Pierce, Enoch	MANS (267, 271)
Phelps, Oliver	HARW (3, 4, 7, 14, 16, 21, 22, 23, 25), HEBR (217, 218)	Pierce, Enoch Junr	MANS (233, 336)
		Pierce, Isaac	CORN (17)
		Pierce, John	CORN (9, 10, 11, 12, 13, 15, 18, 25, 27, 28, 86, 89), LITC (129, 135)
Phelps, Roger	HEBR (218, 220)		
Phelps, Roger Capt	HEBR (233, 245)	Pierce, John Lieut	CORN (2, 10, 23)
Phelps, Ruben	HEBR (217, 234)	Pierce, Joshua	CORN (25)
Phelps, Saml	HARL (42, 52), HARW (4, 22, 534)	Pierce, Joshua Capt	CORN (2, 14, 17, 18, 22, 23, 24)
Phelps, Saml Jur	HARL (52)	Pierce, Joshua Jur	CORN (10, 13, 86)
Phelps, Samuel	HARL (43, 44, 47, 51, 55), HARW (3, 7, 10, 17, 19, 20, 21, 23, 25)	Pierce, Joshua Jur Capt	CORN (10, 12, 13), CORN (14)
Phelps, Samuel jur	HARL (44, 47, 51), HARW (14)	Pierce, Levi	CORN (17)
		Pierce, Moses	GLAS (114)
Phelps, Silas	LEBA (305, 310, 315, 318, 326, 333)	Pierce, Peletiah	HARF (253, 261a, 263, 266, 272), HART (255A)
Phelps, Silus	LEBA (299)	Pierce, Seth	CORN (2, 4, 5, 9, 10, 12, 13, 22, 23, 25, 86)
Phelps, Silvanas	HEBR (245, 247)		
Phelps, Silvenas	HEBR (217)	Pierce, Seth Capt	CORN (1, 2, 10, 11, 12, 18, 19, 24)
Phelps, Solomon Jur	HEBR (246)		

INDEX

Name	Index Pages	Name	Index Pages
Pierce, Seth Ensign	CORN (23)	Pitkin, Thom White	BOLT (146)
Pierce, Stephen	MIDD (363, 365)	Pitkin, Thomas	BOLT (139, 146, 147, 148, 150, 180, 182)
Pierce, Thomas	CANA (21)		
Pierce, Timeus	CANT (160)	Pitkin, Thomas Capt	BOLT (145, 150)
Pierce, William	CORN (9)	Pitkin, Thomas White	BOLT (148)
Pierce, Willm	KILY (87a)	Pitkin, Thos White	EWIN (11)
Pike, Amos	CANT (176)	Pitkin, Timo Revd	FARM (442)
Pine, James	GREE (128)	Pitkin, Timothy	FARM (440)
Pinneo, Jas Cap	LEBA (315)	Pitkin, Timoy Revd	GOSH (123)
Pinneo, James [ ]	LEBA (313)	Pitkin, White	EWIN (12)
Pinneo, James Cap	LEBA (310)	Pitkin, William	DURH (18), EHAR (3), HARF (263A)
Pinneo, James Jur	LEBA (294, 297, 305)		
Pinneo, Jas	LEBA (320)	Pitkin, George Colo	HARF (300)
Pinneo, Jas Jur	LEBA (325)	Pitts, Jno	ASHF (311)
Pinney, David	COLE (1, 4, 5, 113, 115)	Pitts, John	ASHF (203, 210, 232)
Pinney, David Capt	COLE (7, 8, 11, 14)	Plank, John	KILY (12)
Pinney, Eleazer	EWIN (12, 16, 17, 85, 89)	Plank, Robart	KILY (8, 94)
Pinney, Eleazr	EWIN (13)	Plant, Benjn	BRAN (164)
Pinney, Joseph Jur	EWIN (10, 85, 89)	Plant, Ebenezer	DERB (126, 131, 140, 141, 145, 148, 167)
Pinney, Lemuel	EWIN (85, 89)		
Pinnney, David Capt	COLE (10)	Plant, Ebenr	DERB (106)
Pirkins, Capt	ENFD (19, 24, 25, 32, 33, 34)	Plant, Stephen	LITC (139, 141, 146)
		Platt, Benja	DANB (63)
Pirkins, Daniel Capt	ENFD (19, 33)	Platt, Benjamin	MILF (102)
Pirkins, Eliphas	HARL (51)	Platt, Ebenezer	MILF (93)
Pirkins, Eliphaz	HARL (44, 47)	Platt, Isaac	MILF (10, 103)
Pirkins, Gideon	HARL (47)	Platt, Jonas	MILF (85)
Pirkins, Moses	CHES (11)	Platt, Joseph	DANB (47, 93, 104)
Pirkins, Phinehas	HARL (44, 47, 51)	Platt, Joseph Junr	MILF (82, 98, 102, 105, 106)
Pirkins, Phinehas jur	HARL (44, 47)		
Pitkin, [ ]	BOLT (181)	Platt, Nathan Junr	MILF (85, 88)
Pitkin, Ashbel	EHAR (3), HARF (261a, 265, 266, 272, 281, 287, 294, 295)	Platt, Obadiah	FAIR (253, 258, 262, 265, 266, 267)
Pitkin, Daniel	EHAR (2, 3), HARF (253, 255A, 261A, 266, 272, 275, 280, 281, 283, 287, 292, 294, 295, 296, 300)	Platt, Obediah	FAIR (253)
		Platt, Richard	MILF (82, 105)
		Platt, Saml	MILF (98)
		Plum, [ ]	MIDD (344)
		Plum, Aaron	MIDD (345, 363, 365, 370, 381, 394)
Pitkin, Elisha	HARF (255A, 265, 267, 294, 296)	Plum, Abraham	MIDD (363, 365)
		Plum, Abraham Capt	MIDD (366)
Pitkin, Elisha Capt	HARF (272, 281, 289, 290, 297)	Plum, Daniel	MIDD (347, 350, 359, 362, 406)
Pitkin, George	EHAR (2), HARF (250, 258, 261a, 291)	Plum, Danl	MIDD (371, 377, 382, 394, 395, , 416)
Pitkin, George Colo	HARF (299)	Plum, James	MIDD (376, 382)
Pitkin, George Junr	HARF (285, 292)	Plum, Joshua	MIDD (347, 348, 351, 353, 356, 368, 371)
Pitkin, John	EHAR (1), HARF (250, 251, 253, 255A, 258, 259, 260, 261A, 263, 263A, 265, 280, 281, 287, 288, 289, 291, 292, 293, 295)	Plum, Saml	MIDD (372, 382, 388)
		Plum, Saml Junr	MIDD (364)
		Plum, Samuel	MIDD (363, 415)
		Plumb, Benjamin	CHES (4)
Pitkin, John Colo	HARF (290)	Plumb, Benoni	CHES (9)
Pitkin, John Junr	HARF (268, 280, 292, 293)	Plumb, Jos	MILF (85)
		Plumb, Joseph 3d	MILF (88)
Pitkin, Richard	EHAR (2), HARF (250, 253, 256, 258, 261a, 263, 265, 267, 268, 281, 287, 292)	Plumb, Joseph Junr	MILF (103)
		Plumb, Saml	FARM (455)
		Plumb, Samuel	MILF (98, 103, 105)
		Plumbe, Ebenezer	LITC (131, 139, 153, 157
Pitkin, Richard Capt	EHAR (3, 270, 273)	Plumbe, Ezra Junr	LITC (142)
Pitkin, Richard Junr	HARF (292, 298)	Plumer, John	KILY (94)
Pitkin, Richd	HARF (273)		

INDEX

Name	Index Pages	Name	Index Pages
Plummer, Ebenezer	GLAS (60, 66, 70, 78, 80, 82, 87, 100, 101)	Porter, Iaiah	COVE (170)
		Porter, Increas	HEBR (236)
Plummer, Ebenr	GLAS (71, 74, 93, 105, 108, 109, 110, 111, 113, 114)	Porter, Increce	HEBR (218, 220)
		Porter, Increce Jur	HEBR (216, 246)
		Porter, James	HARF (288, 292)
Plummer, Isaac	GLAS (90, 99, 109, 112)	Porter, James Junr	HARF (253)
Plummer, John	KILY (7)	Porter, Jas	FARM (442)
Plump, Simon	FARM (455)	Porter, Joel	HEBR (246)
Polley, John Jur	CHAT (59)	Porter, John	COLE (1, 2, 4, 5, 6, 7, 8, 9, 10, 13, 113, 115), FARM (14, 433, 442, 445, 449), HARL (45, 48)
Polly, John Jur	CHAT (62)		
Polly, Wm	HEBR (216)		
Pomeroy, Eleazer	COVE (314)		
Pomery, Elihu	HEBR (236)	Porter, John Capt	FARM (28, 436, 449, 455)
Pomroy, Adino	MIDD (345, 357, 365, 368, 371, 381, 385, 394, 405, 406, 415)	Porter, Jonah	HEBR (220, 246)
		Porter, Jonathan	COVE (165, 168, 169, 170, 174, 176, 177, 180)
Pomroy, Daniel	COVE (165, 168, 169, 170, 171, 173)	Porter, Jonathan Ens	COVE (314)
		Porter, Jonathan Jur	COVE (168, 170, 172, 174, 176, 178), EWIN (8, 9)
Pomroy, Eleazer	COVE (167, 170, 174, 177, 180)		
Pond, Charles Capt	MILF (94, 95, 96)	Porter, Jonathen	COVE (166)
Pond, Gad	CHES (12)	Porter, Joseph	FARM (2, 3, 438, 445, 449)
Pond, Moses	FARM (433)		
Pond, Zachariah	MILF (102)	Porter, Joseph Capt	FARM (434, 438)
Pool, Micah	DERB (106, 120, 124, 127, 145, 167)	Porter, Joseph Ensn	FARM (435)
		Porter, Josh	FARM (442, 445)
Pool, Micah Capt	DERB (139, 140, 141, 142, 145, 148)	Porter, Joshua Docr	FARM (434)
		Porter, Nathaniel	EWIN (12, 85, 88)
Pope, Rodert	DERB (120)	Porter, Nathaniel Junr	EWIN (16)
Porteer, Elijah	FARM (14)	Porter, Nathl Jur	EWIN (11, 13, 15, 17)
Porter, Thomas	COVE (172)	Porter, Neh[ ]	HEBR (246)
Porter, [ ]	FARM (2), 23)	Porter, Nehemiah	HEBR (217, 220, 236)
Porter, Aaron	HADD (112)	Porter, Noah	COVE (165, 166, 167, 168, 169, 170, 172, 174, 177, 180, 314), FARM (2, 6, 9, 16, 22, 27, 29, 31, 435, 438, 440, 441, 443, 444, 445, 446, 447, 450, 454)
Porter, Abm	LEBA (315)		
Porter, Abner	HADD (112)		
Porter, Asa	FARM (434)		
Porter, Ashbil	HARW (21, 23, 24)		
Porter, Benjamin	HARF (261a)		
Porter, Capt	FARM (8), HADD (126)		
Porter, Danl	FARM (434)	Porter, Noah Ensn	FARM (433)
Porter, Ebenezr	FARM (455)	Porter, Noah Jur	COVE (170, 174, 314)
Porter, Ebenr	FARM (2)	Porter, Richard	FARM (2, 9, 443)
Porter, Edmund	HADD (113, 114, 116, 126)	Porter, Saml	MIDD (350, 354, 356, 368, 369, 371, 381, 393, 404, 412, 415)
Porter, Edmund Capt	HADD (120, 121, 123, 125, 126, 129)	Porter, Samuel	MIDD (345, 347, 359, 361, 380, 390)
Porter, Eleazer	HEBR (218)	Porter, Seth	FARM (23, 449, 455)
Porter, Elijah	FARM (3, 8, 9, 16, 18, 22, 29, 435, 442, 444, 446, 449, 450, 454)	Porter, Thomas	CORN (9, 11, 18, 21, 77, 86, 87, 88, 170, 178, 314)
Porter, Elijah Leut	FARM (11, 434, 438, 445, 446)	Porter, Thomas Capt	CORN (11, 13, 17)
		Porter, Thos	CORN (89, 14)
Porter, Elishama	HARL (45, 46, 48, 50, 51, 59)	Porter, Timo	FARM (442)
		Porter, Timothy	HEBR (220, 236, 246)
Porter, Elisheme	HARL (56, 56)	Porter, Timothy Jur	FARM (3, 6, 434, 438, 445, 449, 456)
Porter, Ezra	HADD (148)		
Porter, Francis	HARL (45)	Porter, William	FARM (28)
Porter, Gaylord	HEBR (234)	Porter, Wm	DANB (68, 70), FARM (9, 449)
Porter, Gideon	FARM (6)		
Porter, Giles	FARM (443), HADD (109)	Portter, Abijah	FARM (436)
		Portter, Elijah	FARM (438)
Porter, Hezekiah	EWIN (85, 88)	Portter, Jas	FARM (17)

INDEX

Name	Index Pages	Name	Index Pages
Portter, John	FARM (14)	Pratt, Noah	KENT (A28, B1, B2, C548, C552, C554, C555, D1, D7, D10, D12, E58, E62)
Portter, Noah	FARM (18, 22)		
Portter, Wm	FARM (436)		
Post, David	HEBR (216)		
Post, Isaiah	FARM (433, 436, 440)	Pratt, Peter	KENT (A26, A28, B3, C547, C548, C552, D1, D3, D5, D7, E58, E62)
Post, James	HEBR (216)		
Post, Jed Capt	HEBR (219)		
Post, Joel	HEBR (235)	Pratt, Saml	GLAS (114)
Post, Jordan Jur	HEBR (233, 245)	Pratt, Stephen	FARM (443)
Post, Jos	LEBA (300)	Pratt, Timothy	HARF (272)
Post, Joseph	LEBA (299)	Pratt, Zachariah	HARF (44, 47, 253, 255A, 259, 265)
Post, Peter	HEBR (218, 236)		
Post, Thos	HEBR (247)	Pratt, Zaciheviah	HARL (52)
Post, Thos Jur	HEBR (234, 246)	Prentice, Amos	GROT [4], [6], [9], [15], [20], [23], [24], [25]
Potes, Philip	ASHF (313)		
Pots, Peter	ASHF (308)	Prentice, Amos Doctr	GROT [1], [18], [19]
Potter, Edward	GLAS (75, 80, 86, 94, 100, 102, 113)	Prentice, Thomas	GROT [6]
		Preston, Asa	HARW (534)
Potter, Jesse	HARW (2, 18)	Preston, Benj	ASHF (311)
Potter, Joel	FARM (443)	Preston, Benja	ASHF (222, 313)
Potter, John	BRAN (170)	Preston, Ephraim	CHES (11)
Potter, Stephen	BRAN (180)	Preston, Jacob	ASHF (202, 205, 210, 213, 311), CANT (181)
Pousley, Samuel	MIDD (363)		
Powe[ ], Timothy	MIDD (362)	Preston, Jno	ASHF (308, 311)
Powel, Jno	MILF (93)	Preston, John	HARW (2, 5, 7, 8, 13, 17, 23, 534)
Powel, John	MILF (97, 104)		
Powell, Stephen	LEBA (299)	Preston, Joshua	CANA (64, 77)
Powells, Stephen	LEBA (298)	Preston, Lieut	ASHF (224, 308)
Power, John	GROT ([23])	Preston, Medina	ASHF (202, 209, 213, 226, 310)
Power, Thos Capt	GUIL (344)		
Power, Thos Liut	GUIL (304, 325, 332)	Preston, Medinah	ASHF (213, 232, 236)
Powers, Edward	MIDD (416)	Preston, Midena	ASHF (308)
Powers, John	GROT ([25])	Preston, Reuben	CHES (A)
Powers, Thomas	MIDD (382)	Preston, Stephen	HARW (3, 4, 5, 7, 10, 17, 533)
Powers, Thos	MIDD (358, 372)		
Prat, Elisha	FARM (456)	Preston, Tiras	MANS (339)
Pratt, Capt	GOSH (131)	Preston, William	LITC (131, 142)
Pratt, Azariah	KENT (C554, E59, E63)	Preston, Zera	ASHF (308)
Pratt, Capt	GOSH (130, 134, 138, 139)	Price, Hez	FAIR (256, 263)
		Price, Samuel	GLAS (93)
Pratt, Cary	COLE (113, 115)	Prichard, James	FARM (28)
Pratt, Daniel	GLAS (108)	Prince	GLAS (82)
Pratt, Daniel Junr	COLC (11)	Prince, [ ]	FAIR (252)
Pratt, George	HARF (292)	Prince, David	MILF (93)
Pratt, Gideon	GOSH (112)	Prince, Ebenezer	KILY (14, 19, 97a)
Pratt, Isaac	GOSH (102, 104, 110, 115, 184)	Prince, Ebenezr	KILY (32)
		Prince, Joseph	ASHF (230), KILY (4)
Pratt, Isaac Liut	GOSH (118)	Prince, Nathan	MILF (104)
Pratt, Jeremiah	HARF (299)	Prince, Saml	FAIR (253, 255, 258, 263, 267)
Pratt, John	COLC (243, 248, 249, 251)		
		Prindle, Charles	HARW (2, 12, 13, 25)
Pratt, Jonathan	MIDD (363, 400)	Prindle, John	DERB (120)
Pratt, Joseph	KENT (D10)	Prindle, Mark	HARW (2, 22, 24)
Pratt, Joseph Capt	KENT (A26, C550, C551, D1, D3, D6, D7, D12, D13)	Prior, Daniel	MIDD (406)
		Prior, Danl	MIDD (368, 371, 382, 395, 416)
Pratt, Joseph Jur	KENT (A28, C548, C555)	Prior, Joel	EWIN (88)
Pratt, Joseph Jur Capt	KENT (E58, E62)	Prior, John	EWIN (9, 12, 85, 88)
Pratt, Joshua	HEBR (217)	Prior, Josiah	MIDD (376, 378, 394)
Pratt, Lt	GOSH (115, 120, 127)	Prior, Zaccheus	ENFD (19)
Pratt, Nathaniel	HARF (292)	Prior, Zacheus	ENFD (30, 32)
		Pritchard, Eunis	DERB (134)

INDEX

Name	Index Pages	Name	Index Pages
Pritchard, James	DERB (132)	Ranney, George Ens	CHAT (40)
Pritchard, James Junr	DERB (120, 134)	Ranney, George Jur	CHAT (30, 39)
Probin, David	ASHF (230)	Ranney, Hezekiah	MIDD (377)
Prout, Darcy	MIDD (364, 365)	Ranney, Joseph Jr	MIDD (363, 413)
Prout, Harris	MIDD (356)	Ranney, Nathl	MIDD (363)
Prout, Harriss	MIDD (362, 365, 373, 384, 394, 404, 413)	Ranney, Stephen	MIDD (364, 421)
Prout, William	MIDD (365)	Ranney, Thomas	CHAT (42, 68), MIDD (347, 351, 359, 382)
Prout, William Jur	MIDD (347, 359)	Ranney, Thos	CHAT (58), MIDD (364, 371)
Prout, Wm Jur	MIDD (363, 371)		
Prudden, Fletcher	MILF (85, 88, 97, 102, 104, 105)	Ransom, Alpheus	COLC (246, 248)
		Ransom, Amasa	COLC (245, 248)
Prudden, Job Revd	MILF (83)	Ransom, Amos	COLC (246, 255)
Prudden, John Lieut	MILF (97, 98)	Ransom, Asahel	COLC (243, 247)
Prudden, Jonathan	MILF (83)	Ransom, Bliss	COLC (255)
Prudden, Joseph	MILF (82, 85)	Ransom, James	COLC (6, 242, 252)
Prudden, Newton	MILF (92, 102, 103, 104)	Ransom, John	KENT (A24, D1, E58)
Prudden, Samuel	MILF (82, 85, 91)	Ransom, John Jur	KENT (A28, B1, B2, C548, C552, C554, C555, D1, D5, D7, D10, D14, E58, E63)
Pryor, Daniel	MIDD (359)		
Pulsefer, Silvester	GLAS (94)		
Pulsefor, Silvester	GLAS (71)		
Pumroy, Noah	COLC (8, 11, 242, 243, 245, 247, 249, 251, 256)	Ransom, John Leiut	KENT (D3)
		Ransom, Joshua Junr	COLC (242)
Pumry, Noah	COLC (4), COLC (254)	Ransom, Peleg	COLC (251)
Purdy, Solomon Capt	GREE (119, 121, 128)	Ransom, Robert	CANT (146, 148, 154), KENT (A28, B3, D3, E62)
Purkens, Eliphas	HARL (61)		
Purple, David	COLC (249)		
Purple, David	COLC (10, 243)	Ransom, Robt	KENT (E58)
Purple, Edward	CHAT (37, 39, 40, 65)	Ranson, Asahel	COLC (245)
Purple, Ezra	CHAT (29, 31, 37, 39), COLC (8, 11)	Ranson, Joshua Junr	COLC (248)
		Rathbun, Abel	COLC (251)
Purple, Josiah	CHAT (43, 50, 51)	Rathbun, Job	COLC (252)
Purson, Abram	KILH (54)	Rathbun, Simeon	COLC (249, 251)
Purson, Abraml	KILH (52)	Rathburn, Job	COLC (8)
Purson, Dodo	KILH (146)	Rathburn, Simeon	COLC (254)
Purson, John	KILH (51, 52, 55, 146)	Rawson, Doct	MIDD (360, 395, 403, 415, 416)
Purson, Saml 2d	KILH (51)		
Purson, Saml 2d Leut	KILH (52)	Rawson, Doctr	MIDD (356)
Purson, Saml Leut	KILH (54)	Rawson, Dutchess	MIDD (391)
R[ ], James	GREE (127)	Rawson, Eliot	MIDD (367, 391)
Ramsey, Alexander	GLAS (100)	Rawson, Eliot Doct	MIDD (348, 404, 405, 409)
Rand, Robert	MIDD (363)		
Randal, [ ]	COLC (253)	Rawson, Eve	MIDD (391)
Randal, Amos	EHAD (45, 47)	Rawson, Francis	MIDD (391)
Randal, Benjamin	COLC (252)	Rawson, Lettice	MIDD (391)
Randal, Benjamin Junr	COLC (246)	Rawson, Phillip	MIDD (391)
Randal, Jonathan	GROT ([9])	Ray, Benja	FARM (9)
Randal, Rufus	COLC (7, 8, 248, 252, 253)	Ray, Isaac	HADD (117, 121, 126, 129, 148)
Randal, Silvester	COLC (12, 243, 248)	Ray, Saml Jur	HADD (148)
Randal, Sylvester	COLC (10, 11)	Raymond, Abraham Jur	KENT (E63)
Randall, Jonathan	GROT [6], [12]		
Randol, Amos	EHAD (65, 79, 84, 87)	Raymond, Comfort	DANB (64)
Randol, Silvester	COLC (245)	Raymond, James	CANT (168, 174)
Ranney, Abijah	MIDD (361, 363, 371, 381, 387, 394, 398, 404, 405, 407, 413, 415)	Raymond, Josiah	KENT (A28, C554, E60)
		Raynolds, John	ENFD (24, 25, 26, 28, 29, 32, 33, 34, 35)
Ranney, Amos	CHAT (55)	Raynolds, Peter	ENFD (17, 25, 26, 28, 29)
Ranney, Ebr Junr	MIDD (364)	Raynsford, David	CANT (161)
Ranney, Frances	CHAT (55, 59)	Raynsford, Jona	CANT (145, 148)
Ranney, Francis	CHAT (42)	Raynsford, Jos	CANT (144, 145, 146)
Ranney, Fransis	CHAT (68)	Raynsford, Jos Capt	CANT (161, 176)

698

INDEX

Name	Index Pages	Name	Index Pages
Raynsford, Joseph	CANT (148)	Rice, Levi	CHES (5)
Raynsford, Joseph Capt	CANT (156, 181)	Rice, Nathaniel	CHES (14)
		Rice, Reuben	CHES (A, 4, 8, 9, 11)
Raynsford, Ricd	CANT (150)	Rice, Robert	CHES (15)
Raynsford, Richard	CANT (145, 148)	Rice, Robert Capt	CHES (4, 9)
Raynsford, Richd	CANT (144)	Rice, Sam	LEBA (339)
Read, Benjamen	HARL (59)	Rice, Saml	GLAS (112)
Read, Ebenezer	EWIN (8, 10, 11, 15, 17, 85, 88)	Rice, Samuel	GLAS (93, 106)
		Rice, Willm	ASHF (204)
Read, Ebenr	EWIN (13)	Rich, Eliakim	MIDD (400)
Read, John	MANS (271, 277, 348)	Rich, Henry	GREE (119)
Read, Silas	EWIN (10, 13, 15, 17)	Rich, James	CHAT (35, 39, 61)
Read, Wm	KILY (19)	Rich, Wm	FARM (9, 444, 456)
Read, Ebenezer	EWIN (12)	Rich, Wm Jur	FARM (455, 456)
Redfield, [ ] Capt	KILH (146)	Richard, John	FARM (436, 440, 442)
Redfield, Constant	KILH (145)	Richard, Samuel Jur	FARM (31)
Redfield, Daniel	KILH (43, 44, 48, 49, 51, 52, 53, 54, 55, 146)	Richards, Eliphaled	FARM (25)
		Richards, Guy	GLAS (107)
Redfield, Eliakim	KILH (145)	Richards, Israel	KILY (21)
Redfield, Jeremiah	KILH (54)	Richards, John	FARM (444, 447, 449)
Redfield, John	GUIL (275)	Richards, Saml	FARM (13)
Redfield, John Doctr	GUIL (275, 344)	Richards, William	KILY (94, 91a, 94)
Redfield, Josiah	KILH (44, 49, 50, 146)	Richardson, Amos	COVE (170, 174, 177, 178, 180)
Redfield, Levi	KILH (51, 52)		
Redfield, Martin	KILH (145)		
Redfield, Saml	KILH (46, 47, 49, 50, 53, 55)	Richardson, Amos Capt	COVE (314)
		Richardson, Amos Jur	COVE (166, 168)
Redfield, Selvester	KILH (44)	Richardson, Andrew	COVE (168)
Redfield, Selvister	KILH (52)	Richardson, Billey	COVE (181)
Redfield, Seth	KILH (52)	Richardson, Capt	COVE (314)
Redfield, Silvester	KILH (55)	Richardson, Eleazer	LEBA (304)
Redfield, Simion	KILH (145)	Richardson, Eleazr	LEBA (302, 311, 327, 334, 341)
Redfield, Sylvester	KILH (145)		
Redfield, Wm	MIDD (388)	Richardson, Jonathan	COVE (167, 180, 314)
Reed, Benjamin	HARL (44, 46, 47)	Richardson, Justus	COVE (167, 314)
Reed, Danl Jur	LEBA (333)	Richardson, Roland	MIDD (363)
Reed, Mathew	ASHF (226, 236)	Richardson, Rowland	MIDD (382)
Reed, Matthew	ASHF (311)	Richardson, William	GLAS (106)
Reede, Benja	HARL (57)	Richmd, Barna	GOSH (104)
Reede, Zeph	HEBR (217)	Richmond, B[ ]	GOSH (184)
Reeve, Tapping	LITC (130, 133, 135, 153)	Richmond, Barnabas	GOSH (112, 120, 130, 137, 139)
Remington, Elehu	HARL (54)		
Remington, Elihu	HARL (52)	Richmond, Oliver	KILY (86a)
Remmenton, Elihu	HARL (47)	Richmond, Phillip	KILY (94, 95, 98)
Remmington, Elihu	HARL (44)	Richmond, Silas	GOSH (102, 104, 109, 110, 115, 119, 120, 124, 127, 129, 130, 131, 137, 138, 139, 184)
Remonton, Elihu	HARL (50)		
Reuby, Thomas	HARL (51)		
Rew, Eliathah	FARM (443)		
Rew, Eliather	FARM (444)	Richmund, Silas	GOSH (114)
Rew, Memucan	FARM (5)	Rieley, Charles	GLAS (92)
Rexford, [ ]	CORN (19)	Riggs, Ebenezer	DERB (133)
Rexford, Daniel	CORN (19)	Riggs, Ebenezer Capt	DERB (148)
Reynold, Timothy	GREE (127)	Riggs, Ebenezer Junr	DERB (124)
Reynolds, Horton	GREE (119, 126, 128)	Riggs, Jeremiah	LITC (131, 135)
Reynolds, John	ENFD (19)	Riggs, John	DERB (133, 134)
Reynolds, Nathaniel junr	GREE (124)	Riggs, John Capt	DERB (127, 131, 132, 135, 137, 140, 145, 167)
Reynolds, Nathl junr	GREE (126, 128)	Riggs, John Junr	DERB (106, 107, 113, 120, 122)
Reynolds, Phillip	GREE (120)		
Rice, Bennet	CHES (4, 11)	Riggs, Jos: Lit	DERB (141)
Rice, David	CHES (A)	Riggs, Joseph	DERB (167)
Rice, Eliphalet	GLAS (92)	Riggs, Joseph [ ]d	DERB (169)

699

INDEX

Name	Index Pages
Riggs, Joseph 3d	DERB (126, 131)
Riggs, Joseph Capt	DERB (106, 107, 114, 120, 122, 124, 125, 126, 127, 131, 140, 145, 167)
Riggs, Joseph Junr	DERB (113, 120, 122, 124, 131, 145)
Riggs, Joseph Lieut	DERB (135, 140, 170)
Riggs, Lowis	DERB (134)
Riggs, Moses	DERB (121, 122)
Right, Job Capt	KILH (49)
Riley, Asher	MIDD (394)
Riley, Charles	GLAS (100, 102)
Riley, John	GOSH (102, 115)
Riley, John Lt	GOSH (112, 117)
Riley, Julias	MIDD (411)
Riley, Julius	MIDD (363, 395, 406, 416)
Riley, Lt	GOSH (104, 110, 115, 120)
Riley, Roger	MIDD (368, 420)
Riley, Roger Capt	MIDD (342, 345, 346, 349, 350, 354, 356, 358, 401)
Rily, John	GOSH (138)
Rily, John Lt	GOSH (183)
Rily, Lt	GOSH (112, 130, 134, 185)
Rimington, Elihu	HARL (56)
Rimmington, Elihu	HARL (55)
Ripler, Jeremiah	COVE (167)
Ripley, Jeremiah	COVE (165, 166, 169, 171, 177)
Ripley, Jeremiah Capt	COVE (173, 177, 178, 179)
Riply, Jeremiah	COVE (164)
Riply, Jeremiah Capt	COVE (314)
Risley, Benjamin	BOLT (158, 181), GLAS (93)
Risley, Benjamin Ensn	BOLT (154, 155, 156, 160, 162, 163)
Risley, Benjn	BOLT (160)
Risley, Gorsom	BOLT (183)
Risley, Job	GLAS (78, 84, 94)
Risley, Reuben	GLAS (86, 114)
Risley, Ruben	GLAS (66, 70, 72, 74, 93)
Risley, Thomas	GLAS (94)
Risley, William	BOLT (182)
Robard, Jabez	FARM (444)
Robards, Nathl	MIDD (365)
Robards, Aaron Jr	MIDD (363)
Robards, Collins Saml	MIDD (373)
Robards, David Jr	MIDD (395, 405, 413)
Robards, Doct	MIDD (364)
Robards, Ebenezer	MIDD (366)
Robards, Ebenr	MIDD (362, 414)
Robards, Hinchman	MIDD (381, 406)
Robards, Hinksman	MIDD (363, 381, 394, 414)
Robards, Jesse	MIDD (363)
Robards, John	MIDD (363, 371, 377, 381, 394, 404, 416)

Name	Index Pages
Robards, John 3d	MIDD (371, 382, 395, 406, 416)
Robards, John Junr	MIDD (370, 380, 382, 393, 404, 413, 414)
Robards, Jona	MIDD (416)
Robards, Jonathan	HARL (51), MIDD (380)
Robards, Jonathan Junr	MIDD (382, 395, 406)
Robards, Nathl	MIDD (364)
Robards, Noah	MIDD (362)
Robards, Noyce	MIDD (363)
Robards, Recompence	MIDD (376, 378)
Robards, Simeon	MIDD (367, 370, 381)
Robards, Simion	MIDD (394)
Robartson, Elijah	KILY (96a)
Robbard, David	FARM (455)
Robbard, Jabez	FARM (438, 449, 456)
Robbards, Collins	MIDD (349)
Robbards, Collins Jur	MIDD (351)
Robbards, Saml	MIDD (346)
Robbards, David	FARM (433, 449, 455)
Robbards, Gideon	FARM (456)
Robbards, Hinksman	MIDD (359)
Robbards, Jabez	FARM (3, 434)
Robbards, Jacob	FARM (433)
Robbards, John Jur	MIDD (349)
Robbards, Jonathan	MIDD (349)
Robbards, Josiah	FARM (455)
Robbards, Seth	FARM (441)
Robbens, Samuel	CANA (11)
Robbins, Ephraim	MANS (283, 285)
Robbins, Esther	CANA (14)
Robbins, Job	ASHF (202, 310)
Robbins, Jobe	ASHF (308)
Robbins, Joseph	ASHF (204), KILY (26)
Robbins, Levi	HARF (255A)
Robbins, Samuel	CANA (11, 12, 14)
Robbins, Zebulon	CANA (77)
Robenson, Capt	COVE (181)
Robenson, Joel	HARL (45, 48, 50)
Roberson, Aaron	GLAS (85)
Roberson, Aron	GLAS (68)
Roberson, David	GLAS (65)
Roberson, Joel	HARL (58, 59)
Roberts, Elias	HARF (253, 255A)
Roberts, Eliphalet	HARF (255A)
Roberts, George	HARF (266)
Roberts, Gideon	FARM (11, 28)
Roberts, John	MIDD (359, 350)
Roberts, John Junr	MIDD (345, 356)
Roberts, Jonathan	HARF (273), HARL (47, 57), MIDD (346, 356)
Roberts, Jothn	HARL (52)
Roberts, Samuel	HARF (266, 275)
Roberts, Seth	HARL (44, 47, 52)
Roberts, Simeon	MIDD (350)
Robertson, Daniel	COVE (166, 168, 172, 174, 180)
Robertson, Daniel Jur	COVE (181)
Robertson, John 3rd	COVE (168, 170)
Robertson, John Junr	COVE (314)
Robertson, Saml Jur Capt	COVE (314)

INDEX

Name	Index Pages
Robertson, Samuel	COVE (165, 172, 178, 180)
Robertson, Samuel Capt	COVE (169, 178)
Robertson, Samuel Jur	COVE (170, 172, 177, 180)
Robertson, Samuel Jur Capt	COVE (177, 179)
Robertson, Samuel Leut	COVE (174)
Robinson, Obediah	KILY (27)
Robins, Josiah	KILY (94a)
Robins, Josiah Leut	KILY (92)
Robins, Samuel	CANA (11)
Robinson, [ ]	CHAT (59, 60, 61)
Robinson, Aaron	GLAS (92)
Robinson, Asher	DURH (12)
Robinson, Ashur	DURH (10, 15, 17, 18, 23
Robinson, Capt	DURH (26)
Robinson, David	CHAT (30, 31, 33, 34, 36, 37, 39, 40, 41, 51, 65, 68, 69)
Robinson, David Lieut	CHAT (45, 50, 64)
Robinson, Ebenr	DURH (11)
Robinson, Ensn	MIDD (358)
Robinson, Icha	LEBA (298, 299, 311, 316, 327, 342)
Robinson, Ichabod	LEBA (305, 334)
Robinson, James Capt	DURH (11, 22, 24)
Robinson, Jas Capt	DURH (14, 23)
Robinson, Joel	HARL (46, 51, 53)
Robinson, John	MIDD (372)
Robinson, Jos	LEBA (310, 315, 316, 326)
Robinson, Saml	GUIL (286, 291, 309, 314, 319, 274)
Robinson, Saml Junr	GUIL (275)
Robinson, Samuel Junr	GUIL (260)
Robinson, Timothy	ASHF (310)
Rock, John	BOLT (183)
Rock, William	BOLT (165)
Rockwell, [ ]	COLE (12)
Rockwell, [ ]ard	MIDD (363)
Rockwell, Abner	EWIN (8, 85, 89)
Rockwell, Amariah	COVE (165, 166, 168, 172, 174, 177, 180, 314, 315)
Rockwell, Amoriah	COVE (170)
Rockwell, Capt	HARL (60)
Rockwell, Daniel	EWIN (8)
Rockwell, Danl	EWIN (10, 85, 88)
Rockwell, David	COLE (13, 113, 115)
Rockwell, Ebenezer	MIDD (345, 349, 356, 370)
Rockwell, Ebenr	MIDD (363)
Rockwell, Ebenr 3d	EWIN (85, 89)
Rockwell, Edward	MIDD (394, 405, 413)
Rockwell, Edward Jr	MIDD (368, 371, 382, 406)
Rockwell, Edward Senior	MIDD (385)
Rockwell, Edwd Junr	MIDD (395)

Name	Index Pages
Rockwell, Elijah	COLE (1, 2, 4, 7, 8, 10, 113, 115)
Rockwell, Ezra	EWIN (85, 89)
Rockwell, Henry	MIDD (363, 388)
Rockwell, Isaac	EWIN (85, 88)
Rockwell, Jabez	DANB (47, 55, 58)
Rockwell, Joel	EWIN (85, 89)
Rockwell, John	COLE (1, 5, 6, 7, 9, 10, 11, 12)
Rockwell, John Junr	MIDD (363)
Rockwell, Jonah	FAIR (255, 259)
Rockwell, Jos	LEBA (312)
Rockwell, Joseph	COLE (11, 113, 115), FAIR (263), KENT (E59)
Rockwell, Joshua	GUIL (324), MIDD (351, 359, 364, 367, 371, 381)
Rockwell, Josiah	LEBA (298, 299, 305, 306, 311, 315, 316, 326, 334, 341)
Rockwell, Josiah Jur	LEBA (305, 321, 326)
Rockwell, Nathaniel	EWIN (89)
Rockwell, Nathl	EWIN (85)
Rockwell, Noadiah	MIDD (413)
Rockwell, Saml	EWIN (10)
Rockwell, Saml Capt	COLE (10, 13, 14)
Rockwell, Samuel Capt	COLE (1, 2, 3, 4, 5, 6, 7, 8, 9, 11, 12)
Rockwell, Silvenus	EWIN (12, 85, 89)
Rockwell, Stephen	KENT (E60)
Rockwell, Sylvenus	EWIN (17)
Rockwell, Timothy	COLE (8, 10, 13, 113, 115)
Rockwill, Jabez	DANB (51)
Rodgers, Edward	CORN (86)
Rodgers, Moses	ASHF (232, 236)
Roe, John	DERB (120)
Roger, Edmd Ct	BRAN (163)
Roger, Noah	CORN (25)
Rogers, Eli	BRAN (170)
Rogers, [ ]	CORN (29), FARM (443)
Rogers, Abijah	BRAN (170, 172, 179)
Rogers, Abraham	BRAN (179)
Rogers, Daniel Junr	COLC (248, 249)
Rogers, David	BRAN (174, 175), FAIR (258)
Rogers, David Doctor	FAIR (251, 257, 260)
Rogers, Ebenezer	BRAN (170, 173, 174, 175, 176, 178, 179), COLC (243, 251)
Rogers, Ebenezr	BRAN (163)
Rogers, Ebenezr Capt	BRAN (166)
Rogers, Ebenezr Ct	BRAN (164)
Rogers, Ebenr	COLC (7, 8, 254)
Rogers, Eber Ct	BRAN (163)
Rogers, Edmd	BRAN (163)
Rogers, Edmond	BRAN (164)
Rogers, Edmund	BRAN (174, 175, 176)
Rogers, Edmund Capt	BRAN (174)
Rogers, Edward	CORN (9, 24, 25, 30)
Rogers, Edward Capt	CORN (1, 2, 6, 7, 9, 11, 15, 16, 17, 21, 22, 26)
Rogers, Edward Lieut	CORN (77)

INDEX

Name	Index Pages	Name	Index Pages
Rogers, Eli	BRAN (166, 172, 174, 178)	Root, Eliakim	BOLT (182)
Rogers, Elihu	BRAN (173, 178)	Root, Elijah	FARM (17, 455)
Rogers, Hezekh	HARW (16)	Root, Elisha	FARM (433, 435)
Rogers, Hezekiah	HARW (8, 14, 17, 25, 523)	Root, Ephraim	COVE (161, 163, 166, 167, 168, 169, 170, 171, 172, 173, 174, 175, 177, 178, 179, 180, 181, 314)
Rogers, Hezh	HARW (3)		
Rogers, Isaiah	EHAD (65, 69, 81)	Root, Gideon	KENT (A28)
Rogers, Ja[ ]	BRAN (168)	Root, Hezh	FARM (436, 443)
Rogers, Jabez	COLC (7, 8, 10, 11, 12, 242, 245, 246, 247, 249), EWIN (8, 15)	Root, James	FARM (5)
		Root, Jesse	HARF (252(2), 255, 263A)
Rogers, Jeremiah	MILF (85)	Root, Jesse Colo	COVE (315)
Rogers, John	BRAN (168, 170), MIDD (345, 349, 356, 362, 366, 369, 379, 380, 393, 403, 404, 412)	Root, Jesse Conl	COVE (175)
		Root, John	COVE (167, 172, 177, 180), FARM (6, 9, 435, 438, 442, 444, 445)
Rogers, John Ensn	MIDD (354)	Root, Jona	FARM (427, 430, 440, 442, 446, 450, 451)
Rogers, John Junr	BRAN (173)		
Rogers, Jonah	ASHF (202)	Root, Jona Jur	FARM (456)
Rogers, Jonathan	MILF (88, 98)	Root, Jonah	HEBR (246)
Rogers, Joseph	BRAN (173, 179), MILF (98)	Root, Jonathan	COVE (174), FARM (19, 21, 30, 453)
Rogers, Josiah	BRAN (175, 176, 177, 178, 179, 181)	Root, Jonth	HEBR (218)
Rogers, Levi Junr	BRAN (175)	Root, Joseph	COVE (166, 169, 170, 171, 173, 174, 178, 180), FARM (6, 449, 450, 456)
Rogers, Moses	ASHF (308, 311)		
Rogers, Noah	CORN (1, 2, 7, 9, 10, 11, 12, 15, 17, 19, 21, 22, 23, 25, 29, 86, 89)	Root, Joseph Capt	COVE (181, 314)
		Root, Madad	COVE (168)
		Root, Medad	COVE (165, 167, 180)
Rogers, Saml	KILH (146)	Root, Moses	CHES (14)
Rogers, Samuel	BRAN (175, 176, 178, 179)	Root, Nathaniel	COVE (174, 177)
		Root, Phinehas	CANA (64)
Rogers, Sarah	CANT (174)	Root, Salmon	FARM (2, 5, 433, 456)
Rogers, Thomas	BRAN (166, 180), CHAT (29, 62)	Root, Saml	CANA (23, 27), FARM (13, 434, 456)
Rogers, Thos	BRAN (179), CHAT (51)	Root, Samuel	BOLT (160, 182)
Rogers, Timothy	CHAT (41, 29, 90)	Root, Simeon	CANA (19, 64)
Rogers, Timothy Doctr	CORN (28)	Root, Thed[ ]	FARM (456)
Rogors, Jabez	COLC (252)	Root, Theodore	FARM (9, 17)
Rollo, Wm	HEBR (216, 217, 218)	Root, Thomas	ENFD (18, 24, 28)
Rolo, Wm	HEBR (219)	Root, Thos	FARM (435)
Rood, David	CANA (28, 64)	Root, Timo	FARM (9, 23, 430, 443)
Rood, Mariner	CANA (28)	Root, Timo Capt	FARM (27)
Rood, Meriner	CANA (23, 28)	Root, Timothy	FARM (2, 6, 8, 11, 14, 17, 19, 21, 30, 433, 435, 436, 445, 447, 449, 450, 454)
Rood, Merinor	CANA (15, 17, 24, 77)		
Rood, Merinor Junr	CANA (12)		
Rood, Robert	GOSH (115, 121, 125, 138, 184)	Root, Timothy Capt	FARM (28, 31)
Rood, Roger	CANA (19)	Root, William	CANA (64)
Roose, Wilm	KENT (E58)	Root, Wm	HEBR (220)
Root, Amos	FARM (436, 442, 444, 449, 450)	Roots, [ ]	HARL (42)
		Roots, Benjn	ENFD (18)
Root, Asa	CANA (64)	Roots, Daniel	KENT (E60, E63)
Root, Asahel	BOLT (151, 167, 180, 182)	Roots, Gideon	KENT (E60)
		Roott, Daniel	BOLT (180)
Root, Benjn	COLC (9)	Roott, Eliakim	BOLT (180)
Root, Caleb	HEBR (216, 245)	Roott, Samuel	BOLT (157, 180)
Root, Daniel	BOLT (167), FARM (433)	Rose , Justus	BRAN (179)
		Rose, Amaziah	BRAN (171, 173)
Root, Danl	FARM (28, 443)	Rose, Ammaziah	BRAN (174)
Root, Ebenr	HEBR (236)		

702

INDEX

Name	Index Pages	Name	Index Pages
Rose, Bille	BRAN (163, 164, 166, 171, 173, 175, 176, 177, 178)	Rowbinson, John	CANA (64)
		Rowbinson, William	CANA (64)
		Rowe, Danl	FARM (2, 433, 442, 455)
Rose, Daniel	BRAN (170, 173, 179)	Rowe, Isaiah	FARM (9)
Rose, Elijah	FARM (29, 443)	Rowe, Joseph	FARM (455)
Rose, Giles	DURH (19)	Rowe, Stepn	FARM (456)
Rose, Jehiel	COVE (174, 177)	Rowel, Robert	FARM (24)
Rose, Joel	GUIL (294, 325, 338)	Rowland, Andrew	FAIR (261, 269)
Rose, Justus	BRAN (163, 175, 176, 178, 180)	Rowland, Andw	FAIR (265, 266, 267)
		Rowland, Jabez	FAIR (255, 258, 260, 263)
Rose, Levi	BRAN (166, 170, 173)	Rowland, Jeremiah	FAIR (253)
Rose, Nathan Junr	BRAN (170)	Rowland, Saml	FAIR (253)
Rose, Reuben	BRAN (176)	Rowland, Saml Jur	FAIR (254, 255, 258)
Rose, Reuben Capt	BRAN (172, 173, 178, 179)	Rowland, Samuel	FAIR (254)
		Rowlee, Abij Capt	HEBR (217)
Rose, Reuben Captain	BRAN (170)	Rowlee, Nathan	HEBR (217)
Rose, Reuben Ct	BRAN (164)	Rowley, Ebenr	CHAT (50)
Rose, Reubin Capt	BRAN (174)	Rowley, Eleazer	EHAD (69, 79, 86)
Rose, Reubin Ct	BRAN (163)	Rowley, Garshom	CHAT (51)
Rose, Robert Junr	GROT [12], [15], [23], [25]	Rowley, Gershom	CHAT (38, 45)
		Rowley, Isachar	KENT (E60)
Rose, Roger	KILH (45)	Rowley, Ithamer	CHAT (58)
Rose, Ruben Ct	BRAN (165)	Rowlson, Ira	CANA (27)
Rose, Sam 2d	BRAN (176)	Royce, Clark	LITC (131)
Rose, Saml	BRAN (164, 165, 166, 175)	Royce, Josiah	GOSH (102, 104, 110, 112, 120, 131, 184)
Rose, Samuel	BRAN (173, 178)	Royce, Nehemiah	FARM (23, 430)
Rose, Samuel 2d	BRAN (175, 176, 178)	Royce, Phinehas	HARW (2)
Rose, Samuel Jur	BRAN (170, 171, 173, 179, 180)	Roys, James Junr	MANS (281)
		Roys, Reuben	CHES (14)
Rose, Solomon	BRAN (166, 173, 176)	Royse, Solomon	MANS (233)
Rose, Timothy	COVE (170)	Royse, Asa	MANS (338)
Rose, William	KENT (E62)	Royse, David Junr	MANS (271, 277, 353)
Ross, Asher	KENT (E59)	Royse, Isaac	MANS (233, 338)
Ross, Timo	ASHF (222)	Royse, James	MANS (281, 328)
Ross, Wm	GREE (128)	Royse, James Junr	MANS (271, 336, 338)
Rosseter, Amos	HARW (3, 7, 10, 533)	Royse, John	MANS (281, 283, 329, 336, 348)
Rosseter, Benj[ ]	KILH (49)		
Rosseter, Benjn	GUIL (269, 287, 294, 300)	Royse, Solomon	MANS (278)
		Rube, Thomas	HARL (45)
Rosseter, Bryan	DURH (10)	Ruby, Thomas	HARL (53)
Rosseter, Bryan Leut	DURH (12)	Ruby, Thos	HARL (50)
Rosseter, John	KILH (46)	Rude, J[ ]	LEBA (315)
Rosseter, Josiah	KILH (49, 51, 145)	Rude, Jos	LEBA (326, 334)
Rosseter, Rowland	DURH (11)	Rude, Joseph	LEBA (341)
Rosseter, Timo	GUIL (313, 315, 318)	Ruggles, Nathl	GUIL (273, 275, 310)
Rosseter, Willm	GUIL (304)	Ruggles, Nathl Junr	GUIL (294, 299)
Rosseter, Wm	GUIL (313)	Rumsey, Benja	FAIR (260, 262, 264, 267)
Rosseter, Wm Lieut	GUIL (286, 309)	Rumsey, Benjamin	FAIR (266)
Rossetor, Benj[ ]	KILH (52)	Rumsey, Jos	FAIR (265)
Rossetor, John	KILH (145)	Rumsey, Joseph	FAIR (253, 255, 258, 259
Rossetor, John 2d	KILH (145)	Rundall, Eli	GREE (119, 128)
Rossetor, Josiah	KILH (44, 48, 54, 55, 146)	Rundall, Eli junr	GREE (124, 126)
Rossetter, Amos	HARW (4)	Rundall, Jeremiah	GREE (124)
Rossetter, Benjamin	GUIL (273)	Rundall, Reuben	GREE (125)
Rossetter, Benjn	GUIL (277)	Rundall, Samuel	GREE (121, 124)
Rossetter, Bryan	DURH (14, 16, 21, 23)	Rundall, Solomon	GREE (128)
Rothbun, Job	CANA (17)	Rundall, Willm	GREE (119)
Rouland, David	CANA (11)	Rundall, Wm	GREE (126)
Rounds, Jeremiah Doctr	KILY (13)	Runford, John	CANA (64)
		Rusell, John Lieut	ASHF (227)
Row, Seth	KENT (C555)	Russ, [ ]	ASHF (239)

703

INDEX

Name	Index Pages	Name	Index Pages
Russ, John Junr	MANS (336, 338, 353, 357, 359)	Russell, Samuel	BRAN (176, 179), DERB (106, 122, 127, 140, 167)
Russ, Timo	ASHF (222)		
Russ, Timothy	ASHF (311)	Russell, Samuel Capt	BRAN (170, 175, 178)
Russ, Timy	ASHF (311)	Russell, Samuel Junr	BRAN (169)
Russel, Capt	MIDD (356, 415)	Russell, Stephen	COLE (113), LITC (146)
Russel, Daniel	KILY (92, 94a, 98), MIDD (364, 402)	Russell, Thomas	ASHF (308), BRAN (178, 179), CORN (9, 11, 15, 19, 22, 87, 88)
Russel, David	KILY (91a)		
Russel, Ebenr	BRAN (180)	Russell, Timothy	BRAN (167, 169, 170, 173)
Russel, Edward	BRAN (172)		
Russel, Jno	ASHF (223, 308)	Russell, Willm	BRAN (166)
Russel, Jno Lieut	ASHF (225)	Russes, Timo	ASHF (223)
Russel, John	ASHF (223), MIDD (367)	Rust, Abel	KENT (E60, E63)
Russel, John Lieut	ASHF (228)	Rust, Amariah	COVE (165, 171)
Russel, Jonathan	BRAN (179)	Rust, Amazia Capt	COVE (177)
Russel, Lieut	ASHF (224)	Rust, Amaziah Capt	COVE (178)
Russel, Nicholas	CHES (8, 12, 15)	Rust, Elisha	FARM (449)
Russel, Nicholes	CHES (9)	Rust, Levi	KENT (D7)
Russel, Noadiah Lt	CHAT (31, 38, 50, 67)	Rust, Simeon	KENT (E59)
Russel, Saml	MIDD (365, 368)	Rutley, Jonah	HADD (130)
Russel, Saml Capt	MIDD (351, 359, 369, 393, 405, 412, 413)	Rutly, Jonah	HADD (117, 129, 130)
		Rutty, John	KILH (49, 145)
Russel, Samuel	DERB (140)	Rutty, Levi	KILH (51, 53, 54, 146)
Russel, Samuel Capt	MIDD (346, 349, 350, 351, 356, 380)	Rutty, Livi	KILH (47)
		Rutty, Tim[ ]	KILH (145)
Russel, Thomas	BRAN (179), CORN (20, 87)	Ryard, Noah	LITC (146)
		S[ ], Elnathan	FARM (433)
Russel, Timothy	BRAN (179), CHAT (51)	S[ ], Josiah	MIDD (344)
Russell, Benjn	ASHF (310)	S[ ], Thos	DANB (39)
Russell, Daniel	KILY (11)	S[ ], Caleb	HARL (48)
Russell, David	KILY (7, 23)	Saber, Jacob	MIDD (378)
Russell, Ebenezer	BRAN (174, 176, 178, 179)	Sabin, Eldad	LEBA (326, 333)
		Sabin, Walter	LEBA (341)
Russell, Ebenezr	BRAN (165, 166)	Sacket, Wilm	KENT (E58)
Russell, Ebenezr Jur	BRAN (165)	Sacket, Jonathan	KENT (A27, A28)
Russell, Edw	BRAN (164, 165)	Sacket, Justus	KENT (A28, B1, B2, C555, D1)
Russell, Edw Col	BRAN (166)		
Russell, Edward	BRAN (167, 170, 171)	Sacket, Justus Capt	KENT (A27, B1, B3, E58, E62)
Russell, Edward Capt	BRAN (179)		
Russell, Edward Col	BRAN (168, 169, 173, 175)	Sacket, Reuben	KENT (A28, C554, C555, E58, E62)
Russell, Edward Major	BRAN (176, 178)	Sacket, William	KENT (E62)
Russell, Ithiel	BRAN (178, 179)	Sackett, Benjamin	KENT (E63)
Russell, Jno	ASHF (222, 311)	Sackett, Alexander	KENT (D1)
Russell, John	ASHF (209, 222, 233, 310), BRAN (173, 174)	Sackett, Alixander	KENT (E63)
		Sackett, Benjamin	KENT (E60)
Russell, John 2d	ASHF (236)	Sackett, Joseph	GREE (121)
Russell, John Capt	BRAN (174, 179)	Sackett, Justus	GREE (121, 126),KENT (C544, C545, C547, C552, D5, D6)
Russell, John Ensn	ASHF (202)		
Russell, John Jur	ASHF (313)		
Russell, John Lieut	ASHF (236)	Sackett, Reuben	KENT (B3, C548, D1, D7, D10)
Russell, Jonathan	BRAN (164, 165, 168)		
Russell, Jonth	BRAN (172, 174, 178)	Sackett, Salmon	KENT (E63)
Russell, Jos	DERB (127)	Sackett, Wilm	KENT (D7)
Russell, Joseph	DERB (120, 132, 141)	Safford, [ ]	CANT (150)
Russell, Noadiah	CHAT (64)	Safford, David	BOLT (163, 164)
Russell, Noadiah Lt	CHAT (37)	Safford, Jos	CANT (146, 150, 162, 163)
Russell, Saml	DERB (124, 131, 145)		
Russell, Saml Capt	BRAN (166, 173, 176)	Safford, Joseph	CANT (154, 156, 165, 176, 180)
Russell, Saml Ct	BRAN (165)		
Russell, Saml Junr	BRAN (169)	Sage, [ ]	MIDD (360)

704

INDEX

Name	Index Pages	Name	Index Pages
Sage, Abraham	MIDD (376, 378)	Sanford, Oliver	LITC (132)
Sage, Amos	MIDD (345, 364, 377, 379, 393)	Sanford, Philemon	GOSH (102, 115, 184)
		Sanford, Philimon	GOSH (104)
Sage, Colo	MIDD (356, 370, 385, 395, 401, 403, 407, 409, 415, 417, 420)	Sanford, Ramond	MILF (82)
		Sanford, Raymond	MILF (102)
		Sanford, Raymond Capt	MILF (97, 100, 105)
Sage, Comfort	MIDD (386)		
Sage, Comfort Colo	MIDD (345, 346, 349), 350, 351, 358, 369, 380, 381, 385, 387, 389, 391, 393, 404, 408, 412, 414)	Sanford, Samuel Capt	MILF (97)
		Sanford, Solomon	LITC (141)
		Sanford, Zadock	MILF (97)
		Sanley, Moses	COVE (170)
Sage, Comft	MIDD (368)	Sargeant, Isaac	MANS (280)
Sage, Comft Colo	MIDD (386, 413)	Sargeant, Isaac Capt	MANS (328, 341, 346)
Sage, David	CHAT (29, 30, 32, 33, 37, 39, 41, 43, 44, 48, 49, 52, 53, 63, 66, 67, 68, 69, 70)	Sargeant, Jacob	MANS (267, 268, 283)
		Sargeant, Saml	MANS (278, 283, 284, 336, 337, 353)
Sage, David Capt	MIDD (366)	Sargeant, Samuel	MANS (268, 272, 272, 283, 328, 347, 348,354 357, 358)
Sage, Ebenezer	MIDD (365)		
Sage, Ebenr	MIDD (363)		
Sage, Elisha	MIDD (364)	Saunders, Ithamar	CORN (7, 16, 18, 23, 87, 91)
Sage, Enoch	CHAT (45, 61)		
Sage, Giles	MIDD (363, 364, 365, 372, 411)	Saunders, Nathan	CORN (88, 91)
		Saunders, Zelotes	CORN (10, 13, 17, 90)
Sage, Giles Junr	MIDD (375, 399)	Savage, Amos	MIDD (404)
Sage, Jedediah	MIDD (347, 358, 368, 393)	Savage, [ ]on	MIDD (363)
		Savage, A Capt	MIDD (372)
Sage, Jedidiah	MIDD (369, 379, 387, 398, 403, 412)	Savage, Abij[ ] Capt	MIDD (358)
		Savage, Abijah	MIDD (414)
Sage, John	MIDD (362)	Savage, Abijah Capt	MIDD (382)
Sage, John Junr	MIDD (375)	Savage, Amos	MIDD (346, 349, 356, 359, 363, 370, 373, 380, 394, 402, 406)
Sage, Joseph	CHAT (38, 39, 42, 43, 58, 59, 60, 64, 67)		
Sage, Joseph Capt	CHAT (66)	Savage, Daniel	MIDD (345)
Sage, Joseph Leiut	CHAT (43, 45, 50, 51)	Savage, Danl	MIDD (363)
Sage, Nathaniel	MIDD (364)	Savage, Elisha	MIDD (358, 368, 370, 394, 395, 405, 413, 415)
Sage, Saml	MIDD (356, 372, 416)		
Sage, Solo Capt	MIDD (361, 366, 395)	Savage, Elisha Lieut	MIDD (358, 382)
Sage, Solomon	MIDD (344, 349, 351, 357, 367)	Savage, Gideon	MIDD (381, 405)
		Savage, John	MIDD (364)
Sage, Solomon Capt	MIDD (342, 345, 346, 355)	Savage, Jonathan	MIDD (364)
		Savage, Josiah	MIDD (346, 362, 365)
Sage, Timo	MIDD (364)	Savage, Luther	MIDD (415)
Sage, William	MIDD (357, 368)	Savage, Nathl	MIDD (364)
Sage, Wm	MIDD (394, 410, 414)	Savage, Saml	MIDD (382)
Salter, John	MANS (255, 258, 262, 263, 267, 270, 271, 273, 275, 276, 277, 278, 279, 282, 285, 324, 328, 333, 335, 337, 338, 341, 342, 246, 249, 351, 352, 353, 354, 355, 356, 357, 359)	Savage, Saml Capt	MIDD (345, 349, 362, 369)
		Savage, Samuel	MIDD (366)
		Savage, Samuel Capt	MIDD (354, 356)
		Savage, Solo Lt	MIDD (401)
		Savage, Solomon	MIDD (394)
		Savage, Stephen	MIDD (389, 395, 405, 413)
Salter, Richard Revd	MANS (338)	Savage, William	MIDD (363)
Sanders, Benjamin	KENT (E59)	Savage, Wm	MIDD (395, 406, 416)
Sanders, Ithamer	CORN (12)	Sawer, Jacob	HARL (52)
Sanders, Zelotes	CORN (23, 25)	Sawney	GLAS (107)
Sandford, Thomas	HARF (266, 288, 293)	Sawyer, [ ]	CORN (23)
Sandors, Ephraim	HARL (44)	Sawyer, Ephraim	HADD (121, 127, 129)
Sanford, John	CHES (11)	Sawyer, Jacob	HARL (54, 57, 58, 59)
Sanford, Jonah	LITC (129, 146, 152)	Sawyer, Nathan	CORN (9, 22, 89, 91)
Sanford, Joseph	LITC (129)	Sawyer, Samuel	CORN (10, 17, 18, 23, 25, 87, 91)
Sanford, Leml	DANB (39)		
Sanford, Moses	LITC (129, 130, 133)		

INDEX

Name	Index Pages	Name	Index Pages
Saxton, James	COLC (7, 255)	Scrantom, Abrm Jur	DURH (10, 14, 17)
Saxton, Simeon	GUIL (316, 328, 333)	Scrantom, Abrm Lt	DURH (24)
Schallenx, Gideon	CHAT (52)	Scrantom, David	DURH (23, 25)
Schellenx, Abraham	CHAT (34)	Scrantom, David Ensn	DURH (24)
Schellinx, Abraham	CHAT (31)	Scrantom, Ensn	DURH (20)
Schovel, Elisha	MIDD (355)	Scrantom, John	GUIL (325)
Schovil, Ezekiel	HARW (17)	Scrantom, Josiah	GUIL (310, 325, 326, 335)
Scot, [ ]	FARM (435)	Scrantom, Lt	DURH (20)
Scott, Adonijah	GLAS (92)	Scrantom, Mehetable	GUIL (327)
Scott, Ebenezer	GLAS (100)	Scrantom, Saml	GUIL (325)
Scott, Ebenr	FARM (2, 433, 438, 445), GLAS (94, 108)	Scrantom, Theo	GUIL (335, 324)
		Scrantom, Theophilus	GUIL (301)
Scott, Elisha	FARM (17, 436, 443, 449)	Scranton, Abraham	GUIL (271)
Scott, Ezekiel	FARM (9)	Scranton, John	GUIL (313, 317, 320)
Scott, George	HARW (534)	Scranton, Josiah	GUIL (269, 270, 277, 287, 293, 294, 300)
Scott, Hezh	FARM (443)		
Scott, Joseph	GLAS (86, 99)	Scranton, Mehetable	GUIL (326)
Scott, Reuben	HARW (534)	Scranton, Saml	GUIL (273)
Scott, Samuel	FARM (433)	Scranton, Saml Junr	GUIL (293, 324)
Scott, Thomas	GLAS (87)	Scranton, Theo	GUIL (290)
Scott, Thos	ASHF (311)	Scranton, Theophilus	GUIL (296)
Scoval, Elisha	COLC (8)	Scranton, Timo	GUIL (300, 310, 327)
Scovel, Elisha	MIDD (363)	Scripture, John	MANS (354)
Scovel, Ezra	FARM (9, 17, 449)	Scripture, Simeon	COVE (171)
Scovel, Jonah	EHAD (69)	Scriptures, John	COVE (171)
Scovel, Micha	HARL (44, 46)	Seabury, Benj Jur	LEBA (326)
Scovel, Samuel	CORN (1, 9, 10, 18)	Seabury, Olivr	LEBA (315)
Scovel, Stephen	EHAD (50, 54, 70)	Seamons, Benjn	KILY (94)
Scovel, Timothy	CORN (9)	Sears, Capt	HADD (113, 119, 121, 123, 129)
Scovell, Ezra	FARM (3, 9, 18, 29, 433, 438, 443, 449)		
		Sears, Charles Capt	HADD (109, 113, 114, 116, 117)
Scovil, Ens	HADD (130)		
Scovil, Ezekiel	HARW (3, 14, 25, 534)	Sears, Ebenr Jur	CHAT (40, 42)
Scovil, Ezra	FARM (445)	Sears, Elias	MIDD (373)
Scovil, John	HADD (125, 148)	Sears, Elkanah	CHAT (37, 38, 40, 43, 51, 59)
Scovil, John [ ]	HADD (148)		
Scovil, Joseph	HADD (3, 23, 148)	Sears, Hezekiah	CHAT (30, 33, 38, 40, 44, 68)
Scovil, Josiah	HADD (109, 121)		
Scovil, Judah	COLC (251)	Sears, Hezekiah Ensn	CHAT (42)
Scovil, Micah	HARL (52)	Sears, Hezh	CHAT (43)
Scovil, Micha	HARL (47)	Sears, Isaac	CHAT (53, 54, 55)
Scovil, Sam Serg	HADD (110)	Sears, John	MIDD (346)
Scovil, Saml	HADD (123, 130)	Sears, Matthew	EHAD (60, 65)
Scovil, Saml Ens	HADD (113, 122, 127)	Sears, Nathan	MIDD (356, 363)
Scovil, Samuel	CORN (12, 13, 16, 86), HADD (109, 110, 113, 116, 117)	Sears, Saml	FARM (24)
		Sears, Stephen	MIDD (362, 380, 394)
Scovil, Samuel Ens	HADD (114, 116, 117, 120, 129)	Seaward, [ ]	GUIL (341)
		Seaward, Ashar	GUIL (334)
		Seaward, Asher	GUIL (340)
Scovil, Timothy	CORN (9)	Seaward, David	GUIL (343)
Scovil, Westal	GUIL (270)	Seaward, David Capt	GUIL (274, 283, 299, 309, 324, 328, 339, 340)
Scovil, William	HADD (110)		
Scovil, William Jur	HADD (116, 117)	Seaward, David Junr	GUIL (274, 286, 293, 299, 309, 322, 340)
Scovil, Willm Jur	HADD (114, 148)		
Scovill, Ezra	FARM (29, 31, 444)	Seaward, Job	KILH (52, 54)
Scovill, Judah	COLC (11, 247)	Seaward, Moses	DURH (16)
Scovill, Samuel	CORN (22)	Seaward, Saml	DURH (17, 24, 26)
Scovill, Timothy	CORN (87)	Seaward, Sutlief	DURH (20)
Scrantom, Abraham	DURH (10, 21)	Seaward, Timo	GUIL (316)
Scrantom, Abraham Jur	DURH (16, 18)	Seaward, Timothy	GUIL (308)
		Sedgwick, Abraham Capt	HARF (275, 282)
Scrantom, Abrm	DURH (24)		

INDEX

Name	Index Pages	Name	Index Pages
Sedgwick, Benjamin	CANA (11, 12)	Seldin, Cephas	HADD (110, 119, 121)
Sedgwick, Benjn	CANA (15, 77)	Seldin, Joseph	HADD (110)
Sedgwick, Jno Major	CORN (84)	Seldin, Joseph Capt	HADD (109, 110)
Sedgwick, John	CORN (9), 25, 88, 91)	Seldin, Thomas	CHAT (51, 64, 67)
Sedgwick, John Colo	CORN (30)	Seldin, Thos Capt	HADD (118)
Sedgwick, John Lieut	CORN (77)	Selding, Thomas	CHAT (42)
Sedgwick, John Major	CORN (1, 2, 9, 12, 14, 16, 17, 19, 20, 22, 23, 24, 25, 26, 28)	Selding, Thos	CHAT (43)
		Seldon, Thomas	CHAT (41)
		Selew, John	GLAS (66, 94)
Sedgwick, Jonathan	HARF (255A)	Selew, Philip	GLAS (66, 77, 79, 105)
Sedgwick, Saml	CANA (64)	Sellew, John	GLAS (112)
Sedgwick, Stephen	FARM (432)	Sellew, Philip	GLAS (111)
Sedgwick, Stepn	FARM (443)	Sely, James	DANB (62)
Seeley, Ezra	FAIR (258)	Sergeant, Saml	MANS (353)
Seeley, Jos	FAIR (258)	Serymour, Daniel	HARF (263)
Seeley, Nathan	FAIR (254, 257, 258)	Sessions, Saml	EWIN (13)
Seeley, Nathaniel Jur	FAIR (257)	Sessions, Samuel	EWIN (8, 12, 15, 17)
Seeley, Nathl	FAIR (257)	Settle, Thomas	CANA (64)
Seeley, Nathl 2d	FAIR (258)	Severy, Solomon	HEBR (219)
Seeley, Nathl 3d	FAIR (254)	Seward, Daniel	HARL (53)
Seeley, Seth	FAIR (258)	Seward, David Capt	GUIL (335)
Seely, [ ]	DANB (64)	Seward, John	HADD (110, 116)
Seely, Ezra	FAIR (252, 253, 255, 256)	Seward, Nathan	CORN (23, 25)
Seely, Isaac	FAIR (253, 259, 260, 263, 266)	Sexton, Ezekiel	EWIN (85, 88)
		Sexton, James	COLC (243)
Seely, James	DANB (39, 49, 51, 56, 59, 60, 61, 62, 63, 65)	Sexton, Jesse	CHAT (55, 64, 68)
		Sexton, Saml	CHAT (40, 58)
Seely, James Lieut	DANB (58)	Sexton, Samuel	CHAT (41, 43)
Seely, Joseph	FAIR (255)	Sexton, Simeon	GUIL (272)
Seely, Nathan	FAIR (252, 256, 259, 260, 262, 263, 265, 267)	Sexton, Thomas	EWIN (8)
		Seymour, Capt	GOSH (119)
Seely, Nathan Capt	FAIR (259)	Seymour, Charles	HARF (255A, 261a, 266, 272, 281, 287)
Seely, Nathaniel 3d	FAIR (252)		
Seely, Nathl 2d	FAIR (258)	Seymour, Daniel	HARF (253, 255A, 256, 266, 267, 273, 281, 288, 293)
Seely, Nathl 3d	FAIR (253, 255, 258, 262, 263)		
Seely, Nathl Capt	FAIR (253, 255, 259, 261, 262, 264)	Seymour, Daniel Capt	HARF (281)
		Seymour, Drake	GREE (128)
Seely, Nathl Jur	FAIR (266, 267)	Seymour, Elisha	HARF (263, 267, 273, 281, 287, 293)
Seely, Saml	FAIR (267)		
Seely, Seth	FAIR (252, 253, 254, 255, 256, 259, 261, 262, 263, 264, 265, 267)	Seymour, Israel	HARF (255A, 266)
		Seymour, John	HARF (261a, 263, 292)
		Seymour, John Lieut	HARF (275)
Segar, Eli	DANB (39, 40, 49, 59)	Seymour, Jonathan	HARF (251(2))
Seger, Eli	DANB (47)	Seymour, Joseph	COLE (11, 113, 115)
Selbey, William	HARL (58)	Seymour, Joseph Ensn	COLE (11)
Selbey, Wilm	HARL (57)	Seymour, Joseph Junr	COLE (7, 11, 115)
Selbey, Wm	HARL (55)	Seymour, Moses	HARF (253, 256, 263), LITC (132, 157)
Selby, [ ]	EHAD (44)		
Selby, Ephraim	EHAD (59)	Seymour, Moses Capt	LITC (129, 157, 158, 159, 161)
Selby, William	EHAD (45, 50, 55, 56, 60, 64, 69, 80, 87), HARL (44, 47, 52, 55, 56, 57, 59, 60, 61)		
		Seymour, Roger	BRAN (169, 178)
		Seymour, Saml	GREE (119, 120, 126, 128)
Selby, Wm	HARL (45, 46)		
Selden, Cephas	HADD (148)	Seymour, Samuel	GREE (121, 125)
Selden, Elias	HADD (117)	Seymour, Samuel Capt	GREE (119)
Selden, Joseph	EHAD (54, 64, 66, 79), FARM (2, 5)	Seymour, Thomas	HARF (250, 258, 263A, 270, 294, 296, 299)
Selden, Thomas	CHAT (40)	Seymour, Thomas Colo	HARF (27, 275, 276, 279, 291, 294, 295, 297, 298, 299, 300)
Selden, Thos	CHAT (45)		
Seldin, [ ] Jur	HADD (109)		

707

INDEX

Name	Index Pages	Name	Index Pages
Seymour, Timothy Junr	HARF (275, 281, 283, 288, 292)	Shepard, Saml	FARM (443), MIDD (368)
Seymour, Zebulon	HARF (251, 255)	Shepard, Squire	CANT (146)
Shailer, Asa	HADD (112)	Shepard, Timothy	HARF (252(2), 256, 263, 267, 273, 281)
Shailer, Asa Sergt	HADD (113, 117)		
Shailer, Bezaleel	HADD (109)	Shepard, Timothy Junr	HARF (281, 288, 293)
Shailer, Bezeleel	HADD (113)	Shepart, Thomas	FARM (22)
Shailer, Ezra	HADD (113, 121, 148)	Shephard, Eldad	HARL (43, 45, 51)
Shailer, Hez	HADD (126)	Shephard, Jared Capt	MIDD (350, 358)
Shailer, Hezh	HADD (121)	Shephard, Saml	MIDD (357)
Shailer, Reuben	HADD (121)	Shephard, Samuel	MIDD (355)
Shailer, Thomas Jur	HADD (110, 125)	Shepherd, [ ]	HARL (50)
Shailer, Thomas Sergt	HADD (117, 120, 124)	Shepherd, Capt	MIDD (415)
Shailer, Thos Jr	HADD (113)	Shepherd, Eldad	HARL (42, 46, 48, 49, 50)
Shailer, Thos Sergt	HADD (121)		
Shapley, Jno	LEBA (309)	Shepherd, Jared Capt	MIDD (366, 381, 387, 394, 396, 397, 405, 407, 409, 415, 416, 420)
Sharp, Isaac	COLE (7)		
Sharper	GROT [17], [24]		
Shattuck, Randale	CHAT (59)	Sherman, [ ]	GOSH (137, 138, 141)
Shattuck, Robert	COLC (11)	Sherman, Daniel	DANB (39), HARW (2, 22)
Shaw, [ ]	GLAS (80)		
Shaw, Daniel	EHAD (64, 84)	Sherman, Josiah	GOSH (137)
Shaw, David	EWIN (85, 89)	Sherman, Josiah Revd	MILF (83), GOSH (129, 132, 133, 136)
Shearwood, Joseph	DERB (120, 122, 140)		
Sheffield, Nathaniel	KILY (87a)	Sherman, Revd	GOSH (127, 128, 134, 137, 141)
Shelby, Reuben	GUIL (269)		
Sheldin, Remembrance	HARL (45, 50)	Shertliff, Silvanus	ASHF (310)
Sheldon, Asher	BRAN (179)	Sherwod, Ebenr	CORN (86)
Sheldon, Daniel	HARF (291)	Sherwood, Albert	FAIR (252, 254, 260, 262, 263, 266, 269)
Sheldon, Isaac	HARF (250)		
Sheldon, John	HARF (257)	Sherwood, Benja	FAIR (260, 262)
Sheldon, John Junr	HARF (272)	Sherwood, Danl 2d	FAIR (252, 253, 256, 257, 258, 259, 260, 262, 263, 264, 265, 266, 267)
Sheldon, Joseph	HARF (263A, 265, 266, 272, 300)		
Sheldon, Samuel	LITC (129, 141, 153)	Sherwood, Jabez Capt	GREE (120)
Shelhar, John	LITC (152)	Sherwood, Jeremiah	FAIR (264, 265, 266, 267, 269)
Shelley, Ebenr	GUIL (304)		
Shelley, John	GUIL (335)	Sherwood, Joseph	DERB (145)
Shelley, Shubal	GUIL (334, 340)	Sherwood, Moses	FAIR (252, 254, 257, 258, 260, 261, 262, 263, 264)
Shelley, Timo	GUIL (290)		
Shepard, Abel	CHAT (42)		
Shepard, Daniel	CHAT (43, 51)	Sherwood, Noah	FAIR (267)
Shepard, Daniel Jur	CHAT (29, 30, 39, 40, 45, 48, 51, 64, 67)	Sherwood, Oliver	GREE (119)
		Sherwood, Saml 2d	FAIR (262)
Shepard, Daniel Lt	CHAT (31, 34, 40, 45, 64, 68)	Sherwood, Saml Jur	FAIR (264)
		Sherwood, Samuel 2d	FAIR (260)
Shepard, Ebenezer	COLE (5, 7, 113)	Sherwood, Seth	FAIR (256, 259, 260, 263)
Shepard, Edward	CHAT (29, 40, 43, 47, 64, 67)	Sherwood, Thos	FAIR (266)
		Shethar, John	LITC (158)
Shepard, Eldad	HARL (53, 56, 59, 61)	Shillenx, Abraham	CHAT (29)
Shepard, Elisha	CHAT (31, 34, 37, 38, 41, 42, 43, 46, 51, 58, 65, 68)	Shipman, Fradrick	HARL (44)
		Shipman, John	GLAS (83, 84, 92)
Shepard, Jared	MIDD (368, 370, 399, 401, 417)	Shipman, Jothan	HARL (52)
		Shipman, Majr	DURH (26)
		Shipman, Stephen	GLAS (93)
Shepard, Jared Capt	MIDD (360)	Shipman, Stephen Jur	GLAS (93, 105, 112)
Shepard, John	CHAT (37, 41, 42, 45, 51, 52, 65), HARF (253, 256, 263, 267, 273, 281, 288, 293)	Shipman, Steven Jur	GLAS (92)
		Shirman, [ ]	GOSH (139)
		Shirtleif, Silvas	ASHF (308)
Shepard, John Jur	CHAT (59)	Shirtliff, William	EWIN (15)
Shepard, Jonathan Jur	EHAD (57)	Shirtliff, Wm	EWIN (10, 13, 17)
Shepard, Joseph	CHAT (42)	Sholes, Abel	GROT [4], [9]

708

INDEX

Name	Index Pages
Short, Siloam	KILY (8, 19)
Shove, Benj[ ]	DANB (39)
Shove, Daniel	DANB (70)
Shove, Daniel Jur	DANB (51)
Shove, Danl Jur	DANB (46)
Shove, Seth	DANB (69)
Shumway, John Capt	MANS (342)
Shurtlif, Salvenus	ASHF (232)
Shurtliff, William	EWIN (9)
Shute, Capt	DANB (66)
Shute, Richard	DANB (49)
Shute, Richd	DANB (39, 40)
Shute, Richd Capt	DANB (65)
Siilliman, Ebenr	FAIR (262)
Sill, Capt	COLE (3), GOSH (119, 120, 130, 138, 139, 184), HARL (60)
Sill, Dr	GOSH (110)
Sill, E Capt	GOSH (138)
Sill, Elisha Capt	GOSH (130, 140)
Sill, Richard Lord	CORN (89, 90)
Sill, Richd L Doct	CORN (1)
Sill, Thomas	HARL (45, 53)
Sill, Thomas Lieut	HARL (48)
Silleck, Gold John	GREE (126)
Silleman, John	KENT (E59)
Sillick, Nathl	DANB (49, 59)
Silliman, Daniel	FAIR (255, 263)
Silliman, David	FAIR (252, 253, 254, 256, 257, 258, 259, 260, 261, 262, 263, 265, 267)
Silliman, Deodate	FAIR (259, 262, 263, 264, 265, 267)
Silliman, Ebenezer	FAIR (269)
Silliman, Ebenr	FAIR (259, 260, 265, 267)
Silliman, G Selleck	FAIR (251, 252, 253, 254), 255, 256, 258, 262)
Silliman, G Selleck Genl	FAIR (263)
Silliman, Genl	FAIR (254)
Silliman, Gold S Colo	FAIR (269)
Silliman, Gold Selleck	FAIR (251, 262, 263, 264, 266, 269)
Silliman, Jonth	FAIR (264, 265, 266)
Silliman, Seth	FAIR (258)
Silliman, Seth Capt	FAIR (256, 257)
Silliman, William	FAIR (253)
Silva	GROT [17], [24]
Simmins, Ebenezer	CORN (87)
Simmons Ebenezer	CORN (17)
Simmons, Asa	CORN (17)
Simmons, Ebenezer	CORN (1, 12, 18, 23, 91)
Simmons, Ebenr	CORN (10, 13)
Simmons, Joshua	HADD (148)
Simmons, Saml	MIDD (363)
Simon, [ ]	COLE (11)
Simon, Abil Junr	ASHF (228)
Simon, Paul	HARL (48)
Simonds, Arad	MANS (340)
Simonds, Eliphalet	MANS (340)
Simonds, Nathan	MANS (338)
Simons, Aaron	COLE (113)

Name	Index Pages
Simons, Abel	ASHF (232)
Simons, Benjn	ENFD (34)
Simons, Hezekiah	COLE (4, 7, 11, 13, 113)
Simons, James	COLE (113)
Simons, Joel	ENFD (34)
Simons, Joseph	GLAS (70, 74, 78, 94)
Simons, Paul	EWIN (85, 88), HARL (43, 44)
Simons, William	COLE (113, 115)
Sims, Edward	LEBA (341)
Sims, George	LEBA (316)
Sims, John	CANT (150)
Simson, Benjn	GLAS (65)
Sizer, Abel	MIDD (362, 374)
Sizer, Jona	MIDD (372)
Sizer, Jonathan	MIDD (382)
Sizer, William	MIDD (364, 366)
Sizer, Wm Capt	MIDD (389, 395)
Skiff, Joseph	KENT (C543, 552)
Skiff, Nathan	KENT (C552, E59, E63)
Skiff, Nathan Jur	KENT (D7, D14, E59, E63)
Skiff, Stephen	KENT (A28, C555, D7, E58, E62)
Skiff, Stephen 3d	KENT (C555)
Skiner, Elijah	BOLT (146)
Skiner, John	BOLT (147, 148, 149, 157)
Skiner, Reuben	BOLT (147)
Skiner, Reubin	BOLT (148)
Skinner, Joseph	COLC (248)
Skinner, Nathaniel	HARF (266)
Skinner, Abijah	EWIN (85, 88)
Skinner, Abiram	EWIN (8, 85, 89)
Skinner, Abraham	GLAS (77, 106)
Skinner, Abraham Jur	GLAS (81, 94)
Skinner, Abram Junr	GLAS (70)
Skinner, Asahel	BOLT (167, 180, 183)
Skinner, Ashbil	HARW (5, 7, 9, 13, 15, 16, 21, 523, 533)
Skinner, Ashbil Jur	HARW (3, 16, 17)
Skinner, Benja	HEBR (235)
Skinner, Benjamin	EWIN (85)
Skinner, Benjn	EWIN (89), GLAS (94)
Skinner, Capt	HEBR (235)
Skinner, Daniel	COVE (165)
Skinner, Daniel Capt	HARF (289)
Skinner, Daniel Junr	HARF (263A, 266, 268, 271, 272, 281, 285, 285A, 286, 287, 288, 289, 290, 292)
Skinner, David	COLC (11), EWIN (10, 85, 88), HEBR (216)
Skinner, Elias	BOLT (181)
Skinner, Elijah	BOLT (154, 157, 160, 165, 166, 180, 182)
Skinner, Ezekiel	GLAS (98)
Skinner, Ezel	GLAS (94)
Skinner, Jno	HEBR (218)

INDEX

Name	Index Pages	Name	Index Pages
Skinner, John	BOLT (151, 153, 155, 160, 167, 180, 182, 183), HARF (251, 255A, 272, 281, 287)	Slosson, Nathan	KENT (C548, C550, D8, D11)
		Smalley, Daniel Junr	LEBA (305)
		Smalley, John Revd	FARM (456)
Skinner, John 2nd	COLC (248)	Smedley, Ephraim Junr	LITC (129, 141, 155)
Skinner, John Capt	HARF (275, 280, 290), HEBR (220, 234, 245)	Smedley, Gideon	LITC (146, 152, 158)
		Smedley, Nathan	LITC (153)
Skinner, John Jur	BOLT (183)	Smedly, John	FAIR (262, 263, 265, 267
Skinner, John Lt	HEBR (217)	Smith, Asher	GOSH (183)
Skinner, Jonathan	BOLT (181, 182), HARF (263, 288, 292)	Smith, [ ]	HADD (113, 119), KILH (146)
Skinner, Jos	COLC (7)	Smith, Aaron	HADD (109, 113, 148)
Skinner, Joseph	COLC (243, 251), HARF (275, 279, 285)	Smith, Aaron Ens	HADD (115, 124, 126)
		Smith, Abijah	LEBA (305, 315)
Skinner, Lieut	LITC (149)	Smith, Abner	MIDD (366)
Skinner, Luther	BOLT (181)	Smith, Abner Capt	MIDD (351, 359)
Skinner, Nathaniel	HARF (255A, 261a)	Smith, Abraham	DERB (106, 107, 124, 127, 132, 141, 145, 167, 168)
Skinner, Noah	COLC (246)		
Skinner, Noah Capt	COLC (246, 248)		
Skinner, Noah Jur	COLC (249, 251, 254)	Smith, Abraham Jnr	DERB (122)
Skinner, Patience	BOLT (181)	Smith, Abraham Leut	DERB (135)
Skinner, Richard	BOLT (180, 182), GLAS (66, 71, 95, 103), HARF (253, 255A, 256, 263, 267, 273, 281, 288, 293)	Smith, Abram	DERB (168)
		Smith, Abram Jnr	DERB (121)
		Smith, Alexander	EWIN (12)
		Smith, Alexr	EWIN (13)
Skinner, Richard Junr	COLC (251)	Smith, Allen	BRAN (173)
Skinner, Ruben	BOLT (146, 155, 158, 160, 162, 164, 166, 167, 180)	Smith, Allen Ensign	BRAN (166, 170)
		Smith, Allin	FARM (17)
		Smith, Allyn	FARM (438)
Skinner, Stephen	COLC (8)	Smith, Amasa	FARM (455)
Skinner, Thomas	EWIN (85, 88), HARW (3, 4, 7, 8, 13, 16, 18, 21, 23, 24)	Smith, Andrew	DERB (106, 113, 121, 122, 141, 145, 168)
		Smith, Asa	ASHF (310), CANT (168), HARL (53, 59), HARW (3, 10, 17)
Skinner, Timo	HARF (252(2))		
Skinner, Timothy	EWIN (8), LITC (131, 134, 135, 139, 141, 142, 143, 145, 146, 147, 148, 152, 153, 157, 158, 159)	Smith, Asa Doctor	HARL (45, 48, 49, 51, 56, 58, 59)
		Smith, Asaph	ASHF (217)
Skinner, Timothy Lt	LITC (155)	Smith, Asaph Capt	ASHF (213, 214, 218, 219, 222, 226, 308)
Skinner, Uriah	BOLT (163, 183)		
Skinner, Zenas	BOLT (162)	Smith, Aseph Capt	ASHF (232, 236)
Slade, James	EWIN (9)	Smith, Assa Dr	HARL (41, 43)
Slade, Thomas	HARF (253)	Smith, B[ ]ton	HADD (148)
Slade, Thos	HARF (285)	Smith, Benja Jur	FAIR (255)
Slafter, Eleazar	MANS (285, 336)	Smith, Benjamin	CHAT (31, 33, 43, 64, 68)
Slafter, Samuel	MANS (328, 338, 348)		
Slason, Nathan	KENT (D5)	Smith, Benjn	CHAT (38, 45), GLAS (85, 93)
Slate, Ebenezer	MANS (262)		
Slate, Sarah	MANS (262)	Smith, Benoni	GLAS (78, 93)
Slate, Thomas	HARF (266)	Smith, Benoni Capt	GLAS (85, 89, 90, 102, 109, 114)
Slater, Samuel	MANS (271)		
Slew, Philip	GLAS (93)	Smith, Caleb	FARM (443), MILF (88)
Sloan, Robert	HARF (273)	Smith, Capt	MIDD (415)
Sloan, Thomas	HARF (253, 256, 263, 263A, 267, 281, 285, 288, 293)	Smith, Challenge	HADD (148, 125)
		Smith, Challenge Sergt	HADD (121)
		Smith, Charles	GROT ([18], [20], [23]), HADD (109, 110, 111, 114), LITC (129, 160)
Slone, Saml	MILF (103)		
Sloper, Ambrose	FARM (442, 449, 452)		
Sloper, Danl	FARM (443, 450, 452)	Smith, Charles Junr	LITC (131, 139, 158)
Sloper, Danl Capt	FARM (435)	Smith, Charles Sergt	HADD (112, 114, 115)
Sloson, Nathan	KENT (A28, C552, E63)	Smith, Cheleab	GOSH (115)

INDEX

Name	Index Pages
Smith, Cheliab	GOSH (112, 120, 130, 183)
Smith, Chileab	GOSH (116, 184)
Smith, Chuliab	GOSH (110)
Smith, Cristepher	DERB (113, 124, 131, 141)
Smith, Daniel	CHAT (51, 55)
Smith, Daniel Jur	HADD (128, 129, 148)
Smith, Danl	FARM (443, 449)
Smith, David	CHAT (33, 39, 45, 47, 50), DERB (138), EWIN (16, 17, 85, 88), FARM (442, 444), GLAS (92)
Smith, David Capt	CHAT (67)
Smith, David Jur	CHAT (39), FARM (456)
Smith, David Lieut	CHAT (32, 39, 45, 53, 56, 58)
Smith, Doctr	HARF (255)
Smith, Dow	BRAN (163, 170, 171, 175, 178, 179)
Smith, Ebenezer	HADD (112, 114, 115, 116, 148)
Smith, Elathn	FARM (6)
Smith, Eli	LITC (131, 135, 139, 146, 147, 153, 159)
Smith, Elias	HADD (129, 148)
Smith, Elihu	FARM (28, 436)
Smith, Elijah	FARM (9, 436, 438, 443, 445), GLAS (60, 63, 66, 67, 70, 71, 75, 88, 93, 114)
Smith, Elijah Capt	CHAT (52, 54, 59, 68), COLC (242)
Smith, Elijah Jur	FARM (438)
Smith, Eliphalet	HADD (123)
Smith, Elnan	FARM (17)
Smith, Elnathan	FARM (7, 8, 9, 433, 440, 441, 449)
Smith, Enoch	CHAT (29, 30, 31, 32, 33, 34, 35, 36, 37, 38, 39, 41, 43, 44, 50, 51, 64), DERB (122)
Smith, Enoch 3d	CHAT (43, 53, 55, 61, 63
Smith, Enoch Jur	CHAT (51, 54, 64)
Smith, Enock	DERB (120)
Smith, Enos	KILH (145)
Smith, Ephraim	CHES (4, 9, 11, 14)
Smith, Ephraim Jur	CHES (8, 11), MILF (85)
Smith, Ezekil	KILY (89)
Smith, Ezra	ASHF (206, 310)
Smith, Ezra Capt	ASHF (211)
Smith, Ezra Leut	ASHF (201, 207, 210, 308)
Smith, Francis	HARF (261a, 281)
Smith, George	HARF (250, 292)
Smith, George Capt	HARF (300)
Smith, Gilbert	GROT [12], [19], [21], [23], [25]
Smith, Heman	GOSH (120, 130, 183, 185)
Smith, Hezekiah	HADD (125, 128), MILF (88, 103, 106)

Name	Index Pages
Smith, Hezh	ASHF (226, 311), MILF (98)
Smith, Hope Capt	KILY (5)
Smith, Ignatious	EHAD (45)
Smith, Isaac	CANA (64, 77), DERB (106, 113, 120, 122, 126, 127, 132, 140, 141, 142, 145), FARM 20, 443, 444), GLAS (66, 70, 74, 75, 78, 82, 93, 98, 105, 111, 114), MILF (82)
Smith, Isaac Capt	DERB (167), MILF (78, 85, 86, 88, 92, 98, 103, 105)
Smith, Isaac Dr	CHAT (42)
Smith, Isaac Jur	CHAT (32, 40, 42, 45. 59
Smith, Isaac Lieut	DERB (132)
Smith, Israel	GLAS (78, 83, 98, 106, 112)
Smith, Israel Jur	GLAS (114)
Smith, Jabez	GROT ([19])
Smith, Jabez Capt	GROT ([4])
Smith, Jabez Junr	GROT ([9])
Smith, Jacob	CANT (180)
Smith, Jacob Jr	CANT (151, 168, 176)
Smith, James	BRAN (165, 166, 170), FARM (443), MIDD (364, 382)
Smith, James Capt	HADD (123)
Smith, James Jur	FARM (455)
Smith, Jeduthun	GLAS (95)
Smith, Jeremiah	FARM (443)
Smith, Jno	ASHF (222)
Smith, Jno Capt	MIDD (408)
Smith, Joel	MILF (82, 106)
Smith, John	CANT (148, 168), EWIN (8, 10, 11, 15, 17), LITC (147), MILF (91, 92)
Smith, John 3d	HADD (125)
Smith, John Capt	GOSH (184), HADD (113, 117, 121, 124, 125), MIDD (409), MILF (102)
Smith, John Lieut	HADD (110), MILF (93, 98)
Smith, Jona	GLAS (98)
Smith, Jona Wait	FARM (444)
Smith, Jonah	GREE (119)
Smith, Jonath	GLAS (70, 83)
Smith, Jonathan	BOLT (146, 147, 157, 180), GLAS (74, 78, 94), HADD (125, 129), LITC (129)
Smith, Jonathan Jur	CHAT (38, 43), LITC (158)
Smith, Jonathn Jur	CHAT (51)
Smith, Jos	CANT (148), FARM (443)

INDEX

Name	Index Pages	Name	Index Pages
Smith, Joseph	BRAN (166, 175, 178), CANT (50), DERB (131), DURH (21, 24, EWIN (10, 85, 88), FAIR (252, 260, 263, 265, 266), FARM (2, 16, 17, 24, 33, 455), MIDD (363, 365, 366)	Smith, Richard	DERB (120, 124), GLAS (95), HARF (299)
		Smith, Saml	EWIN (89), FARM (2, 6, 9, 18, 427, 436, 440, 441, 442, 444, 446, 452, 456), GLAS (111, 115), HADD (148), KILH (145)
Smith, Joseph Lt	DURH (24)	Smith, Saml Jnr	DERB (133)
Smith, Joshua	ASHF (310), GREE (119, 123, 126, 127, 128), LITC (153)	Smith, Samuel	DERB (106, 120), EWIN (85), FARM (3, 7, 15, 28, 31, 438, 455), GLAS (67, 68, 71, 78, 85, 86, 88, 93), HARF (255, 251(2), 261a), KILH (146)
Smith, Joshua Jur	HADD (125, 129, 148)		
Smith, Josiah	DERB (113, 120, 124, 126, 135, 141)		
		Smith, Samuel Capt	EHAR (3)
Smith, Lamberton	MILF (104)	Smith, Samuel Junr	HARF (253, 256)
Smith, Lemuel	CHAT (31, 69), FARM (29)	Smith, Seth Colo	COLE (4), HARL (55)
		Smith, Sim	ASHF (226)
Smith, Lewis	HADD (127)	Smith, Sim Capt	ASHF (224, 225, 308)
Smith, Lt	DURH (20)	Smith, Simeon	ASHF (202, 226, 238, 310), GROT ([19], [23])
Smith, Matthew 2d	EHAD (65, 79)		
Smith, Matthew 3d	EHAD (64)	Smith, Simeon Capt	ASHF (202, 207, 209, 216, 218, 220, 222, 223, 224, 225, 226, 227, 228, 229, 230, 231, 232, 233, 234, 235, 238, 239, 240)
Smith, Matthew Capt	EHAD (49, 53, 54, 55, 56, 57), GOSH (112, 114, 116, 117, 120, 124, 130, 184)		
Smith, Matthew Jr	EHAD (49)	Smith, Simion Capt	ASHF (221)
Smith, Matthew Lt	GOSH (102, 104)	Smith, Simn Capt	ASHF (213)
Smith, Mercy	FARM (19)	Smith, Solomon	ASHF (218, 233, 313), HARF (289, 290)
Smith, Nahum	BOLT (181)		
Smith, Nathan	DERB (167), HADD (148, 116)	Smith, Solomon Doct	HARF (270)
		Smith, Solon	ASHF (311)
Smith, Nathan Capt	DERB (106, 107, 113, 120, 122, 124, 126)	Smith, Step	GOSH (102, 110, 184)
		Smith, Stephen	FAIR (260)
Smith, Nathan Junr	GROT [6], [10]	Smith, Stephen Capt	HADD (110)
Smith, Nathan Major	DERB (135, 167)	Smith, Stephen Jur	HADD (148)
Smith, Nathan Sergt	HADD (115, 123)	Smith, Stepn	GOSH (112)
Smith, Nathaniel 2nd	LITC (152, 158)	Smith, Thankful	FARM (19)
Smith, Nathaniel Junr	MILF (104)	Smith, Thomas	COLC (11)
Smith, Nathl	MIDD (364)	Smith, Thomas 2d	EHAD (65)
Smith, Nehemiah	GROT [4], [18], [25]	Smith, Thomas 3d	FARM (455)
Smith, Noah	CHAT (33, 37, 39, 40, 43, 50, 59, 64, 67, 68), KENT (D1)	Smith, Thos	CHAT (54, 68), FARM (442)
		Smith, Thos Jur	FARM (9, 447, 451)
Smith, Noah Jur	KENT (E60)	Smith, Timothy	CHAT (29, 39, 40, 41, 45, 48)
Smith, Obadiah	CANA (64)		
Smith, Oliver	MANS (278)	Smith, Timt	CHAT (34)
Smith, Peabody	KENT (C548, C552, D1, E58, E63)	Smith, Venture	GLAS (107)
		Smith, Wait	FARM (449, 456)
Smith, Peter	ASHF (223, 233, 311), FAIR (261)	Smith, William	CANA (19, 64), FARM (16, 32), HADD (110, 112, 116, 126), MILF (104)
Smith, Phenihas	FARM (455)		
Smith, Ralph	CHAT (30, 44, 53, 58, 59, 65)		
		Smith, William 3d	GROT ([24])
Smith, Reuben	CANA (19, 64), HADD (110), LITC (128, 130, 133, 134, 138, 139, 140, 141, 146, 149, 150, 152, 156, 158, 159)	Smith, William Lieut	HADD (114, 116, 117)
		Smith, Willm	HADD (129), KILY (4)
		Smith, Wm	FARM (9, 18)
		Smith, Wm Lieut	HADD (121, 123)
		Smith, Ze[ ]h	ASHF (308)
Smith, Reuben Sergt	HADD (121)	Smith, Zoeth	CHAT (31)
Smith, Reubin	CANA (25)	Smith. Willm	FARM (449)
		Smithfield, Elisabeth	COLC (13)

INDEX

Name	Index Pages
Smithson, Robert	DURH (14, 16)
Snell, Thos	ASHF (311)
Snow, Abraham	CANT (160)
Snow, Benja	ASHF (218, 311)
Snow, Ebenezr	MANS (280)
Snow, Ebenr	MANS (281)
Snow, James	ASHF (202)
Snow, Joseph Junr	ASHF (222, 232)
Snow, Robert	ASHF (311)
Snow, Salvenus	ASHF (312)
Snow, Saml	ASHF (202, 203, 208, 209, 211, 218, 222)
Snow, Saml Junr	ASHF (311)
Snow, Samuel	ASHF (213, 236, 311)
Snow, Stephen	ASHF (226, 228, 311)
Snow, William	ASHF (209, 232)
Snow, Wm	ASHF (200, 202, 222, 226, 310)
Sonny	GLAS (86)
Southmaid, Daniel	EHAD (55)
Southmaid, Daniel Doct	EHAD (58)
Southmayd, Daniel	MIDD (344, 357, 363, 381)
Southmayd, Daniel Doct	EHAD (83)
Southmayd, Giles	MIDD (357, 368, 372, 414)
Southmayd, Jonathan	MIDD (363)
Southmayd, Partridge	MIDD (362)
Southmayd, Patridge	MIDD (346, 357)
Southmayd, William	MIDD (365)
Southmayd, Wm	MIDD (362)
Southworth, Asa	MANS (280, 353)
Southworth, Beri	LEBA (311, 341)
Southworth, Beri.	LEBA (326)
Southworth, Beri:h	LEBA (316)
Southworth, Beriah	LEBA (298, 299, 305, 315, 333, 334, 342)
Southworth, Bire	LEBA (327)
Southworth, Con	MANS (267, 271, 278, 279, 280, 281, 282, 328, 333, 335, 338, 339, 347, 353, 357)
Southworth, Const	MANS (255, 271, 328)
Southworth, Constant	MANS (258, 346, 360)
Southworth, Josiah	MANS (271, 280, 328)
Southworth, Nathaniel Junr	MANS (357)
Southworth, Nathl	MANS (277)
Southworth, Nathl Junr	MANS (281, 348)
Southworth, Saml	MANS (336)
Southworth, Samuel	MANS (271, 338)
Spafford, Abraham	MANS (267)
Spafford, Abraham Capt	MANS (273)
Spafford, Nathan	LEBA (311)
Spalding, Davis	KILY (7, 19, 32)
Spalding, Ebenezer Capt	CANT (148)
Spalding, Ebenr	CANT (139)
Spalding, Ebenr Capt	CANT (181)
Spalding, Ebenr Jur	CANT (154, 155, 174)
Spalding, Edward	CANA (64)
Spalding, Jacob	KILY (14)
Spalding, Saml	KILY (32, 34)
Spalding, Zadock	KILY (7, 10, 31, 36, 97a, 98)
Spalding, Zadok	KILY (95)
Sparks, Ruben	GLAS (93)
Sparrow, Nathaniel	EHAD (49, 62, 69, 73, 88, 89)
Sparrow, Richard	EHAD (44, 64, 66, 69, 87)
Spaulden, Josiah Lieut	ASHF (213)
Spaulding, David	KILY (94a)
Spaulding, Davis	KILY (87, 87a, 92. 96a, 97)
Spaulding, Ebenr Jr	CANT (167, 175)
Spaulding, Edward	CANA (15, 64)
Spaulding, Ephraim	ASHF (203, 213, 215, 226, 311)
Spaulding, Jacob	KILY (20, 94, 86a, 97)
Spaulding, John	CANA (11, 15, 16, 28)
Spaulding, Jos Lieut	ASHF (308)
Spaulding, Joseph	MIDD (356, 381)
Spaulding, Josiah	ASHF (206, 207, 209, 210, 218, 223, 226, 233, 236, 310)
Spaulding, Josiah Lieut	ASHF (218, 222)
Spaulding, Lieut	ASHF (224, 232)
Spaulding, Liut	ASHF (207)
Spaulding, Nathaniel	KILY (94)
Spaulding, Nathl	KILY (86a, 91a)
Spaulding, Rufus	MANS (340)
Spaulding, Simon	KILY (86a)
Spaulding, Zadock	KILY (86a, 91, 92, 94, 95, 96a)
Spelman, Phineas	DURH (8, 10)
Spelman, Phinehas	DURH (13, 14, 16, 17, 18, 19, 21, 23)
Spelman, Phins	DURH (15, 20, 22, 25)
Spelman, Richd	DURH (25)
Spence, John	FARM (17)
Spencer, [ ]	MIDD (376)
Spencer, Abigail	HADD (113)
Spencer, Abner	HADD (115, 116, 125)
Spencer, Abner Sergt	HADD (113)
Spencer, Abraham	HADD (126, 148)
Spencer, Ashbel	HARF (263)
Spencer, Caleb	HARL (48)
Spencer, Daniel	HADD (121)
Spencer, David B	EHAD (54)
Spencer, David B Capt	EHAD (68, 87, 80)
Spencer, David B Lieut	EHAD (53, 57)
Spencer, Ebenezer Capt	EHAD (53, 57, 59, 66)
Spencer, Elijah	HARF (287)
Spencer, Eliphas	EHAD (64, 66)
Spencer, Elisha	HADD (148)
Spencer, Gideon	EHAD (60)
Spencer, Ich[ ]	MIDD (394)
Spencer, Ichabod	MIDD (421)
Spencer, Ichd	MIDD (376)

INDEX

Name	Index Pages	Name	Index Pages
Spencer, Isaac	EHAD (44, 64, 86)	Sprauge, Daniel	KILY (92)
Spencer, Isaac 2nd	EHAD (69, 70, 80)	Sprauge, John	KILY (87a, 93, 95)
Spencer, Isaac Lt	EHAD (80)	Sprauge, John Leut	KILY (94a, 97)
Spencer, Israel	EHAD (49, 51, 82)	Spring, Sam	ASHF (308)
Spencer, Israel Capt	EHAD (55, 62, 67)	Spring, Saml	ASHF (310)
Spencer, Jared Capt	EHAD (48)	Spring, Samuel	ASHF (204, 218, 222, 233)
Spencer, Jehiel	DERB (120, 122)		
Spencer, Job	EHAD (44, 53, 54, 57, 59, 64, 69)	Squier, Amy	CORN (22, 27)
		Squier, Danl	FAIR (261)
Spencer, John	EHAD (45, 54, 64, 69, 114, 148), HARF (263), KILH (49, 50, 51, 54)	Squier, Ebenr	FAIR (253, 258, 265, 266, 267)
		Squier, John	FAIR (269)
Spencer, John Junr	HARF (287)	Squier, John 3d	FAIR (252, 257)
Spencer, Joseph	FARM (456)	Squier, John Jur	FAIR (259)
Spencer, Matthias	EHAD (59)	Squier, Jonathan	FAIR (255, 258, 259)
Spencer, Nathl	CHAT (51, 64)	Squier, Jonth	FAIR (257, 260, 267)
Spencer, Reuben	EHAD (59, 64, 79, 87)	Squier, Saml	FAIR (260, 263)
Spencer, Seth	HADD (111)	Squier, Saml Capt	FAIR (260)
Spencer, Shelden	MIDD (395)	Squier, Samuel	FAIR (261, 269)
Spencer, Sheldin	MIDD (398)	Squire, David	DURH (25)
Spencer, Simeon	BOLT (165, 180, 182)	Squire, Elias	MIDD (385)
Spencer, Thomas	HARF (272, 292), HARL (47, 52)	Squire, Jesse	CANA (28)
		Squire, Philip	GLAS (106)
Spencer, Thos	HARL (51)	Squire, Robert	KENT (E61)
Spencer, Timothy	EHAD (85)	St John, Timothy	KENT (B2, C548, C552, C555, D1, D10, D7, E58, E62)
Sperry, Benjamin	DANB (39)		
Sperry, Ebenezer	HARW (6, 9, 10, 14, 17, 533)		
		St[ ], Andrew Revd	GOSH (123)
Sperry, Ebenezr	HARW (3)	St[ ], Josh	FARM (431)
Sperry, Richd	MILF (105)	Stafford, Thomas	COLE (7)
Spicer, Abel	GROT [7], [9], [16], [21]	Stanard, Saml	HADD (148)
Spicer, Abel Capt	GROT [12], [15]	Stanard, Samuel	HADD (112, 116)
Spicer, Edward	GROT [9], [23]	Stanclift, James	CHAT (37, 39)
Spicer, John	GROT [6]	Stand, Saml	FARM (447)
Spicer, Oliver	GROT []7], [9], [10], [12], [16], [18]	Standley, Jiramiah	ASHF (236)
		Standly, Jeremiah	ASHF (311)
Spicer, Oliver Capt	GROT [7], [14], [17], [19]	Stanley, Caleb	COVE (178)
		Stanley, Caleb Jur	COVE (166, 172, 177)
Spier, Abel Capt	GROT [7]	Stanley, Capt	GOSH (102, 104)
Spinning, Levi	GUIL (340, 341)	Stanley, Col	FARM (8, 23, 11, 12, 15, 23)
Spooner, Ebenezer Jur	KENT (D7, D10)		
Spooner, Ebenr	KENT (E59)	Stanley, Elijah	FARM (456)
Spooner, George	MIDD (363, 377)	Stanley, Elisha	HARF (266)
Spooner, Nathl	KENT (E60, E63)	Stanley, Fredrick	LITC (153)
Spooner, William	KENT (C552, D10)	Stanley, Gad	FARM (6, 14, 21, 30, 453
Spooner, William Jur	KENT (E63)	Stanley, Gad Col	FARM (2, 3, 5, 8, 12, 17, 18, 26, 28, 29, 31, 32, 33, 34, 454)
Spooner, Wilm	KENT (D12, E59, E63)		
Spooner, Wilm Jur	KENT (E59)		
Spoulding, Zadock	KILY (91a)	Stanley, Gad Majr	FARM (448, 452, 453)
Sprage, James	KENT (E59)	Stanley, John	FARM (449)
Sprague, Benj	LEBA (325)	Stanley, Jonathan Junr	HARF (253)
Sprague, Benj[ ]	LEBA (299, 329)	Stanley, Lott	FARM (2, 436, 449, 450)
Sprague, Benjamin	LEBA (305)	Stanley, Major	FARM (440, 445, 451, 453)
Sprague, Benjn	LEBA (316)		
Sprague, Dyer	LEBA (342)	Stanley, Moses	COVE (165, 167, 174, 175, 314)
Sprague, Elisha	COVE (314)		
Sprague, John	CANA (77)	Stanley, Nathaniel	CANA (12, 27)
Sprague, John Leut	KILY (10)	Stanley, Noah	FARM (5, 28, 442, 446, 448)
Sprague, John Lt	KILY (14)		
Sprague, Saml	COVE (314, 315)	Stanley, Oliver	CHES (10), FARM (2, 5, 9)
Sprague, Samuel	COVE (170, 172, 178)		
Sprague, Wm Jur	LEBA (326)	Stanley, Saml	FARM (2, 9, 442)

INDEX

Name	Index Pages	Name	Index Pages
Stanley, Seth	FARM (2, 6, 8, 17, 28, 438, 443, 444, 449, 453)	Starkweather, Stephen	KENT (E59)
		Starlin, Simon	EHAD (69)
Stanley, Thomas	FARM (29)	Starns, Elias Isn	KILY (90)
Stanley, Thoms	FARM (9)	Starr, Timo Capt	MIDD (406)
Stanley, Thos	FARM (18)	Starr, William	GROT ([4])
Stanley, Timo	FARM (9)	Starr, [ ]	GOSH (134)
Stanley, Timothy	FARM (3, 5, 16, 442, 452	Starr, Abijah	DANB (47)
Stanly, [ ]	GOSH (104)	Starr, Benajah	DANB (40, 47)
Stanly, Amaziah	HARF (281)	Starr, Daniel	MIDD (370)
Stanly, Ashbel	HARF (299)	Starr, Danl	MIDD (368)
Stanly, Caleb Jur	COVE (180)	Starr, David	MIDD (346, 376, 377, 405)
Stanly, Capt	GOSH (104, 109, 110, 130, 184)	Starr, David Capt	MIDD (382, 387, 395)
Stanly, Earl	GOSH (125)	Starr, Eliakim	DANB (40, 46, 49, 51, 58, 61, 63)
Stanly, Elisha	GOSH (185, 186), HARF (268, 272, 281)	Starr, Elihu	MIDD (347, 349, 350, 351, 353, 356, 357, 359, 365, 368, 369, 373, 380, 386, 393, 406, 414)
Stanly, Erl	GOSH (138)		
Stanly, Gad	FARM (427, 430, 435)		
Stanly, Gad Capt	FARM (433)		
Stanly, Gad Majr	FARM (443, 446)	Starr, Elihus	MIDD (356)
Stanly, Hezekiah	FARM (433)	Starr, Eph	GOSH (104, 111, 112, 123)
Stanly, John	FARM (443), HARF (274)	Starr, Ephm	GOSH (106, 109, 110, 140, 184)
Stanly, Jonathan Jur	EHAR (2, 3), HARF (263, 267, 273, 281, 287, 293)	Starr, Ephraim	GOSH (115, 120, 130)
		Starr, Ezra	DANB (49, 50, 54, 65)
Stanly, Lott	FARM (443)	Starr, Ezra Majr	DANB (65)
Stanly, Major	FARM (450)	Starr, George	MIDD (368)
Stanly, Noah	FARM (430)	Starr, Ichad	MIDD (367)
Stanly, Oliver	FARM (443)	Starr, Jabez	DANB (63)
Stanly, Samuel	HARF (255A, 281)	Starr, Jeh[ ] Majr	MIDD (381, 405)
Stanly, Seth	FARM (433, 435)	Starr, Jehh Majr	MIDD (370)
Stanly, Theodore	EHAR (3), HARF (266, 272, 274)	Starr, Jehoshephat Major	MIDD (342, 346, 350, 358)
Stanly, Thomas	FARM (433)	Starr, John	DANB (39), GUIL (270, 294, 309, 324, 335)
Stanly, Thos	FARM (443)		
Stanly, Timo	FARM (445)	Starr, Jonathan	DANB (43)
Stanly, Timo Jur	GOSH (185)	Starr, Jonth	DANB (47, 58, 60)
Stanly, Timothy	FARM (438)	Starr, Joseph	DANB (39, 40, 59), GROT ([7], [20]), MIDD (367, 376)
Stanly, William	GOSH (112, 120)		
Stanly, Wm	GOSH (185)		
Stanton, Jacob	KENT (B1, E58, E62)	Starr, Joseph 3rd	DANB (43)
Stanton, Joseph	GROT ([4])	Starr, Joseph Capt	DANB (47)
Stanton, Samuel	GROT [18], [23]	Starr, Joshua Jur	DANB (54)
Stanton, William	LITC (128, 129, 130, 133, 134)	Starr, Josiah	MANS (267, 368)
		Starr, Josiah Jur Capt	DANB (40)
Stapels, Benjamin	COLC (13)	Starr, Levi	DANB (63)
Staples, Benjn	COLC (8)	Starr, Ma[ ]	DANB (47)
Staples, Capt	BRAN (162)	Starr, Major	DANB (48) MIDD (394, 415)
Staples, Enoch	BRAN (163, 164, 166, 170, 173, 174, 175, 179)	Starr, Matthh	DANB (53)
Staples, John	FAIR (256, 262, 263)	Starr, Mattw	DANB (40, 43, 64)
Staples, Samuel	DANB (262, 262)	Starr, Nathan	DANB (40, 381, 416)
Staples, Thos	FAIR (265)	Starr, Nathl	DANB (39, 40, 45, 48, 51, 59), MIDD (368)
Star, Ebenezer	KILY (86a)		
Star, Eph	GOSH (119, 122)	Starr, Nathn	MIDD (376, 416)
Stark, Eunice	GLAS (64)	Starr, Nicholas	GROT [12], [15]
Stark, Joshua	MIDD (359)	Starr, Peter Revd	KENT (E58, E62)
Stark, Nathan	GROT ([9])	Starr, Richard	GROT [4], [5], [6]
Stark, Silas	COLC (252, 254)	Starr, Richard Junr	GROT [9]
Starkweather, Charles	MANS (340)	Starr, Saml	MIDD (367)
Starkweather, Joel	MANS (279, 283, 353)	Starr, Thomas	GROT [18]

INDEX

Name	Index Pages	Name	Index Pages
Starr, Thos	DANB (39, 49, 58)	Steel, Timothy	HARF (253, 255A, 256, 263, 267, 273, 281, 288, 293)
Starr, Thos 3d	DANB (51, 63)		
Starr, Thos Capt	DANB (54)		
Starr, Thos Lieut	DANB (52)	Steele, Elijah	CORN (6, 7, 10, 13, 14, 15, 17, 18, 87)
Starr, Timo	MIDD (368, 416)		
Starr, Timo Capt	MIDD (413)	Steevens, [ ]	KILH (145)
Starr, Timothy	MIDD (350, 359)	Steevens, Aaron	KILH (43)
Starr, Timothy Capt	MIDD (347)	Steevens, Aaron Capt	KILH (44, 55)
Starr, William	GROT ([6], [23], [24], [25]), GUIL (299, 302, 339, 343), MIDD (368, 370)	Steevens, Amos	KILH (55)
		Steevens, Christopher	KILH (45)
		Steevens, Daniel Ens	KILH (146)
		Steevens, Eliakim	GUIL (270, 294, 309, 333)
Starr, Wm	GUIL (286, 287, 293, 294, 310, 319, 328), MIDD (394, 415)	Steevens, Eliphelet	KILH (49, 51, 145)
		Steevens, Elipht	KILH (47)
		Steevens, Elipt	KILH (44)
		Steevens, Elnath Capt	KILH (46)
Starr, Wm Capt	MIDD (394, 405)	Steevens, Elnathan	KILH (48, 53)
Starr, Wm Lieut	MIDD (387) DANB (58)	Steevens, Elnathn	KILH (54)
		Steevens, Esrael 2d	KILH (145)
Steadman, Alexander	HARF (273, 281, 285, 285A, 286, 287, 289)	Steevens, Hiel	KILH (51, 145)
		Steevens, Hubbel	KILH (146)
Steadman, Joseph	HARF (253, 266)	Steevens, Hubble	KILH (145)
Steadman, Nathan	HARF (255A, 279, 287, 292)	Steevens, Israel	KILH (51, 53, 146)
		Steevens, Israel 2d	KILH (44, 49, 50)
Steadman, Timothy	HARF (263, 281)	Steevens, James	KILH (146)
Stearman, Saml Jur	FARM (440)	Steevens, Nathan	KILH (44, 145)
Stearns, Boaz	MANS (338)	Steevens, Nathl	GUIL (304), KILH (146)
Stearns, Elias	KILY (94a)	Steevens, Nathl 2d	GUIL (269)
Stearns, Elias Ensign	KILY (32)	Steevens, Nathl Ensn	GUIL (273)
Stearns, Elias Ensn	KILY (7, 91a)	Steevens, Nathl Junr	GUIL (287, 309)
Stearns, Elias Insn	KILY (94a)	Steevens, Orsbon	KILH (145)
Stearns, Samuel Insn	KILY (97)	Steevens, Orsborn	KILH (146)
Stebbins, Josiah	DANB (62)	Steevens, Philip	KILH (145)
Stedman, Justis	HARW (3)	Steevens, Phillip	KILH (54)
Stedman, Lucinda	FARM (19)	Steevens, Ruben	KILH (49, 51, 55)
Stedman, Nathan	EHAD (79)	Steevens, Thomas 2d	KILH (54)
Stedman, Saml	FARM (24)	Steevins, Eliphett	KILH (48)
Stedman, Saml Jur	FARM (436)		
Stedman, Stephen Jr	EWIN (17)	Stent, Eleazar	BRAN (170, 171, 172, 173, 174, 176)
Stedman, Theodore	FARM (19)		
Stedman, Timothy	EHAR (3)	Stent, Eleazer	BRAN (178)
Steel, Ashbel	HARF (255A, 261a, 266, 272, 281, 288, 292)	Stent, Eleazr	BRAN (164, 166, 167)
		Stent, Othniel	BRAN (163, 168, 174)
Steel, Ashbell	DERB (134)	Stephens, [ ]	DERB (146), HARL (45)
Steel, Bradford	DERB (120, 122, 125, 126, 131, 133, 134, 141)	Stephens, Ann	DURH (13)
		Stephens, James Sergt	HADD (119)
Steel, Bradford Capt	DERB (132, 135, 137, 146, 167)	Stephens, Joshua	HARW (2, 14)
		Stephens, Sam	GOSH (104)
Steel, Bradford Leiut	DERB (107, 114, 127)	Stephens, Thankfull	FARM (19)
Steel, Ebenezer	HARF (261a)	Stephens, Thomas	KENT (A28)
Steel, Ebenr	FARM (453)	Sterling, James	CORN (1, 10, 23, 87, 91)
Steel, Ebenr Jur	FARM (453)	Sterne, Thomas Smith	GLAS (109)
Steel, Eliphaz	HARF (266)	Sterns, Elias Ensn	KILY (19)
Steel, James	EWIN (17, 85, 89)	Sterns, Levi	ENFD (20)
Steel, John	HARF (253, 256, 263, 267, 273, 281)	Stetson, Saml	MANS (274, 341)
		Stetson, Saml Ensn	MANS (277)
Steel, Jonathan	HARF (261a, 292)	Stetson, Samuel	MANS (267, 272, 284, 358)
Steel, Leiut	DERB (127)		
Steel, Lemuel	HARF (253, 272)	Stetson, Timothy	MANS (281, 336, 338, 347)
Steel, Moses Junr	HARF (281)		
Steel, Theophilus	HARF (251(2))	Steven, Thos Capt	DANB (51)
Steel, Thomas	HARF (263A, 287, 292, 293)	Stevens, [ ]	KENT (C543)
		Stevens, Abell	CANA (18, 19)

716

INDEX

Name	Index Pages	Name	Index Pages
Stevens, Abil	CANA (28)	Stewart, John	HEBR (216)
Stevens, Andrew	CANA (28)	Stewart, Joseph	EHAD (60)
Stevens, Benj	DANB (39)	Stewart, Nathan	LITC (141)
Stevens, Benjamin	GLAS (93)	Stewart, Samuel	EHAD (64, 69)
Stevens, Benjamin Capt	CANA (15, 16)	Stewart, William	CORN (1, 90)
		Stibbin, Thos	ASHF (218)
Stevens, Benjn Capt	CANA (11, 64, 77)	Stibbins, Thomas	ASHF (232)
Stevens, Benjn Jur	DANB (40)	Stibbins, Thos	ASHF (202)
Stevens, Caleb Jur	DANB (49, 63)	Stibins, Thomas	ASHF (232)
Stevens, Comfort	DANB (51)	Stiles, Aaron	HEBR (236)
Stevens, Daniel	CANA (12, 17, 19, 28, 64)	Stiles, Asahel	EWIN (12)
Stevens, Elijah	GLAS (93, 111)	Stiles, Ebenezer	COVE (168)
Stevens, Elisha	GLAS (99)	Stiles, Reuben	COVE (314)
Stevens, Elnatn	KILH (55)	Stiles, Ruben	COVE (181, 315)
Stevens, Ezra	DANB (39)	Stillman, David	FAIR (258)
Stevens, Forward	DANB (52)	Stilman, Asabel	HADD (148)
Stevens, George	GLAS (96)	Stilman, John	COLE (113, 115)
Stevens, Henery	CANA (64)	Stilman, Roger	COLE (113, 115)
Stevens, Henry jur	CANA (18, 19)	Stocken, Jos	FARM (443)
Stevens, Isaac	CANT (146, 147, 155, 162, 168)	Stocker, John	MIDD (346, 364)
		Stockin, Joseph	FARM (15, 436)
Stevens, Israel	KILH (55)	Stockin, Luther	FARM (9, 16, 433, 443, 449)
Stevens, James	CANA (11, 15, 28, 64), GLAS (99)		
		Stocking, Abner Capt	CHAT (59, 64)
Stevens, John	CANT (180), GLAS (78, 83, ,94)	Stocking, Benjamin	CHAT (34, 42)
		Stocking, Capt	MIDD (408)
Stevens, John Capt	CANA (10, 17, 20, 64, 77)	Stocking, Daniel	MIDD (345, 349, 350, 356, 393, 404)
Stevens, Jonah	DANB (59)		
Stevens, Josiah	GLAS (99)	Stocking, Danl	MIDD (362, 369, 371, 380, 381, 413)
Stevens, Nathl Jur	GUIL (291)		
Stevens, Peter	CANT (151)	Stocking, Elijah	CHAT (31, 42, 65)
Stevens, Phillip	KILH (55)	Stocking, Elisha	MIDD (345, 349, 356)
Stevens, Rebekah	DANB (51)	Stocking, George	CHAT (36)
Stevens, Ruben	CANA (12)	Stocking, George Capt	CHAT (29, 30, 40)
Stevens, Saml	DANB (40, 41, 47)	Stocking, George Junr	GLAS (70, 74)
Stevens, Simon	CANA (15, 64)	Stocking, J[ ]	MIDD (364)
Stevens, Thomas	GLAS (66, 74, 79, 83, 95, 98, 106), KENT (B2, C548, C552, C554, D1, D7, D10, E59, E63)	Stocking, Josh	FARM (17)
		Stocking, Joz[ ]	MIDD (413)
		Stocking, Lamberton	HADD (118, 121)
		Stocking, Nathl	HADD (148)
Stevens, Thomas Capt	DANB (50, 65)	Stocking, Reuben	CHAT (43, 50, 51, 54, 58)
Stevens, Thomas Lieut	GLAS (98, 112)	Stocking, Stephen	CHAT (29)
Stevens, Thoms Capt	DANB (58)	Stocking, Stephen Jur	CHAT (51, 52)
Stevens, Thos	DANB (39, 21)	Stocking, Zebulon	MIDD (364, 365, 370)
Stevens, Thos Capt	DANB (40, 41, 42, 45, 46, 52, 53)	Stockwell, Eleazer	KENT (C554)
		Stoddard, [ ]	ASHF (203, 229)
Stevens, Timothy	GLAS (94, 99, 108)	Stoddard, Briant	LITC (129, 130)
Stevens, Timy	GLAS (99)	Stoddard, Briant Capt	LITC (139, 141, 159)
Stevens, William	GLAS (73, 106)	Stoddard, David	LITC (129, 130, 132, 134, 139, 141, 152)
Stevens, Wm	GLAS (85, 86, 94, 101)		
Stevens, Zebulon	CANA (18)	Stoddard, David Lt	LITC (140, 155)
Stevens, Zebulon Jur	CANA (28, 64)	Stoddard, Ichabod	GROT [9], [15], [16], [23], [24]
Stevenson, Robert	CHAT (32)		
Stevenson, Thomas	CHAT (29)	Stoddard, James	FARM (2, 3, 5, 18, 435, 442, 444, 452), LITC (147, 158)
Stevevs, Simon	CANA (77)		
Steward, Nathan	LITC (135)		
Steward, William	EHAD (44)	Stoddard, James Capt	FARM (2, 442, 449, 452, 454)
Stewart, Daniel	CORN (1, 9, 10, 12, 13, 22, 23, 25, 90), CHAT (60)		
		Stoddard, John	LITC (131, 134, 139, 146)
Stewart, Daniel Capt	CHAT (33, 43, 45, 50, 53)	Stoddard, Moses	LITC (134, 139, 140, 147
Stewart, Henry	CANA (64)	Stoddard, Obed	LITC (129, 131)

INDEX

Name	Index Pages	Name	Index Pages
Stoddard, Ralph	GROT [7], [21]	Stone, Wm	DANB (63, 64), HARW (3, 4)
Stoddard, Ralph Capt	GROT [4], [7], [12], [25]		
Stoddard, Ralph Junr	GROT [12], [14], [25]	Storng, John Colonel	FARM (427)
Stoddard, Robert	GROT [5]	Storrs, Amariah	MANS (338, 353)
Stoddard, Vine	GROT [6], [12], [14], [18], [23]	Storrs, Benjamin	MANS (339, 357)
Stoel, Jonathan	MANS (339)	Storrs, Cornelius	MANS (267, 271, 278, 279, 283, 328, 335, 347, 355)
Stoel, Josiah	MANS (336, 338, 358)		
Stoel, Josiah Capt	MANS (356, 358)	Storrs, Corns Ensn	MANS (277)
Stoel, Josiah Lieut	MANS (328, 351)	Storrs, Dan	MANS (280, 283, 336, 356)
Stone, Aaron	GUIL (286, 295, 300, 309, 324, 335)	Storrs, Ebenezer	MANS (283, 328, 334, 353)
Stone, Abner	GUIL (270)		
Stone, Abrm	GUIL (274)	Storrs, Ebenr	MANS (277, 336)
Stone, Bela	GUIL (304, 312)	Storrs, Exper Colo	MANS (262, 284, 352, 359)
Stone, Benjamin	LITC (129)		
Stone, Caleb	GUIL (271, 287, 300)	Storrs, Experience Colo	MANS (328, 346, 347)
Stone, Daniel	GUIL (274, 300, 325)		
Stone, Ebenr	GUIL (340)	Storrs, Expr Capt	MANS (255, 258)
Stone, Elihu	BRAN (163, 174, 178)	Storrs, Expr Colo	MANS (267, 279, 281, 282, 325, 326, 333, 335, 337, 350, 358, 360)
Stone, Ephraim	MIDD (349, 356, 364, 365, 369, 370, 380, 394, 402, 404)		
		Storrs, Joseph	MANS (275, 280, 281, 341)
Stone, Epm	MIDD (389)		
Stone, Heber	LITC (141, 147, 150, 158, 160)	Storrs, Joseph Junr	MANS (339)
		Storrs, Joseph Majr	MANS (255, 258, 269, 274, 335, 342, 345)
Stone, Isaac	GUIL (319, 326), MILF (82)		
		Storrs, Josiah	MANS (271, 277, 336, 347)
Stone, James	FARM (28), LITC (153)		
Stone, John	GUIL (270)	Storrs, Judah	MANS (277, 283, 356)
Stone, John 2nd	GUIL (270, 335)	Storrs, Majr	MANS (342)
Stone, Jonah	LITC (129)	Storrs, Nathl	MANS (336)
Stone, Joseph	FARM (433, 444, 449), GUIL (297, 335)	Storrs, Saml Capt	MANS (338)
		Storrs, Samuel Junr	MANS (356)
Stone, Josh	FARM (455)	Storrs, Thomas	MANS (271)
Stone, Leman	LITC (133, 146, 147, 148, 149, 152)	Storrs, Thos	MANS (274, 279, 281, 353)
Stone, Levi	DANB (51, 58, 63), LITC (135, 139, 142, 143, 147, 152, 153, 158)	Stoughton, Alexander	EWIN (89)
		Stoughton, Alexr	EWIN (8, 85)
		Stoughton, John	EWIN (8, 85, 89), FARM (433, 435, 436, 438)
Stone, Miles	GUIL (328, 329, 333, 340)		
Stone, Nathl	GUIL (260, 273, 274, 275, 285, 291, 294, 295, 326, 334)	Stoughton, Jonathan	EWIN (85, 89)
		Stoughton, Joseph	EWIN (8)
		Stoughton, Leml Capt	EWIN (8)
Stone, Nathl Liut	GUIL (309)	Stoughton, Leml Majr	EWIN (14, 16)
Stone, Nehemiah	KENT (B6)	Stoughton, Lemuel	EWIN (7)
Stone, Noah	GUIL (320, 324), LITC (139, 146, 158)	Stoughton, Lemuel Capt	EWIN (9)
Stone, Reuben	GUIL (280, 289, 298, 310, 313, 314), LITC (129, 131, 132, 141, 146, 147)	Stoughton, Lemuel Majr	EWIN (10, 12, 13, 14, 16, 85, 88)
		Stoughton, Nathaniel Jur	EWIN (8, 9)
Stone, Reuben Capt	LITC (141, 143, 159, 161)	Stoughton, Nathl Jur	EWIN (10)
Stone, Saml	MILF (106)	Stoughton, Oliver	EWIN (85, 88)
Stone, Samuel	MILF (92)	Stoughton, Russell	EWIN (85, 89)
Stone, Sarah	GUIL (328, 329, 340)	Stoughton, William	EWIN (85)
Stone, Sibble	GUIL (312)	Stoughton, Wm	EWIN (89)
Stone, Stephen	LITC (156)	Stow, Daniel Capt	CHAT (59)
Stone, Thos	GUIL (287)	Stow, David	MIDD (362, 371, 395, 406)
Stone, William	KENT (C548, D1, E58, E62)	Stow, David Lt	MIDD (372)

INDEX

Name	Index Pages
Stow, Elihu	MIDD (346, 349, 351, 362, 366, 371, 373, 381, 387, 390, 394, 395, 396, 405, 409, 415, 416, 418, 420, 421)
Stow, Ichd	MIDD (395, 398)
Stow, Jonathan	MIDD (346, 349, 356, 363, 370, 380, 394, 404, 413)
Stow, Joseph	MIDD (364, 388)
Stow, Leml	CANA (26)
Stow, Nathl	MIDD (363)
Stow, Samuel	CANA (19)
Stow, Solo Jr	MIDD (404)
Stow, Solomon	MIDD (363)
Stow, Solomon Junr	MIDD (363, 365, 399)
Stow, Zeb	MIDD (364)
Stow, Zebulon	MIDD (344)
Strait, [ ]	KILY (98)
Strait, Willm	KILY (11)
Stratton, Corn[ ]	FAIR (253)
Stratton, John	FAIR (253, 258, 259, 267), GLAS (92)
Stratton, Saml	GLAS (70, 112, 113)
Stratton, Saml Jur	GLAS (113)
Stratton, Samuel	GLAS (67, 76, 83, 93)
Street Nehem	FARM (9)
Street, Caleb	BRAN (179)
Street, James	GROT ([4])
Street, Jesse	BRAN (165, 166, 170, 172, 176, 178)
Street, Neheh	FARM (442)
Street, Nehemiah	FARM (433)
Strickland, Abel	CHAT (33, 42, 47, 58)
Strickland, David	MIDD (363)
Strickland, Jonah	BOLT (180, 182)
Strickland, Jonah Jur	BOLT (157, 164, 167, 180, 183)
Strickland, Jonathan	MANS (267)
Strickland, Neheh	GLAS (93)
Strickland, Nehemiah	GLAS (69, 79)
Strickland, Semion	GLAS (92)
Strickland, Simeon	GLAS (109)
Strickland, Stephen	GLAS (83, 93, 98, 106, 112, 113)
Strickland, Stephen Jur	GLAS (91, 102)
Strickland, William	MIDD (364)
Stron, Benjah	COVE (167)
Strong, [ ]	FARM (440), MIDD (413)
Strong, Aaron	BOLT (155, 156, 180, 183)
Strong, Abijah	HEBR (220)
Strong, Adonijah	HEBR (219, 236, 246)
Strong, Ambros	COLC (249, 251)
Strong, Amos	GLAS (70, 73, 74), 93, 108, 112)
Strong, Amos Ensign	GLAS (89, 90)
Strong, Asahel	LITC (135, 139, 141, 143, 146, 147, 150, 151, 152, 153)
Strong, Bela	MIDD (370, 382, 395)

Name	Index Pages
Strong, Benajah	COVE (172, 177, 180, 181, 314, 315)
Strong, Caleb	CHAT (46, 52)
Strong, Charles	BOLT (160, 181)
Strong, Cipryan Revd	CHAT (43)
Strong, Cyprian Reverd	CHAT (37)
Strong, Daniel	LEBA (305)
Strong, Danl	LEBA (296, 318)
Strong, Davd	LEBA (317)
Strong, David	COLC (7, 11, 249, 254), HEBR (217, 234, 246), BOLT (181)
Strong, Eben	COLC (7), 242, 251), KENT (E63)
Strong, Ebenezer	BOLT (180)
Strong, Eliakim	DURH (23)
Strong, Eliakim Leut	DURH (12)
Strong, Elijah	COVE (174, 314)
Strong, Elisha	FARM (2, 443, 450, 451)
Strong, Elisha Leut	FARM (434)
Strong, Ensn	DURH (20)
Strong, Ephraim	MILF (78, 81, 83, 84, 90)
Strong, Ephraim Junr	MILF (104)
Strong, Jed	LEBA (326)
Strong, Jed[ ]	LEBA (342)
Strong, Jedediah	LITC (140)
Strong, Jedh	LEBA (316, 327, 333, 334, 310, 311)
Strong, Jedh Jur	LEBA (298, 299)
Strong, Jedidiah	LEBA (305), LITC (128, 129, 130, 131, 134, 135, 139, 141, 146, 149, 152, 153, 154, 158, 159)
Strong, John	GLAS (6, 109, 112)
Strong, John Col	FARM (430, 433)
Strong, Jona	LEBA (310, 311, 315, 316, 342)
Strong, Joseph	FAIR (253, 255, 257, 258, 260, 262, 266, 267, 269)
Strong, Joshua	CHAT (40, 45)
Strong, Josiah	CHAT (38, 39, 40, 43, 51, 58, 64, 66), COLC (248), DERB (140, 141, 145, 167, 168, 169)
Strong, Judah	BOLT (146, 148, 149, 150, 151, 158, 160, 162, 163, 164, 166, 180, 182)
Strong, Medad	DURH (18, 21, 25)
Strong, Medad Ensn	DURH (24)
Strong, Nathan	BOLT (147, 155, 158, 164, 180, 182), MIDD (367, 399, 405, 410, 412)
Strong, Nathaniel	EWIN (8)
Strong, Nathl	EWIN (85)
Strong, Philip	KENT (B2, C554, D3, D5, E58, E63)
Strong, Philip Jur	KENT (E60, E63)
Strong, Phinehas	COVE (161), EWIN (10, 12, 85, 89), HEBR (234, 246)

INDEX

Name	Index Pages
Strong, Rachel	GLAS (65)
Strong, Simeon	FARM (430)
Strong, Thomas	DURH (12, 18, 19)
Strong, Thomas Jur	DURH (18)
Strong, Thos	DURH (16, 21, 24)
Strong, Thos Jur	DURH (21)
Strong, Thos Jur Col	DURH (15)
Strong, Zebulon	COLC (255)
Stronge, Josiah	CHAT (69)
Strowbridge, Stephen	CORN (26)
Stuart, Alexander	DANB (39)
Stuart, Alexandr	DANB (51)
Stuart, Alexr	DANB (40, 53)
Stuart, Daniel Capt	CHAT (58)
Stuart, Henrey	CANA (64)
Stuart, James	DANB (45, 51, 61), KENT (C548, C552, E58, E62)
Stuart, Luke	KENT (A24, B2)
Stuart, Silas	KENT (B1)
Sturdevant, Peleg	KENT (B1, B2, C548)
Sturdevant, Perez	KENT (A24)
Sturdevent, Peleg	KENT (A28)
Sturdevent, Saml	DANB (40, 47, 49)
Sturges, [ ]	FAIR (267)
Sturges, Abigail	FAIR (253)
Sturges, Andrew	FAIR (253, 256)
Sturges, Hez	FAIR (258, 260, 262, 265, 266, 267)
Sturges, Hez Capt	FAIR (263)
Sturges, Jonath	FAIR (265)
Sturges, Jonathan	FAIR (251, 252, 253, 254, 255, 257, 258, 259, 260, 261, 266, 268, 269)
Sturges, Jonth	FAIR (256, 261, 264, 265, 266, 269)
Sturges, Judgson	FAIR (255, 258, 265)
Sturges, Judson	FAIR (259)
Sturges, Solomon	FAIR (262, 267)
Sturtevant, Peleg	KENT (C550, C552, C555, D1, D7, E58, E62)
Sturtevant, Peleg Capt	KENT (C543, C545)
Sturtevant, Perez	KENT (E58, E62)
Sturtevant, Saml	KENT (E63)
Sturtevant, Zebedy	KENT (E63)
Suard, Daniel	HARL (45)
Suerd, Daniel	HARL (48)
Sullard, Jos	LEBA (334)
Sullard, Joseph Junr	LEBA (305)
Summers, Abel	MILF (98, 102)
Sumner, [ ]	ASHF (225, 234)
Sumner, Ben[ ]	ASHF (231)
Sumner, Bena	ASHF (222)
Sumner, Benj[ ]	ASHF (238)
Sumner, Benja	ASHF (194, 207, 210, 211, 216, 221, 222, 223, 224, 225, 226, 228, 232, 236, 308, 310)
Sumner, Benjamin	ASHF (215, 218, 219, 220, 227, 229, 230, 231, 238)
Sumner, Benjn	ASHF (196, 199, 200, 201, 202, 208, 212, 233, 234, 240)
Sumner, Clap	ASHF (214, 308, 311)
Sumner, Colo	MIDD (417)
Sumner, Daniel	MIDD (345)
Sumner, Danl	MIDD (368)
Sumner, Ebenezer	ASHF (227, 232)
Sumner, Ebenr	ASHF (236), MIDD (367)
Sumner, Ebenr Capt	MIDD (370, 371)
Sumner, Eddd	ASHF (308)
Sumner, Edward	ASHF (220, 223, 226, 229, 230, 231, 232, 238)
Sumner, Edward Jur	ASHF (206, 209, 210, 213, 218, 222, 311)
Sumner, James	ASHF (222)
Sumner, James F	ASHF (209, 210)
Sumner, James Fitch	ASHF (202, 311)
Sumner, Jno	ASHF (217, 311)
Sumner, Jno Capt	ASHF (225)
Sumner, John	MIDD (367)
Sumner, John Capt	ASHF (224, 228, 229, 230, 231)
Sumner, John Colo	MIDD (382)
Sumner, Ruben	HEBR (218, 220, 234, 236)
Sumner, Saml	ASHF (201)
Sumner, Samuel	ASHF (236, 308)
Sutherland, Roger	GREE (124)
Sutleff, Samuel	HARL (59)
Sutlief, Saml	DURH (10), DANB (58)
Sutlief, Samuel	DURH (12), HARL (51)
Sutliff, Samuel	HARL (56, 58)
Sutlis, Salvenus	ASHF (209)
Sutton, Benjamin	GREE (126)
Sutton, Edward	CANA (9)
Suyuard, Daniel	HARL (51)
Swan, Amos	KENT (D7, E59, E63)
Swan, Jabez	EHAD (86)
Sweet, Palmer	FARM (9, 17)
Sweetland, Joel	HEBR (233)
Sweett, Palmer	FARM (5)
Swetland, Aaron	HEBR (236, 246, 248)
Swetland, Az	HEBR (217)
Swetland, Azariah	HEBR (218, 234)
Swetland, Daniel	HARF (266, 272, 288, 292)
Swetland, Joel	HEBR (216, 219, 220, 236, 245)
Swetland, Jonah	LEBA (316, 333)
Swetland, Levi	COVE (314), HEBR (218, 220)
Swetland, Levy	COVE (177, 180)
Swift, Barza	MANS (277)
Swift, Barzalai	KENT (C554)
Swift, Barzilai	KENT (A24)
Swift, Barzillai	MANS (271, 353, 354)
Swift, Charles	LEBA (305)
Swift, Chas	LEBA (320)
Swift, Heman	CORN (9, 11, 76, 77, 79, 89)
Swift, Heman Colonel	CORN (7, 11, 90)

INDEX

Name	Index Pages
Swift, Isaac	CANA (64), CORN (23, 25), KENT (E59)
Swift, Isaac Doct	CORN (1)
Swift, Jairah	KENT (A28)
Swift, Jirai	KENT (A27)
Swift, John	MANS (275, 277), MIDD (389)
Swift, Nathaniel	KENT (E59)
Swift, Nathaniel Capt	KENT (A26)
Swift, Nathaniel Jur	KENT (B3, C552, E62)
Swift, Nathl Cpt	KENT (E63)
Swift, Nathl Jur	KENT (C548, C554, D1, D6, E58)
Swift, Nathl Leiut	KENT (C546)
Swift, Roland	LEBA (297, 299)
Swift, Rowld	LEBA (333)
Swift, Thomas	MANS (284, 334, 356)
Swift, Thomas Junr	MANS (267, 268)
Swift, Thos	MANS (271, 278, 348)
Swift, Wm	LEBA (342)
Swift, Zephaniah	MANS (357)
Swift, Zephh Capt	MANS (360)
Symond, Jona	CANT (178)
Syzer, William	MIDD (344)
Taft, Asahel	KILY (4)
Tafts, Aaron	ASHF (313)
Tailbourn, Daniel	FARM (19)
Tailbourn, Martha	FARM (19)
Tailer, Chiles	HARL (61)
Tailor, Prince Jr	HARL (61)
Tainter, Joseph	COLE (5, 115)
Tainter, Medad	BRAN (168)
Tainter, Micah	BRAN (165)
Tainter, Michael	BRAN (170, 175, 176, 178)
Tainter, Michael Junr	BRAN (170)
Tainton, John	COLC (249)
Taintor, Charles	COLC (246, 249, 255)
Taintor, Charles Capt	COLC (246)
Taintor, John	COLC (8, 10, 243, 247, 248, 251, 255), GLAS (64)
Taintor, Joseph	COLE (5)
Taintor, Mical	BRAN (166)
Taintor, Mical Jur	BRAN (166)
Taintor, Michael	BRAN (164)
Talbut, Jarid Ensn	KILY (14)
Talbut, Jered Isn	KILY (91)
Talcoot, Joseph	COVE (165)
Talcot, Benjn	BOLT (181)
Talcott, Wm	HEBR (246)
Talcott, Asa	GLAS (72, 93)
Talcott, Benjamin	BOLT (139, 146, 148, 150, 155, 157, 160, 163, 165, 166, 167, 180, 182, 183)
Talcott, Benjamin 3d	BOLT (181)
Talcott, Benjamin Capt	BOLT (144, 151, 155, 156)
Talcott, Benjamin Jur	BOLT (139, 145, 152, 153, 155, 164, 180, 182)
Talcott, Benjn	BOLT (181)
Talcott, Caleb	BOLT (155, 161, 164, 180, 182)
Talcott, Colo	HARF (295)
Talcott, David	DURH (14, 19)
Talcott, Elijah	BOLT (167, 181, 183)
Talcott, Elizur	GLAS (63, 67, 74, 93)
Talcott, Elizur Colonel	GLAS (59, 60, 71, 81)
Talcott, Elizur Jur	GLAS (66, 92, 93)
Talcott, Gad	HEBR (217, 220, 248)
Talcott, George	GLAS (75, 93)
Talcott, Job	BOLT (162)
Talcott, John	BOLT (180, 182)
Talcott, Josep Leut	COVE (179)
Talcott, Joseph	COVE (167, 169, 171, 172, 178), GLAS (71, 75, 93)
Talcott, Joseph Capt	COVE (181), HARF (261a, 281)
Talcott, Joseph Jur	COVE (174), HARF (255A, 273)
Talcott, Joshua	BOLT (182, 180)
Talcott, Joshua Jur	BOLT (164, 181, 183)
Talcott, Nathl	GLAS (93)
Talcott, Phenehas	BOLT (183)
Talcott, Samuel	BOLT (181, 183), HARF (250, 258, 291)
Talcott, Samuel Colo	HARF (270, 272)
Talcott, Samuel Junr	HARF (261a)
Talcott, Seth	BOLT (146)
Talcott, William	HEBR (216)
Talcott, Wm	HEBR (234)
Tallcott, [ ]	MIDD (418)
Tallcott, Abraham	GLAS (95, 111)
Tallcott, Colo	GLAS (85) MIDD (358, 360, 374, 395, 406, 410, 420)
Tallcott, Elizur	GLAS (92, 95, 96)
Tallcott, Elizur Col	GLAS (77, 80, 82, 89, 99, 115)
Tallcott, Gad	HEBR (217)
Tallcott, George	GLAS (81, 85, 98, 99, 106, 108)
Tallcott, Hezekiah	MIDD (347, 350, 359, 400, 405)
Tallcott, Hezh	MIDD (414)
Tallcott, Isaac	GLAS (92, 98)
Tallcott, Joseph	GLAS (87, 108)
Tallcott, Joseph Junr	HARF (265)
Tallcott, Matthew	MIDD (344, 346, 367, 368, 375, 377, 378, 384, 388, 389, 390, 391, 392, 409, 412)
Tallcott, Matthew Colo	MIDD (344, 349, 351, 372, 385)
Tallcott, Matthew Major	MIDD (342)
Tallcott, N	GLAS (99)
Tallcott, Nathaniel Jur	GLAS (91, 95, 98)
Tallcott, Nathl Jur	GLAS (105, 106, 109)
Tallcott, Oliver	GLAS (96)
Tallcott, William	HEBR (216)
Tallmage, Josiah	CHES (4)

INDEX

Name	Index Pages	Name	Index Pages
Tallmage, Samuel	CHES (A)	Taylor, Prince	HARL (45, 46, 48, 53, 55, 58, 59)
Tallman, Peter	GUIL (274, 287, 289)		
Talmage, Jacob	FARM (443)	Taylor, Prince Jr	HARL (57, 59)
Talmage, Solomon	BRAN (168, 174, 175)	Taylor, Prince jur	HARL (43, 45, 48, 54, 58)
Tamage, Thos Wm	FARM (455)		
Tanner, Consider	CORN (2, 10, 12, 13, 17, 23, 25, 88, 91)	Taylor, Saml	CHAT (30, 32, 37, 45, 46, 50, 58, 64, 67, 68), DANB (47), FAIR (254)
Tanner, Ebenr	KENT (E64)		
Tanner, Ephm	KENT (C551, C554, E58)	Taylor, Samuel	CHAT (33, 34, 39, 40, 42, 51, 56, 61, 69), DANB (49)
Tanner, Ephraim	KENT (D7, D10, E63)		
Tanner, Thomas	CORN (9)		
Tanner, Thomas Capt	CORN (11, 14, 18, 89)	Taylor, Silas	DANB (47, 59, 63)
Tanner, Trial	CORN (17, 86)	Taylor, Stephen	GLAS (68)
Tanner, Tryal	CORN (23, 25, 27)	Taylor, Theop[ ] Jur	DANB (51)
Tanner, Tryal Lieut	CORN (10)	Taylor, Theopus	DANB (63)
Tanner, William	CORN (22, 87), KENT (E60)	Taylor, Thomas	DANB (47)
		Taylor, Thos	DANB (39, 40, 41, 48, 49, 51)
Tannor, Consider	CORN (91)		
Tarbox, Benjamin	MIDD (363)	Taylor, Wm	GLAS (99)
Tarbox, David Capt	HEBR (219, 233)	Taylor, Zebulon	LITC (129, 147)
Tarbox, Jonathan	HEBR (248)	Taylor, Zebulon Capt	LITC (140, 143)
Tarbox, Jonth	HEBR (219)	Teal, Benjn	GUIL (309)
Tarbox, Sol	HEBR (218)	Teller, Nathl	KILY (86a)
Tarbox, Sol Lt	HEBR (216)	Tembleton, Hendrick	GLAS (65)
Tayler, Benj Jur	HEBR (234, 236)	Temple, Joseph	GLAS (92, 111)
Taylor, Benj[ ]	HEBR (246)	Tenant, John	COLC (251, 252)
Taylor, Benja Jur	HEBR (218, 220)	Tennant, Caleb	GLAS (94)
Taylor, Capt	DANB (70)	Tennant, John	COLC (8)
Taylor, Childs	HARL (51, 53)	Terrell, Samuel	MILF (92)
Taylor, Chiles	HARL (54)	Terrey, Nathanl Colonl	HARL (55)
Taylor, Daniel	DANB (39, 46, 49, 63)	Terril, Samuel Junr	MILF (98)
Taylor, Daniel Capt	DANB (38, 39, 54, 55)	Terril, Thomas	COVE (171)
Taylor, David	BOLT (180, 182), KENT (E58, E62)	Terril, Thomas Capt	COVE (169, 177, 178)
		Terry, [ ]	ENFD (33, 34)
Taylor, David Ensign	BOLT (155, 157)	Terry, Col	ENFD (33)
Taylor, David Jur	BOLT (146, 158, 160, 168, 180, 182)	Terry, Dan	LEBA (305, 341)
		Terry, Daniel	ENFD (24, 28)
Taylor, David Jur Ensn	BOLT (162)	Terry, David	ENFD (19, 26, 28, 29, 30, 34)
Taylor, David Jur Liut	BOLT (167)		
Taylor, Elisha	CHAT (37, 38, 39, 43, 51, 68)	Terry, Ebenezer	ENFD (35)
		Terry, Ebenezar 2d	ENFD (30)
Taylor, Humphrey	COVE (180)	Terry, Ebenezar Junr	ENFD (26, 28)
Taylor, Humphry	COVE (170)	Terry, Ebenezer 3d	ENFD (28)
Taylor, Huphrey	COVE (172)	Terry, Ebenr 2d	ENFD (35)
Taylor, Job	HARL (48)	Terry, Eliphalet	ENFD (18, 24, 25, 26, 27, 28, 29, 32, 34, 35)
Taylor, John	GLAS (93), HEBR (236), KENT (A28)	Terry, Eliphalet Ensn	ENFD (25)
Taylor, Jonath	GLAS (93)	Terry, Eliphat	ENFD (26)
Taylor, Joseph	COLC (245)	Terry, Ely Ensign	ENFD (19)
Taylor, Josiah	MANS (268, 271, 272, 277, 283, 284, 328, 336, 346, 347, 350, 352, 353, 357, 358)	Terry, Ephraim	ENFD (17)
		Terry, Ephraim Junr	ENFD (18)
		Terry, Ephraim Liut	ENFD (24)
		Terry, Isaac	ENFD (35)
Taylor, Major	DANB (38, 39, 40, 41, 46, 49, 51, 57, 58, 62, 63, 65, 198)	Terry, Jacob	ENFD (24)
		Terry, Jonathan	ENFD (19)
		Terry, Majr	ENFD (19, 24)
Taylor, Nathan	DANB (39, 65)	Terry, Nathl	ENFD (17)
Taylor, Nathan Jur	DANB (49)	Terry, Nathl Col	ENFD (28, 31)
Taylor, Noadiah	CHAT (42)	Terry, Selah	ENFD (18, 19, 24, 25, 26, 28, 30, 31, 32, 33, 35)
Taylor, Noadiah Jur	CHAT (61, 62, 67)		
Taylor, Preserved	DANB (51)	Terry, Shadrack	ENFD (18, 19, 26, 30, 35)
		Terry, Shadrick	ENFD (18)

722

INDEX

Name	Index Pages
Teulls, Elijah	MIDD (363)
Teulls, Micajah	MIDD (377)
Thacher, Rhodols	LEBA (298, 299, 316, 341, 342)
Thacher, Rhodophus	LEBA (305)
Thare, Oliver	KENT (C551, C554, C555)
Thare, Zepheriah	BOLT (181)
Thatcher, Rhodolphus	LEBA (297)
Thayre, Jona	MIDD (376)
Thomas, [ ] Jr	HADD (148)
Thomas, Abijah	LEBA (299, 334, 341)
Thomas, Amos	LEBA (296)
Thomas, Amos Jur	LEBA (305, 311, 316, 333)
Thomas, Amos Jur Lt	LEBA (320)
Thomas, Aron	HADD (113)
Thomas, Ebenezer Lieut	HADD (109, 116, 117, 121)
Thomas, Elihu	LEBA (296, 316, 342)
Thomas, Elihu Lt	LEBA (320)
Thomas, Evan	HADD (121)
Thomas, Henry	HADD (148)
Thomas, James	HADD (117, 118, 123, 129, 148)
Thomas, John	HADD (122)
Thomas, Joseph	LITC (153)
Thomas, Malachi	LEBA (298, 303)
Thomas, Malachi Ens	LEBA (320)
Thomas, Malichi	LEBA (304, 305)
Thomas, Peleg	LEBA (297, 299, 305, 310, 315, 325, 326, 333, 342)
Thomas, Peleg Lt	LEBA (341)
Thomas, Richd	HADD (129)
Thomas, Roger	HADD (148)
Thomas, Saml	LEBA (317)
Thompson, Elijah	FARM (436)
Thompson, Havilah	HARW (3, 5, 7, 8, 14, 17, 20, 24)
Thompson, Jabez	DERB (140, 141)
Thompson, Jabez Col	DERB (106, 107)
Thompson, James	GOSH (126)
Thompson, Jno	ASHF (311)
Thompson, Saml	MANS (283, 336)
Thompson, Saml Capt	MANS (277, 346)
Thompson, Samuel	MANS (284, 357, 360)
Thompson, Samuel Capt	MANS (349, 354, 356)
Thompson, Samuel Junr	MANS (339)
Thompson, Sanford	MIDD (364)
Thompson, Sebe	HARW (2, 8, 11, 22)
Thompson, Thomas	COVE (180)
Thomson, Abel	FARM (436)
Thomson, Abell	FARM (17, 443, 444, 455
Thomson, Asa	FARM (5)
Thomson, Barnabas	FARM (5, 449)
Thomson, Barnebas	FARM (443)
Thomson, Benoni	EWIN (12, 85, 89)
Thomson, Daniel	FARM (446), KENT (E6, E63)
Thomson, Danl	FARM (9, 450, 456)
Thomson, David	GOSH (102, 104, 105, 110, 112, 115, 120, 184)
Thomson, E Lt	GOSH (124)
Thomson, Eleazer	KENT (B2, C555, D1)
Thomson, Eli	KENT (C544)
Thomson, Elieazer	KENT (D5)
Thomson, Eliezer	KENT (A28, E58, E62)
Thomson, Elisha	GOSH (110, 115, 116, 119, 122, 128, 130, 134, 138)
Thomson, Elisha Jur	GOSH (186)
Thomson, Elisha Leut	GOSH (102)
Thomson, Elisha Lt	GOSH (102, 104, 112)
Thomson, Elizr	KENT (C548)
Thomson, George	KENT (A24)
Thomson, James	FARM (443), GOSH (104, 112, 114, 115, 116, 119, 121, 123, 125, 128, 129, 130, 131, 133, 134, 136, 141, 184), MILF (86)
Thomson, James 3d	EWIN (8)
Thomson, James Lt	GOSH (104, 105, 117, 119, 120, 129, 130, 133, 138), MILF (104, 106)
Thomson, John	FARM (444, 445, 449)
Thomson, John 3d	EWIN (85, 88)
Thomson, John Jnr	GOSH (185)
Thomson, Jona	FARM (17)
Thomson, Levi	FARM (2, 9, 16, 28, 441, 445, 456)
Thomson, Lt	GOSH (104)
Thomson, Luke	FARM (4, 450)
Thomson, Mathew	ENFD (28)
Thomson, Saml	FARM (442)
Thomson, Solomon	FARM (3, 434, 438, 445, 450)
Thomson, Step	GOSH (104, 184)
Thomson, Stephen	GOSH (102, 112, 115, 124, 125, 128, 139, 141)
Thomson, Stepn	GOSH (104, 105, 110, 120)
Thomson, Thomas	FARM (5, 15)
Thomson, Thos	FARM (6, 9, 12, 17, 436, 444, 449)
Thomson, Timo	FARM (8, 13, 430)
Thomson, Timothy	FARM (435, 440, 449)
Thonson, Resolved	KILY (87a)
Thonson, Uriah	KILY (92)
Thornton, Medad	EHAD (50, 55)
Thorp Saml Jur	FARM (449)
Thorp, [ ]	ASHF (238)
Thorp, Aaron	LEBA (297)
Thorp, Asher	LITC (160)
Thorp, Charles	FARM (443)
Thorp, Eliphalet	FAIR (269)
Thorp, Elipt	FAIR (258, 260, 262, 266, 267)
Thorp, Elipt Capt	FAIR (254, 261)
Thorp, Gershom	FAIR (259)

INDEX

Name	Index Pages	Name	Index Pages
Thorp, Jabez	FAIR (253, 258, 260, 263, 264)	Tiffeny, Humphry	EHAD (50)
		Tiffeny, Nathan	EHAD (44)
Thorp, Jehiel	FAIR (267)	Til[ ], John	HEBR (217)
Thorp, Linds	FARM (436)	Tilden, Danl	LEBA (326, 334, 341)
Thorp, Lines	FARM (455)	Tilden, Danl Cap	LEBA (320, 325, 330, 334, 337, 338)
Thorp, Saml Jur	FAIR (254, 255, 259, 260, 263, 266, 267)	Tildin, Joshua	COVE (165)
Thorp, Samuel Jur	FAIR (262)	Tilletson, Elizur	HEBR (245)
Thorp, Stephen Capt	FAIR (256, 264)	Tillitson, Elizur	HEBR (218, 248)
Thorpe, Aaron	LEBA (305)	Tillotson, [ ]	FARM (16)
Thrall, James	BOLT (165, 167, 181)	Tillotson, Ebenr	FARM (13, 443, 444)
Thrall, Lemme	BOLT (180)	Tillotson, Elizur	HEBR (236)
Thrall, Lemmy Liut	BOLT (160)	Tillotson, John	FARM (5, 9, 12, 17, 28)
Thrall, Moses	BOLT (155, 158, 165, 166, 180, 182)	Tillotson, Josiah	FARM (2)
		Tillotson, Martha	FARM (19)
Thrall, Mosis	BOLT (148)	Tinker, Silvanus	EHAD (51, 53, 57, 58, 64, 71, 74, 85, 89)
Throop, Benj	LEBA (326)		
Throop, Benjamin	LITC (134)	Tirrel, Phins	MILF (92)
Throop, Dan	LEBA (316)	Tirril, Joel	KENT (A28)
Throop, Dyan Colo		Tisdale, Ebener	LEBA (334)
Throop, Dyar	GLAS (107)	Tisdale, Ebenezer	LEBA (305)
Throop, Dyar Col	EHAD (53, 66, 70)	Tisdale, Ebenr	LEBA (298, 311, 316, 342)
Throop, Dyer Major	EHAD (49)		
Throop, Ichabod Capt	EHAD (48)	Tisdale, Ebr	LEBA (299, 327)
Throop, Jos	LEBA (343)	Tisdale, Elka	LEBA (325)
Throope, Benjamin	LEBA (305)	Tisdale, Elkanah	LEBA (299, 304, 313, 321, 323, 324)
Throope, Dan	LEBA (305, 311), LITC (129)		
		Titus, Richard	GREE (119)
Throope, Jos	LEBA (310)	Tod, Timo	GUIL (260)
Throope, Joseph	LEBA (342)	Todd, Daniel	DERB (120, 122, 124, 126)
Ti[ ], Elizer	HEBR (217)		
Tibballs, Arnold	MILF (92, 93)	Todd, Jonathan Doctr	GUIL (340)
Tibballs, Arnold Capt	MILF (86, 88, 89)	Todd, Jonathan Ensn	GUIL (321)
Tibballs, Arnold Junr	MILF (98)	Todd, Jonathan Junr	GUIL (297, 309, 323)
Tibbals, Abel	DURH (25, 26)	Todd, Timo	GUIL (318)
Tibbals, Arnold Capt	MILF (78)	Todd, Timothy	GUIL (260, 273, 275, 317)
Tibbals, David	MILF (97)	Tolbut, Jared	KILY (86a)
Tomson		Tolls, Daniel	MILF (85, 88, 97, 104)
Tibbals, Ebenezer	DURH (10, 12, 16)	Tomlinson, Abm	MILF (82)
Tibbals, Ebenr	DURH (15, 19, 21, 25)	Tomlinson, Agur	DERB (107, 120, 122, 132, 135)
Tibbals, Eber	HADD (111, 113, 114, 125)		
		Tomlinson, Beers	DERB (147)
Tibbals, Nathan	KENT (C555, E59)	Tomlinson, Benjamin	DERB (122)
Tibbells, Arnold	MILF (92)	Tomlinson, Benjn	DERB (107, 120)
Tibbells, Arnold Capt	MILF (85)	Tomlinson, Dan	DERB (120, 122, 124, 126, 131, 140, 141, 145, 167)
Tibbels, Abner Jur	HADD (110)		
Tibbles, Arnold Capt	MILF (84)		
Ticker, Isaac	LEBA (333)	Tomlinson, David	DERB (120, 122, 131, 135, 140, 141, 167)
Tickner, Isaac	LEBA (334)		
Tickner, James	LEBA (298)	Tomlinson, Henry	DERB (107, 120, 125, 131)
Tifany, Consider	HARL (53)		
Tiffaney, Thomas	ASHF (231)	Tomlinson, Isaac	DERB (106, 113, 120, 122, 167)
Tiffany, Consider	HARL (45, 46, 48, 51)		
Tiffany, Ephram	HARL (51)	Tomlinson, John	DERB (141, 145, 106, 134)
Tiffany, Ezeki	ASHF (308)		
Tiffany, Ezekiel	ASHF (311)	Tomlinson, John Capt	DERB (106, 107, 113, 114, 120, 122, 124, 126, 127, 131, 132, 135, 139, 140, 145, 167, 168)
Tiffany, Saml	HARL (53)		
Tiffany, Samuel	HARL (45, 48)		
Tiffany, Simeon	ASHF (232)		
Tiffany, Simon	ASHF (224)	Tomlinson, Jonah	DERB (122)
Tiffany, Thos	ASHF (310)	Tomlinson, Jonas	DERB (121)
Tiffany, Timothy	HARL (45)	Tomlinson, Joseph	DERB (106, 122)

INDEX

Name	Index Pages
Tomlinson, Levi	DERB (106, 113, 120, 122, 124, 126, 132, 141)
Tomlinson, Noah	DERB (107, 120, 122, 127, 132, 135, 140, 141)
Tomlinson, Samuel	DERB (121)
Tomlinson, Webb	DERB (106, 113, 120, 122, 131, 135, 140, 141)
Topliff, Calvin	MANS (271, 280, 281, 283, 336)
Topliff, Calvin Junr	MANS (339)
Torrey, David	ASHF (236)
Torrey, Joseph	KILY (19, 31, 36, 86a, 97a)
Torrey, Samuel	MIDD (363)
Torrey, Wm	LEBA (327, 329, 330, 325, 326)
Torrey, Wm Jur	LEBA (310, 311)
Torry, David	ASHF (313)
Torry, Jos	KILY (92a, 94, 94a, 95, 96a)
Torry, Joseph	KILY (31, 86a, 87, 87a, 91a, 92, 96)
Torry, Wm Jur	LEBA (316)
Tory, Nathl	GLAS (114)
Tory, Saml H	KILY (94a)
Toun[ ], Revd	KILH (146)
Towner, Elisha	GOSH (186)
Towner, Daniel	KILH (50, 145, 146)
Towner, Daniel 2d	KILH (145)
Towner, Elijah	GOSH (185)
Towner, Eph	GOSH (120)
Towner, Jonathan Jur	BRAN (165)
Towner, Ruben	KILH (145, 146)
Towner, Saml	KILH (54)
Towner, Timothy	HADD (129, 148)
Townsend, David	HEBR (216, 218, 233, 249)
Townsend, Jesse	HEBR (217)
Tracey, Uriah	LITC (146)
Tracy, Eliashib	CANT (160, 168)
Tracy, Nehemiah	EHAD (48, 50, 55, 60, 65, 69, 81, 87)
Tracy, Uriah	LITC (158)
Tracy, Zachs	LEBA (298)
Trappe, William	KENT (E63)
Treadway, Amos	MIDD (368, 413)
Treadway, Asa	COLC (248)
Treadway, Davd	LEBA (311, 316, 326)
Treadway, David	LEBA (299)
Treadway, E	MIDD (376, 380)
Treadway, Elijah	CHAT (44), COLC (251, 254), MIDD (356, 365, 367, 368, 369, 377, 378, 395)
Treadwell John	FARM (456)
Treadwell, Capt	FARM (440, 449)
Treadwell, Ephm Capt	FARM (444)
Treadwell, Ephraim	FARM (3, 442)
Treadwell, Ephraim Capt	FARM (438)

Name	Index Pages
Treadwell, John	FARM (3, 4, 5, 6, 7, 8, 10, 12, 13, 18, 21, 23, 26, 27, 29, 30, 31, 33, 34, 427, 430, 432, 434, 435, 440, 441, 442, 444, 445, 446, 448, 450, 451)
Treat, [ ]	MIDD (399)
Treat, Donald	MILF (103)
Treat, Dorotheus	GLAS (95)
Treat, Elisha	GLAS (87)
Treat, Henry Junr	HARF (263)
Treat, Israel Capt	MILF (98)
Treat, John	HARL (59, 61)
Treat, Jonathan	GLAS (92, 111)
Treat, Jos	MILF (86)
Treat, Joseph	MILF (78, 98, 106)
Treat, Mary	GLAS (86, 99)
Treat, Mathias	HARF (287)
Treat, Peter	GLAS (66, 70, 75, 86, 93, 106, 112)
Treat, Philo	MILF (88)
Treat, Robert	MILF (88)
Treat, Saml	MILF (95)
Treat, Saml Capt	MILF (86)
Treat, Samuel	EWIN (17), GLAS (67, 95), MILF (93, 97, 99, 100, 101, 102, 103, 106)
Treat, Samuel Capt	MILF (88, 91)
Treat, Samuel Lieut	MILF (78)
Treat, Stephen	MILF (93, 363)
Treat, Stephen Junr	MIDD (364, 370, 406, 416)
Treawell, Ephram Capt	FARM (434)
Treawell, John	FARM (454)
Tredway, Amos	MIDD (359)
Tredway, Elijah	MIDD (356)
Tredwell, David	FAIR (267)
Treek, John	HARL (43)
Treet, George	HARL (51)
Treet, Jno	HARL (53)
Treet, John	HARL (45, 46, 48, 49, 51, 59)
Treete, John	HARL (57)
Treette, John	HARL (58)
Trip, Hannah	KILY (93)
Trobridge, Benjamin	CHAT (58)
Troop, Joseph	KENT (A24)
Trowbridge, James	DANB (52, 55, 59)
Trowbridge, John	DANB (51, 56, 58, 63)
Trowbridge, John Lut	DANB (46)
Trowbridge, Stephen	DANB (45, 48)
Trowbridge, Stephen Ensn	DANB (43)
Truby, Ansel	FAIR (259)
Trumble, Governour	FARM (6)
Trumble, Benj Revd	GOSH (123)
Trumble, Governor	MIDD (351)
Trumbul, Benjamin Ensign	BOLT (149)
Trumbull, Asaph	HEBR (216, 236)
Trumbull, Asaph Lt	HEBR (218, 220)
Trumbull, Benjamin	BOLT (158, 180, 152)

INDEX

Name	Index Pages	Name	Index Pages
Trumbull, Benjamin Ensign	BOLT (149, 159, 160, 161, 162, 163, 168, 182)	Tucker, Danl Jnr	DERB (106)
		Tucker, Elijah	BOLT (165, 181)
Trumbull, Davd	LEBA (297, 299, 320, 333)	Tucker, Gideon	DERB (113, 148)
		Tucker, John	BOLT (181)
Trumbull, David	EWIN (8, 10, 11, 12, 13, 15, 17, 85, 88), LEBA (298)	Tucker, Joseph Ensign	BOLT (181)
		Tucker, Richard	KILY (19)
		Tucker, Ruben	DERB (126, 127, 131, 167)
Trumbull, Govr	LEBA (290, 296, 301, 304, 310)		
		Tucker, Rusul	ASHF (308)
Trumbull, John	HARF (299)	Tucker, Saml Jnr	DERB (168)
Trumbull, Jona Jur	LEBA (294, 297, 319, 320, 322)	Tucker, Thadus	ASHF (313)
		Tucker, Zephh	DERB (120)
Trumbull, Lt	HEBR (233)	Tuder, Saml	EWIN (13)
Trumbull, Walter	MANS (233)	Tuder, Saml Lt	EWIN (12, 88)
Trumbull, William	MANS (357)	Tuder, Samuel	EWIN (8, 10)
Trumbull, Wm	MANS (278)	Tuder, Samuel Lt	EWIN (16, 85)
Trusdel, Ebenezer Lieut	BRAN (170)	Tudor, Samuel	EWIN (10)
		Tudor, Samuel Lieut	EWIN (11)
Tryon, Amos	MIDD (363, 366, 370, 381, 385, 394, 404, 407, 413, 417)	Tuel, Elijah	MIDD (346, 349, 356)
		Tuells, Benja	MIDD (376)
		Tuells, Elijah	MIDD (370, 388)
Tryon, Amos Capt	MIDD (357, 358, 371, 381, 382, 394, 409)	Tuells, Micajah	MIDD (380)
		Tuells, Saml	MIDD (364)
Tryon, Benjn	GLAS (93)	Tuffs, Aaron	ASHF (213, 226)
Tryon, Benjn Jur	GLAS (109, 114)	Tuffts, Aaron	ASHF (236)
Tryon, Caleb	MIDD (363, 366)	Tufts, Aaron	ASHF (233, 308)
Tryon, Charles	MIDD (382, 395, 406)	Tur[ ]alot, Barnu	KILY (19)
Tryon, Daniel	MIDD (347)	Tur[ ]lott, Mical	KILY (4)
Tryon, David	MIDD (366, 417)	Turner, Amos	GROT ([9])
Tryon, David Lieut	MIDD (342, 346, 349, 353, 354, 355, 358, 361, 373)	Turner, Benj[ ] Jur	KILH (47)
		Turner, Benja	ASHF (225)
		Turner, Caleb	HARF (265, 289, 291)
Tryon, Elijah	HARF (266)	Turner, Daniel	COVE (170, 172, 180, 314)
Tryon, Elizabeth	GLAS (101, 102)		
Tryon, Elizur	GLAS (84, 92, 94)	Turner, Elijah	MANS (339)
Tryon, Ezra	GLAS (94, 114)	Turner, Ezekiel	GROT [4], [6], [9]
Tryon, Jona	MIDD (416)	Turner, Hab[ ]	COVE (174)
Tryon, Joseph	GLAS (94)	Turner, Isaac	MANS (279, 281, 329)
Tryon, Noah	GLAS (70, 73, 78, 83, 84, 93, 108)	Turner, James	LEBA (299)
		Turner, Jethro	COVE (179)
Tryon, Stephen	MIDD (350, 376, 377, 387)	Turner, John	COVE (181)
		Turner, Jonathan	MIDD (346, 349, 357, 368, 373, 395)
Tryon, Thomas	MIDD (368)		
Tryon, William	GLAS (67)	Turner, Joseph	MANS (271, 273)
Tryon, William General	FAIR (261)	Turner, Philip	MANS (233, 277)
		Turner, Phinehas	MANS (280, 281)
Tryon, Wm	GLAS (99), MIDD (363)	Turner, Prince	MANS (281, 357)
Tubb, Amos	FARM (444)	Turner, Rachel	HARF (297)
Tubbs, Amos	FARM (13, 28)	Turner, Robert	COVE (168, 170, 172, 174, 177)
Tubbs, Elisha	FARM (2, 438)		
Tubbs, Eneas	FARM (455)	Turner, Saml	MANS (279, 281, 336)
Tubbs, Ezekiel	GLAS (87, 92)	Turner, Samuel	MANS (348)
Tubbs, Ezekl	GLAS (94)	Turner, Seth	MIDD (376)
Tubbs, Isaac	GLAS (112)	Turner, Stephen	MANS (277, 359),MIDD (376, 395, 406, 413, 416, 421)
Tubbs, Leml	GLAS (102)		
Tubbs, Lemuel	GLAS (80, 94, 102)		
Tubbs, Simon	CANA (11, 15, 19, 23, 27, 28, 64, 77)	Turner, Timothy	MANS (280, 281, 353, 357)
Tubs, Lemuel	CHAT (54)	Turner, Titus	LITC (147, 152)
Tucker, Benjn	GLAS (112)	Turney, Stephen	FAIR (255, 258, 259)
Tucker, Daniel Junr	DERB (106, 113, 126, 145, 168)	Turney, Thomas	FAIR (256)
		Tuttel, Danl	FARM (441)

INDEX

Name	Index Pages
Tuttel, Gershom	FARM (438, 456)
Tuttle, Aaron	GOSH (185)
Tuttle, Ebenezer	CHES (A)
Tuttle, Elisha	GOSH (184)
Tuttle, Ephraim	CHES (11)
Tuttle, Gideon	DERB (121, 126)
Tuttle, Ichabod	CHES (A)
Tuttle, Joel	GUIL (282, 301, 309, 310, 314, 329, 339)
Tuttle, Joseph	HEBR (218)
Tuttle, Lucious	CHES (4)
Tuttle, Lucius	CHES (8, 9, 11, 12, 14, 15, 17)
Tuttle, Noah	GOSH (138, 183, 184)
Tuttle, Samuel	CHES (A)
Tuttle, Step	GOSH (183)
Tuttle, Step Leut	GOSH (104)
Tuttle, Stephen	GOSH (112)
Tuttle, Stepn	GOSH (102, 110)
Twichel, Benjamin	DERB (168)
Twitchel, David	DERB (133)
Tyler, Abraham Capt	HADD (111)
Tyler, Abraham Col	HADD (128)
Tyler, Abraham Major	HADD (112)
Tyler, Abram	HADD (109)
Tyler, Abrm Major	HADD (112, 113)
Tyler, Asahel	BRAN (175)
Tyler, Baird	GOSH (105)
Tyler, Bille	BRAN (164, 167, 170, 175)
Tyler, Capt	HADD (111)
Tyler, Col	HADD (119, 122, 123, 130, 119)
Tyler, D	GOSH (138)
Tyler, Daniel	FARM (17)
Tyler, David	GOSH (111, 112, 115, 120, 130, 138, 139, 184)
Tyler, Elnathan	BRAN (163, 164, 177, 178)
Tyler, Enos	CHES (4, 14, 15)
Tyler, Ezra	HADD (110, 113, 115, 116, 117, 121, 129, 148)
Tyler, Ichabod	BRAN (174)
Tyler, Jacob	HARW (3, 4, 7, 11, 12, 16, 533)
Tyler, Job	ASHF (204, 213, 218, 310)
Tyler, Job Lieut	ASHF (232)
Tyler, Jobe	ASHF (308)
Tyler, Jonathan	BRAN (166, 173, 179), HARW (3, 5, 7, 13, 17, 25)
Tyler, Jonathn	HARW (8)
Tyler, Jonth	BRAN (170, 178)
Tyler, Joseph	BRAN (175), HADD (110, 113)
Tyler, Josiah	BRAN (163, 164)
Tyler, Leut	ASHF (224)
Tyler, Nathan	HADD (109, 110, 116, 121, 129)
Tyler, Nathan Ens	HADD (117, 126)
Tyler, Nathaniel	HADD (114, 116)

Name	Index Pages
Tyler, Obadiah	BRAN (179)
Tyler, Obediah	BRAN (165)
Tyler, Ozias	BRAN (174, 179)
Tyler, Peter	BRAN (164, 165, 173, 178, 179)
Tyler, Peter Jur	BRAN (173)
Tyler, Phinehas	BRAN (174, 175)
Tyler, Roger Junr	BRAN (164, 165, 166, 168, 170, 172, 173, 175, 176, 178, 179)
Tyler, Saml	BRAN (166), HADD (148)
Tyler, Samuel	HADD (110, 113, 118), BRAN (170, 173, 179)
Tyler, Simon	HADD (109)
Tyler, Solomon	BRAN (170, 173, 178)
Tyler, Solon	BRAN (163)
Tyler, Timothy	HADD (113, 116, 148)
Ufford, Eliakem	CHAT (30, 52)
Ufford, Eliakim	CHAT (44)
Ufford, John	CHAT (30, 33, 38, 42, 43, 51, 67)
Ufford, Jonth	CHAT (29)
Underfield, Thomas	CHES (A)
Underwood, Elias	ASHF (308)
Upham, Benjamin	MANS (338)
Upham, Ivory	KILY (7, 32)
Upham, Joseph	MANS (338)
Upham, Luke	KILY (12, 21, 31, 34, 86a, 87, 92, 98)
Upham, Saml	MANS (338)
Uppon, Luke	KILY (94a)
Upsom, Luke	KILY (88)
Upson, Amos	FARM (442, 444)
Upson, Asa	FARM (17, 430, 438, 440, 442, 445, 446, 450)
Upson, Asa Capt	FARM (433, 445, 449, 450, 452, 454)
Upson, Asa Jur	FARM (11, 17, 455)
Upson, Benoni Revd	FARM (455)
Upson, Capt	FARM (8, 10, 23, 445)
Upson, Freeman	FARM (456)
Upson, Freman	FARM (2)
Upson, John	FARM (435)
Upson, John Jur	FARM (5, 443, 450)
Upson, Josiah	FARM (443)
Upson, Thomas	FARM (430, 434, 435, 452)
Upson, Thos	FARM (433, 440, 442, 444, 446, 449)
Upson, Timo	FARM (443, 449)
Usher, Hezekiah	EHAD (49, 59, 81, 86)
Usher, Robert Doct	CHAT (51, 58)
Ussher, Robert	CHAT (39)
Ussher, Robert Doctr	CHAT (64)
Utley, Jno	ASHF (308)
Utley, Joel	ASHF (214, 218, 308, 310)
Utley, John	ASHF (310)
Utley, Landd	ASHF (214)
Utley, Olover	ASHF (308)
Utley, Saml	ASHF (311)

INDEX

Name	Index Pages	Name	Index Pages
Utter, Jedediah	KILY (21, 33)	Wadkins, Ens	GOSH (138)
Utter, Jediah	KILY (94a)	Wadsworth, Asahel	FARM (5, 6, 27, 28, 430, 435, 444, 446, 449, 450)
Utter, Jedidiah	KILY (12, 98)		
Utter, Josiah	GREE (127)	Wadsworth, Asahell	FARM (12), 427, 451, 456)
Utter, Rhoady	KILY (88a)		
Utter, Rhoda	KILY (12, 21, 34, 97a, 98)	Wadsworth, Asal	FARM (2)
		Wadsworth, Capt	DURH (26)
Uttley, John	ASHF (209)	Wadsworth, Colo	DURH (8)
Uttley, Joseph	ASHF (209)	Wadsworth, Eli	HARF (295)
Vail, Joseph	LITC (137)	Wadsworth, Elijah	LITC (129, 131)
Vail, Peter Capt	GUIL (299)	Wadsworth, Eliphalet	FARM (17, 444)
Vaill, Capt	GUIL (338)	Wadsworth, Eliphelet	FARM (9)
Vaill, Peter Capt	GUIL (321, 323)	Wadsworth, Elipt	FARM (28)
Van Horn, Garrit	MILF (78)	Wadsworth, Epaphras	LITC (135, 139, 142, 147, 153, 158, 159)
Van Randts, Cornelious	GREE (125)		
		Wadsworth, Esther	DURH (26)
Van sant, Cristopher	CHAT (31, 34)	Wadsworth, Fenn	FARM (442)
Vansant, Capt	CHAT (64)	Wadsworth, Gad	FARM (28, 433, 442, 443
Vansant, Christopher	CHAT (37)	Wadsworth, General	DURH (12, 26)
Vansant, Christopher	CHAT (51)	Wadsworth, Hez	FARM (21, 444)
Vansant, Cristopher	CHAT (41, 52)	Wadsworth, Hezekiah	FARM (19)
Vansant, Cristr	CHAT (46)	Wadsworth, Hezh	FARM (7, 10, 11, 12, 14, 23, 27, 32, 33, 431, 440, 443, 445, 446, 450, 451)
Vaughan, Jno	LEBA (305, 318)		
Vaughan, Jno Cap	LEBA (320)		
Ventrus, Capt	HADD (123)	Wadsworth, Ichabod Capt	EWIN (10, 14)
Ventrus, Daniel	HADD (123, 130)		
Ventrus, Daniel Lieut	HADD (109, 110, 112, 114)	Wadsworth, James	CORN (1, 18, 87, 91), DURH (11)
Ventrus, David	HADD (129)	Wadsworth, James	DURH (14, 16, 18, 21, 23, 24)
Ventrus, John Capt	HADD (111)	Genl	
Ventrus, John Ens	HADD (109)	Wadsworth, James Jur Colo	DURH (10, 11)
Ventrus, John Lieut	HADD (109, 110)		
Vescy, Eleazer	MIDD (350, 352)	Wadsworth, Jas	DURH (23)
Vescy, Mary	MIDD (357)	Wadsworth, Jedd Capt	EWIN (12, 14)
Vining, Alexander	EWIN (85)	Wadsworth, Jeremiah Colo	HARF (275, 276, 279)
Vining, Alexr	EWIN (17, 88)		
Vining, John	EWIN (8)	Wadsworth, Jno Noyes Jur	DURH (23)
Vining, Josiah	DANB (40)		
W[ ]all, Saml	KILY (31)	Wadsworth, John N Capt	DURH (18, 19, 22, 25)
W[ ], Capt	GOSH (120)		
W[ ], Ezekl	FARM (9)	Wadsworth, John Noyes Capt	DURH (18, 19, 20, 26)
W[ ], Samuel	MILF (106)		
Wa[ ], Aron	HARL (52)	Wadsworth, Joseph	CORN (88, 91)
Wackley, Asa	HADD (114)	Wadsworth, Joseph Junr	HARF (255A)
Wackley, Jonathan	DURH (16, 22)		
Wackley, Solomon	HADD (115)	Wadsworth, Judah Capt	FARM (449)
Wackly, Richard	HADD (112, 113, 129)		
Wackly, Richd	HADD (148)	Wadsworth, Luke	FARM (5)
Wackly, Solomon	HADD (109, 110, 125, 148)	Wadsworth, Nathl	FARM (9, 17, 29, 446, 450)
Wade, Dudley	KILY (86a)	Wadsworth, Saml	CORN (9, 91)
Wadham, Ens	GOSH (112)	Wadsworth, Samuel	CORN (2, 11, 16, 23, 25, 87), HARF (250, 300)
Wadhams, John	GOSH (102)		
Wadhams, Abraham	GOSH (130)	Wadsworth, Seth	FARM (7, 18, 442, 444)
Wadhams, Ens	GOSH (102, 105, 110, 137, 140, 184)	Wadsworth, Thomas Junr	HARF (272, 281)
Wadhams, John	GOSH (104, 112, 119, 138, 184)	Wadsworth, Timo	CANA (28), FARM (455)
		Wadsworth, Timothy	CANA (20), FARM (451)
Wadhams, Seth	GOSH (104, 112, 138)	Wadsworth, William	FARM (23, 444), HARF (255A, 266, 285)
Wadhams, Sol	GOSH (138, 184)		
Wadhams, Solomon	GOSH (113)	Wadsworth, Willm	FARM (11)
Wadhems, Ens	GOSH (110)		

INDEX

Name	Index Pages
Wadsworth, Wm	FARM (2, 6, 8, 12, 433, 435, 436, 438, 442, 445)
Wadworth, James	DURH (20)
Wainwright, Jonathan	CHES (15)
Wait, Martin	GLAS (65)
Wait, Marvin	GLAS (107)
Wait, Marvin G	GLAS (107)
Wait, N	MIDD (364)
Wakeley, Ebenr	GUIL (308, 335, 336)
Wakeley, Jonathan	DURH (12)
Wakely, Ebenr	GUIL (313, 314, 316, 317, 326, 327)
Wakeman, Andrew Capt	FAIR (253, 255)
Wakeman, Andw	FAIR (258, 266, 267)
Wakeman, Andw Capt	FAIR (254, 255)
Wakeman, Ebenr Jur	FAIR (265, 266)
Wakeman, Elipt	FAIR (266, 267)
Wakeman, Gershom	FAIR (256, 258, 259, 260, 262, 263)
Wakeman, Gid	FAIR (255)
Wakeman, Gideon	FAIR (253, 258, 260, 262, 264, 266, 267)
Wakeman, Jesup	FAIR (263)
Wakeman, John	FAIR (259)
Wakeman, John 2d	FAIR (262)
Wakeman, John Jur	FAIR (258, 260, 261, 266, 267)
Wakeman, Jos	FAIR (262)
Wakeman, Joseph	FAIR (258, 259, 260, 261, 266, 267)
Wakeman, Lyman	FAIR (253, 256)
Wakeman, Saml	FAIR (260, 261, 262, 265, 266, 267)
Wakeman, Samuel	FAIR (252, 257, 269)
Wakeman, Stephen	FAIR (256, 260, 261, 262, 267)
Wakeman, Thad	FAIR (261)
Wakeman, Thads	FAIR (255, 258, 259, 260, 267)
Wakeman, Timy	FAIR (267)
Wakeman, William	FAIR (259)
Wakeman, Willm	FAIR (253)
Wakeman, Wm	FAIR (262)
Walbridg, John	COVE (180)
Walbridg, Samuel	COVE (180)
Waldo, Albigene Doctr	KILY (13)
Waldo, Jesse	MANS (267, 283, 339)
Waldo, Jesse Capt	MANS (346, 349, 354, 356, 359, 360)
Waldo, Nathan	CANT (147, 151, 156, 157, 159, 160, 161, 162, 167, 168, 177, 183)
Waldo, Zachariah	CANT (148, 159, 162, 168, 171, 172, 176, 179, 180)
Waldo, Zechh	CANT (157)
Waldow, John	COVE (170)
Waldow, John Doctr	COVE (174)
Wales, [ ]	ASHF (237)
Wales, Capt	ASHF (206, 213, 217, 222, 224)
Wales, Elisha	ASHF (217, 220, 310)
Wales, Elisha Capt	ASHF (194, 208, 209, 210, 213, 214, 216), 218, 219, 220, 230, 308)
Wales, Jos Jur	HEBR (220)
Wales, Nath	ASHF (308)
Wales, Nathan	ASHF (232, 310)
Wales, Smith	ASHF (310)
Wales, Timothy	HEBR (216, 217, 219, 220, 233)
Walker, [ ] widow	ASHF (205)
Walker, Aaron	LEBA (327, 342)
Walker, Benja	ASHF (310)
Walker, Benja Jur	ASHF (310)
Walker, Benjamin	ASHF (218)
Walker, Benjamin Ens	ASHF (205)
Walker, Capt	ASHF (233)
Walker, Comfort	KILY (7, 8, 19, 94)
Walker, Ebenezer	ASHF (206)
Walker, Ebenezer Lieut	ASHF (230)
Walker, Ebenr	ASHF (222)
Walker, Ebenr 3d	ASHF (310)
Walker, Ebenr Capt	ASHF (210, 212)
Walker, Ebenr Junr	ASHF (226)
Walker, Ensn	ASHF (224)
Walker, Ephraim	ASHF (202, 209, 214, 308, 310)
Walker, Er 3d	ASHF (310)
Walker, John Juner	BOLT (181)
Walker, Lieut	ASHF (224)
Walker, Nathaniel	KILY (88a)
Walker, Saml	ASHF (311)
Walker, Walter	LEBA (334)
Walker, William	ASHF (218, 310)
Walker, Willm Insgn	ASHF (229)
Walker, Willm Lieut	ASHF (232, 236, 238, 239)
Walker, Wm	ASHF (310)
Walker, Wm Ens	ASHF (225)
Walkers, Wm	ASHF (313)
Wallace, Abraham	EWIN (11, 12, 85)
Wallace, Richard	LITC (147)
Waller, Elijah	KENT (B1, D7, E63)
Waller, Peter	KENT (B2, C548, C551, C554, C555, D2, D7, D8, E59, E63)
Waller, Phinehas	CORN (6, 25, 89, 90)
Walson, John Capt	COLE (9)
Walson, Saml	KILY (94a)
Walstone, Thos	GUIL (293)
Walter, Aaron	LEBA (316, 334)
Walters, Aaron	LEBA (315)
Walters, Daniel Leut	KILY (91, 92)
Walton, John	CANA (15)
Ward, Ambros	KILH (44, 48, 49, 50, 51, 53, 54, 55, 145, 146)
Ward, Andrew	GUIL (284, 295)
Ward, Andrew Capt	GUIL (260)
Ward, Andrew Col	GUIL (259, 269, 270, 273, 277, 280, 283, 287, 288, 295)

729

INDEX

Name	Index Pages	Name	Index Pages
Ward, Andrew Genl	GUIL (305, 319, 324)	Warker, Ebenr	ASHF (311)
Ward, Andrew Junr Col	GUIL (275)	Warkes, Wm Junr	ASHF (223)
Ward, Asher	MIDD (376)	Warner, Aaron	CANA (77), HARL (44, 48, 58)
Ward, Bilious	GUIL (260)	Warner, Capt	MIDD (405)
Ward, Capt	ASHF (202, 311), MIDD (347)	Warner, Daniel	EHAD (64), EWIN (89)
		Warner, Deliverance	GLAS (64)
Ward, Daniel	GLAS (93)	Warner, Ebenezer	DERB (135, 140)
Ward, David	DURH (26)	Warner, Eleazar	ASHF (213)
Ward, Doct	MIDD (407)	Warner, Eleazer Capt	ASHF (237)
Ward, Edmund	GUIL (302)	Warner, Eleazr Lieut	ASHF (308)
Ward, Edwd	FARM (455)	Warner, Elezar	ASHF (210)
Ward, Elisha	MIDD (414)	Warner, Eli	HARF (292, 299)
Ward, Genl	GUIL (283, 317)	Warner, Ichabod	BOLT (139, 145, 149, 150)
Ward, Hannah	KILH (49)		
Ward, Icabd Capt	ASHF (308)	Warner, Ichabod Doct	BOLT (152, 157, 159, 160, 161, 163, 164, 166, 168, 180, 182)
Ward, Ichabod Capt	ASHF (194, 200, 201)		
Ward, James	KILH (145), MIDD (372, 416)		
		Warner, Jabez 2d	EHAD (87)
Ward, James T	MIDD (382, 406)	Warner, Jno	ASHF (214), MIDD (376)
Ward, James Tapn	MIDD (395)	Warner, John	ASHF (236), EHAD (45, 50), MIDD (413)
Ward, James Tappen	MIDD (362, 377)		
Ward, James Tappin	MIDD (357, 380)	Warner, John 2d	EHAD (69)
Ward, Jno	MIDD (395)	Warner, John 3d	EHAD (84, 87)
Ward, Joel	ASHF (202, 209, 218, 225, 227, 228, 231, 232, 233, 236, 308, 311)	Warner, Joseph	EHAD (69), MIDD (346)
		Warner, Lieut	ASHF (222)
		Warner, Lois	MIDD (348)
Ward, John	CHAT (29, 39, 68), MIDD (368, 372, 382, 405)	Warner, Majr	MIDD (413)
		Warner, Mathew	MANS (336, 355)
		Warner, Matt	MANS (277)
Ward, John 3d	MIDD (357, 362, 370)	Warner, Matthew	MANS (267, 283, 285)
Ward, John 4th	MIDD (362, 378, 382)	Warner, Nath	COLC (11, 249)
Ward, Joseph	MIDD (370, 373, 395, 406, 413, 416)	Warner, Nathan	COLC (255)
		Warner, Nathl	FARM (455)
Ward, Josiah	MIDD (347, 350, 359, 363, 371, 377, 381, 382, 394, 395, 406, 416)	Warner, Oliver [ ]ing	MIDD (362)
		Warner, Oliver Ring	MIDD (365)
		Warner, R Capt	MIDD (372)
		Warner, Robert	MIDD (377)
Ward, Levi	GUIL (274, 285, 288, 294, 296, 306, 318, 323, 325, 340)	Warner, Robt Capt	MIDD (358, 382, 395)
		Warner, Saml	FARM (9, 28, 436, 444)
Ward, Saml	MIDD (380, 384, 407)	Warner, William	MIDD (362, 364, 365, 415)
Ward, Saml 3d	MIDD (387)		
Ward, Samuel	MIDD (347)	Warner, William Charles	BOLT (183)
Ward, Samuel 3d	MIDD (362)		
Ward, Thelus	GUIL (270, 277, 288, 295, 301, 311, 327, 336)	Warren, [ ]	GLAS (88)
		Warren, Abijah	LITC (158)
Ward, Thomas	MIDD (365)	Warren, Capt	KILY (86)
Ward, Thomas Lieut	MIDD (355)	Warren, Daniel	HARF (263)
Ward, Thos Lieut	MIDD (361, 362)	Warren, Eleazer Capt	KILY (98)
Ward, William	MIDD (368)	Warren, Eleazr Capt	KILY (85a)
Ward, William Capt	MIDD (346, 349, 356, 357)	Warren, Elisha Capt	FARM (433)
		Warren, Ephm	KILY (24)
Ward, William Junr	MIDD (377)	Warren, Ephraim	KILY (97)
Ward, Wm	MIDD (380)	Warren, Ephraim Capt	KILY (10, 14, 16, 19, 22, 25, 26, 28, 87a, 98)
Ward, Wm Capt	MIDD (370, 371, 372, 382, 394, 398)		
		Warren, Jno Lieut	ASHF (218, 223, 308)
Ward, Wm Junr	MIDD (368, 371, 381, 382, 405, 413)	Warren, John	ASHF (209, 211, 310)
		Warren, John Leut	ASHF (202, 208, 210, 212)
Ward,, Wm Junr	MIDD (377)		
Warin, Elizer Capt	KILY (89)	Warren, Lieut	ASHF (224, 233)
Waring, Henry	GREE (128)	Warren, Moses	CANT (176)
Warker, Capt	ASHF (311)	Warren, Thomas	HARF (267, 273, 281)

INDEX

Name	Index Pages
Warrin, Capt	KILY (87a)
Warrin, Eleazer Capt	KILY (12, 23, 34)
Warrin, Ephm Capt	KILY (37, 93)
Warrin, Ephraim Capt	KILY (31, 36, 96, 96a, 97, 97a)
Warrin, Ephrom Capt	KILY (90, 91, 92, 94, 94a)
Warriner, Saml	ENFD (25)
Warterman, Ezra	BOLT (146, 151, 167, 180, 182)
Washbond, Bowers	DERB (131)
Washbond, Joseph	DERB (140)
Washbond, Josiah	DERB (134)
Washborn, John	CHAT (30, 65, 67, 68)
Washborn, Joseph	CHAT (30, 51)
Washburn, John	CHAT (29, 50, 52, 64)
Washburn, Noah	HARF (255)
Washington, General	DURH (27), LITC (151)
Wason, John	FAIR (253)
Watarous, John	COLC (251)
Water, Joseph Jur	HEBR (220)
Waterbury, General	FAIR (255)
Waterhous, Jabez	GROT ([15])
Waterman, And Cap	LEBA (320)
Waterman, Andw	LEBA (311, 327)
Waterman, Andw Capt	LEBA (325, 330, 337)
Waterman, David	KENT (C543, C546, C547, E63)
Waterman, Ezra	BOLT (147)
Waterman, Robert	CHAT (50)
Waterman, Robert Leiut	CHAT (67)
Waterman, Saml	MIDD (364)
Waterman, Simeon	LEBA (334, 342)
Waterman, Simion	LEBA (326)
Waterman, Sylvanus	CHAT (47)
Waterman, William	LEBA (305)
Waterman, Wm	LEBA (311)
Waterman, Zebn	COLC (7)
Waterman, Zebulon	COLC (244, 246, 249)
Watermon, Zebulon Capt	COLC (247)
Waterous, [ ]	ASHF (219)
Waterous, Josiah	KILH (146)
Waterous, Sarah	GUIL (293)
Waters, [ ]	HEBR (236)
Waters, Abner	HARL (48, 52)
Waters, Abraham	FARM (14)
Waters, Adam Capt	HEBR (216, 220, 247)
Waters, Capt	HEBR (234)
Waters, Daniel	KILY (87a)
Waters, Hannah	COLC (250, 252)
Waters, Isaac	HEBR (218, 220, 246)
Waters, Israel	MANS (280, 281)
Waters, Jacob	MANS (267, 278, 329, 353)
Waters, Jacob Junr	MANS (233, 278)
Waters, John	GLAS (64), HEBR (246)
Waters, Jos	HEBR (217, 218)
Waters, Joseph	HEBR (248)
Waters, Joseph Jur	HEBR (245)
Waters, Laz	COLC (11)
Waters, Lazarus	COLC (243, 245, 249, 251, 252)
Waters, Lazarus Capt	COLC (254)
Waters, Lydia	HARL (48)
Waters, Timothy	COLC (243, 246, 252)
Waters, William Jur	COLC (243)
Waters, Worthy Capt	HEBR (216)
Watkins, Amasa	ASHF (202, 218, 222)
Watkins, Edward	ASHF (203)
Watkins, Jed	ASHF (202)
Watkins, John	HARW (6, 7, 8, 11, 14, 20, 25, 523, 534)
Watkins, John Capt	HARW (16, 22)
Watkins, Phineas	ASHF (204)
Watrous, [ ]	LEBA (296)
Watrous, Daniel	COLC (10, 11)
Watrous, John	COLC (9, 242, 243, 244, 245, 247, 248)
Watrous, Josiah	KILH (145)
Watson, John Junr	CANA (20)
Watson, Capt	CANA (20, 22, 24)
Watson, Ebenezer Jur	EWIN (8, 12, 15, 16, 85)
Watson, Ebenr Jur	EWIN (10, 11, 13, 17, 88)
Watson, John	CANA (10, 28, 64), EHAD (48, 50, 55, 60, 65, 69, 80, 81, 87), EWIN (17, 85, 88)
Watson, John Capt	CANA (16, 17, 21, 22, 25, 27, 28, 29, 64)
Watson, John Jur	CANA (15, 16, 19, 23)
Watson, Phobe	COLC (8)
Watson, Read	KILY (20)
Watson, Read In	KILY (32)
Watson, Robert	EWIN (17, 85)
Watson, Saml	KILY (85a, 86a, 87a, 92, 93, 93a, 97, 97a)
Watson, Saml Jr	EWIN (17)
Watson, Samuel	KILY (7, 8, 94a, 98)
Watson, Samuel Jur	EWIN (85, 88)
Watson, Samuel Lt	EWIN (85, 88)
Watson, Widw	KILY (21)
Wattles, Andrew	LEBA (305)
Wattles, Benij[ ]	LEBA (326)
Wattles, Charles	LEBA (333)
Wattles, Dan	LEBA (342)
Wattles, Danl	LEBA (326, 327, 334)
Wattles, Denisn	LEBA (311)
Wattles, Denison	LEBA (305, 320, 342)
Wattles, Dennison	LEBA (311, 334)
Wattles, Jno Cap	LEBA (296)
Wattles, Olivr	LEBA (315)
Wattles, Saml	LEBA (297)
Wattles, Sluman	LEBA (310)
Wattles, Wm Lt	LEBA (296)
Waugh, Alexander	LITC (129)
Waugh, Alexander Capt	LITC (143)
Waugh, Joseph	LITC (130)
Waugh, Thomas	LITC (130, 131, 135)
Way, Abel	HARW (2)
Weard, John	FARM (455)
Weard, Seth	FARM (435, 446)

INDEX

Name	Index Pages	Name	Index Pages
Weaver, Jonath	GLAS (64)	Webster, Wm	FARM (433, 444)
Weaver, Thomas Docr	KILY (98)	Webter, Timothy	LITC (147)
Webb, Capt	EWIN (14)	Wedge, Asahel	KENT (E59)
Webb, Jabez	ASHF (226, 236, 310)	Wedge, John	KENT (A28)
Webb, Josiah	KENT (D7, E60, E63)	Wee[ ], Jabez	ASHF (232)
Webb, Richard	GREE (121)	Weed, David	DANB (40)
Webster, [ ]	FARM (443)	Weed, Ebenr	DANB (41, 59)
Webster, Aaron	FARM (443, 453)	Weed, Ephm	DANB (55)
Webster, Abel	LEBA (299, 303)	Weed, Saml	ASHF (313), DANB (39)
Webster, Abraham	HARF (261, 263, 266, 272)	Weeks, Francis	MIDD (364)
Webster, Amos	HARW (3, 5, 8, 13, 17, 25)	Welch, Constant	CHAT (47, 52)
		Welch, David	CORN (88), LITC (134, 135, 137, 141, 146, 147, 152)
Webster, Asahel	BOLT (157, 160, 166, 180, 182)	Welch, David Major	LITC (139, 145)
Webster, Benjamin	LITC (135, 141, 147, 149	Welch, James	BOLT (181)
Webster, Charles	HARW (3, 7)	Welch, John	CHAT (55, 69)
Webster, Cyprian	HARW (5, 6, 10, 11, 15, 20, 21, 23, 24, 523, 533)	Welch, Lydia	BOLT (181)
		Welch, Major	LITC (149)
Webster, Cyprian Ensn	HARW (3)	Welch, Mary	BOLT (181)
Webster, Cyrenus	EWIN (85, 88)	Welch, Moses Cook	MANS (339)
Webster, David	BOLT (146, 147, 148, 180, 182)	Welch, Thomas	MANS (339)
		Welch, William	CHAT (39, 42, 43), COLC (251)
Webster, Elijah	HEBR (236, 245)		
Webster, Ephraim	HARF (281)	Welch, Willm	CHAT (44)
Webster, Gideon	HARF (272)	Weld, Joseph	GUIL (271, 277, 288, 295, 301, 310, 311, 327, 335, 337)
Webster, Isaac	HARF (253, 287)		
Webster, Isaac Junr	HARF (287)		
Webster, James	LEBA (326), LITC (158)	Weldon, Peleg	GLAS (94)
Webster, John	CANA (77), GLAS (94), LITC (135, 153)	Welles, Baze	FARM (28)
		Welles, Benjamin	BOLT (182)
Webster, John Junr	LEBA (305)	Welles, Elihu	HEBR (246)
Webster, Jona	LEBA (315, 333, 326)	Welles, George	GLAS (93)
Webster, Jona Jur	LEBA (315)	Welles, Gideon	CANT (163)
Webster, Jonath	GLAS (93)	Welles, Gideon Docr	CANT (170, 174, 177, 181)
Webster, Jonathan	LEBA (305)		
Webster, Joseph	HARF (292)	Welles, Hezekiah	EWIN (11, 85)
Webster, Joshua	FARM (2, 12, 438, 445, 450, 455)	Welles, Isaac	GLAS (111)
		Welles, John	GLAS (75, 88, 92, 93)
Webster, Josiah	LEBA (297, 299)	Welles, John H	HEBR (246)
Webster, Justis	FARM (2, 18, 438, 450, 455)	Welles, Jona	GLAS (98)
		Welles, Jonathan	GLAS (69, 70, 72, 77, 78, 86, 87, 88, 90, 93, 94, 95, 104, 105, 109, 111, 113)
Webster, Justiss	FARM (9, 29)		
Webster, Mathew	HARF (251(2))		
Webster, Medad	HARF (266, 283, 289)	Welles, Jonathan Capt	GLAS (115)
Webster, Medad Capt	HARF (275)	Welles, Joseph	GLAS (92)
Webster, Moses	HARW (3), MANS (281, 336, 350, 355, 357)	Welles, Lamson	EWIN (10, 89)
		Welles, Saml	GLAS (106)
Webster, Noah	FARM (1, 13), HARF (250, 258, 265, 267, 268, 291)	Welles, Saml Capt	GLAS (108)
		Welles, Saml Jur	GLAS (112)
		Welles, Samuel	GLAS (66)
Webster, Noah Capt	HARF (271, 273)	Welles, Samuel Capt	GLAS (82, 105)
Webster, Pela	LEBA (312)	Welles, Samuel Jur	GLAS (66, 71, 74, 93, 103, 109)
Webster, Robert	FARM (443)		
Webster, Samuel	EWIN (85, 88), HARF (287)	Welles, Thaddeus	GLAS (93, 104)
		Welles, Thaddeus Junr	GLAS (95)
Webster, Samuel Junr	HARF (253)	Welles, Thomas Doctr	CHAT (44, 59, 64)
Webster, Stephen	LITC (141, 152, 154)	Welles, William	GLAS (60, 63, 66, 67, 70, 71, 72, 76, 93)
Webster, Timothy	LITC (142)		
Webster, Timothy Junr	LITC (134, 142)	Welles, Wm	GLAS (65, 82, 88, 89, 91, 94, 98, 115)
Webster, William Jur	FARM (438)		
Webster, Willm	FARM (450)		

INDEX

Name	Index Pages
Wells, [ ]	FARM (22), HADD (109, 110)
Wells, Amos	COLC (243, 245, 246, 248, 249, 251)
Wells, Ashbel	HARF 258, 252(2)
Wells, Ashbell	HARF 252(2)
Wells, Baize	FARM (9)
Wells, Baizel	FARM (5)
Wells, Baze Leut	FARM (31)
Wells, Benjamin	BOLT (166, 181)
Wells, Beze[ ]	FARM (17)
Wells, Capt	HADD (125)
Wells, Ebenezer	HARF (250, 253, 255A, 261a, 266, 272, 281, 287)
Wells, Edmund Capt	HEBR (216, 218)
Wells, Eleazor	CANA (64)
Wells, Elihu	HEBR (248)
Wells, Elisha	FARM (1, 13)
Wells, Elisha Capt	ASHF (211)
Wells, G[ ]ore	FARM (1)
Wells, George	FARM (13)
Wells, Hez Capt	EWIN (14)
Wells, Hezekiah Capt	EWIN (17, 89)
Wells, Isaac	GLAS (96)
Wells, Israel Wyatt	COLC (246)
Wells, Jas Doct	FARM (442)
Wells, Jno Capt	HEBR (218)
Wells, Jo[ ]	HEBR (217)
Wells, John	GLAS (79), HARF (258, 273)
Wells, John Capt	HARF (283), HEBR (220)
Wells, John Ensn	FARM (31)
Wells, John H	HEBR (248, 234)
Wells, John H Capt	HEBR (234, 236)
Wells, John Jur	DURH (27), FARM (444)
Wells, Jona	GLAS (101)
Wells, Jonathan	GLAS (71, 74, 82, 110), HARF (251(2), 253, 255A, 259, 265)
Wells, Jonathan Colonel	HARF (261a, 263, 266, 270, 278, 280, 297)
Wells, Jonn Capt	GLAS (81)
Wells, Jonth	GLAS (95)
Wells, Joseph	FARM (430, 455), GLAS (78), HADD (110)
Wells, Joseph Dr	FARM (444)
Wells, Joseph Jur	FARM (28, 443, 445)
Wells, Josh Dr	FARM (445)
Wells, Josh Jur	FARM (2, 17)
Wells, Joshua	EWIN (8, 12)
Wells, Lamson	EWIN (85, 88)
Wells, Lamson Jur	EWIN (8)
Wells, Livi	COLC (242)
Wells, Moses	EWIN (8, 10, 85, 88)
Wells, Noah	CANA (11, 15, 19, 28), EWIN (89)
Wells, Oliver	HADD (109, 126, 130, 148)
Wells, Oliver Capt	HADD (125, 128)
Wells, Oliver Ens	HADD (113, 115, 116, 121)

Name	Index Pages
Wells, Saml	HEBR (216)
Wells, Samuel	GLAS (78)
Wells, Samuel Captain	GLAS (81, 92, 98)
Wells, Thomas	FARM (1, 13)
Wells, Timo	FARM (2)
Wells, Timothy	FARM (28)
Wells, William	GLAS (74, 77, 78)
Wells, Wm	GLAS (64, 91, 95, 100, 102, 103, 105)
Welman, Zadock	KILH (146)
Welsh, David	CORN (88)
Weltch, Fitch	MILF (93)
Wendon, Thos	FARM (456)
Weng, Thomas	ASHF (205)
Werts, David	COLE (12)
Wessells, Lawrence	LITC (147)
West, Abel	BOLT (160, 180, 182)
West, Able	BOLT (148)
West, David	BOLT (146), CHAT (42), EHAD (50, 54, 70)
West, Gershom	LEBA (311)
West, Hezh	FARM (449, 455)
West, Jabez	LEBA (333)
West, John	CHAT (59)
West, Joshua	LEBA (294, 297, 299, 303, 306, 309, 314, 315, 318, 322, 326, 328, 331)
West, Joshua Jur	LEBA (310)
West, Lemuel	CHAT (67)
West, Moses	CHAT (37, 43, 45)
West, Saml	LEBA (305, 341)
Westcock, James	KILY (97)
Westcut, James Capt	KILY (8)
Weston, Darius	MIDD (371)
Weston, Samuel Jur	HARW (2)
Wetherel, Benjamin	GLAS (93)
Wetherel, Henry	CHAT (58)
Wetheril, Henry	CHAT (54)
Wetmore, Amos	MIDD (347, 350, 394, 406, 414, 367)
Wetmore, Amos Capt	MIDD (357, 358, 359, 371, 398, 401, 407, 415, 416)
Wetmore, Caleb	MIDD (376)
Wetmore, Caleb Capt	MIDD (421)
Wetmore, Daniel	MIDD (345, 381)
Wetmore, Danl	MIDD (362)
Wetmore, Danl Lieut	MIDD (371, 416)
Wetmore, Ethe	MIDD (351, 363, 394)
Wetmore, Ichabod	MIDD (405)
Wetmore, Ichabod Capt	MIDD (357)
Wetmore, Ichd	MIDD (364, 384, 406, 407, 413, 416)
Wetmore, Ichd Capt	MIDD (394, 413)
Wetmore, Jabez	FARM (444)
Wetmore, Jesse	MIDD (376, 421)
Wetmore, Jno	MIDD (401)
Wetmore, Jno Capt	MIDD (362)
Wetmore, John	MIDD (366, 399)

INDEX

Name	Index Pages	Name	Index Pages
Wetmore, John Capt	MIDD (357, 371, 382, 393, 395, 396, 397, 402, 416)	Wheeler, Thos	GUIL (312)
		Wheeler, Thos Jur	FAIR (253, 258, 259, 267
		Wheeler, Timothy	FAIR (253, 260)
Wetmore, Joseph	LITC (131, 158), MIDD (362)	Wheeler, Timy	FAIR (267)
		Wheelock, Revd	LEBA (317)
Wetmore, Oliver	MIDD (359, 368, 370, 381, 390, 394, 395, 405, 413)	Whelden, Jabez	GLAS (93)
		Whelden, Saml	BOLT (160)
		Whelden, Samuel	BOLT (182)
Wetmore, Seth	MIDD (344, 345, 346, 349, 367, 370, 375, 381, 383, 387, 388, 394, 396, 397, 401, 403, 405, 406, 407, 412, 413, 414, 415, 417, 418)	Whelding, Samuel	BOLT (151)
		Wheldon, Samuel	BOLT (181)
		Wheler, Joseph	DERB (120, 124, 132, 137), KILH (53)
		Wheler, Moses	DERB (120, 131, 132, 140)
Wetmore, Seth Junr	MIDD (351, 353, 355, 368)	Wheler, Robert	DERB (106, 122, 126, 132, 141, 142, 145)
Wetmore, Stephen	MIDD (394)	Wheler, Saml	DERB (122)
Wettens, Ebenr	FARM (434)	Wheler, Saml Junr	DERB (107, 113, 120, 122, 124, 138)
Wever, Thos Docr	KILY (92a)		
Whaples, Eleazer	FARM (456)	Wheler, Samuel Leiut	DERB (127)
Whay, [ ]	COLC (253)	Wheler, Simeon	DERB (106)
Whay, John	COLC (10, 245, 249, 251, 252, 255)	Wheler, Willm	FARM (17)
		Wheton, Elijah	ASHF (196)
Whay, Joseph	COLC (243)	Wheton, James	ASHF (213)
Whealding, Jabez	GLAS (99)	Whipple, Joseph	GROT [18]
Whealer, Willm	FARM (431)	Whipple, Luther	GROT [18]
Wheaton, Joseph	KENT (C555)	Whipple, Saml	ASHF (308, 222, 311)
Whedon, Isaac	BRAN (179)	Whitaker, Ephraim	CHAT (66)
Whedon, James	BRAN (175)	Whitaker, Saml	CANA (77)
Whedon, Reuben	BRAN (163, 176)	Whitaker, Samuel	CANA (11, 12, 15, 64)
Whedon, Ruben	BRAN (166)	Whitamor, Phillip	KILY (91a)
Whedon, Solomon	BRAN (164, 170, 173, 178)	Whitcomb, Israel	CHAT (40)
		Whitcomb, Job	FARM (455)
Whedon, Stephen	GUIL (328)	White, [ ]	DANB (69, 70)
Whedon, William	BRAN (166, 170, 173, 176)	White, Aaron	MIDD (346, 349, 361, 368)
Whedon, Willm	BRAN (164, 174)	White, Abner	COVE (166, 168, 170, 172, 174, 177, 180, 314)
Wheelding, Jabez	GLAS (106, 109, 112)		
Wheeler, Benja	FAIR (253, 256, 257, 258, 260, 262, 264, 265, 266)	White, Adonij	HEBR (236)
		White, Adonijah	HEBR (216)
		White, Alexander	HEBR (216)
Wheeler, Benjamin	FAIR (269)	White, Alexr	HEBR (246, 248)
Wheeler, Cyprian	HARW (8)	White, Amos	EHAD (44, 54, 59, 69, 80, 83)
Wheeler, Danl	FAIR (267)		
Wheeler, Danl Jur	FAIR (255)	White, Asa	HEBR (216, 217, 220, 233)
Wheeler, David	FAIR (253)		
Wheeler, David Capt	FAIR (255, 257)	White, Charles	DURH (25)
Wheeler, Elnathan	FAIR (253)	White, Daniel	COVE (168, 172, 178), HEBR (216)
Wheeler, Ichabod	FAIR (258, 259, 260, 262, 266, 267, 269)	White, Daniel Leut	COVE (174, 179)
		White, David	CHAT (30, 33, 37, 39, 40, 45, 50, 58, 64, 68)
Wheeler, Ichabod Capt	FAIR (254, 256, 264)		
Wheeler, Jabez	FAIR (253, 258, 260)	White, Dudly	KILH (145)
Wheeler, James	MILF (104)	White, Ebenezer	CHAT (33, 39, 44)
Wheeler, Jona	CANT (144)	White, Ebenr	CHAT (29, 30, 32, 37, 40, 41, 42, 43, 46, 47, 54, 55, 59, 60, 61, 65, 66, 68)
Wheeler, Joseph	DERB (141)		
Wheeler, Lazarus	GLAS (95)		
Wheeler, Nathan	FAIR (257)		
Wheeler, Nathan Jur	FAIR (252, 253, 255, 256, 257, 258, 259, 260, 261, 262, 263, 264)	White, Ebnr	CHAT (64)
		White, Elias	MIDD (364)
		White, Elijah	BOLT (150, 154, 158)
Wheeler, Phineas	GLAS (104)	White, Elijah Leut	BOLT (151, 163)
Wheeler, Phinehas	GLAS (105)		

734

INDEX

Name	Index Pages
White, Elijah Lieut	BOLT (150, 153, 155, 159, 164, 166, 167, 180, 182)
White, Elisha Capt	KILH (146)
White, Elizur	CANA (64)
White, Enoch	LEBA (298, 299, 311)
White, Hugh	GLAS (65), MIDD (367, 377, 378, 389, 392)
White, Hugh Junr	MIDD (345, 350, 361, 368)
White, Hugh Jur Lieut	MIDD (358)
White, Hugh Lieut	MIDD (354, 355, 369, 379, 387, 402, 403, 412, 415)
White, Isaac	FARM (455)
White, James Jur	HEBR (246)
White, Jedediah	MIDD (368)
White, Jedidiah	MIDD (371, 382)
White, Jo[ ] 2d	HEBR (220)
White, Joel	BOLT (138, 147, 148, 150, 155, 158, 160, 163, 165, 180, 181, 182)
White, Joel Capt	BOLT (144, 146, 149, 151)
White, John	CHAT (30, 37, 40, 42), MIDD (364)
White, Joseph	CHAT (29, 37, 51, 58), HEBR (216, 217, 246)
White, Josiah	CHAT (66, 67, 68)
White, Moses	CHAT (37, 43, 50)
White, Nathl	CHAT (52)
White, Noadiah	CHAT (42)
White, Noadiah Jur	CHAT (29, 37, 39)
White, Stephen	CHAT (61)
White, Stephen Lt	CHAT (59, 60)
White, Timo	MIDD (393, 413)
White, Timothy	MIDD (370, 380, 381, 404)
White, William	LEBA (305), MIDD (345, 346, 349, 350, 351, 356, 357, 362, 369, 377, 380, 404, 413)
White, Wm	LEBA (298, 299, 311, 316, 326, 334, 342), MIDD (358, 393, 412)
Whitehead, Jehiel	FAIR (253, 254, 260, 267)
Whiteing, John	COLE (115)
Whitellsy, Charles	DERB (168)
Whitelsey, Charles	DERB (121, 122)
Whiteman, Solomon	FARM (440)
Whitemore, E Turel	DERB (122)
Whitemore, Ebenr T	DERB (131)
Whitemore, Richard	KILY (96a)
Whitemore, Turel	DERB (120, 135, 141)
Whiteny, Henry	DERB (120)
Whiting, John	COLE (113)
Whiting, William Col	COLC (249)
Whitlock, [ ]	DANB (70)
Whitlock, Joel	KENT (E60)
Whitlock, Nathan	DANB (63)
Whitlock, Saml	KENT (E59)
Whitlock, Saml Jur	KENT (E58, E62)

Name	Index Pages
Whitlock, Thads	FAIR (253, 258)
Whitman, [ ]	FARM (448)
Whitman, Allen	LEBA (310)
Whitman, Allyn	GROT [6], [23]
Whitman, Elnathan	FARM (28)
Whitman, Isaac	GROT [15], [24]
Whitman, John Jur	FARM, (455), HARF (253, 255A, 261a, 265, 266, 292)
Whitman, Salomon	FARM (456)
Whitman, Samuel	HARF (289)
Whitman, Soln	FARM (13, 17, 23, 434, 438, 442, 444, 445, 447, 449, 455, 456)
Whitman, Soln Jur	FARM (16, 433, 438, 442, 444, 447, 448)
Whitman, Solomon	FARM (2, 3, 6, 8, 28, 433, 436, 443, 446, 450)
Whitman, Solomon Jur	FARM (19, 22, 31, 32, 450)
Whitmire, Jacob Capt	MIDD (398)
Whitmore, Daniel	KILY (96a), MIDD (342, 346, 353, 355, 358, 382, 405)
Whitmore, Danl	DURH (11), MIDD (368)
Whitmore, Ebenezer	MIDD (350)
Whitmore, Francis	MIDD (345)
Whitmore, Isaac	KILY (86a, 88)
Whitmore, Jabez	FARM (2, 9)
Whitmore, Jacob	KILY (7, 94, 96a), MIDD (367, 370, 405)
Whitmore, Jacob Capt	MIDD (370)
Whitmore, Jacob Lieut	MIDD (356)
Whitmore, John	KILY (7, 86a, 94a)
Whitmore, John Isn	KILY (90, 92, 93)
Whitmore, Perley	KILY (19)
Whitmore, Saml	KILY (23)
Whitmore, Saml B	HADD (122)
Whitmore, Samuel	KILY (11, 98)
Whitmore, Stephen	MIDD (371, 376, 378, 381, 387, 406, 414)
Whitney, Aaron	FAIR (258, 259, 267)
Whitney, Capt	CANA (12, 18)
Whitney, Elijah	CANA (15, 16, 17, 19, 28, 64, 77)
Whitney, Henry	DERB (122, 145)
Whitney, Henry Capt	DERB (135)
Whitney, John	CANA (9, 10, 11, 12, 13, 14, 15, 16, 17, 18, 21, 23, 64, 77)
Whitney, John Jur	CANA (17, 19, 27, 28)
Whitney, Joshua	CANA (11, 12, 15, 17, 18, 19, 20, 23, 24, 27, 64, 77)
Whitney, Joshua Capt	CANA (26)
Whitney, Peter	ASHF (310), FAIR (258)
Whitney, Ranford	DERB (113, 122, 134, 145, 167)
Whitney, Saml Jur	FAIR (256, 260)
Whitney, Stephen	DERB (126)
Whitney, Tarbull Capt	CANA (9, 10, 11, 12)
Whitny, John	CANA (11)

INDEX

Name	Index Pages	Name	Index Pages
Whiton, [ ]	ASHF (207, 234, 240, 313)	Wickham, Hezh	GLAS (94)
		Wickham, John	GLAS (66, 94, 109)
Whiton, Elijah	ASHF (213, 214, 223, 224, 225, 231, 232, 239, 308, 310)	Wickwire, Solomon	ASHF (228, 308)
		Wier, John	GLAS (106)
		Wightman, Allen	LEBA (297, 299, 343)
Whiton, James	ASHF (202, 308, 310)	Wightman, Timothy	GROT [11]
Whiton, Joseph	ASHF (213, 227, 236, 308)	Wil[ ], Elijah	GOSH (185)
		Wil[ ], Jehiel	HEBR (220, 236)
Whiton, Joseph Jur	ASHF (209, 310)	Wilbour, Uriah	GROT ([10])
Whittelsey, [ ]	MIDD (416, 420)	Wilcocks, Samuel	CORN (12)
Whittelsey, Abner	FARM (455)	Wilcoks, Abel	KILH (48)
Whittelsey, C	MIDD (372)	Wilcoks, Ebenezer	KILH (49, 55)
Whittelsey, Ch	MIDD (367)	Wilcoks, Simeon	KILH (47)
Whittelsey, Chancey	MIDD (382)	Wilcoks, Steeven	KILH (48)
Whittelsey, Chauncey	MIDD (349, 351, 353, 357, 358, 367, 377, 378, 379, 389, 392, 405, 413, 417)	Wilcox, Abel	KILH (55)
		Wilcox, Epm	LEBA (316)
		Wilcox, Ezekiel	GLAS (86)
		Wilcox, Simeon	KILH (50)
Whittelsey, Chy	MIDD (369, 388, 390, 414)	Wilcox, Stephen	KILH (50)
		Wilder, Elijah	HARL (45)
Whittelsey, Dean	MIDD (395)	Wilder, Ephraim	HARL (43, 45, 46, 48, 49, 51, 53, 59, 60, 61)
Whittelsey, Newton	MIDD (364)		
Whittelsey, Samuel	MILF (78, 80, 81)	Wilder, Gamaliel	HARL (43, 45, 48, 51, 53, 59)
Whittelsy, Chy	GLAS (65)		
Whittemore, Aaron Capt	MANS (356)	Wilder, James	HARL (53)
		Wilder, Jno	HARL (53)
Whittemore, Joseph	MANS (267, 348, 353)	Wilder, John	HARL (41, 43, 45, 48, 49, 61)
Whittemore, Joseph Capt	MANS (328, 345, 346, 349, 353, 354)	Wilder, Jonas	HARL (45, 48)
Whittemore, Joseph Lt	MANS (279, 281, 283)	Wilder, Jonathan	HARL (48)
Whittlesay, Roger N	LITC (152)	Wilder, Jonth	HARL (45)
Whittlesey, Abner	FARM (5, 17)	Wilder, Joseph	HARL (42, 43, 44, 45, 46, 48)
Whittlesey, David	KENT (A28, B1, B2, C555, E58, E62)	Wilder, Joseph Lieut	HARL (49)
Whittlesey, Eliphalet Capt	KENT (B3, E58, E62)	Wilder, Joth[ ]	HARL (53)
		Wildes, David	COLC (11)
Whittlesey, John	KENT (A28, B1, C552, C554, E58, E62)	Wildman, Daniel	DANB (39, 61)
		Wildman, Danl	DANB (51, 60)
Whittlesey, Martain	KENT (C552, E59, E63)	Wildman, David	DANB (39)
Whittlesey, Martin	KENT (A28)	Wildman, Joseph	DANB (39, 40, 55)
Whittlesey, Roger N	LITC (135, 158)	Wildman, Saml	DANB (46)
Whittlesey, Roger Newton	LITC (141, 146)	Wileder, Ephram	HARL (58)
		Wileder, Gamaliel	HARL (56)
Whittmore, Aaron	MANS (274, 283, 284, 357)	Wileder, John	HARL (56, 57, 58, 62)
		Wiles, David	GLAS (106)
Whittmore, Aaron Capt	MANS (277, 346, 348, 359)	Wilford, Joseph	BRAN (167)
		Wilke, Hannah	KILY (34)
Whittmore, Joseph Capt	MANS (356)	Wilkenson, Robert	KILH (49)
		Wilkes, Mattw	DANB (45, 48, 65)
Wiand, Seth	FARM (430)	Wilkey, Hannah	KILY (12, 13, 21, 24)
Wiar, James	GLAS (98)	Wilkinson, Amos	FARM (443)
Wiar, John	GLAS (78)	Wilkinson, Thomas	KILH (145)
Wiard, [ ]	FARM (8)	Wilks, [ ] Ensign	DANB (39)
Wiard, John	FARM (440)	Will[ ], Israel Ens	HARL (59)
Wiard, Lemuel	FARM (31)	Will[ ], Joseph	MIDD (382)
Wiard, Seth	FARM (2, 3, 6, 7, 9, 11, 17, 18, 23, 27, 29, 434, 438, 441, 442, 444, 445, 446, 449)	Willard, Elias	GUIL (318)
		Willard, Jared Junr	GUIL (272)
		Willard, Julius	GUIL (308, 325, 341)
		Willard, Nathan	CORN (16)
Wickham, David	GLAS (66, 70, 75, 78, 83, 95, 98, 106, 112)	Willcock, John	HADD (109)
		Willcocks, Saml	CORN (91)
Wickham, Hezekiah	GLAS (95)	Willcocks, Thos	ASHF (313)

736

INDEX

Name	Index Pages	Name	Index Pages
Willcok, Abel	KILH (44)	Willcox, Josiah	FARM (456), MIDD (376)
Willcok, Benj[ ]	KILH (51)		
Willcok, Elijah	KILH (146)	Willcox, Josiah Jur	FARM (17, 436)
Willcok, John	KILH (43)	Willcox, Ju[ ]	MIDD (371)
Willcok, Stephen	KILH (43, 44, 146)	Willcox, Justus	MIDD (405)
Willcoks, Abel	KILH (146, 48)	Willcox, Moses	CHAT (29, 34, 36), HARW (10, 24)
Willcoks, Abram	KILH (146)		
Willcoks, Ad[ ]	KILH (47)	Willcox, Nathan	KILH (51)
Willcoks, Daniel	KILH (49, 53)	Willcox, Nathn	KILH (55, 146)
Willcoks, Ebenezer	KILH (47, 50, 146)	Willcox, Olliver	GOSH (183)
Willcoks, John	KILH (44, 50)	Willcox, Ozias	MIDD (354, 355, 372, 407, 417)
Willcoks, John 2d	KILH (44)		
Willcoks, Moses	HARW (5)	Willcox, Saml	MIDD (381, 394)
Willcoks, Simon	KILH (53)	Willcox, Saml Jr	MIDD (404, 413)
Willcoks, Stephen	KILH (47)	Willcox, Simeon	KILH (51, 53)
Willcoks, Stephen 2d	KILH (47, 49)	Willcox, Simion	KILH (55)
Willcox, Aaron	CHAT (29, 31, 64, 67)	Willcox, Stephen	KILH (51, 55)
Willcox, Abel	KILH (51, 52), MIDD (357, 376, 419)	Willcox, Stephen 2d	KILH (53)
		Willcox, Thos	ASHF (311), GUIL (271, 277, 280)
Willcox, Abel 2d	KILH (51)		
Willcox, Abij[ ]	KILH (145)	Willcox, Thos Ensn	GUIL (275)
Willcox, Bena	FARM (17)	Willcox, Timo	GUIL (318, 326)
Willcox, Benja	FARM (6, 449)	Willcox, William	HADD (121)
Willcox, Danel	MIDD (353)	Willes, B[ ]	HEBR (234)
Willcox, Daniel	KILH (55, MIDD (347, 350, 351, 359, 387, 407)	Willey, Abraham	EHAD (54, 60, 65, 69)
		Willey, Benajah	EHAD (59, 81)
Willcox, Danl	MIDD (366, 371, 373, 382, 417)	Willey, David	EHAD (58, 59, 69)
		Willey, Ephraim	EHAD (64)
Willcox, Ebenezer	KILH (51)	Willey, Ezra	EHAD (50, 59)
Willcox, Ebenezr	KILH (55)	Willey, John 2d	EHAD (50)
Willcox, Edmund	GUIL (294)	Willey, John Capt	EHAD (49, 53, 54, 57, 62)
Willcox, Eleazer	FARM (17)	Willey, John Junr	EHAD (45)
Willcox, Eli	MIDD (405, 411)	Willey, Jonathan	EHAD (45, 50)
Willcox, Elijah	MIDD (362, 394, 411)	Willey, Joseph 2nd	EHAD (44, 65, 70)
Willcox, Elisha	MIDD (357, 363, 380, 395, 411)	Willey, Lemuel	EHAD (59)
		Willey, Noah 2d	EHAD (69, 87)
Willcox, Ely	MIDD (363)	Willey, Samuel	EHAD (44, 66)
Willcox, Ezra	FARM (2, 13, 28), GUIL (335)	Willford, Joseph	BRAN (163, 164, 165, 166, 170, 174)
Willcox, Francis	MIDD (364)	Willford, Joseph Lieut	BRAN (170)
Willcox, Giles	MIDD (363, 381, 413, 419)	William, Benja	FARM (9)
		William, Elnathan	FAIR (259)
Willcox, Hezekiah	MIDD (345)	Williams, [ ]	HARF (296), LEBA (316)
Willcox, J[ ][ ]	MIDD (395)		
Willcox, James	GUIL (325)	Williams, Abraham	EHAD (44, 86)
Willcox, Jehiel	GUIL (303, 304, 310, 313, 325)	Williams, Abrm	HADD (148)
		Williams, Amariah	MANS (263, 275, 282)
Willcox, Jer[ ]	MIDD (382)	Williams, Amariah Capt	MANS (266, 267, 282, 284, 328, 333, 335, 342, 346, 347, 354, 356, 357)
Willcox, Jeremiah	MIDD (347, 350, 359, 376, 394, 406, 419)		
Willcox, Jesse	MIDD (382)	Williams, Ambrose	LEBA (342)
Willcox, John	CHAT (53, 55), FARM (456), GOSH (184), HADD (113, 116, 117, 118, 121, 125), KILH (50, 51), MIDD (353, 363, 377, 382)	Williams, Amos	CHES (4), FAIR (256, 258, 263, 266)
		Williams, Amr Capt	MANS (277, 355)
		Williams, Billy	LEBA (316, 333, 334)
		Williams, Caleb	GROT ([23])
		Williams, Charles	EHAD (44), LEBA (305, 341)
Willcox, John Junr	MIDD (363, 419)		
Willcox, John Sergt	HADD (116)	Williams, Danl	COLC (8)
Willcox, Jonathan	GUIL (272, 299)	Williams, David	FAIR (258, 260, 261, 266)
Willcox, Joseph	KILH (52), MIDD (376)	Williams, Elanth	FAIR (265)
		Williams, Elij Junr	COLC (242)

INDEX

Name	Index Pages	Name	Index Pages
Williams, Elijah Jr	COLC (10, 245, 255)	Williams, Simon	LEBA (298, 299, 311, 326)
Williams, Elisha	GROT [4], [23], [24]		
Williams, Elnath	FAIR (254, 255, 258, 265	Williams, Solomon	HARF (253, 255A, 272, 281, 287)
Williams, Elnathan	FAIR (260, 263, 266)		
Williams, Elnathn	FAIR (267)	Williams, Stephen	BRAN (164, 165, 166, 170, 173)
Williams, Ezra	FAIR (267)		
Williams, George	LEBA (315)	Williams, Thomas	CHAT (30, 33, 36, 37, 39, 40, 43, 45, 50, 67, 69)
Williams, Gideon	FARM (9, 18, 29, 433, 438, 445, 450)	Williams, Thos	CANA (64), LEBA (303, 304, 311, 320, 343)
Williams, Gidion	FARM (2)		
Williams, Henry Capt	GROT ([6])	Williams, Veach	LEBA (297, 299, 326)
Williams, Isa Jur	LEBA (311)	Williams, Veach Cap	LEBA (294)
Williams, Isaac	KENT (C553), LEBA (334)	Williams, Vetch Capt	LEBA (313, 315)
		Williams, W Col	LEBA (341)
Williams, Isaac Capt	LEBA (325, 330, 334, 337)	Williams, Warham Jur	BRAN (164, 170)
		Williams, William	GROT ([1], [2], [3], [4], [5], [6], [7], [8], [9], [10], [11], [13], [14], [15], [17], [18], [20], [21], [22], [23], [24]), HARL (44, 47, 52), LEBA (305)
Williams, Isaiah Jr	CANT (180), LEBA (305)		
Williams, Isl Lt	LEBA (320)		
Williams, Israel	HARL (43, 45, 46, 48, 49, 55, 58, 61), LEBA (334, 342)		
		Williams, William 2d	GROT [4]
Williams, Israel Capt	HARL (62), LEBA (296)	Williams, William Capt	GROT [23]
Williams, Israel Ensign	HARL (50, 56, 58, 59, 60		
Williams, Isrl	LEBA (318, 325, 326)	Williams, William Colo	LEBA (304)
Williams, Jacob	CANA (77), GOSH (184), HARF (255A)	Williams, William Junr	GROT ([20], [25]
Williams, Jeavail	HARL (53)	Williams, William Lieut	GROT ([14], [17], [19]
Williams, Jehiel	LEBA (341), MIDD (362, 414)	Williams, Wm	GROT ([16]), HARL (54, 55), LEBA (294, 297, 299, 310, 313, 314, 315, 318, 326, 330, 333, 336, 339, 340, 341, 343)
Williams, Jeremiah	MANS (265)		
Williams, Jesse	MANS (271, 353)		
Williams, Jesse Doct	MANS (278, 329, 342)		
Williams, Jno	LEBA (299)		
Williams, Jno Jur	LEBA (311, 342)	Williams, Wm Col	LEBA (313, 325, 333, 327)
Williams, John	CHES (A), GROT ([16], [23], [25]), HARF (273), LEBA (304, 305, 316)	Willis, Ebenr	MIDD (382)
		Willis, Ebr	MIDD (372)
Williams, John 3d	GROT [6], [9], [16]	Willis, Joseph	MIDD (395, 405, 413)
Williams, John 3d Capt	GROT [14]	Willis, Joseph Junr	MIDD (363)
Williams, John Capt	GROT [15], [17], [19]	Willis, Samuel Capt	MIDD (345, 349)
Williams, John Jur	LEBA (341)	Willmor, John	COLE (7)
Williams, Jona	LEBA (316, 326, 334, 341)	Willmott, Asa	CHES (15)
		Willoby, Josiah	GOSH (120, 184)
Williams, Jonathan	KILH (53)	Willoby, Westil	GOSH (104, 112, 121, 184)
Williams, Nathan	COLC (254)		
Williams, Nathl	LEBA (318)	Willoby, Westill	GOSH (110, 115, 116, 126, 130)
Williams, Nathl 2d	KILH (145)		
Williams, Neheh	LEBA (305)	Willoby, Wistill	GOSH (110)
Williams, Neheh Cap	LEBA (310)	Willoks, Abel 2d	KILH (49)
Williams, Oliver	KILY (19, 32, 97)	Wills, Israel Wyat	COLC (249)
Williams, Peleg	GROT [4], [6], [24]	Willson, [ ]	HARW (2)
Williams, Philip	EHAD (86)	Willson, Abner	HARW (5, 8, 10, 13, 14, 17, 18, 20, 25, 523)
Williams, Phillip	EHAD (44)		
Williams, Robertson	EHAD (87)	Willson, Abner Capt	HARW (26)
Williams, Saml	FARM (456), GLAS (111)	Willson, Abner Ensn	HARW (3)
		Willson, Daniel	HARW (11)
Williams, Saml 4th	GROT [25]	Willson, Danl	MIDD (368)
Williams, Saml Lieut	GROT [15]	Willson, Edmund	GUIL (324)
Williams, Samuel 2d	GROT [9]	Willson, Eli	HARW (5, 7, 9, 13, 16, 19, 21, 22, 24, 25, 533)
Williams, Samuel Lieut	GROT [18]		
		Willson, Eli Lieut	HARW (3, 12)

INDEX

Name	Index Pages
Willson, Jacob	COVE (170, 177)
Willson, John	HARW (3, 5, 6, 8, 9, 15, 16, 20, 26, 523, 533, 534)
Willson, John Capt	HARW (5)
Willson, John Jur	HARW (3)
Willson, Josiah Jur	FARM (2)
Willson, William	COVE (163, 171)
Willson, William Capt	COVE (167, 177, 178)
Willson, William Leut	COVE (161)
Wilson, [ ]	FAIR (266)
Wilson, Andrew	KILY (7, 94)
Wilson, Daniel	FAIR (252, 253, 255, 269)
Wilson, Danl	FAIR (257, 264, 267)
Wilson, Ebenezer	KILY (94)
Wilson, Eli Lieut	HARW (14)
Wilson, John	FAIR (253, 259, 263, 269), KILY (19, 32)
Wilson, Nathl	FAIR (259, 264)
Wilson, Oliver	KILY (7)
Wilson, Robert	FAIR (252)
Wilson, Saml	FAIR (266)
Wilson, Widow	HARF (255)
Wilton, James	CHAT (31)
Winbon, Prince	MIDD (368)
Winchel, Hezh	FARM (2, 443)
Winchel, Munson	GOSH (183)
Winchel, Soln	FARM (9, 17)
Winchell, Hezh	FARM (433)
Winchester, Amariah	ASHF (311)
Winchester, Andrew	CANT (147)
Winegar, Hendrick	KENT (D1, E60, E63)
Wing, Martha	GUIL (302)
Wing, Thos	ASHF (222, 311)
Winslow, Job	EHAD (64)
Winston, Abraham	FARM (456)
Winston, Abram	FARM (433)
Winstone, Apham	FARM (456)
Winstone, Abrm	FARM (449)
Wintworth, Ebenezer	COVE (168)
Wintworth, Ebenezer Jur	COVE (166)
Wiskell, Da[ ]	FARM (442)
Witkinson, Amos	FARM (436)
Witmore, Jesse	MIDD (364)
Witmore, Jno Capt	MIDD (372)
Witmore, Seth	MIDD (358)
Witon, James	CHAT (32, 33, 34)
Witter, Asa	CANT (139, 144, 146, 155, 157, 158, 160, 168, 172, 174, 175, 180, 181, 184)
Wiyard, Seth	FARM (28)
Wolcot, Benjamin	EWIN (85)
Wolcot, Henry	EWIN (9)
Wolcott, [ ]	EWIN (13)
Wolcott, Albert	EWIN (85, 89)
Wolcott, Arodi	EWIN (85, 89)
Wolcott, Benjamin	EWIN (88)
Wolcott, Ephm	EWIN (85)
Wolcott, Ephraim	EWIN (89)
Wolcott, Erastus	EWIN (6, 7, 85), GLAS (64)
Wolcott, Erastus Capt	EWIN (85)
Wolcott, Erastus Col	EWIN (8)
Wolcott, Erastus General	EWIN (10, 12, 13, 14, 15, 16, 88)
Wolcott, Erastus Jur	EWIN (8, 89)
Wolcott, Genl	LITC (135)
Wolcott, Henry	EWIN (10, 85, 88, 89)
Wolcott, Oliver	LITC (127, 128, 139, 143, 151)
Wolcott, Oliver General	LITC (134, 141)
Wolcott, Samuel	EWIN (8, 10)
Wolcott, Simon	EWIN (11)
Wolcott, Simon Capt	EWIN (13, 14, 85, 88)
Wolcott, William	EWIN (7, 8, 9, 10, 85, 88)
Wolcott, Wm	EWIN (11, 16), GLAS (64)
Wollcott, Solomon	COLC (245)
Woman of Color, Cate	DERB (146)
Woman of Color, Silva	GROT [17], [24]
Womansey, John	GROT ([23])
Wood, Benj	LEBA (327)
Wood, Benj[ ]	LEBA (298, 299, 311, 342)
Wood, Benja	DANB (63), LEBA (334)
Wood, Benjamin	LEBA (305)
Wood, Benjn	DANB (47), LEBA (316)
Wood, Daniel	DANB (39, 49, 55, 59, 63
Wood, Daniel Jur	DANB (39)
Wood, Danl Jur	DANB (56)
Wood, David	DANB (40, 43, 45, 47, 58, 64), GREE (119, 120, 121, 125, 126, 127, 128)
Wood, David Capt	GREE (128)
Wood, Elijah	DANB (53, 59)
Wood, Jabez	CHAT (52)
Wood, Jerh	CHAT (54)
Wood, John	CHAT (65), DANB (50, 54, 65), GROT [6], [9], [15]
Wood, John Doctr	DANB (50, 54)
Wood, Joseph	DANB (47)
Wood, Leml	FAIR (265, 266)
Wood, Leml Jur	DANB (40)
Wood, Lemuel	FAIR (258, 260, 263, 267)
Wood, Robert	EWIN (85, 89)
Wood, Saml	CHAT (54)
Wood, Samuel	MANS (338)
Woodard, Amos	ASHF (218)
Woodard, Jason	ASHF (311)
Woodard, Joseph	ASHF (213, 218, 231, 232)
Woodard, Joseph Jur	ASHF (218, 308)
Woodbrick, Howel	GLAS (64)
Woodbridg, Theodore	GLAS (96)
Woodbridge, Howel	GLAS (64, 66, 71, 94)
Woodbridge, Howel Col	GLAS (86, 90, 99, 101, 103)
Woodbridge, Howel Liet Coln	GLAS (82, 83)

INDEX

Name	Index Pages
Woodbridge, Howel Majr	GLAS (70)
Woodbridge, Howell Col	GLAS (109)
Woodbridge, Russel Junr	HARF (255A)
Woodbridge, Saml Revrnd	HARL (56, 57)
Woodbridge, Theodore	HARL (47)
Woodbridge, Theodore Capt	HARL (48)
Woodbridge, Ward	HARF (253, 255A, 258)
Woodbrige, Theodore Leut	HARL (45)
Woodcock, Saml	ASHF (212), LITC (157)
Woodford, [ ]	FARM (8)
Woodford, Charles	FARM (5)
Woodford, Danl	FARM (436)
Woodford, Dudley	FARM (17, 28, 436)
Woodford, Elijah	FARM (4, 5, 7, 9, 438)
Woodford, Ezekiel	FARM (3, 5, 12, 17, 29, 434, 444, 449)
Woodford, Ezekl	FARM (9, 18, 438, 445)
Woodford, Isaac	FARM (9, 17)
Woodford, John Jur	FARM (13)
Woodford, Jos Capt	FARM (23)
Woodford, Joseph	FARM (6, 27, 440, 444)
Woodford, Joseph Capt	FARM (28, 31, 454)
Woodford, Joseph Jur	FARM (446)
Woodford, Joseph Leut	FARM (433)
Woodford, Josh	FARM (445)
Woodford, Josh Capt	FARM (2, 9, 17, 23)
Woodford, Roger	FARM (2, 28)
Woodford, Soln	FARM (5, 444)
Woodford, Solomon	FARM (449)
Woodford, William	FARM (3, 8, 436, 455)
Woodford, William Capt	FARM (5)
Woodford, William Jur	FARM (436, 449)
Woodford, Willm Ens	FARM (433)
Woodford, Wm	FARM (5, 7, 9, 443, 449)
Woodford, Wm Capt	FARM (440, 444)
Woodford, Wm Jur	FARM (2, 433, 444, 456)
Woodin, Corbun	HARW (23)
Woodin, Hezekiah	DERB (145)
Woodin, Hezekieh	DERB (134)
Woodin, James Jur	LITC (146)
Woodin, Joseph	HARW (3, 7, 8, 10, 534)
Woodman, Saml	GOSH (185)
Woodmansey, John	GROT [6], [12], [19], [25]
Woodmansey, Joseph	GROT [6], [15], [18], [23]
Woodroof, Martin	GLAS (95)
Woodruff, [ ]	KILH (145)
Woodruff, Abell	FARM (5)
Woodruff, Amos	FARM (17)
Woodruff, Appleton	FARM (455)
Woodruff, Asa	FARM (438, 456)
Woodruff, Asahel	FARM (433, 438)
Woodruff, Danl Jur	FARM (433)

Name	Index Pages
Woodruff, David	DERB (113, 124, 126, 131)
Woodruff, Doct	HADD (118)
Woodruff, Eldad	FARM (23, 28, 444, 449)
Woodruff, Elezor	KILH (146)
Woodruff, Elijah	FARM (5, 433)
Woodruff, Elisha	FARM (443, 449)
Woodruff, Enoch	MILF (92)
Woodruff, Enoch Capt	MILF (97, 98, 99, 103)
Woodruff, Ezekl	FARM (17)
Woodruff, Hawkins	FARM (2, 9, 17)
Woodruff, Hezh Jur	FARM (455)
Woodruff, Isaac	FARM (20, 436), 443, 449)
Woodruff, Jacob	LITC (128, 134, 137)
Woodruff, Jacob Junr	LITC (129, 152)
Woodruff, James	LITC (139)
Woodruff, Jesse	FARM (455), HARW (4, 8, 10, 14, 16, 17, 534)
Woodruff, John	FARM (28, 443)
Woodruff, John Jur	FARM (433, 449)
Woodruff, Jona	FARM (443, 453)
Woodruff, Joseph	FARM (9, 13, 28, 443, 450, 435)
Woodruff, Joseph Jur	FARM (433)
Woodruff, Joshua	FARM (23, 443, 444)
Woodruff, Levi	FARM (456)
Woodruff, Lott	FARM (5, 9)
Woodruff, Martin	FARM (2, 13, 28)
Woodruff, Mathew	FARM (16), MILF (106)
Woodruff, Matin	GLAS (94)
Woodruff, Medad	FARM (449)
Woodruff, Micah	FARM (3, 5, 17, 23, 29, 449, 455)
Woodruff, Moses	FARM (2)
Woodruff, Nathaniel	LITC (129, 130, 131, 133, 134, 135, 141, 147, 153, 158)
Woodruff, Noah	FARM (435, 442, 443, 449)
Woodruff, Oliver	FARM (456)
Woodruff, Phineas	FARM (443)
Woodruff, Reuben	FARM (2)
Woodruff, Robert	FARM (455)
Woodruff, Robt	FARM (456)
Woodruff, Saml	FARM (443, 449)
Woodruff, Samuel	LITC (139)
Woodruff, Samuel Junr	LITC (134)
Woodruff, Seth	FARM (435, 450)
Woodruff, Timo	FARM (2, 443)
Woodruff, Timothy	FARM (29, 32), LITC (129, 131, 135)
Woodruff, Wright	LITC (134)
Woodward, Eleazr	LEBA (326)
Woodward, Gaskill	BRAN (170, 176)
Woodward, Gauskin	BRAN (179)
Woodward, Joseph	ASHF (201, 208, 209, 212, 225, 227, 229, 236, 237, 239, 308, 310)
Woodward, Joseph Jur	ASHF (310)
Woodward, Moses	COVE (172)
Woodward, Peter	CANT (150, 151)

INDEX

Name	Index Pages
Woodward, Saml	LEBA (341)
Woodward, Saml Jur	LEBA (299)
Woodworth, Elipt	LEBA (310)
Woodworth, Isaac	FARM (2)
Woodworth, James	LEBA (298, 317)
Woodworth, Jas	LEBA (311)
Woodworth, Lebbeus	LEBA (297, 299, 305, 310, 317)
Woolcott, Joshua	CHAT (47)
Woolcott, Olliver General	GOSH (109)
Woolcott, Solomon	COLC (11, 247, 248)
Wooster, Abram	DERB (134)
Wooster, Eleazer	DERB (121)
Wooster, Elezer	DERB (122)
Wooster, Eliphet	DERB (167)
Wooster, John	DERB (134)
Wooster, John Capt	DERB (142)
Wooster, Jonas	MILF (78, 83, 86, 88)
Wooster, Samuel	DERB (134)
Wooster, Samuel Jnr	DERB (106)
Wooster, Walter	DERB (135)
Word, Edward	FARM (2)
Word, Josiah	MIDD (350, 356)
Word, Saml 3d	MIDD (345)
Word, Wm Capt	MIDD (358)
Worden, James	GROT [4], [6]
Worden, Joseph	GROT [9]
Worden, Sylvester	GROT [12]
Worhington, Elias Jur	COLC (8)
Work, Englesby	ASHF (222)
Work, Inglesbee	ASHF (218)
Work, Ingoldsby	ASHF (210)
Work, Ingolsbe	ASHF (212, 218), 310)
Work, Ingolsby	ASHF (206, 210)
Work, Jno	ASHF (311)
Work, Jno Capt	ASHF (214, 218, 226)
Work, John	ASHF (308)
Work, John Capt	ASHF (210, 228)
Work, Joseph	ASHF (202, 209, 213, 214, 218, 227, 311)
Work, Joseph Jur	ASHF (203, 311)
Works, Inglos	ASHF (308)
Works, Ingolsley	ASHF (313)
Works, Joseph	ASHF (232, 236)
Works, Joseph Jur	ASHF (313)
Worter, Abner	HARL (44)
Worthing, Elias	COLC (250)
Worthing, Elias Jur	COLC (255)
Worthington, [ ]	COLC (4, 8)
Worthington, Dan	COLC (254)
Worthington, Elias	COLC (6, 7, 11, 242, 243, 246, 247, 249, 252, 255)
Worthington, Elias Col	COLC (4, 6, 9, 253)
Worthington, Elias Junr	COLC (6, 7, 13, 243, 247, 248, 249, 250, 251, 253, 255, 254, 256)
Worthington, Elias Major	COLC (250)
Worthington, Elijah	COLC (242, 247)
Worthington, Elijah Capt	COLC (6)
Worthington, Elijah Col	COLC (254)
Worthington, Gad	COLC (249, 251, 256)
Worthington, Joel	COLC (7, 243, 248, 249)
Worthington, John	COLC (242, 243, 247, 251)
Worthington, William	COLC (10, 243, 248, 251)
Wrigh, Elijah	COVE (170)
Wright, [ ]	MIDD (397)
Wright, Abraham	MIDD (368, 394, 404)
Wright, Abraham Lieut	MIDD (355)
Wright, Amazh Capt	MANS (277)
Wright, Amaziah Capt	MANS (342, 352)
Wright, Azariah	COLC (7, 8, 245, 251)
Wright, Capt	GOSH (112, 119, 120, 127, 130, 131, 138)
Wright, Charles	COLE (115), LEBA (342)
Wright, Daniel	DURH (10, 12, 16)
Wright, Danl	DURH (11, 14)
Wright, Dudley	COLC (245)
Wright, Dudley Capt	COLC (10, 13, 241, 242, 243, 244, 245, 247)
Wright, Dudly	COLC (255)
Wright, Dudly Capt	COLC (256)
Wright, Ebenr	ASHF (209, 232, 310)
Wright, Ebnr	ASHF (236, 308)
Wright, Eleazar	MANS (268)
Wright, Eleazer	GLAS (68, 72, 73, 74, 78, 81, 86, 89, 93, 106, 113)
Wright, Eleazur	GLAS (69)
Wright, Elez[ ]	KILH (45)
Wright, Elijah	COVE (172, 173, 176, 178)
Wright, Elizar	ENFD (27)
Wright, Elizer	CANA (21)
Wright, Elizur	CANA (12, 18, 64, 77)
Wright, Ephraim	HARL (51, 52)
Wright, Ezekl	FARM (2, 438, 443)
Wright, Geb Capt	GOSH (111)
Wright, Hezekiah	GLAS (64, 95)
Wright, Hezh	GLAS (105)
Wright, Jabez	GOSH (102, 104)
Wright, Jabez Capt	GOSH (110, 111, 114, 137)
Wright, Jabez Lt	GOSH (184)
Wright, James	GLAS (94), LEBA (298, 299, 305, 311, 316)
Wright, Jeremiah	GLAS (95)
Wright, Jeriah	LEBA (305)
Wright, Job	KILH (55)
Wright, Job Capt	KILH (49, 50, 51, 53, 55)
Wright, Job Leut	KILH (44)
Wright, Joel	LEBA (297, 326)
Wright, John	COLC (7, 11, 245, 248, 249, 250, 251), CORN (1, 86, 87)
Wright, John Junr	CORN (87)
Wright, Jonas	CHAT (42)
Wright, Jonathan	LITC (129, 131, 141, 142, 143, 145)
Wright, Jonathan Ens	LITC (143, 155)
Wright, Jos	FARM (450)

INDEX

Name	Index Pages
Wright, Joseph	ASHF (313), FARM (446), MIDD (399), DURH (25)
Wright, Joseph Jur	DURH (14)
Wright, Judah	FARM (456)
Wright, Moses	COLE (1, 8, 10, 13, 14, 113, 115)
Wright, Nathan	ASHF (311)
Wright, Reuben	FARM (17, 444)
Wright, Saml	CANT (156), HEBR (217)
Wright, Samuel	EHAD (54, 79), GLAS (93), HEBR (218)
Wright, Seth	LEBA (315, 316)
Wright, Seth Capt	LEBA (317)
Wright, Solo	LEBA (326)
Wright, Solomon	LEBA (334, 342)
Wright, Willard	MIDD (394, 412, 413, 417)
Wright, William	CHAT (43)
Wright, Willm	CHAT (54), KILH (146)
Write, Ebenr	ASHF (213)
Wyar, James	GLAS (94)
Wyar, John	GLAS (66, 70, 94)
Wyar, Nehemiah	GLAS (94)
Wyles, John	EHAR (3)
Wyllys, Ephraim	GLAS (94)
Wyllys, George	COLE (3), DANB (42), EHART (2), HARF (253, 255A, 261a, 263A, 266, 272, 281, 282, 287, 292)
Wyllys, George Colo	HARF (287)
Wyllys, Hez	HARF (256)
Wyllys, Hezekiah	HARF (258, 267)
Wyllys, Hezh	HARF (265, 270, 292)
Wyllys, Hezh Colo	HARF (270, 273, 275, 276, 299)
Wyllys, John	GLAS (94), GREE (128)
Wyllys, John Capt	GREE (128)
Wyllys, John Palsgrave	HARF (252(2))
Wyllys, Samuel	HARF (250)
Wyllys, Samuel Colo	HARF (259)
Wyllys, William Capt	GROT ([24])
Wynkoop, Benja	FAIR (258, 264)
Wynkoop, Benjamin	FAIR (259)
Yale, [ ]	FARM (438)
Yale, Abel	FARM (442)
Yale, Abell	FARM (449, 452)
Yale, Asa	FARM (28, 455)
Yale, Asa Capt	FARM (454)
Yale, Asa Jur	FARM (433, 434, 436, 455)
Yale, Elisha	CANA (15, 16, 19, 20, 23, 27, 28, 64, 77)
Yale, Ezra	FARM (27, 433)
Yale, Job	CHES (4)
Yale, Martha	HARW (11)
Yale, Thomas	DERB (106, 107, 113, 120, 125, 134, 140, 145, 146, 167)
Yale, Thos	DERB (122)
Yeamans, David	COLC (244)

Name	Index Pages
Yeamons, David	COLC (11, 242, 245, 248, 249, 251)
Yeamons, Moses	COLC (242)
Yeomans, Daniel	LEBA (298)
Yeomans, Danl	LEBA (316, 333)
Young, Andrew	CORN (1, 2, 5, 7, 9, 11, 12, 14, 15, 16, 17, 18, 19, 21, 23, 24, 25, 28, 29, 30, 77, 87, 89)
Young, Mahiteble	CHAT (41)
Young, Saml	CHAT (30, 38, 40, 43, 54, 64)
Young, Samuel	CHAT (40)
Young, Silvanus	MIDD (345, 368, 370, 415, 416, 417)
Young, Sylvanus	MIDD (345)
Young, widow	CHAT (46)
Younglove, John	KILY (19)
Youngs, James	HADD (109)
Youngs, Mahetable	CHAT (34)
Youngs, Saml	CHAT (33)

www.ingramcontent.com/pod-product-compliance
Lightning Source LLC
Chambersburg PA
CBHW071212290426
44108CB00013B/1168